Maj Canton's

The Complete Reference Guide To Movies and Miniseries Made for TV and Cable 1984-1994

10 Years of TV Movies

Maj Canton's

The Complete Reference Guide To Movies and Miniseries Made for TV and Cable 1984-1994

Published by:

Adams-Blake Publishing
8041 Sierra Street
Fair Oaks, CA 95628
(916) 962-9296

Copyright © 1994 by Maj Canton

First Printing 1994
Printed in the United States of America

ISBN 1-883422-44-2

Library of Congress Catalog Number: 94-78089

ABOUT THE AUTHOR

Maj Canton, the **"Queen of TV Movies,"** started her career as a TV comedy writer. She segued to independent longform production affiliated with Fries Entertainment Inc.,then served as Executive Director of Development at the Larry Thompson Organization.

She is now an independent producer, having recently completed a TV movie for ABC and is currently in development with a feature at Castle Rock Entertainment. Maj Canton has seen over 1,700 television movies and is currently under observation at the UCLA Neurospsychiatric Institute!

She lives in Los Angeles with her two VCRs.

ACKNOWLEDGEMENTS

I would like to thank the following people for their time, assistance and advice in putting this book together:

Alan N. Canton
Bennnet Cohen
Rean Luttrell
Jeff Meshel
Colleen Nihen

TABLE OF CONTENTS

NOTE:

THIS BOOK REQUIRED COUNTLESS HOURS TO COMPILE AND
EDIT. ALL THE LOG LINES WERE WRITTEN BY US, AND WE
TOOK EVERY CARE TO MAKE THEM REFLECT THE FLAVOR OF
THEIR RESPECTIVE MOVIES. FURTHERMORE, WE WOULD HAVE
LIKED TO HAVE INCLUDED EVERYONE INVOLVED WITH EACH
MOVIES LISTED IN THIS BOOK BUT BUDGETARY AND SPACE
CONSIDERATIONS PREVENTED US FROM DOING SO. PLEASE
LET US KNOW IF YOU SHOULD SPOT ANY ERRORS OR
OMISSIONS.

**IF YOU OR YOUR COMPANY WOULD LIKE SPECIFIC DATA
ANALYSIS OR CUSTOM REPORTS PLEASE CALL
(310)-823-1917 FOR RATES.**

Legend of Subject Matters and Abbreviations Used in This Book

ACTION/ADVENTURE
ADDICTION STORY- *Drugs, Alcohol, Food*
AMERICAN INDIANS
BIOGRAPHY
BLACK STORY
BUDDY STORY
CHILDREN/TEENS
COPS/DETECTIVES/LAW ENFORCEMENT
COURTROOM DRAMA
CROSS-CULTURAL STORY-*Involves people of different cultures, nationalities or religions*
DISASTER
DRUG SMUGGLING/DEALING
FAMILY DRAMA
FAMILY VIOLENCE
FARM STORY
FORBIDDEN LOVE- *Love stories involving social or moral conventions*
FOREIGN OR EXOTIC LOCATION
HISTORICAL PIECE
HOLIDAY SPECIAL
HOLLYWOOD
HOMOSEXUALITY
LOVE STORY
MAFIA/MOB
MAN AGAINST THE SYSTEM
MEDICAL/DISEASE/MENTAL ILLNESS
MURDER AND MURDER MYSTERY
NAZIS
PERIOD PIECE
POLITICAL PIECE

PRISON AND PRISON CAMP
PROSTITUTION
PSYCHOLOGICAL THRILLER
RAPE/MOLESTATION
ROMANTIC COMEDY
SCI-FI/SUPERNATURAL/HORROR/FANTASY
SERIES PILOT (2HR.)
SEX/GLITZ
SOCIAL ISSUE-*Adoption, Aging, Anti-Semitism, Child Abuse, Crime, Education, Forced Retirement, Gangs, Gun Control, Homelessness, Illiteracy, Inter-racial Marriage, Juvenile Delinquency, Legal System, Nuclear War, Racism, Teen Pregnancy, Terrorism, Suicide, Vigilantism, Wife Beating, and anything else of social importance.*
SPORTS
SUSPENSE THRILLER
TOXIC WASTE/ENVIRONMENTAL
TRUE CRIME
TRUE STORY
VIETNAM
WESTERN
WOMAN AGAINST THE SYSTEM
WOMAN IN JEOPARDY
WOMAN'S ISSUE/STORY-*Abortion, Abuse, Adultery, Babies, Career, Dating, Marriage, Divorce, Sexism, Health Care*
WORLD WAR II
YOUTH COMEDY

Abbreviations Used in This Book

IAW — *"In Association With"*

PROD. CO. — "Production Company"

A/C — "Against the Competition" - Ranks the movie as to how it performed against the programming on the opposite networks If a movie has an A/C of 1 then you know that the movie came in first against what was being aired during the same time period on the other networks. This information is only listed for movies from 1990-94 and covers only ABC, CBS, NBC, & FBC. If the movie aired multiple times, separate statistics are shown for each airing.

N/A — "Not applicable"

Section A

MOVIES

Movies & Miniseries
Listed Alphabetically

September 1, 1984 to September 1, 1994

AARON'S WAY — NBC
Drama: Family Drama • Man Against The System • Series Pilot (2 hr.) • Cross-Cultural Story • Farm Story
Airdate: 03/09/88
Rating: 19.5/31   A/C:

An Amish man and his family, who move to California to help his late son's pregnant girlfriend with her farming, must cope with the modern world.

Production Company: Blinn/Thorpe Prods. IAW Lorimar Telepictures
Executive Producer .... Jerry Thorpe
Executive Producer .... William Blinn
Producer .... Bonnie Raskin
Director .... Noel Nosseck
Writer .... Rena Down
Writer .... William Blinn
Cast .... Belinda Montgomery
Cast .... Jessica Walter
Cast .... Christopher Gartin
Cast .... Merlin Olsen

ABDUCTION OF KARI SWENSON, THE — NBC

Drama: Woman In Jeopardy • Suspense/Thriller • True Crime
Airdate: 03/08/87
Rating: 21.4/33   A/C:

Based on the true story of a biathlon champion who is abducted by two mountain men, wounded, then rescued. Eventually her captors are hunted down.

Production Company: NBC Prods. Inc.
Executive Producer .... Michael Manheim
Producer .... Andre R. Guttfreund
Director .... Stephen Gyllenhaal
Writer .... William Gray
Cast .... Tracy Pollan
Cast .... Joe Don Baker
Cast .... Ronny Cox

ABRAHAM — TNT
Miniseries/Drama: Historical Piece • Foreign or Exotic Location • Period Piece • Biography
Airdate: 4/3/94 • 4/4/94
Rating: N/A   A/C:

Abram, a shepherd persuades his wife Sar'ai and several others to follow him to the land of Canaan after he hears the voice of god telling him to lead his people and become "the father of nations." Along the way his faith is tested through various ordeals; a repugnant pharaoh, the destruction of Sodom and Gomorrah and his near-sacrifice of his eleven year old son Isaac.

Production Company: Lube Prods. IAW Lux, Betafilm Italiano, Turner Pictures
Executive Producer .... Gerald Rafshoon
Producer .... Lorenzo Minoli
Director .... Joseph Sargent
Writer .... Robert McKee
Cast .... Richard Harris
Cast .... Barbara Hershey
Cast .... Maximilian Schell
Cast .... Vittorio Gassman

ABSOLUTE STRANGERS — CBS
Drama: Man Against The System • Medical/Disease/ Mental Illness • True Story • Courtroom Drama • Social Issue
Airdate: 04/14/91
Rating: 17.7/29   A/C: 1

While his pregnant wife lingers in a coma, NYC businessman Marty Klein must battle hospital administrators, anti-abortion groups and his own conscience when he decides to terminate her pregnancy in order to save her life.

Production Company: Gilbert Cates Productions
Executive Producer .... Gilbert Cates
Producer .... Dennis Doty
Director .... Gilbert Cates
Writer .... Robert Anderson
Cast .... Henry Winkler
Cast .... Richard Kiley
Cast .... Karl Malden
Cast .... Patty Duke

ACCEPTABLE RISKS — ABC
Drama: Toxic Waste/Environmental • Social Issue
Airdate: 03/02/86
Rating: 9.7/15   A/C:

Inspired by the Bhopal tragedy. Disaster strikes an American city when corporate greed results in a calamitous chemical leak.

Production Company: ABC Circle Films
Producer .... R.W. Goodwin
Director .... Rick Wallace
Writer .... Norman Strum
Cast .... Brian Dennehy
Cast .... Kenneth McMillan
Cast .... Cicely Tyson
Cast .... Christine Ebersole

ACCIDENTAL MEETING — USA
Drama: Suspense/Thriller • Murder and Murder Mystery
Airdate: 3/17/94
Rating: N/A   A/C:

A women whose husband is cheating on her and another women whose boss is taking credit for her work, meet and fantasize about murdering the rotten men in their lives. Thinking it was only in fun, one of the women is shocked to find her boss dead and that she is now expected to return the favor and kill the philandering spouse.

Production Company: Wilshire Court Productions
Executive Producer .... Ed Milkovich
Producer .... Walter Klenhard
Director .... Michael Zinberg
Writer .... Pete Best
Writer .... Christopher Horner
Cast .... Linda Gray
Cast .... Linda Purl
Cast .... Leigh McCloskey
Cast .... Kent McCord

ACT OF VENGEANCE — HBO
Drama: True Crime • Man Against The System • Period Piece
Airdate: 4/20/86
Rating: N/A   A/C:

When popular United Mine Workers union official Jock Yablonski, from Clarsksville, Pennsylvania runs for the Presidency of the union against current corrupt boss, Tony Boyle, he becomes the target for assassination by a group of hand picked thugs. When Boyle wins the election is contested by the National Labor Relations Board. Yalbonski and his family are found murdered in their home over the 1969 Christmas holidays.

Production Company: Telepix Canada Corporation Prods.
Executive Producer .... Frank Konigsberg
Executive Producer .... Larry Sanitsky
Producer .... Jack Clements
Director .... John Mackenzie
Writer .... Scott Spencer
Cast .... Charles Bronson
Cast .... Ellen Burstyn
Cast .... Wilford Brimley
Cast .... Ellen Barkin

ADAM: HIS SONG CONTINUES — NBC
Drama: Family Drama • Man Against The System • True Crime • Children/Teens • Social Issue
Airdate: 09/06/86
Rating: 15.9/25   A/C:

Adam Walsh's father, John, throws himself into the cause of missing and abused children, to the detriment of his marriage.

Production Company: Landsburg Co.
Executive Producer .... Alan Landsburg
Executive Producer .... Joan Barnett
Producer .... Linda Otto
Director .... Robert Markowitz
Writer .... Oliver Hailey
Cast .... Daniel J. Travanti
Cast .... JoBeth Williams
Cast .... Richard Masur
Cast .... Lindsey Amelio

ADDICTED TO HIS LOVE — ABC
Drama: Love Story • Woman's Issue/Story
Airdate: 03/28/88
Rating: 18.1/29   A/C:

Past victims get together to take revenge against a parasitic confidence man who exploits women's loneliness to obtain their money and their love.

Production Company: Green/Epstein Prods. IAW Columbia Pictures
Executive Producer .... Jim Green
Executive Producer .... Allen Epstein
Producer .... Danielle Alexandra
Director .... Arthur Allan Seidelman
Writer .... Ronni Simon
Writer .... Richard Alfieri
Cast .... Barry Bostwick
Cast .... Polly Bergen
Cast .... Colleen Camp
Cast .... Erin Gray
Cast .... Linda Purl
Cast .... Dee Wallace Stone

ADRIFT — CBS

Drama: Suspense/Thriller • Foreign or Exotic
Location
Airdate: 4/13/93
Rating: 12.1/20   A/C: 2

A young married couple sailing on a dream vacation encounter two survivors on a sinking yacht. After they rescue the stranded pair, they must fight for their lives when the psychotic duo hijack their boat and plot to kill them.

Production Company: Atlantis Films Ltd. IAW
   WIC, Blue Andre Prods., CTV TV Network
Executive Producer .... Blue Andre
Executive Producer .... Ed Gernon
Executive Producer .... Peter Sussman
Producer .... Jonathan Goodwill
Director .... Christian Duguay
Writer .... Graham Flashner
Writer .... Ed Gernon
Cast .... Kate Jackson
Cast .... Bruce Greenwood
Cast .... Kenneth Welsh
Cast .... Kelly Rowan

ADVENTURES OF BRISCO COUNTY JR., THE — FBC

Comedy: Western • Series Pilot (2 hr.)
Airdate: 8/27/93
Rating: 7.2/14   A/C: 2

A mischievous bounty hunter with a Harvard law degree goes after the bad guys with his loyal sidekick Socrates, a priggish lawyer, and his devoted trick horse, Comet.

Production Company: Boam/Cuse Prods IAW
   Warners TV
Executive Producer .... Jeffrey Boam
Executive Producer .... Carlton Cuse
Co-Producer .... David Simkins
Co-Producer .... Paul Marks
Director .... Bryan Spicer
Writer .... Jeffrey Boam
Writer .... David Simkins
Writer .... Carlton Cuse
Cast .... Bruce Campbell
Cast .... Julius Carry
Cast .... John Astin
Cast .... Ann Tremko

AFTER THE PROMISE — CBS

Drama: Family Drama • Man Against The System •
Children/Teens • Period Piece
Airdate: 10/11/87
Rating: 19.2/30   A/C:

Fact-based drama of a 1930s California carpenter whose run-in with the welfare department led to an eight year fight to recover custody of his four sons.

Production Company: Tamara Asseyev Prods.
   IAW New World TV
Producer .... Tamara Asseyev
Director .... David Greene
Writer .... Robert W. Lenski
Cast .... Mark Harmon
Cast .... Diana Scarwid
Cast .... Rosemary Dunsmore
Cast .... Chance Michael Corbitt

AFTER THE SHOCK — USA

Drama: True Story • Disaster
Airdate: 09/12/90
Rating: N/A   A/C:

Reenactment of heroic deeds by firefighters, rescue workers and ordinary persons, following the October 17, 1989, earthquake in San Francisco.

Production Company: Wilshire Court Productions
Executive Producer .... Ross Albert
Executive Producer .... Gary Sherman
Producer .... Gary Sherman
Director .... Gary Sherman
Writer .... Gary Sherman
Cast .... Rue McClanahan
Cast .... Scott Valentine
Cast .... Jack Scalia
Cast .... Richard Crenna

AFTERBURN — HBO

Drama: Woman Against The System • True Story
Airdate: 05/30/92
Rating: N/A   A/C:

In 1982, an Air Force F-16 test pilot dies on a training mission. His widow, Janet Harduvel, stubbornly refuses to accept the government's finding of pilot error and sues General Dynamics, the plane's designer, to clear her husband's name.

Production Company: Steve Tisch Co.
Executive Producer .... Steve Tisch
Producer .... Paul Kurta
Director .... Robert Markowitz
Writer .... Elizabeth Chandler
Cast .... Laura Dern
Cast .... Robert Loggia
Cast .... Vincent Spano
Cast .... Michael Rooker

AFTERMATH: A TEST OF LOVE — CBS

Drama: Family Drama • Medical/Disease/Mental
Illness • True Story
Airdate: 03/10/91
Rating: 17.3/27   A/C: 1

Based on the book "Victim" by Gary Kinder. An emotionally detached physician must learn to love and help his family heal after a violent crime kills his wife and permanently disables his youngest son.

Production Company: Clandon/Interscope
Executive Producer .... Ted Field
Producer .... Judie Gregg
Producer .... Helena Hacker Rosenberg
Director .... Glenn Jordan
Writer .... Gregory Goodell
Cast .... Richard Chamberlain
Cast .... Michael Learned
Cast .... Zeljko Ivanek
Cast .... Denis Heames

AGAINST HER WILL: AN INCIDENT IN BALTIMORE — CBS

Drama: Medical/Disease/Mental Illness • Period
Piece • Courtroom Drama
Airdate: 01/19/92
Rating: 16.0/25   A/C: 1

In 1947, an uprooted small-town lawyer represents a woman wrongly imprisoned in a state-run mental hospital. He ultimately uncovers a fraudulent scandal and sues the State of Maryland.

Production Company: RHI Entertainment
Executive Producer .... Robert Halmi, Sr.
Producer .... Edwin Self
Director .... Delbert Mann
Writer .... Michael Norell
Writer .... James Norell
Cast .... Walter Matthau
Cast .... Harry Morgan
Cast .... Susan Blakely
Cast .... Brian Kerwin

AGAINST THE WALL — HBO

Drama: True Story • Prison and Prison Camp • Period
Piece • Black Story • Social Issue
Airdate: 3/26/94
Rating: N/A   A/C:

In 1971 New York, inmates at Attica prison rioted against the inhuman conditions and barbaric treatment they received by the brutal guards. One young neophyte guard is wounded and taken hostage during the uprising, refusing to cooperated with his captors. He soon forms a bond of moral courage with a black activist prisoner who tries to stop the bloodbath that resulted in the deaths of 32 convicts and 11 guards.

Production Company: Producers Entertainment
   Group
Executive Producer .... Jonathan Axelrod
Executive Producer .... Irwin Meyer
Executive Producer .... Harvey Bibicoff
Producer .... Steve McGlothen
Director .... John Frankenheimer
Writer .... Ron Hutchinson
Cast .... Kyle MacLachlan
Cast .... Samuel L. Jackson
Cast .... Clarence Williams III
Cast .... Frederic Forrest
Cast .... Harry Dean Stanton

AGATHA CHRISTIE'S DEAD MAN'S FOLLY CBS

Mystery: Murder and Murder Mystery • Cops/Detectives/Law Enforcement • Period Piece • Foreign or Exotic Location
Airdate: 01/08/86
Rating: 14.4/22   A/C:

Belgian detective Hercule Poirot solves all-too-real murders that stem from a murder game played by a clutch of eccentrics on an English estate.

Production Company: Warner Bros. TV
Producer .... Neil Hartley
Director .... Clive Donner
Writer .... Rod Browning
Cast .... Peter Ustinov
Cast .... Tim Pigott-Smith
Cast .... Jean Stapleton

AGATHA CHRISTIE'S MURDER IN THREE ACTS CBS

Mystery: Murder and Murder Mystery • Cops/Detectives/Law Enforcement • Period Piece • Foreign or Exotic Location
Airdate: 09/30/86
Rating: 15.4/25   A/C:

Inspector Poirot solves three murders in Acapulco.

Production Company: Warner Bros. TV
Producer .... Paul Waigner
Director .... Gary Nelson
Writer .... Scott Swanton
Cast .... Tony Curtis
Cast .... Emma Samms
Cast .... Diana Muldaur
Cast .... Peter Ustinov

AGATHA CHRISTIE'S THE MAN IN THE BROWN SUIT CBS

Mystery: Murder and Murder Mystery • Cops/Detectives/Law Enforcement • Action/Adventure • Foreign or Exotic Location
Airdate: 01/04/89
Rating: 15.8/25   A/C:

An American tourist in Egypt becomes involved in a mystery of murder and stolen diamonds aboard a cruise ship.

Production Company: Alan Shayne Prods. Inc. IAW Warner Bros. TV
Executive Producer .... Alan Shayne
Director .... Alan Grint
Writer .... Carla Jean Wagner
Cast .... Stephanie Zimbalist
Cast .... Tony Randall
Cast .... Rue McClanahan
Cast .... Ken Howard
Cast .... Edward Woodward

AGATHA CHRISTIE'S THIRTEEN AT DINNER CBS

Mystery: Murder and Murder Mystery • Cops/Detectives/Law Enforcement • Foreign or Exotic Location
Airdate: 10/19/85
Rating: 12.8/21   A/C:

Based on Agatha Christie's novel about Hercule Poirot's investigation of an English nobleman's murder by his actress wife.

Production Company: Warner Bros. TV
Producer .... Neil Hartley
Director .... Lou Antonio
Writer .... Rod Browning
Cast .... Peter Ustinov
Cast .... Faye Dunaway
Cast .... David Suchet
Cast .... Bill Nighy
Cast .... Diane Keen
Cast .... John Sride

ALAMO: 13 DAYS TO GLORY, THE NBC

Drama: Historical Piece • Western
Airdate: 01/26/87
Rating: 15.7/22   A/C:

Detailed dramatization of the Texans' last stand at the Alamo.

Production Company: Briggle, Hennessy, Carothers Prods. IAW Finnegan Co.
Executive Producer .... Stockton Briggle
Executive Producer .... Richard Carothers
Executive Producer .... Dennis D. Hennessy
Producer .... Bill Finnegan
Producer .... Pat Finnegan
Producer .... Sheldon Pinchuk
Director .... Burt Kennedy
Writer .... Clyde Ware
Writer .... Norman Morrill
Cast .... James Arness
Cast .... Raul Julia
Cast .... Brian Keith
Cast .... Alec Baldwin
Cast .... Lorne Greene

ALEX: THE LIFE OF A CHILD ABC

Drama: Family Drama • Children/Teens • Medical/Disease/Mental Illness • True Story
Airdate: 04/23/86
Rating: 21.7/36   A/C:

Famous sportswriter Frank Deford's true story of the brief life and times of his daughter who died at age eight of cystic fibrosis.

Production Company: Mandy Films
Executive Producer .... Leonard Goldberg
Producer .... Nigel McKeand
Director .... Robert Markowitz
Writer .... Nigel McKeand
Writer .... Carol Evan McKeand
Cast .... Craig T. Nelson
Cast .... Bonnie Bedelia

ALFRED HITCHCOCK PRESENTS NBC

Mystery: Suspense/Thriller • Psychological Thriller
Airdate: 05/05/85
Rating: 18.0/28   A/C:

Four updated episodes from the original show, prefaced by a colorized clip of an Alfred Hitchcock introduction: "Bang! You're Dead - An Unlocked Window - Incident in a Small Town - Man from the South."

Production Company: Universal TV
Executive Producer .... Christopher Crowe
Producer .... Alan Barnette
Producer .... Stephen Cragg
Director .... Steve De Jarnatt
Director .... Fred Walton
Director .... Joel Oliansky
Director .... Randa Haines
Writer .... Harold Swanton
Writer .... James Bridges
Writer .... Steve De Jarnatt
Writer .... Joel Olianski
Cast .... John Huston
Cast .... Melanie Griffith
Cast .... Kim Novak
Cast .... Annette O'Toole
Cast .... Ned Beatty

ALICE IN WONDERLAND CBS

Miniseries/Musical (2 nights): Sci-Fi/Supernatural/Horror/Fantasy
Airdate: 12/09/85 • 12/10/85
Rating: 21.2/31 • 16.8/25   A/C:

A musical retelling of the classic Lewis Carroll tale of Alice's adventures in Wonderland.

Production Company: Irwin Allen Prods. and Procter Gamble Prods. IAW Columbia TV
Producer .... Irwin Allen
Director .... Harry Harris
Writer .... Paul Zindel
Cast .... Natalie Gregory
Cast .... Sheila Allen
Cast .... Scott Baio
Cast .... Red Buttons
Cast .... Sid Caesar

ALONE IN THE NEON JUNGLE CBS

Drama: Cops/Detectives/Law Enforcement • Woman Against The System
Airdate: 01/17/88
Rating: 17.6/28   A/C:

A female police captain assigned to clean up a tough inner-city precinct runs into serious resistance from not only criminals but also her subordinates.

Production Company: Robert Halmi Inc.
Executive Producer .... Bill Brademan
Executive Producer .... Edwin Self
Producer .... Robert Halmi, Sr.
Director .... Georg Stanford Brown
Writer .... Mark Rodgers
Writer .... Stephen Downing
Cast .... Suzanne Pleshette
Cast .... Danny Aiello
Cast .... Frank Converse
Cast .... Georg Stanford Brown

Movies and Miniseries

ALWAYS REMEMBER I LOVE YOU — CBS

Drama: Family Drama • Children/Teens
Airdate: 12/23/90
Rating: 15.3/26   A/C: 1

An anguished teen learns he was kidnapped as an infant by a baby broker. He leaves his adoptive parents and, posing as a runaway, tries to fit in with his biological family.

Production Company: Gross-Weston Prods. IAW Stephen J. Cannell Prods.

Executive Producer	Marcy Gross
Executive Producer	Ann Weston
Producer	Diane Walsh
Director	Michael Miller
Writer	Vivienne Radkoff
Cast	Patty Duke
Cast	Stephen Dorff
Cast	Joan Van Ark
Cast	David Birney

AMELIA EARHART: THE FINAL FLIGHT — TNT

Drama: Biography • True Story • Period Piece • Historical Piece
Airdate: 6/12/94
Rating: N/A   A/C:

Based on the book, "Amelia Earhart: A Biography, by Doris L. Rich. The single-minded introvert from Kansas is transformed by her impresario husband into a media darling and hero after her 1928 Atlantic crossing, the first for a woman, in an airplane. In 1937 the legendary pilot vanished without a trace somewhere over the South Pacific- which to this day is one of this century's greatest mysteries.

Production Company: Avenue Pictures

Executive Producer	Randy Robinson
Producer	Cary Brokaw
Co-Producer	Joseph Kelly
Director	Yves Simoneau
Writer	Anna Sandor
Cast	Diane Keaton
Cast	Rutger Hauer
Cast	Bruce Dern

AMERICAN CLOCK, THE — TNT

Drama: Family Drama • Period Piece • Historical Piece
Airdate: 8/23/93
Rating: N/A   A/C:

Based on the play by Arthur Miller. An upper class, New York family faces economic disaster when the stock market crashes in 1929. Forced to sell their possessions and move in with relatives in Brooklyn they struggle to make ends meet. The son, unable to afford college or find work sets out on the road to chronicle the despair of the nation and the promise of FDR's New Deal.

Production Company: Amblin Ent., Michael Brandman Prods.

Executive Producer	Michael Brandman
Producer	Leanne Moore
Co-Producer	Steven Brandman
Director	Bob Clark
Writer	Frank Galati
Cast	Mary McDonnell
Cast	Darren McGavin
Cast	John Rubinstein
Cast	Loren Dean

AMERICAN GEISHA — CBS

Drama: Cross-Cultural Story • Love Story • True Story • Foreign or Exotic Location
Airdate: 09/11/86
Rating: 11.7/20   A/C:

Fact-based story of an American graduate student who becomes a Japanese geisha and falls in love with a Kabuki actor.

Production Company: Interscope Communications IAW Stonehenge Prods.

Executive Producer	Dick Berg
Executive Producer	Ted Field
Producer	Richard L. O'Connor
Director	Lee Philips
Writer	Judith P. Mitchell
Cast	Robert Ito
Cast	Pam Dawber
Cast	Beulah Quo
Cast	Dorothy McGuire

AMERICAN HARVEST — CBS

Drama: Farm Story • Man Against The System
Airdate: 01/16/87
Rating: 16.4/27   A/C:

A wheat farmer who loses his own crop tries to keep his farm by harvesting for others.

Production Company: Finnegan & Associates

Producer	Ron Roth
Director	Dick Lowry
Writer	Bill Stratton
Cast	John Anderson
Cast	Wayne Rogers
Cast	Earl Holliman
Cast	Jay Kerr

AMERICAN STORY, AN — CBS

Drama: Man Against The System • Period Piece • Political Piece • WWII
Airdate: 11/29/92
Rating: 12.7/20   A/C: 2

Upon returning to their small Texas town, a World War II veteran and his two buddies fight corruption and racism by running for mayor against the greedy town boss and his repugnant sheriff. Challenging the status quo has its price as the town erupts in violence.

Production Company: Signboard Hill Prods. IAW RHI Ent.

Executive Producer	Robert Halmi, Sr.
Co-Producer	Judith Feldman
Co-Producer	Sarah Gallagher
Executive Producer	John Gray
Writer	John Gray
Cast	Brad Johnson
Cast	Kathleen Quinlan
Cast	Tom Sizemore
Cast	Lisa Blount

AMERIKA — ABC

Miniseries/Drama (7 nights): Man Against The System • Suspense/Thriller • Political Piece • Social Issue
Airdate: 02/15/87 • 02/16/87 • 02/17/87 • 02/18/87 • 02/19/87
Rating: 24.7/38 • 20.9/31 • 17.7/26 • 17.8/28 • 15.6/23   A/C:

In 1997, ten years after the Soviet invasion of the U.S., an anti-war activist is released from a concentration camp and inspires a rebellion against the Soviet occupation and the American collaborators.

Production Company: ABC Circle Films

Executive Producer	Donald Wrye
Producer	Richard L. O'Connor
Co-Producer	John Lugar
Director	Donald Wrye
Writer	Donald Wrye
Cast	Mariel Hemingway
Cast	Kris Kristofferson
Cast	Dorian Harewood
Cast	Christine Lahti
Cast	Robert Urich
Cast	Sam Neill
Cast	Cindy Pickett

AMITYVILLE: THE EVIL ESCAPES   NBC
Drama: Suspense/Thriller • Sci-Fi/Supernatural/
Horror/Fantasy
Airdate: 05/12/89
Rating: 8.6/16   A/C:

The satanic evil escapes the famous Amityville house via a lamp which is sent to a family in California. The forces wreak havoc and horror until a priest comes to their aid with an exorcism.

Production Company: Steve White Prods. IAW
    Spectacor Films

Executive Producer .... Steve White
Producer .... Barry Bernardi
Director .... Sandor Stern
Writer .... Sandor Stern
Cast .... Patty Duke
Cast .... Frederic Lehne
Cast .... Norman Lloyd
Cast .... Jane Wyatt

AMOS   CBS
Mystery: Murder and Murder Mystery • Man Against
The System • Suspense/Thriller
Airdate: 09/29/85
Rating: 24.5/37   A/C:

A recent arrival to a nursing home begins to suspect that one of the nurses is murdering the elderly patients.

Production Company: Bryna Co. Prods. IAW
    Vincent Pictures Inc.

Executive Producer .... Peter Douglas
Producer .... Bill Finnegan
Producer .... Sheldon Pinchuk
Director .... Michael Tuchner
Writer .... Richard Kramer
Cast .... Kirk Douglas
Cast .... Elizabeth Montgomery
Cast .... Dorothy McGuire
Cast .... Pat Morita

AMY FISHER: MY STORY   NBC
Drama: Children/Teens • True Crime
Airdate: 12/28/92
Rating: 19.1/30   A/C: 2

Long Island, New York teenager, Amy Fisher, is accused of shooting Mary Jo Buttafuoco, the wife of car mechanic Joey Buttafuoco, who she claimed was her lover for ten months. She is ultimately convicted of attempted murder.

Note: See ABC TV Movie- "Beyond Control and the CBS TV Movie -"Casualties of Love"

Production Company: KLM, Spectacor Films IAW
    Michael Jaffe Films

Executive Producer .... Michael Jaffe
Executive Producer .... Alfred R. Kelman
Producer .... Howard Braunstein
Producer .... Phil Levitan
Co-Producer .... Christine Lynch
Co-Producer .... John Danylkiw
Director .... Bradford May
Writer .... Phil Penningroth
Cast .... Ed Marinaro
Cast .... Noelle Parker
Cast .... Boyd Kestner

AN EARLY FROST   NBC
Drama: Family Drama • Medical/Disease/Mental
Illness • Homosexuality
Airdate: 11/11/85
Rating: 23.3/33   A/C:

When a young Chicago lawyer learns he has AIDS, he goes home to his parents and reveals his homosexuality. His mother helps him through the pain of his illness while his father struggles with his own homophobia.

Production Company: NBC Prods.

Producer .... Perry Lafferty
Co-Producer .... Art Seidel
Director .... John Erman
Writer .... Ron Cowen
Writer .... Daniel Lipman
Cast .... Gena Rowlands
Cast .... Ben Gazzara
Cast .... Sylvia Sidney
Cast .... Aidan Quinn

ANASTASIA: THE MYSTERY OF ANNA   NBC
Miniseries/Drama (2 nights): True Story • Period
Piece • Foreign or Exotic Location • Biography •
Historical Piece
Airdate: 12/07/86 • 12/08/86
Rating: 20.7/32 • 20.9/32   A/C:

True story of Anna Anderson, who strove for over three decades to be acknowledged as the Grand Duchess Anastasia, daughter of the last Russian Tsar, Nicholas II.

Production Company: Telecom Entertainment Inc.

Executive Producer .... Michael Lepiner
Executive Producer .... Ken Kaufman
Producer .... Marvin J. Chomsky
Director .... Marvin J. Chomsky
Writer .... James Goldman
Cast .... Claire Bloom
Cast .... Edward Fox
Cast .... Amy Irving
Cast .... Rex Harrison
Cast .... Susan Lucci

AND THE BAND PLAYED ON   HBO
Drama: Medical/Disease/Mental Illness • Political
Piece • True Story • Homosexuality • Social Issue
Airdate: 9/11/93
Rating: N/A   A/C:

Based on the book by Randy Shilts. In 1981, Dr. Don Francis a devoted medical researcher at the Center For Disease Control battles bureaucratic indifference as he and his team of investigators try to identify a mysterious new ailment that seems to affect gay men. As the AIDS epidemic spreads, egotistical Dr. Robert Gallo of the National Institute of Health competes with the French researchers for the right to be the first to isolate the virus. As the crisis escalates the government reluctantly acknowledges the problem but it is way too late for so many innocent victims.

Production Company: HBO Pictures

Executive Producer .... Aaron Spelling
Executive Producer .... E. Duke Vincent
Producer .... Midge Sanford
Producer .... Sarah Pillsbury
Co-Producer .... Arnold Schulman
Co-Producer .... Edward Teets
Director .... Roger Spottiswoode
Writer .... Arnold Schulman
Cast .... Matthew Modine
Cast .... Alan Alda
Cast .... Patrick Bauchau
Cast .... Ian McKellen

AND THE SEA WILL TELL   CBS
Miniseries/Drama (2 nights): Murder and Murder
Mystery • True Crime • Courtroom Drama • Foreign
or Exotic Location
Airdate: 02/24/91 • 02/26/91
Rating: 20.1/31 • 19.0/29   A/C: 1 • 1

From the book by Vincent Bugliosi and Bruce Henderson. When new evidence arises in an unsolved murder case, famed attorney Bugliosi defends Jennifer Jenkins and her lover, who have been accused of murdering a wealthy couple on a South Pacific Island.

Production Company: Green/Epstein IAW
    Columbia Pictures Television

Executive Producer .... Jim Green
Executive Producer .... Allen Epstein
Producer .... Matthew O'Connor
Director .... Tommy Lee Wallace
Writer .... James S. Henerson
Cast .... Richard Crenna
Cast .... Rachel Ward
Cast .... Hart Bochner
Cast .... James Brolin

... AND THEN SHE WAS GONE   NBC

Drama: Suspense/Thriller • Children/Teens
Airdate: 09/29/91
Rating: 11.7/19   A/C: 3

A self-involved business executive gets caught up in a mother's search for her kidnapped daughter when he inadvertently spots the child on a subway train.

Production Company: Steve White Prods. IAW
     Spectator

Executive Producer	Steve White
Executive Producer	Barry Bernardi
Producer	Chris DeFaria
Director	David Greene
Writer	Matthew Bombeck
Cast	Robert Urich
Cast	Megan Gallagher
Cast	Brett Cullen

AND THEN THERE WAS ONE
LIFETIME

Drama: True Story • Medical/Disease/Mental Illness • Family Drama
Airdate: 3/9/94
Rating: N/A   A/C:

Los Angeles Television writers, Roxy and Vinnie Ventola face the greatest tragedy when they and their infant daughter are diagnosed with AIDS. They try to live each day to the fullest but when first the baby dies and then her husband, Roxy must find the strength to make sense of her loss and fight for political awareness of the disease.

Production Company: Freyda Rothstein Prods.
     IAW Hearst Entertainment Prods.

Executive Producer	Freyda Rothstein
Producer	Angela Bromstad
Director	David Jones
Writer	Rama Laurie Stagner
Cast	Amy Madigan
Cast	Dennis Boutsikaris
Cast	Jane Daly
Cast	Steven Flynn

ANGEL IN GREEN   CBS

Drama: Woman In Jeopardy • Forbidden Love • Foreign or Exotic Location
Airdate: 09/22/87
Rating: 13.1/22   A/C:

A versatile nun doing good works on a South Sea island runs up against a Green Beret captain who arrives to put down a rebellion. Along the way, they fall in love and her faith is tested.

Production Company: Taft Entertainment

Producer	Harry R. Sherman
Director	Marvin J. Chomsky
Writer	Michael Patrick Goodman
Cast	Bruce Boxleitner
Cast	Susan Dey

ANGEL OF DEATH   CBS

Drama: Murder and Murder Mystery • Woman In Jeopardy • Psychological Thriller
Airdate: 10/02/90
Rating: 10.8/18   A/C: 3

A psychotic escapes from prison so he can pursue a beautiful woman and her six-year-old son. He charms his way into their life, destroying anything or anyone that threatens his delusions of family bliss.

Production Company: Once Upon A Time Films

Executive Producer	Stanley Brooks
Producer	R.J. Louis
Producer	Paul Boorstin
Producer	Sharon Boorstin
Director	Bill L. Norton
Writer	Paul Boorstin
Writer	Sharon Boorstin
Cast	Gregory Harrison
Cast	Jane Seymour
Cast	Brian Bonsall
Cast	Grand L. Bush

ANN JILLIAN STORY, THE   NBC

Drama: Medical/Disease/Mental Illness • True Story • Woman's Issue/Story • Hollywood • Biography
Airdate: 01/04/88
Rating: 23.8/35   A/C:

True story of the singer-actress's career, with emphasis on her traumatic double mastectomy and the down-to-earth husband who stood by her.

Production Company: 9J Inc. Prods. IAW ITC

Executive Producer	Andrea Baynes
Producer	Peter Thompson
Director	Corey Allen
Writer	Audrey Davis Levin
Cast	Ann Jillian
Cast	Viveca Lindfors
Cast	Tony Lo Bianco
Cast	Kate Lynch

ANNA KARENINA   CBS

Drama: Love Story • Period Piece • Historical Piece • Foreign or Exotic Location
Airdate: 03/26/85
Rating: 16.6/26   A/C:

Based on Tolstoy's classic novel about an aristocratic 19th century Russian woman who gives up her family and respectability for the love of a dashing soldier.

Production Company: Colgems Prods. & Rastar

Executive Producer	Doreen Bergesen
Producer	Simon Langton
Director	Simon Langton
Writer	James Goldman
Cast	Christopher Reeve
Cast	Paul Scofield
Cast	Ian Ogilvy
Cast	Anna Massey
Cast	Jacqueline Bisset

ANNIHILATOR, THE   NBC

Drama: Action/Adventure • Series Pilot (2 hr.) • Sci-Fi/Supernatural/Horror/Fantasy
Airdate: 04/07/86
Rating: 14.1/23   A/C:

Only a newspaper reporter can save the world from an invasion of space creatures who take over the bodies of their victims.

Production Company: Universal TV

Executive PRODUCER	Roderick Taylor
Director	Michael Chapman
Writer	Bruce A. Taylor
Writer	Roderick Taylor
Cast	Susan Blakely
Cast	Lisa Blount
Cast	Mark Lindsay Chapman

ANOTHER PAIR OF ACES: THREE OF A KIND   CBS

Drama: Cops/Detectives/Law Enforcement • Western • Buddy Story
Airdate: 04/09/91
Rating: 9.9/17   A/C: 3

A gritty Texas ranger and a wise-ass con-man bust a ring of vigilantes and save a friend from a murder rap.

Production Company: Pedernales Films IAW
     Once Upon A Time Films

Executive Producer	Stanley Brooks
Executive Producer	Willie Nelson
Producer	Cyrus Yavneh
Co-Executive Producer	Bud Shrake
Co-Executive Producer	Gary Cartwright
Director	Bill Bixby
Writer	Rob Gilmer
Cast	Willie Nelson
Cast	Kris Kristofferson
Cast	Joan Severance
Cast	Rip Torn

ANYTHING TO SURVIVE   ABC

Drama: Family Drama • True Story • Foreign or Exotic Location • Action/Adventure
Airdate: 02/05/90
Rating: 16.5/26   A/C: 1

Based on the book "Almost Too Late" by Elmo Wortman. Inspiring story of a family's struggle to survive in the Alaskan Wilderness after their boat is capsized in a storm.

Production Company: Saban/Scherick - ATL
     Production IAW B.C. Films

Executive Producer	Edgar J. Scherick
Executive Producer	Haim Saban
Producer	Nick Gillott
Director	Zale Dalen
Writer	Jonathan Rintels
Cast	Robert Conrad
Cast	Emily Perkins
Cast	Matthew LeBlanc
Cast	Ocean Hellman

APOLOGY   HBO

Drama: Suspense/Thriller
Airdate: 7/27/86
Rating: N/A   A/C:

In the New York city artist community of Soho, a sculptress whose experiment in taping anonymous telephone confessions as part of a new art project brings her into deadly contact with a psychotic killer when he confesses his crimes into her answering machine. She soon becomes his next target. With the help of a a thick-skinned homicide detective she is saved from the malignant misogynist.

Production Company: Roger Gimbel Prod. IAW
   Peregrine Entertainment, LTD. IAW A.S.A.P
   Prods.
Executive Producer .... Roger Gimbel
Producer .... Richard Parks
Producer .... Richard Smith
Producer .... Les Alexander
Director .... Robert Bierman
Writer .... Mark Medoff
Cast .... Lesley Ann Warren
Cast .... Peter Weller
Cast .... John Glover

APPEARANCES   NBC

Drama: Family Drama • Series Pilot (2 hr.)
Airdate: 06/17/90
Rating: 9.8/18   A/C: 3

A seemingly normal Ohio family is actually torn apart by feuds, embezzlement in the family business and acrimony stemming from the death of one twin son caused by his grandfather, the patriarch.

Production Company: Walt DISNEY Television
Executive Producer .... William Blinn
Producer .... Frank Fischer
Director .... Win Phelps
Writer .... William Blinn
Cast .... Scott Paulin
Cast .... Ernest Borgnine
Cast .... Wendy Phillips
Cast .... James Handy

APRIL MORNING   CBS

Drama: Children/Teens • Period Piece • Historical
Piece
Airdate: 04/24/88
Rating: 15.2/24   A/C:

Based on Howard Fast's novel. The events surrounding the Revolutionary War's "shot heard 'round the world" in Lexington, 1775, as seen through the maturing experiences of a 15-year-old youth.

Production Company: Samuel Goldwyn Co./
   Robert Halmi Inc.
Executive Producer .... Robert Halmi, Sr.
Executive Producer .... Samuel Goldwyn, Jr.
Producer .... Robert Halmi, Jr.
Producer .... Delbert Mann
Director .... Delbert Mann
Writer .... James Lee Barrett
Cast .... Robert Urich
Cast .... Chad Lowe
Cast .... Susan Blakely
Cast .... Rip Torn
Cast .... Tommy Lee Jones

ARCH OF TRIUMPH   CBS

Drama: Love Story • Period Piece • Foreign or Exotic
Location • WWII
Airdate: 05/29/85
Rating: 9.2/16   A/C:

Remake of the 1948 film, and based on Erich Maria Remarque's classic World War II novel about the Parisian love affair between a German doctor dedicated to helping Jews and the emotionally fragile cabaret singer he saves from suicide.

Production Company: Newland-Raynor Prods.
Executive Producer .... Milton T. Raynor
Executive Producer .... Patrick Dromgoole
Producer .... John Newland
Producer .... Mort Abrahamson
Director .... Waris Hussein
Writer .... Charles Israel
Cast .... Anthony Hopkins
Cast .... Lesley-Anne Down
Cast .... Colleen Nihen

ARCHIE: TO RIVERDALE AND BACK
AGAIN   NBC

Comedy: Buddy Story • Series Pilot (2 hr.)
Airdate: 05/06/90
Rating: 10.6/17   A/C: 3

Archie, Jughead, Betty, and Veronica attend their 15-year high school reunion, still supervised by Mr. Weatherbee and Miss Grundy. But life is no longer simple. Divorce, careers and single parenthood have affected our once carefree crew.

Production Company: Patchett- Kaufman
   Entertainment IAW DIC
Executive Producer .... Ken Kaufman
Executive Producer .... Tom Patchett
Executive Producer .... Andy Heyward
Producer .... Graham Cottle
Director .... Dick Lowry
Writer .... Evan Katz
Cast .... Christopher Rich
Cast .... Lauren Holly
Cast .... Karen Kopins
Cast .... James Noble

ARE YOU LONESOME TONIGHT?   USA

Drama: Cops/Detectives/Law Enforcement •
Suspense/Thriller
Airdate: 01/22/92
Rating: N/A   A/C:

When her husband disappears, a wealthy socialite suspects foul play when she discovers he had a long relationship with a phone sex operator. She hires a cocky detective and together they unravel the mystery.

Production Company: OTML Productions Inc.
   IAW Wilshire Court
Executive Producer .... James E. Mahoney, Jr.
Producer .... Gordon Wolf
Director .... E.W. Swackhamer
Writer .... Wesley Moore
Cast .... Jane Seymour
Cast .... Parker Stevenson
Cast .... Beth Broderick
Cast .... Joel Brooks

ARMED & INNOCENT   CBS

Drama: Family Drama • True Crime • Children/Teens
Airdate: 1/4/94
Rating: 14.9/24   A/C: 2

An eleven year old boy, home alone, guns down two career criminals when they break into his home. He is hailed as a hero especially by his macho father who fails to see the emotional damage done to his frightened son. Suffering from post-traumatic stress syndrome the boy is eventually helped by a empathic Vietnam vet who forces the family to deal honestly with the situation.

Production Company: Gillian Prods. IAW
   Republic Pictures
Executive Producer .... Chuck McLain
Executive Producer .... Christy Welker
Executive Producer .... Kathryn Wallack
Executive Producer .... Barney Cohen
Co-Executive Producer .... Tim Hill
Co-Executive Producer .... Danielle Hill
Producer .... William Beaudine Jr.
Director .... Jack Bender
Writer .... Danielle Hill
Cast .... Gerald McRaney
Cast .... Kate Jackson
Cast .... Andrew Starnes
Cast .... Cotter Smith

AROUND THE WORLD IN 80 DAYS   NBC

Miniseries/Drama (3 nights): Action/Adventure •
Historical Piece • Period Piece • Foreign or Exotic
Location
Airdate: 04/16/89 • 04/17/89 • 04/18/89
Rating: 15.5/24 • 13.2/21 • 13.0/21   A/C:

In this new telling of Jules Verne's story, a wealthy Londoner accepts a bet that he can circle the world in 80 days. While doing so he encounters incredible adventures and even finds himself chased by detectives who think he's a bank thief.

Production Company: Harmony Gold Prods. IAW
   Valente/Baerwald Prods.
Executive Producer .... Renee Valente
Executive Producer .... Paul Baerwald
Co-Producer .... Danielle Lorenzang
Co-Producer .... Frank Agrama
Director .... Buzz Kulik
Writer .... John Gray
Cast .... Pierce Brosnan
Cast .... Julia Nickson
Cast .... Peter Ustinov
Cast .... Henry Gibson
Cast .... John Hillerman
Cast .... Erik Idle

ARTHUR THE KING   CBS
Drama: Action/Adventure • Sci-Fi/Supernatural/
Horror/Fantasy
Airdate: 04/26/85
Rating: 9.5/17   A/C:

An American tourist visiting Stonehenge travels
back in time 1000 years and encounters the
wizard Merlin as well as the rest of King
Arthur's court.

Production Company: Martin Poll Prods. IAW
    Comworld Prods.
Producer .... Martin Poll
Director .... Clive Donner
Writer .... J. David Wyles
Cast .... Malcolm McDowell
Cast .... Candice Bergen
Cast .... Edward Woodward
Cast .... Dyan Cannon

AS SUMMERS DIE   HBO
Drama: Family Drama • Period Piece • Courtroom
Drama
Airdate: 5/18/86
Rating: N/A   A/C:

Based on the novel by Winston Groom. In 1959,
in a small Louisiana town a sympathetic lawyer
takes on the case of and elderly black women
whose property is being stolen out from under
her by the town's wealthiest family. Believing
that the real estate was deeded to her by the
late family patriarch he sets out to uncover the
secrets that have been kept hidden for over thirty
years.

Production Company: Chris-Rose/Baldwin/
    Aldrich Productions IAW Telepictures
Executive Producer .... Frank Konigsberg
Executive Producer .... Larry Sanitsky
Producer .... Bob Christiansen
Producer .... Richard Rosenberg
Co-Producer .... Peter Baldwin
CO-Producer .... Richard Aldrich
Director .... Jean-Cluade Tramont
Writer .... Jeff Andrus
Cast .... Scott Glenn
Cast .... Jamie Lee Curtis
Cast .... Bette Davis
Cast .... Bea Richards

ASSASSIN   CBS
Drama: Suspense/Thriller • Action/Adventure • Sci-
Fi/Supernatural/Horror/Fantasy
Airdate: 03/19/86
Rating: 14.1/23   A/C:

A retired U.S. spy and a young female college
professor battle a high-tech killer robot.

Production Company: Sankan Prods. Inc.
Executive Producer .... Sandor Stern
Producer .... Neil T. Maffeo
Director .... Sandor Stern
Writer .... Sandor Stern
Cast .... Robert Conrad
Cast .... Ben Frank
Cast .... Robert Webber
Cast .... Karen Austin

ASSAULT AND MATRIMONY   NBC
Comedy: Romantic Comedy
Airdate: 09/28/87
Rating: 20.2/32   A/C:

A meek accountant and his dominating wife, in
conflict over the sale of an expensive house,
repeatedly try to murder each other.

Production Company: NBC Prods. Inc.
Executive Producer .... Michael Filerman
Producer .... Karen Moore
Director .... James Frawley
Writer .... John Binder
Cast .... Jill Eikenberry
Cast .... Michael Tucker
Cast .... Michelle Phillips
Cast .... Joe Cortese
Cast .... John Hillerman

ASSAULT AT WEST POINT SHOWTIME
Drama: Black Story • True Story • Period Piece •
Courtroom Drama
Airdate: 2/27/94
Rating: N/A   A/C:

Based on the book "The Court-Martial of
Johnson Whittaker" by John F. Marzalek. In
1880, black West Point cadet, Johnson
Whittaker, is court martialled for mutilating
himself in order to avoid taking a final exam.
His defense attorneys contend that he was
attacked by racist upperclassman and that the
academy covered up the crime to protect it's
own reputation.

Production Company: Ultra Ent. IAW Mosaic
    Group Inc.
Executive Producer .... Bob Rubin
Executive Producer .... Bill Siegler
Producer .... Harry Moses
Director .... Harry Moses
Writer .... Harry Moses
Cast .... Samuel L. Jackson
Cast .... Sam Waterston
Cast .... Seth Gilliam
Cast .... John Glover

AT MOTHER'S REQUEST   CBS
Miniseries/Drama (2 nights): True Crime • Children/
Teens • Family Violence • Murder and Murder
Mystery
Airdate: 01/04/87 • 01/06/87
Rating: 23.3/35 • 22.7/35   A/C:

Fact-based drama of a socially prominent
woman, Frances Schreuder, who induced her
son to murder her father for his money.

Production Company: Vista Films
Executive Producer .... Gabriel Katzka
Executive Producer .... Bob Markell
Producer .... Christopher Morgan
Director .... Michael Tuchner
Writer .... Richard DeLong Adams
Cast .... Stefanie Powers
Cast .... Corey Parker
Cast .... Doug McKeon
Cast .... Frances Sternhagen
Cast .... E.G. Marshall
Cast .... John Woods

ATLANTA CHILD MURDERS, THE   CBS
Miniseries/Drama (2 nights): Cops/Detectives/Law
Enforcement • True Crime • Courtroom Drama •
Black Story • Murder and Murder Mystery
Airdate: 02/10/85 • 02/12/85
Rating: 21.8/31 • 20.9/31   A/C:

Fact based story of the investigation and trial
of Wayne Williams, the accused killer of thirteen
black children in Atlanta.

Production Company: Gerald Rafshoon Comm. &
    Abby Mann Prods. IAW Finnegan Assocs.
Executive Producer .... Abby Mann
Executive Producer .... Gerald Rafshoon
Producer .... Bill Finnegan
Producer .... Sheldon Pinchuk
Director .... John Erman
Writer .... Abby Mann
Cast .... James Earl Jones
Cast .... Rip Torn
Cast .... Morgan Freeman
Cast .... Lynne Moody
Cast .... Jason Robards
Cast .... Martin Sheen

ATTACK OF THE 50FT. WOMAN   HBO
Drama: Sci-Fi/Supernatural/Horror/Fantasy
Airdate: 12/11/93
Rating: N/A   A/C:

Remake of the 1958 B movie. A passive and
obedient housewife who lets her philandering
husband and manipulative father run her life
seeks revenge when she is grows to fifty feet
tall after an encounter with a UFO.

Production Company: HBO Pictures IAW Warner
    Bros.
Executive Producer .... Joseph Dougherty
Producer .... Debra Hill
Co-Producer .... Chuck Binder
Co-Producer .... Daryl Hannah
Director .... Christopher Guest
Writer .... Joseph Dougherty
Cast .... Daryl Hannah
Cast .... Daniel Baldwin
Cast .... William Windom
Cast .... Frances Fisher

ATTACK ON FEAR   CBS
Drama: Man Against The System • Woman Against
The System • True Story • Social Issue
Airdate: 10/10/84
Rating: 10.9/16   A/C:

Based on a true story about a married couple,
both journalists, who win a Pulitzer prize for
their expose on the controversial policies of a
Synanon drug rehabilitation center.

Production Company: Tomorrow Entertainment
Executive Producer .... Thomas W. Moore
Executive Producer .... John D. Backe
Executive Producer .... Phillip D. Fehrle
Producer .... Herbert Hirschman
Director .... Mel Damski
Writer .... T.S. Cook
Cast .... Paul Michael Glaser
Cast .... Linda Kelsey
Cast .... Kevin Conway

ATTIC: THE HIDING OF ANNE FRANK, THE — CBS

Drama: Period Piece • True Story • WWII • Nazis
Airdate: 04/17/88
Rating: 11.5/19   A/C:

The true story of a Catholic woman, Miep Gies, who was instrumental in sheltering Jews from the Nazis in Holland, among them Anne Frank.

Production Company: Telecom Entertainment Inc.
Executive Producer .... Michael Lepiner
Executive Producer .... Ken Kaufman
Co-Executive Producer .... David Cunliffe
Co-Executive Producer .... William Hanley
Producer .... Marjorie Kalins
Producer .... Timothy J. Fee
Producer .... Nick Gillott
Director .... John Erman
Writer .... William Hanley
Cast .... Mary Steenburgen
Cast .... Miriam Karlin
Cast .... Paul Scofield
Cast .... Ronald Pickup

AURORA — NBC

Drama: Love Story • Medical/Disease/Mental Illness • Foreign or Exotic Location
Airdate: 10/22/84
Rating: 18.0/28   A/C:

In an effort to raise money for a sight restoring operation, an Italian woman contacts men from her past and tells each one of them that they fathered her eleven year old blind son. She ends up falling in love with one of them, a lonely American.

Production Company: Roger Gimbel Prods. for Peregrine Prod. Group IAW Sacis S.P.A Roma
Executive Producer .... Roger Gimbel
Executive Producer .... Tony Converse
Producer .... Alex Ponti
Director .... Maurizio Ponti
Writer .... John McGreevey
Writer .... Franco Terrini
Writer .... Gianni Menon
Writer .... Maurizio Ponti
Cast .... Daniel J. Travanti
Cast .... Sophia Loren
Cast .... Edoardo Ponti

BABE RUTH — NBC

Drama: Period Piece • Sports • Biography
Airdate: 10/06/91
Rating: 10.0/16   A/C: 2

Baseball slugger Babe Ruth's life from his early years as an orphan to his glory days with the Boston Red Sox and the New York Yankees from 1914 to 1935.

Production Company: A Lyttle Production Co.
Executive Producer .... Lawrence Lyttle
Producer .... Frank Pace
Director .... Mark Tinker
Writer .... Michael De Guzman
Cast .... Stephen Lang
Cast .... Bruce Weitz
Cast .... Donald Moffat
Cast .... Lisa Zane

BABES IN TOYLAND — NBC

Musical: Holiday Special
Airdate: 12/19/86
Rating: 13.4/22   A/C:

Adaptation of the classic Victor Herbert fantasy operetta in which a young girl is transported to the magical Toyland.

Production Company: Finnegan-Pinchuk Co. IAW Orion TV
Executive Producer .... Sheldon Pinchuk
Executive Producer .... Pat Finnegan
Executive Producer .... Bill Finnegan
Producer .... Tony Ford
Producer .... Neil T. Maffeo
Director .... Clive Donner
Writer .... Paul Zindel
Cast .... Drew Barrymore
Cast .... Richard Mulligan
Cast .... Pat Morita

BABIES — NBC

Drama: Woman's Issue/Story
Airdate: 09/17/90
Rating: 13.5/22   A/C: 3

Three close female friends face the controversies of single parenthood, modern fertilization techniques, and in utero surgery, respectively, as they each strive to have a child.

Production Company: Indieprod Co. & Hearst Entertainment
Executive Producer .... Bruce J. Sallan
Executive Producer .... Lynn Roth
Producer .... Helena Hacker Rosenberg
Producer .... Frank Swertlow
Director .... Michael Rhodes
Writer .... Lynn Roth
Cast .... Lindsay Wagner
Cast .... Dinah Manoff
Cast .... Marcy Walker
Cast .... Adam Arkin

BABY BROKERS — NBC

Drama: True Crime • Woman's Issue/Story • Children/Teens • Social Issue
Airdate: 2/21/94
Rating: 11.4/17   A/C: 2

Debbie Freeman, a single psychologist in her forties is desperate to adopt a baby. Through a classified ad she unknowing becomes the pawn of opportunists who agree to give up their yet unborn baby when she agrees to pay all their living expenses. When the drifters take off she uncovers their scam which had them stringing along and extorting money from numerous couples around the country. Working with the police she eventually brings them to justice.

Production Company: Steinhardt Baer Pictures, bbk Prods. IAW Columbia Pictures TV
Executive Producer .... Robert Dalrymple
Executive Producer .... Craig Anderson
Co-Executive Producer .... Joseph Plager
Producer .... Boris Malden
Co-Producer .... Susan Nanus
Director .... Mimi Leder
Writer .... Susan Nanus
Cast .... Cybil Shepherd
Cast .... Nina Siemaszko
Cast .... Anna Maria Horsford
Cast .... Jeffrey Nordling

BABY GIRL SCOTT — CBS

Drama: Man Against The System • Children/Teens • Medical/Disease/Mental Illness • Social Issue
Airdate: 05/24/87
Rating: 13.2/23   A/C:

Parents face the devastating human and financial cost of caring for an extremely premature baby.

Production Company: Polson Co. Prods. and Finnegan/Pinchuk Co.
Executive Producer .... Beth Polson
Producer .... Nick Lombardo
Director .... John Korty
Writer .... Christopher Knopf
Cast .... John Lithgow
Cast .... Mary Beth Hurt
Cast .... Mimi Kennedy
Cast .... Linda Kelsey

BABY M — ABC

Miniseries/Drama (2 nights): Family Drama • True Story • Children/Teens • Social Issue
Airdate: 05/22/88 • 05/23/88
Rating: 15.0/24 • 17.6/27   A/C:

True story of Mary Beth Whitehead, who reneged on her surrogate-mother contract and fled with the baby she bore for a New Jersey couple.

Production Company: ABC Circle Films
Executive Producer .... Ilene Amy Berg
Producer .... Gordon L. Freedman
Director .... James Sadwith
Writer .... James Sadwith
Cast .... JoBeth Williams
Cast .... John Shea
Cast .... Bruce Weitz
Cast .... Robin Strasser
Cast .... Anne Jackson
Cast .... Dabney Coleman

BABY OF THE BRIDE   CBS
Drama: Family Drama • Woman's Issue/Story
Airdate: 12/22/91
Rating: 15.0/26   A/C: 1

Sequel to the 1990's TV movie "Children Of The Bride." A fifty-three-year-old woman's unexpected pregnancy throws chaos into her relationship with her younger husband, her four grown children and the dramas in their lives.

Production Company: Leonard Hill
Executive Producer .... Leonard Hill
Executive Producer .... Ron Gilbert
Executive Producer .... Joel Fields
Producer .... Bart Baker
Producer .... Cyrus Yavneh
Co-Executive Producer .... Rue McClanahan
Co-Executive Producer .... June Renfrow
Director .... Bill Bixby
Writer .... Bart Baker
Cast .... Rue Mcclanahan
Cast .... Kristy McNichol
Cast .... Ted Shackelford
Cast .... John Wesley Shipp

BABY SNATCHER   CBS
Drama: True Crime • Children/Teens
Airdate: 05/03/92
Rating: 16.3/26   A/C: 1

An unstable woman kidnaps a newborn in an attempt to save her marriage. The infant's real mother must persuade the unsympathetic FBI, who believes she is guilty of killing her own baby, to help in the frantic search to rescue it.

Production Company: Morgan Hill/Hearst
    Entertainment
Executive Producer .... Jennifer Alward
Co-Executive Producer .... Veronica Hamel
Producer .... Carol Trussell
Co-Producer .... Celeste Fremon
Director .... Joyce Chopra
Writer .... Susan Rhinehart
Cast .... Veronica Hamel
Cast .... Nancy McKeon
Cast .... Michael Madsen
Cast .... David Duchovny
Cast .... Penny Fuller

BABYCAKES   CBS
Drama/Comedy: Romantic Comedy • Woman's Issue/Story
Airdate: 02/14/89
Rating: 13.3/22   A/C:

Based on the German film "Sugarbaby". An pretty-but-obese mortuary assistant sets her cap for a subway motorman and wins him over with humor, charm and honesty.

Production Company: Konigsberg/Sanitsky Co.
Executive Producer .... Frank Konigsberg
Executive Producer .... Larry Sanitsky
Producer .... Diana Kerew
Co-Producer .... Joyce Eliason
Director .... Paul Schneider
Writer .... Joyce Eliason
Cast .... Ricki Lake
Cast .... Paul Benedict
Cast .... Betty Buckley
Cast .... John Karlen
Cast .... Craig Sheffer

BABYMAKER: THE DR. CECIL
JACOBSON'S STORY   CBS
Drama: True Story • Woman's Issue/Story • Family Drama • Children/Teens
Airdate: 2/8/94
Rating: 14.0/21   A/C: 2

Prominent fertility specialist, Dr. Cecil Jacobson is indicted for inseminating patients with his own sperm when two women who were victimized by the unscrupulous physician bring him up on charges of fraud.

Production Company: Jaffe/Braunstein Films Inc.
    and Heartstar Prods.
Executive Producer .... Michael Jaffe
Executive PRODUCER .... Howard Braunstein
Producer .... John Danylkiw
Director .... Arlene Sanford
Writer .... Phil Penningroth
Writer .... Sharon Doyle
Cast .... Melissa Gilbert
Cast .... George Dzundza
Cast .... Shanna Reed
Cast .... Tom Verica

BACK HOME   DISNEY
Drama: Children/Teens • Period Piece • Foreign or Exotic Location
Airdate: 06/07/90
Rating: N/A   A/C:

A young English girl evacuated to the U.S. during WWII, returns home to England, completely "Americanized." Her new personality conflicts with proper British culture and she finds herself at odds with both her family and her schoolmates.

Production Company: TVS Prods./Citadel
    Entertainment
Executive Producer .... Graham Benson
Executive Producer .... Dickie Bamber
Executive Producer .... David R. Ginsburg
Producer .... Nigel Pickard
Director .... Piers Haggard
Writer .... David Wood
Cast .... Hayley Mills
Cast .... Hayley Carr

BACK TO HANNIBAL: THE RETURN OF
TOM SAWYER AND HUCK FINN DISNEY
Drama: Murder and Murder Mystery • Period Piece • Courtroom Drama
Airdate: 10/21/90
Rating: N/A   A/C:

Grown-up Huck Finn, reporter, and Tom Sawyer, lawyer, return to Hannibal to come to the aid of ex-slave, Jim, who has been falsely accused of murdering Becky's husband.

Production Company: Gay-Jay Productions IAW
    The DISNEY Channel and Wonderworks
Producer .... Hugh Benson
Producer .... Thomas Lane
Director .... Paul Krasny
Writer .... Roy Johansen
Cast .... Raphael Sbarge
Cast .... Mitchell Anderson
Cast .... Megan Follows
Cast .... William Windom

BACK TO THE STREETS OF SAN
FRANCISCO   NBC
Drama: Murder and Murder Mystery • Cops/Detectives/Law Enforcement
Airdate: 01/27/92
Rating: 13.2/20   A/C: 3

Update of the 1972-77 TV series. Captain Mike Stone takes to the streets and successfully hunts down the murderer of his long-time friend and ex-partner, Steve Keller.

Production Company: Aaron Spelling Prods.
Executive Producer .... William Yates
Executive Producer .... Melissa Goldsmith
Executive Producer .... Aaron Spelling
Executive Producer .... E. Duke Vincent
Director .... Mel Damski
Writer .... William Yates
Cast .... Karl Malden
Cast .... Debrah Farentino
Cast .... Conor O'Farrell
Cast .... Carl Lumbly

BACKFIELD IN MOTION   ABC
Comedy: Woman's Issue/Story • Sports
Airdate: 11/13/91
Rating: 15.0/24   A/C: 1

Controversy erupts in a small suburban town when a wisecracking newly-widowed woman, trying to earn her son's respect, organizes a mother-son football game. A love affair ensues when she enlists the help of the Vice Principal of her son's school.

Production Company: Think Entertainment IAW
    Avnet/Kerner Co.
Executive Producer .... Shelley Duvall
Executive Producer .... Jon Avnet
Executive Producer .... Jordan Kerner
Co-Producer .... Robert Z. Shapiro
Producer .... Bill Borden
Producer .... Barry Rosenbrush
Director .... Richard Michaels
Writer .... Gene O'Neill
Writer .... Noreen Tobin
Writer .... Janet Brownell
Cast .... Roseanne Arnold
Cast .... Tom Arnold
Cast .... Colleen Camp
Cast .... Conchata Ferrell

BAD ATTITUDES   FBC
Comedy: Youth Comedy
Airdate: 09/16/91
Rating: 4.2/6   A/C: 4

Five summer camp escapees stow away on a billionaire's private jet and find themselves in the middle of a hijacking attempt by a pair of bumbling terrorists.

Production Company: FNM Films Inc.
Executive Producer .... Sandy Russell Gartin
Producer .... James A. Dennett
Director .... Alan Myerson
Writer .... Caleb Carr
Cast .... Richard Gilliland
Cast .... Maryedith Burrell
Cast .... Ethan Randall
Cast .... Jack Evans

BAD SEED, THE   ABC

Drama: Suspense/Thriller • Children/Teens
Airdate: 02/07/85
Rating: 12.9/19   A/C:

Remake of the 1956 film. A widow begins to suspect that her sweet and obedient nine year old daughter has a murderous streak in her.

Production Company: Hajeno Prods. IAW Warner
     Bros. TV
Executive Producer .... George Eckstein
Director .... Paul Wendkos
Writer .... George Eckstein
Cast .... Lynn Redgrave
Cast .... David Carradine
Cast .... David Ogden Stiers
Cast .... Richard Kiley
Cast .... Carrie Wells
Cast .... Blair Brown

BADGE OF THE ASSASSIN   CBS

Drama: Murder and Murder Mystery • Cops/
Detectives/Law Enforcement • Period Piece •
Historical Piece • Black Story
Airdate: 11/02/85
Rating: 13.6/23   A/C:

A district attorney and a police detective conduct an arduous and expansive two year search for members of a militant black group suspected of murdering a group of policemen.

Production Company: Blatt-Singer Prods.
Executive Producer .... Daniel H. Blatt
Executive Producer .... Robert Singer
Co-Executive Producer .... Robert K. Tanenbaum
Director .... Mel Damski
Writer .... Lawrence Roman
Cast .... James Woods
Cast .... Alex Rocco
Cast .... David Harris
Cast .... Larry Riley

BAJA OKLAHOMA   HBO

Comedy: Romantic Comedy
Airdate: 2/5/88
Rating: N/A   A/C:

Based on the novel by Dan Jenkins. In a small Texas town a high-spirited barmaid balances her mixed-up love life against her dreams of becoming a famous country singer-songwriter.

Production Company: Rastar Productions.
Executive Producer .... Marykay Powell
Director .... Bobby Roth
Writer .... Bobby Roth
Cast .... Lesley Ann Warren
Cast .... Peter Coyote
Cast .... Swoosie Kurtz
.... William Forsythe

BARBARA TAYLOR BRADFORD'S
REMEMBER   NBC

Miniseries/Drama (2 nights): Foreign or Exotic
Location • Love Story • Suspense/Thriller
Airdate: 10/24/93 • 10/25/93
Rating: 10.9/18 • 13.5/21   A/C: 2 • 3

When her fiance disappears on her wedding day an international television reporter hooks up with an old friend in Amsterdam when she sees news footage of a man she is sure is her absent lover. Together they uncover the truth surrounding her boyfriend's true identity when they become embroiled in a British Intelligence operation and soon become the target of a deadly rogue terrorist who turns out to be her missing beau.

Production Company: List/Estrin Prods and H.R.
     Prods. IAW NBC Prods.
Executive Producer .... Robert Bradford
Executive Producer .... Jonathan Estrin
Executive Producer .... Shelly List
Director .... John Herzfeld
Writer .... Mart Crowley
Writer .... Shelley List
Writer .... John Herzfeld
Cast .... Donna Mills
Cast .... Stephen Collins
Cast .... Claire Bloom
Cast .... Derek De Lint
Cast .... Ian Richardson
Cast .... Gail Strickland
Producer .... Frederick Muller

BARBARIANS AT THE GATE   HBO
EMMY WINNER

Drama: True Story • Social Issue
Airdate: 3/20/93
Rating: N/A   A/C:

Based on the book by Bryan Burrough and John Helyar. In 1988 businessman and CEO F. Ross Johnson sets off a major bidding war for R.J.R. Nabisco when he decides to buy the company. Fighting to gain control of his corporation against leverage-buyout tycoon Henry Kravis he ultimately sets up the largest corporate takeover in Wall Street history.

Production Company: Columbia Pictures, HBO
Executive Producer .... Thomas Hammel
Executive Producer .... Glenn Jordan
Producer .... Ray Stark
Co-Producer .... Marykay Powell
Director .... Glenn Jordan
Writer .... Larry Gelbart
Cast .... James Garner
Cast .... Jonathan Pryce
Cast .... Peter Riegert
Cast .... Joanna Cassidy

BARE ESSENTIALS   CBS

Comedy: Foreign or Exotic Location • Romantic
Comedy
Airdate: 01/08/91
Rating: 13.3/21   A/C: 3

A yuppie New York couple reassess their values and discover the meaning of love when stranded on a Pacific Island with a Robinson Crusoe-type guy and a Polynesian beauty.

Production Company: Republic Pictures
Executive Producer .... Karen Mack
Producer .... Jay Benson
Director .... Martha Coolidge
Writer .... Mark Estrin
Writer .... Allen Estrin
Cast .... Gregory Harrison
Cast .... Mark Linn-Baker
Cast .... Lisa Hartman
Cast .... Charlotte Lewis

BARNUM   CBS

Drama: Period Piece • Biography
Airdate: 11/30/86
Rating: 14.1/25   A/C:

Sweeping biography of the proverbial showman P. T. Barnum, who introduced singer Jenny Lind, midget Tom Thumb and Jumbo the elephant to American audiences.

Production Company: Robert Halmi Prods. IAW
     Filmline International Inc.
Executive Producer .... Robert Halmi, Sr.
Producer .... David Patterson
Director .... Lee Philips
Writer .... Michael Norell
Cast .... Burt Lancaster
Cast .... John Roney
Cast .... Laura Press
Cast .... Bronwen Mantel

BARON AND THE KID, THE   CBS

Drama: Family Drama • Addiction Story
Airdate: 11/21/84
Rating: 10.4/17   A/C:

A hard-drinking, ex-professional pool shark discovers he has a son. As they grow closer, he also discovers his son's life is taking a similar course to his.

Production Company: Telecom Entertainment Inc.
Executive Producer .... Michael Lepiner
Executive Producer .... Ken Kaufman
Producer .... Michael Lepiner
Producer .... Ken Kaufman
Director .... Gene Nelson
Writer .... Bill Stratton
Cast .... Johnny Cash
Cast .... Tracy Pollan
Cast .... Greg Webb
Cast .... Darren McGavin

BASED ON AN UNTRUE STORY   FBC
Comedy: Sex/Glitz
Airdate: 9/20/93
Rating: 3.5/5   A/C: 4

When a professional perfume sniffer loses her sense of smell she opts for a olfactory transplant but first must find her birth mother and her two sisters to be donors. While searching for her dysfunctional family she becomes entangled with a serial killer, a transsexual and a philandering husband.

Production Company: Westgate Prods.
Executive Producer .... Paul Lussier
Producer .... Kevin Reidy
Director .... Jim Drake
Writer .... George McGrath
Cast .... Morgan Fairchild
Cast .... Dyan Cannon
Cast .... Robert Goulet
Cast .... Harvey Korman

BATES MOTEL   NBC
Drama: Suspense/Thriller • Sci-Fi/Supernatural/ Horror/Fantasy
Airdate: 07/05/87
Rating: 14.6/27   A/C:

When a young former mental patient inherits the "Psycho" site from Norman Bates and tries to run it, weird things begin to happen.

Production Company: Universal TV
Executive Producer .... Richard Rothstein
Producer .... Ken Topolsky
Co-Producer .... Henry Kline
Director .... Richard Rothstein
Writer .... Richard Rothstein
Cast .... Jason Bateman
Cast .... Bud Cort
Cast .... Moses Gunn

BATTLING FOR BABY   CBS
Drama: Family Drama • Woman's Issue/Story
Airdate: 01/12/92
Rating: 16.2/26   A/C: 2

Two grandmothers, a concert pianist and a happy homemaker, who once rivaled over the same man in high school, must overcome their longstanding feud when their grown-up kids marry and have a baby.

Production Company: A Brummel Production IAW Von Zerneck/Sertner
Executive Producer .... Frank Von Zerneck
Executive Producer .... Robert M. Sertner
Co-Executive Producer .... Robert Brummel
Producer .... Steve McGlothen
Producer .... Julie Anne Weitz
Director .... Art Wolff
Writer .... Walter Lockwood
Writer .... Nancey Silvers
Cast .... Suzanne Pleshette
Cast .... Debbie Reynolds
Cast .... Courteney Cox
Cast .... John Terlesky

BAY COVEN   NBC
Drama: Suspense/Thriller • Sci-Fi/Supernatural/ Horror/Fantasy
Airdate: 10/25/87
Rating: 13.8/22   A/C:

Supernatural manifestations haunt a couple when they move into an old house off the New England coast with a history of witchcraft and encounter some strange neighbors.

Production Company: Guber-Peters Entertainment Co. IAW Phoenix Entertainment Group
Executive Producer .... Jon Peters
Executive Producer .... Roger Birnbaum
Executive Producer .... Peter Guber
Director .... Carl Schenkel
Writer .... Timothy Kring
Cast .... Barbara Billingsley
Cast .... Woody Harrelson
Cast .... Barbara Billingsley
Cast .... Pamela Sue Martin
Cast .... Tim Matheson

BAYWATCH: PANIC AT MALIBU PIER   NBC
Drama: Action/Adventure • Series Pilot (2 hr.)
Airdate: 04/23/89
Rating: 17.1/28   A/C:

Series pilot about the romances, family lives and daredevil aquatic rescues of a group of L.A. County lifeguards and an amateur lifeguard/ attorney.

Production Company: GTG Entertainment
Executive Producer .... Douglas Schwartz
Executive Producer .... Michael Berk
Producer .... Robert Hargrove
Producer .... Gregory J. Bonnan
Director .... Richard Compton
Writer .... Douglas Schwartz
Writer .... Michael Berk
Cast .... Peter Phelps
Cast .... David Hasselhoff
Cast .... Parker Stevenson

BED OF LIES   ABC
Drama: True Crime • Family Violence
Airdate: 1/20/92
Rating: 16.8/25   A/C: 2

Based on "Deadly Blessing" by Steve Salerno. In mid-70's Texas, waitress Vickie Moore marries wealthy and abusive Price Daniel, Jr. When she kills him in self-defense, her politically powerful in-laws, who believe the crime was premeditated, try to obtain custody of her children.

Production Company: David L. Wolper/Bernard Sofronski IAW Warner Bros.
Executive Producer .... David L. Wolper
Executive Producer .... Bernard Sofronski
Producer .... Andrew Gottlieb
Director .... William A. Graham
Writer .... John Ireland
Cast .... Susan Dey
Cast .... Chris Cooper
Cast .... G.W. Bailey
Cast .... Mary Kay Place
Cast .... Fred Dalton Thompson

BEHIND ENEMY LINES   NBC
Drama: Action/Adventure • Period Piece • WWII • Nazis
Airdate: 12/29/85
Rating: 14.5/23   A/C:

During World War II, a group from the office of strategic service goes on a mission to eliminate a Norwegian physicist who may be a Nazi collaborator.

Production Company: TVS Prods. IAW MTM Enterprises
Executive Producer .... Stephen McPherson
Producer .... Gareth Davies
Director .... Sheldon Larry
Writer .... Stephen McPherson
Cast .... Ray Sharkey
Cast .... Maryam D'Abo
Cast .... Hal Holbrook
Cast .... David McCallum

BEJEWELED   DISNEY
Comedy: Action/Adventure • Foreign or Exotic Location
Airdate: 01/20/90
Rating: N/A   A/C:

Based on the novel by Marion Babson. A curator traveling by plane to England with priceless jewels encounters murder, mayhem and mystery in her efforts to deliver the gems to a London museum.

Production Company: TVS Prods. IAW PWD Prods.
Executive Producer .... Paula Weinstein
Executive Producer .... Graham Benson
Executive Producer .... Wendy Dytman
Producer .... John Price
Producer .... Nigel Pickard
Director .... Terry Marcel
Writer .... Tom J. Astle
Cast .... Emma Samms
Cast .... Denis Lawson
Cast .... Jean Marsh
Cast .... Jerry Hall

BERMUDA GRACE   NBC
Drama: Cops/Detectives/Law Enforcement • Foreign or Exotic Location • Murder and Murder Mystery
Airdate: 1/7/94
Rating: 8.2/14   A/C: 3

A hard drinking Philadelphia detective working on the murder of a showgirl follows the trail to Bermuda, where he teams up with an eager young constable. Together they track down the killers.

Production Company: Catalyst Prods.
Executive Producer .... Sarah Wilson
Executive Producer .... Charles Falzon
Producer .... William Davies
Producer .... William Osborne
Director .... Mark Sobel
Writer .... William Davies
Writer .... William Osborne
Cast .... William Sadler
Cast .... David Harewood
Cast .... Serena Scott Thomas

BERYL MARKHAM: A SHADOW ON THE SUN — CBS

Miniseries/Drama (2 nights): Woman Against The System • Period Piece • Action/Adventure • Foreign or Exotic Location • Biography
Airdate: 05/15/88 • 05/17/88
Rating: 10.4/16 • 7.8/13   A/C:

The life and times of Beryl Markham, famous Kenya-based horse-trainer, aviatrix, writer and lover (she had many famous affairs and was married several times).

Production Company: Tamara Asseyev Prods. IAW New World TV
Executive Producer .... Tamara Asseyev
Producer .... Stefanie Powers
Director .... Tony Richardson
Writer .... Allan Scott
Cast .... Stefanie Powers
Cast .... Claire Bloom
Cast .... James Fox
Cast .... Peter Bowles
Cast .... Frederic Forrest

BETRAYAL OF TRUST — NBC

Drama: Woman's Issue/Story • Medical/Disease/Mental Illness • Woman Against The System
Airdate: 1/3/94
Rating: 13.0/20   A/C: 3

Based on the book "You Must Be Dreaming" by Barbara Noel with Kathryn Watterson. In 1984, Chicago singer Barbara Noel struggles to bring charges against world-renowned psychiatrist, Jules Masserman when she accuses him of raping her after he had sedated her into an unconscious state. After former patients come forward with similar horror stories the eminent doctor loses his license to practice medicine and is suspended for five years from the American Psychiatric Association.

Production Company: Cosgrove-Meurer Prods.
Executive Producer .... Terry Meurer
Executive Producer .... John Cosgrove
Executive Producer .... Stuart Benjamin
Co-Executive Producer .... Carrie Stein
Director .... George Kaczender
Writer .... Suzette Couture
Cast .... Judith Light
Cast .... Betty Buckley
Cast .... Judd Hirsch
Cast .... Kevin Tighe

BETRAYED BY INNOCENCE — CBS

Drama: Family Drama • Forbidden Love • Children/Teens • Rape/Molestation
Airdate: 03/01/86
Rating: 10.8/19   A/C:

A married middle-aged film director and a rebellious sixteen year old girl have a brief affair, which leads to a statutory rape charge.

Production Company: InterPlanetary Limited
Executive Producer .... Max A. Keller
Executive Producer .... Robert Lewis
Producer .... Micheline H. Keller
Co-Producer .... Dennis Considine
Co-Producer .... Charles Hairston
Director .... Elliot Silverstein
Writer .... Ken August
Cast .... Susan Marie Snyder
Cast .... Philip Bruns
Cast .... Barry Bostwick
Cast .... Lee Purcell
Cast .... Paul Sorvino

BETRAYED BY LOVE — ABC

Drama: Cops/Detectives/Law Enforcement • Forbidden Love • Murder and Murder Mystery • True Crime • Woman Against The System
Airdate: 1/17/94
Rating: 10.8/16   A/C: 2

Based on the book "The FBI Killer" by Aphrodite Jones. An ambitious married FBI agent has an affair with a captivating informant. When she tells him she is pregnant he becomes irrational and inadvertently strangles her then hides the body. Her sister, convinced she was murdered by the lawman wages a solitary campaign to bring him to justice and prove his guilt.

Production Company: Greengrass Prods. IAW Edgar J. Scherick Assoc. Inc.
Executive Producer .... Edgar J. Scherick
Producer .... Mitch Engel
CO-Producer .... Rick Baker
Director .... John Power
Writer .... Alan Sharp
Cast .... Mare Winningham
Cast .... Steven Weber
Cast .... Patricia Arquette
Cast .... Perry Lang

BETTER OFF DEAD — LIFETIME

Drama: Woman Against The System • Social Issue
Airdate: 1/12/93
Rating: N/A   A/C:

An ex- District Attorney fights to save the life of a female death row inmate whom she prosecuted in a cop killing case seven years earlier. Realizing she might have made a mistake during the original trail the lawyer attempts to right her previous wrongs. A strong bond develops between the two changed women as they race against time to win a stay of execution.

Production Company: Heller-Steinem Prods. IAW Viacom Prods.
Executive Producer .... Gloria Steinem
Executive Producer .... Rosilyn Heller
Producer .... Rosilyn Heller
Co-Producer .... Randy Baer
Co-Producer .... Grazia Caroselli
Director .... Neema Barnette
Writer .... Marlane Meyers
Cast .... Mare Winningham
Cast .... Tyra Ferrell
Cast .... Kevin Tighe
Cast .... Don Harvey

BETTY FORD STORY, THE — ABC

Drama: Medical/Disease/Mental Illness • Addiction Story • Biography • True Story
Airdate: 03/02/87
Rating: 11.4/16   A/C:

True story of the President's wife, from 1974 through his retirement, with emphasis on her addiction to alcohol and prescription drugs.

Production Company: David L. Wolper Prods. IAW Warner Bros. TV
Executive Producer .... David L. Wolper
Executive Producer .... Robert A. Papazian
Producer .... Mark M. Wolper
Director .... David Greene
Writer .... Karen Hall
Cast .... Gena Rowlands
Cast .... Josef Sommer
Cast .... Nan Woods

BETWEEN LOVE AND HATE — ABC

Drama: Forbidden Love
Airdate: 2/22/93
Rating: 14.2/21   A/C: 2

A rich socialite has an affair with a nineteen year old student. She breaks off the romance when her husband threatens to ruin her financially and the young man then becomes violently obsessive,

Production Company: Cosgrove/Meurer Prods. IAW WIN
Executive Producer .... Terry Meurer
Executive Producer .... John Cosgrove
Producer .... Jay Benson
Co-Producer .... Carrie Stein
Director .... Rod Hardy
Writer .... D. Victor Hawkins
Writer .... Tom Nelson
Cast .... Susan Lucci
Cast .... Patrick Van Horn
Cast .... Barry Bostwick

BETWEEN TWO WOMEN — ABC
Drama: Family Drama
Airdate: 03/10/86
Rating: 16.2/25   A/C:

The stormy fourteen year relationship between a former opera star who, after a stroke, comes to live with her son and daughter-in-law.

Production Company: Jon Avnet Co.
Executive Producer .... Jon Avnet
Producer .... Carol Schreder
Co-Producer .... Polly Platt
Director .... Jon Avnet
Writer .... Larry Grusin
Cast .... Farrah Fawcett
Cast .... Michael Nouri
Cast .... Bronson Pinchot
Cast .... Colleen Dewhurst

BEVERLY HILLS COWGIRL BLUES — CBS
Drama: Murder and Murder Mystery • Cops/Detectives/Law Enforcement • Prostitution
Airdate: 10/05/85
Rating: 12.9/22   A/C:

A Wyoming policewoman goes to Beverly Hills to investigate the murder of a friend, whom she discovers to have been a diamond smuggling prostitute.

Production Company: The Leonard Goldberg Co.
Executive Producer .... Leonard Goldberg
Producer .... Rick Husky
Director .... Corey Allen
Writer .... Rick Husky
Cast .... Lisa Hartman
Cast .... David Hemmings
Cast .... James Brolin

BEVERLY HILLS MADAM — NBC
Drama: Prostitution • Sex/Glitz
Airdate: 03/31/86
Rating: 17.5/27   A/C:

The glamorous but moralistic story of a motherly madam and her high-priced call girls who tend to fall in love with the clients.

Production Company: NLS Prods. IAW Orion TV
Executive Producer .... Nancy Sackett
Director .... Harvey Hart
Writer .... Nancy Sackett
Cast .... Faye Dunaway
Cast .... Melody Anderson
Cast .... Donna Dixon
Cast .... Robin Givens
Cast .... Louis Jourdan

BEYOND CONTROL: THE AMY FISHER STORY — ABC
Drama: True Crime • Sex/Glitz • Children/Teens
Airdate: 1/3/93
Rating: 19.5/30   A/C: 1

In 1992 Amy Fisher, a Long Island NY high school student, has an affair with married car mechanic Joey Buttafuoco. Fisher, in a fit of jealousy, shoots Buttafuoco's wife Mary Jo in the head. A sensational trial ensues and Amy is ultimately convicted of attempted murder. Note: See- Amy Fisher: My Story - NBC & Casualties of Love - CBS

Production Company: Andrew Adelson Co. IAW ABC Prods.
Executive Producer .... Andrew Adelson
Producer .... George Perkins
Director .... Andy Tennant
Writer .... Janet Brownell
Cast .... Drew Barrymore
Cast .... Anthony John Denison
Cast .... Harley Jane Kozak

BEYOND OBSESSION — ABC
Drama: True Crime • Family Violence • Children/Teens
Airdate: 4/4/94
Rating: 13.6/21   A/C: 2

Based on the book by Richard Hammer. An abused teenager manipulates her love sick boyfriend to killing her domineering mother. As the murder investigation proceeds the young man is arrested and confesses to the crime, when he realizes his girlfriend was just using him, he testifies against her. She eventually goes on trial for conspiracy which results in a hung jury and is currently awaiting a retrial.

Production Company: Pacific Motion Pictures, Western Intl. Communications, Green/Epstein Prods. IAW Warner Bros.
Executive Producer .... Bonnie Raskin
Producer .... Matthew O'Connor
Director .... David Greene
Writer .... Eugenia Bostwick Singer
Writer .... Raymond Singer
Cast .... Victoria Principal
Cast .... Henry Thomas
Cast .... Emily Warfield
Cast .... Joe Regalbuto

BEYOND SUSPICION — NBC
Drama: True Crime • Murder and Murder Mystery • Woman Against The System
Airdate: 11/22/93
Rating: 14.4/22   A/C: 2

Based on the book "Appointment For Murder" by Susan Crain Bakos. A charming St. Louis dentist and seemly devoted husband and father is discovered by his wife to have a murderous past. She is rebuffed by the local police, who only see him as a pillar of the community. Determined, she enlists the help of an Federal agent and together they set up a dangerous undercover operation in order to gain a confession. He is eventually convicted of seven murders and sentenced to life in prison.

Production Company: Patricia K. Meyer Prods. IAW Von Zerneck/Sertner Films
Executive Producer .... Patricia K. Meyer
Executive Producer .... Frank Von Zerneck
Executive Producer .... Robert M. Sertner
Co-Producer .... Markie Post
Producer .... Randy Sutter
Co-Producer .... Karen Clark
Director .... William A. Graham
Writer .... Karen Clark
Cast .... Markie Post
Cast .... Corbin Bernsen
Cast .... Don Swayze
Cast .... Jeanne Cooper
Cast .... Kelsey Grammer

BIG ONE: THE GREAT LOS ANGELES EARTHQUAKE, THE — NBC
Miniseries/Drama (2 nights): Disaster
Airdate: 11/11/90 • 11/12/90
Rating: 17.1/26 • 19.5/30   A/C: 1 • 1

A seismologist frantic warnings are widely ignored and silenced until the "Big One" hits, and Los Angeles must struggle to recover from the devastation.

Production Company: Von Zerneck/Sertner Films
Executive Producer .... Frank Von Zerneck
Executive Producer .... Robert M. Sertner
Producer .... Susan Weber-Gold
Producer .... Gregory Prange
Producer .... Stratton Leopold
Producer .... Michael Petryni
Director .... Larry Elikann
Writer .... Bill Bast
Writer .... Paul Huson
Writer .... Michael Petryni
Cast .... Joanna Kerns
Cast .... Ed Begley, Jr.
Cast .... Dan Lauria
Cast .... Bonnie Bartlett

BILLIONAIRE BOYS CLUB   NBC
Miniseries/Drama (2 nights): Murder and Murder
Mystery • True Crime • Courtroom Drama
Airdate: 11/08/87 • 11/09/87
Rating: 20.7/34 • 22.1/34   A/C:

*True story of Joe Hunt's trial for the killing of a
confidence man, and his hypnotic hold on other
young men who believed they were destined to
grow rich.*

Production Company: Donald March/Gross-
    Weston IAW ITC Prods.
Executive Producer .... Donald March
Producer .... Marcy Gross
Producer .... Ann Weston
Director .... Marvin J. Chomsky
Writer .... Gy Waldron
Cast .... Judd Nelson
Cast .... Raphael Sbarge
Cast .... Barry Tubb
Cast .... Ron Silver
Cast .... Frederic Lehne
Cast .... John Stockwell

BIONIC SHOWDOWN: THE 6 MILLION
DOLLAR MAN/BIONIC WOMAN   NBC
Drama: Action/Adventure • Sci-Fi/Supernatural/
Horror/Fantasy
Airdate: 04/30/89
Rating: 17.6/28   A/C:

*The Six Million Dollar Man and the Bionic
Woman are prime suspects when some
important documents are found missing. They
join up with a younger bionic woman to find
an evil cyborg and restore their reputation.*

Production Company: Universal TV
Executive Producer .... Michael Sloan
Producer .... Nigel Watts
Producer .... Bernadette Joyce
Director .... Alan J. Levi
Writer .... Michael Sloan
Cast .... Lindsay Wagner
Cast .... Lee Majors
Cast .... Sandra Bullock
Cast .... Richard Anderson

BIRDS I I: LAND'S END, THE
SHOWTIME
Drama: Sci-Fi/Supernatural/Horror/Fantasy •
Suspense/Thriller
Airdate: 3/19/94
Rating: N/A   A/C:

*Sequel to Alfred Hitchcock's 1963 feature film
"The Birds". Based on the short story by
Daphne du Maurier. Killer seagulls incensed
at environmental destruction begin to terrorize
a family of vacationers as well as the other
inhabitants of a remote island on the East Coast.*

Production Company: Rosemont Prods. IAW
    MTE/Universal.
Executive Producer .... Norman Rosemont
Executive Producer .... David A. Rosemont
Producer .... Ted Kurdyla
Director .... Rick Rosenthal
Writer .... Ken Wheat
Cast .... Brad Johnson
Cast .... Chelsea Field
Cast .... James Naughton
Cast .... Tippi Hedren

BITTER VENGEANCE   USA
Drama: Murder and Murder Mystery • Suspense/
Thriller
Airdate: 7/29/94
Rating: N/A   A/C:

*A bitter ex-cop, reduced to working as a bank
security guard, frames his unsuspecting wife for
"murder" and a bank heist that he commits with
help from a sexy young bank teller. They flee
to Mexico, but his wife tracks him down and
recovers the loot.*

Production Company: Wilshire Court Productins
Producer .... Christopher Griffin
Director .... Stuart Cooper
Writer .... Pablo Fenjves
Cast .... Virginia Madsen
Cast .... Bruce Greenwood

BLACK ICE   USA
Drama: Suspense/Thriller
Airdate: 6/16/93
Rating: N/A   A/C:

*A mysterious woman hires a grubby Detroit cab
driver to help her flee from a sadistic hit man
out to avenge the death of a philandering
politician that she had killed in self defense.*

Production Company: Saban Ent., Prism Pictures
Executive Producer .... Lance Robbins
Producer .... Vonnie Von Helmolt
Producer .... Robert Vince
Co-Executive Producer .... Barry Collier
Director .... Neil Fearnley
Writer .... Arne Olsen
Writer .... John Schwartz
Cast .... Michael Nouri
Cast .... Joanna Pacula
Cast .... Michael Ironside

BLACK MAGIC   SHOWTIME
Drama: Suspense/Thriller • Sci-Fi/Supernatural/
Horror/Fantasy • Murder and Murder Mystery
Airdate: 03/21/92
Rating: N/A   A/C:

*When a man is bullied by his cousin's ghost, he
becomes fatally attracted to an enchanting
sorceress. Together, they are plunged into a
conspiracy of jealousy and murder as he seeks
to unravel the mystery surrounding his cousin's
death.*

Production Company: Point of View/MTE
Executive Producer .... Dan Wigutow
Producer .... Harvey Frand
Director .... Daniel Taplitz
Writer .... Daniel Taplitz
Cast .... Judge Reinhold
Cast .... Rachel Ward
Cast .... Anthony La Paglia
Cast .... Maud Adams
Cast .... Carl Ballantine
Cast .... David Huddleston
.... Peter S. Fischer

BLACK WIDOW MURDERS: THE
BLANCHE TAYLOR MOORE STORY   NBC
Drama: True Crime • Murder and Murder Mystery
Airdate: 5/3/93
Rating: 13.3/21   A/C: 2

*Based on the book, "Preachers Girl" by Jim
Schutze. In 1980s North Carolina, supermarket
checker Blanche Taylor Moore murders her first
husband and then her boyfriend with arsenic.
When her second husband, a minister, succumbs
to the same symptoms the authorities begin to
examine her sordid life. After exhuming the
bodies of her past loves, including her father,
and finding arsenic in all of them, she is arrested
and convicted of murder.*

Production Company: Andrea Baynes Prods.,
    Finnegan/Pinchuk Co., Lorimar TV
Executive Producer .... Andrea Baynes
Executive Producer .... Judith P. Mitchell
Producer .... Pat Finnegan
Producer .... Sheldon Pinchuk
Co-Producer .... Dale Eunson
Director .... Alan Metzger
Writer .... Judith P. Mitchell
Cast .... Elizabeth Montgomery
Cast .... David Clennon
Cast .... Grace Zabriskie
Cast .... John M. Jackson

MOVIES AND MINISERIES

BLACKE'S MAGIC   NBC
Mystery: Cops/Detectives/Law Enforcement •
Suspense/Thriller • Series Pilot (2 hr.) • Murder and
Murder Mystery
Airdate: 01/05/86
Rating: 21.8/32   A/C:

A retired magician is enlisted to help the Los
Angeles police solve the inexplicable murder
of a magician who was found shot to death
during a performance in a sealed trunk
underwater.

Production Company: Universal TV
Executive Producer .... Peter S. Fischer
Producer .... Douglas Benton
Producer .... Cliff Gould
Director .... John Llewellyn Moxey
Writer .... Peter S. Fischer
Cast .... Hal Linden
Cast .... Maud Adams
Cast .... Carl Ballantine
Cast .... David Huddleston
Cast .... Harry Morgan

BLACKMAIL   USA
Drama: Suspense/Thriller
Airdate: 10/02/91
Rating: N/A   A/C:

Based on "Passing for Love" by Bill Crenshaw.
A young couple scams wealthy women by luring
them into affairs and then blackmailing them.
The tables are turned when they become the
victims of a sleazy detective who horns in on
their action.

Production Company: Barry Weitz IAW Wilshire
     Court Prods.
Executive Producer .... Barry Weitz
Producer .... Matthew O'Connor
Director .... Ruben Preuss
Writer .... Miguel Tejada-Flores
Cast .... Dale Midkiff
Cast .... Susan Blakely
Cast .... Mac Davis
Cast .... Beth Toussaint

BLACKOUT   HBO
Drama: Suspense/Thriller
Airdate: 7/28/85
Rating: N/A   A/C:

An embittered ex-cop is haunted by the murder
of a woman and her three children. Obsessed
with the case for seven years, through an
anonymous tip, he goes after a amnesiac who
has had extensive facial surgery after a car
accident. Shaken by the accusation, the lost man
hires a private detective to try to uncover his
past identity.

Production Company: Roger Gimbel Prods.IAW
     Peregrine Entertainment LTD., Lee Rock
     Industries, LTD.
Executive Producer .... Roger Gimbel
Executive Producer .... Freyda Rothstein
Producer .... Les Alexander
Producer .... Richard Smith
Producer .... Richard Parks
Director .... Douglas Hickox
Writer .... David Ambrose
Writer .... Richard Smith
Writer .... Richard Parks
Cast .... Keith Carradine
Cast .... Kathleen Quinlan
Cast .... Richard Widmark

BLADE IN HONG KONG   CBS
Drama: Cops/Detectives/Law Enforcement • Foreign
or Exotic Location
Airdate: 05/15/85
Rating: 10.3/16   A/C:

A Hong Kong private detective tries to free the
kidnapped daughter of a Chinese merchant and
save his own stepfather from a murder attempt.

Production Company: Becker Enterprises Prods.
Producer .... Terry Becker
Director .... Reza Badiyi
Writer .... Gordon Cotler
Cast .... Terry Lester
Cast .... Keye Luke
Cast .... Leslie Nielsen

BLIND FAITH   NBC
Miniseries/Drama (2 nights): Family Drama • Murder
and Murder Mystery • True Crime • Children/Teens
• Family Violence
Airdate: 02/11/90 • 02/13/90
Rating: 19.9/31 • 23.3/36   A/C: 1 • 1

Based on the book by Joe McGinniss.
Contemporary drama about the brutal murder
in Toms River, NJ, of the wife of a seemingly
model husband whose sons learn their father
may have arranged the killing.

Production Company: NBC Productions
Executive Producer .... Susan Baerwald
Executive Producer .... Dan Wigutow
Director .... Paul Wendkos
Writer .... John Gay
Cast .... Robert Urich
Cast .... Joanna Kerns
Cast .... David Barry Gray
Cast .... Dennis Farina

BLIND JUSTICE   CBS
Drama: Man Against The System • True Story
Airdate: 03/09/86
Rating: 19.2/29   A/C:

The true story of an innocent photographer who
struggles against charges of armed robbery,
kidnapping and rape for over a year in an
incredible case of mistaken identity.

Production Company: CBS Entertainment Prods.
Producer .... Andrew Gottlieb
Director .... Rod Holcomb
Writer .... Josephine Cummings
Writer .... Richard Yalem
Cast .... Tim Matheson
Cast .... Mimi Kuzyk
Cast .... Anne Haney
Cast .... Lisa Eichhorn

BLIND JUSTICE   HBO
Drama: Western • Period Piece
Airdate: 6/25/94
Rating: N/A   A/C:

In 1865, a gunfighter of incredible prowess,
engages in a solitary battle against a band of
vicious outlaws while trying to deliver and
orphaned baby to safety.

Production Company: HBO Pictures
Executive Producer .... Neal Moritz
Executive Producer .... David Heyman
Producer .... Rick Nathanson
Director .... Richard Spence
Writer .... Daniel Knauf
Cast .... Armand Assante
Cast .... Elisabeth Shue
Cast .... Robert Davi

BLIND MAN'S BLUFF   USA
Mystery: Murder and Murder Mystery •
Psychological Thriller
Airdate: 02/19/92
Rating: N/A   A/C:

A sensitive but troubled blind professor is
framed for a succession of murders. In order
to clear his name, he sets a trap for the killer,
only to discover it's his best friend.

Production Company: Wilshire Court Prods. IAW
     Pacific Motion Pictures
Producer .... Tom Rowe
Co-Producer .... Robert Urich
Director .... James Quinn
Writer .... Joel Gross
Cast .... Robert Urich
Cast .... Lisa Eilbacher
Cast .... Ron Perlman
Cast .... Patricia Clarkson

BLIND SIDE — HBO
Drama: Murder and Murder Mystery • Foreign or Exotic Location • Suspense/Thriller
Airdate: 1/30/93
Rating: N/A   A/C:

An American couple, vacationing in Mexico, accidentally run over a policeman with their car. After fleeing the scene, the two are then blackmailed by a psycho-killer who witnessed their crime. NOTE: Also aired on NBC-4/26/93

Production Company: Chestnut Hill Prods. IAW HBO Pictures
Executive Producer .... Jeffrey Lurie
Executive Producer .... John Manulis
Executive Producer .... John Marsh
Producer .... Jay Roewe
Director .... Geoff Murphy
Writer .... Stewart Lindh
Writer .... Solomon Weingarten
Writer .... John Carlen
Cast .... Rutger Hauer
Cast .... Ron Silver
Cast .... Rebecca De Mornay
Cast .... Jonathan Banks

BLIND SPOT — CBS
Drama: Family Drama • Addiction Story
Airdate: 5/2/93
Rating: 13.1/20   A/C: 2

When her son-in-law and political aide, dies in a car accident, an aggressive congresswoman discovers that he and her pregnant daughter are addicted to cocaine. The domineering mother takes control of the situation and coerces her only child into rehab where the family painfully confronts long held guilt and recriminations.

Production Company: Signboard Hill Prods. IAW RHI Ent.
Executive Producer .... Robert Halmi, Jr.
Executive Producer .... Richard Welsh
Producer .... Andrew Gottlieb
Director .... Michael Toshiyuki Uno
Writer .... Nina Shengold
Cast .... Joanne Woodward
Cast .... Laura Linney
Cast .... Fritz Weaver
Cast .... Cynthia Martells

BLIND VENGEANCE — USA
Drama: Man Against The System • Suspense/Thriller
Airdate: 08/22/90
Rating: N/A   A/C:

After a former Army hero's son is slain by white supremacists due to the boy's friendship with a black, the Army hero avenges the murder through psychological warfare, culminating in a violent showdown.

Production Company: Spanish Trail IAW MCA TV Entertainment
Executive Producer .... Gerald McRaney
Executive Producer .... Robert Stolfi
Producer .... Albert J. Salzer
Director .... Lee Philips
Writer .... Henri Simoun
Writer .... Curt Allen
Cast .... Gerald McRaney
Cast .... Lane Smith
Cast .... Don Hood
Cast .... Thalmus Rasulala
Cast .... James Parks
Cast .... Marg Helgenberger

BLIND WITNESS — ABC
Drama: Murder and Murder Mystery • Woman In Jeopardy • Suspense/Thriller
Airdate: 11/26/89
Rating: 16.3/25   A/C: 1

A blind woman, whose husband was murdered in her presence, is sure that the wrong men are on trial for the crime. Determined to avenge his death, she sets a trap for his killers.

Production Company: King-Phoenix Entertainment
Executive Producer .... Hans Proppe
Executive Producer .... Victoria Principal
Producer .... Richard Colla
Director .... Richard Colla
Writer .... Edmond Stevens
Writer .... Robert Carrington
Cast .... Victoria Principal
Cast .... Paul LeMat
Cast .... Stephen Macht
Cast .... Matt Clark

BLINDFOLD: ACTS OF OBSESSION — USA
Drama: Suspense/Thriller
Airdate: 5/20/94
Rating: N/A   A/C:

A troubled L.A. wife acts out her sexual fantasies with her impotent husband on the advice of psychiatrist who is under investigation in a series of murders. Turns out the kinky shrink was associated with a murderer in San Francisco who was into blindfolds and handcuffs.

Production Company: Libra Pictures Prods.
Executive Producer .... Lance H. Robbins
Producer .... Ronnie Hadar
Director .... Lawrence L. Simeone
Writer .... Lawrence L. Simeone
Cast .... Judd Nelson
Cast .... Shannen Doherty
Cast .... Kristian Alfonso
Cast .... Michael Woods

BLINDSIDED — USA
Drama: Suspense/Thriller
Airdate: 1/20/93
Rating: N/A   A/C:

A blind ex-cop turned criminal falls in love with a mysterious woman while they are both hiding out in Mexico. When he regains his sight he discovers she is connected to his past and his ex-partner who have conspired to frame him.

Production Company: MTE Prods. IAW Alan Barnette Prods
Executive Producer .... Alan Barnette
Co-Producer .... Mychelle Deschamps
Director .... Tom Donnelly
Writer .... Tom Donnelly
Cast .... Jeff Fahey
Cast .... Mia Sara
Cast .... Ben Gazzara

BLOOD AND ORCHIDS — CBS
Miniseries/Drama (2 nights): Murder and Murder Mystery • Cops/Detectives/Law Enforcement • Foreign or Exotic Location • Period Piece • Courtroom Drama • Rape/Molestation
Airdate: 02/23/86 • 02/24/86
Rating: 22.9/35 • 25.6/38   A/C:

Based on Norman Katkov's novel. A fictional tale inspired by the true story of a young Navy wife who accused four Hawaiians of assaulting her in 1937 Hawaii. The woman's husband kills one of the Hawaiians and is then tried for murder.

Production Company: Lorimar Prods. Inc.
Executive Producer .... Malcolm Stuart
Producer .... Andrew Adelson
Director .... Jerry Thorpe
Writer .... Norman Katkov
Cast .... Jane Alexander
Cast .... Madeline Stowe
Cast .... Matt Salinger
Cast .... Jose Ferrer
Cast .... Kris Kristofferson
Cast .... James Saito
Cast .... Sean Young
Cast .... Susan Blakely

BLOOD RIVER — CBS
Drama: Western
Airdate: 03/17/91
Rating: 13.4/23   A/C: 3

A young man on the run for avenging his parents' death teams up with a cranky, old undercover lawman who repeatedly saves his life and ultimately clears his name.

Production Company: CBS Entertainment Prods. IAW Little Apple Prods.
Executive Producer .... Mel Damski
Executive Producer .... Merrill H. Karpf
Producer .... Andrew Gottlieb
Director .... Mel Damski
Writer .... John Carpenter
Cast .... Rick Schroder
Cast .... Wilford Brimley
Cast .... Adrienne Barbeau

BLOOD TIES   FBC

Drama: Sci-Fi/Supernatural/Horror/Fantasy
Airdate: 05/27/91
Rating: 6.3/11   A/C: 4

A young modern day vampire comes to grips with his supernatural heritage, rescues his step-sister, and avenges the death of his parents by religious fanatics.

Production Company: Richard Shapiro Ent., Inc.
Executive Producer .... Richard Shapiro
Executive Producer .... Esther Shapiro
Producer .... Gene Corman
Co-Producer .... Jim McBride
Director .... Jim McBride
Writer .... Richard Shapiro
Cast .... Harley Venton
Cast .... Patrick Bauchau
Cast .... Bo Hopkins
Cast .... Kim Ulrich

BLOOD VOWS: THE STORY OF A MAFIA WIFE   NBC

Drama: Woman In Jeopardy • Mafia/Mob
Airdate: 01/18/87
Rating: 24.8/37   A/C:

A young woman innocently marries a man she discovers is a member of the Mafia.

Production Company: Louis Rudolph Films IAW
    Fries Entertainment
Executive Producer .... Louis Rudolph
Director .... Paul Wendkos
Writer .... Guerdon Trueblood
Cast .... Melissa Gilbert
Cast .... Joe Penny
Cast .... Tony Franciosa
Cast .... Eileen Brennan
Cast .... Talia Shire

BLOODLINES: MURDER IN THE FAMILY   NBC

Miniseries/Drama (2 nights): True Crime • Family
Drama • Family Violence
Airdate: 3/1/93 • 3/2/93
Rating: 10.7/17 • 13.3/21   A/C: 3 • 2

In 1985, a wealthy, avaricious Los Angeles businessman is arrested for hiring a hit man to kill his millionaire parents, who are gunned down in their home. When her husband is jailed, his once prominent wife struggles to start a new life while her affluent friends shun her and family finances become increasingly tight.

Production Company: Stonehenge Prods. IAW
    Lorimar TV
Executive Producer .... Dick Berg
Executive Producer .... Allan Marcil
Co-Executive Producer .... Michael O'Hara
Producer .... Sam Manners
Co-Producer .... Judith P. Mitchell
Director .... Paul Wendkos
Writer ....Bill Driskill
Writer .... Sara Davidson
Cast .... Elliott Gould
Cast .... Mimi Rogers
Cast .... Clancy Brown
Cast .... Kim Hunter
Cast .... Joe Spano

BLUE BAYOU   NBC

Drama: Murder and Murder Mystery • Woman
Against The System • Series Pilot (2 hr.)
Airdate: 01/15/90
Rating: 12.8/20   A/C: 3

An L.A. lawyer moves to New Orleans so her teen-age son can get to know the father he's never met. After securing a job as an assistant D.A., she and her ex-husband, a policeman, investigate an exotic murder case involving the very rich.

Production Company: Fisher Entertainment IAW
    Touchstone Television
Executive Producer .... Terry Louise Fisher
Producer .... Christopher Morgan
Director .... Karen Arthur
Writer .... Terry Louise Fisher
Cast .... Alfre Woodard
Cast .... Mario Van Peebles
Cast .... Keith Williams
Cast .... Roy Thinnes

BLUE DEVILLE   NBC

Drama: Buddy Story
Airdate: 12/29/86
Rating: 13.4/22   A/C:

Two female friends take to the road in search of adventure in a 1959 Cadillac they win in a contest.

Production Company: B & E Entertainment IAW
    NBC Prods.
Executive Producer .... Brad Buckner
Executive Producer .... Eugenie Ross-Lemming
Producer .... Christopher Nelson
Producer .... Edward D. Markley
Director .... Jim Johnston
Writer .... Brad Buckner
Writer .... Eugenie Ross-Leming
Cast .... Kimberley Pistone
Cast .... Jennifer Runyon
Cast .... Mark Thomas Miller

BLUE LIGHTNING, THE   CBS

Drama: Cops/Detectives/Law Enforcement • Action/
Adventure • Cops/Detectives/Law Enforcement
Airdate: 05/07/86
Rating: 12.1/19   A/C:

A private detective and a criminal vie for a valuable opal in the Australian outback.

Production Company: Alan Sloan Inc. IAW The
    Seven Network & Coote-Carroll
Executive Producer .... Allan Sloane
Executive Producer .... Gregg Coote
Executive Producer .... Matt Carroll
Director .... Lee Philips
Writer .... William Kelly
Cast .... Sam Elliott
Cast .... Rebecca Gilling
Cast .... Robert Culp

BLUEGRASS   CBS

Miniseries/Drama (2 nights): Woman Against The
System • Love Story • Farm Story • Sex/Glitz
Airdate: 02/28/88 • 02/29/88
Rating: 17.6/27 • 18.4/29   A/C:

A once-poor woman establishes a successful Kentucky horse farm while deciding between two suitors and seeking revenge against her next-door neighbor, a judge, who, when they were children, nearly raped her.

Production Company: Landsburg Co.
Executive Producer .... Alan Landsburg
Executive Producer .... Joan Barnett
Producer .... Arthur Fellows
Producer .... Terry Keegan
Director .... Simon Wincer
Writer .... Mart Crowley
Cast .... Cheryl Ladd
Cast .... Wayne Rogers
Cast .... Mickey Rooney
Cast .... Brian Kerwin
Cast .... Anthony Andrews
Cast .... Diane Ladd

BLUFFING IT   ABC

Drama: Family Drama • Social Issue
Airdate: 09/13/87
Rating: 13.4/22   A/C:

A middle-aged factory worker deals with the reactions of his family and co-workers as he struggles to overcome his inability to read.

Production Company: Ohlmeyer Communications
Executive Producer .... Don Ohlmeyer
Producer .... Linda Jonsson
Producer .... Christopher Sands
Co-Producer .... Karen Danaher-Dorr
Director .... James Sadwith
Writer .... James Sadwith
Cast .... Dennis Weaver
Cast .... Michelle Little
Cast .... Janet Carroll

BODY LANGUAGE   USA

Drama: Woman In Jeopardy • Psychological Thriller
Airdate: 07/15/92
Rating: N/A   A/C:

A recently promoted businesswoman hires an assistant who flunked the executive training course. The assistant's jealousy and resentment build, causing her to usurp her boss's identity and resort to murder.

Production Company: Wilshire Court Prods.
Executive Producer .... Dan Gurskis
Producer .... Robert Rolsky
Director .... Arthur Allan Seidelman
Writer .... Dan Gurskis
Writer .... Brian Ross
Cast .... Heather Locklear
Cast .... Linda Purl
Cast .... Edward Albert, Jr.
Cast .... James Acheson

BODY OF EVIDENCE — CBS
Mystery: Murder and Murder Mystery • Woman In Jeopardy • Psychological Thriller
Airdate: 01/24/88
Rating: 18.4/28   A/C:

After a series of events, a nurse begins to suspect that her police pathologist husband may be a serial murderer of attractive young women.

Production Company: CBS Entertainment Prods.
Producer .... Roy Campanella II
Director .... Roy Campanella II
Writer .... Cynthia Whitcomb
Cast .... Barry Bostwick
Cast .... Tony Lo Bianco
Cast .... Margot Kidder

BONANZA: THE RETURN — NBC
Drama: Family Drama • Western • Period Piece
Airdate: 11/28/93
Rating: 17.6/26   A/C: 2

Based on the long running series. In 1905, the offspring of the original Cartwright clan come from hither and yon to help their old beloved cowhand ,who is now running the ranch, to fight off a greedy developer who wants to strip mine the Ponderosa.

Production Company: Legend Ent. IAW NBC Prods.
Executive Producer .... Thomas W. Sarnoff
Co-Executive Producer .... Tom Brinson
Co-Executive Producer .... E.K. Gaylord
Producer .... Kent McCray
Producer .... Gary Wohleben
Director .... Jerry Jameson
Writer .... Michael McGreevey
Cast .... Michael Landon, Jr.
Cast .... Ben Johnson
Cast .... Richard Roundtree
Cast .... Emily Warfield

BONDS OF LOVE — CBS
Drama: Love Story • Medical/Disease/Mental Illness • Social Issue • True Story
Airdate: 1/24/93
Rating: 14.9/23   A/C: 1

When a twice divorced woman falls in love with a mentally retarded man in a small Kansas town his overprotective family and the social welfare department try to keep them apart. Determined to stay together they wage a emotional legal battle which ultimately lets the couple proclaim their love.

Production Company: Hearts Ent. Prods.
Executive Producer .... Harry Chandler
Executive Producer .... Treat Williams
Producer .... Julian Marks
Co-Producer .... Joel Rice
Co-Producer .... Heidi Wall
Director .... Larry Elikann
Writer .... Mary Gallagher
Cast .... Treat Williams
Cast .... Kelly McGillis
Cast .... Steve Railsback
Cast .... Hal Holbrook

BONNIE AND CLYDE: THE TRUE STORY — FBC
Drama: Love Story • True Crime • Period Piece • Historical Piece • Biography
Airdate: 08/17/92
Rating: 8.7/15   A/C:

In 1920's East Texas, a bleak sense of the future and thrill for adventure bring teenagers Bonnie Parker and Clyde Barrow together in love and a violent rampage of robbery and murder. Their childhood friend Sheriff Ted Hinton sets up their ambush.

Production Company: FNM Films IAW Hoffman-Israel Prods.
Executive Producer .... Gary Hoffman
Executive Producer .... Neal Israel
Producer .... Ooty Moorehead
Director .... Gary Hoffman
Writer .... Gary Hoffman
Cast .... Dana Ashbrook
Cast .... Tracey Needham
Cast .... Michelle Joyner
Cast .... Michael Bowen

BORIS AND NATASHA — SHOWTIME
Comedy: Sci-Fi/Supernatural/Horror/Fantasy
Airdate: 04/17/92
Rating: N/A   A/C:

Based on television cartoon series. Pottsylvania agents Boris and Natasha, of "Bullwinkle" fame, bumble through zany bad guys who thwart their pursuit of a lost microchip that holds the secrets of time.

Production Company: MCEG Prods.
Executive Producer .... Jonathan D. Krane
Director .... Charles Martin Smith
Writer .... Charles Fradin
Writer .... Linda Favila
Writer .... Anson Downes
Cast .... Sally Kellerman
Cast .... Dave Thomas
Cast .... Andrea Martin
Cast .... John Calvin

BORN TO RUN — FBC
Drama: Suspense/Thriller • Mafia/Mob
Airdate: 8/2/93
Rating: 3.9/7   A/C: 4

In Brooklyn, New York a street wise drag racer tries to rescue his older brother who crosses the local mob boss while romancing the kingpin's attractive girlfriend.

Production Company: Fox West Pictures
Executive Producer .... Lance Hool
Producer .... Bruce Binkow
Producer .... Peter McAlevey
Co-Producer .... Jerald Silverhardt
Director .... Albert Magnoli
Writer .... Randall Badat
Writer .... Frank Bitetto
Cast .... Richard Grieco
Cast .... Jay Acovone
Cast .... Shelli
Lether
Cast .... Joe Cortese

BORN TOO SOON — NBC
Drama: Family Drama • Children/Teens • Medical/Disease/Mental Illness • True Story
Airdate: 4/25/93
Rating: 10.5/17   A/C: 3

Based on the book by Elizabeth Mehren. Los Angeles Times Reporter, Elizabeth Mehren and her husband New York Times writer Fox Butterfield face emotional and marital turmoil when their daughter is born three months premature and weighs one pound, eleven ounces. As the baby struggles to survive in intensive care, the months of anguish take there toll on the strained couple.

Production Company: Adam Prods. IAW Republic Pictures
Executive Producer .... Robert M. Myman
Producer .... R.W. Goodwin
Co-Producer .... Deirdre Berthrong
Director .... Noel Nosseck
Writer .... Susan Baskin
Cast .... Pamela Reed
Cast .... Michael Moriarty
Cast .... Terry O'Quinn
Cast .... Joanna Gleason

BORROWERS, THE — TNT
Miniseries/Drama (2 nights): Sci-Fi/Supernatural/Horror/Fantasy • Foreign or Exotic Location
Airdate: 11/27/27 • 11/28/93
Rating: N/A   A/C:

Based on the book by Mary Norton. A family of tiny people live under the floor boards of an English country house, where they borrow objects from their human housemates who reside upstairs. When they are eventually discovered they flee into the woods and are ultimately guided to safety by a lonely English schoolboy.

Production Company: Working Title TV, IAW Turner Network TV, BBC's Children Intl., DeFaria Co.
Executive Producer .... Walt DeFaria
Executive Producer .... Tim Bevan
Producer .... Grainne Marmion
Director .... John Hendeerson
Writer .... Richard Carpenter
Cast .... Ian Holm
Cast .... Penolope Wilton
Cast .... Rebecca Callard
Cast .... Paul Cross

BOURNE IDENTITY, THE   ABC

Miniseries/Drama (2 nights): Love Story • Suspense/
Thriller • Foreign or Exotic Location
Airdate: 05/08/88 • 05/09/88
Rating: 18.5/30 • 18.5/29   A/C:

*Based on the Robert Ludlum novel, this is the
thrill-packed adventure of a man whose
amnesia may hide his identity as notorious
terrorist Jason Bourne.*

Production Company: Alan Shayne Prods. IAW
    Warner Bros. TV
Executive Producer .... Alan Shayne
Producer .... Frederick Muller
Co-Producer .... Martin Rabbett
Director .... Roger Young
Writer .... Carol Sobieski
Cast .... Richard Chamberlain
Cast .... Jaclyn Smith
Cast .... Anthony Quayle
Cast .... Donald Moffat
Cast .... Peter Vaughan

BOYS, THE   ABC

Drama: Medical/Disease/Mental Illness • Buddy
Story
Airdate: 04/15/91
Rating: 8.9/15   A/C: 3

*The friendship of two long-time screenwriting
partners meets the ultimate challenge when one
is faced with terminal cancer.*

Production Company: William Link/Papazian-
    Hirsch
Executive Producer .... William Link
Executive Producer .... Robert A. Papazian
Executive Producer .... James G. Hirsch
Producer .... Glenn Jordan
Director .... Glenn Jordan
Writer .... William Link
Cast .... James Woods
Cast .... John Lithgow
Cast .... Joanna Gleason
Cast .... Eve Gordon
Cast .... Bruce Greenwood
Cast .... Greg Kean
Cast .... Arlen Dean Snyder
Cast .... Casey Sander

BRADYS, THE   CBS

Drama: Family Drama
Airdate: 02/09/90
Rating: 12.9/22   A/C: 2

*1970's sitcom "The Brady Bunch" faces life
twenty years later as all of the family members
must cope with assorted crises...alcoholism,
physical handicaps, divorce and unemployment.*

Production Company: Brady Prods. IAW
    Paramount
Executive Producer .... Sherwood Schwartz
Executive producer .... Lloyd J. Schwartz
Producer .... Barry Berg
Director .... Bruce Bilson
Writer .... Sherwood Schwartz
Writer .... Lloyd J. Schwartz
Cast .... Florence Henderson
Cast .... Robert Reed
Cast .... Ann B. Davis
Cast .... Eve Plumb
Cast .... Mike Lookinland
Cast .... Barry Williams

BRAND NEW LIFE: THE HONEYMOON   NBC

Comedy: Children/Teens • Woman's Issue/Story •
Series Pilot (2 hr.)
Airdate: 09/18/89
Rating: 15.9/25   A/C: 2

*A waitress with court-reporter aspirations and
a rich lawyer meet and fall in love. But, a la
Brady Bunch, his three children and her three
children manage to complicate their courtship
and marriage.*

Production Company: NBC Productions
Executive Producer .... Chris Carter
Producer .... George Perkins
Director .... Eric Laneuville
Writer .... Chris Carter
Cast .... Barbara Eden
Cast .... Don Murray
Cast .... Shawnee Smith
Cast .... Jennie Garth

BRASS   CBS

Drama: Cops/Detectives/Law Enforcement • Series
Pilot (2 hr.)
Airdate: 09/11/85
Rating: 12.9/22   A/C:

*The New York City chief of detectives
investigates two separate cases involving
corporate intrigue and a psychotic killer who
stalks the elderly.*

Production Company: Carnan Prods. & Jaygee
    Prods. IAW Orion TV
Executive Producer .... Jerry Golod
Producer .... T.J. Castronova
Director .... Corey Allen
Writer .... Roy Baldwin
Writer .... Matt Harris
Cast .... Carroll O'Connor
Cast .... Lois Nettleton
Cast .... Larry Atlas

BREAKING POINT   TNT

Drama: Suspense/Thriller • Period Piece • WWII •
Nazis
Airdate: 08/18/89
Rating: N/A   A/C:

*Based on the movie "36 Hours." Just before
the Normandy invasion, an American
intelligence officer is kidnapped by the
Germans. They try to learn what he knows by
convincing him he's in an American hospital
two years after the war has ended.*

Production Company: Avnet/Kerner Co.
Producer .... Jon Avnet
Producer .... Jordan Kerner
Director .... Peter Markle
Writer .... Stanley Greenberg
Cast .... Corbin Bernsen
Cast .... John Glover
Cast .... Joanna Pacula

BREAKING THE SILENCE   CBS

Drama: Murder and Murder Mystery • Courtroom
Drama • Rape/Molestation • Family Violence
Airdate: 01/14/92
Rating: 12.8/20   A/C: 2

*A sophisticated criminal attorney's suppressed
memories of his tormented relationship with his
mother surface when he assists his former law
school girlfriend in defending a teenager
accused of killing his violently abusive father.*

Production Company: Permut Presentations Inc.
    IAW Finnegan/Pinchuk Co.
Executive Producer .... David Permut
Executive Producer .... Sheldon Pinchuk
Executive Producer .... Pat Finnegan
Producer .... Lori-Etta Taub
Co-Producer .... Adam Greenman
Director .... Robert Iscove
Writer .... Adam Greenman
Cast .... Gregory Harrison
Cast .... Stephanie Zimbalist
Cast .... Chris Young
Cast .... Kevin Conway

BREATHING LESSONS   CBS

Drama: Family Drama
Airdate: 2/6/94
Rating: 21.6/32   A/C: 1

*Based on the book by Anne Tyler. One day in
the life of a middle-aged Baltimore couple who
have been married for twenty-eight years, as
they drive to a funeral in Pennsylvania. Along
the way they examine their quarrelsome
relationship and try and convince their
estranged ex-daughter-in-law to get back
together with their irresponsible son.*

Production Company: Signboard Hill Prods.
Executive Producer .... Richard Welsh
Producer .... John Erman
Supervising Producer .... Andrew Gottlieb
Director .... John Erman
Writer .... Robert W. Lenski
Cast .... Joanne Woodward
Cast .... James Garner
Cast .... Kathryn Erbe
Cast .... Joyce Van Patten

BRIDE IN BLACK, THE   ABC

Drama: Murder and Murder Mystery • Woman In
Jeopardy • Suspense/Thriller
Airdate: 10/21/90
Rating: 16.7/27   A/C: 1

*A new bride's husband is violently murdered
on their wedding day, and then becomes the next
target when she investigates his mysterious past.*

Production Company: Barry Weitz Films/Street
    Life Prods. IAW New World Television
Executive Producer .... Barry Weitz
Producer .... Brooke Kennedy
Director .... James Goldstone
Writer .... Claire Labine
Cast .... Susan Lucci
Cast .... Reginald VelJohnson
Cast .... Robert Gunton
Cast .... Tom Signorelli

BRIDESMAIDS   CBS
Drama: Woman's Issue/Story
Airdate: 02/21/89
Rating: 14.6/25   A/C:

Twenty years after high school, five female classmates come together for a wedding and a revelatory bull session.

Production Company: Motown IAW Qintex
   Entertainment and Deaun Prods. Inc.
Executive Producer .... Suzanne De Passe
Producer .... Jay Benson
Director .... Lila Garrett
Writer .... Cynthia Cherbak
Cast .... Shelley Hack
Cast .... Brooke Adams
Cast .... Hamilton Camp
Cast .... Sela Ward
Cast .... Jack Coleman

BRIDGE ACROSS TIME   NBC
Drama: Murder and Murder Mystery • Sci-Fi/
Supernatural/Horror/Fantasy • Cops/Detectives/Law
Enforcement
Airdate: 11/22/85
Rating: 13.7/21   A/C:

Jack the Ripper travels through time and goes on a murderous spree in Arizona, where a local detective tracks him down.

Production Company: Charles Fries Prods.
Executive Producer .... Charles Fries
Executive Producer .... Irv Wilson
Producer .... Jack Michon
Producer .... Richard Maynard
Director .... E.W. Swackhamer
Writer .... William F. Nolan
Cast .... David Hasselhoff
Cast .... Stefanie Kramer
Cast .... Adrienne Barbeau
Cast .... Randolph Mantooth

BRIDGE TO SILENCE   CBS
Drama: Family Drama • Children/Teens
Airdate: 04/09/89
Rating: 13.9/24   A/C:

A young deaf widow struggles to overcome the loss of her husband and fights her mother for custody of her four year old daughter.

Production Company: Briggle, Hennessy,
   Carothers & Assocs. IAW Fries Ent. Inc.
Executive Producer .... Charles Fries
Producer .... Stockton Briggle
Producer .... Dennis D. Hennessy
Producer .... Richard Carothers
Director .... Karen Arthur
Writer .... Louis Burns-Bisogno
Cast .... Lee Remick
Cast .... Marlee Matlin
Cast .... Michael O'Keefe

BRING ME THE HEAD OF DOBIE GILLIS   CBS
Comedy: Romantic Comedy
Airdate: 02/21/88
Rating: 15.0/23   A/C:

The cast of the original series is reunited when the glamorous Thalia Menninger returns to offer the whole town cash if Dobie will leave his family for her.

Production Company: 20th Century-Fox TV
Executive Producer .... Stanley Z. Cherry
Producer .... Dwayne Hickman
Producer .... Steve Clements
Producer .... Marc Summers
Writer .... Deborah Zoe Dawson
Writer .... Victoria Johns
Director .... Stanely Z. Cherry
Cast .... Sheila James
Cast .... Connie Stevens
Cast .... William Schallert
Cast .... Bob Denver
Cast .... Steve Franken
Cast .... Dwayne Hickman

BROADWAY BOUND   ABC
Drama: Family Drama • Period Piece
Airdate: 03/23/92
Rating: 8.4/14   A/C: 3

Based on the play by Neil Simon. In 1948 Brooklyn, two brothers' burgeoning success as comedy writers is dampened by the disintegration of their parents' long-suffering marriage.

Production Company: ABC Productions
Executive Producer .... Michael Brandman
Executive Producer .... Emanuel Azenberg
Producer .... Terry Nelson
Director .... Paul Bogart
Writer .... Neil Simon
Cast .... Corey Parker
Cast .... Hume Cronyn
Cast .... Jonathan Silverman
Cast .... Anne Bancroft
Cast .... Jerry Orbach

BROKEN ANGEL   ABC
Drama: Family Drama • Children/Teens • Drug
Smuggling/Dealing • Social Issue
Airdate: 03/14/88
Rating: 16.9/28   A/C:

Runaways, drug dealing, gangs, and battling parents are the background for the story of a middle class high-school girl who disappears on prom night in the aftermath of a fatal urban gang shooting.

Production Company: Stan Margulies Co. IAW
   MGM/UA
Executive Producer .... Stan Margulies
Producer .... Robin S. Clark
Director .... Richard T. Heffron
Writer .... Cynthia Cherbak
Cast .... William Shatner
Cast .... Susan Blakely
Cast .... Jason Horst
Cast .... Millie Perkins
Cast .... Carmen Zapata
Cast .... Brock Peters

BROKEN BADGES   CBS
Drama: Cops/Detectives/Law Enforcement • Action/
Adventure • Series Pilot (2 hr.)
Airdate: 11/24/90
Rating: 9.1/16   A/C: 3

A team of police officers suffering from psychiatric disorders investigates a murder to clear their favorite stool pigeon.

Production Company: Stephen J. Cannell Prods.
Executive Producer .... Stephen J. Cannell
Executive Producer .... Randall Wallace
Producer .... John Peter Kousakis
Director .... Kim Manners
Writer .... Stephen J. Cannell
Writer .... Randall Wallace
Cast .... Miguel Ferrer
Cast .... Eileen Davidson
Cast .... Jay Johnson
Cast .... Ernie Hudson

BROKEN CHAIN   TNT
Drama: American Indians • Historical Piece • Period
Piece
Airdate: 12/12/93
Rating: N/A   A/C:

The Iroquois Confederation, made up of six individual tribes, is torn apart because of conflicting loyalties during the American Revolution. An English educated warrior Joseph Brandt persuades his tribe to support the British while others support the Americans. He eventually see the white man as a threat to his peoples' way of life and fights to keep colonial settlers from his lands.

Production Company: Von Zerneck/Sertner Films,
   TNT
Executive Producer .... Frank Von Zerneck
Executive Producer .... Robert M. Sertner
Producer .... Cleve Landsberg
Producer .... Lamont Johnson
Producer .... Hannay Geigamah
Producer .... Phill Lucas
Producer .... Richard Hill
Director .... Lamont Johnson
Writer .... Earl W. Wallace
Cast .... Eric Schweig
Cast .... Wes Studi
Cast .... Buffy Sainte-Marie
Cast .... Pierce Brosnan

BROKEN CORD, THE   ABC

Drama: Family Drama • Children/Teens • Medical/
Disease/Mental Illness • True Story • Social Issue •
American Indians
Airdate: 02/03/92
Rating: 14.3/22   A/C: 2

*Based on the book by Michael Dorris. When a
college professor learns that his adopted Native
American son suffers from fetal alcohol
syndrome, he becomes an outspoken advocate
as he struggles to help the boy overcome his
limitations.*

Production Company: Carmen Culver Films &
    Alan Barnette Prods.
Executive Producer .... Carmen Culver
Producer .... Alan Barnette
Co-Producer .... Oscar L. Costo
Director .... Ken Olin
Writer .... Ann Beckett
Cast .... Jimmy Smits
Cast .... Kim Delaney
Cast .... Michael Spears
Cast .... Fredrick Leader-Charge

BROKEN PROMISES: TAKING EMILY
BACK   CBS

Drama: Family Drama • Children/Teens • Social Issue
• Woman's Issue/Story • True Story
Airdate: 12/26/93
Rating: 12.6/22   A/C: 1

*An affluent husband and wife face emotional
uncertainty when they try to adopt a toddler
from a shady homeless couple. It is soon
discovered that the indigent duo have a history
of promising their babies to different couples
at the same time, in order to extract cash from
the desperate parents to-be. Unwilling to be
pawns in their scheme, the adoptive mother
fights to keep custody of her new daughter.*

Production Company: Larry Thompson Ent.
Executive Producer .... Larry Thompson
Co-Producer .... Daniel Schneider
Co-PRODUCER .... Christopher Canaan
Co-Producer .... Tyler Tyhurst
Producer .... Donald Wrye
Director .... Donald Wrye
Writer .... Vickie Patik
Writer .... Christopher Canaan
Cast .... Cheryl Ladd
Cast .... Robert Desiderio
Cast .... D. David Morin
Cast .... Kathleeen Wilhoite

BROKEN VOWS   CBS

Drama: Murder and Murder Mystery • Forbidden
Love
Airdate: 01/28/87
Rating: 14.1/22   A/C:

*The priest who gave last rites to a murder victim
begins questioning his vows when he meets the
victim's former lover and becomes involved with
the murder investigation.*

Production Company: Robert Halmi Inc.
Executive Producer .... Peter Zimmer
Executive Producer .... Robert Thompson
Producer .... Bill Brademan
Producer .... Edwin Self
Director .... Jud Taylor
Writer .... Ivan Davis
Cast .... Tommy Lee Jones
Cast .... Annette O'Toole
Cast .... David Groh
Cast .... M. Emmet Walsh

BROTHERHOOD OF JUSTICE, THE   ABC

Drama: Children/Teens • Drug Smuggling/Dealing •
Social Issue
Airdate: 05/18/86
Rating: 11.6/19   A/C:

*High-school seniors overreact by becoming
vigilantes when their principal asks his students
to counter drugs and vandalism.*

Production Company: Guber-Peters IAW Taper
    Forum Media & Phoenix Ent.
Executive Producer .... Hans Proppe
Producer .... Judith James
Producer .... Margo Winchester
Director .... Charles Braverman
Writer .... Noah Jubelirer
Writer .... Jeffrey Bloom
Cast .... Keanu Reeves
Cast .... Joe Spano
Cast .... Kiefer Sutherland

BROTHERHOOD OF THE GUN   CBS

Drama: Series Pilot (2 hr.) • Western • Period Piece
Airdate: 10/05/91
Rating: 7.3/14   A/C: 3

*A gunslinging outlaw turns lawman to seek
revenge on his ex-partner who double-crossed
him and killed his younger brother.*

Production Company: Desperado Pictures IAW
    Universal TV
Executive Producer .... Robert Ward
Producer .... Chuck Sellier
Director .... Vern Gillum
Writer .... Bob Ward
Cast .... Brian Bloom
Cast .... Jamie Rose
Cast .... Jorge Cervera, Jr.
Cast .... David Carradine
Cast .... James Remar
Cast .... Alan Canton

BROTHERHOOD OF THE ROSE   NBC

Miniseries/Drama (2 nights): Suspense/Thriller •
Action/Adventure • Foreign or Exotic Location
Airdate: 01/22/89 • 01/23/89
Rating: 20.9/35 • 19.2/30   A/C:

*Based on David Morrell's novel. A secret spy
organization composed of agents from all over
the world causes three members—a father and
his two adopted sons-to all turn against each
other as layers of a mystery are peeled away.*

Production Company: NBC Prods.
Executive Producer .... Stirling Silliphant
Producer .... Marvin J. Chomsky
Writer .... Gy Waldron
Director .... Marvin J. Chomsky
Cast .... Peter Strauss
Cast .... Connie Sellecca
Cast .... David Morse
Cast .... Robert Mitchum

BROTHERLY LOVE   CBS

Drama: Suspense/Thriller • Psychological Thriller •
Mafia/Mob
Airdate: 05/28/85
Rating: 13.5/22   A/C:

*Based on the novel by William Blankenship.
Upon release from a California asylum, a
murderous psychopath decides to exact revenge
for an alleged wrong done by his identical twin
by making him the leading suspect in a murder.*

Production Company: CBS Entertainment Prods.
Producer .... Andrew Gottlieb
Director .... Jeff Bleckner
Writer .... Ernest Tidyman
Cast .... Judd Hirsch
Cast .... Lori Lethin
Cast .... George Dzundza
Cast .... Karen Carlson

BUMP IN THE NIGHT   CBS

Drama: Family Drama • Children/Teens • Rape/
Molestation • Psychological Thriller • Social Issue
Airdate: 01/06/91
Rating: 16.0/25   A/C: 1

*A former investigative reporter fights the effects
of alcohol withdrawal as she and her ex-
husband search to find her son, who is
kidnapped by a pedophile.*

Production Company: Craig Anderson Prods. IAW
    RHI Entertainment
Executive Producer .... Robert Halmi, Sr.
Producer .... Craig Anderson
Co-Executive Producer .... JoBeth Williams
Co-Executive Producer .... Barry Krost
Director .... Karen Arthur
Writer .... Christopher Lofton
Cast .... Meredith Baxter
Cast .... Christopher Reeve
Cast .... Wings Hauser
Cast .... Corey Carrier

BUNNY'S TALE, A   ABC
Drama: Woman Against The System • True Story •
Woman's Issue/Story • Period Piece
Airdate: 02/25/85
Rating: 17.3/26   A/C:

*Based on a true story by Gloria Steinem, who
in 1963 was assigned to pose as a Playboy
Bunny and write an investigative article. She
discovers that the lives of these hard-working
waitresses is far less glamorous than expected.*

Production Company: Stan Margulies Co.
Executive Producer .... Stan Margulies
Co-Producer .... Joan Marks
Director .... Karen Arthur
Writer .... Deena Goldstone
Cast .... Kirstie Alley
Cast .... Joanna Kerns
Cast .... Lisa Pelikan

BURDEN OF PROOF, THE   ABC
Miniseries/Drama (2 nights): Family Drama •
Suspense/Thriller • Courtroom Drama
Airdate: 02/09/92 • 02/10/92
Rating: 12.8/18 • 15.1/23   A/C: 3 • 2

*Based on the book by Scott Turow. A middle-
aged criminal attorney becomes embroiled in
the mystery of his wife's suicide. As he unravels
the case, he discovers family duplicity and
shocking indiscretions.*

Production Company: Mike Robe Productions
      IAW ABC Video Enterprises
Executive Producer .... Mike Robe
Producer .... John Flynn
Co-Producer .... Benjamin A. Weissman
Director .... Mike Robe
Writer .... John Gay
Cast .... Hector Elizondo
Cast .... Brian Dennehy
Cast .... Mel Harris
Cast .... Stefanie Powers
Cast .... Victoria Principal

BURIED ALIVE   USA
Drama: Murder Mystery • Suspense/Thriller
Airdate: 05/09/90
Rating: N/A   A/C:

*A doctor lusting after a sexy young woman tells
her he'll take her out of the hick town they're
in and gives her poison to kill her husband.
Unfortunately for them, the husband isn't
completely dead, so he climbs out of his grave
to exact revenge.*

Production Company: MCA Entertainment
Producer .... Niki Marvin
Director .... Frank Darabont
Writer .... Mark Patrick Carducci
Cast .... Tim Matheson
Cast .... Jennifer Jason Leigh
Cast .... William Atherton
Cast .... Hoyt Axton

BURNING BED, THE   NBC
Drama: True Crime • Courtroom Drama • Woman's
Issue/Story • Social Issue • Family Violence
Airdate: 10/08/84
Rating: 36.2/52   A/C:

*True story of Francine Huges, wife and mother
of three, whose husband brutally abuses her.
She exacts revenge on him by setting his bed
on fire while he sleeps. She is later tried and
acquitted.*

Production Company: Tisch/Avnet Prods.
Executive Producer .... Jon Avnet
Executive Producer .... Steve Tisch
Producer .... Carol Schreder
Director .... Robert Greenwald
Writer .... Rose Leiman Goldemberg
Cast .... Farrah Fawcett
Cast .... Paul LeMat
Cast .... Richard Masur

BURNING BRIDGES   ABC
Drama: Family Drama • Forbidden Love • Woman's
Issue/Story
Airdate: 05/06/90
Rating: 13.6/22   A/C: 2

*A married woman's refusal to end her love affair
with a doctor tears her family apart and drives
her to a breakdown.*

Production Company: Andrea Baynes Productions
      IAW Lorimar Television
Executive Producer .... Andrea Baynes
Executive Producer .... Judith P. Mitchell
Producer .... Bruce Johnson
Director .... Sheldon Larry
Writer .... Judith P. Mitchell
Cast .... Meredith Baxter
Cast .... Nick Mancuso
Cast .... Lois Chiles

BURNING RAGE   CBS
Drama: Woman Against The System
Airdate: 09/21/84
Rating: 16.5/30   A/C:

*When an Appalachian coal town is poisoned
by an underground coal fire, a Federal
investigator comes to their rescue only to be
thwarted by the greedy and powerful mine
owner.*

Production Company: Gilbert Cates Prods.
Producer .... Gilbert Cates
Director .... Gilbert Cates
Writer .... Karol Ann Hoeffner
Writer .... Clifford Campion
Cast .... Tom Wopat
Cast .... Carol Kane
Cast .... Eddie Albert
Cast .... Barbara Mandrell

BY DAWN'S EARLY LIGHT   HBO
Drama: Suspense/Thriller • Political Piece • Sci-Fi/
Supernatural/Horror/Fantasy • Social Issue
Airdate: 05/19/90
Rating: N/A   A/C:

*The Soviets mistake a nuclear missile fired by
a group of renegade Soviet soldiers for a hostile
attack by the U.S. War is avoided through the
heroic efforts of two American pilots.*

Production Company: HBO Pictures IAW
      Paravision International U.S.A.
Executive Producer .... Bruce Gilbert
Producer .... Thomas Hammel
Director .... Jack Sholder
Writer .... Bruce Gilbert
Cast .... Powers Boothe
Cast .... Rebecca De Mornay
Cast .... Martin Landau

C. A. T. SQUAD   NBC
Drama: Cops/Detectives/Law Enforcement • Action/
Adventure • Series Pilot (2 hr.)
Airdate: 07/26/86
Rating: 17.3/30   A/C:

*A Counter Assault Tactical Squad is created to
capture the serial murderer of NATO defense
scientists.*

Production Company: NBC Prods.
Executive Producer .... William Friedkin
Producer .... David Salven
Director .... William Friedkin
Writer .... Gerald Petievich
Cast .... Jack Youngblood
Cast .... Joseph Cortese
Cast .... Steve James

C. A. T. SQUAD: PYTHON WOLF   NBC
Drama: Cops/Detectives/Law Enforcement • Action/
Adventure
Airdate: 05/23/88
Rating: 12.8/20   A/C:

*The Counter Assault Tactical Squad takes on a
plot involving missing plutonium, a South
African forced-labor camp and technological
espionage.*

Production Company: NBC Prods.
Executive Producer .... William Friedkin
Producer .... David Salven
Writer .... Robert Ward
Cast .... Joe Cortese
Cast .... Jack Youngblood
Cast .... Deborah Van Valkenburgh
Cast .... Miguel Ferrer

CAINE MUTINY COURT - MARTIAL, THE
CBS

Drama: Period Piece • Courtroom Drama
Airdate: 05/08/88
Rating: 9.4/15   A/C:

Based on the Herman Wouk novel about a naval officer who, with the help of a resourceful attorney, defends his decision to relieve his captain of command while at sea.

Production Company: Maltese Companies IAW Wouk/War Prods. and Sandcastle 5 Prods.
Executive Producer .... Ray Volpe
Executive Producer .... Joseph Wouk
Co-Executive Producer .... Edd Griles
Producer .... Robert Altman
Producer .... John Flaxman
Director .... Robert Altman
Writer .... Herman Wouk
Cast .... Jeff Daniels
Cast .... Brad Davis
Cast .... Eric Bogosian

CALENDAR GIRL, COP KILLER? THE BAMBI BEMBENEK STORY
ABC

Drama: Murder and Murder Mystery • True Crime • Family Violence
Airdate: 05/18/92
Rating: 10.7/17   A/C: 3

In 1982, Lawrencia Bembenek, former pin-up girl and ex-Milwaukee cop, is convicted of murdering her husband's ex-wife. Steadfastly claiming her innocence, she escapes nine years later and flees to Canada, only to be caught and sent back to prison. Note: See "Woman on the Run: The Lawrencia Bembenek Story" -NBC

Production Company: Von Zerneck-Sertner Films
Executive Producer .... Frank Von Zerneck
Executive Producer .... Robert M. Sertner
Producer .... Jerry London
Co-Producer .... Robert Engelman
Co-Producer .... Randy Sutter
Director .... Jerry London
Writer .... Larry Barber
Writer .... Paul Barber
Cast .... Lindsay Frost
Cast .... Timothy Busfield
Cast .... John Karlen
Cast .... Linda Blair

CALIFORNIA GIRLS
ABC

Comedy: Romantic Comedy
Airdate: 03/24/85
Rating: 20.3/31   A/C:

In pursuit of a dream, a New Jersey mechanic moves to Southern California and falls in love with the perfect "California girl" only to find out that all that glitters is not gold.

Production Company: ABC Circle Films
Producer ....R.W. Goodwin
Director .... Rick Wallace
Writer .... Charles Rosin
Cast .... Robby Benson
Cast .... Martin Mull
Cast .... Tawny Kitaen

CALL ME ANNA
ABC

Drama: Medical/Disease/Mental Illness • True Story • Biography • Hollywood
Airdate: 11/11/90
Rating: 15.9/24   A/C: 2

Based on the bestselling autobiography by Patty Duke. The account of actress Patty Duke's life including her terrible years as a child star, failed marriages, and her long battle with manic depression.

Production Company: Gilbert Cates/Mianna Pearce/Finnegan-Pinchuk
Executive Producer .... Sheldon Pinchuk
Producer .... Gilbert Cates
Co-Producer .... Anna Duke-Pearce
Director .... Gilbert Cates
Writer .... John McGreevey
Cast .... Patty Duke
Cast .... Timothy Carhart
Cast .... Howard Hesseman
Cast .... Deborah May

CALL OF THE WILD
CBS

Drama: Action/Adventure • Period Piece • Historical Piece
Airdate: 4/25/93
Rating: 18.2/29   A/C: 1

Based on the book by Jack London. In 1897, an enterprising young man stricken with gold rush fever strikes out for the Alaskan Klondike where he rescues an abused sled dog named Buck. The two are soon separated and each faces the harsh realities of life in the Yukon. They are eventually reunited and form a bond that teaches both man and beast the true meaning of trust and loyalty.

Production Company: RHI Ent.
Executive Producer .... Robert Halmi, Sr.
Producer .... Alan Jacobs
Director .... Alan Smithee
Writer .... Christopher Lofton
Cast .... Rick Schroder
Cast .... Gordon Tootoosis
Cast .... Mia Sara
Cast .... Duncan Fraser

CAMILLE
CBS

Drama: Love Story • Period Piece
Airdate: 12/11/84
Rating: 15.2/25   A/C:

Based on the novel by Alexander Dumas as well as a remake of the 1936 classic movie. The story of a provincial French girl who heads for Paris and finds both love and misfortune in 19th Century French high society.

Production Company: Norman Rosemont Prods.
Producer .... Norman Rosemont
Director .... Desmond Davis
Writer .... Blanche Hanalis
Cast .... Greta Scacchi
Cast .... Colin Firth
Cast .... John Gielgud
Cast .... Denholm Elliott

CAMP CUCAMONGA
NBC

Comedy: Youth Comedy
Airdate: 09/23/90
Rating: 8.3/14   A/C: 3

Gregarious teen campers find new friendship, horny counselors find new love, and all join together to save the camp from threatened closure.

Production Company: Richmel Ent. IAW NBC Prods.
Executive Producer .... Richard Melcombe
Producer .... Scott Maitland
Director .... Roger Duchowney
Writer .... Bennett Tramer
Cast .... John Ratzenberger
Cast .... Josh Saviano
Cast .... Danica McKellar
Cast .... Sherman Hemsley

CAN YOU FEEL ME DANCING?
NBC

Drama: Family Drama • Medical/Disease/Mental Illness
Airdate: 10/13/86
Rating: 19.1/30   A/C:

A congenitally blind woman, who first asserts her independence from her overly protective parents with the help of her boyfriend, realizes that the only way to achieve true independence is by herself.

Production Company: Robert Greenwald Prods.
Executive Producer .... Robert Greenwald
Executive Producer .... Jonathan Bernstein
Co-Producer .... Diane Walsh
Co-Producer .... Cleve Landsberg
Director .... Michael Miller
Writer .... J. Miyoko Hensley
Writer .... Steven Hensley
Cast .... Justine Bateman
Cast .... Jason Bateman
Cast .... Max Gail
Cast .... Frances Lee McCain
Cast .... Roger Wilson

CANDLES IN THE DARK
FAMILY

Drama: Foreign or Exotic Location • Cross-Cultural Story • Love Story
Airdate: 12/3/93
Rating: N/A   A/C:

After flunking out of college a young women travels to Estonia to visit her Aunt. She quickly falls in love with a devoted resistance fighter which is then complicated when his old girlfriend, a Russian skater, comes back into his life. Becoming deeply involved in the country's fight for independence from the Soviet Union, she convinces her aunt to stand proud and fight for freedom.

Production Company: Taska Films IAW Kushner-Locke Co. and Family Prods.
Executive Producer .... James M Dowaliby
Producer ....Ilmar Taska
Co-Producer .... Peter Shepherd
Director .... Maximilian Schell
Writer .... Nicholas Niciphor
Cast .... Maximilian Schell
Cast .... Alyssa Milano
Cast .... Chad Lowe
Cast .... Gunther Halmer

© 1994, Reference Guide To Movies & Miniseries For TV & Cable
Page 26

CAPITAL NEWS — ABC
Drama: Series Pilot (2 hr.)
Airdate: 04/09/90
Rating: 10.1/17   A/C: 3

Writers and editors on a Washington, D.C., newspaper investigate stories and each other in the nation's capital.

Production Company: MTM Enterprises Inc.
Executive Producer .... David Milch
Producer .... Allan Arkush
Producer .... Andrew Gottlieb
Co-Producer .... Fred Lyle
Director .... Allan Arkush
Writer .... David Milch
Writer .... Christian Williams
Cast .... Lloyd Bridges
Cast .... Mark Blum
Cast .... Christian Clemenson
Cast .... Kurt Fuller

CAPTAIN COOK — TNT
Drama: Historical Piece • Biography • Period Piece
Airdate: 10/16/89
Rating: N/A   A/C:

This six hour miniseries chronicles the adventures of Captain James Cook the famous English explorer who charted New Zealand and the east coast of Australia (1768-71) and mapped numerous tropical islands. He was murdered in 1779 by natives in Hawaii on his third voyage in search of a northwest passage.

Production Company: Revcom IAW TNT
Producer .... Geoffrey Daniels
Director .... Lawrence G. Clark
Writer .... Peter Yelman
Cast .... Keith Michell
Cast .... John Gregg
Cast .... Erich Hallhuber

CAPTIVE — ABC
Drama: Family Drama • Suspense/Thriller • True Crime
Airdate: 10/13/91
Rating: 12.9/20   A/C: 3

An Oregon couple and their infant child are kidnapped and terrorized by two drug-crazed killers. After surviving the ordeal, they must learn to deal with their feelings of anger and guilt.

Production Company: Capital Cities/ABC IAW Bonny Dore Prods. IAW Ten-Four Prods.
Executive Producer .... Greg Strangis
Executive Producer .... Bonny Dore
Producer .... Michael Rhodes
Producer .... Geoffrey Cowan
Producer .... Julian Fowles
Director .... Michael Tuchner
Writer .... Leonie Sandercock
Cast .... Joanna Kerns
Cast .... Barry Bostwick
Cast .... Chad Lowe
Cast .... John Stamos

CARLY'S WEB — NBC
Drama: Woman Against The System • Action/Adventure • Series Pilot (2 hr.)
Airdate: 07/12/87
Rating: 9.3/17   A/C:

A low-level adventure-seeking Justice Department clerk, pretending to be an agent, unearths corruption using a variety of high-tech and espionage methods.

Production Company: MTM Ent.
Executive Producer .... Michael Gleason
Producer .... Gareth Davies
Director .... Kevin Inch
Writer .... Brad Kern
Cast .... Daphne Ashbrook
Cast .... Vincent Baggetta
Cast .... Peter Billingsley

CAROLINA SKELETONS — NBC
Drama: Murder and Murder Mystery • Man Against The System • Black Story
Airdate: 09/30/91
Rating: 14.7/23   A/C: 3

Based on the book by David Stout. A black Viet Nam Marine officer returns to his rural South Carolina hometown to clear the name of his brother who was executed at the age of fourteen for the murder of two white girls in the 1930's.

Production Company: Kushner-Locke
Executive Producer .... Donald Kushner
Executive Producer .... Peter Locke
Producer .... John Erman
Producer .... Tracy Keenan Wynn
Director .... John Erman
Writer .... Tracy Keenan Wynn
Cast .... Louis Gossett, Jr.
Cast .... Bruce Dern
Cast .... Melissa Leo
Cast .... G.D. Spradlin

CAROLINE? — CBS
EMMY WINNER
Mystery: Family Drama • Children/Teens • Period Piece
Airdate: 04/29/90
Rating: 19.4/30   A/C: 1

Based on the book "Father's Arcane Daughter" by E.L. Konigsberg. A woman presumed dead for fifteen years returns to her family just in time for a large inheritance. Unfortunately, not everyone is convinced of her identity.

Production Company: Barry & Enright Prods.
Executive Producer .... Dan Enright
Executive Producer .... Les Alexander
Executive Producer .... Don Enright
Producer .... Dorothea Petrie
Director .... Joseph Sargent
Writer .... Michael De Guzman
Cast .... Stephanie Zimbalist
Cast .... Pamela Reed
Cast .... George Grizzard
Cast .... Shawn Phelan
Cast .... Patricia Neal

CARTIER AFFAIR, THE — NBC
Drama: Suspense/Thriller
Airdate: 11/04/84
Rating: 17.1/27   A/C:

In order to case her house for a robbery, an ex-convict working for a crime boss, takes a job as a TV star's personal secretary.

Production Company: Hill-Mandelker TV Prods.
Executive Producer .... Leonard Hill
Producer .... Joel Dean
Producer .... Christopher Nelson
Writer .... Brad Buckner
Writer .... Eugenie Ross-Lemming
Director .... Rod Holcomb
Cast .... Joan Collins
Cast .... David Hasselhoff
Cast .... Ed Lauter
Cast .... Telly Savalas

CASANOVA — ABC
Drama: Period Piece • Historical Piece • Foreign or Exotic Location • Biography • Sex/Glitz
Airdate: 03/01/87
Rating: 10.3/15   A/C:

Lighthearted tale of the 18th-century nobleman whose name became a synonym for bed-hopping and other amorous adventures.

Production Company: Konigsberg/Sanitsky Co. IAW Reteitalia
Executive Producer .... Frank Konigsberg
Executive Producer .... Larry Sanitsky
Producer .... Sam Manners
Director .... Simon Langton
Writer .... George MacDonald Fraser
Cast .... Richard Chamberlain
Cast .... Faye Dunaway
Cast .... Ornella Muti
Cast .... Sylvia Kristel
Cast .... Hanna Schygulla

CASE CLOSED — CBS
Drama: Murder and Murder Mystery • Cops/Detectives/Law Enforcement • Action/Adventure • Buddy Story
Airdate: 04/19/88
Rating: 13.0/22   A/C:

A frenetic young policeman teams up with a retired cop to solve a series of killings related to a fifteen year old diamond theft.

Production Company: Houston Motion Picture Ent. Inc. in cooperation with CBS Ent.
Producer .... Andrew Gottlieb
Co-Producer .... Byron Allen
Director .... Dick Lowry
Writer .... Steve Crider
Writer .... Byron Allen
Cast .... Charles Durning
Cast .... Charles Weldon
Cast .... Erica Gimpel
Cast .... Byron Allen

CASE FOR MURDER, A   USA
Drama: Courtroom Drama • Suspense/Thriller
Airdate: 5/19/93
Rating: N/A   A/C:

While preparing for a sensational murder trial, an ambitious young lawyer apprentices herself to a rising attorney, falls in love with him but then uncovers some dirty evidence about his all-too-sudden climb to the top.

Production Company: ..... Bodega Bay Prods. MTE	
Executive Producer	Richard Gitelson
Executive Producer	Eric Freiser
Producer	Michael S. Murphy
Director	Duncan Gibbins
Writer	Pablo Fenjves
Cast	Jennifer Grey
Cast	Peter Berg
Cast	Belinda Bauer

CASE OF DEADLY FORCE, A   CBS
Drama: Courtroom Drama • Man Against The System • True Story • Black Story • Social Issue
Airdate: 04/09/86
Rating: 12.0/20   A/C:

Fact-based story of a Boston ex-cop lawyer who takes the case of a black woman whose husband was killed by police in what turn out to be suspicious circumstances.

Production Company: Telecom Ent. Inc.	
Executive Producer	Michael Lepiner
Executive Producer	Ken Kaufman
Producer	Bruce Pustin
Director	Michael Miller
Writer	Dennis Nemec
Cast	Richard Crenna
Cast	John Shea
Cast	Lorraine Toussaint

CASE OF THE HILLSIDE STRANGLER, THE
                                                NBC
Drama: Cops/Detectives/Law Enforcement • True Crime
Airdate: 04/02/89
Rating: 23.1/36   A/C:

The true story of L.A.'s hillside stranglers, Angelo Buono and his cousin Kenneth Bianchi, who are ultimately brought to justice by officers Grogan and Fernandez of the LAPD.

Production Company: Kenwood Prods. IAW Fries Ent. Inc.	
Executive Producer	Charles Fries
Executive Producer	Mike Rosenfeld
Producer	Carol Coates
Director	Steven Gethers
Writer	Steven Gethers
Cast	Richard Crenna
Cast	Tony Plana
Cast	Billy Zane
Cast	Dennis Farina

CASEY'S GIFT: FOR LOVE OF A CHILD
                                                NBC
Drama: Family Drama • Children/Teens
Airdate: 09/24/90
Rating: 14.0/22   A/C: 2

The lives of two neighboring families are torn apart when the child of one family drowns in the other's swimming pool.

Production Company: American First Run Studios	
Executive Producer	Max A. Keller
Executive Producer	Micheline H. Keller
Executive Producer	Charles Hairston
Producer	Daniel Helfgott
Producer	Norm Lenzer
Producer	Tom Ackerman
Director	Kevin James Dobson
Writer	Allan Sloane
Writer	Phil Penningroth
Cast	Kevin Dobson
Cast	Michael Tucker
Cast	Belinda Montgomery
Cast	Karen Austin

CAST A DEADLY SPELL   HBO
Drama: Cops/Detectives/Law Enforcement • Period Piece • Sci-Fi/Supernatural/Horror/Fantasy
Airdate: 09/07/91
Rating: N/A   A/C:

In 1948 Los Angeles, a private eye finds himself embroiled in black magic when he tries to destroy a menacing plot to rule the world by sinister zombies.

Production Company: Pacific Western Production	
Executive Producer	Gale Anne Hurd
Producer	Ginny Nugent
Director	Martin Campbell
Writer	Joseph Dougherty
Cast	Fred Ward
Cast	David Warner
Cast	Julianne Moore
Cast	Clancy Brown

CAST THE FIRST STONE   NBC
Drama: Woman Against The System • True Story • Rape/Molestation • Woman's Issue/Story
Airdate: 11/13/89
Rating: 17.9/28   A/C: 2

The story of a former Roman Catholic novitiate who is a respected school teacher until she decides to keep the baby conceived during a rape attack. The school board, disbelieving she was attacked, fires her on the grounds of immoral conduct.

Production Company: A Mench Prod. IAW Columbia Pictures Television	
Executive Producer	Sheri Singer
Producer	Mark A. Burley
Director	John Korty
Writer	Brian Ross
Cast	Jill Eikenberry
Cast	Richard Masur
Cast	Joe Spano
Cast	Anne Schedeen

CASUALTIES OF LOVE: THE LONG ISLAND LOLITA STORY   CBS
Drama: True Crime • Children/Teens • Sex/Glitz
Airdate: 1/3/93
Rating: 14.3/22   A/C: 2

In 1992 Amy Fisher, a Long Island NY high school student, has an affair with married car mechanic Joey Buttafuoco. Fisher, in a fit of jealousy, shoots Buttafuoco's wife Mary Jo in the head. A sensational trial ensues and Amy is ultimately convicted of attempted murder. Note: See- "Amy Fisher: My Story" - NBC &"Beyond Control" - ABC

Production Company: Diane Soklow Prods. IAW Tristar TV	
Executive Producer	Diane Sokolow
Producer	John Herzfeld
Producer	Vahan Moosekian
Director	John Herzfeld
Writer	John Herzfeld
Cast	Alyssa Milano
Cast	Jack Scalia
Cast	Phyllis Lyons

CASUALTY OF WAR, A   USA
Drama: Suspense/Thriller • Foreign or Exotic Location
Airdate: 03/14/90
Rating: N/A   A/C:

Based on the Frederick Forsythe novel. A former British intelligence agent is brought back to masquerade as a terrorist arms buyer in order to sabotage a Libyan arms sale to the IRA.

Production Company: F.F.S. Prods. IAW Taurus Film & Blair Communications	
Executive Producer	Frederick Forsyth
Executive Producer	Murray Smith
Executive Producer	Nick Elliot
Producer	Frederick Muller
Director	Tom Clegg
Writer	Murray Smith
Cast	Shelley Hack
Cast	David Threlfall
Cast	Alan Howard
Cast	Bill Bailey

CAUGHT IN THE ACT — USA
Mystery: Romantic Comedy
Airdate: 7/22/93
Rating: N/A   A/C:

A struggling actor discovers ten million dollars in his bank account and at the same time he is framed for murder. He slowly uncovers the fact that he is a pawn in an elaborate embezzlement scheme and that his new romance with an aspiring actress might be the cause of this most unpleasant predicament.

Production Company: Davis Ent. Meltzer/Viviano Prods. IAW MTE Prods.
Executive Producer .... John Davis
Executive Producer .... Merrill H. Karpf
Producer .... Michael Meltzer
Producer .... Bettina Viviano
Co-Producer .... William Fay
Director .... Deborah Reinsch
Writer .... Ken Hixon
Cast .... Gregory Harrison
Cast .... Leslie Hope
Cast .... Patricia Clarkson
Cast .... Kevin Tighe

CELEBRATION FAMILY — ABC
Drama: Family Drama • Cross-Cultural Story • Man Against The System • Children/Teens • Social Issue
Airdate: 05/24/87
Rating: 10.2/17   A/C:

A couple unable to have a third child adopt ten hard-to-place children. Though unsympathetic neighbors try to have the children removed, the family remains together.

Production Company: Frank von Zerneck Films
Executive Producer .... Frank Von Zerneck
Executive Producer .... Stu Samuels
Producer .... Robert M. Sertner
Co-Producer .... Clifford Campion
Director .... Robert Day
Writer .... Richard Lees
Cast .... Stephanie Zimbalist
Cast .... James Read
Cast .... Diane Ladd
Cast .... Ed Begley, Jr.

CHALLENGE OF A LIFETIME — ABC
Drama: Woman's Issue/Story • Sports
Airdate: 02/14/85
Rating: 8.7/13   A/C:

A divorced mother gets a new lease on life when she starts training to compete in a grueling triathlon.

Production Company: Moonlight Prods.
Executive Producer .... Robert Greenwald
Producer .... Robert M. Sertner
Director .... Russ Mayberry
Writer .... Peachy Markowitz
Cast .... Penny Marshall
Cast .... Richard Gilliland
Cast .... Jonathan Silverman

CHALLENGER — ABC
Drama (3 Hours): True Story • Historical Piece
Airdate: 02/25/90
Rating: 12.8/20   A/C: 3

A poignant look into the lives of the seven Challenger crew members during the months before the launch of the ill-fated space shuttle.

Production Company: The Indie Prod. Co. IAW King Phoenix Ent. & George Englund Prod.
Executive Producer .... Bruce J. Sallan
Executive Producer .... George Englund
Producer .... Debbie Robins
Producer .... George Englund, Jr.
Director .... Glenn Jordan
Writer .... George Englund
Cast .... Karen Allen
Cast .... Barry Bostwick
Cast .... Joe Morton
Cast .... Lane Smith

CHAMELEONS — NBC
Comedy: Cops/Detectives/Law Enforcement • Action/Adventure • Series Pilot (2 hr.)
Airdate: 12/29/89
Rating: 9.9/17   A/C: 3

When an eccentric newspaper tycoon is murdered, his two granddaughters discover the bizarre secret life he and his handsome young protege were leading as uniformed, caped crimefighters.

Production Company: Glen A. Larson Productions IAW NBC Productions
Executive Producer .... Glen A. Larson
Executive Producer .... Stephen A. Miller
Producer .... Steven Stafford
Producer .... Janet Curtis-Larson
Director .... Glen A. Larson
Writer .... Glen A. Larson
Writer .... Stephen A. Miller
Cast .... Crystal Bernard
Cast .... Marcus Gilbert
Cast .... Mary Bergmann
Cast .... Richard Burgi

CHANCE OF A LIFETIME — NBC
Comedy: Romantic Comedy
Airdate: 11/18/91
Rating: 14.8/22   A/C: 3

An uptight, overworked widow, given six months to live, decides to have one last fling. She comes face to face with her emotions when she finds herself hopelessly in love, learns she was wrongly diagnosed and is very much alive.

Production Company: Lynn Roth Prods. Inc., Fries Entertainment, Inc.
Executive Producer .... Charles Fries
Executive Producer .... Lynn Roth
Producer .... Lynn Roth
Director .... Jonathan Sanger
Writer .... Lynn Roth
Cast .... Betty White
Cast .... Leslie Nielsen
Cast .... Ed Begley, Jr.
Cast .... Michael Tucci

CHANTILLY LACE — SHOWTIME
Drama: Woman's Issue/Story
Airdate: 7/18/93
Rating: N/A   A/C:

A group of seven women come together on three separate occasions during the course of a year. The first time is for a 40th birthday celebration, the second time is for a bachelorette party and the last time is to mourn a death. During each reunion the women reflect, confess, confront and bond with each other, learning to express long held feelings and emotions.

Production Company: Showtime Productions
Executive Producer .... Steven Hewitt
Producer .... Linda Yellen
Producer .... Rosanne Ehlich
Director .... Linda Yellen
Director .... Rosanne Ehlich
Writer .... Linda Yellen
Cast .... Lindsay Crouse
Cast .... Jill Eikenberry
Cast .... Martha Plimpton
Cast .... Ally Sheedy
Cast .... JoBeth Williams

CHARLES AND DIANA: UNHAPPILY EVER AFTER — ABC
Drama: Family Drama • True Story • Foreign or Exotic Location • Biography
Airdate: 12/13/93
Rating: 12.8/19   A/C: 2

Chronicles the marriage of the Prince and Princess of Wales from their much publicized fairy tale wedding in 1981 to their stormy, turbulent separation in 1992 which rocked Buckingham Palace.

Production Company: Amblin TV IAW Universal TV
Executive Producer .... Jonas McCord
Executive Producer .... Steven Spielberg
Producer .... Gregg Fienberg
Director .... Gregory Hoblit
Writer .... Jonas McCord
Cast .... Christien Anholt
Cast .... Andre Braugher
Cast .... Joshua Lucas

Movies and Miniseries

CHARLEY HANNAH — ABC

Drama: Cops/Detectives/Law Enforcement •
Children/Teens • Period Piece • Mafia/Mob
Airdate: 04/05/86
Rating: 13.4/23   A/C:

Against a 1950s backdrop, a veteran policeman takes an interest in the welfare of a friend of a youth whom he has accidentally killed, protecting the boy from the mob.

Production Company: A. Shane Prods.
Executive Producer .... Joan Conrad
Producer .... Roger Bacon
Director .... Peter H. Hunt
Writer .... David J. Kinghorn
Cast .... Robert Conrad
Cast .... Christian Conrad
Cast .... Shane Conrad

CHASE — CBS

Drama: Woman Against The System • Courtroom
Drama • Social Issue
Airdate: 11/23/85
Rating: 11.7/19   A/C:

When a tough talking lawyer returns to her hometown to defend a migrant worker in an unpopular case, she is ostracized by old friends and lovers.

Production Company: CBS Entertainment Prods.
Producer .... Sam Strangis
Director .... Rod Holcomb
Writer .... David Peckinpah
Cast .... Jennifer O'Neill
Cast .... Robert S. Woods
Cast .... Terence Knox

CHASE, THE — NBC

Drama: Cops/Detectives/Law Enforcement • True
Story
Airdate: 02/10/91
Rating: 14.6/23   A/C: 3

In 1988, a helicopter pilot for a Denver TV station helps police capture a notorious escaped convict.

Production Company: Steve White Prods. IAW
    Spectacor Films
Executive Producer .... Steve White
Producer .... Barry Bernardi
Producer .... Paul Wendkos
Co-Producer ....John Flynn
Director .... Paul Wendkos
Writer .... Guerdon Trueblood
Cast .... Casey Siemaszko
Cast .... Ben Johnson
Cast .... Barry Corbin
Cast .... Ricki Lake

CHERNOBYL: THE FINAL WARNING — TNT

Drama: True Story • Foreign or Exotic Location •
Toxic Waste/Environmental • Medical/Disease/
Mental Illness
Airdate: 04/22/91
Rating: N/A   A/C:

UCLA bone marrow specialist, Dr. Robert Gale, leads a medical team in treating victims of the Soviet nuclear power plant disaster.

Production Company: Roger Gimbel Prods. IAW
    Carolco TV
Executive Producer .... Roger Gimbel
Executive Producer .... Kenneth Locker
Producer .... Phillip Barry
Director .... Anthony Page
Writer .... Ernest Kinoy
Cast .... Jon Voight
Cast .... Jason Robards
Cast .... Sammi Davis
Cast .... Annette Crosbie

CHILD IN THE NIGHT — CBS

Drama: Murder and Murder Mystery • Cops/
Detectives/Law Enforcement • Suspense/Thriller •
Children/Teens
Airdate: 05/01/90
Rating: 9.7/16   A/C: 3

A psychologist, despite her guilt over a patient's suicide, is convinced by a detective to help a traumatized eight-year-old boy remember whom he saw murder his father.

Production Company: Mike Robe Prods.
Executive Producer .... Mike Robe
Producer .... Ira Marvin
Director .... Mike Robe
Writer .... Michael Petryni
Cast .... JoBeth Williams
Cast .... Tom Skerritt
Cast .... Season Hubley
Cast .... Darren McGavin

CHILD LOST FOREVER, A — NBC

Drama: Family Drama • True Crime • Children/Teens
• Social Issue
Airdate: 11/16/93
Rating: 15.4/23   A/C: 3

Seventeen year old Jerry Sherwood was forced to give up her infant son for adoption while serving time in a youth correctional facility. Twenty years later she discovers the boy died under mysterious circumstances. Determined to uncover the truth she enlists the aid of a compassionate journalist. Their investigation culminates in the trial and conviction of Lois Jurgens, her son's adoptive, abusive mother.

Production Company: ERB Prods. IAW Tristar TV
Executive Producer .... Gail Berman
Executive Producer .... Susan Rose
Executive Producer .... Melvyn Estrin
Producer .... Vahan Moosekian
Director .... Claudia Weill
Writer .... Stephanie Liss
Writer .... Judith Parker
Cast .... Beverly D'Angelo
Cast .... Dana Ivey
Cast .... Michael McGrady
Cast .... Max Gail

CHILD OF DARKNESS, CHILD OF LIGHT — USA

Drama: Suspense/Thriller • Sci-Fi/Supernatural/
Horror/Fantasy
Airdate: 05/01/91
Rating: N/A   A/C:

Based on the book "Virgin" by James Patterson. The Vatican sends a young priest to investigate two pregnant virgins carrying both the new Christ and Anti-Christ, respectively, signaling the beginning of the apocalypse.

Production Company: G.C. Group/Wilshire Court
Producer .... Paul L. Tucker
Director .... Marina Sargenti
Writer .... Brian Taggert
Cast .... Anthony John Denison
Cast .... Sela Ward
Cast .... Paxton Whitehead
Cast .... Brad Davis

CHILD OF RAGE — CBS

Drama: Family Drama • Children/Teens • Medical/
Disease/Mental Illness • True Story
Airdate: 9/29/92
Rating: 14.7/24   A/C: 2

A seven year old girl and her younger brother are adopted by a loving minister and his wife. At first the children seem sweet and withdrawn but it soon becomes evident that the little girl is a rage-filled, homicidal, and dishonest child. As the behavior worsens the parents embark on a journey of desperation until they find an unorthodox therapist who is able, through confrontational therapy, to uncover the little girl's prior history of sexual and physical abuse

Production Company: Gilliam Prods., C.M. Two
    Prods. IAW Republic Pictures
Executive Producer .... Christy Welker
Executive Producer .... Chuck McLain
Producer .... David Shepherd
Executive Producer .... Larry Peerce
Writer .... Phil Penningroth
Executive Producer .... Susan Couture
Cast .... Mel Harris
Cast .... Dwight Schultz
Cast .... Ashley Peldon
Cast .... Mariette Hartley

CHILD SAVER, THE   NBC

Drama: Suspense/Thriller • Children/Teens • Drug
Smuggling/Dealing • Social Issue
Airdate: 01/18/88
Rating: 15.8/25   A/C:

*At the expense of her career, a Madison Avenue
executive becomes obsessed with rescuing a
seven year old drug dealer from the dangers of
a life on the street.*

Production Company: Michael Filerman Prods.
 IAW NBC Prods.
Executive Producer .... Michael Filerman
Producer .... Karen Moore
Co-Producer .... Grace Gilroy
Director .... Stan Lathan
Writer .... Charles Rosin
Cast .... Alfre Woodard
Cast .... Michael Warren
Cast .... Mario Van Peebles
Cast .... Martin Balsam

CHILD'S CRY   CBS

Drama: Woman Against The System • Children/Teens
• Social Issue
Airdate: 02/09/86
Rating: 22.7/33   A/C:

*An emtionally-repressed social worker takes a
personal interest in a six year old abused
runaway boy. His father, furious that the boy
has been taken from him, may or may not be
the abuser.*

Production Company: Shoot the Moon Enterprises
 Inc. IAW Phoenix Entertainment Group
Executive Producer .... Kate Jackson
Executive Producer .... Gerald I. Isenberg
Producer .... Gilbert Cates
Director .... Gilbert Cates
Writer .... Jonathan Rintels
Cast .... Lindsay Wagner
Cast .... Marlene Warfield
Cast .... Peter Coyote
Cast .... Talesin Jaffe

CHILDREN IN THE CROSSFIRE   NBC

Drama: Cross-Cultural Story • Children/Teens • True
Story
Airdate: 12/03/84
Rating: 14.8/23   A/C:

*A group of Irish children, Protestant and
Catholic, visit the U.S. for a summer and work
to resolve their nationalistic and religious
differences.*

Production Company: Schaefer-Karpf Prods. &
 Pedengarst-Britcadia Prods. IAW Gaylord
Executive Producer .... Merrill H. Karpf
Producer .... Frank Pendergrast
Producer (USA) .... Charles Haid
Producer (Ireland) .... Aida Young
Producer .... George Schaefer
Director .... George Schaefer
Writer .... Lionel Chetwynd
Cast .... Charles Haid
Cast .... David Huffman
Cast .... Karen Valentine
Cast .... Julia Duffy

CHILDREN OF THE BRIDE   CBS

Drama: Family Drama • Love Story • Romantic
Comedy • Woman's Issue/Story
Airdate: 10/05/90
Rating: 13.6/25   A/C: 1

*When an older woman decides to marry a man
fourteen years her junior, various conflicts arise
for her four grown children when they return
home for the wedding.*

Production Company: Leonard Hill Films
Executive Producer .... Leonard Hill
Executive Producer .... Ron Gilbert
Producer .... Joel Fields
Producer .... Bart Baker
Director .... Jonathan Sanger
Writer .... Bart Baker
Cast .... Rue McClanahan
Cast .... Kristy McNichol
Cast .... Jack Coleman
Cast .... Anne Marie Bobby
Cast .... Patrick Duffy

CHILDREN OF THE DARK   CBS

Drama: Medical/Disease/Mental Illness • Family
Drama • Children/Teens • True Story
Airdate: 4/17/94
Rating: 13.4/22   A/C: 1

*The parents of two little girls who suffer from
the rare genetic disease of xeeroderma
pigmentosum in which they must live in
darkened rooms and avoid exposure to sunlight,
face intolerance and prejudice from their
community. Guilt, anger and self
recriminations at first threaten to destroy the
family but the strength of their love helps them
through the grueling ordeal.*

Production Company: Steve Krantz Prods. IAW
 Multimedia Motion Pictures
Executive Producer .... Steve Krantz
Executive Producer .... Tony Etz
Producer .... Richard L. O'Connor
Co-Producer .... Art Schaefer
Director .... Michael Switzer
Writer .... Jeff Andrus
Writer .... Charles Wilkins
Writer .... Janet Brownell
Cast .... Peter Horton
Cast .... Tracy Pollan
Cast .... Roy Dotrice

CHILDREN OF THE NIGHT   CBS

Drama: Children/Teens • Prostitution
Airdate: 10/26/85
Rating: 12.4/21   A/C:

*A young sociologist devotes herself to helping
teenage Hollywood prostitutes, to the detriment
of her relationship with her boyfriend.*

Production Company: Robert Guenette Prods.
Executive Producer .... Robert Guenette
Producer .... Conrad Holzgang
Director .... Robert Markowitz
Writer .... Vickie Patik
Writer .... Robert Guenette
Cast .... Kathleen Quinlan
Cast .... Mario Van Peebles
Cast .... Lar Park-Lincoln
Cast .... Wally Ward
Cast .... Eddie Velez
Cast .... Nicholas Campbell

CHILDREN OF TIMES SQUARE   ABC

Drama: Woman Against The System • Children/Teens
• Drug Smuggling/Dealing • Social Issue
Airdate: 03/03/86
Rating: 12.5/20   A/C:

*A young teenager runs away to Times Square
and hooks up with a gang lead by a Fagin-like
character. Meanwhile the boy's mother tries to
rescue him as he becomes involved with drug
dealing.*

Production Company: Gross-Weston Prods. IAW
 Fries Entertainment Inc.
Producer .... Marcy Gross
Producer .... Ann Weston
Co-Producer .... Irv Wilson
Director .... Curtis Hanson
Writer .... Curtis Hanson
Cast .... Howard E. Rollins, Jr.
Cast .... Joanna Cassidy
Cast .... Griffin O'Neal
Cast .... Brandon Douglas

CHINA BEACH   ABC

Drama: Medical/Disease/Mental Illness • Period
Piece • Action/Adventure • Series Pilot (2 hr.) •
Vietnam • Foreign or Exotic Location
Airdate: 04/26/88
Rating: 18.0/29   A/C:

*The work-hard, play-hard experiences of an
American military medical unit in the Vietnam
war, focusing on the female nurses.*

Production Company: Sacret Inc. Prods. IAW
 Warner Bros. TV
Executive Producer .... John Sacret Young
Director .... Rod Holcomb
Writer .... John Sacret Young
Cast .... Dana Delany
Cast .... Michael Boatman
Cast .... Marg Helgenberger
Cast .... Robert Picardo
Cast .... Tim Ryan
Cast .... Concetta Tomei
Cast .... Brian Wimmer
Cast .... Chloe Webb
Cast .... Christopher Allport
Cast .... Nan Woods

CHINA LAKE MURDERS, THE — USA

Drama: Murder and Murder Mystery • Cops/
Detectives/Law Enforcement
Airdate: 01/31/90
Rating: N/A   A/C:

*Story of two police officers (one suffering from
his family's alienation due to job pressures, and
one a psychotic killer) who become adversaries
in the investigation of serial killings.*

Production Company: Papazian-Hirsch Ent. for
    MCA TV Ent.
Executive Producer .... Robert A. Papazian
Executive Producer .... James G. Hirsch
Co-Producer .... Beth Tate
Director .... Alan Metzger
Writer .... Nevin Schreiner
Cast .... Tom Skerritt
Cast .... Michael Parks
Cast .... Nancy Everhard
Cast .... Lauren Tewes

CHIPS, THE WAR DOG — DISNEY

Drama: WWII • True Story • Action/Adventure •
Period Piece
Airdate: 03/24/90
Rating: N/A   A/C:

*A family dog is recruited into the U.S. Army's
K-9 Corps. during WWII. Along with his young
army trainer, Chips is awarded both the Silver
Star and the Purple Heart for his wartime
courage.*

Production Company: W.G. Films
Executive Producer .... Fred Weintraub
Producer .... Sandra Weintraub
Director .... Ed Kaplan
Writer .... Michael Pardridge
Writer .... Janice Hickey
Cast .... William Devane
Cast .... Brandon Douglas
Cast .... Paxton Whitehead
Cast .... Ned Vaughn

CHOICES — ABC

Drama: Family Drama • Woman's Issue/Story • Social
Issue
Airdate: 02/17/86
Rating: 18.1/27   A/C:

*A retired judge's nineteen year old unwed
daughter and thirty-eight year old wife, both
pregnant, must each decide whether or not to
have an abortion.*

Production Company: Robert Halmi Prods.
Producer .... Robert Halmi, Sr.
Director .... David Lowell Rich
Writer .... Judith Parker
Cast .... George C. Scott
Cast .... Jacqueline Bisset
Cast .... Melissa Gilbert

CHRISTMAS CAROL, A — CBS

Drama: Holiday Special
Airdate: 12/17/84
Rating: 20.7/30   A/C:

*A retelling of the classic Dickens tale, in which
a miser is convinced by the spirits of Christmas
to partake in kindness and cheer.*

Production Company: Entertainment Partners Inc.
Executive Producer .... Robert E. Fuisz
Producer .... William F. Storke
Producer .... Alfred R. Kelman
Director .... Clive Donner
Writer .... Roger O. Hirson
Cast .... George C. Scott
Cast .... Nigel Davenport
Cast .... Lucy Gutteridge

CHRISTMAS COMES TO WILLOW CREEK — CBS

Drama: Holiday Special
Airdate: 12/20/87
Rating: 19.2/30   A/C:

*Feuding brothers reconcile when they team up
to deliver a load of Christmas presents to a
small Alaskan town.*

Production Company: Blue Andre Prods. IAW
    ITC Prods.
Producer .... Blue Andre
Co-Producer .... Jeffrey Fischgrund
Director .... Richard Lang
Writer .... Michael Norell
Cast .... John Schneider
Cast .... Kim Delaney
Cast .... Tom Wopat
Cast .... Anthony Holland
Cast .... Hoyt Axton

CHRISTMAS EVE — NBC

Drama: Holiday Special
Airdate: 12/22/86
Rating: 21.3/33   A/C:

*A rich widow makes every effort to track down
and bring her three grandchildren home for
Christmas, despite their father's resistance and
his attempts to have her declared incompetent
to handle her own financial affairs.*

Production Company: NBC Prods.
Executive Producer .... Michael Finnerman
Producer .... Karen Moore
Director .... Stuart Cooper
Writer .... Blanche Hanalis
Cast .... Loretta Young
Cast .... Ron Leibman
Cast .... Season Hubley
Cast .... Kate Reid
Cast .... Arthur Hill
Cast .... Trevor Howard

CHRISTMAS GIFT, THE — CBS

Drama: Holiday Special
Airdate: 12/21/86
Rating: 20.2/33   A/C:

*A big-city architect and daughter visit a
Colorado town for Christmas while he buys up
property for condo development. He's touched
by the Christmas spirit and decides not to
destroy the small-town charm with real estate
development.*

Production Company: Rosemont Prods. IAW Sunn
    Classics
Executive Producer .... Norman Rosemont
Producer .... David A. Rosemont
Director .... Michael Pressman
Writer .... Ronald Venable
Writer .... Jeb Rosebrook
Writer .... Christopher Grabenstein
Cast .... John Denver
Cast .... Ed Winter
Cast .... Mary Wickes
Cast .... Jane Kaczmarek
Cast .... Gennie James

CHRISTMAS IN CONNECTICUT — TNT

Comedy: Holiday Special • Romantic Comedy
Airdate: 04/13/92
Rating: N/A   A/C:

*Remake of the 1945 film. A famous TV chef is
forced to reveal her inability as a cook and
homemaker when she falls in love with a
national hero who is guest starring on her
primetime Christmas special.*

Production Company: Once Upon A Time
Executive Producer .... Stanley Brooks
Producer .... Cyrus Yavneh
Director .... Arnold Schwarzenegger
Writer .... Janet Brownell
Cast .... Dyan Cannon
Cast .... Kris Kristofferson
Cast .... Tony Curtis
Cast .... Richard Roundtree

CHRISTMAS ON DIVISION STREET — CBS

Drama: Children/Teens • Holiday Special • Social
Issue
Airdate: 12/15/91
Rating: 16.7/26   A/C: 1

*When a compassionate preppy befriends a
homeless, alcoholic, 80-year-old man, they
form an unusual friendship. Against the wishes
of his snobbish parents, the teenager learns a
valuable lesson in social responsibility.*

Production Company: Guber-Peters Ent. Co.,
    MIC, Morrow/Heus Prods. IAW Columbia
    Picts.
Executive Producer .... Barry Morrow
Executive Producer .... Richard Heus
Producer .... Tony Allard
Producer .... Colleen Nystedt
Director .... George Kaczender
Writer .... Barry Morrow
Cast .... Fred Savage
Cast .... Hume Cronyn
Cast .... Badja Djola

CHRISTOPHER COLUMBUS   CBS
Miniseries/Drama (2 nights): Period Piece • Historical
Piece • Foreign or Exotic Location • Biography
Airdate: 05/19/85 • 05/20/85
Rating: 17.4/29 • 15.8/25   A/C:

*An epic presentation spanning twenty-five years
of Christopher Columbus' life, his struggle to
get funding to explore the Western Ocean, his
triumphant discoveries and his romantic
interludes.*

Production Company: Lorimar IAW RAI &
 Bavaria Atelier
Executive Producer .... Malcolm Stuart
Executive Producer .... Ervin Zavada
Director .... Alberto Lattuada
Writer .... Laurence Heath
Cast .... Gabriel Byrne
Cast .... Rossano Brazzi
Cast .... Virna Lisi
Cast .... Oliver Reed
Cast .... Raf Vallone
Cast .... Max Von Sydow

CHRISTY   CBS
Drama: Period Piece • Woman Against The System •
Children/Teens • Series Pilot (2 hr.)
Airdate: 4/3/94
Rating: 17.7/29   A/C: 1

*Based on the novel by Catherine Marshall. In
1912 Tennessee, a well-bred, educated nineteen
year old woman leaves the security of her
comfortable home in Asheville, North Carolina
and moves to a poverty-stricken Appalachia
backwoods community to teach at a newly built
mission school. She is met with distrust from
the locals but with the help of a sympathetic
minister she sets about to teach the ragged
group of children.*

Production Company: Family Prods. Inc. IAW
 Rosenzweig Co. and MTM Enterprises
Executive Producer .... Ken Wales
Executive Producer .... Barney Rosenzweig
Director .... Michael Rhodes
Writer .... Patricia Green
Cast .... Kellie Martin
Cast .... Tyne Daly
Cast .... Tess Harper
Cast .... Randall Batinkoff
Cast .... Stewart Finlay-McLenna

CHROME SOLDIERS   USA
Drama: Murder and Murder Mystery • Suspense/
Thriller
Airdate: 05/06/92
Rating: N/A   A/C:

*The murder of a businessman and ex-vet
reunites former Vietnam buddies who battle
against small-town collusion to exact
vengeance on the killer.*

Production Company: Wilshire Court Prods.
Producer .... Derek Kavanagh
Co-Producer .... Thomas J. Wright
Co-Producer .... Dori Weiss
Director .... Thomas J. Wright
Writer .... Nick Randall
Cast .... Gary Busey
Cast .... Ray Sharkey
Cast .... William Atherton
Cast .... Yaphet Kotto

CIRCLE OF VIOLENCE: A FAMILY DRAMA   CBS
Drama: Family Drama • Family Violence • Social
Issue
Airdate: 10/21/86
Rating: 15.7/25   A/C:

*When her mother is forced by circumstance to
move in with her, a single mother finds herself
engaging in elder-abuse.*

Production Company: Sheldon Pinchuk &
 Rafshoon Comm. IAW Finnegan Assoc. &
 Telepictures
Executive Producer .... Bill Finnegan
Executive Producer .... Pat Finnegan
Producer .... Sheldon Pinchuk
Director .... David Greene
Writer .... William Wood
Cast .... Tuesday Weld
Cast .... Geraldine Fitzgerald
Cast .... Peter Bonerz
Cast .... River Phoenix

CISCO KID, THE   TNT
Drama: Action/Adventure • Western • Period Piece •
Foreign or Exotic Location
Airdate: 2/6/94
Rating: N/A   A/C:

*Based on characters created by O. Henry and
remake of numerous films and 1950's TV series.
In 1867, the dashing, irreverent adventurer,
Cisco Kid and his sidekick Pancho become
reluctant heroes when they team up to fight the
French military and a his former band of Texas
outlaws during the Mexican Revolution.*

Production Company: Esparza/Katz Prods,
 Goodman/Rosen Prods. IAW Turner Pictures
Executive Producer .... Moctesuma Esparza
Executive Producer .... Robert Katz
Producer .... Gary Goodman
Producer .... Barry Rosen
Director .... Luis Valdez
Writer .... Michael Kane
Writer .... Luis Valdez
Cast .... Jimmy Smits
Cast .... Cheech Marin
Cast .... Sadie Frost
Cast .... Bruce Payne

CITIZEN COHN   HBO
Drama: Historical Piece • Biography • Political Piece
• Courtroom Drama • Period Piece • True Story
Airdate: 08/22/92
Rating: N/A   A/C:

*Based on the Nicholas von Hoffman biography.
Controversial attorney and political gadfly Roy
Cohn's life, from his days as assistant to Sen.
Joe McCarthy during the HUAC hearings
through his disbarment and eventual death from
AIDS.*

Production Company: HBO Pictures IAW
 Breakheart Films and Spring Creek Prods.
Executive Producer .... Linda Gottlieb
Executive Producer .... Paula Weinstein
Executive Producer .... Mark Rosenberg
Producer .... Dora Bachrach
Director .... Frank Pierson
Writer .... David Franzoni
Cast .... James Woods
Cast .... Joe Don Baker
Cast .... Joseph Bologna
Cast .... Lee Grant
Cast .... Frederic Forrest

CITY KILLER   NBC
Drama: Suspense/Thriller
Airdate: 10/28/84
Rating: 14.9/24   A/C:

*A love-mad army vet, spurned by the woman
he loves, goes on a rampage and blows up city
buildings. The woman ultimately helps the
police in their search for the "love bomber."*

Production Company: Stan Shpetner Prods.
Producer .... Stan Shpetner
Director .... Robert Lewis
Writer .... William Wood
Cast .... Gerald McRaney
Cast .... Heather Locklear
Cast .... Terence Knox

CLARENCE   FAMILY CHANNEL
Drama: Sci-Fi/Supernatural/Horror/Fantasy
Airdate: 11/22/90
Rating: N/A   A/C:

*Sequel to "It's A Wonderful Life." A recently
widowed businesswoman becomes suicidal
when she's threatened by a big business
takeover and is rescued by a clumsy, well-
intentioned angel.*

Production Company: Atlantis Films Ltd., South
 Pacific Ltd. IAW North Star Ent. Group
Executive Producer .... Michael MacMillan
Executive Producer .... S. Harry Young
Executive Producer .... Terry A. Botwick
Executive Producer .... Don Reynolds
Producer .... Mary Kahn
Director .... Eric Till
Writer .... Lorne Cameron
Writer .... David Hoselton
Cast .... Robert Carradine
Cast .... Kate Trotter
Cast .... Nicholas Van Burek
Cast .... Jamie Rainey

CLASS CRUISE — NBC

Comedy: Youth Comedy
Airdate: 10/22/89
Rating: 11.4/19   A/C: 3

Students and teachers from a preppy private school and County High class clash on a semester at sea. At stake is County High's continued participation in the program, which the ship's captain, a County High grad himself, helps save.

Production Company: Portoangelo Prods.
Executive Producer .... Larry Thompson
Producer .... Ervin Zavada
Director .... Oz Scott
Writer .... Craig W. Van Sickle
Writer .... Steven Long Mitchell
Cast .... Josh Taylor
Cast .... McLean Stevenson
Cast .... Jane Carr
Cast .... Michael De Luise

CLASSS OF '61 — ABC

Drama: Period Piece • Historical Piece • Series Pilot (2 hr.)
Airdate: 4/13/93
Rating: 8.5/14   A/C: 3

Three best friends from West Point class of 1861 are forced to take sides against each other in the Civil War which causes each personal and family conflict .

Production Company: Amblin TV IAW Universal TV
Executive Producer .... Jonas McCord
Executive Producer .... Steven Speilberg
Producer .... Gregg Fienberg
Director .... Gregory Hoblit
Writer .... Jonas McCord
Cast .... Cristien Anholt
Cast .... Andre Braugher
Cast .... Joshua Lucas
Cast .... Dan Futterman

CLASSIFIED LOVE — CBS

Comedy: Romantic Comedy • Buddy Story
Airdate: 03/08/86
Rating: 9.7/17   A/C:

A trio of ad-agency employees set out to find love through personal classified ads.

Production Company: CBS Entertainment Prods.
Producer .... Don Taylor
Director .... Don Taylor
Writer .... Diane English
Cast .... Dinah Manoff
Cast .... Michele Seyler
Cast .... Michael McKean
Cast .... Matt Craven
Cast .... Stephanie Faracy

CLINTON AND NADINE — HBO

Drama: Action/Adventure • Love Story • Foreign or Exotic Location
Airdate: 5/28/88
Rating: N/A   A/C:

A small-time bird smuggler who, while investigating his lawyer brother's murder, meets up with a high class hooker. Romance and revenge lead them to Central American and a deadly gun-running scheme involving the Contras.

Production Company: HBO Pictures, ITC Entertainment Group
Producer .... Donald March
Director .... Jerry Schatzberg
Writer .... Willard Walpole
Cast .... Andy Garcia
Cast .... Ellen Barkin
Cast .... Morgan Freeman

CLUB MED — ABC

Comedy: Foreign or Exotic Location • Romantic Comedy
Airdate: 01/19/86
Rating: 14.8/23   A/C:

Former and future lovers seek romance, release or reconciliation at the famous Mexican resort.

Production Company: Lorimar Prods.
Executive Producer .... Karen Mack
Producer .... Ervin Zavada
Director .... Bob Giraldi
Writer .... Judith P. Mitchell
Writer .... Jeff Freilich
Cast .... Jack Scalia
Cast .... Linda Hamilton
Cast .... Patrick Macnee
Cast .... Janis Lee Burns

CODENAME: FOXFIRE - SLAY IT AGAIN, SAM — NBC

Drama: Cops/Detectives/Law Enforcement • Suspense/Thriller
Airdate: 01/27/85
Rating: 20.4/29   A/C:

An FBI agent searches for a stolen U.S. missile, which he finds in the possession of a villain who wants to start a war with the Soviet Union.

Production Company: Universal TV
Executive Producer .... Richard Chapman
Executive Producer .... Bill Dial
Executive Producer .... Joel Schumacher
Producer .... Stefanie Staffin Kowal
Producer .... Douglas Benton
Director .... Corey Allen
Writer .... Richard Chapman
Writer .... Bill Dial
Cast .... Joanna Cassidy
Cast .... Henry Jones
Cast .... Sherly Lee Ralph
Cast .... John McCook

COINS IN THE FOUNTAIN — CBS

Drama: Romantic Comedy
Airdate: 09/28/90
Rating: 10.0/19   A/C: 3

Remake of the 1954 film. Three single gals travel to Rome in search of love and romance.

Production Company: Michael Filerman Prods., Konigsberg/Sanitsky Co.,JE Ent., RTL Prods
Executive Producer .... Michael Filerman
Producer .... Tom Reeve
Director .... Tony Wharmby
Writer .... Lindsay Harrison
Cast .... Loni Anderson
Cast .... Stefanie Kramer
Cast .... Shanna Reed
Cast .... Carl Weintraub

COLD SASSY TREE — TNT

Drama: Love Story • Period Piece
Airdate: 10/16/89
Rating: N/A   A/C:

Adapted from Olive Ann Burn's novel, this is the story of a May-December romance that scandalizes a hypocritical southern town.

Production Company: TNT, A Faye Dunaway and Don Ohlmeyer Prod.
Executive Producer .... Don Ohlmeyer
Executive Producer .... Faye Dunaway
Producer .... Karen Danaher-Dorr
Director .... Joan Tewkesbury
Writer .... Joan Tewkesbury
Cast .... Faye Dunaway
Cast .... Richard Widmark
Cast .... Neil Patrick Harris
Cast .... Frances Fisher

COLUMBO: A BIRD IN THE HAND — ABC

Mystery: Cops/Detectives/Law Enforcement • Murder and Murder Mystery
Airdate: 11/22/93
Rating: 12.2/19   A/C: 3

Detective Columbo unravels the mystery of a murdered football team owner, whose wife is having an affair with her husband's nephew, a compulsive gambler.

Production Company: Universal TV
Executive Producer .... Peter Falk
Producer .... Christopher Seiter
Director .... Vincent McEveety
Writer .... Jackson Gillis
Cast .... Peter Falk
Cast .... Tyne Daly
Cast .... Greg Evigan

COLUMBO AND THE MURDER OF A ROCK STAR   ABC

Mystery: Murder and Murder Mystery • Cops/
Detectives/Law Enforcement
Airdate: 04/29/91
Rating: 12.6/19   A/C: 2

*An undefeated defense attorney murders his
unfaithful mistress, frames her musician lover,
and tries to outwit the unrelenting Lt. Columbo
with a perfect alibi.*

Production Company: Universal TV
Executive Producer .... Jon Epstein
Executive Producer .... Peter Falk
Co-Producer .... Todd London
Director .... Alan J. Levi
Writer .... William Read Woodfield
Cast .... Peter Falk
Cast .... Dabney Coleman
Cast .... Shera Danese
Cast .... Cheryl Paris

COLUMBO - CAUTION: MURDER CAN BE HAZARDOUS TO YOUR HEALTH   ABC

Drama: Murder and Murder Mystery • Cops/
Detectives/Law Enforcement
Airdate: 02/20/91
Rating: 11.8/18   A/C: 3

*Lt. Columbo is on the trail of the host of a true
crime drama show, who murdered his chain-
smoking, blackmailing colleague with a
poisoned cigarette.*

Production Company: Universal City Studios
Executive Producer .... Jon Epstein
Executive Producer .... Peter Falk
Co-Producer .... Todd London
Director .... Daryl Duke
Writer .... Sonia Wolf
Writer .... Patricia Ford
Writer .... April Raynell
Cast .... Peter Falk
Cast .... George Hamilton
Cast .... Peter Haskell
Cast .... Penny Johnson

COLUMBO: DEATH HITS THE JACKPOT   ABC

Drama: Murder and Murder Mystery • Cops/
Detectives/Law Enforcement
Airdate: 12/15/91
Rating: 14.2/22   A/C: 2

*Lt. Columbo solves the murder case of a young
lottery winner murdered by his financially
strapped uncle so he can live comfortably with
his girlfriend, who happens to be the dead man's
wife.*

Production Company: Universal Television Prod.
Executive Producer .... Peter Falk
Producer .... Christopher Seiter
Director .... Jeffrey Bloom
Writer .... Vincent McEveety
Cast .... Peter Falk
Cast .... Rip Torn
Cast .... Jamie Rose
Cast .... Gary Kroeger

COLUMBO GOES TO COLLEGE   ABC

Drama: Murder and Murder Mystery • Cops/
Detectives/Law Enforcement
Airdate: 12/09/90
Rating: 14.9/24   A/C: 1

*Lt. Columbo solves the tricky slaying of a
college professor, who was murdered by two
spoiled fraternity boys caught cheating on his
exam.*

Production Company: Universal TV
Executive Producer .... Jon Epstein
Executive Producer .... Peter Falk
Co-Producer .... Todd London
Director .... E.W. Swackhamer
Writer .... Jeffrey Bloom
Cast .... Peter Falk
Cast .... Stephen Caffrey
Cast .... Gary Hershberger
Cast .... James Sutorius

COLUMBO: IT'S ALL IN THE GAME   ABC

Mystery: Cops/Detectives/Law Enforcement •
Murder and Murder Mystery
Airdate: 10/31/93
Rating: 13.4/21   A/C: 1

*A pair of glamorous women plot the murder of
a two-timing gambler who's been courting them
simultaneously. When he turns up dead,
Columbo begins his investigation which finds
him attracted to one of the lethal ladies.*

Production Company: Universal TV
Executive Producer .... Peter Falk
Executive Producer .... Christopher Seiter
Producer .... Christopher Seiter
Director .... Vincent McEveety
Writer .... Peter Falk
Cast .... Peter Falk
Cast .... Faye Dunaway
Cast .... Claudia Christian
Cast .... Bill Macy

COLUMBO: NO TIME TO DIE   ABC

Mystery: Cops/Detectives/Law Enforcement
Airdate: 03/15/92
Rating: 16.5/27   A/C: 1

*Rumpled Lt. Columbo races against time to save
his nephew's super model wife from sinister
kidnappers.*

Production Company: Universal Television
Executive Producer .... Peter Falk
Executive Producer .... Patrick McGoohan
Executive Producer .... Alan J. Levi
Producer .... Christopher Seiter
Director .... Alan J. Levi
Writer .... Robert Van Scoyk
Cast .... Peter Falk
Cast .... Joanna Going
Cast .... Thomas Calabro

COLUMBO: UNDERCOVER   ABC

Drama: Murder and Murder Mystery • Cops/
Detectives/Law Enforcement
Airdate: 5/3/94
Rating: 14.1/22   A/C: 1

*The diligent detective goes undercover to help
an insipid insurance investigator get to the
bottom of a four million dollar bank heist and
a baffling double murder.*

Production Company: Universal Television
Executive Producer .... Peter Falk
Producer .... Christopher Seiter
Producer .... Vincent McEveety
Director .... Vincent McEveety
Writer .... Gerry Day
Cast .... Peter Falk
Cast .... Ed Begley, Jr.
Cast .... Burt Young
Cast .... Harrison Page

COMBAT HIGH   NBC

Comedy: Youth Comedy
Airdate: 11/23/86
Rating: 18.9/29   A/C:

*Two high-schoolers' high jinx get them sent to
military school where they manage to change
everyone's life for the better.*

Production Company: Frank & Julie Films &
     Lynch/Biller Prods. IAW F. von Zemeck Films
Executive Producer .... Frank Von Zemeck
Co-Executive Producer .... Thomas W. Lynch
Co-Executive Producer .... Gary P. Biller
Producer .... Robert M. Sertner
Co-Producer .... Bill Novodor
Director .... Neal Israel
Writer .... Paul W. Shapiro
Cast .... Keith Gordon
Cast .... Wally Ward
Cast .... Jamie Farr
Cast .... Sherman Hemsley
Cast .... Bernie Kopell
Cast .... Robert Culp
Cast .... Dana Hill
Cast .... Richard Moll

COMEBACK, THE   CBS

Drama: Family Drama • Forbidden Love
Airdate: 01/08/89
Rating: 16.6/29   A/C:

*Now in his forties, a former pro football player
returning to his home town to settle down must
deal with his family and friends' reactions to
his history of irresponsibility and his affair with
his son's girlfriend.*

Production Company: CBS Entertainment Prods.
Producer .... Ron Roth
Director .... Jerrold Freedman
Writer .... Percy Granger
Cast .... Robert Urich
Cast .... Chynna Phillips
Cast .... Mitchell Anderson
Cast .... Brynn Thayer
Cast .... Ronny Cox

COMMON GROUND · CBS

Miniseries/Drama (2 nights): Family Drama • Black Story • Historical Piece • Social Issue
Airdate: 03/25/90 • 03/27/90
Rating: 11.0/18 • 10.8/18   A/C: 3 • 3

Drama about three families caught up in the conflict surrounding the court-ordered desegregation of the Boston public schools.

Production Company: Daniel H. Blatt Prods./
     Lorimar
Executive Producer .... Daniel H. Blatt
Producer .... Lynn Raynor
Director .... Mike Newell
Writer .... Edward Hume
Cast .... Jane Curtin
Cast .... CCH Pounder
Cast .... Richard Thomas
Cast .... James Farentino

COMPLEX OF FEAR · CBS

Drama: Cops/Detectives/Law Enforcement • Rape/
Molestation • Woman In Jeopardy • True Crime
Airdate: 1/12/93
Rating: 14.8/23   A/C: 2

A suburban Atlanta apartment complex is terrorized by a serial rapist who police think might be a resident of the building. An earnest young cop who lives in the condominium and feels responsible for his neighbors' safety becomes obsessed with capturing the demented sex offender.

Production Company: Cosgrove-Meurer Prods.
     IAW WIN
Executive Producer .... John Cosgrove
Executive Producer .... Terry Meurer
Executive Producer .... J.C. Shardo
Producer .... John Flynn
Co-Producer .... Carrie Stein
Director .... Brian Grant
Writer .... Dyanne Asimow
Writer .... Matt Dorff
Cast .... Hart Bochner
Cast .... Joe Don Baker
Cast .... Chelsea Field
Cast .... Brett Cullen

COMRADES OF SUMMER · HBO

Comedy: Sports • Foreign or Exotic Location • Cross-
Cultural Story
Airdate: 07/11/92
Rating: N/A   A/C:

Colorful baseball player-manager, fired by the Seattle Mariners, tries to recapture glory by agreeing to coach a novice Russian team. His love of baseball is rekindled as he leads the Soviets to an exhibition victory over his former team.

Production Company: HBO Pictures and
     Grossbart/Barnett Prod.
Executive Producer .... Joan Barnett
Executive Producer .... Jack Grossbart
Producer .... Tim Braine
Producer .... David Pritchard
Director .... Tommy Lee Wallace
Writer .... Robert Rodat
Cast .... Joe Mantegna
Cast .... Natalya Negoda
Cast .... Michael Lerner

CONAGHER · TNT

Drama: Period Piece • Western
Airdate: 07/01/91
Rating: N/A   A/C:

Based on the novel by Louis L'Amour. A frontier widow and her two children brave Indians, loneliness and hard times. She eventually sparks to a wandering cowboy, who has his hands full foiling a bunch of cattle rustlers.

Production Company: Imagine Film Entertainment
Executive Producer .... Sam Elliott
Producer .... John Kuri
Director .... Raynold Villalobos
Writer .... Jeffrey M. Meyer
Writer .... Sam Elliott
Writer .... Katharine Ross
Cast .... Sam Elliott
Cast .... Katharine Ross
Cast .... Barry Corbin

CONDITION: CRITICAL · NBC

Drama: Suspense/Thriller • Series Pilot (2 hr.) •
Medical/Disease/Mental Illness
Airdate: 12/20/92
Rating: 11.0/18   A/C: 3

Two physicians, who were once lovers, race to discover the cause of an epidemic by an unidentified deadly virus. They are hampered in their search by hospital politics and sinister forces.

Production Company: Warner Bros. TV
Executive Producer .... Michael Braverman
Producer .... R.W. Goodwin
Director .... Jerrold Freedman
Writer .... Michael Braverman
Cast .... Christian Haag
Cast .... Kevin Sorbo
Cast .... Mark Blum

CONFESSIONS: TWO FACES OF EVIL · NBC

Drama: True Crime • Murder and Murder Mystery •
Courtroom Drama
Airdate: 1/17/94
Rating: 10.7/16   A/C: 3

The cops, the D.A. and a defense attorney must unravel the truth when two troubled young men separately confess to the Christmas Eve murder of a California police officer.

Production Company: Cates/Doty Prods.
Executive Producer .... Gilbert Cates
Executive Producer .... Dennis Doty
Producer .... Bobbie Edrick
Producer .... Gy Waldron
Writer .... Gy Waldron
Director .... Gilbert Cates
Cast .... Jason Bateman
Cast .... James Wilder
Cast .... James Earl Jones
Cast .... William Converse

CONNECTICUT YANKEE IN KING ARTHUR'S COURT, A · NBC

Drama: Period Piece • Sci-Fi/Supernatural/Horror/
Fantasy • Children/Teens
Airdate: 12/18/89
Rating: 11.5/17   A/C: 2

Inspired by Mark Twain's book. A 1980s child awakens after falling off her horse to find herself in King Arthur's Camelot. She helps Arthur defeat traitors close to him with the help of some 20th-century "magic" and becomes court magician.

Production Company: A Schaeffer/Karpf
     Productions IAW Consolidated
Executive Producer .... Merrill H. Karpf
Producer .... Graham Ford
Producer .... James Pulliam
Director .... Mel Damski
Writer .... Paul Zindel
Cast .... Keshia Knight Pulliam
Cast .... Jean Marsh
Cast .... Rene Auberjonois
Cast .... Emma Samms
Cast .... Michael Gross

CONSENTING ADULT · ABC

Drama: Family Drama • Homosexuality
Airdate: 02/04/85
Rating: 23.1/33   A/C:

Based on the novel by Laura Z. Hobson. When a twenty year old medical student tells his mother that he is gay, she must not only deal with her feelings, but act as a buffer between her son and homophobic husband as well.

Production Company: Starger Co. IAW David
     Lawrence and Ray Aghayan Prods.
Executive Producer .... Martin Starger
Producer .... Ray Aghayan
Producer .... David Lawrence
Director .... Gilbert Cates
Writer .... John McGreevey
Cast .... Marlo Thomas
Cast .... Martin Sheen
Cast .... Barry Tubb

CONSPIRACY OF LOVE · CBS

Drama: Family Drama • Children/Teens
Airdate: 10/18/87
Rating: 14.1/21   A/C:

Based on the book by Lisa Priest. When a deserted wife's divorce becomes final, she and her daughter leave her ex-husband's parents' house. The grandparents and the daughter-in-law begin to compete for the granddaughter, but things turn out fine when the child's father returns.

Production Company: New World Television
Producer .... Nelle Nugent
Director .... Noel Black
Writer .... Barry Morrow
Cast .... Drew Barrymore
Cast .... Robert Young
Cast .... Glynnis O'Connor
Cast .... Elizabeth Wilson

CONSPIRACY OF SILENCE   CBS

Miniseries/Drama (2 nights): Murder and Murder Mystery • Cops/Detectives/Law Enforcement • True Crime • Rape/Molestation • Foreign or Exotic Location • Social Issue
Airdate: 07/26/92 • 07/28/92
Rating: 12.5/21 • 12.2/20   A/C: 2 • 2

In 1971, in a small Canadian town, four young men brutally murder Cree teenager Helen Betty Osborne. They take a vow of silence that lasts for sixteen years until a new member of the Royal Canadian Mounted Police cracks the case.

Production Company: Canadian Broadcasting Corp.
Executive Producer .... Bernard Zukerman
Producer .... Gail Carr
Director .... Francis Mankiewicz
Writer .... Suzette Couture
Cast .... Michael Mahonen
Cast .... Jonathan Potts
Cast .... Ian Tracey
Cast .... Diego Chambers

CONVICTED   ABC

Drama: Man Against The System • True Story • Courtroom Drama • Rape/Molestation
Airdate: 05/12/86
Rating: 17.4/27   A/C:

True story of a Tennessee mailman wrongly jailed for rape whose troubles continue even after the real culprit admits to the crime.

Production Company: Larry Thompson Org.
Executive Producer .... Larry Thompson
Producer .... Paul Pompian
Director .... David Lowell Rich
Writer .... Jonathan Rintels
Cast .... John Larroquette
Cast .... Lindsay Wagner
Cast .... Carroll O'Connor

CONVICTED: A MOTHER'S STORY   NBC

Drama: Family Drama • Children/Teens • Prison and Prison Camp
Airdate: 02/02/87
Rating: 17.4/27   A/C:

A misguided mother steals $10,000 to loan to her boyfriend and is jailed when he disappears with it. Later, her prison record jeopardizes her custody of her children.

Production Company: NBC Prods. Inc.
Executive Producer .... Lucy Antek Johnson
Producer .... Ervin Zavada
Director .... Richard T. Heffron
Writer .... Ellen Kesend
Writer .... Elizabeth Gill
Writer .... Katherine Specktor
Cast .... Ann Jillian
Cast .... Kiel Martin
Cast .... Gloria Loring

CONVICTION OF KITTY DODDS, THE   CBS

Drama: Family Violence • True Crime • Woman's Issue/Story
Airdate: 11/2/93
Rating: 13.2/21   A/C: 2

A Louisiana mother is convicted of having her abusive husband killed, and is sentenced to life in prison. After five years she escapes, changes her name and in time remarries but keeps her past a secret. She is eventually recaptured but with the help of her husband and a sympathetic lawyer gets her controversial case reopened which results in the reduction of her sentence to thirty years. She is finally paroled in December of 1992 after serving seventeen years.

Production Company: Republic Pictures Corp.
Executive Producer .... Helena Hacker Rosenberg
Co-Producer .... Doug Magee
Director .... Michael Tuchner
Writer .... Doug Magee
Cast .... Veronica Hamel
Cast .... Kevin Dobson
Cast .... Lee Garlington

COOPERSTOWN   TNT

Drama: Buddy Story • Sci-Fi/Supernatural/Horror/Fantasy • Sports
Airdate: 1/26/93
Rating: N/A   A/C:

A long retired star pitcher is repeatedly passed over for induction into the Baseball Hall of Fame and goes totally bonkers when his longtime estranged best friend is given the honor. His ex-buddy dies two days before the announcement and comes back in true ghost style to haunt and taunt him. Together they hit the road for Cooperstown and along the way they bury long held resentments and achieve self understanding and inner peace.

Production Company: Amblin Ent., Michael Brandman Prods.
Executive Producer .... Michael Brandman
Producer .... Leanne Moore
Co-Producer .... Steven Brandman
Director .... Charles Haid
Writer .... Lee Blessing
Cast .... Alan Arkin
Cast .... Josh Charles
Cast .... Graham Greene
Cast .... Hope Lange

COPACABANA   CBS

Musical: Period Piece • Love Story
Airdate: 12/03/85
Rating: 12.6/20   A/C:

Inspired by Barry Manilow's pop hit. A pianist and a dancer at a 1940's nightclub fall in love and dream of success together until the wealthy club owner comes between them.

Production Company: Dick Clark Prods. IAW Stiletto Ltd.
Executive Producer .... Dick Clark
Co-Executive Producer .... Dan Paulson
Producer .... R.W. Goodwin
Director .... Waris Hussein
Writer .... James Lipton
Cast .... Barry Manilow
Cast .... Annette O'Toole
Cast .... Ernie Sabella
Cast .... Estelle Getty

CORPSE HAD A FAMILIAR FACE, THE   CBS

Drama: True Crime • Woman Against The System • Biography • Murder and Murder Mystery • Cops/Detectives/Law Enforcement
Airdate: 3/27/94
Rating: 16.4/26   A/C: 1

Inquisitive Pulitzer Prize -winning " Miami Herald" crime reporter Edna Buchanan whose knack for solving crimes leads her to help an emotional father find his missing eighteen year old daughter. After making a grievous mistake in judgment which leads to the death of the girl and the suicide of the father, Buchanan is thrown into a period of self-examination.

Production Company: Von Serneck/Sertner Prods. IAW Touchstone Television
Executive Producer .... Robert M. Sertner
Executive Producer .... Frank von Zerneck
Executive Producer .... Debbie Blum
Executive Producer .... Tony Ganz
Executive Producer .... Barry Krost
Executive Producer .... Doug Chapin
Producer .... Randy Sutter
Director .... Joyce Chopra
Writer .... Derek Marlowe
Writer .... Dennis Turner
Cast .... Elizabeth Montgomery
Cast .... Dennis Farina
Cast .... Lee Horsley
Cast .... Yaphet Kotto

CORSICAN BROTHERS, THE   CBS
Drama: Period Piece • Action/Adventure
Airdate: 02/05/85
Rating: 11.9/18   A/C:

Based on the story by Alexandre Dumas. Siamese twins separated at birth become involved in a family vendetta and a dangerous group of Paris aristocrats in 1820.

Production Company: Norman Rosemont Prods.
Executive Producer .... Norman Rosemont
Producer .... David A. Rosemont
Director .... Ian Sharp
Writer .... Robert Miller
Cast .... Trevor Eve
Cast .... Geraldine Chaplin
Cast .... Olivia Hussey
Cast .... Nicholas Clay
Cast .... Jean Marsh

COSBY MYSTERIES, THE   NBC
Mystery: Murder and Murder Mystery • Cops/Detectives/Law Enforcement
Airdate: 1/31/94
Rating: 14.8/22   A/C: 3

A recently retired New York Police Department forensic expert helps his detective friend solve the murder of a high-powered business executive.

Production Company: SAH Ent. IAW Columbia Pictures TV and NBC Prods.
Executive Producer .... Bill Cosby
Executive Producer .... William Link
Executive Producer .... David Black
Producer .... George E. Cosby
Co-Producer .... Ted Kurdyla
Director .... Jerry London
Writer .... David Black
Writer .... William Link
Cast .... Bill Cosby
Cast .... James Naughton
Cast .... Alice Playten
Cast .... Lynn Whitfield

COUNTERFEIT CONTESSA, THE   FBC
Comedy: Romantic Comedy
Airdate: 4/4/93
Rating: 5.1/8   A/C: 4

A Brooklyn saleswoman in a posh Manhattan gourmet shop falls for a sophisticated society blue blood. When she passes herself off as a wealthy Italian countess he immediately begins to show interest—but it is really her money that has him enthralled. When his black sheep brother discovers her real identify he helps her set a trap for the avaricious snake, despite his own romantic feelings for her.

Production Company: Fox West Pictures IAW Sandord/Pillsbury Prods.
Executive Producer .... Sarah Pillsbury
Executive Producer .... Midge Sanford
Producer .... Iain Paterson
Director .... Ron Lagomarsino
Writer .... Scott Davis Jones
Writer .... Christine Burrill
Writer .... Randi Johnson
Cast .... Tea Leoni
Cast .... D.W. Moffett
Cast .... David Beecroft
Cast .... Karla Tamburrelli

COURAGE   CBS
Drama: Woman In Jeopardy • Woman Against The System • Drug Smuggling/Dealing • Family Drama • True Story
Airdate: 09/24/86
Rating: 12.5/20   A/C:

True story of a woman who volunteers to spy for government anti-drug forces when she discovers her son's drug problem and a friend's trafficking.

Production Company: Highgate IAW New World Television
Producer .... Joel B. Michaels
Director .... Jeremey Kagan
Writer .... E.Jack Neuman
Cast .... Sophia Loren
Cast .... Billy Dee Williams
Cast .... Hector Elizondo
Cast .... Ron Rifkin

COURT - MARTIAL OF JACKIE ROBINSON, THE   TNT
Drama: True Story • Period Piece • Courtroom Drama • Black Story • Biography • WWII
Airdate: 10/15/90
Rating: N/A   A/C:

After being drafted in 1947, young baseball great Jackie Robinson finds himself fighting racism in the U.S. Army. When he defiantly refuses to move to the back of an army bus, he is court-martialled by his bigoted superiors.

Production Company: Von Zerneck Sertner Films and Turner Network Television
Executive Producer .... Frank Von Zerneck
Executive Producer .... Robert M. Sertner
Producer .... Julie Anne Weitz
Producer .... Susan Weber-Gold
Producer .... Cleve Landsberg
Director .... Larry Peerce
Writer .... L. Travis Clark
Writer .... Steve Duncan
Writer .... Clay Frohman
Writer .... Dennis Lynton Clark
Cast .... Andre Braugher
Cast .... Ruby Dee
Cast .... Stan Shaw
Cast .... Kasi Lemmons
Cast .... Daniel Stern
Cast .... J.A. Preston

COVER GIRL AND THE COP, THE   NBC
Comedy: Murder and Murder Mystery • Cops/Detectives/Law Enforcement • Buddy Story
Airdate: 01/16/89
Rating: 18.0/28   A/C:

When a flighty model discovers a double murder, she's assigned a down-to-earth policewoman for protection. The unlikely pair team up to capture the killer.

Production Company: Barry & Enright Prods.
Executive Producer .... Dan Enright
Producer .... Les Alexander
Producer .... Don Enright
Director .... Neal Israel
Writer .... Michael Norell
Cast .... Dinah Manoff
Cast .... David Carradine
Cast .... Parker Stevenson
Cast .... Blair Underwood
Cast .... Danitra Vance
Cast .... Julia Duffy
Cast .... John Karlen

COVER GIRL MURDERS, THE   USA
Drama: Foreign or Exotic Location • Murder and Murder Mystery • Sex/Glitz
Airdate: 10/28/93
Rating: N/A   A/C:

A sleazy publishing tycoon who's magazine is in financial trouble seeks to gain publicity by killing his cover girl models while on swimsuit photo shoot on a remote island.

Production Company: River Enterprises Ltd. IAW Wilshire Court
Producer .... Lance Hool
Director .... James A. Contner
Writer .... Douglas Barr
Writer .... Bernard Maybeck
Cast .... Lee Majors
Cast .... Jennifer O'Neill
Cast .... Beverly Johnson
Cast .... Adrian Paul

COVER UP   CBS
Drama: Murder and Murder Mystery • Foreign or Exotic Location • Series Pilot (2 hr.) • Action/Adventure
Airdate: 09/22/84
Rating: 14.0/26   A/C:

A fashion photographer and a former Green Beret male model travel to Central America under the pretense of a fashion shoot. They are in fact there to find the photographer's husband's killer and stop the illegal sale of U.S. weapons technology.

Production Company: Glenn Larson Prods. IAW 20th Century Fox TV
Executive Producer .... Glen A. Larson
Producer .... Harker Wade
Director .... Peter Crane
Writer .... Glen A. Larson
Cast .... Jennifer O'Neill
Cast .... Richard Anderson
Cast .... Robert Webber
Cast .... Doug McClure
Cast .... John Erik Hexum

COWBOY AND THE BALLERINA, THE   CBS

Drama: Cross-Cultural Story • Love Story
Airdate: 10/23/84
Rating: 12.1/19   A/C:

A recently defected Russian ballerina and a cowboy fall in love while driving cross country to New York to visit her exiled mother.

Production Company: Cowboy Prods.
Executive Producer .... Jerry Weintraub
Executive Producer .... Lee Majors
Producer .... Neil T. Maffeo
Director .... Jerry Jameson
Writer .... Denne Petitclerc
Cast .... Lee Majors
Cast .... Leslie Wing
Cast .... Christopher Lloyd

CRACKED UP   ABC

Drama: Family Drama • Children/Teens • Addiction Story • Sports
Airdate: 05/26/87
Rating: 14.7/23   A/C:

A promising high-school athlete, the son of a middle-class clergyman, begins using crack cocaine. He becomes an addict, then dies at a track meet under the horrified gaze of his family and friends.

Production Company: Aaron Spelling Prods. Inc.
Executive Producer .... Aaron Spelling
Executive Producer .... Douglas S. Cramer
Executive Producer .... Esther Shapiro
Producer .... Peter Lefcourt
Director .... Karen Arthur
Writer .... Peter Lefcourt
Cast .... James Wilder
Cast .... Raphael Sbarge
Cast .... Kim Delaney
Cast .... Edward Asner

CRASH COURSE   NBC

Comedy: Youth Comedy
Airdate: 01/17/88
Rating: 19.9/32   A/C:

A new, streetsmart driving instructor challenges a dictatorial school principal as she teaches road smarts to a motley collection of high-schoolers who must pass in order to graduate.

Production Company: Fries Entertainment Inc.
Executive Producer .... Charles Fries
Producer .... Irv Wilson
Director .... Oz Scott
Writer .... William A. Schwartz
Cast .... Jackee Harry
Cast .... Charlie Robinson
Cast .... Brian Bloom
Cast .... Harvey Korman
Cast .... Alyssa Milano
Cast .... Rob Stone
Cast .... Tina Yothers

CRASH LANDING: THE RESCUE OF
FLIGHT 232   ABC

Drama: True Story • Disaster
Airdate: 02/24/92
Rating: 17.1/26   A/C: 1

In 1989, the combined rescue efforts of the Sioux City Iowa Fire Department, emergency rescue unit, and airport personnel save numerous lives when Capt. Al Haynes and his United Airlines flight crash land in a corn field.

Production Company: Dorothea G. Petrie Prods.,
    Helios Prods., Bob Banner Assoc., Gary L.
    Pudney Co. IAW WIN
Executive Producer .... Dorothea Petrie
Producer .... Bradley Wigor
Producer .... Joseph Maurer
Director .... Lamont Johnson
Writer .... Harve Bennett
Cast .... Charlton Heston
Cast .... Richard Thomas
Cast .... James Coburn
Cast .... Leon Russom

CRASH: THE MYSTERY OF FLIGHT 1501
NBC

Drama: Woman Against The System
Airdate: 11/18/90
Rating: 12.7/20   A/C: 3

When a commercial plane crashes during a thunderstorm, the pilot's wife battles the press and government bureaucracy to absolve him of pilot error in the fatal accident.

Production Company: Schaefer-Karpf Prods.,
    Citadel IAW Consolidated
Executive Producer .... Merrill H. Karpf
Executive Producer .... David R. Ginsburg
Producer .... Lee Rafner
Director .... Philip Saville
Writer .... E. Arthur Kean
Cast .... Cheryl Ladd
Cast .... Jeffrey DeMunn
Cast .... Frederick Coffin
Cast .... Peter Jurasik

CRAZY FROM THE HEART   TNT

Comedy: Romantic Comedy
Airdate: 08/19/91
Rating: N/A   A/C:

An uptight Texas high-school principal finds love and romance, and also gets a lesson in small town bigotry, when she starts dating a Mexican-American janitor at her school.

Production Company: DeMann Ent. IAW
    Papazian/Hirsch
Executive Producer .... James G. Hirsch
Executive Producer .... Freddy DeMann
Executive Producer .... Sherry Mars
Executive Producer .... Robert A. Papazian
Producer .... R.J. Louis
Director .... Thomas Schlamme
Writer .... Linda Voorhees
Cast .... Christine Lahti
Cast .... Ruben Blades
Cast .... William Russ
Cast .... Louise Latham

CRAZY IN LOVE   TNT

Drama: Family Drama • Woman's Issue/Story
Airdate: 8/10/92
Rating: N/A   A/C:

Based on the novel by Luanne Rice. On an island in Puget Sound, a woman's obsessive love for her husband almost destroys her marriage when she imagines he is unfaithful, as her father and grandfather were. A family crisis makes her realize how firm the foundation of her happiness is.

Production Company: Ohlmeyer Communications
    IAW Karen Danaher-Dorr Prods.
Executive Producer .... Don Ohlmeyer
Producer .... Karen Danaher-Dorr
Producer .... Joan Stein
Director .... Martha Coolidge
Writer .... Gerald Ayres
Cast .... Holly Hunter
Cast .... Gena Rowlands
Cast .... Bill Pullman
Cast .... Julian Sands

CRIES UNHEARD: THE DONNA YAKLICH
STORY   CBS

Drama: True Crime • Family Violence • Woman's Issue/Story
Airdate: 2/1/94
Rating: 14.0/22   A/C: 2

In Pueblo, Colorado, an abused wife and mother, in fear for her life, hires two local punks to murder her brutal, irrational, steroid-addicted policeman husband. She is eventually tried and convicted and sentenced to forty years for conspiracy to murder.

Production Company: World International
    Network
Executive Producer .... Felice Gordon
Executive Producer .... Carla Singer
Producer .... Jon Larson
Co-Producer .... Arnie Grossman
Co-Producer .... Christopher Canaan
Director .... Armand Mastroianni
Writer .... Christopher Canaan
Cast .... Jaclyn Smith
Cast .... Brad Johnson
Cast .... Hilary Swank
Cast .... David Lascher

MOVIES AND MINISERIES

CRIME OF INNOCENCE   NBC
Drama: Children/Teens • Prison and Prison Camp
Airdate: 10/27/85
Rating: 17.2/26   A/C:

A high achieving high school student is sentenced to an adult prison for a minor offense and suffers sadistic treatment while incarcerated.

Production Company: Ohlmeyer Communications
Executive Producer .... Don Ohlmeyer
Co-Executive Producer .... Karen Danaher-Dorr
Producer .... Paul Radin
Co-Producer .... Michael Berk
Co-Producer .... Douglas Schwartz
Director .... Michael Miller
Writer .... Michael Berk
Writer .... Douglas Schwartz
Cast .... Diane Ladd
Cast .... Shawnee Smith
Cast .... Jordan Charney
Cast .... Andy Griffith
Cast .... Ralph Waite

CRIMINAL BEHAVIOR   ABC
Drama: Murder and Murder Mystery • Cops/Detectives/Law Enforcement
Airdate: 05/11/92
Rating: 12.1/19   A/C: 3

Based on the book "The Ferguson Affair" by Ross MacDonald. A tough-talking female public defender, trying to clear her client, unravels a murder case that takes her through the streets of L.A., while simultaneously fending off an amorous detective more interested in her than the case.

Production Company: Preston Fischer Co. IAW World Int'l Network & Toliver Prods.
Executive Producer .... Preston Fischer
Producer .... John Flynn
Co-Executive Producer .... Marjorie Schicktanz
Director .... Michael Miller
Writer .... Wendell Mayes
Cast .... Farrah Fawcett
Cast .... A Martinez
Cast .... Morgan Stevens
Cast .... Dakin Matthews

CRIMINAL JUSTICE   HBO
Drama: Courtroom Drama • Social Issue
Airdate: 09/08/90
Rating: N/A   A/C:

An ex-con becomes the victim of an overburdened and ineffective justice system when he is accused of robbing and maiming a prostitute.

Production Company: Elysian Films IAW HBO Showcase
Executive Producer .... Michael Apted
Executive Producer .... Robert O'Connor
Producer .... Michael Nozik
Director .... Andy Wolk
Writer .... Andy Wolk
Cast .... Forest Whitaker
Cast .... Anthony La Paglia
Cast .... Rosie Perez
Cast .... Jennifer Grey

CROSS OF FIRE   NBC
Miniseries/Drama (2 nights): True Crime • Social Issue • Period Piece • Courtroom Drama • Historical Piece
Airdate: 11/05/89 • 11/06/89
Rating: 12.5/20 • 14.7/23   A/C: 3 • 3

The story of the rape and death of a young schoolteacher in 1928 Indiana at the hands of D.C. Stephenson, Grand Dragon of the Ku Klux Klan, whose crime precipitated the Klan's collapse.

Production Company: Leonard Hill Films
Executive Producer .... Leonard Hill
Executive Producer .... Ron Gilbert
Producer .... Joel Fields
Director .... Paul Wendkos
Writer .... Robert Crais
Cast .... John Heard
Cast .... Mel Harris
Cast .... Lloyd Bridges
Cast .... David Morse

CROSSING THE MOB   NBC
Drama: Love Story • Mafia/Mob
Airdate: 10/14/88
Rating: 9.9/17   A/C:

A young car thief's organized-crime aspirations are short-circuited when he falls for his onetime girlfriend and their baby son.

Production Company: Bateman Co. Prods. IAW Interscope Communications Inc.
Executive Producer .... Ted Field
Executive Producer .... Kent Bateman
Executive Producer .... Patricia Clifford
Producer .... Phil Parslow
Director .... Steven H. Stern
Writer .... Lewis Colick
Writer .... Alan Shapiro
Cast .... Jason Bateman
Cast .... Frank Stallone
Cast .... Patti D'Arbanville
Cast .... Maura Tierney

CROSSING TO FREEDOM   CBS
Drama: Man Against The System • Children/Teens • Period Piece • Foreign or Exotic Location • WWII • Nazis
Airdate: 04/08/90
Rating: 10.3/17   A/C: 2

Story of an English lawyer who shepherds seven children to safety in England as the Germans invade France during WWII.

Production Company: Proctor & Gamble Prods. IAW Stan Margulies Prods. & Granada TV
Executive Producer .... Stan Margulies
Executive Producer .... Michael Cox
Producer .... Craig McNeil
Director .... Norman Stone
Writer .... Jerome Kass
Cast .... Peter O'Toole
Cast .... Mare Winningham
Cast .... Susan Wooldridge
Cast .... Michael Kitchen

CROSSINGS   ABC
Miniseries/Drama (3 nights): Period Piece • Foreign or Exotic Location • Sex/Glitz
Airdate: 02/23/86 • 02/24/86 • 02/25/86
Rating: 17.5/27 • 15.0/22 • 17.4/27   A/C:

From the Danielle Steel novel: A married industrialist and a French diplomat's wife overcome barriers to their romance amidst glamorous international settings.

Production Company: Aaron Spelling Prods.
Cast .... Zach Buchholz
Executive Producer .... Aaron Spelling
Executive Producer .... Douglas S. Cramer
Producer .... Howard W. Koch
Director .... Karen Arthur
Writer .... Bill Lamond
Writer .... Jo Lamond
Cast .... Cheryl Ladd
Cast .... Christopher Plummer
Cast .... Joan Fontaine
Cast .... Jane Seymour
Cast .... Horst Buchholz
Cast .... Lee Horsley

CRUCIFIER OF BLOOD, THE   TNT
Mystery: Period Piece • Action/Adventure • Foreign or Exotic Location
Airdate: 11/4/91
Rating: N/A   A/C:

Based on the play by Paul Giovanni. Supersleuth Sherlock Holmes and Dr. Watson are on the trail of a stolen chest of maharaja's jewels that is said to be possessed by an evil curse.

Production Company: Agamemnon/British Lion/TNT
Executive Producer .... Peter Snell
Executive Producer .... Richard Horner
Executive Producer .... Lynne Stuart
Producer .... Fraser C. Heston
Director .... Fraser C. Heston
Writer .... Fraser C. Heston
Cast .... Charlton Heston
Cast .... Richard Johnson
Cast .... Susannah Harker
Cast .... Edward Fox

CRUEL DOUBT   NBC
Miniseries/Drama (2 nights): Family Drama • Murder and Murder Mystery • True Crime • Children/Teens • Family Violence
Airdate: 05/17/92 • 05/17/92
Rating: 16.8/27 • 14.8/24   A/C: 1 • 1

Based on the book by Joe McGinniss. In North Carolina in 1988, greed and Dungeons & Dragons fantasies drive Chris Pritchard to plot to murder his mother and step-father. Bonnie Von Stein survives to see her son stand trial and be convicted of murder. See Honor Thy Mother.

Production Company: Susan Baerwals Prods. IAW NBC Prods.
Executive Producer .... Susan Baerwald
Co-Producer .... Daniel Franklin
Director .... Yves Simoneau
Writer .... John Gay
Cast .... Blythe Danner
Cast .... Matt McGrath
Cast .... Edward Asner
Cast .... Miguel Ferrer
Cast .... Dennis Farina

CRY FOR HELP: THE TRACEY THURMAN STORY, A   NBC
Drama: Family Drama • True Crime • Family Violence • Woman's Issue/Story • Social Issue
Airdate: 10/02/89
Rating: 21.5/33   A/C: 1

Story of a woman who survived her husband's repeated beatings and brutal stabbing. She subsequently sued the city of Torrington, Conn., for negligence in their failure to keep her husband away.

Production Company: Dick Clark Productions
Executive Producer .... Dick Clark
Producer .... Lee Miller
Director .... Robert Markowitz
Writer .... Beth Sullivan
Cast .... Nancy McKeon
Cast .... Dale Midkiff
Cast .... Bruce Weitz
Cast .... Graham Jarvis

CRY IN THE WILD: THE TAKING OF PEGGY ANN   NBC
Drama: Woman In Jeopardy • True Crime • Children/Teens
Airdate: 05/06/91
Rating: 17.2/27   A/C: 1

An eight-day manhunt ensues when a Pennsylvania teen is kidnapped and terrorized by a desperate and lonely mountain man.

Production Company: Ron Gilbert Assoc. IAW Leonard Hill Films
Executive Producer .... Ron Gilbert
Executive Producer .... Leonard Hill
Executive Producer .... Joel Fields
Director .... Charles Correll
Writer .... Durrell Royce Crays
Cast .... David Morse
Cast .... Megan Follows
Cast .... Dion Anderson
Cast .... David Soul

CURIOSITY KILLS   USA
Mystery: Murder and Murder Mystery • Suspense/Thriller
Airdate: 06/27/90
Rating: N/A   A/C:

When a neighbor apparently commits suicide, a skeptical photographer and sculptress suspect that the new occupant of the victim's apartment had something to do with his murder. When they begin to investigate, more bodies start turning up.

Production Company: Dutch Prods.
Executive Producer .... John Davis
Executive Producer .... Andrew Hill
Producer .... Alan Barnette
Director .... Colin Bucksey
Writer .... Joe Batteer
Writer .... John Rice
Cast .... C. Thomas Howell
Cast .... Rae Dawn Chong
Cast .... Courteney Cox
Cast .... Jeff Fahey

DADAH IS DEATH   CBS
Miniseries/Drama (2 nights): Woman Against The System • Drug Smuggling/Dealing • Children/Teens • Foreign or Exotic Location • True Story
Airdate: 10/30/88 • 10/31/88
Rating: 11.3/17 • 10.1/17   A/C:

Fact-based struggle of an Australian mother who fights for the life of her son, who is under death sentence in Malaysia for drug smuggling.

Production Company: Steve Krantz Prods./ Roadshow, Coote & Carroll, Sam Goldwyn TV
Executive Producer .... Steve Krantz
Executive Producer .... Matt Carroll
Producer .... Jerry London
Director .... Jerry London
Writer .... Bill Kerby
Cast .... Julie Christie
Cast .... John Polson
Cast .... Robin Ramsey
Cast .... Kerry Armstrong
Cast .... Victor Banerjee

DADDY   ABC
Drama: Children/Teens • Social Issue • Family Drama
Airdate: 04/05/87
Rating: 17.1/25   A/C:

A high-school couple faces very little encouragement, and some very real problems, when they decide to keep their baby.

Production Company: Robert Greenwald Prods.
Executive Producer .... Robert Greenwald
Producer .... Robert Florio
Producer .... Heidi M. Frey
Co-Producer .... Steve McGlothen
Director .... John Herzfeld
Writer .... John Herzfeld
Cast .... Dermot Mulroney
Cast .... Patricia Arquette
Cast .... John Karlen
Cast .... Tess Harper

DALLAS: THE EARLY YEARS   CBS
Drama: Family Drama • Period Piece
Airdate: 03/23/86
Rating: 21.3/33   A/C:

We learn the origins of the Barnes-Ewing rivalry that has been the centerpiece of the popular TV series.

Production Company: Lorimar-Telepictures
Executive Producer .... David Jacobs
Executive Producer .... Malcolm Stuart
Producer .... Joseph Wallenstein
Director .... Larry Elikann
Writer .... David Jacobs
Cast .... Larry Hagman
Cast .... Geoffrey Lewis
Cast .... David Marshall Grant
Cast .... Hoyt Axton
Cast .... Dale Midkiff

DANCE TILL DAWN   ABC
Comedy: Youth Comedy
Airdate: 10/23/88
Rating: 15.8/26   A/C:

A group of high school seniors and their parents endure the anxieties and dreams of prom night.

Production Company: Konigsber-Sanitsky
Executive Producer .... Frank Konigsberg
Executive Producer .... Larry Sanitsky
Producer .... Whitney Green
Director .... Paul Schneider
Writer .... Andrew Guerdat
Writer .... Steven Kreinberg
Cast .... Alyssa Milano
Cast .... Brian Bloom
Cast .... Tracey Gold
Cast .... Kelsey Grammer

DANCING WITH DANGER   USA
Drama: Murder and Murder Mystery • Suspense/Thriller • Cops/Detectives/Law Enforcement
Airdate: 4/22/94
Rating: N/A   A/C:

In Portland, Oregon a taxi dancer is linked to a series of brutal murders. A hard nosed detective becomes romantically and professionally involved with her when he is hired by her alleged husband to find her. When the supposed spouse turns up dead from a fatal scissor wound, and others associated with the seductive two-stepper also meet untimely ends, her innocence soon comes into question.

Production Company: Fast Track Films IAW Wilshire Court Prods. & USA Network
Producer .... Christopher Griffin
Director .... Stuart Cooper
Writer .... Elisa Bell
Cast .... Cheryl Ladd
Cast .... Ed Marinaro
Cast .... Miguel Sandoval

DANGER DOWN UNDER   NBC

Drama: Family Drama • Suspense/Thriller • Foreign or Exotic Location • Series Pilot (2 hr.)
Airdate: 03/14/88
Rating: 13.3/22   A/C:

An American horse breeder, in Australia to arrange a stud deal, must solve a horse theft, as well as unite his family and save their business when his estranged wife dies.

Production Company: Hoyts Prod. Ltd. IAW
     Weintraub Entertainment Group Inc.
Executive Producer .... Reuben Leder
Executive Producer .... Lee Majors
Producer .... Jane Scott
Director .... Russ Mayberry
Writer .... Reuben Leder
Cast .... Lee Majors
Cast .... William Wallace
Cast .... Bruce Hughes
Cast .... Rebecca Gilling

DANGER ISLAND   NBC

Drama: Sci-Fi/Supernatural/Horror/Fantasy •
Suspense/Thriller
Airdate: 9/20/92
Rating: 11.6/19   A/C: 2

After their plane crashes, a group of Americans struggle to survive on a eerie deserted island. They soon discover the place is alive with evil monsters that are the result of biological experiments gone awry sixteen years earlier.

Production Company: Von Zerneck/Sertner Films
     IAW NBC Prods.
Executive Producer .... Frank Von Zerneck
Executive Producer .... Robert M. Sertner
Producer .... William Bleich
Producer .... Ted Swanson
Director .... Tommy Lee Wallace
Writer .... William Bleich
Cast .... June Lockhart
Cast .... Richard Beymer
Cast .... Kathy Ireland
Cast .... Gary Graham

DANGER OF LOVE, THE   CBS

Drama: Murder and Murder Mystery • True Crime
Airdate: 10/4/92
Rating: 15.9/26   A/C: 1

In 1989, suburban New York school teacher Carolyn Warmus murders her lover's wife in a fit of jealousy. Professing her innocence and that her boyfriend framed her, she is ultimately convicted of second degree murder and sentenced to twenty five years-to-life. NOTE: See "Murderous Affair, A: The Carolyn Warmus Story". -ABC

Production Company: Lois Luger Prods. IAW
     Citadel Pictures Inc.
Executive Producer .... Lois Luger
Executive Producer .... David R. Ginsburg
Producer .... Michael O. Gallant
Director .... Joyce Chopra
Writer .... Ara Watson
Writer .... Sam Blackwell
Cast .... Joe Penny
Cast .... Jenny Robertson
Cast .... Joseph Bologna
Cast .... Richard Lewis

DANGEROUS AFFECTION   NBC

Drama: Murder and Murder Mystery • Woman In Jeopardy • Love Story • Suspense/Thriller • Children/Teens
Airdate: 11/01/87
Rating: 16.4/26   A/C:

A pregnant woman accused of murdering her estranged husband must apprehend the killer who is now after her eyewitness four year old son and along the way she falls in love with the detective assigned to the case.

Production Company: Freyda Rothstein Prods.,
     Litke-Grossbart Prods. and New World TV
Executive Producer .... Freyda Rothstein
Executive Producer .... Jack Grossbart
Producer .... Renee Valente
Director .... Larry Elikann
Writer .... Annabel Davis Goff
Writer .... Susan Rice
Cast .... Judith Light
Cast .... Rhea Perlman
Cast .... Jimmy Smits
Cast .... Michael Parks

DANGEROUS HEART   USA

Drama: Drug Smuggling/Dealing • Suspense/Thriller
Airdate: 2/2/94
Rating: N/A   A/C:

A seedy drug dealer responsible for a undercover cops death, becomes involved with the dead man's grieving widow hoping to find his million dollars that was stolen by her drug-induced husband. When he truly begins to fall in love with her, his odious partners in crime lose patience with his plan and take matters into their own deadly hands.

Production Company: Point of View Prods. IAW
     MCA Televison Ent.
Executive Producer .... Janet Meyers
Producer .... Harvey Frand
Director .... Michael Scott
Writer .... Partick Cirillo
Cast .... Tim Daly
Cast .... Lauren Holly
Cast .... Alice Carter
Cast .... Joe Pantoliano

DANGEROUS PASSION   ABC

Drama: Murder and Murder Mystery • Love Story • Suspense/Thriller • Mafia/Mob
Airdate: 03/25/90
Rating: 11.4/19   A/C: 3

A naive electrician becomes the pawn of a dangerous gangster. When he falls in love with the mobster's abused wife, they are forced to fight their way to freedom.

Production Company: Stormy Weathers Prods.
     IAW Davis Entertainment
Executive Producer .... Andrew Hill
Executive Producer .... John Davis
Producer .... Paul Pompian
Co-Executive Producer .... Carl Weathers
Director .... Michael Miller
Writer .... Brian Taggert
Cast .... Carl Weathers
Cast .... Lonette McKee
Cast .... Billy Dee Williams

DANGEROUS PURSUIT   USA

Drama: Murder and Murder Mystery • Woman In Jeopardy • Suspense/Thriller
Airdate: 02/14/90
Rating: N/A   A/C:

The wife of a cop is hunted down by a political assassin she had a one night stand with three years earlier in New York City.

Production Company: Sankan Prods.
Executive Producer .... Sandor Stern
Producer .... Robert Rolsky
Director .... Sandor Stern
Writer .... Sandor Stern
Cast .... Gregory Harrison
Cast .... Alexandra Powers
Cast .... Brian Wimmer
Cast .... Scott Valentine

DANIELLE STEEL'S CHANGES   NBC

Drama: Family Drama • Love Story • Woman's Issue/Story
Airdate: 04/01/91
Rating: 17.8/28   A/C: 2

Adapted from the novel. When a successful NYC TV reporter falls in love with a widowed L.A. heart surgeon with five kids, she must ultimately decide between career or family.

Production Company: The Cramer Company
Executive Producer .... Douglas S. Cramer
Producer .... Hugh Benson
Director .... Charles Jarrott
Writer .... Susan Nanus
Cast .... Cheryl Ladd
Cast .... Michael Nouri
Cast .... Christie Clark
Cast .... Christopher Gartin

DANIELLE STEEL'S DADDY   NBC

Drama: Family Drama • Love Story
Airdate: 10/23/91
Rating: 19.6/30   A/C:

Based on the novel. A successful advertising executive is forced to keep the emotional stability of his three children together when his wife of eighteen years walks out. In the process, he learns the real values of love, family and commitment.

Production Company: The Cramer Co. IAW NBC
     Prods.
Executive Producer .... Douglas S. Cramer
Co-Producer .... Daniel Franklin
Producer .... Paul Pompian
Director .... Michael Miller
Writer .... L. Virginia Browne
Cast .... Patrick Duffy
Cast .... Kate Mulgrew
Cast .... Lynda Carter
Cast .... John Anderson
Cast .... Ben Affleck

DANIELLE STEEL'S FINE THINGS NBC

Drama: Family Drama • Love Story • Children/Teens
Airdate: 10/16/90
Rating: 18.0/28   A/C: 2

Adapted from the novel. After his wife dies, a loving stepfather is thrown into emotional turmoil when he must battle the biological father for custody of his stepdaughter.

Production Company: The Cramer Company IAW
    NBC Prods.
Executive Producer .... Douglas S. Cramer
Executive Producer .... Hugh Benson
Producer .... Timothy King
Producer .... Ed Milkovich
Director .... Tom Moore
Writer .... Peter Lefcourt
Cast .... D.W. Moffett
Cast .... Tracy Pollan
Cast .... Cloris Leachman
Cast .... Noley Thornton

DANIELLE STEEL'S HEARTBEAT NBC

Drama: Love Story
Airdate: 2/8/93
Rating: 16.8/26   A/C: 1

Based on the book. A pregnant TV news producer is abandoned by her husband because of their premarital agreement not to have a family. In the depths of depression, she is rescued by a charming soap opera producer who sweeps her off her feet into romantic bliss.

Production Company: Cramer Co. IAW NBC
    Prods.
Executive Producer .... Douglas S. Cramer
Co-Producer .... Daniel Dugan
Director .... Michael Miller
Writer .... Jan Worthington
Cast .... John Ritter
Cast .... Polly Draper
Cast .... Michael Lembeck
Cast .... Kevin Kilner

DANIELLE STEEL'S JEWELS NBC

Miniseries/Drama (2 nights): Family Drama • Love Story • Period Piece • Foreign or Exotic Location • WWII
Airdate: 10/18/92 • 10/20/92
Rating: 14.7/22 • 15.6/24   A/C: 2 • 2

Based on the book. When an American divorcee marries a British duke they settle in France and are soon separated by the hardships of World War II. After the war, shrewd business maneuvers enable the family to open a high class jewelry store, turning it into a vast business empire over the years. All of which causes hidden rivalries and family power struggles.

Production Company: List/Estrin Prods. RCS
    Video IAW NBC Prods.
Executive Producer .... Shelly List
Executive Producer .... Jonathan Estrin
Producer .... Hans Proppe
Co-Producer .... Christabel Albrey
Director .... Roger Young
Writer .... Shelley List
Writer .... Jonathan Estrin
Cast .... Annette O'Toole
Cast .... Anthony Andrews
Cast .... Jurgen Prochnow
Cast .... Robert Wagner
Cast .... Corinne Touzet

DANIELLE STEEL'S KALEIDOSCOPE NBC

Drama: Family Drama • Sex/Glitz
Airdate: 10/15/90
Rating: 20.3/32   A/C: 1

Adapted from the novel. A dying attorney hires a P.I. to reunite three orphaned sisters separated in childhood and unveils the true nature of their parents' dark past.

Production Company: The Cramer Company IAW
    NBC Prods.
Executive Producer .... Douglas S. Cramer
Producer .... Elaine Rich
Producer .... James Margellos
Director .... Jud Taylor
Writer .... Karol Ann Hoeffner
Cast .... Jaclyn Smith
Cast .... Perry King
Cast .... Colleen Dewhurst
Cast .... Donald Moffat
Cast .... Patricia Kalember

DANIELLE STEEL'S MESSAGE FROM NAM NBC

Miniseries/Drama (2 nights): Love Story • Foreign or Exotic Location • Period Piece • Vietnam
Airdate: 10/17/93 • 10/19/93
Rating: 11.5/18 • 11.4/18   A/C: 3 • 3

A wealthy Georgia girl defies southern traditions and leaves for journalism school at Berkeley during the radical days of the 1960's. When her fiance is killed in Vietnam she heads off to Saigon as a correspondent for a San Francisco paper. Determined to make sense of the war she soon becomes a well respected reporter and eventually falls in love again with a sergeant who winds up missing in action. Refusing to believe he is dead she sets out on a mission to find her man.

Production Company: Cramer Co. IAW NBC
    Prods.
Executive Producer .... Douglas S. Cramer
Producer .... Hugh Benson
Director .... Paul Wendkos
Writer .... Suzanne Clauser
Cast .... Jenny Robertson
Cast .... Nick Mancuso
Cast .... Rue McClanahan
Cast .... Ed Flanders
Cast .... Ted Marcoux

DANIELLE STEEL'S ONCE IN A LIFETIME NBC

Drama: Love Story
Airdate: 2/15/94
Rating: 11.2/16   A/C: 3

Based on the book. When her husband and daughter die in a fire, a successful novelist becomes devoted to raising her deaf son. Her lonely existence takes a turn for the better when she enrolls the boy in a boarding school, run by a handsome, charming expert on deaf education. Their relationship remains platonic over the course of several years but they ultimately profess their true love for each other when she is almost killed in a car accident.

Production Company: Cramer Co. IAW NBC
    Prods.
Executive Producer .... Douglas S. Cramer
Co-Producer .... Daniel Dugan
Director .... Michael Miller
Writer .... Syrie Astrahan James
Cast .... Lindsay Wagner
Cast .... Barry Bostwick
Cast .... Amy Aquino
Cast .... Duncan Regehr

DANIELLE STEEL'S PALOMINO   NBC
Drama: Love Story • Farm Story
Airdate: 10/21/91
Rating: 18.4/28   A/C:

Based on the novel. A recently-divorced, N.Y. photojournalist, shooting modern-day cowboys, falls in love with a poor but proud ranch hand. The socially-doomed romance eventually blossoms after a dire accident teaches them the real meaning of love.

Production Company: The Cramer Co. IAW NBC
    Prods.
Executive Producer .... Douglas S. Cramer
Co-Producer .... Daniel Franklin
Director .... Michael Miller
Writer .... Karol Ann Hoeffner
Cast .... Lindsay Frost
Cast .... Lee Horsley
Cast .... Eva Marie Saint
Cast .... Rod Taylor

DANIELLE STEEL'S SECRETS   NBC
Drama: Sex/Glitz • Hollywood
Airdate: 04/06/92
Rating: 15.6/24   A/C: 2

Based on the novel. A group of actors brought together to star in a new television series are each haunted by personal demons and secret lies.

Production Company: Cramer Co. Prod. IAW
    NBC Prods.
Executive Producer .... Douglas S. Cramer
Director .... Peter H. Hunt
Writer .... Bill Bast
Writer .... Paul Huson
Cast .... Christopher Plummer
Cast .... Linda Purl
Cast .... Gary Collins
Cast .... Stephanie Beacham

DANIELLE STEEL'S STAR   NBC
Drama: Sex/Glitz • Love Story
Airdate: 9/20/93
Rating: 15.9/24   A/C: 2

Based on the novel. A poor country girl leaves the farm after a family tragedy and goes to San Francisco to pursue a career in singing. While she becomes a big Hollywood star she pines for a married New York lawyer she once met at her sister's wedding and with whom she has an on again-off again romance over the course of fifteen years. They are finally reunited forever when he rids himself of his controlling wife and she gives up the glitter of stardom and returns to her rural roots.

Production Company: Schoolfield Prods.
Executive Producer .... Douglas S. Cramer
Producer .... Elaine Rich
Co-Producer .... Daniel Dugan
Director .... Michael Miller
Writer .... Claire Labine
Cast .... Jennie Garth
Cast .... Craig Bierko
Cast .... Terry Farrell
Cast .... Penny Fuller

DARK HOLIDAY   NBC
Drama: Woman In Jeopardy • True Story • Foreign
or Exotic Location • Prison and Prison Camp
Airdate: 05/01/89
Rating: 11.1/18   A/C:

Based on the book "Never Pass This Way Again" by Gene LePere. True story of an innocent American tourist who is thrown into a dreadful Turkish prison for possessing national antiquities which she bought from roadside peasants.

Production Company: Finnegan-Pinchuck IAW
    Orion TV
Executive Producer .... Lou Antonio
Producer .... Peter Nelson
Director .... Lou Antonio
Writer .... Rose Leiman Goldemberg
Cast .... Lee Remick
Cast .... Norma Aleandro
Cast .... Roy Thinnes

DARK REFLECTION   FBC
Drama: Sci-Fi/Supernatural/Horror/Fantasy
Airdate: 1/10/94
Rating: 4.8/7   A/C: 4

A computer software designer encounters a sinister architect with an uncanny resemblance to himself and a prying interest in his wife and child. Sensing a threat to his family he probes into the man's background and discovers that they were both involved in a bizarre experiment in genetic cloning twenty years earlier and that his clone has a murderous past.

Production Company: Stillwater Prods., WIN IAW
    Fox West Pictures
Executive Producer .... Kiefer Sutherland
Executive Producer .... Charles Weinstock
Producer .... Kevin Ready
Producer .... Bob Lemchen
Director .... Jack Sholder
Writer .... Todd Slavin
Writer .... Darren Swimmer
Cast .... C. Thomas Howell
Cast .... Lisa Zane
Cast .... Miko Hughes

DARK SHADOWS   NBC
Miniseries/Drama (2 nights): Series Pilot (2 hr.) • Sci-
Fi/Supernatural/Horror/Fantasy
Airdate: 01/13/91 • 01/14/91
Rating: 14.6/23 • 13.1/21   A/C: 2 • 3

A reworking of the classic series which has vampire, Barnabus Collins, posing as a long-lost relative visiting his cousins in Maine, falling for their governess, and satisfying his thirst for blood.

Production Company: Dan Curtis Television
    Prods. IAW MGM/UA Telecommunications
Executive Producer .... Dan Curtis
Producer .... Armand Mastroianni
Co-Producer .... Jon Boorstin
Co-Producer .... William Gray
Director .... Dan Curtis
Writer .... Hal Powell
Writer .... Bill Taub
Writer .... Steve Feke
Writer .... Dan Curtis
Writer .... Jon Boorstin
Cast .... Ben Cross
Cast .... Jean Simmons
Cast .... Roy Thinnes
Cast .... Barbara Blackburn

DARKNESS BEFORE DAWN   NBC
Drama: True Story • Addiction Story
Airdate: 2/15/93
Rating: 13.1/20   A/C: 3

Mary Ann Thompson, a nurse at a Las Vegas Clinic who is dependent on alcohol and drugs falls in love and marries a recovering heroin addict. The couple spiral down into an abyss of chemical dependency with brief attempts at sobriety. When she gives birth to a drug addicted baby she realizes she must leave her husband in order to save herself and child. With his wife gone he too finds the strength to clean up his act.

Production Company: Diana Kerew Prods. Polone
    Co. IAW Hearst Ent.
Executive Producer .... Judith A. Polone
Producer .... Diana Kerew
Director .... John Patterson
Writer .... Karen Hall
Cast .... Meredith Baxter
Cast .... Stephen Lang
Cast .... Chelsea Hertford

DAUGHTER OF DARKNESS CBS
Drama: Foreign or Exotic Location • Sci-Fi/Supernatural/Horror/Fantasy
Airdate: 01/26/90
Rating: 10.4/18   A/C: 3

A young woman travels to Romania in search of her father and discovers that he is a 200-year-old vampire prince. When he tries to save her from his fate, he is destroyed by the other vampires.

Production Company: King Phoenix
       Entertainment Inc.
Executive Producer .... Harry Chandler
Executive Producer .... Gerald W. Abrams
Producer .... Andras Hamori
Director .... Stuart Gorden
Writer .... Andrew Laskos
Cast .... Anthony Perkins
Cast .... Mia Sara
Cast .... Jack Coleman
Cast .... Robert Reynolds

DAUGHTER OF THE STREETS ABC
Drama: Family Drama • Children/Teens • Prostitution • Social Issue • True Story
Airdate: 02/26/90
Rating: 14.9/24   A/C: 1

A divorcee who spends most of her time working to help others unwittingly neglects her daughter. When her daughter becomes a prostitute, and the police can't help because she's over 18, the woman is forced to rescue her daughter herself.

Production Company: Adam Productions IAW
       Fox
Executive Producer .... Robert M. Myman
Producer .... Hugh Benson
Director .... Ed Sherin
Writer .... David Abramowitz
Cast .... Jane Alexander
Cast .... Roxana Zal
Cast .... Harris Yulin
Cast .... John Stamos

DAUGHTERS OF PRIVILEGE NBC
Drama: Family Drama • Series Pilot (2 hr.) • Sex/Glitz
Airdate: 03/17/91
Rating: 13.9/23   A/C: 2

A rivalry for men and power engulf the lives of three daughters of a wealthy Florida newspaper magnate.

Production Company: NBC Prods.
Executive Producer .... Michele Gallery
Executive Producer .... Michael Vittes
Director .... Michael Fresco
Writer .... Michele Gallery
Cast .... Dick Van Dyke
Cast .... Daphne Ashbrook
Cast .... Kate Vernon
Cast .... Angela Alvarado

DAVID ABC
Drama: Family Drama • True Crime • Children/Teens • Medical/Disease/Mental Illness • Family Violence
Airdate: 10/25/88
Rating: 19.5/30   A/C:

True story of a six year old New York boy stolen away to California by his estranged ex-con father, who purposely sets fire to him in a motel room. The mother of the grotesquely burned child sees him through his recovery.

Production Company: Tough Boys Inc./Donald
       March IAW ITC Entertainment Group
Producer .... Donald March
Director .... John Erman
Writer .... Stephanie Liss
Cast .... Bernadette Peters
Cast .... John Glover
Cast .... George Grizzard
Cast .... Christopher Allport
Cast .... Matthew Lawrence
Cast .... Dan Lauria

DAVID'S MOTHER CBS
Drama: Family Drama • Medical/Disease/Mental Illness • Love Story
Airdate: 4/10/94
Rating: 16.3/26   A/C: 1

Based on the play by Bob Randall. When an abrasive, divorced mother of an autistic child meets a new man and a head strong social worker, she is forced to face her obsessive devotion to her son as well as her long held guilt and resentment towards herself and family members.

Production Company: Morgan Hill Films IAW
       Hearst Entertainment Prods.
Executive Producer .... Jennifer Alward
Executive Producer .... Bob Randall
Producer .... Julian Marks
Co-Producer .... Fran Bell
Director .... Robert Allan Ackerman
Writer .... Bob Randall
Cast .... Kirstie Alley
Cast .... Sam Waterston
Cast .... Stockard Channing
Cast .... Phylicia Rashad
Cast .... Michael Goorjian

DAY MY PARENTS RAN AWAY, THE FBC
Comedy: Youth Comedy
Airdate: 12/13/93
Rating: 6.0/9   A/C: 4

Frustrated parents of an obnoxious, smart-assed teenager decide to run away from home leaving their son to fend for himself while they take a long deserved rest. Turning his home into party central he becomes the pawn of his destructive friends. The kid ultimately learns the value of family and the meaning of responsibility.

Production Company: Fox West Pitures, New Line
       TV IAW Chanticleer Films
Executive Producer .... Jana Sue Memel
Executive Producer .... Sasha Emerson
Producer .... Thom Colwell
Director .... Martin Nicholson
Writer .... Handel Glassberg
Cast .... Matt Frewer
Cast .... Blair Brown
Cast .... Bobby Jacoby
Cast .... Martin Mull

DAY - O NBC
Drama: Sci-Fi/Supernatural/Horror/Fantasy
Airdate: 05/03/92
Rating: 5.3/10   A/C: 3

A married, successful career woman with low self-esteem reverts to her imaginary childhood friend to help her through an unplanned pregnancy.

Production Company: Steve White Prods. IAW
       Walt Disney TV
Executive Producer .... Steve White
Producer .... Barry Bernardi
Producer .... Ira Shuman
Director .... Michael Schultz
Writer .... Bruce Franklin Singer
Cast .... Delta Burke
Cast .... Elijah Wood

DAY OF RECKONING NBC
Drama: Foreign or Exotic Location • Action/Adventure
Airdate: 3/7/94
Rating: 8.7/14   A/C: 3

An American Special Forces Captain who moved to Bangkok after the Vietnam War is now a rogue travel guide, specializing in expeditions to remote and dangerous locations in Southeast Asia. While escorting two French research scientists into the jungles of northern Burma he encounters a wartime nemesis bent of settling and old score.

Production Company: Dryer Prods. IAW
       Paramount Television
Executive Producer .... Fred Dryer
Executive Producer .... Victor Schiro
Co-Executive Producer .... Stirling Silliphant
Co-Executive Producer .... Robert Ginty
Producer .... Ron Frazier
Director .... Brian Grant
Writer .... Stirling Silliphant
Cast .... Fred Dryer
Cast .... Geoffrey Lewis
Cast .... Patrick Bauchau
Cast .... Assumpta Serna

DAY ONE
CBS

EMMY WINNER

Drama: True Story • Period Piece • Historical Piece • Social Issue
Airdate: 03/05/89
Rating: 15.2/24   A/C:

True story of the invention of the atomic bomb, the project that succeeded in building it, and the planning and reaction to its first use.

Production Company: Aaron Spelling Prods. IAW Paragon Motion Pictures, David W. Rintels
Executive Producer .... Aaron Spelling
Executive Producer .... E. Duke Vincent
Producer .... David W. Rintels
Director .... Joseph Sargent
Writer .... David W. Rintels
Cast .... Brian Dennehy
Cast .... Barnard Hughes
Cast .... Hume Cronyn
Cast .... Hal Holbrook
Cast .... Michael Tucker
Cast .... Richard Dysart

DAYBREAK
HBO

Drama: Medical/Disease/Mental Illness • Sci-Fi/Supernatural/Horror/Fantasy
Airdate: 5/8/93
Rating: N/A   A/C:

Based on the play "Beirut" by Alan Bowne. In the near future, a unnamed virus is devastating the American population and the fascist government has branded and banished all victims to dismal quarantine camps. A young woman joins an underground group whose members rescue people from quarantine and she falls in love with the macho leader of the resistance. Together they fight to expose the truth and save the country from fear and hatred.

Production Company: Foundation Ent. Prods. IAW HBO Showcase
Executive Producer .... Kathryn Galan
Executive Producer .... Colin Callender
Producer .... John Manulis
Director .... Steven Tolkin
Writer .... Steven Tolkin
Cast .... Moira Kelly
Cast .... Cuba Gooding, Jr.
Cast .... Martha Plimpton
Cast .... Omar Epps

DEAD AHEAD: THE EXXON VALDEZ DISASTER
HBO

Drama: True Story • Toxic Waste/Environmental • Disaster
Airdate: 12/12/92
Rating: N/A   A/C:

On March 24, 1989, oil tanker the Exxon Valdez ran aground, spilling eleven million gallons of oil into Alaska's Prince William Sound. Corporate, state and government officials fight with and against each other, creating bureaucratic quagmires that result in costly delays in the clean-up of the most devastating environmental catastrophe in U.S. history.

Production Company: HBO Showcase, BBC
Executive Producer .... Leslie Woodhead
Producer .... David Thompson
Producer .... John Smithson
Director .... Paul Seed
Writer .... Michael Baker
Cast .... John Heard
Cast .... Christopher Lloyd
Cast .... Rip Torn
Cast .... Michael Murphy

DEAD AND ALIVE
ABC

Drama: Murder and Murder Mystery • Cops/Detectives/Law Enforcement • True Crime • Mafia/Mob
Airdate: 11/24/91
Rating: 11.8/18   A/C: 3

A small-time drug dealer becomes the target of a manhunt when he kills a federal agent. The cops want him alive for the murder of their friend and the mob wants him dead for knowing too much.

Production Company: Patchett-Kaufman Ent., Katie Face Prods., World Int'l Network
Executive Producer .... Ken Kaufman
Executive Producer .... Tom Patchett
Producer .... Ken Kaufman
Director .... Peter Markle
Writer .... Dick Beebe
Cast .... Tony Danza
Cast .... Ted Levine
Cast .... Dan Lauria
Cast .... Caroline Aaron

DEAD BEFORE DAWN
ABC

Drama: Family Drama • True Crime • Family Violence • Woman In Jeopardy
Airdate: 1/10/93
Rating: 18.0/26   A/C: 2

When a battered Texas wife files for divorce, her abusive husband hires a hit man to have her killed. With the aid of an FBI agent, she fakes her own death to lay a trap for her scheming spouse.

Production Company: Joel Fields Prods. IAW Leonard Hill Films
Executive Producer .... Joel Fields
Executive Producer .... Leonard Hill
Executive Producer .... Ron Gilbert
Co-Executive Producer .... Ardythe Goergens
Co-Executive Producer .... Bernadette Caulfield
Director .... Charles Correll
Writer .... John Ireland
Cast .... Cheryl Ladd
Cast .... Jameson Parker
Cast .... G.W. Bailey
Cast .... Kim Coates

DEAD IN THE WATER
USA

Drama: Murder and Murder Mystery • Suspense/Thriller
Airdate: 12/04/91
Rating: N/A   A/C:

Based on the novel "Web of Murder" by Harry Whittington. When a successful lawyer becomes disenchanted with his wealthy wife, he and his seductive secretary plot her demise. When the scheme backfires, he is accused of the mysterious murder of his office paramour.

Production Company: Kevin Bright Prods. IAW MTE
Executive Producer .... Dan Wigutow
Producer .... Michael M. Scott
Director .... Bill Condon
Writer .... Eleanor E. Gaver
Writer .... Robert Seidenberg
Writer .... Walter Klenhard
Cast .... Bryan Brown
Cast .... Teri Hatcher
Cast .... Anne DeSalvo
Cast .... Veronica Cartwright

DEAD ON THE MONEY   TNT

Drama: Suspense/Thriller
Airdate: 06/17/91
Rating: N/A   A/C:

Based on the novella "The End of Tragedy" by Rachel Ingalls. An innocent actress falls in love with a master manipulator, who persuades her to marry his wealthy eccentric cousin and expose him in a murderous insurance scam.

Production Company: Perfect Circle Corp. Voyager Prods. IAW Indieprod Co.
Executive Producer .... Bruce J. Sallan
Producer .... John Dolf
Producer .... Victor Simpkins
Co-Producer .... Bob Birnbaum
Director .... Mark Cullingham
Writer .... Gavin Lambert
Cast .... Corbin Bernsen
Cast .... Amanda Pays
Cast .... John Glover
Cast .... Eleanor Parker

DEAD RECKONING   USA

Drama: Murder and Murder Mystery • Suspense/Thriller
Airdate: 05/23/90
Rating: N/A   A/C:

An adulterous wife and a ship's captain plot to kill her wealthy husband when their sailboat is washed up on a desert island.

Production Company: Houston Lady Production Co. for MCA Entertainment
Executive Producer .... Barry Weitz
Producer .... Robert Lewis
Director .... Robert Lewis
Writer .... Neill D. Hicks
Writer .... Andie McCuaig
Cast .... Susan Blakely
Cast .... Cliff Robertson
Cast .... Rick Springfield

DEAD SILENCE   FBC

Drama: Murder and Murder Mystery • Children/Teens
Airdate: 08/26/91
Rating: 6.8/12   A/C: 4

On a drunken joyride in the Palm Springs desert, three college coeds hit and kill a transient. Deciding to cover up the crime, the girls are soon racked with suspicion, paranoia and guilt, which ultimately destroys their friendship.

Production Company: FNM Films
Executive Producer .... Robert Bibb
Executive Producer .... Lewis Goldstein
Producer .... Tony Amatullo
Director .... Peter O'Fallon
Writer .... J. David Miles
Cast .... Renee Estevez
Cast .... Carrie Mitchum
Cast .... Lisanne Falk
Cast .... Tim Russ
Cast .... Steven Brill

DEAD SOLID PERFECT   HBO

Comedy: Sports • Romantic Comedy
Airdate: 12/1/88
Rating: N/A   A/C:

Based on the novel by Dan Jenkins. A golf pro is beset by problems on and off the course.

Production Company: HBO Pictures, David Merrick Prods.
Executive Producer .... Dan Jenkins
Executive Producer .... Etan Merrick
Producer .... Bill Badalato
Director .... Bobby Roth
Writer .... Dan Jenkins
Writer .... Bobby Roth
Cast .... Randy Quaid
Cast .... Jack Warden
Cast .... Kathryn Harrold

DEADBOLT   CBS

Drama: Woman In Jeopardy • Psychological Thriller
Airdate: 6/8/93
Rating: 12.9/23   A/C: 1

A divorced medical student is terrorized and held hostage in her own apartment by her charming, psychopathic roommate.

Production Company: Allegro Films, Image Organizatrion
Executive Producer .... Pierre David
Producer .... Tom Berry
Producer .... Franco Batista
Director .... Douglas Jackson
Writer .... Mara Trafficante
Writer .... Frank Rehwaldt
Cast .... Justine Bateman
Cast .... Adam Baldwin
Cast .... Michele Scarabelli
Cast .... Chris Mulkey

DEADLOCK   HBO

Drama: Suspense/Thriller • Sci-Fi/Supernatural/Horror/Fantasy • Prison and Prison Camp
Airdate: 09/28/91
Rating: N/A   A/C:

A thief sentenced to a futuristic prison is electronically bound to a female prisoner. She convinces him to escape, leading them both on a frenzied chase to retrieve stolen jewels and remove their shackles before they detonate.

Production Company: Frederick S. Pierce, Specatcor Films, HBO
Executive Producer .... Frederick Pierce
Executive Producer .... Michael Jaffe
Producer .... Branko Lustig
Director .... Lewis Teague
Writer .... Broderick Miller
Cast .... Rutger Hauer
Cast .... Mimi Rogers
Cast .... Joan Chen
Cast .... James Remar

DEADLY BETRAYAL: THE BRUCE CURTIS STORY   NBC

Drama: True Crime • Children/Teens • Courtroom
Drama • Foreign or Exotic Location • Family Violence
Airdate: 02/02/92
Rating: 12.9/20   A/C: 3

A naive Canadian teenager stands trial for helping his manipulative New Jersey friend kill both his parents in 1982.

Production Company: Atlantis Film Ltd. and Citadel Films
Executive Producer .... Peter Sussman
Producer .... Seaton McLean
Producer .... Barry Cowling
Director .... Graeme Campbell
Writer .... Keith Ross Leckie
Cast .... Simon Reynolds
Cast .... Jaimz Woolvett
Cast .... Kenneth Welsh

DEADLY BUSINESS, A   CBS

Drama: Man Against The System • True Story • Toxic Waste/Environmental • Mafia/Mob
Airdate: 03/04/86
Rating: 12.3/21   A/C:

True story of a mob-involved waste-disposal man who turns against his employers when he realizes the environmental harm his work is doing.

Production Company: Thebaut/Frey Prods. Inc. IAW Taft Entertainment TV Inc.
Executive Producer .... Jim Thebaut
Producer .... Harry R. Sherman
Director .... John Korty
Writer .... Al Ramrus
Cast .... Alan Arkin
Cast .... Armand Assante
Cast .... Michael Learned

DEADLY CARE   CBS

Drama: Medical/Disease/Mental Illness • Addiction Story
Airdate: 03/22/87
Rating: 18.6/31   A/C:

An intensive-care nurse, seeing the damage being done to her life by her stress-induced substance abuse, seeks help.

Production Company: Universal TV
Executive Producer .... Wendy Riche
Executive Producer .... Paula Rudnick
Executive Producer .... Jon Epstein
Director .... David Anspaugh
Writer .... Lane Slate
Cast .... Cheryl Ladd
Cast .... Richard Evans
Cast .... Peggy McCay
Cast .... Jason Miller

DEADLY DECEPTION   CBS

Mystery: Suspense/Thriller • Children/Teens •
Psychological Thriller
Airdate: 03/08/87
Rating: 19.2/30   A/C:

A year after a man's wife is found dead and his young son missing, a female reporter who has discovered helpful evidence teams up with him to find the boy.

Production Company: CBS Entertainment Prods.
Producer .... Andrew Gottlieb
Director .... John Llewellyn Moxey
Writer .... Gordon Cotler
Cast .... Matt Salinger
Cast .... Lisa Eilbacher
Cast .... Bonnie Bartlett
Cast .... Mildred Natwick

DEADLY DESIRE   USA

Mystery: Murder and Murder Mystery • Cops/
Detectives/Law Enforcement • Suspense/Thriller
Airdate: 01/29/91
Rating: N/A   A/C:

A manipulative, sexy housewife seduces a home security guard into a plot to murder her husband and defraud an insurance company. When he learns the husband is still alive, he tracks the couple down and untangles their web of deceit.

Production Company: Wilshire Court Prods.
Producer .... Vanessa Greene
Writer .... Jerry Ludwig
Cast .... Jack Scalia
Cast .... Kathryn Harrold
Cast .... Will Patton
Cast .... Joe Santos

DEADLY GAME   USA

Drama: Action/Adventure
Airdate: 07/09/91
Rating: N/A   A/C:

Seven strangers are invited to a remote rain forest by a sadistic hunter, who promises them great wealth if they can survive a hunt in which they are the prey.

Production Company: Osiris Prods. IAW Wilshire
   Court Prods.
Producer .... Johanna Persons
Co-Producer .... Thomas J. Wright
Director .... Thomas J. Wright
Writer .... Wes Claridge
Cast .... Roddy McDowall
Cast .... Marc Singer
Cast .... Michael Beck
Cast .... Jenny Seagrove

DEADLY INTENTIONS   ABC

Miniseries/Drama (2 nights): Woman In Jeopardy •
True Crime • Courtroom Drama • Psychological
Thriller
Airdate: 05/19/85 • 05/20/85
Rating: 13.3/22 • 21.3/32   A/C:

True story based on the book by William Randolph Stevens about a young woman's seemingly happy marriage to an intern which dissolves into terror when he begins to exhibit erratic, sadistic and murderous behavior.

Production Company: Green-Epstein Prods.
Executive Producer .... Jim Green
Executive Producer .... Allen Epstein
Producer .... Neil T. Maffeo
Director .... Noel Black
Writer .... Andrew Peter Marin
Cast .... Michael Biehn
Co-Executive Producer .... Cloris Leachman
Cast .... Madolyn Smith Osborne
Cast .... Morgana King
Cast .... Cliff De Young

DEADLY INTENTIONS... AGAIN?   ABC

Drama: Woman In Jeopardy • True Crime • Family
Violence
Airdate: 02/11/91
Rating: 12.8/20   A/C: 3

Sequel to the 1985 TV MOW, "Deadly Intentions." Paroled ex-doctor Charles Raynor was imprisoned for the murder of his first wife. Now he is attempting to kill his second wife as well as the prosecutor who sent him to prison.

Production Company: Green/Epstein Prods. IAW
   Lorimar TV
Executive Producer .... Jim Green
Executive Producer .... Allen Epstein
Supervising Producer .... Matthew O'Connor
Supervising Producer .... Tom Rowe
Director .... James Sadwith
Writer .... William Wood
Cast .... Harry Hamlin
Cast .... Joanna Kerns
Cast .... Conchata Ferrell
Cast .... Eileen Brennan

DEADLY MATRIMONY   NBC

Miniseries/Drama (2 nights): True Crime • Murder
and Murder Mystery • Cops/Detectives/Law
Enforcement • Mafia/Mob • Man Against The System
Airdate: 11/22/92 • 11/23/92
Rating: 16.1/25 • 18.9/29   A/C: 1 • 1

Based on an unpublished manuscript by Barbara Schaaf. A sleazy, Chicago, mob lawyer who bribes judges and fixes trials for organized crime figures, murders his wife in a jealous rage. A diligent detective attempts to expose the loathsome attorney as the killer but is stonewalled by crooked cops, silent witnesses and a corrupt judge. Undaunted, the determined cop uncovers the truth and gets his man.

Production Company: Steve Krantz Prods.,
   Multimedia TV Prods.
Executive Producer .... Steve Krantz
Executive Producer .... Tony Etz
Producer .... Stephanie Austin
Co-Producer .... Stanley Neufeld
Co-Producer .... Andrew Laskos
Director ....John Korty
Writer .... Andrew Laskos
Cast .... Brian Dennehy
Cast .... Lisa Eilbacher
Cast .... Treat Williams
Cast .... Susan Ruttan

DEADLY MEDICINE   NBC

Drama: Murder and Murder Mystery • True Crime •
Children/Teens • Medical/Disease/Mental Illness •
Courtroom Drama
Airdate: 11/11/91
Rating: 15.8/24   A/C: 3

Based on the book by Kelly Moore and Dan Reed. In 1982, Texas pediatrician Kathy Holland, accused of murder, ostracized and losing her practice, fights to prove her innocence. She and the D.A. uncover the incriminating past of her sociopathic nurse who is found guilty of multiple infanticides.

Production Company: Multimedia Entertainment/
   Steve Krantz
Executive Producer .... Steve Krantz
Executive Producer .... Veronica Hamel
Producer .... Harry R. Sherman
Co-Producer .... Stanley Neufeld
Director .... Richard Colla
Writer .... Vicki Polon
Writer .... L. Virginia Browne
Writer .... Andrew Laskos
Cast .... Veronica Hamel
Cast .... Susan Ruttan
Cast .... Stephen Tobolowsky
Cast .... Scott Paulin

DEADLY MESSAGES   ABC
Drama: Murder and Murder Mystery • Woman In Jeopardy • Psychological Thriller
Airdate: 02/21/85
Rating: 11.4/17   A/C:

A young woman witnesses her best friend being murdered by a psychotic killer. She is then pursued by the killer as she tries to solve the crime by using a Ouija board.

Production Company: Columbia TV
Producer .... Paul Pompian
Director .... Jack Bender
Writer .... William Bleich
Cast .... Kathleen Beller
Cast .... Michael Brandon
Cast .... Dennis Franz

DEADLY RELATIONS   ABC
Drama: Family Drama • Family Violence • True Crime • Period Piece
Airdate: 5/22/93
Rating: 10.01/19   A/C: 1

Based on the book by Carol Donahue. A mentally abusive and domineering father, Leonard John Fagot, is obsessed with controlling his four daughters' lives. When they marry against his wishes, he takes out big insurance policies-with himself as beneficiary-on their husbands, who suddenly become prone to fatal accidents. The women eventually find the strength to testify against their father.

Production Company: OTML Prods. IAW Wilshire Court Prods.
Producer .... Ed Milkovich
Director .... Bill Condon
Writer .... Dennis Nemec
Cast .... Robert Urich
Cast .... Shelley Fabares
Cast .... Gwyneth Paltrow
Cast .... Roxana Zal

DEADLY SILENCE, A   ABC
Drama: True Crime • Children/Teens • Rape/Molestation • Family Violence
Airdate: 04/16/89
Rating: 17.9/28   A/C:

Based on Dena Kleiman's book about a teenage girl who hires a school acquaintance to kill her father to end an alleged incestuous relationship. The girl is ultimately arrested and tried.

Production Company: Robert Greenwald Prods.
Executive Producer .... Robert Greenwald
Executive Producer .... Jennifer Miller
Producer .... Philip Kleinbart
Producer .... Paul Lussier
Co-Producer .... Robert Florio
Director .... John Patterson
Writer .... Jennifer Miller
Cast .... Bruce Weitz
Cast .... Charles Haid
Cast .... Heather Fairfield
Cast .... Mike Farrell

DEADLY SURVEILLANCE   SHOWTIME
Drama: Cops/Detectives/Law Enforcement • Suspense/Thriller • Drug Smuggling/Dealing
Airdate: 09/06/91
Rating: N/A   A/C:

A detective discovers evidence linking his former partner's girlfriend to a drug-dealing operation.

Production Company: Westwind Prods.
Executive Producer .... Jean-Marie Malenfant
Producer .... Louis Goyer
Director .... Paul Ziller
Writer .... Hal Salwen
Writer .... Paul Ziller
Cast .... Michael Ironside
Cast .... Christopher Bonoy
Cast .... David Carradine
Cast .... Susan Almgren

DEADMAN'S REVENGE   USA
Drama: Western • Period Piece
Airdate: 4/15/94
Rating: N/A   A/C:

A homesteader sets up and elaborate sting operation to get revenge against the ruthless railroad baron who sent him to prison on trumped-up charges and murdered his wife.

Production Company: MTE Prods. IAW Finnegan/Pinchuk Co.
Executive Producer .... Charmaine Balian
Producer .... Ed Lahti
Co-Producer .... Lori-Etta Taub
Director .... Alan J. Levi
Writer .... Jim Byrnes
Writer .... David Chisholm
Cast .... Bruce Dern
Cast .... Michael Ironside
Cast .... Keith Coulouris
Cast .... Doug McClure

DEATH DREAMS   LIFETIME
Drama: Family Drama • Suspense/Thriller • Children/Teens • Sci-Fi/Supernatural/Horror/Fantasy
Airdate: 06/25/91
Rating: N/A   A/C:

A woman begins to have psychic visions of her dead daughter, who is sending her clues about her suspicious demise. Convinced the child was killed by her wealthy husband, she fights to have him charged with murder.

Production Company: Ultra Entertainment IAW Dick Clark Films and Roni Weisberg Prods.
Executive Producer .... Dick Clark
Executive Producer .... Bob Rubin
Executive Producer .... Bill Seigler
Producer .... Roni Weisberg
Director .... Martin Donovan
Writer .... Robert Glass
Cast .... Christopher Reeve
Cast .... Marg Helgenberger
Cast .... Fionnula Flanagan

DEATH IN CALIFORNIA, A   ABC
Miniseries/Drama (2 nights): Woman In Jeopardy • True Crime • Courtroom Drama • Rape/Molestation
Airdate: 05/12/85 • 05/13/85
Rating: 15.7/25 • 19.2/30   A/C:

Based on the 1973 case of a wealthy socialite who develops a bizarre relationship with the psychopath who murders her boyfriend, rapes her and terrorizes her family.

Production Company: Mace Neufeld Prods. IAW Lorimar
Executive Producer .... Malcolm Stuart
Executive Producer .... Mace Neufeld
Producer .... Richard L. O'Connor
Director .... Delbert Mann
Writer .... E. Jack Neuman
Cast .... Cheryl Ladd
Cast .... Sam Elliott
Cast .... Alexis Smith
Cast .... Fritz Weaver
Cast .... John Ashton
Cast .... Barry Corbin

DEATH OF A SALESMAN   CBS
Drama: Family Drama
Airdate: 09/15/85
Rating: 14.5/23   A/C:

TV adaptation of Arthur Miller's award wining play about Willy Loman, an aging salesman who struggles with his uncertain financial future and troubled family life by daydreaming about his past.

Production Company: Roxbury & Punch Prods.
Executive Producer .... Robert F. Colesberry
Director .... Volker Schlondorff
Writer .... Arthur Miller
Cast .... Dustin Hoffman
Cast .... Kate Reid
Cast .... Stephen Lang
Cast .... Charles Durning
Cast .... Louis Zorich
Cast .... John Malkovich

DEATH OF THE INCREDIBLE HULK, THE   NBC
Drama: Sci-Fi/Supernatural/Horror/Fantasy
Airdate: 02/18/90
Rating: 14.6/22   A/C: 3

Based on the comic books and TV series. David Banner infiltrates a secret government laboratory to find a way to rid himself forever of the Hulk, his uncontrollably violent alter ego. But others at the lab have different plans for the Hulk.

Production Company: Bixby-Brandon Prods Inc. IAW New World TV
Executive Producer .... Bill Bixby
Producer .... Hugh Spencer-Phillips
Producer .... Robert Ewing
Writer .... Gerald Di Pego
Cast .... Bill Bixby
Cast .... Lou Ferrigno
Cast .... Elizabeth Gracen
Cast .... Philip Sterling

MOVIES AND MINISERIES

DEATH TRAIN — USA
Drama: Suspense/Thriller • Foreign or Exotic Location
Airdate: 4/14/93
Rating: N/A — A/C:

Based on the book by Alistair MacLean. A multi-national anti-terrorist organization must stop a hijacked train carrying a nuclear bomb headed for Iraq. The squad rushes to find the mastermind behind the plot, an ex-Soviet general whose intent is to reestablish a Communist Russia power bloc.

Production Company: British Lion Screen Ent., Yorkshire TV
Executive Producer .... Peter Snell
Director .... David S. Jackson
Writer .... David S. Jackson
Cast .... Pierce Brosnan
Cast .... Patrick Stewart
Cast .... Christopheer Lee
Cast .... Alexandra Paul

DECEPTION: A MOTHER'S SECRET — NBC
Drama: Family Drama • Man Against The System • Children/Teens
Airdate: 11/24/91
Rating: 15.6/23 — A/C: 2

A recent widower legally attempts to adopt his step-son and slowly uncovers the horrifying truth that the boy was kidnapped at the age of two by his late wife. He ultimately is torn between keeping the child or returning him to his natural parents.

Production Company: SanKan Prods. Inc.
Executive Producer .... Sandor Stern
Producer .... Kandy Stern
Co-Producer .... Robert Rolsky
Director .... Sandor Stern
Writer .... Sandor Stern
Cast .... Steven Weber
Cast .... Katherine Helmond
Cast .... Mary Page Keller
Cast .... Robert Gorman

DECEPTIONS — SHOWTIME
Drama: Murder and Murder Mystery • Cops/Detectives/Law Enforcement • Love Story • Suspense/Thriller
Airdate: 06/10/90
Rating: N/A — A/C:

When a beautiful woman kills her husband, the police detective who falls head over heels in love with her believes her story of self-defense; his partner is skeptical.

Production Company: Sugar Entertainment & Alpha Entertainment Prod.
Executive Producer .... Ruben Preuss
Executive Producer .... Miguel Tejada-Flores
Producer .... Guy Louthan
Director .... Ruben Preuss
Writer .... Ken Denbow
Writer .... Richard Taylor
Cast .... Harry Hamlin
Cast .... Robert Davi
Cast .... Nicolette Sheridan

DECEPTIONS — NBC
Miniseries/Drama (2 nights): Suspense/Thriller • Foreign or Exotic Location • Sex/Glitz
Airdate: 05/26/85 • 05/27/85
Rating: 19.9/35 • 21.8/35 — A/C:

A wealthy London socialite and her identical twin sister, an unhappy New Jersey housewife, decide to switch places and run into all sorts of trouble in their new lives.

Production Company: Louis Rudolph Prods. for Consolidated Prods. IAW Columbia TV
Executive Producer .... Louis Rudolph
Producer .... William Hill
Director .... Robert Chenault
Director .... Melville Shavelson
Writer .... Melville Shavelson
Cast .... Stefanie Powers
Cast .... Barry Bostwick
Cast .... Gina Lollobrigida
Cast .... Brenda Vaccaro

DECONSTRUCTING SARAH — USA
Drama: Murder and Murder Mystery • Suspense/Thriller
Airdate: 6/17/94
Rating: N/A — A/C:

A high-powered female executive has a secret nightlife that involves casual sex. One of her sexual partners, a volatile trucker, learns her secret and tries to blackmail her. Later, she vanishes and is found dead. Her best friend, a conservative wife and mother, learns of her concealed lifestyle and sets out to find her killer.

Production Company: MTE Universal
Executive Producer .... Lee Rose
Executive Producer .... Carla Singer
Producer .... Sally Young
Director .... Craig Baxley
Writer .... Lee Rose
Cast .... Sheila Kelley
Cast .... A. Martinez
Cast .... Rachel Ticotin

DECORATION DAY — NBC
Drama: Black Story • Historical Piece • Social Issue
Airdate: 12/02/90
Rating: 17.9/28 — A/C: 1

Based on the novella by John William Corrington. A retired Georgia judge overcomes his depression when he investigates the case of a black tenant farmer and old friend, who rejects a belated WWII medal of honor.

Production Company: Marian Rees Associates, Inc.
Executive Producer .... Marian Rees
Producer .... Anne Hopkins
Director .... Robert Markowitz
Writer .... Robert W. Lenski
Cast .... James Garner
Cast .... Bill Cobbs
Cast .... Judith Ivey
Cast .... Ruby Dee

DEEP DARK SECRETS — NBC
Drama: Woman In Jeopardy • Suspense/Thriller • Mafia/Mob
Airdate: 10/26/87
Rating: 15.5/25 — A/C:

When the owner of a country inn dies in a car crash, his new wife is horrified when she learns more about his past, which included adultery and laundered mob money. But she's really in for a surprise when she learns he's not dead after all.

Production Company: Fries Entertainment Inc.
Executive Producer .... Charles M. Fries
Producer .... Marcy Gross
Producer .... Ann Weston
Director .... Robert Lewis
Writer .... Nancy Sackett
Cast .... Melody Anderson
Cast .... James Brolin
Cast .... Pamela Bellwood
Cast .... Morgan Stevens
Cast .... Joe Spano

DEEP TROUBLE — USA
Drama: Cops/Detectives/Law Enforcement • Murder and Murder Mystery • Suspense/Thriller • Foreign or Exotic Location
Airdate: 7/8/93
Rating: N/A — A/C:

Based on a story by Bruno Tardon. When in France, an American salvage diver finds millions of dollars worth of stolen diamonds in a sunken van. Connecting the gems to a villainous mob boss who also murdered his business partner and best friend he soon becomes entangled in a web of intrigue and deadly revenge.

Production Company: Papazian-Hirsch, Ellipse Programme
Executive Producer .... Robert A. Papazian
Executive Producer .... James G. Hirsch
Executive Producer .... Simon Hart
Executive Producer .... Robert Rea
Producer .... Richard L. O'Connor
Director .... Armand Mastroianni
Writer .... James G. Hirsch
Cast .... Robert Wagner
Cast .... Ben Cross
Cast .... Isabelle Pasco

DEFIANT ONE, THE — ABC
Drama: Prison and Prison Camp • Black Story • Action/Adventure • Social Issue
Airdate: 1/5/86
Rating: 18.9/28 — A/C:

Remake of the 1958 feature film. A black and white convict, manacled together during a prison transfer, escape and must endure their mutual racial hatred and struggle for survival.

Production Company: Stormy Weathers Inc., Urich Prods. IAW MGM/UA TV
Executive Producer .... Carl Weathers
Executive Producer .... Robert Urich
Producer .... Robert Lovenheim
Director .... David Lowell Rich
Writer .... James Lee Barrett
Cast .... Carl Weathers
Cast .... Robert Urich

DELIBERATE STRANGER, THE   NBC

Miniseries/Drama (2 nights): Cops/Detectives/Law
Enforcement • Woman In Jeopardy • True Crime
Airdate: 05/04/86 • 05/05/86
Rating: 18.6/28 • 21.7/32   A/C:

*True story of clean-cut mass murderer Ted
Bundy, once a law student. The film explores
his effect on his victims, their associates, and
those who knew him, as well as the massive
detection effort that ended in his capture and
execution.*

Production Company: Stuart/Phoenix Productions
    IAW Lorimar-Telepictures
Executive Producer .... Malcolm Stuart
Producer .... Marvin J. Chomsky
Director .... Marvin J. Chomsky
Writer .... Hesper Anderson
Cast .... Mark Harmon
Cast .... Frederic Forrest
Cast .... Ben Masters
Cast .... Frederick Coffin
Cast .... M. Emmet Walsh
Cast .... Glynnis O'Connor
Cast .... George Grizzard

DELIVER THEM FROM EVIL: THE TAKING OF ALTA VIEW   CBS

Drama: Suspense/Thriller • True Crime
Airdate: 04/28/92
Rating: 16.6/26   A/C: 1

*In 1990, deranged gunman and religious
fundamentalist Richard Worthington takes a
Utah maternity ward hostage in outrage over
his wife's sterilization. A hostage negotiator
clashes with a confused chain of command to
free the terrorized victims.*

Production Company: Citadel Pictures Inc.
Executive Producer .... David R. Ginsburg
Executive Producer .... Mark Sennet
Producer .... Steve McGlothen
Director .... Peter Levin
Writer .... John Miglis
Cast .... Harry Hamlin
Cast .... Teri Garr
Cast .... Terry O'Quinn
Cast .... Gary Frank

DESCENDING ANGEL   HBO

Drama: Nazis • Psychological Thriller • Family
Drama • Foreign or Exotic Location
Airdate: 11/25/90
Rating: N/A   A/C:

*A young man becomes increasingly disturbed
when he learns that his fiancee's father may in
fact have been a murderous fascist during WWII.*

Production Company: Fredya Rosthstein
    Production of a Jeremy Kagan Film
Producer .... Freyda Rothstein
Producer .... Carol Gordon Morra
Producer .... Robert Siegel
Director .... Jeremy Kagan
Writer .... Robert Siegel
Writer .... Grace Woodard
Writer .... Alan Sharp
Cast .... George C. Scott
Cast .... Diane Lane
Cast .... Eric Roberts
Cast .... Jan Rubes

DESPERADO   NBC

Drama: Western
Airdate: 04/26/87
Rating: 19.3/32   A/C:

*In the Old West, a stranger establishes his
gunfighting credentials, upsets the local
establishment, and saves the ranch for a small
landowner and his pretty daughter.*

Production Company: Walter Mirisch Prods.,
    Charles E. Sellier and Universal TV
Executive Producer .... Andrew Mirisch
Producer .... Chuck Sellier
Director .... Virgil W. Vogel
Writer .... Elmore Leonard
Cast .... Alex McArthur
Cast .... Lise Cutter
Cast .... David Warner
Cast .... Robert Vaughn

DESPERADO: BADLANDS JUSTICE   NBC

Drama: Western
Airdate: 12/17/89
Rating: 13.1/21   A/C: 1

*In the Old West, an unjustly accused loner
struggles against mining-town corruption to
cleanse his reputation.*

Production Company: Desperado Productions Inc.
Executive Producer .... Andrew Mirisch
Producer .... Chuck Sellier
Director .... E.W. Swackhamer
Writer .... Les Bohem
Cast .... John Rhys-Davies
Cast .... Alex McArthur
Cast .... James B. Sikking
Cast .... Patricia Charbonneau

DESPERATE CHOICES: TO SAVE MY CHILD   NBC

Drama: Family Drama • Medical/Disease/Mental
Illness • Children/Teens • Courtroom Drama
Airdate: 10/5/92
Rating: 12.4/19   A/C: 3

*A family is torn apart when their teenage
daughter is stricken with leukemia. Her life
could be saved by a bone-marrow transplant
from her seven year old half brother, but
concern for his safety compel his overprotective
mother-and the girl's stepmother, to refuse
permission for the procedure. The father of the
dying girl takes his wife to court, but tragedy is
adverted when she realizes her fears are
unfounded and consents to the operation.*

Production Company: Andrew Adelson Prods.
    IAW ABC Prods.
Executive Producer .... Andrew Adelson
Director .... Andy Tennant
Writer .... Sandra Jennings
Writer .... Maggie Kleinman
Cast .... Joanna Kerns
Cast .... Bruce Davison
Cast .... Reese Witherspoon
Cast .... Joe Mazzello

DESPERATE FOR LOVE   CBS

Drama: Forbidden Love • Love Story • Children/
Teens • True Crime • Murder and Murder Mystery
Airdate: 01/17/89
Rating: 12.0/20   A/C:

*Truth-based story of a girl who seduces the
youth she really loves by going after his best
friend first. When the boy she loves is found
murdered, his friend is put on trial.*

Production Company: Vishudda Prods. IAW
    Andrew Adelson Co. and Lorimar-Telepictures
Executive Producer .... Andrew Adelson
Executive Producer .... Judith P. Mitchell
Producer .... Steve McGlothen
Director .... Michael Tuchner
Writer .... Judith P. Mitchell
Cast .... Brian Bloom
Cast .... Christian Slater
Cast .... Veronica Cartwright
Cast .... Tammy Lauren

DESPERATE JOURNEY: THE ALLISON WILCOX STORY   ABC

Drama: Disaster • True Story
Airdate: 12/5/93
Rating: 9.7/15   A/C: 3

*A single young women who recovers from
leukemia, then becomes pregnant, is determined
to crew on a yacht traveling up the southeast
coast before marrying her boyfriend and
settling down. After setting sail, she soon find
herself and her two male shipmates in the path
of Hurricane Bob which destroys their boat and
leaves them clinging to a small life raft for
twelve grueling days. They are eventually
rescued by the Coast Guard.*

Production Company: D'Antoni Prods. Group
    IAW Viacom Prods.
Executive Producer .... James D'Antoni
Executive Producer .... Chris D'Antoni
Producer .... Harry R. Sherman
Director .... Dan Lerner
Writer .... Jonathan Rintels
Cast .... Mel Harris
Cast .... John Schneider
Cast .... Dana Ashbrook
Cast .... Cotter Smith

DESPERATE RESCUE: THE CATHY MAHONE STORY   NBC
Drama: True Story • Children/Teens • Family Drama • Cross-Cultural Story • Foreign or Exotic Location • Woman Against The System
Airdate: 1/18/93
Rating: 13.3/20   A/C: 3

Based on a magazine article by Neil Livingstone & David Halevy. When her Jordanian ex-husband kidnaps their seven year old daughter to his home in the Middle East an American women hires and accompanies former Army commandos on a desperate rescue mission.

Production Company: Gimble-Adelson Prods. IAW Multimedia TV, WIN
Executive Producer .... Roger Gimbel
Executive Producer .... Orly Adelson
Producer .... David Hamburger
Director .... Richard Colla
Writer .... Guerdon Trueblood
Cast .... Mariel Hemingway
Cast .... Clancy Brown
Cast ....Jeff Kober
Cast .... James Russo

DESTINATION: AMERICA   ABC
Drama: Murder and Murder Mystery
Airdate: 04/03/87
Rating: 8.8/15   A/C:

A billionaire's son who has rejected his origins becomes involved with an abused woman, but soon has serious problems of his own: he's accused of murdering his father.

Production Company: Stephen J. Cannell Prods.
Executive Producer .... Stephen J. Cannell
Executive Producer .... Patrick Hasburgh
Producer .... Steve Beers
Director .... Corey Allen
Writer .... Patrick Hasburgh
Cast .... Rip Torn
Cast .... Alan Autry
Cast .... Bruce Greenwood

DETECTIVE IN THE HOUSE   CBS
Drama: Cops/Detectives/Law Enforcement • Series Pilot (2 hr.)
Airdate: 03/15/85
Rating: 14.4/24   A/C:

A former engineer and present detective investigates a murder plot involving a ex-film star.

Production Company: Lorimar
Executive Producer .... Gary Adelson
Executive Producer .... Gil Grant
Producer .... William L. Young
Director .... Bill Bixby
Writer .... Judy Merl
Writer .... Paul Eric Myers
Cast .... Judd Hirsch
Cast .... Cassie Yates
Cast .... Meeno Peluce
Cast .... Jack Elam

DEVLIN   SHOWTIME
Drama: Cops/Detectives/Law Enforcement • Murder and Murder Mystery • Mafia/Mob • Suspense/Thriller
Airdate: 9/12/92
Rating: N/A   A/C:

Based on the book by Roderick Thorp. A tough New York cop finds himself on the lam from the mob and the police when he is framed for the murder of his brother-in-law, a respected city politician.

Production Company: Viacom Pictures
Executive Producer .... Michael Rauch
Producer .... Paulo De Oliveria
Producer .... Craig Roessler
Director .... Rick Rosenthal
Writer .... David Taylor
Cast .... Bryan Brown
Cast .... Roma Downey
Cast .... Lloyd Bridges
Cast .... Whip Hubley

DIAGNOSIS OF MURDER   CBS
Drama: Murder and Murder Mystery • Cops/Detectives/Law Enforcement • Series Pilot (2 hr.)
Airdate: 01/05/92
Rating: 14.6/23   A/C: 2

An eccentric physician with a knack for solving crimes works to clear his patient accused of murdering a local media mogul.

Production Company: Fred Silverman Co., Dean Hargrove Prods. IAW Viacom Prods.
Executive Producer .... Fred Silverman
Executive Producer .... Dean Hargrove
Producer .... Barry Steinberg
Director .... Christopher Hibler
Writer .... Dean Hargrove
writer .... Joyce Burditt
Cast .... Dick Van Dyke
Cast .... Mariette Hartley
Cast .... Stephen Caffrey
Cast .... Bill Bixby

DIAMOND FLEECE   USA
Drama: Cops/Detectives/Law Enforcement • Suspense/Thriller
Airdate: 06/17/92
Rating: N/A   A/C:

A fabled uncut diamond is purchased by a Beverly Hills jewelry store. When the store owner hires an ex-cat burglar to guard the stone, they have no idea the thief is setting up an elaborate hoax to sting the cop who put him behind bars.

Production Company: Moving Image Prods.
Executive Producer .... Alan Landsburg
Producer .... Stewart Harding
Director .... Al Waxman
Writer .... Michael Norell
Cast .... Ben Cross
Cast .... Kate Nelligan
Cast .... Brian Dennehy

DIAMOND TRAP, THE   CBS
Mystery: Cops/Detectives/Law Enforcement • Suspense/Thriller • Foreign or Exotic Location
Airdate: 11/20/88
Rating: 15.1/24   A/C:

Two New York police detectives investigate inside-job gallery jewel thefts involving violent death, uncertain identities and pairing up with an attractive female in the English countryside.

Production Company: Jay Bernstein Prods. IAW Columbia Pictures TV
Executive Producer .... Jay Bernstein
Supervising Exec. Producer ..... Patrick Dromgoole
Supervising Exec. Producer .... Johnny Goodman
Producer .... Neil T. Maffeo
Co-Producer .... Jeffrey Morton
Director .... Don Taylor
Writer .... David Peckinpah
Cast .... Howard Hesseman
Cast .... Brooke Shields
Cast .... Ed Marinaro
Cast .... Darren McGavin
Cast .... Twiggy

DIANA: HER TRUE STORY   NBC
Miniseries/Drama (2 nights): True Story • Biography • Foreign or Exotic Location • Family Drama
Airdate: 4/4/93 • 4/5/93
Rating: 14.5/23 • 15.6/24   A/C: 2 • 2

Based on the book by Andrew Morton. The stormy relationship between England's Prince and Princess of Wales that eventually caused embarrassment and public scandal to the British Royal family.

Production Company: Martin Poll Prods.
Executive Producer .... Martin Poll
Producer .... Hugh Benson
Director .... Kevin Connor
Writer .... Stephen Zito
Cast .... Serena Scott Thomas
Cast .... David Threlfall
Cast .... Elizabeth Garvie
Cast .... Donald Douglas

DIARY OF A PERFECT MURDER   NBC
Mystery: Courtroom Drama • Murder and Murder Mystery • Series Pilot (2 hr.)
Airdate: 03/03/86
Rating: 20.9/33   A/C:

Pilot for "Matlock": A folksy Georgia man and his sophisticated daughter, both lawyers, take the case of a TV journalist accused of killing his former wife.

Production Company: Viacom Prods. Inc.
Executive Producer .... Fred Silverman
Writer .... Dean Hargrove
Producer .... Joel Steiger
Co-Producer .... Robin S. Clark
Director .... Robert Day
Cast .... Andy Griffith
Cast .... Lori Lethin
Cast .... Lawrence Pressman
Cast .... Jack Bannon

DIFFERENT AFFAIR, A   CBS
Drama: Children/Teens • Social Issue
Airdate: 03/24/87
Rating: 10.8/18   A/C:

When her sponsored "foster child's" real mother becomes ill and the boy decides to move in with her, a radio psychiatrist discovers that caring is more than just sticking a few dollars in an envelope.

Production Company: Rogers/Samuels Prods.
Executive Producer .... Ron Samuels
Executive Producer .... Kenny Rogers
Director .... Noel Nosseck
Writer .... Jodi Rothe
Cast .... Anne Archer
Cast .... Beverly Todd
Cast .... Stuart Pankin
Cast .... Tony Roberts

DILLINGER   ABC
Drama: Cops/Detectives/Law Enforcement • True Crime • Period Piece • Biography
Airdate: 01/06/91
Rating: 14.5/22   A/C: 2

Stylized portrait of Depression-era gangster John Dillinger, who became the FBI's public enemy number one in the 1930's Midwest.

Production Company: David L. Wolper Prods. IAW Bernard Sofronski
Executive Producer .... David L. Wolper
Executive Producer .... Bernard Sofronski
Producer .... Mark M. Wolper
Director .... Rupert Wainwright
Writer .... Paul F. Edwards
Cast .... Mark Harmon
Cast .... Sherilyn Fenn
Cast .... Will Patton
Cast .... Bruce Abbott

DINNER AT EIGHT   TNT
Drama: Family Drama • Sex/Glitz
Airdate: 12/11/89
Rating: N/A   A/C:

Updating of the 1933 classic in which a society woman's elaborate dinner party plans collide with her guests' schemes for love, lust and hostile takeovers.

Production Company: A Think Entertainment Prod.
Executive Producer .... Shelley Duvall
Producer .... Bridget Terry
Director .... Ron Lagomarsino
Writer .... Donald Ogden Stewart
Cast .... Lauren Bacall
Cast .... Charles Durning
Cast .... Ellen Greene
Cast .... Harry Hamlin
Cast .... Marsha Mason

DIRTY DOZEN: THE DEADLY MISSION   NBC
Drama: Action/Adventure • WWII • Nazis
Airdate: 03/01/87
Rating: 18.5/28   A/C:

Another suicide mission for twelve U.S. Army convicts who would rather get shot at by Nazis than do hard time in the stockade.

Production Company: MGM/UA TV Prods.
Executive Producer .... David Gerber
Producer .... Mel Swope
Director .... Lee H. Katzin
Writer .... Mark Rodgers
Cast .... Vince Edwards
Cast .... Bo Svenson
Cast .... Vince Van Patten
Cast .... James Van Patten
Cast .... Telly Savalas
Cast .... Ernest Borgnine

DIRTY DOZEN: THE FATAL MISSION   NBC
Drama: Action/Adventure • WWII • Nazis
Airdate: 02/14/88
Rating: 14.3/22   A/C:

The team of World War II Army convicts must intercept a train full of young Nazi leaders.

Production Company: MGM/UA TV Prods.
Producer .... Mel Swope
Director .... Lee H. Katzin
Writer .... Mark Rodgers
Cast .... Telly Savalas
Cast .... Erik Estrada
Cast .... Ernie Hudson
Cast .... Matthew Burton
Cast .... John Matuszak
Cast .... Ernest Borgnine

DIRTY WORK   USA
Drama: Cops/Detectives/Law Enforcement • Drug Smuggling/Dealing • Mafia/Mob
Airdate: 7/22/92
Rating: N/A   A/C:

A former cop turned bailbondsman finds that his loyalty to his friend and partner has been terribly misplaced when his buddy cons the mob and then set him up to take the rap.

Production Company: Pacific Motion Pictures IAW Wilshire Court Prods.
Executive Producer .... Jeff Heyes
Producer .... Tom Rowe
Director .... John McPherson
Writer .... Aaron Julien
Cast .... Kevin Dobson
Cast .... John Ashton
Cast .... Roxann Biggs

DISAPPEARANCE OF CHRISTINA, The   USA
Mystery: Murder and Murder Mystery • Suspense/Thriller
Airdate: 11/4/93
Rating: N/A   A/C:

When his wife mysteriously vanishes during an outing on his friend's yacht a wealthy businessman is accused of her murder. He is convinced she is still alive when he begins receiving phone calls, and items she was wearing the day of her disappearance are found in his house. He becomes more depressed and thinks he is going crazy until he discovers that his partner's jealous and neglected wife murdered his spouse so she could have him all to herself.

Production Company: B.A.L. Prods. IAW MCA TV Ent. USA Networks
Producer .... Paul Heller
Producer .... Ruth Vitale
Producer .... Barry Berg
Director .... Karen Arthur
Writer .... Camille Thomasson
Cast .... John Stamos
Cast .... Robert Carradine
Cast .... Kim Delaney
Cast .... CCH Pounder

DISAPPEARANCE OF NORA   CBS
Drama: Murder and Murder Mystery • Woman In Jeopardy
Airdate: 3/7/93
Rating: 17.0/27   A/C: 1

When a beautiful young woman wakes up in the Nevada desert with amnesia, a Reno hotel security chief comes to her aid and helps to find her identity. He discovers she is a high powered trial lawyer from California married to a developer and implicated in the murder of her firm's senior partner. Investigating the case together they clear her name and uncover her husband's murderous scheme.

Production Company: Citadel Pictures
Executive Producer .... David R. Ginsburg
Producer .... Lee Rafner
Director .... Joyce Chopra
Writer .... Alan Ormsby
Writer .... Tom Cole
Cast .... Veronica Hamel
Cast .... Dennis Farina
Cast .... Stephen Collins

DISASTER AT SILO 7   ABC

Drama: Suspense/Thriller • True Story • Social Issue
Airdate: 11/27/88
Rating: 10.1/16   A/C:

Based on a real life incident which occurred near Little Rock, Arkansas in 1980. A maintenance accident with a nuclear-tipped guided missile leads to panic in a small town as the Air Force frantically tries to avoid an atomic explosion.

Production Company: Mark Carliner Prods. Inc.
Executive Producer .... Mark Carliner
Producer .... Julian Krainin
Co-Producer .... Lynn H. Guthrie
Director .... Larry Elikann
Writer .... Douglas Lloyd McIntosh
Writer .... Mark Carliner
Cast .... Patricia Charbonneau
Cast .... Dennis Weaver
Cast .... Perry King
Cast .... Joe Spano
Cast .... Michael O'Keefe

DISASTER IN TIME   SHOWTIME

Drama: Suspense/Thriller • Sci-Fi/Supernatural/ Horror/Fantasy
Airdate: 05/09/92
Rating: N/A   A/C:

Based on the novella "Vintage Season" by C.L. Moore. Time travelers from the future descend on a small town in Ohio, giving one man and his daughter the chance to save their community from impending disaster.

Production Company: Wildstreet Pictures
Executive Producer .... Jill Sattinger
Executive Producer .... Paul White
Producer .... John O'Connor
Director .... David N. Twohy
Writer .... David N. Twohy
Cast .... Jeff Daniels
Cast .... Ariana Richards
Cast .... Emilia Crow

DO YOU KNOW THE MUFFIN MAN?   CBS

Drama: Family Drama • Children/Teens • Rape/ Molestation • Social Issue
Airdate: 10/22/89
Rating: 18.4/30   A/C: 1

The devastating effects of preschool child abuse on a suburban, middle-class family who unite to confront the accused ritual sex offenders in court.

Production Company: Jon Avnet/Jordan Kerner Prods.
Executive Producer .... Jon Avnet
Executive Producer .... Jordan Kerner
Producer .... Daniel Freudenberger
Director .... Gilbert Cates
Writer .... Daniel Freudenberger
Cast .... Pam Dawber
Cast .... John Shea
Cast .... Brian Bonsall
Cast .... Stephen Dorff

DO YOU REMEMBER LOVE?   CBS
EMMY WINNER

Drama: Family Drama • Medical/Disease/Mental Illness
Airdate: 05/21/85
Rating: 17.0/28   A/C:

A gifted poet and professor develops Alzheimer's Disease. Her husband, family and friends must deal with the mental and physical deterioration that follows.

Production Company: Dave Bell Prods.
Executive Producer .... Dave Bell
Co-Executive Producer .... Marilyn Hall
Producer .... Wayne Threm
Producer .... James E. Thompson
Co-Producer .... Walter Halsey Davis
Director .... Jeff Bleckner
Writer .... Vickie Patik
Cast .... Joanne Woodward
Cast .... Richard Kiley
Cast .... Geraldine Fitzgerald
Cast .... Jordan Charney

DOING LIFE   NBC

Drama: True Story • Prison and Prison Camp
Airdate: 09/23/86
Rating: 16.8/27   A/C:

True story of Jerry Rosenberg, a murderer who was the first convict to earn a law degree while in jail and ends up fighting for inmates' rights.

Production Company: Castillian Prods.
Executive Producer .... Gene Reynolds
Co-Executive Producer .... Tony Danza
Producer .... Julian Marks
Director .... Gene Reynolds
Writer .... Stephen Bello
Cast .... Tony Danza
Cast .... Dawn Greenhalgh
Cast .... Rocco Sisto
Cast .... Alvin Epstein

DOING TIME ON MAPLE DRIVE   FBC

Drama: Family Drama • Homosexuality
Airdate: 03/16/92
Rating: 9.4/15   A/C: 3

An upper middle-class "all-American" family disintegrates when long-held secrets...one son's homosexuality, another's alcoholism, and a daughter's upcoming abortion...are revealed at a family reunion.

Production Company: FNM Films Inc.
Producer .... Paul Lussier
Director .... Ken Olin
Writer .... James Duff
Cast .... James B. Sikking
Cast .... Bibi Besch
Cast .... William McNamara
Cast .... James Carrey
Cast .... Lori Loughlin

DON'T TALK TO STRANGERS   USA

Drama: Suspense/Thriller
Airdate: 8/12/94
Rating: N/A   A/C:

A midwestern mother is awarded custody of her young son, infuriating her ex-husband, a volatile cop. After a whirlwind romance, she marries a man from Los Angeles. But as she and her child drive cross-country to their new home, they find themselves being stalked by her angry ex-spouse and a mysterious third party.

Production Company: MTE Universal TV
Producer .... Nevin Schreiner
Director .... Robert Lewis
Writer .... Nevin Schreiner
Cast .... Pierce Brosnan
Cast .... Shanna Reed
Cast .... Terry O'Quinn

DON'T TOUCH MY DAUGHTER   NBC

Drama: Woman Against The System • Suspense/ Thriller • Children/Teens • Rape/Molestation
Airdate: 04/07/91
Rating: 14.5/23   A/C: 2

Based on the book "Nightmare" by M. Dorner. A single mother takes the law into her own hands to bring to justice the man who molested her 11-year-old daughter.

Production Company: Patchett- Kaufman Ent. IAW Victoria Principal Prods.
Executive Producer .... Victoria Principal
Executive Producer .... Ken Kaufman
Executive Producer .... Tom Patchett
Producer .... Graham Cottle
Director .... John Pasquin
Writer .... John Robert Bensink
Writer .... Rick Husky
Cast .... Victoria Principal
Cast .... Paul Sorvino
Cast .... Jonathan Banks
Cast .... Danielle Harris

DONATO AND DAUGHTER   CBS

Drama: Family Drama • Cops/Detectives/Law Enforcement • Murder and Murder Mystery
Airdate: 9/21/93
Rating: 14.8/24   A/C: 2

Based on the book by Jack Early. An estranged father and daughter LAPD cop team must confront painful family secrets as well as the devious mind of a psychopath when they pair up to track down a serial killer.

Production Company: Multimedia Motion Pictures
Executive Producer .... Neil Russell
Co-Executive Producer .... Brenda Miao
Producer .... Marian Brayton
Producer .... Annie Carlucci
Director .... Rod Holcomb
Writer .... Robert Pool
Cast .... Charles Bronson
Cast .... Dana Delany
Cast .... Bonnie Bartlett
Cast .... Xander Berkeley

DONOR   CBS

Drama: Woman In Jeopardy • Suspense/Thriller •
Medical/Disease/Mental Illness
Airdate: 12/09/90
Rating: 14.8/24   A/C: 2

*A resident doctor becomes enmeshed in
murderous intrigue when she discovers
suspicious deaths and mysterious experiments
to reverse aging in a big city hospital.*

Production Company: CBS Entertainment Prods.,
   Peter Frankovich, Daniel A. Sherkow Prods
Executive Producer .... Daniel A. Sherkow
Executive Producer .... Peter Frankovich
Producer .... Ken Swor
Director .... Larry Shaw
Writer .... Michael Braverman
Cast .... Melissa Gilbert
Cast .... Jack Scalia
Cast .... Wendy Hughes
Cast .... Gregory Sierra

DOOMSDAY GUN   HBO

Drama: True Story • Suspense/Thriller • Political
Piece
Airdate: 7/23/94
Rating: N/A   A/C:

*Canadian genius Gerald Bull, former director
of a Top-secret NASA project and dealer of arms
to such countries as Israel, South Africa and
China becomes obsessed with building a
supergun that would be the largest ever built.
Desperately seeking a patron for his project,
he finally finds a sponsor in Saddam Hussein.
The deadly agreement sparks international
intrigue and murder as Bull is mysteriously
assassinated in Brussels in 1990.*

Production Company: HBO Showcase
Executive Producer .... Michael Deakin
Executive Producer .... Colin Callender
Producer .... Adam Clapham
Director .... Robert Young
Writer .... Walter Bernstein
Writer .... Lionel Chetwynd
Cast .... Frank Langella
Cast .... Alan Arkin
Cast .... Kevin Spacey
Cast .... James Fox

DOUBLE DECEPTION   NBC

Drama: Murder and Murder Mystery • Cops/
Detectives/Law Enforcement • Series Pilot (2 hr.)
Airdate: 6/21/93
Rating: 9.6/17   A/C: 3

*When a Venice Beach California private eye
investigates the disappearance of a mysterious
woman's ex-husband he also uncovers
information on the murder of his client's sister
ten years earlier. With the help of a cop friend
and a former prostitute the diligent dick solves
the puzzling crime.*

Production Company: NBC Prods., Finnegan-
   Pinchuk
Executive Producer .... Richard Rothstein
Executive Producer .... Lewis B. Chestler
Producer .... Pat Finnegan
Producer .... Bill Finnegan
Producer .... Lori-Etta Taub
Director .... Jan Egelson
Writer .... Richard Rothstein
Cast .... James Russo
Cast .... Alice Krige
Cast .... Burt Young
Cast .... Sally Kirkland

DOUBLE, DOUBLE, TOIL AND TROUBLE
ABC

Comedy: Children/Teens • Sci-Fi/Supernatural/
Horror/Fantasy • Holiday Special
Airdate: 10/30/93
Rating: 10.8/19   A/C: 2

*Two twin girls go after their evil witch Aunt
Agatha who has put a spell on their good, rich
Aunt Sophia in order to get money to save the
family home.*

Production Company: Dualstar Prods., Green/
   Epstein Prods. IAW Warner Bros. TV
Executive Producer .... Jim Green
Executive Producer .... Allen Epstein
Producer .... Adria Later
Producer .... Mark Bacino
Director .... Stuart Margolin
Writer .... Jurgen Wolff
Cast .... Mary Kate Olsen
Cast .... Ashley Olsen
Cast .... Cloris Leachman
Cast .... Meshach Taylor

DOUBLE EDGE   CBS

Drama: Murder and Murder Mystery • Cops/
Detectives/Law Enforcement • Suspense/Thriller
Airdate: 03/22/92
Rating: 17.1/28   A/C: 1

*An FBI agent is teamed with her ex-husband to
track and capture a notorious hit woman who
happens to be her look-a-like.*

Production Company: Konigsberg/Sanitsky Co.
Executive Producer .... Frank Konigsberg
Executive Producer .... Larry Sanitsky
Producer .... Jayne Bieber
Producer .... Carole Bloom
Director .... Stephen Stafford
Writer .... Joe Reb Moffly
Writer .... Otis Jones
Cast .... Susan Lucci
Cast .... Robert Urich
Cast .... Michael Woods

DOUBLE JEOPARDY   SHOWTIME

Drama: Suspense/Thriller • Murder and Murder
Mystery
Airdate: 11/21/92
Rating: N/A   A/C:

*A high powered attorney defends her husband's
ex-girlfriend when she is accused of stabbing
an ex-boyfriend in her apartment. What she
doesn't know is that her amiable spouse is a
witness to the crime, as he was hiding on the
balcony after a passionate romp in her shower.
Note: also aired on CBS -10/24/93 Rating:
12.4/20.*

Production Company: Boxleitner/Bernstein Prods.
   IAW CBS Ent.
Executive Producer .... Jay Bernstein
Executive Producer .... Bruce Boxleitner
Producer .... Jeffrey Morton
Producer .... Lawrence Schiller
Director .... Lawrence Schiller
Writer .... Craig Tepper
Writer .... Monte Stettin
Cast .... Bruce Boxleitner
Cast .... Rachel Ward
Cast .... Sela Ward
Cast .... Sally Kirkland

DOUBLE STANDARD   NBC

Drama: Family Drama • Forbidden Love • Social
Issue
Airdate: 10/17/88
Rating: 21.1/33   A/C:

*A judge is married to two women at once, only
one of whom knows about the other, and has
ten children. He keeps up the charade until
one of his daughters discovers his double life.*

Production Company: Louis Rudolph Prods./
   Fenton Entertainment Group/Fries
   Entertainment
Executive Producer .... Louis Rudolph
Producer .... Robert Fenton
Producer .... S. Bryan Hickox
Director .... Louis Rudolph
Writer .... Robert E. Thompson
Cast .... Robert Foxworth
Cast .... Christianne Hirt
Cast .... Pamela Bellwood
Cast .... Michele Greene

DOUBLE YOUR PLEASURE   NBC

Comedy: Cops/Detectives/Law Enforcement • Buddy
Story
Airdate: 10/29/89
Rating: 10.9/18   A/C: 2

*When an FBI undercover agent is sidelined, her
twin sister assumes her identity to catch a
crooked wheeler dealer.*

Production Company: Steve White Prods.
Executive Producer .... Steve White
Producer .... Barry Bernardi
Director .... Paul Lynch
Writer .... Jeff Cohn
Writer .... Kristi Kane
Cast .... Richard Lawson
Cast .... Harold Sylvester
Cast .... Dan Hedaya
Cast .... Jackee Harry

DOUBLECROSSED   HBO

Drama: True Story • Foreign or Exotic Location • Drug Smuggling/Dealing
Airdate: 07/20/91
Rating: N/A   A/C:

Barry Seal, a former airline pilot, smuggles drugs into the U.S. for the Medellin drug cartel. After he is arrested by the DEA, he turns informant and helps set up his old bosses in Miami and Colombia.

Production Company: Lorimar/Green-Epstein
Executive Producer .... Jim Green
Executive Producer .... Allen Epstein
Executive Producer .... Ronald Tanet
Producer .... Albert J. Salzer
Director .... Roger Young
Writer .... Roger Young
Cast .... Dennis Hopper
Cast .... G.W. Bailey
Cast .... Robert Carradine
Cast .... Adrienne Barbeau

DOUBLETAKE   CBS

Miniseries/Drama (2 nights): Murder and Murder Mystery • Cops/Detectives/Law Enforcement • Suspense/Thriller
Airdate: 11/24/85 • 11/26/85
Rating: 21.1/33 • 18.7/28   A/C:

A psychotic murderer mixes and matches the heads and bodies of two similar looking women whom he murders, baffling a police detective who must piece the clues together one by one in order to solve the mystery.

Production Company: Titus Prods.
Executive Producer .... Herbert Brodkin
Executive Producer .... Robert Berger
Producer .... Thomas De Wolfe
Director .... Jud Taylor
Writer .... John Gay
Cast .... Richard Crenna
Cast .... Beverly D'Angelo
Cast .... Vincent Baggetta
Cast .... Cliff Gorman

DOWNPAYMENT ON MURDER   NBC

Drama: Family Drama • Woman In Jeopardy • True Crime • Family Violence
Airdate: 12/06/87
Rating: 16.1/27   A/C:

Inspired by a true story. When the abused wife of a financially besieged real-estate man leaves him with their two children, he hires a hit man to kill her.

Production Company: Adam Prods. IAW 20th Century Fox TV
Executive Producer .... Robert M. Myman
Producer .... Carole Bloom
Director .... Waris Hussein
Writer .... Barry Schneider
Writer .... Bill Driskill
Cast .... Ben Gazzara
Cast .... Connie Sellecca
Cast .... David Morse
Cast .... Jonathan Banks

DR. QUINN, MEDICINE WOMAN   CBS

Drama: Period Piece • Series Pilot (2 hr.) • Western
Airdate: 1/1/93
Rating: 18.2/29   A/C: 1

In the late 1860s, a woman doctor from Boston travels to the wilds of Colorado Springs to set up a practice. After a patient dies she takes on the responsibilities of raising the woman's three orphaned children while trying to overcome sexism and the hardships of frontier life.

Production Company: Sullivan Co. IAW CBS Ent. Prods.
Executive Producer .... Beth Sullivan
Producer .... Richard L. O'Connor
Co-Producer .... Timothy Johnson
Co-Producer .... Jeremy Kagan
Director .... Jeremy Kagan
Writer .... Beth Sullivan
Cast .... Jane Seymour
Cast .... Joe Lando
Cast .... Chad Allen
Cast .... Guy Boyd

DREAM BREAKERS   CBS

Drama: Family Drama • Mafia/Mob
Airdate: 01/31/89
Rating: 7.4/12   A/C:

Two Chicago brothers—a high-minded priest and a greedy businessman—come into conflict over a real-estate deal in Chicago, and are forced to stand up to the mob.

Production Company: CBS Entertainment Prods.
Producer .... Stuart Millar
Director .... Stuart Millar
Writer .... Victor Levin
Writer .... Stuart Millar
Cast .... Robert Loggia
Cast .... Hal Linden
Cast .... Kyle MacLachlan
Cast .... D.W. Moffett

DREAM DATE   NBC

Comedy: Youth Comedy
Airdate: 10/09/89
Rating: 15.1/24   A/C: 3

A 40-year-old father and his date clandestinely follow his 15-year-old daughter around on her first date, unaware that his friends have taken over his house for a surprise birthday party complete with adult entertainment.

Production Company: Golchan/Kosberg Prod. Hoffman/Israel Prod. IAW Saban International
Executive Producer .... Robert Kosberg
Executive Producer .... Neal Israel
Executive Producer .... Gary Hoffman
Executive Producer .... Frederic Golchan
Producer .... Harry R. Sherman
Director .... Anson Williams
Writer .... Peter Crabbe
Cast .... Tempestt Bledsoe
Cast .... Clifton Davis
Cast .... Kadeem Hardison
Cast .... Anne-Marie Johnson

DREAM WEST   CBS

Miniseries/Drama (3 nights): Action/Adventure • American Indians • Biography • Historical Piece • Western
Airdate: 04/13/86 • 04/15/86 • 04/20/86
Rating: 19.5/29 • 18.1/29 • 20.1/32   A/C:

Fact-based legend of assertive frontier explorer John Fremont, who furthered "manifest destiny" in the American West and became involved with politics in the mid-19th century.

Production Company: Sunn Classic Pictures
Executive Producer .... Chuck McLain
Producer .... Hunt Lowry
Director .... Dick Lowry
Writer .... Evan Hunter
Cast .... Richard Chamberlain
Cast .... John Anderson
Cast .... Alice Krige
Cast .... Ben Johnson
Cast .... Rip Torn
Cast .... Fritz Weaver
Cast .... F.Murray Abraham
Cast .... Mel Ferrer

DREAMER OF OZ, THE   NBC

Drama: Family Drama • Children/Teens • Period Piece • Biography
Airdate: 12/10/90
Rating: 11.8/18   A/C: 3

Failing businessman, L. Frank Baum, escapes the drudgery of his life in 1880s South Dakota through the love and support of his wife and his magical storytelling, which ultimately resulted in the publication of the "Wizard of Oz" books.

Production Company: Bedrock Prods. and Adam Prods. IAW Spelling Entertainment
Executive Producer .... David Kirschner
Executive Producer .... Robert M. Myman
Producer .... Ervin Zavada
Producer .... Laura Moskowitz
Producer .... David Brooks
Director .... Jack Bender
Writer .... Richard Matheson
Cast .... John Ritter
Cast .... Annette O'Toole
Cast .... Rue McClanahan
Cast .... Charles Haid

DREAMS OF GOLD: THE MEL FISHER STORY   CBS

Drama: Man Against The System • True Story • Action/Adventure
Airdate: 11/15/86
Rating: 11.3/20   A/C:

True story of the intensely determined man who sought the sunken treasure-filled Spanish galleon Atosha for seventeen years and finally found it.

Production Company: InterPlanetary Prods.
Executive Producer .... Max A. Keller
Producer .... Charles Hairston
Producer .... Daniel Helfgott
Director .... James Goldstone
Writer .... Stanford Whitmore
Cast .... Cliff Robertson
Cast .... Loretta Swit
Cast .... Ed O'Ross
Cast .... Scott Paulin

DRESS GRAY   NBC

Miniseries/Drama (2 nights): Murder and Murder Mystery • Love Story • Homosexuality • Period Piece • Suspense/Thriller
Airdate: 03/09/86 • 03/10/86
Rating: 17.9/27 • 19.0/30   A/C:

From Lucian Truscott's novel. A 1960's military-school student's family runs up against the school commandant's attempt to cover-up the murder of their cadet son, who was found drowned and raped. With the of an upperclassman the mystery is solved.

Production Company: Frank von Zerneck/Warners Bros. TV Prods.
Executive Producer .... Frank Von Zerneck
Producer .... Glenn Jordan
Director .... Glenn Jordan
Writer .... Gore Vidal
Cast .... Alec Baldwin
Cast .... Susan Hess
Cast .... Eddie Albert
Cast .... Tim Van Patten
Cast .... Alexis Smith
Cast .... Lloyd Bridges
Cast .... Hal Holbrook

DRIVE LIKE LIGHTNING   USA

Drama: Action/Adventure
Airdate: 01/08/92
Rating: N/A   A/C:

An ex-daredevil teams with a female singer on the cross-country delivery of a high tech stunt car to his former rival. Pursued by the mob and local cops, he ultimately steals the thunder from his old nemesis by making the spectacular jump himself.

Production Company: Papazian-Hirsch Prods. IAW Canal Plus
Executive Producer .... Robert A. Papazian
Executive Producer .... James G. Hirsch
Producer .... Bradford May
Director .... Bradford May
Writer .... James G. Hirsch
Cast .... Steven Bauer
Cast .... Cynthia Gibb
Cast .... William Russ
Cast .... James Handy

DROP DEAD GORGEOUS   USA

Drama: Murder and Murder Mystery • Woman In Jeopardy
Airdate: 08/07/91
Rating: N/A   A/C:

A beautiful young girl finds fame and fortune in the modeling world until a string of homicides of people she worked with starts to threaten her very existence.

Production Company: Power Pictures Corp. Prods.
Executive Producer .... Harry Chandler
Executive Producer .... Gerald W. Abrams
Producer .... Julian Marks
Director .... Paul Lynch
Writer .... Thomas Baum
Writer .... Bill Wells
Writer .... Mimi Schapiro
Cast .... Jennifer Rubin
Cast .... Peter Outerbridge
Cast .... Sally Kellerman

DROP-OUT MOTHER   CBS

Comedy: Woman's Issue/Story • Social Issue
Airdate: 01/01/88
Rating: 13.2/22   A/C:

A suburban career woman chucks her job in favor of housewifery, to the disgust of her husband and children.

Production Company: Fries Entertainment Inc. and Comco Prods. Inc.
Executive Producer .... Charles Fries
Executive Producer .... Julie Corman
Producer .... Ann Shanks
Producer .... Bob Shanks
Director .... Charles S. Dubin
Writer .... Bob Shanks
Cast .... Wayne Rogers
Cast .... Valerie Harper
Cast .... Carol Kane

DRUG WARS: THE CAMARENA STORY   NBC

EMMY WINNER

Miniseries/Drama (3 nights): Cops/Detectives/Law Enforcement • Foreign or Exotic Location • Drug Smuggling/Dealing • True Crime
Airdate: 01/07/90 • 01/08/90 • 01/09/90
Rating: 14.4/22 • 15.2/23 • 16.1/25
A/C: 2 • 3 • 2

The story of D.E.A. agent Enrique Camarena's murder and the subsequent U.S. led investigation of the case which uncovered high-level corruption within the Mexican government.

Production Company: ZZY Inc. Productions
Executive Producer .... Michael Mann
Executive Producer .... Richard Brams
Producer .... Branko Lustig
Director .... Brian Gibson
Writer .... Ann Powell
Writer .... Rose Schacht
Writer .... Mel Frohman
Writer .... Christopher Canaan
Cast .... Steven Bauer
Cast .... Craig T. Nelson
Cast .... Treat Williams

DRUG WARS: THE COCAINE CARTEL   NBC

Miniseries/Drama (2 nights): Cops/Detectives/Law Enforcement • True Crime • Foreign or Exotic Location • Drug Smuggling/Dealing
Airdate: 01/19/92 • 01/20/92
Rating: 12.8/20 • 13.2/20   A/C: 3 • 3

Sequel to 1990 miniseries "The Drug Wars: The Camarena Story." A DEA agent and female Colombian judge team up for a sting operation to topple a cartel headed by druglords Don Pablo Escobar Gaviria and Rodriguez Gacha.

Production Company: ZZY I Inc.
Executive Producer .... Michael Mann
Co-Executive Producer .... Richard Brams
Co-Executive Producer .... Gordon Greisman
Director .... Paul Krasny
Writer .... Gordon Greisman
Writer .... Gail Morgan Hickman
Cast .... Alex McArthur
Cast .... Dennis Farina
Cast .... Julie Carmen
Cast .... John Glover
Cast .... Karen Young

DUE SOUTH   CBS

Drama: Cops/Detectives/Law Enforcement • Murder and Murder Mystery • Buddy Story • Series Pilot (2 hr.)
Airdate: 4/23/94
Rating: 11.5/21   A/C: 1

A no nonsense, diligent Canadian Mountie leaves the wilds of the Yukon for the streets of Chicago to catch the man who murdered his father. He is paired with a smart-mouthed, reckless detective who shows him the ropes and helps him get his man.

Production Company: Alliance Communications Corp. IAW CTV Televison Network LTD.
Executive Producer .... Paul Haggis
Producer .... Jeff King
Director .... Fred Gerber
Writer .... Paul Haggis
Cast .... Paul Gross
Cast .... David Marciano
Cast .... Wendel Meldrum
Cast .... Ken Pogue

DUEL OF HEARTS   TNT

Drama: Love Story • Period Piece • Sex/Glitz • Foreign or Exotic Location
Airdate: 02/24/92
Rating: N/A   A/C:

Based on the book by Barbara Cartland. Posing as a commoner and taking a job as a servant to an aristocratic family, a noblewoman unravels the royals' mysterious past to win the man she loves.

Production Company: TNT/The Grade Co./ Gainsborough
Executive Producer .... Lew Grade
Producer .... John Hough
Director .... John Hough
Writer .... Terence Feely
Cast .... Alison Doody
Cast .... Michael York
Cast .... Geraldine Chaplin
Cast .... Benedict Taylor

DUPLICATES — USA

Drama: Suspense/Thriller • Sci-Fi/Supernatural/
Horror/Fantasy
Airdate: 03/18/92
Rating: N/A   A/C:

A couple races against time to save their son who has been kidnapped as part of a government mind reprogramming plot gone astray.

Production Company: Sankan Prods. IAW
    Wilshire Court Prods.
Executive Producer .... Sandor Stern
Producer .... Robert Rolsky
Director .... Sandor Stern
Writer .... Sandor Stern
Writer .... Andrew Neiderman
Cast .... Gregory Harrison
Cast .... Kim Greist
Cast .... Cicely Tyson
Cast .... Kevin McCarthy

DYING TO LOVE YOU — CBS

Drama: Psychological Thriller • True Story
Airdate: 3/16/93
Rating: 15.4/25   A/C: 1

Thinking that he's found the perfect woman in the personal ads, Roger Paulson, a shy businessman, soon discovers that the lady he is falling in love with is a psychotic manipulator, who is wanted by the FBI.

Production Company: Longbow Prods., WIN
Executive Producer .... Ronnie Clemmer
Executive Producer .... Bill Pace
Executive Producer .... Richard Kughn
Producer .... David C. Thomas
Co-Producer .... Robert Iscove
Writer .... John Miglis
Cast .... Tracy Pollan
Cast .... Tim Matheson
Cast .... Christine Ebersole
Cast .... Lee Garlington

DYING TO REMEMBER — USA

Drama: Murder and Murder Mystery • Suspense/
Thriller
Airdate: 12/2/93
Rating: N/A   A/C:

A young fashion designer haunted by nightmares and anxiety attacks, discovers under hypnosis that thirty years ago in a past life she was murdered by being pushed into an empty elevator shaft. Using information from her dreams she travels to San Francisco to investigate her death. As she puts the pieces together she finds the man who killed her is now a wealthy developer with a dark secret that must remain hidden at all costs.

Production Company: Wilshire Court Productions
Executive Producer .... Frank Cardea
Executive Producer .... George Schenck
Producer .... Tom Rowe
Director .... Arthur Allan Seidelman
Writer .... George Schenck
Writer .... Frank Cardea
Cast .... Melissa Gilbert
Cast .... Ted Shackelford
Cast .... Scott Plank
Cast .... Christopher Stone

DYNASTY: THE REUNION — ABC

Miniseries/Drama (2 nights): Family Drama
Airdate: 10/20/91 • 10/22/91
Rating: 16.8/25 • 15.3/23   A/C: 2

The Carringtons and Colbys reunite to destroy a corrupt international business consortium that has conspired to ruin the Carrington empire and dominate world markets.

Production Company: Richard and Esther Shapiro
    Prods. IAW Aaron Spelling Prods., Inc.
Executive Producer .... Aaron Spelling
Executive Producer .... Douglas S. Cramer
Executive Producer .... Richard Shapiro
Executive Producer .... Esther Shapiro
Producer .... Elaine Rich
Director .... Irving J. Moore
Writer .... Robert Pollock
Writer .... Eileen Pollock
Writer .... Richard Shapiro
Writer .... Esther Shapiro
Writer .... Edward De Blasio
Cast .... John Forsythe
Cast .... Joan Collins
Cast .... Linda Evans
Cast .... John James
Cast .... Emma Samms
Cast .... Michael Brandon

E. A. R. T. H. FORCE — CBS

Drama: Toxic Waste/Environmental • Series Pilot (2
hr.)
Airdate: 09/16/90
Rating: 9.9/17   A/C: 2

A team of environmental experts are brought together by a wealthy industrialist to stop a nuclear meltdown caused by a plutonium theft.

Production Company: Paramount Network
    Television
Executive Producer .... Richard Chapman
Executive Producer .... Bill Diaz
Producer .... Arthur Fellows
Producer .... Terry Keegan
Director .... Bill Corcoran
Writer .... Richard Chapman
Writer .... Bill Diaz
Cast .... Gil Gerard
Cast .... Joanna Pacula
Cast .... Tiffany Lamb
Cast .... Robert Knepper

EARTH ANGEL — ABC

Drama: Sci-Fi/Supernatural/Horror/Fantasy
Airdate: 03/04/91
Rating: 11.2/18   A/C: 3

Killed in a 1962 car crash, the ghost of a popular teen queen returns twenty-eight years later to her hometown to play matchmaker and help mend broken hearts.

Production Company: Ron Gilbert Prods. IAW
    Leonard Hill Films
Executive Producer .... Ron Gilbert
Executive Producer .... Leonard Hill
Executive Producer .... Joel Fields
Producer .... Ron Gilbert
Director .... Joe Napolitano
Writer .... Nina Shengold
Cast .... Cindy Williams
Cast .... Cathy Podewell
Cast .... Mark Hamill
Cast .... Erik Estrada

EASY PREY — ABC

Drama: Woman In Jeopardy • True Crime • Rape/
Molestation
Airdate: 10/26/86
Rating: 18.4/29   A/C:

True story of a homicidal kidnapper who captures a teenage girl hitch-hiker and takes her on a long and torturous journey.

Production Company: New World TV-Rene Malo
    Prods.
Executive Producer .... Lawrence Taylor- Mortoff
Executive Producer .... Allan Bodoh
Producer .... Rene Malo
Producer .... Gary Goodman
Producer .... Barry Rosen
Director .... Sandor Stern
Writer .... John Carlen
Cast .... Gerald McRaney
Cast .... Shawnee Smith
Cast .... Kate Lynch

ECHOES IN THE DARKNESS — CBS

Miniseries/Drama (2 nights): Murder and Murder
Mystery • Cops/Detectives/Law Enforcement • True
Crime • Courtroom Drama
Airdate: 11/01/87 • 11/02/87
Rating: 20.1/33 • 22.0/33   A/C:

Based on the book by Joseph Wambaugh. Faculty and students at a Philadelphia high school are involved in the true story of the murder of one of the teachers, the disappearance of her two children and the ensuing seven year investigation.

Production Company: New World Pictures
Executive Producer .... Jack Grossbart
Producer .... Glenn Jordan
Writer .... Joseph Wambaugh
Cast .... Peter Coyote
Cast .... Robert Loggia
Cast .... Peter Boyle
Cast .... Stockard Channing
Cast .... Cindy Pickett
Cast .... Gary Cole
Cast .... Treat Williams

EIGHT IS ENOUGH: A FAMILY REUNION
NBC

Drama: Family Drama
Airdate: 10/18/87
Rating: 22.0/34   A/C:

From the popular TV series. The eight children come home to celebrate the 50th birthday of their father, whose newspaper is about to be sold out from under him.

Production Company: Lorimar-Telepictures
Executive Producer .... William Blinn
Producer .... Frank Fischer
Director .... Harry Harris
Writer .... Gwen Bagni-Dubov
Cast .... Dick Van Patten
Cast .... Mary Frann
Cast .... Willie Aames
Cast .... Brian Patrick Clarke
Cast .... Grant Goodeve
Cast .... Dianne Kay
Cast .... Adam Rich

EIGHT IS ENOUGH WEDDING, AN   NBC

Comedy: Romantic Comedy
Airdate: 10/15/89
Rating: 15.3/25   A/C: 3

Based on the series. Every member of the Bradford family seems to be going through a crisis as they prepare for David, the oldest son's, second wedding.

Production Company: Lorimar Telepictures
Executive Producer .... Greg Strangis
Director .... Stan Lathan
Writer .... Greg Strangis
Cast .... Dick Van Patten
Cast .... Sandy Faison
Cast .... Grant Goodeve
Cast .... Willie Aames

EIGHTY-THREE HOURS 'TIL DAWN   CBS

Drama: Family Drama • True Crime • Psychological Thriller
Airdate: 11/04/90
Rating: 14.2/22   A/C: 2

Based on the book by Barbara Jane Mackle & Gene Miller. A wealthy businessman races the clock to meet the demands of a psychotic sociopath who has kidnapped his daughter and buried her alive.

Production Company: Consolidated Entertainment Inc.
Executive Producer .... Elizabeth Matthews
Executive Producer .... Sue Reiner
Producer .... Joy McMahon
Producer .... Paulette Breen
Director .... Donald Wrye
Writer .... Gale Patrick Hickman
Cast .... Peter Strauss
Cast .... Robert Urich
Cast .... Paul Winfield
Cast .... Elizabeth Gracen

EL DIABLO   HBO

Comedy: Western
Airdate: 07/22/90
Rating: N/A   A/C:

In old Texas, a shy schoolteacher who dreams about the "real wild west" finds himself in the middle of it when a colorful gunfighter helps him rescue a student who's been kidnapped by a Mexican bandit.

Production Company: Wizan/Black Films Prod.
Executive Producer .... Joe Wizan
Executive Producer .... Debra Hill
Executive Producer .... John Carpenter
Producer .... Mickey Borofsky
Producer .... Todd Black
Director .... Peter Markle
Writer .... Tommy Lee Wallace
Writer .... John Carpenter
Writer .... Bill Phillips
Cast .... Anthony Edwards
Cast .... Louis Gossett, Jr.
Cast .... John Glover
Cast .... Joe Pantoliano

ELLIS ISLAND   CBS

Miniseries/Drama (3 nights): Cross-Cultural Story • Period Piece • Historical Piece
Airdate: 11/11/84 • 11/13/84 • 11/14/84
Rating: 23.4/35 • 21.1/33 • 19.0/29   A/C:

Based on the book by Fred Mustard Stewart. The stories of three immigrants (one Russian, one Italian, one Irish) and their struggles to succeed in America after they arrive in New York in 197.

Production Company: Pantheon TV IAW
    Telepictures Prods.
Executive Producer .... Gabriel Katzka
Executive Producer .... Frank Konigsberg
Producer .... Nick Gillott
Director .... Jerry London
Writer .... Fred Mustard Stewart
Writer .... Christopher Newman
Cast .... Peter Riegert
Cast .... Greg Martyn
Cast .... Claire Bloom
Cast .... Kate Burton
Cast .... Joan Greenwood

ELVIS AND ME   ABC

Miniseries/Drama (2 nights): Love Story • Period Piece • Hollywood • Biography
Airdate: 02/07/88 • 02/08/88
Rating: 23.9/35 • 24.9/36   A/C:

Based on the book by Priscilla Presley. True story of the courtship, married life and divorce of Priscilla Beaulieu and Elvis Presley, who began living together when she was fourteen and married seven years later. The story line runs through Elvis's death.

Production Company: New World TV
Executive Producer .... Priscilla Beaulieu Presley
Executive Producer .... Bernard Schwartz
Executive Producer .... Joel Stevens
Producer .... Robert Lovenheim
Director .... Larry Peerce
Writer .... Joyce Eliason
Cast .... Dale Midkiff
Cast .... Ken Gibbel
Cast .... Linda Miller
Cast .... Hugh Gillin
Cast .... Billy Greenbush

ELVIS AND THE COLONEL: THE UNTOLD STORY   NBC

Drama: True Story • Period Piece • Biography • Hollywood
Airdate: 1/10/93
Rating: 9.8/14   A/C: 3

Chronicles the stormy relationship between the King of Rock & Roll, Elvis Presley, and his shifty, domineering manager, Col. Tom Parker. Through Elvis's early years as a teen idol to his drug induced decline and ultimate death the Colonel exerted total control over his naive client.

Production Company: Ultra Ent., ABC Video
    Enterprises IAW Dick Clark Film Group
Executive Producer .... Dick Clark
Executive Producer .... Neil Stearns
Executive Producer .... Bob Rubin
Executive Producer .... Bill Seigler
Producer .... Daniel A. Sherkow
Director .... William A. Graham
Writer .... Phil Penningroth
Cast .... Beau Bridges
Cast .... Rob Youngblood
Cast .... Dan Shor

EMPTY CRADLE — ABC

Drama: True Crime • Children/Teens
Airdate: 10/3/93
Rating: 15.2/24   A/C: 1

A unbalanced obstetrics nurse, determined to keep her boyfriend from leaving, fakes a pregnancy then kidnaps a baby after she induces labor in a drugged out mother and delivers the child. Told her baby was born dead the despondent birth mother refuses to accept the facts surrounding her infant's demise and fights her family, the hospital and the police to uncover the real truth of her baby's disappearance.

Production Company: Bein-Mills Prods. IAW
    Papazian-Hirsch
Executive Producer .... Robert A. Papazian
Executive Producer .... James G. Hirsch
Executive Producer .... Nancy Bein
Executive Producer .... Beth Rickman
Producer .... Steve Mills
Director .... Paul Schneider
Writer .... Rebecca Soladay
Cast .... Kate Jackson
Cast .... Lori Loughlin
Cast .... Don Yesso

ENDLESS GAME, THE — SHOWTIME

Drama: Murder and Murder Mystery • Cops/Detectives/Law Enforcement • Suspense/Thriller • Foreign or Exotic Location
Airdate: 01/21/90
Rating: N/A   A/C:

Based on director Bryan Forbes' book. When his former mistress, prematurely senile after Russian captivity, is killed, a retired British intelligence agent is dragged back into a world where no one is who he says he is and the dead come back to life.

Production Company: Telso International,
    Reteitalia
Executive Producer .... Graham Benson
Executive Producer .... Nicola Carraro
Producer .... Fernando Ghia
Director .... Bryan Forbes
Writer .... Bryan Forbes
Cast .... Albert Finney
Cast .... George Segal
Cast .... Kristin Scott Thomas

ENEMY WITHIN, THE — HBO

Drama: Suspense/Thriller • Political Piece
Airdate: 8/5/94
Rating: N/A   A/C:

Updates the classic 1964 thriller "Seven Days in May" to the 1990's, when military power is on the wane. An officer with the Joint Chiefs of Staff suspects that his commanding officer is masterminding a military coup against a politically shaky president .

Production Company: HBO Pictures
Executive Producer .... Peter Douglas
Producer .... Robert A. Papazian
Director .... Jonathan Darby
Writer .... Ron Bass
Writer .... Darryl Ponicsan
Cast .... Forest Whitaker
Cast .... Sam Waterston
Cast .... Dana Delany
Cast .... Jason Robards

ENTERTAINERS, THE — ABC

Drama: Buddy Story
Airdate: 11/21/91
Rating: 7.0/11   A/C: 4

A veteran vaudevillian and his partner of twenty-five years, an aging chimpanzee, head out to fulfill a lifelong ambition of performing in Las Vegas. A former flame, now a big star, helps him realize his dream.

Production Company: Robert Greenwald
    Productions
Executive Producer .... Robert Greenwald
Executive Producer .... Carla Singer
Producer .... Philip Kleinbart
Co-Executive Producer .... Gabrielle Madelik
Director .... Paul Schneider
Writer .... Charles Leinenweber
Cast .... Bob Newhart
Cast .... Linda Gray
Cast .... Richard Romanus

EQUAL JUSTICE — ABC

Drama: Courtroom Drama • Series Pilot (2 hr.)
Airdate: 03/27/90
Rating: 12.2/23   A/C: 2

Staffers in a big-city District Attorney's office deal with ambition, ethical issues and front-line justice as they prosecute crimes, including a race-related killing and a rape.

Production Company: The Thomas Carter Co.
    IAW Orion Television Entertainment
Executive Producer .... Thomas Carter
Producer .... Peter McIntosh
Co-Executive Producer .... David A. Simons
Co-Executive Producer .... Christopher Knopf
Director .... Thomas Carter
Writer .... Christopher Knopf
Writer .... David A. Simons
Cast .... Sarah Jessica Parker
Cast .... Joe Morton
Cast .... Lise Cutter
Cast .... Debrah Farentino
Cast .... Cotter Smith

ERNEST GREEN STORY, THE — DISNEY

Drama: Children/Teens • True Story • Black Story • Historical Piece • Period Piece • Social Issue
Airdate: 1/17/93
Rating: N/A   A/C:

The year in the life of the only senior among a group of nine black students who integrated Little Rock Central High School in 1957. Facing an angry, all white student body, Green endured intimidation, verbal abuse and threats of violence but with courage and fortitude he became the first black student to graduate.

Production Company: Emmalyn Enterprises
Executive Producer .... Carol Abrams
Executive Producer .... Adrienne Levin
Producer .... Jean Higgins
Director .... Eric Laneuville
Writer .... Lawrence Roman
Cast .... Ossie Davis
Cast .... Morris Chestnut
Cast .... CCH Pounder
Cast .... Ruby Dee

ESCAPE FROM SOBIBOR — CBS

Drama: Period Piece • Nazis • WWII • Historical Piece • Prison and Prison Camp • True Story
Airdate: 04/12/87
Rating: 21.4/34   A/C:

True story of a partially-successful mass escape from a Nazi extermination camp in Poland, attempted against almost insurmountable odds.

Production Company: Rule/Starger Prods. IAW
    Zenith
Executive Producer .... Martin Starger
Producer .... Dennis Doty
Co-Producer .... Howard Alston
Director .... Jack Gold
Writer .... Reginald Rose
Cast .... Alan Arkin
Cast .... Rutger Hauer
Cast .... Joanna Pacula
Cast .... Hartmut Becker

EVERGREEN — NBC

Miniseries/Drama (3 nights): Family Drama • Cross-Cultural Story • Love Story • Period Piece • Historical Piece
Airdate: 02/24/85 • 02/25/85 • 02/26/85
Rating: 22.3/33 • 20.9/32 • 22.9/33   A/C:

Based on the bestseller by Belva Plain. The story of a Polish-Jewish immigrant's ascent from New York's sweatshops to a comfortable life. Heartache, triumph, family secrets, lost loves and unfulfilled dreams unfold in this multi-generational saga.

Production Company: Edgar J. Scherick Assocs.
    IAW Metromedia
Executive Producer .... Edgar J. Scherick
Executive Producer .... Susan Pollock
Producer .... Phillip Barry
Director .... Fielder Cook
Writer .... Jerome Kass
Cast .... Lesley Ann Warren
Cast .... Armand Assante
Cast .... Ian McShane
Cast .... Brian Dennehy
Cast .... Patricia Barry
Cast .... Ron Rifkin

EVERYBODY'S BABY: THE RESCUE OF JESSICA MCCLURE ABC
Drama: Family Drama • Children/Teens • True Story
Airdate: 05/21/89
Rating: 22.2/36   A/C:

The true story of the intensive rescue effort to save eighteen month old Jessica McClure of Midland, Texas from the abandoned water well into which she fell.

Production Company: Stonehenge Prods. IAW
   Interscope Communications
Executive Producer .... Ted Field
Executive Producer .... Dick Berg
Executive Producer .... Patricia Clifford
Producer .... Diana Kerew
Director .... Mel Damski
Writer .... David Eyre, Jr.
Cast .... Beau Bridges
Cast .... Pat Hingle
Cast .... Roxana Zal
Cast .... Will Oldham
Cast .... Patty Duke

EVIL IN CLEAR RIVER ABC
Drama: Family Drama • Woman Against The System • Children/Teens • Social Issue • Foreign or Exotic Location
Airdate: 01/11/88
Rating: 12.9/20   A/C:

A woman in a small western Canadian town fights the anti-Semitism with which the mayor is infecting the townspeople and their children.

Production Company: Steve Tisch Co. & Lionel
   Chetwynd Prods. IAW Phoenix TV Prods. Inc.
Executive Producer .... Steve Tisch
Executive Producer .... Lionel Chetwynd
Producer .... Barbara Black
Director .... Karen Arthur
Writer .... William Schmidt
Cast .... Lindsay Wagner
Cast .... Randy Quaid
Cast .... Thomas Wilson Brown
Cast .... Michael Flynn

EWOK ADVENTURE, THE ABC
Drama: Sci-Fi/Supernatural/Horror/Fantasy • Foreign or Exotic Location
Airdate: 11/25/84
Rating: 24.9/36   A/C:

A young brother and sister become separated from their parents when their spaceship crashes on the moon of Endor. The two children face numerous perils and are ultimately reunited with their family with the help of the local Ewoks.

Production Company: Lucasfilm Ltd. & Korty
   Films Prods.
Executive Producer .... George Lucas
Producer .... Thomas G. Smith
Director .... John Korty
Writer .... Bob Carrau
Cast .... Eric Walker
Cast .... Warwick Davis
Cast .... Fionnula Flanagan
Cast .... Guy Boyd

EWOKS: THE BATTLE FOR ENDOR ABC
Drama: Sci-Fi/Supernatural/Horror/Fantasy • Foreign or Exotic Location
Airdate: 11/24/85
Rating: 18.7/26   A/C:

A little girl and her Ewok friend rescue an Ewok family held captive by a villainous king on the planet Endor.

Production Company: Lucasfilm Ltd.
Executive Producer .... George Lucas
Producer .... Thomas G. Smith
Director .... Jim Wheat
Director .... Ken Wheat
Writer .... Jim Wheat
Writer .... Ken Wheat
Cast .... Aubree Miller
Cast .... Sian Phillips
Cast .... Wilford Brimley
Cast .... Warwick Davis

EXCLUSIVE ABC
Drama: Murder and Murder Mystery • Woman In Jeopardy • Suspense/Thriller
Airdate: 10/4/92
Rating: 10.8/17   A/C: 2

A Los Angeles investigative television reporter is terrorized by a psychopath when she tries to solve a serial killing with the help of her tough detective ex-husband.

Production Company: Hamel-Somers Prods.,
   Freyda Rothstein Prods. IAW Hearst Ent.
Executive Producer .... Freyda Rothstein
Co-Executive Producer .... Suzanne Somers
Co-Executive Producer .... Alan Hamel
Director .... Alan Metzger
Writer .... Bill Wells
Writer .... Mimi Schapiro
Cast .... Suzanne Somers
Cast .... Ed Begley, Jr.
Cast .... Joe Cortese
Cast .... Michael Nouri

EXECUTION, THE NBC
Drama: Murder and Murder Mystery • Suspense/Thriller • Nazis
Airdate: 01/14/84
Rating: 21.4/32   A/C:

A group of women concentration camp survivors living in 1970 Los Angeles, believe that they have located a Nazi torturer living nearby. They dispatch a member of their group to kill him.

Production Company: Newland-Raynord Prods.
   IAW Comworld
Executive Producer .... John Newland
Producer .... Milton T. Raynor
Producer .... Oliver Crawford
Director .... Paul Wendkos
Writer .... William Wood
Writer .... Oliver Crawford
Cast .... Valerie Harper
Cast .... Rip Torn
Cast .... Jessica Walter
Cast .... Sandy Dennis
Cast .... Barbara Barrie
Cast .... Loretta Swit

EXTREME CLOSE-UP NBC
Drama: Family Drama • Children/Teens • Medical/Disease/Mental Illness
Airdate: 10/22/90
Rating: 12.3/20   A/C: 3

A teenage boy discovers that his mother's recent death was no accident but a suicide when he sees her gradual descent into madness in his own home videos.

Production Company: Bedford Falls Prods. IAW
   Robert Greenwald Prods.
Executive Producer .... Edward Zwick
Executive Producer .... Marshall Herskovitz
Producer .... Sarah Caplan
Producer .... Ronald B. Colby
Director .... Peter Horton
Writer .... Marshall Herskowitz
Writer .... Edward Zwick
Cast .... Craig T. Nelson
Cast .... Morgan Weisser
Cast .... Samantha Mathis
Cast .... Kimber Shoop

EYE ON THE SPARROW NBC
Drama: Family Drama • Woman Against The System • Children/Teens • True Story • Social Issue
Airdate: 12/07/87
Rating: 14.3/22   A/C:

Fact-based story of Ethel and James Lee, a blind couple who fight the system for the right to adopt children.

Production Company: Sarabande Prods. IAW
   Republic Pictures
Executive Producer .... David Manson
Producer .... Barbara Turner
Co-Producer .... Cyrus Yavneh
Director .... John Korty
Writer .... Barbara Turner
Cast .... Mare Winningham
Cast .... Keith Carradine
Cast .... Conchata Ferrell
Cast .... Joe Carlin

EYES OF A WITNESS CBS
Drama: Murder and Murder Mystery • Action/Adventure • Foreign or Exotic Location
Airdate: 03/31/91
Rating: 13.0/23   A/C: 2

An arrogant American businessman is arrested in Kenya for a murder he didn't commit. He is freed by evidence supplied by his doctor daughter. Ultimately he serves justice by tracking down the poachers responsible.

Production Company: RHI Entertainment
Executive Producer .... Robert Halmi, Sr.
Producer .... Andrew Gottlieb
Director .... Peter H. Hunt
Writer .... Charles Robert Carner
Writer .... Walter Clayton
Cast .... Daniel J. Travanti
Cast .... Jennifer Grey
Cast .... Carl Lumbly
Cast .... Daniel Gerroll

EYES OF TERROR — NBC

Drama: Cops/Detectives/Law Enforcement • Murder and Murder Mystery
Airdate: 3/18/94
Rating: 10.6/19   A/C: 2

Sequel to the 1993 TV movie "Visions of Murder". A San Francisco psychic psychologist, working with the police department, helps a street cop hunt down the dangerous killer of his long time partner.

Production Company: Bar-Gene Prods., Freyda Rothstein Prods. IAW Hearst Entertainment
Executive Producer .... Freyda Rothstein
Co-Executive Producer .... Gene Schwam
Producer .... James R. McGee
Co-Producer .... Angela Bromstad
Director .... Sam Pillsbury
Writer .... Duane Poole
Cast .... Barbara Eden
Cast .... Michael Nouri
Cast .... Ted Marcoux
Cast .... Missy Crider

FACE OF A STRANGER — CBS

Drama: True Story • Social Issue
Airdate: 12/29/91
Rating: 16.8/27   A/C: 1

Based on an article by Mary Stuart in New York Magazine. A wealthy Seattle woman, recently widowed, befriends a homeless woman with a troubled past. Through this friendship, they both learn to face their lives with renewed awareness and determination.

Production Company: Linda Gottlieb Prods. IAW Viacom Prods.
Executive Producer .... Linda Gottlieb
Producer .... George Perkins
Director .... Claudia Weill
Writer .... Marsha Norman
Cast .... Tyne Daly
Cast .... Gena Rowlands
Cast .... Cynthia Nixon

FACE OF FEAR, THE — CBS

Drama: Murder and Murder Mystery • Cops/Detectives/Law Enforcement • Woman In Jeopardy • Psychological Thriller
Airdate: 9/30/90
Rating: 14.0/23   A/C: 2

Based on a book by Dean Koontz. A mountain climbing psychic and his police psychologist wife are trapped in a NYC high-rise stalked by a serial killer. Daring mountaineering maneuvers outwit the killer and bring him to justice.

Production Company: Papazian-Hirsch Productions
Executive Producer .... Lee Rich
Executive Producer .... Grant Rosenberg
Executive Producer .... Dean Koontz
Producer .... William Beaudine, Jr.
Director .... Farhad Mann
Writer .... Dean Koontz
Writer .... Alan Jay Glueckman
Cast .... Lee Horsley
Cast .... Pam Dawber
Cast .... Kevin Conroy
Cast .... William Sadler

FACE TO FACE — CBS

Drama: Cross-Cultural Story • Love Story • Foreign or Exotic Location
Airdate: 01/24/90
Rating: 14.7/24   A/C: 2

A female American paleontologist and a British miner, mistakenly issued permits for the same Kenya digging site, almost come to blows. But when they unite to help a Masai warrior fight exile from his tribe, they become drawn to each other.

Production Company: Qintex Productions
Executive Producer .... Robert Halmi, Sr.
Producer .... Jim Chory
Director .... Lou Antonio
Writer .... John Sweet
Cast .... Elizabeth Montgomery
Cast .... Robert Foxworth

FACTS OF LIFE DOWN UNDER, THE — NBC

Comedy: Foreign or Exotic Location • Youth Comedy
Airdate: 02/15/87
Rating: 21.4/32   A/C:

From the popular TV Sitcom. Four girl students, their chaperone and a young boy find light crime and scenic wonders on an Australian tour.

Production Company: Embassy TV IAW Crawford Prods.
Executive Producer .... Virginia L. Carter
Producer .... Michael Lake
Director .... Stuart Margolin
Writer .... Gordon Cotler
Cast .... Nancy McKeon
Cast .... Lisa Whelchel
Cast .... Kim Fields
Cast .... Mindy Cohn
Cast .... Cloris Leachman
Cast .... Mackenzie Astin

FADE TO BLACK — USA

Drama: Murder and Murder Mystery • Suspense/Thriller
Airdate: 2/10/93
Rating: N/A   A/C:

A lonely college professor, researching human behavior by videotaping his neighbors becomes involved in a murder case when he inadvertently films what he thinks might be a homicide. Having trouble convincing the police when they can't find a body, he attempts to solve the puzzle himself and prevent the killer from striking again.

Production Company: Francine LeFrak Prods. IAW Wilshire Court Prods
Executive Producer .... Francine LeFrak
Executive Producer .... Robert Kosberg
Producer .... Robert Rolsky
Director .... John McPherson
Writer .... Douglas Barr
Cast .... Timothy Busfield
Cast .... Heather Locklear
Cast .... Cloris Leachman
Cast .... Michael Beck

FALL FROM GRACE — NBC

Miniseries/Drama (2 nights): True Story • Biography • Sex/Glitz
Airdate: 04/29/90
Rating: 17.6/27   A/C: 2

The rise and fall of Jim and Tammy Baker's televangelical empire, which was undermined by sexual scandal and financial mismanagement.

Production Company: NBC Productions
Executive Producer .... Jeff Franklin
Producer .... Richard L. O'Connor
Director .... Karen Arthur
Writer .... Ken Trevey
Cast .... Bernadette Peters
Cast .... Kevin Spacey
Cast .... Richard Herd
Cast .... Beth Grant

FALL FROM GRACE — CBS

Drama: WWII • Foreign or Exotic Location
Airdate: 6/2/94 • 6/3/94
Rating: 7.7/14 • 6.4/13   A/C: 2 • 3

Based on the novel by Larry Collins. A beautiful young English women who is a spy for the Allies, goes into occupied France on a elaborate mission to deceive the German high command into thinking that D-Day would take place in Calais instead of Normandy. Romantic entanglements and dangerous deceptions cause her to make the ultimate sacrifice.

Production Company: Rysher TPE, SFP Prods., Silvio Berlusconi Communications, Sky TV, Banco Prods.
Executive Producer .... Pascale Breugnot
Director .... Waris Hussein
Writer .... David Ambrose
Cast .... Michael York
Cast .... Gary Cole
Cast .... Patsy Kensit
Cast .... Richard Anconina
Cast .... James Fox

FALSE ARREST   ABC
Miniseries/Drama (2 nights): Murder and Murder
Mystery • True Crime • Prison and Prison Camp
Airdate: 11/03/91 • 11/06/91
Rating: 11.5/18 • 16.6/27   A/C: 3 • 1

*Successful Phoenix businesswoman and mother,
Joyce Lukezic, is falsely accused of conspiracy
in the brutal murder of her husband's business
partner. While in prison, she fights to win a
new trial and ultimately her release.*

Production Company: Ron Gilbert Associates
 IAW Leonard Hill Films
Executive Producer .... Ron Gilbert
Executive Producer .... Leonard Hill
Executive Producer .... Joel Fields
Co-Producer .... Andrew Laskos
Co-Producer .... Ardythe Goergens
Director .... Bill L. Norton
Writer .... Andrew Laskos
Cast .... Donna Mills
Cast .... Robert Wagner
Cast .... James Handy
Cast .... Steven Bauer
Cast .... Kiersten Warren
Cast .... Lane Smith

FALSE WITNESS   NBC
Drama: Cops/Detectives/Law Enforcement •
Suspense/Thriller
Airdate: 10/23/89
Rating: 18.7/29   A/C: 2

*Based on Dorothy Uhnak's book. The
relationship between a New Orleans Assist.
D.A. on the fast track and her lover, a
department investigator, deteriorates when they
go after different suspects in the case of a
gruesome attack of a talk-show hostess.*

Production Company: Valente/Kritzer/EPI Prods.
 IAW New World TV
Executive Producer .... Renee Valente
Executive Producer .... Eddie Kritzer
Executive Producer .... Richard Alfieri
Producer .... Renee Valente
Director .... Arthur Allan Seidelman
Writer .... Bill Driskill
Cast .... Phylicia Rashad
Cast .... Philip Michael Thomas
Cast .... Robin Mattson
Cast .... George Grizzard

FAMILY FOR JOE, A   NBC
Drama: Family Drama • Series Pilot (2 hr.) • Children/
Teens
Airdate: 02/25/90
Rating: 15.8/23   A/C: 1

*When four orphans commandeer an old vagrant
to appear as their grandfather so they won't be
taken to a home, they get more than they
bargained for. The vagrant decides that he
really is going to take care of these independent
kids.*

Production Company: Grosso-Jacobson Prods.
Executive Producer .... Sonny Grosso
Executive Producer .... Larry Jacobson
Executive Producer .... Arnold Margolin
Producer .... Richard Learman
Director .... Jeffrey Melman
Writer .... Arnold Margolin
Cast .... Robert Mitchum
Cast .... Chris Furrh
Cast .... Maia Brewton
Cast .... Barbara Babcock

FAMILY OF SPIES   CBS
Miniseries/Drama (2 nights): Family Drama • True
Crime
Airdate: 02/04/90 • 02/06/90
Rating: 14.7/22 • 13.6/21   A/C: 3 • 3

*A depiction of Naval Officer John Walker, who
supplied military secrets to Russia for seventeen
years, using a treacherous web comprised of
his entire family.*

Production Company: King Phoenix
 Entertainment
Executive Producer .... Jennifer Alward
Executive Producer .... Gerald W. Abrams
Producer .... Jonathan Bernstein
Co-Producer .... William Dunne
Director .... Stephen Gyllenhaal
Writer .... Richard DeLong Adams
Cast .... Powers Boothe
Cast .... Lesley Ann Warren
Cast .... Graham Beckel
Cast .... Lili Taylor

FAMILY OF STRANGERS   CBS
Drama: Family Drama • Medical/Disease/Mental
Illness • True Story • Rape/Molestation • Woman's
Issue/Story
Airdate: 2/21/93
Rating: 19.8/29   A/C: 1

*Based on the book "Jody" by Jerry Hulse. In
the need of life saving surgery an adopted
woman must find her biological parents in order
to get vital family medical history prior to the
risky operation. At first reluctant, her real
mother finally accepts her child's situation but
refuses to divulge the circumstances
surrounding the birth father. It is eventually
revealed that she had been raped and has
repressed his identity for many years. Together
they unblock the painful memories and confront
the man responsible.*

Production Company: Alliance Commications
Executive Producer .... Robert Lantos
Executive Producer .... Michael Weisbarth
Producer .... William Gough
Producer .... John Ryan
Co-Executive Producer .... Frank Rosenberg
Director .... Sheldon Larry
Writer .... William Gough
Writer .... Anna Sandor
Cast .... Patty Duke
Cast .... Melissa Gilbert
Cast .... William Shatner

FAMILY PICTURES   ABC
Miniseries/Drama (2 nights): Family Drama •
Children/Teens • Medical/Disease/Mental Illness
Airdate: 3/21/93 • 3/22/93
Rating: 10.1/16 • 11.5/18   A/C: 3 • 3

*Based on the book by Sue Miller. Over a twenty
year period a suburban mother faces guilt,
isolation and recriminations when her total
devotion to her beloved autistic son tears the
family apart .*

Production Company: Alexander, Engriht & Assoc.
 IAW Hearst Ent.
Executive Producer .... Don Enright
Executive Producer .... Les Alexander
Producer .... Joe Broido
Director .... Philip Saville
Writer .... Jennifer Miller
Cast .... Anjelica Huston
Cast .... Sam Neill
Cast .... Kyra Sedgwick
Cast .... Dermot Mulroney

FAMILY SINS — CBS
Drama: Family Drama • Children/Teens • Family Violence • Murder and Murder Mystery
Airdate: 10/25/87
Rating: 12.9/20   A/C:

A family is plunged into tragedy when an eleven year old boy kills his younger, favored brother.

Production Company: London Films Inc.
Executive Producer .... Jerry London
Producer .... Mel A. Bishop
Director .... Jerrold Freedman
Writer .... George Rubino
Cast .... James Farentino
Cast .... Jill Eikenberry
Cast .... Andrew Bednarski
Cast .... Thomas Wilson Brown
Cast .... Mimi Kuzyk
Cast .... Richard Venture

FAMILY TIES VACATION — NBC
Comedy: Youth Comedy • Foreign or Exotic Location
Airdate: 09/23/85
Rating: 22.1/33   A/C:

From the TV Sitcom. The Keaton family decides to vacation in Great Britain while Alex studies at Oxford and inadvertently becomes involved in a spy caper.

Production Company: UBU Prods. IAW Paramount TV
Executive Producer .... Gary David Goldberg
Producer .... Michael J. Weithorn
Producer .... Alan Uger
Line Producer .... Carol Himes
Director .... Will MacKenzie
Writer .... Marc Lawrence
Writer .... Michael J. Weithorn
Writer .... Alan Uger
Cast .... Michael J. Fox
Cast .... Justine Bateman
Cast .... Tina Yothers
Cast .... Meredith Baxter
Cast .... Michael Gross

FAMILY TORN APART, A — NBC
Drama: True Crime • Family Violence • Children/Teens
Airdate: 11/21/93
Rating: 15.1/23   A/C: 2

Based on the book "Sudden Fury" by Leslie Walker. Two teen-age boys are suspects in the murders of their seemingly loving parents. The police investigation first focuses on the eldest of three adopted children, who has a history of wild behavior. They soon uncover the abusive methods the parents employed on their kids which led their other adopted son, who was quiet and obedient, to become totally unhinged and brutally murder his folks.

Production Company: River City Prods. IAW Robert Halmi Inc.
Executive Producer .... Robert Lovenheim
Executive Producer .... John Levoff
Director .... Craig Baxley
Writer .... Matthew Brombeck
Cast .... Neil Patrick Harris
Cast .... Johnny Galecki
Cast .... Gregory Harrison
Cast .... Lisa Banes

FATAL CHARM — SHOWTIME
Drama: Woman In Jeopardy • Suspense/Thriller • Children/Teens • Sex/Glitz
Airdate: 02/22/92
Rating: N/A   A/C:

A teenage girl becomes infatuated with a charming serial killer through an erotic pen-pal relationship while he's in prison. When he escapes, her playful fantasies soon turn to deadly terror.

Production Company: Jonathan D. Krane/Bruce Cohn Curtis Prods.
Executive Producer .... John Strong
Producer .... Bruce Cohn Curtis
Producer .... Jonathan D. Krane
Co-Producer .... Douglass Stewart
Director .... Fritz Kiersch
Writer .... Nicholas Niciphor
Cast .... Christopher Atkins
Cast .... Amanda Peterson
Cast .... Mary Frann
Cast .... Peggy Lipton

FATAL CONFESSION: A FATHER DOWLING MYSTERY — NBC
Mystery: Murder and Murder Mystery • Suspense/Thriller • Series Pilot (2 hr.) • Mafia/Mob
Airdate: 11/30/87
Rating: 15.5/24   A/C:

A mystery-obsessed parish priest and a streetwise nun investigate the apparent suicide of a rich young businessman and discover it was a murder involving the mob.

Production Company: Fred Silverman Co. and Strathmore Prods. IAW Viacom
Executive Producer .... Fred Silverman
Executive Producer .... Dean Hargrove
Producer .... Peter Katz
Director .... Christopher Hibler
Writer .... Donald E. Westlake
Cast .... Tom Bosley
Cast .... Tracy Nelson
Cast .... Mary Wickes
Cast .... Susan Blakely
Cast .... Leslie Nielsen
Cast .... Peter Scolari

FATAL DECEPTION: MRS. LEE HARVEY OSWALD — NBC
Drama: Historical Piece • Biography • Period Piece • Foreign or Exotic Location • Political Piece
Airdate: 11/15/93
Rating: 11.2/18   A/C: 3

The 1961-1963 courtship and marriage of naive Soviet immigrant Marina Oswald to the volatile assassin, Lee Harvey Oswald, which ended with a fatal bullet by Jack Ruby in a Dallas city jail. After the assassination she and her family are hounded by the press and government officials for information surrounding her husband's behavior which eventually drove her into seclusion.

Production Company: David L. Wolper IAW Bernard Sofronski and Warner Bros. TV
Executive Producer .... Bernard Sofronski
Executive Producer .... David L. Wolper
Producer .... Paul Pompian
Producer .... Stephen Bello
Director .... Borter Dornhelm
Writer .... Stephen Bello
Cast .... Helena Bonham Carter
Cast .... Frank Whaley
Cast .... Robert Picardo
Cast .... Bill Bolender

FATAL EXPOSURE — USA
Drama: Cops/Detectives/Law Enforcement • Woman In Jeopardy • Suspense/Thriller
Airdate: 02/06/91
Rating: N/A   A/C:

A vacationing mother and her two children become targets of mob vengeance when she mistakenly picks up incriminating photographs linking certain Chicago police to organized crime.

Production Company: G.C. Group IAW Wilshire Court Prods.
Executive Producer .... Lisa Weinstein
Producer .... Paul L. Tucker
Producer .... Raymond Hartung
Director .... Alan Metzger
Writer .... Raymond Hartung
Cast .... Mare Winningham
Cast .... Nick Mancuso
Cast .... Christopher McDonald
Cast .... Geoffrey Blake

FATAL FRIENDSHIP   NBC
Drama: Suspense/Thriller
Airdate: 12/01/91
Rating: 12.4/19   A/C: 3

A family man becomes suspicious of his life-long friend and neighbor, who he suspects is a cold-blooded hit man. His life becomes endangered when he learns of the man's underworld connections.

Production Company: Papazian Hirsch
   Entertainment
Executive Producer .... Robert A. Papazian
Executive Producer .... James G. Hirsch
Producer .... Hal Galli
Director .... Bradford May
Writer .... Bill Driskill
Cast .... Kevin Dobson
Cast .... Gerald McRaney
Cast .... Kate Mulgrew

FATAL IMAGE, THE   CBS
Drama: Murder and Murder Mystery • Cops/Detectives/Law Enforcement • Woman In Jeopardy • Suspense/Thriller • Foreign or Exotic Location
Airdate: 12/02/90
Rating: 14.1/22   A/C: 2

An American mother and daughter vacationing in Paris unknowingly videotape a murder. Stalked by the killer, they are given protection by a charming French inspector, and together they capture the murderer.

Production Company: Ellipse Programme, Hearst
   Entertainment Prods.
Executive Producer .... Harry Chandler
Executive Producer .... Gerald W. Abrams
Producer .... Ron Roth
Producer .... Steve Verona
Director .... Thomas J. Wright
Writer .... Jeff Andrus
Writer .... Aaron Barzman
Cast .... Michele Lee
Cast .... Justine Bateman
Cast .... Francois Dunoyer
Cast .... Jean-Pierre Cassel

FATAL JUDGMENT   CBS
Drama: Medical/Disease/Mental Illness • True Story • Courtroom Drama
Airdate: 10/18/88
Rating: 15.4/24   A/C:

A conscientious nurse is prosecuted when a terminal patient dies in an apparent mercy killing.

Production Company: Jack Farren Prods. IAW
   Group W Productions
Executive Producer .... Jack Farren
Producer .... Paul Pompian
Director .... Gilbert Cates
Writer .... Gerald Green
Cast .... Patty Duke
Cast .... Joe Regalbuto
Cast .... Jo Henderson
Cast .... Tom Conti

FATAL MEMORIES   NBC
Drama: Family Drama • Woman's Issue/Story • True Crime • Rape/Molestation • Courtroom Drama
Airdate: 11/9/92
Rating: 15.8/24   A/C: 2

In 1990, California housewife, Eileen Franklin suddenly begins to have horrifying flashbacks of childhood violence and sexual abuse that compel her to prosecute her father, whom she hasn't seen in many years. Her long repressed memories lead eventually to her testimony in court that twenty years ago her father raped and murdered her nine year old best friend. In a landmark case, the jury finds him guilty of first degree murder.

Production Company: Green's Point Prods. IAW
   WIC and MGM/UA
Executive Producer .... Georgia Jeffries
Producer .... Daryl Duke
Co-Producer .... Joseph Fimm
Director .... Daryl Duke
Writer .... Audrey Davis Levin
Cast .... Shelley Long
Cast .... Helen Shaver
Cast .... Dean Stockwell

FATAL VISION   NBC
Miniseries/Drama (2 nights): Man Against The System • True Crime • Family Violence • Courtroom Drama • Murder and Murder Mystery
Airdate: 11/18/84 • 11/19/84
Rating: 29.5/44 • 32.7/49   A/C:

From the bestseller. Respected army doctor, Jeffrey MacDonald, is accused of murdering his pregnant wife and two daughters. He is initially exonerated, but his father-in-law reviews the evidence, has the case reopened and MacDonald retried.

Production Company: NBC Prods.
Executive Producer .... Dan Wigutow
Executive Producer .... Mike Rosenfeld
Producer .... Richard L. O'Connor
Director .... David Greene
Writer .... John Gay
Cast .... Gary Cole
Cast .... Karl Malden
Cast .... Eva Marie Saint
Cast .... Barry Newman
Cast .... Andy Griffith

FATHER CLEMENTS STORY, THE   NBC
Drama: Man Against The System • Children/Teens • True Story • Black Story • Social Issue
Airdate: 12/13/87
Rating: 16.7/26   A/C:

True story of a black Chicago priest who meets stiff resistance from his superior when he tries to adopt a homeless boy to set an example for his flock.

Production Company: Zev Braun Prods. IAW
   Interscope Communications Inc.
Executive Producer .... Zev Braun
Executive Producer .... Ted Field
Producer .... Phil Parslow
Co-Producer .... Chet Walker
Director .... Ed Sherin
Writer .... Arthur Heinemann
Writer .... Ted Tally
Cast .... Louis Gossett, Jr.
Cast .... Irv Kupcinet
Cast .... Carroll O'Connor
Cast .... Malcolm-Jamal Warner

FATHER OF HELL TOWN   NBC
Drama: Man Against The System • Children/Teens • Family Violence • Series Pilot (2 hr.)
Airdate: 03/06/85
Rating: 18.2/29   A/C:

A streetwise priest, who serves a parish in a rough neighborhood, helps a young girl get away from her abusive father.

Production Company: Breezy Prods.
Executive Producer .... Lyman P. Docker
Producer .... Alan Godfrey
Director .... Don Medford
Writer .... Robert Blake
Cast .... Robert Blake
Cast .... Whitman Mayo
Cast .... Fran Ryan
Cast .... James Gammon

FATHER & SON: DANGEROUS RELATIONS
                                        NBC
Drama: Family Drama • Prison and Prison Camp
Airdate: 4/19/93
Rating: 14.6/24   A/C: 1

A tenuous relationship forms between a father and son who are paroled into each other's custody after meeting for the first time in prison. Long held resentments by the son for his father, who he feels abandoned him long ago make living together an ordeal both men. Through patience and understanding the two come to terms with each other and establish a loving bond. .

Production Company: Kushne-Locke Co. IAW
   Logo Prods, Gregory/Kahn Prods.
Executive Producer .... Peter Locke
Executive Producer .... Donald Kushner
Co-Executive Producer .... Don Gregory
Co-Producer .... Bernard Kahn
Writer .... Walter Halsey Davis
Director .... Georg Stanford Brown
Cast .... Louis Gossett, Jr.
Cast .... Blair Underwood
Cast .... Rae Dawn Chong

FATHER'S HOMECOMING, A — NBC

Drama: Family Drama • Children/Teens
Airdate: 06/19/88
Rating: 12.5/23   A/C:

A new headmaster at a New England prep school must deal not only with the school's new coed policy, but with local politics and his own teenage children as well.

Production Company: NBC Prods.
Executive Producer .... Willard Huyck
Executive Producer .... Gloria Katz
Producer .... R.W. Goodwin
Director .... Rick Wallace
Writer .... Willard Huyck
Cast .... Michael McKean
Cast .... Jonathan Ward
Cast .... Nana Visitor
Cast .... Brandon Douglas

FATHER'S REVENGE, A — ABC

Drama: Family Drama • Man Against The System • Suspense/Thriller • Foreign or Exotic Location
Airdate: 01/24/88
Rating: 10.4/16   A/C:

A high-school basketball coach organizes and leads a gang of mercenaries to Germany to rescue his daughter, an airline stewardess kidnapped by terrorists.

Production Company: Shadowplay/Rosco Prods.
   IAW Phoenix Entertainment Group
Executive Producer .... Gerald W. Abrams
Producer .... Hans Proppe
Director .... John Herzfeld
Writer .... Mel Frohman
Cast .... Brian Dennehy
Cast .... Ron Silver
Cast .... Anthony Valentine
Cast .... Joanna Cassidy

FAVORITE SON — NBC

Miniseries/Drama (3 nights): Murder and Murder Mystery • Suspense/Thriller • Political Piece • Sex/Glitz
Airdate: 10/30/88 • 10/31/88 • 11/1/88
Rating: 15.9/26 • 15.7/25 • 16.3/26   A/C:

The assassination of a contra leader and wounding of the ambitious Senator accompanying him, rocket the Senator and his beautiful female aide to the top and opens a Pandora's box of high-level Washington intrigue.

Production Company: NBC Prods.
Executive Producer .... Steve Sohmer
Producer .... Jonathan Bernstein
Director .... Jeff Bleckner
Writer .... Steve Sohmer
Cast .... Linda Kozlowski
Cast .... Harry Hamlin
Cast .... James Whitmore
Cast .... John Mahoney
Cast .... Harry Hamlin
Cast .... Lance Guest

FEAR — SHOWTIME

Drama: Murder and Murder Mystery • Cops/Detectives/Law Enforcement • Woman In Jeopardy • Suspense/Thriller • Sci-Fi/Supernatural/Horror/Fantasy
Airdate: 07/15/90
Rating: N/A   A/C:

A psychic who solves notorious killings for the police may have met her match...a killer who's more telepathic than she is.

Production Company: Richard Kobritz/Rockne S. O'Bannon Prod.
Executive Producer .... Mitchell Cannold
Executive Producer .... Diane Nabatoff
Producer .... Richard Kobritz
Director .... Rockne S. O'Bannon
Writer .... Rockne S. O'Bannon
Cast .... Ally Sheedy
Cast .... Lauren Hutton
Cast .... Michael O'Keefe
Cast .... Dina Merrill

FEAR INSIDE, THE — SHOWTIME

Drama: Woman In Jeopardy • Psychological Thriller
Airdate: 08/15/92
Rating: N/A   A/C:

An agoraphobic woman, estranged from her husband, becomes a hostage when she takes in a pair of borders. When her life and the safety of her son are threatened by the criminals, she must overcome her fear.

Production Company: Viacom Pictures
Executive Producer .... Alan Jay Glueckman
Executive Producer .... Judie Gregg
Executive Producer .... Helena Hacker Rosenberg
Producer .... John Broderick
Director .... Leon Ichaso
Writer .... David Birke
Cast .... Christine Lahti
Cast .... Dylan McDermott
Cast .... Jennifer Rubin
Cast .... David Ackroyd

FEAR STALK — CBS

Drama: Woman In Jeopardy • Psychological Thriller
Airdate: 12/17/89
Rating: 11.7/19   A/C: 2

A highly successful television producer is stalked and terrorized by a psychopath after he steals the contents of her purse.

Production Company: Donald March Prod. IAW ITC Prods.
Executive Producer .... Donald March
Producer .... Donald March
Director .... Larry Shaw
Writer .... Ellen Weston
Cast .... Jill Clayburgh
Cast .... Stephen Macht
Cast .... Sada Thompson
Cast .... Mary Ellen Trainor

FERGIE AND ANDREW: BEHIND THE PALACE DOORS — NBC

Drama: Biography • Foreign or Exotic Location • True Story
Airdate: 9/28/92
Rating: 13.6/21   A/C: 3

The courtship, marriage and separation of the Duke and Duchess of York.

Production Company: Rosemont Prods.
Executive Producer .... Norman Rosemont
Executive Producer .... David A. Rosemont
Co-Executive Producer .... Frank Von Zerneck
Co-Executive Producer .... Robert M. Sertner
Co-Executive Producer .... Martin Poll
Producer .... Paul Sarony
Director .... Michael Switzer
Writer .... Stephen Zito
Cast .... Pippa Hinchley
Cast .... Sam Miller
Cast .... Edita Brychta

FEVER — HBO

Drama: Woman In Jeopardy • Love Story • Suspense/Thriller
Airdate: 05/11/91
Rating: N/A   A/C:

A recently released convict reluctantly teams up with a proper English lawyer to rescue a woman they both love from the clutches of a gang of hired hoods.

Production Company: Saban-Scherick Prods.
Executive Producer .... Edgar J. Scherick
Producer .... Nick Gillott
Director .... Larry Elikann
Writer .... Larry Brothers
Cast .... Armand Assante
Cast .... Sam Neill
Cast .... Marcia Gay Harden
Cast .... Joe Spano

FIFTH MISSILE, THE — NBC

Drama: Suspense/Thriller • Psychological Thriller
Airdate: 02/17/86
Rating: 14.7/22   A/C:

An emergency drill threatens to go disastrously awry when a deranged nuclear sub captain supplied with four harmless missiles may fire a fifth, nuclear-armed one.

Production Company: Bercovici/St. Johns Prods.
   IAW MGM/UA TV
Executive Producer .... Eric Bercovici
Producer .... Arthur Fellows
Director .... Larry Peerce
Writer .... Eric Bercovici
Cast .... Robert Conrad
Cast .... Sam Waterston
Cast .... Richard Roundtree
Cast .... Yvette Mimieux
Cast .... David Soul

FIGHT FOR JENNY, A — NBC

Drama: Family Drama • Children/Teens • Black Story • Social Issue
Airdate: 10/13/86
Rating: 20.0/31   A/C:

A mother must fight her ex-husband for the custody of their child after she moves in with, and then marries, a black man.

Production Company: Robert Greenwald Prods.
Executive Producer .... Robert Greenwald
Producer .... Jonathan Bernstein
Co-Producer .... Diane Walsh
Director .... Gilbert Moses
Writer .... Duffy Bart
Writer .... Paul Eric Myers
Writer .... Judy Merl
Cast .... Lesley Ann Warren
Cast .... Philip Michael Thomas
Cast .... Jean Smart

FIGHT FOR LIFE — ABC

Drama: Family Drama • Man Against The System • Children/Teens • Medical/Disease/Mental Illness
Airdate: 03/23/87
Rating: 16.2/26   A/C:

A wealthy optometrist and his wife fight the bureaucracy to obtain a drug that is banned in the U.S. to treat their epileptic six year old daughter.

Production Company: Fries Entertainment Inc.
Executive Producer .... Charles Fries
Executive Producer .... Irv Wilson
Producer .... Ian McDougall
Director .... Elliot Silverstein
Writer .... Scott Nisor
Writer .... Tom Nesi
Cast .... Jerry Lewis
Cast .... Patty Duke
Cast .... Barry Morse
Cast .... Morgan Freeman

FINAL APPEAL — NBC

Drama: True Crime • Courtroom Drama • Family Violence
Airdate: 9/26/93
Rating: 12.7/20   A/C: 2

A alcoholic, down on his luck attorney gets his act together when his sister is accused of murdering her seemingly perfect husband. At first he is reluctant to believe her story of his brother-in-law's drug and physical abuse and that she acted in self defense. With the help of a sympathetic detective he is able to expose police cover-ups and political threats which help to prove his sister's innocence.

Production Company: Republic Pictures TV
Executive Producer .... Laurie Levit
Producer .... Jay Benson
Co-Producer .... George Marshall
Co-Producer .... Melissa Goddard
Co-Producer .... Peter Morgan
Director .... Eric Till
Writer .... Philip Rosenberg
Cast .... Brian Dennehy
Cast .... JoBeth Williams
Cast .... Tom Mason
Cast .... Eddie Jones

FINAL DAYS — ABC

Drama (3 Hours): Period Piece • Historical Piece • Period Piece • Biography
Airdate: 10/29/89
Rating: 10.2/17   A/C: 3

Based on the book by Woodward-Bernstein, a fact-based account of the last year of Richard Nixon's presidency as he tries to cover up his involvement in the Watergate scandal.

Production Company: The Samuels Film Co.
Executive Producer .... Stu Samuels
Producer .... Richard L. O'Connor
Director .... Richard Pearce
Writer .... Hugh Whitemore
Cast .... Lane Smith
Cast .... Richard Kiley
Cast .... David Ogden Stiers
Cast .... Ed Flanders

FINAL JEOPARDY, THE — NBC

Drama: Suspense/Thriller
Airdate: 12/08/85
Rating: 16.5/26   A/C:

A small town couple make their first visit to a big city and are pursued by criminals, drug abusers and derelicts.

Production Company: Frank von Zerneck Films
Executive Producer .... Frank Von Zerneck
Producer .... Robert M. Sertner
Director .... Michael Pressman
Writer .... Shiryl Hendryx
Cast .... Richard Thomas
Cast .... Mary Crosby
Cast .... Jeff Corey

FINAL NOTICE — USA

Mystery: Murder and Murder Mystery • Cops/Detectives/Law Enforcement
Airdate: 11/29/89
Rating: N/A   A/C:

A private detective solves two gruesome murders.

Production Company: Wilshire Court Productions IAW Sharm Hill Prods.
Executive Producer .... Jay Bernstein
Producer .... Paul Freeman
Director .... Steven H. Stern
Writer .... John Gay
Cast .... Gil Gerard
Cast .... Melody Anderson
Cast .... Louise Fletcher
Cast .... David Ogden Stiers

FINAL VERDICT — TNT

Drama: True Story • Period Piece • Courtroom Drama • Biography
Airdate: 09/09/91
Rating: N/A   A/C:

Based on the book by Adela Rogers St. John. In 1919 Los Angeles, a fourteen-year-old girl who idolizes her criminal attorney father, Earl Rogers, becomes disillusioned by his alcoholism, contentious relationship with his father, and self-absorption with his famous trials.

Production Company: Turner Pictures
Executive Produce .... Nelle Nugent
Producer .... George Manasse
Co-Producer .... Victor Simpkins
Director .... Jack Fisk
Writer .... Lawrence Roman
Cast .... Treat Williams
Cast .... Glenn Ford
Cast .... Olivia Burnette
Cast .... Gretchen Corbett

FINDING THE WAY HOME — ABC

Drama: Family Drama • Cross-Cultural Story • Social Issue
Airdate: 08/26/91
Rating: 10.2/18   A/C: 2

Based on the book "Mittleman's Hardware" by George Raphael Small. A down and out Texas hardware store owner loses his memory in an auto accident and finds a new beginning and a sense of self-worth in a community of Latino migrant workers.

Production Company: Peter K. Duchow Enterprises Inc.
Executive Producer .... Peter K. Duchow
Producer .... Peter K. Duchow
Producer .... Rod Holcomb
Producer .... Scott Swanton
Director .... Rod Holcomb
Writer .... Scott Swanton
Cast .... George C. Scott
Cast .... Hector Elizondo
Cast .... Julie Carmen
Cast .... Beverly Garland

FINISH LINE — TNT

Drama: Family Drama • Addiction Story • Sports
Airdate: 1/11/89
Rating: N/A   A/C:

The tensions between a father and his son and the tragic effect steroids have on a young track star's life.

Production Company: Phoenix Films IAW TNT
Producer .... Stanley Brooks
Director .... John Nicolella
Writer .... Norman Morrill
Cast .... James Brolin
Cast .... Josh Brolin

FINNEGAN BEGIN AGAIN — HBO

Drama: Romantic Comedy
Airdate: 2/24/85
Rating: N/A   A/C:

A schoolteacher who is involved in a covert affair with a married funeral director begins a relationship with a lonely hearts newspaper columnist who is unhappily married to an older, senile woman. Their friendship eventually develops into a romance and together they both find a second chance at happiness.

Production Company: Zenith/Consolidated, Jennie Co.

Executive Producer	Michael Deeley
Producer	Gower Frost
Director	Joan Micklin Silver
Writer	Walter Lockwood
Cast	Mary Tyler Moore
Cast	Robert Preston
Cast	Sam Waterston
Cast	Sylvia Sidney

FIRE AND RAIN — USA

Drama: Family Drama • True Story • Disaster
Airdate: 09/13/89
Rating: N/A   A/C:

Based on the book by Jerome Chandler, which tells the story of the crash of Delta Airlines flight 191 at Dallas/Ft. Worth Airport in 1985 which claimed one-hundred-thirty seven lives and yielded fifteen survivors.

Production Company: Wilshire Court Prods.

Producer	Richard Luke Rothschild
Director	Jerry Jameson
Writer	Gary Sherman
Cast	Charles Haid
Cast	Angie Dickinson
Cast	John Beck
Cast	Dean Jones

FIRE IN THE DARK — CBS

Drama: Family Drama • Social Issue
Airdate: 10/06/91
Rating: 14.8/23   A/C: 1

When an aging widow is suddenly afflicted with a crippling disability, she fights to retain her will to live and her family must learn to deal with their own issues of responsibility, duty and guilt.

Production Company: Kushner-Locke Co.

Executive Producer	Peter Locke
Executive Producer	Donald Kushner
Producer	Don Gregory
Producer	Bernie Kahn
Director	David Jones
Writer	David Hill
Cast	Olympia Dukakis
Cast	Lindsay Wagner
Cast	Jean Stapleton
Cast	Edward Herrmann

FIRE NEXT TIME, THE — NBC

Miniseries/Drama (2 nights): Toxic Waste/ Environmental • Sci-Fi/Supernatural/Horror/Fantasy • Disaster
Airdate: 4/18/93 • 4/20/93
Rating: 13.1/22 • 11.0/18   A/C: 1 • 2

In the year 2013 a Louisiana fisherman and his family attempt to make their way to Canada when the United States is stricken by climatic disasters brought about by global warming. As the family makes their way through the country's wasteland they are assaulted by eco-cops, crazed cults and villainous terrorists.

Production Company: RHI Ent., Kirch Group

Executive Producer	Robert Halmi, Jr.
Executive Producer	James S. Henerson
Co-Executive Producer	Larry Strichman
Producer	Edwin Self
Director	Tom McLoughlin
Writer	James S. Henerson
Cast	Craig T. Nelson
Cast	Bonnie Bedelia
Cast	Richard Farnsworth
Cast	Charles Haid
Cast	Jurgen Prochnow
Cast	Justin Whalin

FIRE: TRAPPED ON THE 37TH FLOOR — ABC

Drama: True Story • Action/Adventure • Disaster
Airdate: 02/18/91
Rating: 11.2/17   A/C: 3

Dramatic re-creation of the 1988 fire at the First Interstate Bank building in L.A. Heroic efforts by the Fire Department result in the rescue of two bank executives trapped on the 37th floor.

Production Company: Papazian/Hirsch Prods. IAW Republic Pictures

Executive Producer	Carole Bloom
Executive Producer	Susan Whittaker
Producer	Robert A. Papazian
Producer	James G. Hirsch
Co-Producer	Lisa Friedman Block
Director	Robert Day
Writer	Jeffrey Bloom
Cast	Lisa Hartman
Cast	Peter Scolari
Cast	Lee Majors
Cast	Kim Miyori

FIREFIGHTER — CBS

Drama: Woman Against The System • True Story • Woman's Issue/Story
Airdate: 09/23/86
Rating: 12.6/20   A/C:

True-life story of the first woman to qualify for field duty with the Los Angeles County Fire Department.

Production Company: Embassy TV

Executive Producer	Greg H. Sims
Executive Producer	Nancy McKeon
Director	Robert Lewis
Writer	Kathryn Montgomery
Cast	Nancy McKeon
Cast	Barry Corbin
Cast	Guy Boyd

FIRESTORM: 72 HOURS IN OAKLAND — ABC

Drama: Disaster • True Story
Airdate: 2/7/93
Rating: 11.5/17   A/C: 3

In 1991, the heroic efforts of Oakland, California fire chief, J. Allen Mather are recounted as he risks his life in the conflagration to rescue three trapped families.

Production Company: Gross-Weston Prods. IAW Capitol Cities/ABC Video & Cannell Ent.

Executive Producer	Ann Weston
Executive Producer	Marcy Gross
Producer	Gloria Morrison
Producer	Diane Walsh
Producer	Sam Grogg
Director	Michael Tuchner
Writer	John McGreevey
Cast	Jill Clayburgh
Cast	LeVar Burton
Cast	Michael Gross

FIRST STEPS — CBS

Drama: Children/Teens • True Story
Airdate: 03/19/85
Rating: 14.4/24   A/C:

Based on the true story of Nan Martin, a paraplegic, who with the help of Dr. Jerrold Petrofsky, a bio-engineer, walks again through the use of computerized muscle stimulation.

Production Company: CBS Entertainment

Producer	Ellis A. Cohen
Director	Sheldon Larry
Writer	Rod Browning
Cast	Judd Hirsch
Cast	Amy Steel
Cast	Kim Darby
Cast	Frances Lee McCain

FLASH, THE — CBS

Drama: Series Pilot (2 hr.) • Sci-Fi/Supernatural/ Horror/Fantasy
Airdate: 09/20/90
Rating: 14.2/23   A/C: 2

Based on the comic book character. After being struck by lightning, a police forensics officer gains superhuman speed and uses his new powers to battle criminals.

Production Company: Pet Fly Prods.

Executive Producer	Danny Bilson
Executive Producer	Paul DeMeo
Producer	Don Kurt
Director	Robert Iscove
Writer	Danny Bilson
Writer	Paul DeMeo
Cast	John Wesley Shipp
Cast	Amanda Pays
Cast	Alex Desert
Cast	Paula Marshall

FLIGHT OF BLACK ANGEL SHOWTIME
Drama: Suspense/Thriller • Action/Adventure
Airdate: 02/23/91
Rating: N/A   A/C:

When a top airforce trainee goes insane during training maneuvers, his commander must try and stop him from detonating a nuclear bomb over Las Vegas.

Production Company: Hess-Kallberg Prods.
Executive Producer .... Danielle Doty
Executive Producer .... Michael C. Green
Producer .... Kevin Kallberg
Producer .... Oliver G. Hess
Co-Producer .... Cristen M. Carr
Director .... Jonathan Mostow
Writer .... Henry Dominic
Cast .... Peter Strauss
Cast .... William O'Leary
Cast .... James O'Sullivan

FLOOD: WHO WILL SAVE OUR CHILDREN?   NBC
Drama: Disaster • Children/Teens
Airdate: 10/10/93
Rating: 11.4/18   A/C: 3

In 1987, a flash flood in Texas sweeps away two busloads of Bible students returning from a camping trip near the town of Comfort. The tragedy rips apart the lives of the survivors and the victims' families as they confront the possibly of criminal negligence on the part of the guilt ridden bus driver.

Production Company: Wolper Organization IAW Warner Bros. TV
Executive Producer .... David L. Wolper
Executive Producer .... Jeffery Hayes
Producer .... Donna Kanter
Producer .... Darryl Sheen
Director .... Chris Thomson
Writer .... David J. Kinghorn
Cast .... Joe Spano
Cast .... David Lascher
Cast .... Michael Goorjian
Cast .... Amy Van Nostrand

FLORENCE NIGHTINGALE   NBC
Drama (3 hrs.): Woman Against The System • Medical/Disease/Mental Illness • Period Piece • Foreign or Exotic Location • Biography
Airdate: 04/07/85
Rating: 11.6/19   A/C:

The biography of 19th century British nurse Florence Nightingale who gave up her social position to serve the sick and wounded during the Crimean war. Her admirable actions advanced the cause of nursing everywhere.

Production Company: Cypress Point Prods.
Executive Producer .... Gerald W. Abrams
Producer .... Tony Richmond
Director .... Daryl Duke
Writer .... Ivan Moffat
Writer .... Rose Leiman Goldemberg
Cast .... Jaclyn Smith
Cast .... Timothy Dalton
Cast .... Claire Bloom
Cast .... Jeremy Brett

FLORIDA STRAITS   HBO
Drama: Action/Adventure • Foreign or Exotic Location
Airdate: 10/26/86
Rating: N/A   A/C:

A trio of adventurers brave the treacherous Florida straits and the dense Cuban jungles in search for a fortune in buried gold.

Production Company: HBO Pictures
Executive Producer .... Robert Cooper
Producer .... Stuart B. Rekant
Director .... Mike Hodges
Writer .... Roderick Taylor
Cast .... Raul Julia
Cast .... Fred Ward
Cast .... Daniel Jenkins

FOLLOW YOUR HEART   NBC
Drama: Family Drama • Children/Teens • Series Pilot (2 hr.)
Airdate: 04/02/90
Rating: 14.7/23   A/C: 2

Based on the novel "Walk Me to the Distance" by Percival Everett. A lonely drifter's life takes on new meaning when he gets stuck in a small Wyoming town, and the colorful locals become his family and friends.

Production Company: Force Ten/Jabberwocky/ NBC Productions
Executive Producer .... Dan Fauci
Executive Producer .... John Faunce Roach
Producer .... Marvin Miller
Producer .... Ricka Fisher
Director .... Noel Nosseck
Writer .... John Faunce Roach
Writer .... Dan Fauci
Writer .... Cynthia Whitcomb
Cast .... Patrick Cassidy
Cast .... Frances Sternhagen
Cast .... Catherine Mary Stewart
Cast .... James Stephens

FOR LOVE AND GLORY   CBS
Drama: Family Drama • Period Piece • Historical Piece • Series Pilot (2 hr.)
Airdate: 9/11/93
Rating: 9.4/18   A/C: 1

A wealthy Southern family on a Virginia Plantation is caught up in the drama's of the marriage of their rugged older son to a saucy, working class Irish lass; the father's affair with an understanding slave and the youngest son's involvement with the Confederacy. But soon the family is forever changed as the Civil War wreaks havoc on their insulated, privileged lives.

Production Company: Gerber Co. IAW CBS Ent.
Executive Producer .... David Gerber
Executive Producer .... Georgia Jeffries
Executive Producer .... Richard Fielder
Producer .... Albert J. Salzer
Director .... Roger Young
Writer .... Geoffrey Thomas
Writer .... George Fielder
Cast .... Kate Mulgrew
Cast .... Robert Foxworth
Cast .... Daniel Markel
Cast .... Olivia D'Abo

FOR LOVE OR MONEY   CBS
Comedy: Romantic Comedy
Airdate: 11/20/84
Rating: 12.4/20   A/C:

A man and a woman participate in a game show in which they are brought together for a few weeks and allowed to become romantically involved. They are then asked to choose between receiving one million or staying together.

Production Company: Robert Papazian Prods. IAW Henerson-Hirsch Prods.
Executive Producer .... James S. Henerson
Executive Producer .... James G. Hirsch
Producer .... Robert A. Papazian
Director .... Terry Hughes
Writer .... James S. Henerson
Cast .... Gil Gerard
Cast .... Suzanne Pleshette
Cast .... Ray Walston
Cast .... Jamie Farr

FOR RICHER, FOR POORER   HBO
Comedy: Family Drama
Airdate: 02/28/91
Rating: N/A   A/C:

A wealthy businessman secretly liquidates his business and gives away his money in an effort to evoke renewed passion in his life and marriage and force his lazy son to work for a living.

Production Company: HBO/Citadel/Iron Mountain
Executive Producer .... David R. Ginsburg
Producer .... Richard Rosenbloom
Director .... Jay Sandrich
Writer .... Stan Daniels
Cast .... Jack Lemmon
Cast .... Talia Shire
Cast .... Madeline Kahn
Cast .... Jonathan Silverman

FOR THE LOVE OF AARON   CBS
Drama: Family Drama • Medical/Disease/Mental Illness • Children/Teens
Airdate: 1/1/94
Rating: 12.4/21   A/C: 2

Based on a treatment by Margaret Gibson. Divorced writer Margaret Gibson battles serve bouts of mental illness during which time her eight year old son Aaron becomes her caretaker. The boy's estranged father begins custody hearings on the grounds that his ex-wife is unfit to care for the child. With the help of a new doctor and proper medication, Gibson struggles to regain her emotional health as well as fight for permanent custody of her boy.

Production Company: Paterdale Prods. Inc./The Stroytellers Group IAW Marian Rees Assoc.
Executive Producer .... Marian Rees
Producer .... Bob Gray
Director .... John Kent Harrison
Writer .... Peter Silverman
Cast .... Meredith Baxter
Cast .... Nick Mancuso
Cast .... Keegan MacIntosh
Cast .... John Kapelos

FOR THE LOVE OF MY CHILD: THE ANISSA AYALA STORY   NBC

Drama: Family Drama • Medical/Disease/Mental Illness • True Story • Children/Teens • Social Issue
Airdate: 5/10/93
Rating: 12.8/20   A/C: 3

In 1991, Walnut, California, nineteen year old Anissa Ayala is stricken with leukemia. In need of a bone marrow transplant and unable to find a suitable match, the girl's mother, Mary, decides to have another baby in hope that the infant can provide the life saving cure. While a heated medical and ethical debate ensues, the family continues on with their plans which eventually proves to be medically successful.

Production Company: Viacom IAW Stonehenge
    Prods.
Executive Producer .... Dick Berg
Executive Producer .... Allan Marcil
Producer .... Michelle MacLaren
Director .... Waris Hussein
Writer .... Anna Sandor
Cast .... Priscilla Lopez
Cast .... Teresa Dispina
Cast .... Tony Perez

FOR THE VERY FIRST TIME   NBC

Drama: Forbidden Love • Children/Teens • Period Piece
Airdate: 04/22/91
Rating: 10.8/18   A/C: 2

A Jewish boy and a Catholic girl nurture a secret romance in early 1960s Texas.

Production Company: Lorimar/American Flyer
Executive Producer .... Michael Zinberg
Producer .... Randy Zisk
Co-Producer .... Karen Clark
Director .... Michael Zinberg
Writer .... Karen Clark
Cast .... Corin Nemec
Cast .... Cheryl Pollak
Cast .... Madchen Amick
Cast .... Joe Spano

FOR THEIR OWN GOOD   ABC

Drama: Woman Against The System • True Story • Toxic Waste/Environmental • Woman's Issue/Story • Social Issue
Airdate: 4/5/93
Rating: 10.9/17   A/C: 3

A working mother faces sexual discrimination at the hazardous chemical factory where she works when she is required to be sterilized or lose her job. A brash New York attorney takes the case which leads to a precedent setting decision.

Production Company: Avnet/Kerner Co.
Executive Producer .... Jordan Kerner
Executive Producer .... Jon Avnet
Producer .... Ruthe Benton
Producer .... Tad Devlin
Producer .... Martin Huberty
Producer .... Phyllis Rossheim
Director .... Ed Kaplan
Writer .... Ed Kaplan
Cast .... Elizabeth Perkins
Cast .... Laura San Giacomo
Cast .... Charles Haid
Cast .... CCH Pounder

FORBIDDEN   HBO

Drama: True Story • Love Story • WWII • Foreign or Exotic Location
Airdate: 3/24/85
Rating: N/A   A/C:

Based on the book "The Last Jew In Berlin" by Leonard Gross. During World War II, a German countess risks everything when she falls in love with a Jewish writer. Hiding him from the Gestapo in her apartment, she embarks on a deadly cat and mouse game in the sinister atmosphere of war-torn Berlin.

Production Company: HBO Premiere Films
Executive Producer .... Gerald I. Isenberg
Producer .... Mark Forstater
Co-Executive Producer .... Fritz Buttenstedt
Co-Executive Producer .... Herbert G. Kloiber
Director .... Anthony Page
Writer .... Leonard Gross
Cast .... Jacqueline Bisset
Cast .... Jurgen Prochnow
Cast .... Irene Worth

FORBIDDEN NIGHTS   CBS

Drama: Cross-Cultural Story • Love Story • True Story • Historical Piece • Foreign or Exotic Location • Forbidden Love
Airdate: 04/10/90
Rating: 10.5/17   A/C: 3

Based on Judy Shapiro's 1979 experiences as an American teacher in communist China. She falls in love with a Chinese radical and joins the struggle for democracy and modernization.

Production Company: Tristine Rainer Prods. IAW
    Warner Brothers
Executive Producer .... Tristine Rainer
Producer .... Charles Jennings
Director .... Waris Hussein
Writer .... Tristine Rainer
Cast .... Melissa Gilbert
Cast .... Robin Show
Cast .... Victor K. Wong

FOREIGN AFFAIRS   TNT

Drama: Love Story • Foreign or Exotic Location
Airdate: 3/17/93
Rating: N/A   A/C:

Based on the book by Alison Lurie. A refined New England college professor meets an unsophisticated, loud, sanitation company engineer from Oklahoma while on a plane to London. He is instantly smitten and persists in his conquest even though the lady shows no interest. Opposites eventually attract but the romance is short lived due to his untimely heart attack.

Production Company: Stagescreen Prods.,
    Interscope Commuications.
Executive Producer .... Ted Field
Executive Producer .... Jeffery Taylor
Producer .... Patricia Clifford
Director .... Jim O'Brien
Writer .... Chris Bryant
Cast .... Joanne Woodward
Cast .... Brian Dennehy
Cast .... Eric Stoltz
Cast .... Stephanie Beacham

FORGET ME NOT MURDERS, THE   CBS

Drama: Cops/Detectives/Law Enforcement • Murder and Murder Mystery
Airdate: 3/29/94
Rating: 13.1/21   A/C: 2

Based on the novel "Wallflower" by William Bayer. Sixth TV movie about veteran NYPD homicide detective Frank Janek. When his goddaughter becomes the victim of a brutal serial killer the veteran cop races the FBI to break the case. The investigation leads him to a troubled therapist who is linked to the murder victims.

Production Company: Janek Prods. IAW Pendick
    Entertainment and Spelling Televison
Executive Producer .... Robert Berger
Producer .... Robert Iscove
Producer .... Marilyn Stonehouse
Director .... Robert Iscove
Writer .... Gerald Di Pego
Cast .... Richard Crenna
Cast .... Tyne Daly
Cast .... Cliff Gorman

FORGOTTEN PRISONERS: THE AMNESTY FILE   TNT

Drama: Man Against The System • Foreign or Exotic Location • Political Piece • Social Issue • Prison and Prison Camp
Airdate: 11/19/90
Rating: N/A   A/C:

A dedicated law professor volunteering with Amnesty International travels to Istanbul, and fights government bureaucracy to save the lives of three tortured political prisoners.

Production Company: Robert Greenwald Prods.
Executive Producer .... Philip Kleinbart
Executive Producer .... Carla Singer
Producer .... Steve McGlothen
Producer .... Robert Greenwald
Director .... Robert Greenwald
Writer .... Rex Weiner
Writer .... Cindy Myers
Cast .... Ron Silver
Cast .... Hector Elizondo
Cast .... Roger Daltrey

FORTRESS   HBO

Drama: Woman In Jeopardy • Action/Adventure • Foreign or Exotic Location
Airdate: 11/24/85
Rating: N/A   A/C:

Based on the novel by Gabrielle Lord. An Australian schoolteacher and her nine students are thrust into a primitive struggle for survival when they are kidnapped by a quartet of thugs and transported into the bush country.

Production Company: HBO Premiere Films
Executive Producer .... Hector Crawford
Executive Producer .... Ian Crawford
Executive Producer .... Terry Stapleton
Producer .... Raymond Menmuir
Director .... Arch Nicholson
Writer .... Everett De Roche
Cast .... Rachel Ward
Cast .... Sean Garlick
Cast .... Rebecca Rigg

FOUR EYES AND SIX GUNS   TNT

Comedy: Western
Airdate: 12/7/92
Rating: N/A   A/C:

In 1882, a prissy New York optometrist follows his dream and sets up a practice in Tombstone, Arizona. He is soon disillusioned when he is swindled and his hero Wyatt Earp turns out to be a nearsighted, obnoxious drunk. When the town is threatened by an outlaw gang he shows his mettle with some fancy sharpshooting, saving the day and getting the legendary marshal into a pair of glasses.

Production Company: Firebrand Prods. IAW Saban/ Scherick Prods.
Executive Producer .... Edgar J. Scherick
Producer .... Salli Newman
Co-Producer .... James Margellos
Director .... Piers Haggard
Writer .... Leon Prochnik
Cast .... Judge Reinhold
Cast .... Fred Ward
Cast .... Patricia Clarkson

FOURTH STORY   SHOWTIME

Drama: Cops/Detectives/Law Enforcement • Suspense/Thriller
Airdate: 01/19/90
Rating: N/A   A/C:

A missing persons private investigator hits the mystery trail with a woman whose husband has suddenly disappeared.

Production Company: Viacom Pictures
Executive Producer .... Diana Kerew
Producer .... Frank Konigsberg
Producer .... Larry Sanitsky
Director .... Ivan Passer
Writer .... Andrew Guerdat
Cast .... Mark Harmon
Cast .... Mimi Rogers
Cast .... Paul Gleason
Cast .... Cliff De Young

FOXFIRE   CBS

Drama: Family Drama
Airdate: 12/13/87
Rating: 19.3/30   A/C:

Based on the play by Susan Cooper. An old woman with a country-singer son and a deceased husband who lives on in her dreams looks back on almost a century of Georgia mountain life.

Production Company: Marian Rees Associates
Executive Producer .... Marian Rees
Producer .... Dorothea Petrie
Director .... Jud Taylor
Writer .... Susan Cooper
Cast .... Jessica Tandy
Cast .... Hume Cronyn
Cast .... John Denver
Cast .... Gary Grubbs

FRAMED   HBO

Drama: Suspense/Thriller
Airdate: 6/24/90
Rating: N/A   A/C:

A painter who spent two years in prison for art forgery when his sexy young lover turned him in, finds himself under her spell again and about to go back into his nefarious profession. Not wanting to get burned again he plots to uncover her scheme before he gets framed again.

Production Company: HBO Pictures
Executive Producer .... Neal Moritz
Producer .... Elaine H. Sperber
Director .... Dean Parisot
Writer .... Gary Rosen
Cast .... Jeff Goldblum
Cast .... Kristin Scott Thomas
Cast .... Todd Graff

FRANK NITTI: THE ENFORCER   ABC

Drama: True Crime • Period Piece • Biography • Mafia/Mob
Airdate: 04/17/88
Rating: 17.4/28   A/C:

The blood-spattered career of hitman-gangster Frank Nitti, who was Al Capone's lieutenant and later a mob chieftain in his own right.

Production Company: Len Hill Films Inc.
Executive Producer .... Leonard Hill
Executive Producer .... Robert O'Connor
Co-Producer .... Daniel Cahn
Co-Producer .... Joel Fields
Producer .... Lee David Zlotoff
Director .... Michael Switzer
Writer .... Lee David Zlotoff
Cast .... Anthony La Paglia
Cast .... Mike Starr
Cast .... Michael Moriarty
Cast .... Trini Alvarado

FRANKENSTEIN   TNT

Drama: Sci-Fi/Supernatural/Horror/Fantasy • Foreign or Exotic Location
Airdate: 6/13/93
Rating: N/A   A/C:

Based on the book by Mary Shelley. An obsessed scientist, Dr. Victor Frankenstein creates a monstrous creature in his laboratory which eventually escapes and threatens to destroy him and his fiance.

Production Company: David Wickes Prods.
Executive Producer .... David Wickes
Director .... David Wickes
Writer .... David Wickes
Cast .... Patrick Bergin
Cast .... Randy Quaid
Cast .... John Mills
Cast .... Lambert Wilson

FRANKENSTEIN: THE COLLEGE YEARS   FBC

Comedy: Sci-Fi/Supernatural/Horror/Fantasy • Youth Comedy
Airdate: 10/28/91
Rating: 6.1/9   A/C: 4

Two college science students revive the Frankenstein monster and find themselves helping the big guy adjust to campus life, while trying to protect him from an evil professor out to steal their research.

Production Company: FNM Productions
Executive Producer .... Richard E. Johnson
Executive Producer .... Scott D. Goldstein
Producer .... Robert Engelman
Director .... Tom Shadyac
Writer .... Bryant Christ
Writer .... John Trevor Wolff
Cast .... William Ragsdale
Cast .... Vincent Hammond
Cast .... Christopher Daniel Barnes
Cast .... Larry Miller

FREEDOM FIGHTER   NBC

Drama: Love Story • Suspense/Thriller • Period Piece
Airdate: 01/11/88
Rating: 16.0/25   A/C:

An American soldier helps East Germans escape to the West during the building of the Berlin wall, which disrupts his romance with an East Berlin woman.

Production Company: Bill McCutchen Prods. IAW HTV Limited and Columbia Pictures TV

Executive Producer .... Bill McCutchen
Co-Executive Producer .... Tony Danza
Producer .... Frederic Golchan
Producer .... William Hill
Director .... Desmond Davis
Writer .... Gerald Di Pego
Cast .... Tony Danza
Cast .... David McCallum
Cast .... Colette Stevenson
Cast .... Neil Dickson

FRENCH SILK   ABC

Drama: Murder and Murder Mystery • Cops/ Detectives/Law Enforcement
Airdate: 1/23/94
Rating: 11.3/17   A/C: 2

Based on the novel by Sondra Brown. In New Orleans, a rouge homicide detective becomes romantically involved with a secretive lingerie designer who is a suspect in the murder of a crusading televangelist, who had targeted the businesswoman's sexy lingerie catalog as pornographic. Believing that she is innocent of the crime, he eventually exposes the real killer.

Production Company: Lee Rich Co. IAW von Zerneck/Sertner Films

Executive Producer .... Lee Rich
Executive Producer .... Bruce J. Sallan
Executive Producer .... Frank von Zerneck
Executive Producer .... Robert M. Sertner
Producer .... Gregory Prange
Director .... Noel Nosseck
Writer .... Carol Monpere
Cast .... Susan Lucci
Cast .... Lee Horsley
Cast .... Shari Belafonte
Cast .... R.Lee Ermey

FRESNO   CBS

Miniseries/Comedy (5 nights): Sex/Glitz
Airdate: 11/16/86 • 11/17/86 • 11/18/86 • 11/19/86 • 11/20/86
Rating: 19.7/30 • 15.2/22 • 12.8/19 • 12.5/24 • 12.7/18   A/C:

Lavish sendup of primetime soap genre is set in a California agricultural community, the raisin capital of the world.

Production Company: MTM Prods.

Executive Producer .... Barry Kemp
Producer .... R.W. Goodwin
Director .... Jeff Bleckner
Writer .... Mark Ganzel
Writer .... Michael Petryni
Writer .... Barry Kemp
Cast .... Dabney Coleman
Cast .... Gregory Harrison
Cast .... Teri Garr
Cast .... Charles Grodin
Cast .... Louise Latham
Cast .... Jerry Van Dyke
Cast .... Tom Poston
Cast .... Carol Burnett

FROM THE DEAD OF NIGHT   NBC

Miniseries/Drama (2 nights): Woman In Jeopardy • Sci-Fi/Supernatural/Horror/Fantasy
Airdate: 02/27/89 • 02/28/89
Rating: 11.6/20 • 14.3/22   A/C:

After three eerie near-death experiences, a Los Angeles fashion designer is told that death will come for her unless she is strong enough to fight off the supernatural forces of darkness.

Production Company: Shadowplay Films/Phoenix Entertainment Group

Executive Producer .... Hans Proppe
Co-Producer .... Jody Brockway
Director .... Paul Wendkos
Writer .... William Bleich
Cast .... Lindsay Wagner
Cast .... Bruce Boxleitner
Cast .... Peter Jason
Cast .... Diahann Carroll

FROM THE FILES OF JOSEPH WAMBAUGH: A JURY OF ONE   NBC

Drama: Murder and Murder Mystery • Cops/ Detectives/Law Enforcement • Series Pilot (2 hr.)
Airdate: 11.1.93
Rating: 17/17   A/C: 3

A good cop goes into a deep alcoholic depression after he accidentally kills another officer. While trying to work through his guilt, he and his partner investigate a series of perplexing barrio murders. He starts to turn his life around when he is fixed up with a young attractive widow who understands his pain and dedication to work.

Production Company: Gossbart/Barnett Prods. & Tristar TV

Executive Producer .... Joan Barnett
Executive Producer .... Jack Grossbart
Co-Producer .... Linda Kent
Executive Producer .... Alan Metzger
Writer .... David J. Kinghorn
Cast .... John Spencer
Cast .... Eddie Velez
Cast .... Dan Lauria
Cast .... Rachel Ticotin

FUGITIVE AMONG US   CBS

Drama: Cops/Detectives/Law Enforcement • True Crime
Airdate: 02/04/92
Rating: 14.0/23   A/C: 2

Based on the book "And Deliver Us From Evil" by Mike Cochran. A driven Texas cop turns his obsession with tracking down an escaped rapist into a personal vendetta. However, when a witness proves the cop wrong, he must unflinchingly continue the hunt to clear the escapee's name.

Production Company: Andrew Adelson Co. IAW ABC Prods.

Executive Producer .... Andrew Adelson
Producer .... Blue Andre
Director .... Michael Toshiyuki Uno
Writer .... Gordon Greisman
Cast .... Peter Strauss
Cast .... Eric Roberts
Cast .... Elizabeth Pena
Cast .... Guy Boyd

FUGITIVE NIGHTS: DANGER IN THE DESERT   NBC

Drama: Cops/Detectives/Law Enforcement
Airdate: 11/19/93
Rating: 11.5/20   A/C: 2

Based on the book by Joseph Wambaugh. A brassy cop turned private investigator enlists the aid of a hard drinking local police detective to help her find a fugitive in the resort community of Palm Springs, California.

Production Company: TriStar TV

Executive Producer .... Vahan Moosekian
Executive Producer .... Joseph Wambaugh
Director .... Gary Nelson
Writer .... Joseph Wambaugh
Cast .... Teri Garr
Cast .... Sam Elliott
Cast .... Barbara Babcock
Cast .... Thomas Haden Church

FULFILLMENT OF MARY GRAY, THE CBS
Drama: Family Drama • Forbidden Love • Period Piece
Airdate: 02/19/89
Rating: 16.5/26   A/C:

Based on the novel "The Fulfillment" by La Vyrle Spencer. A sterile farmer induces his reluctant wife and brother to have the child he cannot, and their emotions, once awakened, create problems for everyone.

Production Company: Lee Caplin Prods./Indian Neck Entertainment
Executive Producer .... Howard Baldwin
Executive Producer .... Richard M. Cohen
Executive Producer .... Lee Caplin
Producer .... Harry R. Sherman
Director .... Piers Haggard
Writer .... Laird Koenig
Cast .... Cheryl Ladd
Cast .... Ted Levine
Cast .... Lewis Smith
Cast .... Sheila Kelley

FULL EXPOSURE: THE SEX TAPES SCANDAL NBC
Drama: Murder and Murder Mystery • Cops/Detectives/Law Enforcement • Prostitution • Sex/Glitz
Airdate: 02/05/89
Rating: 16.2/24   A/C:

A policeman and a female D.A. investigate the murders of a prostitute who kept videotape records of her sadomasochistic sessions, which involved a high-ranking political figure.

Production Company: Von Zerneck/Sertner Films
Executive Producer .... Frank Von Zerneck
Executive Producer .... Robert M. Sertner
Producer .... Gregory Prange
Producer .... Stephen Zito
Director .... Noel Nosseck
Writer .... Stephen Zito
Cast .... Lisa Hartman
Cast .... Vanessa Williams
Cast .... Jennifer O'Neill
Cast .... James Avery

GAMBLER RETURNS: THE LUCK OF THE DRAW, THE NBC
Miniseries/Drama (2 nights): Period Piece • Action/Adventure • Western
Airdate: 11/03/91 • 11/04/91
Rating: 18.0/28 • 16.6/25   A/C: 1 • 3

A big stakes poker game in San Francisco makes cardshark Brady Hawks hit the trail from Mexico. He is soon waylaid by bandits, outlaws, hookers and hombres. With the help of some legendary heros of the Old West, he arrives safely to ante up.

Production Company: Kenny Rogers Prods. IAW NBC
Executive Producer .... Ken Kragen
Executive Producer .... Kelly Junkermann
Producer .... Dick Lowry
Co-Producer .... Ann Kindberg
Director .... Dick Lowry
Writer .... Joe Byre
Writer .... Jeb Rosebrook
Cast .... Kenny Rogers
Cast .... Reba McEntire
Cast .... Rick Rossovich
Cast .... Gene Barry
Cast .... Linda Evans
Cast .... Hugh O'Brian

GATHERING OF OLD MEN, A CBS
Drama: Murder and Murder Mystery • Period Piece • Black Story
Airdate: 05/10/87
Rating: 18.4/31   A/C:

Adaptation of Ernest Gaines' novel. When a white plantation supervisor is gunned down, nineteen black men claim responsibility and face vengeance from his relatives.

Production Company: Consolidated, Jennie & Co. Zenith Prods.
Executive Producer .... Michael Deeley
Producer .... Gower Frost
Director .... Volker Schlondorff
Writer .... Charles Fuller
Cast .... Louis Gossett, Jr.
Cast .... Richard Widmark
Cast .... Holly Hunter
Cast .... Will Patton
Cast .... Joe Seneca

GENERATION ABC
Drama: Family Drama • Sci-Fi/Supernatural/Horror/Fantasy • Series Pilot (2 hr.)
Airdate: 05/24/85
Rating: 6.5/12   A/C:

A family drama set in 1999, in which a family matriarch tries to convince her daughter to put aside a dispute with the clan's father and celebrate New Year's eve 1999 with the family.

Production Company: Embassy TV
Executive Producer .... Gerald DiPego
Producer .... Bill Finnegan
Producer .... Pat Finnegan
Director .... Michael Tuchner
Writer .... Gerald Di Pego
Cast .... Richard Beymer
Cast .... Hannah Cutrona
Cast .... Marta Dubois
Cast .... Cristina Raines

GEORGE McKENNA STORY, THE CBS
Drama: Man Against The System • Children/Teens • True Story • Black Story • Social Issue
Airdate: 11/01/86
Rating: 15.5/24   A/C:

True story of a Los Angeles high-school principal who rescued his school from inner-city gangs and drugs.

Production Company: The Landsburg Co.
Executive Producer .... Alan Landsburg
Producer .... Linda Otto
Director .... Eric Laneuville
Writer .... Charles Eric Johnson
Cast .... Denzel Washington
Cast .... Richard Masur
Cast .... Barbara Townsend
Cast .... Akosua Busia

GEORGE WASHINGTON II: THE FORGING OF A NATION CBS
Miniseries/Drama (2 nights): Historical Piece • Biography • Period Piece • Period Piece
Airdate: 09/21/86 • 09/22/86
Rating: 12.6/20 • 9.8/15   A/C:

The first President's life during the decade that included his Presidency.

Production Company: MGM TV
Executive Producer .... David Gerber
Producer .... Richard Fielder
Director .... William A. Graham
Writer .... Richard Fielder
Cast .... Barry Bostwick
Cast .... Patty Duke
Cast .... Penny Fuller
Cast .... Jeffrey Jones

GERONIMO TNT
Drama: American Indians • Historical Piece • Period Piece
Airdate: 12/5/93
Rating: N/A   A/C:

The exciting but often painful life (1829-1909) of the great Apache war chief from his early years as a proud young warrior, his bloody battles against Mexican and American soldiers to his later years as a tragic but dignified U.S. government sideshow attraction.

Production Company: Yorktown Prods. IAW Von Zerneck/Sertner Films
Executive Producer .... Norman Jewison
Executive Producer .... Christopher Cook
Producer .... Ira Marvin
Co-Producer .... Hannay Geiogamah
Director .... Roger Young
Writer .... J.T. Allen
Cast .... Joseph Runningfox
Cast .... Nick Ramus
Cast .... Michelle St. John
Cast .... Michael Greyeyes

GET SMART AGAIN — ABC

Comedy: Cops/Detectives/Law Enforcement • Action/Adventure
Airdate: 02/26/89
Rating: 13.7/21   A/C:

Retired U.S. secret agents Maxwell Smart and his wife Agent 99 return to find and disable KAOS's weather-control machine.

Production Company: IndieProd Co. IAW Phoenix Entertainment Group Inc.
Executive Producer .... Leonard B. Stern
Executive Producer .... Daniel Melnick
Producer .... Burt Nodella
Director .... Gary Nelson
Writer .... Rod Ash
Writer .... Mark Curtiss
Writer .... Leonard B. Stern
Cast .... Don Adams
Cast .... Barbara Feldon
Cast .... Bernie Kopell
Cast .... Dick Gautier
Cast .... Harold Gould

GETTING GOTTI — CBS

Drama: True Crime • Mafia/Mob • Courtroom Drama • Woman Against The System
Airdate: 5/10/94
Rating: 8.3/13   A/C: 3

Assistant U.S. Attorney, Diane Giacalone devotes seven long years to bring New York City mafia kingpin, John Gotti to justice. But the six month, 1987 trial in which she prosecutes the arrogant mob boss results in a acquittal, a verdict that was obtained by jury tampering. It wasn't until 1992 that Gotti was convicted on murder and racketeering charges by another group of prosecutors.

Production Company: Kushner-Locke Co.
Executive Producer .... Peter Locke
Executive Producer .... Donald Kushner
Executive Producer .... Robert Dwek
Producer .... John M. Eckert
Director .... Roger Young
Writer .... James S. Henerson
Cast .... Lorraine Bracco
Cast .... Anthony John Denison
Cast .... Kathleen Lasky
Cast .... Kenneth Welsh

GETTING OUT — ABC

Drama: Family Drama • Children/Teens • Prison and Prison Camp • Woman's Issue/Story
Airdate: 4/25/94
Rating: 11.1/18   A/C: 2

Based on the 1977 play by Marsha Norman. A Georgia woman recently paroled from prison attempts to regain custody of the son she gave birth to while incarcerated. Discovering her mother gave the child up for adoption, she must get on with rebuilding her life which forces her to confront long held resentments against her sexually abusive father and her trashy, belittling mother.

Production Company: Dorothea Petrie Prods. IAW Signboard Hill Prods. and RHI Entertainment
Executive Producer .... Robert Halmi, Sr.
Executive Producer .... Richard Welsh
Producer .... Dorothea Petrie
Co-Producer .... Brent Shields
Director .... John Korty
Writer .... Eugene Corr
Writer .... Ruth Shapiro
Cast .... Rebecca De Mornay
Cast .... Ellen Burstyn
Cast .... Robert Knepper
Cast .... Tandy Cronyn

GETTING UP AND GOING HOME — LIFETIME

Drama: Family Drama • Forbidden Love • Woman's Issue/Story
Airdate: 07/21/92
Rating: N/A   A/C:

Based on the novel by Robert Anderson. A successful lawyer's family life is thrown into conflict when in the midst of a mid-life crisis he has affairs with a married woman and a music student.

Production Company: Polone Company, Carroll Newman Prods. IAW Hearst Ent.
Executive Producer .... Judith A. Polone
Producer .... Carroll Newman
Director .... Steven Schachter
Writer .... Peter Nelson
Cast .... Tom Skerritt
Cast .... Blythe Danner
Cast .... Roma Downey
Cast .... Julianne Phillips

GETTYSBURG — TNT

Miniseries/Drama (2 nights): Historical Piece • Period Piece
Airdate: 6/26/94 • 6/27/94
Rating: N/A   A/C:

Based on the book "Killer Angels" by Michael Shaara. The epic story of the battle of Gettysburg-the bloodiest battle in United States history and the the turning point of the Civil War.

Production Company: Neufeld/Rehme Productions
Executive Producer .... Mace Neufeld
Executive Producer .... Bob Rehme
Producer .... Robert Katz
Producer .... Moctesuma Esparza
Director .... Ron Maxwell
Writer .... Ron Maxwell
Cast .... Jeff Daniels
Cast .... Tom Berenger
Cast .... Martin Sheen
Cast .... Sam Elliott
Cast .... Stephen Lang

GHOST IN MONTE CARLO, A — TNT

Drama: Period Piece • Action/Adventure • Foreign or Exotic Location
Airdate: 03/02/90
Rating: N/A   A/C:

Based on the book by Barbara Cartland. Glitzy tale of a convent-raised young woman entering nineteenth century high society with the help of her flamboyant and conniving aunt.

Production Company: The Grade Co. IAW Gainsborough Pictures
Executive Producer .... Lew Grade
Producer .... John Hough
Director .... John Hough
Writer .... Terence Feely
Cast .... Sarah Miles
Cast .... Oliver Reed
Cast .... Christopher Plummer
Cast .... Samantha Eggar

GHOST MOM — FBC

Comedy: Sci-Fi/Supernatural/Horror/Fantasy
Airdate: 11/1/93
Rating: 6.0/9   A/C: 4

A meddling mother inadvertently acquires a diamond when she sneaks into an operating room to watch her son, the doctor at work. When she suddenly dies and is buried with the priceless gem, a group of Japanese gangsters target her only child. Returning from the grave, she helps her son solve the case as he promises to take her body to Niagara Falls where she must complete some unfinished business before she can rest in peace.

Production Company: Power Pictures Corp., Richard Crystal Co. IAW Hearst Ent.
Executive Producer .... Richard Crystal
Producer .... Daniel Harris
Producer .... Constanitino Magnatta
Director .... Dave Thomas
Writer .... Daniel Harris
Writer .... Constanitino Magnatta
Cast .... Jean Stapleton
Cast .... Geraint Wyn Davies
Cast .... Denis Akiyama

GHOST OF A CHANCE   CBS
Comedy: Sci-Fi/Supernatural/Horror/Fantasy
Airdate: 05/12/87
Rating: 14.4/24   A/C:

A tavern pianist accidentally killed by a policeman returns to earth, determined that the policeman will take care of the pianist's young grandson.

Production Company: Stuart-Phoenix & Thunder Bird Rd. Prods. IAW Lorimar-Telepictures
Executive Producer .... Stuart Sheslow
Executive Producer .... Malcolm Stuart
Producer .... Sam Strangis
Director .... Don Taylor
Writer .... Hank Bradford
Cast .... Redd Foxx
Cast .... Geoffrey Holder
Cast .... Dick Van Dyke
Cast .... Brynn Thayer

GIFTED ONE, THE   NBC
Drama: Series Pilot (2 hr.) • Sci-Fi/Supernatural/ Horror/Fantasy
Airdate: 06/25/89
Rating: 15.5/27   A/C:

A young man with superhuman powers goes on a quest for his natural birth mother and encounters all kinds of perils.

Production Company: Richard Rothstein Prods. IAW NBC Prods.
Executive Producer .... Richard Rothstein
Producer .... Ariel Levy
Director .... Stephen Herek
Writer .... Richard Rothstein
Writer .... Lisa James
Cast .... Pete Kowanko
Cast .... John Rhys-Davies
Cast .... G.W. Bailey
Cast .... Wendy Phillips

GIRL FROM TOMORROW, THE   DISNEY
Drama: Children/Teens • Sci-Fi/Supernatural/Horror/ Fantasy
Airdate: 10/23/91
Rating: N/A   A/C:

A time travel experiment goes awry, trapping a girl from the future in 1990. A sympathetic family helps her retrieve her vehicle from a dastardly time-bandit and return home.

Production Company: Film Australia IAW The Nine Network
Executive Producer .... Ron Saunders
Producer .... Noel Price
Director .... Kathy Mueller
Writer .... Mark Shirrefs
Writer .... John Thomson
Cast .... Katharine Cullen
Cast .... Melissa Marshall
Cast .... James Findlay
Cast .... Helen O'Connor

GIRL WHO CAME BETWEEN THEM, THE   NBC
Drama: Family Drama • Cross-Cultural Story • Children/Teens • Social Issue • Vietnam • True Story
Airdate: 04/01/90
Rating: 13.2/21   A/C: 2

When Vietnam veteran Barry Huntoon discovers years after the war that he fathered a daughter, he brings her to America and his family must deal with old resentments and cultural differences.

Production Company: Saban/Scherick Prods. & Saban International N.V.
Executive Producer .... Edgar J. Scherick
Executive Producer .... Haim Saban
Producer .... Lynn Raynor
Director .... Mel Damski
Writer .... Audrey Davis Levin
Cast .... Cheryl Ladd
Cast .... Anthony John Denison
Cast .... Melissa Chan

GLADIATOR, THE   ABC
Drama: Action/Adventure • Man Against The System • Social Issue
Airdate: 2/2/86
Rating: 15.9/24   A/C:

After his brother is killed by a drunk driver, a man seeks revenge on all motorists, becoming a highway vigilante and ultimately catching his brother's killer.

Production Company: New World TV
Executive Producer .... Jeffrey Walker
Executive Producer .... Michael Chase Walker
Executive Producer .... Tom Schuman
Producer .... Robert Lovenheim
Director .... Abel Ferrara
Writer .... William Bleich
Cast .... Ken Wahl
Cast .... Nancy Allen
Cast .... Robert Culp

GLITTER   ABC
Drama: Series Pilot (2 hr.) • Sex/Glitz
Airdate: 09/13/84
Rating: 15.9/27   A/C:

The Staff of "Glitter," a celebrity oriented magazine, investigates the relationship between a dying madam and a U.S. senator.

Production Company: Aaron Spelling Prods.
Executive Producer .... Aaron Spelling
Executive Producer .... Douglas S. Cramer
Producer .... Lynn Loring
Director .... Jackie Cooper
Writer .... Art Baer
Writer .... Ben Joelson
Writer .... Nancy Sackett
Cast .... David Birney
Cast .... Morgan Brittany
Cast .... Christopher Mayer
Cast .... Tracy Nelson

GLITTER DOME, THE   HBO
Drama: Cops/Detectives/Law Enforcement • Murder and Murder Mystery
Airdate: 11/18/84
Rating: N/A   A/C:

Based on the novel by Joseph Wambaugh. Two Los Angeles cops set out to crack the murder of a film mogul. Their investigation takes them into the seamy side of Hollywood where they uncover a network of hustlers, drug dealers and killers. A sympathetic, hard-living actress aids them in their search.

Production Company: HBO Premiere Films
Executive Producer .... Frank Konigsberg
Producer .... Stuart Margolin
Producer .... Justis Greene
Director .... Stuart Margolin
Writer .... Stanley Kallis
Cast .... James Garner
Cast .... John Lithgow
Cast .... Margot Kidder
Cast .... Colleen Dewhurst

GLITZ   NBC
Drama: Murder and Murder Mystery • Cops/ Detectives/Law Enforcement • Suspense/Thriller • Foreign or Exotic Location
Airdate: 10/21/88
Rating: 14.1/25   A/C:

A Miami police detective recovering from a gunshot wound in Puerto Rico goes after a former girlfriend's killer, who is really stalking him instead.

Production Company: Lorimar-Telepictures/ Robert Cooper Films
Executive Producer .... Gary Adelson
Executive Producer .... Robert Cooper
Executive Producer .... David R. Ginsburg
Producer .... Steve McGlothen
Director .... Sandor Stern
Writer .... Alan Trustman
Writer .... Stephen Zito
Cast .... Jimmy Smits
Cast .... Markie Post
Cast .... John Diehl
Cast .... Robin Strasser

GLORY DAYS   CBS
Drama: Family Drama • Sports
Airdate: 12/11/88
Rating: 11.1/17   A/C:

A driven businessman retires, enrolls in college, and goes out for the football squad.

Production Company: A. Shane Co. with Sibling Rivalries
Executive Producer .... Joan Conrad
Producer .... Roger Bacon
Producer .... Glenn D. Banner
Director .... Robert Conrad
Writer .... Tim Stack
Writer .... Larry B. Williams
Writer .... David J. Kinghorn
Cast .... Robert Conrad
Cast .... Stacy Edwards
Cast .... Jennifer O'Neill
Cast .... Shane Conrad

GO TOWARD THE LIGHT — CBS

Drama: Family Drama • Children/Teens • Medical/Disease/Mental Illness
Airdate: 11/01/88
Rating: 14.9/24   A/C:

The courage of a nine year old hemophiliac dying of AIDS inspires his family and friends to face death as he does.

Production Company: Corapeak Prods. IAW Polson Co.
Executive Producer .... Beth Polson
Producer .... Nick Lombardo
Director .... Mike Robe
Writer .... Susan Nanus
Writer .... Beth Polson
Cast .... Linda Hamilton
Cast .... Piper Laurie
Cast .... Richard Thomas
Cast .... Gary Bayer

GOD BLESS THE CHILD — ABC

Drama: Family Drama • Children/Teens • Social Issue
Airdate: 03/21/88
Rating: 17.7/28   A/C:

The homeless mother of a small child struggles with the challenge of daily survival.

Production Company: IndieProd Prods. IAW Phoenix Entertainment Group Inc.
Executive Producer .... Bruce J. Sallan
Producer .... Andras Hamori
Co-Producer .... Dennis Nemec
Director .... Larry Elikann
Writer .... Dennis Nemec
Cast .... Mare Winningham
Cast .... Dorian Harewood
Cast .... Grace Johnston

GODDESS OF LOVE — NBC

Comedy: Sci-Fi/Supernatural/Horror/Fantasy • Romantic Comedy
Airdate: 11/20/88
Rating: 16.7/26   A/C:

Unless she can find a man who truly loves her, the Goddess Venus will be turned into a statue forever. She goes after an L.A. hairdresser, but when she realizes that he loves someone else, the other gods decide she can return to Mount Olympus.

Production Company: Phil Margo Enterprises Inc.
Executive Producer .... Phil Margo
Producer .... Don Segall
Co-Producer .... Ray Manzella
Director .... Jim Drake
Writer .... Phil Margo
Cast .... Vanna White
Cast .... David Leisure
Cast .... David Naughton
Cast .... Betsy Palmer

GOING FOR THE GOLD: THE BILL JOHNSON STORY — CBS

Drama: True Story • Sports
Airdate: 05/08/85
Rating: 8.9/14   A/C:

The true story of a young Oregon man who goes from being a car thief to winning a gold medal in the '84 Olympic downhill ski event.

Production Company: Goodman-Rosen Prods. & Carter Interests IAW ITC Prods.
Executive Producer .... Judith A. Polone
Producer .... Gary Goodman
Producer .... Barry Rosen
Director .... Don Taylor
Writer .... Maxwell Pitt
Cast .... Anthony Edwards
Cast .... Sarah Jessica Parker
Cast .... Deborah Van Valkenburgh
Cast .... Dennis Weaver
Cast .... Ed Bishop

GOING TO THE CHAPEL — NBC

Comedy: Romantic Comedy
Airdate: 10/09/88
Rating: 15.0/25   A/C:

Friends and family inadvertently do more to tear an engaged couple apart than help them out as their wedding approaches.

Production Company: Furia Organization IAW Finnegan-Pinchuk Co.
Executive Producer .... Barry Oringer
Producer .... Sheldon Pinchuk
Producer .... Pat Finnegan
Producer .... Bill Finnegan
Director .... Paul Lynch
Writer .... Erik Tarloff
Cast .... Barbara Billingsley
Cast .... Michael Talbott
Cast .... Scott Valentine
Cast .... Cloris Leachman
Cast .... Mark Linn-Baker
Cast .... John Ratzenberger
Cast .... Eileen Brennan

GOOD COPS, BAD COPS — NBC

Drama: Cops/Detectives/Law Enforcement • Suspense/Thriller • True Crime
Airdate: 12/09/90
Rating: 8.9/14   A/C: 2

Based on the book "The Cops Are Robbers" by Gerald Clemente and Kevin Stevens. A tough superintendent comes to the Boston police department to snare a pair of bankrobbing cops in the city's biggest bank heist caper.

Production Company: Kushner-Locke IAW Commonwealth Films, Inc.
Executive Producer .... Peter Locke
Executive Producer .... Donald Kushner
Producer .... Fred Whitehead
Producer .... Peter McCann
Producer .... William Bleich
Director .... Paul Wendkos
Writer .... William Bleich
Cast .... Ray Sharkey
Cast .... Steve Railsback
Cast .... Edward Asner
Cast .... James Keach

GOOD FIGHT, THE — LIFETIME

Drama: Social Issue • Woman Against The System • Courtroom Drama • Medical/Disease/Mental Illness
Airdate: 12/15/92
Rating: N/A   A/C:

An attorney and concerned mother sues a chewing tobacco company when a family friend, a star high school baseball player, is diagnosed with oral cancer. Her ex husband, a retired trial attorney, lends his support as they battle their wealthy corporate opponents.

Production Company: Freyda Rothstein Pros. IAW Hearst Ent. Prods.
Executive Producer .... Freyda Rothstein
Producer .... Julian Marks
Director .... John David Coles
Writer .... Beth Gutcheon
Cast .... Christine Lahti
Cast .... Terry O'Quinn
Cast .... Jonathan Crombie

GOOD NIGHT, SWEET WIFE: A MURDER IN BOSTON — CBS

Drama: Family Drama • Murder and Murder Mystery • True Crime • Family Violence
Airdate: 09/25/90
Rating: 14.9/23   A/C: 3

A journalist and a police reporter unearth Charles Stuart's 1989 plot to murder his wife. Stuart's hoax, in which he faked a violent robbery and pinned the blame on an anonymous black street youth, caused an uproar in racially divided Boston.

Production Company: CBS Entertainment Prods., Arnold Shapiro Prods.
Executive Producer .... Arnold Shapiro
Producer .... Jean O'Neill
Co-Producer .... Nancy Jacoby
Co-Producer .... Ken Swor
Director .... Jerrold Freedman
Writer .... Daniel Freudenberger
Cast .... Ken Olin
Cast .... Margaret Colin
Cast .... Annabella Price
Cast .... B.D. Wong

GORE VIDAL'S BILLY THE KID — TNT

Drama: Western • Biography • Period Piece
Airdate: 5/10/89
Rating: N/A   A/C:

The relationship between wild outlaw Billy the Kid and his former sidekick and mentor Pat Garrett, who now under the protection of his Marshall's badge, tracks his old pal down and in a violent confrontation kills him. Thus setting the stage for a new justice in the American West.

Production Company: von Zerneck/Sertner Films IAW TNT
Producer .... Frank von Zerneck
Producer .... Robert M. Sertner
Director .... William A. Graham
Writer .... Gore Vidal
Cast .... Val Kilmer
Cast .... Duncan Regehr
Cast .... Wilford Brimley

GOTHAM — SHOWTIME

Drama: Sci-Fi/Supernatural/Horror/Fantasy • Cops/
Detectives/Law Enforcement
Airdate: 8/21/88
Rating: N/A   A/C:

A down-on-his-luck detective becomes entangled in an erotic web of supernatural danger when he is hired to locate a hauntingly beautiful socialite, whose husband claims that she died tragically, but has returned to torment him. After agreeing to track the "ghost" down he quickly finds himself in over his head, seduced by her powerful allure.

Production Company: Phoenix Entertainment
   Group, Ketih Addis and Associates Production
Executive Producer .... Keith Addis
Executive Producer .... Gerald I. Isenberg
Producer .... David Latt
Co-Producer .... Eli Johnson
Director .... Lloyd Johnson
Writer .... Lloyd Johnson'
Cast .... Tommy Lee Jones
Cast .... Virginia Madsen
Cast .... Colin Bruce
Cast .... Kevin Jarre

GRAND ISLE — TNT

Drama: Forbidden Love • Period Piece • Woman's
Issue/Story
Airdate: 07/14/92
Rating: N/A   A/C:

Based on the book "The Awakening" by Kate Chopin. In the 1800's, a New Orleans socialite's flirtation while vacationing off the Louisiana coast leads to new self-awareness and conflict with her traditional role, resulting in the disintegration of her marriage, her disgrace and eventual suicide.

Production Company: Awakening Inc. IAW TNT
   Films
Executive Producer .... Kelly McGillis
Executive Producer .... Carolyn Pfeiffer
Director .... Mary Lambert
Writer .... Hesper Anderson
Cast .... Kelly McGillis
Cast .... Jon De Vries
Cast .... Adrian Pasdar

GRASS ROOTS — NBC

Miniseries/Drama (2 nights): Family Drama • Murder
and Murder Mystery • Courtroom Drama • Political
Piece
Airdate: 02/24/92 • 02/25/92
Rating: 13.4/20 • 15.1/23   A/C: 3 • 2

Based on the book by Stuart Woods. A Southern senatorial candidate is chosen as defense attorney in a racially-charged murder case. He fights to save his reputation as he is lured by sexual entanglements, haunted by family skeletons, and targeted by white supremacists.

Production Company: Team Cherokee Inc. IAW
   JBS Prods. Inc.
Executive Producer .... Aaron Spelling
Executive Producer .... E. Duke Vincent
Producer .... Martin Manulis
Director .... Jerry London
Writer .... Derek Marlowe
Cast .... Corbin Bernsen
Cast .... Mel Harris
Cast .... John Glover
Cast .... Reginald VelJohnson
Cast .... James Wilder
Cast .... Katherine Helmond

GRAVE SECRETS: THE LEGACY OF HILLTOP DRIVE — CBS

Drama: Family Drama • Sci-Fi/Supernatural/Horror/
Fantasy
Airdate: 03/03/92
Rating: 14.7/23   A/C: 2

Based on the book the "Black Hope Horror" by Ben & Jean Williams. A suburban family and their neighbors are terrified by supernatural occurrences and ghostly undoings. They are forced to move when they discover that their neighborhood sits atop an ancestral burial ground.

Production Company: Freyda Rothstein Prod.
   IAW Hearst Entertainment
Executive Producer .... Freyda Rothstein
Director .... John Patterson
Writer .... Gregory Goodell
Cast .... Patty Duke
Cast .... David Selby
Cast .... Kiersten Warren
Cast .... Blake Clark

GREAT ESCAPE I I: THE UNTOLD STORY, THE — NBC

Miniseries/Drama (2 nights): Action/Adventure •
WWII • Nazis • Prison and Prison Camp
Airdate: 11/06/88 • 11/07/88
Rating: 14.4/23 • 12.3/19   A/C:

An American pilot escapes from a World War II German prison camp and tracks down both the killers of his fellow escapees and the singer who helped him survive his own escape.

Production Company: Michael Jaffe Films Ltd.
   IAW Spectacor Films
Executive Producer .... Michael Jaffe
Producer .... Jud Taylor
Director .... Paul Wendkos
Director .... Jud Taylor
Writer .... Walter Halsey Davis
Cast .... Christopher Reeve
Cast .... Ian McShane
Cast .... Judd Hirsch
Cast .... Donald Pleasence
Cast .... Charles Haid
Cast .... Michael Nader

GREAT EXPECTATIONS — DISNEY

Miniseries/Drama (3 Nights): Period Piece • Children/
Teens • Foreign or Exotic Location • Love Story
Airdate: 07/09/89 • 07/10/89 • 07/11/89
Rating: N/A   A/C:

Charles Dickens' classic story of Pip, a poor young orphan whose life and lowly station are changed forever by an anonymous benefactor and the strange Miss Havisham.

Production Company: Primetime Ent./Harlech
   Television
Producer .... Greg Smith
Director .... Kevin Connor
Writer .... John Goldsmith
Cast .... Anthony Hopkins
Cast .... Jean Simmons
Cast .... John Rhys-Davies

GREAT PRETENDER, THE — NBC

Drama: Murder and Murder Mystery • Man Against
The System • Mafia/Mob
Airdate: 04/14/91
Rating: 8.5/14   A/C: 3

A malcontent prize-winning journalist, with the help of a cub reporter, uncovers corruption and mob alliances, which eventually implicate the publisher of his paper.

Production Company: Stephen J. Cannell Prods.
Executive Producer .... Stephen J. Cannell
Producer .... Art Monterastelli
Director .... Gus Trikonis
Writer .... Stephen J. Cannell
Cast .... Bruce Greenwood
Cast .... Jessica Steen
Cast .... Gregg Henry

GREEN DOLPHIN BEAT   FBC

Drama: Cops/Detectives/Law Enforcement • Series
Pilot (2 hr.)
Airdate: 6/27/94
Rating: 4.4/8   A/C: 4

*A group of offbeat cops in a big city precinct
investigate the murder of a former prostitute.*

Production Company: Robert Ward Prods.,
    Spelling TV
Executive Producer .... Robert Ward
Executive Producer .... Aaron Spelling
Executive Producer .... E. Duke Vincent
Producer .... Christopher Morgan
Director .... Tommy Lee Wallace
Writer .... Robert Ward
Cast .... John Wesley Shipp
Cast .... Jeffrey Sams
Cast .... Troy Evans

GREGORY K   ABC

Drama: Children/Teens • Family Drama • True Story
• Courtroom Drama • Social Issue
Airdate: 2/9/93
Rating: 10.3/16   A/C: 3

*The 1992 ground breaking case of a twelve year
old Florida boy who sues his abusive biological
parents for "divorce" so he can be adopted by
his loving foster family, George and Lizabeth
Russ.*

Note: See CBS Movie- "Place to Be Loved, A"

Production Company: Spectacor Films Ltd. IAW
    Michael Jaffe Films
Executive Producer .... Michael Jaffe
Executive Producer .... Howard Braunstein
Producer .... Linda Otto
Director .... Linda Otto
Writer .... Sharon Doyle
Cast .... Bill Smitrovich
Cast .... Kathleen York
Cast .... Joseph Gordon Levitt

GUARDIAN, THE   HBO

Drama: Suspense/Thriller • Social Issue
Airdate: 10/20/84
Rating: N/A   A/C:

*A group of Manhattan apartment dwellers who,
in the aftermath of a murder within their
building, hire as a security guard, a no-
nonsense ex-military man. Everyone is pleased
with his determination to make the residence
safe except a liberal television director who
begins to wonder if the new guard is a protector
or instigator when a series of strange incidents
happen in the building.*

Production Company: HBO Premiere Films
Executive Producer .... Stanley Chase
Executive Producer .... Richard Levinson
Executive Producer .... William Link
Producer .... Robert Cooper
Director .... David Greene
Writer .... Richard Levinson
Writer .... William Link
Cast .... Martin Sheen
Cast .... Louis Gossett, Jr.
Cast .... Arthur Hill
Cast .... Tandy Cronyn

GUESS WHO'S COMING FOR CHRISTMAS
NBC

Drama: Holiday Special • Sci-Fi/Supernatural/
Fantasy
Airdate: 12/23/90
Rating: 10.9/19   A/C: 2

*An eccentric hardware store owner learns the
true meaning of Christmas through his
friendship with an interstellar visitor.*

Production Company: Corapeake Prods. IAW Fox
    Unicorn Inc.
Executive Producer .... Beth Polson
Producer .... Randy Siegel
Director .... Paul Schneider
Writer .... Blair Ferguson
Cast .... Richard Mulligan
Cast .... Barbara Barrie
Cast .... Paul Dooley
Cast .... Beau Bridges

GUILTY CONSCIENCE   CBS

Mystery: Suspense/Thriller • Sci-Fi/Supernatural/
Horror/Fantasy
Airdate: 04/02/85
Rating: 10.8/18   A/C:

*A adulterous criminal attorney fantasizes about
different ways to kill his wife. We see him play
out in his mind the planning of the perfect crime,
then the trial. Meanwhile, he discovers his wife
has her own plans to do him in.*

Production Company: Levinson-Link Prods. IAW
    Robert Papazian Prods.
Executive Producer .... Richard Levinson
Executive Producer .... William Link
Producer .... Robert A. Papazian
Director .... David Greene
Writer .... Richard Levinson
Writer .... William Link
Cast .... Anthony Hopkins
Cast .... Blythe Danner
Cast .... Swoosie Kurtz

GUILTY OF INNOCENCE: THE LENELL
GETER STORY   CBS

Drama: Black Story • Man Against The System •
Prison and Prison Camp • Social Issue • True Story •
Courtroom Drama
Airdate: 02/03/87
Rating: 15.7/25   A/C:

*True story of a naive black Texas engineer who
was wrongly convicted of robbery despite a
solid alibi and sentenced to life imprisonment.*

Production Company: Embassy TV
Executive Producer .... Sheri Singer
Producer .... Fern Field
Director .... Richard T. Heffron
Writer .... Harold Gast
Cast .... Dorian Harewood
Cast .... Gary Grubbs
Cast .... Dabney Coleman
Cast .... Debbi Morgan
Cast .... Paul Winfield

GUILTY UNTIL PROVEN INNOCENT   NBC

Drama: Man Against The System • True Story •
Courtroom Drama • Social Issue • Prison and Prison
Camp
Airdate: 09/22/91
Rating: 11.8/19   A/C: 2

*High school dropout Bobby McLaughlin is
convicted of a 1979 Brooklyn, N.Y. murder by
the questionable testimony of a 15-year-old
eyewitness. His foster father Harold Honne's
6-year crusade to reopen the case wins his son's
release and love.*

Production Company: Cosgrove/Meurer Prods.
Executive Producer .... Terry Meurer
Executive Producer .... John Cosgrove
Producer .... Jay Benson
Co-Producer .... Cynthia Whitcomb
Director .... Paul Wendkos
Writer .... Cynthia Whitcomb
Cast .... Martin Sheen
Cast .... Brendan Fraser
Cast .... Caroline Kava
Cast .... Zachary Mott

GULAG   HBO

Drama: Prison and Prison Camp • Foreign or Exotic
Location • Action/Adventure
Airdate: 1/13/85
Rating: N/A   A/C:

*An American sportscaster who goes to Moscow
to cover an international sporting event is
railroaded by the KGB into a Russian labor
camp. Unable to adapt to the prison's inhumane
conditions, he plans a daring escape with the
aid of a fellow prisoner.*

Production Company: HBO Premiere Films
Executive Producer .... James Retter
Executive Producer .... Dan Gordon
Producer .... Andrew Adelson
Director .... Roger Young
Writer .... Dan Gordon
Cast .... David Keith
Cast .... Malcolm McDowell
Cast .... David Suchet

GUNSMOKE III: TO THE LAST MAN
CBS

Drama: Period Piece • Western
Airdate: 01/10/92
Rating: 14.2/24   A/C: 1

*As retired Marshal Matt Dillon pursues the man
who stole his cattle and murdered his ranch
foreman, he is drawn into the conflict of the
Pleasant Valley War in the Arizona Territory of
the 1880's.*

Production Company: CBS Entertainment Prods.
Producer .... Ken Swor
Director .... Jerry Jameson
Writer .... Earl W. Wallace
Cast .... James Arness
Cast .... Amy Stock-Poynton
Cast .... Jason Lively
Cast .... Pat Hingle

GUNSMOKE: ONE MAN'S JUSTICE CBS
Drama: Western • Period Piece
Airdate: 2/10/94
Rating: 11.5/17   A/C: 2

The former legendary lawman, Matt Dillon and a traveling salesman team up to help a fifteen year old boy track down the outlaws who killed his mother during a stagecoach robbery.

Production Company: CBS Entertainment Prods.
Executive Producer .... James Arness
Producer .... Norman Powell
Producer .... Jerry Jameson
Director .... Jerry Jameson
Writer .... Harry Longstreet
Writer .... Renee Longstreet
Cast .... James Arness
Cast .... Bruce Boxleitner
Cast .... Kelly Morgan
Cast .... Amy Stock-Poynton

GUNSMOKE: RETURN TO DODGE   CBS
Drama: Western • Period Piece
Airdate: 09/26/87
Rating: 16.6/31   A/C:

Once again, an outlaw has Marshal Dillon in his sights.

Production Company: CBS Entertainment
Producer .... John Mantley
Director .... Vincent McEveety
Writer .... Jim Byrnes
Cast .... James Arness
Cast .... Earl Holliman
Cast .... Amanda Blake
Cast .... Buck Taylor
Cast .... Steve Forrest

GUNSMOKE: THE LAST APACHE   CBS
Drama: Western
Airdate: 03/18/90
Rating: 19.7/32   A/C: 1

It's 1886 and a renegade Apache abducts the daughter Matt Dillon never knew he had. No longer a U.S. Marshal, he takes the law into his own hands.

Production Company: CBS Entertainment IAW
    Galatea Prods., Inc.
Executive Producer .... John Mantley
Producer .... Stan Hough
Director .... Charles Correll
Writer .... Earl W. Wallace
Cast .... James Arness
Cast .... Richard Kiley
Cast .... Michael Learned
Cast .... Geoffrey Lewis

GUNSMOKE: THE LONG RIDE HOME CBS
Drama: Western
Airdate: 5/8/93
Rating: 10.2/19   A/C: 1

Matt Dillon is back in the saddle chasing a band of murdering thieves one of whom is a dead ringer for our hero. The posse is in hot pursuit thinking Matts' the bad dude. Of course the ex-marshall of Dodge gets his man.

Production Company: CBS Ent.
Executive Producer .... James Arness
Producer .... Norman Powell
Director .... Jerry Jameson
Writer .... Bill Statton
Cast .... James Arness
Cast .... James Brolin
Cast .... Ali MacGraw

GUTS AND GLORY: THE RISE AND FALL OF OLIVER NORTH   CBS
Miniseries/Drama (2 nights): True Story • Historical Piece • Biography • Period Piece
Airdate: 04/30/89 • 05/02/89
Rating: 14.0/23 • 9.6/13   A/C:

Based on the book by Ben Bradlee Jr. True story of Col. Oliver North's life from his early years at the Naval Academy to his involvement in the Iran-Contra Affair.

Production Company: Mike Robe Prods. IAW
    Papazian-Hirsch Ent.
Executive Producer .... Mike Robe
Producer .... Robert A. Papazian
Producer .... James G. Hirsch
Director .... Mike Robe
Writer .... Mike Robe
Cast .... David Keith
Cast .... Peter Boyle
Cast .... Amy Stock-Poynton
Cast .... Annette O'Toole

GYPSY   CBS
Musical (3 hrours): Family Drama • Period Piece
Airdate: 12/12/93
Rating: 18.6/28   A/C: 1

Based on the 1959 play by Arthur Laurents, Jule Styne, Stephen Sondheim. During the 1920s and 1930s a hard driving, ambitious stage mother seeks stardom for her two daughters, Rose and June, in the hectic halls of vaudeville. When one of the girls drops out of the act, Mama Rose relentlessly pushes the other child into becoming a burlesque stripper known as Gypsy Rose Lee. Note: 3 hours

Production Company: RHI Ent. Inc.
Executive Producer .... Robert Halmi, Sr.
Executive Producer .... Craig Zadan
Executive Producer .... Neil Meron
Executive Producer .... Bonnie Bruckheimer
Producer .... Emile Ardolino
Producer .... Cindy Gilmore
Director .... Emile Ardolino
Writer .... Arthur Laurents
Cast .... Bette Midler
Cast .... Peter Riegert
Cast .... Cynthia Gibb
Cast .... Edward Asner
Cast .... Christine Ebersole

HABITATION OF DRAGONS, THE   TNT
Drama: Family Drama • Period Piece
Airdate: 9/8/92
Rating: N/A   A/C:

Based on the play by Horton Foote. In the mid 1930's a small town Texas family faces betrayal, sibling rivalry and despair when two of the brothers involve themselves in local politics. When one their wives' extramarital affair is uncovered and one of their children is drowned in an accident, the family is irreparably torn apart.

Production Company: Brandman Prods. IAW
    Amblin Ent.
Executive Producer .... Michael Brandman
Producer .... Donald Borchers
Director .... Michael Lindsay-Hogg
Writer .... Horton Foote
Cast .... Brad Davis
Cast .... Frederic Forrest
Cast .... Maureen O'Sullivan
Cast .... Hallie Foote
Cast .... Jean Stapleton

HANDS OF A MURDERER   CBS
Mystery: Murder and Murder Mystery • Period Piece
Airdate: 05/16/90
Rating: 9.5/17   A/C: 3

Sherlock Holmes rescues his cryptologist brother with the help of Dr. Watson, after his brother is kidnapped by Holmes' nemesis, the evil Moriarty.

Production Company: Storke/Fuisz Prods. IAW
    Yorkshire Television
Executive Producer .... William F. Storke
Executive Producer .... Robert E. Fuisz
Producer .... Norman Foster
Director .... Stuart Orme
Writer .... Charles Edward Pogue
Cast .... Edward Woodward
Cast .... John Hillerman
Cast .... Anthony Andrews
Cast .... Kim Thomson

HANDS OF A STRANGER   NBC
Miniseries/Drama (2 nights): Family Drama • Cops/Detectives/Law Enforcement • Rape/Molestation
Airdate: 05/10/87 • 05/11/87
Rating: 15.2/25 • 17.4/28   A/C:

From Robert Daley's novel about a police detective determined to uncover the truth about his wife's rape. He becomes involved with a female assistant district attorney and learns his wife was raped by the man with whom she was having an affair.

Production Company: Edgar J. Scherick
    Associates Prods. IAW Taft Entertainment TV
Executive Producer .... Edgar J. Scherick
Executive Producer .... Gary Hoffman
Producer .... Lynn Raynor
Director .... Larry Elikann
Writer .... Arthur Kopit
Cast .... Armand Assante
Cast .... Beverly D'Angelo
Cast .... Blair Brown
Cast .... Arliss Howard
Cast .... Michael Lerner

HAREM   ABC

Miniseries/Drama (2 nights): Action/Adventure •
Foreign or Exotic Location • Historical Piece • Period
Piece • Woman In Jeopardy • Sex/Glitz
Airdate: 02/09/86 • 02/10/86
Rating: 16.9/25 • 16.2/23   A/C:

*Around 1900, an American engaged to a British
diplomat is kidnapped and sold into the harem
of the Turkish sultan, where she is endangered
on account of the number one wife's jealousy.
She is finally rescued and the sultan deposed.*

Production Company: Highgate Pictures
Executive Producer .... Martin Manulis
Producer .... Michael Dryhurst
Director .... Billy Hale
Writer .... Karol Ann Hoeffner
Cast .... Omar Sharif
Cast .... Yaphet Kotto
Cast .... Sarah Miles
Cast .... Nancy Travis
Cast .... Ava Gardner

HARMFUL INTENT   CBS

Drama: Suspense/Thriller • Murder and Murder
Mystery
Airdate: 12/14/93
Rating: 12.2/20   A/C: 2

*Based on the book by Dr. Robin Cook. An
anesthesiologist is convicted of the murder of a
pregnant women when she dies on the table
after receiving an overdoes of medication. After
jumping bail he enlists the aid of the wife of an
old medical school buddy who was also
prosecuted for the same crime two years earlier.
Together they uncover a psychotic orderly who
is killing patients for a high power law firm
that is involved in insurance fraud.*

Production Company: Rosemont Prods.
Executive Producer .... Norman Rosemont
Executive Producer .... David A. Rosemont
Executive Producer .... Benjamin Melniker
Executive Producer .... Michael Uslan
Director .... John Patterson
Writer .... Martha Weingartner
Cast .... Tim Matheson
Cast .... Emma Samms
Cast .... Robert Pastorelli

HARRY'S HONG KONG   ABC

Drama: Murder and Murder Mystery • Action/
Adventure • Foreign or Exotic Location • Series Pilot
(2 hr.)
Airdate: 05/08/87
Rating: 6.1/11   A/C:

*While Hong Kong gangsters chase a mercenary
because they think he has the gold his friend
stole, the mercenary must also find an innocent
tourist who has inadvertently become involved,
as well as find his friend's murderer.*

Production Company: Aaron Spelling Prods.
Executive Producer .... Aaron Spelling
Executive Producer .... Douglas S. Cramer
Producer .... Jerry London
Co-Producer .... James L. Conway
Director .... Jerry London
Writer .... Richard Alan Simmons
Cast .... David Soul
Cast .... Julia Nickson
Cast .... David Hemmings
Cast .... Mel Harris

HART TO HART RETURNS   NBC

Drama: Action/Adventure
Airdate: 11/5/93
Rating: 13.1/23   A/C: 2

*From the series. The jet setting crime solvers
are off to find the evil business magnate who is
bent on destroying the Harts financially and
frames them for the murder of a business
competitor.*

Production Company: Papazian-Hirsch Ent.
   Robert Wagner Prods., Columbia Pictures
Executive Producer .... Robert Wagner
Executive Producer .... Robert A. Papazian
Executive Producer .... James G. Hirsch
Executive Producer .... James Veres
Producer .... Stefanie Powers
Producer .... James Polster
Director .... Peter H. Hunt
Writer .... Jack Kaplan
Writer .... Richard Chapman
Writer .... James G. Hirsch
Cast .... Robert Wagner
Cast .... Stefanie Powers
Cast .... Mike Connors
Cast .... Ken Howard

HARVEST FOR THE HEART   FAMILY

Drama: Family Drama • Farm Story
Airdate: 4/16/94
Rating: N/A   A/C:

*After a twenty year absence, a musician returns
to the family farm that his angry brother and
elderly father are trying to keep from going belly
up. While trying to help out, he is forced to
face long held resentments and unresolved
emotional turmoil caused by his lack of
responsibility.*

Production Company: Atlantis Films, Credi Group
   IAW Family Channel, CIDO, CTV, NBC Prods.
Executive Producer .... Derek Mazur
Executive Producer .... Peter Sussman
Executive Producer .... Peter Engel
Producer .... Kim Todd
Director .... Michael Scott
Writer .... Malcolm MacRury
Cast .... Ted Shackelford
Cast .... Ron White
Cast .... Rebecca Jenkins
Cast .... Ken Pogue

HAUNTED BY HER PAST   NBC

Drama: Psychological Thriller • Sci-Fi/Supernatural/
Horror/Fantasy
Airdate: 10/05/87
Rating: 16.7/27   A/C:

*While staying in the room of an old New
England inn, a woman becomes possessed by
the spirit of one of her witch ancestors and tries
to kill her husband.*

Production Company: Norton Wright Prods. IAW
   ITC Prods. Inc.
Executive Producer .... Norton Wright
Producer .... Terry Morse
Director .... Michael Pressman
Writer .... Barry Schneider
Cast .... Susan Lucci
Cast .... Robin Thomas
Cast .... Marcia Strassman
Cast .... John James

HAUNTED, THE   FBC

Drama: Suspense/Thriller • True Story • Sci-Fi/
Supernatural/Horror/Fantasy
Airdate: 05/06/91
Rating: 8.4/13   A/C: 4

*Based on the book by Robert Curran. The
peaceful life of a religious Pennsylvania family
is thrown into turmoil by supernatural forces
hell-bent on their destruction.*

Production Company: FNM Films
Executive Producer .... Bohdan Zachary
Producer .... Daniel Schneider
Director .... Robert Mandel
Writer .... Darrah Cloud
Cast .... Sally Kirkland
Cast .... Jeffrey DeMunn
Cast .... Louise Latham
Cast .... George D. Wallace

HAWAIIAN HEAT — ABC

Drama: Cops/Detectives/Law Enforcement • Series
Pilot (2 hr.) • Foreign or Exotic Location
Airdate: 09/14/84
Rating: 19.1/34   A/C:

Two Chicago police officers move to Hawaii and go to work for the local criminal investigations dept. where they befriend a beautiful helicopter pilot.

Production Company: James D. Parriott Prods.
   IAW Universal TV

Executive Producer	James D. Parriott
Producer	Douglas Green
Producer	Dean Zanetos
Director	Michael Vejar
Writer	James D. Parriott
Cast	Robert Ginty
Cast	Tracy Scoggins
Cast	Mako
Writer	Jeff McCracken

HAZARD OF HEARTS, A — CBS

Drama: Love Story • Period Piece • Action/Adventure
Airdate: 12/27/87
Rating: 15.3/26   A/C:

In this Barbara Cartland novel of Restoration England, a young woman, passed from hand to hand in settlement of gambling debts, discovers a smuggling plot.

Production Company: Grade Co. with
   Gainsborough Pictures

Producer	Albert Fennell
Producer	John Hough
Director	John Hough
Writer	Terence Feely
Cast	Stewart Granger
Cast	Christopher Plummer
Cast	Edward Fox
Cast	Diana Rigg

HE'S FIRED, SHE'S HIRED — CBS

Comedy: Woman's Issue/Story
Airdate: 12/18/84
Rating: 14.2/23   A/C:

When a New York advertising executive loses his job, his homemaker wife gets a job in the same business. Then, while he stays home to write a novel, she becomes a great success using his help and his ideas.

Production Company: CBS Entertainment

Producer	Stan Hough
Director	Marc Daniels
Writer	Bob Shanks
Cast	Wayne Rogers
Cast	Karen Valentine
Cast	Elizabeth Ashley
Cast	Frederick Koehler
Cast	Martha Byrne

HE'S NOT YOUR SON — CBS

Drama: Family Drama • Children/Teens • Medical/Disease/Mental Illness
Airdate: 10/03/84
Rating: 23.2/36   A/C:

Two couples give birth to sons on the same day and at the same hospital and the boys are inadvertently switched. The error is then discovered when one of the boys develops a heart ailment.

Production Company: CBS Entertainment

Producer	Sam Strangis
Co-Producer	Alan Collis
Director	Don Taylor
Writer	Robert Fried
Writer	Alida Van Gores
Writer	Arnold Margolin
Writer	Alan Collis
Cast	Ken Howard
Cast	Donna Mills
Cast	Dorothy Malone
Cast	Ann Dusenberry

HEADS — SHOWTIME

Drama: Murder and Murder Mystery • Suspense/Thriller
Airdate: 1/29/94
Rating: N/A   A/C:

A geek rookie reporter on a small town newspaper tries to make a good impression on his contentious, reprehensible boss by trying to solve a string of grisly murders that has befallen the community.

Production Company: Showtime Ent., Atlantis
   Films Ltd., Credo Group Ltd., Sojourn Pictures
   Ltd., Davis Ent. TV

Executive Producer	Peter Sussman
Executive Producer	Martin Tudor
Executive Producer	Bill Gray
Producer	Jonathan Goodwill
Producer	Derek Mazur
Director	Paul Shapiro
Writer	Jay Stapleton
Writer	Adam Brooks
Cast	Edward Asner
Cast	Jon Cryer
Cast	Jennifer Tilly
Cast	Roddy McDowall

HEARST AND DAVIES AFFAIR, THE — ABC

Drama: Love Story • True Story • Period Piece • Hollywood • Biography
Airdate: 01/14/85
Rating: 16.2/24   A/C:

The true story of the scandalous romance between newspaper tycoon Randolph Hearst and his movie star mistress Marion Davies.

Production Company: ABC Circle Films

Producer	Paul Pompian
Director	David Lowell Rich
Writer	Alison Cross
Writer	David Solomon
Cast	Robert Mitchum
Cast	Virginia Madsen
Cast	Fritz Weaver
Cast	Doris Belack

HEART OF A CHAMPION: THE RAY MANCINI STORY — CBS

Drama: True Story • Sports • Biography
Airdate: 05/01/85
Rating: 10.6/17   A/C:

The true story of Ray "Boom Boom" Mancini, whose supportive family helped him in his struggle to become a lightweight boxing champ.

Production Company: Rare Titles Prods. IAW
   Robert Papazian Prods.

Executive Producer	Sylvester Stallone
Producer	Robert A. Papazian
Co-Producer	Rhonda Young
Director	Richard Michaels
Writer	Dennis Nemec
Cast	Robert Blake
Cast	Doug McKeon
Cast	Tony Burton
Cast	Ray Buktenica

HEART OF A CHILD — NBC

Drama: Family Drama • Medical/Disease/Mental Illness • Children/Teens • Woman's Issue/Story • True Story
Airdate: 5/9/94
Rating: 11.5/18   A/C: 3

Two pregnant women, Karen Schouten and Alice Holc learn that their babies will be born with severe birth defects, one with a defective heart the other with a defective brain-neither is expected to live more than a few hours. Deciding to donate their brain dead daughters heart, the Schouten's provide hope for the Holc family who undergo a landmark infant heart-transplant operation. The surgery is a success and both mothers form an everlasting bond.

Production Company: O'Hara, Horowitz Prods.

Executive Producer	Lawrence Horowitz
Executive Producer	Michael O'Hara
Co-Executive Producer	Susan Nanus
Producer	Michelle MacLaren
Co-Producer	Steven Rosenfeld
Co-Producer	Kathryn McArdle
Director	Steven H. Stern
Writer	Susan Nanus
Cast	Ann Jillian
Cast	Michele Greene
Cast	Terry O'Quinn
Cast	Bruce Greenwood

HEART OF DARKNESS   TNT
Drama: Period Piece • Foreign or Exotic Location •
Action/Adventure
Airdate: 3/13/94
Rating: N/A   A/C:

Based on the novella by Joseph Conrad. In the 1890's an ambitious British steamboat captain commissioned to carry supplies deep into the African jungle and return with precious ivory. On an expedition up the Congo river he discovers a renegade ivory trader who is hoarding a huge cache of ivory and is bent on a maniacal plot to exterminate the local population. Horrified by the death and violence over the amassed treasure, he refuses to bring the ivory out.

Production Company: Chris/Rose Prods. IAW
    Turner Pictures
Executive Producer .... Bob Christiansen
Executive Producer .... Rick Rosenberg
Co-Producer .... James Westman
Director .... Nicolas Roeg
Writer .... Benedict Fitzgerald
Cast .... John Malkovich
Cast .... Tim Roth
Cast .... James Fox
Cast .... Isaach de Bankole

HEART OF JUSTICE, THE   TNT
Drama: Murder and Murder Mystery
Airdate: 2/20/93
Rating: N/A   A/C:

A star reporter investigating a twisted society murder becomes a pawn for the manipulative woman who precipitates the crime.

Production Company: TNT Screenworks
Executive Producer .... Michael Brandman
Executive Producer .... Barbara Corday
Producer .... Donald Borchers
Director .... Bruno Barreto
Writer .... Keith Reddin
Cast .... Eric Stoltz
Cast .... Dennis Hopper
Cast .... Dermot Mulroney
Cast .... Jennifer Connelly

HEARTSOUNDS   ABC
Drama: Family Drama • Medical/Disease/Mental
Illness • True Story
Airdate: 09/30/84
Rating: 18.5/31   A/C:

True story based on Martha Lear's autobiographical book dealing with a doctor and his wife who must deal with the problems caused by his series of heart attacks.

Production Company: Embassy TV
Executive Producer .... Norman Lear
Producer .... Fay Kanin
Producer .... Fern Field
Director .... Glenn Jordan
Writer .... Fay Kanin
Cast .... James Garner
Cast .... Mary Tyler Moore
Cast .... Wendy Crewson
Cast .... Sam Wanamaker

HEAT WAVE   TNT
Drama: True Story • Period Piece • Black Story •
Historical Piece
Airdate: 08/13/90
Rating: N/A   A/C:

Bob Richardson, an aspiring black reporter working as a messenger for the L.A. Times, gets his big break when the city erupts in violence during the infamous 1965 Watts Riots. His coverage resulted in a Pulitzer Prize.

Production Company: Avnet/Kerner IAW
    Propaganda Films
Executive Producer .... Jon Avnet
Executive Producer .... Jordan Kerner
Executive Producer .... Joni Sighvatsson
Executive Producer .... Steve Golin
Co-Executive Producer .... Thomas Carter
Producer .... Jordan Kerner
Director .... Kevin Hooks
Writer .... Michael Lazarou
Cast .... Cicely Tyson
Cast .... Blair Underwood
Cast .... James Earl Jones
Cast .... Sally Kirkland
Cast .... Margaret Avery
Cast .... Adam Arkin

HEIDI   DISNEY
Miniseries/Drama (2 nights): Children/Teens •
Foreign or Exotic Location • Period Piece
Airdate: 7/18/93 • 7/19/93
Rating: N/A   A/C:

Based on the book by Johanna Spyri. A charming little Swiss orphan girl comes to live with her emotionally distant grandfather in a cabin in the mountains. She eventually melts the old mans heart but is soon removed from his home by a sneaky cousin who takes her to Frankfurt to be a companion for a sickly child and is abused by a nasty governess. Grandpa finally wins the child back and Heidi is once again in the Alps living happily ever after.

Production Company: Harmony Gold, Bill
    McCutchen Prods., Silvio Berlusconi Comm.,
    Disney Channel
Executive Producer .... Bill McCutchen
Producer .... Frank Agrama
Producer .... Daniele Lorenzno
Director .... Michael Rhodes
Writer .... Jeanne Rosenberg
Cast .... Jason Robards
Cast .... Jane Seymour
Cast .... Noley Thornton
Cast .... Lexi Randall
Director .... Patricia Neal

HEIST   HBO
Comedy: Suspense/Thriller • Buddy Story
Airdate: 09/16/89
Rating: N/A   A/C:

An innocent man, betrayed into prison by his former racetrack partner, gets out and hatches an elaborate scheme to get revenge against his crooked ex-friend.

Production Company: HBO Pictures, Chris/Rose
    Productions Inc.
Producer .... Rick Rosenberg
Producer .... Bob Christiansen
Director .... Stuart Orme
Writer .... William Irish, Jr.
Writer .... David Fuller
Writer .... Rick Natki
Cast .... Pierce Brosnan
Cast .... Wendy Hughes
Cast .... Tom Skerritt
Cast .... Robert Prosky

HELD HOSTAGE: THE SIS AND JERRY
LEVIN STORY   ABC
Drama: Family Drama • Woman Against The System
• True Story • Foreign or Exotic Location • Political
Piece • Prison and Prison Camp
Airdate: 01/13/91
Rating: 12.0/19   A/C: 3

When reporter Jerry Levin is abducted in 1984 by Muslim fundamentalists in Beirut, his wife, Sis, wages a public campaign for his release.

Production Company: Paragon Entertainment
    Corp. IAW Carol Polakoff Prods.
Executive Producer .... Jon Slan
Producer .... Carol Polakoff
Producer .... Dennis Nemec
Director .... Roger Young
Writer .... Anne Brittany
Writer .... Bruce Hart
Cast .... Marlo Thomas
Cast .... David Dukes
Cast .... G.W. Bailey
Cast .... Ed Winter

HELL HATH NO FURY   NBC
Drama: Murder and Murder Mystery • Woman In
Jeopardy • Psychological Thriller
Airdate: 03/04/91
Rating: 15.2/24   A/C: 2

Based on the novel "Smithereens" by B.W. Batin. A suburban homemaker finds herself widowed and framed when she and her family are terrorized by her husband's college girlfriend.

Production Company: Bar-Gene Prods., Inc. IAW
    Finnegan-Pinchuk Co.
Executive Producer .... Sheldon Pinchuk
Executive Producer .... Bill Finnegan
Executive Producer .... Gene Schwam
Producer .... Pat Finnegan
Director .... Thomas J. Wright
Writer .... Beau Bensink
Cast .... Barbara Eden
Cast .... Loretta Swit
Cast .... David Ackroyd
Cast .... Amanda Peterson

HER FINAL FURY: BETTY BRODERICK, THE LAST CHAPTER   CBS
Drama: True Crime • Courtroom Drama • Woman's Issue/Story
Airdate: 11/1/92
Rating: 14.9/22   A/C: 3

Sequel to the March 1, 1992 TV movie, "A Woman Scorned". Betty Broderick a La Jolla, California socialite, who in a jealous rage, murdered her ex-husband and his young bride in 1989. In 1991, her first emotional trial ended in a hung jury then in the second trial she is found guilty of second-degree murder and sentenced to thirty two years to life.

Production Company: Patchett Kaufman Ent. IAW Lowry/Rawls Prods., WIN
Executive Producer .... Ken Kaufman
Executive Producer .... Tom Patchett
Producer .... Dick Lowry
Producer .... Ann Kindberg
Co-Producer .... Wendell Rawls
Director .... Dick Lowry
Writer .... Joe Cacaci
Cast .... Meredith Baxter
Cast .... Judith Ivey
Cast .... Ray Baker

HER SECRET LIFE   ABC
Drama: Action/Adventure • Foreign or Exotic Location
Airdate: 04/12/87
Rating: 13.7/21   A/C:

Precarious situations arise when a former espionage agent infiltrates Cuba to save a former comrade from captivity while trying to keep her past a secret from her husband.

Production Company: Phoenix Entertainment Group
Executive Producer .... Judith A. Polone
Producer .... Buzz Kulik
Co-Producer .... Carla Jean Wagner
Director .... Buzz Kulik
Writer .... Carla Jean Wagner
Cast .... Kate Capshaw
Cast .... Cliff De Young
Director .... James Sloyan
Cast .... Garette Ratliff

HER WICKED WAYS   NBC
Drama: Psychological Thriller
Airdate: 01/01/91
Rating: 16.9/26   A/C: 2

An experienced Washington news correspondent triumphs over the backstabbing ambition of a cub reporter.

Production Company: Lois Luger Prods., Freyda Rothstein Prods. IAW ITC Ent. Group
Executive Producer .... Lois Luger
Executive Producer .... Freyda Rothstein
Producer .... Gene Schwam
Director .... Richard Michaels
Writer .... Janice Hickey
Writer .... Michael Pardridge
Cast .... Barbara Eden
Cast .... Heather Locklear
Cast .... Stuart Wilson
Cast .... Jed Allan

HEROES OF DESERT STORM   ABC
Drama: True Story • Historical Piece • Foreign or Exotic Location • Period Piece
Airdate: 10/06/91
Rating: 9.9/16   A/C: 4

The heroic battles and sacrifices of American military personnel during the Persian Gulf War.

Production Company: Capital Cities, ABC Video, Ohlmeyer
Executive Producer .... Don Ohlmeyer
Producer .... Johanna Persons
Director .... Don Ohlmeyer
Writer .... Lionel Chetwynd
Cast .... Angela Bassett
Cast .... Daniel Baldwin
Cast .... Kris Kamm
Cast .... Tim Russ

HI HONEY — I'M DEAD   FBC
Comedy: Sci-Fi/Supernatural/Horror/Fantasy
Airdate: 04/22/91
Rating: 6.7/11   A/C: 4

An avaricious real estate developer dies. With the help of an angel, he gets a second chance and is born into the body of an inept housekeeper working for his former wife and child, and, thereby, learns humility and his family's true worth.

Production Company: FNM Films
Producer .... Paula Rudnick
Director .... Alan Myerson
Writer .... Carl Kleinschmitt
Cast .... Curtis Armstrong
Cast .... Catherine Hicks
Cast .... Kevin Conroy
Cast .... Paul Rodriguez

HIDER IN THE HOUSE   USA
Drama: Suspense/Thriller
Airdate: 02/05/92
Rating: N/A   A/C:

A disturbed and violent man moves into the attic of a new house, unbeknownst to the owners. Obsessed with having the family as his own, he plots to do away with the husband, becoming crazed when threatened with disclosure.

Production Company: A Vestron Pictures Production, A Precision Films/Mack-Taylor Prod.
Executive Producer .... Steven Reuther
Executive Producer .... Diane Nabatoff
Producer .... Edward Teets
Producer .... Michael Taylor
Co-Producer .... Stuart Cornfield
Co-Producer .... Lem Dobbs
Director .... Matthew Patrick
Writer .... Lem Dobbs
Cast .... Gary Busey
Cast .... Mimi Rogers
Cast .... Michael McKean

HIGH MOUNTAIN RANGERS   CBS
Drama: Family Drama • Action/Adventure • Series Pilot (2 hr.)
Airdate: 04/19/87
Rating: 19.6/32   A/C:

A former mountain ranger comes out of retirement to help his ranger son catch an escaped murderer. Rescuing a pregnant plane-crash victim provides additional action.

Production Company: Shane Prods.
Executive Producer .... Joan Conrad
Producer .... Roger Bacon
Director .... Robert Conrad
Writer .... David J. Kinghorn
Cast .... Robert Conrad
Cast .... Christian Conrad
Cast .... Shane Conrad
Cast .... Russell Todd

HIGH PRICE OF PASSION, THE   NBC
Drama: Murder and Murder Mystery • True Crime • Prostitution
Airdate: 11/30/86
Rating: 18.6/29   A/C:

The fast-based story of a university anatomy professor who develops an expensive obsession with a money-hungry prostitute, and finally kills her.

Production Company: Edgar Scherick Assocs.
Director .... Larry Elikann
Writer .... Mel Frohman
Cast .... Richard Crenna
Cast .... Karen Young
Cast .... Sean McCann
Cast .... Terry Tweed
Cast .... Steven Flynn

HIGHER GROUND   CBS
Drama: Murder and Murder Mystery • Cops/Detectives/Law Enforcement • Action/Adventure • Series Pilot (2 hr.)
Airdate: 09/04/88
Rating: 13.3/25   A/C:

An FBI agent gives up his career to become an Alaskan bush pilot. When a smuggling-involved friend is killed, he brings those responsible to justice.

Production Company: Green/Epstein Prods. IAW Columbia Pictures TV
Executive Producer .... Jim Green
Executive Producer .... Allen Epstein
Co-Executive Producer .... John Denver
Director .... Robert Day
Writer .... Michael Eric Stein
Cast .... John Denver
Cast .... Martin Kove
Cast .... Meg Wittner
Cast .... Richard Masur

HIGHWAY HEARTBREAKER — CBS
Drama: True Story • Woman's Issue/Story
Airdate: 03/29/92
Rating: 16.0/25   A/C: 2

Three wealthy single women join forces to spin a clever web of revenge when they turn the tables on the smooth-talking con man who has victimized them in love and money.

Production Company: Gross-Weston Prods. IAW Cannell Entertainment
Executive Producer .... Marcy Gross
Executive Producer .... Ann Weston
Producer .... Howard Burkons
Producer .... Diane Walsh
Director .... Paul Schneider
Writer .... Deborah A. Serra
Cast .... John Schneider
Cast .... Linda Gray
Cast .... Heather Locklear
Cast .... Tracy Nelson

HIGHWAY TO HEAVEN — NBC
Drama: Series Pilot (2 hr.) • Sci-Fi/Supernatural/Horror/Fantasy
Airdate: 09/19/84
Rating: 20.6/35   A/C:

Series pilot about an angel who comes down to earth to help a group of retirees face expulsion from their retirement home.

Production Company: Michael Landon Prods.
Executive Producer .... Michael Landon
Producer .... Kent McCray
Director .... Michael Landon
Writer .... Michael Landon
Cast .... Michael Landon
Cast .... Victor French
Cast .... Helen Hayes

HIGHWAYMAN, THE — NBC
Drama: Cops/Detectives/Law Enforcement • Action/Adventure • Series Pilot (2 hr.) • Sci-Fi/Supernatural/Horror/Fantasy
Airdate: 03/04/88
Rating: 13.1/22   A/C:

In an alternative universe controlled by futuristic federal police, Japanese villains conspire to kill American factory workers and replace them with robots.

Production Company: New West Entertainment Inc. IAW Glen A. Larson Prods.
Executive Producer .... Glen A. Larson
Producer .... Mark Jones
Co-Producer .... Scott Levitta
Co-Producer .... J.C. Larson
Director .... Dan Haller
Writer .... Glen A. Larson
Writer .... Mark Jones
Cast .... Sam Jones
Cast .... Jacko
Cast .... Jane Badler
Cast .... Clarence Williams III

HIJACKING OF THE ACHILLE LAURO, THE — NBC
Drama: Suspense/Thriller • True Story • Foreign or Exotic Location • Social Issue • Political Piece
Airdate: 02/13/89
Rating: 12.7/20   A/C:

True story of the 1985 hijacking of a Mediterranean cruise ship by PLO terrorists. Negotiations in Cairo alternate with excruciating shipboard scenes, including the killing of wheelchair-bound American Leon Klinghoffer.

Production Company: Tamara Asseyev Prods./Spectator Films/New World TV
Executive Producer .... Tamara Asseyev
Director .... Robert Collins
Writer .... Robert Collins
Cast .... Lee Grant
Cast .... Karl Malden
Cast .... E. G. Marshall
Cast .... Christina Pickles
Cast .... Vera Miles

HIROSHIMA: OUT OF THE ASHES — NBC
Drama: Period Piece • Historical Piece • Foreign or Exotic Location • WWII
Airdate: 08/06/90
Rating: 11.3/20   A/C: 2

A Japanese family, a Roman Catholic priest and two American P.O.W.'s struggle to survive after the devastating atomic bombing of Hiroshima on August 6, 1945.

Production Company: Robert Greenwald Prods.
Executive Producer .... Robert Greenwald
Producer .... Mark A. Burley
Producer .... Philip Kleinbart
Director .... Peter Werner
Writer .... John McGreevey
Cast .... Max Von Sydow
Cast .... Judd Nelson
Cast .... Mako
Cast .... Tamlyn Tomita
Cast .... Stan Egi
Cast .... Brady Tsurutani

HIT LIST, THE — SHOWTIME
Drama: Murder and Murder Mystery • Suspense/Thriller
Airdate: 1/17/93
Rating: N/A   A/C:

A benevolent hit man who only kills those who "deserve" to die is hired by a sexy young woman to kill a greedy industrialist who she knows masterminded her husbands death.

Production Company: Showtime Ent., Westwind Prods.
Executive Producer .... Robert Mann
Executive Producer .... Rich Goldberg
Producer .... T.R. Conroy
Producer .... William Webb
Director .... William Webb
Writer .... Reed Steiner
Cast .... Jeff Fahey
Cast .... Yancy Butler
Cast .... James Coburn
Cast .... Michael Beach

HITLER'S DAUGHTER — USA
Drama: Murder and Murder Mystery • Cops/Detectives/Law Enforcement • Suspense/Thriller • Nazis
Airdate: 09/26/90
Rating: N/A   A/C:

Based on the novel by Timothy R. Benford. A presidential aide, framed for murder, goes on the run and uncovers a neo-nazi plot to put Hitler's illegitimate, U.S.-born daughter in the White House.

Production Company: O.T.M.L./Wilshire Court Productions
Producer .... Richard Luke Rothschild
Director .... James A. Contner
Writer .... Sherman Gray
Writer .... Christopher Canaan
Cast .... Patrick Cassidy
Cast .... Melody Anderson
Cast .... Veronica Cartwright
Cast .... Kay Lenz

HITLER'S S S: PORTRAIT IN EVIL — NBC
Drama: Family Drama • WWII • Nazis
Airdate: 02/17/85
Rating: 15.8/24   A/C:

The story of a German family set against the rise of Hitler. One of the brothers embraces Nazism and joins the SS, while the other tries to maintain his apolitical, academic life in face of impending danger.

Production Company: Colason Ltd. IAW Edgar Scherick Assocs.
Executive Producer .... Edgar J. Scherick
Producer .... Aida Young
Director .... Jim Goddard
Writer .... Lukas Heller
Cast .... John Shea
Cast .... Bill Nighy
Cast .... Lucy Gutteridge
Cast .... David Warner
Cast .... Jose Ferrer
Cast .... Tony Randall

HOBO'S CHRISTMAS, A — CBS
Drama: Holiday Special
Airdate: 12/06/87
Rating: 19.5/30   A/C:

A once-successful salesman beaten down by business leaves the hobo life to be reunited with his son, a single parent, and meet his two grandchildren.

Production Company: Joe Byrne/Falrose Prods. IAW Phoenix Entertainment Group
Executive Producer .... Joe Byrne
Producer .... Paul Freeman
Director .... Will MacKenzie
Writer .... Jeb Rosebrook
Cast .... Barnard Hughes
Cast .... Gerald McRaney
Cast .... Wendy Crewson
Cast .... William Hickey

HOLLYWOOD WIVES   ABC
Miniseries/Drama (3 nights): Sex/Glitz • Hollywood
Airdate: 02/17/85 • 02/18/85 • 02/19/85
Rating: 22.0/33 • 21.1/32 • 25.2/39   A/C:

Based on Jackie Collins' novel about the lifestyles and infidelities of the rich, famous and up-and-coming in the entertainment industry.

Production Company: Aaron Spelling Prods.
Executive Producer .... Aaron Spelling
Executive Producer .... Douglas S. Cramer
Producer .... Howard W. Koch
Director .... Robert Day
Writer .... Robert McCullough
Cast .... Candice Bergen
Cast .... Joanna Cassidy
Cast .... Mary Crosby
Cast .... Angie Dickinson
Cast .... Steve Forrest
Cast .... Anthony Hopkins

HOME FIRES BURNING   CBS
Drama: Family Drama • Period Piece • WWII
Airdate: 01/29/89
Rating: 18.6/29   A/C:

Toward the end of World War II, a southern newspaper publisher and his family must cope with his shellshocked, estranged son and his pregnant wife.

Production Company: Marian Rees Associates Inc.
Executive Producer .... Marian Rees
Producer .... Glenn Jordan
Director .... Glenn Jordan
Writer .... Robert Inman
Cast .... Robert Prosky
Cast .... Sada Thompson
Cast .... Neil Patrick Harris
Cast .... Barnard Hughes

HOMEFRONT   ABC
Drama: Family Drama • Period Piece • WWII • Series
Pilot (2 hr.)
Airdate: 9/24/91
Rating: 12.2/20   A/C:

The joys and hardships of three families in a small mid-western town after the GI's return from World War II.

Production Company: Laftham/Lechowick,
    Roundplay Prods. IAW Lorimar Television
Executive Producer .... David Jacobs
Executive Producer .... Lynn Marie Latham
Executive Producer .... Bernard Lechowick
Producer .... Christopher Chulack
Director .... Ron Lagomarsino
Writer .... Lynn Marie Latham
Writer .... Bernard Lechowick
Cast .... Wendy Phillips
Cast .... Kyle Chandler
Cast .... David Newsom
Cast .... Jessica Steen
Cast .... Ken Jenkins
Cast .... Mimi Kennedy

HONOR THY FATHER AND MOTHER: THE MENENDEZ MURDERS   FBC
Drama: True Crime • Family Violence • Courtroom Drama
Airdate: 4/18/94
Rating: 10.2/17   A/C: 3

Based on the book "Blood Brothers" by John Johnson & Ronald L. Soble. In 1989, the Beverly Hills murders of wealthy executive Jose Menendez and his wife Kitty result in the arrest of their two spoiled sons, Eric and Lyle. A sensational trial ensues with the brothers claiming their father had sexually abused them for years and they were afraid for their lives. Both cases ended in mistrials with the state of California planning to prosecute the boys again.

Production Company: Saban Entertainment
Executive Producer .... Lance H. Robbins
Producer .... Ronnie Hadar
Director .... Paul Schneider
Writer .... Michael Murray
Cast .... James Farentino
Cast .... Jill Clayburgh
Cast .... Billy Warlock
Cast .... David Beron
Cast .... Susan Blakely

HONOR THY MOTHER   CBS
Drama: Family Drama • True Crime • Family Violence • Murder and Murder Mystery • Children/Teens
Airdate: 04/26/92
Rating: 15.5/24   A/C: 1

Based on the book "Blood Games" by Jerry Bledsoe. In 1988 North Carolina, troubled student Chris Pritchard, involved in drugs, alcohol and "Dungeons & Dragons", plots to murder his mother and step-father for their money. His mother survives and fights to prove his innocence. See Cruel Doubt.

Production Company: A Point Of View Prods.
Executive Producer .... Dan Wigutow
Executive Producer .... Harvey Frand
Director .... David Greene
Writer .... Richard DeLong Adams
Writer .... Robert L. Freedman
Cast .... Sharon Gless
Cast .... William McNamara
Cast .... Paul Scherrer
Cast .... Brian Wimmer

HOOVER   SHOWTIME
Drama: Biography • True Story • Period Piece • Cops/Detectives/Law Enforcement
Airdate: 1/11/87
Rating: N/A   A/C:

Follows the life of J. Edgar Hoover from his turn of the century childhood in a working class section of Washington, D.C., to his tenure as FBI Director that spanned 48 years. Examines the factors that helped him build an unshakable power base that lasted through the administrations of eight presidents.

Production Company: Finnegan Co.
Executive Producer .... Sheldon Pinchuk
Executive Producer .... Bill Finnegan
Executive Producer .... Pat Finnegan
Producer .... Robert Collins
Co-Producer .... Scott Winant
Director .... Robert Collins
Writer .... Robert Collins
Cast .... Treat Williams
Cast .... Rip Torn
Cast .... David Ogden Stiers
Cast .... Louise Fletcher

HOSTAGE   CBS
Drama: Suspense/Thriller • Woman In Jeopardy
Airdate: 02/14/88
Rating: 19.4/29   A/C:

A female teenage convict escapes from prison and holds a rich widow hostage.

Production Company: CBS Entertainment Prods.
Executive Producer .... Diana Kerew
Director .... Peter Levin
Writer .... Stephen H. Foreman
Cast .... Carol Burnett
Cast .... Carrie Hamilton
Cast .... Leon Russom
Cast .... Annette Bening
Cast .... Leon Russom
Cast .... Annette Bening
Executive Producer .... Frank Von Zerneck
Executive Producer .... Robert M. Sertner
Producer .... James Hay

HOSTAGE FLIGHT   NBC
Drama: Suspense/Thriller
Airdate: 11/17/85
Rating: 21.5/32   A/C:

Armed terrorists hijack a commercial flight and the passengers plot to outwit their murderous captors.

Production Company: Shooting Star Prods.
Executive Producer .... Frank Von Zerneck
Executive Producer .... Robert M. Sertner
Producer .... James Hay
Director .... Steven H. Stern
Writer .... Stephen Zito
Writer .... Felix Culver
Cast .... Ned Beatty
Cast .... Dee Wallace Stone
Cast .... Rene Enriquez
Cast .... Barbara Bosson

MOVIES AND MINISERIES

HOSTAGE FOR A DAY   FBC
Comedy: Family Drama
Airdate: 4/25/94
Rating: 6.6/11   A/C: 4

A small town guy stuck in a dead-end job, married to a shrewish wife dreams of moving to Alaska with his former girlfriend. When he fakes his own kidnapping, comical complications ensue which threaten to destroy his misguided plans.

Production Company: Frostback Prods. IAW Once Upon A Time Films Ltd., Fox West Pictures IAW WIC
Executive Producer .... Stanley Brooks
Executive Producer .... John Candy
Producer .... Adam Haight
Co-Producer .... Patrick Whitley
Director .... John Candy
Writer .... Kari Hildebrand
Writer .... Robert Crane
Writer .... Peter Torokvei
Cast .... George Wendt
Cast .... John Vernon
Cast .... Robin Duke

HOSTAGES   HBO
Drama: True Story • Foreign or Exotic Location • Political Piece • Prison and Prison Camp
Airdate: 2/20/93
Rating: N/A   A/C:

The brutal ordeals of six Western hostages-Brian Keenan, John McCarthy, Terry Anderson, Tom Sutherland, Frank Reed and Terry Waite-held captive in Lebanon by Islamic terrorists in the mid 1980s. During the five year nightmare the men are championed by their families who tirelessly campaign for their release.

Production Company: HBO Showcase, Granada Films
Executive Producer .... Colin Callender
Executive Producer .... Ray Fitzwalter
Producer .... Sita Williams
Director .... David Wheatley
Writer .... Bernard MacLaverty
Cast .... Jay O. Sanders
Cast .... Josef Sommer
Cast .... Colin Firth
Cast .... Natasha Richardson
Cast .... Kathy Bates

HOT PAINT   CBS
Comedy: Buddy Story
Airdate: 03/20/88
Rating: 14.1/22   A/C:

An aspiring actor and his friend steal a Renoir painting in an insurance scam, and then try to fence the famous work with comic results.

Production Company: Catalina Prod. Groups Ltd.
Executive Producer .... Franklin R. Levy
Executive Producer .... Gregory Harrison
Producer .... Michael Rauch
Producer .... Matthew Rushton
Writer .... Eliot Wald
Writer .... Matthew Rushton
Director .... Sheldon Larry
Cast .... Gregory Harrison
Cast .... John Larroquette
Cast .... Cyrielle Claire
Cast .... John Glover

HOT PURSUIT   NBC
Drama: Murder and Murder Mystery • Woman In Jeopardy
Airdate: 09/22/84
Rating: 11.2/21   A/C:

When an auto engineer's boss makes a pass at her, his jealous wife frames the engineer for murder. The engineer and her veterinarian husband set forth on a cross country chase for the real murderer.

Production Company: Kenneth Johnson Prods. IAW NBC Prods.
Executive Producer .... Kenneth Johnson
Producer .... Arthur Seidel
Director .... Kenneth Johnson
Writer .... Kenneth Johnson
Cast .... Mike Preston
Cast .... Dina Merrill
Cast .... Kerrie Keanne

HOUSE OF SECRETS   NBC
Drama: Murder and Murder Mystery • Family Violence
Airdate: 11/1/93
Rating: 14.6/23   A/C: 3

Baaed on the book "Celle qui n'etait plus" by Peirre Boileau. In New Orleans a wealthy, frail and abused wife of a seemly charming doctor conspires with his maltreated mistress to murder him during a Mardi Gras celebration. When the deed is done she is shocked to discover his body is missing and he appears to be alive with her partner in crime. Driving her to madness she seeks her revenge with the help of some old Cajun Voodoo.

Production Company: Steve Krantz Prods. IAW Multimedia Motion Pictures
Executive Producer .... Steve Krantz
Executive Producer .... Tony Etz
Producer .... Walter Coblenz
Co-Producer .... Andrew Laskos
Director .... Mimi Leder
Writer .... Andrew Laskos
Cast .... Melissa Gilbert
Cast .... Bruce Boxleitner
Cast .... Kate Vernon
Cast .... Michael Boatman

HOUSE OF SECRETS AND LIES, A   CBS
Drama: Family Drama • Woman's Issue/Story
Airdate: 9/27/92
Rating: 15.5/27   A/C: 1

An insecure, dependent TV reporter becomes obsessed with the thought that her husband is having an affair. Her married life becomes an emotional battlefield leading to a total breakdown when she finally uncovers the truth of his infidelity.

Production Company: Elliot Friedgen & Co., Chris/Rose Prods.
Executive Producer .... Bob Christiansen
Executive Producer .... Rick Rosenberg
Executive Producer .... Linda Schreyer
Executive Producer .... Connie Sellecca
Director .... Paul Schneider
Writer .... Diana Gould
Writer .... Linda Schreyer
Cast .... Connie Sellecca
Cast .... Kevin Dobson
Cast .... Grace Zabriskie

HOUSE ON SYCAMORE STREET, THE   CBS
Mystery: Murder and Murder Mystery • Cops/Detectives/Law Enforcement
Airdate: 05/01/92
Rating: 10.9/20   A/C: 2

Sequel to 1992 TV Movie "Diagnosis of Murder." A successful, if offbeat, doctor and amateur detective is compelled to discover the truth in the questionable suicide of a former student whom he believes was murdered.

Production Company: Fred Silverman Prods. and Dean Hargrove Prods., IAW Viacom
Executive Producer .... Fred Silverman
Executive Producer .... Dean Hargrove
Producer .... Barry Steinberg
Director .... Christian Nyby II
Writer .... Bruce Franklin Singer
Cast .... Dick Van Dyke
Cast .... Cynthia Gibb
Cast .... Stephen Caffrey
Cast .... Barry Van Dyke

HOUSTON: THE LEGEND OF TEXAS   CBS
Drama: Biography • Westem • Historical Piece
Airdate: 11/22/86
Rating: 10.8/18   A/C:

Sam Houston leads Texas's attempt to rid herself of Mexican rule.

Production Company: J. D. Feigelson Prods. IAW Taft Entertainment TV Inc.
Executive Producer .... J. D. Feigelson
Producer .... Frank Q. Dobbs
Director .... Peter Levin
Writer .... John Binder
Cast .... Sam Elliott
Cast .... G. D. Spradlin
Cast .... Michael Beck
Cast .... Claudia Christian
Cast .... Bo Hopkins

HOW TO MURDER A MILLIONAIRE   CBS

Comedy: Romantic Comedy
Airdate: 05/23/90
Rating: 10.2/18   A/C: 3

A Beverly Hills housewife, obsessed with shopping, thinks her husband is trying to kill her. After getting mixed up with bumbling con artists and conniving friends, she lives to shop again.

Production Company: Robert Greenwald Films
Executive Producer .... Robert Greenwald
Executive Producer .... Carla Singer
Producer .... Philip Kleinbart
Director .... Paul Schneider
Writer .... April Kelly
Writer .... Mark Edward Edens
Cast .... Joan Rivers
Cast .... Alex Rocco
Cast .... Morgan Fairchild
Cast .... David Ogden Stiers

HOWARD BEACH: MAKING THE CASE FOR MURDER   NBC

Drama: True Crime • Courtroom Drama • Black Story • Social Issue
Airdate: 12/4/89
Rating: 14.9/24   A/C: 2

In 1986 three black men were attacked by five white youths in Howard Beach, NY, resulting in the death of one black by a hit and run driver. A controversial trial followed, in which the white youths were charged with murder.

Production Company: Patchett-Kaufman Entertainment
Executive Producer .... Tom Patchett
Executive Producer .... Ken Kaufman
Producer .... J. Boyce Harman, Jr.
Director .... Dick Lowry
Writer .... Stephen Bello
Cast .... Daniel J. Travanti
Cast .... William Daniels
Cast .... Joe Morton
Cast .... Dan Lauria

HUNTER   NBC

Drama: Cops/Detectives/Law Enforcement • Series Pilot (2 hr.)
Airdate: 09/18/84
Rating: 20.4/33   A/C:

Series pilot about two tough cops who team up to find a serial killer who is murdering blond, blue-eyed women.

Production Company: Stephen J. Cannell Prods.
Executive Producer .... Stephen J. Cannell
Co-Executive Producer .... Frank Lupo
Director .... Ron Satlof
Writer .... Frank Lupo
Cast .... Fred Dryer
Cast .... Stefanie Kramer
Cast .... James Whitmore, Jr.
Cast .... Brian Dennehy

HUSH LITTLE BABY   USA

Drama: Family Drama • Suspense/Thriller
Airdate: 1/6/94
Rating: N/A   A/C:

A suburban wife and mother unexpectedly learns that she was adopted and is soon reunited with her birth mother. During an extended visit the once charming mom turns into a murderous psychopath who is out to possess her daughter.

Production Company: USA Pictures, Power Pictures, Hearst Ent.
Executive Producer .... Freyda Rothstein
Producer .... Julian Marks
Director .... Jorge Montesi
Writer .... Julie Moskowitz
Writer .... Gary Stephens
Cast .... Diane Ladd
Cast .... Wendel Meldrum
Cast .... Geraint Wyn Davies

I CAN MAKE YOU LOVE ME: THE STALKING OF LAURA BLACK   CBS

Drama: True Crime • Woman In Jeopardy
Airdate: 2/9/93
Rating: 16.1/26   A/C: 1

An attractive, young design engineer takes a new position in Silicon Valley. Her dream job soon becomes a nightmare when she is pursued by a nerdy coworker. Becoming totally obsessed, his behavior becomes more bizarre and he is eventually fired. Plotting revenge, he goes on a murderous rampage at his former company.

Production Company: Joel Fields Prods. IAW Leonard Hill Films
Executive Producer .... Joel Fields
Executive Producer .... Frank Abatemarco
Executive Producer .... Ron Gilbert
Executive Producer .... Leonard Hill
Co-Producer .... Ardythe Goergens
Co-Producer .... Bernadette Caulfield
Director .... Michael Switzer
Writer .... Frank Abatemarco
Cast .... Richard Thomas
Cast .... Brooke Shields

I DREAM OF JEANNIE: 15 YEARS LATER   NBC

Comedy: Sci-Fi/Supernatural/Horror/Fantasy
Airdate: 10/20/85
Rating: 21.4/32   A/C:

A genie with magical powers plots to stop her astronaut husband from going on a space flight with her mischievous sister.

Production Company: Can't Sing Can't Dance Prods. IAW Columbia TV
Executive Producer .... Barbara Corday
Producer .... Hugh Benson
Director .... William Asher
Writer .... Irma Kalish
Cast .... Barbara Eden
Cast .... Bill Daily
Cast .... Hayden Rorke
Cast .... Wayne Rogers

I KNOW MY FIRST NAME IS STEVEN   NBC

Miniseries/Drama (2 nights): Family Drama • True Crime • Children/Teens • Rape/Molestation • Social Issue
Airdate: 05/22/89 • 05/23/89
Rating: 21.6/35 • 27.3/42   A/C:

The true story of seven year old Steven Stayner who was kidnapped by Kenneth Parnell, a child abuser, and held captive for seven years. After escaping and returning to his family, he struggles to readjust.

Production Company: Andrew Adelson Co. IAW Lorimar TV
Executive Producer .... Andrew Adelson
Producer .... Kim C. Friese
Director .... Larry Elikann
Writer .... J.P. Miller
Writer .... Cynthia Whitcomb
Cast .... Corin Nemec
Cast .... Arliss Howard
Cast .... Cindy Pickett
Cast .... John Ashton
Cast .... Ray Walston
Cast .... Pruitt Taylor Vince
Cast .... Luke Edwards

I KNOW MY SON IS ALIVE   NBC

Drama: Family Drama • Psychological Thriller • Children/Teens
Airdate: 2/20/94
Rating: 9.9/15   A/C: 3

A new mother is convinced she is suffering from severe postpartum depression when her baby is repeatedly found in dangerous situations. When the child is kidnapped, she becomes a prime suspect in the case. She eventually exposes her husband's conniving plot to have her declared insane and committed to an institution so he can gain control of her million dollars trust fund.

Production Company: Alexander-Enright & Assoc. IAW WIN
Executive Producer .... Don Enright
Executive Producer .... Les Alexander
Producer .... Joe Broido
Producer .... Julian Marks
Director .... Bill Corcoran
Writer .... Raymond Hartung
Writer .... Joe Broido
Cast .... Corbin Bernsen
Cast .... Amanda Pays
Cast .... Mimi Kuzyk
Cast .... Neve Campbell

Movies and Miniseries

I Love You Perfect — ABC

Drama: Love Story • Medical/Disease/Mental Illness
• True Story
Airdate: 10/08/89
Rating: 13.7/23   A/C: 2

A couple's love draws them closer when the woman learns she has invasive cervical cancer. A subsequent malpractice suit proves that the disease could have been contained if the clinic had informed her of her abnormal Pap test.

Production Company: Gross-Weston and Susan Dey Prod. IAW Stephen J. Cannell Prod.

Executive Producer	Marcy Gross
Executive Producer	Ann Weston
Producer	Susan Dey
Producer	Brenda Friend
Producer	Dalene Young
Director	Harry Winer
Writer	Dalene Young
Cast	Susan Dey
Cast	Anthony John Denison

I Married a Centerfold — NBC

Comedy: Romantic Comedy
Airdate: 11/11/84
Rating: 13.4/21   A/C:

An engineer falls in love with the picture of a magazine centerfold and wagers $500 that he'll not only meet her, but romance her off her feet.

Production Company: Moonlight II Prods.

Executive Producer	Frank Von Zerneck
Producer	Robert M. Sertner
Director	Peter Werner
Writer	Victoria Hochberg
Cast	Teri Copley
Cast	Timothy Daley
Cast	Diane Ladd
Cast	Anson Williams

I Saw What You Did — CBS

Drama: Woman In Jeopardy • Suspense/Thriller •
Children/Teens
Airdate: 05/20/88
Rating: 11.5/21   A/C:

Remake of the 1965 film. Random prank accusatory phone calls get teenage girls in trouble when they coincidentally phone a man who really did do something...murder.

Production Company: Universal TV

Executive Producer	Jon Epstein
Executive Producer	Wendy Riche
Producer	Barry Greenfield
Director	Fred Walton
Writer	Cynthia Cidre
Cast	Shawnee Smith
Cast	Tammy Lauren
Cast	Candace Cameron
Cast	Robert Carradine
Cast	David Carradine

I Spy Returns — CBS

Drama: Cops/Detectives/Law Enforcement • Foreign
or Exotic Location
Airdate: 2/3/94
Rating: 12.4/18   A/C: 2

Sequel to the 1966-68 NBC series. Globe-trotting secret agents, Scotty and Kelly are reunited after twenty-five years when both of their children become rookie agents. The former crime busters now worrywart parents follow the kids to Vienna and find themselves swept up in a cloak-and-dagger espionage adventure.

Production Company: SAH Enterprises Inc., Sheldon Leonard Enterprises Inc. IAW Citadel Ent.

Executive Producer	Sheldon Leonard
Executive Producer	Bill Cosby
Executive Producer	David R. Ginsburg
Producer	Michael O. Gallant
Co-Producer	Stan Robertson
Director	Jerry London
Writer	Michael Norell
Cast	Bill Cosby
Cast	Robert Culp
Cast	George Newbern
Cast	Salli Richardson

I Still Dream Of Jeannie — NBC

Comedy: Sci-Fi/Supernatural/Horror/Fantasy
Airdate: 10/20/91
Rating: 12.3/19   A/C: 3

Jeannie is now raising her teenage son while her astronaut husband is away on a long space mission. Her evil twin sister appears and forces her to follow "Genie Law" and find a new earthly master or she will be sent back to Mesopotamia.

Production Company: Bar-Gene TV Inc., . IAW Columbia Pictures TV

Executive Producer	Carla Singer
Director	Joseph Scanlan
Writer	April Kelly
Cast	Barbara Eden
Cast	Christopher Bolton
Cast	Bill Daily
Cast	Al Waxman

I'll Be Home for Christmas — NBC

Drama: Holiday Special
Airdate: 12/12/88
Rating: 17.9/28   A/C:

A mutually supportive New England family gathers for a Christmas reunion, anxiously awaiting Michael, the oldest son, who is returning from his tour of duty in World War II.

Production Company: NBC Prods.

Executive Producer	Michael Manheim
Producer	Marvin J. Chomsky
Director	Marvin J. Chomsky
Writer	Blanche Hanalis
Cast	Hal Holbrook
Cast	Nancy Travis
Cast	Eva Marie Saint
Cast	Peter Gallagher
Cast	Courteney Cox
Cast	David Moscow

I'll Fly Away — NBC

Drama: Period Piece • Courtroom Drama • Black
Story • Series Pilot (2 hr.) • Family Drama
Airdate: 10/07/91
Rating: 15.4/24   A/C: 3

A principled Southern attorney with three children and a wife in a mental institution faces family problems and the growing civil rights movement with the help of a strong-willed black housekeeper.

Production Company: Falahey/Austin Prods. IAW Lorimar Television

Executive Producer	Joshua Brand
Executive Producer	John Falsey
Producer	Ian Sander
Director	Joshua Brand
Writer	Joshua Brand
Writer	John Falsey
Cast	Sam Waterston
Cast	Regina Taylor
Cast	Jeremy London
Cast	Ashlee Levitch
Cast	John Aaron

I'll Take Manhattan — CBS

Miniseries/Drama (4 nights): Sex/Glitz
Airdate: 03/01/87 • 03/02/87 • 03/03/87 • 03/04/87
Rating: 26.4/40 • 21.3/31 • 21.4/33 • 22.5/36 A/C:

Based on the novel by Judith Krantz. Glamorous adventures of a young but sexually experienced publishing heiress who has a year to put her magazine into the black or she'll lose her entire publishing empire.

Production Company: Steve Krantz Prods.

Executive Producer	Steve Krantz
Producer	Stan Kallis
Director	Douglas Hickox
Director	Richard Michaels
Writer	Sherman Yellen
Writer	Diana Gould
Cast	Valerie Bertinelli
Cast	Barry Bostwick
Cast	Tim Daly
Cast	Jane Kaczmarek
Cast	Ken Olin
Cast	Jack Scalia
Cast	Paul Hecht
Cast	Perry King

I'll Take Romance — ABC

Drama: Love Story • Romantic Comedy
Airdate: 11/25/90
Rating: 13.1/21   A/C: 2

A female meteorologist reluctantly agrees to date the contestants in her TV station's promotional contest. Problems arise when she must choose between her old boyfriend and the contest winner.

Production Company: New World Television

Producer	Harry R. Sherman
Director	Piers Haggard
Writer	James S. Henerson
Writer	James G. Hirsch
Cast	Linda Evans
Cast	Larry Poindexter
Cast	DeLane Matthews
Cast	Heather Tom

I'M DANGEROUS TONIGHT — USA

Drama: Murder and Murder Mystery • Suspense/Thriller • Sci-Fi/Supernatural/Horror/Fantasy
Airdate: 08/08/90
Rating: N/A   A/C:

An ancient ritual red cloak with mysterious origins makes those who wear it into psychotic killers.

Production Company: BBK Prods.
Executive Producer .... Boris Malden
Co-Executive Producer .... Michael Weisbarth
Producer .... Bruce Lansbury
Producer .... Philip John Taylor
Director .... Tobe Hooper
Writer .... Bruce Lansbury
Writer .... Philip John Taylor
Cast .... Anthony Perkins
Cast .... Madchen Amick
Cast .... Corey Parker
Cast .... Daisy Hall
Cast .... Mary Frann
Cast .... Dee Wallace Stone

IF IT'S TUESDAY, IT STILL MUST BE BELGIUM — NBC

Comedy: Foreign or Exotic Location
Airdate: 09/21/87
Rating: 13.4/22   A/C:

An ambitious executive embarks on a European tour to discredit the tour director, but changes his mind and helps the man rescue his daughter from a vicious kidnapper.

Production Company: Eisenstock & Mintz Prods. with the cooperation of Jadran Film
Executive Producer .... John J. McMahon
Executive Producer .... Alan Eisenstock
Executive Producer .... Larry Mintz
Producer .... Mel Swope
Director .... Bob Sweeney
Writer .... Alan Eisenstock
Writer .... Larry Mintz
Cast .... Stephen Furst
Cast .... Tracy Nelson
Cast .... Peter Graves
Cast .... Doris Roberts
Cast .... Kiel Martin
Cast .... Bruce Weitz
Cast .... Claude Akins

IF TOMORROW COMES — CBS

Miniseries/Drama (3 nights): Action/Adventure • Foreign or Exotic Location • Sex/Glitz
Airdate: 03/16/86 • 03/17/86 • 03/18/86
Rating: 21.8/34 • 23.6/37 • 20.8/33   A/C:

A team of elegant con artists prey on rich scoundrels in exotic European locales.

Production Company: CBS Entertainment Prods.
Executive Producer .... Bob Markell
Producer .... Carmen Culver
Producer .... Nick Gillott
Director .... Jerry London
Writer .... Carmen Culver
Cast .... Tom Berenger
Cast .... David Keith
Cast .... John Laughlin
Cast .... Susan Tyrrell
Cast .... Jack Weston
Cast .... Richard Kiley
Cast .... Madolyn Smith Osborne

ILLICIT BEHAVIOR — USA

Drama: Family Drama • Cops/Detectives/Law Enforcement • Murder and Murder Mystery
Airdate: 12/9/92
Rating: N/A   A/C:

A hot-headed cop is under investigation for killing an attempted rapist while in the line of duty. As the stress of his situation increases his home life, personal relationships, and job performance begin to deteriorate.

Production Company: Prism Ent./Promark Ent. Group, Ashok Amritraj Prods.
Executive Producer .... Carl Rossi
Executive Producer .... Barry Collier
Producer .... Ashok Amritraj
Director .... Worth Keeter
Writer .... Michael Potts
Cast .... Jack Scalia
Cast .... Robert Davi
Cast .... Joan Severance
Cast .... James Russo

IMAGE, THE — HBO

Drama: Social Issue
Airdate: 01/27/90
Rating: N/A   A/C:

A hot shot TV reporter-commentator at a TV news magazine is pressured to get higher ratings which leads him to compromise the integrity of the network news.

Production Company: Citadel Entertainment Prods.
Executive Producer .... David R. Ginsburg
Producer .... Steve McGlothen
Director .... Peter Werner
Writer .... Brian Rehak
Cast .... Albert Finney
Cast .... John Mahoney
Cast .... Kathy Baker
Cast .... Swoosie Kurtz

IMPOSTOR, THE — ABC

Drama: Love Story
Airdate: 11/08/84
Rating: 14.2/22   A/C:

In order to win back his girlfriend, who is a teacher, an ex-con lies about his credentials to become the principal of her high school.

Production Company: Gloria Monty Prods. IAW Comworld Prods.
Executive Producer .... Gloria Monty
Producer .... Nancy Malone
Co-Producer .... Terry Morse
Director .... Michael Pressman
Writer .... Eric Hendershot
Writer .... Dori Pierson
Writer .... Marc Rubel
Cast .... Anthony Geary
Cast .... Lorna Patterson
Cast .... Ken Olandt
Cast .... Billy Dee Williams

IN A CHILD'S NAME — CBS

Miniseries/Drama (2 nights): Family Drama • Murder and Murder Mystery • Woman Against The System • True Crime • Children/Teens • Family Violence
Airdate: 11/17/91 • 11/19/91
Rating: 17.8/27 • 21.9/33   A/C: 1 • 1

Based on the book by Peter Maas. In 1984, a New Jersey woman fights to have her sister's husband, Kenneth Taylor, put away for her sister's brutal slaying. She then battles overwhelming odds for custody of her nephew when he is illegally adopted by Taylor's manipulative parents.

Production Company: New World Television
Executive Producer .... Dan Wigutow
Executive Producer .... Helen Verno
Co-Producer .... Donald C. Klune
Co-Producer .... Christopher Canaan
Director .... Tom McLoughlin
Writer .... Bill Phillips
Writer .... Charles Walker
Cast .... Valerie Bertinelli
Cast .... Michael Ontkean
Cast .... Louise Fletcher
Cast .... Timothy Carhart
Cast .... Andy Hirsch
Cast .... John Karlen

IN BROAD DAYLIGHT — NBC

Drama: True Crime • Psychological Thriller • Social Issue
Airdate: 02/03/91
Rating: 13.7/21   A/C: 2

A small Missouri town is driven to vigilantism when a psychopathic town bully uses terror tactics to evade the law.

Production Company: Force Ten Prods. IAW New World Television
Executive Producer .... Freyda Rothstein
Executive Producer .... John Faunce Roach
Co-Executive Producer .... William Hanley
Co-Producer .... Ricka Fisher
Director .... James Sadwith
Writer .... William Hanley
Cast .... Brian Dennehy
Cast .... Cloris Leachman
Cast .... Marcia Gay Harden
Cast .... Chris Cooper

In Defense Of A Married Man   ABC

Drama: Murder and Murder Mystery • Courtroom
Drama • Woman's Issue/Story
Airdate: 10/14/90
Rating: 14.1/23   A/C: 1

*A successful, criminal attorney represents her
philandering husband, who is on trial for the
murder of his mistress. Her exhaustive
investigation ultimately reveals the true
murderer.*

Production Company: The Landsburg Company
Executive Producer .... Alan Landsburg
Producer .... Linda Otto
Director .... Joel Oliansky
Writer .... Norman Morrill
Writer .... Sasha Ferrer
Cast .... Judith Light
Cast .... Michael Ontkean
Cast .... Jerry Orbach
Cast .... Pat Corley

In Like Flynn   ABC

Drama: Woman In Jeopardy • Action/Adventure •
Series Pilot (2 hr.) • Foreign or Exotic Location
Airdate: 09/14/85
Rating: 8.4/15   A/C:

*A woman who writes adventure novels finds a
real life adventure when she tries to stop a
subversive group of U.S. military officials in
the Caribbean.*

Production Company: Astal Film Ent. & Glen
    Larson Prods. IAW 20th Century Fox TV
Executive Producer .... Glen A. Larson
Producer .... Stewart Harding
Producer .... Harker Wade
Director .... Richard Lang
Writer .... Glen A. Larson
Cast .... Jenny Seagrove
Cast .... William Conrad
Cast .... Eddie Albert
Cast .... William Espy

In Love And War   NBC

Drama: Woman Against The System • True Story •
Period Piece • Historical Piece • Vietnam • Prison
and Prison Camp
Airdate: 03/16/87
Rating: 16.7/27   A/C:

*Fact-based story of Jim Stockdale's seven
torturous years as a prisoner of war in Vietnam,
while his wife worked on the home front in
behalf of war prisoners.*

Production Company: Carol Schreder Prods. IAW
    Tisch/Avnet Prods. Inc.
Executive Producer .... Jon Avnet
Executive Producer .... Steve Tisch
Producer .... Carol Schreder
Director .... Paul Aaron
Writer .... Carol Schreder
Cast .... Jane Alexander
Cast .... James Woods
Cast .... Steven Leigh
Cast .... Dr. Hang S. Ngor

In My Daughter's Name   CBS

Drama: Family Drama • Murder and Murder Mystery
• Woman Against The System • Courtroom Drama
Airdate: 05/10/92
Rating: 15.8/27   A/C: 1

*Based on a screenplay by Sharon Michaels.
When her teenage daughter is savagely raped
and murdered and the murderer is acquitted on
the basis of temporary insanity, the distraught
and obsessed mother stalks him and guns him
down, landing herself on trial for murder.*

Production Company: Cates/Doty Prods.
Executive Producer .... Gilbert Cates
Executive Producer .... Donna Mills
Producer .... Dennis Doty
Director .... Jud Taylor
Writer .... Mimi Rothman
Writer .... Bill Wells
Cast .... Donna Mills
Cast .... Lee Grant
Cast .... John Rubinstein
Cast .... Adam Storke

In Self Defense   ABC

Drama: Woman In Jeopardy • Suspense/Thriller •
Courtroom Drama • Social Issue
Airdate: 05/22/87
Rating: 9.2/17   A/C:

*A woman agrees to take the witness stand
against a murderous madman. To her horror,
the trial does not take place and he is free to
terrorize her. She is forced to buy a gun to
protect herself and the results are disastrous.*

Production Company: Leonard Hill Films
Executive Producer .... Leonard Hill
Executive Producer .... Robert O'Connor
Producer .... Ron Gilbert
Co-Producer .... Daniel Cahn
Director .... Bruce Seth Green
Writer .... Robert Crais
Writer .... David Peckinpah
Cast .... Linda Purl
Cast .... Yaphet Kotto
Cast .... Terry Lester

In Sickness And In Health   CBS

Drama: Family Drama • Medical/Disease/Mental
Illness
Airdate: 3/8/92
Rating: 16.3/26   A/C: 1

*When a Texas homemaker contracts multiple
sclerosis, her devoted husband hires a vibrant
young woman to help care for her. Passions
explode when an affair begins, forcing the
family to confront dependencies, expectations
and long-held resentments.*

Production Company: Konigsberg/Sanitsky Co.
Executive Producer .... Frank Konigsberg
Executive Producer .... Larry Sanitsky
Producer .... Jayne Bieber
Director .... Jeff Bleckner
Writer .... Alan Hines
Writer .... Joyce Eliason
Cast .... Lesley Ann Warren
Cast .... Tom Skerritt
Cast .... Marg Helgenberger
Cast .... Lisa Blount

In The Arms Of A Killer   NBC

Drama: Murder and Murder Mystery • Cops/
Detectives/Law Enforcement • Suspense/Thriller
Airdate: 01/05/92
Rating: 14.0/22   A/C: 3

*A female rookie homicide detective's first case
finds her getting romantically involved with a
physician who is one of the murder suspects.*

Production Company: RLC/Monarch/MGM/UA
Executive Producer .... Robert Collins
Producer .... Ronald A. Levinson
Director .... Robert Collins
Writer .... Robert Collins
Cast .... Jaclyn Smith
Cast .... John Spencer
Cast .... Michael Nouri
Cast .... Nina Foch

In The Best Interest Of The Child   CBS

Drama: Family Drama • Children/Teens • Rape/
Molestation • Social Issue
Airdate: 05/20/90
Rating: 11.6/19   A/C: 3

*Story of a young mother's desperate efforts to
protect her daughter from what she believes to
be sexual abuse by her ex-husband, the child's
father.*

Production Company: Papazian-Hirsch
    Entertainment
Executive Producer .... Robert A. Papazian
Executive Producer .... James G. Hirsch
Director .... David Greene
Writer .... Peter Nelson
Writer .... Jud Kinberg
Cast .... Meg Tilly
Cast .... Ed Begley, Jr.
Cast .... Michael O'Keefe

In The Best Interest of the Children   NBC

Drama: Family Drama • Children/Teens • Medical/
Disease/Mental Illness • Family Violence • Social
Issue • True Story
Airdate: 02/16/92
Rating: 16.0/24   A/C: 2

*Manic-depressive Callie Cain loses her five
children to the Iowa Social Services Dept. and
then must fight for their custody when the
appointed foster parents, whom the children
love, want to legally adopt them.*

Production Company: NBC Productions
Executive Producer .... Michael Rhodes
Producer .... Paul Freeman
Director .... Michael Rhodes
Writer .... Hal Sitowitz
Cast .... Sarah Jessica Parker
Cast .... Sally Struthers
Cast .... Elizabeth Ashley
Cast .... Lexi Randall

IN THE BEST OF FAMILIES: MARRIAGE, PRIDE AND MADNESS   CBS

Miniseries/Drama (2 nights): Family Drama • Family Violence • True Crime
Airdate: 1/16/94 • 1/18/94
Rating: 16.1/25 • 17.3/26   A/C: 1 • 1

Based on the book "Bitter Blood" by Jerry Bledsoe. When Susie Leary,the daughter of a prominent North Carolina family is divorced by Tom Leary, her dentist husband, she blocks all his attempts to see their children. As a custody battle ensues she begins an affair with her first cousin, Fritz Klenner an unbalanced gun nut who prepares Susie and her boys for murderous combat against her ex-husband and his family.

Production Company: Ambroco Media Group Inc.
     IAW Dan Wigutow Prods.
Executive Producer .... Dan Wigutow
Producer .... Jeff Bleckner
Co-Producer .... Julie Cohen
Co-Producer .... Robert L. Freedman
Director .... Jeff Bleckner
Writer .... Robert L. Freedman
Cast .... Kelly McGillis
Cast .... Harry Hamlin
Cast .... Keith Carradine
Cast .... Holland Taylor
Cast .... Jayne Brook
Cast .... Louise Latham

IN THE COMPANY OF DARKNESS   CBS

Drama: Cops/Detectives/Law Enforcement • True Crime • Psychological Thriller
Airdate: 1/5/93
Rating: 15.0/24   A/C: 1

A rookie cop, out to prove herself, takes a dangerous undercover assignment to get a confession from a suspected sociopath accused of killing two preteen boys. The closer she gets to the roots of his madness the more she must struggle with her own inner demons.

Production Company: Windy City Prods. IAW
     MCA Television
Executive Producer .... Don Johnson
Executive Producer .... Michele Brustin
Producer .... Richard Brams
Producer .... Joan Marks
Director .... David Anspaugh
Writer .... John Leekley
Cast .... Helen Hunt
Cast .... Steven Weber
Cast .... Jeff Fahey

IN THE DEEP WOODS   NBC

Drama: Murder and Murder Mystery • Cops/Detectives/Law Enforcement • Suspense/Thriller • Woman In Jeopardy
Airdate: 10/26/92
Rating: 14.6/23   A/C: 2

Based on the book by Nicholas Conde. A children's book author is drawn into the web of a psycho-serial killer after he kills a friend of hers. As the murders continue, evidence mounts against her brother while she begins to suspect her boyfriend and a fawning federal agent in charge of the investigation. Also complicating matters is the appearance of a sinister private eye who thinks the young writer can lead him to the killer.

Production Company: Frederic Golchan Prods.
     IAW Leonard Hill Films
Executive Producer .... Joel Fields
Executive Producer .... Ron Gilbert
Executive Producer .... Frederic Golchan
Executive Producer .... Leonard Hill
Director .... Charles Correll
Writer .... Robert Nathan
Writer .... Robert Rosenblum
Cast .... Rosanna Arquette
Cast .... Anthony Perkins
Cast .... Will Patton
Cast .... D.W. Moffett

IN THE EYES OF A STRANGER   CBS

Drama: Cops/Detectives/Law Enforcement • Woman In Jeopardy • Suspense/Thriller
Airdate: 04/07/92
Rating: 14.2/23   A/C: 1

A disreputable murder witness is assigned to the protective custody of a tough young cop who falls in love with her. Ultimately, she betrays him and he's torn between his devotion to her and loyalty to his job.

Production Company: Power Pictures, Avenue
     Entertainment IAW Hearst Entertainment
Executive Producer .... Cary Brokaw
Producer .... Michael Greenburg
Director .... Michael Toshiyuki Uno
Writer .... Warren Taylor
Cast .... Justine Bateman
Cast .... Richard Dean Anderson
Cast .... Cynthia Dale

IN THE HEAT OF THE NIGHT   NBC

Drama: Cops/Detectives/Law Enforcement • Black Story • Series Pilot (2 hr.) • Social Issue • Murder and Murder Mystery
Airdate: 03/06/88
Rating: 18.7/30   A/C:

Based on the 1967 feature film. Detective Tibbs returns to Mississippi and becomes chief of detectives under the still-racist white police chief. When a black youth is arrested for a white girl's murder, Tibbs pushes the investigation farther than others want him to.

Production Company: Fred Silverman Co./
     JADDA Prods. IAW MGM/UA TV
Executive Producer .... Juanita Bartlett
Executive Producer .... Fred Silverman
Producer .... Hugh Benson
Producer .... James Lee Barrett
Director .... David Hemmings
Writer .... James Lee Barrett
Cast .... Howard E. Rollins, Jr.
Cast .... Carroll O'Connor
Cast .... Anne-Marie Johnson
Cast .... Kevin McCarthy
Cast .... David Hart

IN THE LINE OF DUTY: A COP FOR THE KILLING   NBC

Drama: Cops/Detectives/Law Enforcement • True Crime • Drug Smuggling/Dealing
Airdate: 11/25/90
Rating: 14.6/23   A/C: 1

A close-knit narcotics squad is torn apart by fear, anger and grief when one of its officers is killed in a drug bust.

Production Company: Patchett-Kaufman
     Entertainment IAW Brittcadia Prods. and WIN
Executive Producer .... Ken Kaufman
Executive Producer .... Tom Patchett
Producer .... Dick Lowry
Producer .... Charles Haid
Director .... Dick Lowry
Writer .... Philip Rosenberg
Cast .... James Farentino
Cast .... Steven Weber
Cast .... Susan Walters
Cast .... Harold Sylvester

MOVIES AND MINISERIES

IN THE LINE OF DUTY: AMBUSH IN WACO   NBC

Drama: True Crime • Cops/Detectives/Law Enforcement
Airdate: 5/23/93
Rating: 18.8/30   A/C: 1

The standoff between Federal Agents and Branch Davidian cult leader David Koresh at his compound in 1993, Waco, Texas. The ill-fated shootout left four officers dead which eventually led the government to enter by force causing a massive explosion, which killed Koresh and his followers.

Production Company: Patchett-Kaufman Ent.
    IAW WIN
Executive Producer .... Ken Kaufman
Executive Producer .... Tom Patchett
Producer .... Dick Lowry
Co-Producer .... Wendell Rawls
Director .... Dick Lowry
Writer .... Phil Penningroth
Cast .... Tim Daly
Cast .... Dan Lauria
Cast .... William O'Leary

IN THE LINE OF DUTY: MANHUNT IN THE DAKOTAS   NBC

Drama: Murder and Murder Mystery • Cops/Detectives/Law Enforcement • True Crime
Airdate: 05/12/91
Rating: 14.7/26   A/C: 1

Based on the book "Bitter Harvest: Murder In The Heartland" by James Corcoran. FBI honchos track down notorious murderer, cult leader Gordon Kahl in the Midwest after he kills two federal marshals.

Production Company: Patchett-Kaufman
    Entertainment
Executive Producer .... Tom Patchett
Executive Producer .... Ken Kaufman
Producer .... Dick Lowry
Director .... Dick Lowry
Writer .... Michael Petryni
Cast .... Rod Steiger
Cast .... Michael Gross
Cast .... Gary Basaraba

IN THE LINE OF DUTY: STANDOFF AT MARION   NBC

Drama: Cops/Detectives/Law Enforcement • Man Against The System • True Crime
Airdate: 02/10/92
Rating: 13.2/20   A/C: 3

Protesting government infringement, Utah fundamentalist Adam Swapp fire bombs a church and barricades himself in a home with his mother-in-law and nine children, forcing a two-week standoff with the FBI and the authorities.

Production Company: Patchett-Kaufman
    Entertainment
Executive Producer .... Ken Kaufman
Executive Producer .... Tom Patchett
Producer .... Stephanie Hagen
Director .... Charles Haid
Writer .... Rick Husky
Cast .... Kyle Secor
Cast .... Dennis Franz
Cast .... Paul LeMat
Cast .... Tess Harper

IN THE LINE OF DUTY: STREET WAR   NBC

Drama: Cops/Detectives/Law Enforcement • Drug Smuggling/Dealing • True Crime
Airdate: 10/25/92
Rating: 11.9/20   A/C: 2

New York city cops pursue crack dealers turned killers through the drug infested housing projects of Brooklyn. In a brutal attack, one of the officers is slain, leaving his remorseful partner to avenge his death.

Production Company: Patchett Kaufman Ent. IAW
    WIN
Executive Producer .... Ken Kaufman
Executive Producer .... Tom Patchett
Director .... Dick Lowry
Writer .... T.S. Cook
Cast .... Mario Van Peebles
Cast .... Michael Boatman
Cast .... Ray Sharkey
Cast .... Peter Boyle

IN THE LINE OF DUTY: THE FBI MURDERS   NBC

Drama: Murder and Murder Mystery • Cops/Detectives/Law Enforcement • True Crime
Airdate: 11/27/88
Rating: 22.2/34   A/C:

Story about the six months it took the FBI to track down two extremely vicious Florida killers and bank robbers. When they were finally apprehended a bloody massacre ensued.

Production Company: Telecom Entertainment Inc.
    IAW World International Network
Executive Producer .... Ken Kaufman
Executive Producer .... Michael Lepiner
Producer .... David Kappes
Director .... Dick Lowry
Writer .... Tracy Keenan Wynn
Cast .... David Soul
Cast .... Doug Sheehan
Cast .... Bruce Greenwood
Cast .... Ronny Cox
Cast .... Michael Gross
Cast .... Teri Copley

IN THE LINE OF DUTY: THE PRICE OF VENGEANCE   NBC

Drama: True Crime • Cops/Detectives/Law Enforcement
Airdate: 1/23/94
Rating: 10.8/17   A/C: 3

When dedicated Los Angeles police detective, Tom Williams is stalked and killed by a vengeful gang leader, his partner vows to bring the monstrous killer, Johnny Moore to justice and ultimately see him convicted of manslaughter.

Production Company: Patchett-Kaufman Ent.
Executive Producer .... Ken Kaufman
Executive Producer .... Tom Patchett
Producer .... Dick Lowry
Co-Producer .... Arnold S. Friedman
Co-Producer .... Ann Kindberg
Director .... Dick Lowry
Writer .... Keith Ross Leckie
Cast .... Michael Gross
Cast .... Dean Stockwell
Cast .... Mary Kay Place
Cast .... Brent Jennings

IN THE NICK OF TIME   NBC
Drama: Holiday Special • Sci-Fi/Supernatural/Horror/
Fantasy
Airdate: 12/16/91
Rating: 12.9/20   A/C: 3

Approaching mandatory retirement after a 300-year run at the North Pole, Santa Claus has one week to find a worthy replacement or risk Christmas being canceled. He heads to New York and finds some unlikely allies amidst a city of cynicism.

Production Company: Spector Films IAW Walt
    Disney Television
Executive Producer.....................Janet Faust Krusi
Producer.. Michael Jaffe
Co-Producer.................................. John Danylkiw
Co-Producer................................. Christine Sacani
Director .... George Miller
Writer .... Ric Podel
Writer .... Michael Preminger
Writer .... Maryedith Burrell
Cast .... Lloyd Bridges
Cast .... Michael Tucker
Cast .... Alison LaPlaca
Cast .... A Martinez

IN THE SHADOW OF A KILLER   NBC
Drama: Cops/Detectives/Law Enforcement • Man
Against The System • Period Piece • True Story
Airdate: 04/27/92
Rating: 9.5/15   A/C: 3

In 1968, a highly decorated and sensitive NYPD detective, David Mitchell, antagonizes the Department when he refuses to take the stand in support of the death penalty, as he testifies against two Mafioso cop killers.

Production Company: NBC Productions
Executive Producer......................Randy Jurgensen
Producer.. Bob Markell
Director .... Alan Metzger
Writer .... Philip Rosenberg
Cast .... Scott Bakula
Cast .... Lindsay Frost
Cast .... Miguel Ferrer
Cast .... Tony Lo Bianco

IN THE SHADOWS, SOMEONE IS
WATCHING   NBC
Drama: Suspense/Thriller • Children/Teens
Airdate: 10/4/93
Rating: 14.4/22   A/C: 3

Based on the book, "Someone Is Watching" by Judith Kelman. In a peaceful suburban town, a series of unsolved accidents involving certain children propel a suspicious detective and a concerned mother to join forces and solve the mysterious crimes. They finally expose the unbalanced mother of a little boy who wants to make sure her son is the best and the brightest and conveniently removes any and all competition the child might encounter.

Production Company: Arvin Kaufman Prods.
    IAW Saban Ent.
Executive Producer........................ Arvin Kaufman
Executive Producer........................ Lance Robbins
Producer... Henry Colman
Producer... Ronnie Hadar
Director .... Richard Friedman
Writer .... Adam Greenman
Cast .... Joan Van Ark
Cast .... Daniel J. Travanti
Cast .... Christopher Noth
Cast .... Rick Springfield

INCIDENT AT DARK RIVER   TNT
Drama: Family Drama • Man Against The System •
Children/Teens • Toxic Waste/Environmental
Airdate: 12/04/89
Rating: N/A   A/C:

When a youngster is fatally poisoned by a polluted river, her father traces the toxic waste to the factory which is the town's main source of economic support.

Production Company: Farrell/Minoff Prods.
Executive Producer............................ Mike Farrell
Executive Producer......................... Marvin Minoff
Executive Producer............................. David Reiss
Producer .... Marvin Minoff
Director .... Michael Pressman
Writer .... Albert Ruben
Cast .... Mike Farrell
Cast .... Tess Harper
Cast .... Helen Hunt

INCIDENT IN A SMALL TOWN   CBS
Drama: Period Piece • Family Drama • Courtroom
Drama • Murder and Murder Mystery
Airdate: 1/23/94
Rating: 18.7/31   A/C: 1

Sequel to the 1990 TV movie; "The Incident" and the 1992 TV movie; "Against Her Will: An Incident In Baltimore". In 1954 in a small town in Illinois, lawyer Harmon Cobb comes to the aid of his law partner's estranged daughter and her thirteen year old son who are being threatened by the man who sired the child when her raped her years ago. When the brute is found dead, her father takes the rap but it is eventually revealed that the boy, in order to protect his mother from impending violence, dealt the fatal blow.

Production Company: RHI Ent. IAW Procter&
    Gamble
Executive Producer .... Robert Halmi, Sr.
Co-Executive Producer................. Larry Strichman
Producer... Delbert Mann
Director .... Delbert Mann
Writer .... Cindy Myers
Cast .... Walter Matthau
Cast .... Stephanie Zimbalist
Cast .... Harry Morgan
Cast .... Nick Stahl

INCIDENT, THE   CBS
EMMY WINNER
Drama: Murder and Murder Mystery • Period Piece •
Courtroom Drama • WWII • Prison and Prison Camp
Airdate: 03/04/90
Rating: 20.8/33   A/C: 1

In 1944, a broken-down attorney is forced to defend a German P.O.W. accused of murdering an American civilian. As the case proceeds, he uncovers a plot that proves the soldier had been framed.

Production Company: Quintex Entertainment, Inc.
Executive Producer .... Robert Halmi, Sr.
Producer.. Bill Brademan
Producer... Edwin Self
Director .... Joseph Sargent
Writer .... Michael Norell
Writer .... James Norell
Cast .... Walter Matthau
Cast .... Susan Blakely
Cast .... Robert Carradine
Cast .... Barnard Hughes
Cast .... Peter Firth

INCONVENIENT WOMAN, AN   ABC
Miniseries/Drama (2 nights): Family Drama • Murder
and Murder Mystery • Sex/Glitz
Airdate: 05/12/91 • 05/13/91
Rating: 11.7/21 • 12.4/20   A/C: 2 • 2

*Based on the book by Dominick Dunne. An
earthy waitress becomes the mistress of a
wealthy tycoon and is swept up into the dark
world of high society murder, scandal and
blackmail.*

Production Company: ABC Productions
Executive Producer .... Andrew Adelson
Producer .... Cleve Landsberg
Director .... Larry Elikann
Writer .... John Pielmeier
Cast .... Jason Robards
Cast .... Jill Eikenberry
Cast .... Rebecca De Mornay
Cast .... Peter Gallagher

INCREDIBLE HULK RETURNS, THE   NBC
Drama: Action/Adventure • Sci-Fi/Supernatural/
Horror/Fantasy
Airdate: 05/22/88
Rating: 20.2/33   A/C:

*Based on the TV series. The Hulk and alter-
ego Dr. David Banner team up with bumptious
Norse god Thor and his sidekick, the mild-
mannered Dr. Donald Blake, to introduce the
new guy in town to Los Angeles and its varied
crimes.*

Production Company: B&B Prods. IAW New
    World TV
Executive Producer .... Nicholas Corea
Executive Producer .... Bill Bixby
Director .... Nicholas Corea
Writer .... Nicholas Corea
Cast .... Lou Ferrigno
Cast .... Bill Bixby
Cast .... Eric Kramer
Cast .... Lee Purcell

INDECENCY   USA
Drama: Murder and Murder Mystery
Airdate: 9/16/92
Rating: N/A   A/C:

*Not believing her boss' death was a suicide, a
depressed young film editor uncovers scores of
suspects and multiple motives as she seeks to
find the answers to her friends violent demise.
Convinced at first it is was her pals estranged
husband, she shocked to unveil a jealous co-
workers homicidal rage.*

Production Company: Point of View Prods. IAW
    MTE Universal
Executive Producer .... Janet Meyers
Producer .... Harvey Frand
Co-Producer .... Chuck Sloan
Co-Producer .... Holly Sloan
Director .... Marisa Silver
Writer .... Amy Jones
Writer .... Holly Sloan
Writer .... Alan Ormsby
Cast .... Jennifer Beals
Cast .... James Remar
Cast .... Barbara Williams

INDEPENDENCE   NBC
Drama: Western
Airdate: 03/29/87
Rating: 14.5/23   A/C:

*Years after he cleaned up the town of
Independence, the sheriff must face down some
bad guys who are back to break their murderous
friends out of jail.*

Production Company: Sunn Classic Pictures Inc.
Executive Producer .... Gordon Dawson
Producer .... Joseph Wallenstein
Director .... John Patterson
Writer .... Gordon Dawson
Cast .... Isabella Hofmann
Cast .... Anthony Zerbe
Cast .... Macon McCalman
Cast .... Stephanie Dunnam
Cast .... John Bennett Perry

INDISCREET   CBS
Comedy: Love Story • Foreign or Exotic Location •
Romantic Comedy
Airdate: 10/24/88
Rating: 12.0/18   A/C:

*Based on the play by Norman Krasna and
remake of the 1958 film about an English
actress who falls in love with an American
diplomat who pretends to be married.*

Production Company: Republic Pictures
Executive Producer .... Karen Mack
Producer .... John Davis
Director .... Richard Michaels
Writer .... Walter Lockwood
Writer .... Sally Robinson
Cast .... Robert Wagner
Cast .... Maggie Henderson
Cast .... Robert McBain
Cast .... Lesley-Anne Down

INFIDELITY   ABC
Drama: Family Drama • Forbidden Love • Woman's
Issue/Story
Airdate: 04/13/87
Rating: 16.8/27   A/C:

*After his physician-wife miscarries, a
photographer has an affair with her best friend.*

Production Company: Mark/Jett Productions
Executive Producer .... Ilene Amy Berg
Producer .... Tony Mark
Producer .... Sue Jett
Director .... David Lowell Rich
Writer .... Sue Jett
Cast .... Kirstie Alley
Cast .... Vera Lockwood
Cast .... Robert Englund
Cast .... Lee Horsley
Producer .... Michael Carven

INHERIT THE WIND   NBC
EMMY WINNER
Drama: Period Piece • Courtroom Drama • Historical
Piece
Airdate: 03/20/88
Rating: 18.0/29   A/C:

*Fictionalized story based on the classic play
about the Scopes monkey trial which pitted
creationism against Darwinism in the South of
1925.*

Production Company: Vincent Pictures Prods.
    IAW David Greene/Robert Papazian Prods.
Executive Producer .... Peter Douglas
Producer .... Robert A. Papazian
Director .... David Greene
Writer .... John Gay
Cast .... Kirk Douglas
Cast .... Megan Follows
Cast .... Kyle Secor
Cast .... Jean Simmons
Cast .... Jason Robards

INTERNAL AFFAIRS   CBS
Miniseries/Drama (2 nights): Murder and Murder
Mystery • Cops/Detectives/Law Enforcement
Airdate: 11/06/88 • 11/07/88
Rating: 16.1/26 • 13.7/21   A/C:

*A middle-aged New York policeman becomes
involved with a young woman as he investigates
a murder.*

Production Company: Titus Prods. Inc.
Executive Producer .... Herbert Brodkin
Executive Producer .... Robert Berger
Director .... Michael Tuchner
Writer .... William Bayer
Cast .... Richard Crenna
Cast .... Kate Capshaw
Cast .... Cliff Gorman
Cast .... Ronald Hunter

INTERNATIONAL AIRPORT   ABC
Drama: Suspense/Thriller • Series Pilot (2 hr.)
Airdate: 05/25/85
Rating: 13.0/27   A/C:

*The manager of an international airport must
try to avert tragedy when he receives a bomb
threat.*

Production Company: Aaron Spelling Prods.
Executive Producer .... Aaron Spelling
Executive Producer .... Douglas S. Cramer
Producer .... Robert McCullough
Director .... Don Chaffey
Director .... Charles S. Dubin
Writer .... Robert McCullough
Cast .... Gil Gerard
Cast .... Berlinda Tolbert
Cast .... Cliff Potts
Cast .... Pat Crowley

INTIMATE ENCOUNTERS   NBC
Drama: Family Drama • Sex/Glitz
Airdate: 09/28/86
Rating: 14.2/23   A/C:

A couple's marriage begins to fall apart when the wife seeks excitement in sexual fantasy and adultery.

Production Company: Larry Thompson Prods. & Donna Mills Prods. IAW Columbia TV
Executive Producer .... Larry Thompson
Producer .... Jon Andersen
Co-Producer .... Robert Kosberg
Director .... Ivan Nagy
Writer .... Ivan Nagy
Writer .... Dennis Turner
Cast .... Donna Mills
Cast .... James Brolin
Cast .... Cicely Tyson
Cast .... Veronica Cartwright

INTIMATE STRANGER   SHOWTIME
Drama: Psychological Thriller • Sex/Glitz • Woman In Jeopardy
Airdate: 11/15/91
Rating: N/A   A/C:

A phone sex operator is stalked by a murderer after she hears him kill someone during one of her sessions.

Production Company: South Gate Entertainment Prod.
Producer .... Yoram Pelman
Producer .... J.J. Lichauco-Pelman
Director .... Allan Holzman
Writer .... Rob Fresco
Cast .... Deborah Harry
Cast .... Tim Thomerson
Cast .... James Russo

INTIMATE STRANGERS   CBS
Drama: Family Drama • Vietnam
Airdate: 01/01/86
Rating: 26.4/38   A/C:

An army nurse who was a POW in North Vietnam for ten years returns home to her doctor husband and has trouble readjusting to her new life.

Production Company: Nederlander TV and Film Prods. IAW Telepictures
Executive Producer .... John Manulis
Executive Producer .... Gladys Rackmil
Producer .... Kenneth Utt
Director .... Robert Ellis Miller
Writer .... Norman Morrill
Cast .... Teri Garr
Cast .... Stacy Keach
Cast .... Cathy Lee Crosby
Cast .... Priscilla Lopez
Cast .... Max Gail

INTO THE BADLANDS   USA
Drama: Suspense/Thriller • Western
Airdate: 07/24/91
Rating: N/A   A/C:

In his pursuit of a wanted criminal, a hard-bitten bounty hunter guides us on a journey through three separate stories involving eerie occurrences in the Old West.

Production Company: Ogiens/Kane Prods.
Executive Producer .... Michael Ogiens
Executive Producer .... Josh Kane
Producer .... Harvey Frand
Director .... Sam Pillsbury
Writer .... Dick Beebe
Writer .... Gordon Dawson
Writer .... Marjorie David
Cast .... Bruce Dern
Cast .... Mariel Hemingway
Cast .... Dylan McDermott
Cast .... Helen Hunt

INTO THE HOMELAND   HBO
Drama: Suspense/Thriller • Children/Teens
Airdate: 12/26/87
Rating: N/A   A/C:

A hard drinking, ex- L.A. undercover detective learns that his 17 year old daughter is missing in Wyoming. Seeing a photo of the girl with a teenage boy he finds the kid and tails him to the headquarters of the American Liberation Movement. He infiltrates the white supremacist group, kidnaps the young man and forces him to reveal the girls whereabouts. He discovers she was sent East to a youth compound for further indoctrination and together with the F.B.I. she is rescued from the mind controlling organization.

Production Company: HBO Pictures
Executive Producer .... Kevin McCormick
Executive Producer .... Anna Hamilton Phelan
Producer .... Kevin McCormick
Director .... Lesli Glatter
Writer .... Anna Hamilton Phelan
Cast .... Powers Boothe
Cast .... C. Thomas Howell
Cast .... Paul LeMat
Cast .... Cindy Pickett

INTO THIN AIR   CBS
Drama: Family Drama • Children/Teens • Woman Against The System • True Crime • Cops/Detectives/ Law Enforcement
Airdate: 10/29/86
Rating: 15.7/25   A/C:

True story of a mother who doggedly pursues the disappearance of her nineteen year old son, last seen driving from Ottawa to Colorado. Even after his van is found in Maine, she gets little official help and is forced to hire a private eye.

Production Company: Fries Entertainment Inc.
Executive Producer .... Tony Ganz
Executive Producer .... Irv Wilson
Executive Producer .... Ron Howard
Producer .... Joseph Stern
Director .... Roger Young
Writer .... George Rubino
Cast .... Ellen Burstyn
Cast .... Tate Donovan
Cast .... Robert Prosky
Cast .... Nicholas Pryor

INTRIGUE   CBS
Drama: Suspense/Thriller • Action/Adventure • Foreign or Exotic Location
Airdate: 09/11/88
Rating: 8.8/19   A/C:

An American agent goes to eastern Europe to retrieve a CIA defector who now wants to come back.

Production Company: Crew Neck Prods. and Linnea Prods. IAW Columbia Pictures TV
Executive Producer .... John Scheinfeld
Executive Producer .... Jeff Melvoin
Producer .... Nick Gillott
Director .... David Drury
Writer .... Robert Collins
Cast .... Robert Loggia
Cast .... Paul Maxwell
Cast .... Scott Glenn
Cast .... Eleanor Bron
Cast .... William Atherton

INTRUDERS   CBS

Miniseries/Drama (2 nights): Sci-Fi/Supernatural/
Horror/Fantasy
Airdate: 05/17/92 • 05/19/92
Rating: 13.2/21 • 12.9/21   A/C: 2 • 3

*A respected psychiatrist treats two distraught
women who claim they are the victims of UFO
abductions. At first skeptical, he becomes a
devoted advocate when surmounting evidence
validates their experiences.*

Production Company: Osiris Films, Dan Curtis
     Prods. IAW CBS Entertainment Prods.
Executive Producer .... Robert O'Connor
Executive Producer .... Michael Apted
Executive Producer .... Dan Curtis
Producer .... Branko Lustig
Co-Producer .... Mary Benjamin
Co-Producer .... Eric Schiff
Director .... Dan Curtis
Writer .... Barry Oringer
Writer .... Tracy Torme
Cast .... Richard Crenna
Cast .... Mare Winningham
Cast .... Susan Blakely
Cast .... Daphne Ashbrook
Cast .... Alan Autry

INVASION OF PRIVACY   USA

Drama: Woman In Jeopardy • Suspense/Thriller
Airdate: 10/7/92
Rating: N/A   A/C:

*A beautiful magazine writer, doing a story on
ex-cons' rehabilitation, becomes the target of
an obsessed prison inmate after he is released
on parole. Securing a job as her assistant, he
soon becomes totally unhinged when he learns
of her relationship with her sophisticated editor.*

Production Company: Prism Pictures, Promark
     Ent. Group
Executive Producer .... Barry Collier
Executive Producer .... Carol Rossi
Executive Producer .... Bruce Cohn Curtis
Producer .... Ashok Amritraj
Director .... Kevin Meyer
Writer .... Kevin Meyer
Cast .... Jennifer O'Neill
Cast .... Robby Benson
Cast .... Lydie Denier

INVESTIGATION: INSIDE A TERRORIST BOMBING, THE   HBO

Drama: Man Against The System • True Story •
Courtroom Drama • Foreign or Exotic Location •
Social Issue
Airdate: 04/22/90
Rating: N/A   A/C:

*British TV reporters working on a documentary
discover that six alleged IRA members, serving
life sentences in prison for two 1974 pub
bombings that killed twenty one, are innocent.
They then must prove it.*

Production Company: Granada Television
Executive Producer .... Colin Callender
Executive Producer .... Ray Fitzwalter
Producer .... Mike Beckham
Director .... Mike Beckham
Writer .... Rob Ritchie
Cast .... John Hurt
Cast .... Martin Shaw
Cast .... Roger Allam
Cast .... Peter Gowen

IRAN: DAYS OF CRISIS   TNT

Miniseries/Drama (2 nights): True Story • Historical
Piece • Foreign or Exotic Location • Political Piece
Airdate: 09/30/91 • 10/01/91
Rating: N/A   A/C:

*In Iran, an American diplomat and his Iranian
wife are swept up in the political and historical
events leading up to the Shah's overthrow, the
rise of Khomeini, and the 1979-81 hostage
crisis.*

Production Company: Gerald Rafshoon/
     Consolidated Prods. IAW Atlantique Prods.
Executive Producer .... Gerald Rafshoon
Producer .... Tim Sanders
Director .... Kevin Connor
Writer .... Tim Wells
Writer .... Reg Gadney
Cast .... Arliss Howard
Cast .... Jeff Fahey
Cast .... Alice Krige
Cast .... George Grizzard
Cast .... Tony Goldwyn

IRONCLADS   TNT

Drama: Period Piece • Action/Adventure • Historical
Piece
Airdate: 03/11/91
Rating: N/A   A/C:

*The famous 1862 Civil War battle between the
armored gun ships Monitor and Merrimack is
the back drop for this period drama involving
a Southern belle's dangerous games and divided
loyalties.*

Production Company: Rosemont Prods.
Executive Producer .... Norman Rosemont
Producer .... David A. Rosemont
Director .... Delbert Mann
Writer .... Harold Gast
Cast .... Virginia Madsen
Cast .... Alex Hyde-White
Cast .... Fritz Weaver

ISLAND SONS   ABC

Drama: Family Drama • Murder and Murder Mystery
• Action/Adventure • Foreign or Exotic Location •
Series Pilot (2 hr.)
Airdate: 05/15/87
Rating: 7.9/14   A/C:

*In Hawaii, four brothers run their missing
father's businesses as they investigate his
suspicious, crime-related disappearance.*

Production Company: Universal TV
Executive Producer .... James D. Parriott
Co-Executive Producer .... Deanne Barkley
Producer .... Len Kaufman
Director .... Alan J. Levi
Writer .... James Dott
Cast .... Timothy Bottoms
Cast .... Samuel Bottoms
Cast .... Joseph Bottoms
Cast .... Benjamin Bottoms
Cast .... David Wohl

IT'S NOTHING PERSONAL   NBC

Drama: Cops/Detectives/Law Enforcement • Murder
and Murder Mystery • Series Pilot (2 hr.)
Airdate: 2/1/93
Rating: 10.9/17   A/C: 3

*A former Los Angeles cop, haunted by the death
of her brother and a bit over the edge joins up
with a leathery down on his luck bounty hunter.
Together they go after a bail jumper, not
necessarily playing by the rules.*

Production Company: Lee Rich Co. Bruce Sallan
     Prods. IAW Papazian-Hirsch Ent.
Executive Producer .... Bruce J. Sallan
Executive Producer .... Lee Rich
Producer .... Chery Downey
Director .... Bradford May
Writer .... Lee Rose
Cast .... Amanda Donohoe
Cast .... Bruce Dern
Cast .... Yaphet Kotto
Cast .... Claire Bloom

IZZY AND MOE   CBS

Comedy: Period Piece • Buddy Story
Airdate: 09/23/85
Rating: 17.9/27   A/C:

*Two 1920's vaudevillians become Federal
prohibition officers and pursue bootleggers.*

Production Company: Robert Halmi Inc.
Executive Producer .... Robert Halmi, Sr.
Co-Producer .... Robert Boris
Director .... Jackie Cooper
Writer .... Robert Boris
Cast .... Art Carney
Cast .... Jackie Gleason
Cast .... Zohra Lampert
Cast .... Dick Latessa

JFK: RECKLESS YOUTH   ABC

Miniseries/Drama (2 nights): Biography • Period
Piece • Family Drama • Historical Piece
Airdate: 11/21/93 • 11/23/93
Rating: 7.8/12 • 9.5/16   A/C: 4 • 3

*Based on the book by Nigel Hamilton. The life
of John F. Kennedy from the age of 16 to 29.
His years as a charming, rebellious prep school
and Harvard student, his numerous affairs and
his heroic naval career which led him to his
first congressional campaign.*

Production Company: Polone Co. IAW Hearst Ent.
Executive Producer .... Judith A. Polone
Producer .... Harry Winer
Director .... Harry Winer
Writer .... William Broyles, Jr.
Cast .... Patrick Dempsey
Cast .... Terry Kinney
Cast .... Loren Dean
Cast .... Yolanda Jilot
Cast .... Diana Scarwid
Cast .... Robin Tunney

J. O. E. AND THE COLONEL   ABC

Drama: Murder and Murder Mystery • Sci-Fi/
Supernatural/Horror/Fantasy
Airdate: 09/11/85
Rating: 11.0/18   A/C:

*When the friend and confidant of J.O.E., a
cyborg with superhuman powers, is killed,
J.O.E. teams up with a tough colonel to solve
the case. Meanwhile, the army, which has
discovered J.O.E. to be too human, tries to
destroy him.*

Production Company: Mad Dog Prods. IAW
     Universal TV
Executive Producer .... Nicholas Corea
Producer .... Stephen P. Caldwell
Director .... Ron Satlof
Cast .... Nicholas Corea
Cast .... Terence Knox
Cast .... Aimee Eccles
Cast .... William Lucking
Cast .... Gary Kasper

JACK THE RIPPER   CBS

Miniseries/Drama (2 nights): Murder and Murder
Mystery • True Crime • Period Piece • Historical Piece
Airdate: 10/21/88 • 10/23/88
Rating: 14.8/26 • 20.3/31   A/C:

*This fact-based story of the gruesome deeds and
the pursuit of the London serial killer claims to
finally reveal the real Jack.*

Production Company: Euston Films, Thames TV
     IAW Hill-O'Connor Entertainment & Lorimar
Executive Producer .... Lloyd Shirely
Executive Producer .... Robert O'Connor
Executive Producer .... Leonard Hill
Producer .... David Wickes
Director .... David Wickes
Writer .... Derek Marlowe
Cast .... Armand Assante
Cast .... Michael Caine
Cast .... Lewis Collins
Cast .... Susan George
Cast .... Jane Seymour
Cast .... Ray McAnally

JACKIE COLLINS' LADY BOSS   NBC

Miniseries/Drama (2 nights): Sex/Glitz • Hollywood
Airdate: 10/11/92 • 10/12/93
Rating: 12.7/20 • 14.2/22   A/C: 2 • 3

*Based on the book. Sequel to 1990 TV Movie
"Lucky Chances". Shipping heiress Lucky
Santangelo goes up against mob bosses,
Hollywood sleazeballs and avaricious
sycophants when she attempts to take over a
major motion picture studio.*

Production Company: Puma Prods. IAW Von
     Zemeck/Sertner Films
Executive Producer .... Jackie Collins
Executive Producer .... Frank Von Zemeck
Executive Producer .... Robert M. Sertner
Producer .... Steve McGlothen
Co-Producer .... Deborah Edell
Writer .... Jackie Collins
Director .... Charles Jarrott
Cast .... Kim Delaney
Cast .... Jack Scalia
Cast .... Alan Rachins
Cast .... Phil Morris
Cast .... Joe Cortese

JACKIE COLLINS' LUCKY CHANCES   NBC

Miniseries/Drama (3 nights): Family Drama • Period
Piece • Sex/Glitz • Mafia/Mob
Airdate: 10/07/90 • 10/08/90 • 10/9/90
Rating: 14.4/25 • 17.1/26 • 19.5/31
A/C: 2 • 3 • 1

*Based on the novel. Chronicles the lives of an
ambitious, bootlegging immigrant, who rises
to wealth and mob power, and his feisty
daughter, who takes on the family business after
his murder.*

Production Company: NBC Productions
Executive Producer .... Susan Baerwald
Executive Producer .... Jackie Collins
Producer .... Daniel Franklin
Director .... Buzz Kulik
Writer .... Jackie Collins
Cast .... Nicolette Sheridan
Cast .... Vincent Irizarry
Cast .... Michael Nader
Cast .... Anne-Marie Johnson
Cast .... Tim Ryan

JACKSONS: AN AMERICAN DREAM , THE   ABC

Drama: Biography • Family Drama • Hollywood
Airdate: 11/15/93 • 11/18/93
Rating: 21.1/31 • 23.9/36   A/C: 1 • 1

*Chronicles the meteoric rise of the singing
Jackson family, from their working class
background in Gary, Indiana to Motown super
stardom. The boys are constantly driven by
their domineering father Joe which eventually
lead to family conflicts and long held
resentments.*

Production Company: Stan Margulies Co., de
     Passe Ent., Motown Record Co., KJ Films Inc.
Executive Producer .... Stan Margulies
Executive Producer .... Suzanne de Passe
Producer .... Jermanine Jackson
Producer .... Margaret Jackson
Director .... Karen Arthur
Writer .... Joyce Eliason
Cast .... Lawrence-Hilton Jacobs
Cast .... Billy Dee Williams
Cast .... Vanessa Williams
Cast .... Angela Bassett
Cast .... Jason Weaver
Cast .... Wylie Draper

JAILBIRDS   CBS

Comedy: Action/Adventure • Buddy Story
Airdate: 05/16/91
Rating: 12.9/22   A/C: 2

*Tempers flare as two women, an imperious
black L.A. executive and a saucy, white country
seamstress, are on the lam together in Louisiana
after being wrongly accused of crimes they
didn't commit.*

Production Company: Spelling Entertainment, Inc.
Executive Producer .... Aaron Spelling
Executive Producer .... E. Duke Vincent
Producer .... James L. Conway
Director .... Burt Brinckerhoff
Writer .... Craig Heller
Writer .... Guy Shulman
Writer .... Marcia Midkiff
Cast .... Dyan Cannon
Cast .... Phylicia Rashad
Cast .... Dakin Matthews
Cast .... David Knell

JAKE AND THE FATMAN   CBS

Mystery: Murder and Murder Mystery • Foreign or
Exotic Location • Cops/Detectives/Law Enforcement
Airdate: 03/15/89
Rating: 15.8/27   A/C:

*Upon arriving in Hawaii, Jake's best friend is
killed and Jake and the Fatman must go after
the murderer.*

Production Company: Fred Silverman Co. & Dean
     Hargrove Prods.
Executive Producer .... Fred Silverman
Executive Producer .... **Dean Hargrove**
Executive Producer .... Ed Waters
Director .... E.W. Swackhamer
Writer .... Ed Waters
Cast .... Joe Penny
Cast .... William Conrad
Cast .... Amy Steel
Cast .... Alan Campbell

Movies and Miniseries

JAKE SPANNER, PRIVATE EYE USA
Drama: Cops/Detectives/Law Enforcement •
Suspense/Thriller • Drug Smuggling/Dealing
Airdate: 11/15/89
Rating: N/A   A/C:

Based on the novel "The Old Dick" by L. A.
Morse. A retired detective is hired by an old
gangster enemy to help with a ransom drop.
But the kidnapping is a fake, and the detective
discovers that what's really going on is drug
dealing.

Production Company: Scotti Vinnedge Prods. IAW
USA Network
Executive Producer .... Andrew J. Fenady
Producer .... Syd Vinnedge
Producer .... John Vinnedge
Director .... Lee H. Katzin
Writer .... Andrew J. Fenady
Cast .... Robert Mitchum
Cast .... John Mitchum
Cast .... Ernest Borgnine
Cast .... Dick Van Patten

JAMES CLAVELL'S NOBLE HOUSE NBC
Miniseries/Drama (4 nights): Love Story • Action/
Adventure • Foreign or Exotic Location
Airdate: 02/21/88 • 02/22/88 • 02/23/88 • 02/24/88
Rating: 17.9/27 • 15.9/24 • 15.0/22 • 16.3/26
A/C: 1 • 2 • 2 • 2

Based on the novel. The head of a Hong Kong-
based international trading organization,
recently taken public, confronts takeover
attempts, interlocking intrigues and ancient
obligations.

Production Company: Noble House Prods. Ltd.
IAW De Laurentiis Entertainment Group
Executive Producer .... James Clavell
Director .... Gary Nelson
Writer .... Eric Bercovici
Cast .... Pierce Brosnan
Cast .... John Rhys-Davies
Cast .... Julia Nickson
Cast .... Khigh Dhiegh
Cast .... Ben Masters
Cast .... Deborah Raffin
Cast .... Nancy Kwan

JANE'S HOUSE CBS
Drama: Family Drama
Airdate: 1/2/94
Rating: 19.5/29   A/C: 1

Based on the book by Robert Kimmel Smith.
The romance and eventual marriage between
a New York businesswoman and a shy Long
Island, widowed father causes emotional
turmoil for his two children who are still trying
to cope with the loss of their beloved mother.

Production Company: Michael Phillips Prods.
IAW Spelling Television Inc.
Executive Producer .... Aaron Spelling
Executive Producer .... E. Duke Vincent
Executive Producer .... Michael Phillips
Co-Executive Producer .... Debra Greenfield
Producer .... Christopher Morgan
Producer .... Glenn Jordan
Director .... Glenn Jordan
Writer .... Eric Roth
Cast .... James Woods
Cast .... Anne Archer
Cast .... Missy Crider
Cast .... Graham Beckel
Cast .... Jane Schweitzer

JEKYLL & HYDE ABC
Drama: Period Piece • Sci-Fi/Supernatural/Horror/
Fantasy
Airdate: 01/21/90
Rating: 12.2/19   A/C: 3

Adaptation of Robert Louis Stevenson's classic
tale. Dr. Henry Jekyll is a good physician whose
experiments with drugs transforms him into the
evil and murderous Dr. Hyde. He ultimately
kills himself to protect those he loves.

Production Company: David Wickes TV IAW
London Weekend TV and King Phoenix Ent.
Executive Producer .... Nick Elliot
Executive Producer .... David Wickes
Executive Producer .... Gerald W. Abrams
Producer .... Patricia Carr
Director .... David Wickes
Writer .... David Wickes
Cast .... Michael Caine
Cast .... Cheryl Ladd
Cast .... Joss Ackland
Cast .... Ronald Pickup

JERICHO FEVER USA
Drama: Suspense/Thriller • Medical/Disease/Mental
Illness
Airdate: 12/16/93
Rating: N/A   A/C:

A group of deadly terrorists are hunted down
by an FBI agent and doctors from the Centers
for Disease Control when they are discovered
to be the carriers of a lethal virus. When the
leader of the mercenaries becomes the only
survivor of the disease he becomes even more
important in that his blood carries antibodies
that could save thousands from impending
doom.

Production Company: Sankan Prods. IAW
Wilshire Court Prods.
Executive Producer .... Sandor Stern
Producer .... Kandy Stern
Co-Producer .... Terence Donnelly
Director .... Sandor Stern
Writer .... I.C. Rapoport
Cast .... Stephanie Zimbalist
Cast .... Perry King
Cast .... Branscombe Richmond

JESSE CBS
Drama: Woman Against The System • Medical/
Disease/Mental Illness • True Story • Courtroom
Drama
Airdate: 10/04/88
Rating: 19.4/31   A/C:

Fact-based story of a beloved small-town nurse
who is arrested and tried for doctoring without
a license.

Production Company: Turman-Foster Co./Jordan
IAW Republic Pictures
Executive Producer .... Lawrence Turman
Executive Producer .... David Foster
Producer .... Glenn Jordan
Director .... Glenn Jordan
Writer .... James Lee Barrett
Cast .... Lee Remick
Cast .... Kevin Conway
Cast .... Richard Marcus
Cast .... Albert Salmi

JESSE HAWKES CBS
Drama: Action/Adventure • Drug Smuggling/Dealing
• Series Pilot (2 hr.)
Airdate: 04/22/89
Rating: 8.9/17   A/C:

"High Mountain Rangers" protagonist Jesse
Hawkes moves to San Francisco to fight urban
drug crime after his son is paralyzed during an
aborted drug raid.

Production Company: A. Shane Co.
Executive Producer .... Joan Conrad
Producer .... Roger Bacon
Producer .... Tom Blomquist
Producer .... Scott Thomas
Director .... Robert Conrad
Writer .... Stephen A. Miller
Cast .... Robert Conrad
Cast .... Christian Conrad
Cast .... Shane Conrad
Cast .... Maggie Cooper

JESSIE — ABC

Drama: Murder and Murder Mystery • Cops/ Detectives/Law Enforcement • Woman In Jeopardy • Series Pilot (2 hr.)
Airdate: 09/18/84
Rating: 17.7/29   A/C:

A female psychiatrist works with the police department to help find a serial killer of women.

Production Company: Lindsay Wagner Prods. IAW MGM-UA TV

Executive Producer	Felix Culver
Producer	Roger Richard
Director	Richard Michaels
Writer	Felix Culver
Cast	Lindsay Wagner
Cast	Celeste Holm
Cast	Tony Lo Bianco
Cast	Renee Jones
Cast	Tom Nolan

JOHN AND YOKO: A LOVE STORY — NBC

Drama: Love Story • Period Piece • Biography
Airdate: 12/02/85
Rating: 13.4/19   A/C:

The story of Beatle John Lennon and his romance and marriage with Yoko Ono from 1966 to 1980.

Production Company: Carson Prods.

Executive Producer	John J. McMahon
Producer	Aida Yang
Director	Sandor Stern
Writer	Sandor Stern
Cast	Kim Miyori
Cast	Mark McGann
Cast	Peter Capaldi
Cast	Kenneth Price

JOHNNIE MAE GIBSON: F B I — CBS

Drama: Cops/Detectives/Law Enforcement • Woman Against The System • True Story • Black Story
Airdate: 10/21/86
Rating: 13.3/20   A/C:

Fact-based story of a black woman who becomes an active, not deskbound, FBI agent.

Production Company: Foolscap Prods.

Executive Producer	James S. Henerson
Executive Producer	James G. Hirsch
Producer	Jim Begg
Director	Bill Duke
Writer	James G. Hirsch
Cast	Lynn Whitfield
Cast	Howard E. Rollins, Jr.
Cast	Richard Lawson
Cast	John Lehne
Cast	Marta Dubois

JOHNNY BULL — ABC

Drama: Family Drama • Cross-Cultural Story • Period Piece
Airdate: 05/19/86
Rating: 12.7/20   A/C:

A young Englishwoman, her American husband and his Hungarian mother strive to coexist in a Pennsylvania coal town around 1960.

Production Company: Titus Prods.

Executive Producer	Herbert Brodkin
Producer	Thomas De Wolfe
Director	Claudia Weill
Writer	Kathleen Betsko Yale
Cast	Colleen Dewhurst
Cast	Jason Robards
Cast	Kathy Bates
Cast	Peter MacNicol

JOHNNY RYAN — NBC

Drama: Murder and Murder Mystery • Cops/ Detectives/Law Enforcement • Period Piece • Series Pilot (2 hr.) • Mafia/Mob
Airdate: 07/29/90
Rating: 6.6/12   A/C: 4

It's the 1940's and a special police unit, headed by Ryan, has been set up to battle the Mob. While investigating the mysterious fall of a government witness from a very high window, Ryan falls in love with a gangster's girl.

Production Company: Dan Curtis TV Prod. IAW MGM/UA & NBC Prod.

Executive Producer	Dan Curtis
Producer	Christopher Chulack
Director	Robert Collins
Writer	Mark Rodgers
Cast	Clancy Brown
Cast	Bruce Abbott
Cast	Teri Austin
Cast	Eugene Clark

JONATHAN STONE: THREAT OF INNOCENCE — NBC

Drama: Cops/Detectives/Law Enforcement • Murder and Murder Mystery
Airdate: 5/17/94
Rating: 12.2/16   A/C: 4

Boston private eye Jonathan Stone is trying to cope with the death of his wife when he takes up an old friends offer to use his Seattle beach house for a while. When his friend is murdered, Stone becomes the prime suspect. With the help of a friendly neighbor, he must discover who is framing him and who—if anyone—murdered his old buddy.

Production Company: Herkimer Pond Prods.

Executive Producer	Gordon Greisman
Producer	Richard Brams
Director	Michael Switzer
Writer	Gordon Greisman
Cast	Richard Crenna
Cast	Beverly D'Angelo
Cast	Robert Desiderio
Cast	Stephen McHattie

JONATHAN: THE BOY NOBODY WANTED — NBC

Drama: Family Drama • Children/Teens • Medical/ Disease/Mental Illness • True Story • Courtroom Drama • Social Issue
Airdate: 10/19/92
Rating: 13.8/21   A/C: 3

Social worker Ginny Moore, faces a legal battle when she seeks to become the guardian of a Down syndrome teenager who has been institutionalized since infancy and in the need of a heart operation. Blocking her attempts are the boy's selfish parents who forbid Ginny and her husband to have any contact with their son. The court ultimately finds "in the best interest of the child" and awards guardianship to the loving Moore family.

Production Company: Gross-Weston Prods. IAW Cannell Ent.

Executive Producer	Marcy Gross
Executive Producer	Ann Weston
Producer	Peter Nelson
Producer	Doris Silverton
Co-Producer	Diane Walsh
Director	George Kaczender
Writer	Steve Lawson
Writer	Dalene Young
Cast	Chris Burke
Cast	JoBeth Williams
Cast	Alley Mills
Cast	Jeffrey DeMunn

JOSEPHINE BAKER STORY, THE — HBO

Drama: True Story • Period Piece • Black Story • Foreign or Exotic Location • Biography • Hollywood
Airdate: 03/16/91
Rating: N/A   A/C:

Life of the legendary black entertainer focuses on her fight against racism, her self-imposed exile to Paris, and her lifelong devotion to her twelve adopted multi-racial children.

Production Company: HBO-RHI-Anglia

Executive Producer	Robert Halmi, Sr.
Executive Producer	David Puttnam
Producer	John Kemeny
Director	Brian Gibson
Writer	Ron Hutchinson
Cast	Lynn Whitfield
Cast	Ruben Blades
Cast	David Dukes
Cast	Louis Gossett, Jr.

JOSHUA'S HEART · NBC

Drama: Family Drama • Children/Teens • Woman's Issue/Story • Social Issue
Airdate: 09/10/90
Rating: 15.6/26   A/C: 2

A young woman and a lonely ten-year-old boy fight to stay together when her doomed relationship with the boy's father ends.

Production Company: Steve White Prods.,
    Grossbart-Barnett Prods., Spectacor Films
Executive Producer .... Steve White
Executive Producer .... Joan Barnett
Executive Producer .... Jack Grossbart
Co-Executive Producer .... Denise Taylor
Producer .... Barry Bernardi
Director .... Michael Pressman
Writer .... Susan Cuscuna
Cast .... Melissa Gilbert
Cast .... Tim Matheson
Cast ....Matthew Lawrence
Cast .... Lisa Eilbacher

JOURNEY TO THE CENTER OF THE EARTH · NBC

Drama: Sci-Fi/Supernatural/Horror/Fantasy • Series Pilot (2 hr.)
Airdate: 2/28/93
Rating: 13.1/20   A/C: 3

Based on the book by Jules Verne. A team of scientists are trapped in a subterranean world while on a mission below the Earth's surface.

Production Company: High Prods.
Executive Producer .... David Mickey Evans
Executive Producer .... Dale de la Torre
Executive Producer .... William Dear
Producer .... John Ashley
Director .... William Dear
Writer .... David Mickey Evans
Writer .... Robert Gunter
Cast .... David Dundara
Cast .... Farrah Forke
Cast .... Kim Miyori

JUDGMENT · HBO

Drama: Family Drama • True Crime • Children/Teens • Courtroom Drama • Rape/Molestation
Airdate: 10/13/90
Rating: N/A   A/C:

The faith of a small Louisiana town is tested when it is discovered that the local priest has molested several altar boys. Refusing to accept church hush money, one family challenges the Catholic hierarchy in court.

Production Company: Tisch/Wigutow/Hershman
    Productions
Executive Producer .... Steve Tisch
Producer .... Donald C. Klune
Producer .... Dan Wigutow
Producer .... Rob Hershman
Director .... Tom Topor
Writer .... Tom Topor
Cast .... Keith Carradine
Cast .... Blythe Danner
Cast .... Michael Faustino
Cast .... David Strathairn

JUDGMENT DAY: THE JOHN LIST STORY · CBS

Drama: True Crime • Cops/Detectives/Law Enforcement • Murder and Murder Mystery • Family Violence
Airdate: 2/23/93
Rating: 15.8/25   A/C: 1

In 1971, New Jersey accountant, John List, brutally murdered his wife, mother and three children. Assuming a new identity as Robert Clark, he established a new life in Denver for eighteen years. A determined local police chief stayed on the case when other agencies lost interest. He finally gets to see justice served when List is arrested after a segment on the TV show "America's Most Wanted" details the unsolved case.

Production Company: Republic Pictures
Executive Producer .... Chuck McLain
Co-Executive Producer .... Lisa Bloch
Director .... Bobby Roth
Writer .... Dennis Turner
Cast .... Robert Blake
Cast .... Beverly D'Angelo
Cast .... David Caruso
Cast .... Melinda Dillon

JUDITH KRANTZ'S TILL WE MEET AGAIN · CBS

Miniseries/Drama (2 nights): Family Drama • Love Story • Period Piece • Foreign or Exotic Location • WWII • Sex/Glitz
Airdate: 11/19/89 • 11/21/89
Rating: 14.8/23 • 11.7/18   A/C: 2 • 3

Based on the novel. The marriage of a French music-hall performer and a champagne heir produces two daughters, an actress and a stunt pilot, in this glitzy tale of a globe-trotting family spanning two world wars.

Production Company: Steve Krantz Prods. IAW
    Yorkshire TV
Executive Producer .... Steve Krantz
Executive Producer .... Keith Richardson
Producer .... Steve Lanning
Director .... Charles Jarrott
Writer .... Andrew Peter Marin
Cast .... Michael York
Cast .... Courteney Cox
Cast .... Mia Sara
Cast .... Bruce Boxleitner

JURY DUTY: THE COMEDY · ABC

Comedy: Buddy Story
Airdate: 01/14/90
Rating: 11.4/18   A/C: 3

When an unassuming accountant is put on trial for embezzlement, twelve very different jurors...a prostitute, a new age devotee, a no-nonsense businessman, and a woman bent on saving old architecture...are sequestered with hilarious results.

Production Company: A Steve White Productions
    IAW Spectacor
Executive Producer .... Steve White
Producer .... Barry Bernardi
Director .... Michael Schultz
Writer .... Rob Gilmer
Cast .... Lynn Redgrave
Cast .... Heather Locklear
Cast .... Mark Blankfield
Cast .... Barbara Bosson
Cast .... Bronson Pinchot
Cast .... Alan Thicke

JUST ANOTHER SECRET · USA

Drama: Suspense/Thriller • Foreign or Exotic Location • Political Piece
Airdate: 12/13/89
Rating: N/A   A/C:

Based on the Frederick Forsythe novel. When five American spies disappear in East Germany, the American agent investigating the case finds neo-Stalinists plotting to assassinate Mikhail Gorbachev and blame it on the missing agents.

Production Company: F.F.S. Prods. IAW Taurus
    Films and Blair Communications
Executive Producer .... Frederick Forsyth
Executive Producer .... Murray Smith
Producer .... Frederick Muller
Director .... Lawrence G. Clark
Writer .... Murray Smith
Cast .... Beau Bridges
Cast .... Alan Howard
Cast .... Kenneth Cranham
Cast .... James Faulkner

JUST MY IMAGINATION · NBC

Comedy: Romantic Comedy
Airdate: 12/21/92
Rating: 15.5/19   A/C: 3

Based on the book, "Bobby Rex's Greatest Hits" by Marianne Gringher. A small-town teacher has her quiet life turned inside out when a former classmate-turned rock star writes a sexy song about her. Swearing nothing ever happened between them, she finds herself suddenly infamous. Fired from her job, she travels to Los Angeles to confront the lothario and salvage her reputation.

Production Company: Andrea Baynes Prods. IAW
    Lorimar TV
Executive Producer .... Andrea Baynes
Executive Producer .... Lynn Roth
Director .... Jonathan Sanger
Writer .... Lynn Roth
Cast .... Jean Smart
Cast .... Tom Wopat
Cast .... Richard Gilliland

JUST ONE OF THE GIRLS FBC

Comedy: Youth Comedy
Airdate: 9/13/93
Rating: 6.3/10 A/C: 4

When a new high school teen is terrorized by the class bully he starts dressing as a girl in order to avoid a beating. While in his disguise he soon becomes gal pals with the head cheerleader, who he just happens to have a crush on. Matters begin to get out of hand when the bully develops the hots for the "new girl", his parents think he's gay and his gym teacher thinks he's a transvestite. He ultimately comes clean and all is forgiven

Production Company: Entertainment Securities
   Ltd. IAW Saban Ent. & Neal & Gary Prods.
Executive Producer .... Lance Robbins
Executive Producer .... Gary Hoffman
Producer .... Robert Vince
Producer .... Cal Shumlatcher
Director .... Michael Keusch
Writer .... Raul Fernandez
Cast .... Corey Haim
Cast .... Nicole Eggert
Cast .... Cameron Bancroft

KANE AND ABEL CBS

Miniseries/Drama (3 nights): Family Drama • Period Piece • Foreign or Exotic Location
Airdate: 11/17/85 • 11/18/85 • 11/19/85
Rating: 23.2/34 • 23.4/34 • 21.4/32 A/C:

From Jeff Archer's novel about a Boston Brahmin and a Polish immigrant who become enemies due to an unfortunate misunderstanding and finally reach a grudging reconciliation when their respective son and daughter defy them and marry each other.

Production Company: Schreckinger Comm. IAW
   Embassy TV
Executive Producer .... Jud Kinberg
Executive Producer .... Michael Grade
Co-Executive Producer .... Jinny Schreckinger
Producer .... Fern Field
Producer .... Stan Kallis
Director .... Buzz Kulik
Writer .... Robert W. Lenski
Cast .... Peter Strauss
Cast .... Sam Neill
Cast .... Ron Silver
Cast .... David Dukes
Cast .... Fred Gwynne

KAREN CARPENTER STORY, THE CBS

Drama: Medical/Disease/Mental Illness • Addiction Story • Biography • Hollywood
Airdate: 01/01/89
Rating: 26.3/41 A/C: 1

The life and career of the singer, who died young of anorexia nervosa, told from the point of view of her brother and partner, Richard.

Production Company: Weintraub Entertainment
   Prods.
Executive Producer .... Richard Carpenter
Producer .... Robert A. Papazian
Producer .... Hal Galli
Director .... Joseph Sargent
Writer .... Barry Morrow
Cast .... Cynthia Gibb
Cast .... Mitchell Anderson
Cast .... Louise Fletcher
Cast .... James Hong
Cast .... Peter Michael Goetz

KATE'S SECRET NBC

Drama: Family Drama • Medical/Disease/Mental Illness • Addiction Story
Airdate: 11/17/86
Rating: 24.1/36 A/C: 1

A woman who seems to have the perfect life actually suffers from bulimia (the eating/ purging disorder) and undergoes therapy at a clinic with other women to prevent her life and marriage from being destroyed.

Production Company: Andrea Baynes Prods. IAW
   Columbia Pictures TV
Executive Producer .... Andrea Baynes
Executive Producer .... Susan Seeger
Producer .... Stephanie Austin
Producer .... Robert A. Papazian
Director .... Arthur Allan Seidelman
Writer .... Susan Seeger
Writer .... Denise De Garmo
Cast .... Meredith Baxter
Cast .... Ben Masters
Cast .... Tracy Nelson
Cast .... Shari Belafonte
Cast .... Edward Asner

KEEP THE CHANGE TNT

Drama: Family Drama • Farm Story
Airdate: 06/09/92
Rating: N/A A/C:

Based on the novel by Thomas McGuane. A frustrated painter returns home to rescue his family's Montana homestead from a greedy rancher where he encounters romantic entanglements, family squabbles and personal triumphs.

Production Company: The Steve Tisch Co.
Executive Producer .... Steve Tisch
Producer .... Cindy Chvatal
Producer .... William Petersen
Director .... Andy Tennant
Writer .... John Miglis
Cast .... William Petersen
Cast .... Lolita Davidovich
Cast .... Jack Palance
Cast .... Buck Henry
Cast .... Rachel Ticotin

KEEPER OF THE CITY SHOWTIME

Drama: Murder and Murder Mystery • Cops/ Detectives/Law Enforcement
Airdate: 01/25/92
Rating: N/A A/C:

A gritty Chicago detective is on the trail of a serial killer who systematically murders members of the mob.

Production Company: Viacom Pictures
Producer .... Bill McCutchen
Co-Producer .... Paul Kurta
Director .... Bobby Roth
Writer .... Gerald Di Pego
Cast .... Louis Gossett, Jr.
Cast .... Anthony La Paglia
Cast .... Peter Coyote

KEEPING SECRETS ABC

Drama: Family Drama • True Story • Family Violence • Addiction Story • Biography
Airdate: 09/29/91
Rating: 14.2/23 A/C: 2

Based on the book. Actress Suzanne Somers' account of her troubled years growing up in an abusive, alcoholic dysfunctional family and her attempts to overcome her own self-destructive behavior.

Production Company: Freyda Rothstein, Hamel-
   Somers Prods. IAW Finnegan-Pinchuk Prods.
Executive Producer .... Suzanne Somers
Executive Producer .... Alan Hamel
Executive Producer .... Freyda Rothstein
Producer .... Pat Finnegan
Producer .... Sheldon Pinchuk
Director .... John Korty
Writer .... Edmond Stevens
Cast .... Suzanne Somers
Cast .... David Birney
Cast .... Ken Kercheval
Cast .... Michael Learned

KENNEDYS OF MASSACHUSETTS, THE ABC

Miniseries/Drama (3 nights): Family Drama • Period Piece • Historical Piece • Biography • Period Piece • True Story
Airdate: 02/18/90 • 02/19/90 • 02/21/90
Rating: 15.8/24 • 17.6/27 • 16.4/25
A/C: 2 • 1 • 2

Based on Doris Kearn Goodwin's book "The Fitzgeralds and the Kennedys." It chronicles the family saga of the Kennedys, beginning in 1906 with the courtship of Joseph and Rose, and ending in 1961 with JFK's inauguration.

Production Company: Edgar J. Scherick
   Associates IAW Orion
Executive Producer .... Edgar J. Scherick
Executive Producer .... Susan Pollock
Producer .... Lynn Raynor
Director .... Lamont Johnson
Writer .... William Hanley
Cast .... William Petersen
Cast .... Annette O'Toole
Cast .... Charles Durning
Cast .... Steven Weber
Cast .... Mary Jane Buckley

KENNY ROGERS AS THE GAMBLER III: THE LEGEND CONTINUES   CBS

Miniseries/Drama (2 nights): Western • American Indians
Airdate: 11/22/87 • 11/24/87
Rating: 20.9/32 • 17.4/29   A/C: 1 • 2

A gambler and his pal take the side of the Indians against government crooks in old North Dakota.

Production Company: Wild Horses Prods.
Executive Producer .... Ken Kragen
Executive Producer .... Lelan Rogers
Director .... Dick Lowry
Writer .... Jeb Rosebrook
Writer .... Roderick Taylor
Cast .... Kenny Rogers
Cast .... Bruce Boxleitner
Cast .... Linda Gray
Cast .... Melanie Chartoff
Cast .... Matt Clark
Cast .... George Kennedy
Cast .... Dean Stockwell

KEYS, THE   NBC

Drama: Family Drama • Children/Teens • Drug Smuggling/Dealing • Series Pilot (2 hr.)
Airdate: 04/12/92
Rating: 12.1/19   A/C: 2

Two estranged sons attempt to reunite with their father but get caught up in his attempt to stop drug smuggling and corruption in the Florida keys.

Production Company: Riven Rock Prods. IAW Universal Television
Executive Producer .... Maurice Hurley
Executive Producer .... Michele Brustin
Producer .... Michael Hirsh
Producer .... Stan Blum
Director .... Richard Compton
Writer .... Maurice Hurley
Cast .... Brian Bloom
Cast .... Scott Bloom
Cast .... Ben Masters
Cast .... Barry Corbin

KICKS   ABC

Drama: Murder and Murder Mystery • Woman In Jeopardy • Suspense/Thriller
Airdate: 03/11/85
Rating: 13.2/21   A/C:

A rich, thrill-seeking man gets his kicks when he involves an innocent woman in a murder, and then plans to kill her as well after she uncovers evidence related to the crime.

Production Company: ABC Circle Films
Producer .... David Levinson
Director .... William Wiard
Writer .... David Levinson
Cast .... Shelley Hack
Cast .... Anthony Geary
Cast .... Ian Abercrombie
Cast .... Susan Ruttan

KIDS DON'T TELL   CBS

Drama: Children/Teens • Rape/Molestation
Airdate: 03/05/85
Rating: 18.1/29   A/C:

To the detriment of his own family life, a documentary filmmaker becomes obsessed with his filmed interviews of child molesters and their victims.

Production Company: Chris-Rose Prods. IAW Viacom Prods.
Executive Producer .... Bob Christiansen
Executive Producer .... Rick Rosenberg
Co-Producer .... Barry Greenfield
Director .... Sam O'Steen
Writer .... Peter Silverman
Writer .... Maurice Hurley
Cast .... Michael Ontkean
Cast .... JoBeth Williams
Cast .... Leo Rossi
Cast .... Ari Meyers

KIDS LIKE THESE   CBS

Drama: Family Drama • Children/Teens • Medical/ Disease/Mental Illness • True Story
Airdate: 11/08/87
Rating: 16.5/27   A/C:

Based on Emily Kingsley's own story. Despite everyone's urging, the parents of a child with Down Syndrome decide to bring him up themselves rather than institutionalizing him. After their success, they begin spreading the word to other parents.

Production Company: Taft Entertainment/Nexus Prods.
Executive Producer .... Georg Stanford Brown
Producer .... Edward Gold
Director .... Georg Stanford Brown
Writer .... Allan Sloane
Writer .... Emily Perl Kingsley
Cast .... Richard Crenna
Cast .... Tyne Daly
Cast .... Zachary M. Allen
Cast .... Joey McFarland
Cast .... Amy Van Nostrand

KILLER AMONG FRIENDS, A   CBS

Drama: True Crime • Children/Teens • Family Drama
Airdate: 12.8.92
Rating: 16.7/27   A/C: 1

A popular teenager is killed by two jealous high school friends, one of whom moves into the grieving mother's home and tries to be a substitute daughter. The unattractive, manipulative girl gives the determined detective assigned to the case false leads which ultimately leads the cops to suspect her involvement. The devastated mother must face the ugly truth about her dead child's friend and sets a trap to unveil her murderous crime.

Production Company: Bonnie Raskin Prods. IAW Green/Epstein Prods., Lorimar Pictures
Executive Producer .... Bonnie Raskin
Executive Producer .... Jim Green
Executive Producer .... Allen Epstein
Producer .... Mark Bacino
Director .... Charles Robert Carner
Writer .... Christopher Lofton
Writer .... John Miglis
Writer .... Charles Robert Carner
Cast .... Patty Duke
Cast .... Margaret Welsh
Cast .... Tiffani-Amber Thiessen
Cast .... Loretta Swit

KILLER AMONG US, A   NBC

Drama: Murder and Murder Mystery • Woman In Jeopardy • Courtroom Drama
Airdate: 10/29/90
Rating: 13.9/23   A/C: 3

A holdout juror in a murder trial tries to prove the defendant's innocence and becomes a target of the real killer, who turns out to be the jury foreman.

Production Company: Dave Bell Assoc. Inc. Prods.
Executive Producer .... Dave Bell
Producer .... Alan Beattie
Director .... Peter Levin
Writer .... David Westheimer
Cast .... Jasmine Guy
Cast .... Anna Maria Horsford
Cast .... Mykel T. Williamson
Cast .... Dwight Schultz

KILLER IN THE MIRROR   NBC

Drama: Murder and Murder Mystery • Woman In Jeopardy • Psychological Thriller
Airdate: 03/31/86
Rating: 20.4/31   A/C:

When her rich-widow bad twin dies in an accident, the good twin assumes her identity. When the bad twin reappears, the good twin begins to realize that she may have been set up.

Production Company: Litke-Grossbart Prods. IAW Warner Bros. TV
Executive Producer .... Jack Grossbart
Producer .... Michael S. McLean
Director .... Frank De Felitta
Writer .... Frank De Felitta
Cast .... Ann Jillian
Cast .... Max Gail
Cast .... Jessica Walter
Cast .... Len Cariou

KILLER INSTINCT — NBC

Drama: Woman Against The System • Children/Teens • Medical/Disease/Mental Illness
Airdate: 11/22/88
Rating: 12.5/19   A/C:

A hospital psychiatrist becomes so obsessed with curing a violent teenage boy that she destroys her life without helping him at all. He ends up killed by the police.

Production Company: Millar-Bromberg II Prods. with ITC Entertainment

Producer	Stuart Millar
Producer	Conrad Bromberg
Director	Waris Hussein
Writer	Conrad Bromberg
Cast	Melissa Gilbert
Cast	Lane Smith
Cast	Woody Harrelson
Cast	Fernando Lopez

KILLER RULES — NBC

Drama: Suspense/Thriller • Foreign or Exotic Location
Airdate: 1/24/93
Rating: 9.2/14   A/C: 3

When in Rome, a federal agent who is after a murderous mob financier, falls in love with a sensual young women who happens to be the secretary for the man he is pursuing. He eventually discovers she is also having an affair with a mafia hit man who turns out to be his long lost bother and planning on killing them both.

Production Company: Lee Rich Co. IAW Warner Bros. TV

Executive Producer	Joanne Brough
Executive Producer	Bruce J. Sallan
Executive Producer	Lee Rich
Producer	Paul Picard
Director	Robert Ellis Miller
Writer	Paul Monash
Cast	Jamey Sheridan
Cast	Sela Ward
Cast	Peter Dobson
Cast	Riccardo Garrone

KILLING IN A SMALL TOWN — CBS

Drama: Murder and Murder Mystery • True Crime • Courtroom Drama
Airdate: 05/22/90
Rating: 15.8/26   A/C: 1

Based on the book "Evidence of Love." Psychological study of Texas housewife Candy Morrison who was accused of killing her friend Peggy Blankenship with forty-one blows of an axe.

Production Company: Indie Prod./Hearst Entertainment

Executive Producer	Bruce J. Sallan
Producer	Courtney Pledger
Producer	Dan Witt
Director	Stephen Gyllenhaal
Writer	Cynthia Cidre
Cast	Barbara Hershey
Cast	Brian Dennehy
Cast	Richard Gilliland
Cast	John Terry
Cast	Lee Garlington

KILLING MIND, THE — LIFETIME

Drama: Murder and Murder Mystery • Cops/Detectives/Law Enforcement • Suspense/Thriller
Airdate: 04/23/91
Rating: N/A   A/C:

A former FBI investigator, still haunted by childhood memories of a murder scene, joins the L.A.P.D. to solve the twenty-year-old case. She shockingly discovers that the reporter who broke the story also committed the murder.

Production Company: Heart Entertainment Productions

Executive Producer	William W. Forsythe
Executive Producer	Pat A. Victor
Producer	Carroll Newman
Director	Michael Rhodes
Writer	William W. Forsythe
Writer	Pat A. Victor
Cast	Stephanie Zimbalist
Cast	Tony Bill
Cast	Daniel Roebuck

KING OF LOVE, THE — ABC

Drama: Period Piece • Social Issue • Sex/Glitz
Airdate: 11/19/87
Rating: 6.7/11   A/C:

The rise and fall of a hedonistic photographer who creates a slick soft-core sex-magazine empire, promotes free love, defends his first Amendment rights in court, and is ultimately assassinated.

Production Company: Sarabande Prods. with MGM/UA TV Prods.

Executive Producer	David Manson
Producer	Cyrus Yavneh
Director	Anthony Wilkinson
Writer	Donald Freed
Cast	Nick Mancuso
Cast	Rip Torn
Cast	Michael Lerner
Cast	Sela Ward

KISS OF A KILLER — ABC

Drama: Psychological Thriller • Woman In Jeopardy
Airdate: 2/1/93
Rating: 11.5/18   A/C: 2

Based on the book "The Point of Murder" by Margaret Yorke. A psychologically repressed and introverted woman leading a double life as a sexy party girl, is stalked by a rapist who fears she can link him to his crimes.

Production Company: Andrew Adelson Co., John Conboy Prods. IAW ABC Prods.

Executive Producer	Andrew Adelson
Executive Producer	John Conboy
Producer	George Perkins
Director	Larry Elikann
Writer	David Warfield
Cast	Annette O'Toole
Cast	Eva Marie Saint
Cast	Brian Wimmer
Cast	Lee Garlington

KISS SHOT — CBS

Drama: Woman Against The System • Love Story • Sports
Airdate: 04/11/89
Rating: 10.2/16   A/C:

A single mother, struggling to make the balloon payment on her house, returns to professional pool-playing and gets involved with a ne'er-do-well playboy.

Production Company: London Prods. IAW Whoop Inc.

Executive Producer	Jerry London
Producer	Salli Newman
Producer	Mel A. Bishop
Director	Jerry London
Writer	Carl Kleinschmitt
Cast	Whoopi Goldberg
Cast	Dorian Harewood
Cast	Tasha Scott
Cast	Dennis Franz

KISS TO DIE FOR, A — NBC

Drama: Suspense/Thriller • Murder and Murder Mystery
Airdate: 12/6/93
Rating: 10.8/17   A/C: 3

A recently widowed psychology professor falls into a passionate affair with a seductive decorator who the police think might be the prostitute known as "Bedroom Eyes"- responsible for a series of grisly murders.

Production Company: Polone Co. IAW Hearst Ent.

Executive Producer	Judith A. Polone
Producer	Kimberly Myers
Director	Leon Ichaso
Writer	Deborah Dalton
Cast	Tim Matheson
Cast	Mimi Rogers
Cast	William Forsythe
Cast	Carlos Gomez

KISSING PLACE, THE — USA

Drama: Family Drama • Children/Teens • Psychological Thriller • Family Violence
Airdate: 04/11/90
Rating: N/A   A/C:

A ten-year-old boy, snatched by a childless couple when he was three, tries to get back to his real mother, with his psychotic "adoptive" mother in hot pursuit.

Production Company: Cynthia Cherbak Prod. IAW Wilshire Court

Executive Producer	Cynthia Cherbak
Producer	Paul Freeman
Director	Tony Wharmby
Writer	Richard Altabef
Writer	Michael Wing
Writer	Cynthia Cherbak
Cast	Meredith Baxter
Cast	David Ogden Stiers
Cast	Nathaniel Moreau

KNIGHT RIDER 2000   NBC
Drama: Murder and Murder Mystery • Sci-Fi/
Supernatural/Horror/Fantasy
Airdate: 05/19/91
Rating: 16.1/26   A/C: 1

Revival of the old series. Crimefighter Michael Knight with his high-tech computerized car battles renegade cops and gunrunners in the year 2000.

Production Company: Desperado Films Inc.
Executive Producer .... Michele Brustin
Producer .... Rob Hedden
Director .... Alan J. Levi
Writer .... Rob Hedden
Cast .... David Hasselhoff
Cast .... Susan Norman
Cast .... Edward Mulhare

KOJAK: THE BELARUS FILE   CBS
Drama: Murder and Murder Mystery • Cops/
Detectives/Law Enforcement • Nazis
Airdate: 02/16/85
Rating: 18.5/31   A/C:

Detective Kojak investigates the murders of supposed concentration camp victims by Nazi war criminals involved in a U.S. State Department cover-up.

Production Company: Universal TV
Executive Producer .... James McAdams
Producer .... Albert Ruben
Director .... Robert Markowitz
Writer .... Albert Ruben
Cast .... Telly Savalas
Cast .... Max Von Sydow
Cast .... Herbert Berghof
Cast .... Suzanne Pleshette

KOJAK: THE PRICE OF JUSTICE   CBS
Mystery: Murder and Murder Mystery • Cops/
Detectives/Law Enforcement
Airdate: 02/21/87
Rating: 12.0/21   A/C:

Inspector Kojak becomes fascinated with a woman with a scandalous past now accused of killing her two sons.

Production Company: MCA/Universal TV
Executive Producer .... James McAdams
Director .... Alan Metzger
Writer .... Albert Ruben
Cast .... Telly Savalas
Cast .... Kate Nelligan
Cast .... Tony Di Benedetto
Cast .... Pat Hingle

L. A. LAW   NBC
Drama: Courtroom Drama • Series Pilot (2 hr.) •
Social Issue
Airdate: 09/15/86
Rating: 21.2/33   A/C:

The pilot for the series. Members of a small but important Los Angeles law firm take on rape, divorce and an insurance matter while hiring several new interns.

Production Company: 20th Century Fox TV
Executive Producer .... Steven Bochco
Executive Producer .... Terry Louise Fisher
Director .... Gregory Hoblit
Writer .... Steven Bochco
Writer .... Terry Louise Fisher
Cast .... Jill Eikenberry
Cast .... Corbin Bernsen
Cast .... Jimmy Smits
Cast .... Alan Rachins
Cast .... Alfre Woodard
Cast .... Harry Hamlin
Cast .... Richard Dysart

L. A. TAKEDOWN   NBC
Drama: Cops/Detectives/Law Enforcement • Action/
Adventure • Series Pilot (2 hr.)
Airdate: 08/27/89
Rating: 10.4/18   A/C: 2

A hotshot L.A. robbery squad detective, trying to anticipate the moves of a conniving robbery gang leader, uses a computer and street smarts. The two men find they have a lot in common while they attempt to outmaneuver each other.

Production Company: AJAR Inc. IAW Movies
    Film Prods. B.V. and World International Net.
Executive Producer .... Michael Mann
Producer .... Patrick Markey
Director .... Michael Mann
Writer .... Michael Mann
Cast .... Scott Plank
Cast .... Alex McArthur
Cast .... Ely Pouget

L B J: THE EARLY YEARS   NBC
Drama (3 hours): Period Piece • Historical Piece •
Biography • Political Piece • True Story
Airdate: 02/01/87
Rating: 18.4/27   A/C:

Lyndon Johnson's life and political career, from his marriage with Lady Bird through his life in Congress and the Senate, to his assumption of the Presidency.

Production Company: Brice Prods. and Louis
    Rudolph Films IAW Fries Entertainment Inc.
Executive Producer .... Louis Rudolph
Producer .... John Brice
Producer .... Sandra Saxon Brice
Director .... Peter Werner
Writer .... Ken Trevey
Cast .... Randy Quaid
Cast .... Patti LuPone
Cast .... Morgan Brittany
Cast .... Pat Hingle
Cast .... R. G. Armstrong
Cast .... Barry Corbin

LABOR OF LOVE: THE ARLETTE
SCHWEITZER STORY   CBS
Drama: Family Drama • Medical/Disease/Mental
Illness • Woman's Issue/Story
Airdate: 5/9/93
Rating: 14.1/23   A/C: 2

When her daughter, Christa, learns that she cannot bear children, Arlette Schweitzer endues the physical and emotional trauma of in-vitro fertilization in order to give her child the joys of motherhood. Medical history was made when she gave birth to twins.

Production Company: Lauren Film Prods. IAW
    KLM Prods
Executive Producer .... Alfred R. Kelman
Producer .... Michael O. Gallant
Producer .... Phil Levitan
Executive Producer .... Jerry London
Writer .... Susan Baskin
Cast .... Ann Jillian
Cast .... Tracey Gold
Cast .... Bill Smitrovich

LACE II   ABC
Miniseries/Drama (2 nights): Family Drama • Woman
In Jeopardy • Foreign or Exotic Location • Sex/Glitz
Airdate: 05/05/85 • 05/06/85
Rating: 15.3/24 • 16.4/25   A/C:

Sequel to the 1984 miniseries which was based on the novel by Shirley Conran. An international movie star sets out to rescue her mother, an American magazine editor being held hostage in a Far Eastern country. She receives assistance in raising the million dollar ransom from two of her mother's school chums.

Production Company: Lorimar
Executive Producer .... Gary Adelson
Producer .... Preston Fischer
Director .... Billy Hale
Writer .... Elliott Baker
Cast .... Brooke Adams
Cast .... Deborah Raffin
Cast .... Arielle Dombasle
Cast .... Phoebe Cates
Cast .... Anthony Higgins
Cast .... Christopher Cazenove

LADY AGAINST THE ODDS   NBC
Drama: Murder and Murder Mystery • Cops/
Detectives/Law Enforcement • Period Piece
Airdate: 04/20/92
Rating: 11.8/19   A/C: 2

Based on the book "Hand In The Glove" by Rex Stout. Two tough female P.I.'s search for the murderer of a family friend in the backyards of the nouveau riche of 1943 Los Angeles.

Production Company: Robert Greenwald Prods.
    IAW MGM/UA
Executive Producer .... Diane Sokolow
Executive Producer .... Mel Sokolow
Director .... Bradford May
Writer .... Bruce Murkoff
Writer .... Laird Koenig
Cast .... Crystal Bernard
Cast .... Annabeth Gish
Cast .... Rob Estes
Cast .... Dan Castellaneta

Lady and the Highwayman, The   CBS

Drama: Period Piece • Action/Adventure • Foreign or Exotic Location • Sex/Glitz
Airdate: 01/22/89
Rating: 11.1/18   A/C:

In this period romance from a Barbara Cartland novel, a highwayman becomes the protector of a beautiful woman constantly menaced by the men around her.

Production Company: Lord Grade Prods. IAW Gainsborough Pictures

Executive Producer	Laurie Johnson
Producer	Albert Fennell
Director	John Hough
Writer	Terence Feely
Writer	Peter Manley
Cast	Emma Samms
Cast	Christopher Cazenove
Cast	Gordon Jackson
Cast	Claire Bloom
Cast	Michael York
Cast	Oliver Reed

Lady Blue   ABC

Drama: Cops/Detectives/Law Enforcement • Series Pilot (2 hr.)
Airdate: 04/15/85
Rating: 19.8/31   A/C:

A female police officer uses her trademark assertive style to fight crime, including a spur-of-the-moment interception of a bank robbery.

Production Company: David Gerber Prods. IAW MGM TV

Executive Producer	David Gerber
Producer	Herb Wallerstein
Director	Gary Nelson
Writer	Robert Vincent O'Neil
Cast	Jamie Rose
Cast	Danny Aiello
Cast	Jim Brown
Cast	Tony Lo Bianco

Lady Forgets, The   CBS

Drama: Murder and Murder Mystery • Woman In Jeopardy • Psychological Thriller
Airdate: 10/29/89
Rating: 18.5/34   A/C: 1

While trying to find her real identity, an amnesia victim discovers that she has led two lives and is the prime suspect in a murder.

Production Company: Leonard Hill Films

Executive Producer	Leonard Hill
Executive Producer	Robert O'Connor
Producer	Joel Fields
Director	Bradford May
Writer	Durrell Royce Crays
Cast	Donna Mills
Cast	Greg Evigan
Cast	Andrew Robinson
Cast	Roy Dotrice

Lady from Yesterday, The   CBS

Drama: Family Drama • Children/Teens • Vietnam
Airdate: 05/14/85
Rating: 16.0/25   A/C:

A Vietnam vet and his wife are in for a shock when a son that the vet unknowingly fathered in Viet Nam comes to stay with his family in America.

Production Company: The Houston Lady Co. IAW Comworld Prods.

Executive Producer	Barry Weitz
Director	Robert Day
Writer	Tim Maschler
Writer	Ken Pettus
Cast	Wayne Rogers
Cast	Bonnie Bedelia
Cast	Pat Hingle
Cast	Barrie Youngfellow

Lady In A Corner   NBC

Drama: Woman Against The System
Airdate: 12/11/89
Rating: 13.3/21   A/C: 3

A classy fashion magazine editor battles a sleazy publishing magnate when he attempts a corporate takeover.

Production Company: Sagaponack Films/Pantheon Pictures IAW Allan Leicht Prods.

Executive Producer	Stuart Millar
Executive Producer	Gabriel Katzka
Producer	Stuart Millar
Director	Peter Levin
Writer	Allan Leicht
Cast	Loretta Young
Cast	Brian Keith
Cast	Lindsay Frost
Cast	Roscoe Lee Browne

Lady Killer   USA

Drama: Cops/Detectives/Law Enforcement • Murder and Murder Mystery • Woman In Jeopardy • Forbidden Love
Airdate: 08/19/92
Rating: N/A   A/C:

A female police officer becomes successfully involved with a married man through a video dating service. As the affair deepens, the cop discovers her lover may be responsible for a string of serial murders.

Production Company: MCA Television Entertainment

Executive Producer	Dan Wigutow
Producer	Gordon Wolf
Director	Michael Scott
Writer	Shelly Evans
Cast	Mimi Rogers
Cast	John Shea

Lady Mobster   ABC

Drama: Woman In Jeopardy • Mafia/Mob
Airdate: 10/16/88
Rating: 5.9/09   A/C:

The lawyer daughter of a long-dead mob official is imperiled when she quits her lucrative practice to take over the "family" business when the Don dies.

Production Company: Von Zemeck-Samuels

Executive Producer	Frank Von Zerneck
Executive Producer	Stu Samuels
Producer	Robert M. Sertner
Director	John Llewellyn Moxey
Writer	Stephen Zito
Cast	Susan Lucci
Cast	Al Ruscio
Cast	Thom Bray
Cast	Jon Cypher
Cast	Michael Nader

Ladykillers   ABC

Drama: Murder and Murder Mystery • Cops/Detectives/Law Enforcement • Sex/Glitz
Airdate: 11/09/88
Rating: 16.6/27   A/C:

A female police lieutenant and a male rookie, who goes undercover, track down a serial killer who specializes in male strippers at a club called Ladykillers.

Production Company: Barry Weitz Films IAW ABC Circle Films

Executive Producer	Barry Weitz
Producer	Andrew Hill
Director	Robert Lewis
Writer	Greg Dinallo
Cast	Marilu Henner
Cast	Alexandra Borrie
Cast	Lesley-Anne Down
Cast	William Lucking
Cast	Susan Blakely

Laguna Heat   HBO

Drama: Murder and Murder Mystery • Cops/Detectives/Law Enforcement • Mafia/Mob
Airdate: 11/15/87
Rating: N/A   A/C:

A burnt out ex-L.A. detective moves into his father's Laguna Beach house and finds himself investigating the murder of a local stable owner. He eventually uncovers an intricate scheme of corruption and blackmail going back twenty years.

Production Company: HBO Pictures

Executive Producer	Jay Weston
Producer	Bill Badalato
Director	Simon Langton
Writer	Pete Hamill
Writer	David Eyre, Jr.
Writer	David Burton Morris
Cast	Harry Hamlin
Cast	Jason Robards
Cast	Rip Torn
Cast	Catherine Hicks

LAKER GIRLS, THE   CBS
Drama: Sex/Glitz • Sports
Airdate: 4/03/90
Rating: 10.5/17   A/C: 3

Three young women, an overshadowed sibling, an heiress, and a Watts dance teacher, find friendship, fulfillment and romance when they join the cheerleading team of the Los Angeles Lakers.

Production Company: Viacom Prods. IAW The
  Finnegan-Pinchuk Co. & Valente/Hamilton
  Prod.
Executive Producer .... Sheldon Pinchuk
Executive Producer .... Pat Finnegan
Executive Producer .... Bill Finnegan
Producer .... Renee Valente
Co-Executive producer .... Renee Valente
Co-Executive Producer .... Robert Hamilton
Director .... Bruce Seth Green
Writer .... Robert Hamilton
Cast .... Tina Yothers
Cast .... Paris Vaughan
Cast .... Shari Shattuck
Cast .... Paul Johansson
Cast .... Alexandra Paul

LANTERN HILL   DISNEY
Drama: Family Drama • Period Piece • Children/
Teens
Airdate: 01/27/90
Rating: N/A   A/C:

A young girl discovers that her father, whom she has been told was dead, is really alive. Inspired by a mysterious, almost supernatural dream, she sets out to reunite her parents, foiling the constant interventions of her forbidding grandmother.

Production Company: Sullivan Films
Executive Producer .... Kevin Sullivan
Producer .... Trudy Grant
Director .... Kevin Sullivan
Writer .... Kevin Sullivan
Writer .... Fiona McHugh
Cast .... Colleen Dewhurst
Cast .... Sam Waterston

LAS VEGAS STRIP WARS, THE   NBC
Drama: Suspense/Thriller • Mafia/Mob
Airdate: 11/25/84
Rating: 15.2/22   A/C:

The story of revenge and power struggle among wealthy casino operators and a cunning fight promoter.

Production Company: George Englund Prods.
Executive Producer .... George Englund
Producer .... Michael Greenburg
Director .... George Englund
Writer .... George Englund
Cast .... Rock Hudson
Cast .... James Earl Jones
Cast .... Pat Morita

LAST BEST YEAR, THE   ABC
Drama: Medical/Disease/Mental Illness
Airdate: 11/04/90
Rating: 11.1/17   A/C: 3

A repressed, young woman dying of cancer seeks the help of a psychologist. An emotional bond is formed and together they come to terms with the meaning of life and death.

Production Company: David W. Rintels Prods.
  IAW World Entertainment Network
Executive Producer .... Victoria Riskin
Producer .... David W. Rintels
Co-Producer .... Josette Perotta
Director .... John Erman
Writer .... David W. Rintels
Cast .... Mary Tyler Moore
Cast .... Bernadette Peters
Cast .... Brian Bedford
Cast .... Carmen Mathews

LAST DAYS OF FRANK AND JESSE JAMES, THE   NBC
Drama: Biography • Western
Airdate: 02/10/86
Rating: 15.1/22   A/C:

When the James brothers turn from robbery to farming, the wilder Jesse meets a violent death and the milder Frank survives.

Production Company: Joseph Cates Prods.
Executive Producer .... Joe Cates
Producer .... Phillip Cates
Director .... William A. Graham
Writer .... Bill Stratton
Cast .... Johnny Cash
Cast .... Kris Kristofferson
Cast .... Willie Nelson
Cast .... Ed Bruce
Cast .... Gail Youngs
Cast .... June Carter Cash

LAST DAYS OF PATTON, THE   CBS
Drama (3 hours): Biography • Historical Piece •
WWII • Period Piece • Foreign or Exotic Location •
Political Piece
Airdate: 09/14/86
Rating: 19.5/32   A/C:

The last half-year of the general's life. He is removed as military governor of Bavaria for his use of Nazi administrators and his frank anti-Soviet stance. He dies after lingering for several days following an auto accident.

Production Company: Entertainment Partners
Executive Producer .... Robert E. Fuisz
Producer .... William F. Starke
Producer .... Alfred R. Kelman
Director .... Delbert Mann
Writer .... William Luce
Cast .... George C. Scott
Cast .... Eva Marie Saint
Cast .... Richard Dysart
Cast .... Murray Hamilton

LAST ELEPHANT, THE   TNT
Drama: Man Against The System • Foreign or Exotic
Location • Toxic Waste/Environmental • Social Issue
Airdate: 08/20/90
Rating: N/A   A/C:

An alcoholic American novelist is redeemed when he investigates the disappearance of his research assistant who had stumbled upon an illegal ivory poaching operation in Kenya.

Production Company: RHI Entertainment IAW
  Qintex Entertainment
Executive Producer .... Christopher Palmer
Producer .... Robert Halmi, Sr.
Producer .... Jim Chory
Director .... Joseph Sargent
Writer .... Bill Bozzone
Writer .... Richard Guttman
Cast .... John Lithgow
Cast .... Isabella Rossellini
Cast .... James Earl Jones
Cast .... Tony Todd
Cast .... Olek Kruppa

LAST FLIGHT OUT   NBC
Drama: True Story • Period Piece • Foreign or Exotic
Location • Vietnam
Airdate: 05/22/90
Rating: 10.7/18   A/C: 3

The story of how a determined group of private American citizens frantically rescued U.S. civilians and South Vietnamese refugees during the fall of Saigon on April 29, 1975.

Production Company: The Manheim Comp. - Co-
  Star Entertainment IAW NBC Productions
Executive Producer .... Michael Manheim
Producer .... Norman I. Cohen
Director .... Larry Elikann
Writer .... Walter Halsey Davis
Cast .... Richard Crenna
Cast .... James Earl Jones
Cast .... Eric Bogosian
Cast .... Rosalind Chao

LAST FLING, THE   ABC
Comedy: Romantic Comedy
Airdate: 02/09/87
Rating: 15.9/23   A/C:

A ladies' man falls in love with a woman who has just decided to avenge her fiance's infidelity by engaging in a little philandering of her own.

Production Company: Leonard Hill Films
Executive Producer .... Leonard Hill
Director .... Corey Allen
Writer .... Mitchel Lee Katlin
Cast .... Connie Sellecca
Cast .... John Ritter
Cast .... Paul Sand
Cast .... John Bennett Perry

LAST FRONTIER, THE — CBS

Miniseries/Drama (2 nights): Family Drama • Woman Against The System • Cross-Cultural Story • Foreign or Exotic Location
Airdate: 10/05/86 • 10/07/86
Rating: 23.8/36 • 25.0/39   A/C:

Much to the surprise of everyone, an American widow and her four children decide to stay on at her Australian ranch, saving it from enemies and the elements.

Production Company: World Vision Pictures
Executive Producer .... Hal McElroy
Producer .... Tim Sanders
Director ....Simon Wincer
Writer ....Michael Laurence
Writer ....John Misto
Cast .... Linda Evans
Cast .... Jason Robards
Cast .... Judy Morris
Cast .... Jack Thompson

LAST HIT, THE — USA

Drama: Suspense/Thriller
Airdate: 3/31/93
Rating: N/A   A/C:

Based on the book "The Long Kill" by Patrick Ruell. When a ex-CIA assassin hides out, refusing to finish his last lethal assignment, he falls in love with his new neighbor whose father is targeted by the government for elimination. Weary of death and violence, he must kill again in order to protect his new family.

Production Company: MTE Universal
Executive Producer .... Bob Christiansen
Executive Producer .... Rick Rosenberg
Director .... Jan Egelson
Writer .... Walter Klenhard
Writer .... Alan Sharp
Cast .... Bryan Brown
Cast .... Brooke Adams
Cast .... Harris Yulin

LAST INNOCENT MAN, THE — HBO

Drama: Courtroom Drama • Murder and Murder Mystery • Suspense/Thriller
Airdate: 4/14/87
Rating: N/A   A/C:

Based on the novel by Philip Margolin. A brilliant criminal defense attorney, who has the skill to keep his dubious clients out of jail, grows disenchanted and demoralized with the legal profession and decides to quit. He soon gets drawn back in when he becomes enmeshed in a torrid love affair with a seductive woman who persuades him to defend her estranged husband against a charge of murder.

Production Company: HBO Pictures
Executive Producer .... Maurice Singer
Producer .... Ron Silverman
Director .... Roger Spottiswoode
Writer .... Dan Bronson
Cast .... Ed Harris
Cast .... Roxanne Hart
Cast .... David Suchet
Cast .... Bruce McGill

LAST LIGHT — SHOWTIME

Drama: Prison and Prison Camp
Airdate: 8/22/93
Rating: N/A   A/C:

A black prison guard forms a tenuous relationship with a violent, white inmate sentenced to death row. Offering the man some kindness from the abusive treatment dished out by the warden, the convict experiences his first sense of humanity and friendship which helps him come to terms with his destiny.

Production Company: Stillwater Prods., Showtime Ent.
Executive Producer .... Robert Eisele
Producer .... Mary McLaglen
Director .... Kiefer Sutherland
Writer .... Robert Eisele
Cast .... Kiefer Sutherland
Cast .... Forest Whitaker
Cast .... Amanda Plummer
Cast .... Kathleen Quinlan

LAST OF HIS TRIBE, THE — HBO

Drama: True Story • Period Piece • Historical Piece • American Indians • Cross-Cultural Story
Airdate: 03/28/92
Rating: N/A   A/C:

In 1911, anthropologist Dr. Alfred Kroeber discovers the sole survivor of the Yahi Indians, a tribe supposedly eradicated in the 19th Century. As their friendship unfolds, each man learns meaningful lessons from their shared experiences.

Production Company: River City Prods.
Producer .... John Levoff
Producer .... Robert Lovenheim
Co-Producer .... Barbara Bloom
Director .... Harry Hook
Writer .... Steve Harrigan
Cast .... Jon Voight
Cast .... Graham Greene
Cast .... David Ogden Stiers
Cast .... Anne Archer

LAST OUTLAW, THE — HBO

Drama: Western • Period Piece
Airdate: 10/30/93
Rating: N/A   A/C:

An ex- Confederate soldier and his band of rogues take to robbing banks in the old west. They are soon pursued by a Army Lieutenant out to stop the thieving gang. When the beleaguered rebel is finally caught he joins the posse in search of his fellow outlaws and discovers the in helping the law he finds his self-respect.

Production Company: Davis Ent., HBO Pictures
Executive Producer .... Merrill H. Karpf
Executive Producer .... Eric Red
Producer .... John Davis
Director .... Geoff Murphy
Writer .... Eric Red
Cast .... Mickey Rourke
Cast .... Dermot Mulroney
Cast .... Ted Levine

LAST P. O. W? THE BOBBY GARWOOD STORY, THE — ABC

Drama: True Story • Period Piece • Vietnam • Foreign or Exotic Location • Prison and Prison Camp
Airdate: 6/28/93
Rating: 11.5/20   A/C: 1

Vietnam prisoner of war Bobby Garwood's loyalty is in question when he is charged in 1979 with "aiding the enemy" after being captured by the South Vietnamese in 1965 and held captive for more than thirteen years. He is eventually court martialled by the Marine Corps and dishonorably discharged.

Production Company: EME Prods. IAW Nexus Ent., Fries Ent.
Executive Producer .... Georg Stanford Brown
Executive Producer .... John Emr
Producer .... Edward Gold
Producer .... Renee Emr
Director .... Georg Stanford Brown
Writer .... John Pielmeier
Cast .... Ralph Macchio
Cast .... Martin Sheen
Cast .... Noah Blake

LAST PROSTITUTE, THE — LIFETIME

Drama: Love Story • Children/Teens • Prostitution
Airdate: 09/11/91
Rating: N/A   A/C:

Based on the play by William Borden. Two teenage boys set out to lose their virginity to a legendary prostitute, now the owner of an East Texas horse farm. As they pursue their lust, she teaches them lessons in love, respect and growing up.

Production Company: BBK Prods. IAW Carmen Culver Films
Executive Producer .... Carmen Culver
Producer .... Peter Bogart
Director .... Lou Antonio
Writer .... Carmen Culver
Cast .... Sonia Braga
Cast .... Wil Wheaton
Cast .... Cotter Smith
Cast .... David Kaufman

LAST TO GO, THE — ABC

Drama: Family Drama • Woman's Issue/Story
Airdate: 01/21/91
Rating: 11.0/17   A/C: 3

Based on a book by Rand Richards. Chronicles over a twenty-year span the events in the lives of an upscale New England family. The family matriarch is ultimately abandoned by her husband and neglected by her adult children.

Production Company: Freyda Rothstein Productions IAW Interscope Productions, Inc.
Executive Producer .... Freyda Rothstein
Producer .... William Hanley
Producer .... John Erman
Director .... John Erman
Writer .... William Hanley
Cast .... Tyne Daly
Cast .... Terry O'Quinn
Cast .... Annabeth Gish
Cast .... Tim Ransom

LAST WISH — ABC

Drama: Family Drama • Medical/Disease/Mental Illness • True Story • Social Issue
Airdate: 01/12/92
Rating: 10.8/17   A/C: 3

Based on the book by Betty Rollin. Journalist Betty Rollin grapples with the emotional and legal turmoil involved in helping her terminally-ill mother commit suicide.

Production Company: Grossbart-Barnett IAW Spectacor

Executive Producer	Jack Grossbart
Executive Producer	Joan Barnett
Director	Jeff Bleckner
Writer	Jerome Kass
Cast	Patty Duke
Cast	Maureen Stapleton
Cast	Dwight Schultz
Cast	Lee Wallace

LAURA LANSING SLEPT HERE — NBC

Comedy: Social Issue
Airdate: 03/07/88
Rating: 18.9/30   A/C:

To get back in touch with ordinary people, an eminent novelist moves in with an accountant's family, and it's a learning experience all around.

Production Company: Schaefer/Karpf/Eckstein Prods. IAW Gaylord Production Co.

Executive Producer	Merrill H. Karpf
Producer	George Schaefer
Co-Producer	James Prideaux
Director	George Schaefer
Writer	James Prideaux
Cast	Katherine Hepburn
Cast	Joel Higgins
Cast	Karen Austin
Cast	Brenda Forbes

LAUREL AVENUE — HBO

Miniseries/Drama (2 nights): Black Story • Family Drama • Social Issue
Airdate: 7/10/93 • 7/11/93
Rating: N/A   A/C:

The lives of an urban working-class black family during a long busy weekend in St. Paul, Minnesota. The social issues of drugs, guns, racism, single parenthood, crime, and sex beset the household while they celebrate the joys and achievements of various family members.

Production Company: HBO Independent Prods.

Executive Producer	Paul Aaron
Executive Producer	Charles Dutton
Producer	Tony To
Producer	Jesse Beaton
Director	Carl Franklin
Writer	Michael Henry Brown
Cast	Mary Alice
Cast	Jay Brooks
Cast	Juanita Jennings
Cast	Scott Lawrence
Cast	Rhonda Stubbins White

LEAP OF FAITH — CBS

Drama: Family Drama • Medical/Disease/Mental Illness • True Story
Airdate: 10/06/88
Rating: 12.0/20   A/C:

Fact-based story of a woman whose lymphatic cancer went into remission after she tried various nonmedical therapies.

Production Company: Hart, Thomas & Berlin Prods.

Executive Producer	Carole Hart
Executive Producer	Kathie Berlin
Executive Producer	Marlo Thomas
Producer	Ira Marvin
Director	Stephen Gyllenhaal
Writer	Bruce Hart
Cast	Anne Archer
Cast	Sam Neill
Cast	James Tolkan
Cast	Norman Parker
Cast	Michael Constantine

LEAVE OF ABSENCE — NBC

Drama: Family Drama • Forbidden Love • Woman's Issue/Story
Airdate: 5/11/94
Rating: 10.1/15   A/C: 3

A long married, successful architect finds himself having an affair with a business associate. When he learns that she is dying he asks his sympathetic wife for a leave of absence from their marriage to care for his ailing mistress. Long held resentments and unresolved feelings are brought to the surface as his wounded wife finds her inner strength and builds a new life.

Production Company: Grossbart/Barnett IAW NBC

Executive Producer	Joan Barnett
Executive Producer	Jack Grossbart
Executive Producer	Polly Bergen
Producer	Don Goldman
Co-Producer	Linda Kent
Director	Tom McLoughlin
Writer	Betty Goldberg
Cast	Blythe Danner
Cast	Brian Dennehy
Cast	Jacqueline Bisset
Cast	Polly Bergen

LEGACY OF LIES — USA

Drama: Family Drama • Cops/Detectives/Law Enforcement • Mafia/Mob
Airdate: 04/22/92
Rating: N/A   A/C:

During a murder investigation, an honest NY detective finds his father, also a cop, is on the take and his grandfather is a former Mafia don. When his father is killed for turning state's evidence, the son seeks revenge on the guilty mob boss.

Production Company: RAH Prods., MCA Television Entertainment

Executive Producer	James McAdams
Executive Producer	David Black
Producer	Barry Berg
Director	Bradford May
Writer	David Black
Cast	Michael Ontkean
Cast	Martin Landau
Cast	Eli Wallach
Cast	Joe Morton

LENA: MY 100 CHILDREN — NBC

Drama: True Story • Woman Against The System • WWII • Historical Piece • Children/Teens • Foreign or Exotic Location
Airdate: 11/23/87
Rating: 13.4/21   A/C:

Fact-based drama of a woman who sheltered Jewish children in post-World-War-II Poland and fought to take them to Palestine.

Production Company: Robert Greenwald Prods.

Executive Producer	Robert Greenwald
Co-Producer	Tova Laiter
Co-Producer	Steve McGlothen
Director	Ed Sherin
Writer	Jonathan Rintels
Writer	Yabo Yablonsky
Cast	Linda Lavin
Cast	Torquil Campbell
Cast	Leonore Harris
Cast	Cynthia Wilde

LEONA HELMSLEY: THE QUEEN OF MEAN — CBS

Drama: True Story • Biography
Airdate: 09/23/90
Rating: 15.7/26   A/C: 1

Follows the cold-hearted ambitions of the New York hotel-chain Queen from humble beginnings, marriage to real estate tycoon Harry Helmsley, and her eventual conviction for tax evasion.

Production Company: Fries Entertainment IAW Golman/Taylor Ent. Co.

Executive Producer	Charles Fries
Executive Producer	Stuart Goldman
Executive Producer	Jane Ubell
Executive Producer	Mark Malis
Producer	Larry White
Director	Richard Michaels
Writer	Dennis Turner
Cast	Suzanne Pleshette
Cast	Lloyd Bridges
Cast	Joe Regalbuto
Cast	Raymond Singer

LETHAL EXPOSURE NBC
Drama: Murder and Murder Mystery • Suspense/
Thriller • Foreign or Exotic Location
Airdate: 3/28/93
Rating: 8.8/14 A/C: 3

*An a aggressive photojournalist takes a picture
of a murder at an airport. Thinking she has a
scoop on a big story she travels to France to
track down more information, badgering a
charming Parisian detective into helping her
out. Together they put the pieces together, solve
the case and fall in love.*

Production Company: Papazian-Hirsch Ent.,
  Ellipse Programme
Executive Producer .... Allan B. Schwartz
Executive Producer .... Simon Hart
Executive Producer .... Robert Rea
Executive Producer .... Robert A. Papazian
Executive Producer .... James G. Hirsch
Producer .... Richard L. O'Connor
Director .... Kevin Connor
Writer .... James G. Hirsch
Cast .... Ally Sheedy
Cast .... Francois-Eric Gendron

LETTER TO THREE WIVES, A NBC
Drama: Forbidden Love • Psychological Thriller •
Woman's Issue/Story
Airdate: 12/16/85
Rating: 19.3/30 A/C:

*Remake of the 1949 Oscar winner. Three wives,
away for a day's outing, receive a note saying
that one of their husband's has run off with
another woman. They must each weigh the
possibility that it is their husband, and the
reasons why.*

Production Company: Michael Filerman Prods.
  IAW 20th Century Fox TV
Executive Producer .... Michael Filerman
Producer .... Karen Moore
Co-Producer .... Terry Morse
Director .... Larry Elikann
Writer .... Sally Robinson
Cast .... Loni Anderson
Cast .... Michele Lee
Cast .... Stephanie Zimbalist
Cast .... Ben Gazzara
Cast .... Charles Frank
Cast .... Michael Gross

LETTING GO ABC
Comedy: Romantic Comedy
Airdate: 05/11/85
Rating: 15.1/28 A/C:

*Two lonely people who have just come out of a
relationship, one widowed and one abandoned,
become involved with each other after they meet
in a self-help encounter group.*

Production Company: Adam Prods. IAW ITC
  Prods.
Executive Producer .... Judith A. Polone
Co-Executive Producer .... Robert M. Myman
Producer .... Ervin Zavada
Director .... Jack Bender
Writer .... Charlotte Brown
Cast .... John Ritter
Cast .... Sharon Gless
Cast .... Joe Cortese
Cast .... Kit McDonough

LIAR, LIAR CBS
Drama: Family Drama • Children/Teens • Rape/
Molestation • Social Issue
Airdate: 6/22/93
Rating: 14.5/26 A/C: 1

*A precocious eleven year old girl with a
reputation for making up stories to gain
attention, accuses her seemingly perfect father
of sexually abusing her.*

Production Company: CBC Productions
Executive Producer .... Phil Savath
Director .... Jorge Montesi
Writer .... Nancy Isaak
Cast .... Art Hindle
Cast .... Vanessa King
Cast .... Rosemary Dunsmore

LIAR'S EDGE SHOWTIME
Drama: Murder and Murder Mystery • Psychological
Thriller
Airdate: 12/4/92
Rating: N/A A/C:

*When his stuntman father dies, a sixteen year
old boy becomes suicidally depressed. His
mother soon moves in with an abusive low life
which further damages the boys delicate
psychological condition. When he witnesses
the murder of a woman he is not sure if it is a
hallucination or a real homicide. He soon
discovers the killer is not a figment of his
imagination and finds himself in a deadly
confrontation.*

Production Company: Showtime Ent. New Line
  Cinema, Norstar Ent.
Producer .... Ray Sager
Co-Producer .... Ilana Frank
Director .... Ron Oliver
Writer .... Ron Oliver
Cast .... Nicholas Shields
Cast .... Shannon Tweed
Cast .... David Keith
Cast .... Joseph Bottoms

LIBERACE ABC
Drama: Period Piece • Biography • True Story •
Hollywood
Airdate: 10/02/88
Rating: 16.8/27 A/C:

*The authorized biography tracing the keyboard
showman's relationship with his adored mother
and his ultimately tragic death.*

Production Company: Liberace Foundation with
  Dick Clark Pdns. IAW Republic Pictures
Executive Producer .... Joel R. Strote
Executive Producer .... Dick Clark
Producer .... Preston Fischer
Director .... Billy Hale
Writer .... Anthony Lawrence
Writer .... Nancy Lawrence
Cast .... Andrew Robinson
Cast .... Rue McClanahan
Cast .... Deborah Goodrich
Cast .... John Rubinstein

LIBERACE: BEHIND THE MUSIC CBS
Drama: Period Piece • Biography • Homosexuality •
Hollywood • True Story
Airdate: 10/09/88
Rating: 16.6/26 A/C:

*Unauthorized version of the upbringing, career
and decline of the celebrated pianist including
his devoted relationship with his mother and
his homosexuality.*

Production Company: Canadian International
  Studios
Executive Producer .... Linda Yellen
Executive Producer .... Nancy Bein
Producer .... Murray Shostak
Director .... David Greene
Writer .... Gavin Lambert
Cast .... Victor Garber
Cast .... Saul Rubinek
Cast .... Michael Wikes
Cast .... Maureen Stapleton
Cast .... Paul Hipp

LIBERTY NBC
Drama (3 hours): Cross-Cultural Story • Period Piece
• Historical Piece
Airdate: 06/23/86
Rating: 12.0/21 A/C:

*Fiction-packed saga of the conception,
construction and installation of the Statue of
Liberty, with emphasis on the contribution of
the immigrants in New York.*

Production Company: Robert Greenwald Prods.
Executive Producer .... Robert Greenwald
Executive Producer .... Jean Chalopin
Producer .... Paul Pompian
Director .... Richard C. Sarafian
Writer .... Pete Hamill
Cast .... Chris Sarandon
Cast .... Frank Langella
Cast .... LeVar Burton
Cast .... Carrie Fisher
Cast .... George Kennedy
Cast .... Claire Bloom

LIE DOWN WITH LIONS LIFETIME
Drama (4 Hours): Suspense/Thriller • Foreign or
Exotic Location
Airdate: 6/12/94
Rating: N/A   A/C:

*Based on the novel by Ken Follett. An
undercover CIA agent has two missions- to
safely deliver Azerbajan's elusive leader to an
American peace summit and to save the woman
he loves from a certain death at the hands of a
man she now calls her husband. From
Luxembourg to Armenia and Azerbaijan, this
trio becomes unexpectedly intertwined in a web
of passion and deceit that binds them together.
Note: 4 hours*

Production Company: Hannibal Films Ltd. IAW
    Delux Prods. & Anabase Prods.
Executive Producer .... Fabrizio Chiesa
Executive Producer .... Roman Schroeder
Executive Producer .... David J. Evans
Producer .... Geoffrey Reeve
Director .... Jim Goddard
Writer .... Guy Andrews
Writer .... Julian Bond
Cast .... Timothy Dalton
Cast .... Marg Helgenberger
Cast .... Omar Sharif
Cast .... Nigel Havers

LIES AND LULLABIES ABC
Drama: Children/Teens • Addiction Story • Social
Issue
Airdate: 3/14/93
Rating: 10.4/16   A/C: 3

*When a drug addicted single mother gives birth
to a drug dependent baby, the child is quickly
placed in a state facility. In order to get her
baby back she must t fight her own addictions
and a no nonsense social worker.*

Production Company: Susan Dey Prods.,
    Alexander/Enright IAW Hearst Ent.
Executive Producer .... Les Alexander
Executive Producer .... Don Enright
Producer .... Harvey Kahn
Co-Producer .... Susan Dey
Co-Producer .... Barbara Gale
Director .... Rod Hardy
Writer .... Janet Heaney
Writer .... Matthew Eisen
Writer .... Joe Landon
Cast .... Susan Dey
Cast .... Piper Laurie
Cast .... Lorraine Toussaint
Cast .... D.W. Moffett

LIES BEFORE KISSES CBS
Drama: Family Drama • Murder and Murder Mystery
• Suspense/Thriller
Airdate: 03/03/91
Rating: 18.5/29   A/C: 1

*A beautiful woman hires a reporter to
investigate her wealthy husband's infidelity and
uncovers a plot of extortion and murder.*

Production Company: Grossbart-Barnett Prods.
Executive Producer .... Joan Barnett
Executive Producer .... Jack Grossbart
Producer .... Robert Bennett Steinhauer
Director .... Lou Antonio
Writer .... Ellen Weston
Cast .... Jaclyn Smith
Cast .... Ben Gazzara
Cast .... Nick Mancuso
Cast .... Greg Evigan

LIES OF THE HEART: THE STORY OF
LAURIE KELLOGG ABC
Drama: Family Drama • True Crime • Woman's Issue/
Story • Family Violence
Airdate: 1/31/94
Rating: 15.0/23   A/C: 2

*In 1991 Pennsylvania, after suffering ten years
of abuse from her violent, domineering older
husband, a fragile young bride enlists the help
of four local teenagers to murder her dictatorial
spouse. Arrested for the crime, she is eventually
convicted and sentenced to twenty-five years
to life in prison.*

Production Company: MCT Prods., Daniel H.
    Blatt Prods. IAW Warner Bros. TV
Executive Producer .... Daniel H. Blatt
Executive Producer .... Judith P. Mitchell
Producer .... Sam Manners
Director .... Michael Toshiyuki Uno
Writer .... Judith P. Mitchell
Cast .... Jennie Garth
Cast .... Gregory Harrison
Cast .... Steven Keats
Cast .... Francis Guinan

LIES OF THE TWINS USA
Drama: Suspense/Thriller
Airdate: 08/21/91
Rating: N/A   A/C:

*A top fashion model falls in love with both her
sensitive therapist and his abusive vindictive
identical twin brother. Their hatred for each
other ultimately leads to danger and
destruction.*

Production Company: MCA TV Entertainment
Executive Producer .... Craig Baumgarten
Executive Producer .... Gary Adelson
Producer .... Tim Zinnemann
Director .... Tim Hunter
Writer .... Mel Frohman
Writer .... Walter Klenhard
Cast .... Aidan Quinn
Cast .... Isabella Rossellini
Cast .... Iman
Cast .... John Pleshette

LIFE IN THE THEATER, A TNT
DRAMA: Buddy Story
Airdate: 10/9/93
Rating: N/A   A/C:

*Based on the play by David Mamet. The
relationship between two theater actors-a
young man whose career is on the rise and the
other, a seasoned veteran whose career is in its
twilight- during a repertory season of plays.*

Production Company: Beacon Pictures IAW Jalem
    Prods. & Bay Kinescope Prods.
Executive Producer .... Marc Abraham
Executive Producer .... David Mamet
Producer .... Patti Wolff
Producer .... Tom Bliss
Director .... Gregory Mosher
Writer .... David Mamet
Cast .... Jack Lemmon
Cast .... Matthew Broderick

LIFEPOD FBC
Drama: Sci-Fi/Supernatural/Horror/Fantasy
Airdate: 6/28/93
Rating: 6.5/11   A/C: 4

*In the year 2169, survivors of a spaceship
explosion are adrift in a badly damaged lifepod
in outerspace. Of the six passengers and three
crew members it is soon evident that the mother
ship's saboteur is aboard the vessel and out for
blood. Is it the smug politician, a brazen
reporter, an escaped prisoner, a radical medical
technician, a tough shipworker or a blind
philosopher? In a race against time the identity
of the terrorist is revealed and danger averted.*

Production Company: RHI Ent. Trilogy Ent.
    Group Prods.
Executive Producer .... Richard Lewis
Executive Producer .... Pen Densham
Executive Producer .... John Watson
Producer .... Mark Stern
Producer .... Tim Harbert
Producer .... Robert Halmi, Jr.
Co-Producer .... Jay Roach
Director .... Ron Silver
Writer .... Pen Densham
Writer .... Jay Roach
Cast .... Ron Silver
Cast .... Robert Loggia
Cast .... Jessica Tuck
Cast .... CCH Pounder

LIGHTNING INCIDENT, THE   USA

Drama: Children/Teens • Sci-Fi/Supernatural/Horror/
Fantasy
Airdate: 09/11/91
Rating: N/A   A/C:

*A young mother risks her life to save her child
who's been kidnapped by a South American
Indian cult, who has marked the baby to fulfill
an ancient ritual of human sacrifice.*

Production Company: Mark Gordon Co.,
   Christopher Meledandri Prods. IAW Wilshire
   Court
Executive Producer .... Mark Gordon
Executive Producer .... Christopher Meledandri
Producer .... Dori Weiss
Director .... Michael Switzer
Writer .... Michael Murray
Cast .... Nancy McKeon
Cast .... Polly Bergen
Cast .... Tim Ryan

LILY   CBS

Drama: Woman In Jeopardy • Action/Adventure •
Foreign or Exotic Location • Series Pilot (2 hr.)
Airdate: 06/14/86
Rating: 6.6/14   A/C:

*A plucky museum curator pursues the mystery
of an archeological forgery to England and
Mexico, repeatedly dodging attempts to do
away with her.*

Production Company: Platypus Prods. IAW
   Viacom
Executive Producer .... Shelley Duvall
Executive Producer .... Andy Borowitz
Director .... Rick Wallace
Writer .... Robert Folk
Cast .... Shelley Duvall
Cast .... Donald Moffat
Cast .... Peter Jurasik
Cast .... Tom Conti

LINCOLN   NBC

Miniseries/Drama (2 nights): Period Piece • Historical
Piece • Biography • Political Piece • True Story
Airdate: 03/27/88 • 03/28/88
Rating: 16.6/26 • 14.9/24   A/C:

*Based on Gore Vidal's book about Lincoln's
personal and public life during his Presidency.*

Production Company: Chris/Rose Prods. Inc. IAW
   Finnegan/Pinchuk Co.
Executive Producer .... Sheldon Pinchuk
Executive Producer .... Bill Finnegan
Executive Producer .... Pat Finnegan
Producer .... Bob Christiansen
Producer .... Rick Rosenberg
Director .... Lamont Johnson
Writer .... Ernest Kinoy
Cast .... Mary Tyler Moore
Cast .... John Houseman
Cast .... Cleavon Little
Cast .... Sam Waterston
Cast .... Richard Mulligan

LINDA   USA

Drama: Murder and Murder Mystery • Suspense/
Thriller
Airdate: 10/8/93
Rating: N/A   A/C:

*A promiscuous and erotic woman frames her
amiable husband for the murder of her lover's
wife while the two couples are vacationing on
a remote Florida beach. He is convicted of the
crime and sent to death row where he escapes
and sets a trap to expose her murderous
machinations.*

Production Company: Linda Prods. IAW Wilshire
   Court Prods.
Executive Producer .... Bob Roe
Co-Producer .... Nathaniel Gutman
Co-Producer .... Nevin Schreiner
Director .... Nathanie Gutman
Writer .... Nevin Schreiner
Cast .... Virginia Madsen
Cast .... Richard Thomas
Cast .... Ted McGinley
Cast .... Laura Harrington

LINE OF FIRE: THE MORRIS DEES STORY   NBC

Drama: Man Against The System • True Story •
Courtroom Drama • Black Story • Biography • Social
Issue
Airdate: 01/21/91
Rating: 11.3/17   A/C: 2

*In the early 1980s, a white Alabama attorney
battles the powerful Ku Klux Klan and wins a
landmark seven million dollar civil suit for the
lynching of a black youth.*

Production Company: BoJames Entertainment
Executive Producer .... Robert A. Papazian
Executive Producer .... James G. Hirsch
Producer .... Michael Shapiro
Producer .... Ellen Sklarz
Director .... John Korty
Writer .... James G. Hirsch
Writer .... Charles Rosin
Cast .... Corbin Bernsen
Cast .... Jenny Lewis
Cast .... Sandy Bull
Cast .... John M. Jackson

LION OF AFRICA, THE   HBO

Drama: Foreign or Exotic Location • Action/
Adventure
Airdate: 6/28/87
Rating: N/A   A/C:

*A female doctor, who has come into possession
of a priceless gem, and her driver a grizzled
diamond trader are pursued by a ring of local
bandits as they travel the dangerous backroads
of West Africa to pick up medical supplies. After
numerous adventures and some tight spots the
mismatched team eventually fall in love.*

Production Company: HBO Pictures, Lois Luger
   Productions
Executive Producer .... Lois Luger
Producer .... Yoram Ben-Ami
Director .... Kevin Connor
Writer .... Bruce Franklin Singer
Cast .... Brooke Adams
Cast .... Brian Dennehy
Cast .... Joseph Shiloa

LITTLE GIRL LOST   ABC

Drama: Family Drama • Children/Teens • True Story
• Rape/Molestation • Social Issue
Airdate: 04/25/88
Rating: 19.0/31   A/C:

*Fact-based story of a family seeking legal
custody of their foster daughter when they
suspect that her natural father is sexually
abusing her.*

Production Company: Marian Rees Associates
   Prods.
Executive Producer .... Marian Rees
Producer .... Robert Huddleston
Co-Producer .... Angela Shelley
Co-Producer .... C. Scott Alsop
Co-Producer .... David Graham
Director .... Sharron Miller
Writer .... Ann Beckett
Cast .... Tess Harper
Cast .... Christopher McDonald
Cast .... Frederic Forrest
Cast .... Patricia Kalember
Cast .... Lawrence Pressman

LITTLE HOUSE ON THE PRAIRIE - BLESS ALL THE DEAR CHILDREN   NBC

Drama: Period Piece • Holiday Special
Airdate: 12/17/84
Rating: 18.2/27   A/C:

*The characters from "The Little House" series
spend Christmas with friends of different ages,
needs and dispositions.*

Production Company: Ed Friendly IAW NBC
   Prods.
Executive Producer .... Michael Landon
Producer .... Kent McCray
Director .... Victor French
Writer .... Chris Abbott
Cast .... Melissa Gilbert
Cast .... Dean Butler
Cast .... Richard Bull
Cast .... Victor French

LITTLE KIDNAPPERS, THE   DISNEY

Drama: Period Piece • Foreign or Exotic Location •
Children/Teens
Airdate: 08/17/90
Rating: N/A   A/C:

*Two orphans go live with their embittered
grandfather in 1900's Nova Scotia. Failing to
find the love they seek, the boys accidentally
kidnap a baby they can love, further fueling the
feud between their grandfather and a
neighboring Dutch family.*

Production Company: Jones Maple Leaf Prods/
    Rensick and Margellos Prods.
Executive Producer .... Glen R. Jones
Executive Producer .... Noel Resnick
Producer .... James Margellos
Director .... Donald Shebib
Writer .... Coralee Elliott Testar
Cast .... Charlton Heston
Cast .... Bruce Greenwood
Cast .... Leo Wheatley
Cast .... Charles Miller

LITTLE MATCH GIRL, THE   NBC

Drama: Children/Teens • Period Piece • Holiday
Special
Airdate: 12/21/87
Rating: 19.4/30   A/C:

*From "Fairy Tales" by Hans Christian
Andersen. A match-selling orphan is taken into
a rich household and manages to solve the
problems of both servants and masters and
bring Christmas cheer to all.*

Production Company: NBC Prods. Inc.
Executive Producer .... Michael Manheim
Producer .... Robert Hargrove
Director .... Michael Lindsay-Hogg
Writer .... Maryedith Burrell
Cast .... Keshia Knight Pulliam
Cast .... William Daniels
Cast .... John Rhys-Davies
Cast .... Rue McClanahan

LITTLE PIECE OF HEAVEN, A   NBC

Drama: Children/Teens • Holiday Special
Airdate: 12/02/91
Rating: 13.8/21   A/C: 3

*After the death of his parents, a clean-cut
Midwestern teen kidnaps an orphan and a
neighborhood girl to befriend his
developmentally disabled sister during
Christmas, prompting the FBI to search for the
missing kids.*

Production Company: Grossbart-Barnett Prods.
    IAW Spectacor Films
Executive Producer .... Joan Barnett
Executive Producer .... Jack Grossbart
Director .... Mimi Leder
Writer .... Betty Goldberg
Cast .... Kirk Cameron
Cast .... Cloris Leachman
Cast .... Jenny Robertson
Cast .... Chelsea Noble

LITTLE WHITE LIES   NBC

Comedy: Romantic Comedy
Airdate: 11/27/89
Rating: 16.9/26   A/C: 2

*A female police detective and a doctor, both
lying about their jobs for various reasons, meet
on a vacation to Rome and fall in love. On
their return to Philadelphia, however, their jobs
bring them into contact and complications
follow.*

Production Company: Larry Thompson
    Organization IAW New World TV
Executive Producer .... Larry Thompson
Producer .... Kevin Inch
Director .... Anson Williams
Writer .... Janis Hirsch
Cast .... Ann Jillian
Cast .... Tim Matheson

LITTLEST VICTIMS   CBS

Drama: Medical/Disease/Mental Illness • Children/
Teens • Man Against The System • True Story
Airdate: 04/23/89
Rating: 10.9/18   A/C:

*True story of New Jersey doctor James Oleske,
who first spotted the Aids virus in young
children and through continued research
determined it came from contaminated blood
transfusions. He later went on to champion the
cause of Aids research.*

Production Company: CBS Entertainment
Executive Producer .... Marian Brayton
Producer .... Fern Field
Supervising Producer .... Annie Carlucci
Director .... Peter Levin
Writer .... Kenneth Cavender
Writer .... J.J. Towne
Cast .... Tim Matheson
Cast .... Lewis Arit
Cast .... Maryann Plunkett

LIVE: FROM DEATH ROW   FBC

Drama: Woman In Jeopardy • Social Issue • Prison
and Prison Camp
Airdate: 04/03/92
Rating: 6.9/12   A/C: 3

*A TV tabloid reporter's planned death row
interview with a charismatic serial killer
backfires and she finds herself held hostage on
live television.*

Production Company: Charlie Mopic Co.
Executive Producer .... Michael Nolin
Producer .... Julie Ahlberg
Director .... Patrick Duncan
Writer .... Patrick Duncan
Cast .... Bruce Davison
Cast .... Joanna Cassidy
Cast .... Jason Tomlins

LIVING A LIE   NBC

Drama: Family Drama • Social Issue
Airdate: 09/16/91
Rating: 11.0/17   A/C: 3

*The subservient wife of a Southwestern rancher
suspects him of concealing his involvement in
the tragic fire of a Mexican church. Despite
social pressure to stand by her man, she finds
the inner strength to speak the truth.*

Production Company: Bernhardt-Freistat Prods.
    Inc. IAW Cannell Entertainment Inc.
Executive Producer .... Lana Freistat
Executive Producer .... Sharon Bernhardt
Producer .... R.W. Goodwin
Director .... Larry Shaw
Writer .... Dalene Young
Cast .... Jill Eikenberry
Cast .... Peter Coyote
Cast .... Roxanne Hart
Cast .... Jarred Blancard

LOCKED UP: A MOTHER'S RAGE   CBS

Drama: Family Drama • Children/Teens • True Story
• Social Issue • Prison and Prison Camp
Airdate: 10/29/91
Rating: 12.4/20   A/C: 3

*A single mother is wrongfully convicted of
selling drugs, leaving her three children in the
care of her over-burdened sister. While in
prison she battles for freedom and helps expand
the visiting rights of children of incarcerated
mothers.*

Production Company: Steve White Prods.
Executive Producer .... Steve White
Executive Producer .... Pat Foulkrod
Producer .... Barry Bernardi
Director .... Bethany Rooney
Writer .... Robert L. Freedman
Writer .... Selma Thompson
Cast .... Cheryl Ladd
Cast .... Jean Smart
Cast .... Angela Bassett
Cast .... Joshua Harris
Cast .... Diana Muldaur

LOIS & CLARK: THE NEW ADVENTURES OF SUPERMAN ABC

Drama: Series Pilot (2 hr.) • Sci-Fi/Supernatural/
Horror/Fantasy
Airdate: 9/12/93
Rating: 11.2/17   A/C: 2

Intrepid reporter Clark Kent arrives in Metropolis. He lands a job at the Dailey Planet newspaper where the lovely but saucy Lois Lane is investigating a sabotaged space launch. Together the duo come up against the sinister Lex Luthor who is up to his greedy, evil ways and can only be stopped by Superman. Who of course is still fighting for truth, justice and the American way!

Production Company: Roundely Prods. IAW
    Warner Bros. TV
Executive Producer .... David Jacobs
Co-Executive Producer .... Deborah Joy LeVine
Producer .... Mel Efros
Producer .... Thania St. John
Director .... Robert Butler
Writer .... Deborah Joy LeVine
Cast .... Dean Cain
Cast .... Teri Hatcher
Cast .... John Shea
Cast .... Lane Smith

LONDON AND DAVIS IN NEW YORK CBS

Drama: Murder and Murder Mystery
Airdate: 09/19/84
Rating: 9.7/18   A/C:

When the male of the duo becomes a murder target, a pair of successful photojournalists become involved in the investigation of a woman who is offing young bachelors.

Production Company: Bloodworth-Thomason
    Mozark Prods. IAW Columbia TV
Executive Producer .... Harry Thomason
Producer .... Linda Bloodworth Thomason
Director .... Robert Day
Writer .... Linda Bloodworth Thomason
Cast .... Season Hubley
Cast .... James Carroll Jordon
Cast .... Roddy McDowall
Cast .... Richard Crenna

LONESOME DOVE CBS

Miniseries/Drama (4 nights): Western • Period Piece
Airdate: 02/05/89 • 02/06/89 • 02/07/89 • 02/08/89
Rating: 28.5/42 • 23.8/34 • 24.8/41 • 27.3/41 A/C:

Based on the book by Larry McMurty about three former Texas Rangers who go on an epic cattle drive from Texas to Montana.

Production Company: Motown Prods. IAW
    Pangaea and Qintex Entertainment Inc.
Executive Producer .... Suzanne De Passe
Executive Producer .... Bill Wittliff
Co-Executive Producer .... Robert Halmi, Jr.
Director .... Simon Wincer
Writer .... Bill Wittliff
Cast .... Robert Duvall
Cast .... Tommy Lee Jones
Cast .... Frederic Forrest
Cast .... Robert Urich
Cast .... Danny Glover
Cast .... D.B. Sweeney
Cast .... Rick Schroder
Cast .... Anjelica Huston
Cast .... Diane Lane

LONG GONE HBO

Drama: Sports • Romantic Comedy
Airdate: 5/23/87
Rating: N/A   A/C:

Based on a story by Paul Hemphill. The hell-raising, tough-talking manager of a 1950's third-rate minor-league baseball team suddenly finds himself and his hot new rookie players battling for the pennant. A sassy small-town beauty queen plans to turn a one-night stand with brash bachelor into a lifelong commitment.

Production Company: The Landsburg Company
Executive Producer .... Alan Landsburg
Executive Producer .... Joan Barnett
Producer .... Joan Barnett
Director .... Martin Davidson
Writer .... Michael Norell
Cast .... William Petersen
Cast .... Virginia Madsen
Cast .... Dermot Mulroney

LONG HOT SUMMER, THE NBC

Miniseries/Drama (2 nights): Family Drama • Period
Piece
Airdate: 10/06/85 • 10/07/85
Rating: 22.6/34 • 23.8/36   A/C:

Based on Faulkner's "The Hamlet." Remake of 1958 feature film. A mysterious drifter figures in a wealthy small town patriarch's desire to have grandchildren either by his spinster daughter or his milquetoast son.

Production Company: Leonard Hill Films
Executive Producer .... Leonard Hill
Executive Producer .... John Thomas Lenox
Producer .... Dori Weiss
Director .... Stuart Cooper
Writer .... Rita Mae Brown
Writer .... Dennis Turner
Cast .... Ava Gardner
Cast .... Judith Ivey
Cast .... Don Johnson
Cast .... Jason Robards
Cast .... William Russ
Cast .... Cybill Shepherd

LONG JOURNEY HOME, THE CBS

Mystery: Love Story • Suspense/Thriller • Action/
Adventure
Airdate: 11/29/87
Rating: 21.3/34   A/C:

A woman's MIA husband reappears just as she is about to have him declared legally dead. A killer is after him, and the couple flee with new identities.

Production Company: Andrea Baynes Prods. and
    Grail Prods. IAW Lorimar TV
Executive Producer .... Andrea Baynes
Co-Executive Producer .... David Birney
Co-Executive Producer .... Meredith Baxter
Producer .... Ervin Zavada
Director .... Rod Holcomb
Writer .... Karen Clark
Cast .... Daphne Maxwell Reid
Cast .... Kevin McCarthy
Cast .... Meredith Baxter
Cast .... David Birney

LONG ROAD HOME NBC

Drama: Family Drama • Farm Story • Man Against
The System • Period Piece
Airdate: 02/25/91
Rating: 11.8/18   A/C: 3

Based on the book by Ronald B. Taylor. A Depression-era Texas family, forced to move to California, become migrant farm workers and endure the oppression of greedy landowners.

Production Company: Rosemont Prods. Ltd.
Executive Producer .... Norman Rosemont
Producer .... David A. Rosemont
Director .... John Korty
Writer .... Jane-Howard Hammerstein
Cast .... Mark Harmon
Cast .... Lee Purcell
Cast .... Morgan Weisser
Cast .... Leon Russom

LONG TIME GONE · ABC

Drama: Family Drama • Cops/Detectives/Law
Enforcement • Children/Teens • Mafia/Mob
Airdate: 05/23/86
Rating: 7.4/14 · A/C:

*When his eleven year old son comes to live with
him, a mob-involved drifter takes new interest
in his career as a private detective.*

Production Company: Picturemaker Prods. Inc.
with ABC Circle Films
Executive Producer .... Glenn Gordon Caron
Producer .... Jay Daniel
Director .... Robert Butler
Writer .... Glenn Gordon Caron
Cast .... Paul LeMat
Cast .... Eddie Zammit
Cast .... Bill Marcus
Cast .... Deborah Wakeham

LONGARM · ABC

Drama: Western • Period Piece
Airdate: 03/06/88
Rating: 12.3/20 · A/C:

*In this lighthearted drama of the Old West, a
deputy tracks down—and steals the girlfriend
of—a childhood rival who's now a dangerous
robber.*

Production Company: Universal TV
Executive Producer .... David Chisholm
Producer .... Chuck Sellier
Director .... Virgil W. Vogel
Writer .... David Chisholm
Cast .... Whitney Kershaw
Cast .... Shannon Tweed
Cast .... Daphne Ashbrook
Cast .... Rene Auberjonois
Cast .... John Terlesky

LOOKALIKE, THE · USA

Drama: Psychological Thriller
Airdate: 12/12/90
Rating: N/A · A/C:

*A traumatized young woman sees a child who
resembles her dead daughter and a woman who
looks like herself. She unravels her past to learn
the woman is her twin, who she never knew
existed because she was kidnapped at birth.*

Production Company: Gallo-MCA
Executive Producer .... Lillian Gallo
Producer .... Don Goldman
Director .... Gary Nelson
Writer .... Linda Bergman
Writer .... Martin Tahse
Cast .... Melissa Gilbert
Cast .... Diane Ladd
Cast .... Thaao Penghlis
Cast .... Frances Lee McCain

LOST CAPONE, THE · TNT

Drama: Period Piece • Historical Piece • Mafia/Mob
• Biography
Airdate: 09/10/90
Rating: N/A · A/C:

*Chicago gangster Al Capone's younger brother
becomes a lawman, causing emotional turmoil
within the family. Matters are complicated
when he must bust Al's liquor trucks when they
invade his small Nebraska town.*

Production Company: Kenneth Kaufman
Entertainment
Executive Producer .... Ken Kaufman
Executive Producer .... Tom Patchett
Producer .... Eva Fyer
Director .... John Gray
Writer .... John Gray
Cast .... Adrian Pasdar
Cast .... Ally Sheedy
Cast .... Eric Roberts
Cast .... Titus Welliver

LOST IN LONDON · CBS

Drama: Children/Teens • Foreign or Exotic Location
Airdate: 11/20/85
Rating: 13.0/19 · A/C:

*A young boy runs away from his bickering
parents and hooks up with a band of streetwise
children who entertain and steal for a living in
London.*

Production Company: Emmanuel Lewis Ent. IAW
D'Angelo Prods. & Group W. Prods.
Executive Producer .... Bill D'Angelo
Producer .... Peter Manley
Director .... Robert Lewis
Writer .... Ron Rubin
Cast .... Emmanuel Lewis
Cast .... Lynne Moody
Cast .... Ben Vereen

LOVE AMONG THIEVES · ABC

Drama: Suspense/Thriller • Action/Adventure •
Foreign or Exotic Location
Airdate: 02/23/87
Rating: 13.2/21 · A/C:

*A renowned concert pianist and a mysterious,
handsome stranger steal three Faberge eggs
needed to ransom the pianist's kidnapped
fiance.*

Production Company: Robert A. Papazian Prods.
Executive Producer .... Karen Mack
Producer .... Robert A. Papazian
Director .... Roger Young
Writer .... Stephen Black
Writer .... Henry Stern
Cast .... Audrey Hepburn
Cast .... Robert Wagner
Cast .... Jerry Orbach
Cast .... Samantha Eggar

LOVE AND BETRAYAL · CBS

Drama: Family Drama • Woman's Issue/Story
Airdate: 04/16/89
Rating: 16.1/25 · A/C:

*A devoted housewife is forced to develop a new
career, new romantic interests and new self-
esteem when her longtime husband leaves her.*

Production Company: Gross-Weston Prods. IAW
ITC
Producer .... Marcy Gross
Producer .... Ann Weston
Director .... Richard Michaels
Writer .... Laurian Legett
Cast .... Stefanie Powers
Cast .... David Birney
Cast .... Fran Drescher
Cast .... Amanda Peterson

LOVE AND CURSES . . . AND ALL THAT JAZZ · CBS

Mystery: Cops/Detectives/Law Enforcement •
Suspense/Thriller
Airdate: 09/21/91
Rating: 8.5/16 · A/C: 2

*A New Orleans doctor and his psychologist wife
become amateur detectives when they treat a
patient who is catatonic due to an evil voodoo
practitioner.*

Production Company: Delmac Prods.
Executive Producer .... Delta Burke
Executive Producer .... Gerald McRaney
Executive Producer .... Robert Stolfi
Producer .... Albert J. Salzer
Director .... Gerald McRaney
Writer .... Richard C. Okie
Writer .... Rob Gilmer
Cast .... Delta Burke
Cast .... Gerald McRaney
Cast .... Elizabeth Ashley
Cast .... Harold Sylvester

LOVE AND HATE: A MARRIAGE MADE IN HELL · NBC

Miniseries/Drama (2 nights): Family Drama • True
Crime • Foreign or Exotic Location • Family Violence
• Woman's Issue/Story
Airdate: 07/15/90 • 07/16/90
Rating: 13.9/25 • 16.3/28 · A/C: 1 • 1

*The battered wife of a Canadian politician
divorces her husband, taking her younger
children with her. When he can't get custody of
the youngest child, he murders his ex-wife. A
sensational trial eventually proves his guilt.*

Production Company: Canadian Broadcasting
Corp.
Executive Producer .... Bernard Zukerman
Director .... Francis Mankiewicz
Writer .... Suzette Couture
Cast .... Kate Nelligan
Cast .... Kenneth Welsh
Cast .... Leon Pownall
Cast .... Brent Carver

LOVE BOAT: A VALENTINE VOYAGE, THE
CBS

Comedy: Foreign or Exotic Location • Romantic Comedy
Airdate: 02/12/90
Rating: 13.6/22   A/C: 2

"The Love Boat" characters are reunited for a voyage involving a gang of bumbling jewel thieves, an ambitious policeman, and the very pregnant wife of the ship's chef.

Production Company: Aaron Spelling Prods. IAW The Douglas S. Cramer Co.
Executive Producer .... Aaron Spelling
Executive Producer .... Douglas S. Cramer
Producer .... Dennis Hammer
Director .... Ron Satlof
Writer .... Stephanie Garman
Writer .... Hollace White
Writer .... Don Segall
Writer .... Phil Margo
Writer .... Barbara Esenstein
Writer .... James Harmon Brown
Cast .... Gavin MacLeod
Cast .... Bernie Kopell
Cast .... Ted Lange
Cast .... Julia Duffy

LOVE CAN BE MURDER
NBC

Comedy: Murder and Murder Mystery • Sci-Fi/Supernatural/Horror/Fantasy • Romantic Comedy
Airdate: 12/14/92
Rating: 11.4/18   A/C: 3

A successful but restless Los Angeles lawyer gives up her practice to become a private eye. Her new office happens to be inhabited by a mischievous ghost, a detective from the 1940's who wants her to find out who killed him forty years ago—a case that still remains unsolved. Together the gallant gumshoe and the naive neophyte crack the mystery.

Production Company: Konigsberg/Sanitsky Co.
Executive Producer .... Frank Konigsberg
Executive Producer .... Larry Sanitsky
Co-Executive Producer .... Rob Gilmer
Producer .... Jayne Bieber
Director .... Jack Bender
Writer .... Rob Gilmer
Cast .... Jaclyn Smith
Cast .... Corbin Bernsen
Cast .... Cliff De Young
Cast .... Anne Francis

LOVE, CHEAT AND STEAL
SHOWTIME

Drama: Suspense/Thriller
Airdate: 12/5/93
Rating: N/A   A/C:

A successful banker gets involved in a sorted triangle when his wife's ex-husband gets out of prison and seeks revenge on the couple for framing him. While planning to rob the troubled bank the streetwise con is seduced by his ex-wife who is stringing both men along while waiting to make her move.

Production Company: Motion Picture Corp. of America, Showtime Ent.
Producer .... Brad Krevoy
Producer .... Steve Stabler
Producer .... Chad Oman
Director .... William Curran
Writer .... William Curran
Cast .... John Lithgow
Cast .... Eric Roberts
Cast .... Madchen Amick
Cast .... Richard Edson

LOVE, HONOR & OBEY: THE LAST MAFIA MARRIAGE
CBS

Miniseries/Drama (2 nights): Family Drama • Mafia/Mob • True Crime
Airdate: 5/23/93 • 5/25/93
Rating: 12.6/20 • 14.4/24   A/C: 2 • 2

Based on the book, "Mafia Marriage" by Rosalie Bonano. The arranged marriage of Rosalie Profaci to Bill Bonanno marked the alliance of two of the five preeminent NY organized crime families. The young bride soon learns of her Mafia husbands violent ways and struggles to keep her family together.

Production Company: CBS Ent. Prods.
Executive Producer .... Robert Dellinger
Executive Producer .... Larry Strichman
Producer .... Lynn Raynor
Director .... John Patterson
Writer .... Christopher Canaan
Cast .... Eric Roberts
Cast .... Nancy McKeon
Cast .... Ben Gazzara
Cast .... Alex Rocco
Cast .... Phyllis Lyons

LOVE IS NEVER SILENT
NBC
EMMY WINNER

Drama: Family Drama • Period Piece
Airdate: 12/9/85
Rating: 17.3/26   A/C:

In the 1930s and 40s, a young woman serves as the indispensable connection between her deaf parents and the world. Finally the prospect of her marriage forces the entire family to move towards self-sufficiency.

Production Company: Marian Rees Associates
Executive Producer .... Marian Rees
Co-Executive Producer .... Julianna Fjeld
Producer .... Dorothea Petrie
Director .... Joseph Sargent
Writer .... Darlene Craviotto
Cast .... Mare Winningham
Cast .... Phyllis Frelich
Cast .... Frederic Lehne
Cast .... Cloris Leachman
Cast .... Ed Waterstreet

LOVE KILLS
USA

Drama: Woman In Jeopardy • Suspense/Thriller
Airdate: 11/13/91
Rating: N/A   A/C:

A wealthy heiress must uncover the truth between a hit man who claims her husband hired him to kill her and her husband who tries to convince her the man is a pathological liar.

Production Company: Mark Gordon Co., Christopher Meledandri Prods. IAW Wilshire Court
Executive Producer .... Mark Gordon
Executive Producer .... Christopher Meledandri
Producer .... Bob Roe
Director .... Brian Grant
Writer .... Michael Murray
Cast .... Virginia Madsen
Cast .... Lenny Von Dohlen
Cast .... Jim Metzler
Cast .... Erich Anderson

LOVE & LIES
ABC

Drama: Murder and Murder Mystery • Cops/Detectives/Law Enforcement • Love Story • True Crime
Airdate: 03/18/90
Rating: 11.6/18   A/C: 3

A young female private detective must "fall in love" with a murder suspect in order to discover if he committed the crime. While trying to coax the truth out of him, a heated affair develops.

Production Company: Freyda Rothstein Prod., Inc. IAW ITC Entertainment Group
Executive Producer .... Freyda Rothstein
Producer .... Art Levison
Director .... Roger Young
Writer .... Alan Sharp
Cast .... Mare Winningham
Cast .... Peter Gallagher
Cast .... Tom O'Brien
Cast .... M. Emmet Walsh

LOVE, LIES AND MURDER
NBC

Miniseries/Drama (2 nights): Family Drama • Murder and Murder Mystery • True Crime • Children/Teens • Courtroom Drama • Family Violence
Airdate: 02/17/91 • 02/18/91
Rating: 15.5/24 • 20.3/30   A/C: 2 • 1

In 1985, fourteen-year-old Californian Cinnamon Brown takes the rap for her stepmother's murder. Further evidence reveals a bizarre family conspiracy which ultimately leads to the indictment of her manipulative father.

Production Company: Republic Pictures Corp.
Executive Producer .... Laurie Levit
Executive Producer .... Tim Hill
Executive Producer .... Norman Morrill
Producer .... Jay Benson
Director .... Robert Markowitz
Writer .... Danielle Hill
Cast .... Clancy Brown
Cast .... Sheryl Lee
Cast .... Moira Kelly
Cast .... Tom Bower

LOVE LIVES ON   ABC

Drama: Children/Teens • Medical/Disease/Mental Illness • Addiction Story • Social Issue • Family Drama • True Story
Airdate: 04/01/85
Rating: 17.8/26   A/C:

Based on a true story of a fifteen year old girl who overcomes a drug habit, learns she has cancer and becomes pregnant. She decides to stop chemotherapy in order to have her baby.

Production Company: ABC Circle Films
Producer .... April Smith
Co-Producer .... Rod Paul
Co-Producer .... Robert Thompson
Director .... Larry Peerce
Writer .... April Smith
Cast .... Sam Waterston
Cast .... Christine Lahti
Cast .... Louise Latham
Cast .... Ricky Paul Goldin
Cast .... Mary Stuart Masterson

LOVE, MARY   CBS

Drama: Family Drama • Children/Teens • Medical/Disease/Mental Illness • True Story
Airdate: 10/08/85
Rating: 21.5/33   A/C:

A young woman overcomes dyslexia, reform school, teenage motherhood and a stroke to fulfill her dream of becoming a doctor.

Production Company: CBS Entertaiment Prods.
Producer .... Ellis A. Cohen
Director .... Robert Day
Writer .... Clifford Campion
Cast .... Kristy McNichol
Cast .... Matt Clark
Cast .... David Paymer
Cast .... Piper Laurie

LOVE MATTERS   SHOWTIME

Drama: Family Drama
Airdate: 10/3/93
Rating: N/A   A/C:

A workaholic, advertising executive and his distant professor wife realize their ten year old marriage is on its last legs when they are confronted by their best friends adulterous affair. The impact of the illicit behavior forces the couple to reexamine their lives and commitments to each other.

Production Company: Chanticleer Films
Executive Producer .... Jana Sue Memel
Executive Producer .... Jonathan Sanger
Producer .... Laura Stuart
Director .... Eb Lotimer
Writer .... Evan Katz
Writer .... Eb Lotimer
Cast .... Griffin Dunne
Cast .... Tony Goldwyn
Cast .... Annette O'Toole
Cast .... Kate Burton

LOVE ON THE RUN   NBC

Drama: Love Story • True Crime • Prison and Prison Camp
Airdate: 10/21/85
Rating: 15.4/23   A/C:

A woman lawyer falls in love with her convicted murderer client and busts him out of jail. The two flee together with the law hot on their trail.

Production Company: NBC Prods.
Executive Producer .... Sue Grafton
Executive Producer .... Steve Humphrey
Producer .... Jay Benson
Director .... Gus Trikonis
Writer .... Sue Grafton
Writer .... Steve Humphrey
Cast .... Stephanie Zimbalist
Cast .... Alec Baldwin
Cast .... Howard Duff
Cast .... Constance McCashin
Cast .... Ernie Hudson

LOVE ON THE RUN   NBC

Drama: Action/Adventure • Series Pilot (2 hr.) • Foreign or Exotic Location
Airdate: 6/5/94
Rating: 9.3/16   A/C: 2

After exchanging intoxicated marriage vows on whim in Greece a spoiled heiress and a "rogue" adventure seeker come to realize they really don't get along—and decide to divorce. However, sparks fly when the socialites wealthy father orchestrates a clever financial scheme to ensure the two remain partners—in marriage and in "Adventure,Inc.," an operation that allow clients to go anywhere and do anything for a price.

Production Company: Primedia CoProductions Ltd.
Executive Producer .... Aaron Spelling
Executive Producer .... E. Duke Vincent
Executive Producer .... Gary Randall
Executive Producer .... W. Patterson Ferns
Director .... Ted Kotcheff
Writer .... Jim Cruickshank
Writer .... James Orr
Cast .... Anthony Addabbo
Cast .... Noelle Beck
Cast .... Len Cariou

LOVE SHE SOUGHT, THE   NBC

Drama: Love Story • Foreign or Exotic Location
Airdate: 10/21/90
Rating: 12.0/18   A/C: 2

An unfulfilled spinster teacher retires, travels to Ireland in a quest for romance with a long time pen pal, and is crushed to discover he's a priest.

Production Company: Arnold Prods. Inc., An Andrew J. Fenady Production IAW Orion TV
Executive Producer .... Andrew J. Fenady
Executive Producer .... Duke Fenady
Producer .... Richard Rosenbloom
Producer .... Ron Cowen
Producer .... Daniel Lipman
Director .... Joseph Sargent
Writer .... Ron Cowen
Writer .... Daniel Lipman
Cast .... Angela Lansbury
Cast .... Denholm Elliott
Cast .... Cynthia Nixon
Cast .... Gary Hershberger

LUCKY DAY   ABC

Drama: Family Drama • Medical/Disease/Mental Illness
Airdate: 03/11/91
Rating: 9.8/16   A/C: 3

Old family wounds are opened and the patterns of co-dependency are examined when a retarded woman wins the lottery and a custody battle ensues between her caretaker sister and their estranged, recovering alcoholic mother.

Production Company: Hearst Entertainment Prods. IAW Polongo Prods., Inc.
Executive Producer .... Donald Wrye
Producer .... John Lugar
Director .... Donald Wrye
Writer .... John Axness
Writer .... Jennifer Miller
Cast .... Amy Madigan
Cast .... Olympia Dukakis
Cast .... Chloe Webb
Cast .... Terence Knox

LUCY & DESI: BEFORE THE LAUGHTER   CBS

Drama: True Story • Period Piece • Biography • Hollywood
Airdate: 02/10/91
Rating: 16.4/25   A/C: 1

Comedienne Lucille Ball and womanizing Cuban bandleader Desi Arnaz battle over his infidelities, her jealousies, and the pressures of Hollywood through their stormy courtship and eleven-year marriage.

Production Company: Larry Thompson Entertainment
Executive Producer .... Larry Thompson
Producer .... John Thomas Lenox
Director .... Charles Jarrott
Writer .... William Luce
Writer .... Cynthia Cherbak
Cast .... Frances Fisher
Cast .... Maurice Benard
Cast .... Bette Ford

LUSH LIFE   SHOWTIME
Drama: Buddy Story • Medical/Disease/Mental Illness
Airdate: 5/20/94
Rating: N/A   A/C:

Two best friends who are top New York jazz musicians must face the music when one of them is diagnosed with an inoperable brain tumor. Always enjoying the good life together, they plan one last "farewell" bash—although they don't tell their guests just how final it's likely to be.

Production Company: Chanticler Films
Executive Producer .... Jana Sue Memel
Executive Producer .... Jonathan Sanger
Producer .... Thom Colwell
Co-Producer .... Hillary Anne Ripps
Co-Producer .... Ron Colby
Director .... Michael Elias
Writer .... Michael Elias
Cast .... Jeff Goldblum
Cast .... Forest Whitaker
Cast .... Kathy Baker
Cast .... Tracey Needham

MACGYVER : LOST TREASURE OF ATLANTIS   ABC
Drama: Action/Adventure • Foreign or Exotic Location
Airdate: 5/14/94
Rating: 9.1/17   A/C: 2

Based on the long running ABC TV series. Crafty adventurer, MacGyver and his pal, an eccentric archaeologist are off to find the lost treasure of Atlantis

Production Company: Gekko Film Corp. Henry Winkler/John Rich Prods. IAW Paramount Network TV
Executive Producer .... Henry Winkler
Executive Producer .... John Rich
Executive Producer .... Richard Dean Anderson
Producer .... Michael Greenburg
Director .... Michael Vejar
Writer .... John Sheppard
Cast .... Richard Dean Anderson
Cast .... Brian Blessed
Cast .... Sophie Ward

MACSHAYNE: THE FINAL ROLL OF THE DICE   NBC
Drama: Murder and Murder Mystery • Cops/Detectives/Law Enforcement
Airdate: 4/29/94
Rating: 8.3/15   A/C: 3

A Las Vegas hotel casino troubleshooter helps clear a fiery Latin rock singer who is accused of murdering her ex-husband hours before their reunion concert.

Production Company: Larry Levinson Prods., Kenny Rogers IAW Dean Hargrove Prods.
Executive Producer .... Michael Gleason
Executive Producer .... Dean Hargrove
Executive Producer .... Ken Kragen
Producer .... Kelly Junkermann
Writer .... Ernie Wallengren
Director .... E.W. Swackhamer
Cast .... Kenny Rogers
Cast .... Maria Conchita Alonso
Cast .... Wendy Phillips
Cast .... Daniel Hugh Kelly

MACSHAYNE: WINNER TAKE ALL   NBC
Drama: Cops/Detectives/Law Enforcement • Series Pilot (2 hr.)
Airdate: 2/11/94
Rating: 10.7/17   A/C: 3

A charming compulsive gambler, ex petty con and Las Vegas knockabout becomes the security chief of a casino when he foils the attempts of a group of former cops who plan to rob the swanky establishment.

Production Company: Larry Levinson Prods. IAW Kenny Rogers Prods.
Executive Producer .... Ken Kragen
Executive Producer .... Dean Hargrove
Executive Producer .... Michael Gleason
Producer .... Kelly Junkermann
Director .... E.W. Swackhamer
Writer .... Michael Gleason
Cast .... Kenny Rogers
Cast .... Ann Jillian
Cast .... Terry O'Quinn
Cast .... Wendy Phillips

MAFIA PRINCESS   NBC
Drama: Woman In Jeopardy • True Story • Family Violence • Mafia/Mob • Biography
Airdate: 01/19/86
Rating: 24.4/37   A/C:

Fact-based life story of Antoinette Giancana, trying to establish her own identity despite the heavy burden of being the daughter of a Mafia capo.

Production Company: Jack Farren Prods. and Group W Prods.
Executive Producer .... Jack Farren
Producer .... Lew Gallo
Director .... Robert Collins
Writer .... Robert W. Lenski
Cast .... Susan Lucci
Cast .... Louie DiBianco
Cast .... Tony Curtis
Cast .... Tony De Santos

MAID FOR EACH OTHER   NBC
Comedy: Buddy Story • Murder and Murder Mystery
Airdate: 01/13/92
Rating: 13.6/21   A/C: 2

When her deceased husband leaves her penniless, a pampered housewife becomes a maid for a once-famous pop diva. When the singer finds her ex-husband dead in a closet, the two team up to find the killers and get themselves off the hook.

Production Company: Hearst/Alexander-Enright
Executive Producer .... Les Alexander
Executive Producer .... Don Enright
Executive Producer .... Dinah Manoff
Producer .... Don Enright
Producer .... Les Alexander
Co-Producer .... Paul Schneider
Co-Producer .... Rob Gilmer
Director .... Paul Schneider
Writer .... Andrew Smith
Writer .... Rob Gilmer
Cast .... Dinah Manoff
Cast .... Nell Carter
Cast .... Joyce Van Patten
Cast .... Garrett Morris

MAJORITY RULE   LIFETIME
Drama: Woman Against The System • Political Piece
Airdate: 10/27/92
Rating: N/A   A/C:

A female, three star Army General ,who returns a hero from a victorious desert military operation, is catapulted into a campaign for the presidency. With the help of her advisors and the support of her family she is able to change the role of women in the political process.

Production Company: Ultra Ent. IAW Citadel Pictures
Executive Producer .... David R. Ginsburg
Executive Producer .... Bob Rubin
Executive Producer .... Bill Siegler
Producer .... George Perkins
Director .... Gwen Arner
Writer .... David Taylor
Cast .... Blair Brown
Cast .... John Getz
Cast .... John Glover
Cast .... Donald Moffat

Movies and Miniseries

MALICE IN WONDERLAND CBS
Drama: Period Piece • Historical Piece • Biography • Hollywood • True Story
Airdate: 05/12/85
Rating: 18.3/29   A/C:

From 1928 to1944, the lives of powerful Hollywood columnists Hedda Hopper and Lowella Parsons, and the methods they used to influence the stars and their readers.

Production Company: ITC Prods.
Executive Producer .... Judith A. Polone
Producer .... Jay Benson
Director .... Gus Trikonis
Writer .... Jacqueline Feather
Writer .... David Seidler
Cast .... Elizabeth Taylor
Cast .... Jane Alexander
Cast .... Richard Dysart
Cast .... Joyce Van Patten

MAN AGAINST THE MOB NBC
Drama: Murder and Murder Mystery • Cops/ Detectives/Law Enforcement • Period Piece • Mafia/ Mob
Airdate: 01/10/88
Rating: 19.7/32   A/C:

During the 1950s, one honest Los Angeles police sergeant, with the backing of the mayor, must keep the Chicago mob from taking over their city.

Production Company: Frank von Zerneck Films
Executive producer .... Frank Von Zerneck
Executive Producer .... Robert M. Sertner
Producer .... Phillips Wylly, Sr.
Director .... Steven H. Stern
Writer .... David J. Kinghorn
Cast .... George Peppard
Cast .... Kathryn Harrold
Cast .... Max Gail
Cast .... Stella Stevens

MAN AGAINST THE MOB: THE CHINATOWN MURDERS NBC
Drama: Murder and Murder Mystery • Cops/ Detectives/Law Enforcement • Period Piece • Prostitution • Mafia/Mob
Airdate: 12/10/89
Rating: 11.3/18   A/C: 3

Prequel to TV movie "Man against the Mob" (NBC, 1988). In the late 1940s, a Los Angeles police detective fights Mob-involved prostitution and police corruption in Chinatown.

Production Company: Von Zerneck-Sertner Films
Executive producer .... Frank Von Zerneck
Executive Producer .... Robert M. Sertner
Producer .... Susan Weber-Gold
Producer .... Michael Pressman
Director .... Michael Pressman
Writer .... Michael Petryni
Cast .... George Peppard
Cast .... Ursula Andress
Cast .... Charles Haid

MAN FOR ALL SEASON, A TNT
Drama: Period Piece • Historical Piece • Foreign or Exotic Location • Biography
Airdate: 12/7/88
Rating: N/A   A/C:

Remake of the 1966 feature film. When Sir Thomas More refuses to support King Henry VIII in his opposition to the Pope and the formation of t he Church of England he is beheaded in 1535.

Production Company: Agamemnon Films Inc.
  Peter Snell Productions IAW TNT
Producer .... Fraser C. Heston
Producer .... Peter Snell
Director .... Charlton Heston
Writer .... Robert Bolt
Cast .... Charlton Heston
Cast .... Vanessa Redgrave
Cast .... John Gielgud

MAN FROM LEFT FIELD CBS
Drama: Children/Teens • Sports
Airdate: 10/15/93
Rating: 10.5/20   A/C: 2

In Florida, a drifter with amnesia is reluctantly recruited to coach a ragtag Little League team. He pulls the players together and falls in love with a mother of one of the kids. While trying to save a drowning boy he regains his memory and it turns out that he was once a former star slugger for the Kansas City Athletics. While confronting the painful memories of his past he finds a new lease on life with the love from a good woman and his adoring team.

Production Company: Burt Reynolds Prods.
Executive Producer .... Burt Reynolds
Executive Producer .... Lamar Jackson
Executive Producer .... Renee Valente
Producer .... Wayne Rice
Producer .... Rene Valente
Director .... Burt Reynolds
Writer .... Wayne Rice
Cast .... Burt Reynolds
Cast .... Reba McEntire
Cast .... Derek Baxter

MAN UPSTAIRS, THE CBS
Drama: Holiday Special
Airdate: 12/6/92
Rating: 18.8/28   A/C: 1

An escaped jewel thief breaks into and hides out in the wealthy home of a cranky recluse. The two strike up an odd relationship which helps them to both to learn about the true meaning of trust, love and friendship.

Production Company: Burt Reynold Prods.
Executive Producer .... Burt Reynolds
Executive Producer .... John Dayton
Executive Producer .... Lamar Jackson
Producer .... Renee Valente
Producer .... George Schaefer
Director .... George Schaefer
Writer .... James Prideaux
Cast .... Katherine Hepburn
Cast .... Ryan O'Neal
Cast .... Helena Carroll

MAN WHO BROKE 1,000 CHAINS, THE HBO
Drama: True Story • Prison and Prison Camp • Period Piece
Airdate: 10/27/87
Rating: N/A   A/C:

The story of Robert Elliot Burns who sentenced to a brutal prison on a false robbery charge and is forced to endure endless abuse on a chain gang by a sadistic guard. He eventually escapes and is pursued by the ruthless warden of the penitentiary. Note: This story inspired the classic film " I Am a Fugitive from a Chain Gang" .

Production Company: HBO Pictures, Journey Entertainment
Executive Producer .... Michael Campus
Producer .... Yoram Ben-Ami
Director .... Daniel Mann
Writer .... Wendell Mayes
Writer .... Michael Campus
Cast .... Val Kilmer
Cast .... Charles Durning
Cast .... Sonia Braga
Cast .... William Sanderson

MANDELA HBO
Drama: Biography • Black Story • Foreign or Exotic Location • Social Issue • True Story
Airdate: 9/20/87
Rating: N/A   A/C:

The struggle of South African human rights leader Nelson Mandela and his wife Winnie from their courtship and marriage through his involvement with the African National Congress and his imprisonment in 1962 for over twenty-five years -for his outspoken opposition to apartheid.

Production Company: Titus Productions IAW Polymuse, Inc., TVS Ltd. Prods.
Executive Producer .... Herbert Brodkin
Producer .... Robert Berger
Producer .... Dickie Bamber
Director .... Philip Saville
Writer .... Ronald Harwood
Cast .... Danny Glover
Cast .... Alfre Woodard

MANHUNT FOR CLAUDE DALLAS CBS
Drama: Cops/Detectives/Law Enforcement • True Crime
Airdate: 10/28/86
Rating: 14.4/24   A/C:

True story of the sometime folk hero who embraced the unfettered life, murdered two Fish and Game officers, fled, was caught and sentenced to thirty years, and broke jail.

Production Company: London Films, Inc.
Executive Producer .... Jerry London
Producer .... Lee Rafner
Director .... Jerry London
Writer .... John Gay
Cast .... Rip Torn
Cast .... Claude Akins
Cast .... Lois Nettleton
Cast .... Pat Hingle
Cast .... Matt Salinger

ADDENDUM

Maj Canton's Complete Reference Guide to Movies & Miniseries Made For TV and Cable 1984-1994

DUE TO AN OVERSIGHT, THE FOLLOWING TV MOVIE WAS INADVERTENTLY OMITTED FROM THE BOOK. WE SINCERELY APOLOGIZE TO THE PRODUCERS, THE NETWORK AND ALL THOSE INVOLVED FOR THIS UNFORTUNATE ERROR.

Man With Three Wives, The   CBS

Drama:: Family Drama - True Crime - Woman's Issue/Story
Airdate: 3/28/93
Rating: 20.8/33
A/C: 1

A well-respected doctor and family man secretly divides his time between three different spouses over a ten year period.

Production Company: CBS Entertainment Productions IAW Arnold Shapiro Productions.

Executive Producer	Arnold Shapiro
Producer	Jean O'Neill
Co-Producer	Tracy Verna
Director	Peter Levin
Writer	Deborah Serra
Cast	Beau Bridges
Cast	Pam Dawber
Cast	Joanna Kerns
Cast	Kathleen Lloyd

PLEASE NOTE: This Film Was The Highest Rated Two Hour TV Movie For The 1992-1993 Season.

TOP 10 TWO HOUR TV MOVIES 1992-1993 SEASON

1.	The Man With Three Wives	20.8/33	CBS
2.	Skylark	19.9/29	CBS
3.	Family of Strangers	19.8/29	CBS
4.	Men Don't Tell	19.7/31	CBS
5.	Beyond Control: The Amy Fisher Story	19.5/30	ABC
6.	Amy Fisher: My Story	19.1/30	NBC
7.	In the Line of Duty: Ambush in Waco	18.8/30	NBC
8.	The Man Upstairs	18.8/28	CBS
9.	Call of the Wild	18.2/29	CBS
10.	Dr. Quinn, Medicine Woman	18.2/29	CBS

MANHUNT: SEARCH FOR THE NIGHT STALKER — NBC

Drama: Murder and Murder Mystery • Cops/Detectives/Law Enforcement • True Crime
Airdate: 11/12/89
Rating: 15.4/24   A/C: 2

Story of the investigation of the infamous "Night Stalker" murders in Los Angeles in 1985, which led to the apprehension and conviction of Richard Ramirez.

Production Company: Leonard Hill Films
Executive Producer .... Leonard Hill
Executive Producer .... Ron Gilbert
Producer .... Joel Fields
Director .... Bruce Seth Green
Writer .... Joseph Gunn
Cast .... Richard Jordan
Cast .... A Martinez
Cast .... Lisa Eilbacher

MANTIS — FBC

Drama: Sci-Fi/Supernatural/Horror/Fantasy
Airdate: 1/24/94
Rating: 8.5/13   A/C: 4

A paraplegic scientist turns super hero when he invents Mantis (Mechanically Augmented Neuro Transmitter System) a specially designed costume that allows him to walk and to temporarily paralyze any evil-doer in mid-crime.

Production Company: Wilbur Force Prods., Renaissance Pictures IAW Universal TV
Executive Producer .... Sam Hamm
Executive Producer .... Sam Raimi
Executive Producer .... Robert Tapert
Producer .... David Eick
Producer .... Steve Ecclesine
Director .... Eric Laneuville
Writer .... Sam Hamm
Cast .... Carl Lumbly
Cast .... Bobby Hosea
Cast .... Gina Torres
Cast .... Steve James

MANY HAPPY RETURNS — CBS

Comedy: Man Against The System
Airdate: 09/19/86
Rating: 10.2/18   A/C:

A typical taxpayer runs into "your worst nightmare" trouble with an Internal Revenue Service man determined to prove a point.

Production Company: The Many Happy Returns Co.
Executive Producer .... Alan M. Levin
Producer .... Steven H. Stern
Director .... Steven H. Stern
Writer .... Jim Mulholland
Writer .... Michael Barrie
Cast .... George Segal
Cast .... Helen Shaver
Cast .... Ron Leibman
Cast .... Linda Sorenson

MARCUS WELBY, M. D.: A HOLIDAY AFFAIR — NBC

Drama: Love Story • Foreign or Exotic Location
Airdate: 12/19/88
Rating: 13.5/21   A/C:

Based on the 1970's TV series. The retired physician, now a widower, visits France and Switzerland and finds romance.

Production Company: Marstar Ltd. IAW Condor Prods.
Executive Producer .... Martin Starger
Producer .... Howard Alston
Producer .... Peter-Christian Fueter
Producer .... William Hartman
Director .... Steven Gethers
Writer .... Steven Gethers
Cast .... Robert Young
Cast .... Alexis Smith
Cast .... Craig Stevens
Cast .... Delphine Forest

MARGARET BOURKE - WHITE — TNT

Drama: Biography • Period Piece • True Story
Airdate: 4/24/89
Rating: N/A   A/C:

The adventures of the famous Life Magazine photographer, her tumultuous relationship with writer Erskine Caldwell and the conflict caused by her obsession with her work during the 1930's and 40's.

Production Company: Lawrence Schiller Prods. IAW TNT
Producer .... Lawrence Schiller
Producer .... Rob Colby
Director .... Lawrence Schiller
Writer .... Marjorie David
Cast .... Farrah Fawcett
Cast .... Frederic Forrest

MARILYN & BOBBY: HER FINAL AFFAIR — USA

Drama: Hollywood • Sex/Glitz • Period Piece
Airdate: 8/4/93
Rating: N/A   A/C:

A dubious tale of romance and intrigue between movie star Marilyn Monroe and Atorney General Robert F. Kennedy, which culminates on the night of her untimely death in 1962.

Production Company: Barry Weitz Films Inc., Auerbach Co.
Executive Producer .... Barry Weitz
Executive Producer .... Jeffrey Auerbach
Producer .... Lorin Salob
Director .... Bradford May
Writer .... Gerard Macdonald
Cast .... Melody Anderson
Cast .... James Kelly
Cast .... Richard Dysart
Cast .... Thomas Wagner

MARILYN & ME — ABC

Drama: True Story • Period Piece • Biography • Hollywood
Airdate: 09/22/91
Rating: 8.5/14   A/C: 3

Aspiring screenwriter Robert Slatzer recalls his alleged romance and secret five-day marriage in 1952 to movie goddess Marilyn Monroe.

Production Company: World International Network IAW Samuels Film Co.
Executive Producer .... Stu Samuels
Producer .... Robert Boris
Producer .... Susan Weber-Gold
Director .... John Patterson
Writer .... Robert Boris
Cast .... Susan Griffiths
Cast .... Jesse Dabson
Cast .... Joel Grey
Cast .... Sal Landi

MARIO AND THE MOB — ABC

Comedy: Children/Teens • Mafia/Mob
Airdate: 05/16/92
Rating: 7.5/15   A/C: 3

A tough Chicago mobster discovers a soft spot in his heart when he begrudgingly becomes the guardian of his late sister's five children.

Production Company: Black Sheep Prods.
Executive Producer .... Joan Conrad
Producer .... Roger Bacon
Director .... Virgil W. Vogel
Writer .... Nicholas Corea
Cast .... Robert Conrad
Cast .... Ann Jillian

MARIO PUZO'S THE FORTUNATE PILGRIM — NBC

Miniseries/Drama (2 nights): Family Drama • Cross-Cultural Story • Period Piece • Mafia/Mob
Airdate: 04/03/88 • 04/04/88
Rating: 13.1/22 • 13.0/21   A/C:

Based on the novel by Mario Puzo. An Italian woman emigrates to New York in the early 1900s, loses her husband and survives despite a series of Mafia and family involvements.

Production Company: Carlo and Alex Ponti Prods. IAW Reteitalia S.P.A.
Executive Producer .... Carlo Ponti
Producer .... Alex Ponti
Co-Producer .... Norman Brooks
Co-Producer .... Fern Field
Director .... Stuart Cooper
Writer .... John McGreevey
Cast .... Sophia Loren
Cast .... Hal Holbrook
Cast .... Edward James Olmos
Cast .... John Turturro
Cast .... Yorgo Voyagis
Cast .... Anna Strasberg

MARK TWAIN AND ME DISNEY
Drama: Period Piece • Historical Piece • Biography •
Children/Teens • True Story
Airdate: 11/22/91
Rating: N/A   A/C:

*Based on the book "Enchantment" by Dorothy
Quick. In 1907, eleven-year-old Dorothy Quick
befriends seventy-two-year-old Mark Twain.
Their friendship, which continues until his
death, gives Dorothy a confidence she's never
known and Twain a closeness never shared with
his own family.*

Production Company: Chilmark Prods. Inc.
Executive Producer .... Julian Fowles
Executive Producer .... Geoffrey Cowan
Producer .... Daniel Petrie
Director .... Daniel Petrie
Writer .... Cynthia Whitcomb
Cast .... Jason Robards
Cast .... Amy Stewart
Cast .... Talia Shire
Cast .... Fiona Reid

MARKED FOR MURDER NBC
Drama: Cops/Detectives/Law Enforcement •
Suspense/Thriller • Prison and Prison Camp
Airdate: 1/17/93
Rating: 12.4/20   A/C: 2

*In a radical rehabilitation program a hardened
convict is removed from prison and put to work
in the Philadelphia police department, lending
his expertise in fighting crime. With the help of
his skeptical captain the ex-con turns into a
natural supercop-stopping gangsters, drug
lords and slimeballs.*

Production Company: Finnegan/Pinchuk Co. IAW
    NBC Prods.
Executive Producer .... Joel Thurm
Producer .... Sheldon Pinchuk
Producer .... Pat Finnegan
Co-Producer .... Dennis Hackin
Director .... Mimi Leder
Writer .... Dennis Hackin
Cast .... Powers Boothe
Cast .... Laura Johnson
Cast .... Billy Dee Williams
Cast .... Michael Ironside

MARLA HANSON STORY, THE NBC
Drama: Woman In Jeopardy • True Crime • Woman's
Issue/Story • Social Issue
Airdate: 02/04/91
Rating: 15.1/24   A/C: 2

*After a NYC model's face is viciously slashed
after rejecting an obsessed suitor, she must then
endure personal assaults on her reputation
during the subsequent trial.*

Production Company: Citadel
Executive Producer .... David R. Ginsburg
Producer .... Steve McGlothen
Director .... John Gray
Writer .... John Gray
Cast .... Cheryl Pollak
Cast .... Dale Midkiff
Cast .... Kirk Baltz
Cast .... Jack Blessing

MASTERGATE SHOWTIME
Comedy: Political Piece
Airdate: 11/1/92
Rating: N/A   A/C:

*A congressional hearing on the Washington
political scandal known as Mastergate
introduces the country to a bumbling cast of
government officials who come to the defense
of the President; whose involvement in the affair
is being questioned.*

Production Company: Showtime Ent. IAW
    Rollins/Joffe
Executive Producer .... Charles Joffe
Executive Producer .... Bob Weide
Producer .... David Jablin
Director .... Michael Engler
Writer .... Larry Gelbart
Cast .... Ed Begley, Jr.
Cast .... Richard Kiley
Cast .... Ken Howard
Cast .... James Coburn

MATLOCK: THE WITNESS KILLINGS
NBC
Drama: Murder and Murder Mystery • Courtroom
Drama
Airdate: 10/18/91
Rating: 14.0/26   A/C: 2

*Matlock returns to his rural hometown for its
bicentennial celebration and, to the outrage of
his friends and family, finds himself defending
a local man convicted of two murders.*

Production Company: Dean Hargrove and Fred
    Silverman Prods. IAW Viacom Prods. Inc.
Executive Producer .... Fred Silverman
Executive Producer .... Andy Griffith
Producer .... Richard Collins
Producer .... Gerald Sanoff
Director .... Christopher Hibler
Writer .... Anne Collins
Cast .... Andy Griffith
Cast .... Julie Sommars
Cast .... Cyril O'Reilly
Cast .... Anne Haney

MATTER OF JUSTICE, A NBC
Miniseries/Drama (2 nights): True Crime • Woman
Against The System • Children/Teens
Airdate: 11/7/93 • 11/8/93
Rating: 15.2/23 • 19.4/29   A/C: 3 • 1

*In 1978, Chris Brown drops out of high school,
joins the Marines, marries a promiscuous older
woman, has a baby and ends up murdered. His
mother, Mary Brown tirelessly fights to gain
custody of her granddaughter and to prove her
daughter-in-law conspired to have her son
killed. Pressuring the FBI and hiring a private
investigator she finally succeeds in rescuing her
grandchild and prosecuting and convicting her
ex daughter-in-law.*

Production Company: Ron Gilbert Assoc. IAW
    Hill-Fields Ent.
Executive Producer .... Ron Gilbert
Executive Producer .... Leonard Hill
Executive Producer .... Joel Fields
Producer .... Ardythe Goergans
Producer .... Bernadette Caulfield
Producer .... Yvonne Chotzen
Director .... Michael Switzer
Writer .... Dennis Turner
Cast .... Patty Duke
Cast .... Martin Sheen
Cast .... Alenandra Powers
Cast .... Jeff Kober

MATTERS OF THE HEART USA
Drama: Love Story • Medical/Disease/Mental Illness
Airdate: 12/26/90
Rating: N/A   A/C:

*Based on the book "The Country of the Heart"
by Barbara Wersby. A classical pianist virtuoso
falls for her young protege, who is devastated
when he discovers she has terminal cancer.*

Production Company: Tahse-Bergman Prods. IAW
    MCA TV
Executive Producer .... Martin Tahse
Executive Producer .... Linda Bergman
Director .... Michael Rhodes
Writer .... Martin Tahse
Writer .... Linda Bergman
Cast .... Jane Seymour
Cast .... Christopher Gartin
Cast .... James Stacy
Cast .... Geoffrey Lewis

MAX AND HELEN — TNT
Drama: Love Story • True Story • Historical Piece • Foreign or Exotic Location • WWII • Nazis
Airdate: 01/08/90
Rating: N/A   A/C:

Based on Simon Wiesenthal's book. Nazi-hunter, Simon Wiesenthal, must weigh his pursuit of justice against the happiness of two lovers who were separated by the Holocaust and were finally reunited after twenty years.

Production Company: Turner Network Television IAW Hungarian Television Enterprises
Executive Producer .... David R. Ginsburg
Producer .... Steve McGlothen
Director .... Philip Saville
Writer .... Corey Blechman
Cast .... Treat Williams
Cast .... Alice Krige
Cast .... Martin Landau
Cast .... Jonathan Phillips

MAYBE BABY — NBC
Comedy: Woman's Issue/Story
Airdate: 12/05/88
Rating: 17.2/26   A/C:

An advisor to the Mayor of Los Angeles wants to have a baby, but her husband, who already has grown children, doesn't.

Production Company: Perry Lafferty Prods. IAW Von Zerneck/Samuels Prods.
Executive Producer .... Perry Lafferty
Executive Producer .... Frank Von Zerneck
Executive Producer .... Stu Samuels
Producer .... Robert M. Sertner
Director .... Tom Moore
Writer .... Janet Kovalcik
Cast .... Jane Curtin
Cast .... Dabney Coleman
Cast .... Julia Duffy
Cast .... Florence Stanley
Cast .... David Doyle

MAYFLOWER MADAM — CBS
Drama: True Story • Prostitution • Sex/Glitz
Airdate: 11/15/87
Rating: 20.9/34   A/C:

Based on the novel. True story of Sydney Biddle Barrows, the blue-blooded operator of a classy New York prostitution business, who ultimately evades jail by threatening to release her client list.

Production Company: Robert Halmi Inc.
Producer .... Robert Halmi, Sr.
Director .... Lou Antonio
Writer .... Elizabeth Gill
Writer .... Charles Israel
Cast .... Candice Bergen
Cast .... Chris Sarandon
Cast .... Caitlin Clarke
Cast .... Jim Antonio
Cast .... Chita Rivera

MEMORIES OF MURDER — LIFETIME
Drama: Woman In Jeopardy • Psychological Thriller
Airdate: 07/31/90
Rating: N/A   A/C:

While a woman with amnesia tries to find her true identity, a deadly stranger terrorizes her family.

Production Company: The Houston Lady Co. IAW Viacom Prods.
Executive Producer .... Barry Weitz
Producer .... Robert Lewis
Director .... Robert Lewis
Writer .... John Harrison
Writer .... Nevin Schreiner
Cast .... Nancy Allen
Cast .... Robin Thomas
Cast .... Vanity

MEMPHIS — TNT
Drama: Children/Teens • Period Piece • Black Story
Airdate: 01/27/92
Rating: N/A   A/C:

Based on "September, September" by Shelby Foote. Three drifters in 1950's Memphis kidnap the grandson of the town's wealthiest black man. The abduction ultimately fails when one of the kidnappers becomes too attached to the boy, causing dissension and rivalry among her fellow low-lifes.

Production Company: Propaganda Films River Siren Production
Executive Producer .... Cybill Shepherd
Executive Producer .... Sigurjon Sighvatsson
Executive Producer .... Steve Golin
Producer .... Jay Roewe
Director .... Yves Simoneau
Writer .... Larry McMurtry
Writer .... Cybill Shepherd
Writer .... Susan Rhinehart
Cast .... Cybill Shepherd
Cast .... John Laughlin
Cast .... Moses Gunn
Cast .... J.E. Freeman
Cast .... Martin Gardner

MEN DON'T TELL — CBS
Drama: Family Violence • Social Issue
Airdate: 3/14/93
Rating: 19.7/31   A/C: 1

An unhappy wife who was abused as a child, physically beats her passive husband. When she is hospitalized after he defends himself from one of her tirades he is the one who is suspected of wife battering and accused of attempted murder. The true nightmare of their marital relationship unfolds when the whole family is questioned by the police.

Production Company: Daniel H. Blatt Prods., Nancy Bein Prods. IAW Lorimar TV
Executive Producer .... Daniel H. Blatt
Executive Producer .... Nancy Bein
Producer .... Phil Parslow
Director .... Harry Winer
Writer .... Selma Thompson
Writer .... Jeff Andrus
Cast .... Judith Light
Cast .... Peter Strauss
Cast .... Ashley Johnson

MENENDEZ: A KILLING IN BEVERLY HILLS — CBS
Miniseries/Drama (2 nights): True Crime • Family Violence • Murder and Murder Mystery • Courtroom Drama
Airdate: 5/22/94 • 5/24/94
Rating: 9.6/16 • 9.3/15   A/C: 3 • 3

In 1989, teenagers Lyle and Eric Menendez gun down their wealthy, dictatorial father and their alcoholic, passive mother in their Beverly Hills home. A sensational trial ensues with the brothers claiming emotional and sexual abuse and the verdict resulting in a hung jury. NOTE: See "Honor Thy Father and Mother: The True Story of the Menendez Murders" -FBC.

Production Company: Zev Braun Pictures IAW TriStar TV
Executive Producer .... Zev Braun
Co-Executive Producer .... Karen Lamm
Producer .... Vahan Moosekian
Co-Producer .... Philip Krupp
Director .... Larry Elikann
Writer .... Philip Rosenberg
Cast .... Edward James Olmos
Cast .... Beverly D'Angelo
Cast .... Damian Chapa
Cast .... Travis Fine
Cast .... Dwight Schultz

MENU FOR MURDER — CBS
Mystery: Murder and Murder Mystery • Cops/Detectives/Law Enforcement
Airdate: 12/04/90
Rating: 9.7/16   A/C: 3

Based on the novel by Valerie Wolzien. When the president of the P.T.A. in a wealthy L.A. suburb is murdered with a poison croissant, a handsome cop investigates the remaining socialite members of the P.T.A.

Production Company: Patricia K. Meyers Prods. IAW Von Zerneck-Sertner Films
Executive Producer .... Frank Von Zerneck
Executive Producer .... Robert M. Sertner
Producer .... Patricia K. Meyer
Producer .... Susan Weber-Gold
Director .... Larry Peerce
Writer .... Duane Poole
Writer .... Tom Swale
Cast .... Julia Duffy
Cast .... Marla Gibbs
Cast .... Morgan Fairchild
Cast .... Joan Van Ark

Mercy Mission: The Rescue Of Flight 771   NBC

Drama: True Story • Disaster • Foreign or Exotic Location
Airdate: 12/13/93
Rating: 12.2/19   A/C: 3

In 1979, A cavalier pilot, flying from San Francisco to New Zealand in a well-worn Cessna discovers that after fourteen hours in the air he is hopelessly lost, low on fuel and without navigational tools. A senior pilot on a commercial DC-10, with 88 passengers on board, hears his distress call and diverts from his flight plan to search for the lost flyer and guide him to safety.

Production Company: RHI Ent. Inc. IAW Anasazi Prods.

Executive Producer	Robert Benedetti
Producer	Derek Kavanagh
Co-Producer	Peter Stelzer
Director	Roger Young
Writer	George Rubino
Writer	Robert Benedetti
Cast	Robert Loggia
Cast	Scott Bakula
Cast	Rebecca Rigg
Cast	Alan Fletcher

Mercy or Murder?   NBC

Drama: Medical/Disease/Mental Illness • Courtroom Drama • Man Against The System • Social Issue • True Crime
Airdate: 01/11/87
Rating: 23.8/35   A/C:

True story of a Florida man who killed his terminally ill Alzheimer's-diseased wife and was prosecuted for murder.

Production Company: John J. McMahon Prods. IAW MGM-UA TV

Executive Producer	John J. McMahon
Producer	Len Steckler
Director	Steven Gethers
Writer	Steven Gethers
Cast	Robert Young
Cast	Frances Reid
Cast	Michael Learned
Cast	Eddie Albert

Message From Holly   CBS

Drama: Medical/Disease/Mental Illness • Children/Teens • Woman's Issue/Story
Airdate: 12/13/92
Rating: 15.5/24   A/C: 1

A unorthodox artist who is terminally ill asks her old friend, a high powered executive, to bring up her six year old daughter after her death. A roller coaster ride of emotions follow when the two women move into together during the last few remaining months.

Production Company: Corapeake Prods. IAW The Polson Co. and P&G Prods.

Executive Producer	Beth Polson
Producer	Randy Siegel
Director	Rod Holcomb
Writer	Dalene Young
Cast	Shelley Long
Cast	Lindsay Wagner
Cast	Molly Orr
Cast	Cotter Smith

Miami Vice   NBC

Drama: Cops/Detectives/Law Enforcement • Drug Smuggling/Dealing • Series Pilot (2 hr.)
Airdate: 09/16/84
Rating: 22.8/37   A/C:

Series pilot about a New York City police officer who moves to Miami. He joins the vice squad and partners with another cop to fight local drug crime.

Production Company: Michael Mann Co. IAW Universal TV

Executive Producer	Michael Mann
Executive Producer	Anthony Yerkovich
Producer	John Nicolella
Director	Thomas Carter
Writer	Anthony Yeerkovich
Cast	Don Johnson
Cast	Philip Michael Thomas
Cast	Michael Talbott
Cast	Saundra Santiago

Mickey Spillane's Mike Hammer: Murder Takes All   CBS

Drama: Murder and Murder Mystery • Cops/Detectives/Law Enforcement
Airdate: 05/21/89
Rating: 12.8/20   A/C:

Based on the book by Mickey Spillane. Private eye, Mike Hammer, gets involved in a homicide case in Las Vegas.

Production Company: Jay Bernstein Prods. IAW Columbia Pictures TV

Executive Producer	Jay Bernstein
Producer	Jeffrey Morton
Director	John Nicolella
Writer	Mark Edward Edens
Cast	Stacy Keach
Cast	Lynda Carter
Cast	Lindsay Bloom
Cast	Lyle Alzado
Cast	Ed Winter

Middle Ages   CBS

Drama: Buddy Story • Series Pilot (2 hr.)
Airdate: 9/3/92
Rating: 8.7/16   A/C: 3

A group fortysometing guys cope with mid-life crises, aging parents, fears of growing old and unfulfilled fantasies while trying to maintain careers and family relationships.

Production Company: Stan Rogow Prods. IAW Paramount Pictures

Executive Producer	Stan Rogow
Executive Producer	John Byrum
Executive Producer	Peter Werner
Co-Producer	Robin Chamberlin
Director	Sandy Smolan
Writer	John Byrum
Cast	Peter Riegert
Cast	William Russ
Cast	James Gammon
Cast	Ashley Crow

Midnight Hour, The   NBC

Drama: Sci-Fi/Supernatural/Horror/Fantasy
Airdate: 11/01/85
Rating: 10.5/17   A/C:

A group of high school students inadvertently bring a cemetery full of corpses back to life by reading the message on a parchment.

Production Company: ABC Circle Films

Producer	Ervin Zavada
Director	Jack Bender
Writer	William Bleich
Cast	Shari Belafonte
Cast	Levar Burton
Cast	Lee Montgomery
Cast	Dick Van Patten
Cast	Kevin McCarthy

Midnight's Child   Lifetime

Drama: Psychological Thriller • Sci-Fi/Supernatural/Horror/Fantasy
Airdate: 04/21/92
Rating: N/A   A/C:

A sweet, charming Swedish nanny comes to live with a well-to-do Los Angeles couple. The unsuspecting wife fights to protect her family when she discovers the girl is a devil-worshipper who's come to claim her 6-year old daughter's soul for Satan.

Production Company: The Polone Company IAW Hearst Entertainment

Executive Producer	Victoria Principal
Producer	Kimberly Myers
Co-Executive Producer	Jeff Myrow
Co-Executive Producer	David Gottlieb
Director	Colin Bucksey
Writer	David Chaskin
Cast	Marcy Walker
Cast	Olivia D'Abo
Cast	Elisabeth Moss
Cast	Cotter Smith

MILES FROM NOWHERE   CBS

Drama: Family Drama • Medical/Disease/Mental
Illness
Airdate: 01/07/92
Rating: 10.8/17   A/C: 3

*A young man causes an auto accident that
leaves his brother brain damaged. Burdened
by guilt, he fanatically devotes himself to his
brother's rehabilitation, causing his family to
confront unrealistic expectations and long-held
resentments.*

Production Company: Sokolow Prods. - Fast Car
    Prods. - New World Television
Executive Producer .... Diane Sokolow
Executive Producer .... Mel Sokolow
Producer .... Hugh Spencer-Phillips
Director .... Buzz Kulik
Writer .... Steve McGraw
Writer .... Janet Ward
Writer .... Jeff Andrus
Cast .... Rick Schroder
Cast .... Shawn Phelan
Cast .... James Farentino
Cast .... Melora Hardin

MILES TO GO . . .   CBS

Drama: Family Drama • Medical/Disease/Mental
Illness
Airdate: 10/21/86
Rating: 16.5/26   A/C:

*A woman dying of cancer is determined to spend
her last days arranging her husband's future
well-being down to the last detail.*

Production Company: Keating-Shostak Prods.
Executive Producer .... Doris Keating
Producer .... Murray Shostak
Co-Producer .... Robert Baylis
Director .... David Greene
Writer .... Beverly Levitt
Writer .... Stuart Fischoff
Cast .... Jill Clayburgh
Cast .... Tom Skerritt
Cast .... Rosemary Dunsmore
Cast .... Mimi Kuzyk

MIRACLE AT BEEKMAN'S PLACE   NBC

Drama: Family Drama • Medical/Disease/Mental
Illness • Black Story • Social Issue
Airdate: 12/26/88
Rating: 12.3/21   A/C:

*After his wife dies and the trauma center of his
hospital closes, a black doctor quits his hospital
job as chief of staff to open a clinic in the inner
city.*

Production Company: Em/BE Inc. Prods.
Executive Producer .... Scoey Mitchell
Producer .... Donald R. Boyle
Director .... Bernard Kowalski
Writer .... Donald R. Boyle
Writer .... Scoey Mitchlll
Cast .... Scoey Mitchill
Cast .... Robert Costanzo
Cast .... Liz Torres
Cast .... Theresa Merritt

MIRACLE CHILD   NBC

Drama: Children/Teens • Sci-Fi/Supernatural/Horror/
Fantasy
Airdate: 4/6/93
Rating: 11.0/18   A/C: 2

*Based on the book by Patricia Pendergraft. A
recently widowed young woman decides she can
no longer care for her baby daughter. She
leaves the infant on a doorstep, to be raised in
the wonderful town of Clements Pond. In a
short time the child is credited with unexplained
miraculous events and good fortunes. The
mother, having second thoughts returns to be
near her baby and soon finds the warmth and
caring of a loving community for her and the
little girl..*

Production Company: Steve White Prods.,
    DISNEY Family Classics
Executive Producer .... Steve White
Co-Executive Producer .... Cecily Truett
Producer .... Barry Bernardi
Co-Producer .... Irwin Marcus
Director .... Michael Pressman
Writer .... Gerald Di Pego
Cast .... Crystal Bernard
Cast .... Cloris Leachman
Cast .... John Terry
Cast .... Grace Zabriskie

MIRACLE IN THE WILDERNESS   TNT

Drama: Period Piece • Holiday Special • Western •
American Indians • Cross-Cultural Story
Airdate: 12/09/91
Rating: N/A   A/C:

*Based on the novella by Paul Gallico. In 1850's
New Mexico, a pioneer family is held captive
on Christmas eve by Blackfoot Indians. The
tribe is transformed by the re-telling of the
nativity story as a Native American myth.*

Production Company: Ruddy & Morgan
    Production IAW Turner Pictures
Executive Producer .... Albert S. Ruddy
Executive Producer .... Andre Morgan
Producer .... Wayne Morris
Director .... Kevin James Dobson
Writer .... Michael Michaelian
Writer .... Jim Byrnes
Cast .... Kris Kristofferson
Cast .... Kim Cattrall
Cast .... John Dennis Johnston
Cast .... Rino Thunder

MIRACLE LANDING   CBS

Drama: True Story • Action/Adventure • Disaster
Airdate: 02/11/90
Rating: 15.1/23   A/C: 3

*Story of the heroic actions of the pilot and crew
when a mid-air explosion rips away a twenty-
foot section of an Aloha Airlines fuselage at
twenty-four thousand feet.*

Production Company: CBS Entertainment
Producer .... Dick Lowry
Co-Producer .... Alan Crosland
Director .... Dick Lowry
Writer .... Garner Simmons
Cast .... Connie Sellecca
Cast .... Wayne Rogers
Cast .... Nancy Kwan

MIRACLE ON I-880   NBC

Drama: Disaster
Airdate: 2/23/93
Rating: 13.3/20   A/C: 3

*The heroic efforts of rescuers who tried to save
the victims trapped under the collapsed
interstate highway after the devastating,1989
San Francisco Earthquake.*

Production Company: Glen Oak Pros. IAW
    Columbia Pictures
Executive Producer .... Mark Sennet
Executive Producer .... Doris Bacon
Producer .... Mary ' Eilts
Director .... Robert Iscove
Writer .... Leo Arthur
Writer .... Casey Kelly
Cast .... Ruben Blades
Cast .... Len Cariou
Cast .... David Morse
Cast .... Sandy Duncan

MIRRORS   NBC

Drama: Love Story
Airdate: 09/16/85
Rating: 13.8/22   A/C:

*A young ballerina comes to New York to try
her luck and finds herself romantically involved
with a journalist and a handsome ballet dancer.*

Production Company: Leonard Hill Films
Executive Producer .... Leonard Hill
Producer .... James Lipton
Director .... Harry Winer
Writer .... James Lipton
Cast .... Tim Daly
Cast .... Shanna Reed
Cast .... Antony Hamilton

MISFITS OF SCIENCE   NBC

Drama: Action/Adventure • Series Pilot (2 hr.) • Sci-
Fi/Supernatural/Horror/Fantasy
Airdate: 10/04/85
Rating: 14.2/23   A/C:

*A scientist joins an odd group, whose members
include a psychic and a man who can freeze
things with his touch, to stop a greedy
corporation from making a dangerous neutron
weapon.*

Production Company: James. D. Parriott Prods.
    IAW Universal TV
Executive Producer .... James D. Parriott
Producer .... Dean Zanetos
Director .... James D. Parriott
Writer .... James D. Parriott
Cast .... Mark Thomas Miller
Cast .... Courtney Cox
Cast .... Dean Paul Martin
Cast .... Kevin Peter Hall

MISS AMERICA: BEHIND THE CROWN
NBC

Drama: True Story • Biography • Social Issue
Airdate: 9/21/92
Rating: 13.3/20   A/C: 3

While competing in beauty pageants, Carolyn Sapp, Miss Hawaii, suffers physical and mental abuse from her depressed boyfriend, ex- New York Jets football star Nuu Faaola. After extricating herself from his violent behavior she goes on to be crowned Miss America in 1992.

Production Company: Katz/Rush Ent.
Executive Producer .... Raymond Katz
Executive Producer .... Herman Rush
Producer .... Maureen Holmes
Co-Producer .... Don Goldman
Director .... Richard Michaels
Writer .... Karol Ann Hoeffner
Cast .... Carolyn Sapp
Cast .... Ray Bumatai
Cast .... Jack Blessing

MISS ROSE WHITE   NBC
EMMY WINNER

Drama: Family Drama • Period Piece • WWII • Nazis
Airdate: 04/26/92
Rating: 11.0/17   A/C: 3

Based on the play by Barbara Lebow. In 1947 New York, a Jewish woman hides her heritage to pursue a career. The arrival of her sister, a holocaust survivor believed dead, forces her and her traditionalist father to confront guilt, resentments and long-held secrets.

Production Company: Marian Rees Prods. IAW Lorimar Television
Executive Producer .... Marian Rees
Producer .... Anne Hopkins
Co-Executive Producer .... Andrea Baynes
Co-Executive Producer .... Francine LeFrak
Director .... Joseph Sargent
Writer .... Anna Sandor
Cast .... Kyra Sedgwick
Cast .... Maximilan Schell
Cast .... Amanda Plummer
Cast .... Maureen Stapleton

MISSING PERSONS   ABC

Drama: Cops/Detectives/Law Enforcement • Series Pilot (2 hr.)
Airdate: 8/30/93
Rating: 11.4/19   A/C: 1

A veteran cop heads up the missing persons bureau of the Chicago Police Department with the help of a diverse squad of detectives.

Production Company: Stephen J. Cannell Prods.
Executive Producer .... Stephen J. Cannell
Executive Producer .... Gary Sherman
Producer .... Johanna Persons
Director .... Gary Sherman
Writer .... Gary Sherman
Cast .... Daniel J. Travanti
Cast .... Erik King
Cast .... Juan Ramirez
Cast .... Jorjan Fox

MISSION OF THE SHARK   CBS

Drama: True Story • Period Piece • Historical Piece • WWII • Disaster
Airdate: 09/29/91
Rating: 15.6/25   A/C: 1

Returning from a secret mission in 1945, the USS Indianapolis is torpedoed and sunk. The survivors, including Capt. Charles McVay, are left floating 5 days in shark-infested waters. The Navy, embarrassed by the incident, court-martials McVay.

Production Company: Richard Maynard Prods. IAW Fries Entertainment
Executive Producer .... Charles Fries
Producer .... Richard Maynard
Director .... Robert Iscove
Writer .... Alan Sharp
Cast .... Stacy Keach
Cast .... Richard Thomas
Cast .... Don Harvey
Cast .... Steve Landesberg

MISTRAL'S DAUGHTER   CBS

Miniseries/Drama (3 nights): Love Story • Foreign or Exotic Location • Sex/Glitz • Period Piece
Airdate: 09/24/84 • 09/25/84 • 09/26/84
Rating: 18.2/29 • 18.7/30 • 16.3/26   A/C:

Based on the novel by Judith Krantz. Multi-generational story, centering on a temperamentally brilliant French painter and his ex-mistress who eventually opens her own modeling agency in NYC. The painter's life is changed by the coming of WWII and his marriage to a wealthy American.

Production Company: Steve Krantz & R.T.L. Prods. IAW Antenne 2 TV, France
Executive Producer .... Steve Krantz
Producer .... Herbert Hirschman
Producer .... Suzanne Wisenfeld
Director .... Douglas Hickox
Director .... Kevin Connor
Writer .... Rosemary Anne Sisson
Writer .... Terrence Freely
Cast .... Stefanie Powers
Cast .... Lee Remick
Cast .... Stacy Keach
Cast .... Robert Urich
Cast .... Timothy Dalton

MISTRESS   CBS

Drama: Sex/Glitz
Airdate: 10/04/87
Rating: 17.5/29   A/C:

A kept woman, left in the lurch when her middle-aged lover dies, fails to find a real job and is forced to seek a similar position with another married man.

Production Company: Republic Pictures
Executive Producer .... Sherry Lansing
Executive Producer .... Richard Fischoff
Producer .... Stephanie Austin
Director .... Michael Tuchner
Writer .... Joyce Eliason
Cast .... Victoria Principal
Cast .... Don Murray

MOM FOR CHRISTMAS, A   NBC

Drama: Holiday Special • Sci-Fi/Supernatural/Horror/Fantasy
Airdate: 12/17/90
Rating: 17.0/27   A/C: 2

Based on the novel "A Mom by Magic" by Barbara Dillon. A motherless girl's Christmas wish brings a beautiful department store mannequin to life to fulfill her dreams of having a mom.

Production Company: Walt Disney Company
Executive Producer .... Steve White
Producer .... Barry Bernardi
Producer .... Ric Rondell
Director .... George Miller
Writer .... Gerald Di Pego
Cast .... Olivia Newton-John
Cast .... Juliet Sorcey
Cast .... Doug Sheehan
Cast .... Doris Roberts

MOMENT OF TRUTH: A CHILD TOO MANY   NBC

Drama: Family Drama • True Story • Woman's Issue/Story • Children/Teens
Airdate: 10/11/93
Rating: 14.2/22   A/C: 3

When a married, surrogate mother in Michigan gives birth to boy-girl twins she discovers that the adoptive parents, especially the birth father, only wants one of the babies. Refusing to split the children apart she and her husband sue for custody so the infants can stay together. After an exhaustive legal and emotional battle she wins the right to keep the babies in her own family.

Production Company: O'Hara-Horowitz Prods
Executive Producer .... Michael O'Hara
Executive Producer .... Lawrence Horowitz
Producer .... Michelle MacLaren
Director .... Jorge Montesi
Writer .... Jayne Martin
Cast .... Michele Greene
Cast .... Conor O'Farrell
Cast .... Stephen Macht
Cast .... Nancy Stafford

MOMENT OF TRUTH: BROKEN PLEDGES
NBC

Drama: Woman Against The System • Children/Teens
• Social Issue
Airdate: 4/11/94
Rating: 12.6/20   A/C: 2

When her college student son is killed in a fraternity pledge initiation, Eileen Stevens battles the New York state legislature to pass an anti-hazing law. Her one woman campaign eventually results in the passage of a bill outlawing the dangerous behavior.

Production Company: O'Hara/Horowitz Prods.
Executive Producer .... Michael O'Hara
Executive Producer .... Lawrence Horowitz
Producer .... Michelle MacLaren
Co-Producer .... Linda Gray
Co-Producer .... Kathryn McArdle
Director .... Jorge Montesi
Writer .... Sandra Jennings
Cast .... Linda Gray
Cast .... Leon Russom
Cast .... David Lipper
Cast .... Jane Galloway

MOMENT OF TRUTH: CRADLE OF CONSPIRACY
NBC

Drama: Family Drama • Children/Teens • Woman Against The System • True Story
Airdate: 5/2/94
Rating: 13.5/21   A/C: 2

A naive sixteen year old girl gets pregnant by her smooth-talking, dishonest boyfriend and lands up in the seamy underground of a black market baby broker. Her mother, determined to rescue her daughter and grandchild from this well organized ring, battles an inept legal system and eventually brings them to justice.

Production Company: O'Hara-Horowitz Prods.
   IAW NBC
Executive Producer .... Michael O'Hara
Executive Producer .... Lawrence Horowitz
Producer .... Ooty Moorehead
Producer .... Marc B. Lorber
Producer .... Jayne Martin
Producer .... Joseph Plager
Writer .... Jayne Martin
Director .... Gabrielle Beaumont
Cast .... Danica McKellar
Cast .... Dee Wallace Stone
Cast .... Kurt Deutsch

MOMENT OF TRUTH: STALKING BACK
NBC

Drama: Family Drama • Children/Teens • True Crime
• Woman Against The System
Airdate: 10/18/93
Rating: 15.9/25   A/C: 2

For three years, a popular Florida teenager is stalked by young man who was once a friend of the family. As he becomes more aggressive, the young woman becomes a virtual prisoner in her own home with only her parents for protection. Her mother, fed up with the lack of legal remedies available to them, works with a state representative to pass an anti-stalking law.

Production Company: O'Hara-Horowitz Prods.
Executive Producer .... Michael O'Hara
Executive Producer .... Lawrence Horowitz
Producer .... S. Bryan Hickox
Director .... Corey Allen
Writer .... Pricilla English
Cast .... Luanne Ponce
Cast .... Shanna Reed
Cast .... John Martin
Cast .... Tom Kurlander

MOMENT OF TRUTH: TO WALK AGAIN
NBC

Drama: Medical/Disease/Mental Illness • Woman Against The System • Family Drama • True Story
Airdate: 2/16/94
Rating: 8.3/12   A/C: 3

Nineteen year old college dropout, Eddie Keating is forced to join the service by his exasperated parents after he repeatedly gets in trouble with the law. He becomes an outstanding Marine recruit but while on a training mission he is accidentally shot in the head and paralyzed. Placed in a decrepit, understaffed VA hospital his mother, Carole fights the military bureaucracy to have her son transferred to a special rehab facility. With the proper care the boy makes great progress and learns to walk with the help of an experimental electrical stimulation device.

Production Company: O'Hara-Horowitz Prods.
Executive Producer .... Michael O'Hara
Executive Producer .... Lawrence Horowitz
Producer .... Michelle MacLaren
Co-Producer .... Blair Brown
Director .... Randall Zisk
Writer .... George Eckstein
Cast .... Blair Brown
Cast .... Ken Howard
Cast .... Cameron Bancroft

MOMENT OF TRUTH: WHY MY DAUGHTER?
NBC

Drama: Family Drama • Woman Against The System
• Children/Teens • Prostitution
Airdate: 4/28/93
Rating: 14.2/23   A/C: 1

After losing her child to the world of prostitution, Gayle Moffitt, a divorced mother in San Diego goes on a crusade to bring her murdered teenage daughter's boyfriend and pimp to justice.

Production Company: O'Hara-Horowitz Prods.
Executive Producer .... Michael O'Hara
Executive Producer .... Lawrence Horowitz
Co-Producer .... Joseph Plager
Co-Producer .... Scott Martin
Director .... Chuck Bowman
Writer .... Liz Coe
Cast .... Linda Gray
Cast .... Jamie Luner
Cast .... James Eckhouse
Cast .... Antonio Sabato

MONEY, POWER, MURDER
CBS

Drama: Murder and Murder Mystery • Man Against The System • Suspense/Thriller
Airdate: 12/10/89
Rating: 13.4/22   A/C: 2

Based on the book "Dead Air." An ace TV investigative reporter probes the disappearance of an aggressive network anchorwoman which he finds is linked to a murderous conspiracy.

Production Company: Skids Prods. IAW CBS
   Entertainment
Executive Producer .... Susan Dobson
Producer .... Vanessa Greene
Director .... Lee Philips
Writer .... Mike Lupica
Cast .... Kevin Dobson
Cast .... Blythe Danner
Cast .... Josef Sommer
Cast .... Julianne Moore

MONTANA
TNT

Drama: Family Drama • Farm Story • Toxic Waste/Environmental
Airdate: 02/19/90
Rating: N/A   A/C:

Domestic problems flair when the wife of a rancher tries to stop her debt-ridden husband and money-hungry son from selling the family homestead to a strip-mining company.

Production Company: HBO IAW Zoetrope
   Studios & Peter Gimbel Prods.
Executive Producer .... Roger Gimbel
Producer .... Fred Roos
Director .... William A. Graham
Writer .... Larry McMurtry
Cast .... Gena Rowlands
Cast .... Richard Crenna
Cast .... Lea Thompson
Cast .... Justin Deas

MONTE CARLO — CBS

Miniseries/Drama (2 nights): Period Piece • Foreign or Exotic Location • WWII • Suspense/Thriller • Sex/Glitz
Airdate: 11/09/86 • 11/10/86
Rating: 14.6/23 • 12.2/19   A/C:

Based on the novel by Stephen Carlo. In 1940, a femme-fatale British spy dallies with a novelist and intrigues with representatives of the various warring and soon-to-be-warring powers.

Production Company: Phoenix Ent. Group/
  Collins/Holm Prods. IAW Highgate Pictures
Executive Producer .... Joan Collins
Executive Producer .... Peter Holm
Producer .... Gerald W. Abrams
Director .... Anthony Page
Writer .... Peter Lefcourt
Cast .... Joan Collins
Cast .... Robert Carradine
Cast .... Peter Vaughan
Cast .... George Hamilton
Cast .... Malcolm McDowell
Cast .... Lisa Eilbacher

MOONLIGHTING — ABC

Drama: Cops/Detectives/Law Enforcement • Series Pilot (2 hr.)
Airdate: 03/03/85
Rating: 18.3/28   A/C:

An ex-fashion model and an irreverent detective are hired to investigate a case in which a mysterious villain will stop at nothing to obtain a young man's wristwatch.

Production Company: Picturemaker Prods. IAW
  ABC Circle Films
Executive Producer .... Glenn Gordon Caron
Producer .... Jay Daniel
Director .... Robert Butler
Writer .... Glenn Gordon Caron
Cast .... Bruce Willis
Cast .... Cybil Shepherd
Cast .... Dennis Lipscomb
Cast .... Alice Beasly

MORTAL SINS — USA

Drama: Cops/Detectives/Law Enforcement • Suspense/Thriller
Airdate: 11/4/92
Rating: N/A   A/C:

A sensitive Roman Catholic priest hears the confessions of a serial killer. In order to protect the sanctity of the confessional he searches for the killer himself. With only a few clues to go on, he finally puts the pieces together and exposes the psychopath before he can murder again.

Production Company: Blake Edwards TV, Barry
  Weitz Films
Executive Producer .... Jeffrey Auerbach
Executive Producer .... Barry Weitz
Producer .... Tom Rowe
Director .... Bradford May
Writer .... Greg Martinelli
Writer .... Dennis Paoli
Cast .... Christopher Reeve
Cast .... Roxann Biggs
Cast .... Francis Guinan

MOTHER GOOSE ROCK 'N' RHYME — DISNEY

Musical: Sci-Fi/Supernatural/Horror/Fantasy
Airdate: 05/19/90
Rating: N/A   A/C:

In this contemporary musical adaptation of the well known nursery rhymes, Little Bo-Peep and Gordon Goose team up and travel through Rhymeland in search of Mother Goose, who has disappeared.

Production Company: Think Entertainment
Executive Producer .... Shelley Duvall
Producer .... Paula Marcus
Co-Producer .... Thomas Bliss
Director .... Jeff Stein
Writer .... Mark Curtiss
Writer .... Rod Ash
Cast .... Shelley Duvall
Cast .... Jean Stapleton
Cast .... Teri Garr
Cast .... Cyndi Lauper
Cast .... Garry Shandling
Cast .... Paul Simon
Cast .... Little Richard

MOTHER OF THE BRIDE — CBS

Drama: Family Drama
Airdate: 2/27/93
Rating: 9.6/17   A/C: 2

Sequel to "Children of the Bride" and "Baby of the Bride." The matriarch of a unconventional family starts planning a fancy wedding when one of her daughters announces her engagement. Matters get complicated when her long lost ex- husband and the brides father shows up and upsets the well laid plans.

Production Company: Baby Prods. IAW Leonard
  Hill Films
Executive Producer .... Leonard Hill
Executive Producer .... Joel Fields
Executive Producer .... Ron Gilbert
Producer .... Bart Baker
Director .... Charles Correll
Writer .... Bart Baker
Cast .... Rue McClanahan
Cast .... Kristy McNichol
Cast .... Paul Dooley

MOTHER'S JUSTICE, A — NBC

Drama: Family Drama • Woman Against The System • True Crime • Rape/Molestation
Airdate: 11/25/91
Rating: 16.7/25   A/C: 2

A mother becomes obsessed with finding her daughter's rapist. When the police drag their feet in the case, she sets herself up as a decoy on the streets to lure the pervert.

Production Company: Longbow Prods., Green-
  Epstein Prods., Inc. IAW Lorimar Television
Executive Producer .... Jim Green
Executive Producer .... Allen Epstein
Executive Producer .... Bill Pace
Executive Producer .... Ronnie Clemmer
Producer .... Mark Bacino
Director .... Noel Nosseck
Writer .... James S. Henerson
Cast .... Meredith Baxter
Cast .... G.W. Bailey
Cast .... Carrie Hamilton

MOTHERS, DAUGHTERS AND LOVERS — NBC

Drama: Family Drama • Series Pilot (2 hr.)
Airdate: 09/10/89
Rating: 8.4/14   A/C: 3

A single mother combats an unscrupulous land developer to keep her beloved Northwest town from being ruined, while struggling to raise her rebellious teen-age daughters and run her small motel.

Production Company: A Katz/Huyck/Film Prod.
  IAW NBC Prods.
Executive Producer .... Gloria Katz
Executive Producer .... Willard Huyck
Producer .... Kim Kurumada
Director .... Matthew Robbins
Writer .... Gloria Katz
Writer .... Willard Huyck
Cast .... Helen Shaver
Cast .... David McIlwraith
Cast .... Perrey Reeves
Cast .... Claude Akins

MOTHERS REVENGE, A — ABC

Drama: Family Drama • Rape/Molestation • Children/Teens • Courtroom Drama
Airdate: 11/14/93
Rating: 10.6/16   A/C: 3

Based on the book, "Desperate Justice" by Richard Speight. When her twelve year old daughter is raped and beaten by a school janitor, a desperate mother fatally shoots him in the courtroom when he is acquitted on a legal technicality. Facing murder charges, she hires the same defense attorney who defended her child's attacker and together with her shattered family try to convince a jury of her innocence.

Production Company: Martines Prod. Co. IAW
  WIN
Executive Producer .... Carla Singer
Co-Executive Producer .... Maj Canton
Producer .... Jon Larson
Director .... Armand Mastroianni
Writer .... John Robert Bensink
Cast .... Lesley Ann Warren
Cast .... Bruce Davison
Cast .... Annette O'Toole
Cast .... Shirley Knight
Cast .... Missy Crider

MOTHERS' RIGHT, A: THE ELIZABETH MORGAN STORY   ABC
Drama: Children/Teens • Family Drama • True Story
• Rape/Molestation • Social Issue • Woman's Issue/
Story
Airdate: 11/29/92
Rating: 13.6/21   A/C: 1

In 1987, prominent Washington, D.C. physician Elizabeth Morgan faces prosecution when she defies a court order allowing her ex-husband, Eric Foretich visitation rights with their five year old daughter. Claiming he sexually molested the child she hides the little girl and refuses to reveal her whereabouts.

Production Company: Landsburg Co.
Executive Producer .... Alan Landsburg
Executive Producer .... Linda Otto
Director .... Linda Otto
Writer .... Lucretia Baxter
Cast .... Bonnie Bedelia
Cast .... Terence Knox
Cast .... Kenneth Welsh
Cast .... Pam Grier

MOVING TARGET   NBC
Drama: Family Drama • Suspense/Thriller • Children/
Teens
Airdate: 02/08/88
Rating: 17.2/25   A/C:

An accountant's son returns from summer camp to find that his entire family has disappeared. Eluding police and gangsters, he and his friends solve the mystery.

Production Company: Chesler Prods. & Bateman
    Co. Prods. IAW Finnegan/Pinchuk, MGM/UA
    TV
Executive Producer .... Lewis B. Chesler
Executive Producer .... Kent Bateman
Producer .... Bill Finnegan
Producer .... Christopher Morgan
Cast .... Ed Hunsaker
Writer .... Andy Tennant
Director .... Chris Thomson
Cast .... Jason Bateman
Cast .... John Glover
Cast .... Chynna Phillips
Cast .... Jack Wagner
Cast .... Richard Dysart
Cast .... Tom Skerritt

MRS. 'ARRIS GOES TO PARIS   CBS
Drama: Cross-Cultural Story • Period Piece • Foreign
or Exotic Location
Airdate: 12/27/92
Rating: 16.8/28   A/C: 1

Based on the book by Paul Gallico. In 1952, a middle aged, English cleaning woman of modest means scrimps and saves to buy an original Dior gown. At first she is given the snub but her delightful charm and pluck win over the snooty designers at the elite French salon and the lady gets her dress.

Production Company: Accent Films IAW Novo
    Films & Corymore Prods.
Executive Producer .... David Shaw
Producer .... Andras Hamdri
Producer .... Susan Cavan
Co-Producer .... Caroline Hewitt
Co-Producer .... Paul Sandor
Director .... Anthony Shaw
Writer .... John Hawkesworth
Cast .... Angela Lansbury
Cast .... Diana Rigg
Cast .... Omar Sharif

MRS. DELAFIELD WANTS TO MARRY   CBS
Drama: Family Drama • Love Story
Airdate: 03/30/86
Rating: 21.0/35   A/C: 1

A rich WASP widow scandalizes friends and family with her intention to marry her unclassy Jewish doctor.

Production Company: Schaefer/Karpf Prods. IAW
    Gaylord Production Co.
Executive Producer .... Merrill H. Karpf
Producer .... George Schaefer
Director .... George Schaefer
Writer .... James Prideaux
Cast .... Katherine Hepburn
Cast .... Brenda Forbes
Cast .... Harold Gould
Cast .... Bibi Besch
Cast .... Denholm Elliott

MRS. LAMBERT REMEMBERS LOVE   CBS
Drama: Family Drama • Children/Teens • Medical/
Disease/Mental Illness
Airdate: 05/12/91
Rating: 9.9/17   A/C: 3

A grandmother developing Alzheimer's flees the authorities rather than be separated from her nine-year-old grandson.

Production Company: RHI Entertainment
Executive Producer .... Robert Halmi, Sr.
Producer .... Alan Jacobs
Producer .... Charles Matthau
Director .... Charles Matthau
Writer .... Janet Heaney
Cast .... Ellen Burstyn
Cast .... Walter Matthau
Cast .... Ryan Todd
Cast .... William Schallert

MURDER 101   USA
Mystery: Murder and Murder Mystery • Suspense/
Thriller
Airdate: 03/20/91
Rating: N/A   A/C:

A college English professor teaching a mystery writing class challenges his pupils to write the perfect crime story then finds himself the patsy in someone's murder scheme.

Production Company: Alan Barnette/MCA TV
Executive Producer .... Alan Barnette
Producer .... Oscar L. Costo
Director .... Bill Condon
Writer .... Bill Condon
Writer .... Roy Johansen
Cast .... Pierce Brosnan
Cast .... Dey Young
Cast .... Antoni Carone
Cast .... Mark Taylor

MURDER BETWEEN FRIENDS   NBC
Drama: True Crime • Murder and Murder Mystery •
Courtroom Drama • Family Violence
Airdate: 1/10/94
Rating: 12.9/20   A/C: 3

Best buddies, Kerry Meyers and Bill Fontanille give contradictory accounts of the brutal homicide of Meyers' wife, Janet. Each man implicates the other and it becomes the job of assistant district attorney John Thorn to unravel the truth. He eventually uncovers the duplicity of both men and prosecutes each for murder, obtaining a guilty verdict in both cases.

Production Company: Gimbel-Adelson Prods.
    IAW Multimedia TV Prods.
Executive Producer .... Roger Gimbel
Executive Producer .... Orly Adelson
Co-Executive Producer .... Ronald Tanet
Producer .... David Hamburger
Director .... Waris Hussein
Writer .... Philip Rosenberg
Cast .... Timothy Busfield
Cast .... Stephen Lang
Cast .... Martin Kemp
Cast .... Lisa Blount

MURDER BY MOONLIGHT   CBS
Drama: Murder and Murder Mystery • Suspense/
Thriller • Sci-Fi/Supernatural/Horror/Fantasy
Airdate: 05/09/89
Rating: 7.7/12   A/C:

In the year 2015, a NASA security officer and a KGB major work to solve a murder of a security chief at a mining base on the moon.

Production Company: Tamara Asseyev Prods. &
    London Weekend TV
Executive Producer .... Tamara Asseyev
Producer .... Ron Carr
Director .... Michael Lindsay-Hogg
Writer .... Carla Jean Wagner
Cast .... Brigitte Nielsen
Cast .... Gerald McRaney
Cast .... Brian Cox

MURDER BY NIGHT   USA
Mystery: Murder and Murder Mystery • Suspense/
Thriller
Airdate: 07/19/89
Rating: N/A   A/C:

*A witness to a murder gets amnesia and tries to
remember the killer's face, wondering all along
if he himself committed the crime.*

Production Company: Finnegan-Pinchuk
Executive Producer .... Pat Finnegan
Executive Producer .... Sheldon Pinchuk
Producer .... David Rosell
Director .... Paul Lynch
Writer .... Alan McElroy
Cast .... Kay Lenz
Cast .... Robert Urich
Cast .... Jim Metzler
Cast .... Richard Monette

MURDER: BY REASON OF INSANITY CBS
Drama: Woman In Jeopardy • True Story •
Psychological Thriller • Family Violence
Airdate: 10/01/85
Rating: 16.6/26   A/C:

*An abused wife summons up the courage to have
her disturbed husband committed to an
institution, only to have him torment her from
within the asylum.*

Production Company: LS Entertainment Inc.
Executive Producer .... Lawrence Schiller
Director .... Anthony Page
Writer .... Scott Swanton
Cast .... Candice Bergen
Cast .... Jurgen Prochnow
Cast .... Hector Elizondo
Cast .... Eli Wallach

MURDER BY THE BOOK   CBS
Mystery: Murder and Murder Mystery • Sci-Fi/
Supernatural/Horror/Fantasy
Airdate: 03/17/87
Rating: 9.4/15   A/C:

*A successful mystery author's publisher will let
him shed the tough-guy hero he invented only
if he himself can solve a mystery.*

Production Company: Peter Nelson Prods. IAW
   Orion TV
Producer .... Peter Nelson
Director .... Mel Damski
Writer .... Michael Norell
Cast .... Robert Hays
Cast .... Celeste Holm
Cast .... Catherine Mary Stewart
Cast .... Christopher Murney
Cast .... Fred Gwynne

MURDER C. O. D.   NBC
Mystery: Murder and Murder Mystery • Cops/
Detectives/Law Enforcement • Psychological Thriller
Airdate: 09/21/90
Rating: 10.3/19   A/C: 3

*Based on the novel "Kill Fee" by Barbara Paul.
A troubled detective locks horns with a
psychotic hit man who eliminates villainous
characters and then harasses the relieved
beneficiaries into paying his fee.*

Production Company: Perry Lafferty Prods. IAW
   Kushner-Locke Company
Executive Producer .... Perry Lafferty
Executive Producer .... Donald Kushner
Executive Producer .... Peter Locke
Producer .... Fred Whitehead
Director .... Alan Metzger
Writer .... Andrew Peter Marin
Cast .... Patrick Duffy
Cast .... Mariette Hartley
Cast .... William Devane
Cast .... Chelsea Field

MURDER IN BLACK AND WHITE   CBS
Drama: Murder and Murder Mystery • Cops/
Detectives/Law Enforcement
Airdate: 01/07/90
Rating: 17.1/27   A/C: 1

*NYPD detective Frank Janek (from TV movies
"Double Take" and "Internal Affairs")
investigates the murder of his boss, a black
police commissioner. Though it appears to be
race-related, he links the killing to the police
Internal Affairs department.*

Production Company: Titus Productions
Executive Producer .... Robert Berger
Executive Producer .... Herbert Brodkin
Producer .... Thomas De Wolfe
Director .... Robert Iscove
Writer .... Gordon Cotler
Cast .... Richard Crenna
Cast .... Diahann Carroll
Cast .... Cliff Gorman
Cast .... Philip Bosco

MURDER IN HIGH PLACES   NBC
Drama: Murder and Murder Mystery • Cops/
Detectives/Law Enforcement • Series Pilot (2 hr.)
Airdate: 06/02/91
Rating: 12.3/22   A/C: 1

*At a trendy Colorado resort, a hard-drinking
mayor and an ex-Chicago cop team up to solve
the murder of a woman who was linked
romantically to several local power brokers.*

Production Company: Stan Rogow Prods. IAW
   NBC Productions
Executive Producer .... Stan Rogow
Executive Producer .... John Byrum
Producer .... Marvin Miller
Director .... John Byrum
Writer .... John Byrum
Cast .... Adam Baldwin
Cast .... Ted Levine
Cast .... Judith Hoag
Cast .... Jamey Sheridan

MURDER IN MISSISSIPPI   NBC
Drama: Period Piece • Black Story • Historical Piece
• Social Issue • True Story
Airdate: 02/05/90
Rating: 12.4/20   A/C: 3

*The story of three civil rights workers who in
1964 were murdered by white segregationists
while trying to organize black voter registration
in the South.*

Production Company: Warner Bros./Elliot
   Friedgen & Co. - A David L. Wolper Prods.
Executive Producer .... David L. Wolper
Executive Producer .... Bernard Sofronski
Co-Executive Producer .... Tova Laiter
Producer .... Mark M. Wolper
Director .... Roger Young
Writer .... Stanley Weiser
Cast .... Tom Hulce
Cast .... Jennifer Grey
Cast .... Blair Underwood
Cast .... CCH Pounder

MURDER IN NEW HAMPSHIRE: THE PAMELA SMART STORY   CBS
Drama: Murder and Murder Mystery • Forbidden
Love • True Crime • Children/Teens • Courtroom
Drama
Airdate: 09/24/91
Rating: 15.9/26   A/C: 1

*Restless twenty-two-year-old New Hampshire
school teacher Pamela Smart seduces fifteen-
year-old student William Flinn into killing her
newly-wed husband, a conservative insurance
salesman. A sensational trial ultimately proves
her guilty.*

Production Company: Robert Greenwald Prods.
Executive Producer .... Robert Greenwald
Executive Producer .... Carla Singer
Producer .... Philip Kleinbart
Co-Producer .... Don Goldman
Co-Producer .... Rosalyn Wright
Director .... Joyce Chopra
Writer .... Joe Cacaci
Cast .... Helen Hunt
Cast .... Chad Allen
Cast .... Michael Learned
Cast .... Ken Howard
Cast .... Howard Hesseman
Cast .... Larry Drake

MURDER IN PARADISE — NBC
Drama: Murder and Murder Mystery • Cops/
Detectives/Law Enforcement • Foreign or Exotic
Location • Series Pilot (2 hr.)
Airdate: 01/19/90
Rating: 12.6/21   A/C: 3

A burnt out ex-New York cop retreats to Hawaii and is soon involved in a serial murder case which is coincidentally similar to one he was never able to solve back home.

Production Company: A Bill McCutchen
    Production IAW Columbia Pictures Television
Executive Producer .... Bill McCutchen
Director .... Fred Walton
Writer .... Gerald Di Pego
Cast .... Kevin Kilner
Cast .... Maggie Han
Cast .... Mako
Cast .... Yuji Okumoto

MURDER IN THE HEARTLAND — ABC
Miniseries/Drama (2 nights): True Crime • Period
Piece • Children/Teens
Airdate: 5/3/93 • 5/4/93
Rating: 13.2/21 • 14.2/23   A/C: 3 • 1

In 1957 Lincoln, Nebraska, nineteen year old sociopath Charlie Starkweather and his fourteen year old girlfriend, Carol Ann Fugate, went on a shooting spree that killed ten innocent people. They are eventually captured, tried and found guilty of murder. Starkweather was executed and Fugate given life imprisonment.

Production Company: O'Hara-Horowitz Prods.
Executive Producer .... Michael O'Hara
Executive Producer .... Lawrence Horowitz
Producer .... S. Bryan Hickox
Director .... Robert Markowitz
Writer .... Michael O'Hara
Cast .... Tim Roth
Cast .... Fairuza Balk
Cast .... Brian Dennehy
Cast .... Randy Quaid

MURDER OF INNOCENCE — CBS
Drama: Family Drama • True Crime • Medical/
Disease/Mental Illness
Airdate: 11/30/93
Rating: 14.5/22   A/C: 2

A recently married young woman starts to exhibit irrational and bazaar behavior. As she descends into madness her husband desperately tries to find the source of her mental illness. Her rage turns to violence as she goes on a shooting rampage at a elementary school, takes a man a hostage and finally takes her own life.

Production Company: Samuels Film Co. IAW
    Polone Co., Hearst Ent.
Executive Producer .... Stu Samuels
Executive Producer .... Judith A. Polone
Producer .... Carroll Newman
Director .... Tom McLoughlin
Writer .... Philip Rosenberg
Cast .... Valerie Bertinelli
Cast .... Stephen Caffrey
Cast .... Graham Beckel
Cast .... Millie Perkins

MURDER OF MARY PHAGAN, THE — NBC
EMMY WINNER
Miniseries/Drama (2 nights):True Story • Period Piece
• Courtroom Drama • Historical Piece • Social Issue
Airdate: 01/24/88 • 01/26/88
Rating: 18.7/28 • 21.0/34   A/C:

In 1913 Georgia, Leo Frank, a northern Jewish factory owner is convicted of murdering a thirteen year old girl. When the courageous governor interferes in the case, his career is destroyed.

Production Company: George Stevens Jr. Prods.
    IAW Century Tower Prods., Orion Televison
Producer .... George Stevens, Jr.
Director .... Billy Hale
Writer .... Jeffrey Lane
Writer .... George Stevens, Jr.
Cast .... Jack Lemmon
Cast .... Robert Prosky
Cast .... Richard Jordan
Cast .... Peter Gallagher
Cast .... Kathryn Walker

MURDER ORDAINED — CBS
Miniseries/Drama (2 nights): Cops/Detectives/Law
Enforcement • True Crime • Murder and Murder
Mystery
Airdate: 05/03/87 • 05/05/87
Rating: 19.3/29 • 19.8/32   A/C:

Factual account of an affair between a married pastor and a parishioner, and the doggedness of the police officer who determined that their spouses' deaths were murder.

Production Company: Zev Braun Pictures Inc.
Executive Producer .... Zev Braun
Executive Producer .... Ted Field
Producer .... Phil Parslow
Producer .... Patricia Clifford
Director .... Mike Robe
Writer .... James Sadwith
Writer .... Mike Robe
Cast .... Keith Carradine
Cast .... Robert Harper
Cast .... Terence Knox
Cast .... JoBeth Williams
Cast .... Annabella Price
Cast .... M. Emmet Walsh

MURDER, SHE WROTE — CBS
Mystery: Murder and Murder Mystery • Series Pilot
(2 hr.)
Airdate: 09/30/84
Rating: 18.9/29   A/C:

Series pilot about a Maine novelist/substitute teacher turned sleuth who becomes involved in a real-life murder mystery when she visits her publisher's New York estate.

Production Company: Universal TV
Executive Producer .... Peter S. Fischer
Executive Producer .... Richard Levinson
Executive Producer .... William Link
Producer .... Robert F. O'Neill
Director .... Corey Allen
Writer .... Peter S. Fischer
Cast .... Angela Lansbury
Cast .... Arthur Hill
Cast .... Brian Keith
Cast .... Ned Beatty

MURDER TIMES SEVEN — CBS
Drama: Murder and Murder Mystery • Cops/
Detectives/Law Enforcement
Airdate: 10/14/90
Rating: 11.1/18   A/C: 3

NYPD detective Frank Janek gets personally involved in a murder investigation when a serial killer offs Janek's former partner.

Production Company: Titus Productions, Inc. IAW
    Pendick Enterprises, Inc.
Executive Producer .... Robert Berger
Executive Producer .... Herbert Brodkin
Producer .... Thomas De Wolfe
Director .... Jud Taylor
Writer .... Monte Stettin
Cast .... Richard Crenna
Cast .... Susan Blakely
Cast .... Cliff Gorman
Cast .... Moses Gunn

MURDER WITH MIRRORS — CBS
Mystery: Murder and Murder Mystery • Cops/
Detectives/Law Enforcement • Foreign or Exotic
Location
Airdate: 02/20/85
Rating: 15.2/23   A/C:

Based on an Agatha Christie novel about Scotland Yard super sleuth, Miss Marple, who investigates a case involving a series of murders at an old friend's mansion.

Production Company: Hajeno Prods. IAW Warner
    Bros. TV
Executive Producer .... George Eckstein
Producer .... Neil Hartley
Director .... Dick Lowry
Writer .... George Eckstein
Cast .... Bette Davis
Cast .... Helen Hayes
Cast .... Leo McKern
Cast .... John Mills

MURDER WITHOUT MOTIVE: THE EDMUND PERRY STORY — NBC
Drama: Murder and Murder Mystery • True Crime •
Children/Teens • Black Story • Social Issue
Airdate: 01/06/92
Rating: 11.3/18   A/C: 3

Based on the book "Best Intentions" by Robert Sam Anson. Attending a prestigious New England prep school, Edmund Perry, Harlem honor student, struggles to be at home in a world of subtle racism. The resulting emotional chaos culminates in his being shot by a white New York City cop in 1985.

Production Company: Leonard Hill Films
Executive Producer .... Ron Gilbert
Executive Producer .... Leonard Hill
Executive Producer .... Michael Apted
Producer .... Joel Fields
Director .... Kevin Hooks
Writer .... Richard Wesley
Cast .... Curtis McClarin
Cast .... Anna Maria Horsford
Cast .... Carla Gugino
Cast .... Christopher Daniel Barnes

MURDERERS AMONG US: THE SIMON WIESENTHAL STORY   HBO

Drama: Biography • Nazis • WWII • True Story •
Prison and Prison Camp
Airdate: 4/5/89
Rating: N/A   A/C:

*Traces the life of the renowned humanitarian
and Nazi hunter from his imprisonment in a
German concentration camp, his eventual
liberation by an American major- to his life long
obsession to bring Nazi war criminals to justice.*

Production Company: Robert Cooper Prods. IAW
     HBO, TVS Films, Hungarian Television
Executive Producer .... Robert Cooper
Executive Producer .... Abby Mann
Executive Producer .... Graham Benson
Producer .... John Kemeny
Director .... Brian Gibson
Writer .... Abby Mann
Writer .... Lane Slate
Writer .... Ron Hutchinson
Cast .... Ben Kingsley
Cast .... Craig T. Nelson
Cast .... Renee Soutendijk

MURDEROUS AFFAIR, A: THE CAROLYN WARMUS STORY   ABC

Drama: True Crime • Forbidden Love
Airdate: 9/13/92
Rating: 15.0/25   A/C: 1

*In 1989, suburban New York school teacher
Carolyn Warmus murders her lovers' wife in a
fit of jealousy. Professing her innocence and
that her boyfriend framed her, she is ultimately
convicted of second degree murder.*

Note: See "Danger of Love, The" -CBS

Production Company: Steve White Films,
     Spectacor Films
Executive Producer .... Steve White
Executive Producer .... Janet Faust Krusi
Executive Producer .... Michael Jaffe
Producer .... Barry Bernardi
Director .... Martin Davidson
Writer .... Earl W. Wallace
Cast .... Virginia Madsen
Cast .... Chris Sarandon
Cast .... Ned Eisenberg

MURDEROUS VISION   USA

Drama: Murder and Murder Mystery • Cops/
Detectives/Law Enforcement
Airdate: 02/20/91
Rating: N/A   A/C:

*A demoted homicide detective, now working in
missing persons, teams up with a psychic to
capture a psychotic kidnapper who also killed
the officer's best friend.*

Production Company: Gary Sherman/Wilshire
     Court Prods.
Executive Producer .... Gary Sherman
Executive Producer .... Ross Albert
Producer .... Johanna Persons
Director .... Gary Sherman
Writer .... Paul Joseph Gulino
Cast .... Bruce Boxleitner
Cast .... Laura Johnson
Cast .... Robert Culp
Cast .... Joseph D'Angerio

MURDERS IN THE RUE MORGUE, THE   CBS

Mystery: Murder and Murder Mystery • Cops/
Detectives/Law Enforcement • Period Piece
Airdate: 12/07/86
Rating: 17.7/27   A/C:

*Based on the Edgar Allan Poe story. A former
police inspector solves the gruesome murders
of two Parisian women.*

Production Company: Robert Halmi Inc. with
     International Film Productions S.A.
Producer .... Robert Halmi, Sr.
Director .... Jeannot Szwarc
Writer .... David Epstein
Cast .... George C. Scott
Cast .... Rebecca De Mornay
Cast .... Ian McShane
Cast .... Neil Dickson
Cast .... Val Kilmer

MURROW   HBO

Drama: Biography • Period Piece • Historical Piece
Airdate: 1/19/86
Rating: N/A   A/C:

*The life of legendary newsman Edward R.
Murrow for his beginnings as a World War II
radio correspondent and rise as a television
journalist at CBS through his battle with
Senator Joe McCarthy to his tragic death from
lung cancer in 1965.*

Production Company: HBO Premiere Films
Executive Producer .... Herbert Brodkin
Producer .... Robert Berger
Producer .... Dickie Bamber
Director .... Jack Gold
Writer .... Ernest Kinoy
Cast .... Daniel J. Travanti
Cast .... Dabney Coleman
Cast .... Edward Herrmann
Cast .... Kathry Leigh Scott

MUSSOLINI: THE DECLINE AND FALL OF IL DUCE   HBO

Miniseries/Drama (2 nights): Biography • Foreign or
Exotic Location • Period Piece • True Story •
Historical Piece
Airdate: 9/8/85 • 9/9/85
Rating: N/A   A/C:

*As WWII sweeps across Europe, Italy and its
leader Benito Mussolini find themselves drawn
into the conflict. Mussolini feels he must honor
his alliance with Hitler, over the protest of his
Foreign Minister and husband of his beloved
daughter. Eventually overruled by King Victor
Emmanuel III he is arrested and jailed and his
family is forced into hiding. Freed by German
commandos and appointed by Hitler to head a
new fascist regime in German-occupied
northern Italy he is ultimately killed by
partisans in the spring of 1945 after 23 years
of dictatorship.*

Production Company: RAI Channel 1, HBO,
     Antennae 2, Beta Film, TVE and RTSI
Executive Producer .... Thomas M.C. Johnston
Producer .... Mario Gallo
Director .... Alberto Negrin
Writer .... Nicola Badalucco
Writer .... Alberto Negrin
Cast .... Bob Hoskins
Cast .... Susan Sarandon
Cast .... Anthony Hopkins
Cast .... Annie Girardot

MUSSOLINI - THE UNTOLD STORY   NBC

Miniseries/Drama (3 nights): Period Piece • Historical
Piece • Foreign or Exotic Location • Biography •
WWII • Political Piece
Airdate: 11/24/85 • 11/25/85 • 11/26/85
Rating: 17.7/26 • 19.4/29 • 19.6/29   A/C:

*An intimate account of Italy's Benito Mussolini
from his rise to power as a Fascist leader in
the 1920's, through his death in 1945.*

Production Company: Train Prods.
Executive Producer .... Raymond Katz
Executive Producer .... Bernard Sofronski
Producer .... Stirling Silliphant
Producer .... Hal W. Polaire
Director .... William A. Graham
Writer .... Stirling Silliphant
Cast .... George C. Scott
Cast .... Mary Elizabeth Mastrantonio
Cast .... Virginia Madsen
Cast .... Raul Julia
Cast .... Gabriel Byrne
Cast .... Lee Grant

MY BOYFRIEND'S BACK   NBC

Comedy: Woman's Issue/Story • Buddy Story
Airdate: 09/25/89
Rating: 16.1/26   A/C: 2

The story of three women singers from a sixties "girl" group who are reunited after twenty-five years to perform in a network special.

Production Company: Interscope Prods. Inc.
Executive Producer .... Ted Field
Executive Producer .... Patricia Clifford
Producer .... Richard L. O'Connor
Director .... Paul Schneider
Writer .... Lindsay Harrison
Cast .... Sandy Duncan
Cast .... Jill Eikenberry
Cast .... Judith Light
Cast .... Stephen Macht

MY BREAST   CBS

Drama: Medical/Disease/Mental Illness • True Story • Woman's Issue/Story
Airdate: 5/15/94
Rating: 11.4/18   A/C: 3

Based on the book by Joyce Wadler. People Magazine writer Joyce Wadler discovers she has breast cancer. While her live-in, self centered, philandering boyfriend lends her no support she nevertheless faces her fears and battles the disease; refusing to accept a death sentence.

Production Company: Diana Kerew Prods., Polone Co. IAW Hearst Entertainment
Executive Producer .... Diana Kerew
Co-Executive Producer .... Meredith Baxter
Director .... Betty Thomas
Writer .... Joyce Wadler
Cast .... Meredith Baxter
Cast .... Jamey Sheridan
Cast .... James Sutorius
Cast .... Barbara Barrie

MY BROTHER'S WIFE   ABC

Drama: Family Drama • Love Story
Airdate: 12/17/89
Rating: 11.2/18   A/C: 3

Adapted from the play "Middle Ages" by A.R. Gurney. The story of the off-beat son of a wealthy Boston family whose romantic obsessions for his sister-in-law are recounted in flashbacks spanning twenty-seven years.

Production Company: Adam Productions IAW Robert Greenwald Productions
Executive Producer .... Robert Greenwald
Executive Producer .... Robert M. Myman
Producer .... Joan Stein
Director .... Jack Bender
Writer .... Percy Granger
Cast .... John Ritter
Cast .... Mel Harris
Cast .... Polly Bergen
Cast .... Dakin Matthews

MY FATHER, MY SON   CBS

Drama: Family Drama • Medical/Disease/Mental Illness • True Story • Vietnam
Airdate: 05/22/88
Rating: 13.5/22   A/C:

Based on the book by Elmo Zumwalt. True story of Admiral Elmo Zumwalt, Jr., whose order to use Agent Orange in Vietnam apparently caused his own son's later lymphoma and Hodgkin's disease.

Production Company: Fred Weintraub Prods. IAW John J. McMahon Prods.
Executive Producer .... John J. McMahon
Producer .... Fred Weintraub
Director .... Jeff Bleckner
Writer .... Jacqueline Feather
Writer .... David Seidler
Cast .... Keith Carradine
Cast .... Karl Malden
Cast .... Margaret Klenck
Cast .... Michael Horton

MY FIRST LOVE   ABC

Comedy: Romantic Comedy
Airdate: 12/04/88
Rating: 13.7/21   A/C:

A newly widowed older woman looks up an old boyfriend, who is still attracted to her although he's otherwise involved.

Production Company: Avnet/Kerner Co.
Executive Producer .... Jon Avnet
Executive Producer .... Jordan Kerner
Producer .... Gail Mutrux
Writer .... Ed Kaplan
Director .... Gilbert Cates
Cast .... Beatrice Arthur
Cast .... Richard Kiley
Cast .... Joan Van Ark
Cast .... Anne Francis
Cast .... Richard Herd
Cast .... Barbara Barrie

MY NAME IS BILL W.   ABC

Drama: Family Drama • True Story • Period Piece • Addiction Story • Biography
Airdate: 04/30/89
Rating: 15.2/24   A/C:

True story of the founding of Alcoholics Anonymous by Bill Wilson. After years of hard drinking, sanitariums, losing jobs and destroying relationships, Bill finally gets his life together and starts AA with the help of a boozing surgeon.

Production Company: Garner-Duchow Prods.
Executive Producer .... Peter K. Duchow
Executive Producer .... James Garner
Producer .... Daniel Petrie
Director .... Daniel Petrie
Writer .... William G. Borchert
Cast .... James Woods
Cast .... James Garner
Cast .... JoBeth Williams

MY NAME IS KATE   ABC

Drama: Addiction Story • Family Drama
Airdate: 1/24/94
Rating: 11.2/17   A/C: 3

A suburban wife, mother and businesswoman is forced into alcohol treatment when family and friends threaten to desert her. While in a rehabilitation center she confronts her addiction with the help of a diverse group of recovering addicts and begins the long road back to rebuilding her life.

Production Company: a.k.a. Prods., Queen Prods., Donna Mills Prods. IAW ABC Prods.
Executive Producer .... Ilene Amy Berg
Executive Producer .... Donna Mills
Producer .... Harold Tichenor
Director .... Rod Hardy
Writer .... George Eckstein
Cast .... Donna Mills
Cast .... Daniel J. Travanti
Cast .... Nia Peeples
Cast .... Ryan Reynolds

MY SON JOHNNY   CBS

Drama: Family Drama • Murder and Murder Mystery • True Crime • Children/Teens • Courtroom Drama • Family Violence
Airdate: 11/10/91
Rating: 15.6/24   A/C: 1 (TIE)

A sensitive 16-year-old boy murders his violent older brother after years of physical and mental torture. During the trial, his mother finds her denial of her eldest son's behavior is ultimately responsible for her younger son's desperate act.

Production Company: Capital Cities/ABC Video Prods. IAW Citadel Ent.
Executive Producer .... David R. Ginsburg
Executive Producer .... Carla Singer
Producer .... Michael O. Gallant
Producer .... Paul A. Mones
Director .... Peter Levin
Writer .... Peter Nelson
Cast .... Michele Lee
Cast .... Rick Schroder
Cast .... Corin Nemec
Cast .... Rip Torn

MY TWO LOVES   ABC

Drama: Family Drama • Homosexuality
Airdate: 04/07/86
Rating: 17.5/28   A/C:

A middle-aged widow, who can't seem to fall in love with the man she's involved with, is drawn into an affair with a female co-worker. Scandal, indecision and confrontation with her daughter and mother follow.

Production Company: Alvin Cooper Prods. IAW Taft Entertainment TV
Executive Producer .... Alvin Cooperman
Director .... Noel Black
Writer .... Reginald Rose
Writer .... Rita Mae Brown
Cast .... Mariette Hartley
Cast .... Sada Thompson
Cast .... Barry Newman
Cast .... Lynn Redgrave

N. Y. P. D. MOUNTED — CBS

Comedy: Cops/Detectives/Law Enforcement • Action/Adventure • Series Pilot (2 hr.) • Buddy Story
Airdate: 08/03/91
Rating: 6.1/13   A/C: 3

A hard-boiled New York cop is reassigned to the mounted patrol unit and gets partnered with a naive cowboy recently transferred from Montana.

Production Company: P.H. Prods. IAW Orion TV
Executive Producer .... Patrick Hasburgh
Producer .... Mark H. Ovitz
Director .... Mark Tinker
Writer .... Patrick Hasburgh
Cast .... Dennis Franz
Cast .... Dan Gauthier
Cast .... Roxann Biggs
Cast .... Cliff De Young

NAILS — SHOWTIME

Drama: Murder and Murder Mystery • Cops/Detectives/Law Enforcement • Drug Smuggling/Dealing
Airdate: 07/25/92
Rating: N/A   A/C:

A hard-nosed, maverick cop plays by his own rules as he tries to avenge the death of his beloved partner at the hands of Cuban hitman who are involved in a drug-smuggling operation.

Production Company: Viacom Pictures
Executive Producer .... Dale Rosenbloom
Producer .... George Perkins
Director .... John Flynn
Writer .... Larry Ferguson
Cast .... Dennis Hopper
Cast .... Anne Archer
Cast .... Tomas Milian
Cast .... Cliff De Young

NAIROBI AFFAIR — CBS

Drama: Family Drama • Foreign or Exotic Location
Airdate: 10/17/84
Rating: 12.2/20   A/C:

The relationship between a game hunter turned tour guide and his stepson is strained when the son learns his ex-girlfriend is seeing his stepfather.

Production Company: Robert Halmi Inc.
Executive Producer .... Robert Halmi, Sr.
Director .... Marvin J. Chomsky
Writer .... David Epstein
Cast .... Charlton Heston
Cast .... John Savage
Cast .... Maud Adams
Cast .... John Rhys-Davies

NAKED LIE — CBS

Drama: Courtroom Drama • Murder and Murder Mystery • Love Story • Sex/Glitz • Woman In Jeopardy
Airdate: 02/26/89
Rating: 21.2/33   A/C:

An assistant district attorney is sleeping with the judge who is trying her murder case. Worse, the judge is also the killer.

Production Company: Shadowplay Films Inc. with Phoenix Entertainment Group Inc.
Executive Producer .... Victoria Principal
Executive Producer .... Hans Proppe
Producer .... Stephanie Austin
Director .... Richard Colla
Writer .... Timothy Wurtz
Writer .... Glenn M. Benest
Writer .... John Robert Bensink
Cast .... Victoria Principal
Cast .... James Farentino
Cast .... Glenn Withrow
Cast .... William Lucking

NAPOLEON AND JOSEPHINE: A LOVE STORY — ABC

Miniseries/Drama (3 nights): Action/Adventure • Historical Piece • Foreign or Exotic Location • Love Story • Biography • Period Piece
Airdate: 11/10/87 • 11/11/87 • 11/12/87
Rating: 18.6/30 • 16.2/26 • 13.3/21   A/C:

Lavish biography of the French emperor and his fiery wife, covering the years 1794-1814.

Production Company: David L. Wolper Prods. IAW Warner Bros. TV
Executive Producer .... David L. Wolper
Executive Producer .... Bernard Sofronski
Producer .... Alfred R. Kelman
Co-Producer .... Suzanne Wiesenfeld
Director .... Richard T. Heffron
Writer .... James Lee
Cast .... Armand Assante
Cast .... Patrick Cassidy
Cast .... Jean-Pierre Stewart
Cast .... Leigh Taylor-Young
Cast .... William Lucking
Cast .... Stephanie Beacham
Cast .... Anthony Perkins
Cast .... Jacqueline Bisset

NASTY BOYS — NBC

Drama: Cops/Detectives/Law Enforcement • Series Pilot (2 hr.) • Action/Adventure • Drug Smuggling/Dealing
Airdate: 09/22/89
Rating: 15.3/27   A/C: 1

A group of young North Las Vegas cops, hand-picked to resemble their quarry, battle street gangs and other drug peddlers.

Production Company: NBC Prods. IAW Universal TV
Executive Producer .... Dick Wolf
Producer .... Lynn H. Guthrie
Director .... Rick Rosenthal
Writer .... Dick Wolf
Writer .... David Black
Cast .... William Russ
Cast .... Jeff Kaake
Cast .... Benjamin Bratt
Cast .... James Pax

NAZI HUNTER: THE BEATE KLARSFELD STORY — ABC

Drama: Woman Against The System • Woman In Jeopardy • True Story • Nazis
Airdate: 11/23/86
Rating: 13.7/21   A/C:

True story of a German Protestant woman, married to a French Jew, who hunts former Nazis in Europe and South America. Her greatest quarry was Klaus Barbie, who fled to Bolivia.

Production Company: Silver Chalice/Revcom Present. IAW William Kayden Prods. & Orion TV
Executive Producer .... Judith De Paul
Producer .... William Kayden
Director .... Michael Lindsay-Hogg
Writer .... Frederic Hunter
Cast .... Farrah Fawcett
Cast .... Tom Conti
Cast .... Geraldine Page
Cast .... Vincent Gauthier

NECESSITY — CBS

Drama: Family Drama • Woman In Jeopardy • Mafia/Mob • Drug Smuggling/Dealing • Children/Teens
Airdate: 05/03/88
Rating: 15.0/24   A/C:

Based on the novel by Brian Garfield. When a fashion model leaves her husband upon discovering he's a drug-involved mobster, he responds with violent measures. But she returns with a vengeance to recover her baby.

Production Company: 20th Century Fox Film Corp.
Executive Producer .... Dan Enright
Producer .... Les Alexander
Co-Producer .... Ed Fields
Director .... Michael Miller
Writer .... Michael Ahnemann
Cast .... Loni Anderson
Cast .... James Naughton
Cast .... John Heard
Cast .... Harris Laskawy

NED BLESSING: THE STORY OF MY LIFE AND TIMES — CBS

Drama: Western • Period Piece • Series Pilot (2 hr.)
Airdate: 8/18/93
Rating: 11.3/20   A/C: 2

Sequel to 1992 TV movie. The adventures of an ex-bandit turned sheriff in the small western town of Plum Creek, Texas which is faced with a gang of troublemakers hell bent on controlling the streets.

Production Company: Wittliff/Pangaea Prods.,
    Hearst Ent., CBS Ent. Prods.
Executive Producer .... Bill Wittliff
Director .... Jack Bender
Writer .... Bill Wittliff
Cast .... Brad Johnson
Cast .... Luis Avalos
Cast .... Brenda Bakke
Cast .... Tim Scott

NED BLESSING: THE TRUE STORY OF MY LIFE — CBS

Drama: Series Pilot (2 hr.) • Western • Period Piece
Airdate: 04/14/92
Rating: 10.9/18   A/C: 3

A Texas lawman recalls his early days with Mexican banditos, his love for a feisty young actress, and the murder of his father by a ruthless gang of outlaws.

Production Company: Witliff-Pangaea Prods. IAW
    Hearst Entertainment
Executive Producer .... Bill Wittliff
Producer .... William P. Scott
Director .... Peter Werner
Writer .... Bill Wittliff
Cast .... Daniel Baldwin
Cast .... Chris Cooper
Cast .... Luis Avalos
Cast .... Rene Auberjonois

NEON EMPIRE — SHOWTIME

Drama: Period Piece • Historical Piece • Sex/Glitz • Mafia/Mob
Airdate: 12/03/89
Rating: N/A   A/C:

Fictionalized story about the gangster origins of Las Vegas.

Production Company: Fries Entertainment Inc. A
    Richard Maynard Prod.
Executive Producer .... Charles Fries
Producer .... Richard Maynard
Director .... Larry Peerce
Writer .... Pete Hamill
Cast .... Ray Sharkey
Cast .... Linda Fiorentino
Cast .... Dylan McDermott
Cast .... Julie Carmen
Cast .... Martin Landau

NEVER FORGET — TNT

Drama: Man Against The System • True Story • Courtroom Drama • Historical Piece • Social Issue • Nazis
Airdate: 04/08/91
Rating: N/A   A/C:

Concentration camp survivor Mel Mermelstein accepts a neo-nazi revisionist history group's challenge to prove the holocaust really did occur. With the help of his attorney, they devise a strategy whereby the case is ultimately heard in a U.S. court.

Production Company: Nimoy-Radnitz Prods.
Executive Producer .... Leonard Nimoy
Executive Producer .... Robert B. Radnitz
Producer .... Robert B. Radnitz
Director .... Joseph Sargent
Writer .... Ron Rubin
Cast .... Leonard Nimoy
Cast .... Dabney Coleman
Cast .... Blythe Danner
Cast .... Paul Hampton

NEWS AT ELEVEN — CBS

Drama: Man Against The System • Children/Teens • Rape/Molestation • Social Issue
Airdate: 04/02/86
Rating: 13.3/22   A/C:

A news anchorman rebels when his boss demands he take part in predatory trash-journalism in a case of high-school girls allegedly molested by a teacher.

Production Company: Turman/Foster Co. IAW
    Finnegan Associates
Executive Producer .... Lawrence Turman
Executive Producer .... David Foster
Producer .... Bill Finnegan
Director .... Mike Robe
Writer .... Mike Robe
Cast .... Martin Sheen
Cast .... Sheree J. Wilson
Cast .... Barbara Babcock
Cast .... Brooke Bundy
Cast .... Susan Krebs

NICK KNIGHT — CBS

Drama: Cops/Detectives/Law Enforcement • Series Pilot (2 hr.) • Sci-Fi/Supernatural/Horror/Fantasy
Airdate: 08/20/89
Rating: 11.2/19   A/C:

Knight, an L.A. police detective working the night shift because he's a vampire, is tracking a vampire who kills homeless people. The murderer, trying to stop Knight from giving up bloodsucking, frames him for a museum burglary.

Production Company: Cuppa Blood Prods.
Executive Producer .... Roberta F. Becker
Producer .... S. Michael Formica
Director .... Farhad Mann
Writer .... James D. Parriott
Cast .... Rick Springfield
Cast .... John Kapelos
Cast .... Michael Nader
Cast .... Laura Johnson

NIGHT OF COURAGE — ABC

Drama: Man Against The System • Children/Teens • Social Issue
Airdate: 01/12/87
Rating: 12.4/19   A/C:

A high-school teacher learns what really happened when an old man apparently refused to help a Hispanic teenager who was being pursued by a white gang and subsequently beaten to death.

Production Company: Titus Prods.
Executive Producer .... Herbert Brodkin
Executive Producer .... Robert Berger
Producer .... Thomas De Wolfe
Director .... Elliot Silverstein
Writer .... Bryan Williams
Cast .... Barnard Hughes
Cast .... Geraldine Fitzgerald
Cast .... Daniel Hugh Kelly

NIGHT OF THE HUNTER — ABC

Drama: Family Drama • Psychological Thriller
Airdate: 05/05/91
Rating: 13.7/23   A/C: 1

Remake of the 1955 film. A psychopathic ex-con, posing as a preacher in the South, tries to con a cache of stolen money out of a naive widow and her suspecting children with tragic results.

Production Company: Diana Kerew Prods. IAW
    Konigsberg-Sanitsky Co.
Executive Producer .... Diana Kerew
Director .... David Greene
Writer .... Edmond Stevens
Cast .... Richard Chamberlain
Cast .... Diana Scarwid
Cast .... Reid Binion
Cast .... Burgess Meredith

NIGHT OWL — LIFETIME

Drama: Sci-Fi/Supernatural/Horror/Fantasy
Airdate: 8/19/93
Rating: N/A   A/C:

A speech therapist battles a supernatural being who's sexy voice on the radio drives vulnerable men to their deaths with her bewitching, erotic chanting. When the evil demon starts affecting her jazz musician husband she contacts experts in the occult world and together they set a trap to destroy the seductive siren.

Production Company: Morgan Hill Films, Hearst
    Ent.
Executive Producer .... Jennifer Alward
Producer .... Julian Marks
Co-Producer .... Fran Bell
Co-Producer .... Rose Schacht
Co-Producer .... Ann Powell
Director .... Matthew Patrick
Writer .... Rose Schacht
Writer .... Ann Powell
Cast .... Jennifer Beals
Cast .... James Wilder
Cast .... Allison Hossack

NIGHT THEY SAVED CHRISTMAS, THE
ABC

Drama: Holiday Special • Sci-Fi/Supernatural/Horror/Fantasy
Airdate: 12/13/84
Rating: 14.2/22   A/C:

When an oil company plans to drill near Santa's home, an elf enlists the help of a mother and her young children to try and save North Pole City.

Production Company: Robert Halmi Inc.
Executive Producer .... Robert Halmi, Jr.
Executive Producer .... Jack Haley, Jr.
Executive Producer .... David Niven, Jr.
Producer .... David Kappes
Producer .... Robert Halmi, Sr.
Director .... Jackie Cooper
Writer .... James C. Moloney
Writer .... David Niven, Jr.
Cast .... Jaclyn Smith
Cast .... Paul LeMat
Cast .... Mason Adams
Cast .... June Lockhart
Cast .... Paul Williams
Cast .... Art Carney

NIGHT VISIONS
NBC

Drama: Murder and Murder Mystery • Cops/Detectives/Law Enforcement • Sci-Fi/Supernatural/Horror/Fantasy
Airdate: 11/30/90
Rating: 9.8/17   A/C: 3

An alcoholic police sergeant and a traumatized psychic team up to capture a psychotic serial killer loose in Los Angeles.

Production Company: Wes Craven Films, MGM/UA Television
Executive Producer .... Wes Craven
Producer .... Rick Nathanson
Producer .... Thomas Baum
Producer .... Marianne Maddalena
Director .... Wes Craven
Writer .... Wes Craven
Writer .... Thomas Baum
Cast .... Loryn Locklin
Cast .... James Remar
Cast .... Penny Johnson
Cast .... Bruce MacVittie

NIGHT WALK
CBS

Mystery: Murder and Murder Mystery • Cops/Detectives/Law Enforcement • Woman In Jeopardy
Airdate: 10/01/89
Rating: 16.3/27   A/C: 1

A woman witnesses a murder and becomes the unwitting target of the hit men. She and a widowed police officer fall in love and eventually uncover her husband's devious plot to have her killed.

Production Company: CBS Entertainment Prods. IAW Galatea Prods.
Executive Producer .... Harry Longstreet
Executive Producer .... Renee Longstreet
Producer .... Harry Longstreet
Producer .... Renee Longstreet
Director .... Jerrold Freedman
Writer .... Harry Longstreet
Writer .... Renee Longstreet
Cast .... Robert Urich
Cast .... Lesley-Anne Down
Cast .... Mark Joy

NIGHTINGALES
NBC

Drama: Medical/Disease/Mental Illness • Series Pilot (2 hr.) • Sex/Glitz
Airdate: 06/27/88
Rating: 18.9/33   A/C:

The lives and loves of eight student nurses with different backgrounds who live off-campus with their warm-hearted housemother.

Production Company: Aaron Spelling Prods.
Executive Producer .... Aaron Spelling
Executive Producer .... Douglas S. Cramer
Producer .... Dennis Hammer
Producer .... Frank V. Furino
Director .... Mimi Leder
Writer .... Howard Lakin
Cast .... Fran Bennett
Cast .... Chelsea Field
Cast .... Galyn Gorg
Cast .... Mimi Kuzyk
Cast .... John Bennett Perry

NIGHTLIFE
USA

Comedy: Sci-Fi/Supernatural/Horror/Fantasy • Foreign or Exotic Location
Airdate: 08/23/89
Rating: N/A   A/C:

Comedy thriller about a "vampress" who after sleeping for centuries, wakes up and tries to cope in present day Mexico City. She is pursued by her former jealous vampire lover and a curious hematologist who is studying her strange "malady."

Production Company: Cine Enterprises Mexico and MTE
Executive Producer .... Dan Wigutow
Producer .... Robert T. Skodis
Director .... Daniel Taplitz
Writer .... Anne Beatts
Writer .... Daniel Taplitz
Cast .... Maryam D'Abo
Cast .... Ben Cross

NIGHTMAN, THE
NBC

Drama: Suspense/Thriller
Airdate: 03/03/92
Rating: 11.6/18   A/C: 2

From the radio play by Lucille Fletcher. In 1973 Georgia, a Vietnam vet/mother/daughter love triangle ends in the mother's murder. When he takes the blame to protect the daughter, he is imprisoned. Upon his release, he stalks the daughter, forcing her to kill him to keep her secret.

Production Company: Avnet/Kerner
Executive Producer .... Jon Avnet
Executive Producer .... Jordan Kerner
Co-Executive Producer .... Joanna Kerns
Co-Executive Producer .... John Wells
Producer .... Charles Haid
Director .... Charles Haid
Writer .... Lucille Fletcher
Writer .... James Poe
Writer .... John Wells
Cast .... Jenny Robertson
Cast .... Joanna Kerns
Cast .... Ted Marcoux

NIGHTMARE AT BITTER CREEK
CBS

Drama: Woman In Jeopardy • Suspense/Thriller
Airdate: 05/24/88
Rating: 13.1/22   A/C:

While on a camping trip, three city women and their alcoholic guide battle with homicidal neo-Nazis in the woods.

Production Company: Swanton Films IAW Guber-Peters Ent. Co. Prods. IAW Phoenix Ent. Gp.
Executive Producer .... Jon Peters
Executive Producer .... Peter Guber
Producer .... Scott Swanton
Co-Producer .... Stanley Brooks
Director .... Tim Burstall
Writer .... Greg McCarty
Writer .... Scott Swanton
Cast .... Tom Skerritt
Cast .... Constance McCashin
Cast .... Joanna Cassidy
Cast .... Lindsay Wagner

NIGHTMARE IN COLUMBIA COUNTY   CBS

Drama: Murder and Murder Mystery • Cops/Detectives/Law Enforcement • True Crime • Children/Teens
Airdate: 12/10/91
Rating: 14.0/22   A/C: 2

When her younger sister is kidnapped in South Carolina in the mid-1980's, local beauty queen Dawn Smith aids the investigation by luring the psychotic killer into a provocative phone relationship, enabling Sheriff Jim Metts to track and capture him.

Production Company: The Landsburg Co.
Executive Producer .... Alan Landsburg
Producer .... Kay Hoffman
Co-Producer .... Don Goldman
Director .... Roger Young
Writer .... John Robert Bensink
Cast .... William DeVane
Cast .... Jeri Lynn Ryan
Cast .... Michele Abrams

NIGHTMARE IN THE DAYLIGHT   CBS

Drama: Woman In Jeopardy • Suspense/Thriller
Airdate: 11/22/92
Rating: 14.5/23   A/C: 2

A Wisconsin teacher attending a convention in San Francisco with her husband and son is pursued by an obsessed lawyer, thinking she is his long lost wife who was supposedly killed in the 1985 Mexico City earthquake. He frantically tries to prove his case while causing nothing but pure panic in his intended victim.

Production Company: Smith/Richmond Prods.
    IAW Saban/Sherick
Executive Producer .... Barbara Hiser
Executive Producer .... Tony Richmond
Producer .... Henry Colman
Director .... Lou Antonio
Writer .... Frederic Hunter
Cast .... Jaclyn Smith
Cast .... Christopher Reeve
Cast .... Tom Mason
Cast .... Eric Bell

NIGHTMARE ON THE THIRTEENTH FLOOR   USA

Drama: Sci-Fi/Supernatural/Horror/Fantasy
Airdate: 10/31/90
Rating: N/A   A/C:

A travel writer does a story on a Victorian hotel and uncovers a chamber of horrors on a "non-existent" thirteenth floor where an ax-wielding satanist commits heinous sacrifices.

Production Company: GC Group Ltd./Wilshire
    Court Productions
Executive Producer .... Walter Grauman
Director .... Walter Grauman
Writer .... J.D. Feigelson
Writer .... Dan Di Stefano
Cast .... Michele Greene
Cast .... James Brolin
Cast .... Louise Fletcher
Cast .... John Karlen

NIGHTMARE YEARS, THE   TNT

Miniseries/Drama (4 nights): Historical Piece • Biography • WWII • Nazis
Airdate: 09/17/89 • 09/18/89 • 09/19/89 • 09/20/89
Rating: N/A   A/C:

Based on William Shirer's autobiography. American journalist Shirer covers Germany from the rise of Nazism through the beginning of WW II, often working secretly against the regime. Includes footage from Leni Riefenstahl's "Triumph of the Will."

Production Company: Consolidated Productions
    Inc.
Executive Producer .... Gerald Rafshoon
Producer .... Graham Ford
Director .... Anthony Page
Writer .... Bob Woodward
Writer .... Christian Williams
Cast .... Sam Waterston
Cast .... Marthe Keller
Cast .... Kurtwood Smith

NO CHILD OF MINE   CBS

Drama: Family Drama • Medical/Disease/Mental Illness • True Story
Airdate: 10/31/93
Rating: 13.1/21   A/C: 2

The birth of twin sons, one of whom has Down syndrome ignites a legal battle between the child's mother, who feels the baby would be better off with a couple who have devoted their lives to special-needs children, and her controlling, obsessive mother who wants to raise the baby herself. Determined to stop their daughter, the grandparents fight to gain custody of the little boy but the court eventually sides with the birth parents and allows the adoption.

Production Company: Bonnie Raskin Prods.,
    Green/Epstein Prods. IAW Wamr Bros. TV
Executive Producer .... Jim Green
Executive Producer .... Allen Epstein
Executive Producer .... Bonnie Raskin
Producer .... Mark Bacino
Director .... Michael Katleman
Writer .... Selma Thompson
Writer .... Robert L. Freedman
Cast .... Patty Duke
Cast .... Tracy Nelson
Cast .... G.W, Bailey
Cast .... Susan Blakely

NO PLACE LIKE HOME   CBS

Drama: Family Drama • Children/Teens • Social Issue
Airdate: 12/03/89
Rating: 13.3/20   A/C: 3

Made homeless after being burned out of their apartment, a working class family faces the nightmare of life in welfare hotels and ultimately, the street.

Production Company: Feury/Grant Prods. IAW
    Orion Television
Executive Producer .... Joseph Feury
Producer .... Joseph Feury
Director .... Lee Grant
Writer .... Ara Watson
Writer .... Sam Blackwell
Cast .... Christine Lahti
Cast .... Jeff Daniels
Cast .... Lantz Landry
Cast .... Scott Marlowe

NOBODY'S CHILD   CBS

Drama: Medical/Disease/Mental Illness • True Story • Social Issue
Airdate: 04/06/86
Rating: 25.9/39   A/C: 1

True story of, Marie Balter, a woman who spent twenty years in a mental hospital before becoming a successful mental-health professional.

Production Company: Joseph Feury Prods. IAW
    Gaylord Production Co.
Executive Producer .... Dyson Lovell
Producer .... Joseph Feury
Co-Producer .... Milton Justice
Director .... Lee Grant
Writer .... Mary Gallagher
Writer .... Ara Watson
Cast .... Marlo Thomas
Cast .... Ray Baker
Cast .... Caroline Kava
Cast .... Kathy Baker

NOBODY'S CHILDREN   USA

Drama: Foreign or Exotic Location • Children/Teens • Family Drama • Woman Against The System • True Story
Airdate: 3/3/94
Rating: N/A   A/C:

In 1989, Detroit housewife, Carol Stevens, travels to Bucharest, Romania to adopt two children from a squalid state run orphanage. With the help of a dedicated French doctor they fight through endless red-tape and bureaucratic obstinacy to save the abandoned babies from a certain death.

Production Company: Winkler/Daniel Prods.,
    Quinta Communicatons
Executive Producer .... Ann Daniel
Executive Producer .... Henry Winkler
Executive Producer .... Tarak Ben Ammar
Executive Producer .... Peby Guisez
Producer .... Jeffrey White
Producer .... George Dybman
Co-Producer .... Alan Margulies
Co-Producer .... Roger Smith
Director .... David Wheatley
Writer .... Petru Popescu
Writer .... Iris Friedman
Cast .... Ann-Margret
Cast .... Jay O. Sanders
Cast .... Dominique Sanda

NORMAN ROCKWELL'S BREAKING HOME TIES ABC

Drama: Family Drama • Children/Teens • Medical/Disease/Mental Illness • Period Piece
Airdate: 11/26/87
Rating: 9.7/19   A/C:

A boy leaves the ranch for college—and a gentle sexual initiation—while his aging parents deal with the mother's leukemia.

Production Company: John Wilder Prods. IAW Telecom Entertainment Inc.
Executive Producer .... Michael Lepiner
Executive Producer .... Ken Kaufman
Executive Producer .... John Wilder
Producer .... Graham Cottle
Director .... John Wilder
Writer .... John Wilder
Cast .... Eva Marie Saint
Cast .... Claire Trevor
Cast .... Erin Gray
Cast .... Jason Robards

NORTH AND SOUTH ABC

Miniseries/Drama (6 nights): Family Drama • Forbidden Love • Period Piece • Action/Adventure • Historical Piece • Love Story
Airdate: 11/03/85 • 11/05/85 • 11/06/85 • 11/07/85 • 11/09/85
Rating: 25.8/37 • 23.6/34 • 28.0/42 • 25.8/38 • 23.2/37   A/C:

From John Jakes' novel. The Civil War and its travails, as seen through the eyes of two friends, a Southern plantation owner and a Pennsylvania industrialist whose families become more entwined with each other as the years go by.

Production Company: David L. Wolper Prods. IAW Warner Bros. TV
Executive Producer .... David L. Wolper
Executive Producer .... Chuck McLain
Producer .... Paul Freeman
Director .... Richard T. Heffron
Writer .... Paul F. Edwards
Writer .... Patricia Green
Writer .... Douglas Heyes
Writer .... Kathleen A. Shelley
Cast .... Kirstie Alley
Cast .... Patrick Swayze
Cast .... David Carradine
Cast .... James Reed
Cast .... Lesley-Anne Down
Cast .... Genie Francis
Cast .... Philip Casnoff
Cast .... Georg Standford Brown

NORTH AND SOUTH, BOOK 2 ABC

Miniseries/Drama (6 nights): Family Drama • Forbidden Love • Period Piece • Action/Adventure • Historical Piece • Love Story
Airdate: 05/04/86 • 05/05/86 • 05/06/86 • 05/07/86 • 05/08/86
Rating: 19.8/30 • 20.1/30 • 21.6/36 • 22.9/36 • 20.8/32   A/C:

The saga continues with emphasis on the historic Civil War battles and the destruction of the South.

Production Company: David L. Wolper Prods. IAW Warner Bros. TV
Executive Producer .... David L. Wolper
Producer .... Robert A. Papazian
Director .... Kevin Connor
Writer .... Richard Fielder
Cast .... Kirstie Alley
Cast .... Patrick Swayze
Cast .... David Carradine
Cast .... James Reed
Cast .... Philip Casnoff

NORTH AND SOUTH, BOOK 3: HEAVEN AND HELL ABC

Miniseries/Drama (3 nights): Family Drama • Period Piece • Historical Piece
Airdate: 2/27/94 • 2/28/94 • 3/2/94
Rating: 10.1/15 • 9.8/15 • 9.7/15 A/C: 3 • 3 • 3

Based on the book by John Jakes. The continuing saga of the Hazard family from Pennsylvania and the Main family from South Carolina as they rebuild their lives after the Civil War.

Production Company: Wolper Organization, IAW ABC Prods.
Executive Producer .... David L. Wolper
Executive Producer .... Mark M. Wolper
Producer .... Hal Galli
Director .... Larry Peerce
Writer .... Suzanne Clauser
Cast .... Philip Casnoff
Cast .... Lesley-Anne Down
Cast .... James Read
Cast .... Kyle Chandler
Cast .... Terri Garber
Cast .... Cathy Lee Crosby

NORTH BEACH AND RAWHIDE CBS

Miniseries/Drama (2 nights): Man Against The System • Children/Teens
Airdate: 11/12/85 • 11/13/85
Rating: 9.6/14 • 11.4/17   A/C:

The director of a juvenile corrections ranch comes into conflict with a wealthy landowner who is scheming to close down the place and buy the land.

Production Company: CBS Entertainment Prods.
Producer .... Roni Weisberg
Director .... Harry Falk
Writer .... Jimmy Sangster
Writer .... John Beaird
Writer .... George Yanok
Cast .... William Shatner
Cast .... Tate Donovan
Cast .... James Olson
Cast .... Ron O'Neal
Cast .... Conchata Ferrell

NOT A PENNY MORE, NOT A PENNY LESS USA

Miniseries/Comedy: Foreign or Exotic Location • Buddy Story
Airdate: 04/24/90 • 04/25/90
Rating: N/A   A/C:

Based on the novel by Jeffrey Archer. A corrupt financier swindles four men out of their life savings and family fortunes. They all join forces and devise an elaborate scheme to get their money back.

Production Company: BBC IAW Paramount Television Ltd./Revcom
Executive Producer .... Jacqueline Davis
Director .... Clive Donner
Writer .... Sherman Yellen
Cast .... Edward Asner
Cast .... Ed Begley, Jr.
Cast .... Brian Protheroe
Cast .... Maryam D'Abo

NOT IN MY FAMILY ABC

Drama: Family Drama • Rape/Molestation • Family Violence • Woman's Issue/Story
Airdate: 2/28/93
Rating: 15.1/23   A/C: 2

When a successful designer unlocks the repressed childhood memories of her father's repeated sexual abuse, she faces family scorn and denial when she attempts to protect her five year old niece from the same nightmare.

Production Company: Robert Greenwald Films
Executive Producer .... Robert Greenwald
Producer .... Philip Kleinbart
Director .... Linda Otto
Writer .... Michael Love
Writer .... Michael Salinas
Writer .... Joe Cacaci
Cast .... Joanna Kerns
Cast .... Michael Brandon
Cast .... Shelley Hack
Cast .... Richard Gilliland

NOT MY KID — CBS

Drama: Family Drama • Children/Teens • Addiction Story
Airdate: 01/15/84
Rating: 21.6/33   A/C:

The story of a fifteen year old girl whose parents try increasingly drastic measures to stop her drug use.

Production Company: Beth Polson Prods. IAW Finnegan Associates
Executive Producer .... Beth Polson
Producer .... Pat Finnegan
Director .... Michael Tuchner
Writer .... Christopher Knopf
Cast .... George Segal
Cast .... Stockard Channing
Cast .... Andrew Robinson
Cast .... Gary Bayer
Cast .... Nancy Cartwright

NOT OF THIS WORLD — CBS

Drama: Sci-Fi/Supernatural/Horror/Fantasy
Airdate: 02/12/91
Rating: 10.5/17   A/C: 3

An electrical engineer and a local sheriff in a small town team up to battle an alien from outer space who sucks the electricity out of all living beings.

Production Company: Barry & Enright Prods.
Executive Producer .... Les Alexander
Executive Producer .... Don Enright
Producer .... Jonathan Brauer
Director .... Jon Daniel Hess
Writer .... Robert Glass
Cast .... Lisa Hartman
Cast .... A Martinez
Cast .... Pat Hingle
Cast .... Luke Edwards

NOT QUITE HUMAN II — DISNEY

Comedy: Children/Teens • Youth Comedy • Sci-Fi/Supernatural/Horror/Fantasy
Airdate: 09/23/89
Rating: N/A   A/C:

Teenage android, Chip Carson, graduates from high school and goes on to college. When he arrives on campus, he is shocked to learn that the college coed he falls for is also "not quite human."

Production Company: Resnick/Margellos Prods.
Executive Producer .... Noel Resnick
Producer .... James Margellos
Director .... Eric Luke
Writer .... Eric Luke
Cast .... Alan Thicke
Cast .... Jay Underwood
Cast .... Robyn Lively
Cast .... Greg Mullavey
Cast .... Dey Young

NOTORIOUS — LIFETIME

Drama: Suspense/Thriller
Airdate: 01/28/92
Rating: N/A   A/C:

Remake of the Alfred Hitchcock, Ben Hecht 1946 classic. A wanton woman is recruited for spy work and is paired with a CIA agent who falls in love with her. Jealousy prevails when she is assigned to seduce an enemy agent.

Production Company: Hamster-ABC Productions
Executive Producer .... Ilene Amy Berg
Producer .... Sophie Ravard
Director .... Colin Bucksey
Writer .... Douglas Lloyd McIntosh
Cast .... John Shea
Cast .... Jenny Robertson
Cast .... Jean-Pierre Cassel
Cast .... Marisa Berenson

NURSES ON THE LINE: THE CRASH OF FLIGHT 7 — CBS

Drama: Foreign or Exotic Location • Disaster
Airdate: 11/23/93
Rating: 13.2/22   A/C: 1

When one of three light planes carrying doctors and medical supplies crashes in a remote Mexican jungle, student nurses traveling on the other plane fight to rescue the severely injured survivors and get them to a big city hospital.

Production Company: Cosgrove/Meurer Prods. IAW WIN
Executive Producer .... John Cosgrove
Executive Producer .... Terry Meurer
Co-Executive Producer .... Carrie Stein
Producer .... John Flynn
Director .... Larry Shaw
Writer .... Norman Morrill
Writer .... Andrew Laskos
Cast .... Lindsay Wagner
Cast .... Robert Loggia
Cast .... David Clennon
Cast .... Gary Frank

NUTCRACKER: MONEY, MADNESS AND MURDER — NBC

Miniseries/Drama (3 nights): True Crime • Family Violence • Murder and Murder Mystery • Children/Teens • Courtroom Drama
Airdate: 03/22/87 • 03/23/87 • 03/24/87
Rating: 12.2/20 • 11.5/19 • 13.5/22   A/C:

Based on the book by Shana Alexander. True story of, Marc Schreuder, a Utah boy who killed his grandfather at his mercenary mother's request. He later served as a star witness against his mother, the self-style New York socialite Frances Schreuder.

Production Company: Green Arrow Prods. IAW Warner Bros. TV
Executive Producer .... Chuck McLain
Executive Producer .... William Hanley
Producer .... William Beaudine, Jr.
Director .... Paul Bogart
Writer .... William Hanley
Cast .... Lee Remick
Cast .... Tate Donovan
Cast .... Linda Kelsey
Cast .... G. D. Spradlin
Cast .... Zina Bethune
Cast .... Inga Swenson
Cast .... Tony Musante
Cast .... David Ackroyd
Cast .... John Glover

O PIONEERS — CBS

Drama: Love Story • Farm Story • Period Piece
Airdate: 02/02/92
Rating: 18.9/29   A/C: 1

Based on the Willa Cather novel. The daughter of Swedish immigrant parents inherits her family's vast Nebraska plain becoming an heroic early 1900's matriarch. She successfully cultivates the land while denying her romantic needs until her childhood crush returns.

Production Company: Craig Anderson Prods. IAW Lorimar Prods.
Executive Producer .... Craig Anderson
Producer .... Glenn Jordan
Director .... Glenn Jordan
Writer .... Robert W. Lenski
Cast .... Jessica Lange
Cast .... David Strathairn
Cast .... Tom Aldredge
Cast .... Reed Diamond

OBSESSED   ABC

Drama: Suspense/Thriller
Airdate: 9/27/92
Rating: 10.3/16   A/C: 3

A desperately obsessed young woman becomes involved with a divorced older man. When he tries to end the relationship she becomes insanely possessive and violently destructive.

Production Company: Peter Duchow Enterprises
    IAW WIN

Executive Producer	Peter K. Duchow
Producer	S. Bryan Hickox
Director	Jonathan Sanger
Writer	David Peckinpah
Cast	William Devane
Cast	Shannen Doherty
Cast	Clare Carey

OBSESSED WITH A MARRIED WOMAN   ABC

Drama: Forbidden Love • Sex/Glitz
Airdate: 02/11/85
Rating: 14.5/22   A/C:

A man falls in love with his married boss, who strings him along with promises that she will leave her husband and son to be with him.

Production Company: Sidaris/Camhe Prods. IAW
    The Feldman-Meeker Co.

Executive Producer	Edward S. Feldman
Executive Producer	Clyde Phillips
Producer	Beverly J. Camhe
Producer	Arlene Sidaris
Director	Richard Lang
Writer	C. O'Brien
Writer	Dori Pierson
Writer	Marc Rubel
Cast	Jane Seymour
Cast	Tim Matheson
Cast	Richard Masur
Cast	Dori Brenner

OBSESSIVE LOVE   CBS

Drama: Love Story • Psychological Thriller •
Hollywood
Airdate: 10/02/84
Rating: 15.2/25   A/C:

A mentally ill woman moves to Hollywood from a small town to pursue her soap opera idol. As she becomes more and more obsessed, she manages to destroy his life.

Production Company: Ouza Inc. IAW Moonlight
    Prods.

Executive Producer	Frank Von Zerneck
Producer	Robert M. Sertner
Co-Producer	Yvette Mimieux
Director	Steven H. Stern
Writer	Petru Popescu
Writer	Iris Friedman
Cast	Yvette Mimieux
Cast	Simon MacCorkindale
Cast	Constance McCashin
Cast	Kin Shriner

OCEANS OF FIRE   CBS

Drama: Action/Adventure
Airdate: 09/16/86
Rating: 16.1/27   A/C:

The rough-and-tumble life on an offshore oil platform where several convicts have been recruited as divers.

Production Company: LaForche Co.

Executive Producer	Gregory Harrison
Producer	Franklin R. Levy
Producer	Matthew Rushton
Director	Steven Carver
Writer	Walter Halsey Davis
Cast	Gregory Harrison
Cast	David Carradine
Cast	Cynthia Sikes

ODD COUPLE, THE   CBS

Comedy: Buddy Story
Airdate: 9/24/93
Rating: 10.4/19   A/C: 2

Based on the play by Neil Simon. When fussy, Felix Unger is once again thrown out of his home while his wife and daughter prepare for the girls' up coming wedding he moves in with his old messy roommate, Oscar Madison. The sparks fly as Felix helps his depressed friend rehabilitate from throat cancer surgery.

Production Company: Howard W. Koch Prods.
    IAW Paramount TV

Executive Producer	Howard W. Koch
Director	Robert Klane
Writer	Robert Klane
Cast	Tony Randall
Cast	Jack Klugman
Cast	Barbara Barrie
Cast	Penny Marshall

OF PURE BLOOD   CBS

Drama: Woman In Jeopardy • Cross-Cultural Story •
Foreign or Exotic Location • Nazis • Murder and
Murder Mystery
Airdate: 10/19/86
Rating: 20.0/30   A/C:

Based on the book by Marc Hilel & Clarissa Henry. A NYC casting director returns to her native Germany to look into the death of her son. Seeking his infant child, she discovers that the nightmare of her involvement with the infamous Nazi "lebensborn" breeding program has not ended.

Production Company: Warner Bros. TV

Executive Producer	Kip Gowans
Producer	Joseph Sargent
Director	Joseph Sargent
Writer	Michael Zagor
Cast	Lee Remick
Cast	Patrick McGoohan
Cast	Edith Schneider
Cast	Katharina Bohm

OLD MAN & THE SEA, THE   NBC

Drama: Period Piece • Action/Adventure • Foreign
or Exotic Location
Airdate: 03/25/90
Rating: 14.9/24   A/C: 3

Adaptation of Ernest Hemingway's Pulitzer Prize winning novella about a Cuban fisherman who finally lands a mighty marlin.

Production Company: Storke Enterprises Inc. IAW
    Green Pond Prods. & Yorkshire TV

Executive Producer	William F. Storke
Executive Producer	Robert E. Fuisz
Supervising Producer	Norman Foster
Director	Jud Taylor
Writer	Roger O. Hirson
Cast	Anthony Quinn
Cast	Gary Cole
Cast	Valentina Quinn
Cast	Francesco Quinn

OLDEST LIVING CONFEDERATE WIDOW TELLS ALL   CBS

Miniseries/Drama (2 nights): Historical Piece • Period
Piece • Family Drama
Airdate: 5/1/94 • 5/3/94
Rating: 15.7/24 • 13.8/21   A/C: 1 • 2

Based on the novel by Allan Gurgamus. In North Carolina, a centenarian reflects on her unconventional life as a child bride of fifteen who married a fifty year old troubled, eccentric Civil War veteran at the turn of the century.

Production Company: Konigsberg/Sanitsky Co.
    IAW RHI Entertainment

Executive Producer	Frank Konigsberg
Executive Producer	Larry Sanitsky
Producer	Jack Clements
Director	Ken Cameron
Writer	Joyce Eliason
Cast	Donald Sutherland
Cast	Diane Lane
Cast	Cicely Tyson
Cast	Anne Bancroft
Cast	Blythe Danner
Cast	E.G. Marshall

OMEN IV: THE AWAKENING   FBC

Drama: Children/Teens • Sci-Fi/Supernatural/Horror/
Fantasy
Airdate: 05/22/91
Rating: 6.4/11   A/C: 4

The saga of Damien continues as a young congressman and his wife adopt a daughter whose penchant for evil causes murder and mayhem.

Production Company: Harvey Bernhard-Mace
    Neufeld Prods. IAW FNM Films, Inc.

Executive Producer	Mace Neufeld
Producer	Harvey Bernhard
Co-Producer	Robert Anderson
Director	Jorge Montesi
Director	Dominique Girard
Writer	Brian Taggert
Cast	Faye Grant
Cast	Michael Woods
Cast	Michael Lerner
Cast	Madison Mason

ON FIRE — ABC
Drama: Family Drama • Social Issue
Airdate: 01/05/87
Rating: 12.8/20   A/C:

Forced to retire, an arson investigator and his wife face his frustration and anger at being discarded.

Production Company: Robert Greenwald Prods.
Producer .... Jonathan Bernstein
Director .... Robert Greenwald
Writer .... John Herzfeld
Cast .... John Forsythe
Cast .... Carroll Baker
Cast .... Brian McNamara
Cast .... Gordon Jump

ON PROMISED LAND — DISNEY
Drama: Black Story • Period Piece • Historical Piece • Children/Teens
Airdate: 4/17/94
Rating: N/A   A/C:

In 1959 Georgia, an African-American farmer has been promised a piece of land by the white family he has worked for. He sees his dream threatened when his eight year old son accidentally kills the beloved yet vicious dog of the family matriarch, widow of the man who was to give him the land. An unexpected friendship develops between the child and the old woman that ultimately impacts the lives of both families.

Production Company: Anasazi Prods. IAW Walt Disney Co.
Executive Producer .... Robert Benedetti
Producer .... Cleve Landsberg
Co-Producer .... Peter Stelzer
Director .... Joan Tewkesbury
Writer .... Ken Sagoes
Cast .... Joan Plowright
Cast .... Judith Ivey
Cast .... Norman Golden
Cast .... Carl Lumbly

ON THIN ICE: THE TAI BABILONIA STORY — NBC
Drama: True Story • Addiction Story • Biography • Sports
Airdate: 11/05/90
Rating: 13.4/21   A/C: 3

After her partner's injury foils the dreams of an Olympic skater, she sinks into substance abuse, turns suicidal, and with the support of her family skates to recovery.

Production Company: Bernard Rothman Prods. IAW Janet Faust Krusi and Spectacor Films
Executive Producer .... Michael Rosenberg
Producer .... Bernard Rothman
Director .... Zale Dalen
Writer .... Brian Ross
Cast .... Rachael Crawford
Cast .... Charlie Stratton
Cast .... Denise Nicholas
Cast .... Chuck Shamata

ON WINGS OF EAGLES — NBC
Miniseries/Drama (2 nights): True Story • Action/Adventure • Foreign or Exotic Location
Airdate: 05/18/86 • 05/19/86
Rating: 17.0/28 • 21.2/34   A/C:

Based on the book by Ken Follett. Fact-based story of two American businessmen rescued from Iran in a commando raid organized by capitalist H. Ross Perot.

Production Company: Edgar J. Scherick Associates IAW Taft Entertainment TV
Executive Producer .... Edgar J. Scherick
Producer .... Lynn Raynor
Director .... Andrew V. McLaglen
Writer .... Sam Rolfe
Cast .... Richard Crenna
Cast .... Burt Lancaster
Cast .... Esai Morales
Cast .... Paul LeMat

ONCE UPON A TEXAS TRAIN — CBS
Drama: Western • Period Piece
Airdate: 01/03/88
Rating: 21.2/32   A/C:

An aging former train robber and his gang, who want to return some old loot, are hindered by a younger, vicious gang.

Production Company: Robert Papazian Prods. IAW Brigade Prods. and Rastar
Executive Producer .... Doreen Bergesen
Executive Producer .... Robert A. Papazian
Producer .... Burt Kennedy
Director .... Burt Kennedy
Writer .... Burt Kennedy
Cast .... Willie Nelson
Cast .... Jack Elam
Cast .... Chuck Connors
Cast .... Angie Dickinson
Cast .... Richard Widmark
Cast .... Shaun Cassidy

ONE AGAINST THE WIND — CBS
Drama: True Story • Period Piece • Historical Piece • Foreign or Exotic Location • Biography • WWII
Airdate: 12/01/91
Rating: 13.4/21   A/C: 2

British Countess Mary Lindell puts her life at risk as she organizes the daring escapes of Allied soldiers out of World War II Nazi occupied France.

Production Company: Republic Pictures Prods.
Executive Producer .... Karen Mack
Producer .... William Hill
Director .... Larry Elikann
Writer .... Chris Bryant
Cast .... Judy Davis
Cast .... Sam Neill
Cast .... Denholm Elliott
Cast .... Christen Anholt

ONE MORE MOUNTAIN — ABC
Drama: Period Piece • Historical Piece • True Story • Family Drama
Airdate: 3/6/94
Rating: 12.9/20   A/C: 3

In 1846, the Reed family from Illinois leave the comforts of their ranch to head west on the Oregon Trail. While overcoming wild animals and rough terrain they are put to their greatest test when they are stranded in the Sierra Mountains during a crippling blizzard. Alone and facing starvation they are forced to make some hard choices in order to survive.

Production Company: Marian Rees Assoc. IAW Walt Disney Televison
Executive Producer .... Marian Rees
Producer .... John Kuri
Producer .... Anne Hopkins
Director .... Dick Lowry
Writer .... Gerald Di Pego
Cast .... Meredith Baxter
Cast .... Chris Cooper
Cast .... Larry Drake
Cast .... Robert Duncan McNeil

ONE OF HER OWN — ABC
Drama: Woman Against The System • Cops/Detectives/Law Enforcement • Rape/Molestation
Airdate: 5/16/94
Rating: 13.5/21   A/C: 2

A rookie policewoman gets raped by a fellow officer while they're off duty. When she reports the crime she incurs the wrath of the other cops and is eventually fired from the small town police force, despite her excellent performance ratings. Taking her case public she ultimately finds justice in the legal system—winning a rape conviction against her former colleague.

Production Company: Grossbart/Barnett Prods. IAW ABC Televison
Executive Producer .... Joan Barnett
Executive Producer .... Jack Grossbart
Executive Producer .... Sydell Albert
Producer .... Don Goldman
Producer .... Linda Kent
Director .... Armand Mastroianni
Writer .... Valerie West
Cast .... Lori Loughlin
Cast .... Greg Evigan
Cast .... Valerie Landsburg
Cast .... Jeff Yagher

ONE POLICE PLAZA — CBS
Drama: Cops/Detectives/Law Enforcement
Airdate: 11/29/86
Rating: 12.3/22   A/C:

A New York police detective is assigned a case involving police corruption and gun running.

Production Company: CBS Entertainment
Producer .... Stan Hough
Director .... Jerry Jameson
Writer .... Paul King
Cast .... Robert Conrad
Cast .... Anthony Zerbe
Cast .... James Olson
Cast .... George Dzundza

ONE SPECIAL VICTORY   NBC

Drama: Medical/Disease/Mental Illness • Social Issue
• Sports
Airdate: 12/08/91
Rating: 13.1/20   A/C: 2

Based on the book "B-Ball: The Team That Never Lost A Game" by Ron Jones. When an egotistical louse is sentenced to perform community service as a basketball coach to developmentally disabled adults, he learns the meaning of love and respect as he brings them to victory in the Special Olympics.

Production Company: Susan Baerwald, Port Street
    Films, NBC Prods.
Executive Producer .... Susan Baerwald
Executive Producer .... John Larroquette
Co-Producer .... Joseph M. Ellis
Co-Producer .... Rona Edwards
Director .... Stuart Cooper
Writer .... Betty Goldberg
Cast .... John Larroquette
Cast .... Kathy Baker
Cast .... Christine Estabrook
Cast .... Dirk Blocker

ONE TERRIFIC GUY   CBS

Drama: Family Drama • Children/Teens • Rape/
Molestation • Social Issue
Airdate: 02/17/86
Rating: 19.6/30   A/C:

When a young girl accuses a popular high-school coach of molesting his students, including her, the school and town are torn apart.

Production Company: CBS Entertainment Prods.
Producer .... Mike Merrick
Producer .... Joseph Siegman
Director .... Lou Antonio
Writer .... Cynthia Whitcomb
Cast .... Wayne Rogers
Cast .... Susan Rinell
Cast .... Mariette Hartley
Cast .... Laurence Luckinbill
Cast .... Geoffrey Blake
Cast .... Brian Robbins
Cast .... Hildy Brooks

ONE WOMAN'S COURAGE   NBC

Drama: Woman In Jeopardy
Airdate: 2/28/94
Rating: 12.4/19   A/C: 2

A suburban women whose marriage is falling apart, becomes the sole witness in the fatal beating of a young woman. Even though she testifies, the psychotic killer is acquitted of the crime and he soon begins to slowly and relentlessly terrorize her. With the help of a dedicated detective she not only confronts her fears but finds an inner strength that gives her the courage to confront her attacker and begin a new life.

Production Company: Bonnie Raskin Prods. IAW
    NBC Prods.
Executive Producer .... Bonnie Raskin
Producer .... Frank Fischer
Director .... Charles Robert Carner
Writer .... John Steven Owen
Cast .... Patty Duke
Cast .... James Farentino
Cast .... Dennis Farina
Cast .... Keith Szarabajka
Cast .... Margot Kidder

ONLY ONE SURVIVED   CBS

Drama: Action/Adventure • Foreign or Exotic
Location
Airdate: 10/27/90
Rating: 6.5/12   A/C: 3

Based on the book, "Danger Adrift," by Folco Quilici. Four friends on a fishing trip in Brazil turn against one another when they attempt to salvage a boat filled with explosives.

Production Company: CBS Entertainment/RAI TV
Executive Producer .... Vittorio Galiano
Producer .... Arturo La Pegna
Producer .... Paul Picard
Director .... Folco Quilici
Writer .... John Nation
Writer .... Stephen Elkins
Cast .... Perry King
Cast .... Michael Beck
Cast .... Fabio Testi
Cast .... Yuji Okumoto

ONLY WAY OUT, THE   ABC

Drama: Suspense/Thriller
Airdate: 12/19.93
Rating: 12.1/19   A/C: 3

Based on a screenplay by Mick Ford. An architect's ex-wife becomes involved with a manipulative psychopath. When she and their three children turn to him for help his increased involvement causes problems for him at work and with his new girlfriend. The crisis ultimately escalates into a deadly confrontation with the crazed psychotic.

Production Company: Adam Prods. IAW ABC
    Prods.
Executive Producer .... Ilene Amy Berg
Executive Producer .... Robert M. Myman
Co-Executive Producer .... Sarah Lawson
Producer .... Gordon Mark
Director .... Rod Hardy
Writer .... Jerome Kass
Cast .... John Ritter
Cast .... Henry Winkler
Cast .... Stephanie Faracy
Cast .... Sam Mancuso
Cast .... Julianne Phillips

OPEN ADMISSIONS   CBS

Drama: Woman Against System • Woman Against
The System • Black Story • Social Issue
Airdate: 09/08/88
Rating: 7.5/13   A/C:

Adaptation of a Broadway play. A college teacher, burnt out by policies that encourage unqualified students to enter college, is challenged by a ghetto student who really wants to learn and would have otherwise been passed along and out.

Production Company: Mount Co. IAW Viacom
    Prods. Inc.
Executive Producer .... Stevie Phillips
Executive Producer .... Thom Mount
Co-Producer .... J. Boyce Hartman
Director .... Gus Trikonis
Writer .... Shirley Lauro
Cast .... Jane Alexander
Cast .... Dennis Farina
Cast .... Estelle Parsons
Cast .... Michael Beach

OPERATION, THE — CBS
Drama: Love Story • Suspense/Thriller • Sex/Glitz •
Murder and Murder Mystery
Airdate: 01/21/90
Rating: 20.0/30   A/C: 1

A doctor schemes with his patient/lover to
defraud his insurance company with a bogus
malpractice suit. After winning a huge
settlement, their duplicity propels them into
murder when his wife finds out the truth.

Production Company: Moress, Nanas, Golden
Entertainment IAW Viacom

Executive Producer	Herb Nanas
Executive Producer	Peter Golden
Producer	Douglas Stefan Borghi
Producer	Mike Moder
Director	Thomas J. Wright
Writer	Douglas Stefan Borghi
Cast	Joe Penny
Cast	Lisa Hartman
Cast	Jason Beghe
Cast	Kathleen Quinlan

OPPOSITES ATTRACT — NBC
Comedy: Romantic Comedy
Airdate: 10/17/90
Rating: 12.7/21   A/C: 3

A Hollywood Western star and a beautiful
councilwoman are pitted against each other in
a small town mayoral race. As the campaign
heats up, so does their relationship.

Production Company: Bar-Gene Prods. and Rastar
Prods IAW Von Zerneck-Sertner Films

Executive Producer	Frank Von Zerneck
Executive Producer	Robert M. Sertner
Producer	Susan Rice
Producer	Susan Weber-Gold
Director	Noel Nosseck
Writer	Susan Rice
Cast	Barbara Eden
Cast	John Forsythe
Cast	Rebeca Arthur
Cast	Conchata Ferrell

ORDEAL IN THE ARCTIC — ABC
Drama: Foreign or Exotic Location • True Story •
Action/Adventure • Disaster
Airdate: 2/15/93
Rating: 14.0/22   A/C: 2

Based on the book "Death and Deliverance"
by Robert Mason. In 1991, a Canadian
transport plane crashes in the arctic circle,
where Captain John Couch struggles to keep
his crew alive while rescue efforts are hampered
by blizzard conditions.

Production Company: Citadel Pictures IAW
Alliance Comm.

Executive Producer	David R. Ginsburg
Executive Producer	Ronald Cohen
Executive Producer	Robert Lantos
Producer	Jeff King
Producer	R.B. Carney
Director	Mark Sobel
Writer	Paul F. Edwards
Cast	Richard Chamberlain
Cast	Catherine Mary Stewart
Cast	Melanie Mayron
Cast	Scott Hylands

ORIGINAL SIN — NBC
Drama: Family Drama • Mafia/Mob
Airdate: 02/20/89
Rating: 16.8/26   A/C:

When a couple's young son is kidnapped, the
husband must deal with the fact that his father
is a Mafia don.

Production Company: Larry A. Thompson
Organization IAW New World TV

Executive Producer	Larry Thompson
Producer	Ian Sander
Co-Producer	Bruce Savin
Co-Producer	Barbara Title
Co-Producer	Arvin Kaufman
Director	Ron Satlof
Writer	Philip F. Messina
Cast	Ann Jillian
Cast	Charlton Heston
Cast	Robert Desiderio
Cast	Richard Portnow

ORPHEUS DESCENDING — TNT
Drama: Family Drama • Forbidden Love • Period
Piece
Airdate: 09/24/90
Rating: N/A   A/C:

Based on the play by Tennessee Williams. In
1948, life in a sleepy Mississippi backwater
town is ultimately disrupted when a itinerant
musician becomes the object of desire for two
lonely women.

Production Company: Nederlander TV and Film
Prods., Inc.

Executive Producer	Gladys Nederlander
Producer	George Manasse
Director	Peter Hall
Writer	Peter Hall
Cast	Vanessa Redgrave
Cast	Kevin Anderson
Cast	Anne Tubney
Cast	Miriam Margolyes

OTHER LOVER, THE — CBS
Drama: Forbidden Love • Love Story • Sex/Glitz
Airdate: 09/24/85
Rating: 13.8/22   A/C:

A novelist falls in love with a married woman
and becomes the "other man" in her life; not a
situation he is at all familiar or comfortable
with.

Production Company: Larry Thompson Org. IAW
Columbia TV

Executive Producer	Larry Thompson
Producer	Hugh Benson
Co-Producer	Robert Kosberg
Director	Robert Ellis Miller
Writer	Judith Parker
Writer	Susan Title
Cast	Lindsay Wagner
Cast	Jack Scalia
Cast	Max Gail
Cast	Millie Perkins

OTHER WOMEN'S CHILDREN — LIFETIME
Drama: Family Drama • Woman's Issue/Story
Airdate: 10/24/93
Rating: N/A   A/C:

Based on the book by Perri Klass. A
pediatrician, wife and mother struggles to
balance her demanding professional career
with the needs of her child and the desires of
her husband. As she tries to cope with the
pressure, her emotional mental health becomes
increasingly fragile forcing her to reexamine
her true priorities.

Production Company: Crescent Ent., Western Intl.
Comm. & Lifetime TV

Executive Producer	Dale Andrews
Executive Producer	Ilene Amy Berg
Executive Producer	Ellen Collett
Executive Producer	Wendy Dozoretz
Director	Anne Wheeler
Writer	Rama Laurie
Cast	Melanie Mayron
Cast	Geraint Wyn Davies
Cast	Eric Pospil

OUR FAMILY HONOR — ABC
Drama: Family Drama • Cops/Detectives/Law
Enforcement • Series Pilot (2 hr.) • Mafia/Mob
Airdate: 09/17/85
Rating: 15.4/25   A/C:

A feud between the families of a policeman and
a mafia boss is escalated when the mafia
patriarch tries to create a scandal that will
prevent the police patriarch from becoming
commissioner.

Production Company: Lawrence & Charles
Gordon Prods. IAW Lorimar

Executive Producer	Lawrence Gordon
Executive Producer	Charles Gordon
Producer	Ron Frazier
Director	Robert Butler
Writer	John Tanner
Writer	Arthur Bernard Lewis
Writer	Richard Freiman
Cast	Juaning Clay
Cast	Georgann Johnson
Cast	Michael Madsen
Cast	Tom Mason
Cast	Kenneth McMillan
Cast	Barbara Stewart

OUR SONS ABC

Drama: Family Drama • Medical/Disease/Mental Illness • Social Issue • Homosexuality
Airdate: 05/19/91
Rating: 12.8/21   A/C: 3

Two mothers of homosexual sons help each other overcome their guilt and learn acceptance when one of their sons acquires A.I.D.S.

Production Company: Robert Greenwald Prods.
Executive Producer .... Robert Greenwald
Executive Producer .... Carla Singer
Executive Producer .... William Hanley
Producer .... Philip Kleinbart
Producer .... Micki Dickoff
Director .... John Erman
Writer .... William Hanley
Cast .... Julie Andrews
Cast .... Ann-Margret
Cast .... Hugh Grant
Cast .... Zeljko Ivanek

OUT OF THE DARKNESS CBS

Drama: Murder and Murder Mystery • Cops/Detectives/Law Enforcement • True Crime
Airdate: 10/12/85
Rating: 17.6/30   A/C:

The true story of the NYC detectives who investigated and finally caught the "Son of Sam" killer.

Production Company: Gross-Jacobson Prods. IAW Centerpoint Prods.
Executive Producer .... Sonny Grosso
Executive Producer .... Larry Jacobson
Director .... Jud Taylor
Writer .... T.S. Cook
Cast .... Martin Sheen
Cast .... Hector Elizondo
Cast .... Matt Clark
Cast .... Jennifer Salt
Cast .... Eddie Egan

OUT OF THE DARKNESS ABC

Drama: Medical/Disease/Mental Illness
Airdate: 1/16/94
Rating: 12.5/19   A/C: 2

After suffering with schizophrenia for eighteen years a forty-three year old woman is paired with a psychiatric social worker who gets her on the promising new experimental drug, Clozapine. Placed in a group home she begins to make painfully slow progress toward sanity and must face the agonizing realization that she has lost years of her life.

Production Company: Andrew Adelson Co., IAW Anaid Film Prods. IAW ABC Prods.
Executive Producer .... Andrew Adelson
Executive Producer .... Diana Ross
Producer .... George Perkins
Director .... Larry Elikann
Writer .... Barbara Turner
Cast .... Diana Ross
Cast .... Ann Weldon
Cast .... Carl Lumbly
Cast .... Rhonda Stubbins White
Cast .... Lindsay Crouse

OUT OF TIME NBC

Drama: Cops/Detectives/Law Enforcement • Sci-Fi/Supernatural/Horror/Fantasy • Series Pilot (2 hr.)
Airdate: 07/17/88
Rating: 13.8/25   A/C:

Investigating a scientist's murder 100 years in the future, a Los Angeles policeman time-travels back to the present and links up with his great-grandfather, an eccentric cop with a technical sophistication ahead of his time.

Production Company: Columbia Pictures TV
Executive Producer .... Robert Butler
Producer .... David Latt
Director .... Robert Butler
Writer .... Kerry Lenhart
Writer .... Brian Alan Lane
Writer .... John J. Sakhart
Cast .... Bill Maher
Cast .... Rebecca Schaeffer
Cast .... Leo Rossi
Cast .... Adam Ant
Cast .... Bruce Abbott

OUT ON A LIMB ABC

Miniseries/Drama (2 nights): Foreign or Exotic Location • Biography • Sci-Fi/Supernatural/Horror/Fantasy
Airdate: 01/18/87 • 01/19/87
Rating: 13.8/20 • 16.8/25   A/C:

This part of Shirley MacLaine's autobiography includes her affair with an English politician and her growing interest in the supernatural.

Production Company: ABC Circle Films
Producer .... Stan Margulies
Director .... Robert Butler
Writer .... Shirley MacLaine
Writer .... Colin Higgins
Cast .... Shirley MacLaine
Cast .... Charles Dance
Cast .... John Heard
Cast .... Jerry Orbach
Cast .... Anne Jackson

OUT ON THE EDGE CBS

Drama: Family Drama • Children/Teens • Medical/Disease/Mental Illness • Social Issue
Airdate: 05/14/89
Rating: 14.6/23   A/C:

Not able to deal with her troubled teenage son, a mother commits him to a hospital specializing in behavior modification.

Production Company: Rich Dawn Ent. & Steve Tisch Co. IAW King-Phoenix Ent.
Executive Producer .... Steve Tisch
Executive Producer .... Mireille Soria
Producer .... Stephanie Austin
Director .... John Pasquin
Writer .... Rene Balcer
Cast .... Rick Schroder
Cast .... Mary Kay Place
Cast .... Richard Jenkins
Cast .... Natalija Nogulich
Cast .... Dakin Matthews

OUTBACK BOUND CBS

Drama: Action/Adventure • Love Story • Foreign or Exotic Location
Airdate: 10/11/88
Rating: 15.7/25   A/C:

Suddenly bereft of money and men, a glamorous Beverly Hills art gallery owner travels to Australia to sell an inherited opal mine and finds adventure and romance in the outback.

Production Company: Andrew Gottlieb Prods. in cooperation with CBS Entertainment Prods.
Executive Producer .... Robert Silberling
Producer .... Andrew Gottlieb
Director .... John Llewellyn Moxey
Writer .... Elizabeth Comici
Writer .... Luciano Comici
Cast .... Donna Mills
Cast .... John Meillon
Cast .... Andrew Clarke
Cast .... Robert Harper
Cast .... Nina Foch
Cast .... John Schneider

OUTRAGE CBS

Drama: Man Against The System • Courtroom Drama • Social Issue
Airdate: 02/24/86
Rating: 21.7/34   A/C:

From Henry Denker's novel about a hot-shot lawyer who uses questionable tactics to defend an old man tried for the admitted killing of a black man who, he says, would have been convicted of his daughter's rape-murder except for a technicality.

Production Company: Irwin Allen Prods. IAW Columbia Pictures TV
Producer .... Irwin Allen
Director .... Walter Grauman
Writer .... Henry Denker
Cast .... Robert Preston
Cast .... Beau Bridges
Cast .... Burgess Meredith
Cast .... Mel Ferrer
Cast .... William Allen Young
Cast .... Anthony Newley
Cast .... Linda Purl

OUTSIDE WOMAN, THE CBS

Drama: Love Story • True Crime • Prison and Prison Camp
Airdate: 02/12/89
Rating: 14.3/22   A/C:

Fact-based story of Joyce Matox, a woman who visits prisoners with other members of her church, falls in love with an inmate and breaks him out of jail with a helicopter.

Production Company: Green-Epstein Prods.
Executive Producer .... Jim Green
Executive Producer .... Allen Epstein
Producer .... Lou Antonio
Co-Producer .... Leigh Murray
Director .... Lou Antonio
Writer .... William Blinn
Cast .... Sharon Gless
Cast .... Scott Glenn
Cast .... Kyle Secor
Cast .... Max Gail

OVER MY DEAD BODY   CBS

Mystery: Murder and Murder Mystery • Cops/
Detectives/Law Enforcement • Series Pilot (2 hr.) •
Cross-Cultural Story
Airdate: 10/26/90
Rating: 12.4/23   A/C: 2

A Scotland Yard detective-turned-mystery writer confronts corruption in San Francisco when he helps an obituary writer investigate a murder she has witnessed.

Production Company: Universal Television
Executive Producer .... David Chisholm
Executive Producer .... William Link
Producer .... Ken Topolsky
Director .... Bradford May
Writer .... David Chisholm
Cast .... Edward Woodward
Cast .... Jessica Lundy
Cast .... Jill Tracy
Cast .... David Wells

OVEREXPOSED   ABC

Drama: Sex/Glitz • True Story
Airdate: 10/11/92
Rating: 14.4/23   A/C: 1

An unbalanced businessman sets out to destroy his co-worker's wife by sending pornographic video tapes of their illicit liaison to the entire town . Unable to gain police protection or legal support, the outraged husband takes matters into his own hands.

Production Company: LOMO Prods.
Executive Producer .... Oprah Winfrey
Executive Producer .... Debra DiMaio
Director .... Robert Markowitz
Writer .... Christine Berardo
Writer .... Adam Greenman
Writer .... Harlan Woods
Cast .... Marcy Walker
Cast .... Dan Lauria
Cast .... Terence Knox
Cast .... Taylor Miller

OVERKILL: THE AILEEN WUORNOS STORY   CBS

Drama: True Crime • Murder and Murder Mystery
Airdate: 11/17/92
Rating: 15.4/25   A/C: 2

In 1991, America's first convicted female serial killer, Aileen Wuoronos worked as a hooker while hitchhiking around Florida. She murders seven of her customers who she felt abused her, leaving their bodies on rural backroads. Police and FBI agents are stumped at first but eventually arrest the tormented woman who now sits on death row.

Production Company: Republic Pictures IAW
    C.M. Two Prods.
Executive Producer .... Chuck McLain
Producer .... William Beaudine, Jr.
Director .... Peter Levin
Writer .... Fred Mills
Cast .... Jean Smart
Cast .... Park Overall
Cast .... Tim Grimm
Cast .... Ernie Lively

P. S. I LUV U   CBS

Drama: Cops/Detectives/Law Enforcement •
Suspense/Thriller • Series Pilot (2 hr.) • Mafia/Mob
Airdate: 09/15/91
Rating: 15.7/25   A/C: 1

When a New York cop uses a female con artist to bait a trap for a Mafia boss, they are both marked for murder. The government sets them up as husband and wife in a witness protection program in Palm Springs, forcing this odd couple to work together.

Production Company: CBS Entertainment Prods.
    IAW Glen Larson Prods.
Executive Producer .... Glen A. Larson
Producer .... Peter Hunt
Producer .... J.C. Larson
Director .... Peter H. Hunt
Writer .... Glen A. Larson
Writer .... Bob Shayne
Cast .... Connie Sellecca
Cast .... Greg Evigan
Cast .... Earl Holliman
Cast .... Ken Howard

PACK OF LIES   CBS

Drama: Family Drama • Suspense/Thriller • Foreign or Exotic Location • Period Piece
Airdate: 04/26/87
Rating: 18.2/30   A/C:

Adaptation of Hugh Whitemore's stage play. In 1961 England, a British counterintelligence agent prevails on a couple to spy on a another couple who are their closest friends and suspected of espionage.

Production Company: Robert Halmi Inc.
Producer .... Robert Halmi, Sr.
Director .... Anthony Page
Writer .... Ralph Gallup
Cast .... Ellen Burstyn
Cast .... Teri Garr
Cast .... Alan Bates
Cast .... David Corti
Cast .... Daniel Benzali

PAIR OF ACES   CBS

Drama: Murder and Murder Mystery • Cops/
Detectives/Law Enforcement • Western • Buddy Story
Airdate: 01/14/90
Rating: 17.8/28   A/C: 1 (Tie)

When the jails are full, a Texas Ranger is forced to "baby-sit" a convicted safecracker while tracking a serial killer of teen-age girls. To the Ranger's surprise, the safecracker/magician is more help than hindrance.

Production Company: Pedernales Films IAW
    Once Upon A Time Films Ltd.
Executive Producer .... Stanley Brooks
Executive Producer .... Willie Nelson
Producer .... Cyrus Yavneh
Co-Executive Producer .... Bud Shrake
Co-Executive Producer .... Gary Cartwright
Director .... Aaron Lipstadt
Writer .... Bud Shrake
Writer .... Gary Cartwright
Cast .... Willie Nelson
Cast .... Kris Kristofferson
Cast .... Helen Shaver
Cast .... Jane Cameron

PALACE GUARD   CBS

Drama: Suspense/Thriller • Foreign or Exotic Location • Series Pilot (2 hr.) • Cops/Detectives/Law Enforcement
Airdate: 10/18/91
Rating: 7.4/14   A/C: 3

An ex-hotel thief is hired by a posh resort chain to be the new head of security. With the reluctant help of his boss, the PR director, he investigates a suspicious suicide at the Acapulco hotel.

Production Company: Stephen J. Cannell Prods.
Executive Producer .... Stephen J. Cannell
Executive Producer .... Jacob Epstein
Executive Producer .... Ken Solarz
Producer .... Alex Beaton
Co-Producer .... Alan Cassidy
Director .... James A. Contner
Writer .... Stephen J. Cannell
Cast .... D.W. Moffett
Cast .... Marcy Walker
Cast .... Tony Lo Bianco
Cast .... Robert Viharo

PALS   CBS

Comedy: Buddy Story
Airdate: 02/28/87
Rating: 11.1/19   A/C:

Two aging ex-Army pals who live in a trailer park find several million dollars in a car trunk. They experience exciting wealth- and danger-filled adventures before happily returning to their former, simpler life.

Production Company: Robert Halmi Inc.
Executive Producer .... Robert Halmi, Sr.
Director .... Lou Antonio
Writer .... Michael Norell
Cast .... Don Ameche
Cast .... George C. Scott
Cast .... Sylvia Sidney
Cast .... Susan Rinell

PANCHO BARNES   CBS

Drama (3 hours): Woman Against The System • Period Piece • Action/Adventure • Biography
Airdate: 10/24/88
Rating: 11.7/18   A/C:

Biography of the female flier and all-around roughneck who ended up as desert bartender and confidante to supersonic test pilots, including Chuck Yeager.

Production Company: Blue Andre Prods. IAW
    Orion TV
Executive Producer .... Blue Andre
Producer .... Albert J. Salzer
Director .... Richard T. Heffron
Writer .... John Michael Hayes
Cast .... Valerie Bertinelli
Cast .... Todd Allen
Cast .... Ted Wass
Cast .... James Stephens
Cast .... Cynthia Harris
Cast .... Geoffrey Lewis

PAPER DOLLS · ABC

Drama: Series Pilot (2 hr.) · Sex/Glitz
Airdate: 09/23/84
Rating: 18.4/29 · A/C:

The business and private lives of the people connected with the glitz and glamour of the modeling world.

Production Company: Mandy Films Prod. IAW MGM-UA TV

Executive Producer	Leonard Goldberg
Producer	Michele Rappaport
Director	Harry Winer
Writer	Jennifer Miller
Cast	Lloyd Bridges
Cast	Morgan Fairchild
Cast	Jennifer Warren
Cast	Brenda Vaccaro
Cast	Dack Rambo
Cast	Mimi Rogers

PARALLEL LIVES · SHOWTIME

Drama: Romantic Comedy
Airdate: 8/5/94
Rating: N/A · A/C:

When the well-to-do alumni of a college fraternity and sorority are brought together at a reunion weekend, old friendships, romances and rivalries are fondly rekindled. The fun and games come to an abrupt conclusion when a fatal car accident forces the group to confront their lives in ways that change them forever.

Production Company: Linda Yellen Productions IAW Showtime Networks Inc.

Executive Producer	Linda Yellen
Director	Linda Yellen
Writer	Giesela Bernice
Cast	James Belushi
Cast	James Brolin
Cast	Liza Minnelli
Cast	Treat Williams
Cast	Jill Eikenberry

PARIS TROUT · SHOWTIME

Drama: Murder and Murder Mystery · Period Piece · Courtroom Drama · Black Story · Family Violence · Social Issue
Airdate: 04/20/91
Rating: N/A · A/C:

Based on the novel by Pete Dexter. A bigoted white loan shark kills a black girl and begins to go insane when he realizes his wife and the local court are turning against him.

Production Company: Viacom Pictures IAW Konigsberg/Sanitsky

Executive Producer	Diana Kerew
Producer	Frank Konigsberg
Producer	Larry Sanitsky
Director	Stephen Gyllenhaal
Writer	Pete Dexter
Cast	Dennis Hopper
Cast	Barbara Hershey
Cast	Ed Harris
Cast	Eric Lifford

PARKER KANE · NBC

Drama: Murder and Murder Mystery · Cops/Detectives/Law Enforcement · Toxic Waste/Environmental · Series Pilot (2 hr.)
Airdate: 08/05/90
Rating: 8.6/15 · A/C: 4

While a hotshot cop turned P.I. investigates his best friend's murder, he uncovers a toxic waste dumping operation that threatens untold lives.

Production Company: Parker Kane Prods., Silver Pictures TV IAW Orion TV Ent.

Executive Producer	Joel Silver
Producer	Barry Josephson
Co-Producer	Cleve Reinhard
Co-Producer	Peter Lenkov
Director	Steve Perry
Writer	Peter Lenkov
Cast	Jeff Fahey
Cast	Marisa Tomei
Cast	Drew Snyder
Cast	Richard Zobel
Cast	Chino "Fats" Williams
Cast	Amanda Pays

PARTNERS 'N LOVE · FAMILY

Comedy: Romantic Comedy
Airdate: 11/27/92
Rating: N/A · A/C:

A divorced couple who are still business partners discover that due to a clerical error they are still legally married. During a hostile takeover of their company by a corporate weasel, who had a high school crush on the wife, the husband reevaluates his true feelings and vows to save his ex-marriage.

Production Company: Atlantis Films, Barry Jossen Prods. IAW The Family Channel

Executive Producer	Peter Sussman
Executive Producer	Barry Jossen
Producer	Larry Raskin
Director	Eugene Levy
Writer	Josh Goldstein
Cast	Eugene Levy
Cast	Linda Kash
Cast	John James
Cast	Jayne Eastwood

PASSION AND PARADISE · ABC

Miniseries/Drama (2 nights): True Crime · Period Piece · Exotic/Foreign Location · Sex/Glitz · Mafia/Mob · Murder and Murder Mystery
Airdate: 02/19/89 · 02/21/89
Rating: 11.8/19 · 12.5/20 · A/C:

Fact-based story of Alfred de Marigny, a ladies' man who moved to the Bahamas during WWII, married an heiress, and, after alienating the entire Bahamian power structure, was accused of murdering his father-in-law.

Production Company: Picturebase International & Primedia Prods. IAW Leonard Hill Films

Executive Producer	Leonard Hill
Executive Producer	Peter Jeffries
Executive Producer	W. Patterson Ferns
Producer	Michael Custance
Producer	Ian McDougall
Co-Producer	Joel Fields
Director	Harvey Hart
Writer	Andrew Laskos
Cast	Armand Assante
Cast	Michael Sarrazin
Cast	Andrew Ray
Cast	Catherine Mary Stewart
Cast	Linda Griffiths
Cast	Kevin McCarthy
Cast	Wayne Rogers
Cast	Rod Steiger
Cast	Mariette Hartley

PASSION FOR JUSTICE, A: HAZEL BRANNON SMITH STORY · ABC

Drama: Biography · True Story · Woman Against The System · Period Piece · Historical Piece
Airdate: 4/17/94
Rating: 11.1/18 · A/C: 3

In 1950's Mississippi, liberal newspaper editor Hazel Brannon Smith begins publishing articles attacking racism in her hometown. Going up against the bigoted sheriff and local segregationists she becomes a target for violence and intimidation. Her crusading determination and hard hitting journalism ultimately win her the Pulitzer Prize for editorial writing in 1964, the first woman to be so honored.

Production Company: David Brooks Prods. IAW Catfish Prods., Saban/Scherick Prods & Proctor & Gamble Prods.

Executive Producer	Edgar J. Scherick
Executive Producer	David Brooks
Executive Producer	James Keach
Executive Producer	Jane Seymour
Producer	Mitch Engel
Director	James Keach
Writer	Rama Laurie Stagner
Cast	Jane Seymour
Cast	D.W. Moffett
Cast	Lou Walker
Cast	Michelle Joyner

PASSIONS   CBS

Drama: Family Drama • Woman's Issue/Story
Airdate: 10/01/84
Rating: 22.4/34   A/C:

When a man dies, his wife and daughter learn of his adultery and the wife vows revenge on his mistress.

Production Company: Carson Prods.
Executive Producer .... John J. McMahon
Producer .... Bobbi Frank
Director .... Sandor Stern
Writer .... Janet Greek
Writer .... Robin Maxwell
Cast .... Lindsay Wagner
Cast .... Joanne Woodward
Cast .... Richard Crenna
Cast .... Mason Adams

PASSPORT TO MURDER   NBC

Drama: Murder and Murder Mystery • Foreign or Exotic Location
Airdate: 3/7/93
Rating: 11.7/19   A/C: 2

A recently divorced New York socialite travels to Paris on a vacation and gets mixed up in international espionage and murder. She gets romantically involved with a down on his luck private eye out solve the big case.

Production Company: FTM Prods.
Executive Producer .... Anthony Massucci
Producer .... Peter Katz
Director .... David Hemmings
Writer .... Alfred Monacella
Cast .... Connie Sellecca
Cast .... Ed Marinaro
Cast .... Pavel Douglas

PAST TENSE   SHOWTIME

Drama: Cops/Detectives/Law Enforcement • Murder and Murder Mystery • Psychological Thriller
Airdate: 6/12/94
Rating: N/A   A/C:

A veteran cop and aspiring mystery author becomes involved with his provocative new neighbor but when he finds her brutally murdered and begins investigating the crime he is confronted with strange occurrences which begin to haunt him- as reality, imagination, dream and hallucination begin to blur together.

Production Company: Arnold Kopelson Prods.
    IAW Showtime Networks Inc.
Executive Producer .... Arnold Kopelson
Executive Producer .... Anne Kopelson
Producer .... Stephen Brown
Producer .... Nana Greenwald
Co-Producer .... Sanford Panitch
Director .... Graeme Clifford
Writer .... Scott Frost
Writer .... Miguel Tejada-Flores
Cast .... Scott Glenn
Cast .... Anthony LaPaglia
Cast .... Lara Flynn Boyle

PAYOFF   SHOWTIME

Drama: Cops/Detectives/Law Enforcement • Suspense/Thriller • Mafia/Mob
Airdate: 06/22/91
Rating: N/A   A/C:

An ex-cop masterminds a plot to avenge his parents' death, both killed by a high-powered Mafioso.

Production Company: Viacom Pictures, Aurora Prods.
Executive Producer .... Douglas S. Cook
Producer .... William Stuart
Director .... Stuart Cooper
Writer .... Douglas S. Cook
Writer .... David Weisberg
Cast .... Keith Carradine
Cast .... Harry Dean Stanton
Cast .... Kim Greist
Cast .... John Saxon

PENALTY PHASE   CBS

Drama: Courtroom Drama • Social Issue
Airdate: 12/18/86
Rating: 15.8/26   A/C:

When the judge presiding over the penalty phase of a mass murderer's trial hears that the arrest may have been legally flawed, he must decide whether to suppress the evidence or let the man go.

Production Company: Tamara Asseyev Prods.
    IAW New World TV
Producer .... Tamara Asseyev
Director .... Tony Richardson
Writer .... Gale Patrick Hickman
Cast .... Peter Strauss
Cast .... Mitchell Ryan
Cast .... Millie Perkins
Cast .... Jonelle Allen
Cast .... Art LaFleur

PENTHOUSE, THE   ABC

Drama: Woman In Jeopardy • Suspense/Thriller
Airdate: 03/05/89
Rating: 13.4/21   A/C:

A young homicidal fugitive from an insane asylum holds the rich young daughter of a record-company executive hostage in her apartment.

Production Company: Greene-White Prods./
    Spectator Films
Executive Producer .... David Greene
Executive Producer .... Steve White
Co-Executive Producer .... Jerry Reger
Producer .... Harold Tichenor
Director .... David Greene
Writer .... Frank De Felitta
Writer .... William Wood
Cast .... Robin Givens
Cast .... Robert Guillaume
Cast .... Donnelly Rhodes
Cast .... Cedric Smith
Cast .... David Hewlett

PEOPLE ACROSS THE LAKE, THE   NBC

Drama: Family Drama • Murder and Murder Mystery • Suspense/Thriller
Airdate: 10/03/88
Rating: 17.3/27   A/C:

An urban couple and their two children move to a community beside a lake into which a homicidal maniac continues to toss human body parts.

Production Company: Bill McCutcheon Prods.
Executive Producer .... Bill McCutchen
Producer .... Richard L. O'Connor
Director .... Arthur Allan Seidelman
Writer .... Dalene Young
Cast .... Valerie Harper
Cast .... Barry Corbin
Cast .... Tammy Lauren
Cast .... Daryl Anderson
Cast .... Gerald McRaney

PEOPLE LIKE US   NBC

Miniseries/Drama (2 nights): Family Drama • Murder and Murder Mystery • Sex/Glitz • Homosexuality
Airdate: 05/13/90 • 05/14/90
Rating: 9.4/16 • 10.5/17   A/C: 3 • 3

Story based on Dominick Dunne's best-selling novel about an obsessed journalist bent on avenging his daughter's murder and a social-climbing young woman hiding her dangerous past.

Production Company: CM Two Productions IAW
    ITC Productions
Executive Producer .... Chuck McLain
Producer .... William Beaudine, Jr.
Director .... Billy Hale
Writer .... Mart Crowley
Writer .... Kathleen A. Shelley
Cast .... Ben Gazzara
Cast .... Eva Marie Saint
Cast .... Connie Sellecca
Cast .... Dennis Farina

PERCY & THUNDER   TNT

Drama: Buddy Story • Sports
Airdate: 9/7/93
Rating: N/A   A/C:

A retired fighter now a manger-trainer of a hot young middleweight contender tries to keep his protege out of the hands of a manipulative boxing promoter who wants to make big money on the future champ.

Production Company: Amblin TV IAW Brandman Prods.
Executive Producer .... Michael Brandman
Producer .... Leanne Moore
Co-Producer .... Steven Brandman
Director .... Ivan Dixon
Writer .... Art Washington
Cast .... James Earl Jones
Cast .... Billy Dee Williams
Cast .... Courtney Vance
Cast .... Robert Wuhl

Perfect Bride, The — USA

Drama: Suspense/Thriller
Airdate: 06/26/91
Rating: N/A   A/C:

A young woman uncovers the murderous past of her soon to be sister-in-law, who seems just too good to be true.

Production Company: Image Organization and
    Heron Communications

Executive Producer	Glenn Greene
Executive Producer	Jon Turtle
Executive Producer	David Bixler
Producer	Pierre David
Producer	Monica Webb
Director	Terrence O'Hara
Writer	Claire Montgomery
Writer	Monte Montgomery
Cast	Sammi Davis
Cast	Kelly Preston
Cast	Linden Ashby

Perfect Harmony — DISNEY

Drama: Children/Teens • Period Piece • Black Story
• Social Issue
Airdate: 03/31/91
Rating: N/A   A/C:

A choirboy at an all-white Southern prep school befriends a musically-gifted, local black teen and together they overcome racial bigotry through their mutual love of music.

Production Company: Sea Breeze Prods.

Executive Producer	Todd Black
Executive Producer	Joe Wizan
Producer	Mickey Borofsky
Director	Will MacKenzie
Writer	David Obst
Cast	Peter Scolari
Cast	Darren McGavin
Cast	Catherine Mary Stewart
Cast	Moses Gunn

Perfect People — ABC

Comedy: Romantic Comedy
Airdate: 02/29/88
Rating: 13.3/21   A/C:

Twenty years into their marriage, a middle-aged couple launch themselves into the frenzied pursuit of physical rejuvenation.

Production Company: Robert Greenwald Prods.

Executive Producer	Robert Greenwald
Producer	Heidi M. Frey
Director	Bruce Seth Green
Writer	Gregory Goodell
Cast	Lauren Hutton
Cast	Perry King
Cast	Karen Valentine
Cast	David Leisure
Cast	Priscilla Barnes

Perfect Tribute, The — ABC

Drama: Children/Teens • Period Piece • Historical
Piece
Airdate: 04/21/91
Rating: 10.5/18   A/C: 2

Based on a short story by Mary Andrews. During the Civil War, a Southern boy searches for his brother wounded in the battle of Gettysburg and encounters a distraught and beleaguered Lincoln.

Production Company: Dorothea Petrie Prods. IAW
    Proctor & Gamble Prods. & W.I.N.

Executive Producer	Dorothea Petrie
Producer	Joan Kramer
Producer	David Heeley
Director	Jack Bender
Writer	Dennis Brown
Cast	Lukas Haas
Cast	Campbell Scott
Cast	Jason Robards, Jr.
Cast	Katherine Helmond

Perfect Witness — HBO

Drama: Murder and Murder Mystery • Man Against
The System • Social Issue • Mafia/Mob
Airdate: 10/28/89
Rating: N/A   A/C:

When a struggling New York City bar owner witnesses a contract hit, he agrees to testify against the killer, putting himself and his family in jeopardy.

Production Company: HBO with Granger
    Productions

Executive Producer	Wayne Rogers
Executive Producer	Amy H. Rogers
Producer	Elaine H. Sperber
Director	Robert Mandel
Writer	Terry Curtis Fox
Writer	Ron Hutchinson
Cast	Brian Dennehy
Cast	Aidan Quinn
Cast	Stockard Channing

Perry Mason Mystery, A: The Case Of The Lethal Lifestyle — NBC

Mystery: Murder and Murder Mystery • Courtroom
Drama
Airdate: 5/10/94
Rating: 10.8/18   A/C: 2

A former associate of Mason's defends a chess player accused of poisoning a blackmailing TV personality.

Production Company: Dean Hargrove Prods. and
    Fred Silverman Co. IAW Viacom

Executive Producer	Dean Hargrove
Executive Producer	Fred Silverman
Co-Executive Producer	Joel Steiger
Producer	Barry Steinberg
Director	Helaine Head
Writer	Bruce Franklin Singer
Cast	Hal Holbrook
Cast	Barbara Hale
Cast	James Stephens
Cast	Dixie Carter

Perry Mason Mystery: The Case Of The Wicked Wives — NBC

Mystery: Murder and Murder Mystery • Courtroom
Drama
Airdate: 12/17/93
Rating: 10.2/19   A/C: 2

With Perry away in Washington, his old pal, Anthony Caruso is now handling his cases. The opera singing lawyer defends a women accused of of killing her fashion photographer husband while he was shooting a retrospective with his four top models who also were his ex-wives.

Production Company: Fred Silverman Co., Dean
    Hargrove Prods. IAW Viacom

Executive Producer	Dean Hargrove
Executive Producer	Fred Silverman
Co-Executive Producer	Joel Steiger
Producer	Billy Ray Smith
Producer	Barry Steinberg
Director	Christian Nyby II
Writer	Joyce Burditt
Cast	Paul Sorvino
Cast	Barbara Hale
Cast	William R. Moses
Cast	Maud Adams

Perry Mason Returns — NBC

Mystery: Courtroom Drama • Murder and Murder
Mystery
Airdate: 12/01/85
Rating: 27.2/39   A/C:

Perry Mason, now a judge, steps down from the bench to defend his former secretary who is charged with murdering her tycoon boss.

Production Company: Intermedia Prods. &
    Stathmore Prods. IAW Viacom Prods.

Executive Producer	Fred Silverman
Executive Producer	Dean Hargrove
Producer	Barry Steinberg
Director	Ron Satlof
Writer	Dean Hargrove
Cast	Raymond Burr
Cast	William Katt
Cast	Holland Taylor
Cast	Richard Anderson
Cast	Barbara Hale

Perry Mason: The Case of the All-Star Assassin — NBC

Mystery: Murder and Murder Mystery • Courtroom
Drama • Sports
Airdate: 11/19/89
Rating: 16.8/26   A/C: 1

Mason is called in by protege Malansky to help defend an athlete accused of hiring a hit man to kill an unethical team owner. Meanwhile Malansky and his girlfriend track down clues, unearthing a whole slew of people who hated the victim.

Production Company: The Fred Silverman Co. &
    Dean Hargrove Prods. & Viacom

Executive Producer	Fred Silverman
Executive Producer	Dean Hargrove
Producer	Peter Katz
Director	Christian Nyby II
Writer	Robert Hamilton
Cast	Raymond Burr
Cast	Pernell Roberts
Cast	William R. Moses

PERRY MASON: THE CASE OF THE AVENGING ACE — NBC

Mystery: Murder and Murder Mystery • Courtroom Drama
Airdate: 02/28/88
Rating: 17.4/26   A/C:

Mason exonerates an Air Force officer convicted of murdering a land developer's assistant.

Production Company: Fred Silverman Co. & Strathmore Prods. IAW Viacom
Executive Producer .... Dean Hargrove
Executive Producer .... Fred Silverman
Producer .... Peter Katz
Director .... Christian Nyby II
Writer .... Lee David Zlotoff
Cast .... Raymond Burr
Cast .... Barbara Hale
Cast .... William Katt
Cast .... Larry Wilcox
Cast .... Erin Gray
Cast .... David Ogden Stiers
Cast .... Patty Duke

PERRY MASON: THE CASE OF THE DEFIANT DAUGHTER — NBC

Mystery: Murder and Murder Mystery • Courtroom Drama
Airdate: 09/30/90
Rating: 14.7/24   A/C: 1

A precocious thirteen-year-old girl convinces Mason to help defend her father who is framed in a Las Vegas murder.

Production Company: Fred Silverman Co. and Dean Hargrove Prods. IAW Viacom
Executive Producer .... Fred Silverman
Executive Producer .... Dean Hargrove
Executive Producer .... Joel Steiger
Producer .... Billy Ray Smith
Producer .... David Solomon
Director .... Christian Nyby II
Writer .... Anne Collins
Cast .... Raymond Burr
Cast .... Barbara Hale
Cast .... William R. Moses
Cast .... Robert Culp

PERRY MASON: THE CASE OF THE DESPERATE DECEPTION — NBC

Mystery: Murder and Murder Mystery • Courtroom Drama • Foreign or Exotic Location • Nazis
Airdate: 03/11/90
Rating: 17.0/27   A/C: 1

In Paris, a Marine finds a man he believes is the ex-SS officer responsible for killing his relatives in a concentration camp. When the German is shot during their confrontation, Mason defends the Marine.

Production Company: Fred Silverman Co., Dean Hargrove Prods. - Viacom
Executive Producer .... Fred Silverman
Executive Producer .... Dean Hargrove
Producer .... Peter Katz
Director .... Christian Nyby II
Writer .... George Eckstein
Cast .... Ian Bannen
Cast .... Raymond Burr
Cast .... Barbara Hale
Cast .... William R. Moses

PERRY MASON: THE CASE OF THE FATAL FASHION — NBC

Mystery: Murder and Murder Mystery • Courtroom Drama
Airdate: 09/24/91
Rating: 14.6/23   A/C: 2

In New York City, Perry defends an old friend of Della Street's, a fashion magazine editor accused of killing a bitchy competitor.

Production Company: Dean Hargrove Prods., The Fred Silverman Co. and Viacom
Executive Producer .... Dean Hargrove
Executive Producer .... Fred Silverman
Co-Executive Producer .... Joel Steiger
Producer .... Billy Ray Smith
Producer .... David Solomon
Director .... Christian Nyby II
Writer .... Robert Janes
Cast .... Raymond Burr
Cast .... Barbara Hale
Cast .... William R. Moses
Cast .... Valerie Harper
Cast .... Diana Muldaur

PERRY MASON: THE CASE OF THE FATAL FRAMING — NBC

Mystery: Murder and Murder Mystery • Courtroom Drama
Airdate: 03/01/92
Rating: 12.9/20   A/C: 2

Legal eagle Perry Mason defends a photographer framed for the murder of an art world schemer.

Production Company: Viacom Prods., The Fred Silverman Co., Dean Hargrove Prods.
Executive Producer .... Fred Silverman
Executive Producer .... Dean Hargrove
Producer .... Billy Ray Smith
Producer .... David Solomon
Co-Executive Producer .... Joel Steiger
Director .... Christian Nyby II
Writer .... Sean Cholodenko
Cast .... Raymond Burr
Cast .... Barbara Hale
Cast .... William R. Moses
Cast .... David Soul

PERRY MASON: THE CASE OF THE GLASS COFFIN — NBC

Mystery: Murder and Murder Mystery • Courtroom Drama
Airdate: 05/14/91
Rating: 12.8/22   A/C: 2

Perry Mason is on the scene defending a magician accused of murdering his attractive, blackmailing assistant.

Production Company: Fred Silverman Co. and Dean Hargrove Prods. IAW Viacom
Executive Producer .... Dean Hargrove
Executive Producer .... Fred Silverman
Producer .... Billy Ray Smith
Producer .... David Solomon
Producer .... Joel Steiger
Director .... Christian Nyby II
Writer .... Brian Clemens
Cast .... Raymond Burr
Cast .... Barbara Hale
Cast .... William R. Moses
Cast .... Peter Scolari

PERRY MASON: THE CASE OF THE HEARTBROKEN BRIDE — NBC

Mystery: Murder and Murder Mystery • Courtroom Drama
Airdate: 10/30/92
Rating: 12.1/21   A/C: 1

Perry defends a pop singing star for the murder of her soon-to-be husband's obnoxious uncle.

Production Company: Dean Hargrove Prods., Fred Silverman Co. IAW Viacom Enter.
Executive Producer .... Dean Hargrove
Executive Producer .... Fred Silverman
Producer .... Billy Ray Smith
Producer .... Barry Steinberg
Director .... Christian Nyby II
Writer .... Brian Clemens
Writer .... Gerry Conway
Cast .... Raymond Burr
Cast .... Barbara Hale
Cast .... Ronny Cox
Cast .... Linda Blair

PERRY MASON: THE CASE OF THE KILLER KISS NBC

Mystery: Murder and Murder Mystery • Courtroom Drama
Airdate: 11/29/93
Rating: 19.3/29   A/C: 1

Legal eagle, Perry Mason defends a soap opera actress accused of killing her co-star, a repugnant actor who was hated by cast and crew.

Production Company: Dean Hargrove Prods., Fred
    Silverman Co. IAW Viacom Prods.
Executive Producer .... Fred Silverman
Executive Producer .... Dean Hargrove
Co-Executive Producer .... Joel Steiger
Producer .... Billy Ray Smith
Director .... Christian Nyby II
Writer .... Gerry Conway
Cast .... Raymond Burr
Cast .... Barbara Hale
Cast .... Stuart Damon
Cast .... Genie Francis
Cast .... Linda Dano

PERRY MASON: THE CASE OF THE LADY IN THE LAKE NBC

Mystery: Murder and Murder Mystery • Courtroom Drama
Airdate: 05/15/88
Rating: 22.6/35   A/C:

Mason exonerates a man on trial for killing his missing, rich wife.

Production Company: Fred Silverman Co. &
    Strathmore Prods. IAW Viacom
Executive Producer .... Fred Silverman
Executive Producer .... Dean Hargrove
Producer .... Peter Katz
Director .... Ron Satlof
Writer .... Shel Willens
Cast .... Raymond Burr
Cast .... Barbara Hale
Cast .... William Katt
Cast .... David Hasselhoff
Cast .... David Ogden Stiers
Cast .... John Beck
Cast .... Audra Lindley

PERRY MASON: THE CASE OF THE LOST LOVE NBC

Mystery: Murder and Murder Mystery • Courtroom Drama
Airdate: 02/23/87
Rating: 21.3/33   A/C:

Perry defends his old flame's husband on a murder charge.

Production Company: Fred Silverman Co. &
    Strathmore Prods. IAW Viacom
Executive Producer .... Fred Silverman
Executive Producer .... Dean Hargrove
Producer .... Barry Steinberg
Director .... Ron Satlof
Writer .... Anne Collins
Cast .... Raymond Burr
Cast .... Barbara Hale
Cast .... William Katt
Cast .... Gordon Jump
Cast .... Jean Simmons
Cast .... David Ogden Stiers
Cast .... Robert Mandan
Cast .... Gene Barry

PERRY MASON: THE CASE OF THE MALIGNED MOBSTER NBC

Mystery: Murder and Murder Mystery • Courtroom Drama
Airdate: 02/11/91
Rating: 14.0/22   A/C: 2

Perry Mason comes to the aid of an ex-mob boss accused of murdering his wife.

Production Company: Viacom Prods.
Executive Producer .... Fred Silverman
Executive Producer .... Dean Hargrove
Producer .... Billy Ray Smith
Producer .... David Solomon
Director .... Ron Satlof
Writer .... Sean Cholodenko
Cast .... Raymond Burr
Cast .... Barbara Hale
Cast .... William R. Moses
Cast .... Mason Adams

PERRY MASON: THE CASE OF THE MURDERED MADAM NBC

Mystery: Murder and Murder Mystery • Courtroom Drama
Airdate: 10/04/87
Rating: 18.1/29   A/C:

Mason defends a madam's husband who is accused of her murder.

Production Company: Fred Silverman Co. &
    Strathmore Prods. IAW Viacom Prods.
Executive Producer .... Fred Silverman
Director .... Ron Satlof
Writer .... Patricia Green
Cast .... Raymond Burr
Cast .... Barbara Hale
Cast .... William Katt
Cast .... Ann Jillian

PERRY MASON: THE CASE OF THE MUSICAL MURDERS NBC

Mystery: Murder and Murder Mystery • Courtroom Drama
Airdate: 04/09/89
Rating: 17.4/26   A/C:

Perry Mason investigates the murder of a widely disliked stage director. He defends a framed suspect and traps the killer into a confession on the witness stand.

Production Company: Fred Silverman Co. and
    Dean Hargrove Prods. w/Viacom
Executive Producer .... Dean Hargrove
Executive Producer .... Fred Silverman
Producer .... Peter Katz
Co-Producer .... David Solomon
Director .... Christian Nyby II
Writer .... George Eckstein
Cast .... Raymond Burr
Cast .... Alexandra Paul
Cast .... William R. Moses
Cast .... Debbie Reynolds
Cast .... Jerry Orbach

PERRY MASON: THE CASE OF THE NOTORIOUS NUN NBC

Mystery: Murder and Murder Mystery • Courtroom Drama
Airdate: 05/25/86
Rating: 23.3/42   A/C:

Mason defends a nun accused of killing a priest who was looking into the archdiocese's finances.

Production Company: Intermedia & Strathmore
    Prods. IAW Viacom
Executive Producer .... Fred Silverman
Executive Producer .... Dean Hargrove
Producer .... Barry Steinberg
Director .... Ron Satlof
Writer .... Joel Steiger
Cast .... Raymond Burr
Cast .... Barbara Hale
Cast .... Tom Bosley
Cast .... William Katt
Cast .... Michele Greene
Cast .... Arthur Hill
Cast .... Timothy Bottoms

PERRY MASON: THE CASE OF THE POISONED PEN   NBC

Mystery: Murder and Murder Mystery • Courtroom
Drama
Airdate: 01/21/90
Rating: 16.0/24   A/C: 2

When a despised writer is murdered at a mystery writers' convention, everyone's a suspect, including Mason's associates Della and Malansky. When a writer who claimed the victim plagiarized him is put on trial, Mason defends him.

Production Company: Dean Hargrove Productions
    IAW Fred Silverman Company IAW Viacom
Executive Producer .... Dean Hargrove
Executive Producer .... Fred Silverman
Producer .... Joel Steiger
Producer .... Peter Katz
Director .... Christian Nyby II
Writer .... George Eckstein
Cast .... Raymond Burr
Cast .... Barbara Hale
Cast .... William R. Moses
Cast .... Cindy Williams

PERRY MASON: THE CASE OF THE RECKLESS ROMEO   NBC

Mystery: Murder and Murder Mystery • Courtroom
Drama
Airdate: 05/05/92
Rating: 14.7/23   A/C: 2

Perry Mason defends an actress accused of murdering a former lover who has exposed their affair in a scandalous autobiography.

Production Company: The Fred Silverman Co.,
    Viacom Prods., Dean Hargrove Prods.
Executive Producer .... Fred Silverman
Executive Producer .... Dean Hargrove
Producer .... Billy Ray Smith
Producer .... Barry Steinberg
Director .... Christian Nyby II
Writer .... Brian Clemens
Cast .... Raymond Burr
Cast .... Anjanette Comer
Cast .... Leslie Wing
Cast .... Priscilla Barnes
Cast .... Amy Steel

PERRY MASON: THE CASE OF THE RUTHLESS REPORTER   NBC

Mystery: Murder and Murder Mystery • Courtroom
Drama
Airdate: 01/06/91
Rating: 14.0/21   A/C: 3

Mason defends a Denver TV reporter who is charged with the murder of a back-stabbing anchorman.

Production Company: Dean Hargrove Prods. IAW
    Fred Silverman Co. IAW Viacom Prods.
Executive Produer .... Dean Hargrove
Executive Produer .... Fred Silverman
Co-Executive Producer .... Joel Steiger
Producer .... David Solomon
Producer .... Billy Ray Smith
Director .... Christian Nyby II
Writer .... Sean Cholodenko
Cast .... Raymond Burr
Cast .... Barbara Hale
Cast .... William R. Moses
Cast .... John James

PERRY MASON: THE CASE OF THE SCANDALOUS SCOUNDREL   NBC

Mystery: Murder and Murder Mystery • Courtroom
Drama
Airdate: 11/15/87
Rating: 16.6/26   A/C: 1

A female reporter is accused of killing the publisher of a sensationalistic paper.

Production Company: Fred Silverman Co. &
    Strathmore Prods. IAW Viacom
Executive Producer .... Fred Silverman
Executive Producer .... Dean Hargrove
Producer .... Peter Katz
Director .... Christian Nyby II
Writer .... Anthony Spinner
Cast .... Raymond Burr
Cast .... Barbara Hale
Cast .... William Katt
Cast .... Robert Guillaume
Cast .... Morgan Brittany

PERRY MASON: THE CASE OF THE SHOOTING STAR   NBC

Mystery: Murder and Murder Mystery • Courtroom
Drama
Airdate: 11/09/86
Rating: 23.6/37   A/C: 1

Mason defends a movie actor-director who apparently shot a talk-show host on live television.

Production Company: Intermedia Entertainment &
    Strathmore Prods. IAW Viacom
Executive Producer .... Fred Silverman
Executive Producer .... Dean Hargrove
Producer .... Barry Steinberg
Director .... Ron Satlof
Writer .... Anne Collins
Cast .... Raymond Burr
Cast .... Barbara Hale
Cast .... Wendy Crewson
Cast .... David Ogden Stiers
Cast .... Joe Penny
Cast .... Alan Thicke
Cast .... Ivan Dixon
Cast .... William Katt
Cast .... Ron Glass

PERRY MASON: THE CASE OF THE SILENCED SINGER   NBC

Mystery: Murder and Murder Mystery • Courtroom
Drama
Airdate: 05/20/90
Rating: 16.5/27   A/C: 1

When a former student of Mason's is accused of murdering his ex-wife, a flashy rock star, Mason defends him.

Production Company: Dean Hargrove Prods IAW
    Viacom
Executive Producer .... Fred Silverman
Producer .... Peter Katz
Executive Producer .... Dean Hargrove
Director .... Ron Satlof
Writer .... Anne Collins
Cast .... Raymond Burr
Cast .... Tim Reid
Cast .... Vanessa Williams

PERRY MASON: THE CASE OF THE SINISTER SPIRIT   NBC

Mystery: Murder and Murder Mystery • Courtroom
Drama
Airdate: 05/24/87
Rating: 20.5/35   A/C: 1

A publisher is accused of pushing his star chiller-author out a window.

Production Company: Fred Silverman Co. &
    Strathmore Prods. IAW Viacom
Executive Producer .... Fred Silverman
Executive Producer .... Dean Hargrove
Producer .... Barry Steinberg
Director .... Richard Lang
Writer .... Anne Collins
Cast .... Raymond Burr
Cast .... William Katt
Cast .... Barbara Hale
Cast .... David Ogden Stiers
Cast .... Robert Stack
Cast .... Dwight Schultz

PERRY MASON: THE CASE OF THE SKIN-DEEP SCANDAL   NBC

Mystery: Murder and Murder Mystery • Courtroom
Drama
Airdate: 2/19/93
Rating: 13.3/22   A/C: 1

Perry investigates a myriad of suspects when a loathsome cosmetics queen is murdered.

Production Company: Dean Hargrove Prods., Fred
    Silverman Co. IAW Viacom Enter.
Executive Producer .... Dean Hargrove
Executive Producer .... Fred Silverman
Producer .... Billy Ray Smith
Producer .... Barry Steinberg
Director .... Christian Nyby II
Writer .... Robert Schlitt
Cast .... Raymond Burr
Cast .... Barbara Hale
Cast .... Morgan Fairchild
Cast .... Polly Bergen

MOVIES AND MINISERIES

PERRY MASON: THE CASE OF THE TELLTALE TALK SHOW HOST NBC
Mystery: Murder and Murder Mystery • Courtroom Drama
Airdate: 5/21/93
Rating: 13.1/24   A/C: 1

Perry probes the murder of a repugnant radio station owner who angered most of his on-air personalities.

Production Company: Dean Hargrove Prods., Fred Silverman Co. IAW Viacom Enter.
Executive Producer .... Dean Hargrove
Executive Producer .... Fred Silverman
Producer .... Billy Ray Smith
Co-Executive Producer .... Joel Steiger
Director .... Christian Nyby II
Writer .... Joyce Burditt
Cast .... Raymond Burr
Cast .... Barbara Hale
Cast .... Montel Williams
Cast .... Mariette Hartley

PERSONALS USA
Drama: Murder and Murder Mystery • Suspense/Thriller
Airdate: 02/28/90
Rating: N/A   A/C:

A psychotic murderess who culls her victims from the personal pages, kills a freelance writer researching an article. The writer's widow tracks down the killer.

Production Company: Sharmill Productions Inc. IAW Wilshire Court Productions
Producer .... Steven H. Stern
Director .... Steven H. Stern
Writer .... George Franklin
Writer .... Brad Whiting, Jr.
Writer .... Arlene Sanford
Cast .... Stephanie Zimbalist
Cast .... Jennifer O'Neill
Cast .... Robin Thomas
Cast .... Gina Gallego

PETER GUNN ABC
Drama: Cops/Detectives/Law Enforcement • Mafia/Mob
Airdate: 04/23/89
Rating: 14.7/24   A/C:

In this revival of the classic TV series, suave Peter Gunn is retained by a mob boss to discover who killed the head of a rival family.

Production Company: The Blake Edwards Co. IAW New World TV
Executive Producer .... Blake Edwards
Producer .... Tony Adams
Director .... Blake Edwards
Writer .... Blake Edwards
Cast .... Peter Strauss
Cast .... Barbara Williams
Cast .... Charles Cioffi
Cast .... Peter Jurasik

PETER THE GREAT NBC
EMMY WINNER
Miniseries/Drama (4 nights): Biography • Historical Piece • Period Piece • Foreign or Exotic Location
Airdate: 2/2/86 • 2/3/86 • 2/4/86 • 2/5/86
Rating: 19.0/28 • 17.6/26 • 16.6/26 • 17.4/27 A/C:

Based on Robert K. Massey's Book. Lavish biography of the Czar of Russia from 1687 to 1725. Also chronicled his love affair with Caterina Alexandrova as well as the murder of his son and heir, Alexis.

Production Company: PTG Prods. IAW NBC
Executive Producer .... Lawrence Schiller
Producer .... Marvin J. Chomsky
Producer .... Konstantin Thoeren
Director .... Marvin J. Chomsky
Director .... Lawrence Schiller
Writer .... Edward Anhalt
Cast .... Maximilian Schell
Cast .... Vanessa Redgrave
Cast .... Omar Sharif
Cast .... Lawrence Olivier
Cast .... Trevor Howard

PEYTON PLACE: THE NEXT GENERATION NBC
Drama: Murder and Murder Mystery • Suspense/Thriller
Airdate: 05/13/85
Rating: 12.6/20   A/C:

Based on the book by Grace Metalious. Also popular 1960's TV series and 1957 feature film. The daughter of a woman who has been catatonic in a hospital for twenty years, returns to her mother's home and is eventually responsible for her mother's murder.

Production Company: Michael Filerman Prods. IAW 20th Century Fox TV
Executive Producer .... Michael Filerman
Producer .... Terry Morse
Co-Producer .... Karen Moore
Director .... Larry Elikann
Writer .... Rita Lakin
Cast .... Dorothy Malone
Cast .... Barbara Parkins
Cast .... Tim O'Connor
Cast .... Ed Nelson

PHANTOM OF THE OPERA, THE NBC
Miniseries/Drama (2 nights): Love Story • Period Piece • Foreign or Exotic Location
Airdate: 03/18/90 • 03/19/90
Rating: 12.3/19 • 12.3/20 A/C: 2 • 2

From Gaston Leroux's novel. When the new manager makes his untalented wife star of the Paris Opera, the Phantom who lives underneath the opera house turns a young woman into a brilliant singer. Then both sides battle to take control of the Opera.

Production Company: Saban/Scherick
Executive Producer .... Edgar J. Scherick
Executive Producer .... Haim Saban
Producer .... Ross Milloy
Director .... Tony Richardson
Writer .... Arthur Kopit
Cast .... Charles Dance
Cast .... Teri Polo
Cast .... Burt Lancaster

PICKET FENCES CBS
Drama: Family Drama • Cops/Detectives/Law Enforcement • Series Pilot (2 hr.)
Airdate: 9/18/92
Rating: 12.7/24   A/C: 1

A sheriff and his doctor wife deal with unexplained murders, career pressures and family relationships in the quirky small town of Rome, Wisconsin.

Production Company: Twentieth Televison
Executive Producer .... David Kelley
Executive Producer .... Michael Pressman
Producer .... Alice West
Director .... Ron Lagomarsino
Writer .... David Kelley
Cast .... Tom Skerritt
Cast .... Kathy Baker
Cast .... Costas Mandylor
Cast .... Lauren Holly

PICKING UP THE PIECES CBS
Drama: Family Drama • Woman's Issue/Story
Airdate: 10/22/85
Rating: 16.8/25   A/C:

When a a wife and mother decides to terminate her dead-end marriage of seventeen years, she faces the tremendous financial and emotional hardships of being on her own.

Production Company: CBS Entertainment Prods.
Producer .... Dorothea Petrie
Director .... Paul Wendkos
Writer .... Gordon Cotler
Cast .... Margot Kidder
Cast .... David Ackroyd
Cast .... Ari Meyers
Cast .... Joyce Van Patten

PINK LIGHTNING FBC
Drama: Period Piece • Woman's Issue/Story • Buddy Story
Airdate: 07/08/91
Rating: 4.4/8   A/C: 4

A group of five young women, all best friends, share memories and adventures as they come of age in 1962 central California.

Production Company: FNM
Executive Producer .... Marianne Moloney
Producer .... Elliot Rosenblatt
Director .... Carol Monpere
Writer .... Carol Monpere
Cast .... Sarah Buxton
Cast .... Martha Byrne
Cast .... Ray Walston
Cast .... Jennifer Blanc

PLACE FOR ANNIE, A   ABC

Drama: Medical/Disease/Mental Illness • Children/
Teens • Social Issue • Woman's Issue/Story • True
Story
Airdate: 5/1/94
Rating: 14.8/23   A/C: 2

*A single mother and supervisor of a pediatric
intensive-care unit volunteers to become the
foster parent to an abandoned nine week old
baby girl who is born HIV-positive and heroin
addicted. A year later the child's AIDS wracked
mother shows up to legally reclaim her
daughter. Feeling compassion for the
irresponsible woman, she lets her move in to
her home and together they form an uncommon
bond to provide love for the little girl.*

Production Company: Gross-Weston Prods. IAW
    Signboard Hill Prods., Cannell Entertainmnet
Executive Producer .... Marcy Gross
Executive Producer .... Ann Weston
Producer .... Diane Walsh
Co-Producer .... Cathleen Young
Co-Producer .... Lee Guthrie
Director .... John Gray
Writer .... Cathleen Young
Writer .... Lee Guthrie
Cast .... Sissy Spacek
Cast .... Mary Louise Parker
Cast .... Joan Plowright
Cast .... Jack Noseworthy

PLACE TO BE LOVED, A   CBS

Drama: Family Drama • Children/Teens • True Story
• Social Issue
Airdate: 4/4/93
Rating: 13.0/20   A/C: 3

*The 1992 ground breaking case of a twelve year
old Florida boy who sues his abusive biological
parents for "divorce" so he can be adopted by
his loving foster family, George and Lizabeth
Russ.*

Note: See ABC Movie- "Gregory K".

Production Company: Polson Co./Corapeake
    Prods. IAW P&G Prods.
Executive Producer .... Beth Polson
Producer .... Randy Siegel
Director .... Sandy Smolan
Writer .... Blair Ferguson
Cast .... Richard Crenna
Cast .... Rhea Perlman
Cast .... Linda Kelsey
Cast .... Cotter Smith

PLACE TO CALL HOME, A   CBS

Drama: Family Drama • Woman Against The System
• True Story • Foreign or Exotic Location
Airdate: 02/07/87
Rating: 15.4/26   A/C:

*True story of a Texas mother who manages on
the Australian outback with eleven homesick
children, a husband who's never around and
workers who don't want to take orders from a
woman.*

Production Company: Big Deal Inc. and Crawford
    Prods. Intl. IAW Embassy Communications
Executive Producer .... Virginia L. Carter
Executive Producer .... Linda Lavin
Executive Producer .... Marty Litke
Producer .... Michael Lake
Producer .... Ross Mathews
Director .... Russ Mayberry
Writer .... Jeri Taylor
Writer .... Carol Sobieski
Cast .... Linda Lavin
Cast .... Lane Smith
Cast .... Lori Loughlin
Cast .... Robert MacNaughton

PLAYING WITH FIRE   NBC

Drama: Family Drama • Children/Teens • Social Issue
Airdate: 04/14/85
Rating: 16.9/26   A/C:

*A teenager with problems at home vents his
anger by setting fires. His parents and the local
fire chief help him get his life back together.*

Production Company: Zephyr Prods.
Executive Producer .... Lee Levinson
Executive Producer .... Lew Hunter
Producer .... Jim Begg
Director .... Ivan Nagy
Writer .... Lew Hunter
Cast .... Cicely Tyson
Cast .... Gary Coleman
Cast .... Yaphet Kotto
Cast .... Ron O'Neal

PLAZA SUITE   ABC

Comedy: Romantic Comedy
Airdate: 12/03/87
Rating: 8.0/13   A/C:

*Based on the play by Neil Simon. Three couples
occupy the same hotel suite at different times.
First, a reluctant anniversary celebration; then
a Hollywood producer tries to seduce an old
girlfriend; last, a couple try to talk their
daughter out of last-minute pre-wedding jitters.*

Production Company: Kalola Prods.
Executive Producer .... Carol Burnett
Executive Producer .... Kenny Solms
Producer .... George Sunga
Director .... Roger Beatty
Director .... Kenny Solms
Writer .... Neil Simon
Cast .... Carol Burnett
Cast .... Hal Holbrook
Cast .... Tim Conway, Jr.
Cast .... Erin Hamilton
Cast .... Dabney Coleman
Cast .... Richard Crenna
Cast .... Beth Maitland

PLEASURES   ABC

Drama: Foreign or Exotic Location • Sex/Glitz
Airdate: 03/31/86
Rating: 12.9/20   A/C:

*Three women look for summertime love. A
deserted wife becomes involved with her college
sweetheart; her sister throws herself at a rock
star; and her daughter finds a boy who doesn't
speak English.*

Production Company: Catalina Production Group
    Ltd. with Columbia Pictures TV
Executive Producer .... Franklin R. Levy
Executive Producer .... Gregory Harrison
Executive Producer .... Matthew Rushton
Producer .... Peter Katz
Co-Producer .... Jon Andersen
Director .... Sharron Miller
Writer .... Jill Gordon
Cast .... Joanna Cassidy
Cast .... David Paymer
Cast .... Barry Bostwick
Cast .... Tracy Nelson
Cast .... Rick Moses
Cast .... Pamela Segall
Cast .... Linda Purl

PLOT TO KILL HITLER, THE   CBS

Drama: True Story • Period Piece • WWII • Nazis
Airdate: 01/30/90
Rating: 7.2/12   A/C: 3

*Docudrama about the conspiracy to kill Hitler,
involving high-ranking Wehrmacht officers led
by Col. Claus von Stauffenberg. When a bomb
fails to destroy its target, Hitler has the
conspirators killed.*

Production Company: David L. Wolper Prods.
    IAW Bernard Sofronski and Warner Brothers
    TV
Executive Producer .... David L. Wolper
Executive Producer .... Bernard Sofronski
Producer .... Alfred R. Kelman
Director .... Lawrence Schiller
Writer .... Stephen Elkins
Cast .... Brad Davis
Cast .... Madolyn Smith Osborne
Cast .... Ian Richardson
Cast .... Mike Gwilym

PLYMOUTH ABC

Drama: Series Pilot (2 hr.) • Sci-Fi/Supernatural/Horror/Fantasy
Airdate: 05/26/91
Rating: 8.3/17   A/C: 2

When a toxic accident makes a small town in Oregon uninhabitable, the local residents move their community to a mining base on the moon. They soon face personal crises and lunar calamities.

Production Company: Touchstone TV, RAI-Uno, Zlotoff Inc.

Executive Producer	Lee David Zlotoff
Executive Producer	Ralph Winter
Producer	Ian Sander
Director	Lee David Zlotoff
Writer	Lee David Zlotoff
Cast	Cindy Pickett
Cast	Richard Hamilton
Cast	Perrey Reeves
Cast	Dale Midkiff

POISON IVY NBC

Comedy: Youth Comedy
Airdate: 02/10/85
Rating: 19.8/25   A/C:

The hi-jinxs and romances of kids and counselors at a summer camp.

Production Company: NBC Prods.

Executive Producer	Deborah Aal
Producer	Marvin Miller
Director	Larry Elikann
Writer	Bennett Tramer
Cast	Michael J. Fox
Cast	Nancy McKeon
Cast	Caren Kaye
Cast	Adam Baldwin
Cast	Robert Klein

POISONED BY LOVE: THE KERN COUNTY MURDERS CBS

Drama: True Crime • Family Violence
Airdate: 2/2/93
Rating: 14.5/24   A/C: 1

In Kern County, California the ex-wife of low-life womanizer, Steve Catlin, gathers enough evidence to prove that he poisoned two of his former spouses and his mother with Paraquat.

Production Company: Morgan Hill Films IAW Hearst Ent.

Executive Producer	Jennifer Alward
Producer	Richard Biggs
Director	Larry Peerce
Writer	Caliope Brattlestreet
Cast	Harry Hamlin
Cast	Helen Shaver
Cast	Eileen Brennan
Cast	Faith Ford
Writer	Stephen Glanz

POKER ALICE CBS

Drama: Western • Prostitution
Airdate: 05/22/87
Rating: 17.5/32   A/C:

A Boston aristocrat gambles her way across the Old West and ends up the owner of a New Mexico whorehouse.

Production Company: Harvey Matofsky Prods. IAW New World TV

Executive Producer	Harvey Matofsky
Producer	Renee Valente
Director	Arthur Allan Seidelman
Writer	James Lee Barrett
Cast	Elizabeth Taylor
Cast	George Hamilton
Cast	Tom Skerritt
Cast	Richard Mulligan
Cast	Pat Corley
Cast	Paul Drake

POLICE STORY: THE FREEWAY KILLINGS NBC

Drama: Murder and Murder Mystery • Cops/Detectives/Law Enforcement
Airdate: 05/03/87
Rating: 17.3/27   A/C:

Based on the series. Various members of the Los Angeles Police Department deal with their own problems as well as the case of a serial killer who is dumping bodies onto freeways.

Production Company: David Gerber Prods. IAW MGM/UA TV and Columbia Pictures TV

Executive Producer	David Gerber
Producer	Charles B. FitzSimons
Director	William A. Graham
Writer	Mark Rodgers
Cast	Richard Crenna
Cast	Ben Gazzara
Cast	Angie Dickinson
Cast	Don Meredith
Cast	Tony Lo Bianco

POLLY—COMIN' HOME NBC

Musical: Children/Teens • Period Piece • Black Story
Airdate: 11/18/90
Rating: 6.8/10   A/C: 4

A precocious young orphan sings and dances her way to interracial harmony and domestic bliss in a small town in 1950s Alabama.

Production Company: Echo Cove Prods. IAW Walt Disney TV

Executive Producer	William Blinn
Producer	Frank Fischer
Producer	James Pulliam
Director	Debbie Allen
Writer	William Blinn
Cast	Keshia Knight Pulliam
Cast	Phylicia Rashad
Cast	Dorian Harewood
Cast	Barbara Montgomery

POOR LITTLE RICH GIRL: THE BARBARA HUTTON STORY NBC

Miniseries/Drama (2 nights): Biography • True Story • Sex/Glitz • Period Piece • Foreign or Exotic Location • Addiction Story
Airdate: 11/16/87 • 11/17/87
Rating: 21.3/33 • 18.5/30   A/C:

Based on C. David Heymann's best seller. The unhappy life, loves and substance dependencies of one of the wealthiest women in the world, the Woolworth's heiress who married—among others—Cary Grant.

Production Company: Lester Persky Productions IAW ITC

Executive Producer	Lester Persky
Producer	Nick Gillott
Director	Charles Jarrott
Writer	Dennis Turner
Cast	Farrah Fawcett
Cast	James Read
Cast	Kevin McCarthy
Cast	Bruce Davison
Cast	David Ackroyd
Cast	Anne Francis
Cast	Burl Ives

POPEYE DOYLE NBC

Drama: Cops/Detectives/Law Enforcement • Suspense/Thriller • Series Pilot (2 hr.)
Airdate: 09/07/86
Rating: 15.8/26   A/C:

The "French Connection" cop faces terrorists in New York City.

Production Company: 20th Century Fox TV

Producer	Richard Di Lello
Director	Peter Levin
Writer	Richard Di Lello
Cast	Ed O'Neill
Cast	Audrey Landers
Cast	James Handy
Cast	Candy Clark
Cast	Mathew Lawrence

PORTRAIT, THE — TNT
Drama: Family Drama
Airdate: 2/13/93
Rating: N/A   A/C:

Based on the play, "Painting Churches" by Tina Howe. A successful artist returns to her childhood home to paint her parents portrait. She soon discovers that her college professor father is becoming senile and her mother is trying to hide this fact from his colleagues by selling the house and moving from the community. As the painting is being completed the family comes to terms with long held expectations and disappointments, learning to face the challenges of aging.

Production Company: Atticus Corp. IAW Robert Greenwald Prods.
Executive Producer .... Robert Greenwald
Executive Producer .... Gregory P Peck
Producer .... Philip Kleinbart
Co-Producer .... David Haugland
Co-Producer .... Richard Schmiechen
Co-Producer .... Linda Berman
Director .... Arthur Penn
Producer .... Lynn Roth
Cast .... Gregory Peck
Cast .... Lauren Bacall
Cast .... Cecelia Peck

POSING: INSPIRED BY THREE REAL STORIES — CBS
Drama: Woman's Issue/Story • Sex/Glitz
Airdate: 11/05/91
Rating: 11.9/18   A/C: 3

Three women...a mousy stockbroker, a goody two-shoes Yale student, and a neglected housewife...face hypocrisy and ridicule after posing nude for Playboy Magazine.

Production Company: Alta Loma Productions IAW Republic Pictures Prods.
Executive Producer .... Christy Welker
Producer .... Cleve Landsberg
Co-Producer .... Beth Sullivan
Director .... Stephen Stafford
Writer .... Cathleen Young
Cast .... Lynda Carter
Cast .... Michele Greene
Cast .... Amanda Peterson
Cast .... John Finn

POSITIVELY TRUE ADVENTURES OF THE ALLEGED TEXAS CHEERLEADER MURDERING MOM, THE — HBO
Comedy: True Crime
Airdate: 4/10/93
Rating: N/A   A/C:

In 1991, Wanda Holloway a Channelview, Texas housewife is accused of trying to hire her former brother-in-law to knock off the mother of her daughter's cheerleading rival. A sensational trail and media circus ensue which ultimately finds her guilty but she is latter freed on a mistrial. NOTE: See ABC Movie "Willing to Kill"

Production Company: Frederick S. Pierce Company, Sudden Ent. Prods.
Executive Producer .... Frederick Pierce
Executive Producer .... Kyle Heinrich
Producer .... James Manos, Jr.
Director .... Michael Richie
Writer .... Jane Anderson
Cast .... Holly Hunter
Cast .... Beau Bridges
Cast .... Elizabeth Ruscio
Cast .... Swoozie Kurtz

PRAYING MANTIS — USA
Drama: Suspense/Thriller • Murder and Murder Mystery
Airdate: 5/11/93
Rating: N/A   A/C:

An alluring psychopathic woman poisons her husbands on their wedding night. When she meets a wealthy bookshop owner, a widower with a teenage boy, she uses her seductive charms to hook him. His son and former sister-in-law see through her wicked ways and plot to expose her demented past and save the soon-to-be doomed groom.

Production Company: Fast Track Films, Wilshire Court Prods.
Executive Producer .... James Keach
Executive Producer .... Jane Seymour
Producer .... Robert Rolsky
Director .... James Keach
Writer .... William Delligan
Writer .... Duane Poole
Cast .... Jane Seymour
Cast .... Barry Bostwick
Cast .... Frances Fisher
Cast .... Chad Allen

PRECIOUS VICTIMS — CBS
Drama: True Crime • Children/Teens • Murder and Murder Mystery • Courtroom Drama
Airdate: 9/28/93
Rating: 14.6/23   A/C: 2

Based on the book by Charles Bosworth and Don Weber. When two babies from the same household in Illinois disappear and are found dead in the woods, over a three year period, an obsessed detective and tough prosecutor fight to convict the childrens' bizarre parents who claim the kids were kidnapped and murdered by strangers.

Production Company: Laurel Prods.
Executive Producer .... Richard Rubinstein
Executive Producer .... Mitchell Galin
Producer .... Timothy Marx
Director .... Peter Levin
Writer .... Deborah Dalton
Cast .... Park Overall
Cast .... Robby Benson
Cast .... Richard Thomas
Cast .... Frederic Forrest

PREPPIE MURDER, THE — ABC
Drama: Murder and Murder Mystery • Cops/Detectives/Law Enforcement • True Crime • Children/Teens
Airdate: 09/24/89
Rating: 15.2/24   A/C: 2

The notorious Central Park case in which preppie Robert Chambers escaped a murder conviction for the death of eighteen year old Jennifer Levin by claiming her death was accidental due to "rough sex."

Production Company: Jack Grossbart Productions
Executive Producer .... Jack Grossbart
Producer .... Paul Pompian
Producer .... Sydell Albert
Director .... John Herzfeld
Writer .... John Herzfeld
Writer .... Irv Roud
Cast .... Danny Aiello
Cast .... William Baldwin
Cast .... Joanna Kerns
Cast .... William Devane

PRESIDENTS CHILD, THE — CBS
Drama: Suspense/Thriller • Political Piece
Airdate: 10/27/92
Rating: 10.0/17   A/C: 2

Based on the book by Fay Weldon. A former CIA agent, now a political advisor to a presidential contender tries to silence a TV journalist from going public about the candidates illegitimate son she gave birth to seven years ago.

Production Company: Lauren Film Prods.
Executive Producer .... Sandra Saxon
Director .... Sam Pillsbury
Writer .... Edmond Stevens
Cast .... Donna Mills
Cast .... William Devane
Cast .... Trevor Eve

PRICE SHE PAID, THE   CBS
Drama: Woman In Jeopardy • Children/Teens • Rape/
Molestation • Woman's Issue/Story
Airdate: 03/31/92
Rating: 11.7/19   A/C: 3

A convicted rapist returns after twelve years to petition for joint custody of the child he sired with the rape victim. His scheming manipulations ultimately lead to a plot of deadly revenge.

Production Company: Producers Ent. Group,
   Sandy Hook Prods. IAW World Int'l Network
Executive Producer .... Jonathan Axelrod
Executive Producer .... Irwin Meyer
Producer .... John Thomas Lenox
Director .... Fred Walton
Writer .... Robert Foster
Writer .... Phil Penningroth
Cast .... Loni Anderson
Cast .... Anthony John Denison
Cast .... Candy Clark
Cast .... Stephen Meadows

PRIDE AND EXTREME PREJUDICE   USA
Drama: Suspense/Thriller • Foreign or Exotic
Location
Airdate: 01/17/90
Rating: N/A   A/C:

Based on Frederick Forsyth's novel. Bruno Morenz, a German Intelligence officer, is hunted by the CIA and KGB for his involvement in the trade of Soviet military secrets in exchange for a valuable real estate property.

Production Company: USA Network
Executive Producer .... Murray Smith
Executive Producer .... Frederick Forsyth
Executive Producer .... Nick Elliot
Producer .... Frederick Muller
Director .... Ian Sharp
Writer .... Murray Smith
Cast .... Brian Dennehy
Cast .... Alan Howard
Cast .... Simon Cadell
Cast .... Lisa Eichhorn

PRIME TARGET   NBC
Drama: Murder and Murder Mystery • Cops/
Detectives/Law Enforcement
Airdate: 09/29/89
Rating: 12.6/23   A/C: 2

Based on the novel "No Business Being a Cop" by Lillian O'Donnell. Policewomen who fought unfair suspensions are being murdered. Sgt. Kelly Mulcahaney, the next victim, must investigate solo since rogue cops may be involved.

Production Company: RLC Prods. Inc. IAW
   Finnegan Pinchuk Co. and MGM/UA
Executive Producer .... Robert Collins
Producer .... Dennis E. Jones
Director .... Robert Collins
Writer .... Robert Collins
Cast .... Angie Dickinson
Cast .... Charles Durning
Cast .... Mills Watson
Cast .... Joseph Bologna

PRINCE OF BEL AIR   ABC
Drama: Love Story • Sex/Glitz
Airdate: 01/20/86
Rating: 17.5/27   A/C:

An involvement with a beautiful conceptual artist who wants more than a superficial relationship forces a pool (and stud) service entrepreneur to rethink his hedonistic philosophy.

Production Company: Leonard Hill Films
Executive Producer .... Leonard Hill
Producer .... Albert J. Salzer
Co-Producer .... Joseph Akerman
Director .... Charles Braverman
Writer .... Marc Rubel
Writer .... Dori Pierson
Cast .... Mark Harmon
Cast .... Kirstie Alley
Cast .... Robert Vaughn
Cast .... Patrick Laborteaux
Cast .... Deborah Harmon

PRISON FOR CHILDREN   CBS
Drama: Man Against The System • Children/Teens •
Social Issue
Airdate: 03/14/87
Rating: 11.5/20   A/C:

The superintendent of a juvenile facility fights to prevent the jailing of homeless children together with juvenile criminals.

Production Company: Knopf/Simons Prods. IAW
   Viacom Prods.
Executive Producer .... David A. Simons
Producer .... Lee Rafner
Director .... Larry Peerce
Writer .... Christopher Knopf
Cast .... John Ritter
Cast .... Betty Thomas
Cast .... Raphael Sbarge
Cast .... Gordie Wright
Cast .... Josh Brolin

PRISONER OF HONOR   HBO
Drama: True Story • Period Piece • Courtroom Drama
• Historical Piece • Foreign or Exotic Location •
Biography
Airdate: 11/02/91
Rating: N/A   A/C:

In 1890's France, anti-semitic Colonel Picquart is assigned to investigate Jewish officer Alfred Dreyfus's conviction of espionage. He rises above his bigotry when he discovers the truth and exposes the corruption of the military.

Production Company: HBO/Etude
Executive Producer .... Judith James
Executive Producer .... Richard Dreyfuss
Producer .... Ronaldo Vasconcellos
Director .... Ken Russell
Writer .... Ron Hutchinson
Cast .... Richard Dreyfuss
Cast .... Oliver Reed
Cast .... Peter Firth
Cast .... Jeremy Kemp

PRIVATE MATTER, A   HBO
Drama: Period Piece • True Story • Woman's Issue/
Story • Social Issue • Family Drama
Airdate: 06/20/92
Rating: N/A   A/C:

In 1962 Phoenix, "Romper Room" host Sherri Finkbine discovers she is carrying a thalodimide-deformed fetus. Her tragedy becomes a public debate and she is forced to defend her decision in favor of abortion as she struggles for control of her life.

Production Company: Longbow-Mirage-HBO
Executive Producer .... Ronnie Clemmer
Executive Producer .... Bill Pace
Executive Producer .... Sidney Pollock
Executive Producer .... Lindsay Doran
Producer .... David C. Thomas
Director .... Joan Micklin Silver
Writer .... William Nicholson
Cast .... Sissy Spacek
Cast .... Aidan Quinn
Cast .... Estelle Parsons
Cast .... Leon Russom

PRIVATE SESSIONS   NBC
Drama: Medical/Disease/Mental Illness
Airdate: 03/18/85
Rating: 14.9/23   A/C:

The personal problems of a recently divorced psychiatrist are interspersed with those of his patients; among them a nymphomaniac and a cab driver who hears voices.

Production Company: Raven's Claw Prods. &
   Seltzer/Gimbel Prods. IAW Comworld Prods.
Executive Producer .... Deanne Barkley
Executive Producer .... Norman Gimbel
Executive Producer .... Phil Capice
Co-Producer .... Thom Thomas
Director .... Michael Pressman
Writer .... David Seltzer
Writer .... Thom Thomas
Cast .... Mike Farrell
Cast .... Kathryn Walker
Cast .... David Labiosa
Cast .... Maureen Stapleton
Cast .... Denise Miller

PROBE   ABC
Drama: Murder and Murder Mystery • Cops/
Detectives/Law Enforcement • Series Pilot (2 hr.) •
Sci-Fi/Supernatural/Horror/Fantasy
Airdate: 03/07/88
Rating: 14.2/23   A/C:

A computer and engineering genius turns private investigator when a mysterious dead body turns up. The result is a battle of wits with a mad scientist friend and his killer computer.

Production Company: MCA TV Ltd.
Executive Producer .... Alan J. Levi
Executive Producer .... Michael Wagner
Director .... Sandor Stern
Writer .... Michael Wagner
Cast .... Parker Stevenson
Cast .... Ashley Crow
Cast .... Jon Cypher
Cast .... Andy Wood

PROMISE — CBS

EMMY WINNER
Drama: Family Drama • Medical/Disease/Mental Illness
Airdate: 12/14/86
Rating: 19.5/29   A/C:

A man fulfills the promise he made to his now-dead mother: that he would take care of his schizophrenic brother.

Production Company: Warner Bros. TV
Executive Producer .... Peter K. Duchow
Executive Producer .... James Garner
Producer .... Glenn Jordan
Producer .... Nick Gillott
Director .... Glenn Jordan
Writer .... Richard Friedenberg
Cast .... James Garner
Cast .... James Woods
Cast .... Piper Laurie
Cast .... Peter Michael Goetz

PROMISE TO KEEP, A — NBC

Drama: Family Drama • Children/Teens • Woman's Issue/Story • True Story
Airdate: 10/01/90
Rating: 14.3/23   A/C: 3

Based on the memoirs of Jane Yarmolinsky. Middle-class parents, with three children of their own, struggle with their promise to raise four orphaned nephews when the boys' parents suffer tragic deaths.

Production Company: Sacret-Elliott Friedgen-Warner Brothers
Executive Producer .... John Sacret Young
Executive Producer .... Carlton Cuse
Director .... Rod Holcomb
Writer .... Susan Cooper
Writer .... Carlton Cuse
Cast .... Dana Delany
Cast .... William Russ
Cast .... Adam Arkin
Cast .... Frances Fisher

PROMISED A MIRACLE — CBS

Drama: Family Drama • Children/Teens • Medical/Disease/Mental Illness • True Story • Social Issue
Airdate: 05/19/88
Rating: 13.2/22   A/C:

True story of fundamentalist parents who, on the church's advice, withhold insulin from their diabetic child. They then blame the boy's death on Satan, expecting the child to be resurrected, until they realize their tragic mistake at their trial.

Production Company: Roni Weisberg Prods./Dick Clark Cinema Prods. IAW Republic Pictures
Executive Producer .... Preston Fischer
Co-Executive Producer .... Dick Clark
Co-Executive Producer .... Fran La Maina
Producer .... Roni Weisberg
Director .... Stephen Gyllenhaal
Writer .... David Hill
Cast .... Rosanna Arquette
Cast .... Tom Bower
Cast .... Judge Reinhold
Cast .... Vonni Ribisi

PROPHET OF EVIL: THE ERVIL LEBARON STORY — CBS

Drama: Murder and Murder Mystery • Cops/Detectives/Law Enforcement • True Crime
Airdate: 5/4/93
Rating: 9.9/16   A/C: 3

In 1978 Utah, Mormon and self-proclaimed prophet cult leader Ervil LeBaron murders members of his polygamist sect and his own immediate family who attempt to leave the group or question his authority. When LeBaron's brother tips off D.A. investigator Dan Fields the determined lawman eventually gets enough evidence to convict the evil madman.

Production Company: Dream City Films IAW Hearst Ent.
Executive Producer .... Harry Chandler
Co-Executive Producer .... Heidi Wall
Producer .... Anthony Croce
Director .... Jud Taylor
Writer .... Fred Mills
Cast .... Brian Dennehy
Cast .... William Devane
Cast .... Tracey Needham
Cast .... Dee Wallace Stone

PROUD MEN — ABC

Drama: Family Drama • Vietnam
Airdate: 10/01/87
Rating: 9.4/15   A/C:

AWOL from Vietnam for fifteen years, the son of a World War II veteran returns to his western home town to attempt reconciliation with his dying father.

Production Company: Von Zerneck-Samuels Prods.
Executive Producer .... Stu Samuels
Executive Producer .... Frank Von Zerneck
Executive Producer .... Fraser C. Heston
Director .... William A. Graham
Writer .... Jeff Andrus
Cast .... Charlton Heston
Cast .... Peter Strauss
Cast .... Belinda Balaski
Cast .... Nan Martin

PSYCHIC — USA

Drama: Suspense/Thriller • Sci-Fi/Supernatural/Horror/Fantasy
Airdate: 05/20/92
Rating: N/A   A/C:

A college student with clairvoyant powers races to the rescue of his girlfriend after she appears as a victim of a serial killer in one of his psychic nightmares.

Production Company: Trimark Picture
Executive Producer .... William Webb
Producer .... Tom Berry
Co-Executive Producer .... Franco Batista
Co-Executive Producer .... Deborah Thomas
Director .... George Mihalka
Writer .... Miguel Tejada-Flores
Writer .... Paul Kovel
Cast .... Michael Nouri
Cast .... Catherine Mary Stewart
Cast .... Zach Galligan

PSYCHO IV: THE BEGINNING — SHOWTIME

Drama: Murder and Murder Mystery • Psychological Thriller • Family Violence
Airdate: 11/10/90
Rating: N/A   A/C:

The continuing "Psycho" saga unveils the backstory of a newly recovered Norman Bates now married to his therapist and revealing his tortured childhood with his domineering, psychotic mother.

Production Company: Smart Money/MCA
Executive Producer .... Hilton Green
Producer .... George Zaloom
Producer .... Les Mayfield
Director .... Mick Garris
Writer .... Joseph Stefano
Cast .... Anthony Perkins
Cast .... Olivia Hussey
Cast .... Henry Thomas
Cast .... CCH Pounder

QUANTUM LEAP — NBC

Drama: Series Pilot (2 hr.) • Sci-Fi/Supernatural/Horror/Fantasy
Airdate: 03/26/89
Rating: 14.9/25   A/C:

With the help of a mysterious assistant from the future, a time traveler goes back twenty years to an unfamiliar pregnant wife as well as a career as a jet pilot.

Production Company: Belisarius Prods. IAW Universal TV
Executive Producer .... Donald P. Bellisario
Producer .... Harker Wade
Co-Producer .... Deborah Pratt
Director .... David Hemmings
Writer .... Donald P. Bellisario
Cast .... Dean Stockwell
Cast .... Scott Bakula
Cast .... John Allen Nelson
Cast .... Jennifer Runyon

QUEEN — CBS

Miniseries/Drama (3 nights): Biography • Black Story • True Story • Period Piece • Historical Piece
Airdate: 2/14/93 • 2/16/93 • 2/18/93
Rating: 24.7/38 • 24.1/37 • 22.8/34
A/C: 1 • 1 • 1

Based on the story of Alex Haleys' paternal grandmother. Born out of an illicit love affair between a slave and a white plantation owner just before the Civil War, Queen spends most of her life trying to battle racism, poverty and ultimately metal illness.

Production Company: Wolper Organizations IAW Bernard Sofronski Prods.
Executive Producer .... David L. Wolper
Executive Producer .... Bernard Sofronski
Producer .... Mark M. Wolper
Co-Producer .... Hal Galli
Co-Producer .... John Erman
Director .... John Erman
Writer .... David Stevens
Cast .... Halle Berry
Cast .... Jasmine Guy
Cast .... Tim Daly
Cast .... Danny Glover
Cast .... Ann-Margret

Movies and Miniseries

QUEENIE — ABC

Miniseries/Drama (2 nights): Period Piece • Historical Piece • Foreign or Exotic Location • Hollywood
Airdate: 05/10/87 • 05/11/87
Rating: 12.7/21 • 12.9/21   A/C:

Based on the Michael Korda novel apparently inspired by the life of celebrated actress Merle Oberon. In the 1930s, an Anglo-Indian girl with a murder in her past begins in England as a dancer and becomes a movie star.

Production Company: Von Zerneck/Samuels Prods. IAW Highgate Pictures Inc.
Executive Producer .... Frank Von Zerneck
Producer .... John Cutts
Co-Producer .... Robert M. Sertner
Director .... Larry Peerce
Writer .... Winston Beard
Writer .... April Smith
Cast .... Kirk Douglas
Cast .... Mia Sara
Cast .... Martin Balsam
Cast .... Claire Bloom
Cast .... Sarah Miles
Cast .... Topol
Cast .... Joel Grey

QUICK AND THE DEAD, THE — HBO

Drama: Western • Period Piece
Airdate: 2/28/87
Rating: N/A   A/C:

Based on the book by Louis L'Amour. In 1876 Wyoming, A mysterious gunslinger helps a family of novice homesteaders fend off an attack by bandits and becomes their volunteer guide to the lawless ways of the west. His repeated assistance begins to create a threat in the family as the husband feels his wife and son's growing attraction and admiration for the charismatic frontiersman.

Production Company: Joseph Cates Co. Inc.
Executive Producer .... Joe Cates
Producer .... Phillip Cates
Director .... Robert Day
Writer .... James Lee Barrett
Cast .... Sam Elliott
Cast .... Kate Capshaw
Cast .... Tom Conti

QUICKSAND: NO ESCAPE — USA

Drama: Murder and Murder Mystery • Cops/Detectives/Law Enforcement • Suspense/Thriller
Airdate: 03/04/92
Rating: N/A   A/C:

An architect turns the tables on a blackmailing P.I. who framed him for murdering an LAPD vice-cop.

Production Company: Finnegan/Pinchuk Prod. IAW MCA Television
Executive Producer .... Pat Finnegan
Executive Producer .... Sheldon Pinchuk
Producer .... Peter Baloff
Producer .... Dave Wollert
Producer .... Lori-Etta Taub
Director .... Michael Pressman
Writer .... Peter Baloff
Writer .... Dave Wollert
Cast .... Donald Sutherland
Cast .... Tim Matheson
Cast .... Jay Acovone

QUIET KILLER — CBS

Drama: Suspense/Thriller • Medical/Disease/Mental Illness • Disaster
Airdate: 03/24/92
Rating: 11.5/19   A/C: 2

A New York City Public Health physician leads a desperate attempt to quash a sudden outbreak of pneumonic plague.

Production Company: Sunrise Films Ltd. IAW Saban/Scherick Prods.
Executive Producer .... Edgar J. Scherick
Executive Producer .... Lynn Raynor
Executive Producer .... Steve Levitan
Producer .... Paul Saltzman
Director .... Sheldon Larry
Writer .... I.C. Rapoport
Cast .... Kate Jackson
Cast .... Jeffrey Nordling
Cast .... Howard Hesseman
Cast .... Al Waxman

QUIET LITTLE NEIGHBORHOOD, A PERFECT LITTLE MURDER, A — NBC

Comedy: Murder and Murder Mystery
Airdate: 10/14/90
Rating: 12.7/21   A/C: 2

A suburban housewife overhears a supposed murder plot by two of her neighbors and goes on a wild snooping spree when no one else believes her.

Production Company: Molly Ben/Saban/Garry Hoffman & Neil Israel
Executive Producer .... Gary Hoffman
Executive Producer .... Neal Israel
Producer .... Henry Colman
Director .... Anson Williams
Writer .... Mark Stein
Cast .... Teri Garr
Cast .... Robert Urich
Cast .... Jeffrey Tambor
Cast .... Susan Ruttan

QUIET VICTORY: THE CHARLIE WEDEMEYER STORY — CBS

Drama: Family Drama • Medical/Disease/Mental Illness • True Story • Sports
Airdate: 12/26/88
Rating: 14.9/25   A/C:

True story of a football coach who continued to coach despite the crippling and soon-fatal disease ALS.

Production Company: Landsburg Co.
Executive Producer .... Alan Landsburg
Executive Producer .... Joan Barnett
Producer .... Linda Otto
Director .... Roy Campanella II
Writer .... Barry Morrow
Cast .... Michael Nouri
Cast .... Pam Dawber
Cast .... Bess Meyer
Cast .... Noble Willingham

RAGE OF ANGELS: THE STORY CONTINUES — NBC

Miniseries/Drama (2 nights): Sex/Glitz • Mafia/Mob
Airdate: 11/02/86 • 11/03/86
Rating: 15.9/25 • 16.5/25   A/C:

Based on Sidney Sheldon's bestseller. A hotshot female lawyer and her lover, the married Vice President, are blackmailed by a member of the mob who also has personal motivation to destroy the couple.

Production Company: NBC Prods. Inc.
Executive Producer .... Sidney Sheldon
Producer .... Ron Roth
Director .... Paul Wendkos
Writer .... Robert L. Joseph
Cast .... Jaclyn Smith
Cast .... Ken Howard
Cast .... Armand Assante
Cast .... Michael Nouri
Cast .... Angela Lansbury
Cast .... Brad Dourif
Cast .... Susan Sullivan
Cast .... Mason Adams

RAGS TO RICHES — NBC

Drama: Children/Teens • Period Piece • Series Pilot (2 hr.)
Airdate: 03/09/87
Rating: 25.3/36   A/C:

In 1961 Los Angeles, a self-made millionaire with a playboy reputation tries to repair his image by taking two orphan girls into his house.

Production Company: Leonard Hill Films
Executive Producer .... Leonard Hill
Executive Producer .... Bernie Kukoff
Producer .... Ron Gilbert
Director .... Bruce Seth Green
Writer .... Bernie Kukoff
Cast .... Joseph Bologna
Cast .... Douglas Seale
Cast .... Kimiko Gelman
Cast .... Tisha Campbell

RAILWAY STATION MAN, THE   TNT

Drama: Love Story • Foreign or Exotic Location •
Political Piece
Airdate: 10/18/92
Rating: N/A   A/C:

*Based on the book by Jennifer Johnston. In an
Irish coastal town, a middle-aged widow whose
husband was mistakenly killed by the IRA falls
in love with a disabled American railroad man
whose dream is to restore an old railway station.
Their passionate affair is soon troubled when
her son becomes involved in political intrigue
which ultimately ends in a tragic explosion.*

Production Company: First Film Co., Sand Prods.
   IAW TNT & BBC
Executive Producer .... Lauren Sand
Executive Producer .... Mark Shivas
Producer .... Roger Culter
Producer .... Andree Molyneux
Co-Producer .... Amanda Marmot
Director .... Michael Whyte
Writer .... Shelagh Delaney
Cast .... Donald Sutherland
Cast .... Julie Christie

RAINBOW DRIVE   SHOWTIME

Mystery: Murder and Murder Mystery • Suspense/
Thriller • Cops/Detectives/Law Enforcement
Airdate: 09/08/90
Rating: N/A   A/C:

*Based on the novel by Roderick Thorp. When
a Hollywood chief of homicide discovers a
multiple murder, his efforts to solve the case
are hampered by a bizarre cover-up being
orchestrated by an official above him.*

Production Company: Viacom-Dove-ITC
Executive Producer .... Michael Viner
Producer .... John Veitch
Director .... Bobby Roth
Writer .... Bill Phillips
Writer .... Bennett Cohen
Cast .... Peter Weller
Cast .... Sela Ward
Cast .... Bruce Weitz
Cast .... Henry Sanders

RAPE OF DR. WILLIS, THE   CBS

Drama: Murder and Murder Mystery • Woman
Against The System • Courtroom Drama • Rape/
Molestation
Airdate: 11/03/91
Rating: 14.4/23   A/C: 2

*A doctor faces prosecution after she performs
emergency surgery on the man who raped
her...and he dies on the operating table.*

Production Company: Smith/Richmond Prods.
   IAW Saban/Scherick
Executive Producer .... Barbara Hiser
Executive Producer .... Tony Richmond
Executive Producer .... Edgar J. Scherick
Executive Producer .... Haim Saban
Producer .... Henry Colman
Director .... Lou Antonio
Writer .... Steven Gethers
Writer .... Anne Gerard
Cast .... Jaclyn Smith
Cast .... Robin Thomas
Cast .... Lisa Jakub
Cast .... Holland Taylor

RAPE OF RICHARD BECK, THE   ABC

Drama: Cops/Detectives/Law Enforcement • Rape/
Molestation • Social Issue
Airdate: 05/27/85
Rating: 25.2/38   A/C:

*When a tough and insensitive police sergeant
is raped by a pair of criminals, he gets a hard-
won lesson in humility and victimization.*

Production Company: Robert Papazian Prods.
   IAW Henerson-Hirsch Prods.
Executive Producer .... James S. Henerson
Executive Producer .... James G. Hirsch
Producer .... Robert A. Papazian
Director .... Karen Arthur
Writer .... James G. Hirsch
Cast .... Richard Crenna
Cast .... Meredith Baxter
Cast .... Frances Lee McCain
Cast .... Cotter Smith
Cast .... Joanna Kerns

RAY ALEXANDER: A TASTE FOR JUSTICE   NBC

Drama: Cops/Detectives/Law Enforcement • Series
Pilot (2 hr.)
Airdate: 5/13/94
Rating: 8.5/15   A/C: 3

*A San Francisco cafe owner who doubles as a
private eye on high-profile murder cases
uncovers evidence that proves the innocence of
a woman framed for the murder of her wealthy,
psychiatrist husband.*

Production Company: Logo Entertainment and
   Viacom Prods.
Executive Producer .... Dean Hargrove
Co-Executive Producer .... Lou Gossett, Jr.
Co-Executive Producer .... Hillard Elkins
CO-Executive Producer .... Dennis Considine
Producer .... Peter Katz
Co-Producer .... David Solomon
Director .... Gary Nelson
Writer .... Dean Hargrove
Cast .... Louis Gossett, Jr.
Cast .... Ossie Davis
Cast .... James Coburn
Cast .... Tracy Nelson

REARVIEW MIRROR   NBC

Drama: Woman In Jeopardy • Suspense/Thriller
Airdate: 11/26/84
Rating: 19.9/30   A/C:

*After a woman is abducted while hiking, she
must pull out all the stops to outwit her captors
and escape harm as they drive through the
rough and swampy Carolina countryside.*

Production Company: Simon-Asher Entertainment
   Prods. IAW Sunn Classic Pictures
Executive Producer .... Barry Krost
Producer .... Kip Gowans
Producer .... Deborah Simon
Director .... Lou Antonio
Writer .... Lorenzo Semple, Jr.
Cast .... Lee Remick
Cast .... Tony Musante
Cast .... Michael Beck
Cast .... Jim Antonio

REASON FOR LIVING: THE JILL IRELAND STORY   NBC

Drama: Family Drama • Children/Teens • Medical/
Disease/Mental Illness • True Story • Addiction Story
• Biography
Airdate: 05/20/91
Rating: 12.5/21   A/C: 2

*Based on the book "Life Lines" by Jill Ireland.
Late actress Jill Ireland's account of her
struggle to help her adopted son Jason
overcome addiction to heroin while dealing with
her own battle with breast cancer.*

Production Company: Bonny Dore IAW Ten Four
   Prods.
Executive Producer .... Bonny Dore
Executive Producer .... Greg Strangis
Producer .... Sam Strangis
Director .... Michael Rhodes
Writer .... Audrey Davis Levin
Cast .... Jill Clayburgh
Cast .... Lance Henriksen
Cast .... Neill Barry
Cast .... Elizabeth Ashley

REASON TO LIVE, A   NBC

Drama: Family Drama • Children/Teens • Medical/
Disease/Mental Illness • Social Issue
Airdate: 01/07/85
Rating: 15.6/23   A/C:

*A man's business and marriage fall apart and
he sinks into a severe depression. His fourteen
year old son must do all he can to prevent his
father's suicide.*

Production Company: Papazian Prods.
Executive Producer .... Doreen Bergesen
Producer .... Robert A. Papazian
Director .... Robert Lewin
Writer .... Robert Lewin
Cast .... Rick Schroder
Cast .... Peter Fonda
Cast .... Bruce Weitz
Cast .... Carrie Snodgress
Cast .... Tracey Gold
Cast .... Diedre Hall

RED EARTH, WHITE EARTH   CBS

Drama: Family Drama • Social Issue • American
Indians • Farm Story
Airdate: 01/24/89
Rating: 11.9/19   A/C:

*A California businessman who returns to the
Midwest to help with the family farm must deal
not only with family problems, but also with
the intense conflict between whites and Indians
for ownership of the land.*

Production Company: Chris/Rose Prods.
Executive Producer .... Rick Rosenberg
Executive Producer .... Bob Christiansen
Producer .... Murray Shostak
Director .... David Greene
Writer .... Michael De Guzman
Cast .... Genevieve Bujold
Cast .... Tim Daly
Cast .... Ralph Waite
Cast .... Richard Farnsworth

MOVIES AND MINISERIES

RED KING, WHITE KNIGHT HBO
Drama: Suspense/Thriller • Foreign or Exotic
Location • Political Piece
Airdate: 11/25/89
Rating: N/A   A/C:

An ex-CIA agent is re-hired to foil an
assassination attempt against the new liberal
Soviet president, and becomes a marked man
by the KGB.

Production Company: HBO Pictures IAW Zenith,
    A John Kemeny/Citadel Entertainment Prod.
Executive Producer .... David R. Ginsburg
Producer .... John Kemeny
Director .... Geoff Murphy
Writer .... Ron Hutchinson
Cast .... Tom Skerritt
Cast .... Max Von Sydow
Cast .... Helen Mirren

RED RIVER CBS
Drama: Western • Period Piece
Airdate: 04/10/88
Rating: 18.4/29   A/C:

Based on the book "The Chisolm Trail" by
Borden Chase. Remake of the Howard Hawks
film. A cattle drive culminates the rivalry
between a widower and the young man he
raised as his son.

Production Company: Catalina Prods. Group Ltd.
    and MGM/UA TV
Executive Producer .... Franklin R. Levy
Executive Producer .... Gregory Harrison
Producer .... Michael Rauch
Producer .... Matthew Rushton
Director .... Richard Michaels
Writer .... Richard Fielder
Cast .... James Arness
Cast .... Bruce Boxleitner
Cast .... Gregory Harrison
Cast .... Ray Walston

RED SHOES DIARIES SHOWTIME
Drama: Series Pilot (2 hr.) • Sex/Glitz
Airdate: 05/16/92
Rating: N/A   A/C:

To understand his fiancee's suicide, her
distraught lover pours through her diary. In it
he discovers her obsessive passion for another
man which leads him to confront his former
rival.

Production Company: 10 dB Inc.
Executive Producer .... Zalman King
Executive Producer .... Patricia Knop
Executive Producer .... Mark Damon
Producer .... David Saunders
Producer .... Rafeal Eisenman
Director .... Zalman King
Writer .... Patricia Knop
Writer .... Zalman King
Cast .... David Duchovny
Cast .... Brigitte Bako
Cast .... Brenda Vaccaro

RED SPIDER, THE CBS
Drama: Murder and Murder Mystery • Cops/
Detectives/Law Enforcement • Suspense/Thriller
Airdate: 04/21/88
Rating: 15.1/25   A/C:

A police lieutenant investigates the bizarre
murder of a policeman who picked up a woman
in a club, then died with a spider engraved in
his belly.

Production Company: CBS Entertainment Prods.
Producer .... Timothy King
Co-Producer .... Derek Kavanagh
Director .... Jerry Jameson
Writer .... Paul King
Cast .... James Farentino
Cast .... Amy Steel
Cast .... Philip Casnoff
Cast .... Soon-Teck Oh

RED WIND USA
Drama: Woman In Jeopardy • Psychological Thriller
Airdate: 05/15/91
Rating: N/A   A/C:

A therapist, specializing in sadomasochistic
relationships, becomes involved in a lurid
investigation when her patient supposedly
murders her sadistic husband.

Production Company: MCA TV
Executive Producer .... Alan Barnette
Producer .... Tom Noonan
Producer .... Oscar L. Costo
Director .... Alan Metzger
Writer .... Tom Noonan
Cast .... Lisa Hartman
Cast .... Philip Casnoff
Cast .... Christopher McDonald
Cast .... Deanna Lund

RELENTLESS: MIND OF A KILLER NBC
Drama: Murder and Murder Mystery • Cops/
Detectives/Law Enforcement • Psychological Thriller
• Series Pilot (2 hr.)
Airdate: 1/11/93
Rating: 12.8/20   A/C: 2

A distinguished psychiatrist who specializes in
the criminal mind in drawn into a sensational
murder trial that forces him to relive the
nightmare of his wife death at the hands of one
of his jealous, psychotic patients. Able to unlock
the hidden meanings in his troubling dreams
he unravels the mystery of his current case.

Production Company: Universal Television
Executive Producer .... John Badham
Executive Producer .... Rob Cohen
Executive Producer .... Jacob Epstein
Executive Producer .... Ken Solarz
Producer .... Alex Beaton
Director .... John Patterson
Writer .... Ken Solarz
Writer .... Jacob Epstein
Cast .... Tim Matheson
Cast .... Alberta Watson
Cast .... Claudia Christian

REMINGTON STEELE: THE STEELE THAT WOULDN'T DIE NBC
Drama: Murder and Murder Mystery • Cops/
Detectives/Law Enforcement • Romantic Comedy •
Foreign or Exotic Location
Airdate: 01/05/87
Rating: 19.7/28   A/C:

Forced to demonstrate to the Immigration
Service that their marriage is for real, the pair
honeymoon in Mexico, where Steele is charged
with murder.

Production Company: MTM Prods.
Co-Executive Producer .... Michael Gleason
Co-Executive Producer .... Gareth Davies
Producer .... Kevin Inch
Director .... Kevin Inch
Writer .... Brad Kern
Cast .... Pierce Brosnan
Cast .... Stephanie Zimbalist
Cast .... Doris Roberts
Cast .... Jack Scalia

RESTING PLACE CBS
Drama: Black Story • Social Issue • Vietnam
Airdate: 04/27/86
Rating: 22.3/36   A/C:

In 1972 Georgia, a white army officer tries to
ensure that a black Vietnam war hero be buried
in the currently all-white cemetery. In
investigating details of the soldier's heroics, he
discovers a shocking revelation.

Production Company: Marian Rees Associates
Executive Producer .... Marian Rees
Producer .... Robert Huddleston
Director .... John Korty
Writer .... Walter Halsey Davis
Cast .... John Lithgow
Cast .... John Philbin
Cast .... Brian Tarantina
Cast .... Morgan Freeman
Cast .... M. Emmet Walsh
Cast .... G. D. Spradlin

RETURN OF DESPERADO, THE NBC
Drama: Series Pilot (2 hr.) • Western • Black Story •
Period Piece
Airdate: 02/15/88
Rating: 16.0/24   A/C:

McCall, searching for the man who can clear
him of a murder charge, cleans up the town of
Beauty where a con man has the townspeople
hoodwinked and is oppressing black
homesteaders.

Production Company: Walter Mirisch Prods. with
    Charles E. Sellier, Jr. & Universal TV
Executive Producer .... Andrew Mirisch
Producer .... Chuck Sellier
Director .... E.W. Swackhamer
Writer .... John Mankiewicz
Writer .... Charles Grant Craig
Writer .... Daniel Pyne
Cast .... Alex McArthur
Cast .... Robert Foxworth
Cast .... Marcy Walker
Cast .... Victor Love
Cast .... Billy Dee Williams

RETURN OF ELIOT NESS, THE — NBC

Drama: Murder and Murder Mystery • Cops/
Detectives/Law Enforcement • Period Piece • Mafia/
Mob
Airdate: 11/10/91
Rating: 12.7/19   A/C: 2

*In 1947 Chicago, "Untouchable" boss Eliot
Ness comes out of retirement to clear the name
of a former colleague who has been murdered
by the mob.*

Production Company: NBC-Michael Filerman
   Prods.
Executive Producer .... Michael Filerman
Producer .... Joseph Wallenstein
Co-Producer .... John Danylkiw
Co-Producer .... Michael Petryni
Director .... James A. Contner
Writer .... Michael Petryni
Cast .... Robert Stack
Cast .... Jack Coleman
Cast .... Lisa Hartman
Cast .... Philip Bosco

RETURN OF IRONSIDE, THE — NBC

Drama: Murder and Murder Mystery • Cops/
Detectives/Law Enforcement
Airdate: 5/4/93
Rating: 11.6/19   A/C: 2

*Sequel to the 70's series. The retired
wheelchair-bound detective comes to the aid
of his old buddy, now the deputy police chief
when his boss, the Chief of Police of Denver is
murdered. Implicated in the crime is the
daughter of his former assistant.*

Production Company: Riven Rocks Prods., Windy
   City Prods.
Executive Producer .... Michele Brustin
Executive Producer .... James McAdams
Producer .... Richard Brams
Director .... Gene Nelson
Writer .... Rob Hedden
Writer .... William Read Woodfield
Cast .... Raymond Burr
Cast .... Don Galloway
Cast .... Barbara Anderson
Cast .... Dana Wynter

RETURN OF SAM McCLOUD, THE — CBS

Drama: Murder and Murder Mystery • Cops/
Detectives/Law Enforcement • Foreign or Exotic
Location
Airdate: 11/12/89
Rating: 12.9/20   A/C: 3

*From the 1970's TV series. The former U.S.
marshal from the 1970s series, now a U.S.
Senator, goes to London to solve the murder of
his niece, a research scientist at a large drug
company which has something to hide.*

Production Company: Michael Sloan Prods. IAW
   Universal TV
Executive Producer .... Michael Sloan
Executive Producer .... Dennis Weaver
Producer .... Nigel Watts
Producer .... Bernadette Joyce
Director .... Alan J. Levi
Writer .... Michael Sloan
Cast .... Dennis Weaver
Cast .... J.D. Cannon
Cast .... Terry Carter
Cast .... Diana Muldaur

RETURN OF SHERLOCK HOLMES, THE — CBS

Mystery: Murder and Murder Mystery • Cops/
Detectives/Law Enforcement • Foreign or Exotic
Location • Sci-Fi/Supernatural/Horror/Fantasy
Airdate: 01/10/87
Rating: 14.4/24   A/C:

*Thawed by Dr. Watson's great-granddaughter,
a private eye, cryogenically-frozen Holmes
joins her to solve a case in London and Boston
locations.*

Production Company: CBS Entertainment
Director .... Kevin Connor
Writer .... Bob Shayne
Cast .... Margaret Colin
Cast .... William Hootkins
Cast .... Barry Morse
Cast .... Lila Kaye

RETURN OF THE 6 MILLION DOLLAR MAN & BIONIC WOMAN — NBC

Drama: Action/Adventure • Sci-Fi/Supernatural/
Horror/Fantasy
Airdate: 05/17/87
Rating: 20.5/33   A/C:

*From the popular TV series. The two
superheroes and his son foil a villain's attempt
to take over the world.*

Production Company: Michael Sloan Prods. and
   Universal TV
Executive Producer .... Michael Sloan
Producer .... Bernadette Joyce
Director .... Ray Austin
Writer .... Michael Sloan
Cast .... Lindsay Wagner
Cast .... Lee Majors
Cast .... Richard Anderson

RETURN TO GREEN ACRES — CBS

Comedy: Farm Story
Airdate: 05/18/90
Rating: 11.8/22   A/C: 2

*From the popular TV Series. While the series
ended with the Douglases happily ensconced
in Hooterville, now they're moving back to New
York City. But when an unscrupulous land
developer tries to bulldoze the town, the
Douglases return to save Hooterville.*

Production Company: Jaygee Production IAW
   Orion Television Entertainment
Executive Producer .... Jerry Golod
Producer .... Anthony Croce
Director .... William Asher
Writer .... Craig Heller
Writer .... Guy Shulman
Cast .... Eddie Albert
Cast .... Eva Gabor
Cast .... Alvy Moore
Cast .... Pat Buttram

RETURN TO LONESOME DOVE — CBS

Miniseries/Drama (3 nights): Period Piece • Western
• Action/Adventure
Airdate: 11/14/93 • 11/16/93 • 11/18/93
Rating: 18.1/28 • 16.5/25 • 15.2/24   A/C: 1
• 2 • 1

*Sequel to the 1989 CBS Miniseries. In 1870,
Ex-Texas ranger Woodrow Call and his old
buddies drive a heard of wild Mustangs north
to his new ranch in Montana. The trail is
fraught with hardship, romance, rivalries and
desperados but the cowboys persevere in order
to realize their dream.*

Production Company: RHI Ent. IAW de Passe Ent.
   & Nightwatch Prods. Inc.
Executive Producer .... Suzanne de Passe
Executive Producer .... Robert Halmi, Jr.
Executive Producer .... John Wilder
Producer .... Dyson Lovell
Director .... Mike Robe
Writer .... John Wilder
Cast .... Jon Voight
Cast .... Barbara Hershey
Cast .... Rick Schroder
Cast .... Louis Gossett, Jr.
Cast .... Oliver Reed
Cast .... William Petersen

MOVIES AND MINISERIES

RETURN TO MAYBERRY   NBC
Comedy: Buddy Story
Airdate: 04/13/86
Rating: 33.0/49   A/C: 1

From the long running TV series. Opie, Barney, Andy and the Mayberry gang get back together. Andy wants to be Sheriff again, but his old deputy, Barney, is running for the job.

Production Company: Strathmore Prods. IAW Viacom

Executive Producer	Andy Griffith
Executive Producer	Richard O. Linke
Executive Producer	Dean Hargrove
Producer	Robin S. Clark
Director	Bob Sweeney
Writer	Harvey Bullock
Writer	Everett Greenbaum
Cast	Andy Griffith
Cast	Ron Howard
Cast	Howard Morris
Cast	Jack Dodson
Cast	Jim Nabors
Cast	Don Knotts
Cast	George Lindsey

REUNION AT FAIRBOROUGH   HBO
Drama: Love Story • Foreign or Exotic Location
Airdate: 5/12/85
Rating: N/A   A/C:

A sixty year old man whose two failed marriages and forced early retirement cause him to return to the quiet English village where he was a WWII bomber Pilot in the 8th U.S. Air Force. The 40th reunion of his squadron also brings him into contact with his old sweetheart, now a dress shop matron and a grandmother. Old passions are renewed and a family is reunited when he finds out that he has a granddaughter he never knew he had.

Production Company: Wagner/King Productions IAW Columbia Pictures Television

Executive Producer	Alan King
Executive Producer	Alan Wagner
Producer	William Hill
Director	Herbert Wise
Writer	Albert Ruben
Cast	Robert Mitchum
Cast	Deborah Kerr
Cast	Red Buttons
Cast	Barry Morse

REVEALING EVIDENCE   NBC
Drama: Murder and Murder Mystery • Cops/Detectives/Law Enforcement • Foreign or Exotic Location • Series Pilot (2 hr.)
Airdate: 06/03/90
Rating: 14.5/25   A/C: 1

A Honolulu homicide detective is convinced that the latest in a string of apparently serial murders is the work of someone else. Then, after he catches the serial killer, the detective himself is suspected of the copycat killing.

Production Company: T.W.S. Prods. Inc. IAW Universal

Executive Producer	Tom Selleck
Executive Producer	Charles Floyd Johnson
Executive Producer	Chris Abbott
Producer	Rick Weaver
Director	Michael Switzer
Cast	Stanley Tucci
Cast	Mary Page Keller
Cast	Finn Carter
Cast	Perry Lang

REVENGE OF AL CAPONE, THE   NBC
Drama: Mafia/Mob • Period Piece • Historical Piece • Cops/Detectives/Law Enforcement • True Crime • Prison and Prison Camp
Airdate: 02/26/89
Rating: 13.9/22   A/C:

A federal agent attempts to move Al Capone to Alcatraz, where he will no longer be able to rule his criminal empire as he still does from his Chicago jail cell.

Production Company: Unity Prods./River City Prods.

Executive Producer	John Levoff
Executive Producer	Robert Lovenheim
Producer	Vicki Niemi-Gordon
Director	Michael Pressman
Writer	Tracy Keenan Wynn
Cast	Keith Carradine
Cast	Ray Sharkey
Cast	Debrah Farentino
Cast	Charles Haid

REVENGE OF THE NERDS IV: NERDS IN LOVE   FBC
Comedy: Youth Comedy
Airdate: 5/9/94
Rating: 5.9/9   A/C: 4

Based on the 1984 feature film "Revenge of the Nerds". The gang reunites for the wedding of Booger, who is planing to marry the daughter of a disapproving nouveau riche businessman. With the help of his greedy son-in-law, dear old dad plots to put an end to the up-coming nuptials.

Production Company: Zacharias/Buhai Prods. IAW Fox West Pictures

Executive Producer	Steve Zacharias
Executive Producer	Jeff Buhai
Producer	Ooty Moorehead
Co-Producer	Robert Carradine
Director	Steve Zacharias
Writer	Steve Zacharias
Writer	Jeff Buhai
Cast	Robert Carradine
Cast	Curtis Armstrong
Cast	Corinne Bohrer
Cast	Joseph Bologna
Cast	Christina Pickles

REVENGE OF THE NERDS: THE NEXT GENERATION   FBC
Comedy: Youth Comedy
Airdate: 07/13/92
Rating: 7.2/13   A/C: 3

Sequel to the feature film "Revenge Of The Nerds." The nerd alumni of Adams College return to their fraternity to rescue the freshman class of geeks that are once again the target of persecution by thick-headed jocks.

Production Company: FNM Films IAW Zacharias and Guhai Prods.

Executive Producer	Steve Zacharias
Executive Producer	Jeff Buhai
Producer	Robert Engelman
Director	Roland Mesa
Writer	Steve Zacharias
Writer	Jeff Buhai
Cast	Robert Carradine
Cast	Ted McGinley
Cast	Curtis Armstrong
Cast	Morton Downey, Jr.

REVENGE ON THE HIGHWAY   NBC
Drama: True Crime • Man Against The System
Airdate: 12/6/92
Rating: 12.8/19   A/C: 3

When his son is killed in a hit-and-run by an outlaw big rig , Claude Sams who is also a trucker hits the highways in search of revenge. When the police fail to follow up on leads, Sams' takes the law into his own hands and confronts his son's killer while crusading for tougher motor-vehicle laws.

Production Company: Arvin Kaufman Prods.
     IAW Sabin Enter.
Executive Producer .... Arvin Kaufman
Executive Producer .... Lance Robbins
Producer .... Jay Benson
Co-Producer .... Dennis Shryack
Co-Producer .... Michael Blodgett
Director .... Craig Baxley
Writer .... Dennis Shrylack
Writer .... Michael Blodgett
Cast .... Stacy Keach
Cast .... Lisa Banes
Cast .... Sandahl Bergman

REVOLVER   NBC
Drama: Cops/Detectives/Law Enforcement • Suspense/Thriller • Foreign or Exotic Location
Airdate: 04/19/92
Rating: 9.2/16   A/C: 3

In Barcelona, a vengeful FBI agent pursues the assassin who left him paralyzed, uncovering a top-secret plot against the United States.

Production Company: Televisio de Catalunya IAW Columbia Pictures TV, Victoria Prods.
Executive Producer .... Mark Waxman
Executive Producer .... Rift Fournier
Producer .... Christopher Seitz
Director .... Gary Nelson
Writer .... Mark Waxman
Cast .... Robert Urich
Cast .... Dakin Matthews
Cast .... Steven Williams
Cast .... David Ryall

RICH MEN, SINGLE WOMEN   ABC
Comedy: Romantic Comedy
Airdate: 01/29/90
Rating: 14.8/23   A/C: 3

Based on Pamela Beck's book. A N.Y. woman arrives in L.A. with a plan. She and two friends will use a mansion one is supposed to be selling to trap three millionaires into marrying them within sixty days. They find true love...and money, too.

Production Company: Aaron Spelling Productions
Executive Producer .... Aaron Spelling
Producer .... Dennis Hammer
Director .... Elliot Silverstein
Writer .... Barbara Esenstein
Writer .... James Harmon Brown
Writer .... Rita Mae Brown
Cast .... Suzanne Somers
Cast .... Heather Locklear
Cast .... Deborah Adair
Cast .... Larry Wilcox

RICHEST MAN IN THE WORLD: THE ARISTOTLE ONASSIS STORY   ABC
Miniseries/Drama (2 nights): Period Piece • Biography • Love Story • Historical Piece • Sex/Glitz • True Story
Airdate: 05/01/88 • 05/02/88
Rating: 12.1/18 • 13.9/22   A/C:

The life and career of the Greek shipping tycoon, from his youthful adventures onward including his affair with diva Maria Callas, the death of his beloved son and his marriage to former U.S. First Lady Jacqueline Kennedy.

Production Company: Konigsberg/Sanitsky Co.
Executive Producer .... Frank Konigsberg
Executive Producer .... Larry Sanitsky
Producer .... Alfred R. Kelman
Director .... Waris Hussein
Writer .... Jacqueline Feather
Writer .... David Seidler
Cast .... Raul Julia
Cast .... Jane Seymour
Cast .... Anthony Quinn
Cast .... Anthony Zerbe

RIDE WITH THE WIND   ABC
Drama: Medical/Disease/Mental Illness • Children/Teens • Love Story
Airdate: 4/18/94
Rating: 9.0/15   A/C: 4

A burnt out and emotionally crippled motorcycle racer is redeemed by the love of a decent woman and her cancer-stricken son. With their encouragement he finds the courage to enter and win the Grand Nationals.

Production Company: Family Tree Prods. & Peter Frankovich Prods. IAW Hearst Entertainment
Executive Producer .... Peter Frankovich
Executive Producer .... Craig T. Nelson
Executive Producer .... Connie Tavel
Co-Executive Producer .... Harry Grant
Co-Executive Producer .... Dale Rosenbloom
Producer .... Neil Rapp
Co-Producer .... Paul Roman
Director .... Bobby Roth
Writer .... Harry Grant
Cast .... Craig T. Nelson
Cast .... Helen Shaver
Cast .... Bradley Pierce

RIGHT OF THE PEOPLE, THE   ABC
Drama: Family Drama • Man Against The System • Social Issue
Airdate: 01/13/86
Rating: 14.5/22   A/C:

A local prosecuting attorney reacts to the holdup slaughter of his wife and child by supporting a law allowing most adults to carry guns. The results make him realize he really believes in gun control.

Production Company: Big Name Films IAW Fries Entertainment
Executive Producer .... Charles Fries
Producer .... Thomas Fries
Director .... Jeffrey Bloom
Writer .... Jeffrey Bloom
Cast .... Michael Ontkean
Cast .... Billy Dee Williams
Cast .... John Randolph
Cast .... M. Emmet Walsh
Cast .... Jane Kaczmarek

RIGHT TO DIE   NBC
Drama: Family Drama • Medical/Disease/Mental Illness • True Story • Social Issue
Airdate: 10/12/87
Rating: 17.5/28   A/C:

True story of a young psychologist stricken by the incurable degenerative disease ALS. When she realizes she can't fight the disease, she asks her husband to help her commit suicide so that she can die with dignity.

Production Company: Ohlmeyer Communications Co.
Executive Producer .... Don Ohlmeyer
Producer .... Karen Danaher-Dorr
Director .... Paul Wendkos
Writer .... Phil Penningroth
Cast .... Raquel Welch
Cast .... Michael Gross
Cast .... Bonnie Bartlett
Cast .... Peter Michael Goetz
Cast .... Joanna Miles

RIGHT TO KILL?   ABC
Drama: Children/Teens • True Crime • Family Violence • Social Issue • Murder and Murder Mystery
Airdate: 05/22/85
Rating: 19.0/31   A/C: 1

Based on the true story of Richard Jahnke Jr., who after suffering years of physical and mental abuse from his violent father, he finally murders him.

Production Company: Wrye-Konigsberg Prods. & Taper Media Ent. IAW Telepictures Prods.
Executive Producer .... Frank Konigsberg
Executive Producer .... Donald Wrye
Producer .... Jack Clements
Co-Producer .... Elizabeth Daley
Co-Producer .... Gordon Davidson
Director .... John Erman
Writer .... Joyce Eliason
Cast .... Frederic Forrest
Cast .... Christopher Collet
Cast .... Karmin Murcelo
Cast .... Justine Bateman
Cast .... Ann Wedgeworth

RIO DIABLO   CBS
Drama: Western
Airdate: 2/28/93
Rating: 17.3/26   A/C: 1

A bounty hunter with an unsavory past is on the trail of a gang of murdering bank robbers, he is joined by a naive farmer whose sweet young bride has been kidnapped and taken hostage by the odious outlaws.

Production Company: Kenny Rogers Prods. IAW RHI Inc. & WIN
Executive Producer .... Ken Kragen
Executive Producer .... Steven Berman
Executive Producer .... Larry Levinson
Producer .... Kelly Junkermann
Co-Producer .... Frank Q. Dobbs
Director .... Rod Hardy
Writer .... Frank Dobbs
Writer .... David Cass
Writer .... Stephen Lodge
Cast .... Kenny Rogers
Cast .... Travis Tritt
Cast .... Naomi Judd
Cast .... Stacy Keach

RIO SHANON   ABC
Drama: Family Drama • Series Pilot (2 hr.)
Airdate: 8/14/93
Rating: 5.2/11   A/C: 4

Based on the unpublished manuscript by John Egan. A strong willed widow from the city whose desire to rebuild a ramshackle guest ranch in New Mexico is hampered by a medical emergency, her son's ambivalence and a wealthy businessman's sleazy machinations.

Production Company: Sacret Inc. IAW Warner Bros. TV
Executive Producer .... John Sacret Young
Producer .... Linda Bergman
Director .... Mimi Leder
Writer .... Linda Bergman
Cast .... Blair Brown
Cast .... Patrick Van Horn
Cast .... Michael DeLuise
Cast .... Penny Fuller

RISE & WALK: THE DENNIS BYRD STORY
FBC
Drama: True Story • Medical/Disease/Mental Illness • Sports
Airdate: 2/28/94
Rating: 7.1/11   A/C: 4

Based on the book by Dennis Byrd. New York Jets linebacker, Dennis Byrd is paralyzed when he breaks his neck during a 1992 football game. With his loving wife, Angela and his devout religious faith he struggles through a grueling rehabilitation program and triumphantly regains the use of his limbs.

Production Company: Fox West Pictures Inc.
Executive Producer .... Rick Schaeffer
Executive Producer .... Joe Dietz
Producer .... Paul Kurta
Producer .... Michael Dinner
Director .... Michael Dinner
Writer .... Saly Nemeth
Writer .... John Miglis
Writer .... Mark Levin
Cast .... Peter Berg
Cast .... Kathy Morris
Cast .... Carrie Snodgress

RISING SON   TNT
Drama: Family Drama • Social Issue
Airdate: 07/23/90
Rating: N/A   A/C:

A middle-aged factory worker faces two crises at once. When the factory is bought by a Japanese company, he is laid off. And his son, pushed into pre-med studies by his father, decides to drop out.

Production Company: Sarabande Prod.
Executive Producer .... David Manson
Producer .... Fred Berner
Director .... John David Coles
Writer .... Bill Phillips
Cast .... Brian Dennehy
Cast .... Matt Damon
Cast .... Piper Laurie

RIVER OF RAGE: THE TAKING OF
MAGGIE KEENE   CBS
Drama: Woman In Jeopardy
Airdate: 10/3/93
Rating: 12.4/20   A/C: 2

A divorced mother goes on a river rafting trip on the Rio Grande with her new boyfriend and discovers he is involved with a vicious drug dealer. When she witnesses his murder and that of their river guide she is forced to escape from the remote wilderness area while being hunted by the crazed killer and his gang of slimeballs. Her son back home, worried when she doesn't return, convinces the local sheriff to mount a rescue party.

Production Company: David C. Thomas Prods. IAW Longbow
Executive Producer .... Richard Kughn
Executive Producer .... Ronnie Clemmer
Executive Producer .... Bill Pace
Producer .... Robert Iscove
Director .... Robert Iscove
Writer .... Michael Norell
Cast .... Victoria Principal
Cast .... Peter Onorati
Cast .... John Fleck
Cast .... Sean Murray

RIVIERA   ABC
Drama: Suspense/Thriller • Foreign or Exotic Location
Airdate: 05/31/87
Rating: 11.5/17   A/C:

On the French Riviera, a disillusioned American secret agent comes under suspicion for a Vienna bomb blast, and finds he has few friends on either side of the Iron Curtain.

Production Company: MTM Prods.
Executive Producer .... Michael Sloan
Producer .... Robert L. Rosen
Director .... Alan Smithee
Writer .... Michael Sloan
Cast .... Ben Masters
Cast .... Elyssa Davalos
Cast .... Jon Finch
Cast .... Daniel Emilfork

ROAD RAIDERS, THE   CBS
Drama: Period Piece • Action/Adventure • WWII
Airdate: 04/25/89
Rating: 8.5/14   A/C:

Set in Manila circa 1942, a cynical saloon owner romances a nightclub singer as well as an army intelligence officer, then leads a fighting group of misfit G.I.'s against the Japanese.

Production Company: New East Entertainment w/ Universal TV
Executive Producer .... Glen A. Larson
Producer .... Charles F. Engel
Director .... Richard Lang
Writer .... Mark Jones
Writer .... Glen A. Larson
Cast .... Bruce Boxleitner
Cast .... Reed McCants
Cast .... Noble Willingham
Cast .... Susan Diol

ROADRACERS   SHOWTIME
Drama: Period Piece • Children/Teens • Action/
Adventure
Airdate: 7/22/93
Rating: N/A   A/C:

A rebellious, hard living teenage guitar player struggles to find his way in the clashing worlds of the 1950's. Caught between pursuing his dreams as a musician, defending his pride as a gang member and retaining the love of his passionate girlfriend he is ultimately forced to make some tough decisions about his life.

Production Company: Drive-In Classics Cinema
  Production IAW Showtime Networks Inc.
Executive Producer .... Debra Hill
Executive Producer .... Lou Arkoff
Executive Producer .... David Giler
Executive Producer .... Willie Kutner
Co-Producer .... Llewellyn Wells
Director .... Robert Rodriguez
Writer .... Robert Rodriguez
Writer .... Tommy Nix
Cast .... David Arquette
Cast .... Salma Hayek
Cast .... John Hawkes

ROBERT KENNEDY AND HIS TIMES   CBS
Miniseries/Drama (3 nights): True Story • Period
Piece • Biography • Political Piece
Airdate: 01/27/85 • 01/28/85 • 01/29/85
Rating: 19.8/29 • 14.9/21 • 16.9/26   A/C:

The life and political career of Robert F. Kennedy from 1946 to his death in 1968.

Production Company: Chris-Rose Prods. IAW
  Columbia TV
Producer .... Bob Christiansen
Executive Producer .... Rick Rosenberg
Director .... Marvin J. Chomsky
Writer .... Walon Green
Cast .... Brad Davis
Cast .... Veronica Cartwright
Cast .... Cliff De Young
Cast .... Ned Beatty
Cast .... Beatrice Straight
Cast .... G. D. Spradlin

ROBIN HOOD   FBC
Drama: Period Piece • Action/Adventure • Foreign
or Exotic Location
Airdate: 05/13/91
Rating: 6.0/10   A/C: 4

The twelfth century English hero defies oppressive Normans, helps overtaxed peasants and woos the fair maid Marian.

Production Company: 20th Century Fox
Executive Producer .... John McTiernan
Producer .... Sarah Radclyffe
Producer .... Tim Bevan
Director .... John Irvin
Writer .... Mark Allen Smith
Writer .... John McGrath
Cast .... Patrick Bergin
Cast .... Uma Thurman
Cast .... Jurgen Prochnow
Cast .... Edward Fox

ROCK HUDSON   ABC
Drama: True Story • Biography • Homosexuality •
Hollywood
Airdate: 01/08/90
Rating: 15.7/24   A/C: 2

Based on Phyllis Gates' biography "My Husband, Rock Hudson," and court records. The film focuses on Hudson's double life. He became a movie sex symbol while hiding his homosexuality by marrying, then refused to reveal he had AIDS even to his lover.

Production Company: The Konigsberg/Sanitsky
  Co.
Executive Producer .... Frank Konigsberg
Executive Producer .... Larry Sanitsky
Producer .... Renee Palyo
Director .... John Nicolella
Writer .... Dennis Turner
Cast .... Thomas Ian Griffith
Cast .... Daphne Ashbrook
Cast .... William R. Moses
Cast .... Andrew Robinson

ROCKABYE   CBS
Drama: Suspense/Thriller • Children/Teens • Social
Issue • Woman In Jeopardy
Airdate: 01/07/86
Rating: 25.3/38   A/C:

Based on the novel by Laird Koenig. After a woman's toddler is stolen on a New York street, a hard-boiled reporter helps the mother crack a black-market baby ring to get him back.

Production Company: Peregrine Producers Group
  Inc. IAW Bertinelli Prods. Inc.
Executive Producer .... Roger Gimbel
Executive Producer .... Freyda Rothstein
Producer .... Jack Grossbart
Producer .... Marty Litke
Director .... Richard Michaels
Writer .... Laird Koenig
Cast .... Valerie Bertinelli
Cast .... Rachel Ticotin
Cast .... Jonathan Raskin
Cast .... Jason Alexander

ROE VS. WADE   NBC
EMMY WINNER
Drama: Woman Against The System • True Story •
Courtroom Drama • Woman's Issue/Story • Social
Issue
Airdate: 05/15/89
Rating: 17.0/27   A/C:

The true story of Norma McCorvery (Jane Roe), an unwed mother whose case before the Supreme Court led to the legalization of abortion in 1973.

Production Company: The Manheim Co. IAW
  NBC Prods.
Executive Producer .... Michael Manheim
Producer .... Gregory Hoblit
Director .... Gregory Hoblit
Writer .... Alison Cross
Cast .... Holly Hunter
Cast .... Terry O'Quinn
Cast .... Annabella Price
Cast .... Amy Madigan

ROMAN HOLIDAY   NBC
Drama: Love Story • Foreign or Exotic Location
Airdate: 12/28/87
Rating: 17.0/28   A/C:

Remake of the 1953 classic. A raffish American reporter meets and falls in love with an overprotected princess on the lam from her royal guardians in Rome.

Production Company: Jerry Ludwig Enterprises
  Inc. IAW Paramount Network TV
Executive Producer .... Jerry Ludwig
Producer .... Mel Efros
Director .... Noel Nosseck
Writer .... Jerry Ludwig
Cast .... Catherine Oxenberg
Cast .... Ed Begley, Jr.
Cast .... Patrick Allen
Cast .... Tom Conti

ROMANCE ON THE ORIENT EXPRESS NBC
Drama: Love Story • Foreign or Exotic Location
Airdate: 03/04/85
Rating: 15.6/24   A/C:

While riding on the Orient Express, an American magazine editor meets up with the man with whom she had an ill-fated love affair ten years earlier.

Production Company: Frank von Zerneck Films
  IAW Yorkshire TV
Executive Producer .... Frank Von Zerneck
Producer .... James Hay
Producer for Yorkshire TV .... Michael Glynn
Director .... Lawrence Gordon-Clark
Writer .... Jan Worthington
Cast .... Cheryl Ladd
Cast .... Stuart Wilson
Cast .... Renee Asherson
Cast .... John Gielgud

ROOM, THE   ABC
Drama: Suspense/Thriller • Woman In Jeopardy
Airdate: 12/26/87
Rating: 5.5/11   A/C:

From Harold Pinter's one-act stage play. While her truck driver husband is at work, a woman is terrorized by a group of strange visitors.

Production Company: Sandcastle 5 Prods. &
  Secret Castle Prods., Inc.
Executive Producer .... Scott Bushnell
Producer .... Robert Altman
Director .... Robert Altman
Writer .... Harold Pinter
Cast .... Donald Pleasence
Cast .... Annie Lennox
Cast .... Julian Sands
Cast .... Linda Hunt

ROOM UPSTAIRS, THE   CBS

Drama: Love Story
Airdate: 01/31/87
Rating: 14.1/24   A/C:

Based on the novel by Norma Levinson. A lonely learning-therapist keeps a rooming house and falls in love with her cello-playing tenant.

Production Company: Marian Rees Associates Inc.
    IAW Alexander Group Prods. Inc.
Executive Producer .... Marian Rees
Producer .... Robert Huddleston
Director .... Stuart Margolin
Writer .... Steve Lawson
Cast .... Stockard Channing
Cast .... Sam Waterston
Cast .... Linda Hunt
Cast .... Devoreaux White

ROOMMATES   NBC

Drama: Medical/Disease/Mental Illness •
Homosexuality • Buddy Story
Airdate: 5/30/94
Rating: 8.9/15   A/C: 3

In a Seattle AIDS hospice a straight, homophobic ex-con is assigned to share an apartment with a Harvard educated gay man. At first, they form a instant dislike for each other but as they begin to get sicker they forge a compassionate friendship—with each roommate learning the true meaning of tolerance and trust.

Production Company: Pacific Motion Pictures
    Prods. IAW Michael Filerman Prods.
Executive Producer .... Michael Filerman
Producer .... Tom Rowe
Co-Producer .... Jack H. Degelia
Director .... Alan Metzger
Writer .... Robert W. Lenski
Cast .... Randy Quaid
Cast .... Eric Stoltz
Cast .... Elizabeth Pena
Cast .... Charles Durning

ROOTS: THE GIFT   ABC

Drama: Period Piece • Black Story • Holiday Special
Airdate: 12/11/88
Rating: 15.4/24   A/C:

In 1775 Virginia, slave Kunta Kinte is inspired by the efforts of a free black man to help slaves escape to the North and freedom.

Production Company: David L. Wolper Prods.
    IAW Warner Bros. TV
Executive Producer .... David L. Wolper
Executive Producer .... Bernard Sofronski
Producer .... Mark M. Wolper
Director .... Kevin Hooks
Writer .... David Eyre, Jr.
Cast .... Avery Brooks
Cast .... Louis Gossett, Jr.
Cast .... Annabella Price
Cast .... Kate Mulgrew
Cast .... Shaun Cassidy
Cast .... LeVar Burton
Cast .... Michael Learned

ROSE AND THE JACKAL, THE   TNT

Drama: Cops/Detectives/Law Enforcement • Love
Story • True Story • Period Piece • Action/Adventure
• Historical Piece
Airdate: 04/16/90
Rating: N/A   A/C:

As Civil War fever overcomes American politics, Alan Pinkerton, founder of the Secret Service, becomes obsessed with his prisoner, a beautiful and determined Confederate spy.

Production Company: Steve White Prods. IAW
    Spectacor Films and PWD Prods.
Executive Producer .... Steve White
Executive Producer .... Wendy Dytman
Executive Producer .... Paula Weinstein
Producer .... Barry Bernardi
Director .... Jack Gold
Writer .... Eric Edson
Cast .... Christopher Reeve
Cast .... Madolyn Smith Osborne

ROSES ARE FOR THE RICH   CBS

Miniseries/Drama (2 nights): Woman Against The
System • Sex/Glitz
Airdate: 05/17/87 • 05/19/87
Rating: 18.6/30 • 17.8/29   A/C:

Based on Jonell Lawson's novel. To avenge her husband's death in a mine disaster, an Appalachian woman enters the world of business, finance and adultery, and destroys the greedy tycoon she holds responsible for the death of her spouse.

Production Company: Phoenix TV Prods. Inc.
Executive Producer .... Karen Mack
Producer .... Jonathan Bernstein
Director .... Michael Miller
Writer .... Judith P. Mitchell
Cast .... Lisa Hartman
Cast .... Bruce Dern
Cast .... Joe Penny
Cast .... Richard Masur
Cast .... Howard Duff
Cast .... Morgan Stevens
Cast .... Betty Buckley
Cast .... Peggy Pope
Cast .... Kate Mulgrew

ROSWELL   SHOWTIME

Drama: True Story • Period Piece • Historical Piece •
Man Against The System
Airdate: 7/31/94
Rating: N/A   A/C:

In 1947, U.S. Army Air Force intelligence officer Jesse Marcel is forced by the Pentagon to cover up the possible crash of a flying saucer in Roswell, New Mexico—saying it was just a common weather balloon. At an Army reunion in 1977, Marcel begins to ask questions and finds himself reopening the mystery to find out what really happened out there in the desert.

Production Company: Citadel Productions IAW
    Showtime Networks Inc.
Executive Producer .... Paul Davids
Executive Producer .... David R. Ginsburg
Producer .... Ilene Kahn
Producer .... Jeremy Kagan
Director .... Jeremy Kagan
Writer .... Arthur Kopit
Cast .... Kyle Maclachlan
Cast .... J.D. Daniels
Cast .... Doug Wert
Cast .... Dwight Yoakam

ROUND TABLE, THE   NBC

Drama: Series Pilot (2 hr.) • Suspense/Thriller • Cops/
Detectives/Law Enforcement
Airdate: 9/18/92
Rating: 8.3/16   A/C: 3

The lives of six young law enforcement professionals in Washington D.C. are intertwined as they adjust to new jobs, career setbacks, political maneuvering and romantic entanglements in the capitol city.

Production Company: Spelling Televison
Executive Producer .... Aaron Spelling
Executive Producer .... E. Duke Vincent
Executive Producer .... Jeff Bleckner
Producer .... Ann Donahue
Producer .... Christopher Morgan
Director .... Jeff Bleckner
Writer .... Nancy Miller
Cast .... Stacy Haiduk
Cast .... Jessica Walter
Cast .... Roxann Biggs
Cast .... David Ackroyd

ROXANNE: THE PRIZE PULITZER   NBC

Drama: Family Drama • Sex/Glitz • True Story
Airdate: 10/16/89
Rating: 17.3/27   A/C: 2

Based on the autobiography by Roxanne Pulitzer. Herbert Pulitzer's second wife, Roxanne, describes how, as a naive girl, she got caught up in a jet set world, tempestuous marriage, and the famous messy divorce...featuring drug abuse, kinky sex and tabloid headlines.

Production Company: Qintex Entertainment
Executive Producer .... Robert Halmi, Sr.
Producer .... Jim Chory
Director .... Richard Colla
Writer .... Elizabeth Gill
Cast .... Chynna Phillips
Cast .... Perry King
Cast .... Courteney Cox

ROYCE — SHOWTIME

Drama: Suspense/Thriller • Action/Adventure •
Foreign or Exotic Location
Airdate: 4/3/94
Rating: N/A   A/C:

An undercover agent scrambles to foil a band
of disgruntled secret agents who decide to
kidnap a senator's son in order to secure
classified information on Russian nuclear
warheads.

Production Company: Gerber/ITC Prods. IAW
 Showtime
Executive Producer .... David Gerber
Executive Producer .... Paul Bernbaum
Producer .... J. Boyce Harman, Jr.
Producer .... Paul Quigely
Director .... Rod Holcomb
Writer .... Paul Bernbaum
Cast .... James Belushi
Cast .... Peter Boyle
Cast .... Miguel Ferrer
Cast .... Chelsea Field

RUBDOWN — USA

Drama: Suspense/Thriller
Airdate: 9/15/93
Rating: N/A   A/C:

A Beverly Hills masseur who is over his head
in gambling debts is framed for the murder of
his lover's husband who had originally hired
him to sleep with his wife for fifty thousand
dollars in order to break a clause in their
prenuptial agreement.

Production Company: Fast Track Films IAW
 Wilshire Court Prods.
Producer .... Ed Milkovich
Director .... Stuart Cooper
Writer .... Clyde Allen Hayes
Cast .... Michelle Phillips
Cast .... Jack Coleman
Cast .... William Devane
Cast .... Catherine Oxenberg

RUNAWAY FATHER — CBS

Drama: Family Drama • Children/Teens • True Story
• Woman's Issue/Story • Social Issue
Airdate: 09/22/91
Rating: 16.8/27   A/C: 1

Based on the book by Richard Rashke. An
abandoned wife struggles to raise her three
children while searching for her deadbeat
husband. After seventeen years, she finally wins
a precedent-setting legal battle for long-
overdue child support.

Production Company: Polone Co., Bonaparte
 Prods., Lee Levinson Prods. IAW Hearst Ent.
Executive Producer .... Donna Mills
Executive Producer .... Mel A. Bishop
Producer .... Lee Levinson
Producer .... Carroll Newman
Associate Producer .... Howard Rosenstein
Director .... John Nicolella
Writer .... Stephanie Liss
Cast .... Donna Mills
Cast .... Jack Scalia
Cast .... Chris Mulkey
Cast .... Jenny Lewis

RUNNING AGAINST TIME — USA

Drama: Sci-Fi/Supernatural/Horror/Fantasy
Airdate: 11/21/90
Rating: N/A   A/C:

Based on the book "A Time to Remember" by
Stanley Shapiro. A college history professor
goes back in a time machine to prevent
President Kennedy's assassination thinking he
can thereby stop the Vietnam War and his older
brother's subsequent death.

Production Company: Finnegan-Pinchuk Prods.
 IAW MCA TV
Executive Producer .... Pat Finnegan
Executive Producer .... Sheldon Pinchuk
Executive Producer .... Michael Weisbarth
Producer .... David Roessell
Producer .... Lori-Etta Taub
Director .... Bruce Seth Green
Writer .... Stanley Shapiro
Writer .... Robert Glass
Cast .... Robert Hays
Cast .... Catherine Hicks
Cast .... Sam Wanamaker
Cast .... James DiStefano

RUNNING MATES — HBO

Drama: Love Story • Political Piece
Airdate: 10/4/92
Rating: N/A   A/C:

A successful children's book author falls in love
with a presidential candidate. While their
politics are often at odds with each other the
couple go on the campaign trail. They decide
to marry but the honeymoon is short lived when
her radical '60s past is uncovered. Unwilling
to be torn apart by political and media pressure
they confront the issue head on, and find deeper
love and understanding for each other.

Production Company: Marvin Worth Prods.
Executive Producer .... Marvin Worth
Executive Producer .... James Brubaker
Director .... Michael Lindsay-Hogg
Writer .... A.L. Appling
Cast .... Diane Keaton
Cast .... Ed Harris
Cast .... Ed Begley, Jr.
Cast .... Ben Masters

RYAN WHITE STORY, THE — ABC

Drama: Children/Teens • Medical/Disease/Mental
Illness • True Story • Social Issue
Airdate: 01/16/89
Rating: 16.6/26   A/C:

True story of a young hemophiliac boy with
AIDS whose family was forced to leave their
Indiana town by intolerant neighbors.

Production Company: Landsburg Co.
Executive Producer .... Alan Landsburg
Executive Producer .... Joan Barnett
Producer .... Linda Otto
Director .... John Herzfeld
Writer .... Phil Penningroth
Writer .... John Herzfeld
Cast .... Lukas Haas
Cast .... Judith Light
Cast .... Michael Bowen
Cast .... Peter Scolari
Cast .... George C. Scott

SADIE AND SON — CBS

Drama: Cops/Detectives/Law Enforcement • Woman
Against The System • Series Pilot (2 hr.)
Airdate: 10/19/87
Rating: 15.5/25   A/C:

A policewoman believed over the hill arranges
to have her aspiring comedian son join her on
the New York police force despite his obvious
reluctance.

Production Company: Norton Wright Prods./
 Kenny Rogers Organization IAW ITC
Executive Producer .... Norton Wright
Producer .... Richard L. O'Connor
Director .... John Llewellyn Moxey
Writer .... Carl Kleinschmitt
Cast .... Debbie Reynolds
Cast .... Brian McNamara
Cast .... Sam Wanamaker
Cast .... Cynthia Dale
Cast .... David Ferry
Cast .... Robert Morelli
Cast .... Alar Aedma
Cast .... Phil Akin
Cast .... Michael J. Reynolds

SAKHAROV — HBO

Drama: True Story • Biography • Man Against The
System • Foreign or Exotic Location
Airdate: 9/16/84
Rating: N/A   A/C:

Russian nuclear physicist Andrei Sakharov and
his devoted wife, Elena, battle against Soviet
oppression of human rights. For his
courageous support of fellow dissidents he and
his family are repeatedly persecuted by the KGB
.In 1980 is arrested and sent into internal exile
in the closed city of Gorky. For his heroic
actions he was awarded the Nobel Peace Prize

Production Company: HBO Pictures, Titus
 Productions LTD
Executive Producer .... Herbert Brodkin
Producer .... Robert Berger
Director .... Jack Gold
Writer .... David W. Rintels
Cast .... Jason Robards
Cast .... Glenda Jackson
Cast .... Nicol Williamson
Cast .... Frank Finlay

MOVIES AND MINISERIES

SAMARITAN: THE MITCH SNYDER STORY
CBS
Drama: True Story • Biography • Social Issue
Airdate: 05/19/86
Rating: 11.2/18   A/C:

Fact-based story of the Washington, D.C., activist, homeless by choice, who employs fasts as a political tool to help others obtain food and shelter.

Production Company: Levine-Robins IAW Fries Entertainment Inc.
Executive Producer .... Charles Fries
Executive Producer .... Irv Wilson
Producer .... Deborah Joy Levine
Producer .... Debbie Robins
Director .... Richard T. Heffron
Writer .... Clifford Campion
Cast .... Martin Sheen
Cast .... Cicely Tyson
Cast .... Roxanne Hart
Cast .... Joe Seneca

SARAH, PLAIN AND TALL
CBS
Drama: Family Drama • Love Story • Farm Story • Period Piece
Airdate: 02/03/91
Rating: 23.1/35   A/C: 1

Based on Patricia MacLachlan's book. In 1910, an New England woman answers an ad for a wife placed by a widowed Kansas father. She must battle his stubbornness and break through the grief that haunts him and his two children.

Production Company: Self Prods. and Trillium Prods.
Executive Producer .... William Self
Executive Producer .... Glenn Close
Director .... Glenn Jordan
Writer .... Patricia MacLachlan
Writer .... Carol Sobieski
Cast .... Glenn Close
Cast .... Christopher Walken
Cast .... Lexi Randall
Cast .... Christopher Bell

SAVED BY THE BELL-HAWAIIAN STYLE
NBC
Comedy: Youth Comedy • Foreign or Exotic Location
Airdate: 11/27/92
Rating: 9.5/17   A/C: 3

From the Saturday morning series. A group of high school students on summer vacation travel to Hawaii, staying at a hotel of one of their classmate's grandfather. Trouble ensues when greedy land developers try to run pops off his land. The kids do some quick thinking and save the day allowing gramps to live happily ever after.

Production Company: Peter Engel Prods. IAW NBC
Executive Producer .... Peter Engel
Producer .... Franco Bario
Director .... Dan Barnhart
Writer .... Bennett Tramer
Cast .... Mark-Paul Gosselaar
Cast .... Dean Jones
Cast .... Mario Lopez
Cast .... Tiffani-Amber Thiessen

SCANDAL IN A SMALL TOWN
NBC
Drama: Woman Against The System • Children/Teens • Courtroom Drama • Social Issue
Airdate: 04/10/88
Rating: 20.0/31   A/C:

When a cocktail waitress wages a fight against her daughter's high-school instructor's anti-Semitic teachings, her own reputation is torn apart. Despite her daughter's protestations, she takes the teacher to court and stops his hate-mongering.

Production Company: Carliner/Rappoport Prods.
Executive Producer .... Mark Carliner
Executive Producer .... Michele Rappaport
Director .... Anthony Page
Writer .... Robert J. Avrech
Cast .... Raquel Welch
Cast .... Frances Lee McCain
Cast .... Christa Denton
Cast .... Ronny Cox

SCANDAL SHEET
ABC
Drama: Sex/Glitz • Hollywood
Airdate: 01/21/85
Rating: 20.5/32   A/C:

A sleazy editor of a gossip tabloid goes after a famous Hollywood couple who has a secret which if exposed could ruin them.

Production Company: Fair Dinkum Prods.
Executive Producer .... Henry Winkler
Producer .... Roger Birnbaum
Director .... David Lowell Rich
Writer .... Howard Rodman
Cast .... Burt Lancaster
Cast .... Pamela Reed
Cast .... Robert Urich
Cast .... Lauren Hutton

SCATTERED DREAMS: THE KATHRYN MESSENGER STORY
CBS
Drama: Family Drama • Period Piece • Woman Against The System • True Story
Airdate: 12/19/93
Rating: 14.1/22   A/C: 1

In 1951 Florida, dirt poor tenant framers are arrested for an unpaid grocery bill by the towns odious sheriff. They are sentenced to seven years hard labor and their children are made wards of the state and placed in a cruelly run orphanage. With a the help of a benevolent lawyer they eventually win their release but must fight to gain custody of their three daughters. A young reporter takes up their cause, helping them to overturn a corrupt and unlawful system.

Production Company: Robert Greenwald Prods.
Executive Producer .... Robert Greenwald
Producer .... Philip Kleinbart
Co-Producer .... Michael Stroud
Co-Producer .... Joseph Nasser
Co-Producer .... Eddie Velez
Director .... Neema Barnette
Writer .... Karen Croner
Cast .... Tyne Daly
Cast .... Gerald McRaney
Cast .... Sonny Shroyer
Cast .... Andrew Prine

SCENE OF THE CRIME
NBC
Mystery: Murder and Murder Mystery • Psychological Thriller
Airdate: 09/30/84
Rating: 12.5/21   A/C:

The first half on the program features a murder mystery to which the audience and celebrity guests must guess the answer. The second half is a suspense story in which a girl gets revenge against her cruel babysitter.

Production Company: J.E. Prods. IAW Universal TV
Executive Producer .... Jon Epstein
Director .... Walter Grauman
Director .... Rod Holcomb
Writer .... Henry Olek
Writer .... Jeffrey Bloom
Writer .... Carole Wilson Bloom
Cast .... Markie Post
Cast .... Steve Kanaly
Cast .... Greg Evigan
Cast .... Kim Hunter

SCORNED AND SWINDLED
CBS
Drama: True Story • Action/Adventure
Airdate: 10/09/84
Rating: 16.7/26   A/C:

A man and a woman, both conned by the same man, join forces to track him down and end up trekking across the country together.

Production Company: Cypress Point Prods.
Executive Producer .... Gerald W. Abrams
Producer .... Nick Anderson
Director .... Paul Wendkos
Writer .... Karol Ann Hoeffner
Writer .... Jerome Kass
Cast .... Tuesday Weld
Cast .... Keith Carradine
Cast .... Peter Coyote
Cast .... Sheree North
Cast .... Fionnula Flanagan
Cast .... Susan Ruttan

SEA WOLF, THE
TNT
Drama: Action/Adventure • Period Piece
Airdate: 4/18/93
Rating: N/A   A/C:

Based on the book by Jack London. In 1890, a San Francisco aristocrat is shipwrecked and rescued by a sadistic, brutal sea captain who presses him into service aboard his schooner.

Production Company: Bob Banner Prods., Primedia Prods. LTD., Andrew J. Fenady Prods.
Executive Producer .... Andrew J. Fenady
Executive Producer .... Bob Banner
Producer .... W. Patterson Ferns
Producer .... Duke Fenady
Director .... Michael Anderson
Writer .... Andrew J. Fedady
Cast .... Charles Bronson
Cast .... Christopher Reeve
Cast .... Catherine Mary Stewart
Cast .... Marc Singer

SEAQUEST DSV — NBC

Drama: Sci-Fi/Supernatural/Horror/Fantasy • Series Pilot (2 hr.)
Airdate: 9/12/93
Rating: 17.8/28   A/C: 1

In 2018, a retired Naval officer is given the command of a high-tech submarine which is a combination military and scientific research vessel. Their mission is to keep the peace for the United Earth Oceans Organization— an international governing body. With sinister plots to destroy the world the SeaQuest must constantly fight for truth, justice and the American way!

Production Company: Amblin TV IAW Universal
TV
Executive Producer .... Rockne O'Bannnon
Executive Producer .... Steven Spielberg
Executive Producer .... Tommy Thompson
Producer .... Gregg Fienberg
Co-Producer .... David Kemper
Director .... Irvin Kershner
Writer .... Rockne S. O'Bannon
Writer .... Tommy Thompson
Cast .... Roy Scheider
Cast .... Stephanie Beacham
Cast .... John DiAquino
Cast .... Stacy Haiduk

SEARCH AND RESCUE — NBC

Drama: Action/Adventure
Airdate: 3/27/94
Rating: 10.5/17   A/C: 2 (Tie)

The crew chief of a High Sierra volunteer search and rescue team comes to the aid of hapless hikers, stranded skiers and clumsy climbers.

Production Company: Black Sheep Prods. IAW
NBC Prods.
Executive Producer .... Joan Conrad
Producer .... Shane Conrad
Director .... Paul Krasny
Writer .... George Schenck
Writer .... Frank Cardea
Cast .... Robert Conrad
Cast .... Chad McQueen
Cast .... Dee Wallace Stone

SEARCH FOR GRACE — CBS

Drama: Sci-Fi/Supernatural/Horror/Fantasy • Woman In Jeopardy
Airdate: 5/17/94
Rating: 10.5/17   A/C: 2

A Seattle woman is beset with nightmares and visions of a murder that she has no memory of. With the help of a psychologist and hypnosis she uncovers that she has full knowledge of the murder of a woman who lived in Buffalo in the 1920's. She beings to believe that she might have been reincarnated as a warning that she is now in danger of being killed by the controlling man she has recently been obsessed with.

Production Company: CBS Entertainment Prods.
Executive Producer .... Cynthia Whitcomb
Producer .... Vanessa Greene
Co-Producer .... Susan Jeter
Director .... Sam Pillsbury
Writer .... Alex Ayres
Cast .... Lisa Hartman
Cast .... Ken Wahl
Cast .... Richard Masur
Cast .... Don Michael Paul

SEASON OF GIANTS, A — TNT

Miniseries/Drama (2 nights): Period Piece • Historical Piece • Foreign or Exotic Location • Biography
Airdate: 03/17/91 • 3/18/91
Rating: N/A   A/C:

Turbulent renaissance Italy serves as the backdrop for the lives, loves and rivalry between art's great contemporaries: Michelangelo, Leonardo da Vince and Raphael.

Production Company: TNT and RAI-I
Producer .... Vincenzo La Bella
Director .... Jerry London
Writer .... Julian Bond
Writer .... Vincenzo La Bella
Cast .... F. Murray Abraham
Cast .... Steven Berkoff
Cast .... Juliette Caton
Cast .... Mark Frankel

SEASONS OF THE HEART — NBC

Drama: Family Drama • Children/Teens
Airdate: 5/22/94
Rating: 12.9/21   A/C: 2

A successful publisher finds herself caring for her seven year old grandson after he is abandoned by her drug addicted, irresponsible daughter. At first she is resentful and afraid how the child will affect her new marriage to her long-time lover but she ultimately reevaluates her own life and together they all become a loving family.

Production Company: Joseph Feury Prods. IAW
RHI Entertainment
Executive Producer .... Robert Halmi, Jr.
Producer .... Joseph Feury
Co-Producer .... Mary Beth Yarrow
Director .... Lee Grant
Writer .... Robbyn Burger
Cast .... Carol Burnett
Cast .... George Segal
Cast .... Malcolm McDowell
Cast .... Eric Lloyd

SECOND CHANCES — CBS

Drama: Series Pilot (2 hr.) • Woman's Issue/Story
Airdate: 12/2/93
Rating: 9.7/16   A/C: 3

In a small California town three women; a savvy lawyer running for office against a corrupt judge, her younger sister recently dumped by her boyfriend and a young Latina who ran out on her wedding to a law student are all attempting to get their lives in order. But trouble ensues as they all find themselves in jeopardy when the attorney's philandering husband is found murdered..

Production Company: Latham/Lechowick Prods.
Executive Producer .... Lynn Marie Latham
Executive Producer .... Bernard Lechowick
Producer .... Phillips Wylly, Sr.
Writer .... Lynn Marie Latham
Writer .... Bernard Lechowick
Director .... Sharron Miller
Cast .... Connie Sellecca
Cast .... Matt Salinger
Cast .... Megan Follows
Cast .... Jennifer Lopez

SECOND SERVE — CBS

Drama: True Story • Medical/Disease/Mental Illness • Biography • Sports
Airdate: 05/13/86
Rating: 13.6/22   A/C:

Biography of the eminent transsexual surgeon Richard Raskind a.k.a. Renee Richards, focusing on his/her tennis career and relationships with family members.

Production Company: Linda Yellen Prods. IAW
Lorimar-Telepictures
Executive Producer .... Linda Yellen
Director .... Anthony Page
Writer .... Stephanie Liss
Writer .... Gavin Lambert
Cast .... Vanessa Redgrave
Cast .... Richard Venture
Cast .... Martin Balsam
Cast .... Alice Krige

SECRET GARDEN, THE — CBS

Drama: Children/Teens • Period Piece
Airdate: 11/30/88
Rating: 16.7/26   A/C:

Adaptation of the Frances Hodgson Burnett novel about the relationship between an orphaned unpleasant, unhappy little girl and the ill son of her guardian.

Production Company: Rosemont Prods. Ltd.
Executive Producer .... Norman Rosemont
Producer .... Steve Lanning
Director .... Alan Grint
Writer .... Blanche Hanalis
Cast .... Gennie James
Cast .... Derek Jacobi
Cast .... Michael Hordern

MOVIES AND MINISERIES

SECRET LIFE OF ARCHIE'S WIFE, THE — CBS

Comedy: Romantic Comedy
Airdate: 10/28/90
Rating: 13.4/22   A/C: 1

A tragically tormented housewife escapes drudgery when she is kidnapped by a bumbling bank robber and finds herself falling for him.

Production Company: Interscope Prods. IAW Consolidated Prods.
Executive Producer .... Michael Deeley
Executive Producer .... Ted Field
Producer .... Peter Katz
Director .... James Frawley
Writer .... Walter Lockwood
Cast .... Michael Tucker
Cast .... Jill Eikenberry
Cast .... Ray Wise
Cast .... J.C. Quinn

SECRET LIFE OF IAN FLEMING, THE — TNT

Drama: Action/Adventure • Historical Piece • Foreign or Exotic Location • Biography
Airdate: 03/05/90
Rating: N/A   A/C:

The true life adventures of not only the creator of James Bond, but one of the modernizers of the British Secret Service.

Production Company: Saban/Scherick
Executice Producer .... Edgar J. Scherick
Executive Producer .... Haim Saban
Co-Executive Producer .... Gary Hoffman
Co-Producer .... Greg Goldman
Director .... Ferdinand Fairfax
Writer .... Robert J. Avrech
Cast .... Jason Connery
Cast .... Kristin Scott Thomas
Cast .... Joss Ackland
Cast .... Patricia Hodge

SECRET LIFE OF KATHY McCORMICK, THE — NBC

Comedy: Romantic Comedy
Airdate: 10/07/88
Rating: 14.5/26   A/C:

When a supermarket cashier suddenly has an opportunity to crash high society, she tells the rich folk that she works with the market (they think Wall Street) and falls in love with a wealthy man who isn't exactly honest with her either.

Production Company: Tamara Asseyev Prods. Inc. IAW New World TV
Executive Producer .... Tamara Asseyev
Co-Executive Producer .... Barry Weitz
Co-Producer .... Barbara Eden
Co-Producer .... Gloria Goldsmith
Director .... Robert Lewis
Writer .... Jim Brecher
Cast .... Barbara Eden
Cast .... Josh Taylor
Cast .... Dick O'Neill
Cast .... Judy Geeson

SECRET PASSION OF ROBERT CLAYTON, THE — USA

Drama: Murder and Murder Mystery • Courtroom Drama • Sex/Glitz
Airdate: 06/03/92
Rating: N/A   A/C:

A small town Georgia D.A. comes up against his father, a famed criminal attorney, when he prosecutes his lover's husband. Sparks fly when he discovers that he and his father are competing in the bedroom with the same woman.

Production Company: Wilshire Court Productions
Executive Producer .... Irwin Meyer
Executive Producer .... Jonathan Axelrod
Executive Producer .... Harvey Bibicoff
Producer .... Ed Milkovich
Director .... E.W. Swackhamer
Writer .... Brian Ross
Cast .... Scott Valentine
Cast .... John Mahoney
Cast .... Eve Gordon
Cast .... Kevin Conroy

SECRET SINS OF THE FATHER — NBC

Drama: Family Drama • Murder and Murder Mystery • Cops/Detectives/Law Enforcement
Airdate: 1/9/94
Rating: 16.0/24   A/C: 2

In a Nebraska farming community, a small town police chief suspects that his well respected father murdered his mother. As the case goes to trail, family members and townsfolk are torn apart as the anguished cop uncovers family secrets and hidden resentments that prove his father's innocence and his older brother's guilt.

Production Company: UltraEnt, AVC VieeoEnterprises Inc. IAW Dick Clark Film Group Inc.
Executive Producer .... Dick Clark
Executive Producer .... Neil Stearns
Executive Producer .... Bob Rubin
Executive Producer .... Bill Siegler
Producer .... Jeanne Marie Van Cott
Director .... Beau Bridges
Writer .... Lillian Samuel
Cast .... Beau Bridges
Cast .... Lloyd Bridges
Cast .... Lee Purcell
Cast .... Frederick Coffin

SECRET, THE — CBS

Drama: Family Drama • Children/Teens • Medical/Disease/Mental Illness • Social Issue
Airdate: 04/19/92
Rating: 13.3/23   A/C: 1

An old man has spent a lifetime of struggle to keep his dyslexia a secret, alienating his son in the process, but is now forced to confront and accept his problem to help his grandson who suffers the same learning disorder.

Production Company: RHI Entertainment
Executive Producer .... Robert Halmi Sr.
Producer .... Craig Anderson
Director .... Karen Arthur
Writer .... Cynthia Cherbak
Cast .... Kirk Douglas
Cast .... Bruce Boxleitner
Cast .... Brock Peters
Cast .... Messe Tendler

SECRET WEAPON — TNT

Drama: Suspense/Thriller • True Story • Foreign or Exotic Location
Airdate: 03/19/90
Rating: N/A   A/C:

The story of an Israeli nuclear power plant technician who, after he exposes secret atomic weapon production, is hunted by a beautiful Mossad agent and finally captured.

Production Company: Griffin-Elysian Films IAW TVS & ABC-Australia
Executive Producer .... Michael Deakin
Executive Producer .... Graham Benson
Executive Producer .... Penny Chapman
Producer .... Nick Evans
Director .... Ian Sharp
Writer .... Nick Evans
Cast .... Griffin Dunne
Cast .... Karen Allen
Cast .... Joe Petruzzi
Cast .... Jeroen Krabbe

SECRET WEAPONS — NBC

Drama: Suspense/Thriller • Foreign or Exotic Location • Political Piece
Airdate: 03/03/85
Rating: 13.8/21   A/C:

Story of international intrigue, involving a group of young Soviet women trained by the KGB to spy on visiting American businessmen in order to obtain government secrets by using sex and blackmail.

Production Company: Goodman-Rosen Prods. IAW ITC Prods.
Executive Producer .... Judith A. Polone
Producer .... Gary Goodman
Producer .... Barry Rosen
Director .... Don Taylor
Writer .... Thomas Baum
Writer .... Sandor Stern
Cast .... Sally Kellerman
Cast .... Linda Hamilton
Cast .... Hunt Block
Cast .... Viveca Lindfors
Cast .... Geena Davis

SECRETS OF A MARRIED MAN — NBC

Drama: Family Drama • Forbidden Love • Prostitution • Sex/Glitz
Airdate: 09/24/84
Rating: 17.5/27   A/C:

Dissatisfied with his marriage, an aircraft engineer begins to fool around with prostitutes. His life and marriage are destroyed when he falls in love with a street-wise hooker.

Production Company: ITC Prods.
Executive Producer .... Tristine Rainer
Producer .... R.W. Goodwin
Director .... William A. Graham
Writer .... Dennis Nemec
Cast .... William Shatner
Cast .... Michelle Phillips
Cast .... Cybill Shepherd
Cast .... Glynn Turman

SECRETS OF LAKE SUCCESS — NBC

Miniseries/Drama (3 nights): Family Drama • Sex/Glitz
Airdate: 10/1/93 • 10/8/93 • 10/15/93
Rating: 7.7/14 • 7.4/14 • 7.1/13   A/C: 2 • 3 • 3

When the family patriarch dies, his twenty-four year old estranged daughter from a second marriage is willed his two billion pharmaceutical company causing family rivalries, illicit affairs, and long held resentments that threaten to destroy the powerful dynasty.

Production Company: Cramer Co. IAW NBC Prods.
Executive Producer .... Douglas S. Cramer
Executive Producer .... David Stenn
Producer .... Naomi Janzen
Director .... Jonathan Sanger
Director .... Arthur Allan Seidelman
Writer .... David Stenn
Writer .... Naomi Janzen
Cast .... John Bradley
Cast .... Rebeccah Bush
Cast .... Samantha Eggar
Cast .... Lanei Chapman
Cast .... Shawn Huff

SEDUCED — CBS

Drama: Murder and Murder Mystery • Sex/Glitz
Airdate: 03/12/85
Rating: 15.5/25   A/C:

While trying to claim her bequeathment, a millionaire's widow rekindles her affair with an ex-boyfriend, a brash young lawyer who vies for control of her dead husband's corporation. An unexpected murder hinders all their best laid plans.

Production Company: Catalina Prod. Group IAW Comworld Prods.
Executive Producer .... Gregory Harrison
Producer .... Franklin R. Levy
Co-Producer .... Matthew Rushton
Director .... Jerrold Freedman
Writer .... Charles Robert Carner
Cast .... Gregory Harrison
Cast .... Cybill Shepherd
Cast .... Jose Ferrer
Cast .... Michael C. Gwynne

SEDUCED BY EVIL — USA

Drama: Sci-Fi/Supernatural/Horror/Fantasy • Woman In Jeopardy
Airdate: 8/26/94
Rating: N/A   A/C:

Based on the unpublished novel by Jann Arrington Wolcott. A female journalist comes under the influence of a wicked sorcerer, who means to do her and her family harm, and only she can stop him.

Production Company: Wilshire Court Productions
Producer .... Bob Roe
Director .... Tony Wharmby
Writer .... Bill Svanoe
Cast .... Suzanne Somers
Cast .... John Vargas
Cast .... Julie Carmen

SEDUCTION IN TRAVIS COUNTY — CBS

Drama: Murder and Murder Mystery • Suspense/Thriller • True Crime
Airdate: 05/19/91
Rating: 13.9/22   A/C: 2

An acquitted murder suspect becomes obsessed with the attorney who defended her, kills his wife, then implicates him in her deadly conspiracy.

Production Company: Zev Braun Pictures IAW New World Television
Executive Producer .... Zev Braun
Executive Producer .... David Braun
Producer .... Norman I. Cohen
Producer .... Allen Baron
Director .... George Kaczender
Writer .... Christopher Canaan
Cast .... Lesley Ann Warren
Cast .... Peter Coyote
Cast .... Jean Smart
Cast .... Matt Clark

SEDUCTION: THREE TALES FROM THE INNER SANCTUM — ABC

Drama: Forbidden Love • Suspense/Thriller • Sex/Glitz
Airdate: 04/05/92
Rating: 9.4/15   A/C: 2

Based on the radio show "Inner Sanctum" by Hiram Brown. Trio of erotic fantasies seen through the eyes of a businessman and his sexually repressed wife; a tormented artist and his devoted companion; and a fall guy who dies taking the rap for a wife's murderous plot.

Production Company: Victoria Principal-Polone-Hearst
Executive Producer .... Michael Weisbarth
Executive Producer .... Victoria Principal
Producer .... Carroll Newman
Co-Executive Producer .... Barry Brown
Director .... Michael Rhodes
Writer .... Barry Brown
Writer .... Robert Glass
Writer .... Steve Whitney
Cast .... Victoria Principal
Cast .... John Terry
Cast .... John O'Hurley
Cast .... W. Morgan Sheppard

SEEDS OF TRAGEDY — FBC

Drama: Foreign or Exotic Location • Drug Smuggling/Dealing
Airdate: 06/17/91
Rating: 4.6/9   A/C: 4

Follows the perilous journey of a shipment of cocaine; beginning in the impoverished fields of Peru to a hidden processing lab in Columbia, then by way of drug runners into the hands of desperate L.A. street dealers.

Production Company: Sanford/Pillsbury Prods.
Executive Producer .... Sarah Pillsbury
Executive Producer .... Midge Sanford
Producer .... Robert Engelman
Director .... Martin Donovan
Writer .... Alex Lasker
Cast .... Jeff Kaake
Cast .... Norbert Weisser
Cast .... Michael Fernandes

SENTIMENTAL JOURNEY — CBS

Drama: Family Drama • Children/Teens
Airdate: 10/16/84
Rating: 14.0/23   A/C:

Remake of the 1940's movie. After his Broadway producer wife miscarries, an actor finds an orphan for he and his wife to adopt. Complications arise when the boy wants nothing to do with the wife, but becomes attached to the husband.

Production Company: Lucille Ball Prods. & Smith-Richmond Prods. IAW 20th Cent. Fox TV
Executive Producer .... Gary Morton
Executive Producer .... Tony Richmond
Producer .... Harry R. Sherman
Co-Producer .... Lawrence Taylor-Mortoff
Director .... James Goldstone
Writer .... Darlene Craviotto
Writer .... Frank Cavestani
Cast .... Jaclyn Smith
Cast .... David Dukes
Cast .... Maureen Stapleton
Cast .... Jessica Rene Carroll

SEPARATE BUT EQUAL — ABC
EMMY WINNER

Miniseries/Drama (2 nights): Man Against The System • True Story • Period Piece • Courtroom Drama • Black Story • Historical Piece
Airdate: 04/07/91 • 04/08/91
Rating: 11.9/19 • 11.8/19   A/C: 3 • 2

Thurgood Marshall, serving as chief counsel for the NAACP, spearheads the battle which led to the 1954 landmark Supreme Court decision to desegregate schools.

Production Company: New Liberty IAW Republic Pictures/George Stevens, Jr.
Executive Producer .... George Stevens, Jr.
Executive Producer .... Stan Margulies
Director .... George Stevens, Jr.
Writer .... George Stevens, Jr.
Cast .... Sidney Poitier
Cast .... Burt Lancaster
Cast .... Richard Kiley
Cast .... Cleavon Little

MOVIES AND MINISERIES

SEPARATED BY MURDER — CBS
Drama: True Crime • Murder and Murder Mystery • Courtroom Drama
Airdate: 4/12/94
Rating: 11.8/19   A/C: 2

In Memphis, Tennessee brassy, avaricious Holly Faye Walker and her frumpy, churchgoing twin sister, Lily Mae Stokely are indicted for the murder of Holly's wealthy physician husband. A sensational trial ensues where handyman, Jessie Dixon, hired by the sisters to carry out the killing, confesses to the crime. Only Holly is eventually convicted of conspiracy and Lily is proved to have been framed.

Production Company: Larry Thompson Entertainment IAW RHI Entertainment & CBS
Executive Producer .... Larry Thompson
Producer .... Donald Wrye
Producer .... Paulette Breen
Co-Producer .... Daniel Schneider
Director .... Donald Wrye
Writer .... Jeff Andrus
Writer .... Bobby Roth
Cast .... Sharon Gless
Cast .... Steve Railsback
Cast .... Ed Bruce
Cast .... Mark W. Johnson

SETTLE THE SCORE — NBC
Drama: Cops/Detectives/Law Enforcement • Woman In Jeopardy • Rape/Molestation • Psychological Thriller
Airdate: 10/30/89
Rating: 16.8/26   A/C: 2

When a Chicago cop returns to rural Arkansas to find the man who raped her twenty years ago, she discovers that there's an active serial rapist/killer whose m.o. is remarkably like the man who attacked her, and that the rapist is her twisted brother.

Production Company: Steve Sohmer Inc. IAW ITC and Figaro Intl.
Executive Producer .... Steve Sohmer
Producer .... Bob Markell
Director .... Ed Sherin
Writer .... Steve Sohmer
Cast .... Jaclyn Smith
Cast .... Howard Duff
Cast .... Richard Masur
Cast .... Jeffrey DeMunn

SEX, LOVE, AND COLD HARD CASH — USA
Drama: Suspense/Thriller
Airdate: 5/12/93
Rating: N/A   A/C:

A high-priced prostitute enlists the help of an ex-con to track down an embezzler who stole her life savings. The chase leads the couple on a ocean cruise to Rio.

Production Company: Citadel IAW MTE
Executive Producer .... David R. Ginsburg
Producer .... Renee Longstreet
Co-Producer .... Anthony Croce
Director .... Harry Longstreet
Writer .... Harry Longstreet
Cast .... JoBeth Williams
Cast .... Anthony John Denison
Cast .... Richard Sarafian

SEXUAL ADVANCES — ABC
Drama: Woman Against The System • Woman's Issue/Story • Social Issue
Airdate: 05/10/92
Rating: 9.4/16   A/C: 3

When an executive loses a major account to a female co-worker, he retaliates with a vengeful plan of sexual harassment. His scheme ultimately fails when his victim finds the courage to fight the odds and expose the company.

Production Company: Carol Polakoff Prods. IAW Spelling Television
Executive Producer .... Aaron Spelling
Executive Producer .... E. Duke Vincent
Executive Producer .... Carol Polakoff
Producer .... Matthew O'Connor
Director .... Donna Deitch
Writer .... Michele Gallery
Cast .... Stephanie Zimbalist
Cast .... William Russ
Cast .... Terry O'Quinn
Cast .... Patrick James Clarke

SHADOW CHASERS — ABC
Drama: Sci-Fi/Supernatural/Horror/Fantasy
Airdate: 11/14/85
Rating: 6.9/10   A/C:

A tabloid writer and an anthropologist team up to investigate a block of houses that are haunted by a recently deceased spiritualist.

Production Company: Johnson-Grazer Prods. IAW Warner Bros. TV
Executive Producer .... Kenneth Johnson
Executive Producer .... Brian Grazer
Producer .... Craig Schiller
Co-Producer .... Robert Bennett Steinhauer
Director .... Kenneth Johnson
Writer .... Kenneth Johnson
Cast .... Nina Foch
Cast .... Marcia Strassman
Cast .... Avery Schreiber
Cast .... Dennis Dugan
Cast .... Trevor Eve

SHADOW OF A DOUBT — CBS
Drama: Family Drama • Murder and Murder Mystery • Period Piece • Psychological Thriller
Airdate: 04/28/91
Rating: 15.3/24   A/C: 2

Remake of the 1943 Hitchcock film. A small town, California teen is devastated when she discovers that her charming visiting uncle is really the "Merry Widow" serial killer.

Production Company: Rosemont Prods.
Executive Producer .... Norman Rosemont
Producer .... David A. Rosemont
Director .... Karen Arthur
Writer .... John Gay
Cast .... Mark Harmon
Cast .... Margaret Welsh
Cast .... Diane Ladd
Cast .... William Lanteau

SHADOW OF A STRANGER — NBC
Drama: Suspense/Thriller
Airdate: 12/7/92
Rating: 15.1/24   A/C: 2

A high fashion model and her dishonest, lawyer husband come to the aid of a questionable couple shipwrecked just off their weekend beach house. Trouble ensues when a body turns up and they each suspect the other as the cold-blooded killer. Deceit, blackmail and larceny all play apart in the husband's craftily laid plans.

Production Company: Doris Keating Prods. IAW NBC Prods.
Executive Producer .... Doris Keating
Producer .... Hugh Benson
Director .... Richard Friedman
Writer .... Richard Friedman
Cast .... Emma Samms
Cast .... Parker Stevenson
Cast .... Michael Easton

SHADOW OF OBSESSION — NBC
Drama: Psychological Thriller • Woman In Jeopardy • Murder and Murder Mystery
Airdate: 4/10/94
Rating: 11.4/18   A/C: 2

Based on the novel "Unwanted Attentions" by K.K. Beck. A philosophy professor is charged with the murder of a demented student who had been stalking her for years. With the help of a macho private detective and a sympathetic, aggressive lawyer she is able to prove her innocence.

Production Company: Saban Entertainment
Executive Producer .... Lance H. Robbins
Producer .... Ronnie Hadar
Director .... Kevin Connor
Writer .... Ellen Weston
Cast .... Veronica Hamel
Cast .... Jack Scalia
Cast .... Jonathan Banks
Cast .... Sam Behrens

SHADOWHUNTER — SHOWTIME
Drama: Murder and Murder Mystery • Cops/Detectives/Law Enforcement • American Indians
Airdate: 2/10/93
Rating: N/A   A/C:

A burnt out Los Angeles detective is sent to a Navajo reservation to pick up a wanted killer being held by tribal authorities. When his car crashes, the convict escapes into the desert forcing the city cop to learn Native American techniques from the daughter of the tribe's lead tracker. Together they become intertwined in the machinations of cultural differences, survival and romance while both hunting and being hunted.

Production Company: Republic Pictures, Sandstorm Films
Producer .... Carol Kottenbrook
Producer .... Scott Einbinder
Director .... J.S. Cardone
Writer .... J.S. Cardone
Cast .... Scott Glenn
Cast .... Angela Alvarado
Cast .... Benjamin Bratt

SHAKEDOWN ON THE SUNSET STRIP   CBS
Drama: Cops/Detectives/Law Enforcement • True
Story • Period Piece • Hollywood • Prostitution
Airdate: 04/22/88
Rating: 15.0/27   A/C:

*Fact-based story about police corruption in
1940s Hollywood. An honest young cop who
arrests a famous madam is framed as a result.*

Production Company: CBS Entertainment Prods.
Producer .... Walter Grauman
Producer .... Harold Gast
Director .... Walter Grauman
Writer .... Harold Gast
Cast .... Perry King
Cast .... Charles Siebert
Cast .... Season Hubley
Cast .... Michael McGuire
Cast .... Joan Van Ark

SHAME   LIFETIME
Drama: Rape/Molestation • Woman's Issue/Story •
Social Issue • Children/Teens
Airdate: 08/25/92
Rating: N/A   A/C:

*After a woman lawyer's motorcycle breaks
down in a small town in Oregon, she befriends
a teenage rape victim. When the girl is inspired
by the independent woman to file charges
against her attacker, the town erupts in violence.*

Production Company: Viacom
Executive Producer .... Robert Dalrymple
Producer .... Joseph Plager
Producer .... Michelle MacLaren
Co-Producer .... Paul Baron
Director .... Dan Lerner
Writer .... Rebecca Soladay
Cast .... Amanda Donohoe
Cast .... Dean Stockwell
Cast .... Fairuza Balk

SHAMEFUL SECRETS   ABC
Drama: Family Drama • Family Drama • Woman's
Issue/Story • Social Issue
Airdate: 10/10/93
Rating: 13.2/21   A/C: 2

*A battered suburban housewife, unable to cope
with her husband's violent rages flees from the
house, leaving her children behind. When she
tries to regain custody, her husband refuses to
let her see the kids and goes to court to prove
her an unfit mother which turns into a bitter
custody battle.*

Production Company: Steve White Films IAW
    ABC Prods.
Executive Producer .... Steve White
Producer .... Barry Bernardi
Director .... David Carson
Writer .... Stephanie Liss
Co-Producer .... Ken Raskoff
Cast .... Joanna Kerns
Cast .... Tim Matheson
Cast .... La Tanya Richardson
Cast .... Katherine Cortez

SHANNON'S DEAL   NBC
Drama: Suspense/Thriller • Man Against The System
• Drug Smuggling/Dealing • Series Pilot (2 hr.)
Airdate: 06/04/89
Rating: 14.5/25   A/C:

*A former hot shot corporate attorney with heavy
gambling debts opens his own not-so-
glamorous practice. His first case involves him
in a drugs-for-arms deal that pits him against
a Latin American drug lord, freedom fighters
and top U.S. officials.*

Production Company: Stan Rogow Prods. IAW
    NBC Prods.
Executive Producer .... Stan Rogow
Director .... Lewis Teague
Writer .... John Sayles
Cast .... Jamey Sheridan
Cast .... Elizabeth Pena
Cast .... Martin Ferrero
Cast .... Miguel Ferrer

SHARING RICHARD   CBS
Comedy: Romantic Comedy • Woman's Issue/Story
• Buddy Story
Airdate: 04/26/88
Rating: 13.7/22   A/C:

*Without his knowledge, three women arrange
to share a freshly divorced plastic surgeon, but
rivalry and complications ensue.*

Production Company: Houston Motion Picture
    Ent. Inc. in cooperation with CBS Ent.
Producer .... Roni Weisberg
Director .... Peter Bonerz
Writer .... Ann Donahue
Writer .... Marion Zola
Cast .... Ed Marinaro
Cast .... Eileen Davidson
Cast .... Nancy Frangione
Cast .... Janet Carroll
Cast .... Lisa Jane Persky

SHATTERED DREAMS   CBS
Drama: Family Drama • True Story • Family Violence
• Woman's Issue/Story
Airdate: 05/13/90
Rating: 16.8/28   A/C: 1

*The story of Charlotte Fedders, the battered
wife of a prominent Washington official, who
found the courage to end the cycle of physical
violence and reclaim her life.*

Production Company: Roger Gimbel Prods. IAW
    Carolco Television Prods.
Executive Producer .... Roger Gimbel
Executive Producer .... Lindsay Wagner
Producer .... Stephanie Austin
Director .... Robert Iscove
Writer .... David Hill
Cast .... Lindsay Wagner
Cast .... Michael Nouri
Cast .... Georgann Johnson
Cast .... James Karen

SHATTERED IMAGE   USA
Drama: Murder and Murder Mystery • Cops/
Detectives/Law Enforcement • Suspense/Thriller
Airdate: 1/21/94
Rating: N/A   A/C:

*A tenacious FBI agent investigates a former
fashion model who is suspected of staging her
business tycoon husband's kidnapping. While
working on the case he falls in love with the
captivating beauty, only to uncover her
duplicity.*

Production Company: Rysher Prods.
Executive Producer .... Keith Samples
Executive Producer .... Bill Hart
Producer .... Bruce Cohn Curtis
Director .... Fritz Kiersch
Writer .... William Delligan
Cast .... Jack Scalia
Cast .... Bo Derek
Cast .... John Savage
Cast .... David McCallum

SHATTERED INNOCENCE   CBS
Drama: True Story • Addiction Story • Children/Teens
• Social Issue • Hollywood
Airdate: 03/09/88
Rating: 15.2/25   A/C:

*Based on the true story of a midwestern
cheerleader who moves to Hollywood, becomes
a nude model and porno star, is addicted to
cocaine, and ends up committing suicide at age
twenty.*

Production Company: Green/Epstein Prods. IAW
    Lorimar TV
Executive Producer .... Jim Green
Executive Producer .... Allen Epstein
Producer .... Milton Sperling
Director .... Sandor Stern
Writer .... Thanet Richard
Writer .... Sandor Stern
Cast .... Melinda Dillon
Cast .... John Pleshette
Cast .... Kris Kamm
Cast .... Ben Frank
Cast .... Jonna Lee

SHATTERED SPIRITS   ABC
Drama: Family Drama • Addiction Story
Airdate: 01/06/86
Rating: 16.4/25   A/C:

*When his deteriorating behavior begins
destroying his wife and children, an alcoholic
is forced by a judge to leave his family and seek
help from AA.*

Production Company: Sheen/Greenblatt Prods.
    IAW Robert Greenwald Prods.
Executive Producer .... Paul Pompian
Producer .... Robert Greenwald
Director .... Robert Greenwald
Writer .... Gregory Goodell
Cast .... Martin Sheen
Cast .... Matthew Laborteaux
Cast .... Melinda Dillon
Cast .... Lukas Haas

SHATTERED TRUST: THE SHARI KARNEY STORY   NBC

Drama: Family Drama • True Story • Rape/Molestation • Woman Against The System • Woman's Issue/Story
Airdate: 9/27/93
Rating: 16.2/25   A/C: 1

A California attorney working on a child sexual abuse case evokes long suppressed memories of her own incestuous relationship with her father. On the verge of a breakdown she confronts her pain in lengthy therapy sessions. And eventually confronts her family who vehemently deny any wrongdoing. Together with another lawyer she fights to overturn the statue of limitations on incest cases and allow victims the right to sue when they remember the abuse.

Production Company: Heartstar Prods. IAW Spectacor Films, Michael Jaffe Films
Executive Producer .... Janet Faust Krusi
Producer .... John Danylkiw
Co-Executive Producer .... Shari Karney
Director .... Bill Corcoran
Writer .... Susan Nanus
Cast .... Melissa Gilbert
Cast .... Kate Nelligan
Cast .... Patricia Kalember
Cast .... Dick Latessa

SHATTERED VOWS   NBC

Drama: Forbidden Love • True Story
Airdate: 10/29/84
Rating: 21.3/33   A/C:

A naive young nun falls in love with a young priest. Her desires and longing ultimately threaten her sacred vows and she eventually leaves the convent for a new life in New York.

Production Company: Bertinelli-Pequod Prods.
Executive Producer .... Jack Grossbart
Executive Producer .... Marty Litke
Producer .... Robert Lovenheim
Director .... Jack Bender
Writer .... Audrey Davis Levin
Cast .... Valerie Bertinelli
Cast .... David Morse
Cast .... Caroline McWilliams
Cast .... Tom Parsekian
Cast .... Millie Perkins

SHE KNOWS TOO MUCH   NBC

Drama: Cops/Detectives/Law Enforcement • Suspense/Thriller • Action/Adventure
Airdate: 01/29/89
Rating: 17.4/27   A/C:

A female cat burglar is released from prison to help a bumbling government agent investigate a congressman he thinks is involved in burglaries. Then they discover that there's a more complicated plot involving murder and international intrigue.

Production Company: Finnegan/Pinchuk Co., Fred Silverman Co., MGM/UA TV
Executive Producer .... Fred Silverman
Producer .... Pat Finnegan
Producer .... Bill Finnegan
Producer .... Sheldon Pinchuk
Director .... Paul Lynch
Writer .... Michael Norell
Cast .... Meredith Baxter
Cast .... Robert Urich
Cast .... Erik Estrada
Cast .... John Bennett Perry

SHE SAID NO   NBC

Drama: Courtroom Drama • Rape/Molestation • Woman's Issue/Story • Social Issue
Airdate: 09/23/90
Rating: 14.7/23   A/C: 2

After a prominent lawyer rapes an acquaintance, he narrowly beats a court conviction and then coolly sues his victim for malicious prosecution and libel.

Production Company: Steve White/Spectacor
Executive Producer .... Steve White
Executive Producer .... Michael O'Hara
Producer .... Barry Bernardi
Producer .... Paul Kurta
Director .... John Patterson
Writer .... Michael O'Hara
Cast .... Veronica Hamel
Cast .... Judd Hirsch
Cast .... Lee Grant
Cast .... Ray Baker

SHE SAYS SHE'S INNOCENT   NBC

Drama: Family Drama • Murder and Murder Mystery • Children/Teens • Woman Against The System
Airdate: 10/28/91
Rating: 15.0/23   A/C: 3

A single mother, whose rebellious teenage daughter is charged with the homicide of a classmate, refuses to believe her child might be guilty and eventually unmasks the real killer.

Production Company: Robert Greenwald Prods.
Executive Producer .... Robert Greenwald
Executive Producer .... Carl Winger
Producer .... Philip Kleinbart
Co-Producer .... Don Goldman
Director .... Charles Correll
Writer .... Kathleen Rowell
Cast .... Katey Sagal
Cast .... Charlotte Ross
Cast .... Jameson Parker
Cast .... Robert Picardo
Cast .... Alan Rachins

SHE STOOD ALONE   NBC

Drama: Woman Against The System • True Story • Period Piece • Black Story • Historical Piece • Biography
Airdate: 04/15/91
Rating: 10.8/18   A/C: 2

A Connecticut school marm risks community outrage and imprisonment when she insists on educating young, black women at her private school.

Production Company: Mighty Fortress Prods., Inc. IAW Walt Disney Television
Executive Producer .... Steve White
Executive Producer .... Bruce Franklin Singer
Producer .... Barry Bernardi
Director .... Jack Gold
Writer .... Bruce Franklin Singer
Cast .... Mare Winningham
Cast .... Ben Cross
Cast .... Robert Desiderio

SHE WAS MARKED FOR MURDER   NBC

Drama: Woman In Jeopardy • Suspense/Thriller
Airdate: 12/18/88
Rating: 14.8/24   A/C:

A widowed female publisher is introduced to a handsome young man by her assistant, falls in love with him and they marry. Then she discovers that her new husband and her assistant are plotting to murder her.

Production Company: Jack Grossbart Prods.
Executive Producer .... Jack Grossbart
Producer .... Elaine Rich
Director .... Chris Thomson
Writer .... David Stenn
Cast .... Stefanie Powers
Cast .... Polly Bergen
Cast .... Lloyd Bridges
Cast .... Debrah Farentino
Cast .... Hunt Block

SHE WOKE UP   ABC

Drama: Woman In Jeopardy • Suspense/Thriller
Airdate: 01/19/92
Rating: 14.1/22   A/C: 2

When a wealthy society woman awakens from a coma caused by a murder attempt, she struggles to identify her attacker, suspecting various family members. She is forced to kill her husband as he plots to finish her off.

Production Company: Mandy Films Inc. IAW ABC Prods.
Executive Producer .... Leonard Goldberg
Producer .... Terry Nelson
Director .... Waris Hussein
Writer .... Claire Labine
Cast .... Lindsay Wagner
Cast .... David Dukes
Cast .... Frances Sternhagen
Cast .... Maureen Mueller

SHELL SEEKERS, THE   ABC

Drama: Family Drama • Foreign or Exotic Location
Airdate: 12/03/89
Rating: 15.7/24   A/C: 1

Based on the novel by Rosamunde Pilcher. A mature woman on a journey to resolve her life must confront her troubled relationships with her selfish children.

Production Company: Marian Rees Associates
     IAW Central Television
Executive Producer .... Marian Rees
Producer .... Anne Hopkins
Director .... Waris Hussein
Writer .... John Pielmeier
Cast .... Angela Lansbury
Cast .... Christopher Bowen
Cast .... Sam Wanamaker
Cast .... Anna Cateret

SHERLOCK HOLMES RETURNS   CBS

Drama: Sci-Fi/Supernatural/Horror/Fantasy • Series
Pilot (2 hr.)
Airdate: 9/12/93
Rating: 9.7/16   A/C: 3

The British sleuth emerges from a self-induced sleep of nearly a century to find himself befriended by a skeptical doctor in contemporary San Francisco. Together they go after the evil grandson of his old rival, Moriarty who is about to pull of the crime of the millennium.

Production Company: Paragon Ent. Corp. IAW
     Kenneth Johnson
Executive Producer .... Kenneth Johnson
Executive Producer .... Jon Slan
Executive Producer .... Daniel Grodnik
Director .... Kenneth Johnson
Writer .... Kenneth Johnson
Cast .... Anthony Higgins
Cast .... Debrah Farentino
Cast .... Mark Adair

SHOOT FIRST: A COP'S VENGEANCE
     NBC

Drama: Murder and Murder Mystery • Cops/
Detectives/Law Enforcement • True Crime
Airdate: 03/24/91
Rating: 12.6/20   A/C: 3

Two police rookies fight growing crime in San Antonio while one follows the straight and narrow path, the other goes off the deep end and becomes a vigilante.

Production Company: Harvey Kahn Prods. IAW
     Interscope
Executive Producer .... Ted Field
Executive Producer .... Orly Adelson
Executive Producer .... John Kander II
Producer .... Harvey Kahn
Director .... Mel Damski
Writer .... Garry Michael White
Writer .... Joseph Gunn
Cast .... Alex McArthur
Cast .... Dale Midkiff
Cast .... Terry O'Quinn
Cast .... G. D. Spradlin

SHOOTDOWN   NBC

Drama: Family Drama • Woman Against The System
• True Story • Political Piece
Airdate: 11/28/88
Rating: 16.0/25   A/C:

Based on the book "Shootdown: Flight 007" by R.W. Johnson. True story of the mother of one of the victims of the 1983 Soviet downing of Korean Airlines flight 007 who questioned the official explanation of the affair, then took her story to the press to demand a new investigation.

Production Company: Leonard Hill Films
Executive Producer .... Leonard Hill
Executive Producer .... Robert O'Connor
Producer .... Judy Merl
Producer .... Paul Eric Myers
Co-Producer .... Joel Fields
Director .... Michael Pressman
Writer .... Judy Merl
Writer .... Paul Eric Myers
Cast .... Angela Lansbury
Cast .... George Coe
Cast .... Jennifer Savidge
Cast .... Kyle Secor
Cast .... Molly Hagan

SHOOTER   NBC

Drama: Period Piece • Action/Adventure • Vietnam
Airdate: 09/11/88
Rating: 11.3/20   A/C:

The viewpoint of wire-service photographers, along with other newsmen and women, on-site during the war in Vietnam.

Production Company: UBU Prods. IAW
     Paramount
Executive Producer .... Stephen Kline
Executive Producer .... David Hume Kennerly
Producer .... Barry Berg
Co-Producer .... Charles Jennings
Director .... Gary Nelson
Writer .... Stephen Kline
Writer .... David Hume Kennerly
Cast .... Alan Ruck
Cast .... Rosalind Chao
Cast .... Carol Huston
Cast .... Jeffrey Nordling
Cast .... Noble Willingham

SIDE BY SIDE   CBS

Drama: Family Drama • Buddy Story
Airdate: 03/06/88
Rating: 12.4/20   A/C:

Three old men, discarded from the work world, start their own business of clothing made by and for old people, showing up younger men in the process.

Production Company: Avnet/Kerner Prods.
Executive Producer .... Jon Avnet
Executive Producer .... Jordan Kerner
Producer .... Rosemary Edelman
Director .... Jack Bender
Writer .... Sheldon Keller
Writer .... Rosemary Edelman
Cast .... Sid Caesar
Cast .... Danny Thomas
Cast .... Morey Amsterdam
Cast .... Marjorie Lord
cAST .... Milton Berle

SILENCE OF THE HEART   CBS

Drama: Family Drama • Children/Teens • Social Issue
Airdate: 10/30/84
Rating: 21.9/35   A/C:

After a seventeen year old boy commits suicide, his parents and sister are left to sort out their feelings.

Production Company: David A. Simons Prods.
     IAW Tisch/Avnet Prods.
Executive Producer .... Steve Tisch
Executive Producer .... Jon Avnet
Producer .... James O'Fallon
Co-Producer .... David A. Simons
Director .... Richard Michaels
Writer .... Phil Penningroth
Cast .... Mariette Hartley
Cast .... Dana Hill
Cast .... Howard Hesseman
Cast .... Chad Lowe

SILENT CRIES   NBC

Drama: Period Piece • Historical Piece • Foreign or
Exotic Location • WWII • Prison and Prison Camp
Airdate: 3/8/93
Rating: 12.4/20   A/C: 3

Based on the book, "Guests of the Emperor" by Janice Brooks. A diverse group of American and British women are taken captive and brutally treated in a Japanese POW camp on the island of Sumatra during World War II.

Production Company: Sokolow Ent. Prods.,
     Yorkshire Tv, Tristar TV
Executive Producer .... Diane Sokolow
Executive Producer .... Mel Sokolow
Producer .... Carol Williams
Co-Executive Producer .... Keith Richardson
Director .... Anthony Page
Writer .... Walter Halsey Davis
Writer .... Vickie Patik
Cast .... Gena Rowlands
Cast .... Annabeth Gish
Cast .... Chloe Webb
Cast .... Gail Strickland

SILENT MOVIE — LIFETIME

Drama: Murder and Murder Mystery • Woman In Jeopardy • Suspense/Thriller
Airdate: 10/16/91
Rating: N/A   A/C:

A Hollywood screenwriter, famous for murder mysteries, finds herself a suspect and also a target in a series of killings that mimic her own scripts.

Production Company: Viacom Prods. IAW Farrell/Minoff Prods.
Executive Producer .... Mike Farrell
Executive Producer .... Marvin Minoff
Director .... Lee Philips
Writer .... William Bekala
Cast .... Patricia Wettig
Cast .... Mike Farrell
Cast .... Edward Asner
Cast .... Rick Springfield

SILENT WITNESS — NBC

Drama: Family Drama • Courtroom Drama • Rape/Molestation • Family Violence • Woman's Issue/Story
Airdate: 10/14/85
Rating: 22.5/33   A/C:

Loosely based on the famous Massachusetts barroom rape. A woman witnesses a rape by her brother-in-law and is pressured to remain silent by her husband's family.

Production Company: Robert Greenwald Prods.
Executive Producer .... Robert Greenwald
Executive Producer .... Joe Wizan
Producer .... Conrad Bromberg
Director .... Michael Miller
Writer .... Conrad Bromberg
Cast .... Valerie Bertinelli
Cast .... John Savage
Cast .... Melissa Leo
Cast .... Pat Corley

SILENT WITNESS: WHAT A CHILD SAW — USA

Drama: Children/Teens • Social Issue
Airdate: 7/15/94
Rating: N/A   A/C:

A female lawyer joins an anti-crime task force and prosecutes a ruthless gang leader. When he jumps bail, she must find a way to protect her star witness—a nine year old boy.

Production Company: Hearst Entertainment
Executive Producer .... Gerald W. Abrams
Co-Executive Producer .... Richard Maynard
Producer .... Julian Marks
Director .... Bruce Pittman
Writer .... Charles Rosin
Writer .... Paris Qualles
Cast .... Mia Korf
Cast .... Bill Nunn
Cast .... Amir Jamal Williams

SILHOUETTE — USA

Drama: Murder and Murder Mystery • Woman In Jeopardy • Suspense/Thriller
Airdate: 11/28/90
Rating: N/A   A/C:

An architect gets stranded in an eerie New Mexico town where she is the sole witness of a brutal murder of a cocktail waitress. Unable to convince the locals, she ultimately becomes the killer's next target.

Production Company: Dutch Prods. for MCA TV
Executive Producer .... John Davis
Executive Producer .... Andrew Hill
Executive Producer .... Faye Dunaway
Producer .... Chris Chesser
Producer .... Alan Beattie
Director .... Carl Schenkel
Writer .... Jay Wolf
Writer .... Victor Buell
Cast .... Faye Dunaway
Cast .... David Rasche
Cast .... John Terry
Cast .... Carlos Gomez

SIN AND REDEMPTION — CBS

Drama: Rape/Molestation • Family Violence • True Story • Woman's Issue/Story
Airdate: 3/15/94
Rating: 14.0/23   A/C: 2

A young woman from a small town is raped and becomes pregnant, afraid to tell anyone, she is thought to be promiscuous by her father. She unwittingly marries her rapist and only uncovers the truth years later when their daughter is seriously ill, in the need of a kidney donor, and he is a perfect tissue match. While the transplant is successful the marriage is doomed. She finally confronts her anger and gets on with her life.

Production Company: Stonehenge Prods. IAW Viacom Prods.
Executive Producer .... Dick Berg
Executive Producer .... Allan Marcil
Producer .... Loucas George
Co-Producer .... Ellie Ashburn
Director .... Neema Barnette
Writer .... Ellen Weston
Cast .... Richard Grieco
Cast .... Cynthia Gibb
Cast .... Cheryl Pollak
Cast .... Ralph Waite

SIN OF INNOCENCE — CBS

Drama: Family Drama • Forbidden Love • Love Story • Children/Teens
Airdate: 03/24/86
Rating: 12.5/21   A/C:

A stepbrother and sister fall in love much to the horror of their parents.

Production Company: Renee Valente Prods. and A Jeremac Prods. IAW 20th Century Fox TV
Executive Producer .... Renee Valente
Executive Producer .... Jerry McNeely
Director .... Arthur Allan Seidelman
Writer .... Jerry McNeely
Cast .... James Naughton
Cast .... Bill Bixby
Cast .... Dee Wallace Stone
Cast .... Megan Follows
Cast .... Dermot Mulroney

SINATRA — CBS

Miniseries/Drama (2 nights): Biography • True Story • Period Piece • Hollywood
Airdate: 11/8/92 • 11/10/92
Rating: 17.7/26 • 17.2/27   A/C: 1 • 1

The life of singer, actor and chairman on the board, Francis Albert Sinatra from his early days singing in his mothers Hoboken saloon to his meteoric rise as an entertainment legend. Including his stormy marriages and divorces, career setbacks and questionable liaisons with underworld connections.

Production Company: TS Prods. IAW Warner Bros. TV
Executive Producer .... Tina Sinatra
Producer .... Richard Rosenbloom
Co-Producer .... Stanley Neufeld
Director .... James Sadwith
Writer .... William Mastrosimone
Cast .... Philip Casnoff
Cast .... Gina Gershon
Cast .... Olympia Dukakis
Cast .... Joe Santos
Cast .... Rod Steiger
Cast .... Marcia Gay Harden

SINGLE BARS, SINGLE WOMEN — ABC

Drama: Romantic Comedy • Woman's Issue/Story
Airdate: 10/14/84
Rating: 20.0/31   A/C:

The story of a group of single women who frequent a small city singles bar in search of love and romance.

Production Company: Carsey-Werner Co. IAW Sunn Classic Pictures
Executive Producer .... Tom Werner
Executive Producer .... Marcy Carsey
Co-Executive Producer .... Michael O'Donoghue
Producer .... Stuart Cohen
Director .... Harry Winer
Writer .... Michael Bortman
Cast .... Tony Danza
Cast .... Paul Michael Glaser
Cast .... Keith Gordon
Cast .... Shelley Hack
Cast .... Christine Lahti

SINGLE WOMEN, MARRIED MEN — CBS

Drama: Woman's Issue/Story • Sex/Glitz • True Story
• Forbidden Love
Airdate: 10/27/89
Rating: 14.6/26   A/C: 2

Jo Ann Bitner, a San Diego psychologist who, after becoming involved with a married man, organizes a support group for single women caught in these relationships.

Production Company: CBS Entertainment Prods.
Executive Producer .... Michele Lee
Producer .... Elaine Rich
Director .... Nick Havinga
Writer .... Hilma Wolitzer
Cast .... Michele Lee
Cast .... Lee Horsley
Cast .... Mary Frann
Cast .... Julie Harris

SINS — CBS

Miniseries/Drama (3 nights): Woman Against The System • Foreign or Exotic Location • Sex/Glitz • Nazis • Period Piece • Love Story
Airdate: 2/2/86 • 2/3/86 • 2/4/86
Rating: 19.7/29 • 21.9/32 • 20.6/32   A/C:

Based on the book by Judith Gould. A strong-willed woman whose mother was murdered by the Nazis eventually avenges her mother's death by becoming a world-wide publishing mogul and exposing the men responsible. Romantic trysts and corporate intrigue abound.

Production Company: New World TV
Executive Producer .... Bonny Dore
Executive Producer .... Leslie Greif
Producer .... Steve Krantz
Director .... Douglas Hickox
Writer .... Laurence Heath
Cast .... Joan Collins
Cast .... Timothy Dalton
Cast .... Marisa Berenson
Cast .... James Farentino
Cast .... Jean-Pierre Aumont

SINS OF THE FATHER — NBC

Drama: Family Drama • Forbidden Love • Sex/Glitz
Airdate: 1/13/85
Rating: 15.0/23   A/C:

A pretty female attorney falls in love with a wealthy businessman and also has an affair with his unassuming son.

Production Company: Fries Entertainment Inc.
Executive Producer .... Charles Fries
Producer .... Ron Lyon
Producer .... Jack Michon
Director .... Peter Werner
Writer .... Elizabeth Gill
Writer .... Jeff Cohn
Cast .... James Coburn
Cast .... Ted Wass
Cast .... Glynnis O'Connor

SINS OF THE MOTHER — CBS

Drama: Family Drama • True Crime • Rape/ Molestation
Airdate: 02/19/91
Rating: 14.5/23   A/C: 2

Based on the book "Son" by Jack Olsen. The pathological manipulations of a domineering mother drive a young man to terrorize his community with a series of rapes.

Production Company: Corapeake/Polson
Executive Producer .... Beth Polson
Producer .... Randy Siegel
Director .... John Patterson
Writer .... Christopher Lofton
Writer .... Richard Fielder
Writer .... Michael K. Krohn
Cast .... Elizabeth Montgomery
Cast .... Dale Midkiff
Cast .... Heather Fairfield
Cast .... Talia Balsam

SISTER MARGARET AND THE SATURDAY NIGHT LADIES — CBS

Drama: Woman Against The System • Social Issue
Airdate: 01/17/87
Rating: 11.5/19   A/C:

A nun who is also a psychiatrist defeats various obstacles in her struggle to open a halfway house for female parolees.

Production Company: Telepictures
Executive Producer .... Marilyn Shapiro
Producer .... Neil T. Maffeo
Director .... Paul Wendkos
Writer .... Terry Louise Fisher
Writer .... Steve Brown
Cast .... Bonnie Franklin
Cast .... Jon Chardiet
Cast .... Rosemary Clooney
Cast .... Jenetta Arnette
Cast .... Trazana Beverly

SITTER, THE — FBC

Drama: Children/Teens • Psychological Thriller
Airdate: 06/10/91
Rating: 6.7/12   A/C: 4

Based on the novel "Mischief" by Charlotte Armstrong and remake of the 1952 film "Don't Bother to Knock." A little girl is left by her unsuspecting parents with a mentally deranged teen and is soon imperiled by the sitter's dangerous delusions.

Production Company: FNM Films, Inc.
Executive Producer .... Paul Lussier
Producer .... Gina Scheerer
Director .... Rick Berger
Writer .... Rick Berger
Cast .... Kim Meyers
Cast .... Brett Cullen
Cast .... Susan Barnes

SIX AGAINST THE ROCK — NBC

Drama: True Story • Prison and Prison Camp • Period Piece
Airdate: 05/18/87
Rating: 16.4/24   A/C:

Fact-based tale of the long-planned 1946 Alcatraz escape attempt.

Production Company: Schaefer/Karpf/Eckstein Prods. IAW Gaylord Production Co.
Executive Producer .... George Eckstein
Executive Producer .... Merrill H. Karpf
Producer .... Terry Carr
Director .... Paul Wendkos
Writer .... John Gay
Cast .... David Carradine
Cast .... Jan-Michael Vincent
Cast .... Howard Hesseman
Cast .... Charles Haid
Cast .... Richard Dysart
Cast .... David Morse

SKETCH ARTIST — SHOWTIME

Drama: Murder and Murder Mystery • Suspense/ Thriller
Airdate: 06/27/92
Rating: N/A   A/C:

The eyewitness to a designer's murder describes the killer to a police sketch artist, who finds the image looks surprisingly like his wife. When he doctors his sketch to protect her, an innocent photographer is accused, leading to yet another murder.

Production Company: Motion Picture Corporation of America
Producer .... Brad Krevoy
Producer .... Steve Stabler
Co-Producer .... Chad Oman
Director .... Phedon Papamichael
Writer .... Michael Angeli
Cast .... Jeff Fahey
Cast .... Sean Young
Cast .... Drew Barrymore

SKYLARK — CBS

Drama: Family Drama • Farm Story • Period Piece
Airdate: 2/7/93
Rating: 19.9/29   A/C: 1

Sequel to CBS TV Movie, "Sarah, Plain and Tall" by Patricia MacLachlan. In 1912, Kansas, a drought stricken farmer is forced to take her children back to her old home town in Maine while her stoic husband fights to save their scorched land. When they are finally reunited their emotional bonds are deeper and stronger then ever.

Production Company: Self Prods., Trillium Prods. Inc.
Executive Producer .... William Self
Executive Producer .... Glenn Close
Producer .... Joseph Sargent
Director .... Joseph Sargent
Writer .... Patricia MacLachlan
Cast .... Glenn Close
Cast .... Christopher Walken
Cast .... Lexi Randall
Cast .... Christopher Bell

SMALL SACRIFICES   ABC

Miniseries/Drama (2 nights): Murder and Murder
Mystery • True Crime • Children/Teens • Courtroom
Drama • Family Violence
Airdate: 11/12/89 • 11/14/89
Rating: 18.1/28 • 25.2/39   A/C: 1 • 1

*Based on Ann Rule's book. Sociopath Diane
Downs, spurned by a warped passion for her
ex-lover, shoots her three children but claims a
stranger attacked them. Her surviving child
eventually testifies against her and she is
convicted.*

Production Company: Louis Rudolph Films and
     Motown Prods. IAW Larcom Ltd. & Fries Ent.
Executive Producer .... Louis Rudolph
Executive Producer .... Suzanne De Passe
Producer .... S. Bryan Hickox
Director .... David Greene
Writer .... Joyce Eliason
Cast .... Farrah Fawcett
Cast .... John Shea
Cast .... Gordon Clapp
Cast .... Ryan O'Neal

SMOKEY MOUNTAIN CHRISTMAS, A   ABC

Drama: Holiday Special • Love Story
Airdate: 12/14/86
Rating: 23.2/35   A/C:

*A successful country-western singer goes home
to Tennessee, falls in love with a local man, and
ends up adopting a group of homeless children.
She ultimately forsakes her life in the fast lane.*

Production Company: Sandollar Prods.
Executive Producer .... Sandy Gallin
Producer .... Robert Lovenheim
Director .... Henry Winkler
Writer .... William Bleich
Cast .... Dolly Parton
Cast .... Lee Majors
Cast .... Bo Hopkins
Cast .... Anita Morris

SNOW KILL   USA

Drama: Action/Adventure • Murder and Murder
Mystery • Suspense/Thriller
Airdate: 07/25/90
Rating: N/A   A/C:

*A group of corporate executives sent out to a
remote mountain to test their mettle find
themselves stalked by escaped convicts and a
vengeful mountain trapper.*

Production Company: Wilshire Court Prod.
Executive Producer .... Dori Weiss
Executive Producer .... Mark H. Ovitz
Producer .... Raymond Hartung
Director .... Thomas J. Wright
Writer .... Raymond Hartung
Writer .... Harv Zimmel
Cast .... Terence Knox
Cast .... Patti D'Arbanville
Cast .... Jon Cypher
Cast .... Clayton Rohner

SNOWBOUND: THE JIM AND JENNIFER STOLPA STORY   CBS

Drama: True Story • Family Drama • Disaster
Airdate: 1/9/94
Rating: 18.2/27   A/C: 1

*The terrifying ordeal of Jim and Jennifer Stolpa
who along with their infant son were trapped
for eight days in the snowbound Nevada
wilderness. While his wife and baby cling to
life in a cave, young Jim treks for days along
frozen deserted roadways. With sheer
determination he eventually reaches help and
is able to rescue his wife and child from an icy
death.*

Production Company: Pacific Motion Pictures Inc.
     IAW Jaffe/Braunstein Films Ltd.
Executive Producer .... Howard Braunstein
Co-Executive Producer .... Christine Sacani
Producer .... Lisa Richardson
Producer .... Matthew O'Conner
Director .... Christian Duguay
Writer .... Jonathan Rintels
Cast .... Neil Patrick Harris
Cast .... Kelli Williams
Cast .... Susan Clark
Cast .... Michael Gross

SO PROUDLY WE HAIL   CBS

Drama: Social Issue • Nazis • Children/Teens
Airdate: 01/23/90
Rating: 7.5/12   A/C: 3

*A professor's anthropology theories are
exploited by a charismatic leader of a Neo-Nazi
group to legitimize their racists beliefs. Seduced
by the rhetoric, a group of teens are imperiled
by the movement.*

Production Company: Lionel Chetwynd Prods.
     IAW CBS Entertainment Prods.
Executive Producer .... Lionel Chetwynd
Producer .... Jay Benson
Director .... Lionel Chetwynd
Writer .... Lionel Chetwynd
Cast .... Edward Herrmann
Cast .... Chad Lowe
Cast .... David Soul
Cast .... Gloria Carlin

SODBUSTERS   SHOWTIME

Comedy: Farm Story • Period Piece • Western
Airdate: 7/18/94
Rating: N/A   A/C:

*In 1875, Colorado a motley crew of
homesteaders are pressured by a ruthless, land
grabbing cattleman with an eye on the coming
railroad. When a mysterious gunslinger rides
into their midst he turns out to be more deadly
with the ladies than with his gun. Forced to
take matters into their own hands the
determined sodbusters show the spineless
stranger what it takes to be a real hero.*

Production Company: Atlantis Films Ltd. IAW
     Bond Street Prods., The Movie Network, City
     TV
Executive Producer .... Peter Sussman
Executive Producer .... Eugene Levy
Executive Producer .... Stuart Benjamin
Producer .... Brian Parker
Director .... Eugene Levy
Writer .... Eugene Levy
Writer .... John Hemphill
Cast .... Kris Kristofferson
Cast .... John Vernon
Cast .... Fred Willard
Cast .... Max Gail

SOMEBODY HAS TO SHOOT THE PICTURE   HBO

Drama: Man Against The System • Social Issue •
Prison and Prison Camp
Airdate: 09/09/90
Rating: N/A   A/C:

*A photographer, chosen by a death row inmate
to record his execution on film, uncovers new
evidence and struggles to prove the doomed
man's innocence.*

Production Company: Alan Barnette Prods./Frank
     Pierson Films IAW MCA TV Ent./Scholastic
Executive Producer .... William Sackheim
Producer .... Alan Barnette
Co-Producer .... Oscar L. Costo
Director .... Frank Pierson
Writer .... Doug Magee
Cast .... Roy Scheider
Cast .... Bonnie Bedelia
Cast .... Robert Carradine
Cast .... Andre Braugher

SOMEBODY'S DAUGHTER   ABC

Drama: Suspense/Thriller • Murder and Murder
Mystery • Cops/Detectives/Law Enforcement
Airdate: 9/20/92
Rating: 10.2/16   A/C: 3

*A naive stripper becomes entangled in a web
of police coverups when her cop boyfriends's
buddy is accused of murdering her friend and
fellow dancer.*

Production Company: Karen Danaher-Dorr Prods.
     IAW Republic Pictures
Executive Producer .... Karen Danaher-Dorr
Producer .... Joseph Sargent
Director .... Joseph Sargent
Writer .... Barbara Turner
Cast .... Nicolette Sheridan
Cast .... Nick Mancuso
Cast .... Boyd Kestner

SOMETHING IN COMMON   CBS
Comedy: Romantic Comedy
Airdate: 11/02/86
Rating: 18.2/29   A/C:

A middle-aged widow, who dotes on her twenty-two year old son, is horrified when he acquires a forty-two year old girlfriend.

Production Company: Freyda Rothstein/Litke-Grossbart Prods. IAW New World TV
Executive Producer .... Freyda Rothstein
Executive Producer .... Jack Grossbart
Producer .... Glenn Jordan
Director .... Glenn Jordan
Writer .... Susan Rice
Cast .... Ellen Burstyn
Cast .... Tuesday Weld
Cast .... Eli Wallach
Cast .... Don Murray
Cast .... Patrick Cassidy

SOMETHING IS OUT THERE   NBC
Miniseries/Drama (2 nights): Cops/Detectives/Law Enforcement • Series Pilot (2 hr.) • Sci-Fi/Supernatural/Horror/Fantasy
Airdate: 05/08/88 • 05/09/88
Rating: 19.3/31 • 19.0/29   A/C:

An undercover policeman, investigating a series of gruesome murders, discovers a witness who leads him to the extraterrestrial shape-changing monster responsible.

Production Company: Columbia Pictures TV
Executive Producer .... Frank Lupo
Executive Producer .... John Ashley
Director .... Richard Colla
Writer .... Frank Lupo
Cast .... Maryam D'Abo
Cast .... George Dzundza
Cast .... Gregory Sierra
Cast .... Kim Delaney
Cast .... Joe Cortese

SOMETHING TO LIVE FOR: THE ALISON GERTZ STORY   ABC
Drama: Family Drama • Children/Teens • Medical/Disease/Mental Illness • Social Issue • True Story
Airdate: 03/29/92
Rating: 16.2/26   A/C: 1

A twenty-two-year-old, well-to-do New York woman learns she has the AIDS virus. With the emotional support of her family, she battles not only the horrifying effects of the illness, but the ignorance surrounding the disease as well.

Production Company: Grossbart/Barnett Prods.
Executive Producer .... Joan Barnett
Executive Producer .... Jack Grossbart
Director .... Tom McLoughlin
Writer .... Deborah Joy LeVine
Cast .... Molly Ringwald
Cast .... Lee Grant
Cast .... Martin Landau
Cast .... Perry King

SON OF THE MORNING STAR   ABC
Miniseries/Drama (2 nights): True Story • Period Piece • Historical Piece • Biography • Western • American Indians
Airdate: 02/03/91 • 02/04/91
Rating: 11.7/18 • 12.8/20   A/C: 3 • 3

Based on the book by Evan S. Connell. The controversial life of flamboyant General George Armstrong Custer, who forms the U.S. 7th Cavalry and leads them through ten years of the Indian Plain Wars, which eventually results in his legendary defeat at the Battle of Little Bighorn in 1876.

Production Company: Mount Company and Preston Fischer Co. IAW Republic Pictures TV
Executive Producer .... Nicolette Mount
Producer .... Preston Fischer
Producer .... Cyrus Yavneh
Director .... Mike Robe
Writer .... Melissa Mathison
Cast .... Gary Cole
Cast .... Rosanna Arquette
Cast .... Rodney A. Grant
Cast .... Dean Stockwell

SON'S PROMISE, A   ABC
Drama: Family Drama • Children/Teens • True Story
Airdate: 03/05/90
Rating: 16.5/27   A/C: 1

Fifteen-year-old Terry O'Kelly promises his dying mother that he will keep his six younger brothers together. Despite a drunken, resentful father and tremendous odds, Terry triumphs.

Production Company: Marian Rees Associates, Inc.
Executive Producer .... Marian Rees
Producer .... Anne Hopkins
Director .... John Korty
Writer .... Bill Stratton
Writer .... Robert Inman
Cast .... Rick Schroder
Cast .... David Andrews
Cast .... Veronica Cartwright
Cast .... Stephen Dorff

SORRY, WRONG NUMBER   USA
Drama: Woman In Jeopardy • Psychological Thriller
Airdate: 10/01/89
Rating: N/A   A/C:

Based on the radio play by Lucille Fletcher and a remake of the 1948 film. A woman, confined to bed, accidentally overhears a phone conversation involving a planned murder. When the killer learns her identity she must fight for her life.

Production Company: Jack Grossbart Prods IAW Wilshire Court Productions
Executive Producer .... Jack Grossbart
Producer .... Paul Freeman
Director .... Tony Wharmby
Writer .... Ann Louise Bardach
Cast .... Loni Anderson
Cast .... Hal Holbrook
Cast .... Carl Weintraub
Cast .... Patrick MacNee

SOUND AND THE SILENCE, THE   TNT
Miniseries/Drama (2 nights): Biography • Period Piece • Historical Piece
Airdate: 7/18/93 • 7/19/93
Rating: N/A   A/C:

Chronicles the life on inventor Alexander Graham Bell from his early childhood in Scotland, his work with the deaf in Boston, his marriage to a hearing-impaired student, his invention of the telephone to his later career as an aviation pioneer.

Production Company: Screen Star Ent., Atlantis Films, South Pacific Pictures, Kelcom Intl.
Executive Producer .... Michael McMillian
Executive Producer .... Don Reynolds
Executive Producer .... Nicholas Clermont
Executive Producer .... Peter Koonenburg
Producer .... Kim Todd
Producer .... Luciano Lisi
Director .... John Kent Harrison
Writer .... Tony Foster
Writer .... William Schmidt
Writer .... John Kent Harrison
Cast .... John Bach
Cast .... Brenda Fricker
Cast .... Elizabeth Quinn

SOUTH BEACH   NBC
Drama: Cops/Detectives/Law Enforcement • Action/Adventure • Series Pilot (2 hr.)
Airdate: 6/6/93
Rating: 9.8/17   A/C: 2

A sexy Miami con artist reluctantly goes to work as an undercover operative for a hard nosed Federal agent after her shifty brother steals millions of diamonds from the Russian government.

Production Company: Wolf Films IAW Universal TV
Executive Producer .... Robert De Laurentis
Executive Producer .... Dick Wolf
Producer .... Brooke Kennedy
Producer .... Monica Wyatt
Director .... David Greene
Writer .... Robert De Laurentis
Writer .... Glenn Davis
Writer .... William Laurin
Cast .... Yancy Butler
Cast .... John Glover
Cast .... Patti D'Arbanville

Movies and Miniseries

SOUVENIR — SHOWTIME
Drama: Foreign or Exotic Location • WWII
Airdate: 10/30/88
Rating: N/A   A/C:

Based on the novel "The Pork Butcher" by David Hughes. A German ex-soldier, now a naturalized American delicatessen owner, decides to travel to France and return to the small French village where he was stationed during WW II—and fell dangerously in love with a young French girl. Accompanied by his estranged daughter he embarks on a journey of rediscovery only to uncover atrocities of the past as well as hidden guilts of the present.

Production Company: Fancyfree Productions Limited
Producer .... Tom Reeve
Co-Producer .... Bernard Krichefski
Director .... Geoffrey Reeve
Writer .... Paul Wheeler
Cast .... Christopher Plummer
Cast .... Catherine Hicks
Cast .... Michael Lonsdale
Cast .... Christopher Cazenove

SPACE — CBS
Miniseries/Drama (5 nights): Period Piece • Historical Piece • True Story
Airdate: 04/14/85 • 04/15/85 • 04/16/85 • 04/17/85 • 04/18/85
Rating: 19.4/31 • 16.4/26 • 14.7/24 • 17.1/28 • 16.3/26   A/C:

Based on the book by James Michener. This story follows the lives of the astronauts and scientists who develop the space program, starting with WWII all the way up to the 1970's.

Production Company: Stonehenge Prods. IAW Paramount TV
Executive Producer .... Dick Berg
Producer .... Martin Manulis
Co-Producer .... Allan Marcil
Director .... Joseph Sargent
Director .... Lee Philips
Writer .... Stirling Silliphant
Writer .... Dick Berg
Cast .... James Garner
Cast .... Beau Bridges
Cast .... Blair Brown
Cast .... Bruce Dern
Cast .... Melinda Dillon
Cast .... Susan Anspach

SPARKS: THE PRICE OF PASSION — CBS
Drama: Murder and Murder Mystery • Woman In Jeopardy • Love Story • Series Pilot (2 hr.)
Airdate: 02/25/90
Rating: 13.7/21   A/C: 2

With the help of an FBI agent, the mayor of Albuquerque personally pursues a serial murderer while defending herself against ruthless real estate developers who have some compromising photos of her.

Production Company: Shadowplay & Victoria Principal Prods., King Phoenix Ent.
Executive Producer .... Victoria Principal
Executive Producer .... Hans Proppe
Producer .... Bill Svanoe
Producer .... Richard Colla
Director .... Richard Colla
Writer .... John Robert Bensink
Writer .... Bill Svanoe
Cast .... Victoria Principal
Cast .... Ted Wass

SPECIAL FRIENDSHIP, A — CBS
Drama: Action/Adventure • True Story • Period Piece • Black Story • Buddy Story
Airdate: 03/31/87
Rating: 13.7/22   A/C:

True adventure of a Virginia woman and her former slave who spied for the North during the Civil War.

Production Company: Entertainment Partners Inc.
Executive Producer .... Robert E. Fuisz
Producer .... William F. Storke
Producer .... Alfred R. Kelman
Co-Producer .... Phil Levitan
Director .... Fielder Cook
Writer .... Kenneth Cavender
Cast .... Tracy Pollan
Cast .... Akosua Busia
Cast .... Cynthia Harris
Cast .... LeVar Burton

SPECIAL PEOPLE — CBS
Drama: Medical/Disease/Mental Illness • True Story
Airdate: 09/11/84
Rating: 10.7/18   A/C:

Based on the true story of "The Famous People Players," a troupe of mentally impaired black-light puppet performers organized by Canadian Diane Dupuy. The story follows their exploits as they eventually get to perform all over the world.

Production Company: Joe Cates Prods.
Executive Producer .... Bruce Raymond
Producer .... Joe Cates
Co-Producer .... John M. Eckert
Director .... Marc Daniels
Writer .... Corey Blechman
Cast .... Brooke Adams
Cast .... Susan Roman
Cast .... Sandra Ciccone
Cast .... Lesleh Donaldson

SPENSER: CEREMONY — LIFETIME
Drama: Cops/Detectives/Law Enforcement • Children/Teens • Prostitution
Airdate: 7/22/93
Rating: N/A   A/C:

Based on the 1985-88 ABC Series "Spencer For Hire". A Boston novelist and Private Investigator, along with his psychologist girlfriend and streetwise buddy, search for a sixteen year old run away who has become a prostitute. She also happens to be the daughter of a wealthy gubernatorial candidate who doesn't seem overly concerned.

Production Company: Norstar Ent., Boardwalk Ent., Ultra Ent., ABC Video Enterprises
Executive Producer .... Peter Simpson
Executive Producer .... Fred Tarter
Executive Producer .... Alan Wagner
Executive Producer .... Bob Rubin
Producer .... Ray Sager
Director .... Andrew Wild
Writer .... Robert Parker
Writer .... Joan Parker
Cast .... Robert Urich
Cast .... Avery Brooks
Cast .... Barbara Williams
Cast .... Tanya Allen

SPENSER: FOR HIRE — ABC
Drama: Cops/Detectives/Law Enforcement • Series Pilot (2 hr.)
Airdate: 09/20/85
Rating: 14.0/24   A/C:

A Boston private investigator looks into the case of a criminal whose wife has decided to become a bankrobber herself.

Production Company: John Wilder Prods. IAW Warner Bros. TV
Executive Producer .... John Wilder
Producer .... Dick Gallegly
Director .... Lee H. Katzin
Writer .... John Wilder
Cast .... Robert Urich
Cast .... Avery Brooks
Cast .... Geoffrey Lewis
Cast .... Donna Mitchell
Cast .... Ron McLarty
Cast .... Barbara Stock

SPENSER: PALE KINGS AND PRINCES
LIFETIME
Drama: Cops/Detectives/Law Enforcement • Murder and Murder Mystery
Airdate: 1/2/94
Rating: N/A   A/C:

A Boston novelist and private investigator, along with his psychologist girlfriend, try to solve the murder of a nosy reporter and womanizer in a small New England town.

Production Company: Norstar Ent. IAW Boardwalk Ent. IAW Ultra Ent./ABC Video Enterprises.
Executive Producer .... Peter Simpson
Executive Producer .... Fred Tarter
Executive Producer .... Alan Wagner
Executive Producer .... Bob Rubin
Executive Producer .... Bill Siegler
Producer .... Ray Sager
Director .... Vic Sarin
Writer .... Robert Parker
Writer .... Joan Parker
Cast .... Robert Urich
Cast .... Barbara Williams
Cast .... Avery Brooks
Cast .... Jerry Nihen

SPIDER AND THE FLY, THE   USA
Drama: Murder and Murder Mystery • Suspense/Thriller
Airdate: 5/13/94
Rating: N/A   A/C:

Two mystery crime writers who are having a steamy affair challenge each other to design the perfect murder— and the victim is to be someone they both know. The game turns deadly when their publisher is found murdered—and the details matches one of their scenarios.

Production Company: Haft/Nasatir Co. Heartstar Prods. Ltd. IAW Wilshire Court
Executive Producer .... Steven Haft
Executive Producer .... Marcia Nasatir
Producer .... John Danylkiw
Director .... Michael Katleman
Writer .... Alanna Hamill
Writer .... Robert Pucci
Cast .... Mel Harris
Cast .... Ted Shackelford
Cast .... Peggy Lipton
Cast .... Kenneth Welsh

SPIES, LIES AND NAKED THIGHS   CBS
Comedy: Cops/Detectives/Law Enforcement • Buddy Story
Airdate: 11/22/88
Rating: 12.2/19   A/C:

A United Nations interpreter and a bumbling federal agent join forces to go after an assassin.

Production Company: Qintex Entertainment
Executive Producer .... Robert Halmi, Sr.
Executive Producer .... Edwin Self
Executive Producer .... Bill Brademan
Producer .... Robert Halmi, Jr.
Producer .... David Patterson
Director .... James Frawley
Writer .... Ed Self
Cast .... Ed Begley, Jr.
Cast .... Harry Anderson
Cast .... Linda Purl
Cast .... Brent Carver

SPIRIT, THE   ABC
Drama: Murder and Murder Mystery • Cops/Detectives/Law Enforcement • Action/Adventure • Series Pilot (2 hr.) • Sci-Fi/Supernatural/Horror/Fantasy
Airdate: 07/31/87
Rating: 7.0/15   A/C:

A policeman becomes "The Spirit", a masked superhero out to avenge a cop-killing. Based on Will Eisner's 1940s comic book.

Production Company: De Souza Prods. and Von Zerneck/Samuels Prods. IAW Warner Bros. TV
Executive Producer .... Stu Samuels
Executive Producer .... Frank Von Zerneck
Producer .... Paul Aratow
Co-Producer .... William Beaudine, Jr.
Director .... Michael Schultz
Writer .... Steven E. De Souza
Cast .... Sam Jones
Cast .... Nana Visitor
Cast .... Philip Baker Hall
Cast .... Bumper Robinson

SPOILS OF WAR   ABC
Drama: Family Drama • Children/Teens
Airdate: 4/9/94
Rating: 4.9/9   A/C: 4

Based on the 1988 play by Michael Weller. After leaving Colorado and returning to New York City, a lonely, isolated fifteen year old boy orchestrates the reunion of his charismatic mother who has raised him and his cynical, fashion photographer father he has just met for the first time.

Production Company: Evolution Entertainment Prods. IAW Signboard Hill Prods & RHI Entertainment Inc.
Executive Producer .... Robert Halmi, Jr.
Executive Producer .... Richard Walsh
Producer .... Richard Lowry
Director .... David Greene
Writer .... Michael Weller
Cast .... Kate Nelligan
Cast .... Rhea Perlman
Cast .... John Heard
Cast .... Tobey Maguire

SPOONER   DISNEY
Drama: Children/Teens
Airdate: 12/02/89
Rating: N/A   A/C:

An escaped convict assumes the identity of Harry Spooner and takes work as a teacher in a small town. He helps redeem an incorrigible youth and coaches a team of perpetual losers to the district championships in wrestling before he is caught.

Production Company: Pipeline Prods., Inc.
Executive Producer .... Sheldon Pinchuk
Executive Producer .... Bill Finnegan
Co-Producer .... Peter Baloff
Co-Producer .... Dave Wollert
Director .... George Miller
Writer .... Peter Baloff
Writer .... Dave Wollert
Cast .... Robert Urich
Cast .... Jane Kaczmarek
Cast .... Brent Fraser

SPY   USA
Drama: Man Against The System • Suspense/Thriller
Airdate: 12/27/89
Rating: N/A   A/C:

A burnt-out spy fakes his own death and has plastic surgery. When he discovers that his ex-wife is being watched and his only remaining CIA contact is apparently killed, he realizes that the Agency, or someone in it, is after him.

Production Company: Wilshire Court IAW Deadly Prods.
Producer .... Robert Lewis
Director .... Philip F. Messina
Writer .... Philip F. Messina
Cast .... Bruce Greenwood
Cast .... Catherine Hicks
Cast .... Michael Tucker

STAGECOACH   CBS
Drama: Western • Period Piece
Airdate: 05/18/86
Rating: 22.5/36   A/C:

Remake of the John Ford western involving a group of people with little in common heading west through uncivilized territory.

Production Company: Raymond Katz Prods. IAW Heritage Entertainment
Executive Producer .... Raymond Katz
Executive Producer .... Willie Nelson
Senior Producer .... Skip Steloff
Producer .... Hal W. Polaire
Producer .... Jack Thompson
Director .... Ted Post
Writer .... James Lee Barrett
Cast .... Willie Nelson
Cast .... Mary Crosby
Cast .... Johnny Cash
Cast .... Elizabeth Ashley
Cast .... Waylon Jennings
Cast .... Tony Franciosa
Cast .... Kris Kristofferson

STALIN   HBO
EMMY WINNER

Drama (3 hours): Biography • Foreign or Exotic Location • Historical Piece • Period Piece
Airdate: 1/21/92
Rating: N/A   A/C:

The savage rule of Soviet dictator Joseph Stalin from 1924 to 1953. His early days in the communist party to his iron hand leadership of the Russian people which excluded treacherous purges, executions and assassinations. Note: Three Hours.

Production Company: Mark Carliner Prods. IAW Hungarian TV Channel 1
Executive Producer .... Mark Carliner
Co-Producer .... Ilene Kahn
Director .... Ivan Passer
Writer .... Paul Monash
Cast .... Robert Duvall
Cast .... Julia Ormond
Cast .... Joan Plowright
Cast .... Maximilian Schell

STARCROSSED   ABC
Drama: Sci-Fi/Supernatural/Horror/Fantasy
Airdate: 01/31/85
Rating: 11.4/16   A/C:

A man helps an extra-terrestial woman flee a couple of murderers from her planet.

Production Company: Fries Entertainment Inc.
Executive Producer .... Charles Fries
Producer .... Robert Lovenheim
Director .... Jeffrey Bloom
Writer .... Jeffrey Bloom
Cast .... James Spader
Cast .... Peter Kowanko
Cast .... Clark Johnson
Cast .... Jacqueline Brooks
Cast .... Edward Groenenberg
Cast .... Belinda Bauer

STARK   CBS
Drama: Cops/Detectives/Law Enforcement • Woman In Jeopardy
Airdate: 04/10/85
Rating: 14.1/23   A/C:

A detective from Wichita, Kansas, goes to Las Vegas to find his missing sister and teams up with a blackjack dealer who knew her.

Production Company: CBS Entertainment Prods.
Producer .... David H. Balkan
Director .... Rod Holcomb
Writer .... Ernest Tidyman
Writer .... Bill Stratton
Cast .... Marilu Henner
Cast .... Nicolas Surovy
Cast .... Pat Corley
Cast .... Seth Jaffe

STATE OF EMERGENCY   HBO
Drama: Medical/Disease/Mental Illness • Social Issue
Airdate: 2/12/94
Rating: N/A   A/C:

An emergency room doctor at a large inner city hospital tries to cope with the frustration and fatigue of treating endless patients. When a businessman come in with a head trauma, the overworked doctor tries to save the man but fails due to lack of a neurosurgeon or CAT scanner. The dead man's wife then sues the hospital and the attending physician for neglect.

Production Company: Chestnut Hill Prods. for HBO Showcase
Executive Producer .... Jeffrey Lurie
Executive Producer .... Colin Callender
Producer .... John P. Marsh
Producer .... Jay Roewe
Director .... Lesli Glatter
Writer .... Susan Black
Writer .... Lance Gentile
Cast .... Joe Mantegna
Cast .... Lynn Whitfield
Cast .... Melinda Dillon
Cast .... Paul Dooley

STAY THE NIGHT   ABC
Miniseries/Drama (2 nights): Family Drama • Murder and Murder Mystery • Forbidden Love • True Crime • Children/Teens • Family Violence
Airdate: 04/26/92 - 04/27/92
Rating: 13.8/22 • 17.9/28   A/C: 2 • 1

In mid-1980's Georgia, seductive Jimmie Sue Finger manipulates naive 16-year-old Michael Kettman, Jr., into murdering her husband. After his conviction, his distraught mother befriends Finger in an attempt to trick her into revealing her collusion.

Production Company: Stan Margulies-New World
Executive Producer .... Stan Margulies
Executive Producer .... J.C. Shardo
Director .... Harry Winer
Writer .... Daniel Freudenberger
Cast .... Barbara Hershey
Cast .... Jane Alexander
Cast .... Morgan Weisser
Cast .... Fred Dalton Thompson

STAYING AFLOAT   NBC
Drama: Cops/Detectives/Law Enforcement
Airdate: 11/26/93
Rating: 9.5/17   A/C: 3

Disinherited by his billionaire father, a Palm Beach jet setter manages to keep up appearances by helping a bungling federal agent catch bad guys among the rich and famous.

Production Company: Ruddy Moargan Organizations IAW TriStar TV
Executive Producer .... Larry Hagman
Executive Producer .... Gray Frederickson
Executive Producer .... James D. Parriott
Co-Producer .... Jan DeWitt
Director .... Eric Laneuville
Writer .... Michael Sadowski
Cast .... Larry Hagman
Cast .... Gregg Henry
Cast .... Eric Christmas
Cast .... Claire Yarlett

STEAL THE SKY   HBO
Drama: Suspense/Thriller • Foreign or Exotic Location • Forbidden Love
Airdate: 8/5/88
Rating: N/A   A/C:

A female American spy who is trained by Israel's Mossad, orchestrates the theft of a Russian MIG from Iraq, complicating matters is her romantic involvement with a married Iraqi Air Force fighter pilot.

Production Company: HBO Pictures IAW Paramount Pictures
Producer .... Yoram Ben-Ami
Director .... John Hancock
Writer .... Christopher Woods
Writer .... Dorothy Tristan
Cast .... Mariel Hemingway
Cast .... Ben Cross

STEEL JUSTICE   NBC
Drama: Cops/Detectives/Law Enforcement • Series Pilot (2 hr.) • Sci-Fi/Supernatural/Horror/Fantasy
Airdate: 04/05/92
Rating: 8.9/14   A/C: 3

To heal the wounds from the loss of his son, a cop transforms one of his toys into a crime busting robot. He then teams with an ancient time-traveler to capture an illegal arms trader.

Production Company: Universal TV
Executive Producer .... Christopher Crowe
Executive Producer .... Andrew Mirisch
Producer .... Steve Lovejoy
Director .... Christopher Crowe
Writer .... Christopher Crowe
Writer .... John Hill
Cast .... Robert Taylor
Cast .... J.A. Preston
Cast .... Season Hubley
Cast .... Roy Brocksmith

STEPFATHER I I I   HBO

Drama: Woman In Jeopardy • Suspense/Thriller
Airdate: 06/04/92
Rating: N/A   A/C:

Sequel to the feature film. A serial killer undergoes plastic surgery after escaping from prison. He then meets and marries an unsuspecting single mother in a small California town, only to repeat his heinous crimes.

Production Company: ITC Entertainment Group
Producer .... Guy Magar
Producer .... Paul Moen
Director .... Guy Magar
Writer .... Guy Magar
Writer .... Marc Ray
Cast .... Robert Wrightman
Cast .... Priscilla Barnes
Cast .... Season Hubley

STEPFORD CHILDREN, THE   NBC

Drama: Suspense/Thriller • Children/Teens • Sci-Fi/Supernatural/Horror/Fantasy
Airdate: 03/15/87
Rating: 19.2/29   A/C:

Television sequel to the feature film "The Stepford Wives." A couple moves to the suburbs and encounters automaton-acting housewives—and the kids are getting pretty submissive too.

Production Company: Edgar J. Scherick Associates Prods. IAW Taft Entertainment TV
Executive Producer .... Edgar J. Scherick
Executive Producer .... Gary Hoffman
Producer .... Paul Pompian
Director .... Alan J. Levi
Writer .... William Bleich
Cast .... Barbara Eden
Cast .... Randall Batinkoff
Cast .... Richard Anderson
Cast .... Tammy Lauren
Cast .... James Coco

STEPHEN KING'S GOLDEN YEARS   CBS

Drama: Series Pilot (2 hr.) • Sci-Fi/Supernatural/Horror/Fantasy
Airdate: 07/16/91
Rating: 12.2/22   A/C: 1

An elderly janitor, working in a secret government lab, is contaminated during an explosion of unknown chemicals giving him incredible powers of rejuvenation. As he grows younger, sinister government officials move in to exploit the incident.

Production Company: Laurel Entertainment, Inc.
Executive Producer .... Richard Rubinstein
Executive Producer .... Stephen King
Producer .... Mitchell Galin
Producer .... Peter McIntosh
Director .... Ken Fink
Writer .... Stephen King
Cast .... Keith Szarabajka
Cast .... Felicity Huffman
Cast .... Frances Sternhagen
Cast .... Ed Lauter

STEPHEN KING'S IT   ABC

Miniseries/Drama (2 nights): Children/Teens • Sci-Fi/Supernatural/Horror/Fantasy
Airdate: 11/18/90 • 11/20/90
Rating: 18.5/29 • 20.6/33   A/C: 1 • 1

Based on the Stephen King novel. A group of children band together to destroy a child-killing evil being that haunts their small town. Thirty years later "It" returns and the gang comes back home to honor their promise to exterminate the demon.

Production Company: Konigsberg/Sanitsky Prods. and Green/Epstein Prods. IAW Lorimar TV
Executive Producer .... Jim Green
Executive Producer .... Allen Epstein
Director .... Tommy Lee Wallace
Writer .... Lawrence D. Cohen
Writer .... Tommy Lee Wallace
Cast .... John Ritter
Cast .... Richard Thomas
Cast .... Richard Masur
Cast .... Tim Curry

STEPHEN KING'S SOMETIMES THEY COME BACK   CBS

Mystery: Sci-Fi/Supernatural/Horror/Fantasy
Airdate: 05/07/91
Rating: 11.7/19   A/C: 2

Based on a short story by Stephen King. Unsettling events surround a high school teacher's return to his home town where his younger brother was murdered and he is haunted by the three teen killers who also met an untimely demise.

Production Company: Comeback Prods.
Executive Producer .... Dino De Laurentiis
Producer .... Michael S. Murphy
Director .... Tom McLoughlin
Writer .... Lawrence Konner
Writer .... Mark Rosenthal
Cast .... Tim Matheson
Cast .... Brooke Adams
Cast .... Robert Rusler

STEPHEN KING'S THE STAND   ABC

Drama: Sci-Fi/Supernatural/Horror/Fantasy
Airdate: 5/8/94 • 5/9/94 • 5/11/94 • 5/12/94
Rating: 20.1/32 • 21.0/32 • 20.1/31 • 20.0/31 A/C: 1 • 1 • 1 • 1

Based on the 1978 novel by Stephen King. A government biological warfare experiment goes haywire causing a deadly virus to be released into the American population, killing all but a select group of individuals. Haunted by dreams of either a devout old women or a sinister "apostate of hell" the survivors follow their visions which ultimately lead them to confront the forces of good and evil and a cataclysmic battle for the human race.

Production Company: Laurel Entertainmnet IAW Greengrass Prods.
Executive Producer .... Richard Rubinstein
Executive Producer .... Stephen King
Producer .... Mitchell Galin
Director .... Mick Garris
Writer .... Stephen King
Cast .... Gary Sinise
Cast .... Molly Ringwald
Cast .... Jamey Sheridan
Cast .... Laura San Giacomo
Cast .... Ruby Dee
Cast .... Ossie Davis

STILL CRAZY LIKE A FOX   CBS

Comedy: Cops/Detectives/Law Enforcement • Foreign or Exotic Location • Murder and Murder Mystery
Airdate: 04/05/87
Rating: 21.2/31   A/C:

Based on the TV series "Crazy like a Fox". A private eye and his lawyer son, visiting England, become involved in the case of a nobleman's murder.

Production Company: Schenck/Cardea Prods. IAW Columbia Pictures TV
Executive Producer .... George Schenck
Executive Producer .... Frank Cardea
Producer .... William Hill
Director .... Paul Krasny
Writer .... George Schenck
Writer .... Frank Cardea
Cast .... John Rubinstein
Cast .... Penny Peyser
Cast .... Catherine Oxenberg
Cast .... Jack Warden
Cast .... Robby Kiger

STILL NOT QUITE HUMAN   DISNEY

Comedy: Sci-Fi/Supernatural/Horror/Fantasy
Airdate: 05/31/92
Rating: N/A   A/C:

Second sequel to "Not Quite Human." A scientist's android son must join forces with other androids to free his eccentric father from an evil industrialist who has kidnapped him.

Production Company: Resnick-Margellos Prods.
Executive Producer .... Noel Resnick
Producer .... James Margellos
Director .... Eric Luke
Writer .... Eric Luke
Cast .... Alan Thicke
Cast .... Jay Underwood
Cast .... Betsy Palmer

STILLWATCH   CBS

Mystery: Woman In Jeopardy • Suspense/Thriller • Sci-Fi/Supernatural/Horror/Fantasy
Airdate: 02/10/87
Rating: 14.7/23   A/C:

Based on the novel by Mary Higgins Clark. Two women—a TV reporter and the Senator she is profiling—get involved in spooky doings in the Senator's Washington, D.C., mansion, the site of an old murder.

Production Company: Stillwatch Prods.
Producer .... Terry Morse
Director .... Rod Holcomb
Writer .... David Peckinpah
Writer .... Laird Koenig
Cast .... Angie Dickinson
Cast .... Don Murray
Cast .... Stuart Whitman
Cast .... Barry Primus
Cast .... Lynda Carter
Cast .... Bibi Osterwald

STOLEN BABIES   LIFETIME

Drama: True Crime • Children/Teens • Period Piece • Woman Against The System
Airdate: 3/25/93
Rating: N/A   A/C:

From 1924 to 1950 Georgia Tann headed the Tennessee Children's Home Society, a highly respected Orphanage and adoption agency. During her tenure, permanent homes were found for more than 5,000 babies. A determined Memphis welfare worker, Annie Beales exposes the dark secret that a vast majority of these children were actually stolen from their natural parents who were often poor and uneducated.

Production Company: ABC Video Enterprises, Sander/Moses Prods.
Executive Producer .... Ian Sander
Executive Producer .... Kim Moses
Executive Producer .... J. Moses
Producer .... Ann Kindberg
Director .... Eric Laneuville
Writer .... Sharon Doyle
Cast .... Mary Tyler Moore
Cast .... Lea Thompson
Cast .... Kathleen Quinlan

STOLEN: ONE HUSBAND   CBS

Comedy: Romantic Comedy
Airdate: 02/27/90
Rating: 9.5/15   A/C: 3

A wife comes up with ingenious ways to avenge herself on her husband of twenty-five years who's leaving her for a 27-year-old woman. Then, deciding she does look a little old, she visits a plastic surgeon who falls in love with her, lines and all.

Production Company: King Phoenix Entertainment
Executive Producer .... Harry Chandler
Producer .... Carroll Newman
Director .... Catlin Adams
Writer .... Anna Sandor
Writer .... William Gough
Cast .... Valerie Harper
Cast .... Elliott Gould
Cast .... Brenda Vaccaro
Cast .... Sandy Bull

STOMPIN' AT THE SAVOY   CBS

Drama: Period Piece • Black Story • Love Story • Woman's Issue/Story
Airdate: 04/12/92
Rating: 11.2/19   A/C: 3

Four young women from 1939 Harlem belie their menial daytime jobs by stompin' at the Savoy at night, where they encounter relationships that nurture their romantic desires and blinding ambitions.

Production Company: Richard Maynard Prods. IAW Gallant Entertainment
Executive Producer .... Richard Maynard
Producer .... Michael O. Gallant
Director .... Debbie Allen
Writer .... Beverly M. Sawyer
Cast .... Lynn Whitfield
Cast .... Vanessa Williams
Cast .... Jasmine Guy
Cast .... Mario Van Peebles
Cast .... Vanessa Bell Calloway

STONE FOX   NBC

Drama: Farm Story • Period Piece • Action/Adventure • American Indians • Children/Teens
Airdate: 03/30/87
Rating: 15.9/22   A/C:

A twelve year old orphan boy must save his disabled grandfather's farm by winning a dogsled race against a Shoshone Indian and four other men.

Production Company: Hanna-Barbera Prods., Allarcom Ltd. and Taft Entertainment TV
Executive Producer .... William Hanna
Executive Producer .... Joseph Barbera
Executive Producer .... Harry R. Sherman
Producer .... James Anthony Allard
Director .... Harvey Hart
Writer .... Walter Halsey Davis
Cast .... Buddy Ebsen
Cast .... Joey Cramer
Cast .... Belinda Montgomery
Cast .... Gordon Tootoosis
Cast .... Jason Michas

STONE PILLOW   CBS

Drama: Social Issue
Airdate: 11/05/85
Rating: 23.3/33   A/C:

An elderly New York City bag lady befriends a social worker who's posing as a homeless person herself and teaches her about life on the streets.

Production Company: Schaefer-Karpf Prods. IAW The Gaylord Production Co.
Executive Producer .... Merrill H. Karpf
Producer .... George Schaefer
Co-Producer .... Terry Donnelly
Director .... George Schaefer
Writer .... Rose Leiman Goldemberg
Cast .... Lucille Ball
Cast .... William Converse
Cast .... Stephen Lang
Cast .... Daphne Zuniga

STONES OF IBARRA   CBS

Drama: Love Story • Period Piece • Foreign or Exotic Location • Cross-Cultural Story
Airdate: 01/29/88
Rating: 12.4/21   A/C:

Based on the novel by Harriet Doerr. In 1959, an American couple moves to a Mexican village to reopen the copper mine and reverently assimilate the native atmosphere.

Production Company: Titus Prods.
Executive Producer .... Herbert Brodkin
Executive Producer .... Robert Berger
Producer .... Bruce Pustin
Director .... Jack Gold
Writer .... Ernest Kinoy
Cast .... Glenn Close
Cast .... Alfonso Arau
Cast .... Jorge Cervera, Jr.
Cast .... Ron Joseph
Cast .... Keith Carradine

STONING IN FULHAM COUNTY, A   NBC

Drama: Family Drama • Cross-Cultural Story • Man Against The System • Social Issue
Airdate: 10/24/88
Rating: 18.3/28   A/C:

A county prosecutor must convince an Amish farmer to testify against the men who stoned his baby to death just for fun.

Production Company: Landsburg Co.
Executive Producer .... Alan Landsburg
Executive Producer .... Joan Barnett
Producer .... Jud Kinberg
Director .... Larry Elikann
Writer .... Jackson Gillis
Writer .... Jud Kinberg
Cast .... Ken Olin
Cast .... Jill Eikenberry
Cast .... Ron Perlman
Cast .... Gregg Henry

STOP AT NOTHING — LIFETIME

Drama: Family Drama • Children/Teens • Rape/
Molestation • Family Violence • Woman's Issue/Story
• Social Issue
Airdate: 03/12/91
Rating: N/A   A/C:

When a mother hires a woman to help kidnap
her daughter back from her ex-husband, the
bodyguard protecting the girl helps them when
she realizes the father is a child molester.

Production Company: Empty Chair Productions
Executive Producer .... Ilene Amy Berg
Producer .... George Perkins
Director .... Chris Thomson
Writer .... Stephhen Johnson
Cast .... Veronica Hamel
Cast .... David Ackroyd
Cast .... Robert Desiderio
Cast .... Lindsay Frost

STORM AND SORROW — LIFETIME

Drama: True Story • Action/Adventure • Sports •
Woman Against The System
Airdate: 11/22/90
Rating: N/A   A/C:

Based on the book by Robert Craig. In 1974,
Molly Higgins, society deb turned mountain
climber, faces danger and ridicule trying to
prove herself while on an expedition in Russia.

Production Company: Accent Entertainment Corp.
for Hearst Entertainment
Executive Producer .... Hans Proppe
Producer .... Andras Hamori
Producer .... Richard Colla
Director .... Richard Colla
Writer .... Leigh Chapman
Cast .... Rodd Allen
Cast .... Jay Baker
Cast .... Brian McNamara

STORMIN' HOME — CBS

Drama: Family Drama • Action/Adventure • Sports
Airdate: 04/05/85
Rating: 13.1/23   A/C:

An out of work trucker tries his hand at high
stakes motorcycle racing, while trying to patch
things up with his daughter, girlfriend and ex-
wife.

Production Company: CBS Entertainment Prods.
Producer .... Jerry Jameson
Co-Producer .... Jill Trump
Director .... Jerry Jameson
Writer .... George Yanok
Writer .... Jery Jameson
Cast .... Gil Gerard
Cast .... Pat Corley
Cast .... Joanna Kerns
Cast .... Lisa Blount

STORMY WEATHERS — ABC

Drama: Cops/Detectives/Law Enforcement • Action/
Adventure • Drug Smuggling/Dealing
Airdate: 05/04/92
Rating: 10.2/16   A/C: 3

A streetwise female private eye runs into a
convoluted drug smuggling and murder plot
when she's hired to locate the relative of a client
who disappeared sixteen years ago.

Production Company: Haft/Nasatir Co., River
Siren Prods. IAW TriStar TV
Executive Producer .... Steven Haft
Executive Producer .... Marcia Nasatir
Executive Producer .... Cybill Shepherd
Producers .... Vahan Moosekian
Director .... Will MacKenzie
Writer .... Stephan Blom-Cooper
Writer .... V. Phipps Wilson
Writer .... Gerald Ayres
Cast .... Cybill Shepherd
Cast .... Robert Beltran
Cast .... Charlie Schlatter
Cast .... Kurt Fuller

STORY LADY, THE — NBC

Drama: Family Drama • Social Issue
Airdate: 12/09/91
Rating: 15.9/24   A/C: 2

An elderly widow finds success as a local cable
TV children's storyteller. She is discovered by
a driven ad executive who takes her primetime,
knowingly exploits her, but is ultimately forced
to confront the error of her ways.

Production Company: Michael Filerman Prod.
IAW NBC Prods., Jones Programming Partners
Executive Producer .... Michael Filerman
Executive Producer .... Margery Nelson
Producer .... Joseph Wallenstein
Director .... Larry Elikann
Writer .... Robert Zeschin
Cast .... Jessica Tandy
Cast .... Stephanie Zimbalist
Cast .... Tandy Cronyn
Cast .... Richard Masur

STRANDED — NBC

Comedy: Romantic Comedy • Foreign or Exotic
Location
Airdate: 09/22/86
Rating: 24.9/38   A/C:

When two former business partners who are
now rival advertising executives are stranded
together on an island, romance eventually
blossoms.

Production Company: Tim Flack Prods. IAW
Columbia TV
Executive Producer .... Tim Flack
Producer .... Andrew Gottlieb
Co-Producer .... Chan Mahon
Director .... Rod Daniels
Writer .... Janis Hirsch
Writer .... Stephen Black
Writer .... Henry Stern
Cast .... Loni Anderson
Cast .... Perry King
Cast .... Joel Brooks
Cast .... Elaine Strich

STRANGE VOICES — NBC

Drama: Family Drama • Medical/Disease/Mental
Illness
Airdate: 10/19/87
Rating: 21.0/33   A/C:

When a female college student is diagnosed as
schizophrenic, her mother must hold the family
together. The task is complicated by the guilt
and resentment felt by the student's father and
younger sister.

Production Company: Forrest Hills Prods. Inc.
IAW Dacks-Geller Prods. and TLC
Executive Producer .... Alan Landsburg
Executive Producer .... Joan Barnett
Co-Executive Producer .... Greg H. Sims
Co-Executive Producer .... Nancy McKeon
Producer .... Roberta Dacks
Producer .... Nancy Geller
Director .... Arthur Allan Seidelman
Writer .... Donna Dottley Powers
Writer .... Wayne Powers
Cast .... Nancy McKeon
Cast .... Valerie Harper
Cast .... Stephen Macht
Cast .... Tricia Leigh Fisher
Cast .... Millie Perkins
Cast .... Jack Blessing

STRANGER AT MY DOOR — CBS

Drama: Woman In Jeopardy • Suspense/Thriller
Airdate: 09/27/91
Rating: 11.7/22   A/C: 2

After a corrupt politician's wife sees him murder
his mistress, she escapes and takes refuge on a
farm owned by another fugitive in hiding. When
he tries to help her across the state line, they
must elude police controlled by her husband.

Production Company: A Dry Canyon One Inc.
Prods.
Executive Producer .... Peter S. Fischer
Producer .... Kevin Cremin
Director .... Vincent McEveety
Writer .... Peter S. Fischer
Cast .... Robert Urich
Cast .... Markie Post
Cast .... Michael Beck

STRANGER IN MY BED — NBC

Drama: Family Drama • Medical/Disease/Mental
Illness • True Story
Airdate: 10/27/87
Rating: 18.8/29   A/C:

Fact-based drama of a woman who acquires
permanent amnesia after a car accident,
completely losing any memory of her husband
and children. They all struggle to get to know
each other once again.

Production Company: Edgar J. Scherick
Associates Prods. IAW Taft Entertainment TV
Executive Producer .... Edgar J. Scherick
Executive Producer .... Gary Hoffman
Producer .... Lynn Raynor
Director .... Larry Elikann
Writer .... Audrey Davis Levin
Cast .... Lindsay Wagner
Cast .... Armand Assante
Cast .... Doug Sheehan
Cast .... Gabriel Damon

STRANGER IN THE FAMILY, A   ABC

Drama: Family Drama • Children/Teens • Medical/
Disease/Mental Illness • True Story
Airdate: 10/27/91
Rating: 12.7/19   A/C:

Teenager Steve Thompson suffers global amnesia as the result of an auto accident, leaving him to relearn life step by step. The stress of coping with his slow and tedious recovery forces his family to deal with their own dependency, anger and guilt.

Production Company: Polongo Pictures IAW
    Hearst Entertainment

Executive Producer	Donald Wrye
Producer	Russell Vreeland
Co-Producer	Tyler Tyhurst
Director	Donald Wrye
Writer	Rene Balcer
Writer	Hal Sitowitz
Cast	Teri Garr
Cast	Neil Patrick Harris
Cast	Randle Mell

STRANGER IN THE MIRROR, A   ABC

Drama: Hollywood • Sex/Glitz
Airdate: 10/24/93
Rating: 9.6/16   A/C: 3

Based on the book by Sidney Sheldon. An ambitious, arrogant comic and a sweet, captivating actress rise to the top Hollywood stardom. They marry, and ultimately destroy the lives of those around them as well as their own with their insatiable quest for power and status.

Production Company: Sidney Sheldon Prods. IAW
    Paragon Ent. Corp & Spelling TV Inc.

Executive Producer	Aaron Spelling
Executive Producer	E. Duke Vincent
Executive Producer	Jon Slan
Producer	Hugh Spencer-Phillips
Director	Charles Jarrott
Writer	Stirling Silliphant
Cast	Perry King
Cast	Lori Loughlin
Cast	Geordie Johnson
Cast	Juliet Mills

STRANGER ON MY LAND   ABC

Drama: Family Drama • Farm Story • Man Against
The System
Airdate: 01/17/88
Rating: 11.5/18   A/C:

A Vietnam veteran, now a rancher, fights violence with violence when the Air Force starts trying to move local people off their own land.

Production Company: Edgar J. Scherick
    Associates IAW Taft Entertainment TV

Executive Producer	Edgar J. Scherick
Executive Producer	Gary Hoffman
Producer	Michael Barnathan
Director	Edward Hume
Writer	I. C. Rapoport
Writer	Edward Hume
Cast	Tommy Lee Jones
Cast	Dee Wallace Stone
Cast	Ned Romero
Cast	Terry O'Quinn
Cast	Pat Hingle
Director	Ben Johnson

STRANGER WAITS, A   CBS

Drama: Woman In Jeopardy • Suspense/Thriller
Airdate: 03/29/87
Rating: 20.9/33   A/C:

A rich widow, who hires a new caretaker for her estate, takes him to bed not knowing he plans to murder her.

Production Company: B. Lansbury Prods., E.
    Lansbury Prods., Lewisfilm IAW New Century

Executive Producer	Bruce Lansbury
Executive Producer	Edgar Lansbury
Director	Robert Lewis
Writer	Durrell Royce Crays
Cast	Suzanne Pleshette
Cast	Justin Deas
Cast	Jesse Welles
Cast	Paul Benjamin
Cast	Ann Wedgeworth

STRANGER WITHIN, THE   CBS

Drama: Family Drama • Woman In Jeopardy •
Children/Teens • Psychological Thriller
Airdate: 11/27/90
Rating: 15.6/25   A/C: 2

A psychopathic young man wreaks havoc on the life of a still-grieving mother when he shows up on her doorstep claiming to be the son she lost to kidnappers sixteen years ago.

Production Company: Goodman-Rosen Prods.
    IAW New World Television

Executive Producer	Barry Rosen
Executive Producer	Gary Goodman
Producer	Paulette Breen
Director	Tom Holland
Writer	John Pielmeier
Cast	Rick Schroder
Cast	Kate Jackson
Cast	Chris Sarandon
Cast	Clark Sanford

STRAPPED   HBO

Drama: Children/Teens • Black Story • Social Issue
Airdate: 8/2/93
Rating: N/A   A/C:

A virtuous inner city black teen becomes desperate when his pregnant girlfriend is arrested for selling crack. In order to raise bail money he is recruited by a friend to sell illegal guns. A white cop offers him a deal to get his woman out of jail if he agrees to finger his buddies.

Production Company: Osiris Fillms, HBO
    Showcase

Executive Producer	Michael Apted
Executive Producer	Robert O'Connor
Executive Producer	Colin Callender
Producer	Nellie Nugiel
Director	Forest Whitaker
Writer	Dena Kleiman
Cast	Bokeem Woodbine
Cast	Kia Joy Goodwin
Cast	Michael Biehn
Cast	Craig Wasson

STRAYS   USA

Drama: Sci-Fi/Supernatural/Horror/Fantasy •
Suspense/Thriller
Airdate: 12/18/91
Rating: N/A   A/C:

When a city couple moves to an isolated country home, they are terrorized by vicious feral cats who have claimed the house as their own.

Production Company: Niki Marvin Prods. MTE

Producer	Niki Marvin
Co-Producer	Shaun Cassidy
Director	John McPherson
Writer	Shaun Cassidy
Cast	Timothy Busfield
Cast	Kathleen Quinlan
Cast	Claudia Christian

STREET HAWK   ABC

Drama: Cops/Detectives/Law Enforcement • Series
Pilot (2 hr.) • Sci-Fi/Supernatural/Horror/Fantasy
Airdate: 01/04/85
Rating: 17.9/26   A/C:

After he's injured in the line of duty, a policeman is recruited by a special division which utilizes a futuristic motorcycle to fight crime.

Production Company: Limekiln & Templar Prods.
    IAW Universal TV

Executive Producer	Paul W. Belous
Executive Producer	Robert Wolterstorff
Producer	Stephen Cragg
Producer	Burton Armus
Producer	Karen Harris
Director	Virgil W. Vogel
Writer	Bruce Lansbury
Writer	Paul W. Belous
Writer	Robert Wolterstorff
Cast	Rex Smith
Cast	Joe Regalbuto
Cast	Lawrence Pressman
Cast	Jayne Modean

STREET OF DREAMS   CBS
Mystery: Murder and Murder Mystery • Cops/
Detectives/Law Enforcement • Hollywood
Airdate: 10/07/88
Rating: 9.5/17   A/C:

A Hollywood private detective becomes
involved in a murder that was committed to
obtain a valuable screenplay.

Production Company: Bill Stratton/Myrtos Prods.
   IAW Phoenix Entertainment Group
Executive Producer .... Gerald W. Abrams
Producer .... Richard M. Ravin
Director .... William A. Graham
Writer .... Bill Stratton
Cast .... Ben Masters
Cast .... Morgan Fairchild
Cast .... Diane Salinger
Cast .... John Hillerman
Cast .... John Putch

STREETS OF JUSTICE   NBC
Drama: Suspense/Thriller • Social Issue
Airdate: 11/10/85
Rating: 15.4/22   A/C:

When the gang responsible for murdering his
wife and son escape criminal prosecution due
to a technicality, a man goes on a murderous
rampage, in which all criminals become his
target.

Production Company: Universal TV
Executive Producer .... Christopher Crowe
Producer .... Alan Barnette
Director .... Christopher Crowe
Writer .... Christopher Crowe
Cast .... John Laughlin
Cast .... Robert Loggia
Cast .... John Hancock
Cast .... Lance Henriksen

STUCK WITH EACH OTHER   NBC
Comedy: Romantic Comedy
Airdate: 10/20/89
Rating: 8.9/16   A/C: 3

When their boss dies, a salesman and a
secretary discover a million dollars of dirty
money in his open safe. They make off with the
loot, chased by two equally greedy thugs, to
luxurious hideaways, the time of their lives, and,
of course, love.

Production Company: Nexus Prods.
Executive Producer .... Georg Stanford Brown
Producer .... Edward Gold
Director .... Georg Stanford Brown
Writer .... Harold Jack Bloom
Writer .... Howard Albrecht
Cast .... Tyne Daly
Cast .... Richard Crenna
Cast .... Roscoe Lee Browne
Cast .... Eileen Heckart

SUBSTITUTE, THE   USA
Drama: Suspense/Thriller • Murder and Murder
Mystery • Children/Teens
Airdate: 9/22/93
Rating: N/A   A/C:

When a high school teachers discovers her
husband in bed with one of her students she
murders them both and flees to a small town in
Minnesota with a new name and new
appearance. Taking a job as a substitute
teacher she is at first adored by her students
but it soon becomes evident that she is a
deranged psychotic when her behavior turns
lethal.

Production Company: Pacific Motion Pictures
   IAW Wilshire Court Prods.
Executive Producer .... David Kirkpatrick
Producer .... Matthew O'Connor
Director .... Martin Donovan
Writer .... Cynthia Verlaine
Cast .... Amanda Donohoe
Cast .... Marky Mark
Cast .... Natasha Wagner
Cast .... Dalton James

SUBSTITUTE WIFE, THE   NBC
Drama: Period Piece • Family Drama • Medical/
Disease/Mental Illness
Airdate: 5/23/94
Rating: 17.5/27   A/C: 1

In 1869 Nebraska, a dying prairie woman
scours the countryside in search of a new wife
and mother for her homesteader husband and
four children. With a shortage of single women
in the territory she finally convinces a strong-
willed whore to fill her shoes. The laconic
sodbuster is at first cold to the idea but soon
warms up when the brassy working girl turns
out to have a heart of gold.

Production Company: Frederick S. Pierce Co.
Executive Producer .... Frederick Pierce
Executive Producer .... Stan Daniels
Executive Producer .... Keith Pierce
Executive Producer .... Richard Pierce
Producer .... Michael O. Gallant
Director .... Peter Werner
Writer .... Stan Daniels
Cast .... Farrah Fawcett
Cast .... Lea Thompson
Cast .... Peter Weller

SUDIE AND SIMPSON   LIFETIME
Drama: Family Drama • Children/Teens • True Story
• Period Piece • Rape/Molestation • Black Story
Airdate: 09/11/90
Rating: N/A   A/C:

Based on the novel "Sudie" by Sara Flanigan
Carter. A young, white girl forges a deep
friendship with an older black man falsely
accused of child molestation in a small Georgia
town steeped in racial hatred.

Production Company: Freed/Laufer Prods. IAW
   Donald March Prods. & Hearst Ent. Prods.
Executive Producer .... Donald March
Producer .... Richard Freed
Producer .... Ira Laufer
Supervising Producer .... Carroll Newman
Director .... Joan Tewkesbury
Writer .... Sara Flanigan
Cast .... Sara Gilbert
Cast .... John M. Jackson
Cast .... Paige Danahy

SUMMER DREAMS: THE STORY OF THE
BEACH BOYS   ABC
Drama: True Story • Biography • Hollywood
Airdate: 04/29/90
Rating: 10.6/16   A/C: 3

Story of the legendary California band whose
meteoric success was clouded by outrageous
excesses, an embittered father, self-doubt and
family jealousies.

Production Company: Leonard Hill Productions
Executive Producer .... Leonard Hill
Executive Producer .... Ron Gilbert
Producer .... Joel Fields
Director .... Michael Switzer
Writer .... Charles Rosin
Cast .... Bruce Greenwood
Cast .... Greg Kean
Cast .... Arlen Dean Snyder
Cast .... Casey Sander

SUMMER MY FATHER GREW UP, THE
                                            NBC
Drama: Family Drama • Children/Teens
Airdate: 03/03/91
Rating: 10.5/16   A/C: 3

An eleven-year-old boy must heal the deep
psychological wounds left by his parents' bitter
divorce in order to restore a relationship with
his alienated father.

Production Company: Robert Shapiro Prods.
Executive Producer .... Robert Shapiro
Director .... Michael Tuchner
Writer .... Sandra Jennings
Cast .... John Ritter
Cast .... Margaret Whitton
Cast .... Karen Young
Cast .... Matthew Lawrence

SUMMER TO REMEMBER, A — CBS
Drama: Family Drama • Children/Teens
Airdate: 03/27/85
Rating: 13.8/21   A/C:

A young deaf boy and his sister befriend a sign language-trained orangutan whom they eventually try to rescue from a roving carnival.

Production Company: Interplanetary Prods.
Executive Producer .... Max A. Keller
Executive Producer .... Lloyd Lewis
Producer .... Micheline H. Keller
Producer .... Edward Gold
Director .... Robert Lewis
Writer .... Scott Swanton
Cast .... James Farentino
Cast .... Tess Harper
Cast .... Bridgette Anderson
Cast .... Louise Fletcher

SUN ALSO RISES, THE — NBC
Miniseries/Drama (2 nights): Love Story • Period Piece • Foreign or Exotic Location
Airdate: 12/09/84 • 12/10/84
Rating: 13.2/20 • 11.6/18   A/C:

Set in 1923 Paris, Ernest Hemingway's classic story revolves around an impotent expatriate American newsman and the aristocratic British woman that he loves, but can never keep.

Production Company: 20th Century Fox TV
Executive Producer .... John Furia, Jr.
Producer .... Robert L. Joseph
Director .... James Goldstone
Writer .... Robert L. Joseph
Cast .... Hart Bochner
Cast .... Jane Seymour
Cast .... Ian Charleson
Cast .... Robert Carradine
Cast .... Leonard Nimoy

SUNSET BEAT — ABC
Drama: Cops/Detectives/Law Enforcement • Series Pilot (2 hr.)
Airdate: 04/21/90
Rating: 6.5/13   A/C: 3

Young Los Angeles undercover biker cops go after a criminal mastermind who is attempting to extort money from the city.

Production Company: Patrick Hasburgh Prods.
Executive Producer .... Patrick Hasburgh
Director .... Sam Weisman
Writer .... Patrick Hasburgh
Cast .... George Clooney
Cast .... Michael De Luise
Cast .... James Tolkan
Cast .... Markus Flanagan

SUNSTROKE — USA
Drama: Murder and Murder Mystery • Suspense/Thriller
Airdate: 9/25/92
Rating: N/A   A/C:

In the Arizona desert, a recently divorced man meets up with a divorced woman who is searching for her ex-husband and her daughter, whom he kidnapped. He falls hard for the mysterious woman but begins to have serious doubts about her when the body of a hitchhiker she picked up is found dead. The tables turn, and she finds herself in danger when she discovers she has been framed by her new lover who has been secretly hired by her ex-husband to kill her.

Production Company: Wilshire Court Prods.
Executive Producer .... Duane Poole
Executive Producer .... Jane Seymour
Producer .... James Keach
Co-Producer .... Terence Donnelly
Director .... James Keach
Writer .... Duane Poole
Cast .... Jane Seymour
Cast .... Stephen Meadows
Cast .... Steve Railsback

SUPERCARRIER — ABC
Drama: Action/Adventure • Series Pilot (2 hr.)
Airdate: 03/06/88
Rating: 15.0/23   A/C:

A hot-shot Navy pilot evades medical disqualification as officers and subordinates of both sexes interact in this look at peacetime life aboard a huge aircraft carrier.

Production Company: Richard Maynard/Real Tinsel Prods. & Fries Entertainment
Executive Producer .... Charles Fries
Writer .... Steven E. De Souza
Producer .... Richard Maynard
Director .... William A. Graham
Writer .... Stanford Whitmore
Cast .... Robert Hooks
Cast .... Alex Hyde-White
Cast .... Craig Stevens
Cast .... Paul Gleason
Cast .... Richard Jaeckel
Cast .... Denise Nicholas
Cast .... Ken Olandt
Cast .... Cec Verrell
Executive Producer .... Steven E. De Souza

SURVIVE THE NIGHT — USA
Drama: Suspense/Thriller • Woman In Jeopardy
Airdate: 1/13/93
Rating: N/A   A/C:

When their car breaks down in a rough section of the Bronx, three suburban woman are terrorized by a wild group of gang bangers.

Production Company: Heartstar Prods. IAW Once Upon A Time Prods.
Executive Producer .... Stanley Brooks
Executive Producer .... Joseph Cohen
Producer .... John Danylkiw
Director .... Bill Corcoran
Writer .... Steve Whitney
Cast .... Stefanie Powers
Cast .... Helen Shaver
Cast .... Kathleen Robertson
Cast .... Currie Graham

SURVIVE THE SAVAGE SEA — ABC
Drama: Family Drama • True Story • Action/Adventure • Foreign or Exotic Location • Disaster
Airdate: 01/06/92
Rating: 15.6/24   A/C: 2

The odyssey of a farmer-turned-sailor and his family, whose adventure on a schooner in the South Pacific turns into a nightmare when they are stranded for thirty-eight days on a life raft after their boat sinks.

Production Company: Von Zerneck-Sertner Films
Executive Producer .... Frank Von Zerneck
Executive Producer .... Robert M. Sertner
Producer .... Julie Anne Weitz
Producer .... Gregory Prange
Co-Producer .... Max Rosenberg
Co-Producer .... Joseph Strick
Director .... Kevin James Dobson
Writer .... Fred Haines
Writer .... Scott Swanton
Cast .... Robert Urich
Cast .... Ali MacGraw
Cast .... Danielle Von Zerneck
Cast .... Mark Ballou

SURVIVING — ABC
Drama: Family Drama • Children/Teens • Social Issue
Airdate: 02/10/85
Rating: 18.1/26   A/C:

When a teenage boy and girl commit suicide, their families must deal with the loss, and, eventually, the two sets of parents turn to one another for comfort.

Production Company: Telepictures Prods.
Executive Producer .... Frank Konigsberg
Executive Producer .... Larry Sanitsky
Producer .... Hunt Lowry
Director .... Waris Hussein
Writer .... Joyce Eliason
Cast .... Ellen Burstyn
Cast .... Len Cariou
Cast .... Zach Galligan
Cast .... Marsha Mason
Cast .... Molly Ringwald
Cast .... Paul Sorvino

SWEET BIRD OF YOUTH NBC
Drama: Love Story • Period Piece
Airdate: 10/01/89
Rating: 13.0/21   A/C: 3

Based on the play by Tennessee Williams. A beautiful but washed up screen idol seeks to regain her lost youth and virility with the help of a local golden boy with big ambitions and a secret past.

Production Company: Atlantic/Kushner-Locke
  Productions
Executive Producer .... Linda Yellen
Executive Producer .... Laurence Mark
Executive Producer .... Peter Locke
Executive Producer .... Donald Kushner
Producer .... Fred Whitehead
Director .... Nicolas Roeg
Writer .... Gavin Lambert
Cast .... Elizabeth Taylor
Cast .... Mark Harmon
Cast .... Valerie Perrine
Cast .... Kevin Geer

SWEET POISON USA
Drama: Cops/Detectives/Law Enforcement • Woman In Jeopardy • Suspense/Thriller
Airdate: 06/12/91
Rating: N/A   A/C:

A milquetoast man and his provocative wife are kidnapped by an escaped criminal bent on revenge. Swept up by greed and passion, the wife falls for the con, leaving her husband to fight for his life.

Production Company: Smart Money Prods. IAW
  MCA TV Entertainment
Executive Producer .... Hilton Green
Producer .... Michael M. Scott
Executive Producer .... Andrew Mirisch
Director .... Brian Grant
Writer .... Walter Klenhard
Cast .... Steven Bauer
Cast .... Edward Herrmann
Cast .... Patricia Healy

SWEET REVENGE TNT
Comedy: Foreign or Exotic Location • Romantic Comedy
Airdate: 07/09/90
Rating: N/A   A/C:

Legally bound by her promise to support her struggling writer ex-husband until he remarries, a lawyer recruits an actress to lure him into marriage.

Production Company: TNT-Chrysalide-Canal Plus
  - The Movie Group
Executive Producer .... Daniel Marquet
Producer .... Monique Annaud
Director .... Charlotte Brandstrom
Writer .... Janet Brownell
Cast .... Carrie Fisher
Cast .... Rosanna Arquette
Cast .... John Sessions

SWEET REVENGE, A CBS
Drama: Murder and Murder Mystery • Suspense/Thriller
Airdate: 10/31/84
Rating: 10.0/16   A/C:

A woman seeks revenge against an army colonel who is both her husband's superior as well as the man responsible for her brother's death.

Production Company: David Green Prods. IAW
  Robert Papazian Prods. Inc.
Executive Producer .... David Greene
Producer .... Robert A. Papazian
Director .... David Greene
Writer .... Andrew Peter Marin
Cast .... Kevin Dobson
Cast .... Kelly McGillis
Cast .... Alec Baldwin
Cast .... Savannah Smith
Cast .... Wings Hauser
Cast .... Alfre Woodard

SWIMSUIT NBC
Comedy: Foreign or Exotic Location • Sex/Glitz
Airdate: 02/19/89
Rating: 17.3/27   A/C:

Male and female models pose in bathing suits to try to win a lucrative swimsuit company contract.

Production Company: Musifilm Prods. and
  American First Run Studios
Producer .... Max A. Keller
Producer .... Carla Singer
Director .... Chris Thomson
Writer .... Robin Schiff
Cast .... William Katt
Cast .... Catherine Oxenberg
Cast .... Tom Villard
Cast .... Billy Warlock
Cast .... Cyd Charisse

SWITCH, THE CBS
Drama: Medical/Disease/Mental Illness • True Story • Man Against The System
Airdate: 1/17/93
Rating: 11.8/19   A/C: 3

In 1987, despondent quadriplegic, Larry McAfee, battles the state of Georgia to get permission to install a switch on his ventilator that would allow him the right to die when he wished. He comes to the attention of radio talk show host Russ Fine, who becomes his trusted advocate. A deep friendship develops that profoundly change both men.

Production Company: Avnet-Kerner Co. IAW
  Companionway Films
Executive Producer .... T.S. Cook
Executive Producer .... Jordan Kerner
Executive Producer .... Jon Avnet
Producer .... Tad Devlin
Producer .... Martin Huberty
Co-Producer .... Ruthe Benton
Co-Producer .... Ron Schultz
Director .... Bobby Roth
Writer .... T.S. Cook
Cast .... Gary Cole
Cast .... Craig T . Nelson
Cast .... Beverly D'Angelo
Cast .... Kathleen Nolan

SWITCHED AT BIRTH NBC
Miniseries/Drama (2 nights): Family Drama • Children/Teens • Courtroom Drama • True Story
Airdate: 04/28/91 • 04/29/91
Rating: 20.4/32 • 23.1/35   A/C: 1 • 1

The accidental switching of two Florida babies at birth is discovered ten years later; a legal battle ensues as one couple tries to retrieve their biological child.

Production Company: Guber-Peters Entertainment
  IAW Columbia Pictures Television
Executive Producer .... Michael O'Hara
Executive Producer .... Barry Morrow
Producer .... Mark Sennet
Producer .... Ervin Zavada
Executive Producer .... Lawrence Horowitz
Executive Producer .... Richard Heus
Director .... Waris Hussein
Writer .... Michael O'Hara
Cast .... Bonnie Bedelia
Cast .... Brian Kerwin
Cast .... John M. Jackson
Cast .... Edward Asner

SWORD OF GIDEON HBO
Drama: Action/Adventure • Foreign or Exotic Location
Airdate: 11/29/86
Rating: N/A   A/C:

Based on the book "Vengeance" by George Jonas. In 1972, five members of an Israeli anti-terrorist commando team are sent on a mission by the Israeli secret service to hunt down the architects of the Munich Olympic massacre. The clandestine manhunt takes them throughout Europe, endangering them at every turn.

Production Company: Alliance Entertainment
  Corp.
Executive Producer .... Denis Heroux
Executive Producer .... John Kemeny
Producer .... Robert Lantos
Director .... Michael Anderson
Writer .... Chris Bryant
Cast .... Michael York
Cast .... Steven Bauer
Cast .... Rod Steiger
Cast .... Colleen Dewhurst

SWORN TO SILENCE   ABC

Drama: Murder and Murder Mystery • Courtroom Drama • Social Issue
Airdate: 04/06/87
Rating: 16.1/24   A/C:

Two small town lawyers face a quandary when they discover that the man they've been assigned to defend is guilty of several vicious crimes. The issues of lawyer/client confidentiality, as well as "privileged information" are explored.

Production Company: Daniel H. Blatt/Robert Singer Prods.

Executive Producer	Daniel H. Blatt
Executive Producer	Robert Singer
Producer	Ervin Zavada
Director	Peter Levin
Writer	Robert L. Joseph
Cast	Peter Coyote
Cast	Dabney Coleman
Cast	Liam Neeson
Cast	David Spielberg
Cast	Caroline McWilliams

SWORN TO VENGEANCE   CBS

Drama: Murder and Murder Mystery • Cops/Detectives/Law Enforcement • Man Against The System • True Crime
Airdate: 3/23/93
Rating: 15.3/25   A/C: 1

When three Nevada teenagers are murdered, determined police sergeant, Jack Stewart becomes obsessed with bringing the killers to justice. Through unconventional detective work he finally cracks the case.

Production Company: A. Shane Co. IAW RHI Ent.

Executive Producer	Joan Conrad Erwin
Director	Peter H. Hunt
Writer	David Epstein
Writer	John Carlen
Cast	Robert Conrad
Cast	Billy McNamara
Cast	Sharon Farrell
Cast	Peter Breck

T BONE N WESSEL   TNT

Comedy: Buddy Story
Airdate: 11/2/92
Rating: N/A   A/C:

Based on the play by Jon Klein. When a black convict is released from prison he becomes friends with a low life white guy. Together they hit the road in a stolen convertible in search of fast money and good times. The hapless pair get suckered, swindled and ripped-off at every turn —forcing them to reevaluate their wild ways.

Production Company: TNT Productions

Executive Producer	Scott Rosenfelt
Producer	Mark Levinson
Director	Lewis Teague
Writer	Jon Klein
Cast	Gregory Hines
Cast	Christopher Lloyd
Cast	Ned Beatty
Cast	Rip Torn

TAGGET   USA

Drama: Suspense/Thriller • Vietnam • Political Piece
Airdate: 02/14/91
Rating: N/A   A/C:

Based on the novel by Irving A. Greenfield. A disabled Vietnam vet, haunted by flashbacks, seeks vengeance on the C.I.A. operatives who injured him and at the same time uncovers a high-level government plot.

Production Company: Mirisch Films IAW Tagget Prods., Inc.

Executive Producer	Andrew Mirisch
Director	Richard T. Heffron
Writer	Peter S. Fischer
Writer	Janis Diamond
Writer	Richard T. Heffron
Cast	Daniel J. Travanti
Cast	Roxanne Hart
Cast	William Sadler

TAILSPIN: BEHIND THE KOREAN AIRLINES TRAGEDY   HBO

Drama: True Story • Political Piece • Social Issue
Airdate: 08/20/89
Rating: N/A   A/C:

In 1983, when a civilian airliner is shot down over Soviet air space with no survivors, a political power struggle ensues in D.C. between the State Dept., the Pentagon and the National Security Council, all trying to unravel the facts.

Production Company: Darlow Smithson Prods., HBO Showcase, Granada

Executive Producer	Ray Fitzwalter
Executive Producer	Leslie Woodhead
Producer	John Smithson
Director	David Darlow
Writer	Brian Phelan
Cast	Ed O'Ross
Cast	Gavin O'Herlihy
Cast	George Roth

TAINTED BLOOD   USA

Drama: Sci-Fi/Supernatural/Horror/Fantasy • Children/Teens
Airdate: 3/3/93
Rating: N/A   A/C:

A world famous reporter investigates the truth behind a pair of twins who supposedly have been genetically programmed to kill their adoptive parents. When an all American boy kills his parents, she discovers he has a twin sister that he was separated from at birth. Her quest leads her to two girls who live across the street from each other, both of whom were adopted. Through diligent research she uncovers the evil twin before disaster strikes.

Production Company: Fast Track Films IAW Wilshre Court Prods.

Executive Producer	Ed Milkovich
Producer	John Furie
Director	Matthew Partrick
Writer	Kathleen Rowell
Cast	Raquel Welch
Cast	Alley Mills
Cast	Kerri Green
Cast	Natasha Wagner
Cast	Joan Van Ark

TAKE MY DAUGHTERS, PLEASE   NBC

Comedy: Romantic Comedy • Woman's Issue/Story
Airdate: 11/21/88
Rating: 19.9/31   A/C:

Four modern young women endure their mother's attempts to marry them off.

Production Company: NBC Prods.

Executive Producer	Michael Filerman
Producer	Karen Moore
Producer	Penelope Foster
Director	Larry Elikann
Writer	Lindsay Harrison
Cast	Rue McClanahan
Cast	Kim Delaney
Cast	Diedre Hall
Cast	Susan Ruttan

TAKE, THE   USA

Drama: Cops/Detectives/Law Enforcement • Drug Smuggling/Dealing
Airdate: 03/28/90
Rating: N/A   A/C:

A Miami ex-cop, fired for stealing drug money, finds himself in trouble again. Mobsters and the police, some of whom may be dirty, are after him when his involvement with a sleazy TV host implicates him in murder and drug trafficking.

Production Company: Cine-Nevada Inc. Production for MCA-TV Entertainment

Executive Producer	Dan Wigutow
Producer	Boris Malden
Producer	Robert T. Skodis
Producer	Larry Manetti
Writer	Edward Anhalt
Writer	Handel Glassberg
Cast	Ray Sharkey
Cast	Lisa Hartman
Cast	Joe Lala

TAKEN AWAY   CBS

Drama: Family Drama • Children/Teens • Social Issue
Airdate: 11/05/89
Rating: 16.3/25   A/C: 2

A poor single working mother is unjustly charged with parental neglect. She must fight the legal bureaucracy to regain custody of her eight year old daughter.

Production Company: Hart, Thomas & Berlin Prods., Inc.

Executive Producer	Carole Hart
Executive Producer	Marlo Thomas
Executive Producer	Kathie Berlin
Producer	Kimberly Myers
Director	John Patterson
Writer	Selma Thompson
Writer	Robert L. Freedman
Cast	Valerie Bertinelli
Cast	Kevin Dunn
Cast	Anna Maria Horsford
Cast	Juliet Sorcey

TAKING BACK MY LIFE: THE NANCY ZIEGENMEYER STORY   CBS

Drama: Family Drama • Woman Against The System • Rape/Molestation • Woman's Issue/Story • Social Issue
Airdate: 03/15/92
Rating: 15.8/25   A/C: 2

After being brutally raped, an Iowa wife and mother's landmark decision to go public results in a series of Pulitzer Prize-winning articles by the Des Moines Register. Her candid honesty encouraged other victims to shed the shame of rape.

Production Company: Elliot Fredgen Prod., Little/ Heshty Prod. IAW Warner Bros. TV
Executive Producer .... Harry Winer
Executive Producer .... Lawrence Lyttle
Producer .... Andrew Gottlieb
Director .... Harry Winer
Writer .... April Smith
Cast .... Patricia Wettig
Cast .... Stephen Lang
Cast .... Shelley Hack
Cast .... Joanna Cassidy

TAKING OF FLIGHT 847: THE ULI DERICKSON STORY   NBC

Drama: Woman In Jeopardy • Suspense/Thriller • True Story
Airdate: 05/02/88
Rating: 19.7/31   A/C:

True story of the pivotal heroism of a stewardess during the seventeen day Arab hijacking of a TWA plane in 1985 that resulted in the death of a U.S. Navy diver.

Production Company: Columbia Pictures TV
Executive Producer .... Jim Calio
Executive Producer .... David Hume Kennerly
Producer .... Jay Benson
Director ....Paul Wendkos
Writer .... Norman Morrill
Cast .... Lindsay Wagner
Cast .... Eli Danker
Cast .... Sandy McPeak
Cast .... Ray Wise
Cast .... Leslie Easterbrook

TAKING THE HEAT   SHOWTIME

Comedy: Cops/Detectives/Law Enforcement • Mafia/ Mob
Airdate: 6/6/93
Rating: N/A   A/C:

A yuppie, wall street wizard becomes a reluctant observer to a mob Killing. A crusty, female New York City cop is given the assignment to protect him from a bevy of hit men, out to silence the subpoenaed witness. They are grudgingly forced to rely on each other as they evade the gangsters, endure a sweltering Manhattan heat wave, and fight their way through city gridlock.

Production Company: Hoffman/Israel Prods. IAW Viacom Pictures
Executive Producer .... Gary Hoffman
Executive Producer .... Neal Israel
Producer .... Fred Blankfein
Director .... Tom Mankiewicz
Writer .... Dan Gordon
Cast .... Lynn Whitfield
Cast .... Tony Goldwyn
Cast .... Alan Arkin
Cast .... George Segal

TARGET OF SUSPICION   USA

Drama: Foreign or Exotic Location • Murder and Murder Mystery • Suspense/Thriller
Airdate: 6/10/94
Rating: N/A   A/C:

An American visits Paris to oversee a merger between his perfume company and a French firm. A sexy model gives him a tour of the nightlife, after which he is falsely accused of her rape/murder. With help from a female Interpol agent, he finds that his wife and their French partner are the ones behind the false charges.

Production Company: Barry Weitz Films
Executive Producer .... Barry Weitz
Executive Producer .... Simon Hart
Executive Producer .... Robert Rea
Director .... Bob Swaim
Writer .... Brian Ross
Cast .... Tim Matheson
Cast .... Naomi Kocher
Cast .... Lysette Anthony

TARZAN IN MANHATTAN   CBS

Drama: Love Story • Man Against The System • Action/Adventure • Foreign or Exotic Location
Airdate: 04/15/89
Rating: 10.5/19   A/C:

When an unscrupulous scientist kidnaps Cheetah for an animal experiment, Tarzan is forced to leave Africa for New York City where he meets up with Jane, a tough-talking cabbie.

Production Company: American First Run Studios
Executive Producer .... Max A. Keller
Executive Producer .... Micheline H. Keller
Producer .... Charles Hairston
Director .... Michael Schultz
Writer .... Anna Sandor
Writer .... William Gough
Cast .... Joe Lara
Cast .... Kim Crosby
Cast .... Tony Curtis
Cast .... Jan-Michael Vincent

TASTE FOR KILLING, A   USA

Drama: Suspense/Thriller
Airdate: 08/12/92
Rating: N/A   A/C:

College best friends take a summer job working on an off-shore oil rig. They quickly alienate the blue collar workers and are forced to befriend a deadly sociopath.

Production Company: MCA Television Entertainment
Producer .... Barry Greenfield
Producer .... Michael S. Murphy
Director .... Lou Antonio
Writer .... Alan Rucker
Writer .... Dan Bronson
Cast .... Michael Biehn
Cast .... Henry Thomas
Cast .... Jason Bateman

TEAMSTER BOSS: THE JACKIE PRESSER STORY   HBO

Drama: Biography • True Crime • Mafia/Mob
Airdate: 9/12/92
Rating: N/A   A/C:

Based on the book "Mobbed Up" by James Neff. Corrupt, teamster union president, Jackie Presser, who in the early '80s had strong ties to the mob while working as an FBI informant. A womanizer and a thug , Presser becomes an important witness for the government against members of organized crime.

Production Company: HBO Pictures IAW Abby Mann Prods.
Executive Producer .... Abby Mann
Executive Producer .... David R. Ginsburg
Producer .... John Kemeny
Director .... Alastair Reid
Writer .... Abby Mann
Cast .... Brian Dennehy
Cast .... Jeff Daniels
Cast .... Maria Conchita Alonso
Cast .... Eli Wallach

TEARS AND LAUGHTER: THE JOAN AND MIELISSA RIVERS STORY   NBC

Drama: Family Drama • True Story • Hollywood
Airdate: 5/15/94
Rating: 13.1/21   A/C: 2

When her husband Edgar Rosenberg commits suicide in 1987, comedienne Joan Rivers and her daughter Melissa try to deal with their grief, anger and resentments which eventually destroys their mother-daughter relationship. In time, they both learn to trust and love each other again, bringing them closer together.

Production Company: Davis Entertainment
Executive Producer ....John Davis
Executive Producer .... Merrill H. Karpf
Producer .... Tom Rowe
Producer .... George Horie
Director ....Oz Scott
Writer .... Susan Rice
Cast .... Joan Rivers
Cast .... Melissa Rivers
Cast .... Dorothy Lyman
Cast .... Mark Kiely

TED KENNEDY, JR., STORY, THE   NBC
Drama: Children/Teens • Medical/Disease/Mental
Illness • True Story
Airdate: 11/24/86
Rating: 16.8/26   A/C:

*Fact-based story of the Senator's son's mental
and physical recuperation after he lost a leg to
cancer at age twelve.*

Production Company: Entertainment Partners
     Prods.
Executive Producer .... Robert E. Fuisz
Producer .... William F. Storke
Producer .... Alfred R. Kelman
Director .... Delbert Mann
Writer .... Roger O. Hirson
Co-Executive Producer .... Kimber Shoop
Cast .... Craig T. Nelson
Cast .... Susan Blakely
Cast .... Michael J. Shannon

TELLING SECRETS   ABC
Miniseries/Drama (2 nights): Cops/Detectives/Law
Enforcement • Murder and Murder Mystery •
Suspense/Thriller
Airdate: 1/17/93 • 1/18/93
Rating: 13.8/22 • 14.4/21   A/C: 1 • 2

*A Phoenix police detective on a murder case,
discovers that the wife of one of the suspects is
an alluring psychopath who seduces men then
dupes them into murdering for her. After an
international pursuit, the diligent cop lays a
plan to capture her.*

Production Company: Patchett- Kaufman Ent.
     IAW WIN
Executive Producer .... Ken Kaufman
Executive Producer .... Tom Patchett
Producer .... Dan Witt
Producer .... Jennifer Miller
Director .... Marvin J. Chomsky
Writer .... Jennifer Miller
Cast .... Cybill Shepherd
Cast .... Ken Olin
Cast .... Christopher McDonald
Cast .... G.D. Spradlin

TEN MILLION DOLLAR GETAWAY   USA
Drama: True Crime • Mafia/Mob
Airdate: 03/06/91
Rating: N/A   A/C:

*Jimmy "The Gent" Burke and his gang of New
York hoodlums plan and execute the ten million
dollar, 1978, Lufthansa heist at Kennedy
airport.*

Production Company: Alvin Cooperman Prods.
     IAW Wilshire Court Prods.
Producer .... Thomas Kane
Director .... James A. Contner
Writer .... Christopher Canaan
Cast .... John Mahoney
Cast .... Karen Young
Cast .... Tony Lo Bianco
Cast .... Mike Starr

TENTH MAN, THE   CBS
Drama: Suspense/Thriller • Love Story • Period Piece
• Foreign or Exotic Location • WWII
Airdate: 12/04/88
Rating: 13.3/21   A/C:

*Based on a story by Graham Greene. In
occupied France, a lawyer gives his chateau to
the family of a man who takes a convicted man's
name and death sentence. The lawyer becomes
the chateau's handyman and romances his
surrogate's sister until a stranger turns up
claiming to be him.*

Production Company: Rosemont Productions Ltd./
     William Self Prods.
Executive Producer .... Norman Rosemont
Executive Producer .... William Self
Producer .... David A. Rosemont
Director .... Jack Gold
Writer .... Lee Langley
Cast .... Anthony Hopkins
Cast .... Kristin Scott Thomas
Cast .... Derek Jacobi
Cast .... Cyril Cusack

TERROR IN THE NIGHT   CBS
Drama: Woman In Jeopardy • True Crime
Airdate: 1/11/94
Rating: 12.7/20   A/C: 2

*A young woman on a camping trip in the
Arizona mountains is raped and kidnaped by a
sadistic murderer. While she fights for her life,
her boyfriend, who escaped from the
psychopath leads the police on an extensive
manhunt. The killer is eventually captured and
sentenced to life in prison.*

Production Company: Landsburg Co. IAW
     Cinematigue and CBS Ent.
Executive Producer .... Alan Landsburg
Producer .... Kay Hoffman
Co-Producer .... Denise De Garmo
Co-Producer .... Randy Ritchie
Director .... Colin Bucksey
Writer .... Denise De Garmo
Cast .... Justine Bateman
Cast .... Joe Penny
Cast .... Valerie Landsburg
Cast .... Matt Mulhern

TERROR ON HIGHWAY 91   CBS
Drama: Cops/Detectives/Law Enforcement • Man
Against The System
Airdate: 01/03/89
Rating: 16.9/26   A/C:

*A young Southern deputy sheriff, who once
idolized the older policemen, must now battle
to expose their corruption.*

Production Company: Katy Film Prods. Inc.
Producer .... Dan Witt
Producer .... Courtney Pledger
Director .... Jerry Jameson
Writer .... Stuart Schoffman
Cast .... Rick Schroder
Cast .... George Dzundza
Cast .... Matt Clark
Cast .... Lara Flynn Boyle

TERROR ON TRACK 9   CBS
Drama: Murder and Murder Mystery • Cops/
Detectives/Law Enforcement
Airdate: 9/20/92
Rating: 15.4/25   A/C: 1

*NYPD detective, Frank Janek is after a serial
killer lose in Grand Central Station, who is
targeting women by stabbing them with lethal
doses of heroin.*

Production Company: Richard Crenna Prods.
     IAW Spelling Ent.
Executive Producer .... Aaron Spelling
Executive Producer .... E. Duke Vincent
Producer .... Robert Berger
Director .... Robert Iscove
Writer .... Monte Stettin
Cast .... Richard Crenna
Cast .... Joan Van Ark
Cast .... Cliff Gorman
Cast .... Joseph Campanella

TERRORIST ON TRIAL: THE UNITED
STATES VS. SALIM AJAMI   CBS
Drama: Courtroom Drama • Political Piece • Social
Issue
Airdate: 01/10/88
Rating: 13.3/20   A/C:

*A Jewish defense attorney takes the case of a
Palestinian on trial in the U.S. for terrorist
killings overseas.*

Production Company: George Englund Prods.
     IAW Robert Papazian Prods.
Executive Producer .... George Englund
Co-Executive Producer .... William Link
Co-Executive Producer .... Richard Levinson
Producer .... Robert A. Papazian
Director .... Jeff Bleckner
Writer .... William Link
Writer .... Richard Levinson
Cast .... Robert Davi
Cast .... Ron Leibman
Cast .... Sam Waterston
Cast .... Joe Morton
Cast .... Jo Henderson

THANKSGIVING DAY   NBC
Comedy: Family Drama • Holiday Special
Airdate: 11/19/90
Rating: 10.9/17   A/C: 3

*When father dies carving the Thanksgiving
turkey, a quirky, upper middle-class family
moves into their mother's home and drives her
into poverty.*

Production Company: Zacharias/Buhai Prods IAW
     NBC Prods.
Executive Producer .... Steve Zacharias
Executive Producer .... Jeff Buhai
Producer .... Marvin Miller
Director .... Gino Tanasescu
Writer .... Steve Zacharias
Writer .... Jeff Buhai
Cast .... Mary Tyler Moore
Cast .... Jonathon Brandmeier
Cast .... Tony Curtis
Cast .... Kelly Curtis

THAT SECRET SUNDAY   CBS
Drama: Murder and Murder Mystery • Cops/
Detectives/Law Enforcement • Suspense/Thriller •
Man Against The System
Airdate: 11/25/86
Rating: 16.1/26   A/C:

*An investigative reporter discovers that an
apparent serial killing victim actually died in a
shady incident involving some policemen.*

Production Company: CBS Entertainment Prods.
Producer .... Philip Saltzman
Director .... Richard Colla
Writer .... Al Martinez
Writer .... Philip Saltzman
Cast .... George Grizzard
Cast .... Joe Regalbuto
Cast .... Parker Stevenson
Cast .... Daphne Ashbrook
Cast .... James Farentino

THE RACE TO FREEDOM: THE UNDERGROUND RAILROAD   FAMILY
Drama: Black Story • Period Piece • Historical Piece
Airdate: 2/19/94
Rating: N/A   A/C:

*In 1850 North Carolina, four black slaves are
helped by abolitionists as they run away from
their plantation to Canada. But because of the
Fugitive Slave Act, they are hunted by bounty
hunters. In constant danger from the unknown
wilderness, their journey is fraught will peril
and death. With the dedicated guidance from
the Underground Railroad, many survive their
journey to freedom.*

Production Company: Atlantis Films Ltd. IAW
   United Image Ent., BET, CTV Televison
   Network
Executive Producer .... Seaton McLean
Executive Producer .... Tim Reid
Co-Executive Producer .... Peter Sussman
Co-Executive Producer .... Anne Marie La Traverse
Producer .... Daphne Ballon
Producer .... Brian Parker
Director .... Don McBrearty
Writer .... Diana Braithwaite
Writer .... Nancy Botkin
Cast .... Janet Bailey
Cast .... Courtney Vance
Cast .... Dawn Lewis
Cast .... Glynn Turman
Cast .... Tim Reid

THERE ARE NO CHILDREN HERE   ABC
Drama: Family Drama • Black Story • Social Issue •
True Story
Airdate: 11/28/93
Rating: 17.8/26   A/C: 1

*Based on the book by Alex Kotlowitz. In
Chicago's Henry Honer Housing Project, a
crime infested and violent inner city apartment
complex, a devoted mother tries to keep her sons
from joining the gangs. As her twelve year old
boy becomes more infatuated with the" boyz in
the hood" she fights to escape the deplorable
conditions and find a new beginning for her
children.*

Production Company: Harpo Prods., Do We Inc.,
   LOMO Prods.
Executive Producer .... Debra DiMaio
Producer .... Kate Forte
Director .... Anita Addison
Writer .... Bobby Smith, Jr.
Cast .... Oprah Winfrey
Cast .... Keith David
Cast .... Mark Lane
Cast .... Norman Golden
Cast .... Maya Angelou

THERE MUST BE A PONY   ABC
Drama: Family Drama • Love Story • Hollywood
Airdate: 10/05/86
Rating: 12.6/19   A/C:

*Adapted from James Kirkwood's novel. An
over-the-hill, mentally unstable movie star is
trying to remake her career through television,
but events threaten to disrupt her life once more.*

Production Company: Columbia Pictures TV IAW
   R.J. Prods.
Executive Producer .... Robert Wagner
Producer .... Howard Jeffrey
Director .... Joseph Sargent
Writer .... Mart Crowley
Cast .... Elizabeth Taylor
Cast .... Robert Wagner
Cast .... James Coco
Cast .... William Windom
Cast .... Chad Lowe
Cast .... Ken Olin

THERE WAS A LITTLE BOY   CBS
Drama: Family Drama • Children/Teens
Airdate: 5/16/93
Rating: 13.8/22   A/C: 1

*Based on the book by Claire R. Jacobs. A
married couple, who's infant son was kidnapped
fifteen years earlier, feel guilty when they learn
they are expecting a child. While teaching high
school English is a rough neighborhood, the
wife befriends a troubled youth who turns out
to be her long lost boy.*

Production Company: Craig Anderson Prods.
   IAW Lorimar TV
Executive Producer .... Craig Anderson
Producer .... Phil Parslow
Director .... Mimi Leder
Writer .... Wesley Bishop
Cast .... Cybill Shepherd
Cast .... John Heard
Cast .... Scott Bairstow

THEY   SHOWTIME
Drama: Family Drama • Sci-Fi/Supernatural/Horror/
Fantasy
Airdate: 11/14/93
Rating: N/A   A/C:

*Based on the short story by Rudyard Kipling.
After his young daughter dies in an accident, a
self-centered, workaholic father is haunted by
her presence. He seeks the help of a blind
southern spiritualist who is in touch with the
"lost souls" of dead children. She teaches him
the true importance of love, family and life.*

Production Company: Bridget Terry Prods IAW
   Viacom Prods.
Producer .... Bridget Terry
Co-Producer .... Art Seidel
Director .... John Korty
Writer .... Edithe Swenson
Cast .... Patrick Bergin
Cast .... Vanessa Redgrave
Cast .... Valerie Mahaffey

THEY'VE TAKEN OUR CHILDREN: THE CHOWCHILLA KIDNAPPING   ABC
Drama: True Crime • Children/Teens
Airdate: 3/1/93
Rating: 14.5/23   A/C: 2

*Based on the book by Jack Baugh & Jefferson
Morgan. In 1976, Chowchilla, California, bus
driver Ed Ray and a busload of children are
kidnapped and buried alive by three delinquent
teenagers demanding ransom money. Through
the heroic efforts and calming presence of Mr.
Ray, tragedy is averted.*

Production Company: Ron Gilbert Assoc., Joel
   Fields Prods., Leonard Hill Films.
Executive Producer .... Ron Gilbert
Executive Producer .... Joel Fields
Executive Producer .... Leonard Hill
Co-Producer .... Ardythe Goergens
Co-Producer .... Bernadette Caulfield
Director .... Vern Gillum
Writer .... David Eyre, Jr.
Cast .... Karl Malden
Cast .... Tim Ransom
Cast .... Travis Fine
Cast .... Julie Harris

THICKER THAN BLOOD: THE LARRY McLINDEN STORY   CBS

Drama: Family Drama • Children/Teens • Man Against The System • True Story
Airdate: 3/6/94
Rating: 14.5/23   A/C: 1

In 1992 California, Securities broker Larry McLinden sues his former girlfriend for custody of the son they had while living together. His problems are compounded when it is discovered that he is not the boy's biological father, and has no legal grounds to stand on. With the help of an expert attorney the case sets legal precedent when the judge awards him primary custody based on the fact that he has been the child's "psychological father" for five years.

Production Company: Alexander/Enright & Assoc.
Executive Producer .... Don Enright
Executive Producer .... Les Alexander
Co-Executive Producer .... Harvey Kahn
Producer .... Julian Marks
Co-Producer .... Judson Klinger
Director .... Michael Dinner
Writer .... Judson Klinger
Cast .... Peter Strauss
Cast .... Rachel Ticotin
Cast .... Lynn Whitfield

THIRD DEGREE BURN   HBO

Drama: Suspense/Thriller • Murder and Murder Mystery
Airdate: 5/28/89
Rating: N/A   A/C:

Seduced by a wealthy and beautiful woman a young womanizing private eye finds himself framed for the murder of her husband.

Production Company: HBO Pictures IAW MTM Entertainment Inc. and Paramount Pictures
Executive Producer .... Marianne Moloney
Producer .... Fredda Weiss
Director .... Roger Spottiswoode
Writer .... Duncan Gibbins
Writer .... Yale Udoff
Cast .... Treat Williams
Cast .... Virginia Madsen
Cast .... Richard Masur
Cast .... CCH Pounder

THIS CAN'T BE LOVE   CBS

Drama: Love Story • Romantic Comedy
Airdate: 3/13/94
Rating: 17.8/28   A/C: 1

A retired, cranky, legendary actress is reunited with her former leading man, a flamboyant former matinee idol whose career is in the dumps, when he must get her permission to publish his memoirs. Sparks fly and forgotten romance rekindled as they confront old hurts and long held resentments.

Production Company: Davis Entertainment
Executive Producer .... John Dayton
Executive Producer .... Merrill H. Karpf
Executive Producer .... John Davis
Producer .... Tom Rowe
Producer .... George Horie
Director .... Anthony Harvey
Writer .... Duane Poole
Cast .... Katherine Hepburn
Cast .... Anthony Quinn
Cast .... Jason Bateman
Cast .... Jami Gertz

THIS CHILD IS MINE   NBC

Drama: Family Drama • Children/Teens • Woman's Issue/Story • Social Issue
Airdate: 11/04/85
Rating: 21.1/32   A/C:

A seventeen year old unwed mother gives her baby up for adoption, but soon after changes her mind and a legal and emotional battle ensues.

Production Company: Beth Polson Prods. IAW Finnegan Assocs. & Telepictures
Executive Producer .... Beth Polson
Producer .... Pat Finnegan
Director .... David Greene
Writer .... Charles Rosin
Cast .... Lindsay Wagner
Cast .... Chris Sarandon
Cast .... Michael Lerner
Cast .... Nancy McKeon

THIS GUN FOR HIRE   USA

Drama: Murder and Murder Mystery • Cops/ Detectives/Law Enforcement • Suspense/Thriller
Airdate: 01/09/91
Rating: N/A   A/C:

Based on Graham Greene's novel and remake of the 1942 film. A hit man hired to kill a senator by a corporate bigwig is double-crossed sending him into a vengeful rampage across New Orleans.

Production Company: BBK Productions
Executive Producer .... Jon Epstein
Producer .... Peter Ware
Producer .... Boris Malden
Producer .... George Paige
Director .... Lou Antonio
Writer .... Nevin Schreiner
Cast .... Robert Wagner
Cast .... Nancy Everhard
Cast .... John Harkins

THIS PARK IS MINE   HBO

Drama: Vietnam • Social Issue • Man Against The System
Airdate: 10/6/85
Rating: N/A   A/C:

Based on the novel by Stephen Peters. An emotionally shattered Vietnam veteran plants explosive devices in New York City's Central Park and holds it hostage as a protest against the government's indifference to his fellow veterans' plight.

Production Company: HBO Premiere Films, Astral Film Enterprises Inc.
Executive Producer .... Harold Greenberg
Executive Producer .... Claude Heroux
Producer .... Denis Heroux
Director .... Steven H. Stern
Writer .... Lyle Gorsch
Cast .... Tommy Lee Jones
Cast .... Helen Shaver
Cast .... Yaphet Kotto

THIS WIFE FOR HIRE   ABC

Comedy: Woman's Issue/Story
Airdate: 03/18/85
Rating: 15.4/24   A/C:

The story of a wife who rents out her cleaning, cooking, and other homemaking services, and her husband's resentment of her growing independence.

Production Company: The Belle Co. & Guillaume-Margo Prods. IAW Comworld Prods.
Producer .... Phil Margo
Producer .... Don Segall
Director .... Jim Drake
Writer .... Phil Margo
Writer .... Don Segall
Cast .... Pam Dawber
Cast .... Robert Klein
Cast .... Sal Viscuso
Cast .... Laraine Newman
Cast .... Dick Gautier

THOMPSON'S LAST RUN   CBS

Drama: Family Drama • Cops/Detectives/Law Enforcement • Prison and Prison Camp
Airdate: 02/10/86
Rating: 17.4/26   A/C:

A criminal under life sentence is sprung by his niece under the nose of his old lawman nemesis. The criminal and niece he never really knew— who has her own reasons for setting him free— become a real family as the detective pursues them.

Production Company: Cypress Point Prods.
Executive Producer .... Gerald W. Abrams
Producer .... Jennifer Alward
Director .... Jerrold Freedman
Writer .... John Carlen
Cast .... Robert Mitchum
Cast .... Wilford Brimley
Cast .... Kathleen York
Cast .... Susan Tyrrell

THOSE SECRETS — ABC
Drama: Family Drama • Prostitution
Airdate: 03/16/92
Rating: 8.9/14   A/C: 4

An upper middle-class housewife and mother reverts to her former call girl lifestyle when confronted with the infidelities of her husband.

Production Company: Sarabande Prods. IAW MGM/UA
Executive Producer .... David Manson
Producer .... Timothy Marx
Co-Producer .... John Philip Landgraf
Director .... David Manson
Writer .... Lauren Currier
Cast .... Blair Brown
Cast .... Arliss Howard
Cast .... Mare Winningham

THOSE SHE LEFT BEHIND — NBC
Drama: Family Drama • Children/Teens
Airdate: 03/06/89
Rating: 25.1/38   A/C:

After his wife dies unexpectedly while giving birth, a man struggles to bring up their baby daughter. He is forced to seek help from his mother-in-law and wife's best friend, and even considers giving his daughter up for adoption.

Production Company: NBC Prods.
Producer .... R.W. Goodwin
Co-Producer .... Ed Milkovich
Director .... Waris Hussein
Writer .... Michael O'Hara
Cast .... Gary Cole
Cast .... Colleen Dewhurst
Cast .... Joanna Kerns
Cast .... Mary Page Keller

THREE KINGS, THE — ABC
Drama: Holiday Special
Airdate: 12/17/87
Rating: 8.2/13   A/C:

Three mental patients rehearsing their Christmas pageant roles ride their camels into Los Angeles in search of a modern-day Bethlehem.

Production Company: Aaron Spelling Prods. Inc.
Executive Producer .... Aaron Spelling
Executive Producer .... Douglas S. Cramer
Executive Producer .... Esther Shapiro
Producer .... Mel Damski
Producer .... Stirling Silliphant
Director .... Mel Damski
Writer .... Stirling Silliphant
Cast .... Lou Diamond Phillips
Cast .... Vic Tayback
Cast .... Charles Nelson Reilly
Cast .... Jane Kaczmarek
Cast .... Jack Warden
Cast .... Stan Shaw

THREE ON A MATCH — NBC
Drama: Action/Adventure • Series Pilot (2 hr.) • Buddy Story • Prison and Prison Camp
Airdate: 08/02/87
Rating: 14.1/26   A/C:

Three men escape from a southern prison camp run by sadistic guards. They are recaptured in Los Angeles, then escape again.

Production Company: Belisarius with Tri-Star TV
Executive Producer .... Donald P. Bellisario
Producer .... Stuart Segall
Director .... Donald P. Bellisario
Writer .... Donald P. Bellisario
Cast .... Patrick Cassidy
Cast .... Deborah Pratt
Cast .... Bruce A. Young
Cast .... Mitch Pileggi
Cast .... David Hemmings
Cast .... Lance LeGualt

THREE WISHES OF BILLY GRIER, THE — ABC
Drama: Family Drama • Children/Teens • Medical/Disease/Mental Illness
Airdate: 11/01/84
Rating: 13.5/21   A/C:

The title character, who suffers from a rare blood disease which ages him rapidly, goes on the road to reunite with his father in his final days.

Production Company: I & C Prods.
Executive Producer .... Gerald I. Isenberg
Producer .... Jay Benson
Director .... Corey Blechman
Writer .... Corey Blechman
Cast .... Ralph Macchio
Cast .... Hal Holbrook
Cast .... Season Hubley
Cast .... Jeffrey Tambor
Cast .... Lawrence Pressman
Cast .... Betty Buckley

THREESOME — CBS
Comedy: Romantic Comedy • Buddy Story
Airdate: 09/14/84
Rating: 10.3/18   A/C:

A wealthy man decides that he wants to resume his romance with his former girlfriend, despite the fact she has begun dating his best friend.

Production Company: CBS Entertainment
Producer .... Ron Roth
Director .... Lou Antonio
Writer .... Lawrence B. Marcus
Cast .... Stephen Collins
Cast .... Deborah Raffin
Cast .... Joel Higgins
Cast .... Dana Delany

THROUGH THE EYES OF A KILLER — CBS
Drama: Woman In Jeopardy • Suspense/Thriller
Airdate: 12/15/92
Rating: 12.8/21   A/C: 2

Based on the short story "The Master Builder" by Christopher Fowler. A vulnerable woman on the rebound from her two-timing boss becomes romantically involved with a contractor she has hired to remodel her condo. When the relationship starts to go sour she begins to find her home a deadly place— and the intended victim of a psycho-killer.

Production Company: Pacific Motion Pictures, Morgan Hill Films IAW Wilshire Court Prods.
Executive Producer .... Jennifer Alward
Co-Producer .... John Peilmeier
Director .... Peter Markle
Writer .... John Pielmeier
Cast .... Marg Helgenberger
Cast .... Richard Dean Anderson
Cast .... Joe Pantoliano

THUNDERBOAT ROW — ABC
Drama: Cops/Detectives/Law Enforcement • Action/Adventure • Drug Smuggling/Dealing • Series Pilot (2 hr.)
Airdate: 09/10/89
Rating: 13.8/23   A/C: 2

An elite southern Florida law-enforcement squad and a drug runner engage in a high-tech war.

Production Company: Stephan J. Cannell Prods.
Executive Producer .... Stephen J. Cannell
Producer .... Randall Wallace
Director .... Thomas J. Wright
Writer .... Stephen J. Cannell
Cast .... Chad Everett
Cast .... Freddie Simpson
Cast .... Dennis Boutsikaris
Cast .... John J. York

TILL DEATH US DO PART — NBC
Drama: Murder and Murder Mystery • True Crime • Courtroom Drama
Airdate: 02/17/92
Rating: 14.6/21   A/C: 2

Based on the book by Vincent Bugliosi and Ken Hurwitz. In 1966 Los Angeles, Vincent Bugliosi, hotshot assistant DA, uses circumstantial evidence against Alan Palliko, charming womanizer and ex-cop, suspected of killing his mistress' husband and his new bride for insurance money.

Production Company: Saban/Scherick
Executive Producer .... Gary Hoffman
Executive Producer .... Barbara Lieberman
Executive Producer .... Edgar J. Scherick
Producer .... Nick Gillott
Co-Producer .... John Burrows
Director .... Yves Simoneau
Writer .... Philip Rosenberg
Cast .... Arliss Howard
Cast .... Treat Williams
Cast .... Rebecca Jenkins

TIME TO HEAL, A   NBC

Drama: Medical/Disease/Mental Illness • Family
Drama • True Story
Airdate: 4/18/94
Rating: 12.7/21   A/C: 1

*During childbirth, a young wife and mother
suffers a severely debilitating stroke. At first,
she refuses to get physical therapy, choosing
instead to give up. As her family begins to fall
apart she soon realizes that she must face her
condition and begin to regain her life. With
the help of a no-nonsense therapist and her
husband she finds the strength to recover and
reevaluate her priorities.*

Production Company: Susan Baerwald Prods.
   IAW NBC Prods.
Executive Producer .... Susan Baerwald
Co-Producer .... Cathleen Young
Co-Producer .... Lee Guthrie
Co-Producer .... Lewis Abel
Director .... Michael Toshiyuki Uno
Writer .... Cathleen Young
Cast .... Nicolette Sheridan
Cast .... Gary Cole
Cast .... Mara Wilson
Cast .... Annie Corley

TIME TO LIVE, A   NBC

Drama: Family Drama • Children/Teens • Medical/
Disease/Mental Illness • True Story
Airdate: 10/28/85
Rating: 17.1/27   A/C:

*Based on the book by May-Loud Weisman. True
story of a family whose lives are changed
forever when their two year old son is diagnosed
with muscular dystrophy. They try to make his
life as happy as possible until he dies several
years later.*

Production Company: Blue Andre Prods. IAW
   ITC Prods.
Executive Producer .... Judith A. Polone
Producer .... Blue Andre
Director .... Rick Wallace
Writer .... John McGreevey
Cast .... Liza Minnelli
Cast .... Corey Haim
Cast .... Jeffrey DeMunn
Cast .... Swoozie Kurtz

TIME TO TRIUMPH, A   CBS

Drama: Family Drama • Woman Against The System
• True Story • Woman's Issue/Story
Airdate: 01/07/86
Rating: 16.0/25   A/C:

*Fact-based story of, Concetta Hassan, a
housewife who joins the Army after her husband
is no longer able to work due to heart trouble.
She eventually becomes a helicopter pilot and
supports the entire family.*

Production Company: Billos/Kauffman Prods.
   IAW Phoenix Entertainment Group
Executive Producer .... Ethel Winant
Producer .... Fran Billos
Producer .... Judy Kauffman
Director .... Noel Black
Writer .... George Yanok
Writer .... Lavina Dawson
Cast .... Patty Duke
Cast .... Joseph Bologna
Cast .... Dara Modglin
Cast .... Denise B. Mickelbury

TIMESTALKERS   CBS

Drama: Period Piece • Sci-Fi/Supernatural/Horror/
Fantasy • Western
Airdate: 03/10/87
Rating: 12.8/21   A/C:

*A college professor who collects Old West
memorabilia becomes involved in the time
travel track down of a gunslinger.*

Production Company: Fries Entertainment Inc.
   IAW Newland/Raynor Prods. Inc.
Executive Producer .... Charles Fries
Executive Producer .... Milton T. Raynor
Producer .... John Newland
Producer .... Richard Maynard
Director .... Michael Schultz
Writer .... Brian Clemens
Cast .... William Devane
Cast .... James Avery
Cast .... Lauren Hutton
Cast .... John Ratzenberger
Cast .... Klaus Kinski

TO BE THE BEST   CBS

Miniseries/Drama (2 nights): Foreign or Exotic
Location • Family Drama • Suspense/Thriller
Airdate: 08/02/92 • 08/04/92
Rating: 9.3/15 • 7.7/3   A/C: 2 • 3

*Based on the novel by Barbara Taylor Bradford.
A department store heiress is sabotaged by her
vindictive cousin who schemes to overthrow her
empire. Torn between family and career, she
enlists the aid of her loyal director of security
to save her fortune.*

Production Company: Gemmy Production
Executive Producer .... Robert Bradford
Producer .... Aida Young
Director .... Tony Wharmby
Writer .... Elliott Baker
Cast .... Lindsay Wagner
Cast .... Anthony Hopkins
Cast .... Stephanie Beacham
Cast .... Christopher Cazenove
Cast .... James Saito

TO DANCE WITH THE WHITE DOG CBS

Drama: Sci-Fi/Supernatural/Horror/Fantasy • Love
Story
Airdate: 12/5/93
Rating: 21.9/33   A/C: 1

*When his wife of fifty seven years dies, a retired
farmer becomes increasingly despondent until
he befriends a little white dog that strays onto
his property. His children think he is losing his
mind as he is the only one who can see the loving
mutt. When he takes the animal on a journey
to a college reunion the dog is revealed to be
his adoring wife who has come back to help
him accept life's eventualities.*

Production Company: Patricia Clifford Prods.
   IAW Signboard Hill Prods.
Executive Producer .... Patricia Clifford
Executive Producer .... Richard Welsh
Producer .... Glenn Jordan
Director .... Glenn Jordan
Writer .... Susan Cooper
Cast .... Hume Cronyn
Cast .... Jessica Tandy
Cast .... Christine Baranski
Cast .... Esther Rolle

TO GRANDMOTHER'S HOUSE WE GO
                                          ABC

Comedy: Holiday Special • Children/Teens
Airdate: 12/6/92
Rating: 16.9/25   A/C: 2

*Obnoxious twin girls, running away to
grandma's house on Christmas Eve, get
kidnapped by two bumbling criminals out to
make some quick ransom money. They are
rescued by their mother's friend who is after
his winning lottery ticket that the twins happen
to have. All are safely returned in time to enjoy
the holiday festivities.*

Production Company: Green/Epstein Prods. IAW
   Jeff Franklin
Executive Producer .... Allen Epstein
Executive Producer .... Jeff Franklin
Producer .... Mark Bacino
Executive Producer .... Jeff Franklin
Writer .... Jeff Franklin
Writer .... Boyd Hale
Cast .... Ashley Olsen
Cast .... Mary Kate Olsen
Cast .... Rhea Perlman
Cast .... Jerry Van Dyke

TO HEAL A NATION   NBC

Drama: Man Against The System • True Story •
Vietnam
Airdate: 05/29/88
Rating: 10.1/20   A/C:

*True story of Vietnam veteran Jan Scruggs,
whose struggle to create Washington's Vietnam
Veterans Memorial ran into immense
bureaucratic and political resistance.*

Production Company: Lionel Chetwynd Prods.,
    Orion Pictures TV IAW Von Zerneck-Samuels
Executive Producer .... Frank Von Zerneck
Executive Producer .... Stu Samuels
Executive Producer .... Lionel Chetwynd
Producer .... Robert M. Sertner
Co-Producer .... Gordon L. Freedman
Co-Producer .... Ian Sander
Director .... Michael Pressman
Writer .... Lionel Chetwynd
Cast .... Eric Roberts
Cast .... Lee Purcell
Cast .... Scott Paulin
Cast .... Glynnis O'Connor
Cast .... Brock Peters

TO MY DAUGHTER   NBC

Drama: Family Drama • True Story
Airdate: 11/26/90
Rating: 13.5/22   A/C: 3

*An obsessed mother becomes so consumed with
grief when her favorite daughter dies, she
completely ignores her other children, until she
finds solace completing her dead daughter's
unfinished book.*

Production Company: Zacs Prods., Inc., Nugget
    Entertainment
Executive Producer .... William A. Schwartz
Producer .... Ira Shuman
Director .... Larry Shaw
Writer .... William A. Schwartz
Cast .... Rue McClanahan
Cast .... Michele Greene
Cast .... Ty Miller
Cast .... Samantha Mathis

TO MY DAUGHTER WITH LOVE   NBC

Drama: Family Drama • Children/Teens
Airdate: 1/24/94
Rating: 13.8/21   A/C: 2

*A recently widowed young man has trouble
coping with the responsibilities of caring for
his six year old daughter while trying to hold
onto his construction job. At the insistence of
his well-to-do in-laws he agrees to let them raise
the little girl, believing they can give her a better
life. Realizing he has made a terrible mistake,
he gets his act together and proves to his child
that together they can build a new life.*

Production Company: Disney Family Classics
    IAW Steve White Prods.
Executive Producer .... Steve White
Executive Producer .... Sheri Singer
Producer .... Barry Bernardi
Co-Producer .... Terrence A. Donnelly
Director .... Kevin Hooks
Writer .... Michael de Guzman
Cast .... Rick Schroder
Cast .... Linda Gray
Cast .... Lawrence Pressman
Cast .... Ashley Malinger

TO SAVE A CHILD   ABC

Drama: Series Pilot (2 hr.) • Sci-Fi/Supernatural/
Horror/Fantasy
Airdate: 09/08/91
Rating: 9.1/15   A/C: 2

*A young mother gives birth to a stillborn child.
Later, she finds the infant was not really dead,
but had been kidnapped by her husband and
his family of Satanists. She then frantically tries
to rescue her baby from this evil cult.*

Production Company: Konigsberg-Sanitsky/
    Crystal Beach/Isabella
Executive Producer .... Frank Konigsberg
Executive Producer .... Larry Sanitsky
Executive Producer .... Robert Lieberman
Producer .... Larry Sanitsky
Producer .... Jack Clements
Director .... Robert Lieberman
Writer .... Joyce Eliason
Cast .... Marita Geraghty
Cast .... Shirley Knight
Cast .... Anthony Zerbe

TO SAVE THE CHILDREN   CBS

Drama: True Crime • Children/Teens
Airdate: 4/5/94
Rating: 11.6/19   A/C: 2

*Based on the book "When Angels Intervene"
by Hartt and Judene Wixcom. In 1986
Wyoming, demented ex-cop David Young, holds
a small-town elementary school hostage with
a homemade bomb. Before the local authorities
and the FBI are able to act, the explosive device
goes off. Miraculously none of the children or
teachers are killed— only the crazed gunman
and his devoted wife.*

Production Company: Children's Films IAW
    Westcom Entertainment Group & Kushner-
    Locke
Executive Producer .... Janet Faust Krusi
Executive Producer .... Dale Andrews
Producer .... Chris Danton
Director .... Steven H. Stern
Writer .... James S. Henerson
Cast .... Richard Thomas
Cast .... Robert Urich
Cast .... Jessica Steen
Cast .... Wendy Crewson

TOMMYKNOCKERS, THE   ABC

Miniseries/Drama (2 nights): Sci-Fi/Supernatural/
Horror/Fantasy
Airdate: 5/9/93 • 5/10/93
Rating: 15.9/26 • 17.3/27   A/C: 1 • 1

*Based on the book by Stephen King. A
journalist must battle the supernatural when his
girlfriend and the small New England town in
which she lives are possessed by a force buried
deep in the ground that threatens to destroy the
minds and bodies of the community.*

Production Company: Konigsberg/Sanitsky
Executive Producer .... Frank Konigsberg
Executive Producer .... Larry Sanitsky
Producer .... Jayne Bieber
Producer .... Jane Scott
Director .... John Power
Writer .... Lawrence D. Cohen
Cast .... Jimmy Smits
Cast .... Marg Helgenberger
Cast .... Joanna Cassidy
Cast .... John Ashton
Cast .... E.G. Marshall

MOVIES AND MINISERIES

TONIGHT'S THE NIGHT ABC
Drama: Romantic Comedy • Sex/Glitz
Airdate: 02/02/87
Rating: 11.9/19   A/C:

Glimpses of romances between singles hanging out at a Los Angeles night spot.

Production Company: Indie Prod with Phoenix Entertainment Group
Executive Producer .... Ilene Amy Berg
Executive Producer .... Bruce J. Sallan
Producer .... Jack Clements
Director .... Bobby Roth
Writer .... Sue Grafton
Writer .... Steve Humphrey
Cast .... Ed Marinaro
Cast .... Robert Rusler
Cast .... Max Gail
Cast .... Belinda Bauer
Cast .... Tracy Nelson
Cast .... Ken Olin

TONYA & NANCY: THE INSIDE STORY NBC
Drama: True Crime • Sports • Biography
Airdate: 4/30/94
Rating: 10.4/19   A/C: 2

In 1994, the rivalry between Olympic figure skaters Tonya Harding and Nancy Kerrigan erupts into a worldwide scandal when it is discovered that Harding and her husband, Jeff Gillooly, planned the pipe wielding attack on Kerrigan's knee. From personal accounts and public records the backgrounds of the street hardened Harding and the over protected Kerrigan are ultimately revealed.

Production Company: Brian Pike Prods. IAW NBC Prods.
Executive Producer .... Brian Pike
Producer .... Lynn Raynor
Director .... Larry Shaw
Writer .... Phil Penningroth
Cast .... Alexandra Powers
Cast .... James Wilder
Cast .... Heather Langenkamp
Cast .... Susan Clark

TOO GOOD TO BE TRUE NBC
Drama: Family Drama • Psychological Thriller
Airdate: 11/14/88
Rating: 20.9/32   A/C:

Remake of the film "Leave Her to Heaven". A neurotic woman leaves her fiance for a famous novelist. She becomes obsessively jealous, causing the death of his son and ruining their marriage.

Production Company: Newland-Raynor Prods.
Executive Producer .... Milton T. Raynor
Producer .... John Newland
Producer .... Judith Parker
Director .... Christian Nyby II
Writer .... Timothy Bradshaw
Cast .... Loni Anderson
Cast .... Julie Harris
Cast .... Larry Drake
Cast .... Patrick Duffy
Cast .... James B. Sikking
Cast .... Glynnis O'Connor

TOO YOUNG THE HERO CBS
Drama: Children/Teens • True Story • Period Piece • WWII
Airdate: 03/27/88
Rating: 20.7/33   A/C:

True story of Calvin Graham who lied about his age to join the U.S. Navy at age twelve in 1942. He was eventually found out, thrown in the brig and beaten and raped by sadistic guards. He ultimately won his freedom to the Navy's embarrassment.

Production Company: Rick-Dawn Prods. and Pierre Cossette Prods. IAW Landsburg Co.
Executive Producer .... Pierre Cossette
Executive Producer .... Alan Landsburg
Executive Producer .... Joan Barnett
Producer .... Buzz Kulik
Director .... Buzz Kulik
Writer .... David J. Kinghorn
Cast .... Rick Schroder
Cast .... Debra Mooney
Cast .... Mary Louise Parker
Cast .... Rick Warner
Cast .... Jon De Vries

TOO YOUNG TO DIE? NBC
Drama: Murder and Murder Mystery • True Crime • Children/Teens • Social Issue
Airdate: 02/26/90
Rating: 14.5/23   A/C: 3

An abused fifteen year old girl faces the death penalty when she is forced to stand trial as an adult for a brutal murder she was pushed into committing by her low-life boyfriend.

Production Company: Von Zerneck-Sertner Films
Executive Producer .... Frank Von Zerneck
Executive Producer .... Robert M. Sertner
Producer .... Susan Weber-Gold
Producer .... Julie Anne Weitz
Director .... Robert Markowitz
Writer .... David Hill
Writer .... George Rubino
Cast .... Michael Tucker
Cast .... Juliette Lewis
Cast .... Brad Pitt
Cast .... Alan Fudge

TORCH SONG ABC
Drama: Love Story • Addiction Story • Hollywood
Airdate: 5/23/93
Rating: 9.5/15   A/C: 3

Based on the book by Judith Krantz. A fading, alcoholic superstar falls in love with a down-to-earth fireman she meets in a rehab center. Although the road to happiness is a bumpy one, the couple straighten out their lives and finally tie the knot.

Production Company: Steve Krantz Prods. IAW Multimedia Motion Pictures
Executive Producer .... Steve Krantz
Producer .... Stephanie Austin
Co-Executive Producer .... Tony Etz
Co-Producer .... Stanley Neufeld
Director .... Michael Miller
Writer .... Leonora Thuna
Writer .... Janet Brownell
Cast .... Raquel Welch
Cast .... Jack Scalia
Cast .... Alicia Silverstone

TOUCH OF SCANDAL, A CBS
Drama: Woman In Jeopardy • Suspense/Thriller • Prostitution
Airdate: 11/27/84
Rating: 17.0/27   A/C:

A female city council member, who was once involved with a young male prostitute, becomes a target for blackmail and murder.

Production Company: Doris Keating Prods. IAW Columbia TV
Producer .... Doris Keating
Director .... Ivan Nagy
Writer .... Richard Guttman
Cast .... Angie Dickinson
Cast .... Tom Skerritt
Cast .... Jason Miller
Cast .... Don Murray
Cast .... Robert Loggia

TOUGHEST MAN IN THE WORLD, THE CBS
Drama: Action/Adventure
Airdate: 11/07/84
Rating: 12.6/20   A/C:

A ex-marine challenges the so called "toughest man in the world," hoping to win the $100,000 prize in order to help the Chicago youth center where he works.

Production Company: Guber-Peters Prods. IAW Centerpoint Prods.
Executive Producer .... Jon Peters
Executive Producer .... Peter Guber
Producer .... John Cutts
Director .... Dick Lowry
Writer .... Jimmy Sangster
Writer .... Richard Guttman
Cast .... Mr. T
Cast .... Dennis Dugan
Cast .... John Navin
Cast .... Peggy Pope
Cast .... Lynne Moody

TOUGHLOVE ABC
Drama: Family Drama • Children/Teens • Addiction Story • Social Issue
Airdate: 10/13/85
Rating: 20.6/31   A/C:

The parents of a drug abuser son turn to the "Toughlove" parent support group which believes that parents have to stand up to their kids and throw them out of the house, if necessary.

Production Company: Fries Entertainment Inc.
Executive Producer .... Charles Fries
Executive Producer .... Irv Wilson
Producer .... Ervin Zavada
Director .... Glenn Jordan
Writer .... Karen Hall
Cast .... Lee Remick
Cast .... Bruce Dern
Cast .... Jason Patric
Cast .... Eric Schiff

TOWER, THE   FBC
Drama: Suspense/Thriller • Sci-Fi/Supernatural/
Horror/Fantasy
Airdate: 5/16/93
Rating: 6.2/11   A/C: 4

*An office worker must out wit his fully
automated building's central computer when it
runs amok and decides to "delete" him from
the face of the earth. Trapped in the futuristic
Manhattan skyscraper he fights for his life
against the controlling microprocessor.*

Production Company: Catalina Prods. FNM Films
Executive Producer .... Franklin R. Levy
Executive Producer .... Gregory Harrison
Producer .... Matthew Rushton
Director .... Richard Kletter
Writer .... Richard Kletter
Writer .... John Riley
Cast .... Paul Reiser
Cast .... Roger Rees
Cast .... Susan Norman

TOWN BULLY, THE   ABC
Drama: Murder and Murder Mystery • Man Against
The System • Courtroom Drama
Airdate: 04/24/88
Rating: 15.6/25   A/C:

*A small-town district attorney makes an
unpopular decision to enforce the law after five
respected citizens arrange the killing of an ex-
con bully whose death is applauded by the
whole community.*

Production Company: Dick Clark Prods. Inc.
Executive Producer .... Dick Clark
Co-Executive Producer .... Dan Paulson
Producer .... Ian Sander
Co-Producer .... Lisa Demberg
Director .... Noel Black
Writer .... Jonathan Rintels
Cast .... Bruce Boxleitner
Cast .... Ellen Geer
Cast .... Isabella Hofmann
Cast .... David Graf
Cast .... Pat Hingle
Cast .... Tim Scott

TOWN TORN APART, A   NBC
Drama: Man Against The System • Children/Teens •
True Story
Airdate: 11/30/92
Rating: 12.8/20   A/C: 3

*Based on the book, "Doc" by Susan
Kammeraad-Campbell. In Winchester, New
Hampshire, newly hired high school principal,
Dennis Littky, incurs the wrath of the
community when he employs unorthodox
methods to turn around the towns rough,
troubled high school.*

Production Company: Paragon Ent. IAW WIN,
David W. Rintels
Executive Producer .... Victoria Riskin
Executive Producer .... Lyle Poncher
Producer .... Daniel Petrie
Director .... Daniel Petrie
Writer .... Anne Gerard
Cast .... Michael Tucker
Cast .... Jill Eikenberry
Cast .... Carole Galloway
Cast .... Linda Griffiths

TRACKER, THE   HBO
Drama: Western
Airdate: 3/26/88
Rating: N/A   A/C:

*In 1885, a legendary frontier tracker and
Indian fighter who has retired to his ranch in
Arizona joins forces with his estranged son to
hunt down a murderous religious fanatic who
has kidnaped two young women.*

Production Company: HBO Pictures
Executive Producer .... Alan Trustman
Producer .... Lance Hool
Director .... John Guillerman
Writer .... Kevin Jarre
Cast .... Kris Kristofferson
Cast .... Mark Moses
Cast .... David Huddleston

TRADE WINDS   NBC
Miniseries/Drama (4 nights): Family Drama • Foreign
or Exotic Location • Sex/Glitz
Airdate: 8/20/93 • 8/27/93 • 9/10/93 • 9/17/93
Rating: 6.9/13 • 6.2/13 • 5.4/11 • 5.8/11
A/C: 2 • 2 • 3 • 3

*On the Caribbean island of St. Martin, two rival
families form a short lived truce over control
of a luxury hotel and a large rum company.
Illicit affairs, double dealing and long held
resentments, threaten to destroy the tropical
empire.*

Production Company: Cramer Co. IAW NBC
Prods.
Executive Producer .... Douglas S. Cramer
Producer .... Mary Harold
Producer .... Hugh Benson
Director .... Charles Jarrott
Writer .... Hugh Bush
Cast .... Efrem Zimbalist, Jr.
Cast .... John Beck
Cast .... Stephen Meadows
Cast .... Barbara Stock
Cast .... Michael McLafferty
Cast .... Michael Michele

TRAGEDY OF FLIGHT 103: THE INSIDE STORY, THE   HBO
Drama: True Story • Foreign or Exotic Location •
Political Piece • Social Issue • Disaster
Airdate: 12/09/90
Rating: N/A   A/C:

*Details the event surrounding the terrorist
bombing of Pan Am flight 103 over Lockerby,
Scotland on December 21, 1988, which claimed
the lives of two-hundred-and-seventy people.*

Production Company: HBO Showcase, Granada
Film
Executive Producer .... Ray Fitzwalter
Executive Producer .... Colin Callender
Producer .... Leslie Woodhead
Director .... Leslie Woodhead
Writer .... Michael Eaton
Cast .... Ned Beatty
Cast .... Peter Boyle
Cast .... Vincent Gardenia
Cast .... Timothy West

TRAPPED   USA
Drama: Woman In Jeopardy • Suspense/Thriller
Airdate: 06/14/89
Rating: N/A   A/C:

*A psychotic murderer stalks a female executive
and an industrial spy when they all get trapped
overnight in a high-tech office building.*

Production Company: MCA/Cine Enterprises
Executive Producer .... Jon Epstein
Producer .... Robert T. Skodis
Producer .... Joseph Bellotti
Director .... Fred Walton
Writer .... Fred Walton
Writer .... Steve Feke
Cast .... Kathleen Quinlan
Cast .... Bruce Abbott
Cast .... Katy Boyer

TRAPPED IN SILENCE   CBS
Drama: Children/Teens • Medical/Disease/Mental
Illness • Family Violence
Airdate: 05/11/86
Rating: 15.1/24   A/C:

*A psychologist ferrets out the reason why a
sixteen year old boy suffers from elective mutism
(not talking because of emotional trauma).*

Production Company: Reader's Digest
Entertainment
Executive Producer .... Jeff Grant
Producer .... Dick Atkins
Director .... Michael Tuchner
Writer .... Pat A. Victor
Cast .... Marsha Mason
Cast .... Kiefer Sutherland
Cast .... Ron Silver
Cast .... John Mahoney

TRAVELING MAN   HBO
Comedy: Buddy Story
Airdate: 6/25/89
Rating: N/A   A/C:

*A successful , buttton-downed traveling
salesman is teamed up with a young
unscrupulous rookie. Together on the road they
teach each other valuable life lessons which
causes them both to examine the directions of
their lives.*

Production Company: HBO Pictures
Executive Producer .... David Taylor
Producer .... Thomas Hammel
Director .... Irvin Kershner
Writer .... David Taylor
Cast .... John Lithgow
Cast .... Jonathan Silverman
Cast .... John Glover
Cast .... Margaret Colin

Movies and Miniseries

TREACHEROUS CROSSING   USA
Drama: Woman In Jeopardy • Suspense/Thriller •
Period Piece
Airdate: 04/08/92
Rating: N/A   A/C:

*A wealthy woman and former mental patient
becomes the victim of a devious plot when her
husband vanishes on their honeymoon cruise.*

Production Company: Wilshire Court Prods.
Producer .... Bob Roe
Co-Producer .... Ed Milkovich
Director .... Tony Wharmby
Writer .... Elisa Bell
Cast .... Lindsay Wagner
Cast .... Angie Dickinson
Cast .... Jeffrey DeMunn
Cast .... Joseph Bottoms

TREASURE ISLAND   TNT
Drama: Period Piece • Action/Adventure • Foreign
or Exotic Location
Airdate: 01/22/90
Rating: N/A   A/C:

*Based on Robert Louis Stevenson's classic epic
adventure in which pirates battle a mixed band
of Englishmen on an expedition for buried
treasure.*

Production Company: Agamemnon Film Prods.
  IAW British Lion
Executive Producer .... Peter Snell
Producer .... Fraser C. Heston
Director .... Fraser C. Heston
Writer .... Fraser C. Heston
Cast .... Charlton Heston
Cast .... Christian Bale
Cast .... Julian Glover
Cast .... Richard Johnson

TRENCHCOAT IN PARADISE   CBS
Drama: Murder and Murder Mystery • Cops/
Detectives/Law Enforcement • Foreign or Exotic
Location • Series Pilot (2 hr.)
Airdate: 10/17/89
Rating: 12.2/20   A/C: 3

*A New Jersey private detective, who didn't know
he was working for the Mob, escapes to Hawaii,
where he's hired to investigate the murder of a
real-estate developer.*

Production Company: Ogiens/Kane Co.
Executive Producer .... Josh Kane
Executive Producer .... Michael Ogiens
Producer .... Harvey Frand
Director .... Martha Coolidge
Writer .... Tom Dempsey
Cast .... Dirk Benedict
Cast .... Bruce Dern
Cast .... Sydney Walsh
Cast .... Michelle Phillips

TRIAL AND ERROR   USA
Drama: Courtroom Drama • Suspense/Thriller
Airdate: 2/24/93
Rating: N/A   A/C:

*An ambitious Philadelphia district attorney
finds his political future clouded by the
realization that he may have sent an innocent
man to death row.*

Production Company: Alliance Communications
  IAW USA Network
Executive Producer .... David R. Ginsburg
Producer .... Ian McDougall
Director .... Mark Sobel
Writer .... Rick Way
Writer .... Jim Lindsay
Writer .... Nevin Schreiner
Cast .... Tim Matheson
Cast .... Helen Shaver
Cast .... Eugene Clark
Cast .... Ron Small

TRIAL OF THE INCREDIBLE HULK, THE
                                                  NBC
Drama: Action/Adventure • Sci-Fi/Supernatural/
Horror/Fantasy
Airdate: 05/07/89
Rating: 16.2/25   A/C:

*The Hulk teams up with the "Daredevil," a
crime fighter, to foil a sinister mobster
determined to rule the crime world.*

Production Company: Bixby-Brandon Prods. IAW
  New World TV
Executive Producer .... Bill Bixby
Executive Producer .... Gerald DiPego
Producer .... Hugh Spencer-Phillips
Producer .... Robert Ewing
Director .... Bill Bixby
Writer .... Gerald Di Pego
Cast .... Bill Bixby
Cast .... Lou Ferrigno
Cast .... John Rhys Davis

TRIAL: THE PRICE OF PASSION   NBC
Miniseries/Drama (2 nights): Murder and Murder
Mystery • Courtroom Drama • Sex/Glitz
Airdate: 05/03/92 • 05/04/92
Rating: 11.2/18 • 13.2/21   A/C: 2 • 2

*Based on the novel by Clifford Irving. A
tarnished Texas lawyer defends two high stakes
murder cases. As he unravels the truth, he
discovers that his case of a saloon owner
accused of killing her lover is linked to his other
client, a Latino who is also accused of murder.*

Production Company: The Sokolow Co. IAW
  TriStar TV
Executive Producer .... Mel Sokolow
Executive Producer .... Diane Sokolow
Producer .... Harry R. Sherman
Director .... Paul Wendkos
Writer .... John Gay
Cast .... Peter Strauss
Cast .... Beverly D'Angelo
Cast .... Ned Beatty
Cast .... Jill Clayburgh
Cast .... Marco Rodriguez

TRICKS OF THE TRADE   CBS
Drama: Buddy Story • Prostitution • Murder and
Murder Mystery
Airdate: 12/06/88
Rating: 11.6/18   A/C:

*A prostitute and the widow of a man killed in
her bed team up to find the man's murderer.*

Production Company: Leonard Hill Films
Executive Producer .... Leonard Hill
Executive Producer .... Robert O'Connor
Producer .... Ron Gilbert
Director .... Jack Bender
Writer .... Noreen Stone
Cast .... Cindy Williams
Cast .... Markie Post
Cast .... Scott Paulin
Cast .... James Whitmore, Jr.
Cast .... John Ritter

TRIPLECROSS   ABC
Drama: Murder and Murder Mystery • Cops/
Detectives/Law Enforcement • Series Pilot (2 hr.)
Airdate: 03/17/86
Rating: 10.3/16   A/C:

*Three former Los Angeles cops, now millionaire
private eyes, take a case involving the murder
of a rich artist and baseball corruption.*

Production Company: TAP Prods. IAW ABC
  Circle Films
Executive Producer .... Steve Tisch
Executive Producer .... Jon Avnet
Producer .... Dusty Kay
Director .... David Greene
Writer .... Dusty Kay
Cast .... Ted Wass
Cast .... Markie Post
Cast .... Gary Swanson
Cast .... Shannon Wilcox

TRIUMPH OF THE HEART: THE RICKY
BELL STORY   CBS
Drama: Children/Teens • Medical/Disease/Mental
Illness • True Story • Sports
Airdate: 4/2/1991
Rating: 12.5/22   A/C: 2

*Football all-star Ricky Bell's heartwarming
friendship with a handicapped youth in 1981
helps him to confront his own mysterious and
debilitating terminal illness.*

Production Company: Procter & Gamble Prods.
  IAW The Landsburg Company
Executive Producer .... Alan Landsburg
Producer .... David Permut
Producer .... Daniel Levy
Director .... Richard Michaels
Writer .... Jeff Andrus
Cast .... Mario Van Peebles
Cast .... Lane Davis
Cast .... Susan Ruttan
Cast .... Lynn Whitfield

TRIUMPH OVER DISASTER: THE HURRICANE ANDREW STORY   NBC
Drama: True Story • Disaster
Airdate: 5/24/93
Rating: 15.7/25   A/C: 1

The heroic efforts of Miami weatherman, Bryan Norcross and various community members during the long days and nights of Hurricane Andrew that devastated south Florida in 1992.

Production Company: NBC Prods.
Executive Producer .... Brian Pike
Producer .... Marvin J. Chomsky
Director .... Marvin J. Chomsky
Writer .... Casey Kelly
Cast .... Ted Wass
Cast .... Brynn Thayer
Cast .... Brian McNamara

TROUBLE IN PARADISE   CBS
Drama: Action/Adventure • Drug Smuggling/Dealing • Sex/Glitz • Foreign or Exotic Location
Airdate: 05/16/89
Rating: 10.9/18   A/C:

A recently widowed American woman is shipwrecked on a desert island with a hard drinking Aussie sailor. Intrigue begins when her not-so-dead husband shows up to recover the narcotics that were smuggled in his coffin as part of a crooked scheme.

Production Company: Qintex Ent. IAW CBS TV
Executive Producer .... Harvey Matofsky
Producer .... Robert Halmi, Sr.
Director .... Di Drew
Writer .... Robert Sherman
Writer .... Ben Marshall
Cast .... Raquel Welch
Cast .... Jack Thompson
Cast .... Nicholas Hammond

TROUBLE SHOOTERS: TRAPPED BENEATH THE EARTH   NBC
Drama: Disaster
Airdate: 10/3/93
Rating: 9.5/15   A/C: 3

When an eight story apartment building is buried in an earthquake in southern Utah, a family run search and rescue operation attempts to save survivors trapped underground. Complicating matters is the long standing feud between two brothers who must confront their old resentments in order to safely complete the dangerous mission.

Production Company: Ginkgo Prods. IAW Walter Mirisch Prods.
Executive Producer .... Walter Mirisch
Producer .... Ted Kurdyla
Director .... Bradford May
Writer .... Michael Pavone
Writer .... Dave Johnson
Cast .... Kris Kristofferson
Cast .... David Newsom
Cast .... Leigh McCloskey

TRUE BLUE   NBC
Drama: Cops/Detectives/Law Enforcement • Action/Adventure • Series Pilot (2 hr.)
Airdate: 12/03/89
Rating: 14.0/22   A/C: 2

The Emergency Services Unit of the New York City Police Department, an elite troubleshooting group, rescues schoolchildren from terrorists, a potential suicide, and a woman trapped underwater in her car.

Production Company: Grosso-Jacobson Prods.
Executive Producer .... Sonny Grosso
Executive Producer .... Larry Jacobson
Executive Producer .... Michael Fisher
Producer .... Cheryl Quarantiello
Director .... William A. Graham
Writer .... David J. Kinghorn
Cast .... Tony Lo Bianco
Cast .... Amanda Plummer
Cast .... Rich Hall
Cast .... Ally Walker

TURN BACK THE CLOCK   NBC
Drama: Suspense/Thriller • Sci-Fi/Supernatural/Horror/Fantasy
Airdate: 11/20/89
Rating: 13.8/22   A/C: 3

A troubled actress kills her husband at midnight on New Year's Eve and immediately regrets it. Given the opportunity to relive the previous calamitous year, she finds she is powerless to change the final terrible outcome.

Production Company: Michael Filerman Prods. IAW NBC Prods.
Executive Producer .... Michael Filerman
Producer .... Joseph Wallenstein
Director .... Larry Elikann
Writer .... Lee Hutson
Writer .... Lindsay Harrison
Cast .... Connie Sellecca
Cast .... Wendy Kilbourne
Cast .... Jere Burns
Cast .... David Dukes

TWELVE O' ONE (12: 01)   FBC
Drama: Sci-Fi/Supernatural/Horror/Fantasy
Airdate: 7/5/93
Rating: 6.0/12   A/C: 4

Based on the short story by Richard Lupoff. An office worker in a top-secret, high-tech lab finds himself caught in a "time bounce" and relives the same twenty-four hours over and over again. Each time he relives the day he is able to alter events--ultimately saving the women he loves from being murdered and thwarting a sinister plot to destroy company research.

Production Company: Fox West Pictures Inc. IAW New Line TV
Executive Producer .... Jana Sue Memel
Executive Producer .... Sasha Emerson
Producer .... Jonathan Heap
Director .... Jack Sholder
Writer .... Philip Morton
Cast .... Jonathan Silverman
Cast .... Helen Slater
Cast .... Martin Landau
Cast .... Paxton Whitehead

TWIN PEAKS   ABC
Drama: Murder and Murder Mystery • Cops/Detectives/Law Enforcement • Children/Teens • Series Pilot (2 hr.) • Sex/Glitz
Airdate: 04/08/90
Rating: 21.7/33   A/C: 1

A straight-arrow FBI agent joins forces with the local sheriff to probe the murder of a prom queen in lumber country. Everyone in town seems to be hiding something or chasing clues, or both, in this bizarre, unresolved David Lynch pilot.

Production Company: Lynch/Frost Prod. & Propaganda Films IAW Worldvision Enterprises
Executive Producer .... Mark Frost
Executive Producer .... David Lynch
Producer .... David Latt
Director .... David Lynch
Writer .... Mark Frost
Writer .... David Lynch
Cast .... Kyle MacLachlan
Cast .... Michael Ontkean
Cast .... Piper Laurie
Cast .... Joan Chen

TWIST OF FATE   NBC
Miniseries/Drama (2 nights): Nazis • WWII • Historical Piece • Suspense/Thriller • Foreign or Exotic Location • Prison and Prison Camp
Airdate: 01/08/89 • 01/09/89
Rating: 14.3/21 • 15.2/24   A/C:

Based on the novel "Pursuit" by Robert J. Fish. A Nazi SS officer has himself surgically transformed to look like a Jew, takes off for Palestine after the war, and eventually becomes a general in the Israeli army. He is later blackmailed by his old Nazi pals who threaten to reveal his past.

Production Company: Columbia Pictures TV
Executive Producer .... Larry White
Executive Producer .... Henry Plitt
Director .... Ian Sharp
Writer .... Bill Bast
Writer .... Paul Huson
Writer .... Gy Waldron
Cast .... Ben Cross
Cast .... Bruce Greenwood
Cast .... Veronica Hamel
Cast .... John Glover

TWIST OF THE KNIFE, A   CBS
Drama: Cops/Detectives/Law Enforcement • Medical/Disease/Mental Illness
Airdate: 2/13/92
Rating: 10.9/20   A/C: 1

Sequel to CBS TV Movies, "Diagnosis of Murder". Rollerskating, crime-solving Dr. Mark Sloan, investigates a beautiful world renowned surgeon and a suspicious death in the operating room.

Production Company: Dean Hargrove Prods., Fred Silverman Prods.
Executive Producer	Fred Silverman
Executive Producer	Dean Hargrove
Producer	Barry Steinberg
Director	Jerry London
Writer	Gerry Conway
Cast	Dick Van Dyke
Cast	Suzanne Pleshette
Cast	Cynthis Gibb
Cast	Barry Van Dyke

TWO FATHERS' JUSTICE   NBC
Drama: Family Drama • Man Against The System • Children/Teens • Drug Smuggling/Dealing • Social Issue • Murder and Murder Mystery
Airdate: 02/11/85
Rating: 17.9/27   A/C:

The question of vigilantism is explored when a corporate president and a laid-off steelworker, each of whom has lost a child in a drug related murder, join forces and go after the head of the drug ring and exact revenge.

Production Company: A. Shane Co.
Executive Producer	Joan Conrad
Producer	Robert Long
Director	Rod Holcomb
Writer	David J. Kinghorn
Cast	Robert Conrad
Cast	George Hamilton
Cast	Brooke Bundy
Cast	Catherine Corkill

TWO FATHERS: JUSTICE FOR THE INNOCENT   NBC
Drama: Man Against The System • Family Drama • Murder and Murder Mystery
Airdate: 1/14/94
Rating: 10.3/17   A/C: 3

Sequel to the 1985 TV movie, "Two Fathers' Justice". A tough steelworker and a distinguished millionaire team up to capture the escaped convict who they once helped put behind bars after he murdered their children

Production Company: A. Shane Company
Executive Producer	Joan Conrad Irwin
Producer	Shane Conrad
Writer	Steven Meggs
Director	Paul Krasny
Cast	Robert Conrad
Cast	George Hamilton
Cast	Danny Goldring
Cast	Mary Mulligan

TWO MRS. GRENVILLES, THE   NBC
Miniseries/Drama (2 nights): Family Drama • Period Piece • Suspense/Thriller • Murder and Murder Mystery
Airdate: 02/08/87 • 02/09/87
Rating: 23.4/36 • 24.0/35   A/C:

From Dominick Dunne's novel. A rich man's mother teaches his chorus-girl bride how to take advantage of her new status. Her alienated husband, after investigating his bride's background, is shot, and the two women are left with each other.

Production Company: Lorimar
Executive Producer	Susan Pollock
Producer	John Erman
Supervising Producer	Preston Fischer
Cast	Stephen Collins
Cast	Ann-Margret
Cast	Penny Fuller
Cast	John Rubinstein
Cast	Claudette Colbert

TWO THOUSAND MALIBU ROAD   CBS
Drama: Series Pilot (2 hr.) • Sex/Glitz • Suspense/Thriller
Airdate: 8/23/92
Rating: 16.1/28   A/C: 1

A retired prostitute takes in three roommates: a would-be starlet, her manipulative new age sister, and a depressed lawyer, who all get involved in each others lives and loves in the hip beach town of Malibu, California.

Production Company: Spelling TV Inc. IAW Fisher Ent., CGD Prods.
Executive Producer	Terry Louise Fisher
Executive Producer	Joel Schumacher
Executive Producer	Aaron Spelling
Director	Joel Schumacher
Writer	Terry Louise Fisher
Cast	Lisa Hartman
Cast	Drew Barrymore
Cast	Jennifer Beals
Cast	Tuesday Knight
Cast	Brian Bloom

ULTIMATE BETRAYAL   CBS
Drama: Family Violence • Family Drama • Woman Against The System • Woman's Issue/Story • Social Issue • True Story
Airdate: 3/20/94
Rating: 15.6/25   A/C: 1

In 1990 Denver, two adult sisters bring a civil suit against their father, a former FBI child-abuse expert, for the years of sexual, physical and mental abuse he inflicted upon them as children. The ensuing trail pits family members against one another as their father denies all allegations and refuses to attend the proceedings. He is ultimately found guilty in this landmark case.

Production Company: Polongo Prods. IAW Hearst Entertainment
Executive Producer	Donald Wrye
Producer	Julian Marks
Co-Producer	Wendy Kram
Co-Producer	Gregory Goodell
Director	Donald Wrye
Writer	Gregory Goodell
Cast	Marlo Thomas
Cast	Mel Harris
Cast	Kathryn Dowling
Cast	Ally Sheedy

UNCLE TOM'S CABIN   SHOWTIME
Drama: Black Story • Period Piece • Historical Piece
Airdate: 6/14/87
Rating: N/A   A/C:

Based the novel by Harriet Beecher Stowe. The plight of two slaves, Tom and Eliza in the pre-Civil war South as they make their separate and very different ways through the evil system of slavery.

Production Company: Taft Entertainment Televison
Executive Producer	Edgar J. Scherick
Executive Producer	Michael Barnathan
Co-Executive Producer	Gary Hoffman
Producer	Jeff Nelson
Director	Stan Lathan
Writer	John Gay
Cast	Avery Brooks
Cast	Phylicia Rashad
Cast	Edward Woodward
Cast	Bruce Dern

UNCONQUERED   CBS
Drama: Period Piece • Political Piece • True Story • Black Story • Social Issue • Biography
Airdate: 01/15/89
Rating: 17.3/28   A/C:

True story of Richmond Flowers, a white pro-integration Alabama attorney general and his athletic son who are persecuted during the racial turmoil of the 1950s and 1960s.

Production Company: Alexandra Film Prods. Inc./ Double Helix/Dick Lowry Prods.
Producer	Dick Lowry
Director	Dick Lowry
Writer	Pat Conroy
Cast	Dermot Mulroney
Cast	Peter Coyote
Cast	Noble Willingham
Cast	Tess Harper

UNDER COVER   ABC

Drama: Cops/Detectives/Law Enforcement • Action/
Adventure • Foreign or Exotic Location • Series Pilot
(2 hr.)
Airdate: 01/07/91
Rating: 9.9/16   A/C: 3

An undercover agent with the National Intelligence Agency and his ex-agent wife race to foil a plot to assassinate a high-ranking Soviet leader.

Production Company: Sacret Inc. & Paint Rock
    Prods. IAW Warner Bros. Television
Executive Producer .... John Sacret Young
Executive Producer .... William Broyles, Jr.
Producer .... Terry Morse
Director .... Harry Winer
Writer .... William Broyles, Jr.
Cast .... Anthony John Denison
Cast .... Linda Purl
Cast .... John Rhys-Davies
Cast .... John Slattery

UNDER SIEGE   NBC

Drama: Suspense/Thriller • Political Piece • Cops/
Detectives/Law Enforcement
Airdate: 02/09/86
Rating: 17.2/24   A/C:

As terrorist attacks spread across the U.S., only the director of the FBI and the Secretary of Defense advise the President not to attack Iran until they're sure of for whom the terrorists are working.

Production Company: Don Ohlmeyer Prods. IAW
    Telepictures Prods.
Executive Producer .... Don Ohlmeyer
Producer .... Karen Danaher-Dorr
Director .... Roger Young
Writer .... Bob Woodward
Writer .... Christian Williams
Writer .... Alfred Sole
Writer .... Richard Harwood
Cast .... Peter Strauss
Cast .... Thaao Penghlis
Cast .... Mason Adams
Cast .... Victoria Tennant
Cast .... Fritz Weaver
Cast .... E. G. Marshall

UNDER THE INFLUENCE   CBS

Drama: Family Drama • Addiction Story
Airdate: 09/28/86
Rating: 15.4/24   A/C:

A man's alcoholism drives his wife and one daughter to pill-popping and one son to alcohol. His heart attack forces the entire family, including the one son and daughter who have escaped dependency, to face the family's problems.

Production Company: CBS Entertainment
Producer .... Vanessa Greene
Director .... Thomas Carter
Writer .... Joyce Burditt
Cast .... Andy Griffith
Cast .... Season Hubley
Cast .... Keanu Reeves
Cast .... Dana Andersen
Cast .... Joyce Van Patten

UNHOLY MATRIMONY   CBS

Drama: Cops/Detectives/Law Enforcement • True
Crime • Murder and Murder Mystery
Airdate: 10/03/88
Rating: 15.1/24   A/C:

Based on the book by John Dillman. Fact based tale of a mail-order psychologist and a mail-order minister who team up to kill a woman for $300,000 in accident insurance. They are finally caught by an undaunted police detective named John Dillman.

Production Company: Edgar J. Scherick
    Associates IAW Taft Entertainment TV
Executive Producer .... Edgar J. Scherick
Executive Producer .... Gary Hoffman
Producer .... Michael Barnathan
Director .... Jerrold Freedman
Writer .... John McGreevey
Cast .... Patrick Duffy
Cast .... Charles Durning
Cast .... Michael O'Keefe
Cast .... Lisa Blount

UNNATURAL CAUSES   NBC

Drama: Man Against The System • Medical/Disease/
Mental Illness • True Story • Vietnam • Woman
Against The System
Airdate: 11/10/86
Rating: 19.3/31   A/C:

A Veterans Administration employee, Maude DeVictor, and a Vietnam veteran combine to force the government to acknowledge the harm done by Agent Orange to American soldiers in southeast Asia.

Production Company: Blue Andre Prods. IAW
    ITC Prods.
Executive Producer .... Blue Andre
Executive Producer .... Robert M. Myman
Co-Producer .... Steve Doran
Co-Producer .... Marty Goldstein
Director .... Lamont Johnson
Writer .... John Sayles
Cast .... John Ritter
Cast .... Alfre Woodard
Cast .... John Vargas
Cast .... Patti LaBelle

UNSPEAKABLE ACTS   ABC

Drama: True Crime • Children/Teens • Social Issue •
Courtroom Drama • Rape/Molestation
Airdate: 01/15/90
Rating: 15.7/25   A/C: 1

Based on Dan Hollingsworth's book. Dade County husband and wife preschool owners are prosecuted and convicted of child molestation. The work of child development experts Laurie and Joseph Braga help the children testify for the prosecution.

Production Company: Landsburg Productions
Executive Producer .... Alan Landsburg
Executive Producer .... Linda Otto
Producer .... Joan Barnett
Director .... Linda Otto
Writer .... Alan Landsburg
Cast .... Jill Clayburgh
Cast .... Brad Davis
Cast .... Season Hubley
Cast .... Gary Frank

UNTAMED LOVE   LIFETIME

Drama: Children/Teens • Woman Against The System
• True Story
Airdate: 8/3/94
Rating: N/A   A/C:

Based on the book by Torey Hayden. A teacher of emotionally handicapped children is overwhelmed by the addition of a disruptive and violent six year old to her classroom. Eventually bonding with the child, she puts everything aside, including her relationship with her boyfriend, to fight both the child's father and the state to save the little girl from a bleak future.

Production Company: CLC Prods. Carroll
    Newman Prods., The Polone Company IAW
    Hearst Entertainment
Executive Producer .... Judith A. Polone
Executive Producer .... Cathy Lee Crosby
Producer .... Carroll Newman
Director .... Paul Aaron
Writer .... Peter Nelson
Cast .... Cathy Lee Crosby
Cast .... John Getz
Cast .... Gary Frank
Cast .... Ashlee Lauren

US   CBS

Drama: Family Drama • Series Pilot (2 hr.)
Airdate: 09/20/91
Rating: 16.1/29   A/C: 1

An ex-convict, having been cleared of a murder he didn't commit eighteen years ago, tries to reunite with his estranged family.

Production Company: Michael Landon Prods.
    IAW Columbia Pictures Television
Executive Producer .... Michael Landon
Producer .... Kent McCray
Director .... Michael Landon
Writer .... Michael Landon
Cast .... Michael Landon
Cast .... Casey Peterson
Cast .... Barney Martin

VANISHING ACT   CBS

Mystery: Cops/Detectives/Law Enforcement •
Psychological Thriller
Airdate: 05/04/86
Rating: 18.3/27   A/C:

At a ski resort, a woman on her honeymoon disappears. When her husband reports her missing he is confronted with a stranger who claims to be his missing wife.

Production Company: Robert Cooper Prods.
Executive Producer .... Richard Levinson
Executive Producer .... William Link
Producer .... Robert Cooper
Director .... David Greene
Writer .... William Link
Writer .... Richard Levinson
Cast .... Margot Kidder
Cast .... Fred Gwynne
Cast .... Mike Farrell
Cast .... Elliott Gould

VENGEANCE: THE STORY OF TONY CIMO CBS

Drama: Man Against The System • True Crime • Social Issue
Airdate: 11/01/86
Rating: 11.8/21   A/C:

The true story of a young man who, after his parents are killed in a holdup, takes revenge beyond that of the law on the convicted killer.

Production Company: Nederlander TV and Film Prod. Inc. IAW Robirdie Pictures Inc.
Executive Producer .... Roberta F. Becker
Executive Producer .... Gladys Rackmil
Producer .... George Manasse
Director .... Marc Daniels
Writer .... James Lee Barrett
Cast .... Brad Davis
Cast .... Roxanne Hart
Cast .... Brad Dourif
Cast .... William Conrad

VERY BRADY CHRISTMAS, A CBS

Comedy: Holiday Special • Family Drama
Airdate: 12/18/88
Rating: 25.1/39   A/C:

The clan from the TV series "The Brady Bunch" share their problems in a reunion many years after the sitcom.

Production Company: Sherwood Schwartz Co.
Executive Producer .... Sherwood Schwartz
Producer .... Lloyd J. Schwartz
Producer .... Barry Berg
Director .... Peter Baldwin
Writer .... Sherwood Schwartz
Cast .... Robert Reed
Cast .... Ann B. Davis
Cast .... Maureen McCormick
Cast .... Florence Henderson
Cast .... Eve Plumb
Cast .... Barry Williams
Cast .... Maureen McCormick

VESTIGE OF HONOR CBS

Drama: True Story • Foreign or Exotic Location • Vietnam
Airdate: 12/30/90
Rating: 11.0/18   A/C: 3

Two Americans, who served together in Vietnam, fight to save pro-American tribal natives who were abandoned by the U.S. after the fall of Saigon and are now suffering in Thai refugee camps.

Production Company: Desperado Pictures IAW Dan Wigutow, Envoy, and Spanish Trail Prods.
Executive Producer .... Dan Wigutow
Co-Executive Producer .... Gerald McRaney
Producer .... Don Schroeder
Producer .... Elizabeth Daley
Producer .... Patricia Hodges
Producer .... Chuck Sellier
Director .... Jerry London
Writer .... Steve Brown
Cast .... Gerald McRaney
Cast .... Michael Gross
Cast .... Season Hubley
Cast .... Kenny Lao

VICTIM OF LOVE CBS

Drama: Forbidden Love • Suspense/Thriller • Sex/Glitz • Medical/Disease/Mental Illness
Airdate: 05/05/91
Rating: 12.0/20   A/C: 3

A young therapist struggles with her own fears when she suspects that one of her suicidal patients is involved with her boyfriend.

Production Company: Nevermore Prods.
Executive Producer .... Steve Tisch
Co-Executive Producer .... Mireille Soria
Producer .... Leslie Waldman
Producer .... Bernie Goldman
Producer .... Gary Goldstein
Director .... Jerry London
Writer .... James Desmarais
Writer .... Alison Rosenfeld
Writer .... Timothy Kring
Cast .... Pierce Brosnan
Cast .... JoBeth Williams
Cast .... Virginia Madsen

VICTIM OF LOVE: THE SHANNON MOHR STORY NBC

Drama: Family Drama • True Crime • Family Violence
Airdate: 11/9/93
Rating: 13.0/19   A/C: 2

From a story on Unsolved Mysteries. In 1980, Ohio, Shannon Mohr marries captivating Dave Davis after only two months of dating. After making sure his loving wife is fully insured, he cleverly stages a horseback-riding accident. The girls parents insists that their daughter was murdered and fight to bring him to justice. He flees prosecution and ten years later is profiled on "Unsolved Mysteries" and eventually captured and convicted.

Production Company: Cosgrove-Meurer Prods.
Executive Producer .... John Cosgrove
Executive Producer .... Terry Meurer
Producer .... George Perkins
ASSOCIATE PRODUCER ..... Howard Rosenstein
Director .... John Cosgrove
Writer .... Bryce Zabel
Cast .... Bonnie Bartlett
Cast .... Dwight Schultz
Cast .... Andy Romano

VICTIMS FOR VICTIMS - THE THERESA SALDANA STORY NBC

Drama: Woman Against The System • True Crime • Medical/Disease/Mental Illness
Airdate: 11/12/84
Rating: 18.8/28   A/C:

The true story of actress Theresa Saldana, who was herself the victim of a brutal attack and later went on to start a victims support group.

Production Company: Daniel L. Paulson/Loehr Spivey Prods. IAW Orion TV
Executive Producer .... Dan Paulson
Executive Producer .... Loehr Spivey
Producer .... Harry R. Sherman
Director .... Karen Arthur
Writer .... Arthur Heinemann
Cast .... Theresa Saldana
Cast .... Adrian Zmed
Cast .... Leila Goldoni
Cast .... Lawrence Pressman

VIPER NBC

Drama: Sci-Fi/Supernatural/Horror/Fantasy • Action/Adventure • Cops/Detectives/Law Enforcement
Airdate: 1/2/94
Rating: 15.3/23   A/C: 2

In a futuristic city in Southern California, a reprogrammed former criminal and a high tech supercar hit the streets in the ultimate pursuit of crime fighting.

Production Company: Pet Fly Prods. and Paramount Net TV
Executive Producer .... Danny Bilson
Executive Producer .... Paul DeMeo
Co-Executive Producer .... Don Kurt
Producer .... David L. Deanes
Producer .... Michael Lacoe
Director .... Danny Bilson
Writer .... Danny Bilson
Cast .... James McCaffrey
Cast .... Dorian Harewood
Cast .... Joe Nipote

VISIONS OF MURDER NBC

Drama: Woman In Jeopardy • Psychological Thriller
Airdate: 5/7/93
Rating: 10.1/19   A/C: 2

A San Francisco psychotherapist starts having paranormal hallucinations of a recent patient's husband, who she envisions involved in a murder. When the killer begins to stalk her she enlists the aid of her ex husband, a homicide detective, and together they solve the bizarre case.

Production Company: Bar-Gene Prods. Freyda Rothstein Prods. IAW Hearst Ent.
Executive Producer .... Freyda Rothstein
Co-Executive Producer .... Gene Schwam
Co-Producer .... Angela Bromstad
Director .... Michael Rhodes
Writer .... Julie Moskowitz
Writer .... Gary Stephens
Cast .... Barbara Eden
Cast .... James Brolin
Cast .... Joan Pringle
Cast .... Scott Bryce

VITAL SIGNS   CBS
Drama: Family Drama • Addiction Story
Airdate: 02/11/86
Rating: 16.7/26   A/C:

Two doctors, father and son, must fight alcohol and drug dependency together through both conflict and understanding.

Production Company: CBS Entertainment Prods.
Producer .... Stuart Millar
Director .... Stuart Millar
Writer .... Lee Hutson
Cast .... Gary Cole
Cast .... Edward Asner
Cast .... John Randolph
Cast .... James Sloyan
Cast .... Barbara Barrie

VOICES WITHIN: THE LIVES OF TRUDDI CHASE   ABC
Miniseries/Drama (2 nights): Family Drama • Medical/Disease/Mental Illness • True Story • Family Violence
Airdate: 05/20/90 • 05/21/90
Rating: 14.7/24 • 15.5/25   A/C: 2 • 2

Based on the book "When Rabbit Howls" by Truddi Chase. A wife and mother with ninety-two distinct personalities, the result of severe childhood abuses, struggles through therapy to find a cure.

Production Company: Itsbinso Long/P.A./New World
Executive Producer .... E. Jack Neuman
Executive Producer .... Helen Verno
Producer .... Harry R. Sherman
Co-Producer .... Martin Mickelson
Director .... Lamont Johnson
Writer .... E. Jack Neuman
Cast .... Shelley Long
Cast .... Tom Conti
Cast .... John Rubinstein

VOYAGE   USA
Drama: Suspense/Thriller • Foreign or Exotic Location
Airdate: 6/2/93
Rating: N/A   A/C:

A married couple, while on a sailing vacation in the Mediterranean, encounter an old high school friend and his wife. Inviting themselves aboard the ketch bound for Malta, the pair at first seem harmless. As the trip progresses they become abusive and psychopathic, forcing the helpless boaters to fight for their lives.

Production Company: Davis Ent., Qunta Communications
Executive Producer .... Tarak Ben Ammar
Executive Producer .... Peby Guisez
Executive Producer .... John Davis
Executive Producer .... Merrill H. Karpf
Director .... John MacKenzie
Writer .... Mark Montgomery
Cast .... Rutger Hauer
Cast .... Eric Roberts
Cast .... Karen Allen
Cast .... Connie Nielsen

WACO & RHINEHART   ABC
Drama: Cops/Detectives/Law Enforcement • Action/Adventure • Buddy Story
Airdate: 03/27/87
Rating: 7.4/13   A/C:

Two clumsy U.S. marshals, who have a hard time getting along with each other, go after sellers of illegal arms.

Production Company: Touchstone Films TV
Executive Producer .... Daniel Petrie, Jr.
Executive Producer .... Lee David Zlotoff
Director .... Christian Nyby II
Writer .... Lee David Zlotoff
Cast .... William Hootkins
Cast .... Kathleen Lloyd
Cast .... Justin Deas
Cast .... Bob Tzudiker
Cast .... Charles C. Hill

WALKER, TEXAS RANGER   CBS
Drama: Cops/Detectives/Law Enforcement • Action/Adventure • Series Pilot (2 hr.)
Airdate: 4/21/93
Rating: 16.5/27   A/C: 1

A leathery Texas Ranger, who is half Native American, goes after a cop killing bank robber in the city of Fort Worth with his new partner, a computer-wise, ex-football player from Baltimore.

Production Company: Cannon Televison
Executive Producer .... David Moessinger
Executive Producer .... Albert S. Ruddy
Executive Producer .... Leslie Greif
Producer .... Nancy Bond
Director .... Virgil W. Vogel
Writer .... Louise McCarn
Cast .... Chuck Norris
Cast .... Clarence Gilyard
Cast .... Sheree J. Wilson

WALLENBERG: A HERO'S STORY   NBC
Miniseries/Drama (2 nights): Man Against The System • Biography • Historical Piece • Foreign or Exotic Location • WWII • Nazis
Airdate: 04/08/85 • 04/09/85
Rating: 20.2/33 • 19.7/30   A/C:

True story of the Swedish diplomat who saved the lives of thousands of Hungarian Jews from Nazi death camps by daring rescue operations and clever manipulations of political power.

Production Company: Stonehenge Prods. IAW Paramount TV
Executive Producer .... Dick Berg
Producer .... Richard Irving
Director .... Lamont Johnson
Writer .... Gerald Green
Cast .... Richard Chamberlain
Cast .... Melanie Mayron
Cast .... Alice Krige
Cast .... Kenneth Colley
Cast .... Guy Deghy
Cast .... Stuart Wilson

WALTON THANKSGIVING REUNION, A CBS
Drama: Family Drama • Period Piece • Historical Piece
Airdate: 11/21/93
Rating: 20.1/30   A/C: 1

Based on the 1972-1981 drama series. In 1963, the close-knit Virginia family gathers together to celebrate Thanksgiving at the old homestead. Their own personal problems are soon put on hold as the clan reacts to the assassination of President Kennedy, whose death changes the lives of many in the family.

Production Company: Lee Rich Co., Amanda Prods. IAW Warner Bros. TV
Executive Producer .... Earl Hammer
Executive Producer .... Lee Rich
Executive Producer .... Bruce J. Sallan
Producer .... Sam Manners
Director .... Harry Harris
Writer .... Claire Whitaker
Writer .... Rod Peterson
Cast .... Richard Thomas
Cast .... Ralph Waite
Cast .... Michael Learned
Cast .... Judy Norton
Cast .... Mary McDonough

WAR AND REMEMBRANCE   ABC
EMMY WINNER
Miniseries/Drama (7 nights): Foreign or Exotic Location • Historical Piece • Nazis • Period Piece • WWII • Family Drama
Airdate: 11/13/88 • 11/15/88 • 11/16/88 • 11/17/88 • 11/20/88
Rating: 21.8/31 • 19.0/29 • 19.8/31 • 16.8/26 • 17.0/26   A/C:

Based on Herman Wouk's novel. Epic story of WWII and its effects on the family of Navy officer Pug Henry.

Production Company: Dan Curtis Prods.
Executive Producer .... Dan Curtis
Producer .... Barbara Steele
Director .... Dan Curtis
Writer .... Earl W. Wallace
Writer .... Dan Curtis
Writer .... Herman Wouk
Cast .... Robert Mitchum
Cast .... John Gielgud
Cast .... Ian McShane
Cast .... Hart Bochner
Cast .... Robert Morley
Cast .... David Dukes
Cast .... Polly Bergen
Cast .... Jane Seymour
Cast .... Barry Bostwick
Cast .... Victoria Tennant
Cast .... John Rhys-Davies

WAR AND REMEMBRANCE, PART II ABC

Miniseries/Drama (5 nights): Foreign or Exotic
Location • Historical Piece • Nazis • Period Piece •
WWII • Family Drama
Airdate: 05/07/89 • 05/08/89 • 05/09/89 • 05/10/89
• 05/14/89
Rating: 13.4/21 • 14.4/22 • 15.1/24 • 15.7/25 • 15.9/
26   A/C:

*Based on the book by Herman Woulk. The saga
of the Henry family continues through the end
of WWII.*

Production Company: Dan Curtis Prods.

Executive Producer	Dan Curtis
Producer	Barbara Steele
Director	Dan Curtis
Writer	Earl W. Wallace
Writer	Dan Curtis
Writer	Herman Wouk
Cast	Robert Mitchum
Cast	John Gielgud
Cast	Jane Seymour
Cast	Hart Bochner
Cast	Victoria Tennant
Cast	David Dukes

WARM HEARTS, COLD FEET   CBS

Comedy: Romantic Comedy • Woman's Issue/Story
Airdate: 01/18/87
Rating: 15.1/22   A/C:

*A married couple who are rival newspaper
columnists narrate the course of their having a
baby, from conception through delivery.*

Production Company: Lorimar

Executive Producer	Bonnie Raskin
Executive Producer	Andrew Adelson
Director	James Frawley
Writer	Allen Estrin
Writer	Mark Estrin
Cast	Tim Matheson
Cast	Margaret Colin
Cast	Elizabeth Ashley
Cast	Barry Corbin

WATER ENGINE, THE   TNT

Drama: Period Piece • Man Against The System
Airdate: 08/05/92
Rating: N/A   A/C:

*Based on the play by David Mamet. In the
1930's, a genius inventor who inadvertently
revolutionizes manufacturing technology
discovers the dark side of American big
business bent on preserving the status quo.*

Production Company: TNT, Amblin Entertainment
and Michael Brandman Prods.

Producer	Michael Brandman
Director	Steven Schachter
Writer	David Mamet
Cast	Bill Macy
Cast	Treat Williams
Cast	Joe Mantegna
Cast	Patti Lupone

WE ARE THE CHILDREN   ABC

Drama: Love Story • Foreign or Exotic Location •
Social Issue
Airdate: 03/16/87
Rating: 9.1/14   A/C:

*A doctor and a journalist fall in love amidst
the Ethiopian famine as they participate in relief
efforts.*

Production Company: Paulist Pictures IAW Dan
    Fauci/Ted Danson Prods. & Furia Organiz.

Executive Producer	Rev. Ellwood Kieser
Producer	Michael Rhodes
Producer	Lewis Abel
Co-Producer	Ted Danson
Co-Producer	Dan Fauci
Director	Robert Young
Writer	Michael De Guzman
Cast	Ally Sheedy
Cast	Judith Ivey
Cast	Khadija Ali Ahmed
Cast	Ted Danson

WEB OF DECEIT   USA

Drama: Murder and Murder Mystery • Woman
Against The System • Woman In Jeopardy • Suspense/
Thriller • Courtroom Drama
Airdate: 10/17/90
Rating: N/A   A/C:

*A San Francisco attorney, returning to Atlanta
to defend an innocent mechanic accused of rape
and murder reveals a cover-up by wealthy
power brokers of the real murderer.*

Production Company: Sankan Productions for
    Wilshire Court Productions

Executive Producer	Sandor Stern
Producer	Robert Rolsky
Director	Sandor Stern
Writer	Sandor Stern
Cast	Linda Purl
Cast	James Read
Cast	Paul De Souza
Cast	Barbara Rush

WEB OF DECEPTION   NBC

Drama: Murder and Murder Mystery • Psychological
Thriller
Airdate: 4/25/94
Rating: 10.7/17   A/C: 3

*A forensic psychiatrist, whose marriage is
falling apart, is framed for the murder of a
young woman who is obsessed with him. When
he rebuffs her, she commits suicide, staging it
to appear that they were having an affair and
that he killed her. With little support from his
family and the detectives assigned to the case
he eventually proves his innocence in a
contentious trial.*

Production Company: Morgan Hill Films IAW
    Hearst Entertainment

Executive Producer	Jennifer Alward
Producer	Carol Trussell
Co-Producer	Nevin Schreiner
Co-Producer	Fran Bell
Director	Richard Colla
Writer	Nevin Schreiner
Cast	Powers Boothe
Cast	Pam Dawber
Cast	Lisa Collins
Cast	Rosalind Chao

WEEKEND WAR   ABC

Drama: Action/Adventure • Foreign or Exotic
Location
Airdate: 02/01/88
Rating: 14.9/24   A/C:

*California National Guardsmen temporarily
posted to Honduras to repair an airstrip,
instead find themselves embroiled in a power
struggle over a bridge linking Honduras and
Nicaragua.*

Production Company: Pompian/Atamian Prods.
    IAW Columbia Pictures TV

Executive Producer	Paul Pompian
Executive Producer	Gil Atamian
Co-Producer	Gregory Widen
Director	Steven H. Stern
Writer	Dennis Hackin
Writer	Steven Hackin
Writer	Gregory Widen
Cast	Daniel Stern
Cast	James Tolkan
Cast	Charles Kimbrough
Cast	Charles Haid
Cast	Stephen Collins

WELCOME HOME, BOBBY   CBS
Drama: Family Drama • Homosexuality • Children/ Teens
Airdate: 02/17/86
Rating: 12.5/21   A/C:

A teenager faces ostracism after his drug arrest reveals his sexual relationship with a man.

Production Company: Titus Prods. Inc.
Executive Producer .... Herbert Brodkin
Executive Producer .... Robert Berger
Producer .... Thomas De Wolfe
Producer .... Cyma Rubin
Director .... Herbert Wise
Writer .... Conrad Bromberg
Cast .... Timothy Williams
Cast .... John Karlen
Cast .... John Pleshette
Cast .... Tony Lo Bianco

WET GOLD   ABC
Drama: Foreign or Exotic Location • Action/ Adventure
Airdate: 10/28/84
Rating: 18.3/30   A/C:

After hearing a story from an old sailor about sunken gold, a waitress convinces a friend to hunt for the treasure. Soon enough, greed and avarice threaten the expedition.

Production Company: Telepictures Prods.
Executive Producer .... Frank Konigsberg
Executive Producer .... Larry Sanitsky
Producer .... Bill Coker
Director .... Dick Lowry
Writer .... David Sherwin
Writer .... Otis Jones
Cast .... Brooke Shields
Cast .... Burgess Meredith
Cast .... Tom Byrd
Cast .... Brian Kerwin

WHAT EVER HAPPENED TO BABY JANE?   ABC
Drama: Psychological Thriller • Family Violence • Hollywood
Airdate: 02/17/91
Rating: 9.9/15   A/C: 3

Based on the novel by Henry Farrell and remake of the 1962 feature film. A faded film queen, now invalid, fights to survive the sadistic abuses of her demented jealous, former child-actress sister.

Production Company: Steve White Prods. IAW Alrich Group and Spectacor
Executive Producer .... William Aldrich
Executive Producer .... Steve White
Producer .... Barry Bernardi
Director .... David Greene
Writer .... Brian Taggert
Cast .... Vanessa Redgrave
Cast .... Lynn Redgrave
Cast .... John Glover
Cast .... Bruce A. Young

WHAT PRICE VICTORY?   ABC
Drama: Social Issue • Sports
Airdate: 01/18/88
Rating: 10.8/17   A/C:

A fanatical, rich alumnus and a victory-hungry college football coach use money and intimidation to mold a winning football team, with unfortunate results. The players are forced to compete, despite life-theatening injuries and stress.

Production Company: David L. Wolper Prods. IAW Warner Bros. TV
Executive Producer .... David L. Wolper
Executive Producer .... Bernard Sofronski
Producer .... Mark M. Wolper
Director .... Kevin Connor
Writer .... David Eyre, Jr.
Cast .... Robert Culp
Cast .... Susan Hess
Cast .... Nicholas Guest
Cast .... Warren Berlinger
Cast .... George Kennedy
Cast .... Mac Davis

WHAT SHE DOESN'T KNOW   NBC
Drama: Family Drama • Murder and Murder Mystery • Woman Against The System • Mafia/Mob
Airdate: 02/23/92
Rating: 16.6/25   A/C: 1

While investigating a Mafia kingpin, a female DA learns that her detective-father is linked to police corruption and that he used dirty money to put her through Harvard Law School.

Production Company: Two Short Prods. IAW Republic Pictures
Executive Producer .... Laurie Levit
Producer .... Jay Benson
Co-Producer .... Tim Stack
Director .... Kevin James Dobson
Writer .... Andy Tennant
Cast .... Valerie Bertinelli
Cast .... George Dzundza
Cast .... Peter Dobson

WHEELS OF TERROR   USA
Drama: Psychological Thriller • Woman In Jeopardy
Airdate: 07/11/90
Rating: N/A   A/C:

No one believes a school bus driver who says her twelve year old daughter has been kidnapped by a menacing black automobile, so the woman must save her daughter herself.

Production Company: Once Upon A Time/ Wilshire Court
Executive Producer .... Stanley Brooks
Producer .... Richard Learman
Producer .... Mike Cheda
Director .... Chris Cain
Writer .... Alan McElroy
Cast .... Joanna Cassidy
Cast .... Marcie Leeds
Cast .... Arlen Dean Snyder
Cast .... Carlos Cervantes

WHEN A STRANGER CALLS BACK   SHOWTIME
Drama: Suspense/Thriller • Woman In Jeopardy
Airdate: 4/4/93
Rating: N/A   A/C:

Sequel to the 1979 feature "When A Stranger Calls". A woman who was once stalked by a killer is now running a women's crisis center at a major university. When a student is being terrorized, in an all too familiar pattern, she enlists the aid of the police detective who saved her life thirteen years earlier. Together they track down the madman.

Production Company: Krost/Chapin Prods. Producers Ent. Group, MTE
Executive Producer .... Doug Chapin
Executive Producer .... Barry Krost
Producer .... Tom Rowe
Director .... Fred Walton
Writer .... Fred Walton
Cast .... Jill Schoelan
Cast .... Carol Kane
Cast .... Charles Durning
Cast .... Gene Lythgow

WHEN DREAMS COME TRUE   ABC
Drama: Murder and Murder Mystery • Cops/ Detectives/Law Enforcement • Psychological Thriller
Airdate: 05/28/85
Rating: 12.8/21   A/C:

A woman is plagued by premonitional dreams which later become true. Meanwhile, her cop boyfriend tries to shake down a serial killer, who happens to appear in her dreams.

Production Company: I & C Prods.
Executive Producer .... Gerald I. Isenberg
Producer .... Hans Proppe
Director .... John Llewellyn Moxey
Writer .... William Bleich
Cast .... Cindy Williams
Cast .... Jessica Harper
Cast .... Stan Shaw
Cast .... Lee Horsley
Cast .... Norma Young

WHEN HE'S NOT A STRANGER   CBS
Drama: Woman Against The System • Rape/ Molestation • Woman's Issue/Story • Social Issue
Airdate: 11/06/89
Rating: 17.2/26   A/C: 2

A shy college freshman is raped by an acquaintance, the school's football star, after a party. Ostracized by her peers and school authorities when she presses charges, she is forced to seek redress in court.

Production Company: Ohlmeyer Communications
Executive Producer .... Don Ohlmeyer
Producer .... Karen Danaher-Dorr
Producer .... Ian Sander
Director .... John Gray
Writer .... John Gray
Writer .... Beth Sullivan
Cast .... Annabeth Gish
Cast .... John Terlesky
Cast .... Kevin Dillon
Cast .... Kim Meyers
Cast .... Paul Dooley

When Love Kills: The Seduction Of John Hearn — CBS

Miniseries/Drama (2 nights): True Crime
Airdate: 5/18/93 • 5/19/93
Rating: 9.9/16 • 9.5/16   A/C: 3 • 3

Based on the book, "The Soldier Of Fortune Murders" by Ben Green. When Vietnam vet and bodyguard, John Hearn, puts an ad in Soldier of Fortune Magazine it is answered by a seductive woman wanting him to kill her sister's husband. Refusing her initial request, Hearn soon falls victim to her passion and proceeds to do her murderous bidding at any cost.

Production Company: Harvey Kahn Prods.,
    Alexander-Enright & Assoc., McGillen Ent.
Executive Producer .... Les Alexander
Executive Producer .... Patricia Clifford
Executive Producer .... James McGillen
Executive Producer .... Don Enright
Producer .... Harvey Kahn
Director .... Larry Elikann
Writer .... Gregory Goodell
Cast .... Marg Helgenberger
Cast .... Gary Cole
Cast .... Julie Harris
Cast .... Michael Jeter
Cast .... Shirley Knight

When No One Would Listen — CBS

Drama: Family Violence • Woman's Issue/Story •
Social Issue • True Story
Airdate: 11/15/92
Rating: 12.9/19   A/C: 3

A battered wife and mother attempts to escape from her irrational and violent husband. When she finally flees, his homicidal rage intensifies which culminates in holding her hostage.

Production Company: Bruce Sallan Prods. IAW
    Michele Lee Prods., Papazina-Hirsch Ent. &
    Canal Plus
Executive Producer .... Michele Lee
Co-Executive Producer .... Jerry Reger
Director .... Armand Mastroianni
Writer .... Cindy Myers
Cast .... Michele Lee
Cast .... James Farentino
Cast .... John Spencer
Cast .... Lee Garlington

When the Bough Breaks — NBC

Drama: Cops/Detectives/Law Enforcement •
Suspense/Thriller • Children/Teens • Rape/
Molestation
Airdate: 10/12/86
Rating: 22.3/36   A/C:

Based on Jonathan Kellerman's prize-winning novel. A sensitive cop and a child psychologist interviewing a child witness to murder uncover an upscale group of child molesters.

Production Company: TDF Prods. IAW Taft
    Entertainment TV
Executive Producer .... Ted Danson
Executive Producer .... Dan Fauci
Producer .... Rick Husky
Co-Producer .... Ken Koch
Director .... Waris Hussein
Writer .... Phil Penningroth
Cast .... Ted Danson
Cast .... Richard Masur
Cast .... James Noble
Cast .... Kim Miyori
Cast .... David Huddleston

When the Time Comes — ABC

Drama: Family Drama • Medical/Disease/Mental
Illness • Social Issue
Airdate: 05/25/87
Rating: 11.1/18   A/C:

A thirty-four year old woman, suffering greatly as she dies of cancer, attempts to hasten her own death despite the refusal of her husband to help.

Production Company: Jaffe/Lansing Prods. IAW
    Republic Pictures Corp.
Executive Producer .... Sherry Lansing
Executive Producer .... William Hanley
Producer .... John Erman
Co-Producer .... Cyrus Yavneh
Director .... John Erman
Writer .... William Hanley
Cast .... Bonnie Bedelia
Cast .... Judith Doty
Cast .... Mike Shanks
Cast .... Brad Davis

When We Were Young — NBC

Drama: Family Drama • Children/Teens • Period
Piece • Series Pilot (2 hr.)
Airdate: 07/17/89
Rating: 10.9/19   A/C:

A group of eight "Class of 1959" California high school graduates share dreams and fears as they face the future.

Production Company: A Richard and Esther
    Shapiro Entertainment Inc. Production
Executive Producer .... Richard Shapiro
Executive Producer .... Esther Shapiro
Producer .... George Eckstein
Director .... Daryl Duke
Writer .... Richard Shapiro
Writer .... Esther Shapiro
Cast .... Jace Alexander
Cast .... Lindsay Frost
Cast .... Cynthia Gibb

When Will I Be Loved? — NBC

Drama: Woman's Issue/Story
Airdate: 12/03/90
Rating: 12.6/19   A/C: 3

Three very different women meet in a divorce attorney's office and loyally support each other through their respective separations and reconciliations.

Production Company: Nederlander Television and
    Film Prods.
Executive Producer .... Gladys Nederlander
Executive Producer .... Winifred Gorlin
Producer .... Michael Tadross
Director .... Michael Tuchner
Writer .... Nancy Sackett
Cast .... Stefanie Powers
Cast .... Katherine Helmond
Cast .... Crystal Bernard
Cast .... Christopher Meloni

When You Remember Me — ABC

Drama: Man Against The System • Children/Teens •
Medical/Disease/Mental Illness • True Story • Social
Issue
Airdate: 10/07/90
Rating: 14.6/24   A/C: 1

Based on an article by Rena Dictor LeBlanc. Teenager, Michael Patrick, afflicted with terminal muscular dystrophy, fights for the rights of disabled patients when he is abused in a state-run nursing facility.

Production Company: David L. Wolper Prod.;
    Bernard Sofronski and Warner Bros. TV
Executive Producer .... David L. Wolper
Executive Producer .... Bernard Sofronski
Producer .... Vahan Moosekian
Director .... Harry Winer
Writer .... Jerry McNeely
Writer .... Cynthia Whitcomb
Cast .... Fred Savage
Cast .... Kevin Spacey
Cast .... Ellen Burstyn
Cast .... Richard Jenkins

Where Pigeons Go To Die — NBC

Drama: Family Drama • Children/Teens • Period
Piece
Airdate: 01/29/90
Rating: 15.3/24   A/C: 1

Based on the book by R. Wright Campbell. A sentimental tale about a man who returns to sell his grandfather's house and reminisces about how he and his grandfather trained and raced pigeons during the 1940's.

Production Company: Michael Landon
    Productions IAW World International Net.
Executive Producer .... Michael Landon
Producer .... Kent McCray
Director .... Michael Landon
Writer .... Michael Landon
Cast .... Art Carney
Cast .... Cliff De Young
Cast .... Robert Gorman
Cast .... Ronnie Troup

WHERE THE HELL'S THAT GOLD   CBS
Comedy: Western
Airdate: 11/13/88
Rating: 12.1/18   A/C:

Broad adventures of two old cowboys wanted on both sides of the Mexican border.

Production Company: Willie Nelson Prods. & Brigade Prods. with Konigsberg/Sanitsky Co.
Producer .... Burt Kennedy
Director .... Burt Kennedy
Writer .... Burt Kennedy
Cast .... Willie Nelson
Cast .... Delta Burke
Cast .... Jack Elam
Cast .... Gerald McRaney

WHEREABOUTS OF JENNY, THE   ABC
Drama: Family Drama • Man Against The System • Children/Teens • Social Issue
Airdate: 01/14/91
Rating: 15.4/24   A/C: 1

A divorced father battles the FBI to gain custody of his daughter when she is secretly sequestered with her mother in the federal witness-relocation program.

Production Company: Katie Face Prods. IAW Columbia Pictures TV
Executive Producer .... Tony Danza
Executive Producer .... Steve Sauer
Producer .... Gene Reynolds
Co-Producer .... Michael Swerdlick
Director .... Gene Reynolds
Writer .... John Miglis
Cast .... Ed O'Neill
Cast .... Debrah Farentino
Cast .... Mike Farrell
Cast .... Eve Gordon
Cast .... Dan Hedaya

WHICH WAY HOME   TNT
Drama (3 hours): Woman Against The System • Children/Teens • Action/Adventure • Historical Piece • Foreign or Exotic Location • Vietnam
Airdate: 01/28/91
Rating: N/A   A/C:

An American nurse in 1979 Cambodia leads young orphans through the country on a boat captained by a drunken smuggler.

Production Company: McElroy and McElroy IAW Television New Zealand
Executive Producer .... Hal McElroy
Director .... Carl Schultz
Writer .... Michael Laurence
Cast .... Cybill Shepherd
Cast .... John Waters
Cast .... Peta Toppana
Cast .... John Ewart

WHISPER KILLS, A   ABC
Drama: Murder and Murder Mystery • Suspense/Thriller
Airdate: 05/16/88
Rating: 14.7/23   A/C:

A reporter gets to the bottom of a series of stranglings that follow phone threats in a small California town.

Production Company: Sandy Hook Prods., Steve Tisch Co. & Phoenix Entertainment Group
Producer .... Hans Proppe
Co-Producer .... Jody Brockway
Director .... Christian Nyby II
Writer .... John Robert Bensink
Cast .... Loni Anderson
Cast .... Joe Penny
Cast .... James Sutorius
Cast .... June Lockhart
Cast .... Jeremy Slate

WHITE HOT: THE MYSTERIOUS MURDER OF THELMA TODD   NBC
Drama: Murder and Murder Mystery • Period Piece • Hollywood • Mafia/Mob
Airdate: 05/05/91
Rating: 12.3/20   A/C: 2

Based on the book "Hot Todddy" by Andy Edwards. A speculative account that attempts to solve the mysterious, mob-related murder of glamorous '30s film star Thelma Todd.

Production Company: Sandy Hook Prods./Neufeld Keating Prods. IAW Von Zerneck-Sertner
Executive Producer .... Frank Von Zerneck
Executive Producer .... Robert M. Sertner
Producer .... Julie Anne Weitz
Co-Executive Producer .... Mace Neufeld
Co-Executive Producer .... Doris Keating
Director .... Paul Wendkos
Writer .... Robert E. Thompson
Writer .... Lindsay Harrison
Cast .... Loni Anderson
Cast .... Robert Davi
Cast .... Lawrence Pressman
Cast .... Scott Paulin

WHITE LIE   USA
Drama: Black Story • Social Issue
Airdate: 09/25/91
Rating: N/A   A/C:

Based on the book "Louisiana Black" by Samuel Charter. A black New York City political aide travels back to his rural hometown in Georgia to search out the truth behind the lynching of his father, who was accused of raping a white woman in 1957.

Production Company: Alan Barnette Prods. IAW MCA Television Entertainment
Executive Producer .... Larry Thompson
Producer .... Kevin Inch
Executive Producer .... Alan Barnette
Producer .... Oscar L. Costo
Director .... Anson Williams
Director .... Bill Condon
Writer .... Janis Hirsch
Writer .... Nevin Schreiner
Cast .... Ann Jillian
Cast .... Tim Matheson
Cast .... Gregory Hines
Cast .... Annette O'Toole
Cast .... Bill Nunn
Cast .... Gregg Henry

WHITE MILE   HBO
Drama: Action/Adventure
Airdate: 5/21/94
Rating: N/A   A/C:

A ruthless, competitive advertising executive organizes a rugged white water river rafting expedition for his staff and clients, which he thinks will toughen them up for future negotiations. The trip proves fatal for several of the participants and the widow of one of the men sues the agency for damages. Showing little concern for the grieving woman he defends himself and his agency in a tough and aggressive manner.

Production Company: Stonehenge Prods.
Executive Producer .... Dick Berg
Executive Producer .... Allan Marcil
Co-Executive Producer .... Bob Tamarkin
Co-Executive Producer .... Michael Hamilburg
Co-Executive Producer .... Ilene Kahn
Producer .... Anthony Croce
Director .... Robert Butler
Writer .... Michael Butler
Cast .... Alan Alda
Cast .... Robert Loggia
Cast .... Peter Gallagher
Cast .... Fionnula Flanagan

WHO GETS THE FRIENDS?   CBS

Comedy: Woman's Issue/Story
Airdate: 05/10/88
Rating: 11.1/19   A/C:

A longtime married woman, suddenly facing divorce, notices that the friends she thought were hers are actually her husband's.

Production Company: CBS Entertainment Prods.
Producer .... Lila Garrett
Director .... Lila Garrett
Writer .... Lila Garrett
Writer .... Sandy Krinski
Cast .... Jill Clayburgh
Cast .... James Farentino
Cast .... Leigh Taylor-Young
Cast .... Lucie Arnaz
Cast .... Greg Mullavey

WHO IS JULIA?   CBS

Drama: Medical/Disease/Mental Illness • Sci-Fi/Supernatural/Horror/Fantasy
Airdate: 10/26/86
Rating: 18.4/29   A/C:

Based on the novel by Barbara S. Davis. A woman whose brain is damaged as she is rescuing a child receives a brain transplant from the dead mother of the child she saved. She and the husbands of both women must now try to figure out exactly who she is.

Production Company: CBS Entertainment Prods.
Producer .... Phillip Barry
Producer .... Andrew J. Fenady
Director .... Walter Grauman
Writer .... James Sadwith
Cast .... Mare Winningham
Cast .... Ford Rainey
Cast .... Bert Remsen
Cast .... Jonathan Banks
Cast .... Jameson Parker

WHOSE CHILD IS THIS? THE WAR FOR BABY JESSICA   ABC

Drama: Family Drama • Children/Teens • True Story • Social Issue
Airdate: 9/26/93
Rating: 9.6/15   A/C: 3

Based on an article by Lucinda Franks. A highly publicized, two year custody battle ensues when the courts order Jan and Robby DeBoer to return their adopted two year old daughter to her birth parents. It is revealed that the father, Dan Schmidt, who was not married to the birth mother, Cara Clausen, at the time she gave the child up, never consented to the adoption. In 1993, the child was taken from a stable, loving home to a unknown, troubled household.

Production Company: Sofronski Prods. IAW ABC Prods.
Executive Producer .... Bernard Sofronski
Executive Producer .... Dale Andrews
Producer .... Robert Frederick
Director .... John Kent Harrison
Writer .... Jacqueline Feather
Writer .... David Seidler
Cast .... Susan Dey
Cast .... Michael Ontkean
Cast .... Amanda Plummer
Cast .... David Keith

WIFE, MOTHER, MURDERER   ABC

Drama: Murder and Murder Mystery • True Crime • Family Drama
Airdate: 11/10/91
Rating: 15.6/24   A/C: 1(TIE)

In 1975, Marie Hilley from Anniston, Alabama, poisons her husband, attempts to poison her daughter, flees and remarries under an assumed name. Later, she disappears and reappears as her own twin, ending with her capture and trial in 1986.

Production Company: Wilshire Court Productions Inc.
Producer .... Diana Kerew
Producer .... Maj Canton
Director .... Mel Damski
Writer .... David Eyre, Jr.
Cast .... Judith Light
Cast .... David Ogden Stiers
Cast .... Kellie Overbey
Cast .... David Dukes

WILD CARD   USA

Drama: Murder and Murder Mystery
Airdate: 10/28/92
Rating: N/A   A/C:

Based on the book "Preacher" by Ted Thackrey Jr. A one-eyed gambler comes to a small Texas town to find the real cause of an old friends "accidental" death. Nosing around and asking too many questions upset the local powerbrokers who see to it that he is made to feel "unwelcomed". Pursuing the case ultimately leads to the real killer and the exposure of widespread corruption.

Production Company: Davis Ent.
Executive Producer .... John Davis
Executive Producer .... Merrill H. Karpf
Director .... Mel Damski
Writer .... Scobie Richardson
Cast .... Powers Boothe
Cast .... Cindy Pickett
Cast .... Rene Auberjonois
Cast .... Terry O'Quinn

WILD HORSES   CBS

Drama: Man Against The System • Action/Adventure • Farm Story
Airdate: 11/12/85
Rating: 16.7/26   A/C:

A former rodeo champ goes to Wyoming for one last roundup and runs into trouble when he encounters corrupt government officials involved with the wild horses.

Production Company: Wild Horse Prods. IAW Telepictures
Executive Producer .... Ken Kragen
Executive Producer .... Dick Lowry
Producer .... Hunt Lowry
Director .... Dick Lowry
Writer .... Daniel Vining
Writer .... Roderick Taylor
Cast .... Pam Dawber
Cast .... Kenny Rogers
Cast .... Richard Masur
Cast .... David Andrews
Cast .... Ben Johnson

WILD PALMS — ABC

Miniseries/Drama (4 nights): Sci-Fi/Supernatural/
Horror/Fantasy
Airdate: 5/16/93 • 5/17/93 • 5/18/93 • 5/19/93
Rating: 12.3/20 • 9.7/25 • 11.0/19 • 9.9/17
A/C: 2 • 3 • 2 • 2

In the year 2007, murder, mystery and secret societies emerge as a earnest Los Angeles lawyer goes to work for a messianic political leader who runs a Scientology like cult and is out to launch his own virtual reality TV network.

Production Company: Ixlan Corp. IAW
     Greengrass Prods.
Executive Producer .... Oliver Stone
Executive Producer .... Bruce Wagner
Producer .... Michael Rauch
Director .... Peter Hewitt
Director .... Keith Gordon
Director .... Kathryn Bigelow
Director .... Phil Joanou
Writer .... Bruce Wagner
Cast .... James Belushi
Cast .... Dana Delany
Cast .... Robert Loggia
Cast .... Angie Dickinson
Cast .... Ernie Hudson

WILD TEXAS WIND — NBC

Drama: Family Drama • Murder and Murder Mystery
• Family Violence • Woman's Issue/Story • Social
Issue
Airdate: 09/23/91
Rating: 18.0/27   A/C: 3

A country and western singer falls in love with her sweet-talking manager who turns out to be abusive and violent. When he turns up murdered, she takes the rap to protect a life-long friend.

Production Company: Sandollar Television Inc.
Executive Producer .... Sandy Gallin
Executive Producer .... Dolly Parton
Executive Producer .... Candace Ferrell
Producer .... Richard L. O'Connor
Director .... Joan Tewkesbury
Writer .... John Carlen
Cast .... Dolly Parton
Cast .... Gary Busey
Cast .... Ray Benson
Cast .... Willie Nelson

WILDFLOWER — LIFETIME

Drama: Family Drama • Period Piece • Children/
Teens
Airdate: 12/03/91
Rating: N/A   A/C:

Based on the novel "Alice" by Sara Flanigan. In 1938 rural Georgia, a hearing-impaired, epileptic girl is brutalized by her ignorant stepfather who believes she's possessed by the devil. She is rescued by two teenagers who introduce her to the world, awakening her sense of compassion and trust.

Production Company: Freed-Laufer, Carroll
     Newman Prods., Polone Co. IAW Heart Enter.
Executive Producer .... Judith A. Polone
Executive Producer .... Richard Freed
Executive Producer .... Ira Laufer
Producer .... Carroll Newman
Co-Producer .... Dennis Murphy
Co-Producer .... Joseph Kelly
Director .... Diane Keaton
Writer .... Sara Flanigan
Cast .... Beau Bridges
Cast .... Susan Blakely
Cast .... Patricia Arquette
Cast .... William McNamara
Cast .... Reese Witherspoon

WILLING TO KILL: THE TEXAS CHEERLEADER STORY — ABC

Drama: True Crime • Family Drama • Children/Teens
Airdate: 11/8/92
Rating: 14.4/22   A/C: 2

In 1991, Wanda Holloway a Channelview, Texas homemaker conspires to have Verna Heath, the mother of her daughter's cheerleading rival murdered. Convinced this will advance her child's career and fulfill her dreams, she tries to get her unsavory former brother-in -law to hire a hit man. She is turned in and later convicted of solicitation for capital murder but is currently out on bond due to a mistrial.

Production Company: Stockton Briggle Prods.
     IAW David Eagle Prods. & Papazian-Hirsch
     Ent.
Executive Producer .... Stockton Briggle
Executive Producer .... David Eagle
Executive Producer .... Robert A. Papazian
Executive Producer .... James G. Hirsch
Producer .... Alan Stepp
Director .... David Greene
Writer .... Alan Hines
Cast .... Lesley Ann Warren
Cast .... Tess Harper
Cast .... Lauren Woodland
Cast .... Dennis Christopher

WINDMILLS OF THE GODS — CBS

Miniseries/Drama (2 nights): Love Story • Suspense/
Thriller • Foreign or Exotic Location
Airdate: 02/07/88 • 02/08/88
Rating: 19.0/28 • 17.3/27   A/C:

Based on Sidney Sheldon's best seller. A female professor, appointed ambassador to Rumania, must figure out who are the bad guys—who are trying to poison her—and who are the good guys while surrounded by international intrigue.

Production Company: Dove Inc. IAW ITC
     Entertainment Group
Executive Producer .... Sidney Sheldon
Producer .... Michael Viner
Co-Producer .... Deborah Raffin
Director .... Lee Philips
Writer .... John Gay
Cast .... Jaclyn Smith
Cast .... Ruby Dee
Cast .... Robert Wagner
Cast .... Franco Nero
Cast .... Christopher Cazenove
Cast .... David Ackroyd
Cast .... Jean Pierre Aumont

WINNER NEVER QUITS, A — ABC

Drama: Period Piece • Biography • Sports • True Story
Airdate: 04/14/86
Rating: 14.6/24   A/C:

Fact-based story of Pete Gray, who pitched in the major leagues in the 1940s despite having just one arm.

Production Company: Blatt/Singer Prods. IAW
     Columbia Pictures TV
Executive Producer .... Daniel H. Blatt
Executive Producer .... Robert Singer
Producer .... James Keach
Producer .... Lynn Raynor
Director .... Mel Damski
Writer .... Burt Prelutsky
Cast .... Keith Carradine
Cast .... Mare Winningham
Cast .... G.W. Bailey
Cast .... David Haid

WINNIE — NBC

Drama: Medical/Disease/Mental Illness • True Story
• Social Issue
Airdate: 10/10/88
Rating: 16.6/28   A/C:

Fact-based life story of a mildly retarded Iowa woman who longs to leave her institution-home. She and her boyfriend run away and learn that the real world can be both exhilarating and frightening before they are brought back by the police.

Production Company: All Girl Prods. IAW NBC
     Prods.
Executive Producer .... Michael Manheim
Producer .... Andrea Baynes
Director .... John Korty
Writer .... Joyce Eliason
Cast .... Meredith Baxter
Cast .... Peggy McCay
Cast .... David Morse
Cast .... Barbara Barrie

WITH A VENGEANCE   CBS
Drama: Woman In Jeopardy
Airdate: 9/22/92
Rating: 14.7/23   A/C: 2

A amnesiac, working as a nanny for a divorced lawyer, is stalked by a psychopathic whose grisly crime she witnessed six years earlier. With the love and support of her employer and his son she is able to face her horrifying past and out wit the crazed killer.

Production Company: Citadel Pictures
Executive Producer .... David R. Ginsburg
Co-Executive Producer .... Harry Longstreet
Co-Executive Producer .... Renee Longstreet
Producer .... Michael O. Gallant
Director .... Michael Switzer
Writer .... Renee Longstreet
Cast .... Melissa Gilbert
Cast .... Jack Scalia
Cast .... Matthew Lawrence
Cast .... Michael Gross

WITH HOSTILE INTENT   CBS
Drama: Cops/Detectives/Law Enforcement • Woman Against The System • True Story • Woman's Issue/Story
Airdate: 5/11/93
Rating: 12.9/21   A/C: 3

After an extended period of sexual harassment, two Long Beach, California, female police officers bring suit against their male colleagues. The ensuing trial causes both woman intense personal and emotional turmoil.

Production Company: CBS Ent. Prods.
Executive Producer .... Andrew Lack
Producer .... Vanessa Greene
Director .... Paul Schneider
Writer .... Marjorie David
Writer .... Alison Cross
Cast .... Mel Harris
Cast .... Melissa Gilbert
Cast .... Peter Onorati
Cast .... Cotter Smith

WITH INTENT TO KILL   CBS
Drama: Suspense/Thriller • Murder and Murder Mystery
Airdate: 10/24/84
Rating: 11.8/19   A/C:

A young man is put into a mental institution after pleading insanity in the killing of his girlfriend. Four years later he returns to his home town and must deal with the victim's angry father.

Production Company: London Prods.
Executive Producer .... Jerry London
Producer .... Lee Rafner
Director .... Mike Robe
Writer .... Mike Robe
Cast .... Paul Sorvino
Cast .... Shirley Knight
Cast .... Karl Malden
Cast .... Catherine Mary Stewart
Cast .... Holly Hunter
Cast .... Timothy Patrick Murphy

WITH MURDER IN MIND   CBS
Drama: Woman Against The System • True Crime
Airdate: 05/12/92
Rating: 13.3/21   A/C: 2

Gayle Wolfer, a successful real estate agent in a small town near Buffalo is brutally attacked and shot. Shattered, she becomes obsessed with bringing her assailant, a black deputy sheriff, to trial, almost destroying her family relationships.

Production Company: Helios Prods. IAW Bob Banner Assoc.
Executive Producer .... Joseph Maurer
Executive Producer .... Bradley Wigor
Producer .... Robert Huddleston
Director .... Michael Tuchner
Writer .... Daniel Freudenberger
Cast .... Elizabeth Montgomery
Cast .... Robert Foxworth
Cast .... Howard E. Rollins, Jr.
Cast .... Maureen O'Sullivan

WITHOUT A KISS GOODBYE   CBS
Drama: Woman Against The System • True Crime • Medical/Disease/Mental Illness • Children/Teens
Airdate: 3/21/93
Rating: 17.2/29   A/C: 1

A mother faces an emotional and legal nightmare when she is accused and convicted of poisoning her infant with antifreeze. While in prison she finds that she is pregnant and gives birth to a second son who becomes ill with the same symptoms as her first child. The baby is diagnosed with a rare genetic disorder called MMA which mimics antifreeze poisoning. Through the efforts of her husband and a determined lawyer she eventually wins her freedom.

Production Company: Green/Epstein Prods.
Executive Producer .... Jim Green
Executive Producer .... Allen Epstein
Producer .... Mark Bacino
Co-Executive Producer .... Dan Schrier
Director .... Noel Nosseck
Writer .... James Duff
Cast .... Lisa Hartman
Cast .... Christopher Meloni
Cast .... Cloris Leachman
Cast .... David Ogden Stiers

WITHOUT HER CONSENT   NBC
Drama: Courtroom Drama • Rape/Molestation • Woman's Issue/Story • Woman Against The System
Airdate: 01/14/90
Rating: 17.8/28   A/C: 1 (Tie)

After a young woman is raped by a charming and helpful acquaintance, she must suffer the anger of her boyfriend, insensitivities of the courts, and her own misplaced feelings of guilt.

Production Company: Raymond Katz Enterprises IAW Half Pint Prod. and Carla Singer Prod.
Executive Producer .... Raymond Katz
Executive Producer .... Carla Singer
Producer .... Frank Brill
Director .... Sandor Stern
Writer .... Ann Beckett
Cast .... Melissa Gilbert
Cast .... Scott Valentine
Cast .... Barry Tubb
Cast .... Bebe Neuwirth

WITHOUT WARNING: TERROR IN THE TOWERS   NBC
Drama: True Story • Disaster
Airdate: 5/26/93
Rating: 9.3/15   A/C: 3

The heroic efforts and individual dramas surrounding the terrorist bombing of New York City's 110-story World Trade Center on February 26,1993. The accounts include two grade school teacher and their class stuck in a suspended elevator, an office worker who carries a resentful paraplegic down 87 flights and a fireman trapped in a burning basement.

Production Company: Melniker Prods. , Wilshire Court Prods.
Executive Producer .... Charles Melniker
Executive Producer .... Madelson Rosenfeld
Producer .... Robert Rolsky
Producer .... Stephen Downing
Co-Producer .... Duane Poole
Director .... Alan J. Levi
Writer .... Stephen Downing
Writer .... Duane Poole
Cast .... James Avery
Cast .... Susan Ruttan
Cast .... Andre Braugher
Cast .... George Clooney

WITHOUT WARNING: THE JAMES BRADY STORY — HBO
Drama: Family Drama • Medical/Disease/Mental Illness • True Story • Social Issue
Airdate: 06/16/91
Rating: N/A   A/C:

Reagan White House press secretary James Brady is left brain-damaged after an assassination attempt in 1981. He and his wife, Sara, struggle through arduous therapy and ultimately fight for gun control through the passage of the "Brady Bill."

Production Company: HBO Pictures
Executive Producer .... David Puttnam
Producer .... Fred Berner
Director .... Michael Toshiyuki Uno
Writer .... Robert Bolt
Cast .... Beau Bridges
Cast .... Joan Allen
Cast .... Bryan Clark
Cast .... Steven Flynn

WITNESS TO THE EXECUTION — NBC
Drama: Social Issue
Airdate: 2/13/94
Rating: 12.2/17   A/C: 2

In 1999, a brazen television executive, under pressure from her greedy boss to increase revenues at the pay-per-view channel she works at, devises the event of the decade by televising a live execution. She selects a charismatic serial killer who, for a short time, convinces her that he just might be innocent. But the media frenzy and the public's demand for justice helps carry out the sensational execution.

Production Company: Frederick S. Pierce Co.
Executive Producer .... Frederick Pierce
Executive Producer .... Keith Pierce
Executive Producer .... Richard Pierce
Producer .... Casey Lee Justice
Director .... Tommy Lee Wallace
Writer .... Thomas Baum
Cast .... Sean Young
Cast .... Tim Daly
Cast .... Len Cariou
Cast .... Dee Wallace Stone

WOLF — CBS
Drama: Cops/Detectives/Law Enforcement • Drug Smuggling/Dealing • Series Pilot (2 hr.)
Airdate: 09/13/89
Rating: 14.2/25   A/C: 1

A San Francisco policeman unjustly fired reappears two years later. When he's asked to become a private detective, his client turns out to be the man who got him fired. In solving this new case, he clears himself.

Production Company: CBS Entertainment Prods.
Executive Producer .... Rod Holcomb
Executive Producer .... David Peckinpah
Producer .... Ken Swor
Director .... Rod Holcomb
Writer .... David Peckinpah
Cast .... Jack Scalia
Cast .... Mimi Kuzyk
Cast .... Nicolas Surovy
Cast .... Joseph Sirola

WOMAN HE LOVED, THE — CBS
Drama: Period Piece • Historical Piece • Biography • Love Story • Foreign or Exotic Location
Airdate: 04/03/88
Rating: 14.5/25   A/C:

The love story of Wallis Simpson and the man who became King Edward VIII only to abdicate to marry her, told from Mrs. Simpson's point of view.

Production Company: Larry A. Thompson Prods. IAW New World TV
Executive Producer .... Larry Thompson
Producer .... William Hill
Director .... Charles Jarrott
Writer .... William Luce
Cast .... Jane Seymour
Cast .... Anthony Andrews
Cast .... Julie Harris
Cast .... Olivia De Havilland
Cast .... Lucy Gutteridge

WOMAN NAMED JACKIE, A — NBC
EMMY WINNER
Miniseries/Drama (3 nights): Period Piece • Historical Piece • Biography • True Story
Airdate: 10/13/91 • 10/14/91 • 10/15/91
Rating: 15.5/23 • 18.6/28 • 19.1/30
A/C: 1 • 1 • 1

Based on the book by C. David Heymann. The life and times of the famous First Lady, including her privileged childhood, her engagement and marriage to JFK, her devotion to her children, and the troubled years with Aristotle Onassis.

Production Company: Lester Persky Productions
Executive Producer .... Lester Persky
Producer .... Lorin Salob
Co-Producer .... Tomlinson Dean
Director .... Larry Peerce
Writer .... Roger O. Hirson
Cast .... Stephen Collins
Cast .... William DeVane
Cast .... Roma Downey
Cast .... Rosemary Murphy

WOMAN ON THE LEDGE — NBC
Drama: Woman's Issue/Story
Airdate: 3/15/93
Rating: 15.6/24   A/C: 2

While standing on a ledge contemplating suicide an unidentified women recalls her friendship with her two best girlfriends who are all beset with troubling relationships and personal problems. Of the three women, which one is driven to end her life?

Production Company: Louis Rudolph Films, Fenton Ent. Fries Ent.
Executive Producer .... Louis Rudolph
Producer .... Robert Fenton
Director .... Chris Thomson
Writer .... Hal Sitowitz
Cast .... Deidre Hall
Cast .... Leslie Charleson
Cast .... Colleen Pinter
Cast .... Josh Taylor

WOMAN ON THE RUN: THE LAWRENCIA BEMBENEK STORY — NBC
Miniseries/Drama (2 nights): True Crime • Murder and Murder Mystery • Family Violence
Airdate: 5/16/93 • 5/17/93
Rating: 11.1/18 • 15.6/25   A/C: 3 • 1

Lawrencia Bembenek, the ex-model and former Milwaukee policewoman who was convicted in 1981 of killing her husband's ex-wife, then escaped from prison in 1990 and hid out in Canada where she was recaptured after being profiled on the TV show "America's Most Wanted". She steadfastly contends that she was framed by her police detective husband . She was paroled in December of 1992. Note: See ABC TV Movie- "Calendar Girl, Cop Killer?"

Production Company: Alliance Commications, CanWest Global TV IAW NBC Prods.
Executive Producer .... Robert Lantos
Executive Producer .... Michael Weisbarth
Producer .... Ian MacDougall
Director .... Sandor Stern
Writer .... Sandor Stern
Cast .... Tatum O'Neal
Cast .... Bruce Greenwood
Cast .... Peggy McCay
Cast .... Kenneth Welsh
Cast .... Colin Fox

WOMAN SCORNED: THE BETTY BRODERICK STORY, A — CBS
Drama: Family Drama • True Crime • Family Violence • Woman's Issue/Story
Airdate: 03/01/92
Rating: 19.5/30   A/C: 1

In 1989, San Diego socialite Betty Broderick's life becomes unraveled when her lawyer husband of sixteen years divorces her and marries his young assistant. Abandoned, feelings of anger and vindictiveness drive Betty to murder them in their bed.

Production Company: Patchett-Kaufman
Executive Producer .... Tom Patchett
Executive Producer .... Ken Kaufman
Producer .... Dick Lowry
Producer .... Ann Kindberg
Co-Producer .... Wendell Rawls
Director .... Dick Lowry
Writer .... Joe Cacaci
Cast .... Meredith Baxter
Cast .... Stephen Collins
Cast .... Michelle Johnson

MOVIES AND MINISERIES

WOMAN WHO LOVED ELVIS, THE   ABC
Drama: Family Drama
Airdate: 4/18/93
Rating: 12.1/20   A/C: 2

An eccentric single mother on welfare, harbors an obsession for Elvis Presley in which she turns her house into a gaudy shrine. When a prim young social worker is assigned to her case, both women come to realize that in order to find happiness they must give up unrealized fantasies and long held resentments.

Production Company: Wapello County Prods.
    IAW Grossbart/Barnett
Executive Producer .... Tom Arnold
Executive Producer .... Roseanne Arnold
Executive Producer .... Jack Grossbart
Executive Producer .... Joan Barnett
Producer .... Cyrus Yavneh
Director .... Bill Bixby
Writer .... Rita Mae Brown
Cast .... Roseanne Arnold
Cast .... Tom Arnold
Cast .... Sally Kirkland
Cast .... Cynthia Gibb

WOMAN WHO SINNED, THE   ABC
Drama: Murder and Murder Mystery • Forbidden Love • Sex/Glitz
Airdate: 11/17/91
Rating: 12.1/18   A/C: 3

A married woman indulges in an affair with a man who has, unknown to her, killed her best friend. In order to prove her innocence, she must confess the affair to her attorney husband who defends her when she is unjustly accused of the murder.

Production Company: World International
    Network IAW Samuels Film Co.
Executive Producer .... Stu Samuels
Producer .... Susan Weber-Gold
Director .... Michael Switzer
Writer .... Denne Petitclerc
Cast .... Susan Lucci
Cast .... Tim Matheson
Cast .... Michael Dudikoff
Cast .... John Vernon

WOMAN WITH A PAST   NBC
Drama: Family Drama • True Crime • Family Violence
Airdate: 03/02/92
Rating: 17.5/27   A/C: 1

Businesswoman Kay Smith's secret past is revealed with an FBI arrest for her escape from prison ten years earlier. Her husband and lawyer try to prove her crime was committed to save her kids from her abusive ex-husband and she is now rehabilitated.

Production Company: WIN IAW Art Harris
    Prods., Von Zerneck/Sertner, Neal & Gary
    Prods.
Executive Producer .... Gary Hoffman
Executive Producer .... Neal Israel
Executive Producer .... Frank Von Zerneck
Executive Producer .... Robert M. Sertner
Producer .... Julie Anne Weitz
Producer .... Steve Lewis
Producer .... Susan Williams
Co-Producer .... Art Harris
Co-Producer .... Craig Haffner
Director .... Mimi Leder
Writer .... Robert L. Freedman
Writer .... Selma Thompson
Cast .... Pamela Reed
Cast .... Dwight Schultz
Cast .... Richard Lineback
Cast .... Carrie Snodgrass

WOMEN OF BREWSTER PLACE, THE ABC
Miniseries/Drama (2 nights): Period Piece • Woman Against The System • Black Story
Airdate: 03/19/89
Rating: 23.5/36 • 24.5/38   A/C: 1 • 1

Based on the novel by Gloria Naylor about the struggles of a group of women who bond together to help each other through hard times in their impoverished black neighborhood.

Production Company: Harpo Prods. IAW Phoenix
    Ent. Group
Executive Producer .... Carole Isenberg
Executive Producer .... Oprah Winfrey
Producer .... Patricia K. Meyer
Producer .... Reuben Cannon
Director .... Donna Deitch
Writer .... Karen Hall
Cast .... Oprah Winfrey
Cast .... Mary Alice
Cast .... Olivia Cole
Cast .... Robin Givens
Cast .... Moses Gunn
Cast .... Jackee unknown

WOMEN OF VALOR   CBS
Drama: Period Piece • WWII • Woman In Jeopardy • Foreign or Exotic Location • Prison and Prison Camp
Airdate: 11/23/86
Rating: 19.6/32   A/C:

The three year experience of Army nurses and other women held in a brutal Japanese prisoner-of-war camp in the Philippines.

Production Company: Jeni Prods. IAW
    InterPlanetary Ltd.
Executive Producer .... Jonas McCord
Executive Producer .... Phil Parslow
Producer .... Buzz Kulik
Director .... Buzz Kulik
Writer .... Jonas McCord
Cast .... Kristy McNichol
Cast .... Susan Sarandon
Cast .... Patrick Bishop
Cast .... Terry O'Quinn
Cast .... Neva Patterson

WOMEN OF WINDSOR   CBS
Drama (3 hours.): True Story • Biography • Foreign or Exotic Location
Airdate: 10/25/92
Rating: 13.8/22   A/C: 1

The troubled marriages of Princess Diana and Sarah Ferguson set the Windsor household into turmoil. Both women must fight rumor and strict palace protocol while trying to find happiness. Note: 3 hours

Production Company: Sharmhill Prods. IAW
    Samuels Film Co. & WIN
Executive Producer .... Stu Samuels
Producer .... John Danylkiw
Producer .... Steven H. Stern
Co-Executive Producer .... Felice Gordon
Writer .... Peter Lefcourt
Cast .... Sallyanne Law
Cast .... Nicola Formby
Cast .... James Piddock

WORKING TRASH   FBC
Comedy: Buddy Story
Airdate: 11/26/90
Rating: 5.8/9   A/C: 4

Sensitive stock data is retrieved from the garbage by ambitious janitors who use the insider tips to make a fortune.

Production Company: Westgate Prods. IAW
    Auroroa Development Fund & FNM Co.
Producer .... Andrew Sugarman
Director .... Alan Metter
Writer .... Jon Connolly
Cast .... George Carlin
Cast .... Ben Stiller
Cast .... Buddy Ebsen
Cast .... Jack Blessing

WORLD WAR II : WHEN LIONS ROARED
NBC

Miniseries/Drama (2 nights): WWII • Biography •
Historical Piece • True Story • Foreign or Exotic
Location
Airdate: 4/19/94 • 4/20/94
Rating: 9.1/15 • 7.5/12   A/C: 3 • 4

*During WWII, Franklin D. Roosevelt, Winston
Churchill and Joseph Stalin form an uneasy
alliance as they plan stratagem to win the war
and destroy Germany and Italy.*

Production Company: WWII Co. IAW Gideon
  Prods.
Executive Producer ....Ethel Winant
Producer .... David W. Rintels
Co-Producer .... Victoria Riskin
Director .... Joseph Sargent
Writer .... David W. Rintels
Cast .... John Lithgow
Cast .... Michael Caine
Cast .... Bob Hoskins
Cast .... Ed Begley, Jr.
Cast .... Jan Triska

WORLD'S OLDEST LIVING BRIDESMAID, THE
CBS

Drama: Love Story • Woman's Issue/Story
Airdate: 09/21/90
Rating: 11.9/22   A/C: 2

*A beautiful, ambitious and successful attorney
is surprised to find herself involved with her
charming male secretary and craving marital
bliss.*

Production Company: Hearst Entertainment
Executive Producer .... Donna Mills
Producer .... Christopher Morgan
Director .... Joseph Scanlan
Writer .... Janet Kovalcik
Cast .... Donna Mills
Cast .... Brian Wimmer
Cast .... Winston Rekert
Cast .... Art Hindle

WRITER'S BLOCK
USA

Drama: Murder and Murder Mystery • Cops/
Detectives/Law Enforcement • Woman In Jeopardy
Airdate: 10/09/91
Rating: N/A   A/C:

*A murder-mystery writer becomes a suspect in
a serial murder case when the characters in
her book seem to mirror real life occurrences.*

Production Company: Talent Court Productions
  IAW Wilshire Court Prods.
Producer .... Vanessa Greene
Co-Producer .... Gordon Wolf
Co-Producer .... Bradford Pollack
Director .... Charles Correll
Writer .... Elisa Bell
Cast .... Morgan Fairchild
Cast .... Joe Regalbuto
Cast .... Michael Praed
Cast .... Douglas Rowe

WRONG MAN, THE
SHOWTIME

Drama: Murder and Murder Mystery • Suspense/
Thriller
Airdate: 9/5/93
Rating: N/A   A/C:

*An American merchant seaman gets stranded
in a squalid Mexican port town and is framed
for the murder of a Yaqui smuggler. As he flees
from the false charges, he meets up with a wild
itinerant couple and together they hit the road
in search of adventure.*

Production Company: Beattie/Chesser Prods.
Executive Producer .... Fred Schneier
Producer .... Alan Beattie
Producer .... Chris Chesser
Director .... Jim McBride
Writer .... Michael Thoma
Cast .... Kevin Anderson
Cast .... John Lithgow
Cast .... Rosanna Arquette

YARN PRINCESS, THE
ABC

Drama: Family Drama • Medical/Disease/Mental
Illness • Children/Teens • Social Issue
Airdate: 3/27/94
Rating: 10.5/17   A/C: 2 (Tie)

*A developmentally disabled, working class
woman struggles to care for her six kids when
her factory worker husband becomes mentally
ill. A social worker decides she is unable to
care for the unruly children and places them in
foster care. A sympathetic attorney intervenes
and takes the case to court where she eventually
triumphs and regains custody.*

Production Company: Konigsberg/Sanitsky Co.
Executive Producer .... Frank Konigsberg
Executive Producer .... Larry Sanitsky
Producer .... Tyler Tyhurst
Producer .... Gregory Prange
Director .... Tom McLoughlin
Writer .... Dalene Young
Cast .... Jean Smart
Cast .... Robert Pastorelli
Cast .... Lee Garlington
Cast .... Dennis Boutiskaris
Cast .... Luke Edwards

YEARLING, THE
CBS

Drama: Family Drama • Period Piece • Children/
Teens
Airdate: 4/24/94
Rating: 13.2/21   A/C: 1

*Based on the novel by Marjorie Kinnan
Rawlings. Remake of the 1946 feature film. In
the 1930's, a sensitive teenage boy learns the
harsh lessons of life growing up with his dirt
poor family in the backwood swamps of Florida.
After raising an orphaned fawn he is eventually
forced to shoot his beloved pet when the animal
threatens to destroy their crops—and their only
means of support.*

Production Company: RHI Entertainment IAW
  CBS
Executive Producer .... Robert Halmi, Sr.
Executive Producer .... Robert Halmi, Jr.
Executive Producer .... Sandra J. Birnhak
Executive Producer .... David R. Ames
Producer .... Edwin Self
Director .... Rod Hardy
Writer .... Joe Wiesenfeld
Cast .... Peter Strauss
Cast .... Jean Smart
Cast .... Wil Horneff
Cast .... Philip Seymour

YES, VIRGINIA, THERE IS A SANTA CLAUS
ABC

Drama: Children/Teens • Period Piece • Holiday
Special
Airdate: 12/08/91
Rating: 12.2/19   A/C: 3

*In 1897 N.Y., young Virginia O'Hanlan is
advised by her father to write and ask the New
York Sun if Santa is real. Assigned to respond,
reporter Frank Church rediscovers life's
wonders as he brings Christmas cheer to
Virginia and her father.*

Production Company: Andrew J. Fenady Prods.
  IAW Quinta Communications & Paradigm
  Enter.
Executive Producer .... Andrew J. Fenady
Executive Producer .... Bob Banner
Executive Producer .... Gary Pudney
Executive Producer .... Silvio Muraglia
Producer .... Duke Fenady
Co-Producer .... Nick Anderson
Director .... Charles Jarrott
Writer .... Val De Crowl
Writer .... Andrew J. Fenady
Cast .... Charles Bronson
Cast .... Edward Asner
Cast .... Richard Thomas
Cast .... Katharine Isobel

MOVIES AND MINISERIES

YOUNG CATHERINE   TNT
Miniseries/Drama (2 nights): Period Piece • Historical
Piece • Foreign or Exotic Location • Biography
Airdate: 02/17/91 • 2/18/91
Rating: N/A   A/C:

*The rise to the throne of Catherine the Great
from naive Prussian princess in 1744 to grand
Czarina of the Russian Empire.*

Production Company: Consolidated
   Entertainment, Primedia and Lenfilm
Executive Producer .... Michael Deeley
Executive Producer .... Stephen Smallwood
Executive Producer .... W. Patterson Ferns
Producer .... Neville Thompson
Co-Producer .... Chris Bryant
Director .... Michael Anderson
Writer .... Chris Bryant
Cast .... Vanessa Redgrave
Cast .... Christopher Plummer
Cast .... Franco Nero
Cast .... Marthe Keller

YOUNG INDIANA JONES CHRONICLES:
THE CURSE OF THE JACKAL   ABC
Drama: Children/Teens • Period Piece • Action/
Adventure • Historical Piece • Foreign or Exotic
Location • Series Pilot (2 hr.)
Airdate: 03/04/92
Rating: 16.6/26   A/C: 1

*Ninety-three-year-old Indiana Jones recounts
the adventures of his youth as a ten-year-old in
Egypt with Lawrence of Arabia and as a sixteen-
year-old thrill-seeker in Mexico with Pancho
Villa.*

Production Company: Lucasfilm Ltd IAW Amblin
   Television/Paramount
Executive Producer .... George Lucas
Producer .... Rick McCallum
Director .... Carl Schultz
Writer .... Jonathan Hales
Cast .... Sean Patrick Flanery
Cast .... Corey Carrier
Cast .... Margaret Tysack
Cast .... Ronny Coutteure

YOUR MOTHER WEARS COMBAT BOOTS
NBC
Comedy: Buddy Story
Airdate: 03/27/89
Rating: 17.0/28   A/C:

*In an effort to convince her son to leave
airborne training and attend college, a woman
joins the army herself and bumbles through
basic training with the help of two women
recruits.*

Production Company: Kushner-Locke Prods.
Executive Producer .... Peter Locke
Executive Producer .... Donald Kushner
Producer .... Bill Novodor
Director .... Anson Williams
Writer .... Susan Hunter
Cast .... Barbara Eden
Cast .... Hector Elizondo
Cast .... Meagan Fay
Cast .... David Kaufman
Cast .... Richard McGregor
Cast .... Conchata Ferrell

ZELDA   TNT
Drama: Biography • Period Piece • True Story
Airdate: 11/7/93
Rating: N/A   A/C:

*The wild relationship of writer F. Scott
Fitzgerald and his unstable Southern wife,
Zelda. From their first meeting at a Alabama
cotillion in 1918 to their often scandalous,
wanton and decadent lifestyle which ultimately
ended in 1930 when she descends into madness
and is committed to a sanatorium.*

Production Company: Turner Pictures IAW ZDF
   Enterprises, ORF, SRG
Executive Producer .... Robert Greenwald
Producer .... Steven P. Saeta
Producer .... Patricia Saphier
Producer .... Anthony Ivor
Producer .... Benedict Fitzgerald
Director .... Pat O'Connor
Writer .... Anthony Ivor
Writer .... Benedict Fitzgerald
Cast .... Natasha Richardson
Cast .... Timothy Hutton
Cast .... Jon De Vries
Cast .... Spalding Gray

Section B

SUBJECT MATTERS

Movies and Miniseries
Cross-referenced by
Subject Matter
Listed Alphabetically

ACTION/ADVENTURE

Agatha Christie's The Man In The Brown Suit
   CBS 15.8/25
Annihilator, The NBC 14.1/23
Anything To Survive ABC 16.5/26
Around The World In 80 Days NBC 15.5/24
   13.2/21 13.0/21
Arthur The King CBS 9.5/17
Assassin CBS 14.1/23
Baywatch: Panic At Malibu Pier NBC 17.1/28
Behind Enemy Lines NBC 14.5/23
Bejeweled DISNEY
Beryl Markham: A Shadow On The Sun CBS
   10.4/16 7.8/13
Bionic Showdown: The 6 Million Dollar Man/
   Bionic Woman NBC 17.6/28
Blue Lightning, The CBS 12.1/19
Broken Badges CBS 9.1/16
Brotherhood Of The Rose NBC 20.9/35 19.2/30
C. A. T. Squad NBC 17.3/30
C. A. T. Squad: Python Wolf NBC 12.8/20
Call Of The Wild CBS 18.2/29
Carly's Web NBC 9.3/17
Case Closed CBS 13.0/22
Chameleons NBC 9.9/17
China Beach ABC 18.0/29
Chips, The War Dog DISNEY
Cisco Kid, The TNT
Clinton And Nadine HBO
Corsican Brothers, The CBS 11.9/18
Cover Up CBS 14.0/26
Crucifier Of Blood, The TNT
Day Of Reckoning NBC 8.7/14
Deadly Game USA
Defiant One, The ABC 18.9/28
Dirty Dozen: The Deadly Mission NBC 18.5/28
Dirty Dozen: The Fatal Mission NBC 14.3/22
Dream West CBS 19.5/29 18.1/29 20.1/32
Dreams Of Gold: The Mel Fisher Story CBS
   11.3/20
Drive Like Lightning USA
Eyes Of A Witness CBS 13.0/23
Fire: Trapped On The 37th Floor ABC 11.2/17
Flight Of Black Angel SHOWTIME
Florida Straits HBO
Fortress HBO
Gambler Returns: The Luck Of The Draw, The
   NBC 18.0/28 16.6/25
Get Smart Again ABC 13.7/21
Ghost In Monte Carlo, A TNT
Gladiator, The ABC 15.9/24
Great Escape I I: The Untold Story, The NBC
   14.4/23 12.3/19
Gulag HBO
Harem ABC 16.9/25 16.2/23
Harry's Hong Kong ABC 6.1/11
Hart To Hart Returns NBC 13.1/23
Hazard Of Hearts, A CBS 15.3/26
Heart Of Darkness TNT
Her Secret Life ABC 13.7/21
High Mountain Rangers CBS 19.6/32
Higher Ground CBS 13.3/25
Highwayman, The NBC 13.1/22
If Tomorrow Comes CBS 21.8/34 23.6/37
   20.8/33
In Like Flynn ABC 8.4/15
Incredible Hulk Returns, The NBC 20.2/33
Intrigue CBS 8.8/19
Ironclads TNT
Island Sons ABC 7.9/14
Jailbirds CBS 12.9/22

James Clavell's Noble House NBC 17.9/27
   15.9/24 15.0/22 16.3/26
Jesse Hawkes CBS 8.9/17
L. A. Takedown NBC 10.4/18
Lady And The Highwayman, The CBS 11.1/18
Lily CBS 6.6/14
Lion Of Africa, The HBO
Long Journey Home, The CBS 21.3/34
Love Among Thieves ABC 13.2/21
Love On The Run NBC 9.3/16
Macgyver : Lost Treasure Of Atlantis ABC 9.1/17
Miracle Landing CBS 15.1/23
Misfits Of Science NBC 14.2/23
N. Y. P. D. Mounted CBS 6.1/13
Napoleon And Josephine: A Love Story ABC
   18.6/30 16.2/26 13.3/21
Nasty Boys NBC 15.3/27
North And South ABC 25.8/37 23.6/34 28.0/42
   25.8/38 23.2/37
North And South, Book 2 ABC 19.8/30 20.1/30
   21.6/36 22.9/36 20.8/32
Oceans Of Fire CBS 16.1/27
Old Man & The Sea, The NBC 14.9/24
On Wings Of Eagles NBC 17.0/28 21.2/34
Only One Survived CBS 6.5/12
Ordeal In The Arctic ABC 14.0/22
Outback Bound CBS 15.7/25
Pancho Barnes CBS 11.7/18
Return Of The 6 Million Dollar Man & Bionic
   Woman NBC 20.5/33
Return To Lonesome Dove CBS 18.1/28
   16.5/25 15.2/24
Road Raiders, The CBS 8.5/14
Roadracers SHOWTIME
Robin Hood FBC 6.0/10
Rose And The Jackal, The TNT
Royce SHOWTIME
Scorned And Swindled CBS 16.7/26
Sea Wolf, The TNT
Search And Rescue NBC 10.5/17
Secret Life Of Ian Fleming, The TNT
She Knows Too Much NBC 17.4/27
Shooter NBC 11.3/20
Snow Kill USA
South Beach NBC 9.8/17
Special Friendship, A CBS 13.7/22
Spirit, The ABC 7.0/15
Stone Fox NBC 15.9/22
Storm And Sorrow LIFETIME
Stormin' Home CBS 13.1/23
Stormy Weathers ABC 10.2/16
Supercarrier ABC 15.0/23
Survive The Savage Sea ABC 15.6/24
Sword Of Gideon HBO
Tarzan In Manhattan ABC 10.5/19
Three On A Match NBC 14.1/26
Thunderboat Row ABC 13.8/23
Toughest Man In The World, The CBS 12.6/20
Treasure Island TNT
Trial Of The Incredible Hulk, The NBC 16.2/25
Trouble In Paradise CBS 10.9/18
True Blue NBC 14.0/22
Under Cover ABC 9.9/16
Viper NBC 15.3/23
Waco & Rhinehart ABC 7.4/13
Walker, Texas Ranger CBS 16.5/27
Weekend War ABC 14.9/24
Wet Gold ABC 18.3/30
Which Way Home TNT
White Mile HBO
Wild Horses CBS 16.7/26
Young Indiana Jones Chronicles: The Curse Of
   The Jackal ABC 16.6/26

ADDICTION STORY

Baron And The Kid, The CBS 10.4/17
Betty Ford Story, The ABC 11.4/16
Blind Spot CBS 13.1/20
Cracked Up ABC 14.7/23
Darkness Before Dawn NBC 13.1/20
Deadly Care CBS 18.6/31
Finish Line TNT
Karen Carpenter Story, The CBS 26.3/41
Kate's Secret NBC 24.1/36
Keeping Secrets ABC 14.2/23
Lies And Lullabies ABC 10.4/16
Love Lives On ABC 17.8/26
My Name Is Bill W. ABC 15.2/24
My Name Is Kate ABC 11.2/17
Not My Kid CBS 21.6/33
On Thin Ice: The Tai Babilonia Story NBC
   13.4/21
Poor Little Rich Girl: The Barbara Hutton Story
   NBC 21.3/33 18.5/30
Reason For Living: The Jill Ireland Story NBC
   12.5/21
Shattered Innocence CBS 15.2/25
Shattered Spirits ABC 16.4/25
Torch Song ABC 9.5/15
Toughlove ABC 20.6/31
Under The Influence CBS 15.4/24
Vital Signs CBS 16.7/26

AMERICAN INDIANS

Broken Chain TNT
Broken Cord, The ABC 14.3/22
Dream West CBS 19.5/29 ´ 18.1/29 20.1/32
Geronimo TNT
Kenny Rogers As The Gambler I I I: The Legend
   Continues CBS 20.9/32 17.4/29
Last Of His Tribe, The HBO
Miracle In The Wilderness TNT
Red Earth, White Earth CBS 11.9/19
Shadowhunter SHOWTIME
Son Of The Morning Star ABC 11.7/18 12.8/20
Stone Fox NBC 15.9/22

BIOGRAPHY

Abraham TNT
Amelia Earhart: The Final Flight TNT
Anastasia: The Mystery Of Anna NBC 20.7/32
   20.9/32
Ann Jillian Story, The NBC 23.8/35
Babe Ruth NBC 10.0/16
Barnum CBS 14.1/25
Beryl Markham: A Shadow On The Sun CBS
   10.4/16 7.8/13
Betty Ford Story, The ABC 11.4/16
Bonnie And Clyde: The True Story FBC 8.7/15
Call Me Anna ABC 15.9/24
Captain Cook TNT
Casanova ABC 10.3/15
Charles And Diana: Unhappily Ever After ABC
   12.8/19
Christopher Columbus CBS 17.4/29 15.8/25
Citizen Cohn HBO
Corpse Had A Familiar Face, The CBS 16.4/26
Court - Martial Of Jackie Robinson, The TNT

SUBJECT MATTERS
Listed Alphabetically

BIOGRAPHY (CONTINUED)

Diana: Her True Story NBC 14.5/23 15.6/24
Dillinger ABC 14.5/22
Dream West CBS 19.5/29 18.1/29 20.1/32
Dreamer Of Oz, The NBC 11.8/18
Elvis And Me ABC 23.9/35 24.9/36
Elvis And The Colonel: The Untold Story NBC 9.8/14
Fall From Grace NBC 17.6/27
Fatal Deception: Mrs. Lee Harvey Oswald NBC 11.2/18
Fergie And Andrew: Behind The Palace Doors NBC 13.6/21
Final Days ABC 10.2/17
Final Verdict TNT
Florence Nightingale NBC 11.6/19
Frank Nitti: The Enforcer ABC 17.4/28
George Washington I I: The Forging Of A Nation CBS 12.6/20 9.8/15
Gore Vidal's Billy The Kid TNT
Guts And Glory: The Rise And Fall Of Oliver North CBS 14.0/23 9.6/13
Hearst And Davies Affair, The ABC 16.2/24
Heart Of A Champion: The Ray Mancini Story CBS 10.6/17
Hoover SHOWTIME
Houston: The Legend Of Texas CBS 10.8/18
J F K: Reckless Youth ABC 7.8/12 9.5/16
Jacksons: An American Dream , The ABC 21.1/31 23.9/36
John And Yoko: A Love Story NBC 13.4/19
Josephine Baker Story, The HBO
Karen Carpenter Story, The CBS 26.3/41
Keeping Secrets ABC 14.2/23
Kennedys Of Massachusetts, The ABC 15.8/24 17.6/27 16.4/25
L B J: The Early Years NBC 18.4/27
Last Days Of Frank And Jesse James, The NBC 15.1/22
Last Days Of Patton, The CBS 19.5/32
Leona Helmsley: The Queen Of Mean CBS 15.7/26
Liberace ABC 16.8/27
Liberace: Behind The Music CBS 16.6/26
Lincoln NBC 16.6/26 14.9/24
Line Of Fire: The Morris Dees Story NBC 11.3/17
Lost Capone, The TNT
Lucy & Desi: Before The Laughter CBS 16.4/25
Mafia Princess NBC 24.4/37
Malice In Wonderland CBS 18.3/29
Man For All Season, A TNT
Mandela HBO
Margaret Bourke - White TNT
Marilyn & Me ABC 8.5/14
Mark Twain And Me DISNEY
Miss America: Behind The Crown NBC 13.3/20
Murderers Among Us: The Simon Wiesenthal Story HBO
Murrow HBO
Mussolini: The Decline And Fall Of Il Duce HBO
Mussolini - The Untold Story NBC 17.7/26 19.4/29 19.6/29
My Name Is Bill W. ABC 15.2/24
Napoleon And Josephine: A Love Story ABC 18.6/30 16.2/26 13.3/21
Nightmare Years, The TNT
On Thin Ice: The Tai Babilonia Story NBC 13.4/21
One Against The Wind CBS 13.4/21
Out On A Limb ABC 13.8/20 16.8/25
Pancho Barnes CBS 11.7/18

Passion For Justice, A: Hazel Brannon Smith Story ABC 11.1/18
Peter The Great NBC 19.0/28 17.6/26 16.6/26 17.4/27
Poor Little Rich Girl: The Barbara Hutton Story NBC 21.3/33 18.5/30
Prisoner Of Honor HBO
Queen CBS 24.7/38 24.1/37 22.8/34
Reason For Living: The Jill Ireland Story NBC 12.5/21
Richest Man In The World: The Aristotle Onassis Story ABC 12.1/18 13.9/22
Robert Kennedy And His Times CBS 19.8/29 14.9/21 16.9/26
Rock Hudson ABC 15.7/24
Sakharov HBO
Samaritan: The Mitch Snyder Story CBS 11.2/18
Season Of Giants, A TNT
Second Serve CBS 13.6/22
Secret Life Of Ian Fleming, The TNT
She Stood Alone NBC 10.8/18
Sinatra CBS 17.7/26 17.2/27
Son Of The Morning Star ABC 11.7/18 12.8/20
Sound And The Silence, The TNT
Stalin HBO
Summer Dreams: The Story Of The Beach Boys ABC 10.6/16
Teamster Boss: The Jackie Presser Story HBO
Tonya & Nancy: The Inside Story NBC 10.4/19
Unconquered CBS 17.3/28
Wallenberg: A Hero's Story NBC 20.2/33 19.7/30
Winner Never Quits, A ABC 14.6/24
Woman He Loved, The CBS 14.5/25
Woman Named Jackie, A NBC 15.5/23 18.6/28 19.1/30
Women Of Windsor CBS 13.8/22
World War I I : When Lions Roared NBC 9.1/15 7.5/12
Young Catherine TNT
Zelda TNT

BLACK STORY

Against The Wall HBO
Assault At West Point SHOWTIME
Atlanta Child Murders, The CBS 21.8/31 20.9/31
Badge Of The Assassin CBS 13.6/23
Carolina Skeletons NBC 14.7/23
Case Of Deadly Force, A CBS 12.0/20
Common Ground CBS 11.0/18 10.8/18
Court - Martial Of Jackie Robinson, The TNT
Decoration Day NBC 17.9/28
Defiant One, The ABC 18.9/28
Ernest Green Story, The DISNEY
Father Clements Story, The NBC 16.7/26
Fight For Jenny, A NBC 20.0/31
Gathering Of Old Men, A CBS 18.4/31
George Mckenna Story, The CBS 15.5/24
Guilty Of Innocence: The Lenell Geter Story CBS 15.7/25
Heat Wave TNT
Howard Beach: Making The Case For Murder NBC 14.9/24
I'll Fly Away NBC 15.4/24
In The Heat Of The Night NBC 18.7/30
Johnnie Mae Gibson: F B I CBS 13.3/20
Josephine Baker Story, The HBO
Laurel Avenue HBO
Line Of Fire: The Morris Dees Story NBC 11.3/17

Mandela HBO
Memphis TNT
Miracle At Beekman's Place NBC 12.3/21
Murder In Mississippi NBC 12.4/20
Murder Without Motive: The Edmund Perry Story NBC 11.3/18
On Promised Land DISNEY
Open Admissions CBS 7.5/13
Paris Trout SHOWTIME
Perfect Harmony DISNEY
Polly—Comin' Home NBC 6.8/10
Queen CBS 24.7/38 24.1/37 22.8/34
Resting Place CBS 22.3/36
Return Of Desperado, The NBC 16.0/24
Roots: The Gift ABC 15.4/24
Separate But Equal ABC 11.9/19 11.8/19
She Stood Alone NBC 10.8/18
Special Friendship, A CBS 13.7/22
Stompin' At The Savoy CBS 11.2/19
Strapped HBO
Sudie And Simpson LIFETIME
The Race To Freedom: The Underground Railroad FAMILY
There Are No Children Here ABC 17.8/26
Uncle Tom's Cabin SHOWTIME
Unconquered CBS 17.3/28
White Lie USA
Women Of Brewster Place, The ABC 23.5/36 24.5/38

BUDDY STORY

Another Pair Of Aces: Three Of A Kind CBS 9.9/17
Archie: To Riverdale And Back Again NBC 10.6/17
Blue Deville NBC 13.4/22
Boys, The ABC 8.9/15
Case Closed CBS 13.0/22
Classified Love CBS 9.7/17
Cooperstown TNT
Cover Girl And The Cop, The NBC 18.0/28
Double Your Pleasure NBC 10.9/18
Due South CBS 11.5/21
Entertainers, The ABC 7.0/11
Heist HBO
Hot Paint CBS 14.1/22
Izzy And Moe CBS 17.9/27
Jailbirds CBS 12.9/22
Jury Duty: The Comedy ABC 11.4/18
Life In The Theater, A TNT
Lush Life SHOWTIME
Maid For Each Other NBC 13.6/21
Middle Ages CBS 8.7/16
My Boyfriend's Back NBC 16.1/26
N. Y. P. D. Mounted CBS 6.1/13
Not A Penny More, Not A Penny Less USA
Odd Couple, The CBS 10.4/19
Pair Of Aces CBS 17.8/28
Pals CBS 11.1/19
Percy & Thunder TNT
Pink Lightning FBC 4.4/8
Return To Mayberry NBC 33.0/49
Roommates NBC 8.9/15
Sharing Richard CBS 13.7/22
Side By Side CBS 12.4/20
Special Friendship, A CBS 13.7/22
Spies, Lies And Naked Thighs CBS 12.2/19
T Bone N Wessel TNT
Three On A Match NBC 14.1/26
Threesome CBS 10.3/18

BUDDY STORY (CONTINUED)

Traveling Man HBO
Tricks Of The Trade CBS 11.6/18
Waco & Rhinehart ABC 7.4/13
Working Trash FBC 5.8/9
Your Mother Wears Combat Boots NBC 17.0/28

CHILDREN/TEENS

Adam: His Song Continues NBC 15.9/25
After The Promise CBS 19.2/30
Alex: The Life Of A Child ABC 21.7/36
Always Remember I Love You CBS 15.3/26
Amy Fisher: My Story NBC 19.1/30
...And Then She Was Gone NBC 11.7/19
April Morning CBS 15.2/24
Armed & Innocent CBS 14.9/24
At Mother's Request CBS 23.3/35 22.7/35
Baby Brokers NBC 11.4/17
Baby Girl Scott CBS 13.2/23
Baby M ABC 15.0/24 17.6/27
Baby Snatcher CBS 16.3/26
Babymaker: The Dr. Cecil Jacobson's Story CBS 14.0/21
Back Home DISNEY
Bad Seed, The ABC 12.9/19
Betrayed By Innocence CBS 10.8/19
Beyond Control: The Amy Fisher Story ABC 19.5/30
Beyond Obsession ABC 13.6/21
Blind Faith NBC 19.9/31 23.3/36
Born Too Soon NBC 10.5/17
Brand New Life: The Honeymoon NBC 15.9/25
Bridge To Silence CBS 13.9/24
Broken Angel ABC 16.9/28
Broken Cord, The ABC 14.3/22
Broken Promises: Taking Emily Back CBS 12.6/22
Brotherhood Of Justice, The ABC 11.6/19
Bump In The Night CBS 16.0/25
Caroline? CBS 19.4/30
Casey's Gift: For Love Of A Child NBC 14.0/22
Casualties Of Love: The Long Island Lolita Story CBS 14.3/22
Celebration Family ABC 10.2/17
Charley Hannah ABC 13.4/23
Child In The Night CBS 9.7/16
Child Lost Forever, A NBC 15.4/23
Child Of Rage CBS 14.7/24
Child Saver, The NBC 15.8/25
Child's Cry CBS 22.7/33
Children In The Crossfire NBC 14.8/23
Children Of The Dark CBS 13.4/22
Children Of The Night CBS 12.4/21
Children Of Times Square ABC 12.5/20
Christmas On Division Street CBS 16.7/26
Christy CBS 17.7/29
Connecticut Yankee In King Arthur's Court, A NBC 11.5/17
Conspiracy Of Love CBS 14.1/21
Convicted: A Mother's Story NBC 17.4/27
Cracked Up ABC 14.7/23
Crime Of Innocence NBC 17.2/26
Crossing To Freedom CBS 10.3/17
Cruel Doubt NBC 16.8/27 14.8/24
Cry In The Wild: The Taking Of Peggy Ann NBC 17.2/27
Dadah Is Death CBS 11.3/17 10.1/17
Daddy ABC 17.1/25

Dangerous Affection NBC 16.4/26
Danielle Steel's Fine Things NBC 18.0/28
Daughter Of The Streets ABC 14.9/24
David ABC 19.5/30
Dead Silence FBC 6.8/12
Deadly Betrayal: The Bruce Curtis Story NBC 12.9/20
Deadly Deception CBS 19.2/30
Deadly Medicine NBC 15.8/24
Deadly Silence, A ABC 17.9/28
Death Dreams LIFETIME
Deception: A Mother's Secret NBC 15.6/23
Desperate Choices: To Save My Child NBC 12.4/19
Desperate For Love CBS 12.0/20
Desperate Rescue: The Cathy Mahone Story NBC 13.3/20
Different Affair, A CBS 10.8/18
Do You Know The Muffin Man? CBS 18.4/30
Don't Touch My Daughter NBC 14.5/23
Double, Double, Toil And Trouble ABC 10.8/19
Dreamer Of Oz, The NBC 11.8/18
Empty Cradle ABC 15.2/24
Ernest Green Story, The DISNEY
Everybody's Baby: The Rescue Of Jessica Mcclure ABC 22.2/36
Evil In Clear River ABC 12.9/20
Extreme Close-Up NBC 12.3/20
Eye On The Sparrow NBC 14.3/22
Family For Joe, A NBC 15.8/23
Family Pictures ABC 10.1/16 11.5/18
Family Sins CBS 12.9/20
Family Torn Apart, A NBC 15.1/23
Fatal Charm SHOWTIME
Father Clements Story, The NBC 16.7/26
Father Of Hell Town NBC 18.2/29
Father's Homecoming, A NBC 12.5/23
Fight For Jenny, A NBC 20.0/31
Fight For Life ABC 16.2/26
First Steps CBS 14.4/24
Flood: Who Will Save Our Children? NBC 11.4/18
Follow Your Heart NBC 14.7/23
For The Love Of Aaron CBS 12.4/21
For The Love Of My Child: The Anissa Ayala Story NBC 12.8/20
For The Very First Time NBC 10.8/18
George Mckenna Story, The CBS 15.5/24
Getting Out ABC 11.1/18
Girl From Tomorrow, The DISNEY
Girl Who Came Between Them, The NBC 13.2/21
Go Toward The Light CBS 14.9/24
God Bless The Child ABC 17.7/28
Great Expectations DISNEY
Gregory K ABC 10.3/16
He's Not Your Son CBS 23.2/36
Heart Of A Child NBC 11.5/18
Heidi DISNEY
Honor Thy Mother CBS 15.5/24
I Know My First Name Is Steven NBC 21.6/35 27.3/42
I Know My Son Is Alive NBC 9.9/15
I Saw What You Did CBS 11.5/21
In A Child's Name CBS 17.8/27 21.9/33
In The Best Interest Of The Child CBS 11.6/19
In The Best Interest Of The Children NBC 16.0/24
In The Shadows, Someone Is Watching NBC 14.4/22
Incident At Dark River TNT
Into The Homeland HBO
Into Thin Air CBS 15.7/25

Jonathan: The Boy Nobody Wanted NBC 13.8/21
Joshua's Heart NBC 15.6/26
Judgment HBO
Keys, The NBC 12.1/19
Kids Don't Tell CBS 18.1/29
Kids Like These CBS 16.5/27
Killer Among Friends, A CBS 16.7/27
Killer Instinct NBC 12.5/19
Kissing Place, The USA
Lady From Yesterday, The CBS 16.0/25
Lantern Hill DISNEY
Last Prostitute, The LIFETIME
Lena: My 100 Children NBC 13.4/21
Liar, Liar CBS 14.5/26
Lies And Lullabies ABC 10.4/16
Lightning Incident, The USA
Little Girl Lost ABC 19.0/31
Little Kidnappers, The DISNEY
Little Match Girl, The NBC 19.4/30
Little Piece Of Heaven, A NBC 13.8/21
Littlest Victims CBS 10.9/18
Locked Up: A Mother's Rage CBS 12.4/20
Long Time Gone ABC 7.4/14
Lost In London CBS 13.0/19
Love, Lies And Murder NBC 15.5/24 20.3/30
Love Lives On ABC 17.8/26
Love, Mary CBS 21.5/33
Man From Left Field CBS 10.5/20
Mario And The Mob ABC 7.5/15
Mark Twain And Me DISNEY
Matter Of Justice, A NBC 15.2/23 19.4/29
Memphis TNT
Message From Holly CBS 15.5/24
Miracle Child NBC 11.0/18
Moment Of Truth: A Child Too Many NBC 14.2/22
Moment Of Truth: Broken Pledges NBC 12.6/20
Moment Of Truth: Cradle Of Conspiracy NBC 13.5/21
Moment Of Truth: Stalking Back NBC 15.9/25
Moment Of Truth: Why My Daughter? NBC 14.2/23
Mothers Revenge, A ABC 10.6/16
Mothers' Right, A: The Elizabeth Morgan Story ABC 13.6/21
Moving Target NBC 17.2/25
Mrs. Lambert Remembers Love CBS 9.9/17
Murder In New Hampshire: The Pamela Smart Story CBS 15.9/26
Murder In The Heartland ABC 13.2/21 14.2/23
Murder Without Motive: The Edmund Perry Story NBC 11.3/18
My Son Johnny CBS 15.6/24
Necessity CBS 15.0/24
News At Eleven CBS 13.3/22
Night Of Courage ABC 12.4/19
Nightmare In Columbia County CBS 14.0/22
No Place Like Home CBS 13.3/20
Nobody's Children USA
Norman Rockwell's Breaking Home Ties ABC 9.7/19
North Beach And Rawhide CBS 9.6/14 11.4/17
Not My Kid CBS 21.6/33
Not Quite Human I I DISNEY
Nutcracker: Money, Madness And Murder NBC 12.2/20 11.5/19 13.5/22
Omen I V: The Awakening FBC 6.4/11
On Promised Land DISNEY
One Terrific Guy CBS 19.6/30
Out On The Edge CBS 14.6/23
Perfect Harmony DISNEY
Perfect Tribute, The ABC 10.5/18

CHILDREN/TEENS (CONTINUED)

Place For Annie, A ABC 14.8/23
Place To Be Loved, A CBS 13.0/20
Playing With Fire NBC 16.9/26
Polly—Comin' Home NBC 6.8/10
Precious Victims CBS 14.6/23
Preppie Murder, The ABC 15.2/24
Price She Paid, The CBS 11.7/19
Prison For Children CBS 11.5/20
Promise To Keep, A NBC 14.3/23
Promised A Miracle CBS 13.2/22
Rags To Riches NBC 25.3/36
Reason For Living: The Jill Ireland Story NBC 12.5/21
Reason To Live, A NBC 15.6/23
Ride With The Wind ABC 9.0/15
Right To Kill? ABC 19.0/31
Roadracers SHOWTIME
Rockabye CBS 25.3/38
Runaway Father CBS 16.8/27
Ryan White Story, The ABC 16.6/26
Scandal In A Small Town NBC 20.0/31
Seasons Of The Heart NBC 12.9/21
Secret Garden, The CBS 16.7/26
Secret, The CBS 13.3/23
Sentimental Journey CBS 14.0/23
Shame LIFETIME
Shattered Innocence CBS 15.2/25
She Says She's Innocent NBC 15.0/23
Silence Of The Heart CBS 21.9/35
Silent Witness USA
Sin Of Innocence CBS 12.5/21
Sitter, The FBC 6.7/12
Small Sacrifices ABC 18.1/28 25.2/39
So Proudly We Hail CBS 7.5/12
Something To Live For: The Alison Gertz Story ABC 16.2/26
Son's Promise, A ABC 16.5/27
Spenser: Ceremony LIFETIME
Spoils Of War ABC 4.9/9
Spooner DISNEY
Stay The Night ABC 13.8/22 17.9/28
Stepford Children, The NBC 19.2/29
Stephen King's It ABC 18.5/29 20.6/33
Stolen Babies LIFETIME
Stone Fox NBC 15.9/22
Stop At Nothing LIFETIME
Stranger In The Family, A ABC 12.7/19
Stranger Within, The CBS 15.6/25
Strapped HBO
Substitute, The USA
Sudie And Simpson LIFETIME
Summer My Father Grew Up, The NBC 10.5/16
Summer To Remember, A CBS 13.8/21
Surviving ABC 18.1/26
Switched At Birth NBC 20.4/32 23.1/35
Tainted Blood USA
Taken Away CBS 16.3/25
Ted Kennedy, Jr., Story, The NBC 16.8/26
There Was A Little Boy CBS 13.8/22
They've Taken Our Children: The Chowchilla Kidnapping ABC 14.5/23
Thicker Than Blood: The Larry Mclinden Story CBS 14.5/23
This Child Is Mine NBC 21.1/32
Those She Left Behind NBC 25.1/38
Three Wishes Of Billy Grier, The ABC 13.5/21
Time To Live, A NBC 17.1/27
To Grandmother's House We Go ABC 16.9/25
To My Daughter With Love NBC 13.8/21
To Save The Children CBS 11.6/19

Too Young The Hero CBS 20.7/33
Too Young To Die? NBC 14.5/23
Toughlove ABC 20.6/31
Town Torn Apart, A NBC 12.8/20
Trapped In Silence CBS 15.1/24
Triumph Of The Heart: The Ricky Bell Story CBS 12.5/22
Twin Peaks ABC 21.7/33
Two Fathers' Justice NBC 17.9/27
Unspeakable Acts ABC 15.7/25
Untamed Love LIFETIME
Welcome Home, Bobby CBS 12.5/21
When The Bough Breaks NBC 22.3/36
When We Were Young NBC 10.9/19
When You Remember Me ABC 14.6/24
Where Pigeons Go To Die NBC 15.3/24
Whereabouts Of Jenny, The ABC 15.4/24
Which Way Home TNT
Whose Child Is This? The War For Baby Jessica ABC 9.6/15
Wildflower LIFETIME
Willing To Kill: The Texas Cheerleader Story ABC 14.4/22
Without A Kiss Goodbye CBS 17.2/29
Yarn Princess, The ABC 10.5/17
Yearling, The CBS 13.2/21
Yes, Virginia, There Is A Santa Claus ABC 12.2/19
Young Indiana Jones Chronicles: The Curse Of The Jackal ABC 16.6/26

COPS/DETECTIVES/LAW ENFORCEMENT

Agatha Christie's Dead Man's Folly CBS 14.4/22
Agatha Christie's Murder In Three Acts CBS 15.4/25
Agatha Christie's The Man In The Brown Suit CBS 15.8/25
Agatha Christie's Thirteen At Dinner CBS 12.8/21
Alone In The Neon Jungle CBS 17.6/28
Another Pair Of Aces: Three Of A Kind CBS 9.9/17
Are You Lonesome Tonight? USA
Atlanta Child Murders, The CBS 21.8/31 20.9/31
Back To The Streets Of San Francisco NBC 13.2/20
Badge Of The Assassin CBS 13.6/23
Bermuda Grace NBC 8.2/14
Betrayed By Love ABC 10.8/16
Beverly Hills Cowgirl Blues CBS 12.9/22
Blacke's Magic NBC 21.8/32
Blade In Hong Kong CBS 10.3/16
Blood And Orchids CBS 22.9/35 25.6/38
Blue Lightning, The CBS 12.1/19
Blue Lightning, The CBS 12.1/19
Brass CBS 12.9/22
Bridge Across Time NBC 13.7/21
Broken Badges CBS 9.1/16
C. A. T. Squad NBC 17.3/30
C. A. T. Squad: Python Wolf NBC 12.8/20
Case Closed CBS 13.0/22
Case Of The Hillside Strangler, The NBC 23.1/36
Cast A Deadly Spell HBO
Chameleons NBC 9.9/17
Charley Hannah ABC 13.4/23
Chase, The NBC 14.6/23
Child In The Night CBS 9.7/16
China Lake Murders, The USA
Codename: Foxfire - Slay It Again, Sam NBC 20.4/29

Columbo: A Bird In The Hand ABC 12.2/19
Columbo And The Murder Of A Rock Star ABC 12.6/19
Columbo - Caution: Murder Can Be Hazardous To Your Health ABC 11.8/18
Columbo: Death Hits The Jackpot ABC 14.2/22
Columbo Goes To College ABC 14.9/24
Columbo: It's All In The Game ABC 13.4/21
Columbo: No Time To Die ABC 16.5/27
Columbo: Undercover ABC 14.1/22
Complex Of Fear CBS 14.8/23
Conspiracy Of Silence CBS 12.5/21 12.2/20
Corpse Had A Familiar Face, The CBS 16.4/26
Cosby Mysteries, The NBC 14.8/22
Cover Girl And The Cop, The NBC 18.0/28
Criminal Behavior ABC 12.1/19
Dancing With Danger USA
Dead And Alive ABC 11.8/18
Deadly Desire USA
Deadly Matrimony NBC 16.1/25 18.9/29
Deadly Surveillance SHOWTIME
Deceptions SHOWTIME
Deep Trouble USA
Deliberate Stranger, The NBC 18.6/28 21.7/32
Detective In The House CBS 14.4/24
Diagnosis Of Murder CBS 14.6/23
Diamond Fleece USA
Diamond Trap, The CBS 15.1/24
Dillinger ABC 14.5/22
Dirty Work USA
Donato And Daughter CBS 14.8/24
Double Deception NBC 9.6/17
Double Edge CBS 17.1/28
Double Your Pleasure NBC 10.9/18
Doubletake CBS 21.1/33 18.7/28
Drug Wars: The Camarena Story NBC 14.4/22 15.2/23 16.1/25
Drug Wars: The Cocaine Cartel NBC 12.8/20 13.2/20
Due South CBS 11.5/21
Echoes In The Darkness CBS 20.1/33 22.0/33
Endless Game, The SHOWTIME
Eyes Of Terror NBC 10.6/19
Face Of Fear, The CBS 14.0/23
False Witness NBC 18.7/29
Fatal Exposure USA
Fatal Image, The CBS 14.1/22
Fear SHOWTIME
Final Notice USA
Forget Me Not Murders, The CBS 13.1/21
Fourth Story SHOWTIME
French Silk ABC 11.3/17
From The Files Of Joseph Wambaugh: A Jury Of One NBC 17 17
Fugitive Among Us CBS 14.0/23
Fugitive Nights: Danger In The Desert NBC 11.5/20
Full Exposure: The Sex Tapes Scandal NBC 16.2/24
Get Smart Again ABC 13.7/21
Glitter Dome, The HBO
Glitz NBC 14.1/25
Good Cops, Bad Cops NBC 8.9/14
Gotham SHOWTIME
Green Dolphin Beat FBC 4.4/8
Hands Of A Stranger NBC 15.2/25 17.4/28
Hawaiian Heat ABC 19.1/34
Higher Ground CBS 13.3/25
Highwayman, The NBC 13.1/22
Hitler's Daughter USA
Hoover SHOWTIME
House On Sycamore Street, The CBS 10.9/20

COPS/DETECTIVES/LAW ENFORCEMENT (CONTINUED)

Hunter   NBC   20.4/33
I Spy Returns   CBS   12.4/18
Illicit Behavior   USA
In The Arms Of A Killer   NBC   14.0/22
In The Company Of Darkness   CBS   15.0/24
In The Deep Woods   NBC   14.6/23
In The Eyes Of A Stranger   CBS   14.2/23
In The Heat Of The Night   NBC   18.7/30
In The Line Of Duty: A Cop For The Killing   NBC   14.6/23
In The Line Of Duty: Ambush In Waco   NBC   18.8/30
In The Line Of Duty: Manhunt In The Dakotas   NBC   14.7/26
In The Line Of Duty: Standoff At Marion   NBC   13.2/20
In The Line Of Duty: Street War   NBC   11.9/20
In The Line Of Duty: The FBI Murders   NBC   22.2/34
In The Line Of Duty: The Price Of Vengeance   NBC   10.8/17
In The Shadow Of A Killer   NBC   9.5/15
Internal Affairs   CBS   16.1/26   13.7/21
Into Thin Air   CBS   15.7/25
It's Nothing Personal   NBC   10.9/17
Jake And The Fatman   CBS   15.8/27
Jake Spanner, Private Eye   USA
Jessie   ABC   17.7/29
Johnnie Mae Gibson: F B I   CBS   13.3/20
Johnny Ryan   NBC   6.6/12
Jonathan Stone: Threat Of Innocence   NBC   12.2/16
Judgment Day: The John List Story   CBS   15.8/25
Keeper Of The City   SHOWTIME
Killing Mind, The   LIFETIME
Kojak: The Belarus File   CBS   18.5/31
Kojak: The Price Of Justice   CBS   12.0/21
L. A. Takedown   NBC   10.4/18
Lady Against The Odds   NBC   11.8/19
Lady Blue   ABC   19.8/31
Lady Killer   USA
Ladykillers   ABC   16.6/27
Laguna Heat   HBO
Legacy Of Lies   USA
Long Time Gone   ABC   7.4/14
Love And Curses . . . And All That Jazz   CBS   8.5/16
Love & Lies   ABC   11.6/18
Macshayne: The Final Roll Of The Dice   NBC   8.3/15
Macshayne: Winner Take All   NBC   10.7/17
Man Against The Mob   NBC   19.7/32
Man Against The Mob: The Chinatown Murders   NBC   11.3/18
Manhunt For Claude Dallas   CBS   14.4/24
Manhunt: Search For The Night Stalker   NBC   15.4/24
Marked For Murder   NBC   12.4/20
Menu For Murder   CBS   9.7/16
Miami Vice   NBC   22.8/37
Mickey Spillane's Mike Hammer: Murder Takes All   CBS   12.8/20
Missing Persons   ABC   11.4/19
Moonlighting   ABC   18.3/28
Mortal Sins   USA
Murder C. O. D.   NBC   10.3/19
Murder In Black And White   CBS   17.1/27
Murder In High Places   NBC   12.3/22

Murder In Paradise   NBC   12.6/21
Murder Ordained   CBS   19.3/29   19.8/32
Murder Times Seven   CBS   11.1/18
Murder With Mirrors   CBS   15.2/23
Murderous Vision   USA
Murders In The Rue Morgue, The   CBS   17.7/27
N. Y. P. D. Mounted   CBS   6.1/13
Nails   SHOWTIME
Nasty Boys   NBC   15.3/27
Nick Knight   CBS   11.2/19
Night Visions   NBC   9.8/17
Night Walk   CBS   16.3/27
Nightmare In Columbia County   CBS   14.0/22
One Of Her Own   ABC   13.5/21
One Police Plaza   CBS   12.3/22
Our Family Honor   ABC   15.4/25
Out Of The Darkness   CBS   17.6/30
Out Of Time   NBC   13.8/25
Over My Dead Body   CBS   12.4/23
P. S. I Luv U   CBS   15.7/25
Pair Of Aces   CBS   17.8/28
Palace Guard   CBS   7.4/14
Parker Kane   NBC   8.6/15
Past Tense   SHOWTIME
Payoff   SHOWTIME
Peter Gunn   ABC   14.7/24
Picket Fences   CBS   12.7/24
Police Story: The Freeway Killings   NBC   17.3/27
Popeye Doyle   NBC   15.8/26
Preppie Murder, The   ABC   15.2/24
Prime Target   NBC   12.6/23
Probe   ABC   14.2/23
Prophet Of Evil: The Ervil Lebaron Story   CBS   9.9/16
Quicksand: No Escape   USA
Rainbow Drive   SHOWTIME
Rape Of Richard Beck, The   ABC   25.2/38
Ray Alexander: A Taste For Justice   NBC   8.5/15
Red Spider, The   CBS   15.1/25
Relentless: Mind Of A Killer   NBC   12.8/20
Remington Steele: The Steele That Wouldn't Die   NBC   19.7/28
Return Of Eliot Ness, The   NBC   12.7/19
Return Of Ironside, The   NBC   11.6/19
Return Of Sam Mccloud, The   CBS   12.9/20
Return Of Sherlock Holmes, The   CBS   14.4/24
Revealing Evidence   NBC   14.5/25
Revenge Of Al Capone, The   NBC   13.9/22
Revolver   NBC   9.2/16
Rose And The Jackal, The   TNT
Round Table, The   NBC   8.3/16
Sadie And Son   CBS   15.5/25
Secret Sins Of The Father   NBC   16.0/24
Settle The Score   NBC   16.8/26
Shadowhunter   SHOWTIME
Shakedown On The Sunset Strip   CBS   15.0/27
Shattered Image   USA
She Knows Too Much   NBC   17.4/27
Shoot First: A Cop's Vengeance   NBC   12.6/20
Somebody's Daughter   ABC   10.2/16
Something Is Out There   NBC   19.3/31   19.0/29
South Beach   NBC   9.8/17
Spenser: Ceremony   LIFETIME
Spenser: For Hire   ABC   14.0/24
Spenser: Pale Kings And Princes   LIFETIME
Spies, Lies And Naked Thighs   CBS   12.2/19
Spirit, The   ABC   7.0/15
Stark   CBS   14.1/23
Staying Afloat   NBC   9.5/17
Steel Justice   NBC   8.9/14
Still Crazy Like A Fox   CBS   21.2/31
Stormy Weathers   ABC   10.2/16
Street Hawk   ABC   17.9/26

Street Of Dreams   CBS   9.5/17
Sunset Beat   ABC   6.5/13
Sweet Poison   USA
Sworn To Vengeance   CBS   15.3/25
Take, The   USA
Taking The Heat   SHOWTIME
Telling Secrets   ABC   13.8/22   14.4/21
Terror On Highway 91   CBS   16.9/26
Terror On Track 9   CBS   15.4/25
That Secret Sunday   CBS   16.1/26
This Gun For Hire   USA
Thompson's Last Run   CBS   17.4/26
Thunderboat Row   ABC   13.8/23
Trenchcoat In Paradise   CBS   12.2/20
Triplecross   ABC   10.3/16
True Blue   NBC   14.0/22
Twin Peaks   ABC   21.7/33
Twist Of The Knife, A   CBS   10.9/20
Under Cover   ABC   9.9/16
Under Siege   NBC   17.2/24
Unholy Matrimony   CBS   15.1/24
Vanishing Act   CBS   18.3/27
Viper   NBC   15.3/23
Waco & Rhinehart   ABC   7.4/13
Walker, Texas Ranger   CBS   16.5/27
When Dreams Come True   ABC   12.8/21
When The Bough Breaks   NBC   22.3/36
With Hostile Intent   CBS   12.9/21
Wolf   CBS   14.2/25
Writer's Block   USA

COURTROOM DRAMA

Absolute Strangers   CBS   17.7/29
Against Her Will: An Incident In Baltimore   CBS   16.0/25
And The Sea Will Tell   CBS   20.1/31   19.0/29
As Summers Die   HBO
Assault At West Point   SHOWTIME
Atlanta Child Murders, The   CBS   21.8/31   20.9/31
Back To Hannibal: The Return Of Tom Sawyer And Huck Finn   DISNEY
Billionaire Boys Club   NBC   20.7/34   22.1/34
Blood And Orchids   CBS   22.9/35   25.6/38
Breaking The Silence   CBS   12.8/20
Burden Of Proof, The   ABC   12.8/18   15.1/23
Burning Bed, The   NBC   36.2/52
Caine Mutiny Court - Martial, The   CBS   9.4/15
Case For Murder, A   USA
Case Of Deadly Force, A   CBS   12.0/20
Chase   CBS   11.7/19
Citizen Cohn   HBO
Confessions: Two Faces Of Evil   NBC   10.7/16
Convicted   ABC   17.4/27
Court - Martial Of Jackie Robinson, The   TNT
Criminal Justice   HBO
Cross Of Fire   NBC   12.5/20   14.7/23
Deadly Betrayal: The Bruce Curtis Story   NBC   12.9/20
Deadly Intentions   ABC   13.3/22   21.3/32
Deadly Medicine   NBC   15.8/24
Death In California, A   ABC   15.7/25   19.2/30
Desperate Choices: To Save My Child   NBC   12.4/19
Diary Of A Perfect Murder   NBC   20.9/33
Echoes In The Darkness   CBS   20.1/33   22.0/33
Equal Justice   ABC   12.2/23
Fatal Judgment   CBS   15.4/24
Fatal Memories   NBC   15.8/24
Fatal Vision   NBC   29.5/44   32.7/49
Final Appeal   NBC   12.7/20

COURTROOM DRAMA (CONTINUED)

Final Verdict TNT
Getting Gotti CBS 8.3/13
Good Fight, The LIFETIME
Grass Roots NBC 13.4/20 15.1/23
Gregory K ABC 10.3/16
Guilty Of Innocence: The Lenell Geter Story CBS 15.7/25
Guilty Until Proven Innocent NBC 11.8/19
Her Final Fury: Betty Broderick, The Last Chapter CBS 14.9/22
Honor Thy Father And Mother: The Menendez Murders FBC 10.2/17
Howard Beach: Making The Case For Murder NBC 14.9/24
I'll Fly Away NBC 15.4/24
In Defense Of A Married Man ABC 14.1/23
In My Daughter's Name CBS 15.8/27
In Self Defense ABC 9.2/17
Incident In A Small Town CBS 18.7/31
Incident, The CBS 20.8/33
Inherit The Wind NBC 18.0/29
Investigation: Inside A Terrorist Bombing, The HBO
Jesse CBS 19.4/31
Jonathan: The Boy Nobody Wanted NBC 13.8/21
Judgment HBO
Killer Among Us, A NBC 13.9/23
Killing In A Small Town CBS 15.8/26
L. A. Law NBC 21.2/33
Last Innocent Man, The HBO
Line Of Fire: The Morris Dees Story NBC 11.3/17
Love, Lies And Murder NBC 15.5/24 20.3/30
Matlock: The Witness Killings NBC 14.0/26
Menendez: A Killing In Beverly Hills CBS 9.6/16 9.3/15
Mercy Or Murder? NBC 23.8/35
Mothers Revenge, A ABC 10.6/16
Murder Between Friends NBC 12.9/20
Murder In New Hampshire: The Pamela Smart Story CBS 15.9/26
Murder Of Mary Phagan, The NBC 18.7/28 21.0/34
My Son Johnny CBS 15.6/24
Naked Lie CBS 21.2/33
Never Forget TNT
Nutcracker: Money, Madness And Murder NBC 12.2/20 11.5/19 13.5/22
Outrage CBS 21.7/34
Paris Trout SHOWTIME
Penalty Phase CBS 15.8/26
Perry Mason Mystery, A: The Case Of The Lethal Lifestyle NBC 10.8/18
Perry Mason Mystery: The Case Of The Wicked Wives NBC 10.2/19
Perry Mason Returns NBC 27.2/39
Perry Mason: The Case Of The All-Star Assassin NBC 16.8/26
Perry Mason: The Case Of The Avenging Ace NBC 17.4/26
Perry Mason: The Case Of The Defiant Daughter NBC 14.7/24
Perry Mason: The Case Of The Desperate Deception NBC 17.0/27
Perry Mason: The Case Of The Fatal Fashion NBC 14.6/23
Perry Mason: The Case Of The Fatal Framing NBC 12.9/20
Perry Mason: The Case Of The Glass Coffin NBC 12.8/22
Perry Mason: The Case Of The Heartbroken Bride NBC 12.1/21
Perry Mason: The Case Of The Killer Kiss NBC 19.3/29
Perry Mason: The Case Of The Lady In The Lake NBC 22.6/35
Perry Mason: The Case Of The Lost Love NBC 21.3/33
Perry Mason: The Case Of The Maligned Mobster NBC 14.0/22
Perry Mason: The Case Of The Murdered Madam NBC 18.1/29
Perry Mason: The Case Of The Musical Murders NBC 17.4/26
Perry Mason: The Case Of The Notorious Nun NBC 23.3/42
Perry Mason: The Case Of The Poisoned Pen NBC 16.0/24
Perry Mason: The Case Of The Reckless Romeo NBC 14.7/23
Perry Mason: The Case Of The Ruthless Reporter NBC 14.0/21
Perry Mason: The Case Of The Scandalous Scoundrel NBC 16.6/26
Perry Mason: The Case Of The Shooting Star NBC 23.6/37
Perry Mason: The Case Of The Silenced Singer NBC 16.5/27
Perry Mason: The Case Of The Sinister Spirit NBC 20.5/35
Perry Mason: The Case Of The Skin-Deep Scandal NBC 13.3/22
Perry Mason: The Case Of The Telltale Talk Show Host NBC 13.1/24
Precious Victims CBS 14.6/23
Prisoner Of Honor HBO
Rape Of Dr. Willis, The CBS 14.4/23
Roe Vs. Wade NBC 17.0/27
Scandal In A Small Town NBC 20.0/31
Secret Passion Of Robert Clayton, The USA
Separate But Equal ABC 11.9/19 11.8/19
Separated By Murder CBS 11.8/19
She Said No NBC 14.7/23
Silent Witness NBC 22.5/33
Small Sacrifices ABC 18.1/28 25.2/39
Switched At Birth NBC 20.4/32 23.1/35
Sworn To Silence ABC 16.1/24
Terrorist On Trial: The United States Vs. Salim Ajami CBS 13.3/20
Till Death Us Do Part NBC 14.6/21
Town Bully, The ABC 15.6/25
Trial And Error USA
Trial: The Price Of Passion NBC 11.2/18 13.2/21
Unspeakable Acts ABC 15.7/25
Web Of Deceit USA
Without Her Consent NBC 17.8/28

CROSS-CULTURAL STORY

Aaron's Way NBC 19.5/31
American Geisha CBS 11.7/20
Candles In The Dark FAMILY
Celebration Family ABC 10.2/17
Children In The Crossfire NBC 14.8/23
Comrades Of Summer HBO
Cowboy And The Ballerina, The CBS 12.1/19
Desperate Rescue: The Cathy Mahone Story NBC 13.3/20
Ellis Island CBS 23.4/35 21.1/33 19.0/29
Evergreen NBC 22.3/33 20.9/32 22.9/33

Face To Face CBS 14.7/24
Finding The Way Home ABC 10.2/18
Forbidden Nights CBS 10.5/17
Girl Who Came Between Them, The NBC 13.2/21
Johnny Bull ABC 12.7/20
Last Frontier, The CBS 23.8/36 25.0/39
Last Of His Tribe, The HBO
Liberty NBC 12.0/21
Mario Puzo's The Fortunate Pilgrim NBC 13.1/22 13.0/21
Miracle In The Wilderness TNT
Mrs. 'Arris Goes To Paris CBS 16.8/28
Of Pure Blood CBS 20.0/30
Over My Dead Body CBS 12.4/23
Stones Of Ibarra CBS 12.4/21
Stoning In Fulham County, A NBC 18.3/28

DISASTER

After The Shock USA
Big One: The Great Los Angeles Earthquake, The NBC 17.1/26 19.5/30
Crash Landing: The Rescue Of Flight 232 ABC 17.1/26
Dead Ahead: The Exxon Valdez HBO
Desperate Journey: The Allison Wilcox Story ABC 9.7/15
Fire And Rain USA
Fire Next Time, The NBC 13.1/22 11.0/18
Fire: Trapped On The 37th Floor ABC 11.2/17
Firestorm: 72 Hours In Oakland ABC 11.5/17
Flood: Who Will Save Our Children? NBC 11.4/18
Mercy Mission: The Rescue Of Flight 771 NBC 12.2/19
Miracle Landing CBS 15.1/23
Miracle On I-880 NBC 13.3/20
Mission Of The Shark CBS 15.6/25
Nurses On The Line: The Crash Of Flight 7 CBS 13.2/22
Ordeal In The Arctic ABC 14.0/22
Quiet Killer CBS 11.5/19
Snowbound: The Jim And Jennifer Stolpa Story CBS 18.2/27
Survive The Savage Sea ABC 15.6/24
Tragedy Of Flight 103: The Inside Story, The HBO
Triumph Over Disaster: The Hurricane Andrew Story NBC 15.7/25
Trouble Shooters: Trapped Beneath The Earth NBC 9.5/15
Without Warning: Terror In The Towers NBC 9.3/15

DRUG SMUGGLING/DEALING

Broken Angel ABC 16.9/28
Brotherhood Of Justice, The ABC 11.6/19
Child Saver, The NBC 15.8/25
Children Of Times Square ABC 12.5/20
Courage CBS 12.5/20
Dadah Is Death CBS 11.3/17 10.1/17
Dangerous Heart USA
Deadly Surveillance SHOWTIME
Dirty Work USA
Doublecrossed HBO
Drug Wars: The Camarena Story NBC 14.4/22 15.2/23 16.1/25

DRUG SMUGGLING/DEALING (CONTINUED)

Drug Wars: The Cocaine Cartel NBC 12.8/20
    13.2/20
In The Line Of Duty: A Cop For The Killing NBC
    14.6/23
In The Line Of Duty: Street War NBC 11.9/20
Jake Spanner, Private Eye USA
Jesse Hawkes CBS 8.9/17
Keys, The NBC 12.1/19
Miami Vice NBC 22.8/37
Nails SHOWTIME
Nasty Boys NBC 15.3/27
Necessity CBS 15.0/24
Seeds Of Tragedy FBC 4.6/9
Shannon's Deal NBC 14.5/25
Stormy Weathers ABC 10.2/16
Take, The USA
Thunderboat Row ABC 13.8/23
Trouble In Paradise CBS 10.9/18
Two Fathers' Justice NBC 17.9/27
Wolf CBS 14.2/25

FAMILY DRAMA

Aaron's Way NBC 19.5/31
Adam: His Song Continues NBC 15.9/25
After The Promise CBS 19.2/30
Aftermath: A Test Of Love CBS 17.3/27
Alex: The Life Of A Child ABC 21.7/36
Always Remember I Love You CBS 15.3/26
American Clock, The TNT
An Early Frost NBC 23.3/33
And Then There Was One LIFETIME
Anything To Survive ABC 16.5/26
Appearances NBC 9.8/18
Armed & Innocent CBS 14.9/24
As Summers Die HBO
Baby M ABC 15.0/24 17.6/27
Baby Of The Bride CBS 15.0/26
Babymaker: The Dr. Cecil Jacobson's Story CBS
    14.0/21
Baron And The Kid, The CBS 10.4/17
Battling For Baby CBS 16.2/26
Betrayed By Innocence CBS 10.8/19
Between Two Women ABC 16.2/25
Blind Faith NBC 19.9/31 23.3/36
Blind Spot CBS 13.1/20
Bloodlines: Murder In The Family NBC 10.7/17
    13.3/21
Bluffing It ABC 13.4/22
Bonanza: The Return NBC 17.6/26
Born Too Soon NBC 10.5/17
Bradys, The CBS 12.9/22
Breathing Lessons CBS 21.6/32
Bridge To Silence CBS 13.9/24
Broadway Bound ABC 8.4/14
Broken Angel ABC 16.9/28
Broken Cord, The ABC 14.3/22
Broken Promises: Taking Emily Back CBS
    12.6/22
Bump In The Night CBS 16.0/25
Burden Of Proof, The ABC 12.8/18 15.1/23
Burning Bridges ABC 13.6/22
Can You Feel Me Dancing? NBC 19.1/30
Captive ABC 12.9/20
Caroline? CBS 19.4/30
Casey's Gift: For Love Of A Child NBC 14.0/22
Celebration Family ABC 10.2/17
Charles And Diana: Unhappily Ever After ABC
    12.8/19

Child Lost Forever, A NBC 15.4/23
Child Of Rage CBS 14.7/24
Children Of The Bride CBS 13.6/25
Children Of The Dark CBS 13.4/22
Choices ABC 18.1/27
Circle Of Violence: A CBS 15.7/25
Comeback, The CBS 16.6/29
Common Ground CBS 11.0/18 10.8/18
Consenting Adult ABC 23.1/33
Conspiracy Of Love CBS 14.1/21
Convicted: A Mother's Story NBC 17.4/27
Courage CBS 12.5/20
Cracked Up ABC 14.7/23
Crazy In Love TNT
Cruel Doubt NBC 16.8/27 14.8/24
Cry For Help: The Tracey Thurman Story, A NBC
    21.5/33
Daddy ABC 17.1/25
Dallas: The Early Years CBS 21.3/33
Danger Down Under NBC 13.3/22
Danielle Steel's Changes NBC 17.8/28
Danielle Steel's Daddy NBC 19.6/30
Danielle Steel's Fine Things NBC 18.0/28
Danielle Steel's Jewels NBC 14.7/22 15.6/24
Danielle Steel's Kaleidoscope NBC 20.3/32
Daughter Of The Streets ABC 14.9/24
Daughters Of Privilege NBC 13.9/23
David ABC 19.5/30
David's Mother CBS 16.3/26
Dead Before Dawn ABC 18.0/26
Deadly Relations ABC 10.01 19
Death Dreams LIFETIME
Death Of A Salesman CBS 14.5/23
Deception: A Mother's Secret NBC 15.6/23
Descending Angel HBO
Desperate Choices: To Save My Child NBC
    12.4/19
Desperate Rescue: The Cathy Mahone Story
    NBC 13.3/20
Diana: Her True Story NBC 14.5/23 15.6/24
Dinner At Eight TNT
Do You Know The Muffin Man? CBS 18.4/30
Do You Remember Love? CBS 17.0/28
Doing Time On Maple Drive FBC 9.4/15
Donato And Daughter CBS 14.8/24
Double Standard NBC 21.1/33
Downpayment On Murder NBC 16.1/27
Dream Breakers CBS 7.4/12
Dreamer Of Oz, The NBC 11.8/18
Dynasty: The Reunion ABC 16.8/25 15.3/23
Eight Is Enough: A Family Reunion NBC
    22.0/34
Eighty-Three Hours 'til Dawn CBS 14.2/22
Evergreen NBC 22.3/33 20.9/32 22.9/33
Everybody's Baby: The Rescue Of Jessica
    Mcclure ABC 22.2/36
Evil In Clear River ABC 12.9/20
Extreme Close-Up NBC 12.3/20
Eye On The Sparrow NBC 14.3/22
Family For Joe, A NBC 15.8/23
Family Of Spies CBS 14.7/22 13.6/21
Family Of Strangers CBS 19.8/29
Family Pictures ABC 10.1/16 11.5/18
Family Sins CBS 12.9/20
Fatal Memories NBC 15.8/24
Father & Son: Dangerous Relations NBC 14.6/24
Father's Homecoming, A NBC 12.5/23
Father's Revenge, A ABC 10.4/16
Fight For Jenny, A NBC 20.0/31
Fight For Life ABC 16.2/26
Finding The Way Home ABC 10.2/18
Finish Line TNT
Fire And Rain USA

Fire In The Dark CBS 14.8/23
Follow Your Heart NBC 14.7/23
For Love And Glory 9.4/18
For Richer, For Poorer HBO
For The Love Of Aaron CBS 12.4/21
For The Love Of My Child: The Anissa Ayala
    Story NBC 12.8/20
Foxfire CBS 19.3/30
Fulfillment Of Mary Gray, The CBS 16.5/26
Generation ABC 6.5/12
Getting Out ABC 11.1/18
Getting Up And Going Home LIFETIME
Girl Who Came Between Them, The NBC
    13.2/21
Glory Days CBS 11.1/17
Go Toward The Light CBS 14.9/24
God Bless The Child ABC 17.7/28
Good Night, Sweet Wife: A Murder In Boston
    CBS 14.9/23
Grass Roots NBC 13.4/20 15.1/23
Grave Secrets: The Legacy Of Hilltop Drive CBS
    14.7/23
Gregory K ABC 10.3/16
Gypsy CBS 18.6/28
Habitation Of Dragons, The TNT
Hands Of A Stranger NBC 15.2/25 17.4/28
Harvest For The Heart FAMILY
He's Not Your Son CBS 23.2/36
Heart Of A Child NBC 11.5/18
Heartsounds ABC 18.5/31
Held Hostage: The Sis And Jerry Levin Story
    ABC 12.0/19
High Mountain Rangers CBS 19.6/32
Hitler's S S: Portrait In Evil NBC 15.8/24
Home Fires Burning CBS 18.6/29
Homefront ABC 12.2/20
Honor Thy Mother CBS 15.5/24
Hostage For A Day FBC 6.6/11
House Of Secrets And Lies, A CBS 15.5/27
Hush Little Baby USA
I Know My First Name Is Steven NBC 21.6/35
    27.3/42
I Know My Son Is Alive NBC 9.9/15
I'll Fly Away NBC 15.4/24
Illicit Behavior USA
In A Child's Name CBS 17.8/27 21.9/33
In My Daughter's Name CBS 15.8/27
In Sickness And In Health CBS 16.3/26
In The Best Interest Of The Child CBS 11.6/19
In The Best Interest Of The Children NBC
    16.0/24
In The Best Of Families: Marriage, Pride And
    Madness CBS 16.1/25 17.3/26
Incident At Dark River TNT
Incident In A Small Town CBS 18.7/31
Inconvenient Woman, An ABC 11.7/21 12.4/20
Infidelity ABC 16.8/27
Intimate Encounters NBC 14.2/23
Intimate Strangers CBS 26.4/38
Into Thin Air CBS 15.7/25
Island Sons ABC 7.9/14
J F K: Reckless Youth ABC 7.8/12 9.5/16
Jackie Collins' Lucky Chances NBC 14.4/25
    17.1/26 19.5/31
Jacksons: An American Dream , The ABC
    21.1/31 23.9/36
Jane's House CBS 19.5/29
Johnny Bull ABC 12.7/20
Jonathan: The Boy Nobody Wanted NBC 13.8/21
Joshua's Heart NBC 15.6/26
Judgment HBO
Judith Krantz's Till We Meet Again CBS 14.8/23
    11.7/18

FAMILY DRAMA (CONTINUED)

Kane And Abel   CBS   23.2/34   23.4/34   21.4/32
Kate's Secret   NBC   24.1/36
Keep The Change   TNT
Keeping Secrets   ABC   14.2/23
Kennedys Of Massachusetts, The   ABC   15.8/24
   17.6/27   16.4/25
Keys, The   NBC   12.1/19
Kids Like These   CBS   16.5/27
Killer Among Friends, A   CBS   16.7/27
Kissing Place, The   USA
Labor Of Love: The Arlette Schweitzer Story
   CBS   14.1/23
Lace II   ABC   15.3/24   16.4/25
Lady From Yesterday, The   CBS   16.0/25
Lantern Hill   DISNEY
Last Frontier, The   CBS   23.8/36   25.0/39
Last To Go, The   ABC   11.0/17
Last Wish   ABC   10.8/17
Laurel Avenue   HBO
Leap Of Faith   CBS   12.0/20
Leave Of Absence   NBC   10.1/15
Legacy Of Lies   USA
Liar, Liar   CBS   14.5/26
Lies Before Kisses   CBS   18.5/29
Lies Of The Heart: The Story Of Laurie Kellogg
   ABC   15.0/23
Little Girl Lost   ABC   19.0/31
Living A Lie   NBC   11.0/17
Locked Up: A Mother's Rage   CBS   12.4/20
Long Hot Summer, The   NBC   22.6/34   23.8/36
Long Road Home   NBC   11.8/18
Long Time Gone   ABC   7.4/14
Love And Betrayal   CBS   16.1/25
Love And Hate: A Marriage Made In Hell   NBC
   13.9/25   16.3/28
Love, Honor & Obey: The Last Mafia Marriage
   CBS   12.6/20   14.4/24
Love Is Never Silent   NBC   17.3/26
Love, Lies And Murder   NBC   15.5/24   20.3/30
Love Lives On   ABC   17.8/26
Love, Mary   CBS   21.5/33
Love Matters   SHOWTIME
Lucky Day   ABC   9.8/16
Mario Puzo's The Fortunate Pilgrim   NBC
   13.1/22   13.0/21
Miles From Nowhere   CBS   10.8/17
Miles To Go . . .   CBS   16.5/26
Miracle At Beekman's Place   NBC   12.3/21
Miss Rose White   NBC   11.0/17
Moment Of Truth: A Child Too Many   NBC
   14.2/22
Moment Of Truth: Cradle Of Conspiracy   NBC
   13.5/21
Moment Of Truth: Stalking Back   NBC   15.9/25
Moment Of Truth: To Walk Again   NBC   8.3/12
Moment Of Truth: Why My Daughter?   NBC
   14.2/23
Montana   TNT
Mother Of The Bride   CBS   9.6/17
Mother's Justice, A   NBC   16.7/25
Mothers, Daughters And Lovers   NBC   8.4/14
Mothers Revenge, A   ABC   10.6/16
Mothers' Right, A: The Elizabeth Morgan Story
   ABC   13.6/21
Moving Target   NBC   17.2/25
Mrs. Delafield Wants To Marry   CBS   21.0/35
Mrs. Lambert Remembers Love   CBS   9.9/17
Murder Of Innocence   CBS   14.5/22
My Brother's Wife   ABC   11.2/18
My Father, My Son   CBS   13.5/22
My Name Is Bill W.   ABC   15.2/24

My Name Is Kate   ABC   11.2/17
My Son Johnny   CBS   15.6/24
My Two Loves   ABC   17.5/28
Nairobi Affair   CBS   12.2/20
Necessity   CBS   15.0/24
Night Of The Hunter   ABC   13.7/23
No Child Of Mine   CBS   13.1/21
No Place Like Home   CBS   13.3/20
Nobody's Children   USA
Norman Rockwell's Breaking Home Ties   ABC
   9.7/19
North And South   ABC   25.8/37   23.6/34
   28.0/42   25.8/38   23.2/37
North And South, Book 2   ABC   19.8/30   20.1/30
   21.6/36   22.9/36   20.8/32
North And South, Book 3: Heaven And Hell   ABC
   10.1/15   9.8/15   9.7/15
Not In My Family   ABC   15.1/23
Not My Kid   CBS   21.6/33
Oldest Living Confederate Widow Tells All   CBS
   15.7/24   13.8/21
On Fire   ABC   12.8/20
One More Mountain   ABC   12.9/20
One Terrific Guy   CBS   19.6/30
Original Sin   NBC   16.8/26
Orpheus Descending   TNT
Other Women's Children   LIFETIME
Our Family Honor   ABC   15.4/25
Our Sons   ABC   12.8/21
Out On The Edge   CBS   14.6/23
Pack Of Lies   CBS   18.2/30
Passions   CBS   22.4/34
People Across The Lake, The   NBC   17.3/27
People Like Us   NBC   9.4/16   10.5/17
Picket Fences   CBS   12.7/24
Picking Up The Pieces   CBS   16.8/25
Place To Be Loved, A   CBS   13.0/20
Place To Call Home, A   CBS   15.4/26
Playing With Fire   NBC   16.9/26
Portrait, The   TNT
Private Matter, A   HBO
Promise   CBS   19.5/29
Promise To Keep, A   NBC   14.3/23
Promised A Miracle   CBS   13.2/22
Proud Men   ABC   9.4/15
Quiet Victory: The Charlie Wedemeyer Story
   CBS   14.9/25
Reason For Living: The Jill Ireland Story   NBC
   12.5/21
Reason To Live, A   NBC   15.6/23
Red Earth, White Earth   CBS   11.9/19
Right Of The People, The   ABC   14.5/22
Right To Die   NBC   17.5/28
Rio Shanon   ABC   5.2/11
Rising Son   TNT
Roxanne: The Prize Pulitzer   NBC   17.3/27
Runaway Father   CBS   16.8/27
Sarah, Plain And Tall   CBS   23.1/35
Scattered Dreams: The Kathryn Messenger Story
   CBS   14.1/22
Seasons Of The Heart   NBC   12.9/21
Secret Sins Of The Father   NBC   16.0/24
Secret, The   CBS   13.3/23
Secrets Of A Married Man   NBC   17.5/27
Secrets Of Lake Success   NBC   7.7/14   7.4/14
   7.1/13
Sentimental Journey   CBS   14.0/23
Shadow Of A Doubt   CBS   15.3/24
Shameful Secrets   ABC   13.2/21
Shameful Secrets   ABC   13.2/21
Shattered Dreams   CBS   16.8/28
Shattered Spirits   ABC   16.4/25
Shattered Trust: The Shari Karney Story   NBC
   16.2/25

She Says She's Innocent   NBC   15.0/23
Shell Seekers, The   ABC   15.7/24
Shootdown   NBC   16.0/25
Side By Side   CBS   12.4/20
Silence Of The Heart   CBS   21.9/35
Silent Witness   NBC   22.5/33
Sin Of Innocence   CBS   12.5/21
Sins Of The Father   NBC   15.0/23
Sins Of The Mother   CBS   14.5/23
Skylark   CBS   19.9/29
Snowbound: The Jim And Jennifer Stolpa Story
   CBS   18.2/27
Something To Live For: The Alison Gertz Story
   ABC   16.2/26
Son's Promise, A   ABC   16.5/27
Spoils Of War   ABC   4.9/9
Stay The Night   ABC   13.8/22   17.9/28
Stoning In Fulham County, A   NBC   18.3/28
Stop At Nothing   LIFETIME
Stormin' Home   CBS   13.1/23
Story Lady, The   NBC   15.9/24
Strange Voices   NBC   21.0/33
Stranger In My Bed   NBC   18.8/29
Stranger In The Family, A   ABC   12.7/19
Stranger On My Land   ABC   11.5/18
Stranger Within, The   CBS   15.6/25
Substitute Wife, The   NBC   17.5/27
Sudie And Simpson   LIFETIME
Summer My Father Grew Up, The   NBC   10.5/16
Summer To Remember, A   CBS   13.8/21
Survive The Savage Sea   ABC   15.6/24
Surviving   ABC   18.1/26
Switched At Birth   NBC   20.4/32   23.1/35
Taken Away   CBS   16.3/25
Taking Back My Life: The Nancy Ziegenmeyer
   Story   CBS   15.8/25
Tears And Laughter: The Joan And Mielissa Rivers
   Story   NBC   13.1/21
Thanksgiving Day   NBC   10.9/17
There Are No Children Here   ABC   17.8/26
There Must Be A Pony   ABC   12.6/19
There Was A Little Boy   CBS   13.8/22
They   SHOWTIME
Thicker Than Blood: The Larry Mclinden Story
   CBS   14.5/23
This Child Is Mine   NBC   21.1/32
Thompson's Last Run   CBS   17.4/26
Those Secrets   ABC   8.9/14
Those She Left Behind   NBC   25.1/38
Three Wishes Of Billy Grier, The   ABC   13.5/21
Time To Heal, A   NBC   12.7/21
Time To Live, A   NBC   17.1/27
Time To Triumph, A   CBS   16.0/25
To Be The Best   CBS   9.3/15   7.7/3
To My Daughter   NBC   13.5/22
To My Daughter With Love   NBC   13.8/21
Too Good To Be True   NBC   20.9/32
Toughlove   ABC   20.6/31
Trade Winds   NBC   6.9/13   6.2/13   5.4/11   5.8/11
Two Fathers' Justice   NBC   17.9/27
Two Fathers: Justice For The Innocent   NBC
   10.3/17
Two Mrs. Grenvilles, The   NBC   23.4/36   24.0/35
Ultimate Betrayal   CBS   15.6/25
Under The Influence   CBS   15.4/24
Us   CBS   16.1/29
Very Brady Christmas, A   CBS   25.1/39
Victim Of Love: The Shannon Mohr Story   NBC
   13.0/19
Vital Signs   CBS   16.7/26
Voices Within: The Lives Of Truddi Chase   ABC
   14.7/24   15.5/25
Walton Thanksgiving Reunion, A   CBS   20.1/30

FAMILY DRAMA (CONTINUED)

War And Remembrance ABC 21.8/31 19.0/29
  19.8/31 16.8/25 17.0/26
War And Remembrance, Part I I ABC 13.4/21
  14.4/22 15.1/24 15.7/25 15.9/26
Welcome Home, Bobby CBS 12.5/21
What She Doesn't Know NBC 16.6/25
When The Time Comes ABC 11.1/18
When We Were Young NBC 10.9/19
Where Pigeons Go To Die NBC 15.3/24
Whereabouts Of Jenny, The ABC 15.4/24
Whose Child Is This? The War For Baby Jessica
  ABC 9.6/15
Wife, Mother, Murderer ABC 15.6/24
Wild Texas Wind NBC 18.0/27
Wildflower LIFETIME
Willing To Kill: The Texas Cheerleader Story
  ABC 14.4/22
Without Warning: The James Brady Story HBO
Woman Scorned: The Betty Broderick Story, A
  CBS 19.5/30
Woman Who Loved Elvis, The ABC 12.1/20
Woman With A Past NBC 17.5/27
Yarn Princess, The ABC 10.5/17
Yearling, The CBS 13.2/21

FAMILY VIOLENCE

At Mother's Request CBS 23.3/35 22.7/35
Bed Of Lies ABC 16.8/25
Beyond Obsession ABC 13.6/21
Blind Faith NBC 19.9/31 23.3/36
Bloodlines: Murder In The Family NBC 10.7/17
  13.3/21
Breaking The Silence CBS 12.8/20
Burning Bed, The NBC 36.2/52
Calendar Girl, Cop Killer? The Bambi Bembenek
  Story ABC 10.7/17
Circle Of Violence: A CBS 15.7/25
Conviction Of Kitty Dodds, The CBS 13.2/21
Cries Unheard: The Donna Yaklich Story CBS
  14.0/22
Cruel Doubt NBC 16.8/27 14.8/24
Cry For Help: The Tracey Thurman Story, A NBC
  21.5/33
David ABC 19.5/30
Dead Before Dawn ABC 18.0/26
Deadly Betrayal: The Bruce Curtis Story NBC
  12.9/20
Deadly Intentions... Again? ABC 12.8/20
Deadly Relations ABC 10.01 19
Deadly Silence, A ABC 17.9/28
Downpayment On Murder NBC 16.1/27
Family Sins CBS 12.9/20
Family Torn Apart, A NBC 15.1/23
Fatal Vision NBC 29.5/44 32.7/49
Father Of Hell Town NBC 18.2/29
Final Appeal NBC 12.7/20
Good Night, Sweet Wife: A Murder In Boston
  CBS 14.9/23
Honor Thy Father And Mother: The Menendez
  Murders FBC 10.2/17
Honor Thy Mother CBS 15.5/24
House Of Secrets NBC 14.6/23
In A Child's Name CBS 17.8/27 21.9/33
In The Best Interest Of The Children NBC
  16.0/24
In The Best Of Families: Marriage, Pride And
  Madness CBS 16.1/25 17.3/26

Judgment Day: The John List Story CBS
  15.8/25
Keeping Secrets ABC 14.2/23
Kissing Place, The USA
Lies Of The Heart: The Story Of Laurie Kellogg
  ABC 15.0/23
Love And Hate: A Marriage Made In Hell NBC
  13.9/25 16.3/28
Love, Lies And Murder NBC 15.5/24 20.3/30
Mafia Princess NBC 24.4/37
Men Don't Tell CBS 19.7/31
Menendez: A Killing In Beverly Hills CBS
  9.6/16 9.3/15
Murder Between Friends NBC 12.9/20
Murder: By Reason Of Insanity CBS 16.6/26
My Son Johnny CBS 15.6/24
Not In My Family ABC 15.1/23
Nutcracker: Money, Madness And Murder NBC
  12.2/20 11.5/19 13.5/22
Paris Trout SHOWTIME
Poisoned By Love: The Kern County Murders
  CBS 14.5/24
Psycho I V: The Beginning SHOWTIME
Right To Kill? ABC 19.0/31
Shattered Dreams CBS 16.8/28
Silent Witness NBC 22.5/33
Sin And Redemption CBS 14.0/23
Small Sacrifices ABC 18.1/28 25.2/39
Stay The Night ABC 13.8/22 17.9/28
Stop At Nothing LIFETIME
Trapped In Silence CBS 15.1/24
Ultimate Betrayal CBS 15.6/25
Victim Of Love: The Shannon Mohr Story NBC
  13.0/19
Voices Within: The Lives Of Truddi Chase ABC
  14.7/24 15.5/25
What Ever Happened To Baby Jane? ABC
  9.9/15
When No One Would Listen CBS 12.9/19
Wild Texas Wind NBC 18.0/27
Woman On The Run: The Lawrencia Bembenek
  Story NBC 11.1/18 15.6/25
Woman Scorned: The Betty Broderick Story, A
  CBS 19.5/30
Woman With A Past NBC 17.5/27

FARM STORY

Aaron's Way NBC 19.5/31
American Harvest CBS 16.4/27
Bluegrass CBS 17.6/27 18.4/29
Danielle Steel's Palomino NBC 18.4/28
Harvest For The Heart FAMILY
Keep The Change TNT
Long Road Home NBC 11.8/18
Montana TNT
O Pioneers CBS 18.9/29
Red Earth, White Earth CBS 11.9/19
Return To Green Acres CBS 11.8/22
Sarah, Plain And Tall CBS 23.1/35
Skylark CBS 19.9/29
Sodbusters SHOWTIME
Stone Fox NBC 15.9/22
Stranger On My Land ABC 11.5/18
Wild Horses CBS 16.7/26

FORBIDDEN LOVE

Angel In Green CBS 13.1/22
Betrayed By Innocence CBS 10.8/19
Betrayed By Love ABC 10.8/16
Between Love And Hate ABC 14.2/21
Broken Vows CBS 14.1/22
Burning Bridges ABC 13.6/22
Comeback, The CBS 16.6/29
Desperate For Love CBS 12.0/20
Double Standard NBC 21.1/33
For The Very First Time NBC 10.8/18
Forbidden Nights CBS 10.5/17
Fulfillment Of Mary Gray, The CBS 16.5/26
Getting Up And Going Home LIFETIME
Grand Isle TNT
Infidelity ABC 16.8/27
Lady Killer USA
Leave Of Absence NBC 10.1/15
Letter To Three Wives, A NBC 19.3/30
Murder In New Hampshire: The Pamela Smart
  Story CBS 15.9/26
Murderous Affair, A: The Carolyn Warmus Story
  ABC 15.0/25
North And South ABC 25.8/37 23.6/34
  28.0/42 25.8/38 23.2/37
North And South, Book 2 ABC 19.8/30 20.1/30
  21.6/36 22.9/36 20.8/32
Obsessed With A Married Woman ABC 14.5/22
Orpheus Descending TNT
Other Lover, The CBS 13.8/22
Secrets Of A Married Man NBC 17.5/27
Seduction: Three Tales From The Inner Sanctum
  ABC 9.4/15
Shattered Vows NBC 21.3/33
Sin Of Innocence CBS 12.5/21
Single Women, Married Men CBS 14.6/26
Sins Of The Father NBC 15.0/23
Stay The Night ABC 13.8/22 17.9/28
Steal The Sky HBO
Victim Of Love CBS 12.0/20
Woman Who Sinned, The ABC 12.1/18

FOREIGN OR EXOTIC LOCATION

Abraham TNT
Adrift CBS 12.1/20
Agatha Christie's Dead Man's Folly CBS
  14.4/22
Agatha Christie's Murder In Three Acts CBS
  15.4/25
Agatha Christie's The Man In The Brown Suit
  CBS 15.8/25
Agatha Christie's Thirteen At Dinner CBS
  12.8/21
American Geisha CBS 11.7/20
Anastasia: The Mystery Of Anna NBC 20.7/32
  20.9/32
And The Sea Will Tell CBS 20.1/31 19.0/29
Angel In Green CBS 13.1/22
Anna Karenina CBS 16.6/26
Anything To Survive ABC 16.5/26
Arch Of Triumph CBS 9.2/16
Around The World In 80 Days NBC 15.5/24
  13.2/21 13.0/21
Aurora NBC 18.0/28
Back Home DISNEY
Barbara Taylor Bradford's Remember NBC
  10.9/18 13.5/21
Bare Essentials CBS 13.3/21

FOREIGN OR EXOTIC LOCATION
(CONTINUED)

Bejeweled DISNEY
Bermuda Grace NBC 8.2/14
Beryl Markham: A Shadow On The Sun CBS
   10.4/16 7.8/13
Blade In Hong Kong CBS 10.3/16
Blind Side HBO
Blood And Orchids CBS 22.9/35 25.6/38
Borrowers, The TNT
Bourne Identity, The ABC 18.5/30 18.5/29
Brotherhood Of The Rose NBC 20.9/35
   19.2/30
Candles In The Dark FAMILY
Casanova ABC 10.3/15
Casualty Of War, A USA
Charles And Diana: Unhappily Ever After ABC
   12.8/19
Chernobyl: The Final Warning TNT
China Beach ABC 18.0/29
Christopher Columbus CBS 17.4/29 15.8/25
Cisco Kid, The TNT
Clinton And Nadine HBO
Club Med ABC 14.8/23
Comrades Of Summer HBO
Conspiracy Of Silence CBS 12.5/21 12.2/20
Cover Girl Murders, The USA
Cover Up CBS 14.0/26
Crossing To Freedom CBS 10.3/17
Crossings ABC 17.5/27 15.0/22 17.4/27
Crucifier Of Blood, The TNT
Dadah Is Death CBS 11.3/17 10.1/17
Danger Down Under NBC 13.3/22
Danielle Steel's Jewels NBC 14.7/22 15.6/24
Danielle Steel's Message From Nam NBC
   11.5/18 11.4/18
Dark Holiday NBC 11.1/18
Daughter Of Darkness CBS 10.4/18
Day Of Reckoning NBC 8.7/14
Deadly Betrayal: The Bruce Curtis Story NBC
   12.9/20
Death Train USA
Deceptions NBC 19.9/35 21.8/35
Deep Trouble USA
Descending Angel HBO
Desperate Rescue: The Cathy Mahone Story
   NBC 13.3/20
Diamond Trap, The CBS 15.1/24
Diana: Her True Story NBC 14.5/23 15.6/24
Doublecrossed HBO
Drug Wars: The Camarena Story NBC 14.4/22
   15.2/23 16.1/25
Drug Wars: The Cocaine Cartel NBC 12.8/20
   13.2/20
Duel Of Hearts TNT
Endless Game, The SHOWTIME
Evil In Clear River ABC 12.9/20
Ewok Adventure, The ABC 24.9/36
Ewoks: The Battle For Endor ABC 18.7/26
Eyes Of A Witness CBS 13.0/23
Face To Face CBS 14.7/24
Facts Of Life Down Under, The NBC 21.4/32
Fall From Grace CBS 7.7/14 6.4/13
Family Ties Vacation NBC 22.1/33
Fatal Deception: Mrs. Lee Harvey Oswald NBC
   11.2/18
Fatal Image, The CBS 14.1/22
Father's Revenge, A ABC 10.4/16
Fergie And Andrew: Behind The Palace Doors
   NBC 13.6/21

Florence Nightingale NBC 11.6/19
Florida Straits HBO
Forbidden HBO
Forbidden Nights CBS 10.5/17
Foreign Affairs TNT
Forgotten Prisoners: The Amnesty File TNT
Fortress HBO
Frankenstein TNT
Ghost In Monte Carlo, A TNT
Glitz NBC 14.1/25
Great Expectations DISNEY
Gulag HBO
Harem ABC 16.9/25 16.2/23
Harry's Hong Kong ABC 6.1/11
Hawaiian Heat ABC 19.1/34
Heart Of Darkness TNT
Heidi DISNEY
Held Hostage: The Sis And Jerry Levin Story
   ABC 12.0/19
Her Secret Life ABC 13.7/21
Heroes Of Desert Storm ABC 9.9/16
Hijacking Of The Achille Lauro, The NBC
   12.7/20
Hiroshima: Out Of The Ashes NBC 11.3/20
Hostages HBO
I Spy Returns CBS 12.4/18
If It's Tuesday, It Still Must Be Belgium NBC
   13.4/22
If Tomorrow Comes CBS 21.8/34 23.6/37
   20.8/33
In Like Flynn ABC 8.4/15
Indiscreet CBS 12.0/18
Intrigue CBS 8.8/19
Investigation: Inside A Terrorist Bombing, The
   HBO
Iran: Days Of Crisis TNT
Island Sons ABC 7.9/14
Jake And The Fatman CBS 15.8/27
James Clavell's Noble House NBC 17.9/27
   15.9/24 15.0/22 16.3/26
Josephine Baker Story, The HBO
Judith Krantz's Till We Meet Again CBS 14.8/23
   11.7/18
Just Another Secret USA
Kane And Abel CBS 23.2/34 23.4/34 21.4/32
Killer Rules NBC 9.2/14
Lace II ABC 15.3/24 16.4/25
Lady And The Highwayman, The CBS 11.1/18
Last Days Of Patton, The CBS 19.5/32
Last Elephant, The TNT
Last Flight Out NBC 10.7/18
Last Frontier, The CBS 23.8/36 25.0/39
Last P. O. W? The Bobby Garwood Story, The
   ABC 11.5/20
Lena: My 100 Children NBC 13.4/21
Lethal Exposure NBC 8.8/14
Lie Down With Lions LIFETIME
Lily CBS 6.6/14
Lion Of Africa, The HBO
Little Kidnappers, The DISNEY
Lost In London CBS 13.0/19
Love Among Thieves ABC 13.2/21
Love And Hate: A Marriage Made In Hell NBC
   13.9/25 16.3/28
Love Boat: A Valentine Voyage, The CBS
   13.6/22
Love On The Run NBC 9.3/16
Love She Sought, The NBC 12.0/18
Macgyver : Lost Treasure Of Atlantis ABC
   9.1/17
Man For All Season, A TNT
Mandela HBO
Marcus Welby, M. D.: A Holiday Affair NBC
   13.5/21

Max And Helen TNT
Mercy Mission: The Rescue Of Flight 771 NBC
   12.2/19
Mistral's Daughter CBS 18.2/29 18.7/30
   16.3/26
Monte Carlo CBS 14.6/23 12.2/19
Mrs. 'Arris Goes To Paris CBS 16.8/28
Murder In Paradise NBC 12.6/21
Murder With Mirrors CBS 15.2/23
Mussolini: The Decline And Fall Of Il Duce HBO
Mussolini - The Untold Story NBC 17.7/26
   19.4/29 19.6/29
Nairobi Affair CBS 12.2/20
Napoleon And Josephine: A Love Story ABC
   18.6/30 16.2/26 13.3/21
Nightlife USA
Nobody's Children USA
Not A Penny More, Not A Penny Less USA
Nurses On The Line: The Crash Of Flight 7 CBS
   13.2/22
Of Pure Blood CBS 20.0/30
Old Man & The Sea, The NBC 14.9/24
On Wings Of Eagles NBC 17.0/28 21.2/34
One Against The Wind CBS 13.4/21
Only One Survived CBS 6.5/12
Ordeal In The Arctic ABC 14.0/22
Out On A Limb ABC 13.8/20 16.8/25
Outback Bound CBS 15.7/25
Pack Of Lies CBS 18.2/30
Palace Guard CBS 7.4/14
Passion And Paradise ABC 11.8/19 12.5/20
Passport To Murder NBC 11.7/19
Perry Mason: The Case Of The Desperate
   Deception NBC 17.0/27
Peter The Great
   NBC 19.0/28 17.6/26 16.6/26 17.4/27
Phantom Of The Opera, The NBC 12.3/19
   12.3/20
Place To Call Home, A CBS 15.4/26
Pleasures ABC 12.9/20
Poor Little Rich Girl: The Barbara Hutton Story
   NBC 21.3/33 18.5/30
Pride And Extreme Prejudice USA
Prisoner Of Honor HBO
Queenie ABC 12.7/21 12.9/21
Railway Station Man, The TNT
Red King, White Knight HBO
Remington Steele: The Steele That Wouldn't Die
   NBC 19.7/28
Return Of Sam Mccloud, The CBS 12.9/20
Return Of Sherlock Holmes, The CBS 14.4/24
Reunion At Fairborough HBO
Revealing Evidence NBC 14.5/25
Revolver NBC 9.2/16
Riviera ABC 11.5/17
Robin Hood FBC 6.0/10
Roman Holiday NBC 17.0/28
Romance On The Orient Express NBC 15.6/24
Royce SHOWTIME
Sakharov HBO
Saved By The Bell-Hawaiian Style NBC 9.5/17
Season Of Giants, A TNT
Secret Life Of Ian Fleming, The TNT
Secret Weapon TNT
Secret Weapons NBC 13.8/21
Seeds Of Tragedy FBC 4.6/9
Shell Seekers, The ABC 15.7/24
Silent Cries NBC 12.4/20
Sins NBC 19.7/29 21.9/32 20.6/32
Souvenir SHOWTIME
Stalin HBO
Steal The Sky HBO
Still Crazy Like A Fox CBS 21.2/31

FOREIGN OR EXOTIC LOCATION
(CONTINUED)

Stones Of Ibarra CBS 12.4/21
Stranded NBC 24.9/38
Sun Also Rises, The NBC 13.2/20 11.6/18
Survive The Savage Sea ABC 15.6/24
Sweet Revenge TNT
Swimsuit NBC 17.3/27
Sword Of Gideon HBO
Target Of Suspicion USA
Tarzan In Manhattan CBS 10.5/19
Tenth Man, The CBS 13.3/21
To Be The Best CBS 9.3/15 7.7/3
Trade Winds NBC 6.9/13 6.2/13 5.4/11 5.8/11
Tragedy Of Flight 103: The Inside Story, The HBO
Treasure Island TNT
Trenchcoat In Paradise CBS 12.2/20
Trouble In Paradise CBS 10.9/18
Twist Of Fate NBC 14.3/21 15.2/24
Under Cover ABC 9.9/16
Vestige Of Honor CBS 11.0/18
Voyage USA
Wallenberg: A Hero's Story NBC 20.2/33 19.7/30
War And Remembrance ABC 21.8/31 19.0/29 19.8/31 16.8/25 17.0/26
War And Remembrance, Part II ABC 13.4/21 14.4/22 15.1/24 15.7/25 15.9/26
We Are The Children ABC 9.1/14
Weekend War ABC 14.9/24
Wet Gold ABC 18.3/30
Which Way Home TNT
Windmills Of The Gods CBS 19.0/28 17.3/27
Woman He Loved, The CBS 14.5/25
Women Of Valor CBS 19.6/32
Women Of Windsor CBS 13.8/22
World War II: When Lions Roared NBC 9.1/15 7.5/12
Young Catherine TNT
Young Indiana Jones Chronicles: The Curse Of The Jackal ABC 16.6/26

HISTORICAL PIECE

Abraham TNT
Alamo: 13 Days To Glory, The NBC 15.7/22
Amelia Earhart: The Final Flight TNT
American Clock, The TNT
Anastasia: The Mystery Of Anna NBC 20.7/32 20.9/32
Anna Karenina CBS 16.6/26
April Morning CBS 15.2/24
Around The World In 80 Days NBC 15.5/24 13.2/21 13.0/21
Badge Of The Assassin CBS 13.6/23
Bonnie And Clyde: The True Story FBC 8.7/15
Broken Chain TNT
Call Of The Wild CBS 18.2/29
Captain Cook TNT
Casanova ABC 10.3/15
Challenger ABC 12.8/20
Christopher Columbus CBS 17.4/29 15.8/25
Citizen Cohn HBO
Class Of '61 ABC 8.5/14
Common Ground CBS 11.0/18 10.8/18
Cross Of Fire NBC 12.5/20 14.7/23
Day One CBS 15.2/24
Decoration Day NBC 17.9/28
Dream West CBS 19.5/29 18.1/29 20.1/32

Ellis Island CBS 23.4/35 21.1/33 19.0/29
Ernest Green Story, The DISNEY
Escape From Sobibor CBS 21.4/34
Evergreen NBC 22.3/33 20.9/32 22.9/33
Fatal Deception: Mrs. Lee Harvey Oswald NBC 11.2/18
Final Days ABC 10.2/17
For Love And Glory CBS 9.4/18
Forbidden Nights CBS 10.5/17
George Washington II: The Forging Of A Nation CBS 12.6/20 9.8/15
Geronimo TNT
Gettysburg TNT
Guts And Glory: The Rise And Fall Of Oliver North CBS 14.0/23 9.6/13
Harem ABC 16.9/25 16.2/23
Heat Wave TNT
Heroes Of Desert Storm ABC 9.9/16
Hiroshima: Out Of The Ashes NBC 11.3/20
Houston: The Legend Of Texas CBS 10.8/18
In Love And War NBC 16.7/27
Inherit The Wind NBC 18.0/29
Iran: Days Of Crisis TNT
Ironclads TNT
JFK: Reckless Youth ABC 7.8/12 9.5/16
Jack The Ripper CBS 14.8/26 20.3/31
Kennedys Of Massachusetts, The ABC 15.8/24 17.6/27 16.4/25
LBJ: The Early Years NBC 18.4/27
Last Days Of Patton, The CBS 19.5/32
Last Of His Tribe, The HBO
Lena: My 100 Children NBC 13.4/21
Liberty NBC 12.0/21
Lincoln NBC 16.6/26 14.9/24
Lost Capone, The TNT
Malice In Wonderland CBS 18.3/29
Man For All Season, A TNT
Mark Twain And Me DISNEY
Max And Helen TNT
Mission Of The Shark CBS 15.6/25
Murder In Mississippi NBC 12.4/20
Murder Of Mary Phagan, The NBC 18.7/28 21.0/34
Murrow HBO
Mussolini: The Decline And Fall Of Il Duce HBO
Mussolini - The Untold Story NBC 17.7/26 19.4/29 19.6/29
Napoleon And Josephine: A Love Story ABC 18.6/30 16.2/26 13.3/21
Neon Empire SHOWTIME
Never Forget TNT
Nightmare Years, The TNT
North And South ABC 25.8/37 23.6/34 28.0/42 25.8/38 23.2/37
North And South, Book 2 ABC 19.8/30 20.1/30 21.6/36 22.9/36 20.8/32
North And South, Book 3: Heaven And Hell ABC 10.1/15 9.8/15 9.7/15
Oldest Living Confederate Widow Tells All CBS 15.7/24 13.8/21
On Promised Land DISNEY
One Against The Wind CBS 13.4/21
One More Mountain ABC 12.9/20
Passion For Justice, A: Hazel Brannon Smith Story ABC 11.1/18
Perfect Tribute, The ABC 10.5/18
Peter The Great NBC 19.0/28 17.6/26 16.6/26 17.4/27
Prisoner Of Honor HBO
Queen CBS 24.7/38 24.1/37 22.8/34
Queenie ABC 12.7/21 12.9/21
Revenge Of Al Capone, The NBC 13.9/22

Richest Man In The World: The Aristotle Onassis Story ABC 12.1/18 13.9/22
Rose And The Jackal, The TNT
Roswell SHOWTIME
Season Of Giants, A TNT
Secret Life Of Ian Fleming, The TNT
Separate But Equal ABC 11.9/19 11.8/19
She Stood Alone NBC 10.8/18
Silent Cries NBC 12.4/20
Son Of The Morning Star ABC 11.7/18 12.8/20
Sound And The Silence, The TNT
Space CBS 19.4/31 16.4/26 14.7/24 17.1/28 16.3/26
Stalin HBO
The Race To Freedom: The Underground Railroad FAMILY
Twist Of Fate NBC 14.3/21 15.2/24
Uncle Tom's Cabin SHOWTIME
Wallenberg: A Hero's Story NBC 20.2/33 19.7/30
Walton Thanksgiving Reunion, A CBS 20.1/30
War And Remembrance ABC 21.8/31 19.0/29 19.8/31 16.8/25 17.0/26
War And Remembrance, Part II ABC 13.4/21 14.4/22 15.1/24 15.7/25 15.9/26
Which Way Home TNT
Woman He Loved, The CBS 14.5/25
Woman Named Jackie, A NBC 15.5/23 18.6/28 19.1/30
World War II: When Lions Roared NBC 9.1/15 7.5/12
Young Catherine TNT
Young Indiana Jones Chronicles: The Curse Of The Jackal ABC 16.6/26

HOLIDAY SPECIAL

Babes In Toyland NBC 13.4/22
Christmas Carol, A CBS 20.7/30
Christmas Comes To Willow Creek CBS 19.2/30
Christmas Eve NBC 21.3/33
Christmas Gift, The CBS 20.2/33
Christmas In Connecticut TNT
Christmas On Division Street CBS 16.7/26
Double, Double, Toil And Trouble ABC 10.8/19
Guess Who's Coming For Christmas NBC 10.9/19
Hobo's Christmas, A CBS 19.5/30
I'll Be Home For Christmas NBC 17.9/28
In The Nick Of Time NBC 12.9/20
Little House On The Prairie - Bless All The Dear Children NBC 18.2/27
Little Match Girl, The NBC 19.4/30
Little Piece Of Heaven, A NBC 13.8/21
Man Upstairs, The CBS 18.8/28
Miracle In The Wilderness TNT
Mom For Christmas, A NBC 17.0/27
Night They Saved Christmas, The ABC 14.2/22
Roots: The Gift ABC 15.4/24
Smokey Mountain Christmas, A ABC 23.2/35
Thanksgiving Day NBC 10.9/17
Three Kings, The ABC 8.2/13
To Grandmother's House We Go ABC 16.9/25
Very Brady Christmas, A CBS 25.1/39
Yes, Virginia, There Is A Santa Claus ABC 12.2/19

HOLLYWOOD

Ann Jillian Story, The NBC 23.8/35
Call Me Anna ABC 15.9/24
Danielle Steel's Secrets NBC 15.6/24
Elvis And Me ABC 23.9/35 24.9/36
Elvis And The Colonel: The Untold Story NBC
    9.8/14
Hearst And Davies Affair, The ABC 16.2/24
Hollywood Wives ABC 22.0/33 21.1/32
    25.2/39
Jackie Collins' Lady Boss NBC 12.7/20
    14.2/22
Jacksons: An American Dream , The ABC
    21.1/31 23.9/36
Josephine Baker Story, The HBO
Karen Carpenter Story, The CBS 26.3/41
Liberace ABC 16.8/27
Liberace: Behind The Music CBS 16.6/26
Lucy & Desi: Before The Laughter CBS 16.4/25
Malice In Wonderland CBS 18.3/29
Marilyn & Bobby: Her Final Affair USA
Marilyn & Me ABC 8.5/14
Obsessive Love CBS 15.2/25
Queenie ABC 12.7/21 12.9/21
Rock Hudson ABC 15.7/24
Scandal Sheet ABC 20.5/32
Shakedown On The Sunset Strip CBS 15.0/27
Shattered Innocence CBS 15.2/25
Sinatra CBS 17.7/26 17.2/27
Stranger In The Mirror, A ABC 9.6/16
Street Of Dreams CBS 9.5/17
Summer Dreams: The Story Of The Beach Boys
    ABC 10.6/16
Tears And Laughter: The Joan And Mielissa Rivers
    Story NBC 13.1/21
There Must Be A Pony ABC 12.6/19
Torch Song ABC 9.5/15
What Ever Happened To Baby Jane? ABC 9.9/15
White Hot: The Mysterious Murder Of Thelma
    Todd NBC 12.3/20

HOMOSEXUALITY

An Early Frost NBC 23.3/33
And The Band Played On HBO
Consenting Adult ABC 23.1/33
Doing Time On Maple Drive FBC 9.4/15
Dress Gray NBC 17.9/27 19.0/30
Liberace: Behind The Music CBS 16.6/26
My Two Loves ABC 17.5/28
Our Sons ABC 12.8/21
People Like Us NBC 9.4/16 10.5/17
Rock Hudson ABC 15.7/24
Roommates NBC 8.9/15
Welcome Home, Bobby CBS 12.5/21

LOVE STORY

Addicted To His Love ABC 18.1/29
American Geisha CBS 11.7/20
Anna Karenina CBS 16.6/26
Arch Of Triumph CBS 9.2/16
Aurora NBC 18.0/28
Barbara Taylor Bradford's Remember NBC
    10.9/18 13.5/21
Bluegrass CBS 17.6/27 18.4/29
Bonds Of Love CBS 14.9/23

Bonnie And Clyde: The True Story FBC 8.7/15
Bourne Identity, The ABC 18.5/30 18.5/29
Camille CBS 15.2/25
Candles In The Dark FAMILY
Children Of The Bride CBS 13.6/25
Clinton And Nadine HBO
Cold Sassy Tree TNT
Copacabana CBS 12.6/20
Cowboy And The Ballerina, The CBS 12.1/19
Crossing The Mob NBC 9.9/17
Dangerous Affection NBC 16.4/26
Dangerous Passion ABC 11.4/19
Danielle Steel's Changes NBC 17.8/28
Danielle Steel's Daddy NBC 19.6/30
Danielle Steel's Fine Things NBC 18.0/28
Danielle Steel's Heartbeat NBC 16.8/26
Danielle Steel's Jewels NBC 14.7/22 15.6/24
Danielle Steel's Message From Nam NBC
    11.5/18 11.4/18
Danielle Steel's Once In A Lifetime NBC
    11.2/16
Danielle Steel's Palomino NBC 18.4/28
Danielle Steel's Star NBC 15.9/24
David's Mother CBS 16.3/26
Deceptions SHOWTIME
Desperate For Love CBS 12.0/20
Dress Gray NBC 17.9/27 19.0/30
Duel Of Hearts TNT
Elvis And Me ABC 23.9/35 24.9/36
Evergreen NBC 22.3/33 20.9/32 22.9/33
Face To Face CBS 14.7/24
Fever HBO
Forbidden HBO
Forbidden Nights CBS 10.5/17
Foreign Affairs TNT
Freedom Fighter NBC 16.0/25
Great Expectations DISNEY
Hazard Of Hearts, A CBS 15.3/26
Hearst And Davies Affair, The ABC 16.2/24
I Love You Perfect ABC 13.7/23
I'll Take Romance ABC 13.1/21
Impostor, The ABC 14.2/22
Indiscreet CBS 12.0/18
James Clavell's Noble House NBC 17.9/27
    15.9/24 15.0/22 16.3/26
John And Yoko: A NBC 13.4/19
Judith Krantz's Till We Meet Again CBS 14.8/23
    11.7/18
Kiss Shot CBS 10.2/16
Last Prostitute, The LIFETIME
Long Journey Home, The CBS 21.3/34
Love & Lies ABC 11.6/18
Love On The Run NBC 15.4/23
Love She Sought, The NBC 12.0/18
Marcus Welby, M. D.: A Holiday Affair NBC
    13.5/21
Matters Of The Heart USA
Max And Helen TNT
Mirrors NBC 13.8/22
Mistral's Daughter CBS 18.2/29 18.7/30
    16.3/26
Mrs. Delafield Wants To Marry CBS 21.0/35
My Brother's Wife ABC 11.2/18
Naked Lie CBS 21.2/33
Napoleon And Josephine: A ABC 18.6/30
    16.2/26 13.3/21
North And South ABC 25.8/37 23.6/34
    28.0/42 25.8/38 23.2/37
North And South, Book 2 ABC 19.8/30 20.1/30
    21.6/36 22.9/36 20.8/32
O Pioneers CBS 18.9/29
Obsessive Love CBS 15.2/25
Operation, The CBS 20.0/30

Other Lover, The CBS 13.8/22
Outback Bound CBS 15.7/25
Outside Woman, The CBS 14.3/22
Phantom Of The Opera, The NBC 12.3/19
    12.3/20
Prince Of Bel Air ABC 17.5/27
Railway Station Man, The TNT
Reunion At Fairborough HBO
Richest Man In The World: The Aristotle Onassis
    Story ABC 12.1/18 13.9/22
Ride With The Wind ABC 9.0/15
Roman Holiday NBC 17.0/28
Romance On The Orient Express NBC 15.6/24
Room Upstairs, The CBS 14.1/24
Rose And The Jackal, The TNT
Running Mates HBO
Sarah, Plain And Tall CBS 23.1/35
Sin Of Innocence CBS 12.5/21
Sins CBS 19.7/29 21.9/32 20.6/32
Smokey Mountain Christmas, A ABC 23.2/35
Sparks: The Price Of Passion CBS 13.7/21
Stompin' At The Savoy CBS 11.2/19
Stones Of Ibarra CBS 12.4/21
Sun Also Rises, The NBC 13.2/20 11.6/18
Sweet Bird Of Youth NBC 13.0/21
Tarzan In Manhattan CBS 10.5/19
Tenth Man, The CBS 13.3/21
There Must Be A Pony ABC 12.6/19
This Can't Be Love CBS 17.8/28
To Dance With The White Dog CBS 21.9/33
Torch Song ABC 9.5/15
We Are The Children ABC 9.1/14
Windmills Of The Gods CBS 19.0/28 17.3/27
Woman He Loved, The CBS 14.5/25
World's Oldest Living Bridesmaid, The CBS
    11.9/22

MAFIA/MOB

Blood Vows: The Story Of A Mafia Wife NBC
    24.8/37
Born To Run FBC 3.9/7
Brotherly Love CBS 13.5/22
Charley Hannah ABC 13.4/23
Crossing The Mob NBC 9.9/17
Dangerous Passion ABC 11.4/19
Dead And Alive ABC 11.8/18
Deadly Business, A CBS 12.3/21
Deadly Matrimony NBC 16.1/25 18.9/29
Deep Dark Secrets NBC 15.5/25
Devlin SHOWTIME
Dirty Work USA
Dream Breakers CBS 7.4/12
Fatal Confession: A Father Dowling Mystery
    NBC 15.5/24
Frank Nitti: The Enforcer ABC 17.4/28
Getting Gotti CBS 8.3/13
Great Pretender, The NBC 8.5/14
Jackie Collins' Lucky Chances NBC 14.4/25
    17.1/26 19.5/31
Johnny Ryan NBC 6.6/12
Lady Mobster ABC 5.9/09
Laguna Heat HBO
Las Vegas Strip Wars, The NBC 15.2/22
Legacy Of Lies USA
Long Time Gone ABC 7.4/14
Lost Capone, The TNT
Love, Honor & Obey: The Last Mafia Marriage
    CBS 12.6/20 14.4/24

MAFIA/MOB (CONTINUED)

Mafia Princess   NBC   24.4/37
Man Against The Mob   NBC   19.7/32
Man Against The Mob: The Chinatown Murders   NBC   11.3/18
Mario And The Mob   ABC   7.5/15
Mario Puzo's The Fortunate Pilgrim   NBC   13.1/22   13.0/21
Necessity   CBS   15.0/24
Neon Empire   SHOWTIME
Original Sin   NBC   16.8/26
Our Family Honor   ABC   15.4/25
P. S. I Luv U   CBS   15.7/25
Passion And Paradise   ABC   11.8/19   12.5/20
Payoff   SHOWTIME
Perfect Witness   HBO
Peter Gunn   ABC   14.7/24
Rage Of Angels: The Story Continues   NBC   15.9/25   16.5/25
Return Of Eliot Ness, The   NBC   12.7/19
Revenge Of Al Capone, The   NBC   13.9/22
Taking The Heat   SHOWTIME
Teamster Boss: The Jackie Presser Story   HBO
Ten Million Dollar Getaway   USA
What She Doesn't Know   NBC   16.6/25
White Hot: The Mysterious Murder Of Thelma Todd   NBC   12.3/20

MAN AGAINST THE SYSTEM

Aaron's Way   NBC   19.5/31
Absolute Strangers   CBS   17.7/29
Act Of Vengeance   HBO
Adam: His Song Continues   NBC   15.9/25
After The Promise   CBS   19.2/30
American Harvest   CBS   16.4/27
American Story, An   CBS   12.7/20
Amerika   ABC   24.7/38   20.9/31   17.7/26   17.8/28   15.6/23
Amos   CBS   24.5/37
Attack On Fear   CBS   10.9/16
Baby Girl Scott   CBS   13.2/23
Blind Justice   CBS   19.2/29
Blind Vengeance   USA
Carolina Skeletons   NBC   14.7/23
Case Of Deadly Force, A   CBS   12.0/20
Celebration Family   ABC   10.2/17
Convicted   ABC   17.4/27
Crossing To Freedom   CBS   10.3/17
Deadly Business, A   CBS   12.3/21
Deadly Matrimony   NBC   16.1/25   18.9/29
Deception: A Mother's Secret   NBC   15.6/23
Dreams Of Gold: The Mel Fisher Story   CBS   11.3/20
Fatal Vision   NBC   29.5/44   32.7/49
Father Clements Story, The   NBC   16.7/26
Father Of Hell Town   NBC   18.2/29
Father's Revenge, A   ABC   10.4/16
Fight For Life   ABC   16.2/26
Forgotten Prisoners: The Amnesty File   TNT
George Mckenna Story, The   CBS   15.5/24
Gladiator, The   ABC   15.9/24
Great Pretender, The   NBC   8.5/14
Guilty Of Innocence: The Lenell Geter Story   CBS   15.7/25
Guilty Until Proven Innocent   NBC   11.8/19
In The Line Of Duty: Standoff At Marion   NBC   13.2/20
In The Shadow Of A Killer   NBC   9.5/15
Incident At Dark River   TNT

Investigation: Inside A Terrorist Bombing, The   HBO
Last Elephant, The   TNT
Line Of Fire: The Morris Dees Story   NBC   11.3/17
Littlest Victims   CBS   10.9/18
Long Road Home   NBC   11.8/18
Many Happy Returns   CBS   10.2/18
Mercy Or Murder?   NBC   23.8/35
Money, Power, Murder   CBS   13.4/22
Never Forget   TNT
News At Eleven   CBS   13.3/22
Night Of Courage   ABC   12.4/19
North Beach And Rawhide   CBS   9.6/14   11.4/17
Outrage   CBS   21.7/34
Perfect Witness   HBO
Prison For Children   CBS   11.5/20
Revenge On The Highway   NBC   12.8/19
Right Of The People, The   ABC   14.5/22
Roswell   SHOWTIME
Sakharov   HBO
Separate But Equal   ABC   11.9/19   11.8/19
Shannon's Deal   NBC   14.5/25
Somebody Has To Shoot The Picture   HBO
Spy   USA
Stoning In Fulham County, A   NBC   18.3/28
Stranger On My Land   ABC   11.5/18
Switch, The   CBS   11.8/19
Sworn To Vengeance   CBS   15.3/25
Tarzan In Manhattan   CBS   10.5/19
Terror On Highway 91   CBS   16.9/26
That Secret Sunday   CBS   16.1/26
Thicker Than Blood: The Larry Mclinden Story   CBS   14.5/23
This Park Is Mine   HBO
To Heal A Nation   NBC   10.1/20
Town Bully, The   ABC   15.6/25
Town Torn Apart, A   NBC   12.8/20
Two Fathers' Justice   NBC   17.9/27
Two Fathers: Justice For The Innocent   NBC   10.3/17
Unnatural Causes   NBC   19.3/31
Vengeance: The Story Of Tony Cimo   CBS   11.8/21
Wallenberg: A Hero's Story   NBC   20.2/33   19.7/30
Water Engine, The   TNT
When You Remember Me   ABC   14.6/24
Whereabouts Of Jenny, The   ABC   15.4/24
Wild Horses   CBS   16.7/26

MEDICAL/DISEASE/MENTAL ILLNESS

Absolute Strangers   CBS   17.7/29
Aftermath: A Test Of Love   CBS   17.3/27
Against Her Will: An Incident In Baltimore   CBS   16.0/25
Alex: The Life Of A Child   ABC   21.7/36
An Early Frost   NBC   23.3/33
And The Band Played On   HBO
And Then There Was One   LIFETIME
Ann Jillian Story, The   NBC   23.8/35
Aurora   NBC   18.0/28
Baby Girl Scott   CBS   13.2/23
Betrayal Of Trust   NBC   13.0/20
Betty Ford Story, The   ABC   11.4/16
Bonds Of Love   CBS   14.9/23
Born Too Soon   NBC   10.5/17
Boys, The   ABC   8.9/15
Broken Cord, The   ABC   14.3/22

Call Me Anna   ABC   15.9/24
Can You Feel Me Dancing?   NBC   19.1/30
Chernobyl: The Final Warning   TNT
Child Of Rage   CBS   14.7/24
Children Of The Dark   CBS   13.4/22
China Beach   ABC   18.0/29
Condition: Critical   NBC   11.0/18
David   ABC   19.5/30
David's Mother   CBS   16.3/26
Daybreak   HBO
Deadly Care   CBS   18.6/31
Deadly Medicine   NBC   15.8/24
Desperate Choices: To Save My Child   NBC   12.4/19
Do You Remember Love?   CBS   17.0/28
Donor   CBS   14.8/24
Extreme Close-Up   NBC   12.3/20
Family Of Strangers   CBS   19.8/29
Family Pictures   ABC   10.1/16   11.5/18
Fatal Judgment   CBS   15.4/24
Fight For Life   ABC   16.2/26
Florence Nightingale   NBC   11.6/19
For The Love Of Aaron   CBS   12.4/21
For The Love Of My Child: The Anissa Ayala Story   NBC   12.8/20
Go Toward The Light   CBS   14.9/24
Good Fight, The   LIFETIME
He's Not Your Son   CBS   23.2/36
Heart Of A Child   NBC   11.5/18
Heartsounds   ABC   18.5/31
I Love You Perfect   ABC   13.7/23
In Sickness And In Health   ABC   16.3/26
In The Best Interest Of The Children   NBC   16.0/24
Jericho Fever   USA
Jesse   CBS   19.4/31
Jonathan: The Boy Nobody Wanted   NBC   13.8/21
Karen Carpenter Story, The   CBS   26.3/41
Kate's Secret   NBC   24.1/36
Kids Like These   CBS   16.5/27
Killer Instinct   NBC   12.5/19
Labor Of Love: The Arlette Schweitzer Story   CBS   14.1/23
Last Best Year, The   ABC   11.1/17
Last Wish   ABC   10.8/17
Leap Of Faith   CBS   12.0/20
Littlest Victims   CBS   10.9/18
Love Lives On   ABC   17.8/26
Love, Mary   CBS   21.5/33
Lucky Day   ABC   9.8/16
Lush Life   SHOWTIME
Matters Of The Heart   USA
Mercy Or Murder?   NBC   23.8/35
Message From Holly   CBS   15.5/24
Miles From Nowhere   CBS   10.8/17
Miles To Go . . .   CBS   16.5/26
Miracle At Beekman's Place   NBC   12.3/21
Moment Of Truth: To Walk Again   NBC   8.3/12
Mrs. Lambert Remembers Love   CBS   9.9/17
Murder Of Innocence   CBS   14.5/22
My Breast   CBS   11.4/18
My Father, My Son   CBS   13.5/22
Nightingales   NBC   18.9/33
No Child Of Mine   CBS   13.1/21
Nobody's Child   CBS   25.9/39
Norman Rockwell's Breaking Home Ties   ABC   9.7/19
One Special Victory   NBC   13.1/20
Our Sons   ABC   12.8/21
Out Of The Darkness   ABC   12.5/19
Out On The Edge   CBS   14.6/23
Place For Annie, A   ABC   14.8/23

MEDICAL/DISEASE/MENTAL ILLNESS
(CONTINUED)

Private Sessions NBC 14.9/23
Promise CBS 19.5/29
Promised A Miracle CBS 13.2/22
Quiet Killer CBS 11.5/19
Quiet Victory: The Charlie Wedemeyer Story CBS 14.9/25
Reason For Living: The Jill Ireland Story NBC 12.5/21
Reason To Live, A NBC 15.6/23
Ride With The Wind ABC 9.0/15
Right To Die NBC 17.5/28
Rise & Walk: The Dennis Byrd Story FBC 7.1/11
Roommates NBC 8.9/15
Ryan White Story, The ABC 16.6/26
Second Serve CBS 13.6/22
Secret, The CBS 13.3/23
Something To Live For: The Alison Gertz Story ABC 16.2/26
Special People CBS 10.7/18
State Of Emergency HBO
Strange Voices NBC 21.0/33
Stranger In My Bed NBC 18.8/29
Stranger In The Family, A ABC 12.7/19
Substitute Wife, The NBC 17.5/27
Switch, The CBS 11.8/19
Ted Kennedy, Jr., Story, The NBC 16.8/26
Three Wishes Of Billy Grier, The ABC 13.5/21
Time To Heal, A NBC 12.7/21
Time To Live, A NBC 17.1/27
Trapped In Silence CBS 15.1/24
Triumph Of The Heart: The Ricky Bell Story CBS 12.5/22
Twist Of The Knife, A CBS 10.9/20
Unnatural Causes NBC 19.3/31
Victim Of Love CBS 12.0/20
Victims For Victims - The Theresa Saldana Story NBC 18.8/28
Voices Within: The Lives Of Truddi Chase ABC 14.7/24 15.5/25
When The Time Comes ABC 11.1/18
When You Remember Me ABC 14.6/24
Who Is Julia? CBS 18.4/29
Winnie NBC 16.6/28
Without A Kiss Goodbye CBS 17.2/29
Without Warning: The James Brady Story HBO
Yarn Princess, The ABC 10.5/17

MURDER AND MURDER MYSTERY

Accidental Meeting USA
Agatha Christie's Dead Man's Folly CBS 14.4/22
Agatha Christie's Murder In Three Acts CBS 15.4/25
Agatha Christie's The Man In The Brown Suit CBS 15.8/25
Agatha Christie's Thirteen At Dinner CBS 12.8/21
Amos CBS 24.5/37
And The Sea Will Tell CBS 20.1/31 19.0/29
Angel Of Death CBS 10.8/18
At Mother's Request CBS 23.3/35 22.7/35
Atlanta Child Murders, The CBS 21.8/31 20.9/31
Back To Hannibal: The Return Of Tom Sawyer And Huck Finn DISNEY
Back To The Streets Of San Francisco NBC 13.2/20
Badge Of The Assassin CBS 13.6/23

Bermuda Grace NBC 8.2/14
Betrayed By Love ABC 10.8/16
Beverly Hills Cowgirl Blues CBS 12.9/22
Beyond Suspicion NBC 14.4/22
Billionaire Boys Club NBC 20.7/34 22.1/34
Bitter Vengeance USA
Black Magic SHOWTIME
Black Widow Murders: The Blanche Taylor Moore Story NBC 13.3/21
Blacke's Magic NBC 21.8/32
Blind Faith NBC 19.9/31 23.3/36
Blind Man's Bluff USA
Blind Side HBO
Blind Witness ABC 16.3/25
Blood And Orchids CBS 22.9/35 25.6/38
Blue Bayou NBC 12.8/20
Body Of Evidence CBS 18.4/28
Breaking The Silence CBS 12.8/20
Bride In Black, The ABC 16.7/27
Bridge Across Time NBC 13.7/21
Broken Vows CBS 14.1/22
Buried Alive USA
Calendar Girl, Cop Killer? The Bambi Bembenek Story ABC 10.7/17
Carolina Skeletons NBC 14.7/23
Case Closed CBS 13.0/22
Child In The Night CBS 9.7/16
China Lake Murders, The USA
Chrome Soldiers USA
Columbo: A Bird In The Hand ABC 12.2/19
Columbo And The Murder Of A Rock Star ABC 12.6/19
Columbo - Caution: Murder Can Be Hazardous To Your Health ABC 11.8/18
Columbo: Death Hits The Jackpot ABC 14.2/22
Columbo Goes To College ABC 14.9/24
Columbo: It's All In The Game ABC 13.4/21
Columbo: Undercover ABC 14.1/22
Confessions: Two Faces Of Evil NBC 10.7/16
Conspiracy Of Silence CBS 12.5/21 12.2/20
Corpse Had A Familiar Face, The CBS 16.4/26
Cosby Mysteries, The NBC 14.8/22
Cover Girl And The Cop, The NBC 18.0/28
Cover Girl Murders, The USA
Cover Up CBS 14.0/26
Criminal Behavior ABC 12.1/19
Cruel Doubt NBC 16.8/27 14.8/24
Curiosity Kills USA
Dancing With Danger USA
Danger Of Love, The CBS 15.9/26
Dangerous Affection NBC 16.4/26
Dangerous Passion ABC 11.4/19
Dangerous Pursuit USA
Dead And Alive ABC 11.8/18
Dead In The Water USA
Dead Reckoning USA
Deadly Desire USA
Deadly Matrimony NBC 16.1/25 18.9/29
Deadly Medicine NBC 15.8/24
Deadly Messages ABC 11.4/17
Deceptions SHOWTIME
Deconstructing Sarah USA
Deep Trouble USA
Desperate For Love CBS 12.0/20
Destination: America ABC 8.8/15
Devlin SHOWTIME
Diagnosis Of Murder CBS 14.6/23
Diary Of A Perfect Murder NBC 20.9/33
Disappearance Of Christina, The USA
Disappearance Of Nora CBS 17.0/27
Donato And Daughter CBS 14.8/24
Double Deception NBC 9.6/17

Double Edge CBS 17.1/28
Double Jeopardy SHOWTIME
Doubletake CBS 21.1/33 18.7/28
Dress Gray NBC 17.9/27 19.0/30
Drop Dead Gorgeous USA
Due South CBS 11.5/21
Dying To Remember USA
Echoes In The Darkness CBS 20.1/33 22.0/33
Endless Game, The SHOWTIME
Exclusive ABC 10.8/17
Execution, The NBC 21.4/32
Eyes Of A Witness CBS 13.0/23
Eyes Of Terror NBC 10.6/19
Face Of Fear, The CBS 14.0/23
Fade To Black USA
False Arrest ABC 11.5/18 16.6/27
Family Sins CBS 12.9/20
Fatal Confession: A Father Dowling Mystery NBC 15.5/24
Fatal Image, The CBS 14.1/22
Fatal Vision NBC 29.5/44 32.7/49
Favorite Son NBC 15.9/26 15.7/25 16.3/26
Fear SHOWTIME
Final Notice USA
Forget Me Not Murders, The CBS 13.1/21
French Silk ABC 11.3/17
From The Files Of Joseph Wambaugh: A Jury Of One NBC 17 17
Full Exposure: The Sex Tapes Scandal NBC 16.2/24
Gathering Of Old Men, A CBS 18.4/31
Glitter Dome, The HBO
Glitz NBC 14.1/25
Good Night, Sweet Wife: A Murder In Boston CBS 14.9/23
Grass Roots NBC 13.4/20 15.1/23
Great Pretender, The NBC 8.5/14
Hands Of A Murderer CBS 9.5/17
Harmful Intent CBS 12.2/20
Harry's Hong Kong ABC 6.1/11
Heads SHOWTIME
Heart Of Justice, The TNT
Hell Hath No Fury NBC 15.2/24
High Price Of Passion, The NBC 18.6/29
Higher Ground CBS 13.3/25
Hit List, The SHOWTIME
Hitler's Daughter USA
Honor Thy Mother CBS 15.5/24
Hot Pursuit NBC 11.2/21
House Of Secrets NBC 14.6/23
House On Sycamore Street, The CBS 10.9/20
I'm Dangerous Tonight USA
Illicit Behavior USA
In A Child's Name CBS 17.8/27 21.9/33
In Defense Of A Married Man ABC 14.1/23
In My Daughter's Name CBS 15.8/27
In The Arms Of A Killer NBC 14.0/22
In The Deep Woods NBC 14.6/23
In The Heat Of The Night NBC 18.7/30
In The Line Of Duty: Manhunt In The Dakotas NBC 14.7/26
In The Line Of Duty: The FBI Murders NBC 22.2/34
Incident In A Small Town CBS 18.7/31
Incident, The CBS 20.8/33
Inconvenient Woman, An ABC 11.7/21 12.4/20
Indecency USA
Internal Affairs CBS 16.1/26 13.7/21
Island Sons ABC 7.9/14
It's Nothing Personal NBC 10.9/17
J. O. E. And The Colonel ABC 11.0/18

MURDER AND MURDER MYSTERY
(CONTINUED)

Jack The Ripper CBS 14.8/26 20.3/31
Jake And The Fatman CBS 15.8/27
Jessie ABC 17.7/29
Johnny Ryan NBC 6.6/12
Jonathan Stone: Threat Of Innocence NBC
  12.2/16
Judgment Day: The John List Story CBS
  15.8/25
Keeper Of The City SHOWTIME
Kicks ABC 13.2/21
Killer Among Us, A NBC 13.9/23
Killer In The Mirror NBC 20.4/31
Killing In A Small Town CBS 15.8/26
Killing Mind, The LIFETIME
Kiss To Die For, A NBC 10.8/17
Knight Rider 2000 NBC 16.1/26
Kojak: The Belarus File CBS 18.5/31
Kojak: The Price Of Justice CBS 12.0/21
Lady Against The Odds NBC 11.8/19
Lady Forgets, The CBS 18.5/34
Lady Killer USA
Ladykillers ABC 16.6/27
Laguna Heat HBO
Last Innocent Man, The HBO
Lethal Exposure NBC 8.8/14
Liar's Edge SHOWTIME
Lies Before Kisses CBS 18.5/29
Linda USA
London And Davis In New York CBS 9.7/18
Love Can Be Murder NBC 11.4/18
Love & Lies ABC 11.6/18
Love, Lies And Murder NBC 15.5/24 20.3/30
Macshayne: The Final Roll Of The Dice NBC
  8.3/15
Maid For Each Other NBC 13.6/21
Man Against The Mob NBC 19.7/32
Man Against The Mob: The Chinatown Murders
  NBC 11.3/18
Manhunt: Search For The Night Stalker NBC
  15.4/24
Matlock: The Witness Killings NBC 14.0/26
Menendez: A Killing In Beverly Hills CBS
  9.6/16 9.3/15
Menu For Murder CBS 9.7/16
Mickey Spillane's Mike Hammer: Murder Takes
  All CBS 12.8/20
Money, Power, Murder CBS 13.4/22
Murder 101 USA
Murder Between Friends NBC 12.9/20
Murder By Moonlight CBS 7.7/12
Murder By Night USA
Murder By The Book CBS 9.4/15
Murder C. O. D. NBC 10.3/19
Murder In Black And White CBS 17.1/27
Murder In High Places NBC 12.3/22
Murder In New Hampshire: The Pamela Smart
  Story CBS 15.9/26
Murder In Paradise NBC 12.6/21
Murder Ordained CBS 19.3/29 19.8/32
Murder, She Wrote CBS 18.9/29
Murder Times Seven CBS 11.1/18
Murder With Mirrors CBS 15.2/23
Murder Without Motive: The Edmund Perry Story
  NBC 11.3/18
Murderous Vision USA
Murders In The Rue Morgue, The CBS 17.7/27
My Son Johnny CBS 15.6/24
Nails SHOWTIME

Naked Lie CBS 21.2/33
Night Visions NBC 9.8/17
Night Walk CBS 16.3/27
Nightmare In Columbia County CBS 14.0/22
Nutcracker: Money, Madness And Murder NBC
  12.2/20 11.5/19 13.5/22
Of Pure Blood CBS 20.0/30
Operation, The CBS 20.0/30
Out Of The Darkness CBS 17.6/30
Over My Dead Body CBS 12.4/23
Overkill: The Aileen Wuornos Story CBS 15.4/25
Pair Of Aces CBS 17.8/28
Paris Trout SHOWTIME
Parker Kane NBC 8.6/15
Passion And Paradise ABC 11.8/19 12.5/20
Passport To Murder NBC 11.7/19
Past Tense SHOWTIME
People Across The Lake, The NBC 17.3/27
People Like Us NBC 9.4/16 10.5/17
Perfect Witness HBO
Perry Mason Mystery, A: The Case Of The Lethal
  Lifestyle NBC 10.8/18
Perry Mason Mystery: The Case Of The Wicked
  Wives NBC 10.2/19
Perry Mason Returns NBC 27.2/39
Perry Mason: The Case Of The All-Star Assassin
  NBC 16.8/26
Perry Mason: The Case Of The Avenging Ace
  NBC 17.4/26
Perry Mason: The Case Of The Defiant Daughter
  NBC 14.7/24
Perry Mason: The Case Of The Desperate
  Deception NBC 17.0/27
Perry Mason: The Case Of The Fatal Fashion
  NBC 14.6/23
Perry Mason: The Case Of The Fatal Framing
  NBC 12.9/20
Perry Mason: The Case Of The Glass Coffin
  NBC 12.8/22
Perry Mason: The Case Of The Heartbroken Bride
  NBC 12.1/21
Perry Mason: The Case Of The Killer Kiss NBC
  19.3/29
Perry Mason: The Case Of The Lady In The Lake
  NBC 22.6/35
Perry Mason: The Case Of The Lost Love NBC
  21.3/33
Perry Mason: The Case Of The Maligned Mobster
  NBC 14.0/22
Perry Mason: The Case Of The Murdered Madam
  NBC 18.1/29
Perry Mason: The Case Of The Musical Murders
  NBC 17.4/26
Perry Mason: The Case Of The Notorious Nun
  NBC 23.3/42
Perry Mason: The Case Of The Poisoned Pen
  NBC 16.0/24
Perry Mason: The Case Of The Reckless Romeo
  NBC 14.7/23
Perry Mason: The Case Of The Ruthless Reporter
  NBC 14.0/21
Perry Mason: The Case Of The Scandalous
  Scoundrel NBC 16.6/26
Perry Mason: The Case Of The Shooting Star
  NBC 23.6/37
Perry Mason: The Case Of The Silenced Singer
  NBC 16.5/27
Perry Mason: The Case Of The Sinister Spirit
  NBC 20.5/35
Perry Mason: The Case Of The Skin-Deep Scandal
  NBC 13.3/22
Perry Mason: The Case Of The Telltale Talk Show
  Host NBC 13.1/24

Personals USA
Peyton Place: The Next Generation NBC 12.6/20
Police Story: The Freeway Killings NBC 17.3/27
Praying Mantis USA
Precious Victims CBS 14.6/23
Preppie Murder, The ABC 15.2/24
Prime Target NBC 12.6/23
Probe ABC 14.2/23
Prophet Of Evil: The Ervil Lebaron Story CBS
  9.9/16
Psycho I V: The Beginning SHOWTIME
Quicksand: No Escape USA
Quiet Little Neighborhood, A Perfect Little
  Murder, A NBC 12.7/21
Rainbow Drive SHOWTIME
Rape Of Dr. Willis, The CBS 14.4/23
Red Spider, The CBS 15.1/25
Relentless: Mind Of A Killer NBC 12.8/20
Remington Steele: The Steele That Wouldn't Die
  NBC 19.7/28
Return Of Eliot Ness, The NBC 12.7/19
Return Of Ironside, The NBC 11.6/19
Return Of Sam Mccloud, The CBS 12.9/20
Return Of Sherlock Holmes, The CBS 14.4/24
Revealing Evidence NBC 14.5/25
Right To Kill? ABC 19.0/31
Scene Of The Crime NBC 12.5/21
Secret Passion Of Robert Clayton, The USA
Secret Sins Of The Father NBC 16.0/24
Seduced CBS 15.5/25
Seduction In Travis County CBS 13.9/22
Separated By Murder CBS 11.8/19
Shadow Of A Doubt CBS 15.3/24
Shadow Of Obsession NBC 11.4/18
Shadowhunter SHOWTIME
Shattered Image USA
She Says She's Innocent NBC 15.0/23
Shoot First: A Cop's Vengeance NBC 12.6/20
Silent Movie LIFETIME
Silhouette USA
Sketch Artist SHOWTIME
Small Sacrifices ABC 18.1/28 25.2/39
Snow Kill USA
Somebody's Daughter ABC 10.2/16
Sparks: The Price Of Passion CBS 13.7/21
Spenser: Pale Kings And Princes LIFETIME
Spider And The Fly, The USA
Spirit, The ABC 7.0/15
Stay The Night ABC 13.8/22 17.9/28
Still Crazy Like A Fox CBS 21.2/31
Street Of Dreams CBS 9.5/17
Substitute, The USA
Sunstroke USA
Sweet Revenge, A CBS 10.0/16
Sworn To Silence ABC 16.1/24
Sworn To Vengeance CBS 15.3/25
Target Of Suspicion USA
Telling Secrets ABC 13.8/22 14.4/21
Terror On Track 9 CBS 15.4/25
That Secret Sunday CBS 16.1/26
Third Degree Burn HBO
This Gun For Hire USA
Till Death Us Do Part NBC 14.6/21
Too Young To Die? NBC 14.5/23
Town Bully, The ABC 15.6/25
Trenchcoat In Paradise CBS 12.2/20
Trial: The Price Of Passion NBC 11.2/18
  13.2/21
Tricks Of The Trade CBS 11.6/18
Triplecross ABC 10.3/16
Twin Peaks ABC 21.7/33
Two Fathers' Justice NBC 17.9/27
Two Fathers: Justice For The Innocent NBC
  10.3/17

MURDER AND MURDER MYSTERY
(CONTINUED)

Two Mrs. Grenvilles, The   NBC   23.4/36   24.0/35
Unholy Matrimony   CBS   15.1/24
Web Of Deceit   USA
Web Of Deception   NBC   10.7/17
What She Doesn't Know   NBC   16.6/25
When Dreams Come True   ABC   12.8/21
Whisper Kills, A   ABC   14.7/23
White Hot: The Mysterious Murder Of Thelma Todd   NBC   12.3/20
Wife, Mother, Murderer   ABC   15.6/24
Wild Card   USA
Wild Texas Wind   NBC   18.0/27
With Intent To Kill   CBS   11.8/19
Woman On The Run: The Lawrencia Bembenek Story   NBC   11.1/18   15.6/25
Woman Who Sinned, The   ABC   12.1/18
Writer's Block   USA
Wrong Man, The   SHOWTIME

NAZIS

Attic: The Hiding Of Anne Frank, The   CBS   11.5/19
Behind Enemy Lines   NBC   14.5/23
Breaking Point   TNT
Crossing To Freedom   CBS   10.3/17
Descending Angel   HBO
Dirty Dozen: The Deadly Mission   NBC   18.5/28
Dirty Dozen: The Fatal Mission   NBC   14.3/22
Escape From Sobibor   CBS   21.4/34
Execution, The   NBC   21.4/32
Great Escape I I: The Untold Story, The   NBC   14.4/23   12.3/19
Hitler's Daughter   USA
Hitler's S S: Portrait In Evil   NBC   15.8/24
Kojak: The Belarus File   CBS   18.5/31
Max And Helen   TNT
Miss Rose White   NBC   11.0/17
Murderers Among Us: The Simon Wiesenthal Story   HBO
Nazi Hunter: The Beate Klarsfeld Story   ABC   13.7/21
Never Forget   TNT
Nightmare Years, The   TNT
Of Pure Blood   CBS   20.0/30
Perry Mason: The Case Of The Desperate Deception   NBC   17.0/27
Plot To Kill Hitler, The   CBS   7.2/12
Sins   CBS   19.7/29   21.9/32   20.6/32
So Proudly We Hail   CBS   7.5/12
Twist Of Fate   NBC   14.3/21   15.2/24
Wallenberg: A Hero's Story   NBC   20.2/33   19.7/30
War And Remembrance   ABC   21.8/31   19.0/29   19.8/31   16.8/25   17.0/26
War And Remembrance, Part I I   ABC   13.4/21   14.4/22   15.1/24   15.7/25   15.9/26

PERIOD PIECE

Abraham   TNT
Act Of Vengeance   HBO
After The Promise   CBS   19.2/30
Against Her Will: An Incident In Baltimore   CBS   16.0/25
Against The Wall   HBO
Agatha Christie's Dead Man's Folly   CBS   14.4/22
Agatha Christie's Murder In Three Acts   CBS   15.4/25
Amelia Earhart: The Final Flight   TNT
American Clock, The   TNT
American Story, An   CBS   12.7/20
Anastasia: The Mystery Of Anna   NBC   20.7/32   20.9/32
Anna Karenina   CBS   16.6/26
April Morning   CBS   15.2/24
Arch Of Triumph   CBS   9.2/16
Around The World In 80 Days   NBC   15.5/24   13.2/21   13.0/21
As Summers Die   HBO
Assault At West Point   SHOWTIME
Attic: The Hiding Of Anne Frank, The   CBS   11.5/19
Babe Ruth   NBC   10.0/16
Back Home   DISNEY
Back To Hannibal: The Return Of Tom Sawyer And Huck Finn   DISNEY
Badge Of The Assassin   CBS   13.6/23
Barnum   CBS   14.1/25
Behind Enemy Lines   NBC   14.5/23
Beryl Markham: A Shadow On The Sun   CBS   10.4/16   7.8/13
Blind Justice   HBO
Blood And Orchids   CBS   22.9/35   25.6/38
Bonanza: The Return   NBC   17.6/26
Bonnie And Clyde: The True Story   FBC   8.7/15
Breaking Point   TNT
Broadway Bound   ABC   8.4/14
Broken Chain   TNT
Brotherhood Of The Gun   CBS   7.3/14
Bunny's Tale, A   ABC   17.3/26
Caine Mutiny Court - Martial, The   CBS   9.4/15
Call Of The Wild   CBS   18.2/29
Camille   CBS   15.2/25
Captain Cook   TNT
Caroline?   CBS   19.4/30
Casanova   ABC   10.3/15
Cast A Deadly Spell   HBO
Charley Hannah   ABC   13.4/23
China Beach   ABC   18.0/29
Chips, The War Dog   DISNEY
Christopher Columbus   CBS   17.4/29   15.8/25
Christy   CBS   17.7/29
Cisco Kid, The   TNT
Citizen Cohn   HBO
Class Of '61   ABC   8.5/14
Cold Sassy Tree   TNT
Conagher   TNT
Connecticut Yankee In King Arthur's Court, A   NBC   11.5/17
Copacabana   CBS   12.6/20
Corsican Brothers, The   CBS   11.9/18
Court - Martial Of Jackie Robinson, The   TNT
Cross Of Fire   NBC   12.5/20   14.7/23
Crossing To Freedom   CBS   10.3/17
Crossings   ABC   17.5/27   15.0/22   17.4/27
Crucifier Of Blood, The   TNT
Dallas: The Early Years   CBS   21.3/33
Danielle Steel's Jewels   NBC   14.7/22   15.6/24
Danielle Steel's Message From Nam   NBC   11.5/18   11.4/18

Day One   CBS   15.2/24
Deadly Relations   ABC   10.01   19
Deadman's Revenge   USA
Dillinger   ABC   14.5/22
Dr. Quinn, Medicine Woman   CBS   18.2/29
Dreamer Of Oz, The   NBC   11.8/18
Dress Gray   NBC   17.9/27   19.0/30
Duel Of Hearts   TNT
Ellis Island   CBS   23.4/35   21.1/33   19.0/29
Elvis And Me   ABC   23.9/35   24.9/36
Elvis And The Colonel: The Untold Story   NBC   9.8/14
Ernest Green Story, The   DISNEY
Escape From Sobibor   CBS   21.4/34
Evergreen   NBC   22.3/33   20.9/32   22.9/33
Fatal Deception: Mrs. Lee Harvey Oswald   NBC   11.2/18
Final Days   ABC   10.2/17
Final Days   ABC   10.2/17
Final Verdict   TNT
Florence Nightingale   NBC   11.6/19
For Love And Glory   CBS   9.4/18
For The Very First Time   NBC   10.8/18
Frank Nitti: The Enforcer   ABC   17.4/28
Freedom Fighter   NBC   16.0/25
Fulfillment Of Mary Gray, The   CBS   16.5/26
Gambler Returns: The Luck Of The Draw, The   NBC   18.0/28   16.6/25
Gathering Of Old Men, A   CBS   18.4/31
George Washington I I: The Forging Of A Nation   CBS   12.6/20   9.8/15
George Washington I I: The Forging Of A Nation   CBS   12.6/20   9.8/15
Geronimo   TNT
Gettysburg   TNT
Ghost In Monte Carlo, A   TNT
Gore Vidal's Billy The Kid   TNT
Grand Isle   TNT
Great Expectations   DISNEY
Gunsmoke I I I: To The Last Man   CBS   14.2/24
Gunsmoke: One Man's Justice   CBS   11.5/17
Gunsmoke: Return To Dodge   CBS   16.6/31
Guts And Glory: The Rise And Fall Of Oliver North   CBS   14.0/23   9.6/13
Gypsy   CBS   18.6/28
Habitation Of Dragons, The   TNT
Hands Of A Murderer   CBS   9.5/17
Harem   ABC   16.9/25   16.2/23
Hazard Of Hearts, A   CBS   15.3/26
Hearst And Davies Affair, The   ABC   16.2/24
Heart Of Darkness   TNT
Heat Wave   TNT
Heidi   DISNEY
Heroes Of Desert Storm   ABC   9.9/16
Hiroshima: Out Of The Ashes   NBC   11.3/20
Home Fires Burning   CBS   18.6/29
Homefront   ABC   12.2/20
Hoover   SHOWTIME
I'll Fly Away   NBC   15.4/24
In Love And War   NBC   16.7/27
In The Shadow Of A Killer   NBC   9.5/15
Incident In A Small Town   CBS   18.7/31
Incident, The   CBS   20.8/33
Inherit The Wind   NBC   18.0/29
Ironclads   TNT
Izzy And Moe   CBS   17.9/27
J F K: Reckless Youth   ABC   7.8/12   9.5/16
Jack The Ripper   CBS   14.8/26   20.3/31
Jackie Collins' Lucky Chances   NBC   14.4/25   17.1/26   19.5/31
Jekyll & Hyde   ABC   12.2/19
John And Yoko: A   NBC   13.4/19
Johnny Bull   ABC   12.7/20

PERIOD PIECE (CONTINUED)

Johnny Ryan NBC 6.6/12
Josephine Baker Story, The HBO
Judith Krantz's Till We Meet Again CBS 14.8/23
  11.7/18
Kane And Abel CBS 23.2/34 23.4/34 21.4/32
Kennedys Of Massachusetts, The ABC 15.8/24
  17.6/27 16.4/25
Kennedys Of Massachusetts, The ABC 15.8/24
  17.6/27 16.4/25
King Of Love, The ABC 6.7/11
L B J: The Early Years NBC 18.4/27
Lady Against The Odds NBC 11.8/19
Lady And The Highwayman, The CBS 11.1/18
Lantern Hill DISNEY
Last Days Of Patton, The CBS 19.5/32
Last Flight Out NBC 10.7/18
Last Of His Tribe, The HBO
Last Outlaw, The HBO
Last P. O. W.? The Bobby Garwood Story, The
  ABC 11.5/20
Liberace ABC 16.8/27
Liberace: Behind The Music CBS 16.6/26
Liberty NBC 12.0/21
Lincoln NBC 16.6/26 14.9/24
Little House On The Prairie - Bless All The Dear
  Children NBC 18.2/27
Little Kidnappers, The DISNEY
Little Match Girl, The NBC 19.4/30
Lonesome Dove CBS 28.5/42 23.8/34 24.8/37
  27.3/41
Long Hot Summer, The NBC 22.6/34 23.8/36
Long Road Home NBC 11.8/18
Longarm ABC 12.3/20
Lost Capone, The TNT
Love Is Never Silent NBC 17.3/26
Lucy & Desi: Before The Laughter CBS 16.4/25
Malice In Wonderland CBS 18.3/29
Man Against The Mob NBC 19.7/32
Man Against The Mob: The Chinatown Murders
  NBC 11.3/18
Man For All Season, A TNT
Man Who Broke 1,000 Chains, The HBO
Margaret Bourke - White TNT
Marilyn & Bobby: Her Final Affair USA
Marilyn & Me ABC 8.5/14
Mario Puzo's The Fortunate Pilgrim NBC
  13.1/22 13.0/21
Mark Twain And Me DISNEY
Memphis TNT
Miracle In The Wilderness TNT
Miss Rose White NBC 11.0/17
Mission Of The Shark CBS 15.6/25
Mistral's Daughter CBS 18.2/29 18.7/30
  16.3/26
Monte Carlo CBS 14.6/23 12.2/19
Mrs. 'Arris Goes To Paris CBS 16.8/28
Murder In Mississippi NBC 12.4/20
Murder In The Heartland ABC 13.2/21 14.2/23
Murder Of Mary Phagan, The NBC 18.7/28
  21.0/34
Murders In The Rue Morgue, The CBS 17.7/27
Murrow HBO
Mussolini: The Decline And Fall Of Il Duce
  HBO
Mussolini - The Untold Story NBC 17.7/26
  19.4/29 19.6/29
My Name Is Bill W. ABC 15.2/24
Napoleon And Josephine: A ABC 18.6/30
  16.2/26 13.3/21
Ned Blessing: The Story Of My Life And Times
  CBS 11.3/20

Ned Blessing: The True Story Of My Life CBS
  10.9/18
Neon Empire SHOWTIME
Norman Rockwell's Breaking Home Ties ABC
  9.7/19
North And South ABC 25.8/37 23.6/34
  28.0/42 25.8/38 23.2/37
North And South, Book 2 ABC 19.8/30 20.1/30
  21.6/36 22.9/36 20.8/32
North And South, Book 3: Heaven And Hell ABC
  10.1/15 9.8/15 9.7/15
O Pioneers CBS 18.9/29
Old Man & The Sea, The NBC 14.9/24
Oldest Living Confederate Widow Tells All CBS
  15.7/24 13.8/21
On Promised Land DISNEY
Once Upon A Texas Train CBS 21.2/32
One Against The Wind CBS 13.4/21
One More Mountain ABC 12.9/20
Orpheus Descending TNT
Pack Of Lies CBS 18.2/30
Pancho Barnes CBS 11.7/18
Paris Trout SHOWTIME
Passion And Paradise ABC 11.8/19 12.5/20
Passion For Justice, A: Hazel Brannon Smith Story
  ABC 11.1/18
Perfect Harmony DISNEY
Perfect Tribute, The ABC 10.5/18
Peter The Great
  NBC 19.0/28 17.6/26 16.6/26 17.4/27
Phantom Of The Opera, The NBC 12.3/19
  12.3/20
Pink Lightning FBC 4.4/8
Plot To Kill Hitler, The CBS 7.2/12
Polly—Comin' Home NBC 6.8/10
Poor Little Rich Girl: The Barbara Hutton Story
  NBC 21.3/33 18.5/30
Prisoner Of Honor HBO
Private Matter, A HBO
Queen CBS 24.7/38 24.1/37 22.8/34
Queenie ABC 12.7/21 12.9/21
Quick And The Dead, The HBO
Rags To Riches NBC 25.3/36
Red River CBS 18.4/29
Return Of Desperado, The NBC 16.0/24
Return Of Eliot Ness, The NBC 12.7/19
Return To Lonesome Dove CBS 18.1/28
  16.5/25 15.2/24
Revenge Of Al Capone, The NBC 13.9/22
Richest Man In The World: The Aristotle Onassis
  Story ABC 12.1/18 13.9/22
Road Raiders, The CBS 8.5/14
Roadracers SHOWTIME
Robert Kennedy And His Times CBS 19.8/29
  14.9/21 16.9/26
Robin Hood FBC 6.0/10
Roots: The Gift ABC 15.4/24
Rose And The Jackal, The TNT
Roswell SHOWTIME
Sarah, Plain And Tall CBS 23.1/35
Scattered Dreams: The Kathryn Messenger Story
  CBS 14.1/22
Sea Wolf, The TNT
Season Of Giants, A TNT
Secret Garden, The CBS 16.7/26
Separate But Equal ABC 11.9/19 11.8/19
Shadow Of A Doubt CBS 15.3/24
Shakedown On The Sunset Strip CBS 15.0/27
She Stood Alone NBC 10.8/18
Shooter NBC 11.3/20
Silent Cries NBC 12.4/20
Sinatra CBS 17.7/26 17.2/27
Sins CBS 19.7/29 21.9/32 20.6/32

Six Against The Rock NBC 16.4/24
Skylark CBS 19.9/29
Sodbusters SHOWTIME
Son Of The Morning Star ABC 11.7/18 12.8/20
Sound And The Silence, The TNT
Space CBS 19.4/31 16.4/26 14.7/24 17.1/28
  16.3/26
Special Friendship, A CBS 13.7/22
Stagecoach CBS 22.5/36
Stalin HBO
Stolen Babies LIFETIME
Stompin' At The Savoy CBS 11.2/19
Stone Fox NBC 15.9/22
Stones Of Ibarra CBS 12.4/21
Substitute Wife, The NBC 17.5/27
Sudie And Simpson LIFETIME
Sun Also Rises, The NBC 13.2/20 11.6/18
Sweet Bird Of Youth NBC 13.0/21
Tenth Man, The CBS 13.3/21
The Race To Freedom: The Underground Railroad
  FAMILY
Timestalkers CBS 12.8/21
Too Young The Hero CBS 20.7/33
Treacherous Crossing USA
Treasure Island TNT
Two Mrs. Grenvilles, The NBC 23.4/36 24.0/35
Uncle Tom's Cabin SHOWTIME
Unconquered CBS 17.3/28
Walton Thanksgiving Reunion, A CBS 20.1/30
War And Remembrance ABC 21.8/31 19.0/29
  19.8/31 16.8/25 17.0/26
War And Remembrance, Part I I ABC 13.4/21
  14.4/22 15.1/24 15.7/25 15.9/26
Water Engine, The TNT
When We Were Young NBC 10.9/19
Where Pigeons Go To Die NBC 15.3/24
White Hot: The Mysterious Murder Of Thelma
  Todd NBC 12.3/20
Wildflower LIFETIME
Winner Never Quits, A ABC 14.6/24
Woman He Loved, The CBS 14.5/25
Woman Named Jackie, A NBC 15.5/23 18.6/28
  19.1/30
Women Of Brewster Place, The ABC 23.5/36
  24.5/38
Women Of Valor CBS 19.6/32
Yearling, The CBS 13.2/21
Yes, Virginia, There Is A Santa Claus ABC
  12.2/19
Young Catherine TNT
Young Indiana Jones Chronicles: The Curse Of
  The Jackal ABC 16.6/26
Zelda TNT

POLITICAL PIECE

American Story, An CBS 12.7/20
Amerika ABC 24.7/38 20.9/31 17.7/26 17.8/
  28 15.6/23
And The Band Played On HBO
By Dawn's Early Light HBO
Citizen Cohn HBO
Doomsday Gun HBO
Enemy Within, The HBO
Fatal Deception: Mrs. Lee Harvey Oswald NBC
  11.2/18
Favorite Son NBC 15.9/26 15.7/25 16.3/26
Forgotten Prisoners: The Amnesty File TNT
Grass Roots NBC 13.4/20 15.1/23
Held Hostage: The Sis And Jerry Levin Story
  ABC 12.0/19

POLITICAL PIECE (CONTINUED)

Hijacking Of The Achille Lauro, The   NBC   12.7/20
Hostages   HBO
Iran: Days Of Crisis   TNT
Just Another Secret   USA
L B J: The Early Years   NBC   18.4/27
Last Days Of Patton, The   CBS   19.5/32
Lincoln   NBC   16.6/26   14.9/24
Majority Rule   LIFETIME
Mastergate   SHOWTIME
Mussolini - The Untold Story   NBC   17.7/26
   19.4/29   19.6/29
Presidents Child, The   CBS   10.0/17
Railway Station Man, The   TNT
Red King, White Knight   HBO
Robert Kennedy And His Times   CBS   19.8/29
   14.9/21   16.9/26
Running Mates   HBO
Secret Weapons   NBC   13.8/21
Shootdown   NBC   16.0/25
Tagget   USA
Tailspin: Behind The Korean Airlines Tragedy
   HBO
Terrorist On Trial: The United States Vs. Salim
   Ajami   CBS   13.3/20
Tragedy Of Flight 103: The Inside Story, The
   HBO
Unconquered   CBS   17.3/28
Under Siege   NBC   17.2/24

PRISON AND PRISON CAMP

Against The Wall   HBO
Convicted: A Mother's Story   NBC   17.4/27
Crime Of Innocence   NBC   17.2/26
Dark Holiday   NBC   11.1/18
Deadlock   HBO
Defiant One, The   ABC   18.9/28
Doing Life   NBC   16.8/27
Escape From Sobibor   CBS   21.4/34
False Arrest   ABC   11.5/18   16.6/27
Father & Son: Dangerous Relations   NBC
   14.6/24
Forgotten Prisoners: The Amnesty File   TNT
Getting Out   ABC   11.1/18
Great Escape I I: The Untold Story, The   NBC
   14.4/23   12.3/19
Guilty Of Innocence: The Lenell Geter Story
   CBS   15.7/25
Guilty Until Proven Innocent   NBC   11.8/19
Gulag   HBO
Held Hostage: The Sis And Jerry Levin Story
   ABC   12.0/19
Hostages   HBO
In Love And War   NBC   16.7/27
Incident, The   CBS   20.8/33
Last Light   SHOWTIME
Last P. O. W? The Bobby Garwood Story, The
   ABC   11.5/20
Live: From Death Row   FBC   6.9/12
Locked Up: A Mother's Rage   CBS   12.4/20
Love On The Run   NBC   15.4/23
Man Who Broke 1,000 Chains, The   HBO
Marked For Murder   NBC   12.4/20
Murderers Among Us: The Simon Wiesenthal
   Story   HBO
Outside Woman, The   CBS   14.3/22
Revenge Of Al Capone, The   NBC   13.9/22
Silent Cries   NBC   12.4/20

Six Against The Rock   NBC   16.4/24
Somebody Has To Shoot The Picture   HBO
Thompson's Last Run   CBS   17.4/26
Three On A Match   NBC   14.1/26
Twist Of Fate   NBC   14.3/21   15.2/24
Women Of Valor   CBS   19.6/32

PROSTITUTION

Beverly Hills Cowgirl Blues   CBS   12.9/22
Beverly Hills Madam   NBC   17.5/27
Children Of The Night   CBS   12.4/21
Daughter Of The Streets   ABC   14.9/24
Full Exposure: The Sex Tapes Scandal   NBC
   16.2/24
High Price Of Passion, The   NBC   18.6/29
Last Prostitute, The   LIFETIME
Man Against The Mob: The Chinatown Murders
   NBC   11.3/18
Mayflower Madam   CBS   20.9/34
Moment Of Truth: Why My Daughter?   NBC
   14.2/23
Poker Alice   CBS   17.5/32
Secrets Of A Married Man   NBC   17.5/27
Shakedown On The Sunset Strip   CBS   15.0/27
Spenser: Ceremony   LIFETIME
Those Secrets   ABC   8.9/14
Touch Of Scandal, A   CBS   17.0/27
Tricks Of The Trade   CBS   11.6/18

PSYCHOLOGICAL THRILLER

Alfred Hitchcock Presents   NBC   18.0/28
Angel Of Death   CBS   10.8/18
Blind Man's Bluff   USA
Body Language   USA
Body Of Evidence   CBS   18.4/28
Brotherly Love   CBS   13.5/22
Bump In The Night   CBS   16.0/25
Deadbolt   CBS   12.9/23
Deadly Deception   CBS   19.2/30
Deadly Intentions   ABC   13.3/22   21.3/32
Deadly Messages   ABC   11.4/17
Descending Angel   HBO
Dying To Love You   CBS   15.4/25
Eighty-Three Hours 'til Dawn   CBS   14.2/22
Face Of Fear, The   CBS   14.0/23
Fear Inside, The   SHOWTIME
Fear Stalk   CBS   11.7/19
Fifth Missile, The   NBC   14.7/22
Haunted By Her Past   NBC   16.7/27
Hell Hath No Fury   NBC   15.2/24
Her Wicked Ways   NBC   16.9/26
I Know My Son Is Alive   NBC   9.9/15
In Broad Daylight   NBC   13.7/21
In The Company Of Darkness   CBS   15.0/24
Intimate Stranger   SHOWTIME
Killer In The Mirror   NBC   20.4/31
Kiss Of A Killer   ABC   11.5/18
Kissing Place, The   USA
Lady Forgets, The   CBS   18.5/34
Letter To Three Wives, A   NBC   19.3/30
Liar's Edge   SHOWTIME
Lookalike, The   USA
Memories Of Murder   LIFETIME
Midnight's Child   LIFETIME
Murder: By Reason Of Insanity   CBS   16.6/26
Murder C. O. D.   NBC   10.3/19
Night Of The Hunter   ABC   13.7/23
Obsessive Love   CBS   15.2/25

Past Tense   SHOWTIME
Psycho I V: The Beginning   SHOWTIME
Red Wind   USA
Relentless: Mind Of A Killer   NBC   12.8/20
Scene Of The Crime   NBC   12.5/21
Settle The Score   NBC   16.8/26
Shadow Of A Doubt   CBS   15.3/24
Shadow Of Obsession   NBC   11.4/18
Sitter, The   FBC   6.7/12
Sorry, Wrong Number   USA
Stranger Within, The   CBS   15.6/25
Too Good To Be True   NBC   20.9/32
Vanishing Act   CBS   18.3/27
Visions Of Murder   NBC   10.1/19
Web Of Deception   NBC   10.7/17
What Ever Happened To Baby Jane?   ABC   9.9/15
Wheels Of Terror   USA
When Dreams Come True   ABC   12.8/21

RAPE/MOLESTATION

Betrayed By Innocence   CBS   10.8/19
Blood And Orchids   CBS   22.9/35   25.6/38
Breaking The Silence   CBS   12.8/20
Bump In The Night   CBS   16.0/25
Cast The First Stone   NBC   17.9/28
Complex Of Fear   CBS   14.8/23
Conspiracy Of Silence   CBS   12.5/21   12.2/20
Convicted   ABC   17.4/27
Deadly Silence, A   ABC   17.9/28
Death In California, A   ABC   15.7/25   19.2/30
Do You Know The Muffin Man?   CBS   18.4/30
Don't Touch My Daughter   NBC   14.5/23
Easy Prey   ABC   18.4/29
Family Of Strangers   CBS   19.8/29
Fatal Memories   NBC   15.8/24
Hands Of A Stranger   NBC   15.2/25   17.4/28
I Know My First Name Is Steven   NBC   21.6/35
   27.3/42
In The Best Interest Of The Child   CBS   11.6/19
Judgment   HBO
Kids Don't Tell   CBS   18.1/29
Liar, Liar   NBC   14.5/26
Little Girl Lost   ABC   19.0/31
Mother's Justice, A   NBC   16.7/25
Mothers Revenge, A   ABC   10.6/16
Mothers' Right, A: The Elizabeth Morgan Story
   ABC   13.6/21
News At Eleven   CBS   13.3/22
Not In My Family   ABC   15.1/23
One Of Her Own   ABC   13.5/21
One Terrific Guy   CBS   19.6/30
Price She Paid, The   CBS   11.7/19
Rape Of Dr. Willis, The   CBS   14.4/23
Rape Of Richard Beck, The   ABC   25.2/38
Settle The Score   NBC   16.8/26
Shame   LIFETIME
Shattered Trust: The Shari Karney Story   NBC
   16.2/25
She Said No   NBC   14.7/23
Silent Witness   NBC   22.5/33
Sin And Redemption   CBS   14.0/23
Sins Of The Mother   CBS   14.5/23
Stop At Nothing   LIFETIME
Sudie And Simpson   LIFETIME
Taking Back My Life: The Nancy Ziegenmeyer
   Story   CBS   15.8/25
Unspeakable Acts   ABC   15.7/25
When He's Not A Stranger   CBS   17.2/26
When The Bough Breaks   NBC   22.3/36
Without Her Consent   NBC   17.8/28

ROMANTIC COMEDY

Assault And Matrimony NBC 20.2/32
Babycakes CBS 13.3/22
Baja Oklahoma HBO
Bare Essentials CBS 13.3/21
Bring Me The Head Of Dobie Gillis CBS 15.0/23
California Girls ABC 20.3/31
Caught In The Act USA
Chance Of A Lifetime NBC 14.8/22
Children Of The Bride CBS 13.6/25
Christmas In Connecticut TNT
Classified Love CBS 9.7/17
Club Med ABC 14.8/23
Coins In The Fountain CBS 10.0/19
Counterfeit Contessa, The FBC 5.1/8
Crazy From The Heart TNT
Dead Solid Perfect HBO
Eight Is Enough Wedding, An NBC 15.3/25
Finnegan Begin Again HBO
For Love Or Money CBS 12.4/20
Goddess Of Love NBC 16.7/26
Going To The Chapel NBC 15.0/25
How To Murder A Millionaire CBS 10.2/18
I Married A Centerfold NBC 13.4/21
I'll Take Romance ABC 13.1/21
Indiscreet CBS 12.0/18
Just My Imagination NBC 15.5/19
Last Fling, The ABC 15.9/23
Letting Go ABC 15.1/28
Little White Lies NBC 16.9/26
Long Gone HBO
Love Boat: A Valentine Voyage, The CBS 13.6/22
Love Can Be Murder NBC 11.4/18
My First Love ABC 13.7/21
Opposites Attract NBC 12.7/21
Parallel Lives SHOWTIME
Partners 'N Love FAMILY
Perfect People ABC 13.3/21
Plaza Suite ABC 8.0/13
Remington Steele: The Steele That Wouldn't Die NBC 19.7/28
Rich Men, Single Women ABC 14.8/23
Secret Life Of Archie's Wife, The CBS 13.4/22
Secret Life Of Kathy Mccormick, The NBC 14.5/26
Sharing Richard CBS 13.7/22
Single Bars, Single Women ABC 20.0/31
Something In Common CBS 18.2/29
Stolen: One Husband CBS 9.5/15
Stranded NBC 24.9/38
Stuck With Each Other NBC 8.9/16
Sweet Revenge TNT
Take My Daughters, Please NBC 19.9/31
This Can't Be Love CBS 17.8/28
Threesome CBS 10.3/18
Tonight's The Night ABC 11.9/19
Warm Hearts, Cold Feet CBS 15.1/22

SCI-FI/SUPERNATURAL/HORROR/FANTASY

Alice In Wonderland CBS 21.2/31 16.8/25
Amityville: The Evil Escapes NBC 8.6/16
Annihilator, The NBC 14.1/23
Arthur The King CBS 9.5/17
Assassin CBS 14.1/23
Attack Of The 50ft. Woman HBO
Bates Motel NBC 14.6/27
Bay Coven NBC 13.8/22

Bionic Showdown: The 6 Million Dollar Man/Bionic Woman NBC 17.6/28
Birds I I: Land's End, The SHOWTIME
Black Magic SHOWTIME
Blood Ties FBC 6.3/11
Boris And Natasha SHOWTIME
Borrowers, The TNT
Bridge Across Time NBC 13.7/21
By Dawn's Early Light HBO
Cast A Deadly Spell HBO
Child Of Darkness, Child Of Light USA
Clarence FAMILY
Connecticut Yankee In King Arthur's Court, A NBC 11.5/17
Cooperstown TNT
Danger Island NBC 11.6/19
Dark Reflection FBC 4.8/7
Dark Shadows NBC 14.6/23 13.1/21
Daughter Of Darkness CBS 10.4/18
Day - O NBC 5.3/10
Daybreak HBO
Deadlock HBO
Death Dreams LIFETIME
Death Of The Incredible Hulk, The NBC 14.6/22
Disaster In Time SHOWTIME
Double, Double, Toil And Trouble ABC 10.8/19
Duplicates USA
Earth Angel ABC 11.2/18
Ewok Adventure, The ABC 24.9/36
Ewoks: The Battle For Endor ABC 18.7/26
Fear SHOWTIME
Fire Next Time, The NBC 13.1/22 11.0/18
Flash, The CBS 14.2/23
Frankenstein TNT
Frankenstein: The College Years FBC 6.1/9
From The Dead Of Night NBC 11.6/20 14.3/22
Generation ABC 6.5/12
Ghost Mom FBC 6.0/9
Ghost Of A Chance CBS 14.4/24
Gifted One, The NBC 15.5/27
Girl From Tomorrow, The DISNEY
Goddess Of Love NBC 16.7/26
Gotham SHOWTIME
Grave Secrets: The Legacy Of Hilltop Drive CBS 14.7/23
Guess Who's Coming For Christmas NBC 10.9/19
Guilty Conscience CBS 10.8/18
Haunted By Her Past NBC 16.7/27
Haunted, The FBC 8.4/13
Hi Honey — I'm Dead FBC 6.7/11
Highway To Heaven NBC 20.6/35
Highwayman, The NBC 13.1/22
I Dream Of Jeannie: 15 Years Later NBC 21.4/32
I Still Dream Of Jeannie NBC 12.3/19
I'm Dangerous Tonight USA
In The Nick Of Time NBC 12.9/20
Incredible Hulk Returns, The NBC 20.2/33
Intruders CBS 13.2/21 12.9/21
J. O. E. And The Colonel ABC 11.0/18
Jekyll & Hyde ABC 12.2/19
Journey To The Center Of The Earth NBC 13.1/20
Knight Rider 2000 NBC 16.1/26
Lifepod FBC 6.5/11
Lightning Incident, The USA
Lois & Clark: The New Adventures Of Superman ABC 11.2/17
Love Can Be Murder NBC 11.4/18
Mantis FBC 8.5/13
Midnight Hour, The NBC 10.5/17
Midnight's Child LIFETIME

Miracle Child NBC 11.0/18
Misfits Of Science NBC 14.2/23
Mom For Christmas, A NBC 17.0/27
Mother Goose Rock 'n' Rhyme DISNEY
Murder By Moonlight CBS 7.7/12
Murder By The Book CBS 9.4/15
Nick Knight CBS 11.2/19
Night Owl LIFETIME
Night They Saved Christmas, The ABC 14.2/22
Night Visions NBC 9.8/17
Nightlife USA
Nightmare On The Thirteenth Floor USA
Not Of This World CBS 10.5/17
Not Quite Human I I DISNEY
Omen I V: The Awakening FBC 6.4/11
Out Of Time NBC 13.8/25
Out On A Limb ABC 13.8/20 16.8/25
Plymouth ABC 8.3/17
Probe ABC 14.2/23
Psychic USA
Quantum Leap NBC 14.9/25
Return Of Sherlock Holmes, The CBS 14.4/24
Return Of The 6 Million Dollar Man & Bionic Woman NBC 20.5/33
Running Against Time USA
Seaquest Dsv NBC 17.8/28
Search For Grace CBS 10.5/17
Seduced By Evil USA
Shadow Chasers ABC 6.9/10
Sherlock Holmes Returns CBS 9.7/16
Something Is Out There NBC 19.3/31 19.0/29
Spirit, The ABC 7.0/15
Starcrossed ABC 11.4/16
Steel Justice NBC 8.9/14
Stepford Children, The NBC 19.2/29
Stephen King's Golden Years CBS 12.2/22
Stephen King's It ABC 18.5/29 20.6/33
Stephen King's Sometimes They Come Back CBS 11.7/19
Stephen King's The Stand ABC 20.1/32 21.0/32 20.1/31 20.0/31
Still Not Quite Human DISNEY
Stillwatch CBS 14.7/23
Strays USA
Street Hawk ABC 17.9/26
Tainted Blood USA
They SHOWTIME
Timestalkers CBS 12.8/21
To Dance With The White Dog CBS 21.9/33
To Save A Child ABC 9.1/15
Tommyknockers, The ABC 15.9/26 17.3/27
Tower, The FBC 6.2/11
Trial Of The Incredible Hulk, The NBC 16.2/25
Turn Back The Clock NBC 13.8/22
Twelve O' One (12: 01) FBC 6.0/12
Viper NBC 15.3/23
Who Is Julia? CBS 18.4/29
Wild Palms ABC 12.3/20 9.7/15 11.0/19 9.9/17

SERIES PILOT (2 HR.)

Aaron's Way NBC 19.5/31
Adventures Of Brisco County Jr., The FBC 7.2/14
Annihilator, The NBC 14.1/23
Appearances NBC 9.8/18
Archie: To Riverdale And Back Again NBC 10.6/17
Baywatch: Panic At Malibu Pier NBC 17.1/28
Blacke's Magic NBC 21.8/32

SERIES PILOT (2 HR.) (CONTINUED)

Blue Bayou NBC 12.8/20
Brand New Life: The Honeymoon NBC 15.9/25
Brass CBS 12.9/22
Broken Badges CBS 9.1/16
Brotherhood Of The Gun CBS 7.3/14
C. A. T. Squad NBC 17.3/30
Capital News ABC 10.1/17
Carly's Web NBC 9.3/17
Chameleons NBC 9.9/17
China Beach ABC 18.0/29
Christy CBS 17.7/29
Class Of '61 ABC 8.5/14
Condition: Critical NBC 11.0/18
Cover Up CBS 14.0/26
Danger Down Under NBC 13.3/22
Dark Shadows NBC 14.6/23 13.1/21
Daughters Of Privilege NBC 13.9/23
Detective In The House CBS 14.4/24
Diagnosis Of Murder CBS 14.6/23
Diary Of A Perfect Murder NBC 20.9/33
Double Deception NBC 9.6/17
Dr. Quinn, Medicine Woman CBS 18.2/29
Due South CBS 11.5/21
E. A. R. T. H. Force CBS 9.9/17
Equal Justice ABC 12.2/23
Family For Joe, A NBC 15.8/23
Fatal Confession: A Father Dowling Mystery NBC 15.5/24
Father Of Hell Town NBC 18.2/29
Flash, The CBS 14.2/23
Follow Your Heart NBC 14.7/23
For Love And Glory CBS 9.4/18
From The Files Of Joseph Wambaugh: A Jury Of One NBC 17 17
Generation ABC 6.5/12
Gifted One, The NBC 15.5/27
Glitter ABC 15.9/27
Green Dolphin Beat FBC 4.4/8
Harry's Hong Kong ABC 6.1/11
Hawaiian Heat ABC 19.1/34
High Mountain Rangers CBS 19.6/32
Higher Ground CBS 13.3/25
Highway To Heaven NBC 20.6/35
Highwayman, The NBC 13.1/22
Homefront ABC 12.2/20
Hunter NBC 20.4/33
I'll Fly Away NBC 15.4/24
In Like Flynn ABC 8.4/15
In The Heat Of The Night NBC 18.7/30
International Airport ABC 13.0/27
Island Sons ABC 7.9/14
It's Nothing Personal NBC 10.9/17
Jesse Hawkes CBS 8.9/17
Jessie ABC 17.7/29
Johnny Ryan NBC 6.6/12
Journey To The Center Of The Earth NBC 13.1/20
Keys, The NBC 12.1/19
L. A. Law NBC 21.2/33
L. A. Takedown NBC 10.4/18
Lady Blue ABC 19.8/31
Lily CBS 6.6/14
Lois & Clark: The New Adventures Of Superman ABC 11.2/17
Love On The Run NBC 9.3/16
Macshayne: Winner Take All NBC 10.7/17
Miami Vice NBC 22.8/37
Middle Ages CBS 8.7/16
Misfits Of Science NBC 14.2/23
Missing Persons ABC 11.4/19

Moonlighting ABC 18.3/28
Mothers, Daughters And Lovers NBC 8.4/14
Murder In High Places NBC 12.3/22
Murder In Paradise NBC 12.6/21
Murder, She Wrote CBS 18.9/29
N. Y. P. D. Mounted CBS 6.1/13
Nasty Boys NBC 15.3/27
Ned Blessing: The Story Of My Life And Times CBS 11.3/20
Ned Blessing: The True Story Of My Life CBS 10.9/18
Nick Knight CBS 11.2/19
Nightingales NBC 18.9/33
Our Family Honor ABC 15.4/25
Out Of Time NBC 13.8/25
Over My Dead Body CBS 12.4/23
P. S. I Luv U CBS 15.7/25
Palace Guard CBS 7.4/14
Paper Dolls ABC 18.4/29
Parker Kane NBC 8.6/15
Picket Fences CBS 12.7/24
Plymouth ABC 8.3/17
Popeye Doyle NBC 15.8/26
Probe ABC 14.2/23
Quantum Leap NBC 14.9/25
Rags To Riches NBC 25.3/36
Ray Alexander: A Taste For Justice NBC 8.5/15
Red Shoes Diaries SHOWTIME
Relentless: Mind Of A Killer NBC 12.8/20
Return Of Desperado, The NBC 16.0/24
Revealing Evidence NBC 14.5/25
Rio Shanon ABC 5.2/11
Round Table, The NBC 8.3/16
Sadie And Son CBS 15.5/25
Seaquest Dsv NBC 17.8/28
Second Chances CBS 9.7/16
Shannon's Deal NBC 14.5/25
Sherlock Holmes Returns CBS 9.7/16
Something Is Out There NBC 19.3/31 19.0/29
South Beach NBC 9.8/17
Sparks: The Price Of Passion CBS 13.7/21
Spenser: For Hire ABC 14.0/24
Spirit, The ABC 7.0/15
Steel Justice NBC 8.9/14
Stephen King's Golden Years CBS 12.2/22
Street Hawk ABC 17.9/26
Sunset Beat ABC 6.5/13
Supercarrier ABC 15.0/23
Three On A Match NBC 14.1/26
Thunderboat Row ABC 13.8/23
To Save A Child ABC 9.1/15
Trenchcoat In Paradise CBS 12.2/20
Triplecross ABC 10.3/16
True Blue NBC 14.0/22
Twin Peaks ABC 21.7/33
Two Thousand Malibu Road CBS 16.1/28
Under Cover ABC 9.9/16
Us CBS 16.1/29
Walker, Texas Ranger CBS 16.5/27
When We Were Young NBC 10.9/19
Wolf CBS 14.2/25
Young Indiana Jones Chronicles: The Curse Of The Jackal ABC 16.6/26

SEX/GLITZ

Based On An Untrue Story FBC 3.5/5
Beverly Hills Madam NBC 17.5/27
Beyond Control: The Amy Fisher Story ABC 19.5/30
Bluegrass CBS 17.6/27 18.4/29

Casanova ABC 10.3/15
Casualties Of Love: The Long Island Lolita Story CBS 14.3/22
Cover Girl Murders, The USA
Crossings ABC 17.5/27 15.0/22 17.4/27
Danielle Steel's Kaleidoscope NBC 20.3/32
Danielle Steel's Secrets NBC 15.6/24
Danielle Steel's Star NBC 15.9/24
Daughters Of Privilege NBC 13.9/23
Deceptions NBC 19.9/35 21.8/35
Dinner At Eight TNT
Duel Of Hearts TNT
Fall From Grace NBC 17.6/27
Fatal Charm SHOWTIME
Favorite Son NBC 15.9/26 15.7/25 16.3/26
Fresno CBS 19.7/30 15.2/22 12.8/19 12.5/24 12.7/18
Full Exposure: The Sex Tapes Scandal NBC 16.2/24
Glitter ABC 15.9/27
Harem ABC 16.9/25 16.2/23
Hollywood Wives ABC 22.0/33 21.1/32 25.2/39
I'll Take Manhattan CBS 26.4/40 21.3/31 21.4/33 22.5/36
If Tomorrow Comes CBS 21.8/34 23.6/37 20.8/33
Inconvenient Woman, An ABC 11.7/21 12.4/20
Intimate Encounters NBC 14.2/23
Intimate Stranger SHOWTIME
Jackie Collins' Lady Boss NBC 12.7/20 14.2/22
Jackie Collins' Lucky Chances NBC 14.4/25 17.1/26 19.5/31
Judith Krantz's Till We Meet Again CBS 14.8/23 11.7/18
King Of Love, The ABC 6.7/11
Lace I I ABC 15.3/24 16.4/25
Lady And The Highwayman, The CBS 11.1/18
Ladykillers ABC 16.6/27
Laker Girls, The CBS 10.5/17
Marilyn & Bobby: Her Final Affair USA
Mayflower Madam CBS 20.9/34
Mistral's Daughter CBS 18.2/29 18.7/30 16.3/26
Mistress CBS 17.5/29
Monte Carlo CBS 14.6/23 12.2/19
Naked Lie CBS 21.2/33
Neon Empire SHOWTIME
Nightingales NBC 18.9/33
Obsessed With A Married Woman ABC 14.5/22
Operation, The CBS 20.0/30
Other Lover, The CBS 13.8/22
Overexposed ABC 14.4/23
Paper Dolls ABC 18.4/29
Passion And Paradise ABC 11.8/19 12.5/20
People Like Us NBC 9.4/16 10.5/17
Pleasures ABC 12.9/20
Poor Little Rich Girl: The Barbara Hutton Story NBC 21.3/33 18.5/30
Posing: Inspired By Three Real Stories CBS 11.9/18
Prince Of Bel Air ABC 17.5/27
Rage Of Angels: The Story Continues NBC 15.9/25 16.5/25
Red Shoes Diaries SHOWTIME
Richest Man In The World: The Aristotle Onassis Story ABC 12.1/18 13.9/22
Roses Are For The Rich CBS 18.6/30 17.8/29
Roxanne: The Prize Pulitzer NBC 17.3/27
Scandal Sheet ABC 20.5/32
Secret Passion Of Robert Clayton, The USA
Secrets Of A Married Man NBC 17.5/27
Secrets Of Lake Success NBC 7.7/14 7.4/14 7.1/13

SEX/GLITZ (CONTINUED)

Seduced CBS 15.5/25
Seduction: Three Tales From The Inner Sanctum
    ABC 9.4/15
Single Women, Married Men CBS 14.6/26
Sins CBS 19.7/29 21.9/32 20.6/32
Sins Of The Father NBC 15.0/23
Stranger In The Mirror, A ABC 9.6/16
Swimsuit NBC 17.3/27
Tonight's The Night ABC 11.9/19
Trade Winds NBC 6.9/13 6.2/13 5.4/11 5.8/11
Trial: The Price Of Passion NBC 11.2/18 13.2/21
Trouble In Paradise CBS 10.9/18
Twin Peaks ABC 21.7/33
Two Thousand Malibu Road CBS 16.1/28
Victim Of Love CBS 12.0/20
Woman Who Sinned, The ABC 12.1/18

SOCIAL ISSUE

Absolute Strangers CBS 17.7/29
Acceptable Risks ABC 9.7/15
Adam: His Song Continues NBC 15.9/25
Against The Wall HBO
Amerika ABC 24.7/38 20.9/31 17.7/26
    17.8/28 15.6/23
And The Band Played On HBO
Attack On Fear CBS 10.9/16
Baby Brokers NBC 11.4/17
Baby Girl Scott CBS 13.2/23
Baby M ABC 15.0/24 17.6/27
Barbarians At The Gate HBO
Better Off Dead LIFETIME
Bluffing It ABC 13.4/22
Bonds Of Love CBS 14.9/23
Broken Angel ABC 16.9/28
Broken Cord, The ABC 14.3/22
Broken Promises: Taking Emily Back CBS
    12.6/22
Brotherhood Of Justice, The ABC 11.6/19
Bump In The Night CBS 16.0/25
Burning Bed, The NBC 36.2/52
By Dawn's Early Light HBO
Case Of Deadly Force, A CBS 12.0/20
Celebration Family ABC 10.2/17
Chase CBS 11.7/19
Child Lost Forever, A NBC 15.4/23
Child Saver, The NBC 15.8/25
Child's Cry CBS 22.7/33
Children Of Times Square ABC 12.5/20
Choices ABC 18.1/27
Christmas On Division Street CBS 16.7/26
Circle Of Violence: A CBS 15.7/25
Common Ground CBS 11.0/18 10.8/18
Conspiracy Of Silence CBS 12.5/21 12.2/20
Criminal Justice HBO
Cross Of Fire NBC 12.5/20 14.7/23
Cry For Help: The Tracey Thurman Story, A NBC
    21.5/33
Daddy ABC 17.1/25
Daughter Of The Streets ABC 14.9/24
Day One CBS 15.2/24
Decoration Day NBC 17.9/28
Defiant One, The ABC 18.9/28
Different Affair, A CBS 10.8/18
Disaster At Silo 7 ABC 10.1/16
Do You Know The Muffin Man? CBS 18.4/30
Double Standard NBC 21.1/33
Drop-Out Mother CBS 13.2/22
Ernest Green Story, The DISNEY

Evil In Clear River ABC 12.9/20
Eye On The Sparrow NBC 14.3/22
Face Of A Stranger CBS 16.8/27
Father Clements Story, The NBC 16.7/26
Fight For Jenny, A NBC 20.0/31
Finding The Way Home ABC 10.2/18
Fire In The Dark CBS 14.8/23
For The Love Of My Child: The Anissa Ayala
    Story NBC 12.8/20
For Their Own Good ABC 10.9/17
Forgotten Prisoners: The Amnesty File TNT
George Mckenna Story, The CBS 15.5/24
Girl Who Came Between Them, The NBC
    13.2/21
Gladiator, The ABC 15.9/24
God Bless The Child ABC 17.7/28
Good Fight, The LIFETIME
Gregory K ABC 10.3/16
Guardian, The HBO
Guilty Of Innocence: The Lenell Geter Story
    CBS 15.7/25
Guilty Until Proven Innocent NBC 11.8/19
Hijacking Of The Achille Lauro, The NBC
    12.7/20
Howard Beach: Making The Case For Murder
    NBC 14.9/24
I Know My First Name Is Steven NBC 21.6/35
    27.3/42
Image, The HBO
In Broad Daylight NBC 13.7/21
In Self Defense ABC 9.2/17
In The Best Interest Of The Child CBS 11.6/19
In The Best Interest Of The Children NBC
    16.0/24
In The Heat Of The Night NBC 18.7/30
Investigation: Inside A Terrorist Bombing, The
    HBO
Jonathan: The Boy Nobody Wanted NBC
    13.8/21
Joshua's Heart NBC 15.6/26
King Of Love, The ABC 6.7/11
L. A. Law NBC 21.2/33
Last Elephant, The TNT
Last Wish ABC 10.8/17
Laura Lansing Slept Here NBC 18.9/30
Laurel Avenue HBO
Liar, Liar CBS 14.5/26
Lies And Lullabies ABC 10.4/16
Line Of Fire: The Morris Dees Story NBC
    11.3/17
Little Girl Lost ABC 19.0/31
Live: From Death Row FBC 6.9/12
Living A Lie NBC 11.0/17
Locked Up: A Mother's Rage CBS 12.4/20
Love Lives On ABC 17.8/26
Mandela HBO
Marla Hanson Story, The NBC 15.1/24
Men Don't Tell CBS 19.7/31
Mercy Or Murder? NBC 23.8/35
Miracle At Beekman's Place NBC 12.3/21
Miss America: Behind The Crown NBC 13.3/20
Moment Of Truth: Broken Pledges NBC 12.6/20
Mothers' Right, A: The Elizabeth Morgan Story
    ABC 13.6/21
Murder In Mississippi NBC 12.4/20
Murder Of Mary Phagan, The NBC 18.7/28
    21.0/34
Murder Without Motive: The Edmund Perry Story
    NBC 11.3/18
Never Forget TNT
News At Eleven CBS 13.3/22
Night Of Courage ABC 12.4/19
No Place Like Home CBS 13.3/20

Nobody's Child CBS 25.9/39
On Fire ABC 12.8/20
One Special Victory NBC 13.1/20
One Terrific Guy CBS 19.6/30
Open Admissions CBS 7.5/13
Our Sons ABC 12.8/21
Out On The Edge CBS 14.6/23
Outrage CBS 21.7/34
Paris Trout SHOWTIME
Penalty Phase CBS 15.8/26
Perfect Harmony DISNEY
Perfect Witness HBO
Place For Annie, A ABC 14.8/23
Place To Be Loved, A CBS 13.0/20
Playing With Fire NBC 16.9/26
Prison For Children CBS 11.5/20
Private Matter, A HBO
Promised A Miracle CBS 13.2/22
Rape Of Richard Beck, The ABC 25.2/38
Reason To Live, A NBC 15.6/23
Red Earth, White Earth CBS 11.9/19
Resting Place CBS 22.3/36
Right Of The People, The ABC 14.5/22
Right To Die NBC 17.5/28
Right To Kill? ABC 19.0/31
Rising Son TNT
Rockabye CBS 25.3/38
Roe Vs. Wade NBC 17.0/27
Runaway Father CBS 16.8/27
Ryan White Story, The ABC 16.6/26
Samaritan: The Mitch Snyder Story CBS
    11.2/18
Scandal In A Small Town NBC 20.0/31
Secret, The CBS 13.3/23
Sexual Advances ABC 9.4/16
Shame LIFETIME
Shameful Secrets ABC 13.2/21
Shattered Innocence CBS 15.2/25
She Said No NBC 14.7/23
Silence Of The Heart CBS 21.9/35
Sister Margaret And The Saturday Night Ladies
    CBS 11.5/19
So Proudly We Hail CBS 7.5/12
Somebody Has To Shoot The Picture HBO
Something To Live For: The Alison Gertz Story
    ABC 16.2/26
State Of Emergency HBO
Stone Pillow CBS 23.3/33
Stoning In Fulham County, A NBC 18.3/28
Stop At Nothing LIFETIME
Story Lady, The NBC 15.9/24
Strapped HBO
Streets Of Justice NBC 15.4/22
Surviving ABC 18.1/26
Sworn To Silence ABC 16.1/24
Tailspin: Behind The Korean Airlines Tragedy
    HBO
Taken Away CBS 16.3/25
Taking Back My Life: The Nancy Ziegenmeyer
    Story CBS 15.8/25
Terrorist On Trial: The United States Vs. Salim
    Ajami CBS 13.3/20
There Are No Children Here ABC 17.8/26
This Child Is Mine NBC 21.1/32
This Park Is Mine HBO
Too Young To Die? NBC 14.5/23
Toughlove ABC 20.6/31
Tragedy Of Flight 103: The Inside Story, The
    HBO
Two Fathers' Justice NBC 17.9/27
Ultimate Betrayal CBS 15.6/25
Unconquered CBS 17.3/28
Unspeakable Acts ABC 15.7/25

SOCIAL ISSUE (CONTINUED)

Vengeance: The Story Of Tony Cimo   CBS
   11.8/21
We Are The Children   ABC   9.1/14
What Price Victory?   ABC   10.8/17
When He's Not A Stranger   CBS   17.2/26
When No One Would Listen   CBS   12.9/19
When The Time Comes   ABC   11.1/18
When You Remember Me   ABC   14.6/24
Whereabouts Of Jenny, The   ABC   15.4/24
White Lie   USA
Whose Child Is This? The War For Baby Jessica
   ABC   9.6/15
Wild Texas Wind   NBC   18.0/27
Winnie   NBC   16.6/28
Without Warning: The James Brady Story   HBO
Witness To The Execution   NBC   12.2/17
Yarn Princess, The   ABC   10.5/17

SPORTS

Babe Ruth   NBC   10.0/16
Backfield In Motion   ABC   15.0/24
Challenge Of A Lifetime   ABC   8.7/13
Comrades Of Summer   HBO
Cooperstown   TNT
Cracked Up   ABC   14.7/23
Dead Solid Perfect   HBO
Finish Line   TNT
Glory Days   CBS   11.1/17
Going For The Gold: The Bill Johnson Story
   CBS   8.9/14
Heart Of A Champion: The Ray Mancini Story
   CBS   10.6/17
Kiss Shot   CBS   10.2/16
Laker Girls, The   CBS   10.5/17
Long Gone   HBO
Man From Left Field   CBS   10.5/20
On Thin Ice: The Tai Babilonia Story   NBC
   13.4/21
One Special Victory   NBC   13.1/20
Percy & Thunder   TNT
Perry Mason: The Case Of The All-Star Assassin
   NBC   16.8/26
Quiet Victory: The Charlie Wedemeyer Story
   CBS   14.9/25
Rise & Walk: The Dennis Byrd Story   FBC
   7.1/11
Second Serve   CBS   13.6/22
Storm And Sorrow   LIFETIME
Stormin' Home   CBS   13.1/23
Tonya & Nancy: The Inside Story   NBC   10.4/19
Triumph Of The Heart: The Ricky Bell Story   CBS
   12.5/22
What Price Victory?   ABC   10.8/17
Winner Never Quits, A   ABC   14.6/24

SUSPENSE/THRILLER

Abduction Of Kari Swenson, The   NBC   21.4/33
Accidental Meeting   USA
Adrift   CBS   12.1/20
Alfred Hitchcock Presents   NBC   18.0/28
Amerika   ABC   24.7/38   20.9/31   17.7/26   17.8/
   28   15.6/23
Amityville: The Evil Escapes   NBC   8.6/16
Amos   CBS   24.5/37

... And Then She Was Gone   NBC   11.7/19
Apology   HBO
Are You Lonesome Tonight?   USA
Assassin   CBS   14.1/23
Bad Seed, The   ABC   12.9/19
Barbara Taylor Bradford's Remember   NBC
   10.9/18   13.5/21
Bates Motel   NBC   14.6/27
Bay Coven   NBC   13.8/22
Birds I I: Land's End, The   SHOWTIME
Bitter Vengeance   USA
Black Ice   USA
Black Magic   SHOWTIME
Blacke's Magic   NBC   21.8/32
Blackmail   USA
Blackout   HBO
Blind Side   HBO
Blind Vengeance   USA
Blind Witness   ABC   16.3/25
Blindfold: Acts Of Obsession   USA
Blindsided   USA
Born To Run   FBC   3.9/7
Bourne Identity, The   ABC   18.5/30   18.5/29
Breaking Point   TNT
Bride In Black, The   ABC   16.7/27
Brotherhood Of The Rose   NBC   20.9/35   19.2/30
Brotherly Love   CBS   13.5/22
Burden Of Proof, The   ABC   12.8/18   15.1/23
Buried Alive   USA
By Dawn's Early Light   HBO
Captive   ABC   12.9/20
Cartier Affair, The   NBC   17.1/27
Case For Murder, A   USA
Casualty Of War, A   USA
Child In The Night   CBS   9.7/16
Child Of Darkness, Child Of Light   USA
Child Saver, The   NBC   15.8/25
Chrome Soldiers   USA
City Killer   NBC   14.9/24
Codename: Foxfire - Slay It Again, Sam   NBC
   20.4/29
Condition: Critical   NBC   11.0/18
Curiosity Kills   USA
Dancing With Danger   USA
Danger Down Under   NBC   13.3/22
Danger Island   NBC   11.6/19
Dangerous Affection   NBC   16.4/26
Dangerous Heart   USA
Dangerous Passion   ABC   11.4/19
Dangerous Pursuit   USA
Dead In The Water   USA
Dead On The Money   TNT
Dead Reckoning   USA
Deadlock   HBO
Deadly Deception   CBS   19.2/30
Deadly Desire   USA
Deadly Surveillance   SHOWTIME
Death Dreams   LIFETIME
Death Train   USA
Deceptions   SHOWTIME
Deceptions   NBC   19.9/35   21.8/35
Deconstructing Sarah   USA
Deep Dark Secrets   NBC   15.5/25
Deep Trouble   USA
Deliver Them From Evil: The Taking Of Alta
   View   CBS   16.6/26
Devlin   SHOWTIME
Diamond Fleece   USA
Diamond Trap, The   CBS   15.1/24
Disappearance Of Christina, The   USA
Disaster At Silo 7   ABC   10.1/16
Disaster In Time   SHOWTIME
Don't Talk To Strangers   USA

Don't Touch My Daughter   NBC   14.5/23
Donor   CBS   14.8/24
Doomsday Gun   HBO
Double Edge   CBS   17.1/28
Double Jeopardy   SHOWTIME
Doubletake   CBS   21.1/33   18.7/28
Dress Gray   NBC   17.9/27   19.0/30
Duplicates   USA
Dying To Remember   USA
Endless Game, The   SHOWTIME
Enemy Within, The   HBO
Exclusive   ABC   10.8/17
Execution, The   NBC   21.4/32
Fade To Black   USA
False Witness   NBC   18.7/29
Fatal Charm   SHOWTIME
Fatal Confession: A Father Dowling Mystery
   NBC   15.5/24
Fatal Exposure   USA
Fatal Friendship   NBC   12.4/19
Fatal Image, The   CBS   14.1/22
Father's Revenge, A   ABC   10.4/16
Favorite Son   NBC   15.9/26   15.7/25   16.3/26
Fear   SHOWTIME
Fever   HBO
Fifth Missile, The   NBC   14.7/22
Final Jeopardy, The   NBC   16.5/26
Flight Of Black Angel   SHOWTIME
Fourth Story   SHOWTIME
Framed   HBO
Freedom Fighter   NBC   16.0/25
Glitz   NBC   14.1/25
Good Cops, Bad Cops   NBC   8.9/14
Guardian, The   HBO
Guilty Conscience   CBS   10.8/18
Harmful Intent   CBS   12.2/20
Haunted, The   FBC   8.4/13
Heads   SHOWTIME
Heist   HBO
Hider In The House   USA
Hijacking Of The Achille Lauro, The   NBC
   12.7/20
Hit List, The   SHOWTIME
Hitler's Daughter   USA
Hostage   CBS   19.4/29
Hostage Flight   NBC   21.5/32
Hush Little Baby   USA
I Saw What You Did   CBS   11.5/21
I'm Dangerous Tonight   USA
In Self Defense   ABC   9.2/17
In The Arms Of A Killer   NBC   14.0/22
In The Deep Woods   NBC   14.6/23
In The Eyes Of A Stranger   CBS   14.2/23
In The Shadows, Someone Is Watching   NBC
   14.4/22
International Airport   ABC   13.0/27
Into The Badlands   USA
Into The Homeland   HBO
Intrigue   CBS   8.8/19
Invasion Of Privacy   USA
Jake Spanner, Private Eye   USA
Jericho Fever   USA
Just Another Secret   USA
Kicks   ABC   13.2/21
Killer Rules   NBC   9.2/14
Killing Mind, The   LIFETIME
Kiss To Die For, A   NBC   10.8/17
Las Vegas Strip Wars, The   NBC   15.2/22
Last Hit, The   USA
Last Innocent Man, The   HBO
Lethal Exposure   NBC   8.8/14
Lie Down With Lions   LIFETIME

SUSPENSE/THRILLER (CONTINUED)

Lies Before Kisses CBS 18.5/29
Lies Of The Twins USA
Linda USA
Long Journey Home, The CBS 21.3/34
Love Among Thieves ABC 13.2/21
Love And Curses . . . And All That Jazz CBS
    8.5/16
Love, Cheat And Steal SHOWTIME
Love Kills USA
Marked For Murder NBC 12.4/20
Money, Power, Murder CBS 13.4/22
Monte Carlo CBS 14.6/23 12.2/19
Mortal Sins USA
Moving Target NBC 17.2/25
Murder 101 USA
Murder By Moonlight CBS 7.7/12
Murder By Night USA
Nightman, The NBC 11.6/18
Nightmare At Bitter Creek CBS 13.1/22
Nightmare In The Daylight CBS 14.5/23
Notorious LIFETIME
Obsessed ABC 10.3/16
Only Way Out, The ABC 12.1/19
Operation, The CBS 20.0/30
P. S. I Luv U CBS 15.7/25
Pack Of Lies CBS 18.2/30
Palace Guard CBS 7.4/14
Payoff SHOWTIME
Penthouse, The ABC 13.4/21
People Across The Lake, The NBC 17.3/27
Perfect Bride, The USA
Personals USA
Peyton Place: The Next Generation NBC 12.6/20
Popeye Doyle NBC 15.8/26
Praying Mantis USA
Presidents Child, The CBS 10.0/17
Pride And Extreme Prejudice USA
Psychic USA
Quicksand: No Escape USA
Quiet Killer CBS 11.5/19
Rainbow Drive SHOWTIME
Rearview Mirror NBC 19.9/30
Red King, White Knight HBO
Red Spider, The CBS 15.1/25
Revolver NBC 9.2/16
Riviera ABC 11.5/17
Rockabye CBS 25.3/38
Room, The ABC 5.5/11
Round Table, The NBC 8.3/16
Royce SHOWTIME
Rubdown USA
Secret Weapon TNT
Secret Weapons NBC 13.8/21
Seduction In Travis County CBS 13.9/22
Seduction: Three Tales From The Inner Sanctum
    ABC 9.4/15
Sex,Love, And Cold Hard Cash USA
Shadow Of A Stranger NBC 15.1/24
Shannon's Deal NBC 14.5/25
Shattered Image USA
She Knows Too Much NBC 17.4/27
She Was Marked For Murder NBC 14.8/24
She Woke Up ABC 14.1/22
Silent Movie LIFETIME
Silent Witness USA
Silhouette USA
Sketch Artist SHOWTIME
Snow Kill USA
Somebody's Daughter ABC 10.2/16
Spider And The Fly, The USA

Spy USA
Steal The Sky HBO
Stepfather I I I HBO
Stepford Children, The NBC 19.2/29
Stillwatch CBS 14.7/23
Stranger At My Door CBS 11.7/22
Stranger Waits, A CBS 20.9/33
Strays USA
Streets Of Justice NBC 15.4/22
Substitute, The USA
Sunstroke USA
Survive The Night USA
Sweet Poison USA
Sweet Revenge, A CBS 10.0/16
Tagget USA
Taking Of Flight 847: The Uli Derickson Story
    NBC 19.7/31
Target Of Suspicion USA
Taste For Killing, A USA
Telling Secrets ABC 13.8/22 14.4/21
Tenth Man, The CBS 13.3/21
That Secret Sunday CBS 16.1/26
Third Degree Burn HBO
This Gun For Hire USA
Through The Eyes Of A Killer CBS 12.8/21
To Be The Best CBS 9.3/15 7.7/3
Touch Of Scandal, A CBS 17.0/27
Tower, The FBC 6.2/11
Trapped USA
Treacherous Crossing USA
Trial And Error USA
Turn Back The Clock NBC 13.8/22
Twist Of Fate NBC 14.3/21 15.2/24
Two Mrs. Grenvilles, The NBC 23.4/36 24.0/35
Two Thousand Malibu Road CBS 16.1/28
Under Siege NBC 17.2/24
Victim Of Love CBS 12.0/20
Voyage USA
Web Of Deceit USA
When A Stranger Calls Back SHOWTIME
When The Bough Breaks NBC 22.3/36
Whisper Kills, A ABC 14.7/23
Windmills Of The Gods CBS 19.0/28 17.3/27
With Intent To Kill CBS 11.8/19
Wrong Man, The SHOWTIME

TOXIC WASTE/ENVIRONMENTAL

Acceptable Risks ABC 9.7/15
Chernobyl: The Final Warning TNT
Dead Ahead: The Exxon Valdez HBO
Deadly Business, A CBS 12.3/21
E. A. R. T. H. Force CBS 9.9/17
Fire Next Time, The NBC 13.1/22 11.0/18
For Their Own Good ABC 10.9/17
Incident At Dark River TNT
Last Elephant, The TNT
Montana TNT
Parker Kane NBC 8.6/15

TRUE CRIME

Abduction Of Kari Swenson, The NBC 21.4/33
Act Of Vengeance HBO
Adam: His Song Continues NBC 15.9/25
Amy Fisher: My Story NBC 19.1/30
And The Sea Will Tell CBS 20.1/31 19.0/29
Armed & Innocent CBS 14.9/24
At Mother's Request CBS 23.3/35 22.7/35

Atlanta Child Murders, The CBS 21.8/31 20.9/31
Baby Brokers NBC 11.4/17
Baby Snatcher CBS 16.3/26
Bed Of Lies ABC 16.8/25
Betrayed By Love ABC 10.8/16
Beyond Control: The Amy Fisher Story ABC
    19.5/30
Beyond Obsession ABC 13.6/21
Beyond Suspicion NBC 14.4/22
Billionaire Boys Club NBC 20.7/34 22.1/34
Black Widow Murders: The Blanche Taylor
    Moore Story NBC 13.3/21
Blind Faith NBC 19.9/31 23.3/36
Bloodlines: Murder In The Family NBC 10.7/17
    13.3/21
Bonnie And Clyde: The True Story FBC 8.7/15
Burning Bed, The NBC 36.2/52
Calendar Girl, Cop Killer? The Bambi Bembenek
    Story ABC 10.7/17
Captive ABC 12.9/20
Case Of The Hillside Strangler, The NBC 23.1/36
Casualties Of Love: The Long Island Lolita Story
    CBS 14.3/22
Child Lost Forever, A NBC 15.4/23
Complex Of Fear CBS 14.8/23
Confessions: Two Faces Of Evil NBC 10.7/16
Conspiracy Of Silence CBS 12.5/21 12.2/20
Conviction Of Kitty Dodds, The CBS 13.2/21
Corpse Had A Familiar Face, The CBS 16.4/26
Cries Unheard: The Donna Yaklich Story CBS
    14.0/22
Cross Of Fire NBC 12.5/20 14.7/23
Cruel Doubt NBC 16.8/27 14.8/24
Cry For Help: The Tracey Thurman Story, A NBC
    21.5/33
Cry In The Wild: The Taking Of Peggy Ann NBC
    17.2/27
Danger Of Love, The CBS 15.9/26
David ABC 19.5/30
Dead And Alive ABC 11.8/18
Dead Before Dawn ABC 18.0/26
Deadly Betrayal: The Bruce Curtis Story NBC
    12.9/20
Deadly Intentions ABC 13.3/22 21.3/32
Deadly Intentions... Again? ABC 12.8/20
Deadly Matrimony NBC 16.1/25 18.9/29
Deadly Medicine NBC 15.8/24
Deadly Relations ABC 10.01 19
Deadly Silence, A ABC 17.9/28
Death In California, A ABC 15.7/25 19.2/30
Deliberate Stranger, The NBC 18.6/28 21.7/32
Deliver Them From Evil: The Taking Of Alta
    View CBS 16.6/26
Desperate For Love CBS 12.0/20
Dillinger ABC 14.5/22
Downpayment On Murder NBC 16.1/27
Drug Wars: The Camarena Story NBC 14.4/22
    15.2/23 16.1/25
Drug Wars: The Cocaine Cartel NBC 12.8/20
    13.2/20
Easy Prey ABC 18.4/29
Echoes In The Darkness CBS 20.1/33 22.0/33
Eighty-Three Hours 'til Dawn CBS 14.2/22
Empty Cradle ABC 15.2/24
False Arrest ABC 11.5/18 16.6/27
Family Of Spies CBS 14.7/22 13.6/21
Family Torn Apart, A NBC 15.1/23
Fatal Memories NBC 15.8/24
Fatal Vision NBC 29.5/44 32.7/49
Final Appeal NBC 12.7/20
Frank Nitti: The Enforcer ABC 17.4/28
Fugitive Among Us CBS 14.0/23

TRUE CRIME (CONTINUED)

Getting Gotti CBS 8.3/13
Good Cops, Bad Cops NBC 8.9/14
Good Night, Sweet Wife: A Murder In Boston CBS 14.9/23
Her Final Fury: Betty Broderick, The Last Chapter CBS 14.9/22
High Price Of Passion, The NBC 18.6/29
Honor Thy Father And Mother: The Menendez Murders FBC 10.2/17
Honor Thy Mother CBS 15.5/24
Howard Beach: Making The Case For Murder NBC 14.9/24
I Can Make You Love Me: The Stalking Of Laura Black CBS 16.1/26
I Know My First Name Is Steven NBC 21.6/35 27.3/42
In A Child's Name CBS 17.8/27 21.9/33
In Broad Daylight NBC 13.7/21
In The Best Of Families: Marriage, Pride And Madness CBS 16.1/25 17.3/26
In The Company Of Darkness CBS 15.0/24
In The Line Of Duty: A Cop For The Killing NBC 14.6/23
In The Line Of Duty: Ambush In Waco NBC 18.8/30
In The Line Of Duty: Manhunt In The Dakotas NBC 14.7/26
In The Line Of Duty: Standoff At Marion NBC 13.2/20
In The Line Of Duty: Street War NBC 11.9/20
In The Line Of Duty: The FBI Murders NBC 22.2/34
In The Line Of Duty: The Price Of Vengeance NBC 10.8/17
Into Thin Air CBS 15.7/25
Jack The Ripper CBS 14.8/26 20.3/31
Judgment HBO
Judgment Day: The John List Story CBS 15.8/25
Killer Among Friends, A CBS 16.7/27
Killing In A Small Town CBS 15.8/26
Lies Of The Heart: The Story Of Laurie Kellogg ABC 15.0/23
Love And Hate: A Marriage Made In Hell NBC 13.9/25 16.3/28
Love, Honor & Obey: The Last Mafia Marriage CBS 12.6/20 14.4/24
Love & Lies ABC 11.6/18
Love, Lies And Murder NBC 15.5/24 20.3/30
Love On The Run NBC 15.4/23
Manhunt For Claude Dallas CBS 14.4/24
Manhunt: Search For The Night Stalker NBC 15.4/24
Marla Hanson Story, The NBC 15.1/24
Matter Of Justice, A NBC 15.2/23 19.4/29
Menendez: A Killing In Beverly Hills CBS 9.6/16 9.3/15
Mercy Or Murder? NBC 23.8/35
Moment Of Truth: Stalking Back NBC 15.9/25
Mother's Justice, A NBC 16.7/25
Murder Between Friends NBC 12.9/20
Murder In New Hampshire: The Pamela Smart Story CBS 15.9/26
Murder In The Heartland ABC 13.2/21 14.2/23
Murder Of Innocence CBS 14.5/22
Murder Ordained CBS 19.3/29 19.8/32
Murder Without Motive: The Edmund Perry Story NBC 11.3/18
Murderous Affair, A: The Carolyn Warmus Story ABC 15.0/25
My Son Johnny CBS 15.6/24

Nightmare In Columbia County CBS 14.0/22
Nutcracker: Money, Madness And Murder NBC 12.2/20 11.5/19 13.5/22
Out Of The Darkness CBS 17.6/30
Outside Woman, The CBS 14.3/22
Overkill: The Aileen Wuornos Story CBS 15.4/25
Passion And Paradise ABC 11.8/19 12.5/20
Poisoned By Love: The Kern County Murders CBS 14.5/24
Positively True Adventures Of The Alleged Texas Cheerleader Murdering Mom, The HBO
Precious Victims CBS 14.6/23
Preppie Murder, The ABC 15.2/24
Prophet Of Evil: The Ervil Lebaron Story CBS 9.9/16
Revenge Of Al Capone, The NBC 13.9/22
Revenge On The Highway NBC 12.8/19
Right To Kill? ABC 19.0/31
Seduction In Travis County CBS 13.9/22
Separated By Murder CBS 11.8/19
Shoot First: A Cop's Vengeance NBC 12.6/20
Sins Of The Mother CBS 14.5/23
Small Sacrifices ABC 18.1/28 25.2/39
Stay The Night ABC 13.8/22 17.9/28
Stolen Babies LIFETIME
Sworn To Vengeance CBS 15.3/25
Teamster Boss: The Jackie Presser Story HBO
Ten Million Dollar Getaway USA
Terror In The Night CBS 12.7/20
They've Taken Our Children: The Chowchilla Kidnapping ABC 14.5/23
Till Death Us Do Part NBC 14.6/21
To Save The Children NBC 11.6/19
Tonya & Nancy: The Inside Story NBC 10.4/19
Too Young To Die? NBC 14.5/23
Unholy Matrimony CBS 15.1/24
Unspeakable Acts ABC 15.7/25
Vengeance: The Story Of Tony Cimo CBS 11.8/21
Victim Of Love: The Shannon Mohr Story NBC 13.0/19
Victims For Victims - The Theresa Saldana Story NBC 18.8/28
When Love Kills: The Seduction Of John Hearn CBS 9.9/16 9.5/16
Wife, Mother, Murderer ABC 15.6/24
Willing To Kill: The Texas Cheerleader Story ABC 14.4/22
With Murder In Mind CBS 13.3/21
Without A Kiss Goodbye CBS 17.2/29
Woman On The Run: The Lawrencia Bembenek Story NBC 11.1/18 15.6/25
Woman Scorned: The Betty Broderick Story, A CBS 19.5/30
Woman With A Past NBC 17.5/27

TRUE STORY

Absolute Strangers CBS 17.7/29
After The Shock USA
Afterburn HBO
Aftermath: A Test Of Love CBS 17.3/27
Against The Wall HBO
Alex: The Life Of A Child ABC 21.7/36
Amelia Earhart: The Final Flight TNT
American Geisha CBS 11.7/20
Anastasia: The Mystery Of Anna NBC 20.7/32 20.9/32
And The Band Played On HBO
And Then There Was One LIFETIME
Ann Jillian Story, The NBC 23.8/35

Anything To Survive ABC 16.5/26
Assault At West Point SHOWTIME
Attack On Fear CBS 10.9/16
Attic: The Hiding Of Anne Frank, The CBS 11.5/19
Baby M ABC 15.0/24 17.6/27
Babymaker: The Dr. Cecil Jacobson's Story CBS 14.0/21
Barbarians At The Gate HBO
Betty Ford Story, The ABC 11.4/16
Blind Justice CBS 19.2/29
Bonds Of Love CBS 14.9/23
Born Too Soon NBC 10.5/17
Broken Cord, The ABC 14.3/22
Broken Promises: Taking Emily Back CBS 12.6/22
Bunny's Tale, A ABC 17.3/26
Call Me Anna ABC 15.9/24
Case Of Deadly Force, A CBS 12.0/20
Cast The First Stone NBC 17.9/28
Challenger ABC 12.8/20
Charles And Diana: Unhappily Ever After ABC 12.8/19
Chase, The NBC 14.6/23
Chernobyl: The Final Warning TNT
Child Of Rage CBS 14.7/24
Children In The Crossfire NBC 14.8/23
Children Of The Dark CBS 13.4/22
Chips, The War Dog DISNEY
Citizen Cohn HBO
Convicted ABC 17.4/27
Courage CBS 12.5/20
Court - Martial Of Jackie Robinson, The TNT
Crash Landing: The Rescue Of Flight 232 ABC 17.1/26
Dadah Is Death CBS 11.3/17 10.1/17
Dark Holiday NBC 11.1/18
Darkness Before Dawn NBC 13.1/20
Daughter Of The Streets ABC 14.9/24
Day One CBS 15.2/24
Dead Ahead: The Exxon Valdez HBO
Deadly Business, A CBS 12.3/21
Desperate Journey: The Allison Wilcox Story ABC 9.7/15
Desperate Rescue: The Cathy Mahone Story NBC 13.3/20
Diana: Her NBC 14.5/23 15.6/24
Disaster At Silo 7 ABC 10.1/16
Doing Life NBC 16.8/27
Doomsday Gun HBO
Doublecrossed HBO
Dreams Of Gold: The Mel Fisher Story CBS 11.3/20
Dying To Love You CBS 15.4/25
Elvis And The Colonel: The Untold Story NBC 9.8/14
Ernest Green Story, The DISNEY
Escape From Sobibor CBS 21.4/34
Everybody's Baby: The Rescue Of Jessica Mcclure ABC 22.2/36
Eye On The Sparrow NBC 14.3/22
Face Of A Stranger CBS 16.8/27
Fall From Grace NBC 17.6/27
Family Of Strangers CBS 19.8/29
Fatal Judgment CBS 15.4/24
Father Clements Story, The NBC 16.7/26
Fergie And Andrew: Behind The Palace Doors NBC 13.6/21
Final Verdict TNT
Fire And Rain USA
Fire: Trapped On The 37th Floor ABC 11.2/17
Firefighter CBS 12.6/20
Firestorm: 72 Hours In Oakland ABC 11.5/17

TRUE STORY (CONTINUED)

First Steps CBS 14.4/24

For The Love Of My Child: The Anissa Ayala Story NBC 12.8/20

For Their Own Good ABC 10.9/17

Forbidden HBO

Forbidden Nights CBS 10.5/17

George Mckenna Story, The CBS 15.5/24

Girl Who Came Between Them, The NBC 13.2/21

Going For The Gold: The Bill Johnson Story CBS 8.9/14

Gregory K ABC 10.3/16

Guilty Of Innocence: The Lenell Geter Story CBS 15.7/25

Guilty Until Proven Innocent NBC 11.8/19

Guts And Glory: The Rise And Fall Of Oliver North CBS 14.0/23 9.6/13

Haunted, The FBC 8.4/13

Hearst And Davies Affair, The ABC 16.2/24

Heart Of A Champion: The Ray Mancini Story CBS 10.6/17

Heart Of A Child NBC 11.5/18

Heartsounds ABC 18.5/31

Heat Wave TNT

Held Hostage: The Sis And Jerry Levin Story ABC 12.0/19

Heroes Of Desert Storm ABC 9.9/16

Highway Heartbreaker CBS 16.0/25

Hijacking Of The Achille Lauro, The NBC 12.7/20

Hoover SHOWTIME

Hostages HBO

I Love You Perfect ABC 13.7/23

In Love And War NBC 16.7/27

In The Best Interest Of The Children NBC 16.0/24

In The Shadow Of A Killer NBC 9.5/15

Investigation: Inside A Terrorist Bombing, The HBO

Iran: Days Of Crisis TNT

Jesse CBS 19.4/31

Johnnie Mae Gibson: F B I CBS 13.3/20

Jonathan: The Boy Nobody Wanted NBC 13.8/21

Josephine Baker Story, The HBO

Keeping Secrets ABC 14.2/23

Kennedys Of Massachusetts, The ABC 15.8/24 17.6/27 16.4/25

Kids Like These CBS 16.5/27

L B J: The Early Years NBC 18.4/27

Last Flight Out NBC 10.7/18

Last Of His Tribe, The HBO

Last P. O. W? The Bobby Garwood Story, The ABC 11.5/20

Last Wish ABC 10.8/17

Leap Of Faith CBS 12.0/20

Lena: My 100 Children NBC 13.4/21

Leona Helmsley: The Queen Of Mean CBS 15.7/26

Liberace ABC 16.8/27

Liberace: Behind The Music CBS 16.6/26

Lincoln NBC 16.6/26 14.9/24

Line Of Fire: The Morris Dees Story NBC 11.3/17

Little Girl Lost ABC 19.0/31

Littlest Victims CBS 10.9/18

Locked Up: A Mother's Rage CBS 12.4/20

Love Lives On ABC 17.8/26

Love, Mary CBS 21.5/33

Lucy & Desi: Before The Laughter CBS 16.4/25

Mafia Princess NBC 24.4/37

Malice In Wonderland CBS 18.3/29

Man Who Broke 1,000 Chains, The HBO

Mandela HBO

Margaret Bourke - White TNT

Marilyn & Me ABC 8.5/14

Mark Twain And Me DISNEY

Max And Helen TNT

Mayflower Madam CBS 20.9/34

Mercy Mission: The Rescue Of Flight 771 NBC 12.2/19

Miracle Landing CBS 15.1/23

Miss America: Behind The Crown NBC 13.3/20

Mission Of The Shark CBS 15.6/25

Moment Of Truth: A Child Too Many NBC 14.2/22

Moment Of Truth: Cradle Of Conspiracy NBC 13.5/21

Moment Of Truth: To Walk Again NBC 8.3/12

Mothers' Right, A: The Elizabeth Morgan Story ABC 13.6/21

Murder: By Reason Of Insanity CBS 16.6/26

Murder In Mississippi NBC 12.4/20

Murder Of Mary Phagan, The NBC 18.7/28 21.0/34

Murderers Among Us: The Simon Wiesenthal Story HBO

Mussolini: The Decline And Fall Of Il Duce HBO

My Breast CBS 11.4/18

My Father, My Son CBS 13.5/22

My Name Is Bill W. ABC 15.2/24

Nazi Hunter: The Beate Klarsfeld Story ABC 13.7/21

Never Forget TNT

No Child Of Mine CBS 13.1/21

Nobody's Child CBS 25.9/39

Nobody's Children USA

On Thin Ice: The Tai Babilonia Story NBC 13.4/21

On Wings Of Eagles NBC 17.0/28 21.2/34

One Against The Wind CBS 13.4/21

One More Mountain ABC 12.9/20

Ordeal In The Arctic ABC 14.0/22

Overexposed ABC 14.4/23

Passion For Justice, A: Hazel Brannon Smith Story ABC 11.1/18

Place For Annie, A ABC 14.8/23

Place To Be Loved, A CBS 13.0/20

Place To Call Home, A CBS 15.4/26

Plot To Kill Hitler, The CBS 7.2/12

Poor Little Rich Girl: The Barbara Hutton Story NBC 21.3/33 18.5/30

Prisoner Of Honor HBO

Private Matter, A HBO

Promise To Keep, A NBC 14.3/23

Promised A Miracle CBS 13.2/22

Queen CBS 24.7/38 24.1/37 22.8/34

Quiet Victory: The Charlie Wedemeyer Story CBS 14.9/25

Reason For Living: The Jill Ireland Story NBC 12.5/21

Richest Man In The World: The Aristotle Onassis Story ABC 12.1/18 13.9/22

Right To Die NBC 17.5/28

Rise & Walk: The Dennis Byrd Story FBC 7.1/11

Robert Kennedy And His Times CBS 19.8/29 14.9/21 16.9/26

Rock Hudson ABC 15.7/24

Roe Vs. Wade NBC 17.0/27

Rose And The Jackal, The TNT

Roswell SHOWTIME

Roxanne: The Prize Pulitzer NBC 17.3/27

Runaway Father CBS 16.8/27

Ryan White Story, The ABC 16.6/26

Sakharov HBO

Samaritan: The Mitch Snyder Story CBS 11.2/18

Scattered Dreams: The Kathryn Messenger Story CBS 14.1/22

Scorned And Swindled CBS 16.7/26

Second Serve CBS 13.6/22

Secret Weapon TNT

Separate But Equal ABC 11.9/19 11.8/19

Shakedown On The Sunset Strip CBS 15.0/27

Shattered Dreams CBS 16.8/28

Shattered Innocence CBS 15.2/25

Shattered Trust: The Shari Karney Story NBC 16.2/25

Shattered Vows NBC 21.3/33

She Stood Alone NBC 10.8/18

Shootdown NBC 16.0/25

Sin And Redemption CBS 14.0/23

Sinatra CBS 17.7/26 17.2/27

Single Women, Married Men CBS 14.6/26

Six Against The Rock NBC 16.4/24

Snowbound: The Jim And Jennifer Stolpa Story CBS 18.2/27

Something To Live For: The Alison Gertz Story ABC 16.2/26

Son Of The Morning Star ABC 11.7/18 12.8/20

Son's Promise, A ABC 16.5/27

Space CBS 19.4/31 16.4/26 14.7/24 17.1/28 16.3/26

Special Friendship, A CBS 13.7/22

Special People CBS 10.7/18

Storm And Sorrow LIFETIME

Stranger In My Bed NBC 18.8/29

Stranger In The Family, A ABC 12.7/19

Sudie And Simpson LIFETIME

Summer Dreams: The Story Of The Beach Boys ABC 10.6/16

Survive The Savage Sea ABC 15.6/24

Switch, The CBS 11.8/19

Switched At Birth NBC 20.4/32 23.1/35

Tailspin: Behind The Korean Airlines Tragedy HBO

Taking Of Flight 847: The Uli Derickson Story NBC 19.7/31

Tears And Laughter: The Joan And Mielissa Rivers Story NBC 13.1/21

Ted Kennedy, Jr., Story, The NBC 16.8/26

There Are No Children Here ABC 17.8/26

Thicker Than Blood: The Larry Mclinden Story CBS 14.5/23

Time To Heal, A NBC 12.7/21

Time To Live, A NBC 17.1/27

Time To Triumph, A CBS 16.0/25

To Heal A Nation NBC 10.1/20

To My Daughter NBC 13.5/22

Too Young The Hero NBC 20.7/33

Town Torn Apart, A NBC 12.8/20

Tragedy Of Flight 103: The Inside Story, The HBO

Triumph Of The Heart: The Ricky Bell Story CBS 12.5/22

Triumph Over Disaster: The Hurricane Andrew Story NBC 15.7/25

Ultimate Betrayal CBS 15.6/25

Unconquered CBS 17.3/28

Unnatural Causes NBC 19.3/31

Untamed Love LIFETIME

Vestige Of Honor NBC 11.0/18

Voices Within: The Lives Of Truddi Chase ABC 14.7/24 15.5/25

When No One Would Listen CBS 12.9/19

When You Remember Mc ABC 14.6/24

Whose Child Is This? The War For Baby Jessica ABC 9.6/15

TRUE STORY (CONTINUED)

Winner Never Quits, A ABC 14.6/24
Winnie NBC 16.6/28
With Hostile Intent CBS 12.9/21
Without Warning: Terror In The Towers NBC 9.3/15
Without Warning: The James Brady Story HBO
Woman Named Jackie, A NBC 15.5/23 18.6/28 19.1/30
Women Of Windsor CBS 13.8/22
World War I I : When Lions Roared NBC 9.1/15 7.5/12
Zelda TNT

VIETNAM

China Beach ABC 18.0/29
Danielle Steel's Message From Nam NBC 11.5/18 11.4/18
Girl Who Came Between Them, The NBC 13.2/21
In Love And War NBC 16.7/27
Intimate Strangers CBS 26.4/38
Lady From Yesterday, The CBS 16.0/25
Last Flight Out NBC 10.7/18
Last P. O. W? The Bobby Garwood Story, The ABC 11.5/20
My Father, My Son CBS 13.5/22
Proud Men ABC 9.4/15
Resting Place CBS 22.3/36
Shooter NBC 11.3/20
Tagget USA
This Park Is Mine HBO
To Heal A Nation NBC 10.1/20
Unnatural Causes NBC 19.3/31
Vestige Of Honor CBS 11.0/18
Which Way Home TNT

WESTERN

Adventures Of Brisco County Jr., The FBC 7.2/14
Alamo: 13 Days To Glory, The NBC 15.7/22
Another Pair Of Aces: Three Of A Kind CBS 9.9/17
Blind Justice HBO
Blood River CBS 13.4/23
Bonanza: The Return NBC 17.6/26
Brotherhood Of The Gun CBS 7.3/14
Cisco Kid, The TNT
Conagher TNT
Deadman's Revenge USA
Desperado NBC 19.3/32
Desperado: Badlands Justice NBC 13.1/21
Dr. Quinn, Medicine Woman CBS 18.2/29
Dream West CBS 19.5/29 18.1/29 20.1/32
El Diablo HBO
Four Eyes And Six Guns TNT
Gambler Returns: The Luck Of The Draw, The NBC 18.0/28 16.6/25
Gore Vidal's Billy The Kid TNT
Gunsmoke I I I: To The Last Man CBS 14.2/24
Gunsmoke: One Man's Justice CBS 11.5/17
Gunsmoke: Return To Dodge CBS 16.6/31
Gunsmoke: The Last Apache CBS 19.7/32
Gunsmoke: The Long Ride Home CBS 10.2/19
Houston: The Legend Of Texas CBS 10.8/18

Independence NBC 14.5/23
Into The Badlands USA
Kenny Rogers As The Gambler I I I: The Legend Continues CBS 20.9/32 17.4/29
Last Days Of Frank And Jesse James, The NBC 15.1/22
Last Outlaw, The HBO
Lonesome Dove CBS 28.5/42 23.8/34 24.8/37 27.3/41
Longarm ABC 12.3/20
Miracle In The Wilderness TNT
Ned Blessing: The Story Of My Life And Times CBS 11.3/20
Ned Blessing: The True Story Of My Life CBS 10.9/18
Once Upon A Texas Train CBS 21.2/32
Pair Of Aces CBS 17.8/28
Poker Alice CBS 17.5/32
Quick And The Dead, The HBO
Red River CBS 18.4/29
Return Of Desperado, The NBC 16.0/24
Return To Lonesome Dove CBS 18.1/28 16.5/25 15.2/24
Rio Diablo CBS 17.3/26
Sodbusters SHOWTIME
Son Of The Morning Star ABC 11.7/18 12.8/20
Stagecoach CBS 22.5/36
Timestalkers CBS 12.8/21
Tracker, The HBO
Where The Hell's That Gold CBS 12.1/18

WOMEN AGAINST THE SYSTEM

Afterburn HBO
Alone In The Neon Jungle CBS 17.6/28
Attack On Fear CBS 10.9/16
Beryl Markham: A Shadow On The Sun CBS 10.4/16 7.8/13
Betrayal Of Trust NBC 13.0/20
Betrayed By Love ABC 10.8/16
Better Off Dead LIFETIME
Beyond Suspicion NBC 14.4/22
Blue Bayou NBC 12.8/20
Bluegrass CBS 17.6/27 18.4/29
Bunny's Tale, A ABC 17.3/26
Burning Rage CBS 16.5/30
Carly's Web NBC 9.3/17
Cast The First Stone NBC 17.9/28
Chase CBS 11.7/19
Child's Cry CBS 22.7/33
Children Of Times Square ABC 12.5/20
Christy CBS 17.7/29
Corpse Had A Familiar Face, The CBS 16.4/26
Courage CBS 12.5/20
Crash: The Mystery Of Flight 1501 NBC 12.7/20
Dadah Is Death CBS 11.3/17 10.1/17
Desperate Rescue: The Cathy Mahone Story NBC 13.3/20
Don't Touch My Daughter NBC 14.5/23
Evil In Clear River ABC 12.9/20
Eye On The Sparrow NBC 14.3/22
Firefighter CBS 12.6/20
Florence Nightingale NBC 11.6/19
For Their Own Good ABC 10.9/17
Getting Gotti CBS 8.3/13
Good Fight, The LIFETIME
Held Hostage: The Sis And Jerry Levin Story ABC 12.0/19
In A Child's Name CBS 17.8/27 21.9/33
In Love And War NBC 16.7/27
In My Daughter's Name CBS 15.8/27

Into Thin Air CBS 15.7/25
Jesse CBS 19.4/31
Johnnie Mae Gibson: F B I CBS 13.3/20
Killer Instinct NBC 12.5/19
Kiss Shot CBS 10.2/16
Lady In A Corner NBC 13.3/21
Last Frontier, The CBS 23.8/36 25.0/39
Lena: My 100 Children NBC 13.4/21
Majority Rule LIFETIME
Matter Of Justice, A NBC 15.2/23 19.4/29
Moment Of Truth: Broken Pledges NBC 12.6/20
Moment Of Truth: Cradle Of Conspiracy NBC 13.5/21
Moment Of Truth: Stalking Back NBC 15.9/25
Moment Of Truth: To Walk Again NBC 8.3/12
Moment Of Truth: Why My Daughter? NBC 14.2/23
Mother's Justice, A NBC 16.7/25
Nazi Hunter: The Beate Klarsfeld Story ABC 13.7/21
Nobody's Children USA
One Of Her Own ABC 13.5/21
Open Admissions CBS 7.5/13
Pancho Barnes CBS 11.7/18
Passion For Justice, A: Hazel Brannon Smith Story ABC 11.1/18
Place To Call Home, A CBS 15.4/26
Rape Of Dr. Willis, The CBS 14.4/23
Roe Vs. Wade NBC 17.0/27
Roses Are For The Rich CBS 18.6/30 17.8/29
Sadie And Son CBS 15.5/25
Scandal In A Small Town NBC 20.0/31
Scattered Dreams: The Kathryn Messenger Story CBS 14.1/22
Sexual Advances ABC 9.4/16
Shattered Trust: The Shari Karney Story NBC 16.2/25
She Says She's Innocent NBC 15.0/23
She Stood Alone NBC 10.8/18
Shootdown NBC 16.0/25
Sins CBS 19.7/29 21.9/32 20.6/32
Sister Margaret And The Saturday Night Ladies CBS 11.5/19
Stolen Babies LIFETIME
Storm And Sorrow LIFETIME
Taking Back My Life: The Nancy Ziegenmeyer Story CBS 15.8/25
Time To Triumph, A CBS 16.0/25
Ultimate Betrayal CBS 15.6/25
Unnatural Causes NBC 19.3/31
Untamed Love LIFETIME
Victims For Victims - The Theresa Saldana Story NBC 18.8/28
Web Of Deceit USA
What She Doesn't Know NBC 16.6/25
When He's Not A Stranger CBS 17.2/26
Which Way Home TNT
With Hostile Intent CBS 12.9/21
With Murder In Mind CBS 13.3/21
Without A Kiss Goodbye CBS 17.2/29
Without Her Consent NBC 17.8/28
Women Of Brewster Place, The ABC 23.5/36 24.5/38

WOMAN IN JEOPARDY

Abduction Of Kari Swenson, The NBC 21.4/33
Angel In Green CBS 13.1/22
Angel Of Death CBS 10.8/18
Blind Witness ABC 16.3/25
Blood Vows: The Story Of A Mafia Wife NBC 24.8/37
Body Language USA
Body Of Evidence CBS 18.4/28
Bride In Black, The ABC 16.7/27
Complex Of Fear CBS 14.8/23
Courage CBS 12.5/20
Cry In The Wild: The Taking Of Peggy Ann NBC 17.2/27
Dangerous Affection NBC 16.4/26
Dangerous Pursuit USA
Dark Holiday NBC 11.1/18
Dead Before Dawn ABC 18.0/26
Deadbolt CBS 12.9/23
Deadly Intentions ABC 13.3/22 21.3/32
Deadly Intentions... Again? ABC 12.8/20
Deadly Messages ABC 11.4/17
Death In California, A ABC 15.7/25 19.2/30
Deep Dark Secrets NBC 15.5/25
Deliberate Stranger, The NBC 18.6/28 21.7/32
Disappearance Of Nora CBS 17.0/27
Donor CBS 14.8/24
Downpayment On Murder NBC 16.1/27
Drop Dead Gorgeous USA
Easy Prey ABC 18.4/29
Exclusive ABC 10.8/17
Face Of Fear, The CBS 14.0/23
Fatal Charm SHOWTIME
Fatal Exposure USA
Fatal Image, The CBS 14.1/22
Fear SHOWTIME
Fear Inside, The SHOWTIME
Fear Stalk CBS 11.7/19
Fever HBO
Fortress HBO
From The Dead Of Night NBC 11.6/20 14.3/22
Harem ABC 16.9/25 16.2/23
Hell Hath No Fury NBC 15.2/24
Hostage CBS 19.4/29
Hot Pursuit NBC 11.2/21
I Can Make You Love Me: The Stalking Of Laura Black CBS 16.1/26
I Saw What You Did CBS 11.5/21
In Like Flynn ABC 8.4/15
In Self Defense ABC 9.2/17
In The Deep Woods NBC 14.6/23
In The Eyes Of A Stranger CBS 14.2/23
Intimate Stranger SHOWTIME
Invasion Of Privacy USA
Jessie ABC 17.7/29
Kicks ABC 13.2/21
Killer Among Us, A NBC 13.9/23
Killer In The Mirror NBC 20.4/31
Kiss Of A Killer ABC 11.5/18
Lace I I ABC 15.3/24 16.4/25
Lady Forgets, The CBS 18.5/34
Lady Killer USA
Lady Mobster ABC 5.9/09
Lily CBS 6.6/14
Live: From Death Row FBC 6.9/12
Love Kills USA
Mafia Princess NBC 24.4/37
Marla Hanson Story, The NBC 15.1/24
Memories Of Murder LIFETIME
Murder: By Reason Of Insanity CBS 16.6/26
Naked Lie CBS 21.2/33

Nazi Hunter: The Beate Klarsfeld Story ABC 13.7/21
Necessity CBS 15.0/24
Night Walk CBS 16.3/27
Nightmare At Bitter Creek CBS 13.1/22
Nightmare In The Daylight CBS 14.5/23
Of Pure Blood CBS 20.0/30
One Woman's Courage NBC 12.4/19
Penthouse, The ABC 13.4/21
Price She Paid, The CBS 11.7/19
Rearview Mirror NBC 19.9/30
Red Wind USA
River Of Rage: The Taking Of Maggie Keene CBS 12.4/20
Rockabye CBS 25.3/38
Room, The ABC 5.5/11
Search For Grace CBS 10.5/17
Seduced By Evil USA
Settle The Score NBC 16.8/26
Shadow Of Obsession NBC 11.4/18
She Was Marked For Murder NBC 14.8/24
She Woke Up ABC 14.1/22
Silent Movie LIFETIME
Silent Witness USA
Silhouette USA
Sorry, Wrong Number USA
Sparks: The Price Of Passion CBS 13.7/21
Stark CBS 14.1/23
Stepfather I I I HBO
Stillwatch CBS 14.7/23
Stranger At My Door CBS 11.7/22
Stranger Waits, A CBS 20.9/33
Stranger Within, The CBS 15.6/25
Survive The Night USA
Sweet Poison USA
Taking Of Flight 847: The Uli Derickson Story NBC 19.7/31
Terror In The Night CBS 12.7/20
Through The Eyes Of A Killer CBS 12.8/21
Touch Of Scandal, A CBS 17.0/27
Trapped USA
Treacherous Crossing USA
Visions Of Murder NBC 10.1/19
Web Of Deceit USA
Wheels Of Terror USA
When A Stranger Calls Back SHOWTIME
With A Vengeance CBS 14.7/23
Women Of Valor CBS 19.6/32
Writer's Block USA

WOMAN'S ISSUE/STORY

Addicted To His Love ABC 18.1/29
Ann Jillian Story, The NBC 23.8/35
Babies NBC 13.5/22
Baby Brokers NBC 11.4/17
Baby Of The Bride CBS 15.0/26
Babycakes CBS 13.3/22
Babymaker: The Dr. Cecil Jacobson's Story CBS 14.0/21
Backfield In Motion ABC 15.0/24
Battling For Baby CBS 16.2/26
Betrayal Of Trust NBC 13.0/20
Brand New Life: The Honeymoon NBC 15.9/25
Bridesmaids CBS 14.6/25
Broken Promises: Taking Emily Back CBS 12.6/22
Bunny's Tale, A ABC 17.3/26
Burning Bed, The NBC 36.2/52
Burning Bridges ABC 13.6/22
Cast The First Stone NBC 17.9/28

Challenge Of A Lifetime ABC 8.7/13
Chantilly Lace SHOWTIME
Children Of The Bride CBS 13.6/25
Choices ABC 18.1/27
Conviction Of Kitty Dodds, The CBS 13.2/21
Crazy In Love TNT
Cries Unheard: The Donna Yaklich Story CBS 14.0/22
Cry For Help: The Tracey Thurman Story, A NBC 21.5/33
Danielle Steel's Changes NBC 17.8/28
Drop-Out Mother CBS 13.2/22
Family Of Strangers CBS 19.8/29
Fatal Memories NBC 15.8/24
Firefighter CBS 12.6/20
For Their Own Good ABC 10.9/17
Getting Out ABC 11.1/18
Getting Up And Going Home LIFETIME
Grand Isle TNT
He's Fired, She's Hired CBS 14.2/23
Heart Of A Child NBC 11.5/18
Her Final Fury: Betty Broderick, The Last Chapter CBS 14.9/22
Highway Heartbreaker CBS 16.0/25
House Of Secrets And Lies, A CBS 15.5/27
In Defense Of A Married Man ABC 14.1/23
Infidelity ABC 16.8/27
Joshua's Heart NBC 15.6/26
Labor Of Love: The Arlette Schweitzer Story CBS 14.1/23
Last To Go, The ABC 11.0/17
Leave Of Absence NBC 10.1/15
Letter To Three Wives, A NBC 19.3/30
Lies Of The Heart: The Story Of Laurie Kellogg ABC 15.0/23
Love And Betrayal CBS 16.1/25
Love And Hate: A Marriage Made In Hell NBC 13.9/25 16.3/28
Marla Hanson Story, The NBC 15.1/24
Maybe Baby NBC 17.2/26
Message From Holly CBS 15.5/24
Moment Of Truth: A Child Too Many NBC 14.2/22
Mothers' Right, A: The Elizabeth Morgan Story ABC 13.6/21
My Boyfriend's Back NBC 16.1/26
My Breast CBS 11.4/18
Not In My Family ABC 15.1/23
Other Women's Children LIFETIME
Passions CBS 22.4/34
Picking Up The Pieces CBS 16.8/25
Pink Lightning FBC 4.4/8
Place For Annie, A ABC 14.8/23
Posing: Inspired By Three Real Stories CBS 11.9/18
Price She Paid, The CBS 11.7/19
Private Matter, A HBO
Promise To Keep, A NBC 14.3/23
Roe Vs. Wade NBC 17.0/27
Runaway Father CBS 16.8/27
Second Chances CBS 9.7/16
Sexual Advances ABC 9.4/16
Shame LIFETIME
Shameful Secrets ABC 13.2/21
Sharing Richard CBS 13.7/22
Shattered Dreams CBS 16.8/28
Shattered Trust: The Shari Karney Story NBC 16.2/25
She Said No NBC 14.7/23
Silent Witness NBC 22.5/33
Sin And Redemption CBS 14.0/23
Single Bars, Single Women ABC 20.0/31
Single Women, Married Men CBS 14.6/26

WOMAN'S ISSUE/STORY (CONTINUED)

Stompin' At The Savoy   CBS   11.2/19
Stop At Nothing   LIFETIME
Take My Daughters, Please   NBC   19.9/31
Taking Back My Life: The Nancy Ziegenmeyer
   Story   CBS   15.8/25
This Child Is Mine   NBC   21.1/32
This Wife For Hire   ABC   15.4/24
Time To Triumph, A   CBS   16.0/25
Ultimate Betrayal   CBS   15.6/25
Warm Hearts, Cold Feet   CBS   15.1/22
When He's Not A Stranger   CBS   17.2/26
When No One Would Listen   CBS   12.9/19
When Will I Be Loved?   NBC   12.6/19
Who Gets The Friends?   CBS   11.1/19
Wild Texas Wind   NBC   18.0/27
With Hostile Intent   CBS   12.9/21
Without Her Consent   NBC   17.8/28
Woman On The Ledge   NBC   15.6/24
Woman Scorned: The Betty Broderick Story, A
   CBS   19.5/30
World's Oldest Living Bridesmaid, The   CBS
   11.9/22

WWII

American Story, An   CBS   12.7/20
Arch Of Triumph   CBS   9.2/16
Attic: The Hiding Of Anne Frank, The   CBS
   11.5/19
Behind Enemy Lines   NBC   14.5/23
Breaking Point   TNT
Chips, The War Dog   DISNEY
Court - Martial Of Jackie Robinson, The   TNT
Crossing To Freedom   CBS   10.3/17
Danielle Steel's Jewels   NBC   14.7/22   15.6/24
Dirty Dozen: The Deadly Mission   NBC   18.5/28
Dirty Dozen: The Fatal Mission   NBC   14.3/22
Escape From Sobibor   CBS   21.4/34
Fall From Grace   CBS   7.7/14   6.4/13
Forbidden   HBO
Great Escape I I: The Untold Story, The   NBC
   14.4/23   12.3/19
Hiroshima: Out Of The Ashes   NBC   11.3/20
Hitler's S S: Portrait In Evil   NBC   15.8/24
Home Fires Burning   CBS   18.6/29
Homefront   ABC   12.2/20
Incident, The   CBS   20.8/33
Judith Krantz's Till We Meet Again   CBS   14.8/23
   11.7/18
Last Days Of Patton, The   CBS   19.5/32
Lena: My 100 Children   NBC   13.4/21
Max And Helen   TNT
Miss Rose White   NBC   11.0/17
Mission Of The Shark   CBS   15.6/25
Monte Carlo   CBS   14.6/23   12.2/19
Murderers Among Us: The Simon Wiesenthal
   Story   HBO
Mussolini - The Untold Story   NBC   17.7/26
   19.4/29   19.6/29
Nightmare Years, The   TNT
One Against The Wind   CBS   13.4/21
Plot To Kill Hitler, The   CBS   7.2/12
Road Raiders, The   CBS   8.5/14
Silent Cries   NBC   12.4/20
Souvenir   SHOWTIME
Tenth Man, The   CBS   13.3/21
Too Young The Hero   CBS   20.7/33

Twist Of Fate   NBC   14.3/21   15.2/24
Wallenberg: A Hero's Story   NBC   20.2/33
   19.7/30
War And Remembrance   ABC   21.8/31   19.0/29
   19.8/31   16.8/25   17.0/26
War And Remembrance, Part I I   ABC   13.4/21
   14.4/22   15.1/24   15.7/25   15.9/26
Women Of Valor   CBS   19.6/32
World War I I : When Lions Roared   NBC   9.1/15
   7.5/12

YOUTH COMEDY

Bad Attitudes   FBC   4.2/6
Camp Cucamonga   NBC   8.3/14
Class Cruise   NBC   11.4/19
Combat High   NBC   18.9/29
Crash Course   NBC   19.9/32
Dance Till Dawn   ABC   15.8/26
Day My Parents Ran Away, The   FBC   6.0/9
Dream Date   NBC   15.1/24
Facts Of Life Down Under, The   NBC   21.4/32
Family Ties Vacation   NBC   22.1/33
Frankenstein: The College Years   FBC   6.1/9
Just One Of The Girls   FBC   6.3/10
Not Quite Human I I   DISNEY
Poison Ivy   NBC   19.8/25
Revenge Of The Nerds I V: Nerds In Love   FBC
   5.9/9
Revenge Of The Nerds: The Next Generation
   FBC   7.2/13
Saved By The Bell-Hawaiian Style   NBC   9.5/17

Section C

RATINGS & EMMY WINNERS

Movies & Miniseries
Listed by Descending Rating/Share

September 1, 1984 to September 1, 1994

PLEASE NOTE: Cable movies were purposely left out
as they do not have ratings.

Movies are listed by descending rating. Miniseries are listed by descending average of ratings. Cable movies are not listed as they are not rated.

50 TOP RANKING NETWORK MOVIES — 1984-1985 SEASON

1	Burning Bed, The	36.2/52	NBC
2	Rape Of Richard Beck, The	25.2/38	ABC
3	Ewok Adventure, The	24.9/36	ABC
4	He's Not Your Son	23.2/36	CBS
5	Consenting Adult	23.1/33	ABC
6	Miami Vice	22.8/37	NBC
7	Passions	22.4/34	CBS
8	Silence Of The Heart	21.9/35	CBS
9	Shattered Vows	21.3/33	NBC
10	Christmas Carol, A	20.7/30	CBS
11	Highway To Heaven	20.6/35	NBC
12	Scandal Sheet	20.5/32	ABC
13	Codename: Foxfire - Slay It Again, Sam	20.4/29	NBC
14	Hunter	20.4/33	NBC
15	California Girls	20.3/31	ABC
16	Single Bars, Single Women	20.0/31	ABC
17	Rearview Mirror	19.9/30	NBC
18	Lady Blue	19.8/31	ABC
19	Poison Ivy	19.8/25	NBC
20	Hawaiian Heat	19.1/34	ABC
21	Right To Kill?	19.0/31	ABC
22	Murder, She Wrote	18.9/29	CBS
23	Victims For Victims - The Theresa Saldana Story	18.8/28	NBC
24	Heartsounds	18.5/31	ABC
25	Kojak: The Belarus File	18.5/31	CBS
26	Paper Dolls	18.4/29	ABC
27	Malice In Wonderland	18.3/29	CBS
28	Moonlighting	18.3/28	ABC
29	Wet Gold	18.3/30	ABC
30	Father Of Hell Town	18.2/29	NBC
31	Little House On The Prairie - Bless All The Dear Children	18.2/27	NBC
32	Kids Don't Tell	18.1/29	CBS
33	Surviving	18.1/26	ABC
34	Alfred Hitchcock Presents	18.0/28	NBC
35	Aurora	18.0/28	NBC
36	Street Hawk	17.9/26	ABC
37	Two Fathers' Justice	17.9/27	NBC
38	Love Lives On	17.8/26	ABC
39	Jessie	17.7/29	ABC
40	Secrets Of A Married Man	17.5/27	NBC
41	Bunny's Tale, A	17.3/26	ABC
42	Cartier Affair, The	17.1/27	NBC
43	Do You Remember Love?	17.0/28	CBS
44	Touch Of Scandal, A	17.0/27	CBS
45	Playing With Fire	16.9/26	NBC
46	Scorned And Swindled	16.7/26	CBS
47	Anna Karenina	16.6/26	CBS
48	Burning Rage	16.5/30	CBS
49	Hearst And Davies Affair, The	16.2/24	ABC
50	Lady From Yesterday, The	16.0/25	CBS

50 TOP RANKING NETWORK MOIVES — 1985-1986 SEASON

1	Return To Mayberry	33.0/49	NBC
2	Perry Mason Returns	27.2/39	NBC
3	Intimate Strangers	26.4/38	CBS
4	Nobody's Child	25.9/39	CBS
5	Rockabye	25.3/38	CBS
6	Amos	24.5/37	CBS
7	Mafia Princess	24.4/37	NBC
8	An Early Frost	23.3/33	NBC
9	Perry Mason: The Case Of The Notorious Nun	23.3/42	NBC
10	Stone Pillow	23.3/33	CBS
11	Child's Cry	22.7/33	CBS
12	Silent Witness	22.5/33	NBC
13	Stagecoach	22.5/36	CBS
14	Resting Place	22.3/36	CBS
15	Family Ties Vacation	22.1/33	NBC
16	Blacke's Magic	21.8/32	NBC
17	Alex: The Life Of A Child	21.7/36	ABC
18	Outrage	21.7/34	CBS
19	Hostage Flight	21.5/32	NBC
20	Love, Mary	21.5/33	CBS
21	I Dream Of Jeannie: 15 Years Later	21.4/32	NBC
22	Dallas: The Early Years	21.3/33	CBS
23	This Child Is Mine	21.1/32	NBC
24	Mrs. Delafield Wants To Marry	21.0/35	CBS
25	Diary Of A Perfect Murder	20.9/33	NBC
26	Toughlove	20.6/31	ABC
27	Killer In The Mirror	20.4/31	NBC
28	One Terrific Guy	19.6/30	CBS
29	Letter To Three Wives, A	19.3/30	NBC
30	Blind Justice	19.2/29	CBS
31	Defiant One, The	18.9/28	ABC
32	Ewoks: The Battle For Endor	18.7/26	ABC
33	Vanishing Act	18.3/27	CBS
34	Choices	18.1/27	ABC
35	Izzy And Moe	17.9/27	CBS
36	Out Of The Darkness	17.6/30	CBS
37	Beverly Hills Madam	17.5/27	NBC
38	My Two Loves	17.5/28	ABC
39	Prince Of Bel Air	17.5/27	ABC
40	Convicted	17.4/27	ABC
41	Thompson's Last Run	17.4/26	CBS
42	C. A. T. Squad	17.3/30	NBC
43	Love Is Never Silent	17.3/26	NBC
44	Crime Of Innocence	17.2/26	NBC
45	Under Siege	17.2/24	NBC
46	Time To Live, A	17.1/27	NBC
47	Picking Up The Pieces	16.8/25	CBS
48	Vital Signs	16.7/26	CBS
49	Wild Horses	16.7/26	CBS
50	Murder: By Reason Of Insanity	16.6/26	CBS

Movies are listed by descending rating. Miniseries are listed by descending average of ratings. Cable movies are not listed as they are not rated.

50 TOP RANKING NETWORK MOVIES — 1986-1987 SEASON

1	Rags To Riches	25.3/36	NBC
2	Stranded	24.9/38	NBC
3	Blood Vows: The Story Of A Mafia Wife	24.8/37	NBC
4	Kate's Secret	24.1/36	NBC
5	Mercy Or Murder?	23.8/35	NBC
6	Perry Mason: The Case Of The Shooting Star	23.6/37	NBC
7	Smokey Mountain Christmas, A	23.2/35	ABC
8	When The Bough Breaks	22.3/36	NBC
9	Abduction Of Kari Swenson, The	21.4/33	NBC
10	Escape From Sobibor	21.4/34	CBS
11	Facts Of Life Down Under, The	21.4/32	NBC
12	Christmas Eve	21.3/33	NBC
13	Perry Mason: The Case Of The Lost Love	21.3/33	NBC
14	L. A. Law	21.2/33	NBC
15	Still Crazy Like A Fox	21.2/31	CBS
16	Stranger Waits, A	20.9/33	CBS
17	Perry Mason: The Case Of The Sinister Spirit	20.5/35	NBC
18	Return Of The 6 Million Dollar Man & Bionic Woman	20.5/33	NBC
19	Christmas Gift, The	20.2/33	CBS
20	Fight For Jenny, A	20.0/31	NBC
21	Of Pure Blood	20.0/30	CBS
22	Remington Steele: The Steele That Wouldn't Die	19.7/28	NBC
23	High Mountain Rangers	19.6/32	CBS
24	Women Of Valor	19.6/32	CBS
25	Last Days Of Patton, The	19.5/32	CBS
26	Promise	19.5/29	CBS
27	Desperado	19.3/32	NBC
28	Unnatural Causes	19.3/31	NBC
29	Deadly Deception	19.2/30	CBS
30	Stepford Children, The	19.2/29	NBC
31	Can You Feel Me Dancing?	19.1/30	NBC
32	Combat High	18.9/29	NBC
33	Deadly Care	18.6/31	CBS
34	High Price Of Passion, The	18.6/29	NBC
35	Dirty Dozen: The Deadly Mission	18.5/28	NBC
36	Easy Prey	18.4/29	ABC
37	Gathering Of Old Men, A	18.4/31	CBS
38	L B J: The Early Years	18.4/27	NBC
39	Who Is Julia?	18.4/29	CBS
40	Pack Of Lies	18.2/30	CBS
41	Something In Common	18.2/29	CBS
42	Murders In The Rue Morgue, The	17.7/27	CBS
43	Poker Alice	17.5/32	CBS
44	Convicted: A Mother's Story	17.4/27	NBC
45	Police Story: The Freeway Killings	17.3/27	NBC
46	Daddy	17.1/25	ABC
47	Doing Life	16.8/27	NBC
48	Infidelity	16.8/27	ABC
49	Ted Kennedy, Jr., Story, The	16.8/26	NBC
50	In Love And War	16.7/27	NBC

50 TOP RANKING NETWORK MOVIES — 1987-1988 SEASON

1	Ann Jillian Story, The	23.8/35	NBC
2	Perry Mason: The Case Of The Lady In The Lake	22.6/35	NBC
3	Eight Is Enough: A Family Reunion	22.0/34	NBC
4	Long Journey Home, The	21.3/34	CBS
5	Once Upon A Texas Train	21.2/32	CBS
6	Strange Voices	21.0/33	NBC
7	Mayflower Madam	20.9/34	CBS
8	Too Young The Hero	20.7/33	CBS
9	Assault And Matrimony	20.2/32	NBC
10	Incredible Hulk Returns, The	20.2/33	NBC
11	Scandal In A Small Town	20.0/31	NBC
12	Crash Course	19.9/32	NBC
13	Man Against The Mob	19.7/32	NBC
14	Taking Of Flight 847: The Uli Derickson Story	19.7/31	NBC
15	Aaron's Way	19.5/31	NBC
16	Hobo's Christmas, A	19.5/30	CBS
17	Hostage	19.4/29	CBS
18	Little Match Girl, The	19.4/30	NBC
19	Foxfire	19.3/30	CBS
20	After The Promise	19.2/30	CBS
21	Christmas Comes To Willow Creek	19.2/30	CBS
22	Little Girl Lost	19.0/31	ABC
23	Laura Lansing Slept Here	18.9/30	NBC
24	Nightingales	18.9/33	NBC
25	Stranger In My Bed	18.8/29	NBC
26	In The Heat Of The Night	18.7/30	NBC
27	Body Of Evidence	18.4/28	CBS
28	Red River	18.4/29	CBS
29	Addicted To His Love	18.1/29	ABC
30	Perry Mason: The Case Of The Murdered Madam	18.1/29	NBC
31	China Beach	18.0/29	ABC
32	Inherit The Wind	18.0/29	NBC
33	God Bless The Child	17.7/28	ABC
34	Alone In The Neon Jungle	17.6/28	CBS
35	Mistress	17.5/29	CBS
36	Right To Die	17.5/28	NBC
37	Frank Nitti: The Enforcer	17.4/28	ABC
38	Perry Mason: The Case Of The Avenging Ace	17.4/26	NBC
39	Moving Target	17.2/25	NBC
40	Roman Holiday	17.0/27	NBC
41	Broken Angel	16.9/28	ABC
42	Father Clements Story, The	16.7/26	NBC
43	Haunted By Her Past	16.7/27	NBC
44	Gunsmoke: Return To Dodge	16.6/31	CBS
45	Perry Mason: The Case Of The Scandalous Scoundrel	16.6/26	NBC
46	Kids Like These	16.5/27	CBS
47	Dangerous Affection	16.4/26	NBC
48	Downpayment On Murder	16.1/27	NBC
49	Freedom Fighter	16.0/25	NBC
50	Return Of Desperado, The	16.0/24	NBC

Movies are listed by descending rating. Miniseries are listed by descending average of ratings. Cable movies are not listed as they are not rated.

50 TOP RANKING NETWORK MOVIES — 1988-1989 SEASON

1 Karen Carpenter Story, The .... 26.3/41 .... CBS
2 Those She Left Behind .... 25.1/38 .... NBC
3 Very Brady Christmas, A .... 25.1/39 .... CBS
4 Case Of The Hillside Strangler, The .... 23.1/36 .... NBC
5 Everybody's Baby: The Rescue Of Jessica Mcclure .. 22.2/36 .... ABC
6 In The Line Of Duty: The Fbi Murders .... 22.2/34 .... NBC
7 Naked Lie .... 21.2/33 .... CBS
8 Double Standard .... 21.1/33 .... NBC
9 Too Good To Be True .... 20.9/32 .... NBC
10 Take My Daughters, Please .... 19.9/31 .... NBC
11 David .... 19.5/30 .... ABC
12 Jesse .... 19.4/31 .... CBS
13 Home Fires Burning .... 18.6/29 .... CBS
14 Stoning In Fulham County, A .... 18.3/28 .... NBC
15 Cover Girl And The Cop, The .... 18.0/28 .... NBC
16 Deadly Silence, A .... 17.9/28 .... ABC
17 I'll Be Home For Christmas .... 17.9/28 .... NBC
18 Bionic Showdown: The 6 Million Dollar Man/
    Bionic Woman .... 17.6/28 .... NBC
19 Perry Mason: The Case Of The Musical Murders ..... 17.4/26 .... NBC
20 She Knows Too Much .... 17.4/27 .... NBC
21 People Across The Lake, The .... 17.3/27 .... NBC
22 Swimsuit .... 17.3/27 .... NBC
23 Unconquered .... 17.3/28 .... CBS
24 Maybe Baby .... 17.2/27 .... NBC
25 Baywatch: Panic At Malibu Pier .... 17.1/28 .... NBC
26 Roe Vs. Wade .... 17.0/27 .... NBC
27 Your Mother Wears Combat Boots .... 17.0/28 .... NBC
28 Terror On Highway 91 .... 16.9/26 .... CBS
29 Liberace .... 16.8/27 .... ABC
30 Original Sin .... 16.8/26 .... NBC
31 Goddess Of Love .... 16.7/26 .... NBC
32 Secret Garden, The .... 16.7/26 .... CBS
33 Comeback, The .... 16.6/29 .... CBS
34 Ladykillers .... 16.6/27 .... ABC
35 Liberace: Behind The Music .... 16.6/26 .... CBS
36 Ryan White Story, The .... 16.6/26 .... ABC
37 Winnie .... 16.6/28 .... NBC
38 Fulfillment Of Mary Gray, The .... 16.5/26 .... CBS
39 Full Exposure: The Sex Tapes Scandal .... 16.2/24 .... NBC
40 Trial Of The Incredible Hulk, The .... 16.2/25 .... NBC
41 Love And Betrayal .... 16.1/25 .... CBS
42 Shootdown .... 16.0/25 .... NBC
43 Agatha Christie's The Man In The Brown Suit .... 15.8/25 .... CBS
44 Dance Till Dawn .... 15.8/26 .... ABC
45 Jake And The Fatman .... 15.8/27 .... CBS
46 Outback Bound .... 15.7/25 .... CBS
47 Gifted One, The .... 15.5/27 .... NBC
48 Fatal Judgment .... 15.4/24 .... CBS
49 Roots: The Gift .... 15.4/24 .... ABC
50 Day One .... 15.2/24 .... CBS

50 TOP RANKING NETWORK MOVIES — 1989-1990 SEASON

1 Twin Peaks .... 21.7/33 .... ABC
2 Cry For Help: The Tracey Thurman Story, A .... 21.5/33 .... NBC
3 Incident, The .... 20.8/33 .... CBS
4 Operation, The .... 20.0/30 .... CBS
5 Gunsmoke: The Last Apache .... 19.7/32 .... CBS
6 Caroline? .... 19.4/30 .... CBS
7 False Witness .... 18.7/29 .... NBC
8 Lady Forgets, The .... 18.5/34 .... CBS
9 Do You Know The Muffin Man? .... 18.4/30 .... CBS
10 Cast The First Stone .... 17.9/28 .... NBC
11 Pair Of Aces .... 17.8/28 .... CBS
12 Without Her Consent .... 17.8/28 .... NBC
13 Fall From Grace .... 17.6/27 .... NBC
14 Roxanne: The Prize Pulitzer .... 17.3/27 .... NBC
15 When He's Not A Stranger .... 17.2/26 .... CBS
16 Murder In Black And White .... 17.1/27 .... CBS
17 Perry Mason: The Case Of The Desperate Deception . 17.0/27 .... NBC
18 Little White Lies .... 16.9/26 .... NBC
19 Perry Mason: The Case Of The All-Star Assassin ..... 16.8/26 .... NBC
20 Settle The Score .... 16.8/26 .... NBC
21 Shattered Dreams .... 16.8/28 .... CBS
22 Anything To Survive .... 16.5/26 .... ABC
23 Perry Mason: The Case Of The Silenced Singer ...... 16.5/27 .... NBC
24 Son's Promise, A .... 16.5/27 .... ABC
25 Blind Witness .... 16.3/25 .... ABC
26 Night Walk .... 16.3/27 .... CBS
27 Taken Away .... 16.3/25 .... CBS
28 My Boyfriend's Back .... 16.1/26 .... NBC
29 Perry Mason: The Case Of The Poisoned Pen .... 16.0/24 .... NBC
30 Brand New Life: The Honeymoon .... 15.9/25 .... NBC
31 Family For Joe, A .... 15.8/23 .... NBC
32 Killing In A Small Town .... 15.8/26 .... CBS
33 Rock Hudson .... 15.7/24 .... ABC
34 Shell Seekers, The .... 15.7/24 .... ABC
35 Unspeakable Acts .... 15.7/25 .... ABC
36 Manhunt: Search For The Night Stalker .... 15.4/24 .... NBC
37 Eight Is Enough Wedding, An .... 15.3/25 .... NBC
38 Nasty Boys .... 15.3/27 .... NBC
39 Where Pigeons Go To Die .... 15.3/24 .... NBC
40 Preppie Murder, The .... 15.2/24 .... ABC
41 Dream Date .... 15.1/24 .... NBC
42 Miracle Landing .... 15.1/23 .... CBS
43 Daughter Of The Streets .... 14.9/24 .... ABC
44 Howard Beach: Making The Case For Murder .... 14.9/24 .... NBC
45 Old Man & The Sea, The .... 14.9/24 .... NBC
46 Rich Men, Single Women .... 14.8/23 .... ABC
47 Face To Face .... 14.7/24 .... CBS
48 Follow Your Heart .... 14.7/23 .... NBC
49 Death Of The Incredible Hulk, The .... 14.6/22 .... NBC
50 Single Women, Married Men .... 14.6/26 .... CBS

RATINGS

Movies are listed by descending rating. Miniseries are listed by descending average of ratings. Cable movies are not listed as they are not rated.

50 TOP RANKING NETWORK MOVIES — 1990-1991 SEASON

1	Sarah, Plain And Tall	23.1/35	CBS
2	Danielle Steel's Kaleidoscope	20.3/32	NBC
3	Lies Before Kisses	18.5/29	CBS
4	Danielle Steel's Fine Things	18.0/28	NBC
5	Decoration Day	17.9/28	NBC
6	Danielle Steel's Changes	17.8/28	NBC
7	Absolute Strangers	17.7/29	CBS
8	Aftermath: A Test Of Love	17.3/27	CBS
9	Cry In The Wild: The Taking Of Peggy Ann	17.2/27	NBC
10	Mom For Christmas, A	17.0/27	NBC
11	Her Wicked Ways	16.9/26	NBC
12	Bride In Black, The	16.7/27	ABC
13	Lucy & Desi: Before The Laughter	16.4/25	CBS
14	Knight Rider 2000	16.1/26	NBC
15	Bump In The Night	16.0/25	CBS
16	Call Me Anna	15.9/24	ABC
17	Leona Helmsley: The Queen Of Mean	15.7/26	CBS
18	Joshua's Heart	15.6/26	NBC
19	Stranger Within, The	15.6/25	CBS
20	Whereabouts Of Jenny, The	15.4/24	ABC
21	Always Remember I Love You	15.3/26	CBS
22	Shadow Of A Doubt	15.3/24	CBS
23	Hell Hath No Fury	15.2/24	NBC
24	Marla Hanson Story, The	15.1/24	NBC
25	Columbo Goes To College	14.9/24	ABC
26	Good Night, Sweet Wife: A Murder In Boston	14.9/23	CBS
27	Donor	14.8/24	CBS
28	In The Line Of Duty: Manhunt In The Dakotas	14.7/26	NBC
29	Perry Mason: The Case Of The Defiant Daughter	14.7/24	NBC
30	She Said No	14.7/23	NBC
31	Chase, The	14.6/23	NBC
32	In The Line Of Duty: A Cop For The Killing	14.6/23	NBC
33	When You Remember Me	14.6/24	ABC
34	Dillinger	14.5/22	ABC
35	Don't Touch My Daughter	14.5/23	NBC
36	Sins Of The Mother	14.5/23	CBS
37	Promise To Keep, A	14.3/23	NBC
38	Eighty-Three Hours 'til Dawn	14.2/22	CBS
39	Flash, The	14.2/23	CBS
40	Fatal Image, The	14.1/22	CBS
41	In Defense Of A Married Man	14.1/23	ABC
42	Casey's Gift: For Love Of A Child	14.0/22	NBC
43	Face Of Fear, The	14.0/23	CBS
44	Perry Mason: The Case Of The Maligned Mobster	14.0/22	NBC
45	Perry Mason: The Case Of The Ruthless Reporter	14.0/21	NBC
46	Daughters Of Privilege	13.9/23	NBC
47	Killer Among Us, A	13.9/23	NBC
48	Seduction In Travis County	13.9/22	CBS
49	In Broad Daylight	13.7/21	NBC
50	Night Of The Hunter	13.7/23	ABC

50 TOP RANKING NETWORK MOVIES — 1991-1992 SEASON

1	Danielle Steel's Daddy	19.6/30	NBC
2	Woman Scorned: The Betty Broderick Story, A	19.5/30	CBS
3	O Pioneers	18.9/29	CBS
4	Danielle Steel's Palomino	18.4/28	NBC
5	Wild Texas Wind	18.0/27	NBC
6	Woman With A Past	17.5/27	NBC
7	Crash Landing: The Rescue Of Flight 232	17.1/26	ABC
8	Double Edge	17.1/28	CBS
9	Bed Of Lies	16.8/25	ABC
10	Face Of A Stranger	16.8/27	CBS
11	Runaway Father	16.8/27	CBS
12	Christmas On Division Street	16.7/26	CBS
13	Mother's Justice, A	16.7/25	NBC
14	Deliver Them From Evil: The Taking Of Alta View	16.6/26	CBS
15	What She Doesn't Know	16.6/25	NBC
16	Young Indiana Jones Chronicles: The Curse Of The Jackal	16.6/26	ABC
17	Columbo: No Time To Die	16.5/27	ABC
18	Baby Snatcher	16.3/26	CBS
19	In Sickness And In Health	16.3/26	CBS
20	Battling For Baby	16.2/26	CBS
21	Something To Live For: The Alison Gertz Story	16.2/26	ABC
22	Us	16.1/29	CBS
23	Against Her Will: An Incident In Baltimore	16.0/25	CBS
24	Highway Heartbreaker	16.0/25	CBS
25	In The Best Interest Of The Children	16.0/24	NBC
26	Murder In New Hampshire: The Pamela Smart Story	15.9/26	CBS
27	Story Lady, The	15.9/24	NBC
28	Deadly Medicine	15.8/24	NBC
29	In My Daughter's Name	15.8/27	CBS
30	Taking Back My Life: The Nancy Ziegenmeyer Story	15.8/25	CBS
31	P. S. I Luv U	15.7/25	CBS
32	Danielle Steel's Secrets	15.6/24	NBC
33	Deception: A Mother's Secret	15.6/23	NBC
34	Mission Of The Shark	15.6/25	CBS
35	My Son Johnny	15.6/24	CBS
36	Survive The Savage Sea	15.6/24	ABC
37	Wife, Mother, Murderer	15.6/24	ABC
38	Honor Thy Mother	15.5/24	CBS
39	I'll Fly Away	15.4/24	NBC
40	Baby Of The Bride	15.0/26	CBS
41	Backfield In Motion	15.0/24	ABC
42	She Says She's Innocent	15.0/23	NBC
43	Chance Of A Lifetime	14.8/22	NBC
44	Fire In The Dark	14.8/23	CBS
45	Carolina Skeletons	14.7/23	NBC
46	Grave Secrets: The Legacy Of Hilltop Drive	14.7/23	CBS
47	Perry Mason: The Case Of The Reckless Romeo	14.7/23	NBC
48	Diagnosis Of Murder	14.6/23	CBS
49	Perry Mason: The Case Of The Fatal Fashion	14.6/23	NBC
50	Till Death Us Do Part	14.6/21	NBC

Movies are listed by descending rating. Miniseries are listed by descending average of ratings. Cable movies are not listed as they are not rated.

ALL NETWORK MOVIES — 1992-1993 SEASON

1	Skylark	19.9/29	CBS
2	Family Of Strangers	19.8/29	CBS
3	Men Don't Tell	19.7/31	CBS
4	Beyond Control: The Amy Fisher Story	19.5/30	ABC
5	Amy Fisher: My Story	19.1/30	NBC
6	In The Line Of Duty: Ambush In Waco	18.8/30	NBC
7	Man Upstairs, The	18.8/28	CBS
8	Call Of The Wild	18.2/29	CBS
9	Dr. Quinn, Medicine Woman	18.2/29	CBS
10	Dead Before Dawn	18.0/26	ABC
11	Rio Diablo	17.3/26	CBS
12	Without A Kiss Goodbye	17.2/29	CBS
13	Disappearance Of Nora	17.0/27	CBS
14	From The Files Of Joseph Wambaugh: A Jury Of One	17.0/17	NBC
15	To Grandmother's House We Go	16.9/25	ABC
16	Danielle Steel's Heartbeat	16.8/26	NBC
17	Mrs. 'Arris Goes To Paris	16.8/28	CBS
18	Killer Among Friends, A	16.7/27	CBS
19	Walker, Texas Ranger	16.5/27	CBS
20	I Can Make You Love Me: The Stalking Of Laura Black	16.1/26	CBS
21	Two Thousand Malibu Road	16.1/28	CBS
22	Danger Of Love, The	15.9/26	CBS
23	Fatal Memories	15.8/24	NBC
24	Judgment Day: The John List Story	15.8/25	CBS
25	Triumph Over Disaster: The Hurricane Andrew Story	15.7/25	NBC
26	Woman On The Ledge	15.6/24	NBC
27	House Of Secrets And Lies, A	15.5/27	CBS
28	Just My Imagination	15.5/19	NBC
29	Message From Holly	15.5/24	CBS
30	Child Lost Forever, A	15.4/23	NBC
31	Dying To Love You	15.4/25	CBS
32	Overkill: The Aileen Wuornos Story	15.4/25	CBS
33	Terror On Track 9	15.4/25	CBS
34	Sworn To Vengeance	15.3/25	CBS
35	Not In My Family	15.1/23	ABC
36	Shadow Of A Stranger	15.1/24	NBC
37	In The Company Of Darkness	15.0/24	CBS
38	Murderous Affair, A: The Carolyn Warmus Story	15.0/25	ABC
39	Bonds Of Love	14.9/23	CBS
40	Her Final Fury: Betty Broderick, The Last Chapter	14.9/22	CBS
41	Complex Of Fear	14.8/23	CBS
42	Child Of Rage	14.7/24	CBS
43	With A Vengeance	14.7/23	CBS
44	Father & Son: Dangerous Relations	14.6/24	NBC
45	In The Deep Woods	14.6/23	NBC
46	Liar, Liar	14.5/26	CBS
47	Nightmare In The Daylight	14.5/23	CBS
48	Poisoned By Love: The Kern County Murders	14.5/24	CBS
49	They've Taken Our Children: The Chowchilla Kidnapping	14.5/23	ABC
50	Overexposed	14.4/23	ABC
51	Willing To Kill: The Texas Cheerleader Story	14.4/22	ABC
52	Casualties Of Love: The Long Island Lolita Story	14.3/22	CBS
53	Between Love And Hate	14.2/21	ABC
54	Moment Of Truth: Why My Daughter?	14.2/23	NBC
55	Labor Of Love: The Arlette Schweitzer Story	14.1/23	CBS
56	Ordeal In The Arctic	14.0/22	ABC
57	Jonathan: The Boy Nobody Wanted	13.8/21	NBC
58	There Was A Little Boy	13.8/22	CBS
59	Women Of Windsor	13.8/22	CBS
60	Fergie And Andrew: Behind The Palace Doors	13.6/21	NBC
61	Mothers' Right, A: The Elizabeth Morgan Story	13.6/21	ABC
62	Black Widow Murders: The Blanche Taylor Moore Story	13.3/21	NBC
63	Desperate Rescue: The Cathy Mahone Story	13.3/20	NBC
64	Miracle On I-880	13.3/20	NBC
65	Miss America: Behind The Crown	13.3/20	NBC
66	Perry Mason: The Case Of The Skin-Deep Scandal	13.3/22	NBC
67	Blind Spot	13.1/20	CBS
68	Darkness Before Dawn	13.1/20	NBC
69	Journey To The Center Of The Earth	13.1/20	NBC
70	Perry Mason: The Case Of The Telltale Talk Show Host	13.1/24	NBC
71	Place To Be Loved, A	13.0/20	CBS
72	Deadbolt	12.9/23	CBS
73	When No One Would Listen	12.9/19	CBS
74	With Hostile Intent	12.9/21	CBS
75	Charles And Diana: Unhappily Ever After	12.8/19	ABC
76	For The Love Of My Child: The Anissa Ayala Story	12.8/20	NBC
77	Relentless: Mind Of A Killer	12.8/20	NBC
78	Revenge On The Highway	12.8/19	NBC
79	Through The Eyes Of A Killer	12.8/21	CBS
80	Town Tom Apart, A	12.8/20	NBC
81	American Story, An	12.7/20	CBS
82	Picket Fences	12.7/24	CBS
83	Desperate Choices: To Save My Child	12.4/19	NBC
84	Marked For Murder	12.4/20	NBC
85	Silent Cries	12.4/20	NBC
86	Columbo: A Bird In The Hand	12.2/19	ABC
87	Adrift	12.1/20	CBS
88	Perry Mason: The Case Of The Heartbroken Bride	12.1/21	NBC
89	Woman Who Loved Elvis, The	12.1/20	ABC
90	In The Line Of Duty: Street War	11.9/20	NBC
91	Switch, The	11.8/19	CBS
92	Passport To Murder	11.7/19	NBC
93	Danger Island	11.6/19	NBC
94	Return Of Ironside, The	11.6/19	NBC
95	Firestorm: 72 Hours In Oakland	11.5/17	ABC
96	Kiss Of A Killer	11.5/18	ABC
97	Last P. O. W? The Bobby Garwood Story, The	11.5/20	ABC
98	Love Can Be Murder	11.4/18	NBC
99	Ned Blessing: The Story Of My Life And Times	11.3/20	CBS
100	Condition: Critical	11.0/18	NBC
101	Miracle Child	11.0/18	NBC
102	For Their Own Good	10.9/17	ABC
103	It's Nothing Personal	10.9/17	NBC
104	Twist Of The Knife, A	10.9/20	CBS
105	Exclusive	10.8/17	ABC
106	Born Too Soon	10.5/17	NBC
107	Lies And Lullabies	10.4/16	ABC
108	Gregory K	10.3/16	ABC
109	Obsessed	10.3/16	ABC
110	Gunsmoke: The Long Ride Home	10.2/19	CBS
111	Somebody's Daughter	10.2/16	ABC
112	Visions Of Murder	10.1/19	NBC
113	Deadly Relations	10.0/19	ABC
114	Presidents Child, The	10.0/17	CBS
115	Prophet Of Evil: The Ervil Lebaron Story	9.9/16	CBS
116	Elvis And The Colonel: The Untold Story	9.8/14	NBC
117	South Beach	9.8/17	NBC
118	Double Deception	9.6/17	NBC
119	Mother Of The Bride	9.6/17	CBS
120	Saved By The Bell-Hawaiian Style	9.5/17	NBC
121	Torch Song	9.5/15	ABC
122	Without Warning: Terror In The Towers	9.3/15	NBC
123	Killer Rules	9.2/14	NBC
124	Lethal Exposure	8.8/14	NBC
125	Middle Ages	8.7/16	CBS
126	Class Of '61	8.5/14	ABC
127	Round Table, The	8.3/16	NBC
128	Lifepod	6.5/11	FBC
129	Tower, The	6.2/11	FBC
130	Twelve O' One (12: 01)	6.0/12	FBC
131	Rio Shanon	5.2/11	ABC
132	Born To Run	3.9/7	FBC

Movies are listed by descending rating. Miniseries are listed by descending average of ratings. Cable movies are not listed as they are not rated.

All Network Movies — 1993-1994 Season

1	To Dance With The White Dog	21.9/33	CBS
2	Breathing Lessons	21.6/32	CBS
3	Walton Thanksgiving Reunion, A	20.1/30	CBS
4	Jane's House	19.5/29	CBS
5	Perry Mason: The Case Of The Killer Kiss	19.3/29	NBC
6	Incident In A Small Town	18.7/31	CBS
7	Gypsy	18.6/28	CBS
8	Snowbound: The Jim And Jennifer Stolpa Story	18.2/27	CBS
9	Seaquest Dsv	17.8/28	NBC
10	There Are No Children Here	17.8/26	ABC
11	This Can't Be Love	17.8/28	CBS
12	Christy	17.7/29	CBS
13	Bonanza: The Return	17.6/26	NBC
14	Substitute Wife, The	17.5/27	NBC
15	Corpse Had A Familiar Face, The	16.4/26	CBS
16	David's Mother	16.3/26	CBS
17	Shattered Trust: The Shari Karney Story	16.2/25	NBC
18	Secret Sins Of The Father	16.0/24	NBC
19	Danielle Steel's Star	15.9/24	NBC
20	Moment Of Truth: Stalking Back	15.9/25	NBC
21	Ultimate Betrayal	15.6/25	CBS
22	Viper	15.3/23	NBC
23	Empty Cradle	15.2/24	ABC
24	Family Torn Apart, A	15.1/23	NBC
25	Lies Of The Heart: The Story Of Laurie Kellogg	15.0/23	ABC
26	Armed & Innocent	14.9/24	CBS
27	Cosby Mysteries, The	14.8/22	NBC
28	Donato And Daughter	14.8/24	CBS
29	Place For Annie, A	14.8/23	ABC
30	House Of Secrets	14.6/23	NBC
31	Precious Victims	14.6/23	CBS
32	Murder Of Innocence	14.5/22	CBS
33	Thicker Than Blood: The Larry Mclinden Story	14.5/23	CBS
34	Beyond Suspicion	14.4/22	NBC
35	In The Shadows, Someone Is Watching	14.4/22	NBC
36	Moment Of Truth: A Child Too Many	14.2/22	NBC
37	Columbo: Undercover	14.1/22	ABC
38	Scattered Dreams: The Kathryn Messenger Story	14.1/22	CBS
39	Babymaker: The Dr. Cecil Jacobson's Story	14.0/21	CBS
40	Cries Unheard: The Donna Yaklich Story	14.0/22	CBS
41	Sin And Redemption	14.0/23	CBS
42	To My Daughter With Love	13.8/21	NBC
43	Beyond Obsession	13.6/21	ABC
44	Moment Of Truth: Cradle Of Conspiracy	13.5/21	NBC
45	One Of Her Own	13.5/21	ABC
46	Children Of The Dark	13.4/22	CBS
47	Columbo: It's All In The Game	13.4/21	ABC
48	Conviction Of Kitty Dodds, The	13.2/21	CBS
49	Nurses On The Line: The Crash Of Flight 7	13.2/22	CBS
50	Shameful Secrets	13.2/21	ABC
51	Yearling, The	13.2/21	CBS
52	Forget Me Not Murders, The	13.1/21	CBS
53	Hart To Hart Returns	13.1/23	NBC
54	No Child Of Mine	13.1/21	CBS
55	Tears And Laughter: The Joan And Mielissa Rivers Story	13.1/21	NBC
56	Betrayal Of Trust	13.0/20	NBC
57	Victim Of Love: The Shannon Mohr Story	13.0/19	NBC
58	Murder Between Friends	12.9/20	NBC
59	One More Mountain	12.9/20	ABC
60	Seasons Of The Heart	12.9/21	NBC
61	Final Appeal	12.7/20	NBC
62	Terror In The Night	12.7/20	CBS
63	Time To Heal, A	12.7/21	NBC
64	Broken Promises: Taking Emily Back	12.6/22	CBS
65	Moment Of Truth: Broken Pledges	12.6/20	NBC
66	Out Of The Darkness	12.5/19	ABC
67	For The Love Of Aaron	12.4/21	CBS
68	I Spy Returns	12.4/18	CBS
69	One Woman's Courage	12.4/19	NBC
70	River Of Rage: The Taking Of Maggie Keene	12.4/20	CBS
71	Harmful Intent	12.2/20	CBS
72	Jonathan Stone: Threat Of Innocence	12.2/16	NBC
73	Mercy Mission: The Rescue Of Flight 771	12.2/19	NBC
74	Witness To The Execution	12.2/17	NBC
75	Only Way Out, The	12.1/19	ABC
76	Separated By Murder	11.8/19	CBS
77	To Save The Children	11.6/19	CBS
78	Due South	11.5/21	CBS
79	Fugitive Nights: Danger In The Desert	11.5/20	NBC
80	Gunsmoke: One Man's Justice	11.5/17	CBS
81	Heart Of A Child	11.5/18	NBC
82	Baby Brokers	11.4/17	NBC
83	Flood: Who Will Save Our Children?	11.4/18	NBC
84	Missing Persons	11.4/19	ABC
85	My Breast	11.4/18	CBS
86	Shadow Of Obsession	11.4/18	NBC
87	French Silk	11.3/17	ABC
88	Danielle Steel's Once In A Lifetime	11.2/16	NBC
89	Fatal Deception: Mrs. Lee Harvey Oswald	11.2/18	NBC
90	Lois & Clark: The New Adventures Of Superman	11.2/17	ABC
91	My Name Is Kate	11.2/17	ABC
92	Getting Out	11.1/18	ABC
93	Passion For Justice, A: Hazel Brannon Smith Story	11.1/18	ABC
94	Betrayed By Love	10.8/16	ABC
95	Double, Double, Toil And Trouble	10.8/19	ABC
96	In The Line Of Duty: The Price Of Vengeance	10.8/17	NBC
97	Kiss To Die For, A	10.8/17	NBC
98	Perry Mason Mystery, A: The Case Of The Lethal Lifestyle	10.8/18	NBC
99	Confessions: Two Faces Of Evil	10.7/16	NBC
100	Macshayne: Winner Take All	10.7/17	NBC
101	Web Of Deception	10.7/17	NBC
102	Eyes Of Terror	10.6/19	NBC
103	Mothers Revenge, A	10.6/16	ABC
104	Man From Left Field	10.5/20	CBS
105	Search And Rescue	10.5/17	NBC
106	Search For Grace	10.5/17	CBS
107	Yarn Princess, The	10.5/17	ABC
108	Odd Couple, The	10.4/19	CBS
109	Tonya & Nancy: The Inside Story	10.4/19	NBC
110	Two Fathers: Justice For The Innocent	10.3/17	NBC
111	Honor Thy Father And Mother: The Menendez Murders	10.2/17	FBC
112	Perry Mason Mystery:The Case Of The Wicked Wives	10.2/19	NBC
113	Leave Of Absence	10.1/15	NBC
114	I Know My Son Is Alive	9.9/15	NBC
115	Desperate Journey: The Allison Wilcox Story	9.7/15	ABC
116	Second Chances	9.7/16	CBS
117	Sherlock Holmes Returns	9.7/16	CBS
118	Stranger In The Mirror, A	9.6/16	ABC
119	Whose Child Is This? The War For Baby Jessica	9.6/15	ABC
120	Staying Afloat	9.5/17	NBC
121	Trouble Shooters: Trapped Beneath The Earth	9.5/15	NBC
122	For Love And Glory	9.4/18	CBS
123	Love On The Run	9.3/16	NBC
124	Macgyver : Lost Treasure Of Atlantis	9.1/17	ABC
125	Ride With The Wind	9.0/15	ABC
126	Roommates	8.9/15	NBC
127	Day Of Reckoning	8.7/14	NBC
128	Mantis	8.5/13	FBC
129	Ray Alexander: A Taste For Justice	8.5/15	NBC
130	Getting Gotti	8.3/13	CBS
131	Macshayne: The Final Roll Of The Dice	8.3/15	NBC
132	Moment Of Truth: To Walk Again	8.3/12	NBC
133	Bermuda Grace	8.2/14	NBC
134	Adventures Of Brisco County Jr., The	7.2/14	FBC
135	Rise & Walk: The Dennis Byrd Story	7.1/11	FBC
136	Hostage For A Day	6.6/11	FBC
137	Just One Of The Girls	6.3/10	FBC
138	Day My Parents Ran Away, The	6.0/9	FBC
139	Ghost Mom	6.0/9	FBC
140	Revenge Of The Nerds I V: Nerds In Love	5.9/9	FBC
141	Counterfeit Contessa, The	5.1/8	FBC
142	Spoils Of War	4.9/9	ABC
143	Dark Reflection	4.8/7	FBC
144	Green Dolphin Beat	4.4/8	ABC
145	Based On An Untrue Story	3.5/5	FBC

Movies are listed by descending rating. Miniseries are listed by descending average of ratings. Cable movies are not listed as they are not rated.

ALL NETWORK MOVIES — 1984-1994

1	Burning Bed, The	36.2/52	NBC
2	Return To Mayberry	33.0/49	NBC
3	Perry Mason Returns	27.2/39	NBC
4	Intimate Strangers	26.4/38	CBS
5	Karen Carpenter Story, The	26.3/41	CBS
6	Nobody's Child	25.9/39	CBS
7	Rags To Riches	25.3/36	NBC
8	Rockabye	25.3/38	CBS
9	Rape Of Richard Beck, The	25.2/38	ABC
10	Those She Left Behind	25.1/38	NBC
11	Very Brady Christmas, A	25.1/39	CBS
12	Ewok Adventure, The	24.9/36	ABC
13	Stranded	24.9/38	NBC
14	Blood Vows: The Story Of A Mafia Wife	24.8/37	NBC
15	Amos	24.5/37	CBS
16	Mafia Princess	24.4/37	NBC
17	Kate's Secret	24.1/36	NBC
18	Ann Jillian Story, The	23.8/35	NBC
19	Mercy Or Murder?	23.8/35	NBC
20	Perry Mason: The Case Of The Shooting Star	23.6/37	NBC
21	An Early Frost	23.3/33	NBC
22	Perry Mason: The Case Of The Notorious Nun	23.3/42	NBC
23	Stone Pillow	23.3/33	CBS
24	He's Not Your Son	23.2/36	CBS
25	Smokey Mountain Christmas, A	23.2/35	ABC
26	Case Of The Hillside Strangler, The	23.1/36	NBC
27	Consenting Adult	23.1/33	ABC
28	Sarah, Plain And Tall	23.1/35	CBS
29	Miami Vice	22.8/37	NBC
30	Child's Cry	22.7/33	CBS
31	Perry Mason: The Case Of The Lady In The Lake	22.6/35	NBC
32	Silent Witness	22.5/33	NBC
33	Stagecoach	22.5/36	CBS
34	Passions	22.4/34	CBS
35	Resting Place	22.3/36	CBS
36	When The Bough Breaks	22.3/36	NBC
37	Everybody's Baby: The Rescue Of Jessica Mcclure	22.2/36	ABC
38	In The Line Of Duty: The Fbi Murders	22.2/34	NBC
39	Family Ties Vacation	22.1/33	NBC
40	Eight Is Enough: A Family Reunion	22.0/34	NBC
41	Silence Of The Heart	21.9/35	CBS
42	To Dance With The White Dog	21.9/33	CBS
43	Blacke's Magic	21.8/32	NBC
44	Alex: The Life Of A Child	21.7/36	ABC
45	Outrage	21.7/34	CBS
46	Twin Peaks	21.7/33	ABC
47	Breathing Lessons	21.6/32	CBS
48	Not My Kid	21.6/33	CBS
49	Cry For Help: The Tracey Thurman Story, A	21.5/33	NBC
50	Hostage Flight	21.5/32	NBC
51	Love, Mary	21.5/33	CBS
52	Abduction Of Kari Swenson, The	21.4/33	NBC
53	Escape From Sobibor	21.4/34	CBS
54	Execution, The	21.4/32	NBC
55	Facts Of Life Down Under, The	21.4/32	NBC
56	I Dream Of Jeannie: 15 Years Later	21.4/32	NBC
57	Christmas Eve	21.3/33	NBC
58	Dallas: The Early Years	21.3/33	CBS
59	Long Journey Home, The	21.3/34	CBS
60	Perry Mason: The Case Of The Lost Love	21.3/33	NBC
61	Shattered Vows	21.3/33	NBC
62	L. A. Law	21.2/33	NBC
63	Naked Lie	21.2/33	CBS
64	Once Upon A Texas Train	21.2/32	CBS
65	Still Crazy Like A Fox	21.2/31	CBS
66	Double Standard	21.1/33	NBC
67	This Child Is Mine	21.1/32	NBC
68	Mrs. Delafield Wants To Marry	21.0/35	CBS
69	Strange Voices	21.0/33	NBC
70	Diary Of A Perfect Murder	20.9/33	NBC
71	Mayflower Madam	20.9/34	CBS
72	Stranger Waits, A	20.9/33	CBS
73	Too Good To Be True	20.9/32	NBC
74	Incident, The	20.8/33	CBS
75	Christmas Carol, A	20.7/30	CBS
76	Too Young The Hero	20.7/33	CBS
77	Highway To Heaven	20.6/35	NBC
78	Toughlove	20.6/31	ABC
79	Perry Mason: The Case Of The Sinister Spirit	20.5/35	NBC
80	Return Of The 6 Million Dollar Man & Bionic Woman	20.5/33	NBC
81	Scandal Sheet	20.5/32	ABC
82	Codename: Foxfire - Slay It Again, Sam	20.4/29	NBC
83	Hunter	20.4/33	NBC
84	Killer In The Mirror	20.4/31	NBC
85	California Girls	20.3/31	ABC
86	Danielle Steel's Kaleidoscope	20.3/32	NBC
87	Assault And Matrimony	20.2/32	NBC
88	Christmas Gift, The	20.2/33	CBS
89	Incredible Hulk Returns, The	20.2/33	NBC
90	Walton Thanksgiving Reunion, A	20.1/30	CBS
91	Fight For Jenny, A	20.0/31	NBC
92	Of Pure Blood	20.0/30	CBS
93	Operation, The	20.0/30	CBS
94	Scandal In A Small Town	20.0/31	NBC
95	Single Bars, Single Women	20.0/31	ABC
96	Crash Course	19.9/32	NBC
97	Rearview Mirror	19.9/30	NBC
98	Skylark	19.9/29	CBS
99	Take My Daughters, Please	19.9/31	NBC
100	Family Of Strangers	19.8/29	CBS
101	Lady Blue	19.8/31	ABC
102	Poison Ivy	19.8/25	NBC
103	Gunsmoke: The Last Apache	19.7/32	CBS
104	Man Against The Mob	19.7/32	NBC
105	Men Don't Tell	19.7/31	CBS
106	Remington Steele: The Steele That Wouldn't Die	19.7/28	NBC
107	Taking Of Flight 847: The Uli Derickson Story	19.7/31	NBC
108	Danielle Steel's Daddy	19.6/30	NBC
109	High Mountain Rangers	19.6/32	CBS
110	One Terrific Guy	19.6/30	CBS
111	Women Of Valor	19.6/32	CBS
112	Aaron's Way	19.5/31	NBC
113	Beyond Control: The Amy Fisher Story	19.5/30	ABC
114	David	19.5/30	ABC
115	Hobo's Christmas, A	19.5/30	CBS
116	Jane's House	19.5/29	CBS
117	Last Days Of Patton, The	19.5/32	CBS
118	Promise	19.5/29	CBS
119	Woman Scorned: The Betty Broderick Story, A	19.5/30	CBS
120	Caroline?	19.4/30	CBS
121	Hostage	19.4/29	CBS
122	Jesse	19.4/31	CBS
123	Little Match Girl, The	19.4/30	NBC
124	Desperado	19.3/32	NBC
125	Foxfire	19.3/30	CBS
126	Letter To Three Wives, A	19.3/30	NBC
127	Perry Mason: The Case Of The Killer Kiss	19.3/29	NBC
128	Unnatural Causes	19.3/31	NBC
129	After The Promise	19.2/30	CBS
130	Blind Justice	19.2/29	CBS
131	Christmas Comes To Willow Creek	19.2/30	CBS
132	Deadly Deception	19.2/30	CBS
133	Stepford Children, The	19.2/29	NBC
134	Amy Fisher: My Story	19.1/30	NBC
135	Can You Feel Me Dancing?	19.1/30	NBC
136	Hawaiian Heat	19.1/34	ABC
137	Little Girl Lost	19.0/31	ABC
138	Right To Kill?	19.0/31	ABC
139	Combat High	18.9/29	NBC
140	Defiant One, The	18.9/28	ABC
141	Laura Lansing Slept Here	18.9/30	NBC
142	Murder, She Wrote	18.9/29	CBS
143	Nightingales	18.9/33	NBC
144	O Pioneers	18.9/29	CBS
145	In The Line Of Duty: Ambush In Waco	18.8/30	NBC

ALL NETWORK MOVIES — 1984-1994 (CONTINUED)

146 Man Upstairs, The .... 18.8/28 .... CBS
147 Stranger In My Bed .... 18.8/29 .... NBC
148 Victims For Victims - The Theresa Saldana Story ...... 18.8/28 .... NBC
149 Ewoks: The Battle For Endor .... 18.7/26 .... ABC
150 False Witness .... 18.7/29 .... NBC
151 In The Heat Of The Night .... 18.7/30 .... NBC
152 Incident In A Small Town .... 18.7/31 .... CBS
153 Deadly Care .... 18.6/31 .... CBS
154 Gypsy .... 18.6/28 .... CBS
155 High Price Of Passion, The .... 18.6/29 .... NBC
156 Home Fires Burning .... 18.6/29 .... CBS
157 Dirty Dozen: The Deadly Mission .... 18.5/28 .... NBC
158 Heartsounds .... 18.5/31 .... ABC
159 Kojak: The Belarus File .... 18.5/31 .... CBS
160 Lady Forgets, The .... 18.5/34 .... CBS
161 Lies Before Kisses .... 18.5/29 .... CBS
162 Body Of Evidence .... 18.4/28 .... CBS
163 Danielle Steel's Palomino .... 18.4/28 .... NBC
164 Do You Know The Muffin Man? .... 18.4/30 .... CBS
165 Easy Prey .... 18.4/29 .... ABC
166 Gathering Of Old Men, A .... 18.4/31 .... CBS
167 L B J: The Early Years .... 18.4/27 .... NBC
168 Paper Dolls .... 18.4/29 .... ABC
169 Red River .... 18.4/29 .... CBS
170 Who Is Julia? .... 18.4/29 .... CBS
171 Malice In Wonderland .... 18.3/29 .... CBS
172 Moonlighting .... 18.3/28 .... ABC
173 Stoning In Fulham County, A .... 18.3/28 .... NBC
174 Vanishing Act .... 18.3/27 .... CBS
175 Wet Gold .... 18.3/30 .... ABC
176 Call Of The Wild .... 18.2/29 .... CBS
177 Dr. Quinn, Medicine Woman .... 18.2/29 .... CBS
178 Father Of Hell Town .... 18.2/29 .... NBC
179 Little House On The Prairie -
     Bless All The Dear Children .... 18.2/27 .... NBC
180 Pack Of Lies .... 18.2/30 .... CBS
181 Snowbound: The Jim And Jennifer Stolpa Story ...... 18.2/27 .... CBS
182 Something In Common .... 18.2/29 .... CBS
183 Addicted To His Love .... 18.1/29 .... ABC
184 Choices .... 18.1/27 .... ABC
185 Kids Don't Tell .... 18.1/29 .... CBS
186 Perry Mason: The Case Of The Murdered Madam .... 18.1/29 .... NBC
187 Surviving .... 18.1/26 .... ABC
188 Alfred Hitchcock Presents .... 18.0/28 .... NBC
189 Aurora .... 18.0/28 .... NBC
190 China Beach .... 18.0/29 .... ABC
191 Cover Girl And The Cop, The .... 18.0/28 .... NBC
192 Danielle Steel's Fine Things .... 18.0/28 .... NBC
193 Dead Before Dawn .... 18.0/26 .... ABC
194 Inherit The Wind .... 18.0/29 .... NBC
195 Wild Texas Wind .... 18.0/27 .... NBC
196 Cast The First Stone .... 17.9/28 .... NBC
197 Deadly Silence, A .... 17.9/28 .... ABC
198 Decoration Day .... 17.9/28 .... NBC
199 I'll Be Home For Christmas .... 17.9/28 .... NBC
200 Izzy And Moe .... 17.9/27 .... CBS
201 Street Hawk .... 17.9/26 .... ABC
202 Two Fathers' Justice .... 17.9/27 .... NBC
203 Danielle Steel's Changes .... 17.8/28 .... NBC
204 Love Lives On .... 17.8/26 .... ABC
205 Pair Of Aces .... 17.8/28 .... CBS
206 Seaquest Dsv .... 17.8/28 .... NBC
207 There Are No Children Here .... 17.8/26 .... ABC
208 This Can't Be Love .... 17.8/28 .... CBS
209 Without Her Consent .... 17.8/28 .... NBC
210 Absolute Strangers .... 17.7/29 .... CBS
211 Christy .... 17.7/29 .... CBS
212 God Bless The Child .... 17.7/28 .... ABC
213 Jessie .... 17.7/29 .... ABC
214 Murders In The Rue Morgue, The .... 17.7/27 .... CBS
215 Alone In The Neon Jungle .... 17.6/28 .... CBS
216 Bionic Showdown: The 6 Million Dollar Man/
     Bionic Woman .... 17.6/28 .... NBC
217 Bonanza: The Return .... 17.6/26 .... NBC
218 Fall From Grace .... 17.6/27 .... NBC
219 Out Of The Darkness .... 17.6/30 .... CBS
220 Beverly Hills Madam .... 17.5/27 .... NBC
221 Mistress .... 17.5/29 .... CBS
222 My Two Loves .... 17.5/28 .... ABC
223 Poker Alice .... 17.5/32 .... CBS
224 Prince Of Bel Air .... 17.5/27 .... ABC
225 Right To Die .... 17.5/28 .... NBC
226 Secrets Of A Married Man .... 17.5/27 .... NBC
227 Substitute Wife, The .... 17.5/27 .... NBC
228 Woman With A Past .... 17.5/27 .... NBC
229 Convicted .... 17.4/27 .... ABC
230 Convicted: A Mother's Story .... 17.4/27 .... NBC
231 Frank Nitti: The Enforcer .... 17.4/28 .... ABC
232 Perry Mason: The Case Of The Avenging Ace ...... 17.4/26 .... NBC
233 Perry Mason: The Case Of The Musical Murders .... 17.4/26 .... NBC
234 She Knows Too Much .... 17.4/27 .... NBC
235 Thompson's Last Run .... 17.4/26 .... CBS
236 Aftermath: A Test Of Love .... 17.3/27 .... CBS
237 Bunny's Tale, A .... 17.3/26 .... ABC
238 C. A. T. Squad .... 17.3/30 .... NBC
239 Love Is Never Silent .... 17.3/26 .... NBC
240 People Across The Lake, The .... 17.3/27 .... NBC
241 Police Story: The Freeway Killings .... 17.3/27 .... NBC
242 Rio Diablo .... 17.3/26 .... CBS
243 Roxanne: The Prize Pulitzer .... 17.3/27 .... NBC
244 Swimsuit .... 17.3/27 .... NBC
245 Unconquered .... 17.3/28 .... CBS
246 Crime Of Innocence .... 17.2/26 .... NBC
247 Cry In The Wild: The Taking Of Peggy Ann .... 17.2/27 .... NBC
248 Maybe Baby .... 17.2/26 .... NBC
249 Moving Target .... 17.2/25 .... NBC
250 Under Siege .... 17.2/24 .... NBC
251 When He's Not A Stranger .... 17.2/26 .... CBS
252 Without A Kiss Goodbye .... 17.2/29 .... CBS
253 Baywatch: Panic At Malibu Pier .... 17.1/28 .... NBC
254 Cartier Affair, The .... 17.1/27 .... NBC
255 Crash Landing: The Rescue Of Flight 232 ...... 17.1/26 .... ABC
256 Daddy .... 17.1/25 .... ABC
257 Double Edge .... 17.1/28 .... CBS
258 Murder In Black And White .... 17.1/27 .... CBS
259 Time To Live, A .... 17.1/27 .... NBC
260 Disappearance Of Nora .... 17.0/27 .... CBS
261 Do You Remember Love? .... 17.0/28 .... CBS
262 From The Files Of Joseph Wambaugh:
     A Jury Of One .... 17.0/17 .... NBC
263 Mom For Christmas, A .... 17.0/27 .... NBC
264 Perry Mason: The Case Of The Desperate Deception . 17.0/27 .... NBC
265 Roe Vs. Wade .... 17.0/27 .... NBC
266 Roman Holiday .... 17.0/28 .... ABC
267 Touch Of Scandal, A .... 17.0/27 .... CBS
268 Your Mother Wears Combat Boots .... 17.0/28 .... NBC
269 Broken Angel .... 16.9/28 .... ABC
270 Her Wicked Ways .... 16.9/26 .... NBC
271 Little White Lies .... 16.9/26 .... NBC
272 Playing With Fire .... 16.9/26 .... NBC
273 Terror On Highway 91 .... 16.9/26 .... CBS
274 To Grandmother's House We Go .... 16.9/25 .... ABC
275 Bed Of Lies .... 16.8/25 .... ABC
276 Danielle Steel's Heartbeat .... 16.8/26 .... NBC
277 Doing Life .... 16.8/27 .... NBC
278 Face Of A Stranger .... 16.8/27 .... CBS
279 Infidelity .... 16.8/27 .... ABC
280 Liberace .... 16.8/27 .... ABC
281 Mrs. 'Arris Goes To Paris .... 16.8/28 .... CBS
282 Original Sin .... 16.8/26 .... NBC
283 Perry Mason: The Case Of The All-Star Assassin ...... 16.8/26 .... NBC
284 Picking Up The Pieces .... 16.8/25 .... CBS
285 Runaway Father .... 16.8/27 .... CBS
286 Settle The Score .... 16.8/26 .... NBC
287 Shattered Dreams .... 16.8/28 .... CBS

Movies are listed by descending rating. Miniseries are listed by descending average of ratings. Cable movies are not listed as they are not rated.

ALL NETWORK MOVIES — 1984-1994 (CONTINUED)

288	Ted Kennedy, Jr., Story, The	16.8/26	NBC
289	Bride In Black, The	16.7/27	ABC
290	Christmas On Division Street	16.7/26	CBS
291	Father Clements Story, The	16.7/26	NBC
292	Goddess Of Love	16.7/26	NBC
293	Haunted By Her Past	16.7/27	NBC
294	In Love And War	16.7/27	NBC
295	Killer Among Friends, A	16.7/27	CBS
296	Mother's Justice, A	16.7/25	NBC
297	Scorned And Swindled	16.7/26	CBS
298	Secret Garden, The	16.7/26	CBS
299	Vital Signs	16.7/26	CBS
300	Wild Horses	16.7/26	CBS
301	Anna Karenina	16.6/26	CBS
302	Comeback, The	16.6/29	CBS
303	Deliver Them From Evil: The Taking Of Alta View	16.6/26	CBS
304	Gunsmoke: Return To Dodge	16.6/31	CBS
305	Ladykillers	16.6/27	ABC
306	Liberace: Behind The Music	16.6/26	CBS
307	Murder: By Reason Of Insanity	16.6/26	CBS
308	Perry Mason: The Case Of The Scandalous Scoundrel	16.6/26	NBC
309	Ryan White Story, The	16.6/26	ABC
310	What She Doesn't Know	16.6/25	NBC
311	Winnie	16.6/28	NBC
312	Young Indiana Jones Chronicles: The Curse Of The Jackal	16.6/26	ABC
313	Anything To Survive	16.5/26	ABC
314	Burning Rage	16.5/30	CBS
315	Columbo: No Time To Die	16.5/27	ABC
316	Final Jeopardy, The	16.5/26	NBC
317	Fulfillment Of Mary Gray, The	16.5/26	CBS
318	Kids Like These	16.5/27	CBS
319	Miles To Go . . .	16.5/26	CBS
320	Perry Mason: The Case Of The Silenced Singer	16.5/27	NBC
321	Son's Promise, A	16.5/27	ABC
322	Walker, Texas Ranger	16.5/27	CBS
323	American Harvest	16.4/27	CBS
324	Corpse Had A Familiar Face, The	16.4/26	CBS
325	Dangerous Affection	16.4/26	NBC
326	Lucy & Desi: Before The Laughter	16.4/25	CBS
327	Shattered Spirits	16.4/25	ABC
328	Six Against The Rock	16.4/24	NBC
329	Baby Snatcher	16.3/26	CBS
330	Blind Witness	16.3/25	ABC
331	David's Mother	16.3/26	CBS
332	In Sickness And In Health	16.3/26	CBS
333	Night Walk	16.3/27	CBS
334	Taken Away	16.3/25	CBS
335	Battling For Baby	16.2/26	CBS
336	Between Two Women	16.2/25	ABC
337	Fight For Life	16.2/26	ABC
338	Full Exposure: The Sex Tapes Scandal	16.2/24	NBC
339	Hearst And Davies Affair, The	16.2/24	ABC
340	Shattered Trust: The Shari Karney Story	16.2/25	NBC
341	Something To Live For: The Alison Gertz Story	16.2/26	ABC
342	Trial Of The Incredible Hulk, The	16.2/25	NBC
343	Downpayment On Murder	16.1/27	NBC
344	I Can Make You Love Me: The Stalking Of Laura Black	16.1/26	CBS
345	Knight Rider 2000	16.1/26	NBC
346	Love And Betrayal	16.1/25	CBS
347	My Boyfriend's Back	16.1/26	NBC
348	Oceans Of Fire	16.1/27	CBS
349	Sworn To Silence	16.1/24	ABC
350	That Secret Sunday	16.1/26	CBS
351	Two Thousand Malibu Road	16.1/28	CBS
352	Us	16.1/29	CBS
353	Against Her Will: An Incident In Baltimore	16.0/25	CBS
354	Bump In The Night	16.0/25	CBS
355	Freedom Fighter	16.0/25	NBC
356	Highway Heartbreaker	16.0/25	CBS
357	In The Best Interest Of The Children	16.0/24	NBC
358	Lady From Yesterday, The	16.0/25	CBS
359	Perry Mason: The Case Of The Poisoned Pen	16.0/24	NBC
360	Return Of Desperado, The	16.0/24	NBC
361	Secret Sins Of The Father	16.0/24	NBC
362	Shootdown	16.0/25	NBC
363	Time To Triumph, A	16.0/25	CBS
364	Adam: His Song Continues	15.9/25	NBC
365	Brand New Life: The Honeymoon	15.9/25	NBC
366	Call Me Anna	15.9/24	ABC
367	Danger Of Love, The	15.9/26	CBS
368	Danielle Steel's Star	15.9/24	NBC
369	Gladiator, The	15.9/24	ABC
370	Glitter	15.9/27	ABC
371	Last Fling, The	15.9/23	ABC
372	Moment Of Truth: Stalking Back	15.9/25	NBC
373	Murder In New Hampshire: The Pamela Smart Story	15.9/26	CBS
374	Stone Fox	15.9/22	NBC
375	Story Lady, The	15.9/24	NBC
376	Agatha Christie's The Man In The Brown Suit	15.8/25	CBS
377	Child Saver, The	15.8/25	NBC
378	Dance Till Dawn	15.8/26	ABC
379	Deadly Medicine	15.8/24	NBC
380	Family For Joe, A	15.8/23	NBC
381	Fatal Memories	15.8/24	NBC
382	Hitler's S S: Portrait In Evil	15.8/24	NBC
383	In My Daughter's Name	15.8/27	CBS
384	Jake And The Fatman	15.8/27	CBS
385	Judgment Day: The John List Story	15.8/25	CBS
386	Killing In A Small Town	15.8/26	CBS
387	Penalty Phase	15.8/26	CBS
388	Popeye Doyle	15.8/26	NBC
389	Taking Back My Life: The Nancy Ziegenmeyer Story	15.8/25	CBS
390	Alamo: 13 Days To Glory, The	15.7/22	NBC
391	Circle Of Violence: A Family Drama	15.7/25	CBS
392	Guilty Of Innocence: The Lenell Geter Story	15.7/25	CBS
393	Into Thin Air	15.7/25	CBS
394	Leona Helmsley: The Queen Of Mean	15.7/26	CBS
395	Outback Bound	15.7/25	CBS
396	P. S. I Luv U	15.7/25	CBS
397	Rock Hudson	15.7/24	ABC
398	Shell Seekers, The	15.7/24	ABC
399	Triumph Over Disaster: The Hurricane Andrew Story	15.7/25	NBC
400	Unspeakable Acts	15.7/25	ABC
401	Danielle Steel's Secrets	15.6/24	NBC
402	Deception: A Mother's Secret	15.6/23	NBC
403	Joshua's Heart	15.6/26	NBC
404	Mission Of The Shark	15.6/25	CBS
405	My Son Johnny	15.6/24	CBS
406	Reason To Live, A	15.6/23	NBC
407	Romance On The Orient Express	15.6/24	NBC
408	Stranger Within, The	15.6/25	CBS
409	Survive The Savage Sea	15.6/24	ABC
410	Town Bully, The	15.6/25	ABC
411	Ultimate Betrayal	15.6/25	CBS
412	Wife, Mother, Murderer	15.6/24	ABC
413	Woman On The Ledge	15.6/24	NBC
414	Deep Dark Secrets	15.5/25	NBC
415	Fatal Confession: A Father Dowling Mystery	15.5/24	NBC
416	George Mckenna Story, The	15.5/24	CBS
417	Gifted One, The	15.5/27	NBC
418	Honor Thy Mother	15.5/24	CBS
419	House Of Secrets And Lies, A	15.5/27	CBS
420	Just My Imagination	15.5/19	NBC
421	Message From Holly	15.5/24	CBS
422	Sadie And Son	15.5/25	CBS
423	Seduced	15.5/25	CBS
424	Agatha Christie's Murder In Three Acts	15.4/25	CBS
425	Child Lost Forever, A	15.4/23	NBC
426	Dying To Love You	15.4/25	CBS
427	Fatal Judgment	15.4/24	CBS
428	I'll Fly Away	15.4/24	NBC

Movies are listed by descending rating. Miniseries are listed by descending average of ratings. Cable movies are not listed as they are not rated.

ALL NETWORK MOVIES — 1984-1994 (CONTINUED)

429	Love On The Run	15.4/23	NBC
430	Manhunt: Search For The Night Stalker	15.4/24	NBC
431	Our Family Honor	15.4/25	ABC
432	Overkill: The Aileen Wuornos Story	15.4/25	CBS
433	Place To Call Home, A	15.4/26	CBS
434	Roots: The Gift	15.4/24	ABC
435	Streets Of Justice	15.4/22	NBC
436	Terror On Track 9	15.4/25	CBS
437	This Wife For Hire	15.4/24	ABC
438	Under The Influence	15.4/24	CBS
439	Whereabouts Of Jenny, The	15.4/24	ABC
440	Always Remember I Love You	15.3/26	CBS
441	Eight Is Enough Wedding, An	15.3/25	NBC
442	Hazard Of Hearts, A	15.3/26	CBS
443	Nasty Boys	15.3/27	NBC
444	Shadow Of A Doubt	15.3/24	CBS
445	Sworn To Vengeance	15.3/25	CBS
446	Viper	15.3/23	NBC
447	Where Pigeons Go To Die	15.3/24	NBC
448	April Morning	15.2/24	CBS
449	Camille	15.2/25	CBS
450	Day One	15.2/24	CBS
451	Empty Cradle	15.2/24	ABC
452	Hell Hath No Fury	15.2/24	NBC
453	Las Vegas Strip Wars, The	15.2/22	NBC
454	Murder With Mirrors	15.2/23	CBS
455	My Name Is Bill W.	15.2/24	ABC
456	Obsessive Love	15.2/25	CBS
457	Preppie Murder, The	15.2/24	ABC
458	Shattered Innocence	15.2/25	CBS
459	Diamond Trap, The	15.1/24	CBS
460	Dream Date	15.1/24	NBC
461	Family Tom Apart, A	15.1/23	NBC
462	Last Days Of Frank And Jesse James, The	15.1/22	NBC
463	Letting Go	15.1/28	ABC
464	Marla Hanson Story, The	15.1/24	NBC
465	Miracle Landing	15.1/23	CBS
466	Not In My Family	15.1/23	ABC
467	Red Spider, The	15.1/25	CBS
468	Shadow Of A Stranger	15.1/24	NBC
469	Trapped In Silence	15.1/24	CBS
470	Unholy Matrimony	15.1/24	CBS
471	Warm Hearts, Cold Feet	15.1/22	CBS
472	Baby Of The Bride	15.0/26	CBS
473	Backfield In Motion	15.0/24	ABC
474	Bring Me The Head Of Dobie Gillis	15.0/23	CBS
475	Going To The Chapel	15.0/25	NBC
476	In The Company Of Darkness	15.0/24	CBS
477	Lies Of The Heart: The Story Of Laurie Kellogg	15.0/23	ABC
478	Murderous Affair, A: The Carolyn Warmus Story	15.0/25	ABC
479	Necessity	15.0/24	CBS
480	Shakedown On The Sunset Strip	15.0/27	CBS
481	She Says She's Innocent	15.0/25	NBC
482	Sins Of The Father	15.0/23	NBC
483	Supercarrier	15.0/23	ABC
484	Armed & Innocent	14.9/24	CBS
485	Bonds Of Love	14.9/23	CBS
486	City Killer	14.9/24	NBC
487	Columbo Goes To College	14.9/24	ABC
488	Daughter Of The Streets	14.9/24	ABC
489	Go Toward The Light	14.9/24	CBS
490	Good Night, Sweet Wife: A Murder In Boston	14.9/23	CBS
491	Her Final Fury: Betty Broderick, The Last Chapter	14.9/22	CBS
492	Howard Beach: Making The Case For Murder	14.9/24	NBC
493	Old Man & The Sea, The	14.9/24	NBC
494	Private Sessions	14.9/23	NBC
495	Quantum Leap	14.9/25	NBC
496	Quiet Victory: The Charlie Wedemeyer Story	14.9/25	CBS
497	Weekend War	14.9/24	ABC
498	Chance Of A Lifetime	14.8/22	NBC
499	Children In The Crossfire	14.8/23	NBC
500	Club Med	14.8/23	ABC
501	Complex Of Fear	14.8/23	CBS
502	Cosby Mysteries, The	14.8/22	NBC
503	Donato And Daughter	14.8/24	CBS
504	Donor	14.8/24	CBS
505	Fire In The Dark	14.8/23	CBS
506	Place For Annie, A	14.8/23	ABC
507	Rich Men, Single Women	14.8/23	ABC
508	She Was Marked For Murder	14.8/24	NBC
509	Carolina Skeletons	14.7/23	NBC
510	Child Of Rage	14.7/24	CBS
511	Cracked Up	14.7/23	ABC
512	Face To Face	14.7/24	CBS
513	Fifth Missile, The	14.7/22	NBC
514	Follow Your Heart	14.7/23	NBC
515	Grave Secrets: The Legacy Of Hilltop Drive	14.7/23	CBS
516	In The Line Of Duty: Manhunt In The Dakotas	14.7/26	NBC
517	Perry Mason: The Case Of The Defiant Daughter	14.7/24	NBC
518	Perry Mason: The Case Of The Reckless Romeo	14.7/23	NBC
519	Peter Gunn	14.7/24	ABC
520	She Said No	14.7/23	NBC
521	Stillwatch	14.7/23	CBS
522	Whisper Kills, A	14.7/23	ABC
523	With A Vengeance	14.7/23	CBS
524	Bates Motel	14.6/27	NBC
525	Bridesmaids	14.6/25	CBS
526	Chase, The	14.6/23	NBC
527	Death Of The Incredible Hulk, The	14.6/22	NBC
528	Diagnosis Of Murder	14.6/23	CBS
529	Father & Son: Dangerous Relations	14.6/24	NBC
530	House Of Secrets	14.6/23	NBC
531	In The Deep Woods	14.6/23	NBC
532	In The Line Of Duty: A Cop For The Killing	14.6/23	NBC
533	Out On The Edge	14.6/23	CBS
534	Perry Mason: The Case Of The Fatal Fashion	14.6/23	NBC
535	Precious Victims	14.6/23	CBS
536	Single Women, Married Men	14.6/26	CBS
537	Till Death Us Do Part	14.6/21	NBC
538	When You Remember Me	14.6/24	ABC
539	Winner Never Quits, A	14.6/24	ABC
540	Behind Enemy Lines	14.5/23	NBC
541	Death Of A Salesman	14.5/23	CBS
542	Dillinger	14.5/22	ABC
543	Don't Touch My Daughter	14.5/23	NBC
544	Independence	14.5/23	NBC
545	Liar, Liar	14.5/26	CBS
546	Murder Of Innocence	14.5/22	CBS
547	Nightmare In The Daylight	14.5/23	CBS
548	Obsessed With A Married Woman	14.5/22	ABC
549	Poisoned By Love: The Kern County Murders	14.5/24	CBS
550	Revealing Evidence	14.5/25	NBC
551	Right Of The People, The	14.5/22	ABC
552	Secret Life Of Kathy Mccormick, The	14.5/26	NBC
553	Shannon's Deal	14.5/25	NBC
554	Sins Of The Mother	14.5/23	CBS
555	They've Taken Our Children: The Chowchilla Kidnapping	14.5/23	ABC
556	Thicker Than Blood: The Larry Mclinden Story	14.5/23	CBS
557	Too Young To Die?	14.5/23	NBC
558	Woman He Loved, The	14.5/25	CBS
559	Agatha Christie's Dead Man's Folly	14.4/22	CBS
560	Beyond Suspicion	14.4/22	NBC
561	Detective In The House	14.4/24	CBS
562	First Steps	14.4/24	CBS
563	Ghost Of A Chance	14.4/24	CBS
564	In The Shadows, Someone Is Watching	14.4/22	NBC
565	Manhunt For Claude Dallas	14.4/24	CBS
566	Overexposed	14.4/23	ABC
567	Rape Of Dr. Willis, The	14.4/23	CBS
568	Return Of Sherlock Holmes, The	14.4/24	CBS
569	Willing To Kill: The Texas Cheerleader Story	14.4/22	ABC
570	Broken Cord, The	14.3/22	ABC
571	Casualties Of Love: The Long Island Lolita Story	14.3/22	CBS
572	Dirty Dozen: The Fatal Mission	14.3/22	NBC
573	Eye On The Sparrow	14.3/22	NBC

Movies are listed by descending rating. Miniseries are listed by descending average of ratings. Cable movies are not listed as they are not rated.

ALL NETWORK MOVIES — 1984-1994 (CONTINUED)

574	Outside Woman, The	14.3/22	CBS
575	Promise To Keep, A	14.3/23	NBC
576	Between Love And Hate	14.2/21	ABC
577	Columbo: Death Hits The Jackpot	14.2/22	ABC
578	Eighty-Three Hours 'til Dawn	14.2/22	CBS
579	Flash, The	14.2/23	CBS
580	Gunsmoke I I I: To The Last Man	14.2/24	CBS
581	He's Fired, She's Hired	14.2/23	CBS
582	Impostor, The	14.2/22	ABC
583	In The Eyes Of A Stranger	14.2/23	CBS
584	Intimate Encounters	14.2/23	NBC
585	Keeping Secrets	14.2/23	ABC
586	Misfits Of Science	14.2/23	NBC
587	Moment Of Truth: A Child Too Many	14.2/22	NBC
588	Moment Of Truth: Why My Daughter?	14.2/23	NBC
589	Night They Saved Christmas, The	14.2/22	ABC
590	Probe	14.2/22	ABC
591	Wolf	14.2/25	CBS
592	Annihilator, The	14.1/23	NBC
593	Assassin	14.1/23	CBS
594	Barnum	14.1/25	CBS
595	Broken Vows	14.1/22	CBS
596	Columbo: Undercover	14.1/22	ABC
597	Conspiracy Of Love	14.1/21	CBS
598	Fatal Image, The	14.1/22	CBS
599	Glitz	14.1/25	NBC
600	Hot Paint	14.1/22	CBS
601	In Defense Of A Married Man	14.1/23	ABC
602	Labor Of Love: The Arlette Schweitzer Story	14.1/23	CBS
603	Room Upstairs, The	14.1/24	CBS
604	Scattered Dreams: The Kathryn Messenger Story	14.1/22	CBS
605	She Woke Up	14.1/22	ABC
606	Stark	14.1/23	CBS
607	Three On A Match	14.1/26	NBC
608	Babymaker: The Dr. Cecil Jacobson's Story	14.0/21	CBS
609	Casey's Gift: For Love Of A Child	14.0/22	NBC
610	Cover Up	14.0/26	CBS
611	Cries Unheard: The Donna Yaklich Story	14.0/22	CBS
612	Face Of Fear, The	14.0/23	CBS
613	Fugitive Among Us	14.0/23	CBS
614	In The Arms Of A Killer	14.0/22	NBC
615	Matlock: The Witness Killings	14.0/26	NBC
616	Nightmare In Columbia County	14.0/22	CBS
617	Ordeal In The Arctic	14.0/22	ABC
618	Perry Mason: The Case Of The Maligned Mobster	14.0/22	NBC
619	Perry Mason: The Case Of The Ruthless Reporter	14.0/21	NBC
620	Sentimental Journey	14.0/23	CBS
621	Sin And Redemption	14.0/23	CBS
622	Spenser: For Hire	14.0/24	ABC
623	True Blue	14.0/22	NBC
624	Bridge To Silence	13.9/24	CBS
625	Daughters Of Privilege	13.9/23	NBC
626	Killer Among Us, A	13.9/23	NBC
627	Revenge Of Al Capone, The	13.9/22	NBC
628	Seduction In Travis County	13.9/22	CBS
629	Bay Coven	13.8/22	NBC
630	Jonathan: The Boy Nobody Wanted	13.8/21	NBC
631	Little Piece Of Heaven, A	13.8/21	NBC
632	Mirrors	13.8/22	NBC
633	Other Lover, The	13.8/22	CBS
634	Out Of Time	13.8/25	NBC
635	Secret Weapons	13.8/21	NBC
636	Summer To Remember, A	13.8/21	CBS
637	There Was A Little Boy	13.8/22	CBS
638	Thunderboat Row	13.8/23	ABC
639	To My Daughter With Love	13.8/21	NBC
640	Turn Back The Clock	13.8/22	NBC
641	Women Of Windsor	13.8/22	CBS
642	Bridge Across Time	13.7/21	NBC
643	Get Smart Again	13.7/21	ABC
644	Her Secret Life	13.7/21	ABC
645	I Love You Perfect	13.7/23	ABC
646	In Broad Daylight	13.7/21	NBC
647	My First Love	13.7/21	ABC
648	Nazi Hunter: The Beate Klarsfeld Story	13.7/21	ABC
649	Night Of The Hunter	13.7/23	ABC
650	Sharing Richard	13.7/22	CBS
651	Sparks: The Price Of Passion	13.7/21	CBS
652	Special Friendship, A	13.7/22	CBS
653	Badge Of The Assassin	13.6/23	CBS
654	Beyond Obsession	13.6/21	ABC
655	Burning Bridges	13.6/22	ABC
656	Children Of The Bride	13.6/25	CBS
657	Fergie And Andrew: Behind The Palace Doors	13.6/21	NBC
658	Love Boat: A Valentine Voyage, The	13.6/22	CBS
659	Maid For Each Other	13.6/21	NBC
660	Mothers' Right, A: The Elizabeth Morgan Story	13.6/21	ABC
661	Second Serve	13.6/22	CBS
662	Babies	13.5/22	NBC
663	Brotherly Love	13.5/22	CBS
664	Marcus Welby, M. D.: A Holiday Affair	13.5/21	NBC
665	Moment Of Truth: Cradle Of Conspiracy	13.5/21	NBC
666	My Father, My Son	13.5/22	CBS
667	One Of Her Own	13.5/21	ABC
668	Three Wishes Of Billy Grier, The	13.5/21	ABC
669	To My Daughter	13.5/22	NBC
670	Babes In Toyland	13.4/22	NBC
671	Blood River	13.4/23	CBS
672	Blue Deville	13.4/22	NBC
673	Bluffing It	13.4/22	ABC
674	Charley Hannah	13.4/23	ABC
675	Children Of The Dark	13.4/22	CBS
676	Columbo: It's All In The Game	13.4/21	ABC
677	I Married A Centerfold	13.4/22	NBC
678	If It's Tuesday, It Still Must Be Belgium	13.4/22	NBC
679	John And Yoko: A Love Story	13.4/19	NBC
680	Lena: My 100 Children	13.4/21	NBC
681	Money, Power, Murder	13.4/22	CBS
682	On Thin Ice: The Tai Babilonia Story	13.4/21	NBC
683	One Against The Wind	13.4/21	CBS
684	Penthouse, The	13.4/22	ABC
685	Secret Life Of Archie's Wife, The	13.4/22	CBS
686	Babycakes	13.3/22	CBS
687	Bare Essentials	13.3/21	CBS
688	Black Widow Murders: The Blanche Taylor Moore Story	13.3/21	NBC
689	Danger Down Under	13.3/22	NBC
690	Desperate Rescue: The Cathy Mahone Story	13.3/20	NBC
691	Higher Ground	13.3/25	CBS
692	Johnnie Mae Gibson: F B I	13.3/20	CBS
693	Lady In A Corner	13.3/21	NBC
694	Miracle On I-880	13.3/20	NBC
695	Miss America: Behind The Crown	13.3/20	NBC
696	News At Eleven	13.3/22	CBS
697	No Place Like Home	13.3/20	CBS
698	Perfect People	13.3/21	ABC
699	Perry Mason: The Case Of The Skin-Deep Scandal	13.3/22	NBC
700	Secret, The	13.3/23	CBS
701	Tenth Man, The	13.3/21	CBS
702	Terrorist On Trial: The United States Vs. Salim Ajami	13.3/20	CBS
703	With Murder In Mind	13.3/21	CBS
704	Baby Girl Scott	13.2/23	CBS
705	Back To The Streets Of San Francisco	13.2/20	NBC
706	Conviction Of Kitty Dodds, The	13.2/21	CBS
707	Drop-Out Mother	13.2/22	CBS
708	Girl Who Came Between Them, The	13.2/21	NBC
709	In The Line Of Duty: Standoff At Marion	13.2/20	NBC
710	Kicks	13.2/21	ABC
711	Love Among Thieves	13.2/21	ABC
712	Nurses On The Line: The Crash Of Flight 7	13.2/22	CBS
713	Promised A Miracle	13.2/22	CBS
714	Shameful Secrets	13.2/21	ABC
715	Yearling, The	13.2/21	CBS
716	Angel In Green	13.1/22	CBS
717	Blind Spot	13.1/20	CBS

ALL NETWORK MOVIES — 1984-1994 (CONTINUED)

#	Title	Rating	Network
718	Darkness Before Dawn	13.1/20	NBC
719	Desperado: Badlands Justice	13.1/21	NBC
720	Forget Me Not Murders, The	13.1/21	CBS
721	Hart To Hart Returns	13.1/23	NBC
722	Highwayman, The	13.1/22	NBC
723	I'll Take Romance	13.1/21	ABC
724	Journey To The Center Of The Earth	13.1/20	NBC
725	Nightmare At Bitter Creek	13.1/22	CBS
726	No Child Of Mine	13.1/21	CBS
727	One Special Victory	13.1/20	NBC
728	Perry Mason: The Case Of The Telltale Talk Show Host	13.1/24	NBC
729	Stormin' Home	13.1/23	CBS
730	Tears And Laughter: The Joan And Mielissa Rivers Story	13.1/21	NBC
731	Betrayal Of Trust	13.0/20	NBC
732	Case Closed	13.0/22	CBS
733	Eyes Of A Witness	13.0/23	CBS
734	International Airport	13.0/27	ABC
735	Lost In London	13.0/19	CBS
736	Place To Be Loved, A	13.0/20	CBS
737	Sweet Bird Of Youth	13.0/21	NBC
738	Victim Of Love: The Shannon Mohr Story	13.0/19	NBC
739	Bad Seed, The	12.9/19	ABC
740	Beverly Hills Cowgirl Blues	12.9/22	CBS
741	Bradys, The	12.9/22	CBS
742	Brass	12.9/22	CBS
743	Captive	12.9/20	ABC
744	Deadbolt	12.9/23	CBS
745	Deadly Betrayal: The Bruce Curtis Story	12.9/20	NBC
746	Evil In Clear River	12.9/20	ABC
747	Family Sins	12.9/20	CBS
748	In The Nick Of Time	12.9/20	NBC
749	Jailbirds	12.9/22	CBS
750	Murder Between Friends	12.9/20	NBC
751	One More Mountain	12.9/20	ABC
752	Perry Mason: The Case Of The Fatal Framing	12.9/20	NBC
753	Pleasures	12.9/20	ABC
754	Return Of Sam Mccloud, The	12.9/20	CBS
755	Seasons Of The Heart	12.9/21	NBC
756	When No One Would Listen	12.9/19	CBS
757	With Hostile Intent	12.9/21	CBS
758	Agatha Christie's Thirteen At Dinner	12.8/21	CBS
759	Blue Bayou	12.8/20	NBC
760	Breaking The Silence	12.8/20	CBS
761	C. A. T. Squad: Python Wolf	12.8/20	NBC
762	Challenger	12.8/20	ABC
763	Charles And Diana: Unhappily Ever After	12.8/19	ABC
764	Deadly Intentions... Again?	12.8/20	ABC
765	For The Love Of My Child: The Anissa Ayala Story	12.8/20	NBC
766	Mickey Spillane's Mike Hammer: Murder Takes All	12.8/20	CBS
767	On Fire	12.8/20	ABC
768	Our Sons	12.8/21	ABC
769	Perry Mason: The Case Of The Glass Coffin	12.8/22	NBC
770	Relentless: Mind Of A Killer	12.8/20	NBC
771	Revenge On The Highway	12.8/19	NBC
772	Through The Eyes Of A Killer	12.8/21	CBS
773	Timestalkers	12.8/21	CBS
774	Town Torn Apart, A	12.8/20	NBC
775	When Dreams Come True	12.8/21	ABC
776	American Story, An	12.7/20	CBS
777	Crash: The Mystery Of Flight 1501	12.7/20	NBC
778	Final Appeal	12.7/20	NBC
779	Hijacking Of The Achille Lauro, The	12.7/20	NBC
780	Johnny Bull	12.7/20	ABC
781	Opposites Attract	12.7/21	NBC
782	Picket Fences	12.7/24	CBS
783	Quiet Little Neighborhood, A Perfect Little Murder, A	12.7/21	NBC
784	Return Of Eliot Ness, The	12.7/19	NBC
785	Stranger In The Family, A	12.7/19	ABC
786	Terror In The Night	12.7/20	CBS
787	Time To Heal, A	12.7/21	NBC
788	Broken Promises: Taking Emily Back	12.6/22	CBS
789	Columbo And The Murder Of A Rock Star	12.6/19	ABC
790	Copacabana	12.6/20	CBS
791	Firefighter	12.6/20	CBS
792	Moment Of Truth: Broken Pledges	12.6/20	NBC
793	Murder In Paradise	12.6/21	NBC
794	Peyton Place: The Next Generation	12.6/20	NBC
795	Prime Target	12.6/23	NBC
796	Shoot First: A Cop's Vengeance	12.6/20	NBC
797	There Must Be A Pony	12.6/19	ABC
798	Toughest Man In The World, The	12.6/20	CBS
799	When Will I Be Loved?	12.6/19	NBC
800	Children Of Times Square	12.5/20	ABC
801	Courage	12.5/20	CBS
802	Father's Homecoming, A	12.5/23	NBC
803	Killer Instinct	12.5/19	NBC
804	Out Of The Darkness	12.5/19	ABC
805	Reason For Living: The Jill Ireland Story	12.5/21	NBC
806	Scene Of The Crime	12.5/21	NBC
807	Sin Of Innocence	12.5/21	CBS
808	Triumph Of The Heart: The Ricky Bell Story	12.5/22	CBS
809	Welcome Home, Bobby	12.5/21	CBS
810	Children Of The Night	12.4/21	CBS
811	Desperate Choices: To Save My Child	12.4/19	NBC
812	Fatal Friendship	12.4/19	NBC
813	For Love Or Money	12.4/20	CBS
814	For The Love Of Aaron	12.4/21	CBS
815	I Spy Returns	12.4/18	CBS
816	Locked Up: A Mother's Rage	12.4/20	CBS
817	Marked For Murder	12.4/20	NBC
818	Murder In Mississippi	12.4/20	NBC
819	Night Of Courage	12.4/19	ABC
820	One Woman's Courage	12.4/19	NBC
821	Over My Dead Body	12.4/23	CBS
822	River Of Rage: The Taking Of Maggie Keene	12.4/20	CBS
823	Side By Side	12.4/20	CBS
824	Silent Cries	12.4/20	NBC
825	Stones Of Ibarra	12.4/21	CBS
826	Deadly Business, A	12.3/21	CBS
827	Extreme Close-Up	12.3/20	NBC
828	I Still Dream Of Jeannie	12.3/19	NBC
829	Longarm	12.3/20	ABC
830	Miracle At Beekman's Place	12.3/21	NBC
831	Murder In High Places	12.3/22	NBC
832	One Police Plaza	12.3/22	CBS
833	White Hot: The Mysterious Murder Of Thelma Todd	12.3/20	NBC
834	Columbo: A Bird In The Hand	12.2/19	ABC
835	Equal Justice	12.2/23	ABC
836	Harmful Intent	12.2/20	CBS
837	Homefront	12.2/20	ABC
838	Jekyll & Hyde	12.2/19	ABC
839	Jonathan Stone: Threat Of Innocence	12.2/16	NBC
840	Mercy Mission: The Rescue Of Flight 771	12.2/19	NBC
841	Nairobi Affair	12.2/20	CBS
842	Spies, Lies And Naked Thighs	12.2/19	CBS
843	Stephen King's Golden Years	12.2/22	CBS
844	Trenchcoat In Paradise	12.2/20	CBS
845	Witness To The Execution	12.2/17	NBC
846	Yes, Virginia, There Is A Santa Claus	12.2/19	ABC
847	Adrift	12.1/20	CBS
848	Blue Lightning, The	12.1/19	CBS
849	Cowboy And The Ballerina, The	12.1/19	CBS
850	Criminal Behavior	12.1/19	ABC
851	Keys, The	12.1/19	NBC
852	Only Way Out, The	12.1/19	ABC
853	Perry Mason: The Case Of The Heartbroken Bride	12.1/21	NBC
854	Where The Hell's That Gold	12.1/18	CBS
855	Woman Who Loved Elvis, The	12.1/20	ABC
856	Woman Who Sinned, The	12.1/18	ABC
857	Case Of Deadly Force, A	12.0/20	CBS
858	Desperate For Love	12.0/20	CBS
859	Held Hostage: The Sis And Jerry Levin Story	12.0/19	ABC
860	Indiscreet	12.0/18	CBS

Movies are listed by descending rating. Miniseries are listed by descending average of ratings. Cable movies are not listed as they are not rated.

ALL NETWORK MOVIES — 1984-1994 (CONTINUED)

861	Kojak: The Price Of Justice	12.0/21	CBS
862	Leap Of Faith	12.0/20	CBS
863	Liberty	12.0/21	NBC
864	Love She Sought, The	12.0/18	NBC
865	Victim Of Love	12.0/19	CBS
866	Corsican Brothers, The	11.9/18	CBS
867	In The Line Of Duty: Street War	11.9/20	NBC
868	Posing: Inspired By Three Real Stories	11.9/18	CBS
869	Red Earth, White Earth	11.9/19	CBS
870	Tonight's The Night	11.9/19	ABC
871	World's Oldest Living Bridesmaid, The	11.9/22	CBS
872	Columbo - Caution: Murder Can Be Hazardous To Your Health	11.8/18	ABC
873	Dead And Alive	11.8/18	ABC
874	Dreamer Of Oz, The	11.8/18	NBC
875	Guilty Until Proven Innocent	11.8/19	NBC
876	Lady Against The Odds	11.8/19	NBC
877	Long Road Home	11.8/18	NBC
878	Return To Green Acres	11.8/22	CBS
879	Separated By Murder	11.8/19	CBS
880	Switch, The	11.8/19	CBS
881	Vengeance: The Story Of Tony Cimo	11.8/21	CBS
882	With Intent To Kill	11.8/19	CBS
883	American Geisha	11.7/20	CBS
884	. . . And Then She Was Gone	11.7/19	NBC
885	Chase	11.7/19	CBS
886	Fear Stalk	11.7/19	CBS
887	Pancho Barnes	11.7/18	CBS
888	Passport To Murder	11.7/19	NBC
889	Price She Paid, The	11.7/19	CBS
890	Stephen King's Sometimes They Come Back	11.7/19	CBS
891	Stranger At My Door	11.7/22	CBS
892	Brotherhood Of Justice, The	11.6/19	ABC
893	Danger Island	11.6/19	NBC
894	Florence Nightingale	11.6/19	NBC
895	In The Best Interest Of The Child	11.6/19	CBS
896	Love & Lies	11.6/18	ABC
897	Nightman, The	11.6/18	NBC
898	Return Of Ironside, The	11.6/19	NBC
899	To Save The Children	11.6/19	CBS
900	Tricks Of The Trade	11.6/18	CBS
901	Attic: The Hiding Of Anne Frank, The	11.5/19	CBS
902	Connecticut Yankee In King Arthur's Court, A	11.5/17	NBC
903	Due South	11.5/21	CBS
904	Firestorm: 72 Hours In Oakland	11.5/17	ABC
905	Fugitive Nights: Danger In The Desert	11.5/20	NBC
906	Gunsmoke: One Man's Justice	11.5/17	CBS
907	Heart Of A Child	11.5/18	NBC
908	I Saw What You Did	11.5/21	CBS
909	Kiss Of A Killer	11.5/18	ABC
910	Last P. O. W? The Bobby Garwood Story, The	11.5/20	ABC
911	Prison For Children	11.5/20	CBS
912	Quiet Killer	11.5/19	CBS
913	Riviera	11.5/17	ABC
914	Sister Margaret And The Saturday Night Ladies	11.5/19	CBS
915	Stranger On My Land	11.5/18	ABC
916	Baby Brokers	11.4/17	NBC
917	Betty Ford Story, The	11.4/16	ABC
918	Class Cruise	11.4/19	NBC
919	Dangerous Passion	11.4/19	ABC
920	Deadly Messages	11.4/17	ABC
921	Flood: Who Will Save Our Children?	11.4/18	NBC
922	Jury Duty: The Comedy	11.4/18	ABC
923	Love Can Be Murder	11.4/18	NBC
924	Missing Persons	11.4/19	ABC
925	My Breast	11.4/18	CBS
926	Shadow Of Obsession	11.4/18	NBC
927	Starcrossed	11.4/16	ABC
928	Dreams Of Gold: The Mel Fisher Story	11.3/20	CBS
929	French Silk	11.3/17	ABC
930	Hiroshima: Out Of The Ashes	11.3/20	NBC
931	Line Of Fire: The Morris Dees Story	11.3/17	NBC
932	Man Against The Mob: The Chinatown Murders	11.3/18	NBC
933	Murder Without Motive: The Edmund Perry Story	11.3/18	NBC
934	Ned Blessing: The Story Of My Life And Times	11.3/20	CBS
935	Shooter	11.3/20	NBC
936	Danielle Steel's Once In A Lifetime	11.2/16	NBC
937	Earth Angel	11.2/18	ABC
938	Fatal Deception: Mrs. Lee Harvey Oswald	11.2/18	NBC
939	Fire: Trapped On The 37th Floor	11.2/17	ABC
940	Hot Pursuit	11.2/21	NBC
941	Lois & Clark: The New Adventures Of Superman	11.2/17	ABC
942	My Brother's Wife	11.2/18	ABC
943	My Name Is Kate	11.2/18	ABC
944	Nick Knight	11.2/19	CBS
945	Samaritan: The Mitch Snyder Story	11.2/18	CBS
946	Stompin' At The Savoy	11.2/19	CBS
947	Dark Holiday	11.1/18	NBC
948	Getting Out	11.1/18	ABC
949	Glory Days	11.1/17	CBS
950	Lady And The Highwayman, The	11.1/18	CBS
951	Last Best Year, The	11.1/17	ABC
952	Murder Times Seven	11.1/18	CBS
953	Pals	11.1/19	CBS
954	Passion For Justice, A: Hazel Brannon Smith Story	11.1/18	ABC
955	When The Time Comes	11.1/18	ABC
956	Who Gets The Friends?	11.1/19	CBS
957	Condition: Critical	11.0/18	NBC
958	J. O. E. And The Colonel	11.0/18	ABC
959	Last To Go, The	11.0/17	ABC
960	Living A Lie	11.0/17	NBC
961	Miracle Child	11.0/18	NBC
962	Miss Rose White	11.0/17	NBC
963	Vestige Of Honor	11.0/18	CBS
964	Attack On Fear	10.9/16	CBS
965	Double Your Pleasure	10.9/18	NBC
966	For Their Own Good	10.9/17	ABC
967	Guess Who's Coming For Christmas	10.9/19	NBC
968	House On Sycamore Street, The	10.9/20	CBS
969	It's Nothing Personal	10.9/17	NBC
970	Littlest Victims	10.9/18	CBS
971	Ned Blessing: The True Story Of My Life	10.9/18	CBS
972	Thanksgiving Day	10.9/17	NBC
973	Trouble In Paradise	10.9/18	CBS
974	Twist Of The Knife, A	10.9/20	CBS
975	When We Were Young	10.9/19	NBC
976	Angel Of Death	10.8/18	CBS
977	Betrayed By Innocence	10.8/19	CBS
978	Betrayed By Love	10.8/16	ABC
979	Different Affair, A	10.8/18	CBS
980	Double, Double, Toil And Trouble	10.8/19	ABC
981	Exclusive	10.8/17	ABC
982	For The Very First Time	10.8/18	NBC
983	Guilty Conscience	10.8/18	CBS
984	Houston: The Legend Of Texas	10.8/18	CBS
985	In The Line Of Duty: The Price Of Vengeance	10.8/17	NBC
986	Kiss To Die For, A	10.8/17	NBC
987	Last Wish	10.8/17	ABC
988	Miles From Nowhere	10.8/17	CBS
989	Perry Mason Mystery, A: The Case Of The Lethal Lifestyle	10.8/18	NBC
990	She Stood Alone	10.8/18	NBC
991	What Price Victory?	10.8/17	ABC
992	Calendar Girl, Cop Killer? The Bambi Bembenek Story	10.7/17	ABC
993	Confessions: Two Faces Of Evil	10.7/16	NBC
994	Last Flight Out	10.7/18	NBC
995	Macshayne: Winner Take All	10.7/17	NBC
996	Special People	10.7/17	CBS
997	Web Of Deception	10.7/17	NBC
998	Archie: To Riverdale And Back Again	10.6/17	NBC
999	Eyes Of Terror	10.6/19	NBC
1000	Heart Of A Champion: The Ray Mancini Story	10.6/17	CBS
1001	Mothers Revenge, A	10.6/16	ABC
1002	Summer Dreams: The Story Of The Beach Boys	10.6/16	ABC
1003	Born Too Soon	10.5/17	NBC

ALL NETWORK MOVIES — 1984-1994 (CONTINUED)

1004	Forbidden Nights	10.5/17	CBS
1005	Laker Girls, The	10.5/17	CBS
1006	Man From Left Field	10.5/20	CBS
1007	Midnight Hour, The	10.5/17	NBC
1008	Not Of This World	10.5/17	CBS
1009	Perfect Tribute, The	10.5/18	ABC
1010	Search And Rescue	10.5/17	NBC
1011	Search For Grace	10.5/17	CBS
1012	Summer My Father Grew Up, The	10.5/16	NBC
1013	Tarzan In Manhattan	10.5/19	CBS
1014	Yarn Princess, The	10.5/17	ABC
1015	Baron And The Kid, The	10.4/17	CBS
1016	Daughter Of Darkness	10.4/18	CBS
1017	Father's Revenge, A	10.4/16	ABC
1018	L. A. Takedown	10.4/18	NBC
1019	Lies And Lullabies	10.4/16	ABC
1020	Odd Couple, The	10.4/19	CBS
1021	Tonya & Nancy: The Inside Story	10.4/19	NBC
1022	Blade In Hong Kong	10.3/16	CBS
1023	Casanova	10.3/15	ABC
1024	Crossing To Freedom	10.3/17	CBS
1025	Gregory K	10.3/16	ABC
1026	Murder C. O. D.	10.3/19	NBC
1027	Obsessed	10.3/16	ABC
1028	Threesome	10.3/18	CBS
1029	Triplecross	10.3/16	ABC
1030	Two Fathers: Justice For The Innocent	10.3/17	NBC
1031	Celebration Family	10.2/17	ABC
1032	Final Days	10.2/17	ABC
1033	Finding The Way Home	10.2/18	ABC
1034	Gunsmoke: The Long Ride Home	10.2/19	CBS
1035	Honor Thy Father And Mother: The Menendez Murders	10.2/17	FBC
1036	How To Murder A Millionaire	10.2/18	CBS
1037	Kiss Shot	10.2/16	CBS
1038	Many Happy Returns	10.2/18	CBS
1039	Perry Mason Mystery: The Case Of The Wicked Wives	10.2/19	NBC
1040	Somebody's Daughter	10.2/16	ABC
1041	Stormy Weathers	10.2/16	ABC
1042	Capital News	10.1/17	ABC
1043	Disaster At Silo 7	10.1/16	ABC
1044	Leave Of Absence	10.1/15	NBC
1045	To Heal A Nation	10.1/20	NBC
1046	Visions Of Murder	10.1/19	NBC
1047	Deadly Relations	10.0/16	ABC
1048	Babe Ruth	10.0/16	NBC
1049	Coins In The Fountain	10.0/19	CBS
1050	Presidents Child, The	10.0/17	CBS
1051	Sweet Revenge, A	10.0/16	CBS
1052	Another Pair Of Aces: Three Of A Kind	9.9/17	CBS
1053	Chameleons	9.9/17	NBC
1054	Crossing The Mob	9.9/17	NBC
1055	E. A. R. T. H. Force	9.9/17	CBS
1056	Heroes Of Desert Storm	9.9/16	ABC
1057	I Know My Son Is Alive	9.9/15	NBC
1058	Mrs. Lambert Remembers Love	9.9/17	CBS
1059	Prophet Of Evil: The Ervil Lebaron Story	9.9/16	CBS
1060	Under Cover	9.9/16	ABC
1061	What Ever Happened To Baby Jane?	9.9/15	ABC
1062	Appearances	9.8/18	NBC
1063	Elvis And The Colonel: The Untold Story	9.8/14	NBC
1064	Lucky Day	9.8/16	ABC
1065	Night Visions	9.8/17	NBC
1066	South Beach	9.8/17	NBC
1067	Acceptable Risks	9.7/15	ABC
1068	Child In The Night	9.7/16	CBS
1069	Classified Love	9.7/17	CBS
1070	Desperate Journey: The Allison Wilcox Story	9.7/15	ABC
1071	London And Davis In New York	9.7/18	CBS
1072	Menu For Murder	9.7/16	CBS
1073	Norman Rockwell's Breaking Home Ties	9.7/19	ABC
1074	Second Chances	9.7/16	CBS
1075	Sherlock Holmes Returns	9.7/16	CBS
1076	Double Deception	9.6/17	NBC
1077	Mother Of The Bride	9.6/17	CBS
1078	Stranger In The Mirror, A	9.6/16	ABC
1079	Whose Child Is This? The War For Baby Jessica	9.6/15	ABC
1080	Arthur The King	9.5/17	CBS
1081	Hands Of A Murderer	9.5/17	CBS
1082	In The Shadow Of A Killer	9.5/15	NBC
1083	Saved By The Bell-Hawaiian Style	9.5/17	NBC
1084	Staying Afloat	9.5/17	NBC
1085	Stolen: One Husband	9.5/15	CBS
1086	Street Of Dreams	9.5/17	CBS
1087	Torch Song	9.5/15	ABC
1088	Trouble Shooters: Trapped Beneath The Earth	9.5/15	NBC
1089	Caine Mutiny Court - Martial, The	9.4/15	CBS
1090	Doing Time On Maple Drive	9.4/15	FBC
1091	For Love And Glory	9.4/18	CBS
1092	Murder By The Book	9.4/15	CBS
1093	Proud Men	9.4/15	ABC
1094	Seduction: Three Tales From The Inner Sanctum	9.4/15	ABC
1095	Sexual Advances	9.4/16	ABC
1096	Carly's Web	9.3/17	NBC
1097	Love On The Run	9.3/16	NBC
1098	Without Warning: Terror In The Towers	9.3/15	NBC
1099	Arch Of Triumph	9.2/16	CBS
1100	In Self Defense	9.2/17	ABC
1101	Killer Rules	9.2/14	NBC
1102	Revolver	9.2/16	NBC
1103	Broken Badges	9.1/16	CBS
1104	Macgyver : Lost Treasure Of Atlantis	9.1/17	ABC
1105	To Save A Child	9.1/15	ABC
1106	We Are The Children	9.1/14	ABC
1107	Ride With The Wind	9.0/15	ABC
1108	Boys, The	8.9/15	ABC
1109	Going For The Gold: The Bill Johnson Story	8.9/14	CBS
1110	Good Cops, Bad Cops	8.9/14	NBC
1111	Jesse Hawkes	8.9/17	CBS
1112	Roommates	8.9/15	NBC
1113	Steel Justice	8.9/14	NBC
1114	Stuck With Each Other	8.9/16	NBC
1115	Those Secrets	8.9/14	ABC
1116	Destination: America	8.8/15	ABC
1117	Intrigue	8.8/19	CBS
1118	Lethal Exposure	8.8/14	NBC
1119	Bonnie And Clyde: The True Story	8.7/15	FBC
1120	Challenge Of A Lifetime	8.7/13	ABC
1121	Day Of Reckoning	8.7/14	NBC
1122	Middle Ages	8.7/16	CBS
1123	Amityville: The Evil Escapes	8.6/16	NBC
1124	Parker Kane	8.6/15	NBC
1125	Class Of '61	8.5/14	ABC
1126	Great Pretender, The	8.5/14	NBC
1127	Love And Curses . . . And All That Jazz	8.5/16	CBS
1128	Mantis	8.5/13	FBC
1129	Marilyn & Me	8.5/14	ABC
1130	Ray Alexander: A Taste For Justice	8.5/15	NBC
1131	Road Raiders, The	8.5/14	CBS
1132	Broadway Bound	8.4/14	ABC
1133	Haunted, The	8.4/13	FBC
1134	In Like Flynn	8.4/15	ABC
1135	Mothers, Daughters And Lovers	8.4/14	NBC
1136	Camp Cucamonga	8.3/14	NBC
1137	Getting Gotti	8.3/13	CBS
1138	Macshayne: The Final Roll Of The Dice	8.3/15	NBC
1139	Moment Of Truth: To Walk Again	8.3/12	NBC
1140	Plymouth	8.3/13	ABC
1141	Round Table, The	8.3/16	NBC
1142	Bermuda Grace	8.2/14	NBC
1143	Three Kings, The	8.2/13	ABC
1144	Plaza Suite	8.0/13	ABC
1145	Island Sons	7.9/14	ABC
1146	Murder By Moonlight	7.7/12	CBS
1147	Mario And The Mob	7.5/15	ABC

Movies are listed by descending rating. Miniseries are listed by descending average of ratings. Cable movies are not listed as they are not rated.

ALL NETWORK MOVIES — 1984-1994 (CONTINUED)

1148	Open Admissions	7.5/13	CBS
1149	So Proudly We Hail	7.5/12	CBS
1150	Dream Breakers	7.4/12	CBS
1151	Long Time Gone	7.4/14	ABC
1152	Palace Guard	7.4/14	CBS
1153	Waco & Rhinehart	7.4/13	ABC
1154	Brotherhood Of The Gun	7.3/14	CBS
1155	Adventures Of Brisco County Jr., The	7.2/14	FBC
1156	Plot To Kill Hitler, The	7.2/12	CBS
1157	Revenge Of The Nerds: The Next Generation	7.2/13	FBC
1158	Rise & Walk: The Dennis Byrd Story	7.1/11	FBC
1159	Entertainers, The	7.0/11	ABC
1160	Spirit, The	7.0/15	ABC
1161	Live: From Death Row	6.9/12	FBC
1162	Shadow Chasers	6.9/10	ABC
1163	Dead Silence	6.8/12	FBC
1164	Polly—Comin' Home	6.8/10	NBC
1165	Hi Honey — I'm Dead	6.7/11	FBC
1166	King Of Love, The	6.7/11	ABC
1167	Sitter, The	6.7/12	FBC
1168	Hostage For A Day	6.6/11	FBC
1169	Johnny Ryan	6.6/12	NBC
1170	Lily	6.6/14	CBS
1171	Generation	6.5/12	ABC
1172	Lifepod	6.5/11	FBC
1173	Only One Survived	6.5/12	CBS
1174	Sunset Beat	6.5/13	ABC
1175	Omen IV: The Awakening	6.4/11	FBC
1176	Blood Ties	6.3/11	FBC
1177	Just One Of The Girls	6.3/10	FBC
1178	Tower, The	6.2/11	FBC
1179	Frankenstein: The College Years	6.1/9	FBC
1180	Harry's Hong Kong	6.1/11	ABC
1181	N. Y. P. D. Mounted	6.1/13	CBS
1182	Day My Parents Ran Away, The	6.0/9	FBC
1183	Ghost Mom	6.0/9	FBC
1184	Robin Hood	6.0/10	FBC
1185	Twelve O' One (12: 01)	6.0/12	FBC
1186	Lady Mobster	5.9/9	ABC
1187	Revenge Of The Nerds IV: Nerds In Love	5.9/9	FBC
1188	Working Trash	5.8/9	FBC
1189	Room, The	5.5/11	ABC
1190	Day - O	5.3/10	NBC
1191	Rio Shanon	5.2/11	ABC
1192	Counterfeit Contessa, The	5.1/8	FBC
1193	Spoils Of War	4.9/9	ABC
1194	Dark Reflection	4.8/7	FBC
1195	Seeds Of Tragedy	4.6/9	FBC
1196	Green Dolphin Beat	4.4/8	FBC
1197	Pink Lightning	4.4/8	FBC
1198	Bad Attitudes	4.2/6	FBC
1199	Born To Run	3.9/7	FBC
1200	Based On An Untrue Story	3.5/5	FBC

ALL NETWORK MINISERIES — 1984-1994

1	Fatal Vision	31.1/47	NBC
2	Lonesome Dove	26.1/39	CBS
3	North And South	25.3/38	ABC
4	I Know My First Name Is Steven	24.5/39	NBC
5	Elvis And Me	24.4/36	ABC
6	Last Frontier, The	24.4/38	CBS
7	Blood And Orchids	24.3/37	CBS
8	Women Of Brewster Place, The	24.0/37	ABC
9	Queen	23.9/36	CBS
10	Two Mrs. Grenvilles, The	23.7/36	NBC
11	Long Hot Summer, The	23.2/35	NBC
12	At Mother's Request	23.0/35	CBS
13	I'll Take Manhattan	22.9/35	CBS
14	Hollywood Wives	22.8/35	ABC
15	Kane And Abel	22.7/33	CBS
16	Jacksons: An American Dream , The	22.5/34	ABC
17	If Tomorrow Comes	22.1/35	CBS
18	Evergreen	22.0/33	NBC
19	Switched At Birth	21.8/34	NBC
20	Small Sacrifices	21.7/34	ABC
21	Blind Faith	21.6/34	NBC
22	Billionaire Boys Club	21.4/34	NBC
23	Atlanta Child Murders, The	21.4/31	CBS
24	Ellis Island	21.2/32	CBS
25	Echoes In The Darkness	21.1/33	CBS
26	North And South, Book 2	21.0/33	ABC
27	Deceptions	20.9/35	NBC
28	Anastasia: The Mystery Of Anna	20.8/32	NBC
29	Sins	20.7/31	CBS
30	Stephen King's The Stand	20.3/32	ABC
31	Deliberate Stranger, The	20.2/30	NBC
32	Brotherhood Of The Rose	20.1/33	NBC
33	Wallenberg: A Hero's Story	20.0/32	NBC
34	Doubletake	19.9/31	CBS
35	Poor Little Rich Girl: The Barbara Hutton Story	19.9/32	NBC
36	In A Child's Name	19.9/30	CBS
37	Murder Of Mary Phagan, The	19.9/31	NBC
38	And The Sea Will Tell	19.6/30	CBS
39	Murder Ordained	19.6/31	CBS
40	Stephen King's It	19.6/31	ABC
41	Amerika	19.3/29	ABC
42	Dream West	19.2/30	CBS
43	Kenny Rogers As The Gambler I I I: The Legend Continues	19.2/31	CBS
44	Something Is Out There	19.2/30	NBC
45	On Wings Of Eagles	19.1/31	NBC
46	Alice In Wonderland	19.0/28	CBS
47	Mussolini - The Untold Story	18.9/28	NBC
48	War And Remembrance	18.9/28	ABC
49	Bourne Identity, The	18.5/30	ABC
50	Dress Gray	18.5/29	NBC
51	Big One: The Great Los Angeles Earthquake, The	18.3/28	NBC
52	Roses Are For The Rich	18.2/30	CBS
53	Windmills Of The Gods	18.2/28	CBS
54	Bluegrass	18.0/28	CBS
55	Love, Lies And Murder	17.9/27	NBC
56	Mistral's Daughter	17.7/28	CBS
57	Woman Named Jackie, A	17.7/27	NBC
58	Peter The Great	17.7/27	NBC
59	Jack The Ripper	17.6/29	CBS
60	Deadly Matrimony	17.5/27	NBC
61	Death In California, A	17.5/28	ABC
62	Sinatra	17.5/27	CBS
63	Deadly Intentions	17.3/27	ABC
64	Gambler Returns: The Luck Of The Draw, The	17.3/27	NBC
65	Matter Of Justice, A	17.3/26	NBC
66	Robert Kennedy And His Times	17.2/25	CBS
67	Jackie Collins' Lucky Chances	17.0/27	NBC
68	Space	16.8/27	CBS
69	In The Best Of Families: Marriage, Pride And Madness	16.7/26	CBS
70	Crossings	16.6/25	ABC

RATINGS

Movies are listed by descending rating. Miniseries are listed by descending average of ratings. Cable movies are not listed as they are not rated.

ALL NETWORK MINISERIES — 1984-1994 (CONTINUED)

71 Christopher Columbus .... 16.6/27 .... CBS
72 Kennedys Of Massachusetts, The .... 16.6/25 .... ABC
73 Return To Lonesome Dove .... 16.6/26 .... CBS
74 Tommyknockers, The .... 16.6/27 .... ABC
75 Harem .... 16.6/24 .... ABC
76 Baby M .... 16.3/26 .... ABC
77 Hands Of A Stranger .... 16.3/27 .... NBC
78 James Clavell's Noble House .... 16.3/25 .... NBC
79 Rage Of Angels: The Story Continues .... 16.2/25 .... NBC
80 Dynasty: The Reunion .... 16.1/24 .... ABC
81 Napoleon And Josephine: A Love Story .... 16.0/26 .... ABC
82 Favorite Son .... 16.0/26 .... NBC
83 Lace I I .... 15.9/25 .... ABC
84 Stay The Night .... 15.9/25 .... ABC
85 Cruel Doubt .... 15.8/26 .... NBC
86 Lincoln .... 15.8/25 .... NBC
87 Out On A Limb .... 15.3/23 .... ABC
88 Drug Wars: The Camarena Story .... 15.2/23 .... NBC
89 Danielle Steel's Jewels .... 15.2/23 .... NBC
90 Love And Hate: A Marriage Made In Hell ..... 15.1/27 .... NBC
91 Voices Within: The Lives Of Truddi Chase .... 15.1/25 .... ABC
92 Diana: Her True Story .... 15.1/24 .... NBC
93 Internal Affairs .... 14.9/24 .... CBS
94 War And Remembrance, Part I I .... 14.9/24 .... ABC
95 Oldest Living Confederate Widow Tells All ... 14.8/23 .... CBS
96 Twist Of Fate .... 14.8/23 .... NBC
97 Fresno .... 14.6/23 .... CBS
98 Grass Roots .... 14.3/22 .... NBC
99 Family Of Spies .... 14.2/22 .... CBS
100 Telling Secrets .... 14.1/22 .... ABC
101 False Arrest .... 14.1/23 .... ABC
102 Burden Of Proof, The .... 14.0/21 .... ABC
103 Around The World In 80 Days .... 13.9/22 .... NBC
104 Dark Shadows .... 13.9/22 .... NBC
105 Murder In The Heartland .... 13.7/22 .... ABC
106 Cross Of Fire .... 13.6/22 .... NBC
107 Love, Honor & Obey: The Last Mafia Marriage ...... 13.5/22 .... CBS
108 Jackie Collins' Lady Boss .... 13.5/21 .... NBC
109 Monte Carlo .... 13.4/21 .... CBS
110 Great Escape I I: The Untold Story, The ...... 13.4/21 .... NBC
111 Woman On The Run:
     The Lawrencia Bembenek Story .... 13.4/22 .... NBC
112 Judith Krantz's Till We Meet Again .... 13.3/21 .... CBS
113 Intruders .... 13.1/21 .... CBS
114 Mario Puzo's The Fortunate Pilgrim .... 13.1/22 .... NBC
115 Drug Wars: The Cocaine Cartel .... 13.0/20 .... NBC
116 Richest Man In The World:
     The Aristotle Onassis Story .... 13.0/20 .... ABC
117 From The Dead Of Night .... 13.0/21 .... NBC
118 Queenie .... 12.8/21 .... ABC
119 Nutcracker: Money, Madness And Murder ..... 12.4/20 .... NBC
120 Sun Also Rises, The .... 12.4/19 .... NBC
121 Conspiracy Of Silence .... 12.4/21 .... CBS
122 Phantom Of The Opera, The .... 12.3/20 .... NBC
123 Son Of The Morning Star .... 12.3/19 .... ABC
124 Barbara Taylor Bradford's Remember .... 12.2/20 .... NBC
125 Trial: The Price Of Passion .... 12.2/20 .... NBC
126 Passion And Paradise .... 12.2/20 .... ABC
127 Fire Next Time, The .... 12.1/20 .... NBC
128 Inconvenient Woman, An .... 12.1/21 .... ABC
129 Bloodlines: Murder In The Family .... 12.0/19 .... NBC
130 Separate But Equal .... 11.9/19 .... ABC
131 Guts And Glory: The Rise And Fall Of Oliver North . 11.8/18 .... CBS
132 Danielle Steel's Message From Nam .... 11.5/18 .... NBC
133 George Washington I I: The Forging Of A Nation ..... 11.2/18 .... CBS
134 Common Ground .... 10.9/18 .... CBS
135 Family Pictures .... 10.8/17 .... ABC
136 Wild Palms .... 10.7/18 .... ABC
137 Dadah Is Death .... 10.7/17 .... CBS
138 North Beach And Rawhide .... 10.5/16 .... CBS
139 People Like Us .... 10.0/17 .... NBC
140 North And South, Book 3: Heaven And Hell ... 9.9/15 .... ABC

141 When Love Kills: The Seduction Of John Hearn .... 9.7/16 .... CBS
142 Menendez: A Killing In Beverly Hills .... 9.5/16 .... CBS
143 Beryl Markham: A Shadow On The Sun .... 9.1/15 .... CBS
144 J F K: Reckless Youth .... 8.7/14 .... ABC
145 To Be The Best .... 8.5/9 .... CBS
146 World War I I: When Lions Roared .... 8.3/14 .... NBC
147 Secrets Of Lake Success .... 7.4/14 .... NBC
148 Fall From Grace .... 7.1/14 .... CBS
149 Trade Winds .... 6.1/12 .... NBC

ALL NETWORK MINISERIES — 1992-1993 SEASON

1 Queen .... 23.9/36 .... CBS
2 Jacksons: An American Dream, The .... 22.5/34 .... ABC
3 Deadly Matrimony .... 17.5/27 .... NBC
4 Sinatra .... 17.5/27 .... CBS
5 Tommyknockers, The .... 16.6/27 .... ABC
6 Danielle Steel's Jewels .... 15.2/23 .... NBC
7 Diana: Her True Story .... 15.1/24 .... NBC
8 Telling Secrets .... 14.1/22 .... ABC
9 Murder In The Heartland .... 13.7/22 .... ABC
10 Love, Honor & Obey: The Last Mafia Marriage ...... 13.5/22 .... CBS
11 Jackie Collins' Lady Boss .... 13.5/21 .... NBC
12 Woman On The Run:
    The Lawrencia Bembenek Story .... 13.4/22 .... NBC
13 Fire Next Time, The .... 12.1/20 .... NBC
14 Bloodlines: Murder In The Family .... 12.0/19 .... NBC
15 Family Pictures .... 10.8/17 .... ABC
16 Wild Palms .... 10.7/18 .... ABC
17 When Love Kills: The Seduction Of John Hearn .... 9.7/16 .... CBS

ALL NETWORK MINISERIES — 1993-1994 SEASON

1 Stephen King's The Stand .... 20.3/32 .... ABC
2 Matter Of Justice, A .... 17.3/26 .... NBC
3 In The Best Of Families:
   Marriage, Pride And Madness .... 16.7/26 .... CBS
4 Return To Lonesome Dove .... 16.6/26 .... CBS
5 Oldest Living Confederate Widow Tells All ... 14.8/23 .... CBS
6 Barbara Taylor Bradford's Remember .... 12.2/20 .... NBC
7 Danielle Steel's Message From Nam .... 11.5/18 .... NBC
8 North And South, Book 3: Heaven And Hell ... 9.9/15 .... ABC
9 Menendez: A Killing In Beverly Hills .... 9.5/16 .... CBS
10 J F K: Reckless Youth .... 8.7/14 .... ABC
11 World War I I: When Lions Roared .... 8.3/14 .... NBC
12 Secrets Of Lake Success .... 7.4/14 .... NBC
13 Fall From Grace .... 7.1/14 .... CBS
14 Trade Winds .... 6.1/12 .... NBC

EMMY WINNERS

MOVIE OR MINI SERIERS	SEASON
Do You Remember Love-(CBS)	1984-1985
Peter The Great -(NBC)	1985-1986
Love Is Never Silent- (NBC)	1985-1986
A Year In the Life- (NBC)	1986-1987
Promise-(CBS)	1986-1987
Murder of Mary Phagan -(NBC)	1987-1988
Inherit The Wind- (NBC)	1987-1988
War And Remembrance -(ABC)	1988-1989
Day One- (CBS)	1988-1989
Roe VS. Wade-(NBC)	1988-1989
Drug Wars: The Camarena Story- (NBC)	1989-1990
Caroline?-(CBS)	1989-1990
The Incident-(CBS)	1989-1990
Separate But Equal -(ABC)	1990-1991
A Woman Named Jackie-(NBC)	1991-1992
Miss Rose White- (NBC)	1991-1992
Prime Suspect 2-(PBS)	1992-1993
Barbarians At The Gate -(HBO)	1992-1993
Stalin- (HBO)	1992-1993

Section D

NETWORKS

ABC

North And South 25.8/37 23.6/34 28.0/42
 25.8/38 23.2/37
Rape Of Richard Beck, The 25.2/38
Ewok Adventure, The 24.9/36
Elvis And Me 23.9/35 24.9/36
Women Of Brewster Place, The 23.5/36 24.5/38
Smokey Mountain Christmas, A 23.2/35
Consenting Adult 23.1/33
Hollywood Wives 22.0/33 21.1/32 25.2/39
Jacksons: An American Dream , The 21.1/31
 23.9/36
Everybody's Baby: The Rescue Of Jessica
 Mcclure 22.2/36
Alex: The Life Of A Child 21.7/36
Twin Peaks 21.7/33
Small Sacrifices 18.1/28 25.2/39
North And South, Book 2 19.8/30 20.1/30
 21.6/36 22.9/36 20.8/32
Toughlove 20.6/31
Scandal Sheet 20.5/32
California Girls 20.3/31
Stephen King's The Stand 20.1/32 21.0/32
 20.1/31 20.0/31
Single Bars, Single Women 20.0/31
Lady Blue 19.8/31
Stephen King's It 18.5/29 20.6/33
Beyond Control: The Amy Fisher Story 19.5/30
David 19.5/30
Amerika 24.7/38 20.9/31 17.7/26 17.8/28
 15.6/23
Hawaiian Heat 19.1/34
Little Girl Lost 19.0/31
Right To Kill? 19.0/31
Defiant One, The 18.9/28
War And Remembrance 21.8/31 19.0/29
 19.8/31 16.8/25 17.0/26
Ewoks: The Battle For Endor 18.7/26
Bourne Identity, The 18.5/30 18.5/29
Heartsounds 18.5/31
Easy Prey 18.4/29
Paper Dolls 18.4/29
Moonlighting 18.3/28
Wet Gold 18.3/30
Addicted To His Love 18.1/29
Choices 18.1/27
Surviving 18.1/26
China Beach 18.0/29
Dead Before Dawn 18.0/26
Deadly Silence, A 17.9/28
Street Hawk 17.9/26
Love Lives On 17.8/26
There Are No Children Here 17.8/26
God Bless The Child 17.7/28
Jessie 17.7/29
My Two Loves 17.5/28
Prince Of Bel Air 17.5/27
Death In California, A 15.7/25 19.2/30
Convicted 17.4/27
Frank Nitti: The Enforcer 17.4/28
Bunny's Tale, A 17.3/26
Deadly Intentions 13.3/22 21.3/32
Crash Landing: The Rescue Of Flight 232 17.1/26
Daddy 17.1/25
Broken Angel 16.9/28
To Grandmother's House We Go 16.9/25
Bed Of Lies 16.8/25
Infidelity 16.8/27

Liberace 16.8/27
Bride In Black, The 16.7/27
Crossings 17.5/27 15.0/22 17.4/27
Kennedys Of Massachusetts, The 15.8/24 17.6/27
 16.4/25
Ladykillers 16.6/27
Ryan White Story, The 16.6/26
Tommyknockers, The 15.9/26 17.3/27
Young Indiana Jones Chronicles: The Curse Of
 The Jackal 16.6/26
Harem 16.9/25 16.2/23
Anything To Survive 16.5/26
Columbo: No Time To Die 16.5/27
Son's Promise, A 16.5/27
Shattered Spirits 16.4/25
Baby M 15.0/24 17.6/27
Blind Witness 16.3/25
Between Two Women 16.2/25
Fight For Life 16.2/26
Hearst And Davies Affair, The 16.2/24
Something To Live For: The Alison Gertz Story
 16.2/26
Sworn To Silence 16.1/24
Dynasty: The Reunion 16.8/25 15.3/23
Napoleon And Josephine: A Love Story 18.6/30
 16.2/26 13.3/21
Call Me Anna 15.9/24
Gladiator, The 15.9/24
Glitter 15.9/27
Last Fling, The 15.9/23
Lace I I 15.3/24 16.4/25
Stay The Night 13.8/22 17.9/28
Dance Till Dawn 15.8/26
Rock Hudson 15.7/24
Shell Seekers, The 15.7/24
Unspeakable Acts 15.7/25
Survive The Savage Sea 15.6/24
Town Bully, The 15.6/25
Wife, Mother, Murderer 15.6/24
Our Family Honor 15.4/25
Roots: The Gift 15.4/24
This Wife For Hire 15.4/24
Whereabouts Of Jenny, The 15.4/24
Out On A Limb 13.8/20 16.8/25
Empty Cradle 15.2/24
My Name Is Bill W. 15.2/24
Preppie Murder, The 15.2/24
Letting Go 15.1/28
Not In My Family 15.1/23
Voices Within: The Lives Of Truddi Chase
 14.7/24 15.5/25
Backfield In Motion 15.0/24
Lies Of The Heart: The Story Of Laurie Kellogg
 15.0/23
Murderous Affair, A: The Carolyn Warmus Story
 15.0/25
Supercarrier 15.0/23
Columbo Goes To College 14.9/24
Daughter Of The Streets 14.9/24
War And Remembrance, Part I I 13.4/21 14.4/22
 15.1/24 15.7/25 15.9/26
Weekend War 14.9/24
Club Med 14.8/23
Place For Annie, A 14.8/23
Rich Men, Single Women 14.8/23
Cracked Up 14.7/23
Peter Gunn 14.7/24
Whisper Kills, A 14.7/23
When You Remember Me 14.6/24
Winner Never Quits, A 14.6/24

Dillinger 14.5/22
Obsessed With A Married Woman 14.5/22
Right Of The People, The 14.5/22
They've Taken Our Children: The Chowchilla
 Kidnapping 14.5/23
Overexposed 14.4/23
Willing To Kill: The Texas Cheerleader Story
 14.4/22
Broken Cord, The 14.3/22
Between Love And Hate 14.2/21
Columbo: Death Hits The Jackpot 14.2/22
Impostor, The 14.2/22
Keeping Secrets 14.2/23
Night They Saved Christmas, The 14.2/22
Probe 14.2/23
Columbo: Undercover 14.1/22
In Defense Of A Married Man 14.1/23
She Woke Up 14.1/22
Telling Secrets 13.8/22 14.4/21
False Arrest 11.5/18 16.6/27
Ordeal In The Arctic 14.0/22
Spenser: For Hire 14.0/24
Burden Of Proof, The 12.8/18 15.1/23
Thunderboat Row 13.8/23
Get Smart Again 13.7/21
Her Secret Life 13.7/21
I Love You Perfect 13.7/23
Murder In The Heartland 13.2/21 14.2/23
My First Love 13.7/21
Nazi Hunter: The Beate Klarsfeld Story 13.7/21
Night Of The Hunter 13.7/23
Beyond Obsession 13.6/21
Burning Bridges 13.6/22
Mothers' Right, A: The Elizabeth Morgan Story
 13.6/21
One Of Her Own 13.5/21
Three Wishes Of Billy Grier, The 13.5/21
Bluffing It 13.4/22
Charley Hannah 13.4/23
Columbo: It's All In The Game 13.4/21
Penthouse, The 13.4/21
Perfect People 13.3/21
Kicks 13.2/21
Love Among Thieves 13.2/21
Shameful Secrets 13.2/21
I'll Take Romance 13.1/21
International Airport 13.0/27
Richest Man In The World: The Aristotle Onassis
 Story 12.1/18 13.9/22
Bad Seed, The 12.9/19
Captive 12.9/20
Evil In Clear River 12.9/20
One More Mountain 12.9/20
Pleasures 12.9/20
Challenger 12.8/20
Charles And Diana: Unhappily Ever After 12.8/19
Deadly Intentions... Again? 12.8/20
On Fire 12.8/20
Our Sons 12.8/21
Queenie 12.7/21 12.9/21
When Dreams Come True 12.8/21
Johnny Bull 12.7/20
Stranger In The Family, A 12.7/19
Columbo And The Murder Of A Rock Star 12.6/19
There Must Be A Pony 12.6/19
Children Of Times Square 12.5/20
Out Of The Darkness 12.5/19
Night Of Courage 12.4/19
Longarm 12.3/20
Son Of The Morning Star 11.7/18 12.8/20

ABC CONTINUED

Columbo: A Bird In The Hand   12.2/19
Equal Justice   12.2/23
Homefront   12.2/20
Jekyll & Hyde   12.2/19
Yes, Virginia, There Is A Santa Claus   12.2/19
Passion And Paradise   11.8/19   12.5/20
Criminal Behavior   12.1/19
Only Way Out, The   12.1/19
Woman Who Loved Elvis, The   12.1/20
Woman Who Sinned, The   12.1/18
Inconvenient Woman, An   11.7/21   12.4/20
Held Hostage: The Sis And Jerry Levin Story
     12.0/19
Tonight's The Night   11.9/19
Separate But Equal   11.9/19   11.8/19
Columbo - Caution: Murder Can Be Hazardous To
     Your Health   11.8/18
Dead And Alive   11.8/18
Brotherhood Of Justice, The   11.6/19
Love & Lies   11.6/18
Firestorm: 72 Hours In Oakland   11.5/17
Kiss Of A Killer   11.5/18
Last P. O. W? The Bobby Garwood Story, The
     11.5/20
Riviera   11.5/17
Stranger On My Land   11.5/18
Betty Ford Story, The   11.4/16
Dangerous Passion   11.4/19
Deadly Messages   11.4/17
Jury Duty: The Comedy   11.4/18
Missing Persons   11.4/19
Starcrossed   11.4/16
French Silk   11.3/17
Earth Angel   11.2/18
Fire: Trapped On The 37th Floor   11.2/17
Lois & Clark: The New Adventures Of Superman
     11.2/17
My Brother's Wife   11.2/18
My Name Is Kate   11.2/17
Getting Out   11.1/18
Last Best Year, The   11.1/17
Passion For Justice, A: Hazel Brannon Smith Story
     11.1/18
When The Time Comes   11.1/18
J. O. E. And The Colonel   11.0/18
Last To Go, The   11.0/17
For Their Own Good   10.9/17
Betrayed By Love   10.8/16
Double, Double, Toil And Trouble   10.8/19
Exclusive   10.8/17
Family Pictures   10.1/16   11.5/18
Last Wish   10.8/17
What Price Victory?   10.8/17
Wild Palms   12.3/20   9.7/15   11.0/19   9.9/17
Calendar Girl, Cop Killer? The Bambi Bembenek
     Story   10.7/17
Mothers Revenge, A   10.6/16
Summer Dreams: The Story Of The Beach Boys
     10.6/16
Perfect Tribute, The   10.5/18
Yarn Princess, The   10.5/17
Father's Revenge, A   10.4/16
Lies And Lullabies   10.4/16
Casanova   10.3/15
Gregory K   10.3/16
Obsessed   10.3/16
Triplecross   10.3/16

Celebration Family   10.2/17
Final Days   10.2/17
Finding The Way Home   10.2/18
Somebody's Daughter   10.2/16
Stormy Weathers   10.2/16
Capital News   10.1/17
Disaster At Silo 7   10.1/16
Deadly Relations   10.01/19
Heroes Of Desert Storm   9.9/16
Under Cover   9.9/16
What Ever Happened To Baby Jane?   9.9/15
North And South, Book 3: Heaven And Hell
     10.1/15   9.8/15   9.7/15
Lucky Day   9.8/16
Acceptable Risks   9.7/15
Desperate Journey: The Allison Wilcox Story
     9.7/15
Norman Rockwell's Breaking Home Ties   9.7/19
Stranger In The Mirror, A   9.6/16
Whose Child Is This? The War For Baby Jessica
     9.6/15
Torch Song   9.5/15
Proud Men   9.4/15
Seduction: Three Tales From The Inner Sanctum
     9.4/15
Sexual Advances   9.4/16
In Self Defense   9.2/17
Macgyver : Lost Treasure Of Atlantis   9.1/17
To Save A Child   9.1/15
We Are The Children   9.1/14
Ride With The Wind   9.0/15
Boys, The   8.9/15
Those Secrets   8.9/14
Destination: America   8.8/15
Challenge Of A Lifetime   8.7/13
J F K: Reckless Youth   7.8/12   9.5/16
Class Of '61   8.5/14
Marilyn & Me   8.5/14
Broadway Bound   8.4/14
In Like Flynn   8.4/15
Plymouth   8.3/17
Three Kings, The   8.2/13
Plaza Suite   8.0/13
Island Sons   7.9/14
Mario And The Mob   7.5/15
Long Time Gone   7.4/14
Waco & Rhinehart   7.4/13
Entertainers, The   7.0/11
Spirit, The   7.0/15
Shadow Chasers   6.9/10
King Of Love, The   6.7/11
Generation   6.5/12
Sunset Beat   6.5/13
Harry's Hong Kong   6.1/11
Lady Mobster   5.9/09
Room, The   5.5/11
Rio Shanon   5.2/11
Spoils Of War   4.9/9

CBS

Intimate Strangers   26.4/38
Karen Carpenter Story, The   26.3/41
Lonesome Dove   28.5/42   23.8/34   24.8/37
     27.3/41
Nobody's Child   25.9/39
Rockabye   25.3/38
Very Brady Christmas, A   25.1/39
Amos   24.5/37
Last Frontier, The   23.8/36   25.0/39
Blood And Orchids   22.9/35   25.6/38
Queen   24.7/38   24.1/37   22.8/34
Stone Pillow   23.3/33
He's Not Your Son   23.2/36
Sarah, Plain And Tall   23.1/35
At Mother's Request   23.3/35   22.7/35
I'll Take Manhattan   26.4/40   21.3/31   21.4/33
     22.5/36
Child's Cry   22.7/33
Kane And Abel   23.2/34   23.4/34   21.4/32
Stagecoach   22.5/36
Passions   22.4/34
Resting Place   22.3/36
If Tomorrow Comes   21.8/34   23.6/37   20.8/33
Silence Of The Heart   21.9/35
To Dance With The White Dog   21.9/33
Outrage   21.7/34
Breathing Lessons   21.6/32
Not My Kid   21.6/33
Love, Mary   21.5/33
Escape From Sobibor   21.4/34
Atlanta Child Murders, The   21.8/31   20.9/31
Dallas: The Early Years   21.3/33
Long Journey Home, The   21.3/34
Naked Lie   21.2/33
Once Upon A Texas Train   21.2/32
Still Crazy Like A Fox   21.2/31
Ellis Island   23.4/35   21.1/33   19.0/29
Echoes In The Darkness   20.1/33   22.0/33
Mrs. Delafield Wants To Marry   21.0/35
Mayflower Madam   20.9/34
Stranger Waits, A   20.9/33
Incident, The   20.8/33
Sins   19.7/29   21.9/32   20.6/32
Christmas Carol, A   20.7/30
Too Young The Hero   20.7/33
Christmas Gift, The   20.2/33
Walton Thanksgiving Reunion, A   20.1/30
Of Pure Blood   20.0/30
Operation, The   20.0/30
Doubletake   21.1/33   18.7/28
Skylark   19.9/29
In A Child's Name   17.8/27   21.9/33
Family Of Strangers   19.8/29
Gunsmoke: The Last Apache   19.7/32
Men Don't Tell   19.7/31
High Mountain Rangers   19.6/32
One Terrific Guy   19.6/30
Women Of Valor   19.6/32
And The Sea Will Tell   20.1/31   19.0/29
Murder Ordained   19.3/29   19.8/32
Hobo's Christmas, A   19.5/30
Jane's House   19.5/29
Last Days Of Patton, The   19.5/32
Promise   19.5/29
Woman Scorned: The Betty Broderick Story, A
     19.5/30
Caroline?   19.4/30

NETWORKS

Rated Movies are listed by descending rating. Rated miniseries are listed by descending average of ratings. Unrated productions are listed alphabetically.

CBS CONTINUED

Hostage 19.4/29
Jesse 19.4/31
Foxfire 19.3/30
Dream West 19.5/29 18.1/29 20.1/32
After The Promise 19.2/30
Blind Justice 19.2/29
Christmas Comes To Willow Creek 19.2/30
Deadly Deception 19.2/30
Kenny Rogers As The Gambler I I I: The Legend
　　Continues 20.9/32 17.4/29
Alice In Wonderland 21.2/31 16.8/25
Murder, She Wrote 18.9/29
O Pioneers 18.9/29
Man Upstairs, The 18.8/28
Incident In A Small Town 18.7/31
Deadly Care 18.6/31
Gypsy 18.6/28
Home Fires Burning 18.6/29
Kojak: The Belarus File 18.5/31
Lady Forgets, The 18.5/34
Lies Before Kisses 18.5/29
Body Of Evidence 18.4/28
Do You Know The Muffin Man? 18.4/30
Gathering Of Old Men, A 18.4/31
Red River 18.4/29
Who Is Julia? 18.4/29
Malice In Wonderland 18.3/29
Vanishing Act 18.3/27
Call Of The Wild 18.2/29
Dr. Quinn, Medicine Woman 18.2/29
Pack Of Lies 18.2/30
Roses Are For The Rich 18.6/30 17.8/29
Snowbound: The Jim And Jennifer Stolpa Story
　　18.2/27
Something In Common 18.2/29
Windmills Of The Gods 19.0/28 17.3/27
Kids Don't Tell 18.1/29
Bluegrass 17.6/27 18.4/29
Izzy And Moe 17.9/27
Pair Of Aces 17.8/28
This Can't Be Love 17.8/28
Mistral's Daughter 18.2/29 18.7/30 16.3/26
Absolute Strangers 17.7/29
Christy 17.7/29
Murders In The Rue Morgue, The 17.7/27
Alone In The Neon Jungle 17.6/28
Out Of The Darkness 17.6/30
Jack The Ripper 14.8/26 20.3/31
Mistress 17.5/29
Poker Alice 17.5/32
Sinatra 17.7/26 17.2/27
Thompson's Last Run 17.4/26
Aftermath: A Test Of Love 17.3/27
Rio Diablo 17.3/26
Unconquered 17.3/28
Robert Kennedy And His Times 19.8/29 14.9/21
　　16.9/26
When He's Not A Stranger 17.2/26
Without A Kiss Goodbye 17.2/29
Double Edge 17.1/28
Murder In Black And White 17.1/27
Disappearance Of Nora 17.0/27
Do You Remember Love? 17.0/28
Touch Of Scandal, A 17.0/27
Terror On Highway 91 16.9/26
Face Of A Stranger 16.8/27
Mrs. 'Arris Goes To Paris 16.8/28

Picking Up The Pieces 16.8/25
Runaway Father 16.8/27
Shattered Dreams 16.8/28
Space 19.4/31 16.4/26 14.7/24 17.1/28 16.3/26
Christmas On Division Street 16.7/26
In The Best Of Families: Marriage, Pride And
　　Madness 16.1/25 17.3/26
Killer Among Friends, A 16.7/27
Scorned And Swindled 16.7/26
Secret Garden, The 16.7/26
Vital Signs 16.7/26
Wild Horses 16.7/26
Anna Karenina 16.6/26
Christopher Columbus 17.4/29 15.8/25
Comeback, The 16.6/29
Deliver Them From Evil: The Taking Of Alta
　　View 16.6/26
Gunsmoke: Return To Dodge 16.6/31
Liberace: Behind The Music 16.6/26
Murder: By Reason Of Insanity 16.6/26
Return To Lonesome Dove 18.1/28 16.5/25
　　15.2/24
Burning Rage 16.5/30
Fulfillment Of Mary Gray, The 16.5/26
Kids Like These 16.5/27
Miles To Go . . . 16.5/26
Walker, Texas Ranger 16.5/27
American Harvest 16.4/27
Corpse Had A Familiar Face, The 16.4/26
Lucy & Desi: Before The Laughter 16.4/25
Baby Snatcher 16.3/26
David's Mother 16.3/26
In Sickness And In Health 16.3/26
Night Walk 16.3/27
Taken Away 16.3/25
Battling For Baby 16.2/26
I Can Make You Love Me: The Stalking Of Laura
　　Black 16.1/26
Love And Betrayal 16.1/25
Oceans Of Fire 16.1/27
That Secret Sunday 16.1/26
Two Thousand Malibu Road 16.1/28
Us 16.1/29
Against Her Will: An Incident In Baltimore
　　16.0/25
Bump In The Night 16.0/25
Highway Heartbreaker 16.0/25
Lady From Yesterday, The 16.0/25
Time To Triumph, A 16.0/25
Danger Of Love, The 15.9/26
Murder In New Hampshire: The Pamela Smart
　　Story 15.9/26
Agatha Christie's The Man In The Brown Suit
　　15.8/25
In My Daughter's Name 15.8/27
Jake And The Fatman 15.8/27
Judgment Day: The John List Story 15.8/25
Killing In A Small Town 15.8/26
Penalty Phase 15.8/26
Taking Back My Life: The Nancy Ziegenmeyer
　　Story 15.8/25
Circle Of Violence: A Family Drama 15.7/25
Guilty Of Innocence: The Lenell Geter Story
　　15.7/25
Into Thin Air 15.7/25
Leona Helmsley: The Queen Of Mean 15.7/26
Outback Bound 15.7/25
P. S. I Luv U 15.7/25
Mission Of The Shark 15.6/25
My Son Johnny 15.6/24

Stranger Within, The 15.6/25
Ultimate Betrayal 15.6/25
George Mckenna Story, The 15.5/24
Honor Thy Mother 15.5/24
House Of Secrets And Lies, A 15.5/27
Message From Holly 15.5/24
Sadie And Son 15.5/25
Seduced 15.5/25
Agatha Christie's Murder In Three Acts 15.4/25
Dying To Love You 15.4/25
Fatal Judgment 15.4/24
Overkill: The Aileen Wuornos Story 15.4/25
Place To Call Home, A 15.4/26
Terror On Track 9 15.4/25
Under The Influence 15.4/24
Always Remember I Love You 15.3/26
Hazard Of Hearts, A 15.3/26
Shadow Of A Doubt 15.3/24
Sworn To Vengeance 15.3/25
April Morning 15.2/24
Camille 15.2/25
Day One 15.2/24
Murder With Mirrors 15.2/23
Obsessive Love 15.2/25
Shattered Innocence 15.2/25
Diamond Trap, The 15.1/24
Miracle Landing 15.1/23
Red Spider, The 15.1/25
Trapped In Silence 15.1/24
Unholy Matrimony 15.1/24
Warm Hearts, Cold Feet 15.1/22
Baby Of The Bride 15.0/26
Bring Me The Head Of Dobie Gillis 15.0/23
In The Company Of Darkness 15.0/24
Necessity 15.0/24
Shakedown On The Sunset Strip 15.0/27
Armed & Innocent 14.9/24
Bonds Of Love 14.9/23
Go Toward The Light 14.9/24
Good Night, Sweet Wife: A Murder In Boston
　　14.9/23
Her Final Fury: Betty Broderick, The Last Chapter
　　14.9/22
Internal Affairs 16.1/26 13.7/21
Quiet Victory: The Charlie Wedemeyer Story
　　14.9/25
Complex Of Fear 14.8/23
Donato And Daughter 14.8/24
Donor 14.8/24
Fire In The Dark 14.8/23
Oldest Living Confederate Widow Tells All
　　15.7/24 13.8/21
Child Of Rage 14.7/24
Face To Face 14.7/24
Grave Secrets: The Legacy Of Hilltop Drive
　　14.7/23
Stillwatch 14.7/23
With A Vengeance 14.7/23
Bridesmaids 14.6/25
Diagnosis Of Murder 14.6/23
Out On The Edge 14.6/23
Precious Victims 14.6/23
Single Women, Married Men 14.6/26
Fresno 19.7/30 15.2/22 12.8/1 12.5/24 12.7/18
Death Of A Salesman 14.5/23
Liar, Liar 14.5/26
Murder Of Innocence 14.5/22
Nightmare In The Daylight 14.5/23
Poisoned By Love: The Kern County Murders
　　14.5/24

CBS CONTINUED

Sins Of The Mother 14.5/23
Thicker Than Blood: The Larry Mclinden Story 14.5/23
Woman He Loved, The 14.5/25
Agatha Christie's Dead Man's Folly 14.4/22
Detective In The House 14.4/24
First Steps 14.4/24
Ghost Of A Chance 14.4/24
Manhunt For Claude Dallas 14.4/24
Rape Of Dr. Willis, The 14.4/23
Return Of Sherlock Holmes, The 14.4/24
Casualties Of Love: The Long Island Lolita Story 14.3/22
Outside Woman, The 14.3/22
Eighty-Three Hours 'til Dawn 14.2/22
Flash, The 14.2/23
Gunsmoke I I I: To The Last Man 14.2/24
He's Fired, She's Hired 14.2/23
In The Eyes Of A Stranger 14.2/23
Wolf 14.2/25
Family Of Spies 14.7/22 13.6/21
Assassin 14.1/23
Barnum 14.1/25
Broken Vows 14.1/22
Conspiracy Of Love 14.1/21
Fatal Image, The 14.1/22
Hot Paint 14.1/22
Labor Of Love: The Arlette Schweitzer Story 14.1/23
Room Upstairs, The 14.1/24
Scattered Dreams: The Kathryn Messenger Story 14.1/22
Stark 14.1/23
Babymaker: The Dr. Cecil Jacobson's Story 14.0/21
Cover Up 14.0/26
Cries Unheard: The Donna Yaklich Story 14.0/22
Face Of Fear, The 14.0/23
Fugitive Among Us 14.0/23
Nightmare In Columbia County 14.0/22
Sentimental Journey 14.0/23
Sin And Redemption 14.0/23
Bridge To Silence 13.9/24
Seduction In Travis County 13.9/22
Other Lover, The 13.8/22
Summer To Remember, A 13.8/21
There Was A Little Boy 13.8/22
Women Of Windsor 13.8/22
Sharing Richard 13.7/22
Sparks: The Price Of Passion 13.7/21
Special Friendship, A 13.7/22
Badge Of The Assassin 13.6/23
Children Of The Bride 13.6/25
Love Boat: A Valentine Voyage, The 13.6/22
Second Serve 13.6/22
Brotherly Love 13.5/22
Love, Honor & Obey: The Last Mafia Marriage 12.6/20 14.4/24
My Father, My Son 13.5/22
Blood River 13.4/23
Children Of The Dark 13.4/22
Money, Power, Murder 13.4/22
Monte Carlo 14.6/23 12.2/19
One Against The Wind 13.4/21
Secret Life Of Archie's Wife, The 13.4/22
Babycakes 13.3/22
Bare Essentials 13.3/21

Higher Ground 13.3/25
Johnnie Mae Gibson: F B I 13.3/20
News At Eleven 13.3/22
No Place Like Home 13.3/20
Secret, The 13.3/23
Tenth Man, The 13.3/21
Terrorist On Trial: The United States Vs. Salim Ajami 13.3/20
With Murder In Mind 13.3/21
Judith Krantz's Till We Meet Again 14.8/23 11.7/18
Baby Girl Scott 13.2/23
Conviction Of Kitty Dodds, The 13.2/21
Drop-Out Mother 13.2/22
Nurses On The Line: The Crash Of Flight 7 13.2/22
Promised A Miracle 13.2/22
Yearling, The 13.2/21
Angel In Green 13.1/22
Blind Spot 13.1/20
Forget Me Not Murders, The 13.1/21
Nightmare At Bitter Creek 13.1/22
No Child Of Mine 13.1/21
Stormin' Home 13.1/23
Intruders 13.2/21 12.9/21
Case Closed 13.0/22
Eyes Of A Witness 13.0/23
Lost In London 13.0/19
Place To Be Loved, A 13.0/20
Beverly Hills Cowgirl Blues 12.9/22
Bradys, The 12.9/22
Brass 12.9/22
Deadbolt 12.9/23
Family Sins 12.9/20
Jailbirds 12.9/22
Return Of Sam Mccloud, The 12.9/20
When No One Would Listen 12.9/19
With Hostile Intent 12.9/21
Agatha Christie's Thirteen At Dinner 12.8/21
Breaking The Silence 12.8/20
Mickey Spillane's Mike Hammer: Murder Takes All 12.8/20
Through The Eyes Of A Killer 12.8/21
Timestalkers 12.8/21
American Story, An 12.7/20
Picket Fences 12.7/24
Terror In The Night 12.7/20
Broken Promises: Taking Emily Back 12.6/22
Copacabana 12.6/20
Firefighter 12.6/20
Toughest Man In The World, The 12.6/20
Courage 12.5/20
Sin Of Innocence 12.5/21
Triumph Of The Heart: The Ricky Bell Story 12.5/22
Welcome Home, Bobby 12.5/21
Children Of The Night 12.4/21
For Love Or Money 12.4/20
For The Love Of Aaron 12.4/21
I Spy Returns 12.4/18
Locked Up: A Mother's Rage 12.4/20
Over My Dead Body 12.4/23
River Of Rage: The Taking Of Maggie Keene 12.4/20
Side By Side 12.4/20
Stones Of Ibarra 12.4/21
Conspiracy Of Silence 12.5/21 12.2/20
Deadly Business, A 12.3/21
One Police Plaza 12.3/22
Harmful Intent 12.2/20

Nairobi Affair 12.2/20
Spies, Lies And Naked Thighs 12.2/19
Stephen King's Golden Years 12.2/22
Trenchcoat In Paradise 12.2/20
Adrift 12.1/20
Blue Lightning, The 12.1/19
Cowboy And The Ballerina, The 12.1/19
Where The Hell's That Gold 12.1/18
Case Of Deadly Force, A 12.0/20
Desperate For Love 12.0/20
Indiscreet 12.0/18
Kojak: The Price Of Justice 12.0/21
Leap Of Faith 12.0/20
Victim Of Love 12.0/20
Corsican Brothers, The 11.9/18
Posing: Inspired By Three Real Stories 11.9/18
Red Earth, White Earth 11.9/19
World's Oldest Living Bridesmaid, The 11.9/22
Guts And Glory: The Rise And Fall Of Oliver North 14.0/23 9.6/13
Return To Green Acres 11.8/22
Separated By Murder 11.8/19
Switch, The 11.8/19
Vengeance: The Story Of Tony Cimo 11.8/21
With Intent To Kill 11.8/19
American Geisha 11.7/20
Chase 11.7/19
Fear Stalk 11.7/19
Pancho Barnes 11.7/18
Price She Paid, The 11.7/19
Stephen King's Sometimes They Come Back 11.7/19
Stranger At My Door 11.7/22
In The Best Interest Of The Child 11.6/19
To Save The Children 11.6/19
Tricks Of The Trade 11.6/18
Attic: The Hiding Of Anne Frank, The 11.5/19
Due South 11.5/21
Gunsmoke: One Man's Justice 11.5/17
I Saw What You Did 11.5/21
Prison For Children 11.5/20
Quiet Killer 11.5/19
Sister Margaret And The Saturday Night Ladies 11.5/19
My Breast 11.4/18
Dreams Of Gold: The Mel Fisher Story 11.3/20
Ned Blessing: The Story Of My Life And Times 11.3/20
George Washington I I: The Forging Of A Nation 12.6/20 9.8/15
Nick Knight 11.2/19
Samaritan: The Mitch Snyder Story 11.2/18
Stompin' At The Savoy 11.2/19
Glory Days 11.1/17
Lady And The Highwayman, The 11.1/18
Murder Times Seven 11.1/18
Pals 11.1/19
Who Gets The Friends? 11.1/19
Vestige Of Honor 11.0/18
Attack On Fear 10.9/16
Common Ground 11.0/18 10.8/18
House On Sycamore Street, The 10.9/20
Littlest Victims 10.9/18
Ned Blessing: The True Story Of My Life 10.9/18
Trouble In Paradise 10.9/18
Twist Of The Knife, A 10.9/20
Angel Of Death 10.8/18
Betrayed By Innocence 10.8/19
Different Affair, A 10.8/18
Guilty Conscience 10.8/18

NETWORKS

Rated Movies are listed by descending rating. Rated miniseries are listed by descending average of ratings. Unrated productions are listed alphabetically.

CBS CONTINUED

Houston: The Legend Of Texas 10.8/18
Miles From Nowhere 10.8/17
Dadah Is Death 11.3/17 10.1/17
Special People 10.7/18
Heart Of A Champion: The Ray Mancini Story
    10.6/17
Forbidden Nights 10.5/17
Laker Girls, The 10.5/17
Man From Left Field 10.5/20
North Beach And Rawhide 9.6/14 11.4/17
Not Of This World 10.5/17
Search For Grace 10.5/17
Tarzan In Manhattan 10.5/19
Baron And The Kid, The 10.4/17
Daughter Of Darkness 10.4/18
Odd Couple, The 10.4/19
Blade In Hong Kong 10.3/16
Crossing To Freedom 10.3/17
Threesome 10.3/18
Gunsmoke: The Long Ride Home 10.2/19
How To Murder A Millionaire 10.2/18
Kiss Shot 10.2/16
Many Happy Returns 10.2/18
Coins In The Fountain 10.0/19
Presidents Child, The 10.0/17
Sweet Revenge, A 10.0/16
Another Pair Of Aces: Three Of A Kind 9.9/17
E. A. R. T. H. Force 9.9/17
Mrs. Lambert Remembers Love 9.9/17
Prophet Of Evil: The Ervil Lebaron Story 9.9/16
Child In The Night 9.7/16
Classified Love 9.7/17
London And Davis In New York 9.7/18
Menu For Murder 9.7/16
Second Chances 9.7/16
Sherlock Holmes Returns 9.7/16
When Love Kills: The Seduction Of John Hearn
    9.9/16 9.5/16
Mother Of The Bride 9.6/17
Arthur The King 9.5/17
Hands Of A Murderer 9.5/17
Stolen: One Husband 9.5/15
Street Of Dreams 9.5/17
Menendez: A Killing In Beverly Hills 9.6/16
    9.3/15
Caine Mutiny Court - Martial, The 9.4/15
For Love And Glory 9.4/18
Murder By The Book 9.4/15
Arch Of Triumph 9.2/16
Beryl Markham: A Shadow On The Sun 10.4/16
    7.8/13
Broken Badges 9.1/16
Going For The Gold: The Bill Johnson Story
    8.9/14
Jesse Hawkes 8.9/17
Intrigue 8.8/19
Middle Ages 8.7/16
Love And Curses . . . And All That Jazz 8.5/16
Road Raiders, The 8.5/14
To Be The Best 9.3/15 7.7/3
Getting Gotti 8.3/13
Murder By Moonlight 7.7/12
Open Admissions 7.5/13
So Proudly We Hail 7.5/12
Dream Breakers 7.4/12
Palace Guard 7.4/14
Brotherhood Of The Gun 7.3/14

Plot To Kill Hitler, The 7.2/12
Fall From Grace 7.7/14 6.4/13
Lily 6.6/14
Only One Survived 6.5/12
N. Y. P. D. Mounted 6.1/13

DISNEY CHANNEL

Back Home
Back To Hannibal: The Return Of Tom Sawyer
    And Huck Finn
Bejeweled
Chips, The War Dog
Ernest Green Story, The
Girl From Tomorrow, The
Great Expectations
Heidi
Lantern Hill
Little Kidnappers, The
Mark Twain And Me
Mother Goose Rock 'n' Rhyme
Not Quite Human I I
On Promised Land
Perfect Harmony
Spooner
Still Not Quite Human

FAMILY CHANNEL

Candles In The Dark
Clarence
Harvest For The Heart
Partners 'N Love
The Race To Freedom: The Underground Railroad

FBC

Honor Thy Father And Mother: The Menendez
    Murders 10.2/17
Doing Time On Maple Drive 9.4/15
Bonnie And Clyde: The True Story 8.7/15
Mantis 8.5/13
Haunted, The 8.4/13
Adventures Of Brisco County Jr., The 7.2/14
Revenge Of The Nerds: The Next Generation
    7.2/13
Rise & Walk: The Dennis Byrd Story 7.1/11
Live: From Death Row 6.9/12
Dead Silence 6.8/12
Hi Honey — I'm Dead 6.7/11
Sitter, The 6.7/12
Hostage For A Day 6.6/11
Lifepod 6.5/11
Omen I V: The Awakening 6.4/11
Blood Ties 6.3/11
Just One Of The Girls 6.3/10
Tower, The 6.2/11
Frankenstein: The College Years 6.1/9
Day My Parents Ran Away, The 6.0/9
Ghost Mom 6.0/9

Robin Hood 6.0/10
Twelve O' One (12: 01) 6.0/12
Revenge Of The Nerds I V: Nerds In Love 5.9/9
Working Trash 5.8/9
Counterfeit Contessa, The 5.1/8
Dark Reflection 4.8/7
Seeds Of Tragedy 4.6/9
Green Dolphin Beat 4.4/8
Pink Lightning 4.4/8
Bad Attitudes 4.2/6
Born To Run 3.9/7
Based On An Untrue Story 3.5/5

HBO

Act Of Vengeance
Afterburn
Against The Wall
And The Band Played On
Apology
As Summers Die
Attack Of The 50ft. Woman
Baja Oklahoma
Barbarians At The Gate
Blackout
Blind Justice
Blind Side
By Dawn's Early Light
Cast A Deadly Spell
Citizen Cohn
Clinton And Nadine
Comrades Of Summer
Criminal Justice
Daybreak
Dead Ahead: The Exxon Valdez Disaster
Dead Solid Perfect
Deadlock
Descending Angel
Doomsday Gun
Doublecrossed
El Diablo
Enemy Within, The
Fever
Finnegan Begin Again
Florida Straits
For Richer, For Poorer
Forbidden
Fortress
Framed
Glitter Dome, The
Guardian, The
Gulag
Heist
Hostages
Image, The
Into The Homeland
Investigation: Inside A Terrorist Bombing, The
Josephine Baker Story, The
Judgment
Laguna Heat
Last Innocent Man, The
Last Of His Tribe, The
Last Outlaw, The
Laurel Avenue
Lion Of Africa, The
Long Gone

HBO CONTINUED

Man Who Broke 1,000 Chains, The
Mandela
Murderers Among Us: The Simon Wiesenthal
    Story
Murrow
Mussolini: The Decline And Fall Of Il Duce
Perfect Witness
Positively True Adventures Of The Alleged Texas
    Cheerleader Murdering Mom, The
Prisoner Of Honor
Private Matter, A
Quick And The Dead, The
Red King, White Knight
Reunion At Fairborough
Running Mates
Sakharov
Somebody Has To Shoot The Picture
Stalin
State Of Emergency
Steal The Sky
Stepfather I I I
Strapped
Sword Of Gideon
Tailspin: Behind The Korean Airlines Tragedy
Teamster Boss: The Jackie Presser Story
Third Degree Burn
This Park Is Mine
Tracker, The
Tragedy Of Flight 103: The Inside Story, The
Traveling Man
White Mile
Without Warning: The James Brady Story

LIFETIME

And Then There Was One
Better Off Dead
Death Dreams
Getting Up And Going Home
Good Fight, The
Killing Mind, The
Last Prostitute, The
Lie Down With Lions
Majority Rule
Memories Of Murder
Midnight's Child
Night Owl
Notorious
Other Women's Children
Shame
Silent Movie
Spenser: Ceremony
Spenser: Pale Kings And Princes
Stolen Babies
Stop At Nothing
Storm And Sorrow
Sudie And Simpson
Untamed Love
Wildflower

NBC

Burning Bed, The   36.2/52
Return To Mayberry   33.0/49
Fatal Vision   29.5/44   32.7/49
Perry Mason Returns   27.2/39
Rags To Riches   25.3/36
Those She Left Behind   25.1/38
Stranded   24.9/38
Blood Vows: The Story Of A Mafia Wife   24.8/37
I Know My First Name Is Steven   21.6/35
    27.3/42
Mafia Princess   24.4/37
Kate's Secret   24.1/36
Ann Jillian Story, The   23.8/35
Mercy Or Murder?   23.8/35
Two Mrs. Grenvilles, The   23.4/36   24.0/35
Perry Mason: The Case Of The Shooting Star
    23.6/37
An Early Frost   23.3/33
Perry Mason: The Case Of The Notorious Nun
    23.3/42
Long Hot Summer, The   22.6/34   23.8/36
Case Of The Hillside Strangler, The   23.1/36
Miami Vice   22.8/37
Perry Mason: The Case Of The Lady In The Lake
    22.6/35
Silent Witness   22.5/33
When The Bough Breaks   22.3/36
In The Line Of Duty: The FBI Murders   22.2/34
Family Ties Vacation   22.1/33
Evergreen   22.3/33   20.9/32   22.9/33
Eight Is Enough: A Family Reunion   22.0/34
Blacke's Magic   21.8/32
Switched At Birth   20.4/32   23.1/35
Blind Faith   19.9/31   23.3/36
Cry For Help: The Tracey Thurman Story, A
    21.5/33
Hostage Flight   21.5/32
Abduction Of Kari Swenson, The   21.4/33
Billionaire Boys Club   20.7/34   22.1/34
Execution, The   21.4/32
Facts Of Life Down Under, The   21.4/32
I Dream Of Jeannie: 15 Years Later   21.4/32
Christmas Eve   21.3/33
Perry Mason: The Case Of The Lost Love
    21.3/33
Shattered Vows   21.3/33
L. A. Law   21.2/33
Double Standard   21.1/33
This Child Is Mine   21.1/32
Strange Voices   21.0/33
Diary Of A Perfect Murder   20.9/33
Too Good To Be True   20.9/32
Deceptions   19.9/35   21.8/35
Anastasia: The Mystery Of Anna   20.7/32
    20.9/32
Highway To Heaven   20.6/35
Perry Mason: The Case Of The Sinister Spirit
    20.5/35
Return Of The 6 Million Dollar Man & Bionic
    Woman   20.5/33
Codename: Foxfire - Slay It Again, Sam   20.4/29
Hunter   20.4/33
Killer In The Mirror   20.4/31
Danielle Steel's Kaleidoscope   20.3/32
Assault And Matrimony   20.2/32
Incredible Hulk Returns, The   20.2/33
Deliberate Stranger, The   18.6/28   21.7/32

Brotherhood Of The Rose   20.9/35   19.2/30
Fight For Jenny, A   20.0/31
Scandal In A Small Town   20.0/31
Wallenberg: A Hero's Story   20.2/33   19.7/30
Crash Course   19.9/32
Poor Little Rich Girl: The Barbara Hutton Story
    21.3/33   18.5/30
Rearview Mirror   19.9/30
Take My Daughters, Please   19.9/31
Murder Of Mary Phagan, The   18.7/28   21.0/34
Poison Ivy   19.8/25
Man Against The Mob   19.7/32
Remington Steele: The Steele That Wouldn't Die
    19.7/28
Taking Of Flight 847: The Uli Derickson Story
    19.7/31
Danielle Steel's Daddy   19.6/30
Aaron's Way   19.5/31
Little Match Girl, The   19.4/30
Desperado   19.3/32
Letter To Three Wives, A   19.3/30
Perry Mason: The Case Of The Killer Kiss
    19.3/29
Unnatural Causes   19.3/31
Stepford Children, The   19.2/29
Something Is Out There   19.3/31   19.0/29
Amy Fisher: My Story   19.1/30
Can You Feel Me Dancing?   19.1/30
On Wings Of Eagles   17.0/28   21.2/34
Combat High   18.9/29
Laura Lansing Slept Here   18.9/30
Mussolini - The Untold Story   17.7/26   19.4/29
    19.6/29
Nightingales   18.9/33
In The Line Of Duty: Ambush In Waco   18.8/30
Stranger In My Bed   18.8/29
Victims For Victims - The Theresa Saldana Story
    18.8/28
False Witness   18.7/29
In The Heat Of The Night   18.7/30
High Price Of Passion, The   18.6/29
Dirty Dozen: The Deadly Mission   18.5/28
Dress Gray   17.9/27   19.0/30
Danielle Steel's Palomino   18.4/28
L B J: The Early Years   18.4/27
Big One: The Great Los Angeles Earthquake, The
    17.1/26   19.5/30
Stoning In Fulham County, A   18.3/28
Father Of Hell Town   18.2/29
Little House On The Prairie - Bless All The Dear
    Children   18.2/27
Perry Mason: The Case Of The Murdered Madam
    18.1/29
Alfred Hitchcock Presents   18.0/28
Aurora   18.0/28
Cover Girl And The Cop, The   18.0/28
Danielle Steel's Fine Things   18.0/28
Inherit The Wind   18.0/29
Wild Texas Wind   18.0/27
Cast The First Stone   17.9/28
Decoration Day   17.9/28
I'll Be Home For Christmas   17.9/28
Love, Lies And Murder   15.5/24   20.3/30
Two Fathers' Justice   17.9/27
Danielle Steel's Changes   17.8/28
Seaquest Dsv   17.8/28
Without Her Consent   17.8/28
Woman Named Jackie, A   15.5/23   18.6/28
    19.1/30
Peter The Great   19.0/28   17.6/26   16.6/26   17.4/27

Rated Movies are listed by descending rating. Rated miniseries are listed by descending average of ratings. Unrated productions are listed alphabetically.

NBC CONTINUED

Bionic Showdown: The 6 Million Dollar Man/
  Bionic Woman 17.6/28
Bonanza: The Return 17.6/26
Fall From Grace 17.6/27
Beverly Hills Madam 17.5/27
Deadly Matrimony 16.1/25 18.9/29
Right To Die 17.5/28
Secrets Of A Married Man 17.5/27
Substitute Wife, The 17.5/27
Woman With A Past 17.5/27
Convicted: A Mother's Story 17.4/27
Perry Mason: The Case Of The Avenging Ace
  17.4/26
Perry Mason: The Case Of The Musical Murders
  17.4/26
She Knows Too Much 17.4/27
C. A. T. Squad 17.3/30
Gambler Returns: The Luck Of The Draw, The
  18.0/28 16.6/25
Love Is Never Silent 17.3/26
Matter Of Justice, A 15.2/23 19.4/29
People Across The Lake, The 17.3/27
Police Story: The Freeway Killings 17.3/27
Roxanne: The Prize Pulitzer 17.3/27
Swimsuit 17.3/27
Crime Of Innocence 17.2/26
Cry In The Wild: The Taking Of Peggy Ann
  17.2/27
Maybe Baby 17.2/26
Moving Target 17.2/25
Under Siege 17.2/24
Baywatch: Panic At Malibu Pier 17.1/28
Cartier Affair, The 17.1/27
Time To Live, A 17.1/27
From The Files Of Joseph Wambaugh: A Jury Of
  One 17/17
Jackie Collins' Lucky Chances 14.4/25 17.1/26
  19.5/31
Mom For Christmas, A 17.0/27
Perry Mason: The Case Of The Desperate
  Deception 17.0/27
Roe Vs. Wade 17.0/27
Roman Holiday 17.0/28
Your Mother Wears Combat Boots 17.0/28
Her Wicked Ways 16.9/26
Little White Lies 16.9/26
Playing With Fire 16.9/26
Danielle Steel's Heartbeat 16.8/26
Doing Life 16.8/27
Original Sin 16.8/26
Perry Mason: The Case Of The All-Star Assassin
  16.8/26
Settle The Score 16.8/26
Ted Kennedy, Jr., Story, The 16.8/26
Father Clements Story, The 16.7/26
Goddess Of Love 16.7/26
Haunted By Her Past 16.7/27
In Love And War 16.7/27
Mother's Justice, A 16.7/25
Perry Mason: The Case Of The Scandalous
  Scoundrel 16.6/26
What She Doesn't Know 16.6/25
Winnie 16.6/28
Final Jeopardy, The 16.5/26
Perry Mason: The Case Of The Silenced Singer
  16.5/27
Dangerous Affection 16.4/26

Six Against The Rock 16.4/24
Hands Of A Stranger 15.2/25 17.4/28
James Clavell's Noble House 17.9/27 15.9/24
  15.0/22 16.3/26
Full Exposure: The Sex Tapes Scandal 16.2/24
Rage Of Angels: The Story Continues 15.9/25
  16.5/25
Shattered Trust: The Shari Karney Story 16.2/25
Trial Of The Incredible Hulk, The 16.2/25
Downpayment On Murder 16.1/27
Knight Rider 2000 16.1/26
My Boyfriend's Back 16.1/26
Freedom Fighter 16.0/25
In The Best Interest Of The Children 16.0/24
Perry Mason: The Case Of The Poisoned Pen
  16.0/24
Return Of Desperado, The 16.0/24
Secret Sins Of The Father 16.0/24
Shootdown 16.0/25
Favorite Son 15.9/26 15.7/25 16.3/26
Adam: His Song Continues 15.9/25
Brand New Life: The Honeymoon 15.9/25
Danielle Steel's Star 15.9/24
Moment Of Truth: Stalking Back 15.9/25
Stone Fox 15.9/24
Story Lady, The 15.9/24
Child Saver, The 15.8/25
Cruel Doubt 16.8/27 14.8/24
Deadly Medicine 15.8/24
Family For Joe, A 15.8/23
Fatal Memories 15.8/24
Hitler's S S: Portrait In Evil 15.8/24
Popeye Doyle 15.8/26
Lincoln 16.6/26 14.9/24
Alamo: 13 Days To Glory, The 15.7/22
Triumph Over Disaster: The Hurricane Andrew
  Story 15.7/25
Danielle Steel's Secrets 15.6/24
Deception: A Mother's Secret 15.6/23
Joshua's Heart 15.6/26
Reason To Live, A 15.6/23
Romance On The Orient Express 15.6/24
Woman On The Ledge 15.6/24
Deep Dark Secrets 15.5/25
Fatal Confession: A Father Dowling Mystery
  15.5/24
Gifted One, The 15.5/27
Just My Imagination 15.5/19
Child Lost Forever, A 15.4/23
I'll Fly Away 15.4/24
Love On The Run 15.4/23
Manhunt: Search For The Night Stalker 15.4/24
Streets Of Justice 15.4/22
Eight Is Enough Wedding, An 15.3/25
Nasty Boys 15.3/27
Viper 15.3/23
Where Pigeons Go To Die 15.3/24
Drug Wars: The Camarena Story 14.4/22
  15.2/23 16.1/25
Hell Hath No Fury 15.2/24
Las Vegas Strip Wars, The 15.2/22
Danielle Steel's Jewels 14.7/22 15.6/24
Dream Date 15.1/24
Family Torn Apart, A 15.1/23
Last Days Of Frank And Jesse James, The 15.1/22
Love And Hate: A Marriage Made In Hell 13.9/25
  16.3/28
Marla Hanson Story, The 15.1/24
Shadow Of A Stranger 15.1/24
Diana: Her True Story 14.5/23 15.6/24

Going To The Chapel 15.0/25
She Says She's Innocent 15.0/23
Sins Of The Father 15.0/23
City Killer 14.9/24
Howard Beach: Making The Case For Murder
  14.9/24
Old Man & The Sea, The 14.9/24
Private Sessions 14.9/23
Quantum Leap 14.9/25
Chance Of A Lifetime 14.8/22
Children In The Crossfire 14.8/23
Cosby Mysteries, The 14.8/22
She Was Marked For Murder 14.8/24
Twist Of Fate 14.3/21 15.2/24
Carolina Skeletons 14.7/23
Fifth Missile, The 14.7/22
Follow Your Heart 14.7/23
In The Line Of Duty: Manhunt In The Dakotas
  14.7/26
Perry Mason: The Case Of The Defiant Daughter
  14.7/24
Perry Mason: The Case Of The Reckless Romeo
  14.7/23
She Said No 14.7/23
Bates Motel 14.6/27
Chase, The 14.6/23
Death Of The Incredible Hulk, The 14.6/22
Father & Son: Dangerous Relations 14.6/24
House Of Secrets 14.6/23
In The Deep Woods 14.6/23
In The Line Of Duty: A Cop For The Killing
  14.6/23
Perry Mason: The Case Of The Fatal Fashion
  14.6/23
Till Death Us Do Part 14.6/21
Behind Enemy Lines 14.5/23
Don't Touch My Daughter 14.5/23
Independence 14.5/23
Revealing Evidence 14.5/25
Secret Life Of Kathy Mccormick, The 14.5/26
Shannon's Deal 14.5/25
Too Young To Die? 14.5/23
Beyond Suspicion 14.4/22
In The Shadows, Someone Is Watching 14.4/22
Dirty Dozen: The Fatal Mission 14.3/22
Eye On The Sparrow 14.3/22
Promise To Keep, A 14.3/23
Grass Roots 13.4/20 15.1/23
Intimate Encounters 14.2/23
Misfits Of Science 14.2/23
Moment Of Truth: A Child Too Many 14.2/22
Moment Of Truth: Why My Daughter? 14.2/23
Annihilator, The 14.1/23
Glitz 14.1/25
Three On A Match 14.1/26
Casey's Gift: For Love Of A Child 14.0/22
In The Arms Of A Killer 14.0/22
Matlock: The Witness Killings 14.0/26
Perry Mason: The Case Of The Maligned Mobster
  14.0/22
Perry Mason: The Case Of The Ruthless Reporter
  14.0/21
True Blue 14.0/22
Around The World In 80 Days 15.5/24 13.2/21
  13.0/21
Daughters Of Privilege 13.9/23
Killer Among Us, A 13.9/23
Revenge Of Al Capone, The 13.9/22
Dark Shadows 14.6/23 13.1/21
Bay Coven 13.8/22

Rated Movies are listed by descending rating. Rated miniseries are listed by descending average of ratings. Unrated productions are listed alphabetically.

NBC CONTINUED

Jonathan: The Boy Nobody Wanted 13.8/21
Little Piece Of Heaven, A 13.8/21
Mirrors 13.8/22
Out Of Time 13.8/25
Secret Weapons 13.8/21
To My Daughter With Love 13.8/21
Turn Back The Clock 13.8/22
Bridge Across Time 13.7/21
In Broad Daylight 13.7/21
Cross Of Fire 12.5/20 14.7/23
Fergie And Andrew: Behind The Palace Doors 13.6/21
Maid For Each Other 13.6/21
Babies 13.5/22
Marcus Welby, M. D.: A Holiday Affair 13.5/21
Moment Of Truth: Cradle Of Conspiracy 13.5/21
To My Daughter 13.5/22
Jackie Collins' Lady Boss 12.7/20 14.2/22
Babes In Toyland 13.4/22
Blue Deville 13.4/22
I Married A Centerfold 13.4/21
If It's Tuesday, It Still Must Be Belgium 13.4/22
John And Yoko: A Love Story 13.4/19
Lena: My 100 Children 13.4/21
On Thin Ice: The Tai Babilonia Story 13.4/21
Great Escape I I: The Untold Story, The 14.4/23 12.3/19
Woman On The Run: The Lawrencia Bembenek Story 11.1/18 15.6/25
Black Widow Murders: The Blanche Taylor Moore Story 13.3/21
Danger Down Under 13.3/22
Desperate Rescue: The Cathy Mahone Story 13.3/20
Lady In A Corner 13.3/21
Miracle On I-880 13.3/20
Miss America: Behind The Crown 13.3/20
Perry Mason: The Case Of The Skin-Deep Scandal 13.3/22
Back To The Streets Of San Francisco 13.2/20
Girl Who Came Between Them, The 13.2/21
In The Line Of Duty: Standoff At Marion 13.2/20
Darkness Before Dawn 13.1/20
Desperado: Badlands Justice 13.1/21
Hart To Hart Returns 13.1/23
Highwayman, The 13.1/22
Journey To The Center Of The Earth 13.1/20
One Special Victory 13.1/20
Perry Mason: The Case Of The Telltale Talk Show Host 13.1/24
Tears And Laughter: The Joan And Mielissa Rivers Story 13.1/21
Mario Puzo's The Fortunate Pilgrim 13.1/22 13.0/21
Betrayal Of Trust 13.0/20
Drug Wars: The Cocaine Cartel 12.8/20 13.2/20
Sweet Bird Of Youth 13.0/21
Victim Of Love: The Shannon Mohr Story 13.0/19
From The Dead Of Night 11.6/20 14.3/22
Deadly Betrayal: The Bruce Curtis Story 12.9/20
In The Nick Of Time 12.9/20
Murder Between Friends 12.9/20
Perry Mason: The Case Of The Fatal Framing 12.9/20
Seasons Of The Heart 12.9/21
Blue Bayou 12.8/20
C. A. T. Squad: Python Wolf 12.8/20

For The Love Of My Child: The Anissa Ayala Story 12.8/20
Perry Mason: The Case Of The Glass Coffin 12.8/22
Relentless: Mind Of A Killer 12.8/20
Revenge On The Highway 12.8/19
Town Tom Apart, A 12.8/20
Crash: The Mystery Of Flight 1501 12.7/20
Final Appeal 12.7/20
Hijacking Of The Achille Lauro, The 12.7/20
Opposites Attract 12.7/21
Quiet Little Neighborhood, A Perfect Little Murder, A 12.7/21
Return Of Eliot Ness, The 12.7/19
Time To Heal, A 12.7/21
Moment Of Truth: Broken Pledges 12.6/20
Murder In Paradise 12.6/21
Peyton Place: The Next Generation 12.6/20
Prime Target 12.6/23
Shoot First: A Cop's Vengeance 12.6/20
When Will I Be Loved? 12.6/19
Father's Homecoming, A 12.5/23
Killer Instinct 12.5/19
Reason For Living: The Jill Ireland Story 12.5/21
Scene Of The Crime 12.5/21
Desperate Choices: To Save My Child 12.4/19
Fatal Friendship 12.4/19
Marked For Murder 12.4/20
Murder In Mississippi 12.4/20
Nutcracker: Money, Madness And Murder 12.2/20 11.5/19 13.5/22
One Woman's Courage 12.4/19
Silent Cries 12.4/20
Sun Also Rises, The 13.2/20 11.6/18
Extreme Close-Up 12.3/20
I Still Dream Of Jeannie 12.3/19
Miracle At Beekman's Place 12.3/21
Murder In High Places 12.3/22
Phantom Of The Opera, The 12.3/19 12.3/20
White Hot: The Mysterious Murder Of Thelma Todd 12.3/20
Barbara Taylor Bradford's Remember 10.9/18 13.5/21
Jonathan Stone: Threat Of Innocence 12.2/16
Mercy Mission: The Rescue Of Flight 771 12.2/19
Trial: The Price Of Passion 11.2/18 13.2/21
Witness To The Execution 12.2/17
Keys, The 12.1/19
Perry Mason: The Case Of The Heartbroken Bride 12.1/21
Fire Next Time, The 13.1/22 11.0/18
Bloodlines: Murder In The Family 10.7/17 13.3/21
Liberty 12.0/21
Love She Sought, The 12.0/18
In The Line Of Duty: Street War 11.9/20
Dreamer Of Oz, The 11.8/18
Guilty Until Proven Innocent 11.8/19
Lady Against The Odds 11.8/19
Long Road Home 11.8/18
. . . And Then She Was Gone 11.7/19
Passport To Murder 11.7/19
Danger Island 11.6/19
Florence Nightingale 11.6/19
Nightman, The 11.6/18
Return Of Ironside, The 11.6/19
Connecticut Yankee In King Arthur's Court, A 11.5/17
Fugitive Nights: Danger In The Desert 11.5/20
Heart Of A Child 11.5/18

Danielle Steel's Message From Nam 11.5/18 11.4/18
Baby Brokers 11.4/17
Class Cruise 11.4/19
Flood: Who Will Save Our Children? 11.4/18
Love Can Be Murder 11.4/18
Shadow Of Obsession 11.4/18
Hiroshima: Out Of The Ashes 11.3/20
Line Of Fire: The Morris Dees Story 11.3/17
Man Against The Mob: The Chinatown Murders 11.3/18
Murder Without Motive: The Edmund Perry Story 11.3/18
Shooter 11.3/20
Danielle Steel's Once In A Lifetime 11.2/16
Fatal Deception: Mrs. Lee Harvey Oswald 11.2/18
Hot Pursuit 11.2/21
Dark Holiday 11.1/18
Condition: Critical 11.0/18
Living A Lie 11.0/17
Miracle Child 11.0/18
Miss Rose White 11.0/17
Double Your Pleasure 10.9/18
Guess Who's Coming For Christmas 10.9/19
It's Nothing Personal 10.9/17
Thanksgiving Day 10.9/17
When We Were Young 10.9/19
For The Very First Time 10.8/18
In The Line Of Duty: The Price Of Vengeance 10.8/17
Kiss To Die For, A 10.8/17
Perry Mason Mystery, A: The Case Of The Lethal Lifestyle 10.8/18
She Stood Alone 10.8/18
Confessions: Two Faces Of Evil 10.7/16
Last Flight Out 10.7/18
Macshayne: Winner Take All 10.7/17
Web Of Deception 10.7/17
Archie: To Riverdale And Back Again 10.6/17
Eyes Of Terror 10.6/19
Born Too Soon 10.5/17
Midnight Hour, The 10.5/17
Search And Rescue 10.5/17
Summer My Father Grew Up, The 10.5/16
L. A. Takedown 10.4/18
Tonya & Nancy: The Inside Story 10.4/19
Murder C. O. D. 10.3/19
Two Fathers: Justice For The Innocent 10.3/17
Perry Mason Mystery: The Case Of The Wicked Wives 10.2/19
Leave Of Absence 10.1/15
To Heal A Nation 10.1/20
Visions Of Murder 10.1/19
Babe Ruth 10.0/16
People Like Us 9.4/16 10.5/17
Chameleons 9.9/17
Crossing The Mob 9.9/17
I Know My Son Is Alive 9.9/15
Appearances 9.8/18
Elvis And The Colonel: The Untold Story 9.8/14
Night Visions 9.8/17
South Beach 9.8/17
Double Deception 9.6/17
In The Shadow Of A Killer 9.5/15
Saved By The Bell-Hawaiian Style 9.5/17
Staying Afloat 9.5/17
Trouble Shooters: Trapped Beneath The Earth 9.5/15
Carly's Web 9.3/17
Love On The Run 9.3/16

NBC CONTINUED

Without Warning: Terror In The Towers 9.3/15
Killer Rules 9.2/14
Revolver 9.2/16
Good Cops, Bad Cops 8.9/14
Roommates 8.9/15
Steel Justice 8.9/14
Stuck With Each Other 8.9/16
Lethal Exposure 8.8/14
Day Of Reckoning 8.7/14
Amityville: The Evil Escapes 8.6/16
Parker Kane 8.6/15
Great Pretender, The 8.5/14
Ray Alexander: A Taste For Justice 8.5/15
Mothers, Daughters And Lovers 8.4/14
Camp Cucamonga 8.3/14
Macshayne: The Final Roll Of The Dice 8.3/15
Moment Of Truth: To Walk Again 8.3/12
Round Table, The 8.3/16
World War I I : When Lions Roared 9.1/15 7.5/12
Bermuda Grace 8.2/14
Secrets Of Lake Success 7.7/14 7.4/14 7.1/13
Polly—Comin' Home 6.8/10
Johnny Ryan 6.6/12
Trade Winds 6.9/13 6.2/13 5.4/11 5.8/11
Day - O 5.3/10

SHOWTIME

Assault At West Point
Birds I I: Land's End, The
Black Magic
Boris And Natasha
Chantilly Lace
Deadly Surveillance
Deceptions
Devlin
Disaster In Time
Double Jeopardy
Endless Game, The
Fatal Charm
Fear
Fear Inside, The
Flight Of Black Angel
Fourth Story
Gotham
Heads
Hit List, The
Hoover
Intimate Stranger
Keeper Of The City
Last Light
Liar's Edge
Love, Cheat And Steal
Love Matters
Lush Life
Mastergate
Nails
Neon Empire
Parallel Lives
Paris Trout
Past Tense
Payoff
Psycho I V: The Beginning
Rainbow Drive

Red Shoes Diaries
Roadracers
Roswell
Royce
Shadowhunter
Sketch Artist
Sodbusters
Souvenir
Taking The Heat
They
Uncle Tom's Cabin
When A Stranger Calls Back
Wrong Man, The

TNT

Abraham
Amelia Earhart: The Final Flight
American Clock, The
Borrowers, The
Breaking Point
Broken Chain
Captain Cook
Chernobyl: The Final Warning
Christmas In Connecticut
Cisco Kid, The
Cold Sassy Tree
Conagher
Cooperstown
Court - Martial Of Jackie Robinson, The
Crazy From The Heart
Crazy In Love
Crucifier Of Blood, The
Dead On The Money
Dinner At Eight
Duel Of Hearts
Final Verdict
Finish Line
Foreign Affairs
Forgotten Prisoners: The Amnesty File
Four Eyes And Six Guns
Frankenstein
Geronimo
Gettysburg
Ghost In Monte Carlo, A
Gore Vidal's Billy The Kid
Grand Isle
Habitation Of Dragons, The
Heart Of Darkness
Heart Of Justice, The
Heat Wave
Incident At Dark River
Iran: Days Of Crisis
Ironclads
Keep The Change
Last Elephant, The
Life In The Theater, A
Lost Capone, The
Man For All Season, A
Margaret Bourke - White
Max And Helen
Memphis
Miracle In The Wilderness
Montana
Never Forget
Nightmare Years, The
Orpheus Descending

Percy & Thunder
Portrait, The
Railway Station Man, The
Rising Son
Rose And The Jackal, The
Sea Wolf, The
Season Of Giants, A
Secret Life Of Ian Fleming, The
Secret Weapon
Sound And The Silence, The
Sweet Revenge
T Bone N Wessel
Treasure Island
Water Engine, The
Which Way Home
Young Catherine
Zelda

USA

Accidental Meeting
After The Shock
Are You Lonesome Tonight?
Bitter Vengeance
Black Ice
Blackmail
Blind Man's Bluff
Blind Vengeance
Blindfold: Acts Of Obsession
Blindsided
Body Language
Buried Alive
Case For Murder, A
Casualty Of War, A
Caught In The Act
Child Of Darkness, Child Of Light
China Lake Murders, The
Chrome Soldiers
Cover Girl Murders, The
Curiosity Kills
Dancing With Danger
Dangerous Heart
Dangerous Pursuit
Dead In The Water
Dead Reckoning
Deadly Desire
Deadly Game
Deadman's Revenge
Death Train
Deconstructing Sarah
Deep Trouble
Diamond Fleece
Dirty Work
Disappearance Of Christina, The
Don't Talk To Strangers
Drive Like Lightning
Drop Dead Gorgeous
Duplicates
Dying To Remember
Fade To Black
Fatal Exposure
Final Notice
Fire And Rain
Hider In The House
Hitler's Daughter
Hush Little Baby
I'm Dangerous Tonight

USA CONTINUED

Illicit Behavior
Indecency
Into The Badlands
Invasion Of Privacy
Jake Spanner, Private Eye
Jericho Fever
Just Another Secret
Kissing Place, The
Lady Killer
Last Hit, The
Legacy Of Lies
Lies Of The Twins
Lightning Incident, The
Linda
Lookalike, The
Love Kills
Marilyn & Bobby: Her Final Affair
Matters Of The Heart
Mortal Sins
Murder 101
Murder By Night
Murderous Vision
Nightlife
Nightmare On The Thirteenth Floor
Nobody's Children
Not A Penny More, Not A Penny Less
Perfect Bride, The
Personals
Praying Mantis
Pride And Extreme Prejudice
Psychic
Quicksand: No Escape
Red Wind
Rubdown
Running Against Time
Secret Passion Of Robert Clayton, The
Seduced By Evil
Sex,Love, And Cold Hard Cash
Shattered Image
Silent Witness
Silhouette
Snow Kill
Sorry, Wrong Number
Spider And The Fly, The
Spy
Strays
Substitute, The
Sunstroke
Survive The Night
Sweet Poison
Tagget
Tainted Blood
Take, The
Target Of Suspicion
Taste For Killing, A
Ten Million Dollar Getaway
This Gun For Hire
Trapped
Treacherous Crossing
Trial And Error
Voyage
Web Of Deceit
Wheels Of Terror
White Lie
Wild Card
Writer's Block

Section E

TV MOVIES BASED ON BOOKS, PLAYS AND ARTICLES

TITLE OF BOOK/PLAY	AUTHOR	TVMOVIE/MINI
A Time To Remember	Stanley Shapiro	Running Against Time-USA
Alex: The Life of a Child	Frank Deford	Alex: The Life of a Child-ABC
Alice In Wonderland	Lewis Caroll	Alice in Wonderland -CBS
Alice	Sara Flanigan	Wildflower-Lifetime
Almost Too Late	Elmo Wortman	Anything To Survive-ABC
Alter Ego	Mel Arrighi	Murder By the Book-CBS
Amelia Earhart: A Biography	Doris L. Rich	Amelia Earhart: The Final Flight-TNT
American Clock, The (Play)	Arthur Miller	American Clock, The-TNT
Amityville: The Evil Escapes	John G.Jones	Amityville:The Evils Escapes-ABC
And Deliver Us From Evil	Mike Cochran	Fugitive Among Us-CBS
And The Band Played On	Randy Shilts	And The Band Played On-HBO
And The Sea Will Tell	Vincent Bugliosi	And The Sea Will Tell-CBS
Anna Karenia	Leo Tolstoy	Anna Karenina -CBS
Anne Frank Remembered	Miep Gies, Alison Gold	The Attic: Hiding Of Anne Frank -CBS
Appointment For Murder	Susan C. Bakos	Beyond Suspicion- NBC
April Morning	Howard Fast	April Morning-CBS
Arch of Triumph	Erich Remarque	Arch of Triumph-CBS
Ari: The Life & Times Of Aristotle Onassis	Peter Evans	The Richest Man in the World-ABC
Around the World In 80 Days	Jules Verne	Around the World In 80 Days-NBC
As Summers Die	Winston Groom	As Suimmers Die-HBO
Assault and Matrimony	James Anderson	Assault and Matrimony-NBC
At Mothers Request	Jonathan Coleman	At Mothers Request CBS
Awakening, The	Kate Chopin	Grand Isle-TNT
B-Ball	Ron Jones	One Special Victory-NBC
Babes In Toyland	Victor Herbet	Babes In Toyland-NBC
Barbarians At The Gate	B. Burrough & J. Helyar	Barbarians At The Gate-HBO
Beirut (Play)	Alan Bowne	Daybreak -HBO
Bejeweled	Marion Babson	Bejeweled-Disney
Best Intentions	Robert Anson	Murder Without Motive-NBC
Beyound Obsession	Richard Hammar	Beyound Obsession-ABC
Billionaire Boys Club	Sue Horton	Billionaire Boys Club-NBC
Bitter Blood	Jerry Bledsoe	In the Best of Families-CBS
Bitter Harvest: Murder In The Heartland	James Corcoran	In The Line of Duty: Manhunt Dakotas-NBC
Black Hope Horror	Ben & Jean Williams	Grave Secrets- NBC
Blind Faith	Joe McGuinniss	Blind Faith-NBC
Blood and Orchids	Norman Katkov	Blood and Orchids -CBS
Blood Brothers	John Johnson & Ron Soble	Honor Thy Father and Mother-FBC
Blood Games	Jerry Bledsoe	Honor Thy Mother-CBS
Bluegrass	Borden Deal	Bluegrass-CBS
Bobby Rex's Greatest Hits	Marianne Gringher	Just My Imagination-NBC
Born Too Soon	Elizabeth Mehren	Born Too Soon-NBC
Borrowers, The	Mary Norton	Borrowers, The - TNT
Bourne Identity	Robert Ludlum	Bourne Identity-ABC
Breathing Lessons	Anne Tyler	Breathing Lessons-CBS
Broadway Bound(Play)	Neil Simon	Broadway Bound-ABC
Broken Cord, The	Michael Dorris	Broken Cord, The -ABC
Brotherhood of the Rose	David Morrell	Brotherhood of the Rose-NBC
Brotherly Love	William Blankenship	Brotherly Love-CBS
Bundy: The Deliberate Stranger	Richard W. Larsen	Deliberate Stranger-NBC
Bunny's Tale	Gloria Steinem	Bunny's Tale, A -ABC
Burden Of Proof, The	Scott Turow	Burden of Proof, The-ABC
Cabin B-13 (Radio Play)	John Dickson	Treacherous Crossing-USA
Caine Mutiny Court Martial	Herman Wouk	Caine Mutiny Court Martial-CBS
Call Of The Wild	Jack London	Call Of The Wild-CBS
Camile	Alexander Dumas	Camile-CBS
Carolina Skeletons	David Stout	Carolina Skeletons-NBC
Casualty of War, A	Frederick Forsyth	Casualty of War, A-USA
Celle Qui N'etait Plus	Pierre Boileau	House of Secrets - NBC
Changes	Danielle Steel	Changes NBC
Chisolm Trail , The	Borden Chase	Red River-CBS
Christmas Carol, A	Charles Dickens	A Christmas Carol-CBS
Christy	Catherine Marshall	Christy-CBS
Citizen Cohen	Nicholas von Hoffman	Citizen Cohen-HBO
Cold Sassy Tree	Olive Ann Burn	Cold Sassy Tree-TNT

MOVIES AND MINISERIES BASED ON BOOKS

TITLE OF BOOK/PLAY	AUTHOR	TVMOVIE/MINI
Conagher	Louis L'Amour	Conagher-TNT
Connecticut Yankee In King Arthur's Court	Mark Twain	Connecticut Yankee In King Arthur's Court-NBC
Consenting Adult	Laura Hobson	Consenting Adult-ABC
Conspiracy of Silence	Lisa Priest	Conspiracy of Silence-CBS
Cops Are Robbers,The	Gerald Clemente	Good Cops, Bad Cops-NBC
Corsican Brothers, The	Alexandre Dumas	The Corsican Brothers-CBS
Country Of The Heart, The	Barbara Wersby	Matters Of The Heart-USA
Court-Martial of Johnson Whittaker	John F. Marszalek	Assault At West Point- SHOWTIME
Crazy In Love	Luanne Rice	Crazy In Love- TNT
Crucifer Of Blood, The(Play)	Paul Gioavanni	Crucifer of Blood-TNT
Cruel Doubt	Joe McGinniss	Cruel Doubt-NBC
Cupid Rides Pillion	Barbara Cartland	Lady and the Highwayman CBS
Danger Adrift	Folco Quilici	Only One Survived-CBS
David's Mother (Play)	Bob Randall	David's Mother-CBS
Dead Air	Mike Lupica	Money, Power, Murder-CBS
Dead Solid Perfect	Dan Jenkins	Dead Solid Perfect-HBO
Deadly Blessing	Steve Salerno	Bed Of Lies-ABC
Deadly Intentions	William R. Stevens	Deadly Intentions -ABC
Deadly Relations	Carol Donahue	Deadly Relations-ABC
Deadly Silence, A	Dena Kleiman	Deadly Silence,A -ABC
Death And Deliverance	Robert Mason	Ordeal In The Arctic-ABC
Death In California	Joan Barthel	Death In California-ABC
Death of A Salesman	Arthur Miller	Death of A Salesman-CBS
Death Train	Alistair MacLean	Death Train-USA
Deceptions	Judith Mitchell	Deceptions-NBC
Decoration Day	John William Corrington	Decoration Day-NBC
Deep Trouble	Bruno Tardon	Deep Trouble-USA
Desperate Justice	Richard Speight	Mothers Revenge, A- ABC
Desperate Rescue (Article)	N.Livingstone & D Halevy	Desperate Rescue-NBC
Devlin	Roderick Thorp	Devlin-Showtime
Diana: Her True Story	Andrew Morton	Diana: Her True Story-NBC
Doc	Susan K.Campbell	Town Torn Apart, A -NBC
Donato And Daughter	Jack Early	Donato And Daughter-CBS
Dress Gray	Lucian Truscott	Dress Grey-NBC
Duel of Hearts	Barbara Cartland	Duel of Hearts-TNT
Echoes In the Darkness	Joseph Wambaugh	Echoes In the Darkness-CBS
Eighty-Three Hours Till Dawn	B. Mackie, G. Miller	Eighty-Three Hours Till Dawn-CBS
Ellis Island	Fred Mustard Stewart	Ellis Island-CBS
Elvis and Me	Priscillia Presley	Elvis and Me -ABC
Enchantment	Dorothy Quick	Mark Twain And Me-Disney
End Of Tragedy, The	Rachel Ingalls	Dead On the Money-TNT
Endless Game, The	Bryan Forbes	Endless Game, The -SHOWTIME
Escape From Sobibor	Richard Rashke	Escape From Sobibor-CBS
Evergreen	Belva Plain	Evergreen-NBC
Evidence of Love	John Bloom	Killing In A Small Town-CBS
Eye of the Beholder	Seymour Epstein	Comeback,The -CBS
Face of A Stranger (Article)	Mary Stuart	Face of A Stranger-CBS
Face of Fear, The	Dean Koontz	Face of Fear, The-CBS
Fairy Tales	Hans Christian Andersen	Litte Match Girl, The-NBC
Fall From Grace	Larry Collins	Fall From Grace-CBS
False Witness	Dorothy Uhnak	False Witness-NBC
Family Pictures	Sue Miller	Family Pictures-ABC
Fatal Dosage	Gary Provost	Fatal Judgment-CBS
Fatal Vision	Joe McGinniss	Fatal Vision-NBC
Fathers Arcane Daughter	E.L. Konigsberg	Caroline?-CBS
Ferguson Affair,The	Ross MacDonald	Criminal Behavior-ABC
Final Days	Woodward & Bernstein	Final Days-ABC
Final Verdict	Adela Rogers St. John	Final Verdict-TNT
Fire And Rain	Jerome Chandler	Fire And Rain-USA
Fitzgeralds And The Kennedy's, The	Doris Kearn Goodwin	Kennedy's of Massachusetts ABC
Foreign Affairs	Alison Lurie	Foreign Affairs-TNT
Fortress	Gabrielle Lord	Fortress-HBO
Fortunate Pilgrim, The	Mario Puzo	Mario Puzo's Fortunate Pilgrim-NBC
Foxfire (Play)	Susan Cooper	Foxfire-CBS

TITLE OF BOOK/PLAY	AUTHOR	TVMOVIE/MINI
Frankenstein	Mary Shelley	Frankenstein-TNT
French Silk	Sondra Brown	French Silk-ABC
Fugitive Nights: Danger in the Desert	Joseph Wambaugh	Fugitive Nights: Danger in the Desert-NBC
Fulfillment, The	La Vyrle Spencer	The Fulfillment of Mary Gray CBS
Gathering of Old Men, A	Ernest Gaines	Gathering of Old Men,A -CBS
George Washington II	James T. Flexner	George Washington: The Forging Of A Nation-CBS
Getting Out (Play)	Marsha Norman	Getting Out-ABC
Getting Up And Going Home	Robert Anderson	Getting Up And Going Home-LIFETIME
Ghost in Monte Carlo, A	Barbara Cartland	Ghost in Monte Carlo,A-TNT
God Crew, The	Thomas N. Scortia	The Fifth Missile-NBC
Graced Land	Laura Kalpakian	Woman Who Loved Elvis-ABC
Grass Roots	Stuart Woods	Grass Roots-NBC
Great Diamond Robbery, The	John Minahan	The Diamond Trap-CBS
Great Expectations	Charles Dickens	Great Expectations-Disney
Guests Of The Emperor	Janice Brooks	Silent Cries-NBC
Guts & Glory: Rise and Fall Of Oliver North	Ben Bradlee Jr.	Guts and Glory-CBS
Gypsy (Play)	Arthur Laurents	Gypsy-CBS
Habitation Of Dragons, The(Play)	Horton Foote	Habitation Of Dragons-TNT
Hamlet, The	William Faulkner	Long Hot Summer-NBC
Hand In The Glove	Rex Stout	Lady Against The Odds-NBC
Hands of A Stranger	Robert Daley	Hands of A Stranger-NBC
Harmful Intent	Robin Cook	Harmful Intent-CBS
Haunted, The	Rober Curran	Haunted, The -FBC
Hazard of Hearts, A	Barbara Cartland	Hazard of Hearts-CBS
Heart Of Darkness	Joseph Conrad	Heart Of Darkness-TNT
Heartbeat	Danielle Steel	Danielle Steel's Heartbeat-NBC
Heartsounds	Martha Lear	Heartsounds-ABC
Heaven and Hell: North & South	John Jakes	North and South Part 3-ABC
Hedda and Louella	George Eells	Malice in Wonderland-CBS
Heidi	Johanna Spyri	Heidi-Disney
Hitler's Daughter	Timothy R. Benford	Hitler's Daughter-USA
Hot Toddy	Andy Edwards	White Hot: Murder of Thelma Todd-NBC
I'll Take Manhattan	Judith Krantz	I'll Take Manhattan-CBS
In A Child's Name	Peter Maas	In A Child's Name-CBS
In Love And War	Jim &Sybil Stockdale	In Love And War-NBC
In The Deep Woods	Nicholas Conde	In The Deep Woods-NBC
In The Glitter Dome	Joseph Wambaugh	In The Glitter Dome-HB0
In This Sign	Joanne Greenberg	Love Is Never Silent-NBC
Inconvenient Woman, An	Dominick Dunne	Inconvenient Woman, An-ABC
Indiscreet -(Play)	Norman Krasna	Indiscreet-CBS
Inherit The Wind (Play)	J. Lawrence & R.E. Lee	Inherit The Wind-NBC
Intensive Care	Mary-Lou Weisman	A Time To Live-NBC
Investigation, The	Dorothy Uhnaks	Kojak:The Price of Justice - CBS
It	Stephen King	Stephen King's It-ABC
Jane's House	Robert Kimmel Smith	Jane's House, CBS
Jewels	Danielle Steel	Danielle Steel's Jewels-NBC
JFK: Reckless Youth	Nigel Hamilton	JFK: Reckless Youth - ABC
Jody	Jerry Hulse	Family Of Strangers-CBS
Journey To The Center Of The Earth	Jules Verne	Journey To Center Of The Earth-NBC
Just Another Secret	Frederick Forsyth	Just Another Secret-USA
Kane And Abel	Jeffrey Archer	Kane And Abel-CBS
Keep The Change	Thomas McGuane	Keep The Change-TNT
Keeping Secrets	Suzanne Somers	Keeping Secrets-ABC
Kill Fee	Barbara Paul	Murder C.O.D.-NBC
Killer Angels	Michael Shaara	Gettysburg-TNT
Lace	Shirley Conran	Lace II-ABC
Lady Boss	Jackie Collins	Jackie Collin's Lady Boss-NBC
Laguna Heat	T. Jefferson Parker	Laguna Heat-HBO
Last Days of Patton	Ladislas Farago	Last Days of Patton-CBS
Last Innocent Man, The	Philip Margolin	Last Innocent Man, The-HBO
Last Jews in Berlin, The	Leonard Gross	Forbidden-HB0
Last Prostitute, The (Play)	William Border	Last Prostitute, The - LIFETIME
Last Stop, The	Matt Benjamin	And Than She Was Gone-NBC
Last To Go, The	Rand Richards	Last To Go, The -ABC

MOVIES AND MINISERIES BASED ON BOOKS

TITLE OF BOOK/PLAY	AUTHOR	TVMOVIE/MINI
Last Wish	Betty Rollin	Last Wish-ABC
Lie Down With Lions	Ken Follett	Lie Down With Lions-LIFETIME
Life In The Theater, A (Play)	David Mamet	Life In The Theater, A - TNT
Life Lines	Jill Ireland	Reason For Living-NBC
Lincoln	Gore Vidal	Lincoln-NBC
Little Match Girl,The	Hans C. Anderson	Little Match Girl-NBC
Lonesome Dove	Larry McMurtry	Lonesome Dove-CBS
Long Hot Summer	William Faulkner	Long Hot Summer-NBC
Long Kill, The	Partrick Ruell	Last Hit, The-USA
Long Road Home	Ronald B. Taylor	Long Road Home-NBC
Lost Hero: The Mystery Of Raoul Wallenberg	F.E. Werbell, T. Clarke	Wallenburg: A Hero's Story-NBC
Louisiana Black	Samuel Charter	White Lie-USA
Lucky Chances	Jackie Collins	Lucky Chances-NBC
Mafia Marriage	Rosalie Bonanno	Love, Honor And Obey-CBS
Man in the Brown Suit	Agatha Christie	Man in the Brown Suit-CBS
Master Builder, The (Short Story)	Christopher Fowler	Through The Eyes Of A Killer-CBS
Max And Helen	Simon Wisenthal	Max And Helen-TNT
Mayflower Madam	Sydney B.Barrows	Mayflower Madam-CBS
Menu For Murder	Valerie Wolzien	Menu For Murder-CBS
Message From Nam	Danielle Steel	Danielle Steel's Message From Nam-NBC
Middle Ages	A.R. Gurney	My Brother's Wife-ABC
Mike Hammer:Murder Takes All	Mickey Spillane	Mickey Spillane's Mike Hammer-CBS
Miracle Child	Patricia Pendergraft	Miracle Child-NBC
Miracle In The Wilderness	Paul Gallico	Miracle In The Wilderness-TNT
Mischief	Charlotte Armstrong	Sitter, The-FBC
Miss Rose White(Play)	Barbara Lebow	Miss Rose White-NBC
Mistral's Daughter	Judith Krantz	Mistral's Daughter-CBS
Mittleman's Hardware	George R. Small	Finding the Way Home-ABC
Mobbed Up	James Neff	Teamster Boss: J.Presser Story-HBO
Mom By Magic, A	Barbara Dillon	Mom For Christmas -NBC
Monte Carlo	Stephen Carlo	Monte Carlo-CBS
Mrs. 'Arris Goes To Paris	Paul Gallico	Mrs. 'Arris Goes To Paris-CBS
Murder in Three Acts	Agatha Christie	Murder in Three Acts-CBS
Murders in the Rue Morgue	Edgar Allan Poe	Murders in the Rue Morgue-CBS
My Breast	Joyce Wadler	My Breast-CBS
My Father, My Son	Elmo Zumwalt	My Father, My Son-CBS
My Husband, Rock Hudson	Phyllis Gates	Rock Hudson-ABC
Necessity	Brian Garfield	Necessity-CBS
Never Pass This Way Again	Gene LePere	Dark Holiday-NBC
Nightmare	M. Dorner	Don't Touch My Daughter NBC
Nightmare Years, The	William Shirer	Nightmare Years-TNT
No Business Being A Cop	Lillian O'Donnell	Prime Target-NBC
Noble House	James Clavell	James Clavell's Nobel House-NBC
North And South	John Jakes	North And South-ABC
Not A Penny More, Not A Penny Less	Jeffrey Archer	Not A Penny More, Not a...USA
Nutcracker:Money, Madness, Murder	Shana Alexander	Nutcracker:Money, Madness, Murder - NBC
O Pioneers!	Willa Cather	O Pioneers! -CBS
Odd Couple	Neil Simon	Odd Couple-CBS
Of Pure Blood	Marc Hillel,Clarissa Henry	Of Pure Blood-CBS
Old Dick, The	L.A. Morse	Jake Spanner: Private Eye-USA
Old Man & The Sea	Ernest Hemmingway	Old Man & The Sea- NBC
Oldest Living Confederate Widow Tells All	Allan Gurganus	Oldest Living Confederate Widow Tells All-CBS
On Wings of Eagles	Ken Follett	On Wings of Eagles-NBC
Once In a Life Time	Danielle Steel	Danielle Steel's Once in a Lifetime-NBC
Orpheus Descending	Tennessee Williams	Orpheus Descending-TNT
Other Women's Children	Perri Klass	Other Women's Children-LIFETIME
Out On A Limb	Shirley MacLaine	Out On a Limb -ABC
Outrage	Henry Denker	Outrage-CBS
Pack of Lies (Play)	Hugh Whitemore	Pack of Lies-CBS
Painting Churches (Play)	Tina Howe	Portrait, The-TNT
Paris Trout	Pete Dexter	Paris Trout-SHOWTIME
Passing For Love	Bill Crenshaw	Blackmail-USA
Penthouse, The	Elleston Trevor	The Penthouse-ABC
People Like Us	Dominick Dunne	People Like Us-NBC

TITLE OF BOOK/PLAY	AUTHOR	TVMOVIE/MINI
Perfect Tribute, The	Mary Andrews	Perfect Tribute, The-ABC
Peter The Great	Robert K. Massey	Peter The Great- NBC
Phantom Of The Opera	Gaston Leroux	Phantom Of The Opera-NBC
Plaza Suite (Play)	Neil Simon	Plaza Suite-ABC
Point of Murder, The	Margaret Yorke	Kiss Of A Killer-ABC
Poor Little Rich Girl	C. David Heymann	Poor Little Rich Girl-NBC
Pork Butcher, The	David Hughes	Souvenir-SHOWTIME
Preacher	Ted Thackrey Jr.	Wild Card-USA
Preachers Girl	Jim Schutze	Black Widow Murders-NBC
Precious Victims	C.Bosworth, D.Weber	Precious Victims-CBS
President's Child, The	Fay Weldon	President's Child, The, CBS
Pride And Extreme Prejudice	Frederick Forsyth	Pride & Extreme Prejudice-USA
Promise To Keep, A	Jane Yarmolinsky	Promise To Keep,A-NBC
Pursuit	Robert J. Fish	Twist of Fate-NBC
Queen	Alex Haley	Queen-CBS
Queenie	Michael Korda	Queenie-ABC
Quick and the Dead	Louis L'Amour	Quick and the Dead-HBO
Railway Station Man, The	Jennifer Johnson	Railway Station Man, The-TNT
Rainbow Drive	Roderick Thorp	Rainbow Drive-SHOWTIME
Remember	Barbara Taylor Bradford	Barbara T. Bradford's Remember-NBC
Rich Men, Single Women	Pamela Beck	Rich Men, Single Women-ABC
Rise & Walk	Dennis Byrd	Rise & Walk-FBC
Rockabye	Laird Koenig	Rockabye-CBS
Room Upstairs, The	Norma Levinson	The Room Upstairs-CBS
Room, The (play)	Harold Pinter	The Room-ABC
Roses Are For the Rich	Jonell Lawson	Roses Are For The Rich CBS
Roxanne: The Prize Pulitzer	Roxanne Pulitzer	Roxanne: The Prize Pulitzer-NBC
Runaway Father	Richard Rashke	Runaway Father-CBS
Sarah, Plain And Tall	Patricia MacLochlan	Sarah, Plain And Tall-CBS
Sea Wolf, The	Jack London	Sea Wolf, The-TNT
Second Serve	Renee Richards	Second Serve-CBS
Secret Garden,The	Frances Hodgson Burnett	The Secret Garden-CBS
September, September	Shelby Foote	Memphis- TNT
Shell Seekers, The	Rosamunde Pilcher	Shell Seekers, The-ABC
Shootdown: Flight 007	R.W.Johnson	Shootdown-NBC
Sins	Judith Gould	Sins-CBS
Small Sacrifices	Ann Rule	Small Sacrifices-ABC
Smithereens	B.W. Batin	Hell Hath No Fury-NBC
Solider Of Fortune Murders, The	Ben Green	When Love Kills-CBS
Someone's Watching	Judith Kelman	In The Shadows... NBC
Sometimes They Come Back	Stephen King	S.King's Sometime They...CBS
Son Also Rises,The	Ernest Hemmingway	Sun Also Rises-NBC
Son Of The Morning Star	Evan S. Connell	Son Of The Morning Star-ABC
Sorry Wrong Number (Radio Play)	Lucite Fletcher	Sorry Wrong Number-USA
Space	James Michener	Space-CBS
Spoils of War (Play)	Michael Weller	Spoils of War-ABC
Stand, The	Stephen King	Stephen King's The Stand-ABC
Star	Danielle Steel	Danielle Steel's Star-NBC
Stillwatcch	Mary Higgins Clark	Stillwatch-CBS
Stone of Ibarra	Harriet Doerr	Stone of Ibarra-CBS
Storm And Sorrow	Robert Craig	Storm And Sorrow-LIFETIME
Sudden Fury	Leslie Walker	Family Torn Apart, A - NBC
Sudie	Sara Flanigan Carter	Sudie and Simpson-LIFETIME
Sweet Bird of Youth (Play)	Tennessee Williams	Sweet Bird of Youth-NBC
T Bone and Weasel (Play)	Jon Klein	T Bone and Weasel-TNT
Tagget	Irving A. Greenfield	Tagget-USA
Tainted Blood	Ginny Cerrella	Tainted Blood-USA
Tenth Man, The	Graham Greene	Tenth Man, The-CBS
There Are No Children Here	Alex Kotlowitz	There Are No Children Here-ABC
There Must Be A Pony	James Kirkwood	There Must Be A Pony-ABC
There Was A Little Boy	Claire R. Jacobs	There Was A Little Boy-CBS
They	Rudyard Kipling	They- SHOWTIME
Thirteen At Dinner	Agatha Christie	Agatha Christie's Thirteen At Dinner-CBS
Thirteen Days to Glory:Siege Of The Alamo	Lon Tinkle	Alamo: Thirteen Days to Glory-NBC

MOVIES AND MINISERIES BASED ON BOOKS

TITLE OF BOOK/PLAY	AUTHOR	TVMOVIE/MINI
This Gun For Hire	Graham Greene	This Gun For Hire-USA
This Park Is Mine	Stephen Peters	This Park Is Mine-HBO
Till Death Do Us Part	Vincent Buglisosi	Till Death Do Us Part-NBC
Till We Meet Again	Judith Krantz	Till We Meet Again-CBS
Time of My Life, The	Betty Ford &Chris Chase	The Betty Ford Story-ABC
Tintype, The	Ray Brown	Timestalkers-CBS
To Be The Best	Barbara Taylor Bradford	To Be The Best-CBS
To Heal A Nation	Jan Scruggs,	To Heal A Nation-NBC
Tommyknockers,The	Stephen King	S. King's Tommyknockers-ABC
Torch Song	Judith Krantz	Torch Song-ABC
Treasure Island	Robert L. Stevenson	Treasure Island-TNT
Trial	Clifford Irving	Trial: Price of Passion-NBC
Two Mrs. Grenvilles, The	Dominick Dunne	Two Mrs. Grenvilles-NBC
Uncle Tom's Cabin	Harriet Beecher Stowe	Uncle Tom's Cabin-SHOWTIME
Unholy Matrimony	John Dillman	Unholy Matrimony-CBS
Unspeakable Acts	Dan Hollingsworth	Unspeakable Acts-ABC
Untamed Love	Torey Hayden	Untamed Love- LIFETIME
Unwanted Attentions	K.K. Beck	Shadow of Obsession-NBC
Vengeance	George Jonas	Sword Of Gideon-HBO
Victim	Gary Kinder	Aftermath:A Test Of Love CBS
Vintage Season	C. L. Moore	Disaster In Time-SHOWTIME
Virgin	James Patterson	Child of Darkness, Child Of Light-USA
Walk Me To The Distance	Percival Evertt	Follow Your Heart-NBC
Walkers	Gary Brandner	From the Dead Of Night-NBC
Wallflower	William Bayer	Forget Me Not Murders, The-CBS
War And Remembrance	Herman Wouk	War And Remembrance-ABC
Water Engine, The (Play)	David Mamet	Water Engine, The -TNT
We Let Our Son Die	Larry Parker	Promised A Miracle-CBS
What Ever Happened to Baby Jane	Henry Farrell	What Ever Happened to Baby Jane-ABC
When Angels Intervene	Hartt & Judene Wixcom	To Save the Children-CBS
When Rabbit Howls	Truddi Chase	Voices Within-ABC
When The Bough Breaks	Jonathan Kellerman	When The Bough Breaks-NBC
When You Remember Me(Article)	Rena LeBlanc	When You Remember Me-ABC
Where Pigeons Go To Die	R. Wright Campbell	Where Pigeons Go To Die-NBC
Where the Streets Go Dark	Dorothy S. Davis	Broken Vows-CBS
Who is Julia?	Barbara S. Harris	Who is Julia?-CBS
Whose Child Is This ? (Article)	Lucindia Franks	Whose Child Is This?-ABC
Why Have They Taken Our Children	J. Baugh,J.Mogan	They've Taken Our Children-ABC
Windmills of the Gods	Sidney Sheldon	Windmill of the Gods-CBS
Woman Named Jackie, A	C. David Heymann	Woman Named Jackie, A-NBC
Women of Brewster Place	Gloria Naylor	Women of Brewster Place-ABC
Wrong Man, The	Roy Carlson	Wrong Man, The-SHOWTIME
Yearling, The	Marjorie K. Rawlings	Yearling, The-CBS
You Must Be Dreaming	B. Noel, K. Watterson	Betrayal Of Trust-NBC

Section F

WRITERS

Cross-referenced by
Produced Credits

ABATEMARCO, FRANK
I Can Make You Love Me: The Stalking Of
....Laura Black

ABBOTT, CHRIS
Little House On The Prairie - Bless All The
....Dear Children

ABRAMOWITZ, DAVID
Daughter Of The Streets

ADAMS, RICHARD DeLONG
At Mother's Request
Family Of Spies
Honor Thy Mother

AHNEMANN, MICHAEL
Necessity

ALBRECHT, HOWARD
Stuck With Each Other

ALFIERI, RICHARD
Addicted To His Love

ALLEN, BYRON
Case Closed

ALLEN, CURT
Blind Vengeance

ALLEN, J.T.
Geronimo

ALTABEF, RICHARD
Kissing Place, The

AMBROSE, DAVID
Blackout
Fall From Grace

ANDERSON, HESPER
Deliberate Stranger, The
Grand Isle

ANDERSON, JANE
Positively True Adventures Of The Alleged
Texas Cheerleader Murdering Mom, The

ANDERSON, ROBERT
Absolute Strangers

ANDREWS, GUY
Lie Down With Lions

ANDRUS, JEFF
As Summers Die
Children Of The Dark
Fatal Image, The
Men Don't Tell
Miles From Nowhere
Proud Men
Separated By Murder
Triumph Of The Heart: The Ricky Bell Story

ANGELI, MICHAEL
Sketch Artist

ANHALT, EDWARD
Peter The Great
Take, The

APPLING, A.L.
Running Mates

ARTHUR, LEO
Miracle On I-880

ASH, ROD
Get Smart Again
Mother Goose Rock 'n' Rhyme

ASIMOW, DYANNE
Complex Of Fear

ASTLE, TOM J.
Bejeweled

AUGUST, KEN
Betrayed By Innocence

AVRECH, ROBERT J.
Scandal In A Small Town
Secret Life Of Ian Fleming, The

AXNESS, JOHN
Lucky Day

AYRES, ALEX
Search For Grace

AYRES, GERALD
Crazy In Love
Stormy Weathers

BADALUCCO, NICOLA
Mussolini: The Decline And Fall Of Il Duce

BADAT, RANDALL
Born To Run

BAER, ART
Glitter

BAGNI-DUBOV, GWEN
Eight Is Enough: A Family Reunion

BAKER, BART
Baby Of The Bride
Children Of The Bride
Mother Of The Bride

BAKER, ELLIOTT
Lace I I
To Be The Best

BAKER, MICHAEL
Dead Ahead: The Exxon Valdez Disaster

BALCER, RENE
Out On The Edge
Stranger In The Family, A

BALDWIN, ROY
Brass

BALOFF, PETER
Quicksand: No Escape
Spooner

BARBER, LARRY
Calendar Girl, Cop Killer? The Bambi
....Bembenek Story

BARBER, PAUL
Calendar Girl, Cop Killer? The Bambi
....Bembenek Story

BARDACH, ANN LOUISE
Sorry, Wrong Number

BARR, DOUGLAS
Cover Girl Murders, The
Fade To Black

BARRETT, JAMES LEE
April Morning
Defiant One, The
In The Heat Of The Night
Jesse
Poker Alice
Quick And The Dead, The
Stagecoach
Vengeance: The Story Of Tony Cimo

BARRIE, MICHAEL
Many Happy Returns

BART, DUFFY
Fight For Jenny, A

BARZMAN, AARON
Fatal Image, The

BASKIN, SUSAN
Born Too Soon
Labor Of Love: The Arlette Schweitzer Story

BASS, RON
Enemy Within, The

BAST, BILL
Big One: The Great Los Angeles Earthquake
Danielle Steel's Secrets
Twist Of Fate

BATTEER, JOE
Curiosity Kills

BAUM, THOMAS
Drop Dead Gorgeous
Night Visions
Secret Weapons
Witness To The Execution

BAXTER, LUCRETIA
Mothers' Right, A: The Elizabeth Morgan
....Story

BAYER, WILLIAM
Internal Affairs

BEAIRD, JOHN
North Beach And Rawhide

BEARD, WINSTON
Queenie

BEATTS, ANNE
Nightlife

BECKETT, ANN
Broken Cord, The
Little Girl Lost
Without Her Consent

BEEBE, DICK
Dead And Alive
Into The Badlands

BEKALA, WILLIAM
Silent Movie

BELL, ELISA
Dancing With Danger

Treacherous Crossing
Writer's Block

BELLISARIO, DONALD P.
Quantum Leap
Three On A Match

BELLO, STEPHEN
Doing Life
Fatal Deception: Mrs. Lee Harvey Oswald
Howard Beach: Making The Case For Murder

BELOUS, PAUL W.
Street Hawk

BENEDETTI, ROBERT
Mercy Mission: The Rescue Of Flight 771

BENEST, GLENN M.
Naked Lie

BENNETT, HARVE
Crash Landing: The Rescue Of Flight 232

BENSINK, BEAU
Hell Hath No Fury

BENSINK, JOHN ROBERT
Don't Touch My Daughter
Mothers Revenge, A
Naked Lie
Nightmare In Columbia County
Sparks: The Price Of Passion
Whisper Kills, A

BERARDO, CHRISTINE
Overexposed

BERCOVICI, ERIC
Fifth Missile, The
James Clavell's Noble House

BERG, DICK
Space

BERGER, RICK
Sitter, The

BERGMAN, LINDA
Lookalike, The
Matters Of The Heart
Rio Shanon

BERK, MICHAEL
Baywatch: Panic At Malibu Pier
Crime Of Innocence

BERNBAUM, PAUL
Royce

BERNICE, GIESELA
Parallel Lives

BERNSTEIN, WALTER
Doomsday Gun

BEST, PETE
Accidental Meeting

BILSON, DANNY
Flash, The
Viper

BINDER, JOHN
Assault And Matrimony
Houston: The Legend Of Texas

BIRKE, DAVID
Fear Inside, The

BISHOP, WESLEY
There Was A Little Boy

BITETTO, FRANK
Born To Run

BLACK, DAVID
Cosby Mysteries, The
Legacy Of Lies
Nasty Boys

BLACK, STEPHEN
Love Among Thieves
Stranded

BLACK, SUSAN
State Of Emergency

BLACKWELL, SAM
Danger Of Love, The
No Place Like Home

BLAKE, ROBERT
Father Of Hell Town

BLECHMAN, COREY
Max And Helen
Special People
Three Wishes Of Billy Grier, The

BLEICH, WILLIAM
Danger Island
Deadly Messages
From The Dead Of Night
Gladiator, The
Good Cops, Bad Cops
Midnight Hour, The
Smokey Mountain Christmas, A
Stepford Children, The
When Dreams Come True

BLESSING, LEE
Cooperstown

BLINN, WILLIAM
Aaron's Way
Appearances
Outside Woman, The
Polly--Comin' Home

BLODGETT, MICHAEL
Revenge On The Highway

BLOM-COOPER, STEPHAN
Stormy Weathers

BLOODWORTH, LINDA
London And Davis In New York

BLOOM, HAROLD JACK
Stuck With Each Other

BLOOM, JEFFREY
Brotherhood Of Justice, The
Columbo Goes To College
Fire: Trapped On The 37th Floor
Right Of The People, The
Scene Of The Crime
Starcrossed

BOAM, JEFFREY
Adventures Of Brisco County Jr., The

BOCHCO, STEVEN
L. A. Law

BOHEM, LES
Desperado: Badlands Justice

BOLT, ROBERT
Man For All Season, A
Without Warning: The James Brady Story

BOMBECK, MATTHEW
And Then She Was Gone

BOND, JULIAN
Lie Down With Lions
Season Of Giants, A

BOORSTIN, JON
Dark Shadows

BOORSTIN, PAUL
Angel Of Death

BOORSTIN, SHARON
Angel Of Death

BORCHERT, WILLIAM G.
My Name Is Bill W.

BORGHI, DOUGLAS STEFAN
Operation, The

BORIS, ROBERT
Izzy And Moe
Marilyn & Me

BORTMAN, MICHAEL
Single Bars, Single Women

BOTKIN, NANCY
The Race To Freedom: The Underground
....Railroad

BOYLE, DONALD R.
Miracle At Beekman's Place

BOZZONE, BILL
Last Elephant, The

BRADFORD, HANK
Ghost Of A Chance

BRADSHAW, TIMOTHY
Too Good To Be True

BRAITHWAITE, DIANA
The Race To Freedom: The Underground
....Railroad

BRAND, JOSHUA
I'll Fly Away

BRATTLESTREET, CALIOPE
Poisoned By Love: The Kern County Murders

BRAVERMAN, MICHAEL
Condition: Critical
Donor

BRECHER, JIM
Secret Life Of Kathy Mccormick, The

BRIDGES, JAMES
Alfred Hitchcock Presents

BRITTANY, ANNE
Held Hostage: The Sis And Jerry Levin Story

BROIDO, JOE
I Know My Son Is Alive

BROMBECK, MATTHEW
Family Torn Apart, A

BROMBERG, CONRAD
Killer Instinct
Silent Witness
Welcome Home, Bobby

BRONSON, DAN
Last Innocent Man, The
Taste For Killing, A

BROOKS, ADAM
Heads

BROTHERS, LARRY
Fever

BROWN, BARRY
Seduction: Three Tales From The Inner Sanctum

BROWN, CHARLOTTE
Letting Go

BROWN, DENNIS
Perfect Tribute, The

BROWN, JAMES HARMON
Love Boat: A Valentine Voyage, The
Rich Men, Single Women

BROWN, MICHAEL HENRY
Laurel Avenue

BROWN, RITA MAE
Long Hot Summer, The
My Two Loves
Rich Men, Single Women
Woman Who Loved Elvis, The

BROWN, STEVE
Sister Margaret And The Saturday Night ....Ladies
Vestige Of Honor

BROWNE, L. VIRGINIA
Danielle Steel's Daddy
Deadly Medicine

BROWNELL, JANET
Backfield In Motion
Beyond Control: The Amy Fisher Story
Children Of The Dark
Christmas In Connecticut
Sweet Revenge
Torch Song

BROWNING, ROD
Agatha Christie's Dead Man's Folly
Agatha Christie's Thirteen At Dinner
First Steps

BROYLES, JR., WILLIAM
J F K: Reckless Youth
Under Cover

BRYANT, CHRIS
Foreign Affairs
One Against The Wind
Sword Of Gideon
Young Catherine

BUCKNER, BRAD
Blue Deville
Cartier Affair, The

BUELL, VICTOR
Silhouette

BUHAI, JEFF
Revenge Of The Nerds I V: Nerds In Love
Revenge Of The Nerds: The Next Generation
Thanksgiving Day

BULLOCK, HARVEY
Return To Mayberry

BURDITT, JOYCE
Diagnosis Of Murder
Perry Mason Mystery: The Case Of The Wicked Wives
Perry Mason: The Case Of The Telltale Talk Show Host
Under The Influence

BURGER, ROBBYN
Seasons Of The Heart

BURNS-BISOGNO, LOUIS
Bridge To Silence

BURRELL, MARYEDITH
In The Nick Of Time
Little Match Girl, The

BURRILL, CHRISTINE
Counterfeit Contessa, The

BUSH, HUGH
Trade Winds

BUTLER, MICHAEL
White Mile

BYRE, JOE
Gambler Returns: The Luck Of The Draw

BYRNES, JIM
Deadman's Revenge
Gunsmoke: Return To Dodge
Miracle In The Wilderness

BYRUM, JOHN
Middle Ages
Murder In High Places

CACACI, JOE
Her Final Fury: Betty Broderick, The Last ....Chapter
Murder In New Hampshire: The Pamela ....Smart Story
Not In My Family
Woman Scorned: The Betty Broderick Story

CAMERON, LORNE
Clarence

CAMPION, CLIFFORD
Burning Rage
Love, Mary

Samaritan: The Mitch Snyder Story

CAMPUS, MICHAEL
Man Who Broke 1,000 Chains, The

CANAAN, CHRISTOPHER
Broken Promises: Taking Emily Back
Cries Unheard: The Donna Yaklich Story
Drug Wars: The Camarena Story
Hitler's Daughter
Love, Honor & Obey: The Last Mafia ....Marriage
Seduction In Travis County
Ten Million Dollar Getaway

CANNELL, STEPHEN J.
Broken Badges
Great Pretender, The
Palace Guard
Thunderboat Row

CARDEA, FRANK
Dying To Remember
Search And Rescue
Still Crazy Like A Fox

CARDONE, J.S.
Shadowhunter

CARDUCCI, MARK PATRICK
Buried Alive

CARLEN, JOHN
Blind Side
Easy Prey
Sworn To Vengeance
Thompson's Last Run
Wild Texas Wind

CARLINER, MARK
Disaster At Silo 7

CARNER, CHARLES ROBERT
Eyes Of A Witness
Killer Among Friends, A
Seduced

CARON, GLENN GORDON
Long Time Gone
Moonlighting

CARPENTER, JOHN
Blood River
El Diablo

CARPENTER, RICHARD
Borrowers, The

CARR, CALEB
Bad Attitudes

CARRAU, BOB
Ewok Adventure, The

CARRINGTON, ROBERT
Blind Witness

CARTER, CHRIS
Brand New Life: The Honeymoon

CARTWRIGHT, GARY
Pair Of Aces

CASS, DAVID
Rio Diablo

CASSIDY, SHAUN
Strays

CAVENDER, KENNETH
Littlest Victims
Special Friendship, A

CAVESTANI, FRANK
Sentimental Journey

CHANDLER, ELIZABETH
Afterburn

CHAPMAN, LEIGH
Storm And Sorrow

CHAPMAN, RICHARD
Codename: Foxfire - Slay It Again, Sam
E. A. R. T. H. Force
Hart To Hart Returns

CHASKIN, DAVID
Midnight's Child

CHERBAK, CYNTHIA
Bridesmaids
Broken Angel
Kissing Place, The
Lucy & Desi: Before The Laughter
Secret, The

CHETWYND, LIONEL
Children In The Crossfire
Doomsday Gun
Heroes Of Desert Storm
So Proudly We Hail
To Heal A Nation

CHISHOLM, DAVID
Deadman's Revenge
Longarm
Over My Dead Body

CHOLODENKO, SEAN
Perry Mason: The Case Of The Fatal Framing
Perry Mason: The Case Of The Maligned Mobster
Perry Mason: The Case Of The Ruthless Reporter

CHRIST, BRYANT
Frankenstein: The College Years

CIDRE, CYNTHIA
I Saw What You Did
Killing In A Small Town

CIRILLO, PARTICK
Dangerous Heart

CLARIDGE, WES
Deadly Game

CLARK, DENNIS LYNTON
Court - Martial Of Jackie Robinson, The

CLARK, KAREN
Beyond Suspicion
For The Very First Time
Long Journey Home, The

CLARK, L. TRAVIS
Court - Martial Of Jackie Robinson, The

CLAUSER, SUZANNE
Danielle Steel's Message From Nam
North And South, Book 3: Heaven And Hell

CLAYTON, WALTER
Eyes Of A Witness

CLEMENS, BRIAN
Perry Mason: The Case Of The Glass Coffin
Perry Mason: The Case Of The Heartbroken Bride
Perry Mason: The Case Of The Reckless Romeo
Timestalkers

CLOUD, DARRAH
Haunted, The

COE, LIZ
Moment Of Truth: Why My Daughter?

COHEN, BENNETT
Rainbow Drive

COHEN, LAWRENCE D.
Stephen King's It
Tommyknockers, The

COHN, JEFF
Double Your Pleasure
Sins Of The Father

COLE, TOM
Disappearance Of Nora

COLICK, LEWIS
Crossing The Mob

COLLINS, ANNE
Matlock: The Witness Killings
Perry Mason: The Case Of The Defiant Daughter
Perry Mason: The Case Of The Lost Love
Perry Mason: The Case Of The Shooting Star
Perry Mason: The Case Of The Silenced Singer
Perry Mason: The Case Of The Sinister Spirit

COLLINS, JACKIE
Jackie Collins' Lady Boss
Jackie Collins' Lucky Chances

COLLINS, ROBERT
Hijacking Of The Achille Lauro, The
Hoover
In The Arms Of A Killer
Intrigue
Prime Target

COLLIS, ALAN
He's Not Your Son

COMICI, ELIZABETH
Outback Bound

COMICI, LUCIANO
Outback Bound

CONDON, BILL
Murder 101

CONNOLLY, JON
Working Trash

CONROY, PAT
Unconquered

CONWAY, GERRY
Perry Mason: The Case Of The Heartbroken Bride
Perry Mason: The Case Of The Killer Kiss
Twist Of The Knife, A

COOK, DOUGLAS S.
Payoff

COOK, T.S.
Attack On Fear
In The Line Of Duty: Street War
Out Of The Darkness
Switch, The

COOPER, SUSAN
Foxfire
Promise To Keep, A
To Dance With The White Dog

COREA, NICHOLAS
Incredible Hulk Returns, The
Mario And The Mob

CORR, EUGENE
Getting Out

COTLER, GORDON
Blade In Hong Kong
Deadly Deception
Facts Of Life Down Under, The
Murder In Black And White
Picking Up The Pieces

COUTURE, SUZETTE
Betrayal Of Trust
Conspiracy Of Silence
Love And Hate: A Marriage Made In Hell

COWEN, RON
An Early Frost
Love She Sought, The

CRABBE, PETER
Dream Date

CRAIG, CHARLES GRANT
Return Of Desperado, The

CRAIS, ROBERT
Cross Of Fire
In Self Defense

CRANE, ROBERT
Hostage For A Day

CRAVEN, WES
Night Visions

CRAVIOTTO, DARLENE
Love Is Never Silent
Sentimental Journey

CRAWFORD, OLIVER
Execution, The

CRAYS, DURRELL ROYCE
Cry In The Wild: The Taking Of Peggy Ann
Lady Forgets, The
Stranger Waits, A

CRIDER, STEVE
Case Closed

CRONER, KAREN
Scattered Dreams: The Kathryn Messenger
....Story

CROSS, ALISON
Hearst And Davies Affair, The
Roe Vs. Wade
With Hostile Intent

CROWE, CHRISTOPHER
Steel Justice
Streets Of Justice

CROWLEY, MART
Barbara Taylor Bradford's Remember
Bluegrass
People Like Us
There Must Be A Pony

CRUICKSHANK, JIM
Love On The Run

CULVER, CARMEN
If Tomorrow Comes
Last Prostitute, The

CULVER, FELIX
Hostage Flight
Jessie

CUMMINGS, JOSEPHINE
Blind Justice

CURRAN, WILLIAM
Love, Cheat And Steal

CURRIER, LAUREN
Those Secrets

CURTIS, DAN
Dark Shadows
War And Remembrance
War And Remembrance, Part I I

CURTISS, MARK
Get Smart Again
Mother Goose Rock 'n' Rhyme

CUSCUNA, SUSAN
Joshua's Heart

CUSE, CARLTON
Adventures Of Brisco County Jr., The
Promise To Keep, A

DALTON, DEBORAH
Kiss To Die For, A
Precious Victims

DANIELS, STAN
For Richer, For Poorer
Substitute Wife, The

DAVID, MARJORIE
Into The Badlands
Margaret Bourke - White
With Hostile Intent

DAVIDSON, SARA
Bloodlines: Murder In The Family

DAVIES, WILLIAM
Bermuda Grace

DAVIS, GLENN
South Beach

DAVIS, IVAN
Broken Vows

DAVIS, WALTER HALSEY
Father & Son: Dangerous Relations
Great Escape I I: The Untold Story, The
Last Flight Out
Oceans Of Fire
Resting Place
Silent Cries
Stone Fox

DAWSON, DEBORAH ZOE
Bring Me The Head Of Dobie Gillis

DAWSON, GORDON
Independence
Into The Badlands

DAWSON, LAVINA
Time To Triumph, A

DAY, GERRY
Columbo: Undercover

DE BLASIO, EDWARD
Dynasty: The Reunion

DE CROWL, VAL
Yes, Virginia, There Is A Santa Claus

DE FELITTA, FRANK
Killer In The Mirror
Penthouse, The

DE GARMO, DENISE
Kate's Secret
Terror In The Night

DE GUZMAN, MICHAEL
Babe Ruth
Caroline?
Red Earth, White Earth
To My Daughter With Love
We Are The Children

DE JARNATT, STEVE
Alfred Hitchcock Presents

DE LAURENTIS, ROBERT
South Beach

DE ROCHE, EVERETT
Fortress

DE SOUZA, STEVEN E.
Spirit, The
Supercarrier

DELANEY, SHELAGH
Railway Station Man, The

DELLIGAN, WILLIAM
Praying Mantis
Shattered Image

DeMEO, PAUL
Flash, The

DEMPSEY, TOM
Trenchcoat In Paradise

DENBOW, KEN
Deceptions

DENKER, HENRY
Outrage

DENSHAM, PEN
Lifepod

DESMARAIS, JAMES
Victim Of Love

DEXTER, PETE
Paris Trout

DI LELLO, RICHARD
Popeye Doyle

DI PEGO, GERALD
Death Of The Incredible Hulk, The
Forget Me Not Murders, The
Freedom Fighter
Generation
Keeper Of The City
Miracle Child
Mom For Christmas, A
Murder In Paradise
One More Mountain
Trial Of The Incredible Hulk, The

DI STEFANO, DAN
Nightmare On The Thirteenth Floor

DIAL, BILL
Codename: Foxfire - Slay It Again, Sam

DIAMOND, JANIS
Tagget

DIAZ, BILL
E. A. R. T. H. Force

DINALLO, GREG
Ladykillers

DOBBS, FRANK
Rio Diablo

DOBBS, LEM
Hider In The House

DOMINIC, HENRY
Flight Of Black Angel

DONAHUE, ANN
Sharing Richard

DONNELLY, TOM
Blindsided

DORFF, MATT
Complex Of Fear

DOTT, JAMES
Island Sons

DOUGHERTY, JOSEPH
Attack Of The 50ft. Woman
Cast A Deadly Spell

DOWN, RENA
Aaron's Way

DOWNES, ANSON
Boris And Natasha

DOWNING, STEPHEN
Alone In The Neon Jungle
Without Warning: Terror In The Towers

DOYLE, SHARON
Babymaker: The Dr. Cecil Jacobson's Story
Gregory K
Stolen Babies

DRISKILL, BILL
Bloodlines: Murder In The Family
Downpayment On Murder
False Witness
Fatal Friendship

DUFF, JAMES
Doing Time On Maple Drive
Without A Kiss Goodbye

DUNCAN, PATRICK
Live: From Death Row

DUNCAN, STEVE
Court - Martial Of Jackie Robinson, The

EATON, MICHAEL
Tragedy Of Flight 103: The Inside Story, The

ECKSTEIN, GEORGE
Bad Seed, The
Moment Of Truth: To Walk Again
Murder With Mirrors
My Name Is Kate
Perry Mason: The Case Of The Desperate
Deception
Perry Mason: The Case Of The Musical
Murders
Perry Mason: The Case Of The Poisoned Pen

EDELMAN, ROSEMARY
Side By Side

EDENS, MARK EDWARD
How To Murder A Millionaire
Mickey Spillane's Mike Hammer: Murder
....Takes All

EDSON, ERIC
Rose And The Jackal, The

EDWARDS, BLAKE
Peter Gunn

EDWARDS, PAUL F.
Dillinger
North And South
Ordeal In The Arctic

EISELE, ROBERT
Last Light

EISEN, MATTHEW
Lies And Lullabies

EISENSTOCK, ALAN
If It's Tuesday, It Still Must Be Belgium

ELIAS, MICHAEL
Lush Life

ELIASON, JOYCE
Babycakes
Elvis And Me
In Sickness And In Health
Jacksons: An American Dream , The
Mistress
Oldest Living Confederate Widow Tells All
Right To Kill?
Small Sacrifices
Surviving
To Save A Child
Winnie

ELKINS, STEPHEN
Only One Survived
Plot To Kill Hitler, The

ELLIOTT, SAM
Conagher

ENGLISH, DIANE
Classified Love

ENGLISH, PRICILLA
Moment Of Truth: Stalking Back

ENGLUND, GEORGE
Challenger
Las Vegas Strip Wars, The

EPSTEIN, DAVID
Murders In The Rue Morgue, The
Nairobi Affair
Sworn To Vengeance

EPSTEIN, JACOB
Relentless: Mind Of A Killer

ESENSTEIN, BARBARA
Love Boat: A Valentine Voyage, The
Rich Men, Single Women

ESTRIN, ALLEN
Bare Essentials
Warm Hearts, Cold Feet

ESTRIN, JONATHAN
Danielle Steel's Jewels

ESTRIN, MARK
Bare Essentials
Warm Hearts, Cold Feet

EVANS, DAVID MICKEY
Journey To The Center Of The Earth

EVANS, NICK
Secret Weapon

EVANS, SHELLY
Lady Killer

EYRE, JR., DAVID
Everybody's Baby: The Rescue Of Jessica
....Mcclure
Laguna Heat
Roots: The Gift
They've Taken Our Children: The Chowchilla
....Kidnapping
What Price Victory?
Wife, Mother, Murderer

FALK, PETER
Columbo: It's All In The Game

FALSEY, JOHN
I'll Fly Away

FAUCI, DAN
Follow Your Heart

FAVILA, LINDA
Boris And Natasha

FEATHER, JACQUELINE
Malice In Wonderland
My Father, My Son
Richest Man In The World: The Aristotle
....Onassis Story
Whose Child Is This? The War For Baby
....Jessica

FEDADY, ANDREW J.
Sea Wolf, The

FEELY, TERENCE
Duel Of Hearts
Ghost In Monte Carlo, A
Hazard Of Hearts, A
Lady And The Highwayman, The

FEIGELSON, J.D.
Nightmare On The Thirteenth Floor

FEKE, STEVE
Dark Shadows
Trapped

FENADY, ANDREW J.
Jake Spanner, Private Eye
Yes, Virginia, There Is A Santa Claus

FENJVES, PABLO
Bitter Vengeance
Case For Murder, A

FERGUSON, BLAIR
Guess Who's Coming For Christmas
Place To Be Loved, A

FERGUSON, LARRY
Nails

FERNANDEZ, RAUL
Just One Of The Girls

FERRER, SASHA
In Defense Of A Married Man

FIELDER, GEORGE
For Love And Glory

FIELDER, RICHARD
George Washington I I: The Forging Of A
....Nation
North And South, Book 2
Red River
Sins Of The Mother

FISCHER, PETER S.
Blacke's Magic
Murder, She Wrote
Stranger At My Door
Tagget

FISCHOFF, STUART
Miles To Go . . .

FISHER, TERRY LOUISE
Blue Bayou
L. A. Law
Sister Margaret And The Saturday Night
....Ladies
Two Thousand Malibu Road

FITZGERALD, BENEDICT
Heart Of Darkness
Zelda

FLANIGAN, SARA
Sudie And Simpson
Wildflower

FLASHNER, GRAHAM
Adrift

FLETCHER, LUCILLE
Nightman, The

FOLK, ROBERT
Lily

FOOTE, HORTON
Habitation Of Dragons, The

FORBES, BRYAN
Endless Game, The

FORD, PATRICIA
Columbo - Caution: Murder Can Be
....Hazardous To Your Health

FOREMAN, STEPHEN H.
Hostage

FORSYTHE, WILLIAM W.
Killing Mind, The

FOSTER, ROBERT
Price She Paid, The

FOSTER, TONY
Sound And The Silence, The

FOX, TERRY CURTIS
Perfect Witness

FRADIN, CHARLES
Boris And Natasha

FRANKLIN, GEORGE
Personals

FRANKLIN, JEFF
To Grandmother's House We Go

FRANZONI, DAVID
Citizen Cohn

FRASER, GEORGE MACDONALD
Casanova

FREED, DONALD
King Of Love, The

FREEDMAN, ROBERT L.
Honor Thy Mother
In The Best Of Families: Marriage, Pride And
....Madness
Locked Up: A Mother's Rage
No Child Of Mine

Taken Away
Woman With A Past

FREELY, TERRENCE
Mistral's Daughter

FREILICH, JEFF
Club Med

FREIMAN, RICHARD
Our Family Honor

FRESCO, ROB
Intimate Stranger

FREUDENBERGER, DANIEL
Do You Know The Muffin Man?
Good Night, Sweet Wife: A Murder In Boston
Stay The Night
With Murder In Mind

FRIED, ROBERT
He's Not Your Son

FRIEDENBERG, RICHARD
Promise

FRIEDMAN, IRIS
Nobody's Children
Obsessive Love

FRIEDMAN, RICHARD
Shadow Of A Stranger

FROHMAN, CLAY
Court - Martial Of Jackie Robinson, The

FROHMAN, MEL
Drug Wars: The Camarena Story
Father's Revenge, A
High Price Of Passion, The
Lies Of The Twins

FROST, MARK
Twin Peaks

FROST, SCOTT
Past Tense

FULLER, CHARLES
Gathering Of Old Men, A

FULLER, DAVID
Heist

GADNEY, REG
Iran: Days Of Crisis

GALATI, FRANK
American Clock, The

GALLAGHER, MARY
Bonds Of Love
Nobody's Child

GALLERY, MICHELE
Daughters Of Privilege
Sexual Advances

GALLUP, RALPH
Pack Of Lies

GANZEL, MARK
Fresno

GARMAN, STEPHANIE
Love Boat: A Valentine Voyage, The

GARRETT, LILA
Who Gets The Friends?

GAST, HAROLD
Guilty Of Innocence: The Lenell Geter Story
Ironclads
Shakedown On The Sunset Strip

GAVER, ELEANOR E.
Dead In The Water

GAY, JOHN
Blind Faith
Burden Of Proof, The
Cruel Doubt
Doubletake
Fatal Vision
Final Notice
Inherit The Wind
Manhunt For Claude Dallas
Shadow Of A Doubt
Six Against The Rock
Trial: The Price Of Passion
Uncle Tom's Cabin
Windmills Of The Gods

GELBART, LARRY
Barbarians At The Gate
Mastergate

GENTILE, LANCE
State Of Emergency

GERARD, ANNE
Rape Of Dr. Willis, The
Town Torn Apart, A

GERNON, ED
Adrift

GETHERS, STEVEN
Case Of The Hillside Strangler, The
Marcus Welby, M. D.: A Holiday Affair
Mercy Or Murder?
Rape Of Dr. Willis, The

GIBBINS, DUNCAN
Third Degree Burn

GILBERT, BRUCE
By Dawn's Early Light

GILL, ELIZABETH
Convicted: A Mother's Story
Mayflower Madam
Roxanne: The Prize Pulitzer
Sins Of The Father

GILLIS, JACKSON
Columbo: A Bird In The Hand
Stoning In Fulham County, A

GILMER, ROB
Another Pair Of Aces: Three Of A Kind
Jury Duty: The Comedy
Love And Curses . . . And All That Jazz
Love Can Be Murder
Maid For Each Other

GLANZ, STEPHEN
Poisoned By Love: The Kern County Murders

GLASS, ROBERT
Death Dreams
Not Of This World
Running Against Time
Seduction: Three Tales From The Inner
Sanctum

GLASSBERG, HANDEL
Day My Parents Ran Away, The
Take, The

GLEASON, MICHAEL
Macshayne: Winner Take All

GLUECKMAN, ALAN JAY
Face Of Fear, The

GOFF, ANNABEL DAVIS
Dangerous Affection

GOLDBERG, BETTY
Leave Of Absence
Little Piece Of Heaven, A
One Special Victory

GOLDEMBERG, ROSE LEIMAN
Burning Bed, The
Dark Holiday
Florence Nightingale
Stone Pillow

GOLDMAN, JAMES
Anastasia: The Mystery Of Anna
Anna Karenina

GOLDSMITH, JOHN
Great Expectations

GOLDSTEIN, JOSH
Partners 'N Love

GOLDSTONE, DEENA
Bunny's Tale, A

GOODELL, GREGORY
Aftermath: A Test Of Love
Grave Secrets: The Legacy Of Hilltop Drive
Perfect People
Shattered Spirits
Ultimate Betrayal
When Love Kills: The Seduction Of John
....Hearn

GOODMAN, MICHAEL PATRICK
Angel In Green

GORDON, DAN
Gulag
Taking The Heat

GORDON, JILL
Pleasures

GORSCH, LYLE
This Park Is Mine

GOUGH, WILLIAM
Family Of Strangers
Stolen: One Husband
Tarzan In Manhattan

GOULD, DIANA
House Of Secrets And Lies, A
I'll Take Manhattan

GRABENSTEIN, CHRISTOPHER
Christmas Gift, The

GRAFTON, SUE
Love On The Run
Tonight's The Night

GRANGER, PERCY
Comeback, The
My Brother's Wife

GRANT, HARRY
Ride With The Wind

GRAY, JOHN
American Story, An
Around The World In 80 Days
Lost Capone, The
Marla Hanson Story, The
When He's Not A Stranger

GRAY, SHERMAN
Hitler's Daughter

GRAY, WILLIAM
Abduction Of Kari Swenson, The

GREEK, JANET
Passions

GREEN, GERALD
Fatal Judgment
Wallenberg: A Hero's Story

GREEN, PATRICIA
Christy
North And South
Perry Mason: The Case Of The Murdered
Madam

GREEN, WALON
Robert Kennedy And His Times

GREENBAUM, EVERETT
Return To Mayberry

GREENBERG, STANLEY
Breaking Point

GREENMAN, ADAM
Breaking The Silence
In The Shadows, Someone Is Watching
Overexposed

GREISMAN, GORDON
Drug Wars: The Cocaine Cartel
Fugitive Among Us
Jonathan Stone: Threat Of Innocence

GROSS, JOEL
Blind Man's Bluff

GROSS, LEONARD
Forbidden

GRUSIN, LARRY
Between Two Women

GUENETTE, ROBERT
Children Of The Night

GUERDAT, ANDREW
Dance Till Dawn
Fourth Story

GULINO, PAUL JOSEPH
Murderous Vision

GUNN, JOSEPH
Manhunt: Search For The Night Stalker
Shoot First: A Cop's Vengeance

GUNTER, ROBERT
Journey To The Center Of The Earth

GURSKIS, DAN
Body Language

GUTCHEON, BETH
Good Fight, The

GUTHRIE, LEE
Place For Annie, A

GUTTMAN, RICHARD
Last Elephant, The
Touch Of Scandal, A
Toughest Man In The World, The

HACKIN, DENNIS
Marked For Murder
Weekend War

HACKIN, STEVEN
Weekend War

HAGGIS, PAUL
Due South

HAILEY, OLIVER
Adam: His Song Continues

HAINES, FRED
Survive The Savage Sea

HALE, BOYD
To Grandmother's House We Go

HALES, JONATHAN
Young Indiana Jones Chronicles: The Curse
....Of The Jackal

HALL, KAREN
Betty Ford Story, The
Darkness Before Dawn
Toughlove
Women Of Brewster Place, The

HALL, PETER
Orpheus Descending

HAMILL, ALANNA
Spider And The Fly, The

HAMILL, PETE
Laguna Heat
Liberty
Neon Empire

HAMILTON, ROBERT
Laker Girls, The
Perry Mason: The Case Of The All-Star
Assassin

HAMM, SAM
Mantis

HAMMERSTEIN, JANE-HOWARD
Long Road Home

HANALIS, BLANCHE
Camille
Christmas Eve
I'll Be Home For Christmas
Secret Garden, The

HANLEY, WILLIAM
Attic: The Hiding Of Anne Frank, The
In Broad Daylight
Kennedys Of Massachusetts, The
Last To Go, The
Nutcracker: Money, Madness And Murder
Our Sons
When The Time Comes

HANSON, CURTIS
Children Of Times Square

HARGROVE, DEAN
Diagnosis Of Murder
Diary Of A Perfect Murder
Perry Mason Returns
Ray Alexander: A Taste For Justice

HARRIGAN, STEVE
Last Of His Tribe, The

HARRIS, DANIEL
Ghost Mom

HARRIS, MATT
Brass

HARRISON, JOHN
Memories Of Murder

HARRISON, JOHN KENT
Sound And The Silence, The

HARRISON, LINDSAY
Coins In The Fountain
My Boyfriend's Back
Take My Daughters, Please
Turn Back The Clock
White Hot: The Mysterious Murder Of
....Thelma Todd

HART, BRUCE
Held Hostage: The Sis And Jerry Levin Story
Leap Of Faith

HARTUNG, RAYMOND
Fatal Exposure
I Know My Son Is Alive
Snow Kill

HARWOOD, RICHARD
Under Siege

HARWOOD, RONALD
Mandela

HASBURGH, PATRICK
Destination: America
N. Y. P. D. Mounted
Sunset Beat

HAWKESWORTH, JOHN
Mrs. 'Arris Goes To Paris

HAWKINS, D. VICTOR
Between Love And Hate

HAYES, CLYDE ALLEN
Rubdown

HAYES, JOHN MICHAEL
Pancho Barnes

HEANEY, JANET
Lies And Lullabies
Mrs. Lambert Remembers Love

HEATH, LAURENCE
Christopher Columbus
Sins

HEDDEN, ROB
Knight Rider 2000
Return Of Ironside, The

HEFFRON, RICHARD T.
Tagget

HEINEMANN, ARTHUR
Father Clements Story, The
Victims For Victims - The Theresa Saldana
....Story

HELLER, CRAIG
Jailbirds
Return To Green Acres

HELLER, LUKAS
Hitler's S S: Portrait In Evil

HEMPHILL, JOHN
Sodbusters

HENDERSHOT, ERIC
Impostor, The

HENDRYX, SHIRYL
Final Jeopardy, The

HENERSON, JAMES S.
And The Sea Will Tell
Fire Next Time, The
For Love Or Money
Getting Gotti
I'll Take Romance
Mother's Justice, A
To Save The Children

HENSLEY, J. MIYOKO
Can You Feel Me Dancing?

HENSLEY, STEVEN
Can You Feel Me Dancing?

HERSKOWITZ, MARSHALL
Extreme Close-Up

HERZFELD, JOHN
Barbara Taylor Bradford's Remember
Casualties Of Love: The Long Island Lolita
....Story
Daddy
On Fire
Preppie Murder, The
Ryan White Story, The

HESTON, FRASER C.
Crucifier Of Blood, The
Treasure Island

HEYES, DOUGLAS
North And South

HICKEY, JANICE
Chips, The War Dog
Her Wicked Ways

HICKMAN, GAIL MORGAN
Drug Wars: The Cocaine Cartel

HICKMAN, GALE PATRICK
Eighty-Three Hours 'til Dawn
Penalty Phase

HICKS, NEILL D.
Dead Reckoning

HIGGINS, COLIN
Out On A Limb

HILDEBRAND, KARI
Hostage For A Day

HILL, DANIELLE
Armed & Innocent
Love, Lies And Murder

HILL, DAVID
Fire In The Dark
Promised A Miracle
Shattered Dreams
Too Young To Die?

HILL, JOHN
Steel Justice

HINES, ALAN
In Sickness And In Health
Willing To Kill: The Texas Cheerleader Story

HIRSCH, JAMES G.
Deep Trouble
Drive Like Lightning
Hart To Hart Returns
I'll Take Romance
Johnnie Mae Gibson: F B I
Lethal Exposure
Line Of Fire: The Morris Dees Story
Rape Of Richard Beck, The

HIRSCH, JANIS
Little White Lies
Stranded
White Lie

HIRSON, ROGER O.
Christmas Carol, A
Old Man & The Sea, The
Ted Kennedy, Jr., Story, The
Woman Named Jackie, A

HIXON, KEN
Caught In The Act

HOCHBERG, VICTORIA
I Married A Centerfold

HOEFFNER, KAROL ANN
Burning Rage
Danielle Steel's Kaleidoscope
Danielle Steel's Palomino
Harem
Miss America: Behind The Crown

Scorned And Swindled

HOFFMAN, GARY
Bonnie And Clyde: The True Story

HORNER, CHRISTOPHER
Accidental Meeting

HOSELTON, DAVID
Clarence

HUME, EDWARD
Common Ground
Stranger On My Land

HUMPHREY, STEVE
Love On The Run
Tonight's The Night

HUNTER, EVAN
Dream West

HUNTER, FREDERIC
Nazi Hunter: The Beate Klarsfeld Story
Nightmare In The Daylight

HUNTER, LEW
Playing With Fire

HUNTER, SUSAN
Your Mother Wears Combat Boots

HURLEY, MAURICE
Keys, The
Kids Don't Tell

HUSKY, RICK
Beverly Hills Cowgirl Blues
Don't Touch My Daughter
In The Line Of Duty: Standoff At Marion

HUSON, PAUL
Big One: The Great Los Angeles Earthquake
Danielle Steel's Secrets
Twist Of Fate

HUTCHINSON, RON
Against The Wall
Josephine Baker Story, The
Murderers Among Us: The Simon Wiesenthal
....Story
Perfect Witness
Prisoner Of Honor
Red King, White Knight

HUTSON, LEE
Turn Back The Clock
Vital Signs

HUYCK, WILLARD
Father's Homecoming, A
Mothers, Daughters And Lovers

INMAN, ROBERT
Home Fires Burning
Son's Promise, A

IRELAND, JOHN
Bed Of Lies
Dead Before Dawn

IRISH, JR., WILLIAM
Heist

ISAAK, NANCY
Liar, Liar

ISRAEL, CHARLES
Arch Of Triumph
Mayflower Madam

IVOR, ANTHONY
Zelda

JACKSON, DAVID S.
Death Train

JACOBS, DAVID
Dallas: The Early Years

JAMES, LISA
Gifted One, The

JAMES, SYRIE ASTRAHAN
Danielle Steel's Once In A Lifetime

JAMESON, JERY
Stormin' Home

JANES, ROBERT
Perry Mason: The Case Of The Fatal Fashion

JANZEN, NAOMI
Secrets Of Lake Success

JARRE, KEVIN
Tracker, The

JENKINS, DAN
Dead Solid Perfect

JENNINGS, SANDRA
Desperate Choices: To Save My Child
Moment Of Truth: Broken Pledges
Summer My Father Grew Up, The

JETT, SUE
Infidelity

JOELSON, BEN
Glitter

JOHANSEN, ROY
Back To Hannibal: The Return Of Tom
Sawyer And Huck Finn
Murder 101

JOHNS, VICTORIA
Bring Me The Head Of Dobie Gillis

JOHNSON, CHARLES ERIC
George Mckenna Story, The

JOHNSON, DAVE
Trouble Shooters: Trapped Beneath The
....Earth

JOHNSON, KENNETH
Hot Pursuit
Shadow Chasers
Sherlock Holmes Returns

JOHNSON`, LLOYD
Gotham

JOHNSON, RANDI
Counterfeit Contessa, The

JOHNSON, STEPHHEN
Stop At Nothing

JONES, AMY
Indecency

JONES, MARK
Highwayman, The
Road Raiders, The

JONES, OTIS
Double Edge
Wet Gold

JONES, SCOTT DAVIS
Counterfeit Contessa, The

JOSEPH, ROBERT L.
Rage Of Angels: The Story Continues
Sun Also Rises, The
Sworn To Silence

JUBELIRER, NOAH
Brotherhood Of Justice, The

JULIEN, AARON
Dirty Work

KALISH, IRMA
I Dream Of Jeannie: 15 Years Later

KALLIS, STANLEY
Glitter Dome, The

KANE, KRISTI
Double Your Pleasure

KANE, MICHAEL
Cisco Kid, The

KANIN, FAY
Heartsounds

KAPLAN, ED
For Their Own Good
My First Love

KAPLAN, JACK
Hart To Hart Returns

KASS, JEROME
Crossing To Freedom
Evergreen
Last Wish
Only Way Out, The
Scorned And Swindled

KATKOV, NORMAN
Blood And Orchids

KATLIN, MITCHEL LEE
Last Fling, The

KATZ, EVAN
Archie: To Riverdale And Back Again
Love Matters

KATZ, GLORIA
Mothers, Daughters And Lovers

KAY, DUSTY
Triplecross

KEAN, E. ARTHUR
Crash: The Mystery Of Flight 1501

KELLER, SHELDON
Side By Side

KELLEY, DAVID
Picket Fences

KELLY, APRIL
How To Murder A Millionaire
I Still Dream Of Jeannie

KELLY, CASEY
Miracle On I-880
Triumph Over Disaster: The Hurricane
....Andrew Story

KELLY, WILLIAM
Blue Lightning, The

KEMP, BARRY
Fresno

KENNEDY, BURT
Once Upon A Texas Train
Where The Hell's That Gold

KENNERLY, DAVID HUME
Shooter

KERBY, BILL
Dadah Is Death

KERN, BRAD
Carly's Web
Remington Steele: The Steele That Wouldn't
....Die

KESEND, ELLEN
Convicted: A Mother's Story

KINBERG, JUD
In The Best Interest Of The Child
Stoning In Fulham County, A

KING, PAUL
One Police Plaza
Red Spider, The

KING, STEPHEN
Stephen King's Golden Years
Stephen King's The Stand

KING, ZALMAN
Red Shoes Diaries

KINGHORN, DAVID J.
Charley Hannah
Flood: Who Will Save Our Children?
From The Files Of Joseph Wambaugh: A Jury
Of One
Glory Days
High Mountain Rangers
Man Against The Mob
Too Young The Hero
True Blue
Two Fathers' Justice

KINGSLEY, EMILY PERL
Kids Like These

KINOY, ERNEST
Chernobyl: The Final Warning
Lincoln
Murrow
Stones Of Ibarra

KLANE, ROBERT
Odd Couple, The

KLEIMAN, DENA
Strapped

KLEIN, JON
T Bone N Wessel

KLEINMAN, MAGGIE
Desperate Choices: To Save My Child

KLEINSCHMITT, CARL
Hi Honey -- I'm Dead
Kiss Shot
Sadie And Son

KLENHARD, WALTER
Dead In The Water
Last Hit, The
Lies Of The Twins
Sweet Poison

KLETTER, RICHARD
Tower, The

KLINE, STEPHEN
Shooter

KLINGER, JUDSON
Thicker Than Blood: The Larry Mclinden
....Story

KNAUF, DANIEL
Blind Justice

KNOP, PATRICIA
Red Shoes Diaries

KNOPF, CHRISTOPHER
Baby Girl Scott
Equal Justice
Not My Kid
Prison For Children

KOENIG, LAIRD
Fulfillment Of Mary Gray, The
Lady Against The Odds
Rockabye
Stillwatch

KONNER, LAWRENCE
Stephen King's Sometimes They Come Back

KOONTZ, DEAN
Face Of Fear, The

KOPIT, ARTHUR
Hands Of A Stranger
Phantom Of The Opera, The
Roswell

KOVALCIK, JANET
Maybe Baby
World's Oldest Living Bridesmaid, The

KOVEL, PAUL
Psychic

KRAMER, RICHARD
Amos

KREINBERG, STEVEN
Dance Till Dawn

KRING, TIMOTHY
Bay Coven
Victim Of Love

KRINSKI, SANDY
Who Gets The Friends?

KROHN, MICHAEL K.
Sins Of The Mother

KUKOFF, BERNIE
Rags To Riches

LA BELLA, VINCENZO
Season Of Giants, A

LABINE, CLAIRE
Bride In Black, The
Danielle Steel's Star
She Woke Up

LAKIN, HOWARD
Nightingales

LAKIN, RITA
Peyton Place: The Next Generation

LAMBERT, GAVIN
Dead On The Money
Liberace: Behind The Music
Second Serve
Sweet Bird Of Youth

LAMOND, BILL
Crossings

LAMOND, JO
Crossings

LANDON, JOE
Lies And Lullabies

LANDON, MICHAEL
Highway To Heaven
Us
Where Pigeons Go To Die

LANDSBURG, ALAN
Unspeakable Acts

LANE, BRIAN ALAN
Out Of Time

LANE, JEFFREY
Murder Of Mary Phagan, The

LANGLEY, LEE
Tenth Man, The

LANSBURY, BRUCE
I'm Dangerous Tonight
Street Hawk

LARSON, GLEN A.
Chameleons
Cover Up
Highwayman, The
In Like Flynn
P. S. I Luv U
Road Raiders, The

LASKER, ALEX
Seeds Of Tragedy

LASKOS, ANDREW
Daughter Of Darkness
Deadly Matrimony
Deadly Medicine
False Arrest

House Of Secrets
Nurses On The Line: The Crash Of Flight 7
Passion And Paradise

LATHAM, LYNN MARIE
Homefront
Second Chances

LAURENCE, MICHAEL
Last Frontier, The
Which Way Home

LAURENTS, ARTHUR
Gypsy

LAURIE, RAMA
Other Women's Children

LAURIN, WILLIAM
South Beach

LAURO, SHIRLEY
Open Admissions

LAWRENCE, ANTHONY
Liberace

LAWRENCE, MARC
Family Ties Vacation

LAWRENCE, NANCY
Liberace

LAWSON, STEVE
Jonathan: The Boy Nobody Wanted
Room Upstairs, The

LAZAROU, MICHAEL
Heat Wave

LECHOWICK, BERNARD
Homefront
Second Chances

LECKIE, KEITH ROSS
Deadly Betrayal: The Bruce Curtis Story
In The Line Of Duty: The Price Of
....Vengeance

LEDER, REUBEN
Danger Down Under

LEE, JAMES
Napoleon And Josephine: A Love Story

LEEKLEY, JOHN
In The Company Of Darkness

LEES, RICHARD
Celebration Family

LEFCOURT, PETER
Cracked Up
Danielle Steel's Fine Things
Monte Carlo
Women Of Windsor

LEGETT, LAURIAN
Love And Betrayal

LEICHT, ALLAN
Lady In A Corner

LEINENWEBER, CHARLES
Entertainers, The

LENHART, KERRY
Out Of Time

LENKOV, PETER
Parker Kane

LENSKI, ROBERT W.
After The Promise
Breathing Lessons
Decoration Day
Kane And Abel
Mafia Princess
O Pioneers
Roommates

LEONARD, ELMORE
Desperado

LEVIN, AUDREY DAVIS
Ann Jillian Story, The
Fatal Memories
Girl Who Came Between Them, The
Reason For Living: The Jill Ireland Story
Shattered Vows
Stranger In My Bed

LEVIN, MARK
Rise & Walk: The Dennis Byrd Story

LEVIN, VICTOR
Dream Breakers

LeVINE, DEBORAH JOY
Lois & Clark: The New Adventures Of
....Superman
Something To Live For: The Alison Gertz
....Story

LEVINSON, DAVID
Kicks

LEVINSON, RICHARD
Guardian, The
Guilty Conscience
Terrorist On Trial: The United States Vs.
Salim
Vanishing Act

LEVITT, BEVERLY
Miles To Go...

LEVY, EUGENE
Sodbusters

LEWIN, ROBERT
Reason To Live, A

LEWIS, ARTHUR BERNARD
Our Family Honor

LINDH, STEWART
Blind Side

LINDSAY, JIM
Trial And Error

LINK, WILLIAM
Boys, The
Cosby Mysteries, The
Guardian, The
Guilty Conscience
Terrorist On Trial: The United States Vs.
Salim

Vanishing Act

LIPMAN, DANIEL
An Early Frost
Love She Sought, The

LIPTON, JAMES
Copacabana
Mirrors

LISS, STEPHANIE
Child Lost Forever, A
David
Runaway Father
Second Serve
Shameful Secrets

LIST, SHELLEY
Barbara Taylor Bradford's Remember
Danielle Steel's Jewels

LOCKWOOD, WALTER
Battling For Baby
Finnegan Begin Again
Indiscreet
Secret Life Of Archie's Wife, The

LODGE, STEPHEN
Rio Diablo

LOFTON, CHRISTOPHER
Bump In The Night
Call Of The Wild
Killer Among Friends, A
Sins Of The Mother

LONGSTREET, HARRY
Gunsmoke: One Man's Justice
Night Walk
Sex, Love, And Cold Hard Cash

LONGSTREET, RENEE
Gunsmoke: One Man's Justice
Night Walk
With A Vengeance

LOTIMER, EB
Love Matters

LOVE, MICHAEL
Not In My Family

LUCE, WILLIAM
Last Days Of Patton, The
Lucy & Desi: Before The Laughter
Woman He Loved, The

LUDWIG, JERRY
Deadly Desire
Roman Holiday

LUKE, ERIC
Not Quite Human I I
Still Not Quite Human

LUPICA, MIKE
Money, Power, Murder

LUPO, FRANK
Hunter
Something Is Out There

LYNCH, DAVID
Twin Peaks

MACDONALD, GERARD
Marilyn & Bobby: Her Final Affair

MACLACHLAN, PATRICIA
Sarah, Plain And Tall
Skylark

MACLAINE, SHIRLEY
Out On A Limb

MACLAVERTY, BERNARD
Hostages

MACRURY, MALCOLM
Harvest For The Heart

MAGAR, GUY
Stepfather I I I

MAGEE, DOUG
Conviction Of Kitty Dodds, The
Somebody Has To Shoot The Picture

MAGNATTA, CONSTANITINO
Ghost Mom

MAMET, DAVID
Life In The Theater, A
Water Engine, The

MANKIEWICZ, JOHN
Return Of Desperado, The

MANLEY, PETER
Lady And The Highwayman, The

MANN, ABBY
Atlanta Child Murders, The
Murderers Among Us: The Simon Wiesenthal
....Story
Teamster Boss: The Jackie Presser Story

MANN, MICHAEL
L. A. Takedown

MARCUS, LAWRENCE B.
Threesome

MARGO, PHIL
Goddess Of Love
Love Boat: A Valentine Voyage, The
This Wife For Hire

MARGOLIN, ARNOLD
Family For Joe, A
He's Not Your Son

MARIN, ANDREW PETER
Deadly Intentions
Judith Krantz's Till We Meet Again
Murder C. O. D.
Sweet Revenge, A

MARKOWITZ, PEACHY
Challenge Of A Lifetime

MARLOWE, DEREK
Corpse Had A Familiar Face, The
Grass Roots
Jack The Ripper

MARSHALL, BEN
Trouble In Paradise

MARTIN, JAYNE
Moment Of Truth: A Child Too Many
Moment Of Truth: Cradle Of Conspiracy

MARTINELLI, GREG
Mortal Sins

MARTINEZ, AL
That Secret Sunday

MASCHLER, TIM
Lady From Yesterday, The

MASTROSIMONE, WILLIAM
Sinatra

MATHESON, RICHARD
Dreamer Of Oz, The

MATHISON, MELISSA
Son Of The Morning Star

MAXWELL, ROBIN
Passions

MAXWELL, RON
Gettysburg

MAYBECK, BERNARD
Cover Girl Murders, The

MAYES, WENDELL
Criminal Behavior
Man Who Broke 1,000 Chains, The

MCCARN, LOUISE
Walker, Texas Ranger

MCCARTY, GREG
Nightmare At Bitter Creek

MCCORD, JONAS
Charles And Diana: Unhappily Ever After
Class Of '61
Women Of Valor

MCCRACKEN, JEFF
Hawaiian Heat

MCCUAIG, ANDIE
Dead Reckoning

MCCULLOUGH, ROBERT
Hollywood Wives
International Airport

MCELROY, ALAN
Murder By Night
Wheels Of Terror

MCEVEETY, VINCENT
Columbo: Death Hits The Jackpot

MCGRATH, GEORGE
Based On An Untrue Story

MCGRATH, JOHN
Robin Hood

MCGRAW, STEVE
Miles From Nowhere

MCGREEVEY, JOHN
Aurora
Call Me Anna
Consenting Adult

Firestorm: 72 Hours In Oakland
Hiroshima: Out Of The Ashes
Mario Puzo's The Fortunate Pilgrim
Time To Live, A
Unholy Matrimony

MCGREEVEY, MICHAEL
Bonanza: The Return

MCHUGH, FIONA
Lantern Hill

MCINTOSH, DOUGLAS LLOYD
Disaster At Silo 7
Notorious

MCKEAND, CAROL EVAN
Alex: The Life Of A Child

MCKEAND, NIGEL
Alex: The Life Of A Child

MCKEE, ROBERT
Abraham

MCMURTRY, LARRY
Memphis
Montana

MCNEELY, JERRY
Sin Of Innocence
When You Remember Me

MCPHERSON, STEPHEN
Behind Enemy Lines

MEDOFF, MARK
Apology

MEGGS, STEVEN
Two Fathers: Justice For The Innocent

MENON, GIANNI
Aurora

MERL, JUDY
Detective In The House
Fight For Jenny, A
Shootdown

MESSINA, PHILIP F.
Original Sin
Spy

MEYER, JEFFREY M.
Conagher

MEYER, KEVIN
Invasion Of Privacy

MEYERS, MARLANE
Better Off Dead

MICHAELIAN, MICHAEL
Miracle In The Wilderness

MIDKIFF, MARCIA
Jailbirds

MIGLIS, JOHN
Deliver Them From Evil: The Taking Of Alta
....View
Dying To Love You
Keep The Change
Killer Among Friends, A
Rise & Walk: The Dennis Byrd Story

Whereabouts Of Jenny, The

MILCH, DAVID
Capital News

MILES, J. DAVID
Dead Silence

MILLAR, STUART
Dream Breakers

MILLER, ARTHUR
Death Of A Salesman

MILLER, BRODERICK
Deadlock

MILLER, J.P.
I Know My First Name Is Steven

MILLER, JENNIFER
Deadly Silence, A
Family Pictures
Lucky Day
Paper Dolls
Telling Secrets

MILLER, NANCY
Round Table, The

MILLER, ROBERT
Corsican Brothers, The

MILLER, STEPHEN A.
Chameleons
Jesse Hawkes

MILLS, FRED
Overkill: The Aileen Wuornos Story
Prophet Of Evil: The Ervil Lebaron Story

MINTZ, LARRY
If It's Tuesday, It Still Must Be Belgium

MISTO, JOHN
Last Frontier, The

MITCHELL, JUDITH P.
American Geisha
Black Widow Murders: The Blanche Taylor
....Moore Story
Burning Bridges
Club Med
Desperate For Love
Lies Of The Heart: The Story Of Laurie
....Kellogg
Roses Are For The Rich

MITCHELL, STEVEN LONG
Class Cruise

MITCHLLL, SCOEY
Miracle At Beekman's Place

MOFFAT, IVAN
Florence Nightingale

MOFFLY, JOE REB
Double Edge

MOLONEY, JAMES C.
Night They Saved Christmas, The

MONACELLA, ALFRED
Passport To Murder

MONASH, PAUL
Killer Rules
Stalin

MONPERE, CAROL
French Silk
Pink Lightning

MONTGOMERY, CLAIRE
Perfect Bride, The

MONTGOMERY, KATHRYN
Firefighter

MONTGOMERY, MARK
Voyage

MONTGOMERY, MONTE
Perfect Bride, The

MOORE, WESLEY
Are You Lonesome Tonight?

MORRILL, NORMAN
Alamo: 13 Days To Glory, The
Finish Line
In Defense Of A Married Man
Intimate Strangers
Nurses On The Line: The Crash Of Flight 7
Taking Of Flight 847: The Uli Derickson
....Story

MORRIS, DAVID BURTON
Laguna Heat

MORROW, BARRY
Christmas On Division Street
Conspiracy Of Love
Karen Carpenter Story, The
Quiet Victory: The Charlie Wedemeyer Story

MORTON, PHILIP
Twelve O' One (12: 01)

MOSES, HARRY
Assault At West Point

MOSKOWITZ, JULIE
Hush Little Baby
Visions Of Murder

MULHOLLAND, JIM
Many Happy Returns

MURKOFF, BRUCE
Lady Against The Odds

MURRAY, MICHAEL
Honor Thy Father And Mother: The
....Menendez Murders
Lightning Incident, The
Love Kills

MUSTARD STEWART, FRED
Ellis Island

MYERS, CINDY
Forgotten Prisoners: The Amnesty File
Incident In A Small Town
When No One Would Listen

MYERS, PAUL ERIC
Detective In The House
Fight For Jenny, A

Shootdown

NAGY, IVAN
Intimate Encounters

NANUS, SUSAN
Baby Brokers
Danielle Steel's Changes
Go Toward The Light
Heart Of A Child
Shattered Trust: The Shari Karney Story

NATHAN, ROBERT
In The Deep Woods

NATION, JOHN
Only One Survived

NATKI, RICK
Heist

NEGRIN, ALBERTO
Mussolini: The Decline And Fall Of Il Duce

NEIDERMAN, ANDREW
Duplicates

NELSON, PETER
Getting Up And Going Home
In The Best Interest Of The Child
My Son Johnny
Untamed Love

NELSON, TOM
Between Love And Hate

NEMEC, DENNIS
Case Of Deadly Force, A
Deadly Relations
God Bless The Child
Heart Of A Champion: The Ray Mancini Story
Secrets Of A Married Man

NEMETH, SALY
Rise & Walk: The Dennis Byrd Story

NESI, TOM
Fight For Life

NEUMAN, E.JACK
Courage
Death In California, A
Voices Within: The Lives Of Truddi Chase

NEWMAN, CHRISTOPHER
Ellis Island

NICHOLSON, WILLIAM
Private Matter, A

NICIPHOR, NICHOLAS
Candles In The Dark
Fatal Charm

NISOR, SCOTT
Fight For Life

NIVEN, JR., DAVID
Night They Saved Christmas, The

NIX, TOMMY
Roadracers

NOLAN, WILLIAM F.
Bridge Across Time

NOONAN, TOM
Red Wind

NORELL, JAMES
Against Her Will: An Incident In Baltimore
Incident, The

NORELL, MICHAEL
Against Her Will: An Incident In Baltimore
Barnum
Christmas Comes To Willow Creek
Cover Girl And The Cop, The
Diamond Fleece
I Spy Returns
Incident, The
Long Gone
Murder By The Book
Pals
River Of Rage: The Taking Of Maggie
....Keene
She Knows Too Much

NORMAN, MARSHA
Face Of A Stranger

O'BANNON, ROCKNE S.
Fear
Seaquest Dsv

O'BRIEN, C.
Obsessed With A Married Woman

O'HARA, MICHAEL
Murder In The Heartland
She Said No
Switched At Birth
Those She Left Behind

O'NEIL, ROBERT VINCENT
Lady Blue

O'NEILL, GENE
Backfield In Motion

OBST, DAVID
Perfect Harmony

OKIE, RICHARD C.
Love And Curses ... And All That Jazz

OLEK, HENRY
Scene Of The Crime

OLIANSKI, JOEL
Alfred Hitchcock Presents

OLIVER, RON
Liar's Edge

OLSEN, ARNE
Black Ice

ORINGER, BARRY
Intruders

ORMSBY, ALAN
Disappearance Of Nora
Indecency

ORR, JAMES
Love On The Run

OSBORNE, WILLIAM
Bermuda Grace

OWEN, JOHN STEVEN
One Woman's Courage

PAOLI, DENNIS
Mortal Sins

PARDRIDGE, MICHAEL
Chips, The War Dog
Her Wicked Ways

PARKER, JOAN
Spenser: Ceremony
Spenser: Pale Kings And Princes

PARKER, JUDITH
Child Lost Forever, A
Choices
Other Lover, The

PARKER, ROBERT
Spenser: Ceremony
Spenser: Pale Kings And Princes

PARKS, RICHARD
Blackout

PARRIOTT, JAMES D.
Hawaiian Heat
Misfits Of Science
Nick Knight

PATIK, VICKIE
Broken Promises: Taking Emily Back
Children Of The Night
Do You Remember Love?
Silent Cries

PAVONE, MICHAEL
Trouble Shooters: Trapped Beneath The
....Earth

PECKINPAH, DAVID
Chase
Diamond Trap, The
In Self Defense
Obsessed
Stillwatch
Wolf

PENNINGROTH, PHIL
Amy Fisher: My Story
Babymaker: The Dr. Cecil Jacobson's Story
Casey's Gift: For Love Of A Child
Child Of Rage
Elvis And The Colonel: The Untold Story
In The Line Of Duty: Ambush In Waco
Price She Paid, The
Right To Die
Ryan White Story, The
Silence Of The Heart
Tonya & Nancy: The Inside Story
When The Bough Breaks

PETERSON, ROD
Walton Thanksgiving Reunion, A

PETIEVICH, GERALD
C. A. T. Squad

PETITCLERC, DENNE
Cowboy And The Ballerina, The
Woman Who Sinned, The

PETRYNI, MICHAEL
Big One: The Great Los Angeles Earthquake
Child In The Night
Fresno
In The Line Of Duty: Manhunt In The
....Dakotas
Man Against The Mob: The Chinatown
....Murders
Return Of Eliot Ness, The

PETTUS, KEN
Lady From Yesterday, The

PHELAN, ANNA HAMILTON
Into The Homeland

PHELAN, BRIAN
Tailspin: Behind The Korean Airlines Tragedy

PHILLIPS, BILL
El Diablo
In A Child's Name
Rainbow Drive
Rising Son

PIELMEIER, JOHN
Inconvenient Woman, An
Last P. O. W? The Bobby Garwood Story
Shell Seekers, The
Stranger Within, The
Through The Eyes Of A Killer

PIERSON, DORI
Impostor, The
Obsessed With A Married Woman
Prince Of Bel Air

PINTER, HAROLD
Room, The

PITT, MAXWELL
Going For The Gold: The Bill Johnson Story

PODEL, RIC
In The Nick Of Time

POE, JAMES
Nightman, The

POGUE, CHARLES EDWARD
Hands Of A Murderer

POLLOCK, EILEEN
Dynasty: The Reunion

POLLOCK, ROBERT
Dynasty: The Reunion

POLON, VICKI
Deadly Medicine

POLSON, BETH
Go Toward The Light

PONICSAN, DARRYL
Enemy Within, The

PONTI, MAURIZIO
Aurora

POOL, ROBERT
Donato And Daughter

POOLE, DUANE
Eyes Of Terror

Menu For Murder
Praying Mantis
Sunstroke
This Can't Be Love
Without Warning: Terror In The Towers

POPESCU, PETRU
Nobody's Children
Obsessive Love

POTTS, MICHAEL
Illicit Behavior

POWELL, ANN
Drug Wars: The Camarena Story
Night Owl

POWELL, HAL
Dark Shadows

POWERS, DONNA DOTTLEY
Strange Voices

POWERS, WAYNE
Strange Voices

PRELUTSKY, BURT
Winner Never Quits, A

PREMINGER, MICHAEL
In The Nick Of Time

PRIDEAUX, JAMES
Laura Lansing Slept Here
Man Upstairs, The
Mrs. Delafield Wants To Marry

PROCHNIK, LEON
Four Eyes And Six Guns

PUCCI, ROBERT
Spider And The Fly, The

PYNE, DANIEL
Return Of Desperado, The

QUALLES, PARIS
Silent Witness: What A Child Saw

RADKOFF, VIVIENNE
Always Remember I Love You

RAINER, TRISTINE
Forbidden Nights

RAMRUS, AL
Deadly Business, A

RANDALL, BOB
David's Mother

RANDALL, NICK
Chrome Soldiers

RAPOPORT, I.C.
Jericho Fever
Quiet Killer
Stranger On My Land

RAY, MARC
Stepfather III

RAYNELL, APRIL
Columbo - Caution: Murder Can Be
....Hazardous To Your Health

RED, ERIC
Last Outlaw, The

REDDIN, KEITH
Heart Of Justice, The

REHAK, BRIAN
Image, The

REHWALDT, FRANK
Deadbolt

RHINEHART, SUSAN
Baby Snatcher
Memphis

RICE, JOHN
Curiosity Kills

RICE, SUSAN
Dangerous Affection
Opposites Attract
Something In Common
Tears And Laughter: The Joan And Mielissa
....Rivers Story

RICE, WAYNE
Man From Left Field

RICHARD, THANET
Shattered Innocence

RICHARDSON, SCOBIE
Wild Card

RILEY, JOHN
Tower, The

RINTELS, DAVID W.
Day One
Last Best Year, The
Sakharov
World War II: When Lions Roared

RINTELS, JONATHAN
Anything To Survive
Child's Cry
Convicted
Desperate Journey: The Allison Wilcox Story
Lena: My 100 Children
Snowbound: The Jim And Jennifer Stolpa
....Story
Town Bully, The

RITCHIE, ROB
Investigation: Inside A Terrorist Bombing

ROACH, JAY
Lifepod

ROACH, JOHN FAUNCE
Follow Your Heart

ROBE, MIKE
Guts And Glory: The Rise And Fall Of Oliver
....North
Murder Ordained
News At Eleven
With Intent To Kill

ROBINSON, SALLY
Indiscreet
Letter To Three Wives, A

RODAT, ROBERT
Comrades Of Summer

RODGERS, MARK
Alone In The Neon Jungle
Dirty Dozen: The Deadly Mission
Dirty Dozen: The Fatal Mission
Johnny Ryan
Police Story: The Freeway Killings

RODMAN, HOWARD
Scandal Sheet

RODRIGUEZ, ROBERT
Roadracers

ROLFE, SAM
On Wings Of Eagles

ROMAN, LAWRENCE
Badge Of The Assassin
Ernest Green Story, The
Final Verdict

ROSE, LEE
Deconstructing Sarah
It's Nothing Personal

ROSE, REGINALD
Escape From Sobibor
My Two Loves

ROSEBROOK, JEB
Christmas Gift, The
Gambler Returns: The Luck Of The Draw
Hobo's Christmas, A
Kenny Rogers As The Gambler III: The
....Legend Continues

ROSEN, GARY
Framed

ROSENBERG, JEANNE
Heidi

ROSENBERG, PHILIP
Final Appeal
In The Line Of Duty: A Cop For The Killing
In The Shadow Of A Killer
Menendez: A Killing In Beverly Hills
Murder Between Friends
Murder Of Innocence
Till Death Us Do Part

ROSENBLUM, ROBERT
In The Deep Woods

ROSENFELD, ALISON
Victim Of Love

ROSENTHAL, MARK
Stephen King's Sometimes They Come Back

ROSIN, CHARLES
California Girls
Child Saver, The
Line Of Fire: The Morris Dees Story
Silent Witness: What A Child Saw
Summer Dreams: The Story Of The Beach
....Boys
This Child Is Mine

ROSS, BRIAN
Body Language
Cast The First Stone
On Thin Ice: The Tai Babilonia Story
Secret Passion Of Robert Clayton, The
Target Of Suspicion

ROSS, KATHARINE
Conagher

ROSS-LEMING, EUGENIE
Blue Deville

ROSS-LEMMING, EUGENIE
Cartier Affair, The

ROTH, BOBBY
Baja Oklahoma
Dead Solid Perfect
Separated By Murder

ROTH, ERIC
Jane's House

ROTH, LYNN
Babies
Chance Of A Lifetime
Just My Imagination

ROTHE, JODI
Different Affair, A

ROTHMAN, MIMI
In My Daughter's Name

ROTHSTEIN, RICHARD
Bates Motel
Double Deception
Gifted One, The

ROUD, IRV
Preppie Murder, The

ROWELL, KATHLEEN
She Says She's Innocent
Tainted Blood

RUBEL, MARC
Impostor, The
Obsessed With A Married Woman
Prince Of Bel Air

RUBEN, ALBERT
Incident At Dark River
Kojak: The Belarus File
Kojak: The Price Of Justice
Reunion At Fairborough

RUBIN, RON
Lost In London
Never Forget

RUBINO, GEORGE
Family Sins
Into Thin Air
Mercy Mission: The Rescue Of Flight 771
Too Young To Die?

RUCKER, ALAN
Taste For Killing, A

RUSHTON, MATTHEW
Hot Paint

SACKETT, NANCY
Beverly Hills Madam
Deep Dark Secrets
Glitter
When Will I Be Loved?

SADOWSKI, MICHAEL
Staying Afloat

SADWITH, JAMES
Baby M
Bluffing It
Murder Ordained
Who Is Julia?

SAGOES, KEN
On Promised Land

SAKHART, JOHN J.
Out Of Time

SALINAS, MICHAEL
Not In My Family

SALTZMAN, PHILIP
That Secret Sunday

SALWEN, HAL
Deadly Surveillance

SAMUEL, LILLIAN
Secret Sins Of The Father

SANDERCOCK, LEONIE
Captive

SANDOR, ANNA
Amelia Earhart: The Final Flight
Family Of Strangers
For The Love Of My Child: The Anissa
....Ayala Story
Miss Rose White
Stolen: One Husband
Tarzan In Manhattan

SANFORD, ARLENE
Personals

SANGSTER, JIMMY
North Beach And Rawhide
Toughest Man In The World, The

SAWYER, BEVERLY M.
Stompin' At The Savoy

SAYLES, JOHN
Shannon's Deal
Unnatural Causes

SCHACHT, ROSE
Drug Wars: The Camarena Story
Night Owl

SCHAPIRO, MIMI
Drop Dead Gorgeous
Exclusive

SCHENCK, GEORGE
Dying To Remember
Search And Rescue
Still Crazy Like A Fox

SCHIFF, ROBIN
Swimsuit

SCHLITT, ROBERT
Perry Mason: The Case Of The Skin-Deep
Scandal

SCHMIDT, WILLIAM
Evil In Clear River
Sound And The Silence, The

SCHNEIDER, BARRY
Downpayment On Murder
Haunted By Her Past

SCHOFFMAN, STUART
Terror On Highway 91

SCHREDER, CAROL
In Love And War

SCHREINER, NEVIN
China Lake Murders, The
Don't Talk To Strangers
Linda
Memories Of Murder
This Gun For Hire
Trial And Error
Web Of Deception
White Lie

SCHREYER, LINDA
House Of Secrets And Lies, A

SCHULMAN, ARNOLD
And The Band Played On

SCHWARTZ, DOUGLAS
Baywatch: Panic At Malibu Pier
Crime Of Innocence

SCHWARTZ, JOHN
Black Ice

SCHWARTZ, LLOYD J.
Bradys, The

SCHWARTZ, SHERWOOD
Bradys, The
Very Brady Christmas, A

SCHWARTZ, WILLIAM A.
Crash Course
To My Daughter

SCOTT, ALLAN
Beryl Markham: A Shadow On The Sun

SEEGER, SUSAN
Kate's Secret

SEGALL, DON
Love Boat: A Valentine Voyage, The
This Wife For Hire

SEIDENBERG, ROBERT
Dead In The Water

SEIDLER, DAVID
Malice In Wonderland
My Father, My Son
Richest Man In The World: The Aristotle
....Onassis Story
Whose Child Is This? The War For Baby
....Jessica

SELF, ED
Spies, Lies And Naked Thighs

SELTZER, DAVID
Private Sessions

SEMPLE, JR., LORENZO
Rearview Mirror

SERRA, DEBORAH A.
Highway Heartbreaker

SHANKS, BOB
Drop-Out Mother
He's Fired, She's Hired

SHAPIRO, ALAN
Crossing The Mob

SHAPIRO, ESTHER
Dynasty: The Reunion
When We Were Young

SHAPIRO, PAUL W.
Combat High

SHAPIRO, RICHARD
Blood Ties
Dynasty: The Reunion
When We Were Young

SHAPIRO, RUTH
Getting Out

SHAPIRO, STANLEY
Running Against Time

SHARP, ALAN
Betrayed By Love
Descending Angel
Last Hit, The
Love & Lies
Mission Of The Shark

SHAVELSON, MELVILLE
Deceptions

SHAYNE, BOB
P. S. I Luv U
Return Of Sherlock Holmes, The

SHELLEY, KATHLEEN A.
North And South
People Like Us

SHENGOLD, NINA
Blind Spot
Earth Angel

SHEPHERD, CYBILL
Memphis

SHEPPARD, JOHN
Macgyver : Lost Treasure Of Atlantis

SHERMAN, GARY
After The Shock
Fire And Rain
Missing Persons

SHERMAN, ROBERT
Trouble In Paradise

SHERWIN, DAVID
Wet Gold

SHIRREFS, MARK
Girl From Tomorrow, The

SHRAKE, BUD
Pair Of Aces

SHRYLACK, DENNIS
Revenge On The Highway

SHULMAN, GUY
Jailbirds
Return To Green Acres

SIEGEL, ROBERT
Descending Angel

SILLIPHANT, STIRLING
Day Of Reckoning
Mussolini - The Untold Story
Space
Stranger In The Mirror, A
Three Kings, The

SILVERMAN, PETER
For The Love Of Aaron
Kids Don't Tell

SILVERS, NANCEY
Battling For Baby

SIMEONE, LAWRENCE L.
Blindfold: Acts Of Obsession

SIMKINS, DAVID
Adventures Of Brisco County Jr., The

SIMMONS, GARNER
Miracle Landing

SIMMONS, RICHARD ALAN
Harry's Hong Kong

SIMON, NEIL
Broadway Bound
Plaza Suite

SIMON, RONNI
Addicted To His Love

SIMONS, DAVID A.
Equal Justice

SIMOUN, HENRI
Blind Vengeance

SINGER, BRUCE FRANKLIN
Day - O
House On Sycamore Street, The
Lion Of Africa, The
Perry Mason Mystery, A: The Case Of The Lethal
She Stood Alone

SINGER, EUGENIA BOSTWICK
Beyond Obsession

SINGER, RAYMOND
Beyond Obsession

SISSON, ROSEMARY ANNE
Mistral's Daughter

SITOWITZ, HAL
In The Best Interest Of The Children
Stranger In The Family, A

Woman On The Ledge

SLATE, LANE
Deadly Care
Murderers Among Us: The Simon Wiesenthal ....Story

SLAVIN, TODD
Dark Reflection

SLOAN, HOLLY
Indecency

SLOAN, MICHAEL
Bionic Showdown: The 6 Million Dollar ....Man/Bionic Woman
Return Of Sam Mccloud, The
Return Of The 6 Million Dollar Man & Bionic ....Woman
Riviera

SLOANE, ALLAN
Casey's Gift: For Love Of A Child
Kids Like These

SMITH, ANDREW
Maid For Each Other

SMITH, APRIL
Love Lives On
Queenie
Taking Back My Life: The Nancy ....Ziegenmeyer Story

SMITH, JR., BOBBY
There Are No Children Here

SMITH, MARK ALLEN
Robin Hood

SMITH, MURRAY
Casualty Of War, A
Just Another Secret
Pride And Extreme Prejudice

SMITH, RICHARD
Blackout

SOBIESKI, CAROL
Bourne Identity, The
Place To Call Home, A
Sarah, Plain And Tall

SOHMER, STEVE
Favorite Son
Settle The Score

SOLADAY, REBECCA
Empty Cradle
Shame

SOLARZ, KEN
Relentless: Mind Of A Killer

SOLE, ALFRED
Under Siege

SOLOMON, DAVID
Hearst And Davies Affair, The

SPECKTOR, KATHERINE
Convicted: A Mother's Story

SPENCER, SCOTT
Act Of Vengeance

SPINNER, ANTHONY
Perry Mason: The Case Of The Scandalous
Scoundrel

STACK, TIM
Glory Days

STAGNER, RAMA LAURIE
And Then There Was One
Passion For Justice, A: Hazel Brannon Smith
....Story

STAPLETON, JAY
Heads

STATTON, BILL
Gunsmoke: The Long Ride Home

STEFANO, JOSEPH
Psycho I V: The Beginning

STEIGER, JOEL
Perry Mason: The Case Of The Notorious Nun

STEIN, MARK
Quiet Little Neighborhood, A Perfect Little
....Murder, A

STEIN, MICHAEL ERIC
Higher Ground

STEINER, REED
Hit List, The

STENN, DAVID
Secrets Of Lake Success
She Was Marked For Murder

STEPHENS, GARY
Hush Little Baby
Visions Of Murder

STERN, HENRY
Love Among Thieves
Stranded

STERN, LEONARD B.
Get Smart Again

STERN, SANDOR
Amityville: The Evil Escapes
Assassin
Dangerous Pursuit
Deception: A Mother's Secret
Duplicates
John And Yoko: A Love Story
Secret Weapons
Shattered Innocence
Web Of Deceit
Woman On The Run: The Lawrencia
....Bembenek Story

STETTIN, MONTE
Double Jeopardy
Murder Times Seven
Terror On Track 9

STEVENS, DAVID
Queen

STEVENS, EDMOND
Blind Witness
Keeping Secrets
Night Of The Hunter

Presidents Child, The

STEVENS, JR., GEORGE
Murder Of Mary Phagan, The
Separate But Equal

STEWART, DONALD OGDEN
Dinner At Eight

STONE, NOREEN
Tricks Of The Trade

STRANGIS, GREG
Eight Is Enough Wedding, An

STRATTON, BILL
American Harvest
Baron And The Kid, The
Last Days Of Frank And Jesse James, The
Son's Promise, A
Stark
Street Of Dreams

STRUM, NORMAN
Acceptable Risks

SULLIVAN, BETH
Cry For Help: The Tracey Thurman Story, A
Dr. Quinn, Medicine Woman
When He's Not A Stranger

SULLIVAN, KEVIN
Lantern Hill

SVANOE, BILL
Seduced By Evil
Sparks: The Price Of Passion

SWALE, TOM
Menu For Murder

SWANTON, HAROLD
Alfred Hitchcock Presents

SWANTON, SCOTT
Agatha Christie's Murder In Three Acts
Finding The Way Home
Murder: By Reason Of Insanity
Nightmare At Bitter Creek
Summer To Remember, A
Survive The Savage Sea

SWEET, JOHN
Face To Face

SWENSEN, EDITHE
They

SWIMMER, DARREN
Dark Reflection

TAGGERT, BRIAN
Child Of Darkness, Child Of Light
Dangerous Passion
Omen I V: The Awakening
What Ever Happened To Baby Jane?

TAHSE, MARTIN
Lookalike, The
Matters Of The Heart

TALLY, TED
Father Clements Story, The

TANNER, JOHN
Our Family Honor

TAPLITZ, DANIEL
Black Magic
Nightlife

TARLOFF, ERIK
Going To The Chapel

TAUB, BILL
Dark Shadows

TAYLOR, BRUCE A.
Annihilator, The

TAYLOR, DAVID
Devlin
Majority Rule
Traveling Man

TAYLOR, JERI
Place To Call Home, A

TAYLOR, PHILIP JOHN
I'm Dangerous Tonight

TAYLOR, RICHARD
Deceptions

TAYLOR, RODERICK
Annihilator, The
Florida Straits
Kenny Rogers As The Gambler I I I: The
....Legend Continues
Wild Horses

TAYLOR, WARREN
In The Eyes Of A Stranger

TEJADA-FLORES, MIGUEL
Blackmail
Past Tense
Psychic

TENNANT, ANDY
Moving Target
What She Doesn't Know

TEPPER, CRAIG
Double Jeopardy

TERRINI, FRANCO
Aurora

TESTAR, CORALEE ELLIOTT
Little Kidnappers, The

TEWKESBURY, JOAN
Cold Sassy Tree

THOMA, MICHAEL
Wrong Man, The

THOMAS, GEOFFREY
For Love And Glory

THOMAS, THOM
Private Sessions

THOMASSON, CAMILLE
Disappearance Of Christina, The

THOMPSON, ROBERT E.
Double Standard

White Hot: The Mysterious Murder Of
....Thelma Todd

THOMPSON, SELMA
Locked Up: A Mother's Rage
Men Don't Tell
No Child Of Mine
Taken Away
Woman With A Past

THOMPSON, TOMMY
Seaquest Dsv

THOMSON, JOHN
Girl From Tomorrow, The

THUNA, LEONORA
Torch Song

TIDYMAN, ERNEST
Brotherly Love
Stark

TITLE, SUSAN
Other Lover, The

TOBIN, NOREEN
Backfield In Motion

TOLKIN, STEVEN
Daybreak

TOPOR, TOM
Judgment

TORME, TRACY
Intruders

TOROKVEI, PETER
Hostage For A Day

TOWNE, J.J.
Littlest Victims

TRAFFICANTE, MARA
Deadbolt

TRAMER, BENNETT
Camp Cucamonga
Poison Ivy
Saved By The Bell-Hawaiian Style

TREVEY, KEN
Fall From Grace
L B J: The Early Years

TRISTAN, DOROTHY
Steal The Sky

TRUEBLOOD, GUERDON
Blood Vows: The Story Of A Mafia Wife
Chase, The
Desperate Rescue: The Cathy Mahone Story

TRUSTMAN, ALAN
Glitz

TURNER, BARBARA
Eye On The Sparrow
Out Of The Darkness
Somebody's Daughter

TURNER, DENNIS
Corpse Had A Familiar Face, The
Intimate Encounters
Judgment Day: The John List Story

Leona Helmsley: The Queen Of Mean
Long Hot Summer, The
Matter Of Justice, A
Poor Little Rich Girl: The Barbara Hutton
....Story
Rock Hudson

TWOHY, DAVID N.
Disaster In Time

UDOFF, YALE
Third Degree Burn

UGER, ALAN
Family Ties Vacation

VALDEZ, LUIS
Cisco Kid, The

VAN GORES, ALIDA
He's Not Your Son

VAN SCOYK, ROBERT
Columbo: No Time To Die

VAN SICKLE, CRAIG W.
Class Cruise

VENABLE, RONALD
Christmas Gift, The

VERLAINE, CYNTHIA
Substitute, The

VICTOR, PAT A.
Killing Mind, The
Trapped In Silence

VIDAL, GORE
Dress Gray
Gore Vidal's Billy The Kid

VINING, DANIEL
Wild Horses

VOORHEES, LINDA
Crazy From The Heart

WADLER, JOYCE
My Breast

WAGNER, BRUCE
Wild Palms

WAGNER, CARLA JEAN
Agatha Christie's The Man In The Brown Suit
Her Secret Life
Murder By Moonlight

WAGNER, MICHAEL
Probe

WALD, ELIOT
Hot Paint

WALDRON, GY
Billionaire Boys Club
Brotherhood Of The Rose
Confessions: Two Faces Of Evil
Twist Of Fate

WALKER, CHARLES
In A Child's Name

WALLACE, EARL W.
Broken Chain

Gunsmoke I I I: To The Last Man
Gunsmoke: The Last Apache
Murderous Affair, A: The Carolyn Warmus
....Story
War And Remembrance
War And Remembrance, Part I I

WALLACE, RANDALL
Broken Badges

WALLACE, TOMMY LEE
El Diablo
Stephen King's It

WALLENGREN, ERNIE
Macshayne: The Final Roll Of The Dice

WALPOLE, WILLARD
Clinton And Nadine

WALTON, FRED
Trapped
When A Stranger Calls Back

WAMBAUGH, JOSEPH
Echoes In The Darkness
Fugitive Nights: Danger In The Desert

WARD, BOB
Brotherhood Of The Gun

WARD, JANET
Miles From Nowhere

WARD, ROBERT
C. A. T. Squad: Python Wolf
Green Dolphin Beat

WARE, CLYDE
Alamo: 13 Days To Glory, The

WARFIELD, DAVID
Kiss Of A Killer

WASHINGTON, ART
Percy & Thunder

WATERS, ED
Jake And The Fatman

WATSON, ARA
Danger Of Love, The
No Place Like Home
Nobody's Child

WAXMAN, MARK
Revolver

WAY, RICK
Trial And Error

WEINER, REX
Forgotten Prisoners: The Amnesty File

WEINGARTEN, SOLOMON
Blind Side

WEINGARTNER, MARTHA
Harmful Intent

WEISBERG, DAVID
Payoff

WEISER, STANLEY
Murder In Mississippi

WEITHORN, MICHAEL J.
Family Ties Vacation

WELLER, MICHAEL
Spoils Of War

WELLS, BILL
Drop Dead Gorgeous
Exclusive
In My Daughter's Name

WELLS, JOHN
Nightman, The

WELLS, TIM
Iran: Days Of Crisis

WESLEY, RICHARD
Murder Without Motive: The Edmund Perry
....Story

WEST, VALERIE
One Of Her Own

WESTHEIMER, DAVID
Killer Among Us, A

WESTLAKE, DONALD E.
Fatal Confession: A Father Dowling Mystery

WESTON, ELLEN
Fear Stalk
Lies Before Kisses
Shadow Of Obsession
Sin And Redemption

WHEAT, JIM
Ewoks: The Battle For Endor

WHEAT, KEN
Birds I I: Land's End, The
Ewoks: The Battle For Endor

WHEELER, PAUL
Souvenir

WHITAKER, CLAIRE
Walton Thanksgiving Reunion, A

WHITCOMB, CYNTHIA
Body Of Evidence
Follow Your Heart
Guilty Until Proven Innocent
I Know My First Name Is Steven
Mark Twain And Me
One Terrific Guy
When You Remember Me

WHITE, GARRY MICHAEL
Shoot First: A Cop's Vengeance

WHITE, HOLLACE
Love Boat: A Valentine Voyage, The

WHITEMORE, HUGH
Final Days

WHITING, JR., BRAD
Personals

WHITMORE, STANFORD
Dreams Of Gold: The Mel Fisher Story
Supercarrier

WHITNEY, STEVE
Seduction: Three Tales From The Inner
Sanctum
Survive The Night

WICKES, DAVID
Frankenstein
Jekyll & Hyde

WIDEN, GREGORY
Weekend War

WIESENFELD, JOE
Yearling, The

WILDER, JOHN
Norman Rockwell's Breaking Home Ties
Return To Lonesome Dove
Spenser: For Hire

WILKINS, CHARLES
Children Of The Dark

WILLENS, SHEL
Perry Mason: The Case Of The Lady In The
Lake

WILLIAMS, BRYAN
Night Of Courage

WILLIAMS, CHRISTIAN
Capital News
Nightmare Years, The
Under Siege

WILLIAMS, LARRY B.
Glory Days

WILSON BLOOM, CAROLE
Scene Of The Crime

WILSON, V. PHIPPS
Stormy Weathers

WING, MICHAEL
Kissing Place, The

WITTLIFF, BILL
Lonesome Dove
Ned Blessing: The Story Of My Life And
....Times
Ned Blessing: The True Story Of My Life

WOLF, DICK
Nasty Boys

WOLF, JAY
Silhouette

WOLF, SONIA
Columbo - Caution: Murder Can Be
....Hazardous To Your Health

WOLFF, JOHN TREVOR
Frankenstein: The College Years

WOLFF, JURGEN
Double, Double, Toil And Trouble

WOLITZER, HILMA
Single Women, Married Men

WOLK, ANDY
Criminal Justice

WOLLERT, DAVE
Quicksand: No Escape
Spooner

WOLTERSTORFF, ROBERT
Street Hawk

WOOD, DAVID
Back Home

WOOD, WILLIAM
Circle Of Violence: A Family Drama
City Killer
Deadly Intentions... Again?
Execution, The
Penthouse, The

WOODARD, GRACE
Descending Angel

WOODFIELD, WILLIAM READ
Columbo And The Murder Of A Rock Star
Return Of Ironside, The

WOODS, CHRISTOPHER
Steal The Sky

WOODS, HARLAN
Overexposed

WOODWARD, BOB
Nightmare Years, The
Under Siege

WORTHINGTON, JAN
Danielle Steel's Heartbeat
Romance On The Orient Express

WOUK, HERMAN
Caine Mutiny Court - Martial, The
War And Remembrance
War And Remembrance, Part I I

WRYE, DONALD
Amerika

WURTZ, TIMOTHY
Naked Lie

WYLES, J. DAVID
Arthur The King

WYNN, TRACY KEENAN
Carolina Skeletons
In The Line Of Duty: The FBI Murders
Revenge Of Al Capone, The

YABLONSKY, YABO
Lena: My 100 Children

YALE, KATHLEEN BETSKO
Johnny Bull

YALEM, RICHARD
Blind Justice

YANOK, GEORGE
North Beach And Rawhide
Stormin' Home
Time To Triumph, A

YATES, WILLIAM
Back To The Streets Of San Francisco

YEERKOVICH, ANTHONY
Miami Vice

YELLEN, LINDA
Chantilly Lace

YELLEN, SHERMAN
I'll Take Manhattan
Not A Penny More, Not A Penny Less

YELMAN, PETER
Captain Cook

YOUNG, CATHLEEN
Place For Annie, A
Posing: Inspired By Three Real Stories
Time To Heal, A

YOUNG, DALENE
I Love You Perfect
Jonathan: The Boy Nobody Wanted
Living A Lie
Message From Holly
People Across The Lake, The
Yarn Princess, The

YOUNG, JOHN SACRET
China Beach

YOUNG, ROGER
Doublecrossed

ZABEL, BRYCE
Victim Of Love: The Shannon Mohr Story

ZACHARIAS, STEVE
Revenge Of The Nerds I V: Nerds In Love
Revenge Of The Nerds: The Next Generation
Thanksgiving Day

ZAGOR, MICHAEL
Of Pure Blood

ZESCHIN, ROBERT
Story Lady, The

ZILLER, PAUL
Deadly Surveillance

ZIMMEL, HARV
Snow Kill

ZINDEL, PAUL
Alice In Wonderland
Babes In Toyland
Connecticut Yankee In King Arthur's Court, A

ZITO, STEPHEN
Diana: Her True Story
Fergie And Andrew: Behind The Palace
....Doors
Full Exposure: The Sex Tapes Scandal
Glitz
Hostage Flight
Lady Mobster

ZLOTOFF, LEE DAVID
Frank Nitti: The Enforcer
Perry Mason: The Case Of The Avenging Ace
Plymouth
Waco & Rhinehart

ZOLA, MARION
Sharing Richard

ZWICK, EDWARD
Extreme Close-Up

Section G

DIRECTORS

Cross-referenced by
Produced Credits

AARON, PAUL
In Love And War
Untamed Love

ACKERMAN, ROBERT ALLAN
David's Mother

ADAMS, CATLIN
Stolen: One Husband

ADDISON, ANITA
There Are No Children Here

ALLEN, COREY
Ann Jillian Story, The
Beverly Hills Cowgirl Blues
Brass
Codename: Foxfire - Slay It Again, Sam
Destination: America
Last Fling, The
Moment Of Truth: Stalking Back
Murder, She Wrote

ALLEN, DEBBIE
Polly--Comin' Home
Stompin' At The Savoy

ALTMAN, ROBERT
Caine Mutiny Court - Martial, The
Room, The

ANDERSON, MICHAEL
Sea Wolf, The
Sword Of Gideon
Young Catherine

ANSPAUGH, DAVID
Deadly Care
In The Company Of Darkness

ANTONIO, LOU
Agatha Christie's Thirteen At Dinner
Dark Holiday
Face To Face
Last Prostitute, The
Lies Before Kisses
Mayflower Madam
Nightmare In The Daylight
One Terrific Guy
Outside Woman, The
Pals
Rape Of Dr. Willis, The
Rearview Mirror
Taste For Killing, A
This Gun For Hire
Threesome

ARDOLINO, EMILE
Gypsy

ARKUSH, ALLAN
Capital News

ARNER, GWEN
Majority Rule

ARTHUR, KAREN
Blue Bayou
Bridge To Silence
Bump In The Night
Bunny's Tale, A
Cracked Up

Crossings
Disappearance Of Christina, The
Evil In Clear River
Fall From Grace
Jacksons: An American Dream , The
Rape Of Richard Beck, The
Secret, The
Shadow Of A Doubt
Victims For Victims - The Theresa Saldana
....Story

ASHER, WILLIAM
I Dream Of Jeannie: 15 Years Later
Return To Green Acres

AUSTIN, RAY
Return Of The 6 Million Dollar Man & Bionic
....Woman

AVNET, JON
Between Two Women

BADIYI, REZA
Blade In Hong Kong

BALDWIN, PETER
Very Brady Christmas, A

BARNETTE, NEEMA
Better Off Dead
Scattered Dreams: The Kathryn Messenger
....Story
Sin And Redemption

BARNHART, DAN
Saved By The Bell-Hawaiian Style

BARRETO, BRUNO
Heart Of Justice, The

BAXLEY, CRAIG
Deconstructing Sarah
Family Torn Apart, A
Revenge On The Highway

BEATTY, ROGER
Plaza Suite

BEAUMONT, GABRIELLE
Moment Of Truth: Cradle Of Conspiracy

BECKHAM, MIKE
Investigation: Inside A Terrorist Bombing

BELLISARIO, DONALD P.
Three On A Match

BENDER, JACK
Armed & Innocent
Deadly Messages
Dreamer Of Oz, The
Letting Go
Love Can Be Murder
Midnight Hour, The
My Brother's Wife
Ned Blessing: The Story Of My Life And
....Times
Perfect Tribute, The
Shattered Vows
Side By Side
Tricks Of The Trade

BERGER, RICK
Sitter, The

BIERMAN, ROBERT
Apology

BIGELOW, KATHRYN
Wild Palms

BILSON, BRUCE
Bradys, The

BILSON, DANNY
Viper

BIXBY, BILL
Another Pair Of Aces: Three Of A Kind
Baby Of The Bride
Detective In The House
Trial Of The Incredible Hulk, The
Woman Who Loved Elvis, The

BLACK, NOEL
Conspiracy Of Love
Deadly Intentions
My Two Loves
Time To Triumph, A
Town Bully, The

BLECHMAN, COREY
Three Wishes Of Billy Grier, The

BLECKNER, JEFF
Brotherly Love
Do You Remember Love?
Favorite Son
Fresno
In Sickness And In Health
In The Best Of Families: Marriage, Pride And
....Madness
Last Wish
My Father, My Son
Round Table, The
Terrorist On Trial: The United States Vs.
Salim

BLOOM, JEFFREY
Columbo: Death Hits The Jackpot
Right Of The People, The
Starcrossed

BOGART, PAUL
Broadway Bound
Nutcracker: Money, Madness And Murder

BONERZ, PETER
Sharing Richard

BOWMAN, CHUCK
Moment Of Truth: Why My Daughter?

BRAND, JOSHUA
I'll Fly Away

BRANDSTROM, CHARLOTTE
Sweet Revenge

BRAVERMAN, CHARLES
Brotherhood Of Justice, The
Prince Of Bel Air

BRIDGES, BEAU
Secret Sins Of The Father

BRINCKERHOFF, BURT
Jailbirds

BROWN, GEORG STANFORD
Alone In The Neon Jungle
Father & Son: Dangerous Relations
Kids Like These
Last P. O. W? The Bobby Garwood Story
Stuck With Each Other

BUCKSEY, COLIN
Curiosity Kills
Midnight's Child
Notorious
Terror In The Night

BURSTALL, TIM
Nightmare At Bitter Creek

BUTLER, ROBERT
Lois & Clark: The New Adventures Of
....Superman
Long Time Gone
Moonlighting
Our Family Honor
Out Of Time
Out On A Limb
White Mile

BYRUM, JOHN
Murder In High Places

CAIN, CHRIS
Wheels Of Terror

CAMERON, KEN
Oldest Living Confederate Widow Tells All

CAMPANELLA II, ROY
Body Of Evidence
Quiet Victory: The Charlie Wedemeyer Story

CAMPBELL, GRAEME
Deadly Betrayal: The Bruce Curtis Story

CAMPBELL, MARTIN
Cast A Deadly Spell

CANDY, JOHN
Hostage For A Day

CARDONE, J.S.
Shadowhunter

CARNER, CHARLES ROBERT
Killer Among Friends, A
One Woman's Courage

CARSON, DAVID
Shameful Secrets

CARTER, THOMAS
Equal Justice
Miami Vice
Under The Influence

CARVER, STEVEN
Oceans Of Fire

CATES, GILBERT
Absolute Strangers
Burning Rage
Call Me Anna
Child's Cry

Confessions: Two Faces Of Evil
Consenting Adult
Do You Know The Muffin Man?
Fatal Judgment
My First Love

CHAFFEY, DON
International Airport

CHAPMAN, MICHAEL
Annihilator, The

CHENAULT, ROBERT
Deceptions

CHERRY, STANELY Z.
Bring Me The Head Of Dobie Gillis

CHETWYND, LIONEL
So Proudly We Hail

CHOMSKY, MARVIN J.
Anastasia: The Mystery Of Anna
Angel In Green
Billionaire Boys Club
Brotherhood Of The Rose
Deliberate Stranger, The
I'll Be Home For Christmas
Nairobi Affair
Peter The Great
Robert Kennedy And His Times
Telling Secrets
Triumph Over Disaster: The Hurricane
....Andrew Story

CHOPRA, JOYCE
Baby Snatcher
Corpse Had A Familiar Face, The
Danger Of Love, The
Disappearance Of Nora
Murder In New Hampshire: The Pamela
....Smart Story

CLARK, BOB
American Clock, The

CLARK, LAWRENCE G.
Captain Cook
Just Another Secret

CLEGG, TOM
Casualty Of War, A

CLIFFORD, GRAEME
Past Tense

COLES, JOHN DAVID
Good Fight, The
Rising Son

COLLA, RICHARD
Blind Witness
Deadly Medicine
Desperate Rescue: The Cathy Mahone Story
Naked Lie
Roxanne: The Prize Pulitzer
Something Is Out There
Sparks: The Price Of Passion
Storm And Sorrow
That Secret Sunday
Web Of Deception

COLLINS, ROBERT
Hijacking Of The Achille Lauro, The
Hoover
In The Arms Of A Killer
Johnny Ryan
Mafia Princess
Prime Target

COMPTON, RICHARD
Baywatch: Panic At Malibu Pier
Keys, The

CONDON, BILL
Dead In The Water
Deadly Relations
Murder 101
White Lie

CONNOR, KEVIN
Diana: Her True Story
Great Expectations
Iran: Days Of Crisis
Lethal Exposure
Lion Of Africa, The
Mistral's Daughter
North And South, Book 2
Return Of Sherlock Holmes, The
Shadow Of Obsession
What Price Victory?

CONRAD, ROBERT
Glory Days
High Mountain Rangers
Jesse Hawkes

CONTNER, JAMES A.
Cover Girl Murders, The
Hitler's Daughter
Palace Guard
Return Of Eliot Ness, The
Ten Million Dollar Getaway

COOK, FIELDER
Evergreen
Special Friendship, A

COOLIDGE, MARTHA
Bare Essentials
Crazy In Love
Trenchcoat In Paradise

COOPER, JACKIE
Glitter
Izzy And Moe
Night They Saved Christmas, The

COOPER, STUART
Bitter Vengeance
Christmas Eve
Dancing With Danger
Long Hot Summer, The
Mario Puzo's The Fortunate Pilgrim
One Special Victory
Payoff
Rubdown

CORCORAN, BILL
E. A. R. T. H. Force
I Know My Son Is Alive
Shattered Trust: The Shari Karney Story

Survive The Night

COREA, NICHOLAS
Incredible Hulk Returns, The

CORRELL, CHARLES
Cry In The Wild: The Taking Of Peggy Ann
Dead Before Dawn
Gunsmoke: The Last Apache
In The Deep Woods
Mother Of The Bride
She Says She's Innocent
Writer's Block

COSGROVE, JOHN
Victim Of Love: The Shannon Mohr Story

CRANE, PETER
Cover Up

CRAVEN, WES
Night Visions

CROWE, CHRISTOPHER
Steel Justice
Streets Of Justice

CULLINGHAM, MARK
Dead On The Money

CURRAN, WILLIAM
Love, Cheat And Steal

CURTIS, DAN
Dark Shadows
Intruders
War And Remembrance
War And Remembrance, Part I I

DALEN, ZALE
Anything To Survive
On Thin Ice: The Tai Babilonia Story

DAMSKI, MEL
Attack On Fear
Back To The Streets Of San Francisco
Badge Of The Assassin
Blood River
Connecticut Yankee In King Arthur's Court, A
Everybody's Baby: The Rescue Of Jessica
....Mcclure
Girl Who Came Between Them, The
Murder By The Book
Shoot First: A Cop's Vengeance
Three Kings, The
Wife, Mother, Murderer
Wild Card
Winner Never Quits, A

DANIELS, MARC
He's Fired, She's Hired
Special People
Vengeance: The Story Of Tony Cimo

DANIELS, ROD
Stranded

DARABONT, FRANK
Buried Alive

DARBY, JONATHAN
Enemy Within, The

DARLOW, DAVID
Tailspin: Behind The Korean Airlines Tragedy

DAVIDSON, MARTIN
Long Gone
Murderous Affair, A: The Carolyn Warmus
....Story

DAVIS, DESMOND
Camille
Freedom Fighter

DAY, ROBERT
Celebration Family
Diary Of A Perfect Murder
Fire: Trapped On The 37th Floor
Higher Ground
Hollywood Wives
Lady From Yesterday, The
London And Davis In New York
Love, Mary
Quick And The Dead, The

DE FELITTA, FRANK
Killer In The Mirror

DE JARNATT, STEVE
Alfred Hitchcock Presents

DEAR, WILLIAM
Journey To The Center Of The Earth

DEITCH, DONNA
Sexual Advances
Women Of Brewster Place, The

DINNER, MICHAEL
Rise & Walk: The Dennis Byrd Story
Thicker Than Blood: The Larry Mclinden
....Story

DIXON, IVAN
Percy & Thunder

DOBSON, KEVIN JAMES
Casey's Gift: For Love Of A Child
Miracle In The Wilderness
Survive The Savage Sea
What She Doesn't Know

DONNELLY, TOM
Blindsided

DONNER, CLIVE
Agatha Christie's Dead Man's Folly
Arthur The King
Babes In Toyland
Christmas Carol, A
Not A Penny More, Not A Penny Less

DONOVAN, MARTIN
Death Dreams
Seeds Of Tragedy
Substitute, The

DORNHELM, BORTER
Fatal Deception: Mrs. Lee Harvey Oswald

DRAKE, JIM
Based On An Untrue Story
Goddess Of Love
This Wife For Hire

DREW, DI
Trouble In Paradise

DRURY, DAVID
Intrigue

DUBIN, CHARLES S.
Drop-Out Mother
International Airport

DUCHOWNEY, ROGER
Camp Cucamonga

DUGUAY, CHRISTIAN
Adrift
Snowbound: The Jim And Jennifer Stolpa
....Story

DUKE, BILL
Johnnie Mae Gibson: F B I

DUKE, DARYL
Columbo - Caution: Murder Can Be
....Hazardous To Your Health
Fatal Memories
Florence Nightingale
When We Were Young

DUNCAN, PATRICK
Live: From Death Row

EDWARDS, BLAKE
Peter Gunn

EGELSON, JAN
Double Deception
Last Hit, The

EHLICH, ROSANNE
Chantilly Lace

ELIAS, MICHAEL
Lush Life

ELIKANN, LARRY
Big One: The Great Los Angeles Earthquake
Bonds Of Love
Dallas: The Early Years
Dangerous Affection
Disaster At Silo 7
Fever
God Bless The Child
Hands Of A Stranger
High Price Of Passion, The
I Know My First Name Is Steven
Inconvenient Woman, An
Kiss Of A Killer
Last Flight Out
Letter To Three Wives, A
Menendez: A Killing In Beverly Hills
One Against The Wind
Out Of The Darkness
Peyton Place: The Next Generation
Poison Ivy
Stoning In Fulham County, A
Story Lady, The
Stranger In My Bed
Take My Daughters, Please
Turn Back The Clock
When Love Kills: The Seduction Of John
....Hearn

ENGLER, MICHAEL
Mastergate

ENGLUND, GEORGE
Las Vegas Strip Wars, The

ERMAN, JOHN
An Early Frost
Atlanta Child Murders, The
Attic: The Hiding Of Anne Frank, The
Breathing Lessons
Carolina Skeletons
David
Last Best Year, The
Last To Go, The
Our Sons
Queen
Right To Kill?
When The Time Comes

FAIRFAX, FERDINAND
Secret Life Of Ian Fleming, The

FALK, HARRY
North Beach And Rawhide

FEARNLEY, NEIL
Black Ice

FERRARA, ABEL
Gladiator, The

FINK, KEN
Stephen King's Golden Years

FISK, JACK
Final Verdict

FLYNN, JOHN
Nails

FORBES, BRYAN
Endless Game, The

FRANKENHEIMER, JOHN
Against The Wall

FRANKLIN, CARL
Laurel Avenue

FRAWLEY, JAMES
Assault And Matrimony
Secret Life Of Archie's Wife, The
Spies, Lies And Naked Thighs
Warm Hearts, Cold Feet

FREEDMAN, JERROLD
Comeback, The
Condition: Critical
Family Sins
Good Night, Sweet Wife: A Murder In Boston
Night Walk
Seduced
Thompson's Last Run
Unholy Matrimony

FRENCH, VICTOR
Little House On The Prairie - Bless All The
....Dear Children

FRESCO, MICHAEL
Daughters Of Privilege

FRIEDKIN, WILLIAM
C. A. T. Squad

FRIEDMAN, RICHARD
In The Shadows, Someone Is Watching
Shadow Of A Stranger

GARRETT, LILA
Bridesmaids
Who Gets The Friends?

GARRIS, MICK
Psycho I V: The Beginning
Stephen King's The Stand

GERBER, FRED
Due South

GETHERS, STEVEN
Case Of The Hillside Strangler, The
Marcus Welby, M. D.: A Holiday Affair
Mercy Or Murder?

GIBBINS, DUNCAN
Case For Murder, A

GIBSON, BRIAN
Drug Wars: The Camarena Story
Josephine Baker Story, The
Murderers Among Us: The Simon Wiesenthal
....Story

GILLUM, VERN
Brotherhood Of The Gun
They've Taken Our Children: The Chowchilla
....Kidnapping

GIRALDI, BOB
Club Med

GIRARD, DOMINIQUE
Omen I V: The Awakening

GLATTER, LESLI
Into The Homeland
State Of Emergency

GODDARD, JIM
Hitler's S S: Portrait In Evil
Lie Down With Lions

GOLD, JACK
Escape From Sobibor
Murrow
Rose And The Jackal, The
Sakharov
She Stood Alone
Stones Of Ibarra
Tenth Man, The

GOLDSTONE, JAMES
Bride In Black, The
Dreams Of Gold: The Mel Fisher Story
Sentimental Journey
Sun Also Rises, The

GORDEN, STUART
Daughter Of Darkness

GORDON, KEITH
Wild Palms

GORDON-CLARK, LAWRENCE
Romance On The Orient Express

GRAHAM, WILLIAM A.
Bed Of Lies
Beyond Suspicion
Elvis And The Colonel: The Untold Story
George Washington I I: The Forging Of A
....Nation
Gore Vidal's Billy The Kid
Last Days Of Frank And Jesse James, The
Montana
Mussolini - The Untold Story
Police Story: The Freeway Killings
Proud Men
Secrets Of A Married Man
Street Of Dreams
Supercarrier
True Blue

GRANT, BRIAN
Complex Of Fear
Day Of Reckoning
Love Kills
Sweet Poison

GRANT, LEE
No Place Like Home
Nobody's Child
Seasons Of The Heart

GRAUMAN, WALTER
Nightmare On The Thirteenth Floor
Outrage
Scene Of The Crime
Shakedown On The Sunset Strip
Who Is Julia?

GRAY, JOHN
Lost Capone, The
Marla Hanson Story, The
Place For Annie, A
When He's Not A Stranger

GREEN, BRUCE SETH
In Self Defense
Laker Girls, The
Manhunt: Search For The Night Stalker
Perfect People
Rags To Riches
Running Against Time

GREENE, DAVID
After The Promise
And Then She Was Gone
Betty Ford Story, The
Beyond Obsession
Circle Of Violence: A Family Drama
Fatal Vision
Guardian, The
Guilty Conscience
Honor Thy Mother
In The Best Interest Of The Child
Inherit The Wind
Liberace: Behind The Music
Miles To Go . . .
Night Of The Hunter
Penthouse, The
Red Earth, White Earth
Small Sacrifices
South Beach

Spoils Of War
Sweet Revenge, A
This Child Is Mine
Triplecross
Vanishing Act
What Ever Happened To Baby Jane?
Willing To Kill: The Texas Cheerleader Story

GREENWALD, ROBERT
Burning Bed, The
Forgotten Prisoners: The Amnesty File
On Fire
Shattered Spirits

GRINT, ALAN
Agatha Christie's The Man In The Brown Suit
Secret Garden, The

GUEST, CHRISTOPHER
Attack Of The 50ft. Woman

GUILLERMAN, JOHN
Tracker, The

GUTMAN, NATHANIE
Linda

GYLLENHAAL, STEPHEN
Abduction Of Kari Swenson, The
Family Of Spies
Killing In A Small Town
Leap Of Faith
Paris Trout
Promised A Miracle

HAGGARD, PIERS
Back Home
Four Eyes And Six Guns
Fulfillment Of Mary Gray, The
I'll Take Romance

HAID, CHARLES
Cooperstown
In The Line Of Duty: Standoff At Marion
Nightman, The

HAINES, RANDA
Alfred Hitchcock Presents

HALE, BILLY
Harem
Lace I I
Liberace
Murder Of Mary Phagan, The
People Like Us

HALL, PETER
Orpheus Descending

HALLER, DAN
Highwayman, The

HANCOCK, JOHN
Steal The Sky

HANSON, CURTIS
Children Of Times Square

HARDY, ROD
Between Love And Hate
Lies And Lullabies
My Name Is Kate
Only Way Out, The

Rio Diablo
Yearling, The

HARRIS, HARRY
Alice In Wonderland
Eight Is Enough: A Family Reunion
Walton Thanksgiving Reunion, A

HARRISON, JOHN KENT
For The Love Of Aaron
Sound And The Silence, The
Whose Child Is This? The War For Baby
....Jessica

HART, HARVEY
Beverly Hills Madam
Passion And Paradise
Stone Fox

HARVEY, ANTHONY
This Can't Be Love

HAVINGA, NICK
Single Women, Married Men

HEAD, HELAINE
Perry Mason Mystery, A: The Case Of The
Lethal

HEFFRON, RICHARD T.
Broken Angel
Convicted: A Mother's Story
Guilty Of Innocence: The Lenell Geter Story
Napoleon And Josephine: A Love Story
North And South
Pancho Barnes
Samaritan: The Mitch Snyder Story
Tagget

HEMMINGS, DAVID
In The Heat Of The Night
Passport To Murder
Quantum Leap

HENDEERSON, JOHN
Borrowers, The

HEREK, STEPHEN
Gifted One, The

HERZFELD, JOHN
Barbara Taylor Bradford's Remember
Casualties Of Love: The Long Island Lolita
....Story
Daddy
Father's Revenge, A
Preppie Murder, The
Ryan White Story, The

HESS, JON DANIEL
Not Of This World

HESTON, CHARLTON
Man For All Season, A

HESTON, FRASER C.
Crucifier Of Blood, The
Treasure Island

HEWITT, PETER
Wild Palms

HIBLER, CHRISTOPHER
Diagnosis Of Murder

Fatal Confession: A Father Dowling Mystery
Matlock: The Witness Killings

HICKOX, DOUGLAS
Blackout
I'll Take Manhattan
Mistral's Daughter
Sins

HOBLIT, GREGORY
Charles And Diana: Unhappily Ever After
Class Of '61
L. A. Law
Roe Vs. Wade

HODGES, MIKE
Florida Straits

HOFFMAN, GARY
Bonnie And Clyde: The True Story

HOLCOMB, ROD
Blind Justice
Cartier Affair, The
Chase
China Beach
Donato And Daughter
Finding The Way Home
Long Journey Home, The
Message From Holly
Promise To Keep, A
Royce
Scene Of The Crime
Stark
Stillwatch
Two Fathers' Justice
Wolf

HOLLAND, TOM
Stranger Within, The

HOLZMAN, ALLAN
Intimate Stranger

HOOK, HARRY
Last Of His Tribe, The

HOOKS, KEVIN
Heat Wave
Murder Without Motive: The Edmund Perry
....Story
Roots: The Gift
To My Daughter With Love

HOOPER, TOBE
I'm Dangerous Tonight

HORTON, PETER
Extreme Close-Up

HOUGH, JOHN
Duel Of Hearts
Ghost In Monte Carlo, A
Hazard Of Hearts, A
Lady And The Highwayman, The

HUGHES, TERRY
For Love Or Money

HUME, EDWARD
Stranger On My Land

HUNT, PETER H.
Charley Hannah
Danielle Steel's Secrets
Eyes Of A Witness
Hart To Hart Returns
P. S. I Luv U
Sworn To Vengeance

HUNTER, TIM
Lies Of The Twins

HUSSEIN, WARIS
Arch Of Triumph
Copacabana
Downpayment On Murder
Fall From Grace
For The Love Of My Child: The Anissa
....Ayala Story
Forbidden Nights
Killer Instinct
Murder Between Friends
Richest Man In The World: The Aristotle
....Onassis Story
She Woke Up
Shell Seekers, The
Surviving
Switched At Birth
Those She Left Behind
When The Bough Breaks

ICHASO, LEON
Fear Inside, The
Kiss To Die For, A

INCH, KEVIN
Carly's Web
Remington Steele: The Steele That Wouldn't
....Die

IRVIN, JOHN
Robin Hood

ISCOVE, ROBERT
Breaking The Silence
Flash, The
Forget Me Not Murders, The
Miracle On I-880
Mission Of The Shark
Murder In Black And White
River Of Rage: The Taking Of Maggie
....Keene
Shattered Dreams
Terror On Track 9

ISRAEL, NEAL
Combat High
Cover Girl And The Cop, The

JACKSON, DAVID S.
Death Train

JACKSON, DOUGLAS
Deadbolt

JAMESON, JERRY
Bonanza: The Return
Cowboy And The Ballerina, The
Fire And Rain
Gunsmoke III: To The Last Man
Gunsmoke: One Man's Justice

Gunsmoke: The Long Ride Home
One Police Plaza
Red Spider, The
Stormin' Home
Terror On Highway 91

JARROTT, CHARLES
Danielle Steel's Changes
Jackie Collins' Lady Boss
Judith Krantz's Till We Meet Again
Lucy & Desi: Before The Laughter
Poor Little Rich Girl: The Barbara Hutton
....Story
Stranger In The Mirror, A
Trade Winds
Woman He Loved, The
Yes, Virginia, There Is A Santa Claus

JOANOU, PHIL
Wild Palms

JOHNSON, BEN
Stranger On My Land

JOHNSON, KENNETH
Hot Pursuit
Shadow Chasers
Sherlock Holmes Returns

JOHNSON, LAMONT
Broken Chain
Crash Landing: The Rescue Of Flight 232
Kennedys Of Massachusetts, The
Lincoln
Unnatural Causes
Voices Within: The Lives Of Truddi Chase
Wallenberg: A Hero's Story

JOHNSON, LLOYD
Gotham

JOHNSTON, JIM
Blue Deville

JONES, DAVID
And Then There Was One
Fire In The Dark

JORDAN, GLENN
Aftermath: A Test Of Love
Barbarians At The Gate
Boys, The
Challenger
Dress Gray
Heartsounds
Home Fires Burning
Jane's House
Jesse
O Pioneers
Promise
Sarah, Plain And Tall
Something In Common
To Dance With The White Dog
Toughlove

KACZENDER, GEORGE
Betrayal Of Trust
Christmas On Division Street
Jonathan: The Boy Nobody Wanted
Seduction In Travis County

KAGAN, JEREMY
Courage
Descending Angel
Dr. Quinn, Medicine Woman
Roswell

KAPLAN, ED
Chips, The War Dog
For Their Own Good

KATLEMAN, MICHAEL
No Child Of Mine
Spider And The Fly, The

KATZIN, LEE H.
Dirty Dozen: The Deadly Mission
Dirty Dozen: The Fatal Mission
Jake Spanner, Private Eye
Spenser: For Hire

KEACH, JAMES
Passion For Justice, A: Hazel Brannon Smith
....Story
Praying Mantis
Sunstroke

KEATON, DIANE
Wildflower

KEETER, WORTH
Illicit Behavior

KENNEDY, BURT
Alamo: 13 Days To Glory, The
Once Upon A Texas Train
Where The Hell's That Gold

KERSHNER, IRVIN
Seaquest Dsv
Traveling Man

KEUSCH, MICHAEL
Just One Of The Girls

KIERSCH, FRITZ
Fatal Charm
Shattered Image

KING, ZALMAN
Red Shoes Diaries

KLANE, ROBERT
Odd Couple, The

KLETTER, RICHARD
Tower, The

KORTY, JOHN
Baby Girl Scott
Cast The First Stone
Deadly Business, A
Deadly Matrimony
Ewok Adventure, The
Eye On The Sparrow
Getting Out
Keeping Secrets
Line Of Fire: The Morris Dees Story
Long Road Home
Resting Place
Son's Promise, A
They
Winnie

KOTCHEFF, TED
Love On The Run

KOWALSKI, BERNARD
Miracle At Beekman's Place

KRASNY, PAUL
Back To Hannibal: The Return Of Tom Sawyer And Huck Finn
Drug Wars: The Cocaine Cartel
Search And Rescue
Still Crazy Like A Fox
Two Fathers: Justice For The Innocent

KULIK, BUZZ
Around The World In 80 Days
Her Secret Life
Jackie Collins' Lucky Chances
Kane And Abel
Miles From Nowhere
Too Young The Hero
Women Of Valor

LAGOMARSINO, RON
Counterfeit Contessa, The
Dinner At Eight
Homefront
Picket Fences

LAMBERT, MARY
Grand Isle

LANDON, MICHAEL
Highway To Heaven
Us
Where Pigeons Go To Die

LANEUVILLE, ERIC
Brand New Life: The Honeymoon
Ernest Green Story, The
George Mckenna Story, The
Mantis
Staying Afloat
Stolen Babies

LANG, RICHARD
Christmas Comes To Willow Creek
In Like Flynn
Obsessed With A Married Woman
Perry Mason: The Case Of The Sinister Spirit
Road Raiders, The

LANGTON, SIMON
Anna Karenina
Casanova
Laguna Heat

LARRY, SHELDON
Behind Enemy Lines
Burning Bridges
Family Of Strangers
First Steps
Hot Paint
Quiet Killer

LARSON, GLEN A.
Chameleons

LATHAN, STAN
Child Saver, The
Eight Is Enough Wedding, An

Uncle Tom's Cabin

LATTUADA, ALBERTO
Christopher Columbus

LEDER, MIMI
Baby Brokers
House Of Secrets
Little Piece Of Heaven, A
Marked For Murder
Nightingales
Rio Shanon
There Was A Little Boy
Woman With A Past

LERNER, DAN
Desperate Journey: The Allison Wilcox Story
Shame

LEVI, ALAN J.
Bionic Showdown: The 6 Million Dollar ....Man/Bionic Woman
Columbo And The Murder Of A Rock Star
Columbo: No Time To Die
Deadman's Revenge
Island Sons
Knight Rider 2000
Return Of Sam Mccloud, The
Stepford Children, The
Without Warning: Terror In The Towers

LEVIN, PETER
Deliver Them From Evil: The Taking Of Alta ....View
Hostage
Houston: The Legend Of Texas
Killer Among Us, A
Lady In A Corner
Littlest Victims
My Son Johnny
Overkill: The Aileen Wuornos Story
Popeye Doyle
Precious Victims
Sworn To Silence

LEVY, EUGENE
Partners 'N Love
Sodbusters

LEWIN, ROBERT
Reason To Live, A

LEWIS, ROBERT
City Killer
Dead Reckoning
Deep Dark Secrets
Don't Talk To Strangers
Firefighter
Ladykillers
Lost In London
Memories Of Murder
Secret Life Of Kathy Mccormick, The
Stranger Waits, A
Summer To Remember, A

LIEBERMAN, ROBERT
To Save A Child

LINDSAY-HOGG, MICHAEL
Habitation Of Dragons, The
Little Match Girl, The

Murder By Moonlight
Nazi Hunter: The Beate Klarsfeld Story
Running Mates

LIPSTADT, AARON
Pair Of Aces

LONDON, JERRY
Calendar Girl, Cop Killer? The Bambi ....Bembenek Story
Cosby Mysteries, The
Dadah Is Death
Ellis Island
Grass Roots
Harry's Hong Kong
I Spy Returns
If Tomorrow Comes
Kiss Shot
Manhunt For Claude Dallas
Season Of Giants, A
Twist Of The Knife, A
Vestige Of Honor
Victim Of Love

LONGSTREET, HARRY
Sex,Love, And Cold Hard Cash

LOTIMER, EB
Love Matters

LOWRY, DICK
American Harvest
Archie: To Riverdale And Back Again
Case Closed
Dream West
Gambler Returns: The Luck Of The Draw
Her Final Fury: Betty Broderick, The Last ....Chapter
Howard Beach: Making The Case For Murder
In The Line Of Duty: A Cop For The Killing
In The Line Of Duty: Ambush In Waco
In The Line Of Duty: Manhunt In The ....Dakotas
In The Line Of Duty: Street War
In The Line Of Duty: The FBI Murders
In The Line Of Duty: The Price Of ....Vengeance
Kenny Rogers As The Gambler I I I: The ....Legend Continues
Miracle Landing
Murder With Mirrors
One More Mountain
Toughest Man In The World, The
Unconquered
Wet Gold
Wild Horses
Woman Scorned: The Betty Broderick Story

LUKE, ERIC
Not Quite Human I I
Still Not Quite Human

LYNCH, DAVID
Twin Peaks

LYNCH, PAUL
Double Your Pleasure
Drop Dead Gorgeous
Going To The Chapel
Murder By Night

She Knows Too Much

MACKENZIE, JOHN
Act Of Vengeance
Voyage

MACKENZIE, WILL
Family Ties Vacation
Hobo's Christmas, A
Perfect Harmony
Stormy Weathers

MAGAR, GUY
Stepfather I I I

MAGNOLI, ALBERT
Born To Run

MANDEL, ROBERT
Haunted, The
Perfect Witness

MANKIEWICZ, FRANCIS
Conspiracy Of Silence
Love And Hate: A Marriage Made In Hell

MANKIEWICZ, TOM
Taking The Heat

MANN, DANIEL
Man Who Broke 1,000 Chains, The

MANN, DELBERT
Against Her Will: An Incident In Baltimore
April Morning
Death In California, A
Incident In A Small Town
Ironclads
Last Days Of Patton, The
Ted Kennedy, Jr., Story, The

MANN, FARHAD
Face Of Fear, The
Nick Knight

MANN, MICHAEL
L. A. Takedown

MANNERS, KIM
Broken Badges

MANSON, DAVID
Those Secrets

MARCEL, TERRY
Bejeweled

MARGOLIN, STUART
Double, Double, Toil And Trouble
Facts Of Life Down Under, The
Glitter Dome, The
Room Upstairs, The

MARKLE, PETER
Breaking Point
Dead And Alive
El Diablo
Through The Eyes Of A Killer

MARKOWITZ, ROBERT
Adam: His Song Continues
Afterburn
Alex: The Life Of A Child
Children Of The Night

Cry For Help: The Tracey Thurman Story, A
Decoration Day
Kojak: The Belarus File
Love, Lies And Murder
Murder In The Heartland
Overexposed
Too Young To Die?

MASTROIANNI, ARMAND
Cries Unheard: The Donna Yaklich Story
Deep Trouble
Mothers Revenge, A
One Of Her Own
When No One Would Listen

MATTHAU, CHARLES
Mrs. Lambert Remembers Love

MAXWELL, RON
Gettysburg

MAY, BRADFORD
Amy Fisher: My Story
Drive Like Lightning
Fatal Friendship
It's Nothing Personal
Lady Against The Odds
Lady Forgets, The
Legacy Of Lies
Marilyn & Bobby: Her Final Affair
Mortal Sins
Over My Dead Body
Trouble Shooters: Trapped Beneath The
....Earth

MAYBERRY, RUSS
Challenge Of A Lifetime
Danger Down Under
Place To Call Home, A

MCBREARTY, DON
The Race To Freedom: The Underground
....Railroad

MCBRIDE, JIM
Blood Ties
Wrong Man, The

MCEVEETY, VINCENT
Columbo: A Bird In The Hand
Columbo: It's All In The Game
Columbo: Undercover
Gunsmoke: Return To Dodge
Stranger At My Door

MCLAGLEN, ANDREW V.
On Wings Of Eagles

MCLOUGHLIN, TOM
Fire Next Time, The
In A Child's Name
Leave Of Absence
Murder Of Innocence
Something To Live For: The Alison Gertz
....Story
Stephen King's Sometimes They Come Back
Yarn Princess, The

MCPHERSON, JOHN
Dirty Work
Fade To Black

Strays

MCRANEY, GERALD
Love And Curses . . . And All That Jazz

MEDFORD, DON
Father Of Hell Town

MELMAN, JEFFREY
Family For Joe, A

MESA, ROLAND
Revenge Of The Nerds: The Next Generation

MESSINA, PHILIP F.
Spy

METTER, ALAN
Working Trash

METZGER, ALAN
Black Widow Murders: The Blanche Taylor
....Moore Story
China Lake Murders, The
Exclusive
Fatal Exposure
In The Shadow Of A Killer
Kojak: The Price Of Justice
Murder C. O. D.
Red Wind
Roommates

MEYER, KEVIN
Invasion Of Privacy

MICHAELS, RICHARD
Backfield In Motion
Heart Of A Champion: The Ray Mancini Story
Her Wicked Ways
I'll Take Manhattan
Indiscreet
Jessie
Leona Helmsley: The Queen Of Mean
Love And Betrayal
Miss America: Behind The Crown
Red River
Rockabye
Silence Of The Heart
Triumph Of The Heart: The Ricky Bell Story

MIHALKA, GEORGE
Psychic

MILLAR, STUART
Dream Breakers
Vital Signs

MILLER, GEORGE
In The Nick Of Time
Mom For Christmas, A
Spooner

MILLER, MICHAEL
Always Remember I Love You
Can You Feel Me Dancing?
Case Of Deadly Force, A
Crime Of Innocence
Criminal Behavior
Dangerous Passion
Danielle Steel's Daddy
Danielle Steel's Heartbeat
Danielle Steel's Once In A Lifetime

Danielle Steel's Palomino
Danielle Steel's Star
Necessity
Roses Are For The Rich
Silent Witness
Torch Song

MILLER, ROBERT ELLIS
Intimate Strangers
Killer Rules
Other Lover, The

MILLER, SHARRON
Little Girl Lost
Pleasures
Second Chances

MONPERE, CAROL
Pink Lightning

MONTESI, JORGE
Hush Little Baby
Liar, Liar
Moment Of Truth: A Child Too Many
Moment Of Truth: Broken Pledges
Omen I V: The Awakening

MOORE, IRVING J.
Dynasty: The Reunion

MOORE, TOM
Danielle Steel's Fine Things
Maybe Baby

MOSES, GILBERT
Fight For Jenny, A

MOSES, HARRY
Assault At West Point

MOSHER, GREGORY
Life In The Theater, A

MOSTOW, JONATHAN
Flight Of Black Angel

MOXEY, JOHN LLEWELLYN
Blacke's Magic
Deadly Deception
Lady Mobster
Outback Bound
Sadie And Son
When Dreams Come True

MUELLER, KATHY
Girl From Tomorrow, The

MURPHY, GEOFF
Blind Side
Last Outlaw, The
Red King, White Knight

MYERSON, ALAN
Bad Attitudes
Hi Honey -- I'm Dead

NAGY, IVAN
Intimate Encounters
Playing With Fire
Touch Of Scandal, A

NAPOLITANO, JOE
Earth Angel

NEAL, PATRICIA
Heidi

NEGRIN, ALBERTO
Mussolini: The Decline And Fall Of Il Duce

NELSON, GARY
Agatha Christie's Murder In Three Acts
Fugitive Nights: Danger In The Desert
Get Smart Again
James Clavell's Noble House
Lady Blue
Lookalike, The
Ray Alexander: A Taste For Justice
Revolver
Shooter

NELSON, GENE
Baron And The Kid, The
Return Of Ironside, The

NEWELL, MIKE
Common Ground

NICHOLSON, ARCH
Fortress

NICHOLSON, MARTIN
Day My Parents Ran Away, The

NICOLELLA, JOHN
Finish Line
Mickey Spillane's Mike Hammer: Murder ....Takes All
Rock Hudson
Runaway Father

NORTON, BILL L.
Angel Of Death
False Arrest

NOSSECK, NOEL
Aaron's Way
Born Too Soon
Different Affair, A
Follow Your Heart
French Silk
Full Exposure: The Sex Tapes Scandal
Mother's Justice, A
Opposites Attract
Roman Holiday
Without A Kiss Goodbye

NYBY II, CHRISTIAN
House On Sycamore Street, The
Perry Mason Mystery: The Case Of The Wicked Wives
Perry Mason: The Case Of The All-Star Assassin
Perry Mason: The Case Of The Avenging Ace
Perry Mason: The Case Of The Defiant Daughter
Perry Mason: The Case Of The Desperate Deception
Perry Mason: The Case Of The Fatal Fashion
Perry Mason: The Case Of The Fatal Framing
Perry Mason: The Case Of The Glass Coffin
Perry Mason: The Case Of The Heartbroken Bride
Perry Mason: The Case Of The Killer Kiss

Perry Mason: The Case Of The Musical Murders
Perry Mason: The Case Of The Poisoned Pen
Perry Mason: The Case Of The Reckless Romeo
Perry Mason: The Case Of The Ruthless Reporter
Perry Mason: The Case Of The Scandalous Scoundrel
Perry Mason: The Case Of The Skin-Deep Scandal
Perry Mason: The Case Of The Telltale Talk Show Host
Too Good To Be True
Waco & Rhinehart
Whisper Kills, A

O'BANNON, ROCKNE S.
Fear

O'BRIEN, JIM
Foreign Affairs

O'CONNOR, PAT
Zelda

O'FALLON, PETER
Dead Silence

O'HARA, TERRENCE
Perfect Bride, The

O'STEEN, SAM
Kids Don't Tell

OHLMEYER, DON
Heroes Of Desert Storm

OLIANSKY, JOEL
Alfred Hitchcock Presents
In Defense Of A Married Man

OLIN, KEN
Broken Cord, The
Doing Time On Maple Drive

OLIVER, RON
Liar's Edge

ORME, STUART
Hands Of A Murderer
Heist

OTTO, LINDA
Gregory K
Mothers' Right, A: The Elizabeth Morgan ....Story
Not In My Family
Unspeakable Acts

PAGE, ANTHONY
Chernobyl: The Final Warning
Forbidden
Monte Carlo
Murder: By Reason Of Insanity
Nightmare Years, The
Pack Of Lies
Scandal In A Small Town
Second Serve
Silent Cries

PAPAMICHAEL, PHEDON
Sketch Artist

PARISOT, DEAN
Framed

PARRIOTT, JAMES D.
Misfits Of Science

PARTRICK, MATTHEW
Tainted Blood

PASQUIN, JOHN
Don't Touch My Daughter
Out On The Edge

PASSER, IVAN
Fourth Story
Stalin

PATRICK, MATTHEW
Hider In The House
Night Owl

PATTERSON, JOHN
Darkness Before Dawn
Deadly Silence, A
Grave Secrets: The Legacy Of Hilltop Drive
Harmful Intent
Independence
Love, Honor & Obey: The Last Mafia
....Marriage
Marilyn & Me
Relentless: Mind Of A Killer
She Said No
Sins Of The Mother
Taken Away

PEARCE, RICHARD
Final Days

PEERCE, LARRY
Court - Martial Of Jackie Robinson, The
Elvis And Me
Fifth Missile, The
Love Lives On
Menu For Murder
Neon Empire
North And South, Book 3: Heaven And Hell
Poisoned By Love: The Kern County Murders
Prison For Children
Queenie
Woman Named Jackie, A

PENN, ARTHUR
Portrait, The

PERRY, STEVE
Parker Kane

PETRIE, DANIEL
Mark Twain And Me
My Name Is Bill W.
Town Torn Apart, A

PHELPS, WIN
Appearances

PHILIPS, LEE
American Geisha
Barnum
Blind Vengeance
Blue Lightning, The
Money, Power, Murder
Silent Movie

Space
Windmills Of The Gods

PIERSON, FRANK
Citizen Cohn
Somebody Has To Shoot The Picture

PILLSBURY, SAM
Eyes Of Terror
Into The Badlands
Presidents Child, The
Search For Grace

PITTMAN, BRUCE
Silent Witness: What A Child Saw

PONTI, MAURIZIO
Aurora

POST, TED
Stagecoach

POWER, JOHN
Betrayed By Love
Tommyknockers, The

PRESSMAN, MICHAEL
Christmas Gift, The
Final Jeopardy, The
Haunted By Her Past
Impostor, The
Incident At Dark River
Joshua's Heart
Man Against The Mob: The Chinatown
....Murders
Miracle Child
Private Sessions
Quicksand: No Escape
Revenge Of Al Capone, The
Shootdown
To Heal A Nation

PREUSS, RUBEN
Blackmail
Deceptions

QUILICI, FOLCO
Only One Survived

QUINN, JAMES
Blind Man's Bluff

REEVE, GEOFFREY
Souvenir

REID, ALASTAIR
Teamster Boss: The Jackie Presser Story

REINSCH, DEBORAH
Caught In The Act

REYNOLDS, BURT
Man From Left Field

REYNOLDS, GENE
Doing Life
Whereabouts Of Jenny, The

RHODES, MICHAEL
Babies
Christy
Heidi
In The Best Interest Of The Children
Killing Mind, The

Matters Of The Heart
Reason For Living: The Jill Ireland Story
Seduction: Three Tales From The Inner
Sanctum
Visions Of Murder

RICH, DAVID LOWELL
Choices
Convicted
Defiant One, The
Hearst And Davies Affair, The
Infidelity
Scandal Sheet

RICHARDSON, TONY
Beryl Markham: A Shadow On The Sun
Penalty Phase
Phantom Of The Opera, The

RICHIE, MICHAEL
Positively True Adventures Of The Alleged
Texas Cheerleader Murdering Mom, The

ROBBINS, MATTHEW
Mothers, Daughters And Lovers

ROBE, MIKE
Burden Of Proof, The
Child In The Night
Go Toward The Light
Guts And Glory: The Rise And Fall Of Oliver
....North
Murder Ordained
News At Eleven
Return To Lonesome Dove
Son Of The Morning Star
With Intent To Kill

RODRIGUEZ, ROBERT
Roadracers

ROEG, NICOLAS
Heart Of Darkness
Sweet Bird Of Youth

ROONEY, BETHANY
Locked Up: A Mother's Rage

ROSENTHAL, RICK
Birds I I: Land's End, The
Devlin
Nasty Boys

ROTH, BOBBY
Baja Oklahoma
Dead Solid Perfect
Judgment Day: The John List Story
Keeper Of The City
Rainbow Drive
Ride With The Wind
Switch, The
Tonight's The Night

ROTHSTEIN, RICHARD
Bates Motel

RUDOLPH, LOUIS
Double Standard

RUSSELL, KEN
Prisoner Of Honor

SADWITH, JAMES
Baby M
Bluffing It
Deadly Intentions... Again?
In Broad Daylight
Sinatra

SANDRICH, JAY
For Richer, For Poorer

SANFORD, ARLENE
Babymaker: The Dr. Cecil Jacobson's Story

SANGER, JONATHAN
Chance Of A Lifetime
Children Of The Bride
Just My Imagination
Obsessed
Secrets Of Lake Success

SARAFIAN, RICHARD C.
Liberty

SARGENT, JOSEPH
Abraham
Caroline?
Day One
Incident, The
Karen Carpenter Story, The
Last Elephant, The
Love Is Never Silent
Love She Sought, The
Miss Rose White
Never Forget
Of Pure Blood
Skylark
Somebody's Daughter
Space
There Must Be A Pony
World War I I : When Lions Roared

SARGENTI, MARINA
Child Of Darkness, Child Of Light

SARIN, VIC
Spenser: Pale Kings And Princes

SATLOF, RON
Hunter
J. O. E. And The Colonel
Love Boat: A Valentine Voyage, The
Original Sin
Perry Mason Returns
Perry Mason: The Case Of The Lady In The Lake
Perry Mason: The Case Of The Lost Love
Perry Mason: The Case Of The Maligned Mobster
Perry Mason: The Case Of The Murdered Madam
Perry Mason: The Case Of The Notorious Nun
Perry Mason: The Case Of The Shooting Star
Perry Mason: The Case Of The Silenced Singer

SAVILLE, PHILIP
Crash: The Mystery Of Flight 1501
Family Pictures
Mandela
Max And Helen

SCANLAN, JOSEPH
I Still Dream Of Jeannie
World's Oldest Living Bridesmaid, The

SCHACHTER, STEVEN
Getting Up And Going Home
Water Engine, The

SCHAEFER, GEORGE
Children In The Crossfire
Laura Lansing Slept Here
Man Upstairs, The
Mrs. Delafield Wants To Marry
Stone Pillow

SCHATZBERG, JERRY
Clinton And Nadine

SCHELL, MAXIMILIAN
Candles In The Dark

SCHENKEL, CARL
Bay Coven
Silhouette

SCHILLER, LAWRENCE
Double Jeopardy
Margaret Bourke - White
Peter The Great
Plot To Kill Hitler, The

SCHLAMME, THOMAS
Crazy From The Heart

SCHLONDORFF, VOLKER
Death Of A Salesman
Gathering Of Old Men, A

SCHNEIDER, PAUL
Babycakes
Dance Till Dawn
Empty Cradle
Entertainers, The
Guess Who's Coming For Christmas
Highway Heartbreaker
Honor Thy Father And Mother: The ....Menendez Murders
House Of Secrets And Lies, A
How To Murder A Millionaire
Maid For Each Other
My Boyfriend's Back
With Hostile Intent

SCHULTZ, CARL
Which Way Home
Young Indiana Jones Chronicles: The Curse ....Of The Jackal

SCHULTZ, MICHAEL
Day - O
Jury Duty: The Comedy
Spirit, The
Tarzan In Manhattan
Timestalkers

SCHUMACHER, JOEL
Two Thousand Malibu Road

SCHWARZENEGGER, ARNOLD
Christmas In Connecticut

SCOTT, MICHAEL
Dangerous Heart
Harvest For The Heart
Lady Killer

SCOTT, OZ
Class Cruise
Crash Course
Tears And Laughter: The Joan And Mielissa ....Rivers Story

SEED, PAUL
Dead Ahead: The Exxon Valdez Disaster

SEIDELMAN, ARTHUR ALLAN
Addicted To His Love
Body Language
Dying To Remember
False Witness
Kate's Secret
People Across The Lake, The
Poker Alice
Secrets Of Lake Success
Sin Of Innocence
Strange Voices

SHADYAC, TOM
Frankenstein: The College Years

SHAPIRO, PAUL
Heads

SHARP, IAN
Corsican Brothers, The
Pride And Extreme Prejudice
Secret Weapon
Twist Of Fate

SHAVELSON, MELVILLE
Deceptions

SHAW, ANTHONY
Mrs. 'Arris Goes To Paris

SHAW, LARRY
Donor
Fear Stalk
Living A Lie
Nurses On The Line: The Crash Of Flight 7
To My Daughter
Tonya & Nancy: The Inside Story

SHEBIB, DONALD
Little Kidnappers, The

SHERIN, ED
Daughter Of The Streets
Father Clements Story, The
Lena: My 100 Children
Settle The Score

SHERMAN, GARY
After The Shock
Missing Persons
Murderous Vision

SHOLDER, JACK
By Dawn's Early Light
Dark Reflection
Twelve O' One (12: 01)

SILVER, JOAN MICKLIN
Finnegan Begin Again
Private Matter, A

SILVER, MARISA
Indecency

SILVER, RON
Lifepod

SILVERSTEIN, ELLIOT
Betrayed By Innocence
Fight For Life
Night Of Courage
Rich Men, Single Women

SIMEONE, LAWRENCE L.
Blindfold: Acts Of Obsession

SIMONEAU, YVES
Amelia Earhart: The Final Flight
Cruel Doubt
Memphis
Till Death Us Do Part

SLOYAN, JAMES
Her Secret Life

SMITH, CHARLES MARTIN
Boris And Natasha

SMITHEE, ALAN
Call Of The Wild
Riviera

SMOLAN, SANDY
Middle Ages
Place To Be Loved, A

SOBEL, MARK
Bermuda Grace
Ordeal In The Arctic
Trial And Error

SOLMS, KENNY
Plaza Suite

SPENCE, RICHARD
Blind Justice

SPICER, BRYAN
Adventures Of Brisco County Jr., The

SPOTTISWOODE, ROGER
And The Band Played On
Last Innocent Man, The
Third Degree Burn

STAFFORD, STEPHEN
Double Edge
Posing: Inspired By Three Real Stories

STEIN, JEFF
Mother Goose Rock 'n' Rhyme

STERN, SANDOR
Amityville: The Evil Escapes
Assassin
Dangerous Pursuit
Deception: A Mother's Secret
Duplicates
Easy Prey
Glitz
Jericho Fever

John And Yoko: A Love Story
Passions
Probe
Shattered Innocence
Web Of Deceit
Without Her Consent
Woman On The Run: The Lawrencia
....Bembenek Story

STERN, STEVEN H.
Crossing The Mob
Final Notice
Heart Of A Child
Hostage Flight
Man Against The Mob
Many Happy Returns
Obsessive Love
Personals
This Park Is Mine
To Save The Children
Weekend War

STEVENS, JR., GEORGE
Separate But Equal

STONE, NORMAN
Crossing To Freedom

SULLIVAN, KEVIN
Lantern Hill

SUTHERLAND, KIEFER
Last Light

SWACKHAMER, E.W.
Are You Lonesome Tonight?
Bridge Across Time
Columbo Goes To College
Desperado: Badlands Justice
Jake And The Fatman
Macshayne: The Final Roll Of The Dice
Macshayne: Winner Take All
Return Of Desperado, The
Secret Passion Of Robert Clayton, The

SWAIM, BOB
Target Of Suspicion

SWEENEY, BOB
If It's Tuesday, It Still Must Be Belgium
Return To Mayberry

SWITZER, MICHAEL
Children Of The Dark
Fergie And Andrew: Behind The Palace
....Doors
Frank Nitti: The Enforcer
I Can Make You Love Me: The Stalking Of
....Laura Black
Jonathan Stone: Threat Of Innocence
Lightning Incident, The
Matter Of Justice, A
Revealing Evidence
Summer Dreams: The Story Of The Beach
....Boys
With A Vengeance
Woman Who Sinned, The

SZWARC, JEANNOT
Murders In The Rue Morgue, The

TANASESCU, GINO
Thanksgiving Day

TAPLITZ, DANIEL
Black Magic
Nightlife

TAYLOR, DON
Classified Love
Diamond Trap, The
Ghost Of A Chance
Going For The Gold: The Bill Johnson Story
He's Not Your Son
Secret Weapons

TAYLOR, JUD
Broken Vows
Danielle Steel's Kaleidoscope
Doubletake
Foxfire
Great Escape I I: The Untold Story, The
In My Daughter's Name
Murder Times Seven
Old Man & The Sea, The
Out Of The Darkness
Prophet Of Evil: The Ervil Lebaron Story

TEAGUE, LEWIS
Deadlock
Shannon's Deal
T Bone N Wessel

TENNANT, ANDY
Beyond Control: The Amy Fisher Story
Desperate Choices: To Save My Child
Keep The Change

TEWKESBURY, JOAN
Cold Sassy Tree
On Promised Land
Sudie And Simpson
Wild Texas Wind

THOMAS, BETTY
My Breast

THOMAS, DAVE
Ghost Mom

THOMSON, CHRIS
Flood: Who Will Save Our Children?
Moving Target
She Was Marked For Murder
Stop At Nothing
Swimsuit
Woman On The Ledge

THORPE, JERRY
Blood And Orchids

TILL, ERIC
Clarence
Final Appeal

TINKER, MARK
Babe Ruth
N. Y. P. D. Mounted

TOLKIN, STEVEN
Daybreak

TOPOR, TOM
Judgment

TRAMONT, JEAN-CLUADE
As Summers Die

TRIKONIS, GUS
Great Pretender, The
Love On The Run
Malice In Wonderland
Open Admissions

TUCHNER, MICHAEL
Amos
At Mother's Request
Captive
Conviction Of Kitty Dodds, The
Desperate For Love
Firestorm: 72 Hours In Oakland
Generation
Internal Affairs
Mistress
Not My Kid
Summer My Father Grew Up, The
Trapped In Silence
When Will I Be Loved?
With Murder In Mind

TWOHY, DAVID N.
Disaster In Time

UNO, MICHAEL TOSHIYUKI
Blind Spot
Fugitive Among Us
In The Eyes Of A Stranger
Lies Of The Heart: The Story Of Laurie
....Kellogg
Time To Heal, A
Without Warning: The James Brady Story

VALDEZ, LUIS
Cisco Kid, The

VEJAR, MICHAEL
Hawaiian Heat
Macgyver : Lost Treasure Of Atlantis

VILLALOBOS, RAYNOLD
Conagher

VOGEL, VIRGIL W.
Desperado
Longarm
Mario And The Mob
Street Hawk
Walker, Texas Ranger

WAINWRIGHT, RUPERT
Dillinger

WALLACE, RICK
Acceptable Risks
California Girls
Father's Homecoming, A
Lily
Time To Live, A

WALLACE, TOMMY LEE
And The Sea Will Tell
Comrades Of Summer
Danger Island

Green Dolphin Beat
Stephen King's It
Witness To The Execution

WALTON, FRED
Alfred Hitchcock Presents
I Saw What You Did
Murder In Paradise
Price She Paid, The
Trapped
When A Stranger Calls Back

WAXMAN, AL
Diamond Fleece

WEBB, WILLIAM
Hit List, The

WEILL, CLAUDIA
Child Lost Forever, A
Face Of A Stranger
Johnny Bull

WEISMAN, SAM
Sunset Beat

WENDKOS, PAUL
Bad Seed, The
Blind Faith
Blood Vows: The Story Of A Mafia Wife
Bloodlines: Murder In The Family
Chase, The
Cross Of Fire
Danielle Steel's Message From Nam
Execution, The
From The Dead Of Night
Good Cops, Bad Cops
Great Escape I I: The Untold Story, The
Guilty Until Proven Innocent
Picking Up The Pieces
Rage Of Angels: The Story Continues
Right To Die
Scorned And Swindled
Sister Margaret And The Saturday Night
....Ladies
Six Against The Rock
Taking Of Flight 847: The Uli Derickson
....Story
Trial: The Price Of Passion
White Hot: The Mysterious Murder Of
....Thelma Todd

WERNER, PETER
Hiroshima: Out Of The Ashes
I Married A Centerfold
Image, The
L B J: The Early Years
Ned Blessing: The True Story Of My Life
Sins Of The Father
Substitute Wife, The

WHARMBY, TONY
Coins In The Fountain
Kissing Place, The
Seduced By Evil
Sorry, Wrong Number
To Be The Best
Treacherous Crossing

WHEAT, JIM
Ewoks: The Battle For Endor

WHEAT, KEN
Ewoks: The Battle For Endor

WHEATLEY, DAVID
Hostages
Nobody's Children

WHEELER, ANNE
Other Women's Children

WHITAKER, FOREST
Strapped

WHYTE, MICHAEL
Railway Station Man, The

WIARD, WILLIAM
Kicks

WICKES, DAVID
Frankenstein
Jack The Ripper
Jekyll & Hyde

WILD, ANDREW
Spenser: Ceremony

WILDER, JOHN
Norman Rockwell's Breaking Home Ties

WILKINSON, ANTHONY
King Of Love, The

WILLIAMS, ANSON
Dream Date
Little White Lies
Quiet Little Neighborhood, A Perfect Little
....Murder, A
White Lie
Your Mother Wears Combat Boots

WINCER, SIMON
Bluegrass
Last Frontier, The
Lonesome Dove

WINER, HARRY
I Love You Perfect
J F K: Reckless Youth
Men Don't Tell
Mirrors
Paper Dolls
Single Bars, Single Women
Stay The Night
Taking Back My Life: The Nancy
....Ziegenmeyer Story
Under Cover
When You Remember Me

WINKLER, HENRY
Smokey Mountain Christmas, A

WISE, HERBERT
Reunion At Fairborough
Welcome Home, Bobby

WOLFF, ART
Battling For Baby

WOLK, ANDY
Criminal Justice

WOODHEAD, LESLIE
Tragedy Of Flight 103: The Inside Story, The

WRIGHT, THOMAS J.
Chrome Soldiers
Deadly Game
Fatal Image, The
Hell Hath No Fury
Operation, The
Snow Kill
Thunderboat Row

WRYE, DONALD
Amerika
Broken Promises: Taking Emily Back
Eighty-Three Hours 'til Dawn
Lucky Day
Separated By Murder
Stranger In The Family, A
Ultimate Betrayal

YELLEN, LINDA
Chantilly Lace
Parallel Lives

YOUNG, ROBERT
Doomsday Gun
We Are The Children

YOUNG, ROGER
Bourne Identity, The
Danielle Steel's Jewels
Doublecrossed
For Love And Glory
Geronimo
Getting Gotti
Gulag
Held Hostage: The Sis And Jerry Levin Story
Into Thin Air
Love Among Thieves
Love & Lies
Mercy Mission: The Rescue Of Flight 771
Murder In Mississippi
Nightmare In Columbia County
Under Siege

ZACHARIAS, STEVE
Revenge Of The Nerds I V: Nerds In Love

ZILLER, PAUL
Deadly Surveillance

ZINBERG, MICHAEL
Accidental Meeting
For The Very First Time

ZISK, RANDALL
Moment Of Truth: To Walk Again

ZLOTOFF, LEE DAVID
Plymouth

Section H

PRODUCERS

Cross-referenced by
Produced Credits

AAL, DEBORAH
Poison Ivy

AARON, PAUL
Laurel Avenue

ABATEMARCO, FRANK
I Can Make You Love Me: The Stalking Of ....Laura Black

ABBOTT, CHRIS
Revealing Evidence

ABEL, LEWIS
Time To Heal, A
We Are The Children

ABRAHAM, MARC
Life In The Theater, A

ABRAHAMSON, MORT
Arch Of Triumph

ABRAMS, CAROL
Ernest Green Story, The

ABRAMS, GERALD W.
Daughter Of Darkness
Drop Dead Gorgeous
Family Of Spies
Fatal Image, The
Father's Revenge, A
Florence Nightingale
Jekyll & Hyde
Monte Carlo
Scorned And Swindled
Silent Witness: What A Child Saw
Street Of Dreams
Thompson's Last Run

ACKERMAN, TOM
Casey's Gift: For Love Of A Child

ADAMS, TONY
Peter Gunn

ADDIS, KEITH
Gotham

ADELSON, ANDREW
Beyond Control: The Amy Fisher Story
Blood And Orchids
Desperate Choices: To Save My Child
Desperate For Love
Fugitive Among Us
Gulag
I Know My First Name Is Steven
Inconvenient Woman, An
Kiss Of A Killer
Out Of The Darkness
Warm Hearts, Cold Feet

ADELSON, GARY
Detective In The House
Glitz
Lace I I
Lies Of The Twins

ADELSON, ORLY
Desperate Rescue: The Cathy Mahone Story
Murder Between Friends
Shoot First: A Cop's Vengeance

AGHAYAN, RAY
Consenting Adult

AGRAMA, FRANK
Around The World In 80 Days
Heidi

AHLBERG, JULIE
Live: From Death Row

AKERMAN, JOSEPH
Prince Of Bel Air

ALBERT, ROSS
After The Shock
Murderous Vision

ALBERT, SYDELL
One Of Her Own
Preppie Murder, The

ALBREY, CHRISTABEL
Danielle Steel's Jewels

ALDRICH, RICHARD
As Summers Die

ALDRICH, WILLIAM
What Ever Happened To Baby Jane?

ALEXANDER, LES
Apology
Blackout
Caroline?
Cover Girl And The Cop, The
Family Pictures
I Know My Son Is Alive
Lies And Lullabies
Maid For Each Other
Maid For Each Other
Necessity
Not Of This World
Thicker Than Blood: The Larry Mclinden ....Story
When Love Kills: The Seduction Of John ....Hearn

ALEXANDRA, DANIELLE
Addicted To His Love

ALFIERI, RICHARD
False Witness

ALLARD, JAMES ANTHONY
Stone Fox

ALLARD, TONY
Christmas On Division Street

ALLEN, BYRON
Case Closed

ALLEN, IRWIN
Alice In Wonderland
Outrage

ALSOP, C. SCOTT
Little Girl Lost

ALSTON, HOWARD
Escape From Sobibor
Marcus Welby, M. D.: A Holiday Affair

ALTMAN, ROBERT
Caine Mutiny Court - Martial, The
Room, The

ALWARD, JENNIFER
Baby Snatcher
David's Mother
Family Of Spies
Night Owl
Poisoned By Love: The Kern County Murders
Thompson's Last Run
Through The Eyes Of A Killer
Web Of Deception

AMATULLO, TONY
Dead Silence

AMES, DAVID R.
Yearling, The

AMMAR, TARAK BEN
Nobody's Children
Voyage

AMRITRAJ, ASHOK
Illicit Behavior
Invasion Of Privacy

ANDERSEN, JON
Intimate Encounters
Pleasures

ANDERSON, CRAIG
Baby Brokers
Bump In The Night
O Pioneers
Secret, The
There Was A Little Boy

ANDERSON, NICK
Scorned And Swindled
Yes, Virginia, There Is A Santa Claus

ANDERSON, RICHARD DEAN
Macgyver : Lost Treasure Of Atlantis

ANDERSON, ROBERT
Omen I V: The Awakening

ANDRE, BLUE
Adrift
Christmas Comes To Willow Creek
Fugitive Among Us
Pancho Barnes
Time To Live, A
Unnatural Causes

ANDREWS, DALE
Other Women's Children
To Save The Children
Whose Child Is This? The War For Baby ....Jessica

ANNAUD, MONIQUE
Sweet Revenge

ANTONIO, LOU
Dark Holiday
Outside Woman, The

APTED, MICHAEL
Criminal Justice
Intruders

Murder Without Motive: The Edmund Perry
....Story
Strapped

ARATOW, PAUL
Spirit, The

ARDOLINO, EMILE
Gypsy

ARKOFF, LOU
Roadracers

ARKUSH, ALLAN
Capital News

ARMUS, BURTON
Street Hawk

ARNESS, JAMES
Gunsmoke: One Man's Justice
Gunsmoke: The Long Ride Home

ARNOLD, ROSEANNE
Woman Who Loved Elvis, The

ARNOLD, TOM
Woman Who Loved Elvis, The

ASHBURN, ELLIE
Sin And Redemption

ASHLEY, JOHN
Journey To The Center Of The Earth
Something Is Out There

ASSEYEV, TAMARA
After The Promise
Beryl Markham: A Shadow On The Sun
Hijacking Of The Achille Lauro, The
Murder By Moonlight
Penalty Phase
Secret Life Of Kathy Mccormick, The

ATAMIAN, GIL
Weekend War

ATKINS, DICK
Trapped In Silence

AUERBACH, JEFFREY
Marilyn & Bobby: Her Final Affair
Mortal Sins

AUSTIN, STEPHANIE
Deadly Matrimony
Kate's Secret
Mistress
Naked Lie
Out On The Edge
Shattered Dreams
Torch Song

AVNET, JON
Backfield In Motion
Between Two Women
Breaking Point
Burning Bed, The
Do You Know The Muffin Man?
For Their Own Good
Heat Wave
In Love And War
My First Love
Nightman, The

Side By Side
Silence Of The Heart
Switch, The
Triplecross

AXELROD, JONATHAN
Against The Wall
Price She Paid, The
Secret Passion Of Robert Clayton, The

AZENBERG, EMANUEL
Broadway Bound

BACHRACH, DORA
Citizen Cohn

BACINO, MARK
Double, Double, Toil And Trouble
Killer Among Friends, A
Mother's Justice, A
No Child Of Mine
To Grandmother's House We Go
Without A Kiss Goodbye

BACKE, JOHN D.
Attack On Fear

BACON, DORIS
Miracle On I-880

BACON, ROGER
Charley Hannah
Glory Days
High Mountain Rangers
Jesse Hawkes
Mario And The Mob

BADALATO, BILL
Dead Solid Perfect
Laguna Heat

BADHAM, JOHN
Relentless: Mind Of A Killer

BAER, RANDY
Better Off Dead

BAERWALD, PAUL
Around The World In 80 Days

BAERWALD, SUSAN
Blind Faith
Cruel Doubt
Jackie Collins' Lucky Chances
One Special Victory
Time To Heal, A

BAKER, BART
Baby Of The Bride
Children Of The Bride
Mother Of The Bride

BAKER, RICK
Betrayed By Love

BALDWIN, HOWARD
Fulfillment Of Mary Gray, The

BALDWIN, PETER
As Summers Die

BALIAN, CHARMAINE
Deadman's Revenge

BALKAN, DAVID H.
Stark

BALLON, DAPHNE
The Race To Freedom: The Underground
....Railroad

BALOFF, PETER
Quicksand: No Escape
Spooner

BAMBER, DICKIE
Back Home
Mandela
Murrow

BANNER, BOB
Sea Wolf, The
Yes, Virginia, There Is A Santa Claus

BANNER, GLENN D.
Glory Days

BARBERA, JOSEPH
Stone Fox

BARIO, FRANCO
Saved By The Bell-Hawaiian Style

BARKLEY, DEANNE
Island Sons
Private Sessions

BARNATHAN, MICHAEL
Stranger On My Land
Uncle Tom's Cabin
Unholy Matrimony

BARNETT, JOAN
Adam: His Song Continues
Bluegrass
Comrades Of Summer
From The Files Of Joseph Wambaugh: A Jury
Of One
Joshua's Heart
Last Wish
Leave Of Absence
Lies Before Kisses
Little Piece Of Heaven, A
Long Gone
Long Gone
One Of Her Own
Quiet Victory: The Charlie Wedemeyer Story
Ryan White Story, The
Something To Live For: The Alison Gertz
....Story
Stoning In Fulham County, A
Strange Voices
Too Young The Hero
Unspeakable Acts
Woman Who Loved Elvis, The

BARNETTE, ALAN
Alfred Hitchcock Presents
Blindsided
Broken Cord, The
Curiosity Kills
Murder 101
Red Wind
Somebody Has To Shoot The Picture
Streets Of Justice

White Lie

BARON, ALLEN
Seduction In Travis County

BARON, PAUL
Shame

BARRETT, JAMES LEE
In The Heat Of The Night

BARRY, PHILLIP
Chernobyl: The Final Warning
Evergreen
Who Is Julia?

BARTLETT, JUANITA
In The Heat Of The Night

BATEMAN, KENT
Crossing The Mob
Moving Target

BATISTA, FRANCO
Deadbolt
Psychic

BAUM, THOMAS
Night Visions

BAUMGARTEN, CRAIG
Lies Of The Twins

BAXTER, MEREDITH
Long Journey Home, The
My Breast

BAYLIS, ROBERT
Miles To Go . . .

BAYNES, ANDREA
Ann Jillian Story, The
Black Widow Murders: The Blanche Taylor
....Moore Story
Burning Bridges
Just My Imagination
Kate's Secret
Long Journey Home, The
Miss Rose White
Winnie

BEATON, ALEX
Palace Guard
Relentless: Mind Of A Killer

BEATON, JESSE
Laurel Avenue

BEATTIE, ALAN
Killer Among Us, A
Silhouette
Wrong Man, The

BEAUDINE JR., WILLIAM
Armed & Innocent
Face Of Fear, The
Nutcracker: Money, Madness And Murder
Overkill: The Aileen Wuornos Story
People Like Us
Spirit, The

BECKER, ROBERTA F.
Nick Knight
Vengeance: The Story Of Tony Cimo

BECKER, TERRY
Blade In Hong Kong

BECKHAM, MIKE
Investigation: Inside A Terrorist Bombing

BEERS, STEVE
Destination: America

BEGG, JIM
Johnnie Mae Gibson: F B I
Playing With Fire

BEIN, NANCY
Empty Cradle
Liberace: Behind The Music
Men Don't Tell

BELL, DAVE
Do You Remember Love?
Killer Among Us, A

BELL, FRAN
David's Mother
Night Owl
Web Of Deception

BELLISARIO, DONALD P.
Quantum Leap
Three On A Match

BELLO, STEPHEN
Fatal Deception: Mrs. Lee Harvey Oswald

BELLOTTI, JOSEPH
Trapped

BELOUS, PAUL W.
Street Hawk

BEN-AMI, YORAM
Lion Of Africa, The
Man Who Broke 1,000 Chains, The
Steal The Sky

BENEDETTI, ROBERT
Mercy Mission: The Rescue Of Flight 771
On Promised Land

BENJAMIN, MARY
Intruders

BENJAMIN, STUART
Betrayal Of Trust
Sodbusters

BENSON, GRAHAM
Back Home
Bejeweled
Endless Game, The
Murderers Among Us: The Simon Wiesenthal
....Story
Secret Weapon

BENSON, HUGH
Back To Hannibal: The Return Of Tom
Sawyer And Huck Finn
Danielle Steel's Changes
Danielle Steel's Fine Things
Danielle Steel's Message From Nam
Daughter Of The Streets
Diana: Her True Story
I Dream Of Jeannie: 15 Years Later

In The Heat Of The Night
Other Lover, The
Shadow Of A Stranger
Trade Winds

BENSON, JAY
Bare Essentials
Between Love And Hate
Bridesmaids
Final Appeal
Guilty Until Proven Innocent
Love, Lies And Murder
Love On The Run
Malice In Wonderland
Revenge On The Highway
So Proudly We Hail
Taking Of Flight 847: The Uli Derickson
....Story
Three Wishes Of Billy Grier, The
What She Doesn't Know

BENTON, DOUGLAS
Blacke's Magic
Codename: Foxfire - Slay It Again, Sam

BENTON, RUTHE
For Their Own Good
Switch, The

BERCOVICI, ERIC
Fifth Missile, The

BERG, BARRY
Bradys, The
Disappearance Of Christina, The
Legacy Of Lies
Shooter
Very Brady Christmas, A

BERG, DICK
American Geisha
Bloodlines: Murder In The Family
Everybody's Baby: The Rescue Of Jessica
....Mcclure
For The Love Of My Child: The Anissa
....Ayala Story
Sin And Redemption
Space
Wallenberg: A Hero's Story
White Mile

BERG, ILENE AMY
Baby M
Infidelity
My Name Is Kate
Notorious
Only Way Out, The
Other Women's Children
Stop At Nothing
Tonight's The Night

BERGEN, POLLY
Leave Of Absence

BERGER, ROBERT
Doubletake
Forget Me Not Murders, The
Internal Affairs
Mandela
Murder In Black And White

Murder Times Seven
Murrow
Night Of Courage
Sakharov
Stones Of Ibarra
Terror On Track 9
Welcome Home, Bobby

BERGESEN, DOREEN
Anna Karenina
Once Upon A Texas Train
Reason To Live, A

BERGMAN, LINDA
Matters Of The Heart
Rio Shanon

BERK, MICHAEL
Baywatch: Panic At Malibu Pier
Crime Of Innocence

BERLIN, KATHIE
Leap Of Faith
Taken Away

BERMAN, GAIL
Child Lost Forever, A

BERMAN, LINDA
Portrait, The

BERMAN, STEVEN
Rio Diablo

BERNARDI, BARRY
Amityville: The Evil Escapes
And Then She Was Gone
Chase, The
Day - O
Double Your Pleasure
Joshua's Heart
Jury Duty: The Comedy
Locked Up: A Mother's Rage
Miracle Child
Mom For Christmas, A
Murderous Affair, A: The Carolyn Warmus
....Story
Rose And The Jackal, The
Shameful Secrets
She Said No
She Stood Alone
To My Daughter With Love
What Ever Happened To Baby Jane?

BERNBAUM, PAUL
Royce

BERNER, FRED
Rising Son
Without Warning: The James Brady Story

BERNHARD, HARVEY
Omen IV: The Awakening

BERNHARDT, SHARON
Living A Lie

BERNSTEIN, JAY
Diamond Trap, The
Double Jeopardy
Final Notice

Mickey Spillane's Mike Hammer: Murder
....Takes All

BERNSTEIN, JONATHAN
Can You Feel Me Dancing?
Family Of Spies
Favorite Son
Fight For Jenny, A
On Fire
Roses Are For The Rich

BERRY, TOM
Deadbolt
Psychic

BERTHRONG, DEIRDRE
Born Too Soon

BEVAN, TIM
Borrowers, The
Robin Hood

BIBB, ROBERT
Dead Silence

BIBICOFF, HARVEY
Against The Wall
Secret Passion Of Robert Clayton, The

BIEBER, JAYNE
Double Edge
In Sickness And In Health
Love Can Be Murder
Tommyknockers, The

BIGGS, RICHARD
Poisoned By Love: The Kern County Murders

BILLER, GARY P.
Combat High

BILLOS, FRAN
Time To Triumph, A

BILSON, DANNY
Flash, The
Viper

BINDER, CHUCK
Attack Of The 50ft. Woman

BINKOW, BRUCE
Born To Run

BIRNBAUM, BOB
Dead On The Money

BIRNBAUM, ROGER
Bay Coven
Scandal Sheet

BIRNEY, DAVID
Long Journey Home, The

BIRNHAK, SANDRA J.
Yearling, The

BISHOP, MEL A.
Family Sins
Kiss Shot
Runaway Father

BIXBY, BILL
Death Of The Incredible Hulk, The
Incredible Hulk Returns, The

Trial Of The Incredible Hulk, The

BIXLER, DAVID
Perfect Bride, The

BLACK, BARBARA
Evil In Clear River

BLACK, DAVID
Cosby Mysteries, The
Legacy Of Lies

BLACK, TODD
El Diablo
Perfect Harmony

BLANKFEIN, FRED
Taking The Heat

BLATT, DANIEL H.
Badge Of The Assassin
Common Ground
Lies Of The Heart: The Story Of Laurie
....Kellogg
Men Don't Tell
Sworn To Silence
Winner Never Quits, A

BLECKNER, JEFF
In The Best Of Families: Marriage, Pride And
....Madness
Round Table, The

BLEICH, WILLIAM
Danger Island
Good Cops, Bad Cops

BLINN, WILLIAM
Aaron's Way
Appearances
Eight Is Enough: A Family Reunion
Polly--Comin' Home

BLISS, THOMAS
Mother Goose Rock 'n' Rhyme

BLISS, TOM
Life In The Theater, A

BLOCH, LISA
Fire: Trapped On The 37th Floor
Judgment Day: The John List Story

BLODGETT, MICHAEL
Revenge On The Highway

BLOMQUIST, TOM
Jesse Hawkes

BLOODWORTH, LINDA
London And Davis In New York

BLOOM, BARBARA
Last Of His Tribe, The

BLOOM, CAROLE
Double Edge
Downpayment On Murder
Fire: Trapped On The 37th Floor

BLUM, DEBBIE
Corpse Had A Familiar Face, The

BLUM, STAN
Keys, The

BOAM, JEFFREY
Adventures Of Brisco County Jr., The

BOCHCO, STEVEN
L. A. Law

BODOH, ALLAN
Easy Prey

BOGART, PETER
Last Prostitute, The

BOND, NANCY
Walker, Texas Ranger

BONNAN, GREGORY J.
Baywatch: Panic At Malibu Pier

BOORSTIN, JON
Dark Shadows

BOORSTIN, PAUL
Angel Of Death

BOORSTIN, SHARON
Angel Of Death

BORCHERS, DONALD
Habitation Of Dragons, The
Heart Of Justice, The

BORDEN, BILL
Backfield In Motion

BORGHI, DOUGLAS STEFAN
Operation, The

BORIS, ROBERT
Izzy And Moe
Marilyn & Me

BOROFSKY, MICKEY
El Diablo
Perfect Harmony

BOROWITZ, ANDY
Lily

BOTWICK, TERRY A.
Clarence

BOXLEITNER, BRUCE
Double Jeopardy

BOYLE, DONALD R.
Miracle At Beekman's Place

BRADEMAN, BILL
Alone In The Neon Jungle
Broken Vows
Incident, The
Spies, Lies And Naked Thighs

BRADFORD, ROBERT
Barbara Taylor Bradford's Remember
To Be The Best

BRAINE, TIM
Comrades Of Summer

BRAMS, RICHARD
Drug Wars: The Camarena Story
Drug Wars: The Cocaine Cartel
In The Company Of Darkness
Jonathan Stone: Threat Of Innocence
Return Of Ironside, The

BRAND, JOSHUA
I'll Fly Away

BRANDMAN, MICHAEL
American Clock, The
Broadway Bound
Cooperstown
Habitation Of Dragons, The
Heart Of Justice, The
Percy & Thunder
Water Engine, The

BRANDMAN, STEVEN
American Clock, The
Cooperstown
Percy & Thunder

BRAUER, JONATHAN
Not Of This World

BRAUN, DAVID
Seduction In Travis County

BRAUN, ZEV
Father Clements Story, The
Menendez: A Killing In Beverly Hills
Murder Ordained
Seduction In Travis County

BRAUNSTEIN, HOWARD
Amy Fisher: My Story
Babymaker: The Dr. Cecil Jacobson's Story
Gregory K
Snowbound: The Jim And Jennifer Stolpa
....Story

BRAVERMAN, MICHAEL
Condition: Critical

BRAYTON, MARIAN
Donato And Daughter
Littlest Victims

BREEN, PAULETTE
Eighty-Three Hours 'til Dawn
Separated By Murder
Stranger Within, The

BREUGNOT, PASCALE
Fall From Grace

BRICE, JOHN
L B J: The Early Years

BRICE, SANDRA SAXON
L B J: The Early Years

BRIGGLE, STOCKTON
Alamo: 13 Days To Glory, The
Bridge To Silence
Willing To Kill: The Texas Cheerleader Story

BRILL, FRANK
Without Her Consent

BRINSON, TOM
Bonanza: The Return

BROCKWAY, JODY
From The Dead Of Night
Whisper Kills, A

BRODERICK, JOHN
Fear Inside, The

BRODKIN, HERBERT
Doubletake
Internal Affairs
Johnny Bull
Mandela
Murder In Black And White
Murder Times Seven
Murrow
Night Of Courage
Sakharov
Stones Of Ibarra
Welcome Home, Bobby

BROIDO, JOE
Family Pictures
I Know My Son Is Alive

BROKAW, CARY
Amelia Earhart: The Final Flight
In The Eyes Of A Stranger

BROMBERG, CONRAD
Killer Instinct
Silent Witness

BROMSTAD, ANGELA
And Then There Was One
Eyes Of Terror
Visions Of Murder

BROOKS, DAVID
Dreamer Of Oz, The
Passion For Justice, A: Hazel Brannon Smith
....Story

BROOKS, NORMAN
Mario Puzo's The Fortunate Pilgrim

BROOKS, STANLEY
Angel Of Death
Another Pair Of Aces: Three Of A Kind
Christmas In Connecticut
Finish Line
Hostage For A Day
Nightmare At Bitter Creek
Pair Of Aces
Survive The Night
Wheels Of Terror

BROUGH, JOANNE
Killer Rules

BROWN, BARRY
Seduction: Three Tales From The Inner
Sanctum

BROWN, BLAIR
Moment Of Truth: To Walk Again

BROWN, GEORG STANFORD
Kids Like These
Last P. O. W? The Bobby Garwood Story
Stuck With Each Other

BROWN, STEPHEN
Past Tense

BROYLES, JR., WILLIAM
Under Cover

BRUBAKER, JAMES
Running Mates

BRUCKHEIMER, BONNIE
Gypsy

BRUMMEL, ROBERT
Battling For Baby

BRUSTIN, MICHELE
In The Company Of Darkness
Keys, The
Knight Rider 2000
Return Of Ironside, The

BRYANT, CHRIS
Young Catherine

BUCKNER, BRAD
Blue Deville

BUHAI, JEFF
Revenge Of The Nerds I V: Nerds In Love
Revenge Of The Nerds: The Next Generation
Thanksgiving Day

BURKE, DELTA
Love And Curses . . . And All That Jazz

BURKONS, HOWARD
Highway Heartbreaker

BURLEY, MARK A.
Cast The First Stone
Hiroshima: Out Of The Ashes

BURNETT, CAROL
Plaza Suite

BURROWS, JOHN
Till Death Us Do Part

BUSHNELL, SCOTT
Room, The

BUTLER, ROBERT
Out Of Time

BUTTENSTEDT, FRITZ
Forbidden

BYRNE, JOE
Hobo's Christmas, A

BYRUM, JOHN
Middle Ages
Murder In High Places

CAHN, DANIEL
Frank Nitti: The Enforcer
In Self Defense

CALDWELL, STEPHEN P.
J. O. E. And The Colonel

CALIO, JIM
Taking Of Flight 847: The Uli Derickson
....Story

CALLENDER, COLIN
Daybreak
Doomsday Gun
Hostages
Investigation: Inside A Terrorist Bombing
State Of Emergency
Strapped
Tragedy Of Flight 103: The Inside Story, The

CAMHE, BEVERLY J.
Obsessed With A Married Woman

CAMPANELLA II, ROY
Body Of Evidence

CAMPION, CLIFFORD
Celebration Family

CAMPUS, MICHAEL
Man Who Broke 1,000 Chains, The

CANAAN, CHRISTOPHER
Broken Promises: Taking Emily Back
Cries Unheard: The Donna Yaklich Story
In A Child's Name

CANDY, JOHN
Hostage For A Day

CANNELL, STEPHEN J.
Broken Badges
Destination: America
Great Pretender, The
Hunter
Missing Persons
Palace Guard
Thunderboat Row

CANNOLD, MITCHELL
Fear

CANNON, REUBEN
Women Of Brewster Place, The

CANTON, MAJ
Mothers Revenge, A
Wife, Mother, Murderer

CAPICE, PHIL
Private Sessions

CAPLAN, SARAH
Extreme Close-Up

CAPLIN, LEE
Fulfillment Of Mary Gray, The

CARDEA, FRANK
Dying To Remember
Still Crazy Like A Fox

CARLINER, MARK
Disaster At Silo 7
Scandal In A Small Town
Stalin

CARLUCCI, ANNIE
Donato And Daughter
Littlest Victims

CARNEY, R.B.
Ordeal In The Arctic

CAROSELLI, GRAZIA
Better Off Dead

CAROTHERS, RICHARD
Alamo: 13 Days To Glory, The
Bridge To Silence

CARPENTER, JOHN
El Diablo

CARPENTER, RICHARD
Karen Carpenter Story, The

CARR, CRISTEN M.
Flight Of Black Angel

CARR, GAIL
Conspiracy Of Silence

CARR, PATRICIA
Jekyll & Hyde

CARR, RON
Murder By Moonlight

CARR, TERRY
Six Against The Rock

CARRADINE, ROBERT
Revenge Of The Nerds I V: Nerds In Love

CARRARO, NICOLA
Endless Game, The

CARROLL, MATT
Blue Lightning, The
Dadah Is Death

CARSEY, MARCY
Single Bars, Single Women

CARTER, CHRIS
Brand New Life: The Honeymoon

CARTER, THOMAS
Equal Justice
Heat Wave

CARTER, VIRGINIA L.
Facts Of Life Down Under, The
Place To Call Home, A

CARTWRIGHT, GARY
Another Pair Of Aces: Three Of A Kind
Pair Of Aces

CARVEN, MICHAEL
Infidelity

CASSIDY, ALAN
Palace Guard

CASSIDY, SHAUN
Strays

CASTRONOVA, T.J.
Brass

CATES, GILBERT
Absolute Strangers
Burning Rage
Call Me Anna
Child's Cry
Confessions: Two Faces Of Evil
In My Daughter's Name

CATES, JOE
Last Days Of Frank And Jesse James, The
Quick And The Dead, The
Special People

CATES, PHILLIP
Last Days Of Frank And Jesse James, The
Quick And The Dead, The

CAULFIELD, BERNADETTE
Dead Before Dawn
I Can Make You Love Me: The Stalking Of
....Laura Black
Matter Of Justice, A
They've Taken Our Children: The Chowchilla
....Kidnapping

CAVAN, SUSAN
Mrs. 'Arris Goes To Paris

CHALOPIN, JEAN
Liberty

CHAMBERLIN, ROBIN
Middle Ages

CHANDLER, HARRY
Bonds Of Love
Daughter Of Darkness
Drop Dead Gorgeous
Fatal Image, The
Prophet Of Evil: The Ervil Lebaron Story
Stolen: One Husband

CHAPIN, DOUG
Corpse Had A Familiar Face, The
When A Stranger Calls Back

CHAPMAN, PENNY
Secret Weapon

CHAPMAN, RICHARD
Codename: Foxfire - Slay It Again, Sam
E. A. R. T. H. Force

CHASE, STANLEY
Guardian, The

CHEDA, MIKE
Wheels Of Terror

CHERBAK, CYNTHIA
Kissing Place, The

CHERRY, STANLEY Z.
Bring Me The Head Of Dobie Gillis

CHESLER, LEWIS B.
Double Deception
Moving Target

CHESSER, CHRIS
Silhouette
Wrong Man, The

CHETWYND, LIONEL
Evil In Clear River
So Proudly We Hail
To Heal A Nation

CHIESA, FABRIZIO
Lie Down With Lions

CHISHOLM, DAVID
Longarm
Over My Dead Body

CHOMSKY, MARVIN J.
Anastasia: The Mystery Of Anna
Brotherhood Of The Rose
Deliberate Stranger, The
I'll Be Home For Christmas
Peter The Great

Triumph Over Disaster: The Hurricane
....Andrew Story

CHORY, JIM
Face To Face
Last Elephant, The
Roxanne: The Prize Pulitzer

CHOTZEN, YVONNE
Matter Of Justice, A

CHRISTIANSEN, BOB
As Summers Die
Heart Of Darkness
Heist
House Of Secrets And Lies, A
Kids Don't Tell
Last Hit, The
Lincoln
Red Earth, White Earth
Robert Kennedy And His Times

CHULACK, CHRISTOPHER
Homefront
Johnny Ryan

CHVATAL, CINDY
Keep The Change

CLAPHAM, ADAM
Doomsday Gun

CLARK, DICK
Copacabana
Cry For Help: The Tracey Thurman Story, A
Death Dreams
Elvis And The Colonel: The Untold Story
Liberace
Promised A Miracle
Secret Sins Of The Father
Town Bully, The

CLARK, KAREN
Beyond Suspicion
For The Very First Time

CLARK, ROBIN S.
Broken Angel
Diary Of A Perfect Murder
Return To Mayberry

CLAVELL, JAMES
James Clavell's Noble House

CLEMENTS, JACK
Act Of Vengeance
Oldest Living Confederate Widow Tells All
Right To Kill?
To Save A Child
Tonight's The Night

CLEMENTS, STEVE
Bring Me The Head Of Dobie Gillis

CLEMMER, RONNIE
Dying To Love You
Mother's Justice, A
Private Matter, A
River Of Rage: The Taking Of Maggie
....Keene

CLERMONT, NICHOLAS
Sound And The Silence, The

CLIFFORD, PATRICIA
Crossing The Mob
Everybody's Baby: The Rescue Of Jessica
....Mcclure
Foreign Affairs
Murder Ordained
My Boyfriend's Back
To Dance With The White Dog
When Love Kills: The Seduction Of John
....Hearn

CLOSE, GLENN
Sarah, Plain And Tall
Skylark

COATES, CAROL
Case Of The Hillside Strangler, The

COBLENZ, WALTER
House Of Secrets

COHEN, BARNEY
Armed & Innocent

COHEN, ELLIS A.
First Steps
Love, Mary

COHEN, JOSEPH
Survive The Night

COHEN, JULIE
In The Best Of Families: Marriage, Pride And
....Madness

COHEN, NORMAN I.
Last Flight Out
Seduction In Travis County

COHEN, RICHARD M.
Fulfillment Of Mary Gray, The

COHEN, ROB
Relentless: Mind Of A Killer

COHEN, RONALD
Ordeal In The Arctic

COHEN, STUART
Single Bars, Single Women

COKER, BILL
Wet Gold

COLBY, ROB
Margaret Bourke - White

COLBY, RON
Lush Life

COLBY, RONALD B.
Extreme Close-Up

COLESBERRY, ROBERT F.
Death Of A Salesman

COLLA, RICHARD
Blind Witness
Sparks: The Price Of Passion
Storm And Sorrow

COLLETT, ELLEN
Other Women's Children

COLLIER, BARRY
Black Ice
Illicit Behavior
Invasion Of Privacy

COLLINS, JACKIE
Jackie Collins' Lady Boss
Jackie Collins' Lucky Chances

COLLINS, JOAN
Monte Carlo

COLLINS, RICHARD
Matlock: The Witness Killings

COLLINS, ROBERT
Hoover
In The Arms Of A Killer
Prime Target

COLLIS, ALAN
He's Not Your Son

COLMAN, HENRY
In The Shadows, Someone Is Watching
Nightmare In The Daylight
Quiet Little Neighborhood, A Perfect Little
....Murder, A
Rape Of Dr. Willis, The

COLWELL, THOM
Day My Parents Ran Away, The
Lush Life

CONBOY, JOHN
Kiss Of A Killer

CONRAD, JOAN
Charley Hannah
Glory Days
High Mountain Rangers
Jesse Hawkes
Mario And The Mob
Search And Rescue
Sworn To Vengeance
Two Fathers' Justice
Two Fathers: Justice For The Innocent

CONRAD, SHANE
Search And Rescue
Two Fathers: Justice For The Innocent

CONROY, T.R.
Hit List, The

CONSIDINE, DENNIS
Betrayed By Innocence
Ray Alexander: A Taste For Justice

CONVERSE, TONY
Aurora

CONWAY, JAMES L.
Harry's Hong Kong
Jailbirds

COOK, CHRISTOPHER
Geronimo

COOK, DOUGLAS S.
Payoff

COOK, T.S.
Switch, The

COOPER, ROBERT
Florida Straits
Glitz
Guardian, The
Murderers Among Us: The Simon Wiesenthal
....Story
Vanishing Act

COOPERMAN, ALVIN
My Two Loves

COOTE, GREGG
Blue Lightning, The

CORDAY, BARBARA
Heart Of Justice, The
I Dream Of Jeannie: 15 Years Later

COREA, NICHOLAS
Incredible Hulk Returns, The
J. O. E. And The Colonel

CORMAN, GENE
Blood Ties

CORMAN, JULIE
Drop-Out Mother

CORNFIELD, STUART
Hider In The House

COSBY, BILL
Cosby Mysteries, The
I Spy Returns

COSBY, GEORGE E.
Cosby Mysteries, The

COSGROVE, JOHN
Betrayal Of Trust
Between Love And Hate
Complex Of Fear
Guilty Until Proven Innocent
Nurses On The Line: The Crash Of Flight 7
Victim Of Love: The Shannon Mohr Story

COSSETTE, PIERRE
Too Young The Hero

COSTO, OSCAR L.
Broken Cord, The
Murder 101
Red Wind
Somebody Has To Shoot The Picture
White Lie

COTTLE, GRAHAM
Archie: To Riverdale And Back Again
Don't Touch My Daughter
Norman Rockwell's Breaking Home Ties

COUTURE, SUSAN
Child Of Rage

COWAN, GEOFFREY
Captive
Mark Twain And Me

COWEN, RON
Love She Sought, The

COWLING, BARRY
Deadly Betrayal: The Bruce Curtis Story

COX, MICHAEL
Crossing To Freedom

CRAGG, STEPHEN
Alfred Hitchcock Presents
Street Hawk

CRAMER, DOUGLAS S.
Cracked Up
Crossings
Danielle Steel's Changes
Danielle Steel's Daddy
Danielle Steel's Fine Things
Danielle Steel's Heartbeat
Danielle Steel's Kaleidoscope
Danielle Steel's Message From Nam
Danielle Steel's Once In A Lifetime
Danielle Steel's Palomino
Danielle Steel's Secrets
Danielle Steel's Star
Dynasty: The Reunion
Glitter
Harry's Hong Kong
Hollywood Wives
International Airport
Love Boat: A Valentine Voyage, The
Nightingales
Secrets Of Lake Success
Three Kings, The
Trade Winds

CRAVEN, WES
Night Visions

CRAWFORD, HECTOR
Fortress

CRAWFORD, IAN
Fortress

CRAWFORD, OLIVER
Execution, The

CREMIN, KEVIN
Stranger At My Door

CROCE, ANTHONY
Prophet Of Evil: The Ervil Lebaron Story
Return To Green Acres
Sex,Love, And Cold Hard Cash
White Mile

CROSBY, CATHY LEE
Untamed Love

CROSLAND, ALAN
Miracle Landing

CROWE, CHRISTOPHER
Alfred Hitchcock Presents
Steel Justice
Streets Of Justice

CRYSTAL, RICHARD
Ghost Mom

CULTER, ROGER
Railway Station Man, The

CULVER, CARMEN
Broken Cord, The
If Tomorrow Comes

Last Prostitute, The

CULVER, FELIX
Jessie

CUNLIFFE, DAVID
Attic: The Hiding Of Anne Frank, The

CURTIS, BRUCE COHN
Fatal Charm
Invasion Of Privacy
Shattered Image

CURTIS, DAN
Dark Shadows
Intruders
Johnny Ryan
War And Remembrance
War And Remembrance, Part I I

CURTIS-LARSON, JANET
Chameleons

CUSE, CARLTON
Adventures Of Brisco County Jr., The
Promise To Keep, A

CUSTANCE, MICHAEL
Passion And Paradise

CUTTS, JOHN
Queenie
Toughest Man In The World, The

D'ANGELO, BILL
Lost In London

D'ANTONI, CHRIS
Desperate Journey: The Allison Wilcox Story

D'ANTONI, JAMES
Desperate Journey: The Allison Wilcox Story

DACKS, ROBERTA
Strange Voices

DALEY, ELIZABETH
Right To Kill?
Vestige Of Honor

DALRYMPLE, ROBERT
Baby Brokers
Shame

DAMON, MARK
Red Shoes Diaries

DAMSKI, MEL
Blood River
Three Kings, The

DANAHER-DORR, KAREN
Bluffing It
Cold Sassy Tree
Crazy In Love
Crime Of Innocence
Right To Die
Somebody's Daughter
Under Siege
When He's Not A Stranger

DANIEL, ANN
Nobody's Children

DANIEL, JAY
Long Time Gone
Moonlighting

DANIELS, GEOFFREY
Captain Cook

DANIELS, STAN
Substitute Wife, The

DANSON, TED
We Are The Children
When The Bough Breaks

DANTON, CHRIS
To Save The Children

DANYLKIW, JOHN
Amy Fisher: My Story
Babymaker: The Dr. Cecil Jacobson's Story
In The Nick Of Time
Return Of Eliot Ness, The
Shattered Trust: The Shari Karney Story
Spider And The Fly, The
Survive The Night
Women Of Windsor

DANZA, TONY
Doing Life
Freedom Fighter
Whereabouts Of Jenny, The

DAVID, PIERRE
Deadbolt
Perfect Bride, The

DAVIDS, PAUL
Roswell

DAVIDSON, GORDON
Right To Kill?

DAVIES, GARETH
Behind Enemy Lines
Carly's Web
Remington Steele: The Steele That Wouldn't
....Die

DAVIES, WILLIAM
Bermuda Grace

DAVIS, JACQUELINE
Not A Penny More, Not A Penny Less

DAVIS, JOHN
Caught In The Act
Curiosity Kills
Dangerous Passion
Indiscreet
Last Outlaw, The
Silhouette
Tears And Laughter: The Joan And Mielissa
....Rivers Story
This Can't Be Love
Voyage
Wild Card

DAVIS, WALTER HALSEY
Do You Remember Love?

DAWSON, GORDON
Independence

DAYTON, JOHN
Man Upstairs, The
This Can't Be Love

DE GARMO, DENISE
Terror In The Night

DE LA TORRE, DALE
Journey To The Center Of The Earth

DE LAURENTIIS, DINO
Stephen King's Sometimes They Come Back

DE LAURENTIS, ROBERT
South Beach

DE OLIVERIA, PAULO
Devlin

DE PASSE, SUZANNE
Bridesmaids
Jacksons: An American Dream , The
Lonesome Dove
Return To Lonesome Dove
Small Sacrifices

DE PAUL, JUDITH
Nazi Hunter: The Beate Klarsfeld Story

DE SOUZA, STEVEN E.
Supercarrier

DE WOLFE, THOMAS
Doubletake
Johnny Bull
Murder In Black And White
Murder Times Seven
Night Of Courage
Welcome Home, Bobby

DEAKIN, MICHAEL
Doomsday Gun
Secret Weapon

DEAN, JOEL
Cartier Affair, The

DEAN, TOMLINSON
Woman Named Jackie, A

DEANES, DAVID L.
Viper

DEAR, WILLIAM
Journey To The Center Of The Earth

DEELEY, MICHAEL
Finnegan Begin Again
Gathering Of Old Men, A
Secret Life Of Archie's Wife, The
Young Catherine

DeFARIA, CHRIS
And Then She Was Gone

DeFARIA, WALT
Borrowers, The

DEGELIA, JACK H.
Roommates

DELLINGER, ROBERT
Love, Honor & Obey: The Last Mafia
....Marriage

DEMANN, FREDDY
Crazy From The Heart

DEMBERG, LISA
Town Bully, The

DEMEO, PAUL
Flash, The
Viper

DENNETT, JAMES A.
Bad Attitudes

DENSHAM, PEN
Lifepod

DENVER, JOHN
Higher Ground

DESCHAMPS, MYCHELLE
Blindsided

DEVLIN, TAD
For Their Own Good
Switch, The

DEWITT, JAN
Staying Afloat

DEY, SUSAN
I Love You Perfect
Lies And Lullabies

DI LELLO, RICHARD
Popeye Doyle

DIAL, BILL
Codename: Foxfire - Slay It Again, Sam

DIAZ, BILL
E. A. R. T. H. Force

DICKOFF, MICKI
Our Sons

DIETZ, JOE
Rise & Walk: The Dennis Byrd Story

DIMAIO, DEBRA
Overexposed
There Are No Children Here

DINNER, MICHAEL
Rise & Walk: The Dennis Byrd Story

DIPEGO, GERALD
Generation
Trial Of The Incredible Hulk, The

DOBBS, FRANK Q.
Houston: The Legend Of Texas
Rio Diablo

DOBBS, LEM
Hider In The House

DOBSON, SUSAN
Money, Power, Murder

DOCKER, LYMAN P.
Father Of Hell Town

DOLF, JOHN
Dead On The Money

DONAHUE, ANN
Round Table, The

DONNELLY, TERENCE
Jericho Fever
Stone Pillow
Sunstroke
To My Daughter With Love

DORAN, LINDSAY
Private Matter, A

DORAN, STEVE
Unnatural Causes

DORE, BONNY
Captive
Reason For Living: The Jill Ireland Story
Sins

DOTY, DANIELLE
Flight Of Black Angel

DOTY, DENNIS
Absolute Strangers
Confessions: Two Faces Of Evil
Escape From Sobibor
In My Daughter's Name

DOUGHERTY, JOSEPH
Attack Of The 50ft. Woman

DOUGLAS, PETER
Amos
Enemy Within, The
Inherit The Wind

DOWALIBY, JAMES M
Candles In The Dark

DOWNEY, CHERY
It's Nothing Personal

DOWNING, STEPHEN
Without Warning: Terror In The Towers

DOZORETZ, WENDY
Other Women's Children

DREYFUSS, RICHARD
Prisoner Of Honor

DROMGOOLE, PATRICK
Arch Of Triumph
Diamond Trap, The

DRYER, FRED
Day Of Reckoning

DRYHURST, MICHAEL
Harem

DUCHOW, PETER K.
Finding The Way Home
Finding The Way Home
My Name Is Bill W.
Obsessed
Promise

DUGAN, DANIEL
Danielle Steel's Heartbeat
Danielle Steel's Once In A Lifetime
Danielle Steel's Star

DUKE, DARYL
Fatal Memories

DUKE-PEARCE, ANNA
Call Me Anna

DUNAWAY, FAYE
Cold Sassy Tree
Silhouette

DUNNE, WILLIAM
Family Of Spies

DUTTON, CHARLES
Laurel Avenue

DUVALL, SHELLEY
Backfield In Motion
Dinner At Eight
Lily
Mother Goose Rock 'n' Rhyme

DWEK, ROBERT
Getting Gotti

DYBMAN, GEORGE
Nobody's Children

DYTMAN, WENDY
Bejeweled
Rose And The Jackal, The

EAGLE, DAVID
Willing To Kill: The Texas Cheerleader Story

ECCLESINE, STEVE
Mantis

ECKERT, JOHN M.
Getting Gotti
Special People

ECKSTEIN, GEORGE
Bad Seed, The
Murder With Mirrors
Six Against The Rock
When We Were Young

EDELL, DEBORAH
Jackie Collins' Lady Boss

EDELMAN, ROSEMARY
Side By Side

EDEN, BARBARA
Secret Life Of Kathy Mccormick, The

EDRICK, BOBBIE
Confessions: Two Faces Of Evil

EDWARDS, BLAKE
Peter Gunn

EDWARDS, RONA
One Special Victory

EFROS, MEL
Lois & Clark: The New Adventures Of
....Superman
Roman Holiday

EHLICH, ROSANNE
Chantilly Lace

EICK, DAVID
Mantis

EILTS, MARY `
Miracle On I-880

EINBINDER, SCOTT
Shadowhunter

EISELE, ROBERT
Last Light

EISENMAN, RAFEAL
Red Shoes Diaries

EISENSTOCK, ALAN
If It's Tuesday, It Still Must Be Belgium

ELIASON, JOYCE
Babycakes

ELKINS, HILLARD
Ray Alexander: A Taste For Justice

ELLIOT, NICK
Casualty Of War, A
Jekyll & Hyde
Pride And Extreme Prejudice

ELLIOTT, SAM
Conagher

ELLIS, JOSEPH M.
One Special Victory

EMERSON, SASHA
Day My Parents Ran Away, The
Twelve O' One (12: 01)

EMR, JOHN
Last P. O. W? The Bobby Garwood Story

EMR, RENEE
Last P. O. W? The Bobby Garwood Story

ENGEL, CHARLES F.
Road Raiders, The

ENGEL, MITCH
Betrayed By Love
Passion For Justice, A: Hazel Brannon Smith
....Story

ENGEL, PETER
Harvest For The Heart
Saved By The Bell-Hawaiian Style

ENGELMAN, ROBERT
Calendar Girl, Cop Killer? The Bambi
....Bembenek Story
Frankenstein: The College Years
Revenge Of The Nerds: The Next Generation
Seeds Of Tragedy

ENGLUND, GEORGE
Challenger
Las Vegas Strip Wars, The
Terrorist On Trial: The United States Vs.
Salim

ENGLUND, JR., GEORGE
Challenger

ENRIGHT, DAN
Caroline?
Cover Girl And The Cop, The
Necessity

ENRIGHT, DON
Caroline?
Cover Girl And The Cop, The

Family Pictures
I Know My Son Is Alive
Lies And Lullabies
Maid For Each Other
Maid For Each Other
Not Of This World
Thicker Than Blood: The Larry Mclinden
....Story
When Love Kills: The Seduction Of John
....Hearn

EPSTEIN, ALLEN
Addicted To His Love
And The Sea Will Tell
Deadly Intentions
Deadly Intentions... Again?
Double, Double, Toil And Trouble
Doublecrossed
Higher Ground
Killer Among Friends, A
Mother's Justice, A
No Child Of Mine
Outside Woman, The
Shattered Innocence
Stephen King's It
To Grandmother's House We Go
Without A Kiss Goodbye

EPSTEIN, JACOB
Palace Guard
Relentless: Mind Of A Killer

EPSTEIN, JON
Columbo And The Murder Of A Rock Star
Columbo - Caution: Murder Can Be
....Hazardous To Your Health
Columbo Goes To College
Deadly Care
I Saw What You Did
Scene Of The Crime
This Gun For Hire
Trapped

ERMAN, JOHN
Breathing Lessons
Carolina Skeletons
Last To Go, The
Queen
Two Mrs. Grenvilles, The
When The Time Comes

ESPARZA, MOCTESUMA
Cisco Kid, The
Gettysburg

ESTRIN, JONATHAN
Barbara Taylor Bradford's Remember
Danielle Steel's Jewels

ESTRIN, MELVYN
Child Lost Forever, A

ETZ, TONY
Children Of The Dark
Deadly Matrimony
House Of Secrets
Torch Song

EUNSON, DALE
Black Widow Murders: The Blanche Taylor
....Moore Story

EVANS, DAVID J.
Lie Down With Lions

EVANS, DAVID MICKEY
Journey To The Center Of The Earth

EVANS, NICK
Secret Weapon

EWING, ROBERT
Death Of The Incredible Hulk, The
Trial Of The Incredible Hulk, The

FALK, PETER
Columbo: A Bird In The Hand
Columbo And The Murder Of A Rock Star
Columbo - Caution: Murder Can Be
....Hazardous To Your Health
Columbo: Death Hits The Jackpot
Columbo Goes To College
Columbo: It's All In The Game
Columbo: No Time To Die
Columbo: Undercover

FALSEY, JOHN
I'll Fly Away

FALZON, CHARLES
Bermuda Grace

FARRELL, MIKE
Incident At Dark River
Silent Movie

FARREN, JACK
Fatal Judgment
Mafia Princess

FAUCI, DAN
Follow Your Heart
We Are The Children
When The Bough Breaks

FAUST KRUSI, JANET
In The Nick Of Time
Murderous Affair, A: The Carolyn Warmus
....Story
Shattered Trust: The Shari Karney Story
To Save The Children

FAY, WILLIAM
Caught In The Act

FEE, TIMOTHY J.
Attic: The Hiding Of Anne Frank, The

FEHRLE, PHILLIP D.
Attack On Fear

FEIGELSON, J. D.
Houston: The Legend Of Texas

FELDMAN, EDWARD S.
Obsessed With A Married Woman

FELDMAN, JUDITH
American Story, An

FELLOWS, ARTHUR
Bluegrass

E. A. R. T. H. Force
Fifth Missile, The

FENADY, ANDREW J.
Jake Spanner, Private Eye
Love She Sought, The
Sea Wolf, The
Who Is Julia?
Yes, Virginia, There Is A Santa Claus

FENADY, DUKE
Love She Sought, The
Sea Wolf, The
Yes, Virginia, There Is A Santa Claus

FENNELL, ALBERT
Hazard Of Hearts, A
Lady And The Highwayman, The

FENTON, ROBERT
Double Standard
Woman On The Ledge

FERNS, W. PATTERSON
Love On The Run
Passion And Paradise
Sea Wolf, The
Young Catherine

FERRELL, CANDACE
Wild Texas Wind

FEURY, JOSEPH
No Place Like Home
No Place Like Home
Nobody's Child
Seasons Of The Heart

FIELD, FERN
Guilty Of Innocence: The Lenell Geter Story
Heartsounds
Kane And Abel
Littlest Victims
Mario Puzo's The Fortunate Pilgrim

FIELD, TED
Aftermath: A Test Of Love
American Geisha
Crossing The Mob
Everybody's Baby: The Rescue Of Jessica
....Mcclure
Father Clements Story, The
Foreign Affairs
Murder Ordained
My Boyfriend's Back
Secret Life Of Archie's Wife, The
Shoot First: A Cop's Vengeance

FIELDER, RICHARD
For Love And Glory
George Washington I I: The Forging Of A
....Nation

FIELDS, ED
Necessity

FIELDS, JOEL
Baby Of The Bride
Children Of The Bride
Cross Of Fire
Cry In The Wild: The Taking Of Peggy Ann
Dead Before Dawn

Earth Angel
False Arrest
Frank Nitti: The Enforcer
I Can Make You Love Me: The Stalking Of
....Laura Black
In The Deep Woods
Lady Forgets, The
Manhunt: Search For The Night Stalker
Matter Of Justice, A
Mother Of The Bride
Murder Without Motive: The Edmund Perry
....Story
Passion And Paradise
Shootdown
Summer Dreams: The Story Of The Beach
....Boys
They've Taken Our Children: The Chowchilla
....Kidnapping

FIENBERG, GREGG
Charles And Diana: Unhappily Ever After
Class Of '61
Seaquest Dsv

FILERMAN, MICHAEL
Assault And Matrimony
Child Saver, The
Coins In The Fountain
Letter To Three Wives, A
Peyton Place: The Next Generation
Return Of Eliot Ness, The
Roommates
Story Lady, The
Take My Daughters, Please
Turn Back The Clock

FIMM, JOSEPH
Fatal Memories

FINNEGAN, BILL
Alamo: 13 Days To Glory, The
Amos
Atlanta Child Murders, The
Babes In Toyland
Circle Of Violence: A Family Drama
Double Deception
Generation
Going To The Chapel
Hell Hath No Fury
Hoover
Laker Girls, The
Lincoln
Moving Target
News At Eleven
She Knows Too Much
Spooner

FINNEGAN, PAT
Alamo: 13 Days To Glory, The
Babes In Toyland
Black Widow Murders: The Blanche Taylor
....Moore Story
Breaking The Silence
Circle Of Violence: A Family Drama
Double Deception
Generation
Going To The Chapel
Hell Hath No Fury

Hoover
Keeping Secrets
Laker Girls, The
Lincoln
Marked For Murder
Murder By Night
Not My Kid
Quicksand: No Escape
Running Against Time
She Knows Too Much
This Child Is Mine

FINNERMAN, MICHAEL
Christmas Eve

FISCHER, FRANK
Appearances
Eight Is Enough: A Family Reunion
One Woman's Courage
Polly--Comin' Home

FISCHER, PETER S.
Blacke's Magic
Murder, She Wrote
Stranger At My Door

FISCHER, PRESTON
Criminal Behavior
Lace I I
Liberace
Promised A Miracle
Son Of The Morning Star
Two Mrs. Grenvilles, The

FISCHGRUND, JEFFREY
Christmas Comes To Willow Creek

FISCHOFF, RICHARD
Mistress

FISHER, MICHAEL
True Blue

FISHER, RICKA
Follow Your Heart
In Broad Daylight

FISHER, TERRY LOUISE
Blue Bayou
L. A. Law
Two Thousand Malibu Road

FITZGERALD, BENEDICT
Zelda

FITZSIMONS, CHARLES B.
Police Story: The Freeway Killings

FITZWALTER, RAY
Hostages
Investigation: Inside A Terrorist Bombing
Tailspin: Behind The Korean Airlines Tragedy
Tragedy Of Flight 103: The Inside Story, The

FJELD, JULIANNA
Love Is Never Silent

FLACK, TIM
Stranded

FLAXMAN, JOHN
Caine Mutiny Court - Martial, The

FLORIO, ROBERT
Daddy
Deadly Silence, A

FLYNN, JOHN
Burden Of Proof, The
Chase, The
Complex Of Fear
Criminal Behavior
Nurses On The Line: The Crash Of Flight 7

FORD, GRAHAM
Connecticut Yankee In King Arthur's Court, A
Nightmare Years, The

FORD, TONY
Babes In Toyland

FORMICA, S. MICHAEL
Nick Knight

FORSTATER, MARK
Forbidden

FORSYTH, FREDERICK
Casualty Of War, A
Just Another Secret
Pride And Extreme Prejudice

FORSYTHE, WILLIAM W.
Killing Mind, The

FORTE, KATE
There Are No Children Here

FOSTER, DAVID
Jesse
News At Eleven

FOSTER, NORMAN
Hands Of A Murderer
Old Man & The Sea, The

FOSTER, PENELOPE
Take My Daughters, Please

FOULKROD, PAT
Locked Up: A Mother's Rage

FOURNIER, RIFT
Revolver

FOWLES, JULIAN
Captive
Mark Twain And Me

FRAND, HARVEY
Black Magic
Dangerous Heart
Honor Thy Mother
Indecency
Into The Badlands
Trenchcoat In Paradise

FRANK, BOBBI
Passions

FRANK, ILANA
Liar's Edge

FRANKLIN, DANIEL
Cruel Doubt
Danielle Steel's Daddy
Danielle Steel's Palomino

Jackie Collins' Lucky Chances

FRANKLIN, JEFF
Fall From Grace
To Grandmother's House We Go
To Grandmother's House We Go

FRANKOVICH, PETER
Donor
Ride With The Wind

FRAZIER, RON
Day Of Reckoning
Our Family Honor

FREDERICK, ROBERT
Whose Child Is This? The War For Baby
....Jessica

FREDERICKSON, GRAY
Staying Afloat

FREED, RICHARD
Sudie And Simpson
Wildflower

FREEDMAN, GORDON L.
Baby M
To Heal A Nation

FREEDMAN, ROBERT L.
In The Best Of Families: Marriage, Pride And
....Madness

FREEMAN, PAUL
Final Notice
Hobo's Christmas, A
In The Best Interest Of The Children
Kissing Place, The
North And South
Sorry, Wrong Number

FREISER, ERIC
Case For Murder, A

FREISTAT, LANA
Living A Lie

FREMON, CELESTE
Baby Snatcher

FREUDENBERGER, DANIEL
Do You Know The Muffin Man?

FREY, HEIDI M.
Daddy
Perfect People

FRIEDKIN, WILLIAM
C. A. T. Squad
C. A. T. Squad: Python Wolf

FRIEDMAN, ARNOLD S.
In The Line Of Duty: The Price Of
....Vengeance

FRIEND, BRENDA
I Love You Perfect

FRIES, CHARLES
Bridge Across Time
Bridge To Silence
Case Of The Hillside Strangler, The
Chance Of A Lifetime
Crash Course

Drop-Out Mother
Fight For Life
Leona Helmsley: The Queen Of Mean
Mission Of The Shark
Neon Empire
Right Of The People, The
Samaritan: The Mitch Snyder Story
Sins Of The Father
Starcrossed
Supercarrier
Timestalkers
Toughlove

FRIES, CHARLES M.
Deep Dark Secrets

FRIES, THOMAS
Right Of The People, The

FRIESE, KIM C.
I Know My First Name Is Steven

FROST, GOWER
Finnegan Begin Again
Gathering Of Old Men, A

FROST, MARK
Twin Peaks

FUETER, PETER-CHRISTIAN
Marcus Welby, M. D.: A Holiday Affair

FUISZ, ROBERT E.
Christmas Carol, A
Hands Of A Murderer
Last Days Of Patton, The
Old Man & The Sea, The
Special Friendship, A
Ted Kennedy, Jr., Story, The

FURIA, JR., JOHN
Sun Also Rises, The

FURIE, JOHN
Tainted Blood

FURINO, FRANK V.
Nightingales

FYER, EVA
Lost Capone, The

GALAN, KATHRYN
Daybreak

GALE, BARBARA
Lies And Lullabies

GALIANO, VITTORIO
Only One Survived

GALIN, MITCHELL
Precious Victims
Stephen King's Golden Years
Stephen King's The Stand

GALLAGHER, SARAH
American Story, An

GALLANT, MICHAEL O.
Danger Of Love, The
I Spy Returns
Labor Of Love: The Arlette Schweitzer Story
My Son Johnny

Stompin' At The Savoy
Substitute Wife, The
With A Vengeance

GALLEGLY, DICK
Spenser: For Hire

GALLERY, MICHELE
Daughters Of Privilege

GALLI, HAL
Fatal Friendship
Karen Carpenter Story, The
North And South, Book 3: Heaven And Hell
Queen

GALLIN, SANDY
Smokey Mountain Christmas, A
Wild Texas Wind

GALLO, LEW
Mafia Princess

GALLO, LILLIAN
Lookalike, The

GALLO, MARIO
Mussolini: The Decline And Fall Of Il Duce

GANZ, TONY
Corpse Had A Familiar Face, The
Into Thin Air

GARNER, JAMES
My Name Is Bill W.
Promise

GARRETT, LILA
Who Gets The Friends?

GARTIN, SANDY RUSSELL
Bad Attitudes

GAST, HAROLD
Shakedown On The Sunset Strip

GAYLORD, E.K.
Bonanza: The Return

GEIOGAMAH, HANNAY
Broken Chain
Geronimo

GELLER, NANCY
Strange Voices

GEORGE, LOUCAS
Sin And Redemption

GERBER, DAVID
Dirty Dozen: The Deadly Mission
For Love And Glory
George Washington I I: The Forging Of A
....Nation
Lady Blue
Police Story: The Freeway Killings
Royce

GERNON, ED
Adrift

GHIA, FERNANDO
Endless Game, The

GILBERT, BRUCE
By Dawn's Early Light

GILBERT, RON
Baby Of The Bride
Children Of The Bride
Cross Of Fire
Cry In The Wild: The Taking Of Peggy Ann
Dead Before Dawn
Earth Angel
Earth Angel
False Arrest
I Can Make You Love Me: The Stalking Of
....Laura Black
In Self Defense
In The Deep Woods
Manhunt: Search For The Night Stalker
Matter Of Justice, A
Mother Of The Bride
Murder Without Motive: The Edmund Perry
....Story
Rags To Riches
Summer Dreams: The Story Of The Beach
....Boys
They've Taken Our Children: The Chowchilla
....Kidnapping
Tricks Of The Trade

GILER, DAVID
Roadracers

GILLOTT, NICK
Anything To Survive
Attic: The Hiding Of Anne Frank, The
Ellis Island
Fever
If Tomorrow Comes
Intrigue
Poor Little Rich Girl: The Barbara Hutton
....Story
Promise
Till Death Us Do Part

GILMER, ROB
Love Can Be Murder
Maid For Each Other

GILMORE, CINDY
Gypsy

GILROY, GRACE
Child Saver, The

GIMBEL, NORMAN
Private Sessions

GIMBEL, ROGER
Apology
Aurora
Blackout
Chernobyl: The Final Warning
Desperate Rescue: The Cathy Mahone Story
Montana
Murder Between Friends
Rockabye
Shattered Dreams

GINSBURG, DAVID R.
Back Home
Crash: The Mystery Of Flight 1501
Danger Of Love, The
Deliver Them From Evil: The Taking Of Alta
....View
Disappearance Of Nora
For Richer, For Poorer
Glitz
I Spy Returns
Image, The
Majority Rule
Marla Hanson Story, The
Max And Helen
My Son Johnny
Ordeal In The Arctic
Red King, White Knight
Roswell
Sex,Love, And Cold Hard Cash
Teamster Boss: The Jackie Presser Story
Trial And Error
With A Vengeance

GINTY, ROBERT
Day Of Reckoning

GITELSON, RICHARD
Case For Murder, A

GLEASON, MICHAEL
Carly's Web
Macshayne: The Final Roll Of The Dice
Macshayne: Winner Take All
Remington Steele: The Steele That Wouldn't
....Die

GLUECKMAN, ALAN JAY
Fear Inside, The

GLYNN, MICHAEL
Romance On The Orient Express

GODDARD, MELISSA
Final Appeal

GODFREY, ALAN
Father Of Hell Town

GOERGENS, ARDYTHE
Dead Before Dawn
False Arrest
I Can Make You Love Me: The Stalking Of
....Laura Black
Matter Of Justice, A
They've Taken Our Children: The Chowchilla
....Kidnapping

GOLCHAN, FREDERIC
Dream Date
Freedom Fighter
In The Deep Woods

GOLD, EDWARD
Kids Like These
Last P. O. W? The Bobby Garwood Story
Stuck With Each Other
Summer To Remember, A

GOLDBERG, GARY DAVID
Family Ties Vacation

GOLDBERG, LEONARD
Alex: The Life Of A Child
Beverly Hills Cowgirl Blues
Paper Dolls
She Woke Up

GOLDBERG, RICH
Hit List, The

GOLDEN, PETER
Operation, The

GOLDMAN, BERNIE
Victim Of Love

GOLDMAN, DON
Leave Of Absence
Lookalike, The
Miss America: Behind The Crown
Murder In New Hampshire: The Pamela
....Smart Story
Nightmare In Columbia County
One Of Her Own
She Says She's Innocent

GOLDMAN, GREG
Secret Life Of Ian Fleming, The

GOLDMAN, STUART
Leona Helmsley: The Queen Of Mean

GOLDSMITH, GLORIA
Secret Life Of Kathy Mccormick, The

GOLDSMITH, MELISSA
Back To The Streets Of San Francisco

GOLDSTEIN, GARY
Victim Of Love

GOLDSTEIN, LEWIS
Dead Silence

GOLDSTEIN, MARTY
Unnatural Causes

GOLDSTEIN, SCOTT D.
Frankenstein: The College Years

GOLDWYN, JR., SAMUEL
April Morning

GOLIN, STEVE
Heat Wave
Memphis

GOLOD, JERRY
Brass
Return To Green Acres

GOODELL, GREGORY
Ultimate Betrayal

GOODMAN, GARY
Cisco Kid, The
Easy Prey
Going For The Gold: The Bill Johnson Story
Secret Weapons
Stranger Within, The

GOODMAN, JOHNNY
Diamond Trap, The

GOODWILL, JONATHAN
Adrift
Heads

GOODWIN, R.W.
Acceptable Risks
Born Too Soon
California Girls

Condition: Critical
Copacabana
Father's Homecoming, A
Fresno
Living A Lie
Secrets Of A Married Man
Those She Left Behind

GORDON CARON, GLENN
Long Time Gone
Moonlighting

GORDON, CHARLES
Our Family Honor

GORDON, DAN
Gulag

GORDON, FELICE
Cries Unheard: The Donna Yaklich Story
Women Of Windsor

GORDON, LAWRENCE
Our Family Honor

GORDON, MARK
Lightning Incident, The
Love Kills

GORLIN, WINIFRED
When Will I Be Loved?

GOSSETT, JR., LOU
Ray Alexander: A Taste For Justice

GOTTLIEB, ANDREW
Bed Of Lies
Blind Justice
Blind Spot
Blood River
Breathing Lessons
Brotherly Love
Capital News
Case Closed
Deadly Deception
Eyes Of A Witness
Outback Bound
Stranded
Taking Back My Life: The Nancy
....Ziegenmeyer Story

GOTTLIEB, DAVID
Midnight's Child

GOTTLIEB, LINDA
Citizen Cohn
Face Of A Stranger

GOUGH, WILLIAM
Family Of Strangers

GOULD, CLIFF
Blacke's Magic

GOWANS, KIP
Of Pure Blood
Rearview Mirror

GOYER, LOUIS
Deadly Surveillance

GRADE, LEW
Duel Of Hearts
Ghost In Monte Carlo, A

GRADE, MICHAEL
Kane And Abel

GRAFTON, SUE
Love On The Run

GRAHAM, DAVID
Little Girl Lost

GRANT, GIL
Detective In The House

GRANT, HARRY
Ride With The Wind

GRANT, JEFF
Trapped In Silence

GRANT, TRUDY
Lantern Hill

GRAUMAN, WALTER
Nightmare On The Thirteenth Floor
Shakedown On The Sunset Strip

GRAY, BILL
Heads

GRAY, BOB
For The Love Of Aaron

GRAY, JOHN
American Story, An

GRAY, LINDA
Moment Of Truth: Broken Pledges

GRAY, WILLIAM
Dark Shadows

GRAZER, BRIAN
Shadow Chasers

GREEN, DOUGLAS
Hawaiian Heat

GREEN, HILTON
Psycho I V: The Beginning
Sweet Poison

GREEN, JIM
Addicted To His Love
And The Sea Will Tell
Deadly Intentions
Deadly Intentions... Again?
Double, Double, Toil And Trouble
Doublecrossed
Higher Ground
Killer Among Friends, A
Mother's Justice, A
No Child Of Mine
Outside Woman, The
Shattered Innocence
Stephen King's It
Without A Kiss Goodbye

GREEN, MICHAEL C.
Flight Of Black Angel

GREEN, WHITNEY
Dance Till Dawn

GREENBERG, HAROLD
This Park Is Mine

GREENBURG, MICHAEL
In The Eyes Of A Stranger
Las Vegas Strip Wars, The
Macgyver : Lost Treasure Of Atlantis

GREENE, DAVID
Penthouse, The
Sweet Revenge, A

GREENE, GLENN
Perfect Bride, The

GREENE, JUSTIS
Glitter Dome, The

GREENE, VANESSA
Deadly Desire
Money, Power, Murder
Search For Grace
Under The Influence
With Hostile Intent
Writer's Block

GREENFIELD, BARRY
I Saw What You Did
Kids Don't Tell
Taste For Killing, A

GREENFIELD, DEBRA
Jane's House

GREENMAN, ADAM
Breaking The Silence

GREENWALD, NANA
Past Tense

GREENWALD, ROBERT
Can You Feel Me Dancing?
Challenge Of A Lifetime
Daddy
Deadly Silence, A
Entertainers, The
Fight For Jenny, A
Forgotten Prisoners: The Amnesty File
Hiroshima: Out Of The Ashes
How To Murder A Millionaire
Lena: My 100 Children
Liberty
Murder In New Hampshire: The Pamela
....Smart Story
My Brother's Wife
Not In My Family
Our Sons
Perfect People
Portrait, The
Scattered Dreams: The Kathryn Messenger
....Story
Shattered Spirits
She Says She's Innocent
Silent Witness
Zelda

GREGG, JUDIE
Aftermath: A Test Of Love
Fear Inside, The

GREGORY, DON
Father & Son: Dangerous Relations
Fire In The Dark

GREIF, LESLIE
Sins
Walker, Texas Ranger

GREISMAN, GORDON
Drug Wars: The Cocaine Cartel
Jonathan Stone: Threat Of Innocence

GRIFFIN, CHRISTOPHER
Bitter Vengeance
Dancing With Danger

GRIFFITH, ANDY
Matlock: The Witness Killings
Return To Mayberry

GRILES, EDD
Caine Mutiny Court - Martial, The

GRODNIK, DANIEL
Sherlock Holmes Returns

GROGG, SAM
Firestorm: 72 Hours In Oakland

GROSS, MARCY
Always Remember I Love You
Billionaire Boys Club
Children Of Times Square
Deep Dark Secrets
Firestorm: 72 Hours In Oakland
Highway Heartbreaker
I Love You Perfect
Jonathan: The Boy Nobody Wanted
Love And Betrayal
Place For Annie, A

GROSSBART, JACK
Comrades Of Summer
Dangerous Affection
Echoes In The Darkness
From The Files Of Joseph Wambaugh: A Jury
Of One
Joshua's Heart
Killer In The Mirror
Last Wish
Leave Of Absence
Lies Before Kisses
Little Piece Of Heaven, A
One Of Her Own
Preppie Murder, The
Rockabye
Shattered Vows
She Was Marked For Murder
Something In Common
Something To Live For: The Alison Gertz
....Story
Sorry, Wrong Number
Woman Who Loved Elvis, The

GROSSMAN, ARNIE
Cries Unheard: The Donna Yaklich Story

GROSSO, SONNY
Family For Joe, A
Out Of The Darkness
True Blue

GUBER, PETER
Bay Coven
Nightmare At Bitter Creek

Toughest Man In The World, The

GUENETTE, ROBERT
Children Of The Night

GUISEZ, PEBY
Nobody's Children
Voyage

GURSKIS, DAN
Body Language

GUTHRIE, LEE
Place For Annie, A
Time To Heal, A

GUTHRIE, LYNN H.
Disaster At Silo 7
Nasty Boys

GUTMAN, NATHANIEL
Linda

GUTTFREUND, ANDRE R.
Abduction Of Kari Swenson, The

HACKIN, DENNIS
Marked For Murder

HADAR, RONNIE
Blindfold: Acts Of Obsession
Honor Thy Father And Mother: The
....Menendez Murders
In The Shadows, Someone Is Watching
Shadow Of Obsession

HAFFNER, CRAIG
Woman With A Past

HAFT, STEVEN
Spider And The Fly, The
Stormy Weathers

HAGEN, STEPHANIE
In The Line Of Duty: Standoff At Marion

HAGGIS, PAUL
Due South

HAGMAN, LARRY
Staying Afloat

HAID, CHARLES
Children In The Crossfire
In The Line Of Duty: A Cop For The Killing
Nightman, The

HAIGHT, ADAM
Hostage For A Day

HAIRSTON, CHARLES
Betrayed By Innocence
Casey's Gift: For Love Of A Child
Dreams Of Gold: The Mel Fisher Story
Tarzan In Manhattan

HALEY, JR., JACK
Night They Saved Christmas, The

HALL, MARILYN
Do You Remember Love?

HALMI, JR., ROBERT
April Morning
Blind Spot
Fire Next Time, The

Lifepod
Lonesome Dove
Night They Saved Christmas, The
Return To Lonesome Dove
Seasons Of The Heart
Spies, Lies And Naked Thighs
Spoils Of War
Yearling, The

HALMI, SR., ROBERT
Against Her Will: An Incident In Baltimore
Alone In The Neon Jungle
American Story, An
April Morning
Barnum
Bump In The Night
Call Of The Wild
Choices
Eyes Of A Witness
Face To Face
Getting Out
Gypsy
Incident In A Small Town
Incident, The
Izzy And Moe
Josephine Baker Story, The
Last Elephant, The
Mayflower Madam
Mrs. Lambert Remembers Love
Murders In The Rue Morgue, The
Nairobi Affair
Night They Saved Christmas, The
Pack Of Lies
Pals
Roxanne: The Prize Pulitzer
Secret, The
Spies, Lies And Naked Thighs
Trouble In Paradise
Yearling, The

HAMBURGER, DAVID
Desperate Rescue: The Cathy Mahone Story
Murder Between Friends

HAMDRI, ANDRAS
Mrs. 'Arris Goes To Paris

HAMEL, ALAN
Exclusive
Keeping Secrets

HAMEL, VERONICA
Baby Snatcher
Deadly Medicine

HAMILBURG, MICHAEL
White Mile

HAMILTON, ROBERT
Laker Girls, The

HAMM, SAM
Mantis

HAMMEL, THOMAS
Barbarians At The Gate
By Dawn's Early Light
Traveling Man

HAMMER, DENNIS
Love Boat: A Valentine Voyage, The

Nightingales
Rich Men, Single Women

HAMMER, EARL
Walton Thanksgiving Reunion, A

HAMORI, ANDRAS
Daughter Of Darkness
God Bless The Child
Storm And Sorrow

HANLEY, WILLIAM
Attic: The Hiding Of Anne Frank, The
In Broad Daylight
Last To Go, The
Nutcracker: Money, Madness And Murder
Our Sons
When The Time Comes

HANNA, WILLIAM
Stone Fox

HANNAH, DARYL
Attack Of The 50ft. Woman

HARBERT, TIM
Lifepod

HARDING, STEWART
Diamond Fleece
In Like Flynn

HARGROVE, DEAN
Diagnosis Of Murder
Fatal Confession: A Father Dowling Mystery
House On Sycamore Street, The
Jake And The Fatman
Macshayne: The Final Roll Of The Dice
Macshayne: Winner Take All
Perry Mason Mystery, A: The Case Of The Lethal
Perry Mason Mystery: The Case Of The Wicked Wives
Perry Mason Returns
Perry Mason: The Case Of The All-Star Assassin
Perry Mason: The Case Of The Avenging Ace
Perry Mason: The Case Of The Defiant Daughter
Perry Mason: The Case Of The Desperate Deception
Perry Mason: The Case Of The Fatal Fashion
Perry Mason: The Case Of The Fatal Framing
Perry Mason: The Case Of The Glass Coffin
Perry Mason: The Case Of The Heartbroken Bride
Perry Mason: The Case Of The Killer Kiss
Perry Mason: The Case Of The Lady In The Lake
Perry Mason: The Case Of The Lost Love
Perry Mason: The Case Of The Maligned Mobster
Perry Mason: The Case Of The Musical Murders
Perry Mason: The Case Of The Notorious Nun
Perry Mason: The Case Of The Poisoned Pen
Perry Mason: The Case Of The Reckless Romeo
Perry Mason: The Case Of The Ruthless Reporter

Perry Mason: The Case Of The Scandalous Scoundrel
Perry Mason: The Case Of The Shooting Star
Perry Mason: The Case Of The Silenced Singer
Perry Mason: The Case Of The Sinister Spirit
Perry Mason: The Case Of The Skin-Deep Scandal
Perry Mason: The Case Of The Telltale Talk Show Host
Ray Alexander: A Taste For Justice
Return To Mayberry
Twist Of The Knife, A

HARGROVE, ROBERT
Baywatch: Panic At Malibu Pier
Little Match Girl, The

HARMAN, JR., J. BOYCE
Howard Beach: Making The Case For Murder
Royce

HAROLD, MARY
Trade Winds

HARRIS, ART
Woman With A Past

HARRIS, DANIEL
Ghost Mom

HARRIS, KAREN
Street Hawk

HARRISON, GREGORY
Hot Paint
Oceans Of Fire
Pleasures
Red River
Seduced
Tower, The

HART, BILL
Shattered Image

HART, CAROLE
Leap Of Faith
Taken Away

HART, SIMON
Deep Trouble
Lethal Exposure
Target Of Suspicion

HARTLEY, NEIL
Agatha Christie's Dead Man's Folly
Agatha Christie's Thirteen At Dinner
Murder With Mirrors

HARTMAN, J. BOYCE
Open Admissions

HARTMAN, WILLIAM
Marcus Welby, M. D.: A Holiday Affair

HARTUNG, RAYMOND
Fatal Exposure
Snow Kill

HASBURGH, PATRICK
Destination: America
N. Y. P. D. Mounted
Sunset Beat

HAUGLAND, DAVID
Portrait, The

HAY, JAMES
Hostage Flight
Romance On The Orient Express

HAYES, JEFFREY
Dirty Work
Flood: Who Will Save Our Children?

HEAP, JONATHAN
Twelve O' One (12: 01)

HEDDEN, ROB
Knight Rider 2000

HEELEY, DAVID
Perfect Tribute, The

HEINRICH, KYLE
Positively True Adventures Of The Alleged
Texas Cheerleader Murdering Mom, The

HELFGOTT, DANIEL
Casey's Gift: For Love Of A Child
Dreams Of Gold: The Mel Fisher Story

HELLER, PAUL
Disappearance Of Christina, The

HELLER, ROSILYN
Better Off Dead
Better Off Dead

HENERSON, JAMES S.
Fire Next Time, The
For Love Or Money
Johnnie Mae Gibson: F B I
Rape Of Richard Beck, The

HENNESSY, DENNIS D.
Alamo: 13 Days To Glory, The
Bridge To Silence

HEROUX, CLAUDE
This Park Is Mine

HEROUX, DENIS
Sword Of Gideon
This Park Is Mine

HERSHMAN, ROB
Judgment

HERSKOVITZ, MARSHALL
Extreme Close-Up

HERZFELD, JOHN
Casualties Of Love: The Long Island Lolita
....Story

HESS, OLIVER G.
Flight Of Black Angel

HESTON, FRASER C.
Crucifier Of Blood, The
Man For All Season, A
Proud Men
Treasure Island

HEUS, RICHARD
Christmas On Division Street
Switched At Birth

HEWITT, CAROLINE
Mrs. 'Arris Goes To Paris

HEWITT, STEVEN
Chantilly Lace

HEYMAN, DAVID
Blind Justice

HEYWARD, ANDY
Archie: To Riverdale And Back Again

HICKMAN, DWAYNE
Bring Me The Head Of Dobie Gillis

HICKOX, S. BRYAN
Double Standard
Moment Of Truth: Stalking Back
Murder In The Heartland
Obsessed
Small Sacrifices

HIGGINS, JEAN
Ernest Green Story, The

HILL, ANDREW
Curiosity Kills
Dangerous Passion
Ladykillers
Silhouette

HILL, DANIELLE
Armed & Innocent

HILL, DEBRA
Attack Of The 50ft. Woman
El Diablo
Roadracers

HILL, LEONARD
Baby Of The Bride
Cartier Affair, The
Children Of The Bride
Cross Of Fire
Cry In The Wild: The Taking Of Peggy Ann
Dead Before Dawn
Earth Angel
False Arrest
Frank Nitti: The Enforcer
I Can Make You Love Me: The Stalking Of
....Laura Black
In Self Defense
In The Deep Woods
Jack The Ripper
Lady Forgets, The
Last Fling, The
Long Hot Summer, The
Manhunt: Search For The Night Stalker
Matter Of Justice, A
Mirrors
Mother Of The Bride
Murder Without Motive: The Edmund Perry
....Story
Passion And Paradise
Prince Of Bel Air
Rags To Riches
Shootdown
Summer Dreams: The Story Of The Beach
....Boys

They've Taken Our Children: The Chowchilla
....Kidnapping
Tricks Of The Trade

HILL, RICHARD
Broken Chain

HILL, TIM
Armed & Innocent
Love, Lies And Murder

HILL, WILLIAM
Deceptions
Freedom Fighter
One Against The Wind
Reunion At Fairborough
Still Crazy Like A Fox
Woman He Loved, The

HIMES, CAROL
Family Ties Vacation

HIRSCH, JAMES G.
Boys, The
China Lake Murders, The
Crazy From The Heart
Deep Trouble
Drive Like Lightning
Empty Cradle
Fatal Friendship
Fire: Trapped On The 37th Floor
For Love Or Money
Guts And Glory: The Rise And Fall Of Oliver
....North
Hart To Hart Returns
In The Best Interest Of The Child
Johnnie Mae Gibson: F B I
Lethal Exposure
Line Of Fire: The Morris Dees Story
Rape Of Richard Beck, The
Willing To Kill: The Texas Cheerleader Story

HIRSCHMAN, HERBERT
Attack On Fear
Mistral's Daughter

HIRSH, MICHAEL
Keys, The

HISER, BARBARA
Nightmare In The Daylight
Rape Of Dr. Willis, The

HOBLIT, GREGORY
Roe Vs. Wade

HODGES, PATRICIA
Vestige Of Honor

HOFFMAN, GARY
Bonnie And Clyde: The True Story
Dream Date
Hands Of A Stranger
Just One Of The Girls
Quiet Little Neighborhood, A Perfect Little
....Murder, A
Secret Life Of Ian Fleming, The
Stepford Children, The
Stranger In My Bed
Stranger On My Land
Taking The Heat

Till Death Us Do Part
Uncle Tom's Cabin
Unholy Matrimony
Woman With A Past

HOFFMAN, KAY
Nightmare In Columbia County
Terror In The Night

HOLCOMB, ROD
Finding The Way Home
Wolf

HOLM, PETER
Monte Carlo

HOLMES, MAUREEN
Miss America: Behind The Crown

HOLZGANG, CONRAD
Children Of The Night

HOOL, LANCE
Born To Run
Cover Girl Murders, The
Tracker, The

HOPKINS, ANNE
Decoration Day
Miss Rose White
One More Mountain
Shell Seekers, The
Son's Promise, A

HORIE, GEORGE
Tears And Laughter: The Joan And Mielissa
....Rivers Story
This Can't Be Love

HORNER, RICHARD
Crucifier Of Blood, The

HOROWITZ, LAWRENCE
Heart Of A Child
Moment Of Truth: A Child Too Many
Moment Of Truth: Broken Pledges
Moment Of Truth: Cradle Of Conspiracy
Moment Of Truth: Stalking Back
Moment Of Truth: To Walk Again
Moment Of Truth: Why My Daughter?
Murder In The Heartland
Switched At Birth

HOUGH, JOHN
Duel Of Hearts
Ghost In Monte Carlo, A
Hazard Of Hearts, A

HOUGH, STAN
Gunsmoke: The Last Apache
He's Fired, She's Hired
One Police Plaza

HOWARD, RON
Into Thin Air

HUBERTY, MARTIN
For Their Own Good
Switch, The

HUDDLESTON, ROBERT
Little Girl Lost
Resting Place

Room Upstairs, The
With Murder In Mind

HUMPHREY, STEVE
Love On The Run

HUNT, PETER
P. S. I Luv U

HUNTER, LEW
Playing With Fire

HURD, GALE ANNE
Cast A Deadly Spell

HURLEY, MAURICE
Keys, The

HUSKY, RICK
Beverly Hills Cowgirl Blues
When The Bough Breaks

HUYCK, WILLARD
Father's Homecoming, A
Mothers, Daughters And Lovers

INCH, KEVIN
Little White Lies
Remington Steele: The Steele That Wouldn't
....Die
White Lie

IRVING, RICHARD
Wallenberg: A Hero's Story

ISCOVE, ROBERT
Dying To Love You
Forget Me Not Murders, The
River Of Rage: The Taking Of Maggie
....Keene

ISENBERG, CAROLE
Women Of Brewster Place, The

ISENBERG, GERALD I.
Child's Cry
Forbidden
Gotham
Three Wishes Of Billy Grier, The
When Dreams Come True

ISRAEL, NEAL
Bonnie And Clyde: The True Story
Dream Date
Quiet Little Neighborhood, A Perfect Little
....Murder, A
Taking The Heat
Woman With A Past

IVOR, ANTHONY
Zelda

JABLIN, DAVID
Mastergate

JACKSON, JERMANINE
Jacksons: An American Dream , The

JACKSON, KATE
Child's Cry

JACKSON, LAMAR
Man From Left Field
Man Upstairs, The

JACKSON, MARGARET
Jacksons: An American Dream , The

JACOBS, ALAN
Call Of The Wild
Mrs. Lambert Remembers Love

JACOBS, DAVID
Dallas: The Early Years
Homefront
Lois & Clark: The New Adventures Of
....Superman

JACOBSON, LARRY
Family For Joe, A
Out Of The Darkness
True Blue

JACOBY, NANCY
Good Night, Sweet Wife: A Murder In Boston

JAFFE, MICHAEL
Amy Fisher: My Story
Babymaker: The Dr. Cecil Jacobson's Story
Deadlock
Great Escape I I: The Untold Story, The
Gregory K
In The Nick Of Time
Murderous Affair, A: The Carolyn Warmus
....Story

JAMES, JUDITH
Brotherhood Of Justice, The
Prisoner Of Honor

JAMESON, JERRY
Gunsmoke: One Man's Justice
Stormin' Home

JANZEN, NAOMI
Secrets Of Lake Success

JEFFREY, HOWARD
There Must Be A Pony

JEFFRIES, GEORGIA
Fatal Memories
For Love And Glory

JEFFRIES, PETER
Passion And Paradise

JENKINS, DAN
Dead Solid Perfect

JENNINGS, CHARLES
Forbidden Nights
Shooter

JETER, SUSAN
Search For Grace

JETT, SUE
Infidelity

JEWISON, NORMAN
Geronimo

JOFFE, CHARLES
Mastergate

JOHNSON, BRUCE
Burning Bridges

JOHNSON, CHARLES FLOYD
Revealing Evidence

JOHNSON, DON
In The Company Of Darkness

JOHNSON, ELI
Gotham

JOHNSON, KENNETH
Hot Pursuit
Shadow Chasers
Sherlock Holmes Returns

JOHNSON, LAMONT
Broken Chain

JOHNSON, LAURIE
Lady And The Highwayman, The

JOHNSON, LUCY ANTEK
Convicted: A Mother's Story

JOHNSON, RICHARD E.
Frankenstein: The College Years

JOHNSON, TIMOTHY
Dr. Quinn, Medicine Woman

JOHNSTON, THOMAS M.C.
Mussolini: The Decline And Fall Of Il Duce

JONES, DENNIS E.
Prime Target

JONES, GLEN R.
Little Kidnappers, The

JONES, MARK
Highwayman, The

JONSSON, LINDA
Bluffing It

JORDAN, GLENN
Barbarians At The Gate
Boys, The
Dress Gray
Echoes In The Darkness
Home Fires Burning
Jane's House
Jesse
O Pioneers
Promise
Something In Common
To Dance With The White Dog

JOSEPH, ROBERT L.
Sun Also Rises, The

JOSEPHSON, BARRY
Parker Kane

JOSSEN, BARRY
Partners 'N Love

JOYCE, BERNADETTE
Bionic Showdown: The 6 Million Dollar
....Man/Bionic Woman
Return Of Sam Mccloud, The
Return Of The 6 Million Dollar Man & Bionic
....Woman

JUNKERMANN, KELLY
Gambler Returns: The Luck Of The Draw

Macshayne: The Final Roll Of The Dice
Macshayne: Winner Take All
Rio Diablo

JURGENSEN, RANDY
In The Shadow Of A Killer

JUSTICE, CASEY LEE
Witness To The Execution

JUSTICE, MILTON
Nobody's Child

KAGAN, JEREMY
Dr. Quinn, Medicine Woman
Roswell

KAHN, BERNARD
Father & Son: Dangerous Relations

KAHN, BERNIE
Fire In The Dark

KAHN, HARVEY
Lies And Lullabies
Shoot First: A Cop's Vengeance
Thicker Than Blood: The Larry Mclinden
....Story
When Love Kills: The Seduction Of John
....Hearn

KAHN, ILENE
Roswell
Stalin
White Mile

KAHN, MARY
Clarence

KALINS, MARJORIE
Attic: The Hiding Of Anne Frank, The

KALLBERG, KEVIN
Flight Of Black Angel

KALLIS, STAN
I'll Take Manhattan
Kane And Abel

KANDER II, JOHN
Shoot First: A Cop's Vengeance

KANE, JOSH
Into The Badlands
Trenchcoat In Paradise

KANE, THOMAS
Ten Million Dollar Getaway

KANIN, FAY
Heartsounds

KANTER, DONNA
Flood: Who Will Save Our Children?

KAPPES, DAVID
In The Line Of Duty: The FBI Murders
Night They Saved Christmas, The

KARNEY, SHARI
Shattered Trust: The Shari Karney Story

KARPF, MERRILL H.
Blood River
Caught In The Act
Children In The Crossfire

Connecticut Yankee In King Arthur's Court, A
Crash: The Mystery Of Flight 1501
Last Outlaw, The
Laura Lansing Slept Here
Mrs. Delafield Wants To Marry
Six Against The Rock
Stone Pillow
Tears And Laughter: The Joan And Mielissa
....Rivers Story
This Can't Be Love
Voyage
Wild Card

KATZ, GLORIA
Father's Homecoming, A
Mothers, Daughters And Lovers

KATZ, PETER
Fatal Confession: A Father Dowling Mystery
Passport To Murder
Perry Mason: The Case Of The All-Star
Assassin
Perry Mason: The Case Of The Avenging Ace
Perry Mason: The Case Of The Desperate
Deception
Perry Mason: The Case Of The Lady In The
Lake
Perry Mason: The Case Of The Musical
Murders
Perry Mason: The Case Of The Poisoned Pen
Perry Mason: The Case Of The Scandalous
Scoundrel
Perry Mason: The Case Of The Silenced
Singer
Pleasures
Ray Alexander: A Taste For Justice
Secret Life Of Archie's Wife, The

KATZ, RAYMOND
Miss America: Behind The Crown
Mussolini - The Untold Story
Stagecoach
Without Her Consent

KATZ, ROBERT
Cisco Kid, The
Gettysburg

KATZKA, GABRIEL
At Mother's Request
Ellis Island
Lady In A Corner

KAUFFMAN, JUDY
Time To Triumph, A

KAUFMAN, ARVIN
In The Shadows, Someone Is Watching
Original Sin
Revenge On The Highway

KAUFMAN, KEN
Anastasia: The Mystery Of Anna
Archie: To Riverdale And Back Again
Attic: The Hiding Of Anne Frank, The
Baron And The Kid, The
Baron And The Kid, The
Case Of Deadly Force, A
Dead And Alive
Dead And Alive

Don't Touch My Daughter
Her Final Fury: Betty Broderick, The Last
....Chapter
Howard Beach: Making The Case For Murder
In The Line Of Duty: A Cop For The Killing
In The Line Of Duty: Ambush In Waco
In The Line Of Duty: Manhunt In The
....Dakotas
In The Line Of Duty: Standoff At Marion
In The Line Of Duty: Street War
In The Line Of Duty: The FBI Murders
In The Line Of Duty: The Price Of
....Vengeance
Lost Capone, The
Norman Rockwell's Breaking Home Ties
Telling Secrets
Woman Scorned: The Betty Broderick Story

KAUFMAN, LEN
Island Sons

KAVANAGH, DEREK
Chrome Soldiers
Mercy Mission: The Rescue Of Flight 771
Red Spider, The

KAY, DUSTY
Triplecross

KAYDEN, WILLIAM
Nazi Hunter: The Beate Klarsfeld Story

KEACH, JAMES
Passion For Justice, A: Hazel Brannon Smith
....Story
Praying Mantis
Sunstroke
Winner Never Quits, A

KEATING, DORIS
Miles To Go . . .
Shadow Of A Stranger
Touch Of Scandal, A
White Hot: The Mysterious Murder Of
....Thelma Todd

KEEGAN, TERRY
Bluegrass
E. A. R. T. H. Force

KELLER, MAX A.
Betrayed By Innocence
Casey's Gift: For Love Of A Child
Dreams Of Gold: The Mel Fisher Story
Summer To Remember, A
Swimsuit
Tarzan In Manhattan

KELLER, MICHELINE H.
Betrayed By Innocence
Casey's Gift: For Love Of A Child
Summer To Remember, A
Tarzan In Manhattan

KELLEY, DAVID
Picket Fences

KELLY, JOSEPH
Amelia Earhart: The Final Flight
Wildflower

KELMAN, ALFRED R.
Amy Fisher: My Story
Christmas Carol, A
Labor Of Love: The Arlette Schweitzer Story
Last Days Of Patton, The
Napoleon And Josephine: A Love Story
Plot To Kill Hitler, The
Richest Man In The World: The Aristotle
....Onassis Story
Special Friendship, A
Ted Kennedy, Jr., Story, The

KEMENY, JOHN
Josephine Baker Story, The
Murderers Among Us: The Simon Wiesenthal
....Story
Red King, White Knight
Sword Of Gideon
Teamster Boss: The Jackie Presser Story

KEMP, BARRY
Fresno

KEMPER, DAVID
Seaquest Dsv

KENNEDY, BROOKE
Bride In Black, The
South Beach

KENNEDY, BURT
Once Upon A Texas Train
Where The Hell's That Gold

KENNERLY, DAVID HUME
Shooter
Taking Of Flight 847: The Uli Derickson
....Story

KENT, LINDA
From The Files Of Joseph Wambaugh: A Jury
Of One
Leave Of Absence
One Of Her Own

KEREW, DIANA
Babycakes
Darkness Before Dawn
Everybody's Baby: The Rescue Of Jessica
....Mcclure
Fourth Story
Hostage
My Breast
Night Of The Hunter
Paris Trout
Wife, Mother, Murderer

KERNER, JORDAN
Backfield In Motion
Breaking Point
Do You Know The Muffin Man?
For Their Own Good
Heat Wave
Heat Wave
My First Love
Nightman, The
Side By Side
Switch, The

KERNS, JOANNA
Nightman, The

KIESER, REV. ELLWOOD
We Are The Children

KINBERG, JUD
Kane And Abel
Stoning In Fulham County, A

KINDBERG, ANN
Gambler Returns: The Luck Of The Draw
Her Final Fury: Betty Broderick, The Last
....Chapter
In The Line Of Duty: The Price Of
....Vengeance
Stolen Babies
Woman Scorned: The Betty Broderick Story

KING, ALAN
Reunion At Fairborough

KING, JEFF
Due South
Ordeal In The Arctic

KING, STEPHEN
Stephen King's Golden Years
Stephen King's The Stand

KING, TIMOTHY
Danielle Steel's Fine Things
Red Spider, The

KING, ZALMAN
Red Shoes Diaries

KIRKPATRICK, DAVID
Substitute, The

KIRSCHNER, DAVID
Dreamer Of Oz, The

KLEINBART, PHILIP
Deadly Silence, A
Entertainers, The
Forgotten Prisoners: The Amnesty File
Hiroshima: Out Of The Ashes
How To Murder A Millionaire
Murder In New Hampshire: The Pamela
....Smart Story
Not In My Family
Our Sons
Portrait, The
Scattered Dreams: The Kathryn Messenger
....Story
She Says She's Innocent

KLENHARD, WALTER
Accidental Meeting

KLINE, HENRY
Bates Motel

KLINE, STEPHEN
Shooter

KLINGER, JUDSON
Thicker Than Blood: The Larry Mclinden
....Story

KLOIBER, HERBERT G.
Forbidden

KLUNE, DONALD C.
In A Child's Name
Judgment

KNOP, PATRICIA
Red Shoes Diaries

KNOPF, CHRISTOPHER
Equal Justice

KOBRITZ, RICHARD
Fear

KOCH, HOWARD W.
Crossings
Hollywood Wives
Odd Couple, The

KOCH, KEN
When The Bough Breaks

KONIGSBERG, FRANK
Act Of Vengeance
As Summers Die
Babycakes
Casanova
Dance Till Dawn
Double Edge
Ellis Island
Fourth Story
Glitter Dome, The
In Sickness And In Health
Love Can Be Murder
Oldest Living Confederate Widow Tells All
Paris Trout
Richest Man In The World: The Aristotle
....Onassis Story
Right To Kill?
Rock Hudson
Surviving
To Save A Child
Tommyknockers, The
Wet Gold
Yarn Princess, The

KOONENBURG, PETER
Sound And The Silence, The

KOONTZ, DEAN
Face Of Fear, The

KOPELSON, ANNE
Past Tense

KOPELSON, ARNOLD
Past Tense

KOSBERG, ROBERT
Dream Date
Fade To Black
Intimate Encounters
Other Lover, The

KOTTENBROOK, CAROL
Shadowhunter

KOUSAKIS, JOHN PETER
Broken Badges

KRAGEN, KEN
Gambler Returns: The Luck Of The Draw

Kenny Rogers As The Gambler I I I: The
....Legend Continues
Macshayne: The Final Roll Of The Dice
Macshayne: Winner Take All
Rio Diablo
Wild Horses

KRAININ, JULIAN
Disaster At Silo 7

KRAM, WENDY
Ultimate Betrayal

KRAMER, JOAN
Perfect Tribute, The

KRANE, JONATHAN D.
Boris And Natasha
Fatal Charm

KRANTZ, STEVE
Children Of The Dark
Dadah Is Death
Deadly Matrimony
Deadly Medicine
House Of Secrets
I'll Take Manhattan
Judith Krantz's Till We Meet Again
Mistral's Daughter
Sins
Torch Song

KREVOY, BRAD
Love, Cheat And Steal
Sketch Artist

KRICHEFSKI, BERNARD
Souvenir

KRITZER, EDDIE
False Witness

KROST, BARRY
Bump In The Night
Corpse Had A Familiar Face, The
Rearview Mirror
When A Stranger Calls Back

KRUPP, PHILIP
Menendez: A Killing In Beverly Hills

KUGHN, RICHARD
Dying To Love You
River Of Rage: The Taking Of Maggie
....Keene

KUKOFF, BERNIE
Rags To Riches

KULIK, BUZZ
Her Secret Life
Too Young The Hero
Women Of Valor

KURDYLA, TED
Birds I I: Land's End, The
Cosby Mysteries, The
Trouble Shooters: Trapped Beneath The
....Earth

KURI, JOHN
Conagher
One More Mountain

KURT, DON
Flash, The
Viper

KURTA, PAUL
Afterburn
Keeper Of The City
Rise & Walk: The Dennis Byrd Story
She Said No

KURUMADA, KIM
Mothers, Daughters And Lovers

KUSHNER, DONALD
Carolina Skeletons
Father & Son: Dangerous Relations
Fire In The Dark
Getting Gotti
Good Cops, Bad Cops
Murder C. O. D.
Sweet Bird Of Youth
Your Mother Wears Combat Boots

KUTNER, WILLIE
Roadracers

LA BELLA, VINCENZO
Season Of Giants, A

LA MAINA, FRAN
Promised A Miracle

LA PEGNA, ARTURO
Only One Survived

LA TRAVERSE, ANNE MARIE
The Race To Freedom: The Underground
....Railroad

LACK, ANDREW
With Hostile Intent

LACOE, MICHAEL
Viper

LAFFERTY, PERRY
An Early Frost
Maybe Baby
Murder C. O. D.

LAHTI, ED
Deadman's Revenge

LAITER, TOVA
Lena: My 100 Children
Murder In Mississippi

LAKE, MICHAEL
Facts Of Life Down Under, The
Place To Call Home, A

LAMM, KAREN
Menendez: A Killing In Beverly Hills

LANDGRAF, JOHN PHILIP
Those Secrets

LANDON, MICHAEL
Highway To Heaven
Little House On The Prairie - Bless All The
....Dear Children
Us
Where Pigeons Go To Die

LANDSBERG, CLEVE
Broken Chain
Can You Feel Me Dancing?
Court - Martial Of Jackie Robinson, The
Inconvenient Woman, An
On Promised Land
Posing: Inspired By Three Real Stories

LANDSBURG, ALAN
Adam: His Song Continues
Bluegrass
Diamond Fleece
George Mckenna Story, The
In Defense Of A Married Man
Long Gone
Mothers' Right, A: The Elizabeth Morgan
....Story
Nightmare In Columbia County
Quiet Victory: The Charlie Wedemeyer Story
Ryan White Story, The
Stoning In Fulham County, A
Strange Voices
Terror In The Night
Too Young The Hero
Triumph Of The Heart: The Ricky Bell Story
Unspeakable Acts

LANE, THOMAS
Back To Hannibal: The Return Of Tom
Sawyer And Huck Finn

LANGTON, SIMON
Anna Karenina

LANNING, STEVE
Judith Krantz's Till We Meet Again
Secret Garden, The

LANSBURY, BRUCE
I'm Dangerous Tonight
Stranger Waits, A

LANSBURY, EDGAR
Stranger Waits, A

LANSING, SHERRY
Mistress
When The Time Comes

LANTOS, ROBERT
Family Of Strangers
Ordeal In The Arctic
Sword Of Gideon
Woman On The Run: The Lawrencia
....Bembenek Story

LARROQUETTE, JOHN
One Special Victory

LARSON, GLEN A.
Chameleons
Cover Up
Highwayman, The
In Like Flynn
P. S. I Luv U
Road Raiders, The

LARSON, J.C.
Highwayman, The
P. S. I Luv U

LARSON, JON
Cries Unheard: The Donna Yaklich Story
Mothers Revenge, A

LASKOS, ANDREW
Deadly Matrimony
False Arrest
House Of Secrets

LATER, ADRIA
Double, Double, Toil And Trouble

LATHAM, LYNN MARIE
Homefront
Second Chances

LATT, DAVID
Gotham
Out Of Time
Twin Peaks

LAUFER, IRA
Sudie And Simpson
Wildflower

LAVIN, LINDA
Place To Call Home, A

LAWRENCE, DAVID
Consenting Adult

LAWSON, SARAH
Only Way Out, The

LEACHMAN, CLORIS
Deadly Intentions

LEAR, NORMAN
Heartsounds

LEARMAN, RICHARD
Family For Joe, A
Wheels Of Terror

LECHOWICK, BERNARD
Homefront
Second Chances

LEDER, REUBEN
Danger Down Under

LEE, MICHELE
Single Women, Married Men
When No One Would Listen

LEFCOURT, PETER
Cracked Up

LeFRAK, FRANCINE
Fade To Black
Miss Rose White

LEMCHEN, BOB
Dark Reflection

LENKOV, PETER
Parker Kane

LENOX, JOHN THOMAS
Long Hot Summer, The
Lucy & Desi: Before The Laughter
Price She Paid, The

LENZER, NORM
Casey's Gift: For Love Of A Child

LEONARD, SHELDON
I Spy Returns

LEOPOLD, STRATTON
Big One: The Great Los Angeles Earthquake

LEPINER, MICHAEL
Anastasia: The Mystery Of Anna
Attic: The Hiding Of Anne Frank, The
Baron And The Kid, The
Baron And The Kid, The
Case Of Deadly Force, A
In The Line Of Duty: The FBI Murders
Norman Rockwell's Breaking Home Ties

LEVI, ALAN J.
Columbo: No Time To Die
Probe

LEVIN, ADRIENNE
Ernest Green Story, The

LEVIN, ALAN M.
Many Happy Returns

LeVINE, DEBORAH JOY
Lois & Clark: The New Adventures Of
....Superman
Samaritan: The Mitch Snyder Story

LEVINSON, DAVID
Kicks

LEVINSON, LARRY
Rio Diablo

LEVINSON, LEE
Playing With Fire
Runaway Father

LEVINSON, MARK
T Bone N Wessel

LEVINSON, RICHARD
Guardian, The
Guilty Conscience
Murder, She Wrote
Terrorist On Trial: The United States Vs.
Salim
Vanishing Act

LEVINSON, RONALD A.
In The Arms Of A Killer

LEVISON, ART
Love & Lies

LEVIT, LAURIE
Final Appeal
Love, Lies And Murder
What She Doesn't Know

LEVITAN, PHIL
Amy Fisher: My Story
Labor Of Love: The Arlette Schweitzer Story
Special Friendship, A

LEVITAN, STEVE
Quiet Killer

LEVITTA, SCOTT
Highwayman, The

LEVOFF, JOHN
Family Torn Apart, A
Last Of His Tribe, The
Revenge Of Al Capone, The

LEVY, ARIEL
Gifted One, The

LEVY, DANIEL
Triumph Of The Heart: The Ricky Bell Story

LEVY, EUGENE
Sodbusters

LEVY, FRANKLIN R.
Hot Paint
Oceans Of Fire
Pleasures
Red River
Seduced
Tower, The

LEWIS, LLOYD
Summer To Remember, A

LEWIS, RICHARD
Lifepod

LEWIS, ROBERT
Betrayed By Innocence
Dead Reckoning
Memories Of Murder
Spy

LEWIS, STEVE
Woman With A Past

LICHAUCO-PELMAN, J.J.
Intimate Stranger

LIEBERMAN, BARBARA
Till Death Us Do Part

LIEBERMAN, ROBERT
To Save A Child

LINK, WILLIAM
Boys, The
Cosby Mysteries, The
Guardian, The
Guilty Conscience
Murder, She Wrote
Over My Dead Body
Terrorist On Trial: The United States Vs. Salim
Vanishing Act

LINKE, RICHARD O.
Return To Mayberry

LIPMAN, DANIEL
Love She Sought, The

LIPTON, JAMES
Mirrors

LISI, LUCIANO
Sound And The Silence, The

LIST, SHELLY
Barbara Taylor Bradford's Remember
Danielle Steel's Jewels

LITKE, MARTY
Place To Call Home, A
Rockabye
Shattered Vows

LOCKE, PETER
Carolina Skeletons
Father & Son: Dangerous Relations
Fire In The Dark
Getting Gotti
Good Cops, Bad Cops
Murder C. O. D.
Sweet Bird Of Youth
Your Mother Wears Combat Boots

LOCKER, KENNETH
Chernobyl: The Final Warning

LOMBARDO, NICK
Baby Girl Scott
Go Toward The Light

LONDON, JERRY
Calendar Girl, Cop Killer? The Bambi
....Bembenek Story
Dadah Is Death
Family Sins
Harry's Hong Kong
Kiss Shot
Labor Of Love: The Arlette Schweitzer Story
Manhunt For Claude Dallas
With Intent To Kill

LONDON, TODD
Columbo And The Murder Of A Rock Star
Columbo - Caution: Murder Can Be
....Hazardous To Your Health
Columbo Goes To College

LONG, ROBERT
Two Fathers' Justice

LONGSTREET, HARRY
Night Walk
Night Walk
With A Vengeance

LONGSTREET, RENEE
Night Walk
Night Walk
Sex,Love, And Cold Hard Cash
With A Vengeance

LORBER, MARC B.
Moment Of Truth: Cradle Of Conspiracy

LORENZANO, DANIELE
Around The World In 80 Days
Heidi

LORING, LYNN
Glitter

LOUIS, R.J.
Angel Of Death
Crazy From The Heart

LOUTHAN, GUY
Deceptions

LOVEJOY, STEVE
Steel Justice

LOVELL, DYSON
Nobody's Child
Return To Lonesome Dove

LOVENHEIM, ROBERT
Defiant One, The
Elvis And Me
Family Torn Apart, A
Gladiator, The
Last Of His Tribe, The
Revenge Of Al Capone, The
Shattered Vows
Smokey Mountain Christmas, A
Starcrossed

LOWRY, DICK
Gambler Returns: The Luck Of The Draw
Her Final Fury: Betty Broderick, The Last
....Chapter
In The Line Of Duty: A Cop For The Killing
In The Line Of Duty: Ambush In Waco
In The Line Of Duty: Manhunt In The
....Dakotas
In The Line Of Duty: The Price Of
....Vengeance
Miracle Landing
Unconquered
Wild Horses
Woman Scorned: The Betty Broderick Story

LOWRY, HUNT
Dream West
Surviving
Wild Horses

LOWRY, RICHARD
Spoils Of War

LUCAS, GEORGE
Ewok Adventure, The
Ewoks: The Battle For Endor
Young Indiana Jones Chronicles: The Curse
....Of The Jackal

LUCAS, PHILL
Broken Chain

LUDWIG, JERRY
Roman Holiday

LUGAR, JOHN
Amerika
Lucky Day

LUGER, LOIS
Danger Of Love, The
Her Wicked Ways
Lion Of Africa, The

LUPO, FRANK
Hunter
Something Is Out There

LURIE, JEFFREY
Blind Side
State Of Emergency

LUSSIER, PAUL
Based On An Untrue Story
Deadly Silence, A
Doing Time On Maple Drive

Sitter, The

LUSTIG, BRANKO
Deadlock
Drug Wars: The Camarena Story
Intruders

LYLE, FRED
Capital News

LYNCH, CHRISTINE
Amy Fisher: My Story

LYNCH, DAVID
Twin Peaks

LYNCH, THOMAS W.
Combat High

LYON, RON
Sins Of The Father

LYTTLE, LAWRENCE
Babe Ruth
Taking Back My Life: The Nancy
....Ziegenmeyer Story

MACDOUGALL, IAN
Woman On The Run: The Lawrencia
....Bembenek Story

MACK, KAREN
Bare Essentials
Club Med
Indiscreet
Love Among Thieves
One Against The Wind
Roses Are For The Rich

MACLAREN, MICHELLE
For The Love Of My Child: The Anissa
....Ayala Story
Heart Of A Child
Moment Of Truth: A Child Too Many
Moment Of Truth: Broken Pledges
Moment Of Truth: To Walk Again
Shame

MACMILLAN, MICHAEL
Clarence

MADDALENA, MARIANNE
Night Visions

MADELIK, GABRIELLE
Entertainers, The

MAFFEO, NEIL T.
Assassin
Babes In Toyland
Cowboy And The Ballerina, The
Deadly Intentions
Diamond Trap, The
Sister Margaret And The Saturday Night
....Ladies

MAGAR, GUY
Stepfather I I I

MAGEE, DOUG
Conviction Of Kitty Dodds, The

MAGNATTA, CONSTANITINO
Ghost Mom

MAHON, CHAN
Stranded

MAHONEY, JR., JAMES E.
Are You Lonesome Tonight?

MAITLAND, SCOTT
Camp Cucamonga

MAJORS, LEE
Cowboy And The Ballerina, The
Danger Down Under

MALDEN, BORIS
Baby Brokers
I'm Dangerous Tonight
Take, The
This Gun For Hire

MALENFANT, JEAN-MARIE
Deadly Surveillance

MALIS, MARK
Leona Helmsley: The Queen Of Mean

MALO, RENE
Easy Prey

MALONE, NANCY
Impostor, The

MAMET, DAVID
Life In The Theater, A

MANASSE, GEORGE
Final Verdict
Orpheus Descending
Vengeance: The Story Of Tony Cimo

MANETTI, LARRY
Take, The

MANHEIM, MICHAEL
Abduction Of Kari Swenson, The
I'll Be Home For Christmas
Last Flight Out
Little Match Girl, The
Roe Vs. Wade
Winnie

MANLEY, PETER
Lost In London

MANN, ABBY
Atlanta Child Murders, The
Murderers Among Us: The Simon Wiesenthal
....Story
Teamster Boss: The Jackie Presser Story

MANN, DELBERT
April Morning
Incident In A Small Town

MANN, MICHAEL
Drug Wars: The Camarena Story
Drug Wars: The Cocaine Cartel
L. A. Takedown
Miami Vice

MANN, ROBERT
Hit List, The

MANNERS, SAM
Bloodlines: Murder In The Family

Casanova
Lies Of The Heart: The Story Of Laurie
....Kellogg
Walton Thanksgiving Reunion, A

MANOFF, DINAH
Maid For Each Other

MANOS, JR., JAMES
Positively True Adventures Of The Alleged
Texas Cheerleader Murdering Mom, The

MANSON, DAVID
Eye On The Sparrow
King Of Love, The
Rising Son
Those Secrets

MANTLEY, JOHN
Gunsmoke: Return To Dodge
Gunsmoke: The Last Apache

MANULIS, JOHN
Blind Side
Daybreak
Intimate Strangers

MANULIS, MARTIN
Grass Roots
Harem
Space

MANZELLA, RAY
Goddess Of Love

MARCH, DONALD
Billionaire Boys Club
Clinton And Nadine
David
Fear Stalk
Fear Stalk
Sudie And Simpson

MARCIL, ALLAN
Bloodlines: Murder In The Family
For The Love Of My Child: The Anissa
....Ayala Story
Sin And Redemption
Space
White Mile

MARCUS, IRWIN
Miracle Child

MARCUS, PAULA
Mother Goose Rock 'n' Rhyme

MARGELLOS, JAMES
Danielle Steel's Kaleidoscope
Four Eyes And Six Guns
Little Kidnappers, The
Not Quite Human I I
Still Not Quite Human

MARGO, PHIL
Goddess Of Love
This Wife For Hire

MARGOLIN, ARNOLD
Family For Joe, A

MARGOLIN, STUART
Glitter Dome, The

MARGULIES, ALAN
Nobody's Children

MARGULIES, STAN
Broken Angel
Bunny's Tale, A
Crossing To Freedom
Jacksons: An American Dream , The
Out On A Limb
Separate But Equal
Stay The Night

MARK, GORDON
Only Way Out, The

MARK, LAURENCE
Sweet Bird Of Youth

MARK, TONY
Infidelity

MARKELL, BOB
At Mother's Request
If Tomorrow Comes
In The Shadow Of A Killer
Settle The Score

MARKEY, PATRICK
L. A. Takedown

MARKLEY, EDWARD D.
Blue Deville

MARKS, JOAN
Bunny's Tale, A
In The Company Of Darkness

MARKS, JULIAN
Bonds Of Love
David's Mother
Doing Life
Drop Dead Gorgeous
Good Fight, The
Hush Little Baby
I Know My Son Is Alive
Night Owl
Silent Witness: What A Child Saw
Thicker Than Blood: The Larry Mclinden
....Story
Ultimate Betrayal

MARKS, PAUL
Adventures Of Brisco County Jr., The

MARMION, GRAINNE
Borrowers, The

MARMOT, AMANDA
Railway Station Man, The

MARQUET, DANIEL
Sweet Revenge

MARS, SHERRY
Crazy From The Heart

MARSH, JOHN
Blind Side
State Of Emergency

MARSHALL, GEORGE
Final Appeal

MARTIN, JAYNE
Moment Of Truth: Cradle Of Conspiracy

MARTIN, SCOTT
Moment Of Truth: Why My Daughter?

MARVIN, IRA
Child In The Night
Geronimo
Leap Of Faith

MARVIN, NIKI
Buried Alive
Strays

MARX, TIMOTHY
Precious Victims
Those Secrets

MASSUCCI, ANTHONY
Passport To Murder

MASTROIANNI, ARMAND
Dark Shadows

MATHEWS, ROSS
Place To Call Home, A

MATOFSKY, HARVEY
Poker Alice
Trouble In Paradise

MATTHAU, CHARLES
Mrs. Lambert Remembers Love

MATTHEWS, ELIZABETH
Eighty-Three Hours 'til Dawn

MAURER, JOSEPH
Crash Landing: The Rescue Of Flight 232
With Murder In Mind

MAY, BRADFORD
Drive Like Lightning

MAYFIELD, LES
Psycho I V: The Beginning

MAYNARD, RICHARD
Bridge Across Time
Mission Of The Shark
Neon Empire
Silent Witness: What A Child Saw
Stompin' At The Savoy
Supercarrier
Timestalkers

MAZUR, DEREK
Harvest For The Heart
Heads

MCADAMS, JAMES
Kojak: The Belarus File
Kojak: The Price Of Justice
Legacy Of Lies
Return Of Ironside, The

MCALEVEY, PETER
Born To Run

MCARDLE, KATHRYN
Heart Of A Child
Moment Of Truth: Broken Pledges

MCBRIDE, JIM
Blood Ties

MCCALLUM, RICK
Young Indiana Jones Chronicles: The Curse
....Of The Jackal

MCCANN, PETER
Good Cops, Bad Cops

MCCLANAHAN, RUE
Baby Of The Bride

MCCORD, JONAS
Charles And Diana: Unhappily Ever After
Class Of '61
Women Of Valor

MCCORMICK, KEVIN
Into The Homeland
Into The Homeland

MCCRAY, KENT
Bonanza: The Return
Highway To Heaven
Little House On The Prairie - Bless All The
....Dear Children
Us
Where Pigeons Go To Die

MCCULLOUGH, ROBERT
International Airport

MCCUTCHEN, BILL
Freedom Fighter
Heidi
Keeper Of The City
Murder In Paradise
People Across The Lake, The

MCDOUGALL, IAN
Fight For Life
Passion And Paradise
Trial And Error

MCELROY, HAL
Last Frontier, The
Which Way Home

MCEVEETY, VINCENT
Columbo: Undercover

MCGEE, JAMES R.
Eyes Of Terror

MCGILLEN, JAMES
When Love Kills: The Seduction Of John
....Hearn

MCGILLIS, KELLY
Grand Isle

MCGLOTHEN, STEVE
Against The Wall
Battling For Baby
Daddy
Deliver Them From Evil: The Taking Of Alta
....View
Desperate For Love
Forgotten Prisoners: The Amnesty File
Glitz
Image, The
Jackie Collins' Lady Boss

Lena: My 100 Children
Marla Hanson Story, The
Max And Helen

McGoohan, Patrick
Columbo: No Time To Die

McIntosh, Peter
Equal Justice
Stephen King's Golden Years

McKeand, Nigel
Alex: The Life Of A Child

McKeon, Nancy
Firefighter
Strange Voices

McLaglen, Mary
Last Light

McLain, Chuck
Armed & Innocent
Child Of Rage
Dream West
Judgment Day: The John List Story
North And South
Nutcracker: Money, Madness And Murder
Overkill: The Aileen Wuornos Story
People Like Us

McLean, Michael S.
Killer In The Mirror

McLean, Seaton
Deadly Betrayal: The Bruce Curtis Story
The Race To Freedom: The Underground
....Railroad

McMahon, John J.
If It's Tuesday, It Still Must Be Belgium
John And Yoko: A Love Story
Mercy Or Murder?
My Father, My Son
Passions

McMahon, Joy
Eighty-Three Hours 'til Dawn

McMillian, Michael
Sound And The Silence, The

McNeely, Jerry
Sin Of Innocence

McNeil, Craig
Crossing To Freedom

McPherson, Stephen
Behind Enemy Lines

McRaney, Gerald
Blind Vengeance
Love And Curses . . . And All That Jazz
Vestige Of Honor

McTiernan, John
Robin Hood

Melcombe, Richard
Camp Cucamonga

Meledandri, Christopher
Lightning Incident, The
Love Kills

Melnick, Daniel
Get Smart Again

Melniker, Benjamin
Harmful Intent

Melniker, Charles
Without Warning: Terror In The Towers

Meltzer, Michael
Caught In The Act

Melvoin, Jeff
Intrigue

Memel, Jana Sue
Day My Parents Ran Away, The
Love Matters
Lush Life
Twelve O' One (12: 01)

Menmuir, Raymond
Fortress

Merl, Judy
Shootdown

Meron, Neil
Gypsy

Merrick, Etan
Dead Solid Perfect

Merrick, Mike
One Terrific Guy

Metzger, Alan
From The Files Of Joseph Wambaugh: A Jury
Of One

Meurer, Terry
Betrayal Of Trust
Between Love And Hate
Complex Of Fear
Guilty Until Proven Innocent
Nurses On The Line: The Crash Of Flight 7
Victim Of Love: The Shannon Mohr Story

Meyer, Irwin
Against The Wall
Price She Paid, The
Secret Passion Of Robert Clayton, The

Meyer, Patricia K.
Beyond Suspicion
Menu For Murder
Women Of Brewster Place, The

Meyers, Janet
Dangerous Heart
Indecency

Miao, Brenda
Donato And Daughter

Michaels, Joel B.
Courage

Michon, Jack
Bridge Across Time
Sins Of The Father

Mickelson, Martin
Voices Within: The Lives Of Truddi Chase

Milch, David
Capital News

Milkovich, Ed
Accidental Meeting
Danielle Steel's Fine Things
Deadly Relations
Rubdown
Secret Passion Of Robert Clayton, The
Tainted Blood
Those She Left Behind
Treacherous Crossing

Millar, Stuart
Dream Breakers
Killer Instinct
Lady In A Corner
Lady In A Corner
Vital Signs

Miller, Jennifer
Deadly Silence, A
Telling Secrets

Miller, Lee
Cry For Help: The Tracey Thurman Story, A

Miller, Marvin
Follow Your Heart
Murder In High Places
Poison Ivy
Thanksgiving Day

Miller, Stephen A.
Chameleons

Milloy, Ross
Phantom Of The Opera, The

Mills, Donna
In My Daughter's Name
My Name Is Kate
Runaway Father
World's Oldest Living Bridesmaid, The

Mills, Steve
Empty Cradle

Mimieux, Yvette
Obsessive Love

Minoff, Marvin
Incident At Dark River
Incident At Dark River
Silent Movie

Minoli, Lorenzo
Abraham

Mintz, Larry
If It's Tuesday, It Still Must Be Belgium

Mirisch, Andrew
Desperado
Desperado: Badlands Justice
Return Of Desperado, The
Steel Justice
Sweet Poison
Tagget

Mirisch, Walter
Trouble Shooters: Trapped Beneath The
....Earth

MITCHELL, JUDITH P.

Black Widow Murders: The Blanche Taylor ....Moore Story
Bloodlines: Murder In The Family
Burning Bridges
Desperate For Love
Lies Of The Heart: The Story Of Laurie ....Kellogg

MITCHELL, SCOEY

Miracle At Beekman's Place

MODER, MIKE

Operation, The

MOEN, PAUL

Stepfather I I I

MOESSINGER, DAVID

Walker, Texas Ranger

MOLONEY, MARIANNE

Pink Lightning
Third Degree Burn

MOLYNEUX, ANDREE

Railway Station Man, The

MONES, PAUL A.

My Son Johnny

MONTERASTELLI, ART

Great Pretender, The

MONTY, GLORIA

Impostor, The

MOORE, KAREN

Assault And Matrimony
Child Saver, The
Christmas Eve
Letter To Three Wives, A
Peyton Place: The Next Generation
Take My Daughters, Please

MOORE, LEANNE

American Clock, The
Cooperstown
Percy & Thunder

MOORE, THOMAS W.

Attack On Fear

MOOREHEAD, OOTY

Bonnie And Clyde: The True Story
Moment Of Truth: Cradle Of Conspiracy
Revenge Of The Nerds I V: Nerds In Love

MOOSEKIAN, VAHAN

Casualties Of Love: The Long Island Lolita ....Story
Child Lost Forever, A
Fugitive Nights: Danger In The Desert
Menendez: A Killing In Beverly Hills
Stormy Weathers
When You Remember Me

MORGAN, ANDRE

Miracle In The Wilderness

MORGAN, CHRISTOPHER

At Mother's Request
Blue Bayou

Green Dolphin Beat
Jane's House
Moving Target
Round Table, The
World's Oldest Living Bridesmaid, The

MORGAN, PETER

Final Appeal

MORITZ, NEAL

Blind Justice
Framed

MORRA, CAROL GORDON

Descending Angel

MORRILL, NORMAN

Love, Lies And Murder

MORRIS, WAYNE

Miracle In The Wilderness

MORRISON, GLORIA

Firestorm: 72 Hours In Oakland

MORROW, BARRY

Christmas On Division Street
Switched At Birth

MORSE, TERRY

Haunted By Her Past
Impostor, The
Letter To Three Wives, A
Peyton Place: The Next Generation
Stillwatch
Under Cover

MORTOFF, LAWRENCE TAYLOR-

Easy Prey
Sentimental Journey

MORTON, GARY

Sentimental Journey

MORTON, JEFFREY

Diamond Trap, The
Double Jeopardy
Mickey Spillane's Mike Hammer: Murder ....Takes All

MOSES, HARRY

Assault At West Point

MOSES, J.

Stolen Babies

MOSES, KIM

Stolen Babies

MOSKOWITZ, LAURA

Dreamer Of Oz, The

MOUNT, NICOLETTE

Son Of The Morning Star

MOUNT, THOM

Open Admissions

MULLER, FREDERICK

Barbara Taylor Bradford's Remember
Bourne Identity, The
Casualty Of War, A
Just Another Secret
Pride And Extreme Prejudice

MURAGLIA, SILVIO

Yes, Virginia, There Is A Santa Claus

MURPHY, DENNIS

Wildflower

MURPHY, MICHAEL S.

Case For Murder, A
Stephen King's Sometimes They Come Back
Taste For Killing, A

MURRAY, LEIGH

Outside Woman, The

MUTRUX, GAIL

My First Love

MYERS, KIMBERLY

Kiss To Die For, A
Midnight's Child
Taken Away

MYERS, PAUL ERIC

Shootdown

MYMAN, ROBERT M.

Born Too Soon
Daughter Of The Streets
Downpayment On Murder
Dreamer Of Oz, The
Letting Go
My Brother's Wife
Only Way Out, The
Unnatural Causes

MYROW, JEFF

Midnight's Child

NABATOFF, DIANE

Fear
Hider In The House

NANAS, HERB

Operation, The

NANUS, SUSAN

Baby Brokers
Heart Of A Child

NASATIR, MARCIA

Spider And The Fly, The
Stormy Weathers

NASSER, JOSEPH

Scattered Dreams: The Kathryn Messenger ....Story

NATHANSON, RICK

Blind Justice
Night Visions

NEDERLANDER, GLADYS

Orpheus Descending
When Will I Be Loved?

NELSON, CHRISTOPHER

Blue Deville
Cartier Affair, The

NELSON, CRAIG T.

Ride With The Wind

NELSON, JEFF

Uncle Tom's Cabin

NELSON, MARGERY
Story Lady, The

NELSON, PETER
Dark Holiday
Jonathan: The Boy Nobody Wanted
Murder By The Book

NELSON, TERRY
Broadway Bound
She Woke Up

NELSON, WILLIE
Another Pair Of Aces: Three Of A Kind
Pair Of Aces
Stagecoach

NEMEC, DENNIS
God Bless The Child
Held Hostage: The Sis And Jerry Levin Story

NEUFELD, MACE
Death In California, A
Gettysburg
Omen I V: The Awakening
White Hot: The Mysterious Murder Of
....Thelma Todd

NEUFELD, STANLEY
Deadly Matrimony
Deadly Medicine
Sinatra
Torch Song

NEUMAN, E. JACK
Voices Within: The Lives Of Truddi Chase

NEWLAND, JOHN
Arch Of Triumph
Execution, The
Timestalkers
Too Good To Be True

NEWMAN, CARROLL
Getting Up And Going Home
Killing Mind, The
Murder Of Innocence
Runaway Father
Seduction: Three Tales From The Inner
Sanctum
Stolen: One Husband
Sudie And Simpson
Untamed Love
Wildflower

NEWMAN, SALLI
Four Eyes And Six Guns
Kiss Shot

NICOLELLA, JOHN
Miami Vice

NIEMI-GORDON, VICKI
Revenge Of Al Capone, The

NIMOY, LEONARD
Never Forget

NIVEN, JR., DAVID
Night They Saved Christmas, The

NODELLA, BURT
Get Smart Again

NOLIN, MICHAEL
Live: From Death Row

NOONAN, TOM
Red Wind

NOVODOR, BILL
Combat High
Your Mother Wears Combat Boots

NOZIK, MICHAEL
Criminal Justice

NUGENT, GINNY
Cast A Deadly Spell

NUGENT, NELLE
Conspiracy Of Love
Final Verdict

NUGIEL, NELLIE
Strapped

NYSTEDT, COLLEEN
Christmas On Division Street

O'BANNNON, ROCKNE
Seaquest Dsv

O'CONNER, MATTHEW
Snowbound: The Jim And Jennifer Stolpa
....Story

O'CONNOR, JOHN
Disaster In Time

O'CONNOR, MATTHEW
And The Sea Will Tell
Beyond Obsession
Blackmail
Deadly Intentions... Again?
Sexual Advances
Substitute, The

O'CONNOR, RICHARD L.
American Geisha
Amerika
Children Of The Dark
Death In California, A
Deep Trouble
Dr. Quinn, Medicine Woman
Fall From Grace
Fatal Vision
Final Days
Lethal Exposure
My Boyfriend's Back
People Across The Lake, The
Sadie And Son
Wild Texas Wind

O'CONNOR, ROBERT
Criminal Justice
Frank Nitti: The Enforcer
In Self Defense
Intruders
Jack The Ripper
Lady Forgets, The
Shootdown
Strapped
Tricks Of The Trade

O'DONOGHUE, MICHAEL
Single Bars, Single Women

O'FALLON, JAMES
Silence Of The Heart

O'HARA, MICHAEL
Bloodlines: Murder In The Family
Heart Of A Child
Moment Of Truth: A Child Too Many
Moment Of Truth: Broken Pledges
Moment Of Truth: Cradle Of Conspiracy
Moment Of Truth: Stalking Back
Moment Of Truth: To Walk Again
Moment Of Truth: Why My Daughter?
Murder In The Heartland
She Said No
Switched At Birth

O'NEILL, JEAN
Good Night, Sweet Wife: A Murder In Boston

O'NEILL, ROBERT F.
Murder, She Wrote

OGIENS, MICHAEL
Into The Badlands
Trenchcoat In Paradise

OHLMEYER, DON
Bluffing It
Cold Sassy Tree
Crazy In Love
Crime Of Innocence
Heroes Of Desert Storm
Right To Die
Under Siege
When He's Not A Stranger

OMAN, CHAD
Love, Cheat And Steal
Sketch Artist

ORINGER, BARRY
Going To The Chapel

OSBORNE, WILLIAM
Bermuda Grace

OTTO, LINDA
Adam: His Song Continues
George Mckenna Story, The
Gregory K
In Defense Of A Married Man
Mothers' Right, A: The Elizabeth Morgan
....Story
Quiet Victory: The Charlie Wedemeyer Story
Ryan White Story, The
Unspeakable Acts

OVITZ, MARK H.
N. Y. P. D. Mounted
Snow Kill

PACE, BILL
Dying To Love You
Mother's Justice, A
Private Matter, A
River Of Rage: The Taking Of Maggie
....Keene

PACE, FRANK
Babe Ruth

PAIGE, GEORGE
This Gun For Hire

PALMER, CHRISTOPHER
Last Elephant, The

PALYO, RENEE
Rock Hudson

PANITCH, SANFORD
Past Tense

PAPAZIAN, ROBERT A.
Betty Ford Story, The
Boys, The
China Lake Murders, The
Crazy From The Heart
Deep Trouble
Drive Like Lightning
Empty Cradle
Enemy Within, The
Fatal Friendship
Fire: Trapped On The 37th Floor
For Love Or Money
Guilty Conscience
Guts And Glory: The Rise And Fall Of Oliver
....North
Hart To Hart Returns
Heart Of A Champion: The Ray Mancini Story
In The Best Interest Of The Child
Inherit The Wind
Karen Carpenter Story, The
Kate's Secret
Lethal Exposure
Line Of Fire: The Morris Dees Story
Love Among Thieves
North And South, Book 2
Once Upon A Texas Train
Rape Of Richard Beck, The
Reason To Live, A
Sweet Revenge, A
Terrorist On Trial: The United States Vs.
Salim
Willing To Kill: The Texas Cheerleader Story

PARKER, BRIAN
Sodbusters
The Race To Freedom: The Underground
....Railroad

PARKER, JUDITH
Too Good To Be True

PARKS, RICHARD
Apology
Blackout

PARRIOTT, JAMES D.
Hawaiian Heat
Island Sons
Misfits Of Science
Staying Afloat

PARSLOW, PHIL
Crossing The Mob
Father Clements Story, The
Men Don't Tell

Murder Ordained
There Was A Little Boy
Women Of Valor

PARTON, DOLLY
Wild Texas Wind

PATCHETT, TOM
Archie: To Riverdale And Back Again
Dead And Alive
Don't Touch My Daughter
Her Final Fury: Betty Broderick, The Last
....Chapter
Howard Beach: Making The Case For Murder
In The Line Of Duty: A Cop For The Killing
In The Line Of Duty: Ambush In Waco
In The Line Of Duty: Manhunt In The
....Dakotas
In The Line Of Duty: Standoff At Marion
In The Line Of Duty: Street War
In The Line Of Duty: The Price Of
....Vengeance
Lost Capone, The
Telling Secrets
Woman Scorned: The Betty Broderick Story

PATERSON, IAIN
Counterfeit Contessa, The

PATTERSON, DAVID
Barnum
Spies, Lies And Naked Thighs

PAUL, ROD
Love Lives On

PAULSON, DAN
Copacabana
Town Bully, The
Victims For Victims - The Theresa Saldana
....Story

PECK, GREGORY P
Portrait, The

PECKINPAH, DAVID
Wolf

PEERCE, LARRY
Child Of Rage

PEILMEIER, JOHN
Through The Eyes Of A Killer

PELMAN, YORAM
Intimate Stranger

PENDERGRAST, FRANK
Children In The Crossfire

PERKINS, GEORGE
Beyond Control: The Amy Fisher Story
Brand New Life: The Honeymoon
Face Of A Stranger
Kiss Of A Killer
Majority Rule
Nails
Out Of The Darkness
Stop At Nothing
Victim Of Love: The Shannon Mohr Story

PERMUT, DAVID
Breaking The Silence

Triumph Of The Heart: The Ricky Bell Story

PEROTTA, JOSETTE
Last Best Year, The

PERSKY, LESTER
Poor Little Rich Girl: The Barbara Hutton
....Story
Woman Named Jackie, A

PERSONS, JOHANNA
Deadly Game
Heroes Of Desert Storm
Missing Persons
Murderous Vision

PETERS, JON
Bay Coven
Nightmare At Bitter Creek
Toughest Man In The World, The

PETERSEN, WILLIAM
Keep The Change

PETRIE, DANIEL
Mark Twain And Me
My Name Is Bill W.
Town Torn Apart, A

PETRIE, DOROTHEA
Caroline?
Crash Landing: The Rescue Of Flight 232
Foxfire
Getting Out
Love Is Never Silent
Perfect Tribute, The
Picking Up The Pieces

PETRIE, JR., DANIEL
Waco & Rhinehart

PETRYNI, MICHAEL
Big One: The Great Los Angeles Earthquake
Return Of Eliot Ness, The

PFEIFFER, CAROLYN
Grand Isle

PHELAN, ANNA HAMILTON
Into The Homeland

PHILLIPS, CLYDE
Obsessed With A Married Woman

PHILLIPS, MICHAEL
Jane's House

PHILLIPS, STEVIE
Open Admissions

PICARD, PAUL
Killer Rules
Only One Survived

PICKARD, NIGEL
Back Home
Bejeweled

PIERCE, FREDERICK
Deadlock
Positively True Adventures Of The Alleged
Texas Cheerleader Murdering Mom, The
Substitute Wife, The
Witness To The Execution

PIERCE, KEITH
Substitute Wife, The
Witness To The Execution

PIERCE, RICHARD
Substitute Wife, The
Witness To The Execution

PIKE, BRIAN
Tonya & Nancy: The Inside Story
Triumph Over Disaster: The Hurricane
....Andrew Story

PILLSBURY, SARAH
And The Band Played On
Counterfeit Contessa, The
Seeds Of Tragedy

PINCHUK, SHELDON
Alamo: 13 Days To Glory, The
Amos
Atlanta Child Murders, The
Babes In Toyland
Black Widow Murders: The Blanche Taylor
....Moore Story
Breaking The Silence
Call Me Anna
Circle Of Violence: A Family Drama
Going To The Chapel
Hell Hath No Fury
Hoover
Keeping Secrets
Laker Girls, The
Lincoln
Marked For Murder
Murder By Night
Quicksand: No Escape
Running Against Time
She Knows Too Much
Spooner

PLAGER, JOSEPH
Baby Brokers
Moment Of Truth: Cradle Of Conspiracy
Moment Of Truth: Why My Daughter?
Shame

PLATT, POLLY
Between Two Women

PLEDGER, COURTNEY
Killing In A Small Town
Terror On Highway 91

PLITT, HENRY
Twist Of Fate

POLAIRE, HAL W.
Mussolini - The Untold Story
Stagecoach

POLAKOFF, CAROL
Held Hostage: The Sis And Jerry Levin Story
Sexual Advances

POLL, MARTIN
Arthur The King
Diana: Her True Story
Fergie And Andrew: Behind The Palace
....Doors

POLLACK, BRADFORD
Writer's Block

POLLOCK, SIDNEY
Private Matter, A

POLLOCK, SUSAN
Evergreen
Kennedys Of Massachusetts, The
Two Mrs. Grenvilles, The

POLONE, JUDITH A.
Darkness Before Dawn
Getting Up And Going Home
Going For The Gold: The Bill Johnson Story
Her Secret Life
J F K: Reckless Youth
Kiss To Die For, A
Letting Go
Malice In Wonderland
Murder Of Innocence
Secret Weapons
Time To Live, A
Untamed Love
Wildflower

POLSON, BETH
Baby Girl Scott
Go Toward The Light
Guess Who's Coming For Christmas
Message From Holly
Not My Kid
Place To Be Loved, A
Sins Of The Mother
This Child Is Mine

POLSTER, JAMES
Hart To Hart Returns

POMPIAN, PAUL
Convicted
Dangerous Passion
Danielle Steel's Daddy
Deadly Messages
Fatal Deception: Mrs. Lee Harvey Oswald
Fatal Judgment
Hearst And Davies Affair, The
Liberty
Preppie Murder, The
Shattered Spirits
Stepford Children, The
Weekend War

PONCHER, LYLE
Town Torn Apart, A

PONTI, ALEX
Aurora
Mario Puzo's The Fortunate Pilgrim

PONTI, CARLO
Mario Puzo's The Fortunate Pilgrim

POOLE, DUANE
Sunstroke
Without Warning: Terror In The Towers

POST, MARKIE
Beyond Suspicion

POWELL, ANN
Night Owl

POWELL, MARYKAY
Baja Oklahoma
Barbarians At The Gate

POWELL, NORMAN
Gunsmoke: One Man's Justice
Gunsmoke: The Long Ride Home

POWERS, STEFANIE
Beryl Markham: A Shadow On The Sun
Hart To Hart Returns

PRANGE, GREGORY
Big One: The Great Los Angeles Earthquake
French Silk
Full Exposure: The Sex Tapes Scandal
Survive The Savage Sea
Yarn Princess, The

PRATT, DEBORAH
Quantum Leap

PRESLEY, PRISCILLA BEAULIEU
Elvis And Me

PRESSMAN, MICHAEL
Man Against The Mob: The Chinatown
....Murders
Picket Fences

PREUSS, RUBEN
Deceptions

PRICE, JOHN
Bejeweled

PRICE, NOEL
Girl From Tomorrow, The

PRIDEAUX, JAMES
Laura Lansing Slept Here

PRINCIPAL, VICTORIA
Blind Witness
Don't Touch My Daughter
Midnight's Child
Naked Lie
Seduction: Three Tales From The Inner
Sanctum
Sparks: The Price Of Passion

PRITCHARD, DAVID
Comrades Of Summer

PROPPE, HANS
Blind Witness
Brotherhood Of Justice, The
Danielle Steel's Jewels
Father's Revenge, A
From The Dead Of Night
Naked Lie
Sparks: The Price Of Passion
Storm And Sorrow
When Dreams Come True
Whisper Kills, A

PUDNEY, GARY
Yes, Virginia, There Is A Santa Claus

PULLIAM, JAMES
Connecticut Yankee In King Arthur's Court, A
Polly--Comin' Home

PUSTIN, BRUCE
Case Of Deadly Force, A
Stones Of Ibarra

PUTTNAM, DAVID
Josephine Baker Story, The
Without Warning: The James Brady Story

QUARANTIELLO, CHERYL
True Blue

QUIGLELY, PAUL
Royce

RABBETT, MARTIN
Bourne Identity, The

RACKMIL, GLADYS
Intimate Strangers
Vengeance: The Story Of Tony Cimo

RADCLYFFE, SARAH
Robin Hood

RADIN, PAUL
Crime Of Innocence

RADNITZ, ROBERT B.
Never Forget
Never Forget

RAFFIN, DEBORAH
Windmills Of The Gods

RAFNER, LEE
Crash: The Mystery Of Flight 1501
Disappearance Of Nora
Manhunt For Claude Dallas
Prison For Children
With Intent To Kill

RAFSHOON, GERALD
Abraham
Atlanta Child Murders, The
Iran: Days Of Crisis
Nightmare Years, The

RAIMI, SAM
Mantis

RAINER, TRISTINE
Forbidden Nights
Secrets Of A Married Man

RANDALL, BOB
David's Mother

RANDALL, GARY
Love On The Run

RAPP, NEIL
Ride With The Wind

RAPPAPORT, MICHELE
Paper Dolls
Scandal In A Small Town

RASKIN, BONNIE
Aaron's Way
Beyond Obsession
Killer Among Friends, A

No Child Of Mine
One Woman's Courage
Warm Hearts, Cold Feet

RASKIN, LARRY
Partners 'N Love

RASKOFF, KEN
Shameful Secrets

RAUCH, MICHAEL
Devlin
Hot Paint
Red River
Wild Palms

RAVARD, SOPHIE
Notorious

RAVIN, RICHARD M.
Street Of Dreams

RAWLS, WENDELL
Her Final Fury: Betty Broderick, The Last
....Chapter
In The Line Of Duty: Ambush In Waco
Woman Scorned: The Betty Broderick Story

RAYMOND, BRUCE
Special People

RAYNOR, LYNN
Common Ground
Girl Who Came Between Them, The
Hands Of A Stranger
Kennedys Of Massachusetts, The
Love, Honor & Obey: The Last Mafia
....Marriage
On Wings Of Eagles
Quiet Killer
Stranger In My Bed
Tonya & Nancy: The Inside Story
Winner Never Quits, A

RAYNOR, MILTON T.
Arch Of Triumph
Execution, The
Timestalkers
Too Good To Be True

REA, ROBERT
Deep Trouble
Lethal Exposure
Target Of Suspicion

READY, KEVIN
Dark Reflection

RED, ERIC
Last Outlaw, The

REES, MARIAN
Decoration Day
For The Love Of Aaron
Foxfire
Home Fires Burning
Little Girl Lost
Love Is Never Silent
Miss Rose White
One More Mountain
Resting Place
Room Upstairs, The

Shell Seekers, The
Son's Promise, A

REEVE, GEOFFREY
Lie Down With Lions

REEVE, TOM
Coins In The Fountain
Souvenir

REGER, JERRY
Penthouse, The
When No One Would Listen

REHME, BOB
Gettysburg

REID, TIM
The Race To Freedom: The Underground
....Railroad

REIDY, KEVIN
Based On An Untrue Story

REINER, SUE
Eighty-Three Hours 'til Dawn

REINHARD, CLEVE
Parker Kane

REISS, DAVID
Incident At Dark River

REKANT, STUART B.
Florida Straits

RENFROW, JUNE
Baby Of The Bride

RESNICK, NOEL
Little Kidnappers, The
Not Quite Human I I
Still Not Quite Human

RETTER, JAMES
Gulag

REUTHER, STEVEN
Hider In The House

REYNOLDS, BURT
Man From Left Field
Man Upstairs, The

REYNOLDS, DON
Clarence
Sound And The Silence, The

REYNOLDS, GENE
Doing Life
Whereabouts Of Jenny, The

RHODES, MICHAEL
Captive
In The Best Interest Of The Children
We Are The Children

RICE, JOEL
Bonds Of Love

RICE, SUSAN
Opposites Attract

RICE, WAYNE
Man From Left Field

RICH, ELAINE
Danielle Steel's Kaleidoscope
Danielle Steel's Star
Dynasty: The Reunion
She Was Marked For Murder
Single Women, Married Men

RICH, JOHN
Macgyver : Lost Treasure Of Atlantis

RICH, LEE
Face Of Fear, The
French Silk
It's Nothing Personal
Killer Rules
Walton Thanksgiving Reunion, A

RICHARD, ROGER
Jessie

RICHARDSON, KEITH
Judith Krantz's Till We Meet Again
Silent Cries

RICHARDSON, LISA
Snowbound: The Jim And Jennifer Stolpa
....Story

RICHE, WENDY
Deadly Care
I Saw What You Did

RICHMOND, TONY
Florence Nightingale
Nightmare In The Daylight
Rape Of Dr. Willis, The
Sentimental Journey

RICKMAN, BETH
Empty Cradle

RINTELS, DAVID W.
Day One
Last Best Year, The
World War I I : When Lions Roared

RIPPS, HILLARY ANNE
Lush Life

RISKIN, VICTORIA
Last Best Year, The
Town Torn Apart, A
World War I I : When Lions Roared

RITCHIE, RANDY
Terror In The Night

ROACH, JAY
Lifepod

ROACH, JOHN FAUNCE
Follow Your Heart
In Broad Daylight

ROBBINS, LANCE
Black Ice
Blindfold: Acts Of Obsession
Honor Thy Father And Mother: The
....Menendez Murders
In The Shadows, Someone Is Watching
Just One Of The Girls
Revenge On The Highway
Shadow Of Obsession

ROBE, MIKE
Burden Of Proof, The
Child In The Night
Guts And Glory: The Rise And Fall Of Oliver
....North

ROBERTSON, STAN
I Spy Returns

ROBINS, DEBBIE
Challenger
Samaritan: The Mitch Snyder Story

ROBINSON, RANDY
Amelia Earhart: The Final Flight

ROE, BOB
Linda
Love Kills
Seduced By Evil
Treacherous Crossing

ROESSELL, DAVID
Running Against Time

ROESSLER, CRAIG
Devlin

ROEWE, JAY
Blind Side
Memphis
State Of Emergency

ROGERS, AMY H.
Perfect Witness

ROGERS, KENNY
Different Affair, A

ROGERS, LELAN
Kenny Rogers As The Gambler I I I: The
....Legend Continues

ROGERS, WAYNE
Perfect Witness

ROGOW, STAN
Middle Ages
Murder In High Places
Shannon's Deal

ROLSKY, ROBERT
Body Language
Dangerous Pursuit
Deception: A Mother's Secret
Duplicates
Fade To Black
Praying Mantis
Web Of Deceit
Without Warning: Terror In The Towers

ROMAN, PAUL
Ride With The Wind

RONDELL, RIC
Mom For Christmas, A

ROOS, FRED
Montana

ROSE, LEE
Deconstructing Sarah

ROSE, SUSAN
Child Lost Forever, A

ROSELL, DAVID
Murder By Night

ROSEMONT, DAVID A.
Birds I I: Land's End, The
Christmas Gift, The
Corsican Brothers, The
Fergie And Andrew: Behind The Palace
....Doors
Harmful Intent
Ironclads
Long Road Home
Shadow Of A Doubt
Tenth Man, The

ROSEMONT, NORMAN
Birds I I: Land's End, The
Camille
Christmas Gift, The
Corsican Brothers, The
Fergie And Andrew: Behind The Palace
....Doors
Harmful Intent
Ironclads
Long Road Home
Secret Garden, The
Shadow Of A Doubt
Tenth Man, The

ROSEN, BARRY
Cisco Kid, The
Easy Prey
Going For The Gold: The Bill Johnson Story
Secret Weapons
Stranger Within, The

ROSEN, ROBERT L.
Riviera

ROSENBERG, FRANK
Family Of Strangers

ROSENBERG, GRANT
Face Of Fear, The

ROSENBERG, HELENA HACKER
Aftermath: A Test Of Love
Babies
Conviction Of Kitty Dodds, The
Fear Inside, The

ROSENBERG, MARK
Citizen Cohn

ROSENBERG, MAX
Survive The Savage Sea

ROSENBERG, MICHAEL
On Thin Ice: The Tai Babilonia Story

ROSENBERG, RICK
As Summers Die
Heart Of Darkness
Heist
House Of Secrets And Lies, A
Kids Don't Tell
Last Hit, The
Lincoln

Red Earth, White Earth
Robert Kennedy And His Times

ROSENBLATT, ELLIOT
Pink Lightning

ROSENBLOOM, DALE
Nails
Ride With The Wind

ROSENBLOOM, RICHARD
For Richer, For Poorer
Love She Sought, The
Sinatra

ROSENBRUSH, BARRY
Backfield In Motion

ROSENFELD, MADELSON
Without Warning: Terror In The Towers

ROSENFELD, MIKE
Case Of The Hillside Strangler, The
Fatal Vision

ROSENFELD, STEVEN
Heart Of A Child

ROSENFELT, SCOTT
T Bone N Wessel

ROSENSTEIN, HOWARD
Runaway Father
Victim Of Love: The Shannon Mohr Story

ROSENZWEIG, BARNEY
Christy

ROSS, DIANA
Out Of The Darkness

ROSS-LEMMING, EUGENIE
Blue Deville

ROSSHEIM, PHYLLIS
For Their Own Good

ROSSI, CARL
Illicit Behavior

ROSSI, CAROL
Invasion Of Privacy

ROTH, LYNN
Babies
Chance Of A Lifetime
Chance Of A Lifetime
Just My Imagination
Portrait, The

ROTH, RON
American Harvest
Comeback, The
Fatal Image, The
Rage Of Angels: The Story Continues
Threesome

ROTHMAN, BERNARD
On Thin Ice: The Tai Babilonia Story

ROTHSCHILD, RICHARD LUKE
Fire And Rain
Hitler's Daughter

ROTHSTEIN, FREYDA
And Then There Was One

Blackout
Dangerous Affection
Descending Angel
Exclusive
Eyes Of Terror
Good Fight, The
Grave Secrets: The Legacy Of Hilltop Drive
Her Wicked Ways
Hush Little Baby
In Broad Daylight
Keeping Secrets
Last To Go, The
Love & Lies
Rockabye
Something In Common
Visions Of Murder

ROTHSTEIN, RICHARD
Bates Motel
Double Deception
Gifted One, The

ROWE, TOM
Blind Man's Bluff
Deadly Intentions... Again?
Dirty Work
Dying To Remember
Mortal Sins
Roommates
Tears And Laughter: The Joan And Mielissa
....Rivers Story
This Can't Be Love
When A Stranger Calls Back

RUBEN, ALBERT
Kojak: The Belarus File

RUBIN, BOB
Assault At West Point
Death Dreams
Elvis And The Colonel: The Untold Story
Majority Rule
Secret Sins Of The Father
Spenser: Ceremony
Spenser: Pale Kings And Princes

RUBIN, CYMA
Welcome Home, Bobby

RUBINSTEIN, RICHARD
Precious Victims
Stephen King's Golden Years
Stephen King's The Stand

RUDDY, ALBERT S.
Miracle In The Wilderness
Walker, Texas Ranger

RUDNICK, PAULA
Deadly Care
Hi Honey -- I'm Dead

RUDOLPH, LOUIS
Blood Vows: The Story Of A Mafia Wife
Deceptions
Double Standard
L B J: The Early Years
Small Sacrifices
Woman On The Ledge

RUSH, HERMAN
Miss America: Behind The Crown

RUSHTON, MATTHEW
Hot Paint
Oceans Of Fire
Pleasures
Red River
Seduced
Tower, The

RUSSELL, NEIL
Donato And Daughter

RYAN, JOHN
Family Of Strangers

SABAN, HAIM
Anything To Survive
Girl Who Came Between Them, The
Phantom Of The Opera, The
Rape Of Dr. Willis, The
Secret Life Of Ian Fleming, The

SACANI, CHRISTINE
In The Nick Of Time
Snowbound: The Jim And Jennifer Stolpa
....Story

SACKETT, NANCY
Beverly Hills Madam

SACKHEIM, WILLIAM
Somebody Has To Shoot The Picture

SAETA, STEVEN P.
Zelda

SAGER, RAY
Liar's Edge
Spenser: Ceremony
Spenser: Pale Kings And Princes

SALLAN, BRUCE J.
Babies
Challenger
Dead On The Money
French Silk
God Bless The Child
It's Nothing Personal
Killer Rules
Killing In A Small Town
Tonight's The Night
Walton Thanksgiving Reunion, A

SALOB, LORIN
Marilyn & Bobby: Her Final Affair
Woman Named Jackie, A

SALTZMAN, PAUL
Quiet Killer

SALTZMAN, PHILIP
That Secret Sunday

SALVEN, DAVID
C. A. T. Squad
C. A. T. Squad: Python Wolf

SALZER, ALBERT J.
Blind Vengeance
Doublecrossed
For Love And Glory

Love And Curses . . . And All That Jazz
Pancho Barnes
Prince Of Bel Air

SAMPLES, KEITH
Shattered Image

SAMUELS, RON
Different Affair, A

SAMUELS, STU
Celebration Family
Final Days
Lady Mobster
Marilyn & Me
Maybe Baby
Murder Of Innocence
Proud Men
Spirit, The
To Heal A Nation
Woman Who Sinned, The
Women Of Windsor

SAND, LAUREN
Railway Station Man, The

SANDER, IAN
I'll Fly Away
Original Sin
Plymouth
Stolen Babies
To Heal A Nation
Town Bully, The
When He's Not A Stranger

SANDERS, TIM
Iran: Days Of Crisis
Last Frontier, The

SANDOR, PAUL
Mrs. 'Arris Goes To Paris

SANDS, CHRISTOPHER
Bluffing It

SANFORD, MIDGE
And The Band Played On
Counterfeit Contessa, The
Seeds Of Tragedy

SANGER, JONATHAN
Love Matters
Lush Life

SANITSKY, LARRY
Act Of Vengeance
As Summers Die
Babycakes
Casanova
Dance Till Dawn
Double Edge
Fourth Story
In Sickness And In Health
Love Can Be Murder
Oldest Living Confederate Widow Tells All
Paris Trout
Richest Man In The World: The Aristotle
....Onassis Story
Rock Hudson
Surviving
To Save A Child

To Save A Child
Tommyknockers, The
Wet Gold
Yarn Princess, The

SANOFF, GERALD
Matlock: The Witness Killings

SAPHIER, PATRICIA
Zelda

SARGENT, JOSEPH
Of Pure Blood
Skylark
Somebody's Daughter

SARNOFF, THOMAS W.
Bonanza: The Return

SARONY, PAUL
Fergie And Andrew: Behind The Palace
....Doors

SATTINGER, JILL
Disaster In Time

SAUER, STEVE
Whereabouts Of Jenny, The

SAUNDERS, DAVID
Red Shoes Diaries

SAUNDERS, RON
Girl From Tomorrow, The

SAVATH, PHIL
Liar, Liar

SAVIN, BRUCE
Original Sin

SAXON, SANDRA
Presidents Child, The

SCHACHT, ROSE
Night Owl

SCHAEFER, ART
Children Of The Dark

SCHAEFER, GEORGE
Children In The Crossfire
Laura Lansing Slept Here
Man Upstairs, The
Mrs. Delafield Wants To Marry
Stone Pillow

SCHAEFFER, RICK
Rise & Walk: The Dennis Byrd Story

SCHEERER, GINA
Sitter, The

SCHEINFELD, JOHN
Intrigue

SCHENCK, GEORGE
Dying To Remember
Still Crazy Like A Fox

SCHERICK, EDGAR J.
Anything To Survive
Betrayed By Love
Evergreen
Fever
Four Eyes And Six Guns

Girl Who Came Between Them, The
Hands Of A Stranger
Hitler's S S: Portrait In Evil
Kennedys Of Massachusetts, The
On Wings Of Eagles
Passion For Justice, A: Hazel Brannon Smith
....Story
Phantom Of The Opera, The
Quiet Killer
Rape Of Dr. Willis, The
Secret Life Of Ian Fleming, The
Stepford Children, The
Stranger In My Bed
Stranger On My Land
Till Death Us Do Part
Uncle Tom's Cabin
Unholy Matrimony

SCHICKTANZ, MARJORIE
Criminal Behavior

SCHIFF, ERIC
Intruders

SCHILLER, CRAIG
Shadow Chasers

SCHILLER, LAWRENCE
Double Jeopardy
Margaret Bourke - White
Murder: By Reason Of Insanity
Peter The Great

SCHIRO, VICTOR
Day Of Reckoning

SCHMIECHEN, RICHARD
Portrait, The

SCHNEIDER, DANIEL
Broken Promises: Taking Emily Back
Haunted, The
Separated By Murder

SCHNEIDER, PAUL
Maid For Each Other

SCHNEIER, FRED
Wrong Man, The

SCHRECKINGER, JINNY
Kane And Abel

SCHREDER, CAROL
Between Two Women
Burning Bed, The
In Love And War

SCHREINER, NEVIN
Don't Talk To Strangers
Linda
Web Of Deception

SCHREYER, LINDA
House Of Secrets And Lies, A

SCHRIER, DAN
Without A Kiss Goodbye

SCHROEDER, DON
Vestige Of Honor

SCHROEDER, ROMAN
Lie Down With Lions

SCHULMAN, ARNOLD
And The Band Played On

SCHULTZ, RON
Switch, The

SCHUMACHER, JOEL
Codename: Foxfire - Slay It Again, Sam
Two Thousand Malibu Road

SCHUMAN, TOM
Gladiator, The

SCHWAM, GENE
Eyes Of Terror
Hell Hath No Fury
Her Wicked Ways
Visions Of Murder

SCHWARTZ, ALLAN B.
Lethal Exposure

SCHWARTZ, BERNARD
Elvis And Me

SCHWARTZ, DOUGLAS
Baywatch: Panic At Malibu Pier
Crime Of Innocence

SCHWARTZ, LLOYD J.
Bradys, The
Very Brady Christmas, A

SCHWARTZ, SHERWOOD
Bradys, The
Very Brady Christmas, A

SCHWARTZ, WILLIAM A.
To My Daughter

SCOTT, JANE
Danger Down Under
Tommyknockers, The

SCOTT, MICHAEL M.
Dead In The Water
Sweet Poison

SCOTT, WILLIAM P.
Ned Blessing: The True Story Of My Life

SEEGER, SUSAN
Kate's Secret

SEGALL, DON
Goddess Of Love
This Wife For Hire

SEGALL, STUART
Three On A Match

SEIDEL, ART
An Early Frost
Hot Pursuit
They

SEIGLER, BILL
Death Dreams
Elvis And The Colonel: The Untold Story

SEITER, CHRISTOPHER
Columbo: A Bird In The Hand
Columbo: Death Hits The Jackpot
Columbo: It's All In The Game
Columbo: It's All In The Game

Columbo: No Time To Die
Columbo: Undercover

SEITZ, CHRISTOPHER
Revolver

SELF, EDWIN
Against Her Will: An Incident In Baltimore
Alone In The Neon Jungle
Broken Vows
Fire Next Time, The
Incident, The
Spies, Lies And Naked Thighs
Yearling, The

SELF, WILLIAM
Sarah, Plain And Tall
Skylark
Tenth Man, The

SELLECCA, CONNIE
House Of Secrets And Lies, A

SELLECK, TOM
Revealing Evidence

SELLIER, CHUCK
Brotherhood Of The Gun
Desperado
Desperado: Badlands Justice
Longarm
Return Of Desperado, The
Vestige Of Honor

SENNET, MARK
Deliver Them From Evil: The Taking Of Alta
....View
Miracle On I-880
Switched At Birth

SERTNER, ROBERT M.
Battling For Baby
Beyond Suspicion
Big One: The Great Los Angeles Earthquake
Broken Chain
Calendar Girl, Cop Killer? The Bambi
....Bembenek Story
Celebration Family
Challenge Of A Lifetime
Combat High
Corpse Had A Familiar Face, The
Court - Martial Of Jackie Robinson, The
Danger Island
Fergie And Andrew: Behind The Palace
....Doors
Final Jeopardy, The
French Silk
Full Exposure: The Sex Tapes Scandal
Gore Vidal's Billy The Kid
Hostage Flight
I Married A Centerfold
Jackie Collins' Lady Boss
Lady Mobster
Man Against The Mob
Man Against The Mob: The Chinatown
....Murders
Maybe Baby
Menu For Murder
Obsessive Love
Opposites Attract

Queenie
Survive The Savage Sea
To Heal A Nation
Too Young To Die?
White Hot: The Mysterious Murder Of
....Thelma Todd
Woman With A Past

SEYMOUR, JANE
Passion For Justice, A: Hazel Brannon Smith
....Story
Praying Mantis
Sunstroke

SHANKS, ANN
Drop-Out Mother

SHANKS, BOB
Drop-Out Mother

SHAPIRO, ARNOLD
Good Night, Sweet Wife: A Murder In Boston

SHAPIRO, ESTHER
Blood Ties
Cracked Up
Dynasty: The Reunion
Three Kings, The
When We Were Young

SHAPIRO, MARILYN
Sister Margaret And The Saturday Night
....Ladies

SHAPIRO, MICHAEL
Line Of Fire: The Morris Dees Story

SHAPIRO, RICHARD
Blood Ties
Dynasty: The Reunion
When We Were Young

SHAPIRO, ROBERT
Summer My Father Grew Up, The

SHAPIRO, ROBERT Z.
Backfield In Motion

SHARDO, J.C.
Complex Of Fear
Stay The Night

SHAW, DAVID
Mrs. 'Arris Goes To Paris

SHAYNE, ALAN
Agatha Christie's The Man In The Brown Suit
Bourne Identity, The

SHEEN, DARRYL
Flood: Who Will Save Our Children?

SHELDON, SIDNEY
Rage Of Angels: The Story Continues
Windmills Of The Gods

SHELLEY, ANGELA
Little Girl Lost

SHEPHERD, CYBILL
Memphis
Stormy Weathers

SHEPHERD, DAVID
Child Of Rage

SHEPHERD, PETER
Candles In The Dark

SHERKOW, DANIEL A.
Donor
Elvis And The Colonel: The Untold Story

SHERMAN, GARY
After The Shock
After The Shock
Missing Persons
Murderous Vision

SHERMAN, HARRY R.
Angel In Green
Deadly Business, A
Deadly Medicine
Desperate Journey: The Allison Wilcox Story
Dream Date
Fulfillment Of Mary Gray, The
I'll Take Romance
Sentimental Journey
Stone Fox
Trial: The Price Of Passion
Victims For Victims - The Theresa Saldana ....Story
Voices Within: The Lives Of Truddi Chase

SHESLOW, STUART
Ghost Of A Chance

SHIELDS, BRENT
Getting Out

SHIRELY, LLOYD
Jack The Ripper

SHIVAS, MARK
Railway Station Man, The

SHOOP, KIMBER
Ted Kennedy, Jr., Story, The

SHOSTAK, MURRAY
Liberace: Behind The Music
Miles To Go . . .
Red Earth, White Earth

SHPETNER, STAN
City Killer

SHRAKE, BUD
Another Pair Of Aces: Three Of A Kind
Pair Of Aces

SHRYACK, DENNIS
Revenge On The Highway

SHUMAN, IRA
Day - O
To My Daughter

SHUMLATCHER, CAL
Just One Of The Girls

SIDARIS, ARLENE
Obsessed With A Married Woman

SIEGEL, RANDY
Guess Who's Coming For Christmas
Message From Holly
Place To Be Loved, A
Sins Of The Mother

SIEGEL, ROBERT
Descending Angel

SIEGLER, BILL
Assault At West Point
Majority Rule
Secret Sins Of The Father
Spenser: Pale Kings And Princes

SIEGMAN, JOSEPH
One Terrific Guy

SIGHVATSSON, JONI
Heat Wave

SIGHVATSSON, SIGURJON
Memphis

SILBERLING, ROBERT
Outback Bound

SILLIPHANT, STIRLING
Brotherhood Of The Rose
Day Of Reckoning
Mussolini - The Untold Story
Three Kings, The

SILVER, JOEL
Parker Kane

SILVERHARDT, JERALD
Born To Run

SILVERMAN, FRED
Diagnosis Of Murder
Diary Of A Perfect Murder
Fatal Confession: A Father Dowling Mystery
House On Sycamore Street, The
In The Heat Of The Night
Jake And The Fatman
Matlock: The Witness Killings
Perry Mason Mystery, A: The Case Of The Lethal
Perry Mason Mystery: The Case Of The Wicked Wives
Perry Mason Returns
Perry Mason: The Case Of The All-Star Assassin
Perry Mason: The Case Of The Avenging Ace
Perry Mason: The Case Of The Defiant Daughter
Perry Mason: The Case Of The Desperate Deception
Perry Mason: The Case Of The Fatal Fashion
Perry Mason: The Case Of The Fatal Framing
Perry Mason: The Case Of The Glass Coffin
Perry Mason: The Case Of The Heartbroken Bride
Perry Mason: The Case Of The Killer Kiss
Perry Mason: The Case Of The Lady In The Lake
Perry Mason: The Case Of The Lost Love
Perry Mason: The Case Of The Maligned Mobster
Perry Mason: The Case Of The Murdered Madam
Perry Mason: The Case Of The Musical Murders
Perry Mason: The Case Of The Notorious Nun
Perry Mason: The Case Of The Poisoned Pen

Perry Mason: The Case Of The Reckless Romeo
Perry Mason: The Case Of The Ruthless Reporter
Perry Mason: The Case Of The Scandalous Scoundrel
Perry Mason: The Case Of The Shooting Star
Perry Mason: The Case Of The Silenced Singer
Perry Mason: The Case Of The Sinister Spirit
Perry Mason: The Case Of The Skin-Deep Scandal
Perry Mason: The Case Of The Telltale Talk Show Host
She Knows Too Much
Twist Of The Knife, A

SILVERMAN, RON
Last Innocent Man, The

SILVERTON, DORIS
Jonathan: The Boy Nobody Wanted

SIMKINS, DAVID
Adventures Of Brisco County Jr., The

SIMON, DEBORAH
Rearview Mirror

SIMONS, DAVID A.
Equal Justice
Prison For Children
Silence Of The Heart

SIMPKINS, VICTOR
Dead On The Money
Final Verdict

SIMPSON, PETER
Spenser: Ceremony
Spenser: Pale Kings And Princes

SIMS, GREG H.
Firefighter
Strange Voices

SINATRA, TINA
Sinatra

SINGER, BRUCE FRANKLIN
She Stood Alone

SINGER, CARLA
Cries Unheard: The Donna Yaklich Story
Deconstructing Sarah
Entertainers, The
Forgotten Prisoners: The Amnesty File
How To Murder A Millionaire
I Still Dream Of Jeannie
Mothers Revenge, A
Murder In New Hampshire: The Pamela ....Smart Story
My Son Johnny
Our Sons
Swimsuit
Without Her Consent

SINGER, MAURICE
Last Innocent Man, The

SINGER, ROBERT
Badge Of The Assassin

Sworn To Silence
Winner Never Quits, A

SINGER, SHERI
Cast The First Stone
Guilty Of Innocence: The Lenell Geter Story
To My Daughter With Love

SKLARZ, ELLEN
Line Of Fire: The Morris Dees Story

SKODIS, ROBERT T.
Nightlife
Take, The
Trapped

SLAN, JON
Held Hostage: The Sis And Jerry Levin Story
Sherlock Holmes Returns
Stranger In The Mirror, A

SLOAN, CHUCK
Indecency

SLOAN, HOLLY
Indecency

SLOAN, MICHAEL
Bionic Showdown: The 6 Million Dollar
....Man/Bionic Woman
Return Of Sam Mccloud, The
Return Of The 6 Million Dollar Man & Bionic
....Woman
Riviera

SLOANE, ALLAN
Blue Lightning, The

SMALLWOOD, STEPHEN
Young Catherine

SMITH, APRIL
Love Lives On

SMITH, BILLY RAY
Perry Mason Mystery: The Case Of The
Wicked Wives
Perry Mason: The Case Of The Defiant
Daughter
Perry Mason: The Case Of The Fatal Fashion
Perry Mason: The Case Of The Fatal Framing
Perry Mason: The Case Of The Glass Coffin
Perry Mason: The Case Of The Heartbroken
Bride
Perry Mason: The Case Of The Killer Kiss
Perry Mason: The Case Of The Maligned
Mobster
Perry Mason: The Case Of The Reckless
Romeo
Perry Mason: The Case Of The Ruthless
Reporter
Perry Mason: The Case Of The Skin-Deep
Scandal
Perry Mason: The Case Of The Telltale Talk
Show Host

SMITH, GREG
Great Expectations

SMITH, MURRAY
Casualty Of War, A
Just Another Secret

Pride And Extreme Prejudice

SMITH, RICHARD
Apology
Blackout

SMITH, ROGER
Nobody's Children

SMITH, THOMAS G.
Ewok Adventure, The
Ewoks: The Battle For Endor

SMITHSON, JOHN
Dead Ahead: The Exxon Valdez Disaster
Tailspin: Behind The Korean Airlines Tragedy

SNELL, PETER
Crucifier Of Blood, The
Death Train
Man For All Season, A
Treasure Island

SOFRONSKI, BERNARD
Bed Of Lies
Dillinger
Fatal Deception: Mrs. Lee Harvey Oswald
Murder In Mississippi
Mussolini - The Untold Story
Napoleon And Josephine: A Love Story
Plot To Kill Hitler, The
Queen
Roots: The Gift
What Price Victory?
When You Remember Me
Whose Child Is This? The War For Baby
....Jessica

SOHMER, STEVE
Favorite Son
Settle The Score

SOKOLOW, DIANE
Casualties Of Love: The Long Island Lolita
....Story
Lady Against The Odds
Miles From Nowhere
Silent Cries
Trial: The Price Of Passion

SOKOLOW, MEL
Lady Against The Odds
Miles From Nowhere
Silent Cries
Trial: The Price Of Passion

SOLARZ, KEN
Palace Guard
Relentless: Mind Of A Killer

SOLMS, KENNY
Plaza Suite

SOLOMON, DAVID
Perry Mason: The Case Of The Defiant
Daughter
Perry Mason: The Case Of The Fatal Fashion
Perry Mason: The Case Of The Fatal Framing
Perry Mason: The Case Of The Glass Coffin
Perry Mason: The Case Of The Maligned
Mobster

Perry Mason: The Case Of The Musical
Murders
Perry Mason: The Case Of The Ruthless
Reporter
Ray Alexander: A Taste For Justice

SOMERS, SUZANNE
Exclusive
Keeping Secrets

SORIA, MIREILLE
Out On The Edge
Victim Of Love

SPEILBERG, STEVEN
Class Of '61

SPELLING, AARON
And The Band Played On
Back To The Streets Of San Francisco
Cracked Up
Crossings
Day One
Dynasty: The Reunion
Glitter
Grass Roots
Green Dolphin Beat
Harry's Hong Kong
Hollywood Wives
International Airport
Jailbirds
Jane's House
Love Boat: A Valentine Voyage, The
Love On The Run
Nightingales
Rich Men, Single Women
Round Table, The
Sexual Advances
Stranger In The Mirror, A
Terror On Track 9
Three Kings, The
Two Thousand Malibu Road

SPENCER-PHILLIPS, HUGH
Death Of The Incredible Hulk, The
Miles From Nowhere
Stranger In The Mirror, A
Trial Of The Incredible Hulk, The

SPERBER, ELAINE H.
Framed
Perfect Witness

SPERLING, MILTON
Shattered Innocence

SPIELBERG, STEVEN
Charles And Diana: Unhappily Ever After
Seaquest Dsv

SPIVEY, LOEHR
Victims For Victims - The Theresa Saldana
....Story

ST. JOHN, THANIA
Lois & Clark: The New Adventures Of
....Superman

STABLER, STEVE
Love, Cheat And Steal
Sketch Artist

STACK, TIM
What She Doesn't Know

STAFFIN KOWAL, STEFANIE
Codename: Foxfire - Slay It Again, Sam

STAFFORD, STEVEN
Chameleons

STALLONE, SYLVESTER
Heart Of A Champion: The Ray Mancini Story

STAPLETON, TERRY
Fortress

STARGER, MARTIN
Consenting Adult
Escape From Sobibor
Marcus Welby, M. D.: A Holiday Affair

STARK, RAY
Barbarians At The Gate

STEARNS, NEIL
Elvis And The Colonel: The Untold Story
Secret Sins Of The Father

STECKLER, LEN
Mercy Or Murder?

STEELE, BARBARA
War And Remembrance
War And Remembrance, Part I I

STEIGER, JOEL
Diary Of A Perfect Murder
Perry Mason Mystery, A: The Case Of The Lethal
Perry Mason Mystery: The Case Of The Wicked Wives
Perry Mason: The Case Of The Defiant Daughter
Perry Mason: The Case Of The Fatal Fashion
Perry Mason: The Case Of The Fatal Framing
Perry Mason: The Case Of The Glass Coffin
Perry Mason: The Case Of The Killer Kiss
Perry Mason: The Case Of The Poisoned Pen
Perry Mason: The Case Of The Ruthless Reporter
Perry Mason: The Case Of The Telltale Talk Show Host

STEIN, CARRIE
Betrayal Of Trust
Between Love And Hate
Complex Of Fear
Nurses On The Line: The Crash Of Flight 7

STEIN, JOAN
Crazy In Love
My Brother's Wife

STEINBERG, BARRY
Diagnosis Of Murder
House On Sycamore Street, The
Perry Mason Mystery, A: The Case Of The Lethal
Perry Mason Mystery: The Case Of The Wicked Wives
Perry Mason Returns
Perry Mason: The Case Of The Heartbroken Bride

Perry Mason: The Case Of The Lost Love
Perry Mason: The Case Of The Notorious Nun
Perry Mason: The Case Of The Reckless Romeo
Perry Mason: The Case Of The Shooting Star
Perry Mason: The Case Of The Sinister Spirit
Perry Mason: The Case Of The Skin-Deep Scandal
Twist Of The Knife, A

STEINEM, GLORIA
Better Off Dead

STEINHAUER, ROBERT BENNETT
Lies Before Kisses
Shadow Chasers

STELOFF, SKIP
Stagecoach

STELZER, PETER
Mercy Mission: The Rescue Of Flight 771
On Promised Land

STENN, DAVID
Secrets Of Lake Success

STEPP, ALAN
Willing To Kill: The Texas Cheerleader Story

STERN, JOSEPH
Into Thin Air

STERN, KANDY
Deception: A Mother's Secret
Jericho Fever

STERN, LEONARD B.
Get Smart Again

STERN, MARK
Lifepod

STERN, SANDOR
Assassin
Dangerous Pursuit
Deception: A Mother's Secret
Duplicates
Jericho Fever
Web Of Deceit

STERN, STEVEN H.
Many Happy Returns
Personals
Women Of Windsor

STEVENS, JOEL
Elvis And Me

STEVENS, JR., GEORGE
Murder Of Mary Phagan, The
Separate But Equal

STEWART, DOUGLASS
Fatal Charm

STOLFI, ROBERT
Blind Vengeance
Love And Curses . . . And All That Jazz

STONE, OLIVER
Wild Palms

STONEHOUSE, MARILYN
Forget Me Not Murders, The

STORKE, WILLIAM F.
Christmas Carol, A
Hands Of A Murderer
Last Days Of Patton, The
Old Man & The Sea, The
Special Friendship, A
Ted Kennedy, Jr., Story, The

STRANGIS, GREG
Captive
Eight Is Enough Wedding, An
Reason For Living: The Jill Ireland Story

STRANGIS, SAM
Chase
Ghost Of A Chance
He's Not Your Son
Reason For Living: The Jill Ireland Story

STRICHMAN, LARRY
Fire Next Time, The
Incident In A Small Town
Love, Honor & Obey: The Last Mafia
....Marriage

STRICK, JOSEPH
Survive The Savage Sea

STRONG, JOHN
Fatal Charm

STROTE, JOEL R.
Liberace

STROUD, MICHAEL
Scattered Dreams: The Kathryn Messenger
....Story

STUART, LAURA
Love Matters

STUART, LYNNE
Crucifier Of Blood, The

STUART, MALCOLM
Blood And Orchids
Christopher Columbus
Dallas: The Early Years
Death In California, A
Deliberate Stranger, The
Ghost Of A Chance

STUART, WILLIAM
Payoff

SUGARMAN, ANDREW
Working Trash

SULLIVAN, BETH
Dr. Quinn, Medicine Woman
Posing: Inspired By Three Real Stories

SULLIVAN, KEVIN
Lantern Hill

SUMMERS, MARC
Bring Me The Head Of Dobie Gillis

SUNGA, GEORGE
Plaza Suite

SUSSMAN, PETER
Adrift
Deadly Betrayal: The Bruce Curtis Story

Harvest For The Heart
Heads
Partners 'N Love
Sodbusters
The Race To Freedom: The Underground
....Railroad

SUTHERLAND, KIEFER
Dark Reflection

SUTTER, RANDY
Beyond Suspicion
Calendar Girl, Cop Killer? The Bambi
....Bembenek Story
Corpse Had A Familiar Face, The

SVANOE, BILL
Sparks: The Price Of Passion

SWANSON, TED
Danger Island

SWANTON, SCOTT
Finding The Way Home
Nightmare At Bitter Creek

SWERDLICK, MICHAEL
Whereabouts Of Jenny, The

SWERTLOW, FRANK
Babies

SWOPE, MEL
Dirty Dozen: The Deadly Mission
Dirty Dozen: The Fatal Mission
If It's Tuesday, It Still Must Be Belgium

SWOR, KEN
Donor
Good Night, Sweet Wife: A Murder In Boston
Gunsmoke I I I: To The Last Man
Wolf

TADROSS, MICHAEL
When Will I Be Loved?

TAHSE, MARTIN
Matters Of The Heart

TAMARKIN, BOB
White Mile

TANENBAUM, ROBERT K.
Badge Of The Assassin

TANET, RONALD
Doublecrossed
Murder Between Friends

TAPERT, ROBERT
Mantis

TARTER, FRED
Spenser: Ceremony
Spenser: Pale Kings And Princes

TASKA, ILMAR
Candles In The Dark

TATE, BETH
China Lake Murders, The

TAUB, LORI-ETTA
Breaking The Silence
Deadman's Revenge

Double Deception
Quicksand: No Escape
Running Against Time

TAVEL, CONNIE
Ride With The Wind

TAYLOR, DAVID
Traveling Man

TAYLOR, DENISE
Joshua's Heart

TAYLOR, DON
Classified Love

TAYLOR, JEFFERY
Foreign Affairs

TAYLOR, JUD
Great Escape I I: The Untold Story, The

TAYLOR, MICHAEL
Hider In The House

TAYLOR, PHILIP JOHN
I'm Dangerous Tonight

TAYLOR, RODERICK
Annihilator, The

TEETS, EDWARD
And The Band Played On
Hider In The House

TEJADA-FLORES, MIGUEL
Deceptions

TERRY, BRIDGET
Dinner At Eight
They

THEBAUT, JIM
Deadly Business, A

THOEREN, KONSTANTIN
Peter The Great

THOMAS, DAVID C.
Dying To Love You
Private Matter, A

THOMAS, DEBORAH
Psychic

THOMAS, MARLO
Leap Of Faith
Taken Away

THOMAS, SCOTT
Jesse Hawkes

THOMAS, THOM
Private Sessions

THOMASON, HARRY
London And Davis In New York

THOMPSON, DAVID
Dead Ahead: The Exxon Valdez Disaster

THOMPSON, JACK
Stagecoach

THOMPSON, JAMES E.
Do You Remember Love?

THOMPSON, LARRY
Broken Promises: Taking Emily Back
Class Cruise
Convicted
Intimate Encounters
Little White Lies
Lucy & Desi: Before The Laughter
Original Sin
Other Lover, The
Separated By Murder
White Lie
Woman He Loved, The

THOMPSON, NEVILLE
Young Catherine

THOMPSON, PETER
Ann Jillian Story, The

THOMPSON, ROBERT
Broken Vows
Love Lives On

THOMPSON, TOMMY
Seaquest Dsv

THORPE, JERRY
Aaron's Way

THREM, WAYNE
Do You Remember Love?

THURM, JOEL
Marked For Murder

TICHENOR, HAROLD
My Name Is Kate
Penthouse, The

TISCH, STEVE
Afterburn
Burning Bed, The
Evil In Clear River
In Love And War
Judgment
Keep The Change
Out On The Edge
Silence Of The Heart
Triplecross
Victim Of Love

TITLE, BARBARA
Original Sin

TO, TONY
Laurel Avenue

TODD, KIM
Harvest For The Heart
Sound And The Silence, The

TOPOLSKY, KEN
Bates Motel
Over My Dead Body

TRUETT, CECILY
Miracle Child

TRUMP, JILL
Stomin' Home

TRUSSELL, CAROL
Baby Snatcher

Web Of Deception

TRUSTMAN, ALAN
Tracker, The

TUCKER, PAUL L.
Child Of Darkness, Child Of Light
Fatal Exposure

TUDOR, MARTIN
Heads

TURMAN, LAWRENCE
Jesse
News At Eleven

TURNER, BARBARA
Eye On The Sparrow

TURTLE, JON
Perfect Bride, The

TYHURST, TYLER
Broken Promises: Taking Emily Back
Stranger In The Family, A
Yarn Princess, The

UBELL, JANE
Leona Helmsley: The Queen Of Mean

UGER, ALAN
Family Ties Vacation

URICH, ROBERT
Blind Man's Bluff
Defiant One, The

USLAN, MICHAEL
Harmful Intent

UTT, KENNETH
Intimate Strangers

VALENTE, RENEE
Around The World In 80 Days
Dangerous Affection
False Witness
False Witness
Laker Girls, The
Laker Girls, The
Man From Left Field
Man From Left Field
Man Upstairs, The
Poker Alice
Sin Of Innocence

VAN COTT, JEANNE MARIE
Secret Sins Of The Father

VASCONCELLOS, RONALDO
Prisoner Of Honor

VEITCH, JOHN
Rainbow Drive

VELEZ, EDDIE
Scattered Dreams: The Kathryn Messenger
....Story

VERES, JAMES
Hart To Hart Returns

VERNO, HELEN
In A Child's Name
Voices Within: The Lives Of Truddi Chase

VERONA, STEVE
Fatal Image, The

VICTOR, PAT A.
Killing Mind, The

VINCE, ROBERT
Black Ice
Just One Of The Girls

VINCENT, E. DUKE
And The Band Played On
Back To The Streets Of San Francisco
Day One
Grass Roots
Green Dolphin Beat
Jailbirds
Jane's House
Love On The Run
Round Table, The
Sexual Advances
Stranger In The Mirror, A
Terror On Track 9

VINER, MICHAEL
Rainbow Drive
Windmills Of The Gods

VINNEDGE, JOHN
Jake Spanner, Private Eye

VINNEDGE, SYD
Jake Spanner, Private Eye

VITALE, RUTH
Disappearance Of Christina, The

VITTES, MICHAEL
Daughters Of Privilege

VIVIANO, BETTINA
Caught In The Act

VOLPE, RAY
Caine Mutiny Court - Martial, The

VON HELMOLT, VONNIE
Black Ice

VON ZERNECK, FRANK
Battling For Baby
Beyond Suspicion
Big One: The Great Los Angeles Earthquake
Broken Chain
Calendar Girl, Cop Killer? The Bambi
....Bembenek Story
Celebration Family
Combat High
Corpse Had A Familiar Face, The
Court - Martial Of Jackie Robinson, The
Danger Island
Dress Gray
Fergie And Andrew: Behind The Palace
....Doors
Final Jeopardy, The
French Silk
Full Exposure: The Sex Tapes Scandal
Gore Vidal's Billy The Kid
Hostage Flight
I Married A Centerfold
Jackie Collins' Lady Boss

Lady Mobster
Man Against The Mob
Man Against The Mob: The Chinatown
....Murders
Maybe Baby
Menu For Murder
Obsessive Love
Opposites Attract
Proud Men
Queenie
Romance On The Orient Express
Spirit, The
Survive The Savage Sea
To Heal A Nation
Too Young To Die?
White Hot: The Mysterious Murder Of
....Thelma Todd
Woman With A Past

VREELAND, RUSSELL
Stranger In The Family, A

WADE, HARKER
Cover Up
In Like Flynn
Quantum Leap

WAGNER, ALAN
Reunion At Fairborough
Spenser: Ceremony
Spenser: Pale Kings And Princes

WAGNER, BRUCE
Wild Palms

WAGNER, CARLA JEAN
Her Secret Life

WAGNER, LINDSAY
Shattered Dreams

WAGNER, MICHAEL
Probe

WAGNER, ROBERT
Hart To Hart Returns
There Must Be A Pony

WAIGNER, PAUL
Agatha Christie's Murder In Three Acts

WALDMAN, LESLIE
Victim Of Love

WALDRON, GY
Confessions: Two Faces Of Evil

WALES, KEN
Christy

WALKER, CHET
Father Clements Story, The

WALKER, JEFFREY
Gladiator, The

WALKER, MICHAEL CHASE
Gladiator, The

WALL, HEIDI
Bonds Of Love
Prophet Of Evil: The Ervil Lebaron Story

WALLACE, RANDALL
Broken Badges
Thunderboat Row

WALLACK, KATHRYN
Armed & Innocent

WALLENSTEIN, JOSEPH
Dallas: The Early Years
Independence
Return Of Eliot Ness, The
Story Lady, The
Turn Back The Clock

WALLERSTEIN, HERB
Lady Blue

WALSH, DIANE
Always Remember I Love You
Can You Feel Me Dancing?
Fight For Jenny, A
Firestorm: 72 Hours In Oakland
Highway Heartbreaker
Jonathan: The Boy Nobody Wanted
Place For Annie, A

WALSH, RICHARD
Spoils Of War

WAMBAUGH, JOSEPH
Fugitive Nights: Danger In The Desert

WARD, ROBERT
Brotherhood Of The Gun
Green Dolphin Beat

WARE, PETER
This Gun For Hire

WATERS, ED
Jake And The Fatman

WATSON, JOHN
Lifepod

WATTS, NIGEL
Bionic Showdown: The 6 Million Dollar
....Man/Bionic Woman
Return Of Sam Mccloud, The

WAXMAN, MARK
Revolver

WEATHERS, CARL
Dangerous Passion
Defiant One, The

WEAVER, DENNIS
Return Of Sam Mccloud, The

WEAVER, RICK
Revealing Evidence

WEBB, MONICA
Perfect Bride, The

WEBB, WILLIAM
Hit List, The
Psychic

WEBER-GOLD, SUSAN
Big One: The Great Los Angeles Earthquake
Court - Martial Of Jackie Robinson, The

Man Against The Mob: The Chinatown
....Murders
Marilyn & Me
Menu For Murder
Opposites Attract
Too Young To Die?
Woman Who Sinned, The

WEIDE, BOB
Mastergate

WEINSTEIN, LISA
Fatal Exposure

WEINSTEIN, PAULA
Bejeweled
Citizen Cohn
Rose And The Jackal, The

WEINSTOCK, CHARLES
Dark Reflection

WEINTRAUB, FRED
Chips, The War Dog
My Father, My Son

WEINTRAUB, JERRY
Cowboy And The Ballerina, The

WEINTRAUB, SANDRA
Chips, The War Dog

WEISBARTH, MICHAEL
Family Of Strangers
I'm Dangerous Tonight
Running Against Time
Seduction: Three Tales From The Inner
Sanctum
Woman On The Run: The Lawrencia
....Bembenek Story

WEISBERG, RONI
Death Dreams
North Beach And Rawhide
Promised A Miracle
Sharing Richard

WEISS, DORI
Chrome Soldiers
Lightning Incident, The
Long Hot Summer, The
Snow Kill

WEISS, FREDDA
Third Degree Burn

WEISSMAN, BENJAMIN A.
Burden Of Proof, The

WEITHORN, MICHAEL J.
Family Ties Vacation

WEITZ, BARRY
Blackmail
Bride In Black, The
Dead Reckoning
Lady From Yesterday, The
Ladykillers
Marilyn & Bobby: Her Final Affair
Memories Of Murder
Mortal Sins
Secret Life Of Kathy Mccormick, The
Target Of Suspicion

WEITZ, JULIE ANNE
Battling For Baby
Court - Martial Of Jackie Robinson, The
Survive The Savage Sea
Too Young To Die?
White Hot: The Mysterious Murder Of
....Thelma Todd
Woman With A Past

WELKER, CHRISTY
Armed & Innocent
Child Of Rage
Posing: Inspired By Three Real Stories

WELLS, JOHN
Nightman, The

WELLS, LLEWELLYN
Roadracers

WELSH, RICHARD
Blind Spot
Breathing Lessons
Getting Out
To Dance With The White Dog

WENDKOS, PAUL
Chase, The

WERNER, PETER
Middle Ages

WERNER, TOM
Single Bars, Single Women

WEST, ALICE
Picket Fences

WESTMAN, JAMES
Heart Of Darkness

WESTON, ANN
Always Remember I Love You
Billionaire Boys Club
Children Of Times Square
Deep Dark Secrets
Firestorm: 72 Hours In Oakland
Highway Heartbreaker
I Love You Perfect
Jonathan: The Boy Nobody Wanted
Love And Betrayal
Place For Annie, A

WESTON, JAY
Laguna Heat

WHITCOMB, CYNTHIA
Guilty Until Proven Innocent
Search For Grace

WHITE, JEFFREY
Nobody's Children

WHITE, LARRY
Leona Helmsley: The Queen Of Mean
Twist Of Fate

WHITE, PAUL
Disaster In Time

WHITE, STEVE
Amityville: The Evil Escapes
And Then She Was Gone

Chase, The
Day - O
Double Your Pleasure
Joshua's Heart
Jury Duty: The Comedy
Locked Up: A Mother's Rage
Miracle Child
Mom For Christmas, A
Murderous Affair, A: The Carolyn Warmus
....Story
Penthouse, The
Rose And The Jackal, The
Shameful Secrets
She Said No
She Stood Alone
To My Daughter With Love
What Ever Happened To Baby Jane?

WHITEHEAD, FRED
Good Cops, Bad Cops
Murder C. O. D.
Sweet Bird Of Youth

WHITLEY, PATRICK
Hostage For A Day

WHITTAKER, SUSAN
Fire: Trapped On The 37th Floor

WICKES, DAVID
Frankenstein
Jack The Ripper
Jekyll & Hyde

WIDEN, GREGORY
Weekend War

WIESENFELD, SUZANNE
Napoleon And Josephine: A Love Story

WIGOR, BRADLEY
Crash Landing: The Rescue Of Flight 232
With Murder In Mind

WIGUTOW, DAN
Black Magic
Blind Faith
Dead In The Water
Fatal Vision
Honor Thy Mother
In A Child's Name
In The Best Of Families: Marriage, Pride And
....Madness
Judgment
Lady Killer
Nightlife
Take, The
Vestige Of Honor

WILDER, JOHN
Norman Rockwell's Breaking Home Ties
Return To Lonesome Dove
Spenser: For Hire

WILLIAMS, CAROL
Silent Cries

WILLIAMS, JOBETH
Bump In The Night

WILLIAMS, SITA
Hostages

WILLIAMS, SUSAN
Woman With A Past

WILLIAMS, TREAT
Bonds Of Love

WILSON, IRV
Bridge Across Time
Children Of Times Square
Crash Course
Fight For Life
Into Thin Air
Samaritan: The Mitch Snyder Story
Toughlove

WILSON, SARAH
Bermuda Grace

WINANT, ETHEL
Time To Triumph, A
World War I I : When Lions Roared

WINANT, SCOTT
Hoover

WINCHESTER, MARGO
Brotherhood Of Justice, The

WINER, HARRY
J F K: Reckless Youth
Taking Back My Life: The Nancy
....Ziegenmeyer Story

WINFREY, OPRAH
Overexposed
Women Of Brewster Place, The

WINGER, CARL
She Says She's Innocent

WINKLER, HENRY
Macgyver : Lost Treasure Of Atlantis
Nobody's Children
Scandal Sheet

WINTER, RALPH
Plymouth

WISENFELD, SUZANNE
Mistral's Daughter

WITT, DAN
Killing In A Small Town
Telling Secrets
Terror On Highway 91

WITTLIFF, BILL
Lonesome Dove
Ned Blessing: The Story Of My Life And
....Times
Ned Blessing: The True Story Of My Life

WIZAN, JOE
El Diablo
Perfect Harmony
Silent Witness

WOHLEBEN, GARY
Bonanza: The Return

WOLF, DICK
Nasty Boys
South Beach

WOLF, GORDON
Are You Lonesome Tonight?
Lady Killer
Writer's Block

WOLFF, PATTI
Life In The Theater, A

WOLLERT, DAVE
Quicksand: No Escape
Spooner

WOLPER, DAVID L.
Bed Of Lies
Betty Ford Story, The
Dillinger
Fatal Deception: Mrs. Lee Harvey Oswald
Flood: Who Will Save Our Children?
Murder In Mississippi
Napoleon And Josephine: A Love Story
North And South
North And South, Book 2
North And South, Book 3: Heaven And Hell
Plot To Kill Hitler, The
Queen
Roots: The Gift
What Price Victory?
When You Remember Me

WOLPER, MARK M.
Betty Ford Story, The
Dillinger
Murder In Mississippi
North And South, Book 3: Heaven And Hell
Queen
Roots: The Gift
What Price Victory?

WOLTERSTORFF, ROBERT
Street Hawk

WOODHEAD, LESLIE
Dead Ahead: The Exxon Valdez Disaster
Tailspin: Behind The Korean Airlines Tragedy
Tragedy Of Flight 103: The Inside Story, The

WORTH, MARVIN
Running Mates

WOUK, JOSEPH
Caine Mutiny Court - Martial, The

WRIGHT, NORTON
Haunted By Her Past
Sadie And Son

WRIGHT, ROSALYN
Murder In New Hampshire: The Pamela
....Smart Story

WRIGHT, THOMAS J.
Chrome Soldiers
Deadly Game

WRYE, DONALD
Amerika
Broken Promises: Taking Emily Back
Lucky Day
Right To Kill?
Separated By Murder
Stranger In The Family, A

Ultimate Betrayal

WYATT, MONICA
South Beach

WYLLY, SR., PHILLIPS
Man Against The Mob
Second Chances

WYNN, TRACY KEENAN
Carolina Skeletons

YANG, AIDA
John And Yoko: A Love Story

YARROW, MARY BETH
Seasons Of The Heart

YATES, WILLIAM
Back To The Streets Of San Francisco

YAVNEH, CYRUS
Another Pair Of Aces: Three Of A Kind
Baby Of The Bride
Christmas In Connecticut
Eye On The Sparrow
King Of Love, The
Pair Of Aces
Son Of The Morning Star
When The Time Comes
Woman Who Loved Elvis, The

YELLEN, LINDA
Chantilly Lace
Liberace: Behind The Music
Parallel Lives
Second Serve
Sweet Bird Of Youth

YERKOVICH, ANTHONY
Miami Vice

YOUNG, AIDA
Children In The Crossfire
Hitler's S S: Portrait In Evil
To Be The Best

YOUNG, CATHLEEN
Place For Annie, A
Time To Heal, A

YOUNG, DALENE
I Love You Perfect

YOUNG, JOHN SACRET
China Beach
Promise To Keep, A
Rio Shanon
Under Cover

YOUNG, RHONDA
Heart Of A Champion: The Ray Mancini Story

YOUNG, S. HARRY
Clarence

YOUNG, SALLY
Deconstructing Sarah

YOUNG, WILLIAM L.
Detective In The House

ZACHARIAS, STEVE
Revenge Of The Nerds I V: Nerds In Love
Revenge Of The Nerds: The Next Generation

Thanksgiving Day

ZACHARY, BOHDAN
Haunted, The

ZADAN, CRAIG
Gypsy

ZALOOM, GEORGE
Psycho I V: The Beginning

ZANETOS, DEAN
Hawaiian Heat
Misfits Of Science

ZAVADA, ERVIN
Christopher Columbus
Class Cruise
Club Med
Convicted: A Mother's Story
Dreamer Of Oz, The
Letting Go
Long Journey Home, The
Midnight Hour, The
Switched At Birth
Sworn To Silence
Toughlove

ZIMMER, PETER
Broken Vows

ZINBERG, MICHAEL
For The Very First Time

ZINNEMANN, TIM
Lies Of The Twins

ZISK, RANDY
For The Very First Time

ZITO, STEPHEN
Full Exposure: The Sex Tapes Scandal

ZLOTOFF, LEE DAVID
Frank Nitti: The Enforcer
Plymouth
Waco & Rhinehart

ZUKERMAN, BERNARD
Conspiracy Of Silence
Love And Hate: A Marriage Made In Hell

ZWICK, EDWARD
Extreme Close-Up

Section I

CAST

Cross-referenced by
Produced Credits

AAMES, WILLIE
Eight Is Enough: A Family Reunion
Eight Is Enough Wedding, An

AARON, CAROLINE
Dead And Alive

AARON, JOHN
I'll Fly Away

ABBOTT, BRUCE
Dillinger
Johnny Ryan
Out Of Time
Trapped

ABERCROMBIE, IAN
Kicks

ABRAHAM, F.MURRAY
Dream West
Season Of Giants, A

ABRAMS, MICHELE
Nightmare In Columbia County

ACHESON, JAMES
Body Language

ACKLAND, JOSS
Jekyll & Hyde
Secret Life Of Ian Fleming, The

ACKROYD, DAVID
Fear Inside, The
Hell Hath No Fury
Nutcracker: Money, Madness And Murder
Picking Up The Pieces
Poor Little Rich Girl: The Barbara Hutton
....Story
Round Table, The
Stop At Nothing
Windmills Of The Gods

ACOVONE, JAY
Born To Run
Quicksand: No Escape

ADAIR, DEBORAH
Rich Men, Single Women

ADAIR, MARK
Sherlock Holmes Returns

ADAMS, BROOKE
Bridesmaids
Lace I I
Last Hit, The
Lion Of Africa, The
Special People
Stephen King's Sometimes They Come Back

ADAMS, DON
Get Smart Again

ADAMS, MASON
Night They Saved Christmas, The
Passions
Perry Mason: The Case Of The Maligned
Mobster
Rage Of Angels: The Story Continues
Under Siege

ADAMS, MAUD
Blacke's Magic
Nairobi Affair
Perry Mason Mystery: The Case Of The
Wicked Wives

ADDABBO, ANTHONY
Love On The Run

AEDMA, ALAR
Sadie And Son

AFFLECK, BEN
Danielle Steel's Daddy

AHMED, KHADIJA ALI
We Are The Children

AIELLO, DANNY
Alone In The Neon Jungle
Lady Blue
Preppie Murder, The

AKIN, PHIL
Sadie And Son

AKINS, CLAUDE
If It's Tuesday, It Still Must Be Belgium
Manhunt For Claude Dallas
Mothers, Daughters And Lovers

AKIYAMA, DENIS
Ghost Mom

ALBERT, EDDIE
Burning Rage
Dress Gray
In Like Flynn
Mercy Or Murder?
Return To Green Acres

ALBERT, JR., EDWARD
Body Language

ALDA, ALAN
And The Band Played On
White Mile

ALDREDGE, TOM
O Pioneers

ALEANDRO, NORMA
Dark Holiday

ALEXANDER, JACE
When We Were Young

ALEXANDER, JANE
Blood And Orchids
Daughter Of The Streets
In Love And War
Malice In Wonderland
Open Admissions
Stay The Night

ALEXANDER, JASON
Rockabye

ALFONSO, KRISTIAN
Blindfold: Acts Of Obsession

ALICE, MARY
Laurel Avenue
Women Of Brewster Place, The

ALLAM, ROGER
Investigation: Inside A Terrorist Bombing

ALLAN, JED
Her Wicked Ways

ALLEN, BYRON
Case Closed

ALLEN, CHAD
Dr. Quinn, Medicine Woman
Murder In New Hampshire: The Pamela
....Smart Story
Praying Mantis

ALLEN, JOAN
Without Warning: The James Brady Story

ALLEN, JONELLE
Penalty Phase

ALLEN, KAREN
Challenger
Secret Weapon
Voyage

ALLEN, NANCY
Gladiator, The
Memories Of Murder

ALLEN, PATRICK
Roman Holiday

ALLEN, RODD
Storm And Sorrow

ALLEN, SHEILA
Alice In Wonderland

ALLEN, TANYA
Spenser: Ceremony

ALLEN, TODD
Pancho Barnes

ALLEN, ZACHARY M.
Kids Like These

ALLEY, KIRSTIE
Bunny's Tale, A
David's Mother
Infidelity
North And South
North And South, Book 2
Prince Of Bel Air

ALLPORT, CHRISTOPHER
China Beach
David

ALMGREN, SUSAN
Deadly Surveillance

ALONSO, MARIA CONCHITA
Macshayne: The Final Roll Of The Dice
Teamster Boss: The Jackie Presser Story

ALVARADO, ANGELA
Daughters Of Privilege
Shadowhunter

ALVARADO, TRINI
Frank Nitti: The Enforcer

ALZADO, LYLE
Mickey Spillane's Mike Hammer: Murder
....Takes All

AMECHE, DON
Pals

AMELIO, LINDSEY
Adam: His Song Continues

AMICK, MADCHEN
For The Very First Time
I'm Dangerous Tonight
Love, Cheat And Steal

AMSTERDAM, MOREY
Side By Side

ANCONINA, RICHARD
Fall From Grace

ANDERSEN, DANA
Under The Influence

ANDERSON, BARBARA
Return Of Ironside, The

ANDERSON, BRIDGETTE
Summer To Remember, A

ANDERSON, DARYL
People Across The Lake, The

ANDERSON, DION
Cry In The Wild: The Taking Of Peggy Ann

ANDERSON, ERICH
Love Kills

ANDERSON, HARRY
Spies, Lies And Naked Thighs

ANDERSON, JOHN
American Harvest
Danielle Steel's Daddy
Dream West

ANDERSON, KEVIN
Orpheus Descending
Wrong Man, The

ANDERSON, LONI
Coins In The Fountain
Letter To Three Wives, A
Necessity
Price She Paid, The
Sorry, Wrong Number
Stranded
Too Good To Be True
Whisper Kills, A
White Hot: The Mysterious Murder Of
....Thelma Todd

ANDERSON, MELODY
Beverly Hills Madam
Deep Dark Secrets
Final Notice
Hitler's Daughter
Marilyn & Bobby: Her Final Affair

ANDERSON, MITCHELL
Back To Hannibal: The Return Of Tom
Sawyer And Huck Finn
Comeback, The

Karen Carpenter Story, The

ANDERSON, RICHARD
Bionic Showdown: The 6 Million Dollar
....Man/Bionic Woman
Cover Up
Perry Mason Returns
Return Of The 6 Million Dollar Man & Bionic
....Woman
Stepford Children, The

ANDERSON, RICHARD DEAN
In The Eyes Of A Stranger
Macgyver : Lost Treasure Of Atlantis
Through The Eyes Of A Killer

ANDRESS, URSULA
Man Against The Mob: The Chinatown
....Murders

ANDREWS, ANTHONY
Bluegrass
Danielle Steel's Jewels
Hands Of A Murderer
Woman He Loved, The

ANDREWS, DAVID
Son's Promise, A
Wild Horses

ANDREWS, JULIE
Our Sons

ANGELOU, MAYA
There Are No Children Here

ANHOLT, CHRISTEN
One Against The Wind

ANHOLT, CHRISTIEN
Charles And Diana: Unhappily Ever After

ANHOLT, CRISTIEN
Class Of '61

ANN-MARGRET,
Nobody's Children
Our Sons
Queen
Two Mrs. Grenvilles, The

ANSPACH, SUSAN
Space

ANT, ADAM
Out Of Time

ANTHONY, LYSETTE
Target Of Suspicion

ANTONIO, JIM
Mayflower Madam
Rearview Mirror

AQUINO, AMY
Danielle Steel's Once In A Lifetime

ARAU, ALFONSO
Stones Of Ibarra

ARCHER, ANNE
Different Affair, A
Jane's House
Last Of His Tribe, The
Leap Of Faith

Nails

ARIT, LEWIS
Littlest Victims

ARKIN, ADAM
Babies
Heat Wave
Promise To Keep, A

ARKIN, ALAN
Cooperstown
Deadly Business, A
Doomsday Gun
Escape From Sobibor
Taking The Heat

ARMSTRONG, CURTIS
Hi Honey -- I'm Dead
Revenge Of The Nerds I V: Nerds In Love
Revenge Of The Nerds: The Next Generation

ARMSTRONG, KERRY
Dadah Is Death

ARMSTRONG, R. G.
L B J: The Early Years

ARNAZ, LUCIE
Who Gets The Friends?

ARNESS, JAMES
Alamo: 13 Days To Glory, The
Gunsmoke I I I: To The Last Man
Gunsmoke: One Man's Justice
Gunsmoke: Return To Dodge
Gunsmoke: The Last Apache
Gunsmoke: The Long Ride Home
Red River

ARNETTE, JENETTA
Sister Margaret And The Saturday Night
....Ladies

ARNOLD, ROSEANNE
Backfield In Motion
Woman Who Loved Elvis, The

ARNOLD, TOM
Backfield In Motion
Woman Who Loved Elvis, The

ARQUETTE, DAVID
Roadracers

ARQUETTE, PATRICIA
Betrayed By Love
Daddy
Wildflower

ARQUETTE, ROSANNA
In The Deep Woods
Promised A Miracle
Son Of The Morning Star
Sweet Revenge
Wrong Man, The

ARTHUR, BEATRICE
My First Love

ARTHUR, REBECA
Opposites Attract

ASHBROOK, DANA
Bonnie And Clyde: The True Story
Desperate Journey: The Allison Wilcox Story

ASHBROOK, DAPHNE
Carly's Web
Daughters Of Privilege
Intruders
Longarm
Rock Hudson
That Secret Sunday

ASHBY, LINDEN
Perfect Bride, The

ASHERSON, RENEE
Romance On The Orient Express

ASHLEY, ELIZABETH
He's Fired, She's Hired
In The Best Interest Of The Children
Love And Curses . . . And All That Jazz
Reason For Living: The Jill Ireland Story
Stagecoach
Warm Hearts, Cold Feet

ASHTON, JOHN
Death In California, A
Dirty Work
I Know My First Name Is Steven
Tommyknockers, The

ASNER, EDWARD
Cracked Up
Cruel Doubt
Good Cops, Bad Cops
Gypsy
Heads
Kate's Secret
Not A Penny More, Not A Penny Less
Silent Movie
Switched At Birth
Vital Signs
Yes, Virginia, There Is A Santa Claus

ASSANTE, ARMAND
Blind Justice
Deadly Business, A
Evergreen
Fever
Hands Of A Stranger
Jack The Ripper
Napoleon And Josephine: A Love Story
Passion And Paradise
Rage Of Angels: The Story Continues
Stranger In My Bed

ASTIN, JOHN
Adventures Of Brisco County Jr., The

ASTIN, MACKENZIE
Facts Of Life Down Under, The

ATHERTON, WILLIAM
Buried Alive
Chrome Soldiers
Intrigue

ATKINS, CHRISTOPHER
Fatal Charm

ATLAS, LARRY
Brass

AUBERJONOIS, RENE
Connecticut Yankee In King Arthur's Court, A
Longarm
Ned Blessing: The True Story Of My Life
Wild Card

AUMONT, JEAN PIERRE
Windmills Of The Gods

AUMONT, JEAN-PIERRE
Sins

AUSTIN, KAREN
Assassin
Casey's Gift: For Love Of A Child
Laura Lansing Slept Here

AUSTIN, TERI
Johnny Ryan

AUTRY, ALAN
Destination: America
Intruders

AVALOS, LUIS
Ned Blessing: The Story Of My Life And
....Times
Ned Blessing: The True Story Of My Life

AVERY, JAMES
Full Exposure: The Sex Tapes Scandal
Timestalkers
Without Warning: Terror In The Towers

AVERY, MARGARET
Heat Wave

AXTON, HOYT
Buried Alive
Christmas Comes To Willow Creek
Dallas: The Early Years

BABCOCK, BARBARA
Family For Joe, A
Fugitive Nights: Danger In The Desert
News At Eleven

BACALL, LAUREN
Dinner At Eight
Portrait, The

BACH, JOHN
Sound And The Silence, The

BADLER, JANE
Highwayman, The

BAGGETTA, VINCENT
Carly's Web
Doubletake

BAILEY, BILL
Casualty Of War, A

BAILEY, G.W.
Bed Of Lies
Dead Before Dawn
Doublecrossed
Gifted One, The
Held Hostage: The Sis And Jerry Levin Story
Mother's Justice, A

No Child Of Mine
Winner Never Quits, A

BAILEY, JANET
The Race To Freedom: The Underground
....Railroad

BAIO, SCOTT
Alice In Wonderland

BAIRSTOW, SCOTT
There Was A Little Boy

BAKER, CARROLL
On Fire

BAKER, JAY
Storm And Sorrow

BAKER, JOE DON
Abduction Of Kari Swenson, The
Citizen Cohn
Complex Of Fear

BAKER, KATHY
Image, The
Lush Life
Nobody's Child
One Special Victory
Picket Fences

BAKER, RAY
Her Final Fury: Betty Broderick, The Last
....Chapter
Nobody's Child
She Said No

BAKKE, BRENDA
Ned Blessing: The Story Of My Life And
....Times

BAKO, BRIGITTE
Red Shoes Diaries

BAKULA, SCOTT
In The Shadow Of A Killer
Mercy Mission: The Rescue Of Flight 771
Quantum Leap

BALASKI, BELINDA
Proud Men

BALDWIN, ADAM
Deadbolt
Murder In High Places
Poison Ivy

BALDWIN, ALEC
Alamo: 13 Days To Glory, The
Dress Gray
Love On The Run
Sweet Revenge, A

BALDWIN, DANIEL
Attack Of The 50ft. Woman
Heroes Of Desert Storm
Ned Blessing: The True Story Of My Life

BALDWIN, WILLIAM
Preppie Murder, The

BALE, CHRISTIAN
Treasure Island

BALK, FAIRUZA
Murder In The Heartland
Shame

BALL, LUCILLE
Stone Pillow

BALLANTINE, CARL
Blacke's Magic

BALLOU, MARK
Survive The Savage Sea

BALSAM, MARTIN
Child Saver, The
Queenie
Second Serve

BALSAM, TALIA
Sins Of The Mother

BALTZ, KIRK
Marla Hanson Story, The

BANCROFT, ANNE
Broadway Bound
Oldest Living Confederate Widow Tells All

BANCROFT, CAMERON
Just One Of The Girls
Moment Of Truth: To Walk Again

BANERJEE, VICTOR
Dadah Is Death

BANES, LISA
Family Torn Apart, A
Revenge On The Highway

BANKS, JONATHAN
Blind Side
Don't Touch My Daughter
Downpayment On Murder
Shadow Of Obsession
Who Is Julia?

BANNEN, IAN
Perry Mason: The Case Of The Desperate
Deception

BANNON, JACK
Diary Of A Perfect Murder

BARANSKI, CHRISTINE
To Dance With The White Dog

BARBEAU, ADRIENNE
Blood River
Bridge Across Time
Doublecrossed

BARKIN, ELLEN
Act Of Vengeance
Clinton And Nadine

BARNES, CHRISTOPHER DANIEL
Frankenstein: The College Years
Murder Without Motive: The Edmund Perry
....Story

BARNES, PRISCILLA
Perfect People
Perry Mason: The Case Of The Reckless
Romeo

Stepfather I I I

BARNES, SUSAN
Sitter, The

BARRIE, BARBARA
Execution, The
Guess Who's Coming For Christmas
My Breast
My First Love
Odd Couple, The
Vital Signs
Winnie

BARRY, GENE
Gambler Returns: The Luck Of The Draw
Perry Mason: The Case Of The Lost Love

BARRY, NEILL
Reason For Living: The Jill Ireland Story

BARRY, PATRICIA
Evergreen

BARRYMORE, DREW
Babes In Toyland
Beyond Control: The Amy Fisher Story
Conspiracy Of Love
Sketch Artist
Two Thousand Malibu Road

BARTLETT, BONNIE
Big One: The Great Los Angeles Earthquake
Deadly Deception
Donato And Daughter
Right To Die
Victim Of Love: The Shannon Mohr Story

BASARABA, GARY
In The Line Of Duty: Manhunt In The
....Dakotas

BASSETT, ANGELA
Heroes Of Desert Storm
Jacksons: An American Dream , The
Locked Up: A Mother's Rage

BATEMAN, JASON
Bates Motel
Can You Feel Me Dancing?
Confessions: Two Faces Of Evil
Crossing The Mob
Moving Target
Taste For Killing, A
This Can't Be Love

BATEMAN, JUSTINE
Can You Feel Me Dancing?
Deadbolt
Family Ties Vacation
Fatal Image, The
In The Eyes Of A Stranger
Right To Kill?
Terror In The Night

BATES, ALAN
Pack Of Lies

BATES, KATHY
Hostages
Johnny Bull

BATINKOFF, RANDALL
Christy
Stepford Children, The

BAUCHAU, PATRICK
And The Band Played On
Blood Ties
Day Of Reckoning

BAUER, BELINDA
Case For Murder, A
Starcrossed
Tonight's The Night

BAUER, STEVEN
Drive Like Lightning
Drug Wars: The Camarena Story
False Arrest
Sweet Poison
Sword Of Gideon

BAXTER, DEREK
Man From Left Field

BAXTER , MEREDITH
Bump In The Night
Burning Bridges
Darkness Before Dawn
Family Ties Vacation
For The Love Of Aaron
Her Final Fury: Betty Broderick, The Last
....Chapter
Kate's Secret
Kissing Place, The
Long Journey Home, The
Mother's Justice, A
My Breast
One More Mountain
Rape Of Richard Beck, The
She Knows Too Much
Winnie
Woman Scorned: The Betty Broderick Story

BAYER, GARY
Go Toward The Light
Not My Kid

BEACH, MICHAEL
Hit List, The
Open Admissions

BEACHAM, STEPHANIE
Danielle Steel's Secrets
Foreign Affairs
Napoleon And Josephine: A Love Story
Seaquest Dsv
To Be The Best

BEALS, JENNIFER
Indecency
Night Owl
Two Thousand Malibu Road

BEASLY, ALICE
Moonlighting

BEATTY, NED
Alfred Hitchcock Presents
Hostage Flight
Murder, She Wrote
Robert Kennedy And His Times

T Bone N Wessel
Tragedy Of Flight 103: The Inside Story, The
Trial: The Price Of Passion

BECK, JOHN
Fire And Rain
Perry Mason: The Case Of The Lady In The Lake
Trade Winds

BECK, MICHAEL
Deadly Game
Fade To Black
Houston: The Legend Of Texas
Only One Survived
Rearview Mirror
Stranger At My Door

BECK, NOELLE
Love On The Run

BECKEL, GRAHAM
Family Of Spies
Jane's House
Murder Of Innocence

BECKER, HARTMUT
Escape From Sobibor

BEDELIA, BONNIE
Alex: The Life Of A Child
Fire Next Time, The
Lady From Yesterday, The
Mothers' Right, A: The Elizabeth Morgan ....Story
Somebody Has To Shoot The Picture
Switched At Birth
When The Time Comes

BEDFORD, BRIAN
Last Best Year, The

BEDNARSKI, ANDREW
Family Sins

BEECROFT, DAVID
Counterfeit Contessa, The

BEGHE, JASON
Operation, The

BEGLEY, JR., ED
Big One: The Great Los Angeles Earthquake
Celebration Family
Chance Of A Lifetime
Columbo: Undercover
Exclusive
In The Best Interest Of The Child
Mastergate
Not A Penny More, Not A Penny Less
Roman Holiday
Running Mates
Spies, Lies And Naked Thighs
World War I I : When Lions Roared

BEHRENS, SAM
Shadow Of Obsession

BELACK, DORIS
Hearst And Davies Affair, The

BELAFONTE, SHARI
French Silk

Kate's Secret
Midnight Hour, The

BELL, CHRISTOPHER
Sarah, Plain And Tall
Skylark

BELL, ERIC
Nightmare In The Daylight

BELLER, KATHLEEN
Deadly Messages

BELLWOOD, PAMELA
Deep Dark Secrets
Double Standard

BELTRAN, ROBERT
Stormy Weathers

BELUSHI, JAMES
Parallel Lives
Royce
Wild Palms

BENARD, MAURICE
Lucy & Desi: Before The Laughter

BENEDICT, DIRK
Trenchcoat In Paradise

BENEDICT, PAUL
Babycakes

BENING, ANNETTE
Hostage

BENJAMIN, PAUL
Stranger Waits, A

BENNETT, FRAN
Nightingales

BENSON, RAY
Wild Texas Wind

BENSON, ROBBY
California Girls
Invasion Of Privacy
Precious Victims

BENZALI, DANIEL
Pack Of Lies

BERENGER, TOM
Gettysburg
If Tomorrow Comes

BERENSON, MARISA
Notorious
Sins

BERG, PETER
Case For Murder, A
Rise & Walk: The Dennis Byrd Story

BERGEN, CANDICE
Arthur The King
Hollywood Wives
Mayflower Madam
Murder: By Reason Of Insanity

BERGEN, POLLY
Addicted To His Love
Leave Of Absence
Lightning Incident, The

My Brother's Wife
Perry Mason: The Case Of The Skin-Deep Scandal
She Was Marked For Murder
War And Remembrance

BERGHOF, HERBERT
Kojak: The Belarus File

BERGIN, PATRICK
Frankenstein
Robin Hood
They

BERGMAN, SANDAHL
Revenge On The Highway

BERGMANN, MARY
Chameleons

BERKELEY, XANDER
Donato And Daughter

BERKOFF, STEVEN
Season Of Giants, A

BERLE, MILTON
Side By Side

BERLINGER, WARREN
What Price Victory?

BERNARD, CRYSTAL
Chameleons
Lady Against The Odds
Miracle Child
When Will I Be Loved?

BERNSEN, CORBIN
Beyond Suspicion
Breaking Point
Dead On The Money
Grass Roots
I Know My Son Is Alive
L. A. Law
Line Of Fire: The Morris Dees Story
Love Can Be Murder

BERON, DAVID
Honor Thy Father And Mother: The ....Menendez Murders

BERRY, HALLE
Queen

BERTINELLI, VALERIE
I'll Take Manhattan
In A Child's Name
Murder Of Innocence
Pancho Barnes
Rockabye
Shattered Vows
Silent Witness
Taken Away
What She Doesn't Know

BESCH, BIBI
Doing Time On Maple Drive
Mrs. Delafield Wants To Marry

BETHUNE, ZINA
Nutcracker: Money, Madness And Murder

BEVERLY, TRAZANA
Sister Margaret And The Saturday Night
....Ladies

BEYMER, RICHARD
Danger Island
Generation

BIEHN, MICHAEL
Deadly Intentions
Strapped
Taste For Killing, A

BIERKO, CRAIG
Danielle Steel's Star

BIGGS, ROXANN
Dirty Work
Mortal Sins
N. Y. P. D. Mounted
Round Table, The

BILL, TONY
Killing Mind, The

BILLINGSLEY, BARBARA
Bay Coven
Bay Coven
Going To The Chapel

BILLINGSLEY, PETER
Carly's Web

BINION, REID
Night Of The Hunter

BIRNEY, DAVID
Always Remember I Love You
Glitter
Keeping Secrets
Long Journey Home, The
Love And Betrayal

BISHOP, ED
Going For The Gold: The Bill Johnson Story

BISHOP, PATRICK
Women Of Valor

BISSET, JACQUELINE
Anna Karenina
Choices
Forbidden
Leave Of Absence
Napoleon And Josephine: A Love Story

BIXBY, BILL
Death Of The Incredible Hulk, The
Diagnosis Of Murder
Incredible Hulk Returns, The
Sin Of Innocence
Trial Of The Incredible Hulk, The

BLACKBURN, BARBARA
Dark Shadows

BLADES, RUBEN
Crazy From The Heart
Josephine Baker Story, The
Miracle On I-880

BLAIR, LINDA
Calendar Girl, Cop Killer? The Bambi
....Bembenek Story
Perry Mason: The Case Of The Heartbroken
Bride

BLAKE, AMANDA
Gunsmoke: Return To Dodge

BLAKE, GEOFFREY
Fatal Exposure
One Terrific Guy

BLAKE, NOAH
Last P. O. W? The Bobby Garwood Story

BLAKE, ROBERT
Father Of Hell Town
Heart Of A Champion: The Ray Mancini Story
Judgment Day: The John List Story

BLAKELY, SUSAN
Against Her Will: An Incident In Baltimore
Annihilator, The
April Morning
Blackmail
Blood And Orchids
Broken Angel
Dead Reckoning
Fatal Confession: A Father Dowling Mystery
Honor Thy Father And Mother: The
....Menendez Murders
Incident, The
Intruders
Ladykillers
Murder Times Seven
No Child Of Mine
Ted Kennedy, Jr., Story, The
Wildflower

BLANC, JENNIFER
Pink Lightning

BLANCARD, JARRED
Living A Lie

BLANKFIELD, MARK
Jury Duty: The Comedy

BLEDSOE, TEMPESTT
Dream Date

BLESSED, BRIAN
Macgyver : Lost Treasure Of Atlantis

BLESSING, JACK
Marla Hanson Story, The
Miss America: Behind The Crown
Strange Voices
Working Trash

BLOCK, HUNT
Secret Weapons
She Was Marked For Murder

BLOCKER, DIRK
One Special Victory

BLOOM, BRIAN
Brotherhood Of The Gun
Crash Course
Dance Till Dawn

Desperate For Love
Keys, The
Two Thousand Malibu Road

BLOOM, CLAIRE
Anastasia: The Mystery Of Anna
Barbara Taylor Bradford's Remember
Beryl Markham: A Shadow On The Sun
Ellis Island
Florence Nightingale
It's Nothing Personal
Lady And The Highwayman, The
Liberty
Queenie

BLOOM, LINDSAY
Mickey Spillane's Mike Hammer: Murder
....Takes All

BLOOM, SCOTT
Keys, The

BLOUNT, LISA
American Story, An
Annihilator, The
In Sickness And In Health
Murder Between Friends
Stormin' Home
Unholy Matrimony

BLUM, MARK
Capital News
Condition: Critical

BOATMAN, MICHAEL
China Beach
House Of Secrets
In The Line Of Duty: Street War

BOBBY, ANNE MARIE
Children Of The Bride

BOCHNER, HART
And The Sea Will Tell
Complex Of Fear
Sun Also Rises, The
War And Remembrance
War And Remembrance, Part I I

BOGOSIAN, ERIC
Caine Mutiny Court - Martial, The
Last Flight Out

BOHM, KATHARINA
Of Pure Blood

BOHRER, CORINNE
Revenge Of The Nerds I V: Nerds In Love

BOLENDER, BILL
Fatal Deception: Mrs. Lee Harvey Oswald

BOLOGNA, JOSEPH
Citizen Cohn
Danger Of Love, The
Prime Target
Rags To Riches
Revenge Of The Nerds I V: Nerds In Love
Time To Triumph, A

BOLTON, CHRISTOPHER
I Still Dream Of Jeannie

BONERZ, PETER
Circle Of Violence: A Family Drama

BONOY, CHRISTOPHER
Deadly Surveillance

BONSALL, BRIAN
Angel Of Death
Do You Know The Muffin Man?

BOOTHE, POWERS
By Dawn's Early Light
Family Of Spies
Into The Homeland
Marked For Murder
Web Of Deception
Wild Card

BORGNINE, ERNEST
Appearances
Dirty Dozen: The Deadly Mission
Dirty Dozen: The Fatal Mission
Jake Spanner, Private Eye

BORRIE, ALEXANDRA
Ladykillers

BOSCO, PHILIP
Murder In Black And White
Return Of Eliot Ness, The

BOSLEY, TOM
Fatal Confession: A Father Dowling Mystery
Perry Mason: The Case Of The Notorious Nun

BOSSON, BARBARA
Hostage Flight
Jury Duty: The Comedy

BOSTWICK, BARRY
Addicted To His Love
Betrayed By Innocence
Between Love And Hate
Body Of Evidence
Captive
Challenger
Danielle Steel's Once In A Lifetime
Deceptions
George Washington I I: The Forging Of A
....Nation
I'll Take Manhattan
Pleasures
Praying Mantis
War And Remembrance

BOTTOMS, BENJAMIN
Island Sons

BOTTOMS, JOSEPH
Island Sons
Liar's Edge
Treacherous Crossing

BOTTOMS, SAMUEL
Island Sons

BOTTOMS, TIMOTHY
Island Sons
Perry Mason: The Case Of The Notorious Nun

BOUTISKARIS, DENNIS
Yarn Princess, The

BOUTSIKARIS, DENNIS
And Then There Was One
Thunderboat Row

BOWEN, CHRISTOPHER
Shell Seekers, The

BOWEN, MICHAEL
Bonnie And Clyde: The True Story
Ryan White Story, The

BOWER, TOM
Love, Lies And Murder
Promised A Miracle

BOWLES, PETER
Beryl Markham: A Shadow On The Sun

BOXLEITNER, BRUCE
Angel In Green
Double Jeopardy
From The Dead Of Night
Gunsmoke: One Man's Justice
House Of Secrets
Judith Krantz's Till We Meet Again
Kenny Rogers As The Gambler I I I: The
....Legend Continues
Murderous Vision
Red River
Road Raiders, The
Secret, The
Town Bully, The

BOYD, GUY
Dr. Quinn, Medicine Woman
Ewok Adventure, The
Firefighter
Fugitive Among Us

BOYER, KATY
Trapped

BOYLE, LARA FLYNN
Past Tense
Terror On Highway 91

BOYLE, PETER
Echoes In The Darkness
Guts And Glory: The Rise And Fall Of Oliver
....North
In The Line Of Duty: Street War
Royce
Tragedy Of Flight 103: The Inside Story, The

BRACCO, LORRAINE
Getting Gotti

BRADLEY, JOHN
Secrets Of Lake Success

BRAGA, SONIA
Last Prostitute, The
Man Who Broke 1,000 Chains, The

BRANDMEIER, JONATHON
Thanksgiving Day

BRANDON, MICHAEL
Deadly Messages
Dynasty: The Reunion
Not In My Family

BRATT, BENJAMIN
Nasty Boys
Shadowhunter

BRAUGHER, ANDRE
Charles And Diana: Unhappily Ever After
Class Of '61
Court - Martial Of Jackie Robinson, The
Somebody Has To Shoot The Picture
Without Warning: Terror In The Towers

BRAY, THOM
Lady Mobster

BRAZZI, ROSSANO
Christopher Columbus

BRECK, PETER
Sworn To Vengeance

BRENNAN, EILEEN
Blood Vows: The Story Of A Mafia Wife
Deadly Intentions... Again?
Going To The Chapel
Poisoned By Love: The Kern County Murders

BRENNER, DORI
Obsessed With A Married Woman

BRETT, JEREMY
Florence Nightingale

BREWTON, MAIA
Family For Joe, A

BRIDGES, BEAU
Elvis And The Colonel: The Untold Story
Everybody's Baby: The Rescue Of Jessica
....Mcclure
Guess Who's Coming For Christmas
Just Another Secret
Outrage
Positively True Adventures Of The Alleged
Texas Cheerleader Murdering Mom, The
Secret Sins Of The Father
Space
Wildflower
Without Warning: The James Brady Story

BRIDGES, LLOYD
Capital News
Cross Of Fire
Devlin
Dress Gray
In The Nick Of Time
Leona Helmsley: The Queen Of Mean
Paper Dolls
Secret Sins Of The Father
She Was Marked For Murder

BRILL, STEVEN
Dead Silence

BRIMLEY, WILFORD
Act Of Vengeance
Blood River
Ewoks: The Battle For Endor
Gore Vidal's Billy The Kid
Thompson's Last Run

BRITTANY, MORGAN
Glitter

L B J: The Early Years
Perry Mason: The Case Of The Scandalous
Scoundrel

BROCKSMITH, ROY
Steel Justice

BRODERICK, BETH
Are You Lonesome Tonight?

BRODERICK, MATTHEW
Life In The Theater, A

BROLIN, JAMES
And The Sea Will Tell
Beverly Hills Cowgirl Blues
Deep Dark Secrets
Finish Line
Gunsmoke: The Long Ride Home
Intimate Encounters
Nightmare On The Thirteenth Floor
Parallel Lives
Visions Of Murder

BROLIN, JOSH
Finish Line
Prison For Children

BRON, ELEANOR
Intrigue

BRONSON, CHARLES
Act Of Vengeance
Donato And Daughter
Sea Wolf, The
Yes, Virginia, There Is A Santa Claus

BROOK, JAYNE
In The Best Of Families: Marriage, Pride And
....Madness

BROOKS, AVERY
Roots: The Gift
Spenser: Ceremony
Spenser: For Hire
Spenser: Pale Kings And Princes
Uncle Tom's Cabin

BROOKS, HILDY
One Terrific Guy

BROOKS, JACQUELINE
Starcrossed

BROOKS, JAY
Laurel Avenue

BROOKS, JOEL
Are You Lonesome Tonight?
Stranded

BROSNAN, PIERCE
Around The World In 80 Days
Broken Chain
Death Train
Don't Talk To Strangers
Heist
James Clavell's Noble House
Murder 101
Remington Steele: The Steele That Wouldn't
....Die
Victim Of Love

BROWN, BLAIR
Bad Seed, The
Day My Parents Ran Away, The
Hands Of A Stranger
Majority Rule
Moment Of Truth: To Walk Again
Rio Shanon
Space
Those Secrets

BROWN, BRYAN
Dead In The Water
Devlin
Last Hit, The

BROWN, CLANCY
Bloodlines: Murder In The Family
Cast A Deadly Spell
Desperate Rescue: The Cathy Mahone Story
Johnny Ryan
Love, Lies And Murder

BROWN, GEORG STANFORD
Alone In The Neon Jungle
North And South

BROWN, JIM
Lady Blue

BROWN, THOMAS WILSON
Evil In Clear River
Family Sins

BROWNE, ROSCOE LEE
Lady In A Corner
Stuck With Each Other

BRUCE, COLIN
Gotham

BRUCE, ED
Last Days Of Frank And Jesse James, The
Separated By Murder

BRUNS, PHILIP
Betrayed By Innocence

BRYCE, SCOTT
Visions Of Murder

BRYCHTA, EDITA
Fergie And Andrew: Behind The Palace
....Doors

BUCHHOLZ, HORST
Crossings

BUCHHOLZ, ZACH
Crossings

BUCKLEY, BETTY
Babycakes
Betrayal Of Trust
Roses Are For The Rich
Three Wishes Of Billy Grier, The

BUCKLEY, MARY JANE
Kennedys Of Massachusetts, The

BUJOLD, GENEVIEVE
Red Earth, White Earth

BUKTENICA, RAY
Heart Of A Champion: The Ray Mancini Story

BULL, RICHARD
Little House On The Prairie - Bless All The
....Dear Children

BULL, SANDY
Line Of Fire: The Morris Dees Story
Stolen: One Husband

BULLOCK, SANDRA
Bionic Showdown: The 6 Million Dollar
....Man/Bionic Woman

BUMATAI, RAY
Miss America: Behind The Crown

BUNDY, BROOKE
News At Eleven
Two Fathers' Justice

BURGI, RICHARD
Chameleons

BURKE, CHRIS
Jonathan: The Boy Nobody Wanted

BURKE, DELTA
Day - O
Love And Curses . . . And All That Jazz
Where The Hell's That Gold

BURNETT, CAROL
Fresno
Hostage
Plaza Suite
Seasons Of The Heart

BURNETTE, OLIVIA
Final Verdict

BURNS, JANIS LEE
Club Med

BURNS, JERE
Turn Back The Clock

BURR, RAYMOND
Perry Mason Returns
Perry Mason: The Case Of The All-Star
Assassin
Perry Mason: The Case Of The Avenging Ace
Perry Mason: The Case Of The Defiant
Daughter
Perry Mason: The Case Of The Desperate
Deception
Perry Mason: The Case Of The Fatal Fashion
Perry Mason: The Case Of The Fatal Framing
Perry Mason: The Case Of The Glass Coffin
Perry Mason: The Case Of The Heartbroken
Bride
Perry Mason: The Case Of The Killer Kiss
Perry Mason: The Case Of The Lady In The
Lake
Perry Mason: The Case Of The Lost Love
Perry Mason: The Case Of The Maligned
Mobster
Perry Mason: The Case Of The Murdered
Madam
Perry Mason: The Case Of The Musical
Murders
Perry Mason: The Case Of The Notorious Nun
Perry Mason: The Case Of The Poisoned Pen

Perry Mason: The Case Of The Reckless Romeo
Perry Mason: The Case Of The Ruthless Reporter
Perry Mason: The Case Of The Scandalous Scoundrel
Perry Mason: The Case Of The Shooting Star
Perry Mason: The Case Of The Silenced Singer
Perry Mason: The Case Of The Sinister Spirit
Perry Mason: The Case Of The Skin-Deep Scandal
Perry Mason: The Case Of The Telltale Talk Show Host
Return Of Ironside, The

BURRELL, MARYEDITH
Bad Attitudes

BURSTYN, ELLEN
Act Of Vengeance
Getting Out
Into Thin Air
Mrs. Lambert Remembers Love
Pack Of Lies
Something In Common
Surviving
When You Remember Me

BURTON, KATE
Ellis Island
Love Matters

BURTON, LEVAR
Firestorm: 72 Hours In Oakland
Liberty
Midnight Hour, The
Roots: The Gift
Special Friendship, A

BURTON, MATTHEW
Dirty Dozen: The Fatal Mission

BURTON, TONY
Heart Of A Champion: The Ray Mancini Story

BUSEY, GARY
Chrome Soldiers
Hider In The House
Wild Texas Wind

BUSFIELD, TIMOTHY
Calendar Girl, Cop Killer? The Bambi ....Bembenek Story
Fade To Black
Murder Between Friends
Strays

BUSH, GRAND L.
Angel Of Death

BUSH, REBECCAH
Secrets Of Lake Success

BUSIA, AKOSUA
George Mckenna Story, The
Special Friendship, A

BUTLER, DEAN
Little House On The Prairie - Bless All The ....Dear Children

BUTLER, YANCY
Hit List, The
South Beach

BUTTONS, RED
Alice In Wonderland
Reunion At Fairborough

BUTTRAM, PAT
Return To Green Acres

BUXTON, SARAH
Pink Lightning

BYRD, TOM
Wet Gold

BYRNE, GABRIEL
Christopher Columbus
Mussolini - The Untold Story

BYRNE, MARTHA
He's Fired, She's Hired
Pink Lightning

CADELL, SIMON
Pride And Extreme Prejudice

CAESAR, SID
Alice In Wonderland
Side By Side

CAFFREY, STEPHEN
Columbo Goes To College
Diagnosis Of Murder
House On Sycamore Street, The
Murder Of Innocence

CAIN, DEAN
Lois & Clark: The New Adventures Of ....Superman

CAINE, MICHAEL
Jack The Ripper
Jekyll & Hyde
World War I I : When Lions Roared

CALABRO, THOMAS
Columbo: No Time To Die

CALLARD, REBECCA
Borrowers, The

CALLOWAY, VANESSA BELL
Stompin' At The Savoy

CALVIN, JOHN
Boris And Natasha

CAMERON, CANDACE
I Saw What You Did

CAMERON, JANE
Pair Of Aces

CAMERON, KIRK
Little Piece Of Heaven, A

CAMP, COLLEEN
Addicted To His Love
Backfield In Motion

CAMP, HAMILTON
Bridesmaids

CAMPANELLA, JOSEPH
Terror On Track 9

CAMPBELL, ALAN
Jake And The Fatman

CAMPBELL, BRUCE
Adventures Of Brisco County Jr., The

CAMPBELL, NEVE
I Know My Son Is Alive

CAMPBELL, NICHOLAS
Children Of The Night

CAMPBELL, TISHA
Rags To Riches

CAMPBELL, TORQUIL
Lena: My 100 Children

CANNON, DYAN
Arthur The King
Based On An Untrue Story
Christmas In Connecticut
Jailbirds

CANNON, J.D.
Return Of Sam Mccloud, The

CAPALDI, PETER
John And Yoko: A Love Story

CAPSHAW, KATE
Her Secret Life
Internal Affairs
Quick And The Dead, The

CAREY, CLARE
Obsessed

CARHART, TIMOTHY
Call Me Anna
In A Child's Name

CARIOU, LEN
Killer In The Mirror
Love On The Run
Miracle On I-880
Surviving
Witness To The Execution

CARLIN, GEORGE
Working Trash

CARLIN, GLORIA
So Proudly We Hail

CARLIN, JOE
Eye On The Sparrow

CARLSON, KAREN
Brotherly Love

CARMEN, JULIE
Drug Wars: The Cocaine Cartel
Finding The Way Home
Neon Empire
Seduced By Evil

CARNEY, ART
Izzy And Moe
Night They Saved Christmas, The
Where Pigeons Go To Die

CARONE, ANTONI
Murder 101

CARR, HAYLEY
Back Home

CARR, JANE
Class Cruise

CARRADINE, DAVID
Bad Seed, The
Brotherhood Of The Gun
Cover Girl And The Cop, The
Deadly Surveillance
I Saw What You Did
North And South
North And South, Book 2
Oceans Of Fire
Six Against The Rock

CARRADINE, KEITH
Blackout
Eye On The Sparrow
In The Best Of Families: Marriage, Pride And
....Madness
Judgment
Murder Ordained
My Father, My Son
Payoff
Revenge Of Al Capone, The
Scorned And Swindled
Stones Of Ibarra
Winner Never Quits, A

CARRADINE, ROBERT
Clarence
Disappearance Of Christina, The
Doublecrossed
I Saw What You Did
Incident, The
Monte Carlo
Revenge Of The Nerds I V: Nerds In Love
Revenge Of The Nerds: The Next Generation
Somebody Has To Shoot The Picture
Sun Also Rises, The

CARREY, JAMES
Doing Time On Maple Drive

CARRIER, COREY
Bump In The Night
Young Indiana Jones Chronicles: The Curse
....Of The Jackal

CARROLL, DIAHANN
From The Dead Of Night
Murder In Black And White

CARROLL, HELENA
Man Upstairs, The

CARROLL, JANET
Bluffing It
Sharing Richard

CARROLL, JESSICA RENE
Sentimental Journey

CARRY, JULIUS
Adventures Of Brisco County Jr., The

CARTER, ALICE
Dangerous Heart

CARTER, DIXIE
Perry Mason Mystery, A: The Case Of The
Lethal

CARTER, FINN
Revealing Evidence

CARTER, HELENA BONHAM
Fatal Deception: Mrs. Lee Harvey Oswald

CARTER, LYNDA
Danielle Steel's Daddy
Mickey Spillane's Mike Hammer: Murder
....Takes All
Posing: Inspired By Three Real Stories
Stillwatch

CARTER, NELL
Maid For Each Other

CARTER, TERRY
Return Of Sam Mccloud, The

CARTWRIGHT, NANCY
Not My Kid

CARTWRIGHT, VERONICA
Dead In The Water
Desperate For Love
Hitler's Daughter
Intimate Encounters
Robert Kennedy And His Times
Son's Promise, A

CARUSO, DAVID
Judgment Day: The John List Story

CARVER, BRENT
Love And Hate: A Marriage Made In Hell
Spies, Lies And Naked Thighs

CASH, JOHNNY
Baron And The Kid, The
Last Days Of Frank And Jesse James, The
Stagecoach

CASH, JUNE CARTER
Last Days Of Frank And Jesse James, The

CASNOFF, PHILIP
North And South
North And South, Book 2
North And South, Book 3: Heaven And Hell
Red Spider, The
Red Wind
Sinatra

CASSEL, JEAN-PIERRE
Fatal Image, The
Notorious

CASSIDY, JOANNA
Barbarians At The Gate
Children Of Times Square
Codename: Foxfire - Slay It Again, Sam
Father's Revenge, A
Hollywood Wives
Live: From Death Row
Nightmare At Bitter Creek
Pleasures

Taking Back My Life: The Nancy
....Ziegenmeyer Story
Tommyknockers, The
Wheels Of Terror

CASSIDY, PATRICK
Follow Your Heart
Hitler's Daughter
Napoleon And Josephine: A Love Story
Something In Common
Three On A Match

CASSIDY, SHAUN
Once Upon A Texas Train
Roots: The Gift

CASTELLANETA, DAN
Lady Against The Odds

CATERET, ANNA
Shell Seekers, The

CATES, PHOEBE
Lace I I

CATON, JULIETTE
Season Of Giants, A

CATTRALL, KIM
Miracle In The Wilderness

CAZENOVE, CHRISTOPHER
Lace I I
Lady And The Highwayman, The
Souvenir
To Be The Best
Windmills Of The Gods

CERVANTES, CARLOS
Wheels Of Terror

CERVERA, JR., JORGE
Brotherhood Of The Gun
Stones Of Ibarra

CHAMBERLAIN, RICHARD
Aftermath: A Test Of Love
Bourne Identity, The
Casanova
Dream West
Night Of The Hunter
Ordeal In The Arctic
Wallenberg: A Hero's Story

CHAMBERS, DIEGO
Conspiracy Of Silence

CHAN, MELISSA
Girl Who Came Between Them, The

CHANDLER, KYLE
Homefront
North And South, Book 3: Heaven And Hell

CHANNING, STOCKARD
David's Mother
Echoes In The Darkness
Not My Kid
Perfect Witness
Room Upstairs, The

CHAO, ROSALIND
Last Flight Out
Shooter

Web Of Deception

CHAPA, DAMIAN
Menendez: A Killing In Beverly Hills

CHAPLIN, GERALDINE
Corsican Brothers, The
Duel Of Hearts

CHAPMAN, LANEI
Secrets Of Lake Success

CHAPMAN, MARK LINDSAY
Annihilator, The

CHARBONNEAU, PATRICIA
Desperado: Badlands Justice
Disaster At Silo 7

CHARDIET, JON
Sister Margaret And The Saturday Night
....Ladies

CHARISSE, CYD
Swimsuit

CHARLES, JOSH
Cooperstown

CHARLESON, IAN
Sun Also Rises, The

CHARLESON, LESLIE
Woman On The Ledge

CHARNEY, JORDAN
Crime Of Innocence
Do You Remember Love?

CHARTOFF, MELANIE
Kenny Rogers As The Gambler I I I: The
....Legend Continues

CHEN, JOAN
Deadlock
Twin Peaks

CHESTNUT, MORRIS
Ernest Green Story, The

CHILES, LOIS
Burning Bridges

CHONG, RAE DAWN
Curiosity Kills
Father & Son: Dangerous Relations

CHRISTIAN, CLAUDIA
Columbo: It's All In The Game
Houston: The Legend Of Texas
Relentless: Mind Of A Killer
Strays

CHRISTIE, JULIE
Dadah Is Death
Railway Station Man, The

CHRISTMAS, ERIC
Staying Afloat

CHRISTOPHER, DENNIS
Willing To Kill: The Texas Cheerleader Story

CHURCH, THOMAS HADEN
Fugitive Nights: Danger In The Desert

CICCONE, SANDRA
Special People

CIOFFI, CHARLES
Peter Gunn

CLAIRE, CYRIELLE
Hot Paint

CLAPP, GORDON
Small Sacrifices

CLARK, BLAKE
Grave Secrets: The Legacy Of Hilltop Drive

CLARK, BRYAN
Without Warning: The James Brady Story

CLARK, CANDY
Popeye Doyle
Price She Paid, The

CLARK, CHRISTIE
Danielle Steel's Changes

CLARK, EUGENE
Johnny Ryan
Trial And Error

CLARK, MATT
Blind Witness
Kenny Rogers As The Gambler I I I: The
....Legend Continues
Love, Mary
Out Of The Darkness
Seduction In Travis County
Terror On Highway 91

CLARK, SUSAN
Snowbound: The Jim And Jennifer Stolpa
....Story
Tonya & Nancy: The Inside Story

CLARKE, ANDREW
Outback Bound

CLARKE, BRIAN PATRICK
Eight Is Enough: A Family Reunion

CLARKE, CAITLIN
Mayflower Madam

CLARKE, PATRICK JAMES
Sexual Advances

CLARKSON, PATRICIA
Blind Man's Bluff
Caught In The Act
Four Eyes And Six Guns

CLAY, JUANING
Our Family Honor

CLAY, NICHOLAS
Corsican Brothers, The

CLAYBURGH, JILL
Fear Stalk
Firestorm: 72 Hours In Oakland
Honor Thy Father And Mother: The
....Menendez Murders
Miles To Go . . .
Reason For Living: The Jill Ireland Story
Trial: The Price Of Passion

Unspeakable Acts
Who Gets The Friends?

CLEMENSON, CHRISTIAN
Capital News

CLENNON, DAVID
Black Widow Murders: The Blanche Taylor
....Moore Story
Nurses On The Line: The Crash Of Flight 7

CLOONEY, GEORGE
Sunset Beat
Without Warning: Terror In The Towers

CLOONEY, ROSEMARY
Sister Margaret And The Saturday Night
....Ladies

CLOSE, GLENN
Sarah, Plain And Tall
Skylark
Stones Of Ibarra

COATES, KIM
Dead Before Dawn

COBBS, BILL
Decoration Day

COBURN, JAMES
Crash Landing: The Rescue Of Flight 232
Hit List, The
Mastergate
Ray Alexander: A Taste For Justice
Sins Of The Father

COCO, JAMES
Stepford Children, The
There Must Be A Pony

COE, GEORGE
Shootdown

COFFIN, FREDERICK
Crash: The Mystery Of Flight 1501
Deliberate Stranger, The
Secret Sins Of The Father

COHN, MINDY
Facts Of Life Down Under, The

COLBERT, CLAUDETTE
Two Mrs. Grenvilles, The

COLE, GARY
Echoes In The Darkness
Fall From Grace
Fatal Vision
Old Man & The Sea, The
Son Of The Morning Star
Switch, The
Those She Left Behind
Time To Heal, A
Vital Signs
When Love Kills: The Seduction Of John
....Hearn

COLE, OLIVIA
Women Of Brewster Place, The

COLEMAN, DABNEY
Baby M
Columbo And The Murder Of A Rock Star

Fresno
Guilty Of Innocence: The Lenell Geter Story
Maybe Baby
Murrow
Never Forget
Plaza Suite
Sworn To Silence

COLEMAN, GARY
Playing With Fire

COLEMAN, JACK
Bridesmaids
Children Of The Bride
Daughter Of Darkness
Return Of Eliot Ness, The
Rubdown

COLIN, MARGARET
Good Night, Sweet Wife: A Murder In Boston
Return Of Sherlock Holmes, The
Traveling Man
Warm Hearts, Cold Feet

COLLET, CHRISTOPHER
Right To Kill?

COLLEY, KENNETH
Wallenberg: A Hero's Story

COLLINS, GARY
Danielle Steel's Secrets

COLLINS, JOAN
Cartier Affair, The
Dynasty: The Reunion
Monte Carlo
Sins

COLLINS, LEWIS
Jack The Ripper

COLLINS, LISA
Web Of Deception

COLLINS, STEPHEN
Barbara Taylor Bradford's Remember
Disappearance Of Nora
Threesome
Two Mrs. Grenvilles, The
Weekend War
Woman Named Jackie, A
Woman Scorned: The Betty Broderick Story

COMER, ANJANETTE
Perry Mason: The Case Of The Reckless Romeo

CONNELLY, JENNIFER
Heart Of Justice, The

CONNERY, JASON
Secret Life Of Ian Fleming, The

CONNORS, CHUCK
Once Upon A Texas Train

CONNORS, MIKE
Hart To Hart Returns

CONRAD, CHRISTIAN
Charley Hannah
High Mountain Rangers
Jesse Hawkes

CONRAD, ROBERT
Anything To Survive
Assassin
Charley Hannah
Fifth Missile, The
Glory Days
High Mountain Rangers
Jesse Hawkes
Mario And The Mob
One Police Plaza
Search And Rescue
Sworn To Vengeance
Two Fathers' Justice
Two Fathers: Justice For The Innocent

CONRAD, SHANE
Charley Hannah
Glory Days
High Mountain Rangers
Jesse Hawkes

CONRAD, WILLIAM
In Like Flynn
Jake And The Fatman
Vengeance: The Story Of Tony Cimo

CONROY, KEVIN
Face Of Fear, The
Hi Honey -- I'm Dead
Secret Passion Of Robert Clayton, The

CONSTANTINE, MICHAEL
Leap Of Faith

CONTI, TOM
Fatal Judgment
Lily
Nazi Hunter: The Beate Klarsfeld Story
Quick And The Dead, The
Roman Holiday
Voices Within: The Lives Of Truddi Chase

CONVERSE, FRANK
Alone In The Neon Jungle

CONVERSE, WILLIAM
Confessions: Two Faces Of Evil
Stone Pillow

CONWAY, JR., TIM
Plaza Suite

CONWAY, KEVIN
Attack On Fear
Breaking The Silence
Jesse

COOPER, CHRIS
Bed Of Lies
In Broad Daylight
Ned Blessing: The True Story Of My Life
One More Mountain

COOPER, JEANNE
Beyond Suspicion

COOPER, MAGGIE
Jesse Hawkes

COPLEY, TERI
I Married A Centerfold
In The Line Of Duty: The FBI Murders

CORBETT, GRETCHEN
Final Verdict

CORBIN, BARRY
Chase, The
Conagher
Death In California, A
Firefighter
Keys, The
L B J: The Early Years
People Across The Lake, The
Warm Hearts, Cold Feet

CORBITT, CHANCE MICHAEL
After The Promise

COREA, NICHOLAS
J. O. E. And The Colonel

COREY, JEFF
Final Jeopardy, The

CORKILL, CATHERINE
Two Fathers' Justice

CORLEY, ANNIE
Time To Heal, A

CORLEY, PAT
In Defense Of A Married Man
Poker Alice
Silent Witness
Stark
Stomin' Home

CORT, BUD
Bates Motel

CORTESE, JOE
Assault And Matrimony
Born To Run
C. A. T. Squad: Python Wolf
Exclusive
Jackie Collins' Lady Boss
Letting Go
Something Is Out There

CORTESE, JOSEPH
C. A. T. Squad

CORTEZ, KATHERINE
Shameful Secrets

CORTI, DAVID
Pack Of Lies

COSBY, BILL
Cosby Mysteries, The
I Spy Returns

COSTANZO, ROBERT
Miracle At Beekman's Place

COULOURIS, KEITH
Deadman's Revenge

COUTTEURE, RONNY
Young Indiana Jones Chronicles: The Curse
....Of The Jackal

COX, BRIAN
Murder By Moonlight

COX, COURTENEY
Battling For Baby
Curiosity Kills
I'll Be Home For Christmas
Judith Krantz's Till We Meet Again
Roxanne: The Prize Pulitzer

COX, COURTNEY
Misfits Of Science

COX, RONNY
Abduction Of Kari Swenson, The
Comeback, The
In The Line Of Duty: The FBI Murders
Perry Mason: The Case Of The Heartbroken Bride
Scandal In A Small Town

COYOTE, PETER
Baja Oklahoma
Child's Cry
Echoes In The Darkness
Keeper Of The City
Living A Lie
Scorned And Swindled
Seduction In Travis County
Sworn To Silence
Unconquered

CRAMER, JOEY
Stone Fox

CRANHAM, KENNETH
Just Another Secret

CRAVEN, MATT
Classified Love

CRAWFORD, RACHAEL
On Thin Ice: The Tai Babilonia Story

CRENNA, RICHARD
After The Shock
And The Sea Will Tell
Case Of Deadly Force, A
Case Of The Hillside Strangler, The
Doubletake
Forget Me Not Murders, The
High Price Of Passion, The
Internal Affairs
Intruders
Jonathan Stone: Threat Of Innocence
Kids Like These
Last Flight Out
London And Davis In New York
Montana
Murder In Black And White
Murder Times Seven
On Wings Of Eagles
Passions
Place To Be Loved, A
Plaza Suite
Police Story: The Freeway Killings
Rape Of Richard Beck, The
Stuck With Each Other
Terror On Track 9

CREWSON, WENDY
Heartsounds
Hobo's Christmas, A

Perry Mason: The Case Of The Shooting Star
To Save The Children

CRIDER, MISSY
Eyes Of Terror
Jane's House
Mothers Revenge, A

CROMBIE, JONATHAN
Good Fight, The

CRONYN, HUME
Broadway Bound
Christmas On Division Street
Day One
Foxfire
To Dance With The White Dog

CRONYN, TANDY
Getting Out
Guardian, The
Story Lady, The

CROSBIE, ANNETTE
Chernobyl: The Final Warning

CROSBY, CATHY LEE
Intimate Strangers
North And South, Book 3: Heaven And Hell
Untamed Love

CROSBY, KIM
Tarzan In Manhattan

CROSBY, MARY
Final Jeopardy, The
Hollywood Wives
Stagecoach

CROSS, BEN
Dark Shadows
Deep Trouble
Diamond Fleece
Nightlife
She Stood Alone
Steal The Sky
Twist Of Fate

CROSS, PAUL
Borrowers, The

CROUSE, LINDSAY
Chantilly Lace
Out Of The Darkness

CROW, ASHLEY
Middle Ages
Probe

CROW, EMILIA
Disaster In Time

CROWLEY, PAT
International Airport

CRYER, JON
Heads

CULLEN, BRETT
And Then She Was Gone
Complex Of Fear
Sitter, The

CULLEN, KATHARINE
Girl From Tomorrow, The

CULP, ROBERT
Blue Lightning, The
Combat High
Gladiator, The
I Spy Returns
Murderous Vision
Perry Mason: The Case Of The Defiant Daughter
What Price Victory?

CURRY, TIM
Stephen King's It

CURTIN, JANE
Common Ground
Maybe Baby

CURTIS, JAMIE LEE
As Summers Die

CURTIS, KELLY
Thanksgiving Day

CURTIS, TONY
Agatha Christie's Murder In Three Acts
Christmas In Connecticut
Mafia Princess
Tarzan In Manhattan
Thanksgiving Day

CUSACK, CYRIL
Tenth Man, The

CUTRONA, HANNAH
Generation

CUTTER, LISE
Desperado
Equal Justice

CYPHER, JON
Lady Mobster
Probe
Snow Kill

D'ABO, MARYAM
Behind Enemy Lines
Nightlife
Not A Penny More, Not A Penny Less
Something Is Out There

D'ABO, OLIVIA
For Love And Glory
Midnight's Child

D'ANGELO, BEVERLY
Child Lost Forever, A
Doubletake
Hands Of A Stranger
Jonathan Stone: Threat Of Innocence
Judgment Day: The John List Story
Menendez: A Killing In Beverly Hills
Switch, The
Trial: The Price Of Passion

D'ANGERIO, JOSEPH
Murderous Vision

D'ARBANVILLE, PATTI
Crossing The Mob

Snow Kill
South Beach

DABSON, JESSE
Marilyn & Me

DAILY, BILL
I Dream Of Jeannie: 15 Years Later
I Still Dream Of Jeannie

DALE, CYNTHIA
In The Eyes Of A Stranger
Sadie And Son

DALEY, TIMOTHY
I Married A Centerfold

DALTON, TIMOTHY
Florence Nightingale
Lie Down With Lions
Mistral's Daughter
Sins

DALTREY, ROGER
Forgotten Prisoners: The Amnesty File

DALY, JANE
And Then There Was One

DALY, TIM
Dangerous Heart
I'll Take Manhattan
In The Line Of Duty: Ambush In Waco
Mirrors
Queen
Red Earth, White Earth
Witness To The Execution

DALY, TYNE
Christy
Columbo: A Bird In The Hand
Face Of A Stranger
Forget Me Not Murders, The
Kids Like These
Last To Go, The
Scattered Dreams: The Kathryn Messenger
....Story
Stuck With Each Other

DAMON, GABRIEL
Stranger In My Bed

DAMON, MATT
Rising Son

DAMON, STUART
Perry Mason: The Case Of The Killer Kiss

DANAHY, PAIGE
Sudie And Simpson

DANCE, CHARLES
Out On A Limb
Phantom Of The Opera, The

DANESE, SHERA
Columbo And The Murder Of A Rock Star

DANIELS, J.D.
Roswell

DANIELS, JEFF
Caine Mutiny Court - Martial, The
Disaster In Time

Gettysburg
No Place Like Home
Teamster Boss: The Jackie Presser Story

DANIELS, WILLIAM
Howard Beach: Making The Case For Murder
Little Match Girl, The

DANKER, ELI
Taking Of Flight 847: The Uli Derickson
....Story

DANNER, BLYTHE
Cruel Doubt
Getting Up And Going Home
Guilty Conscience
Judgment
Leave Of Absence
Money, Power, Murder
Never Forget
Oldest Living Confederate Widow Tells All

DANO, LINDA
Perry Mason: The Case Of The Killer Kiss

DANSON, TED
We Are The Children
When The Bough Breaks

DANZA, TONY
Dead And Alive
Doing Life
Freedom Fighter
Single Bars, Single Women

DARBY, KIM
First Steps

DAVALOS, ELYSSA
Riviera

DAVENPORT, NIGEL
Christmas Carol, A

DAVI, ROBERT
Blind Justice
Deceptions
Illicit Behavior
Terrorist On Trial: The United States Vs.
Salim
White Hot: The Mysterious Murder Of
....Thelma Todd

DAVID, KEITH
There Are No Children Here

DAVIDOVICH, LOLITA
Keep The Change

DAVIDSON, EILEEN
Broken Badges
Sharing Richard

DAVIES, GERAINT WYN
Ghost Mom
Hush Little Baby
Other Women's Children

DAVIS, ANN B.
Bradys, The
Very Brady Christmas, A

DAVIS, BETTE
As Summers Die

Murder With Mirrors

DAVIS, BRAD
Caine Mutiny Court - Martial, The
Child Of Darkness, Child Of Light
Habitation Of Dragons, The
Plot To Kill Hitler, The
Robert Kennedy And His Times
Unspeakable Acts
Vengeance: The Story Of Tony Cimo
When The Time Comes

DAVIS, CLIFTON
Dream Date

DAVIS, GEENA
Secret Weapons

DAVIS, JOHN RHYS
Trial Of The Incredible Hulk, The

DAVIS, JUDY
One Against The Wind

DAVIS, LANE
Triumph Of The Heart: The Ricky Bell Story

DAVIS, MAC
Blackmail
What Price Victory?

DAVIS, OSSIE
Ernest Green Story, The
Ray Alexander: A Taste For Justice
Stephen King's The Stand

DAVIS, SAMMI
Chernobyl: The Final Warning
Perfect Bride, The

DAVIS, WARWICK
Ewok Adventure, The
Ewoks: The Battle For Endor

DAVISON, BRUCE
Desperate Choices: To Save My Child
Live: From Death Row
Mothers Revenge, A
Poor Little Rich Girl: The Barbara Hutton
....Story

DAWBER, PAM
American Geisha
Do You Know The Muffin Man?
Face Of Fear, The
Quiet Victory: The Charlie Wedemeyer Story
This Wife For Hire
Web Of Deception
Wild Horses

DE BANKOLE, ISAACH
Heart Of Darkness

DE HAVILLAND, OLIVIA
Woman He Loved, The

DE LINT, DEREK
Barbara Taylor Bradford's Remember

DE LUISE, MICHAEL
Class Cruise
Sunset Beat

DE MORNAY, REBECCA
Blind Side
By Dawn's Early Light
Getting Out
Inconvenient Woman, An
Murders In The Rue Morgue, The

DE SANTOS, TONY
Mafia Princess

DE SOUZA, PAUL
Web Of Deceit

DE VRIES, JON
Grand Isle
Too Young The Hero
Zelda

DE YOUNG, CLIFF
Deadly Intentions
Fourth Story
Her Secret Life
Love Can Be Murder
N. Y. P. D. Mounted
Nails
Robert Kennedy And His Times
Where Pigeons Go To Die

DEAN, LOREN
American Clock, The
J F K: Reckless Youth

DEAS, JUSTIN
Montana
Stranger Waits, A
Waco & Rhinehart

DEE, RUBY
Court - Martial Of Jackie Robinson, The
Decoration Day
Ernest Green Story, The
Stephen King's The Stand
Windmills Of The Gods

DEGHY, GUY
Wallenberg: A Hero's Story

DELANEY, KIM
Broken Cord, The
Christmas Comes To Willow Creek
Cracked Up
Disappearance Of Christina, The
Jackie Collins' Lady Boss
Something Is Out There
Take My Daughters, Please

DELANY, DANA
China Beach
Donato And Daughter
Enemy Within, The
Promise To Keep, A
Threesome
Wild Palms

DeLUISE, MICHAEL
Rio Shanon

DEMPSEY, PATRICK
J F K: Reckless Youth

DeMUNN, JEFFREY
Crash: The Mystery Of Flight 1501

Haunted, The
Jonathan: The Boy Nobody Wanted
Settle The Score
Time To Live, A
Treacherous Crossing

DENIER, LYDIE
Invasion Of Privacy

DENISON, ANTHONY JOHN
Beyond Control: The Amy Fisher Story
Child Of Darkness, Child Of Light
Getting Gotti
Girl Who Came Between Them, The
I Love You Perfect
Price She Paid, The
Sex,Love, And Cold Hard Cash
Under Cover

DENNEHY, BRIAN
Acceptable Risks
Burden Of Proof, The
Day One
Deadly Matrimony
Diamond Fleece
Evergreen
Father's Revenge, A
Final Appeal
Foreign Affairs
Hunter
In Broad Daylight
Killing In A Small Town
Leave Of Absence
Lion Of Africa, The
Murder In The Heartland
Perfect Witness
Pride And Extreme Prejudice
Prophet Of Evil: The Ervil Lebaron Story
Rising Son
Teamster Boss: The Jackie Presser Story

DENNIS, SANDY
Execution, The

DENTON, CHRISTA
Scandal In A Small Town

DENVER, BOB
Bring Me The Head Of Dobie Gillis

DENVER, JOHN
Christmas Gift, The
Foxfire
Higher Ground

DEREK, BO
Shattered Image

DERN, BRUCE
Amelia Earhart: The Final Flight
Carolina Skeletons
Deadman's Revenge
Into The Badlands
It's Nothing Personal
Roses Are For The Rich
Space
Toughlove
Trenchcoat In Paradise
Uncle Tom's Cabin

DERN, LAURA
Afterburn

DeSALVO, ANNE
Dead In The Water

DESERT, ALEX
Flash, The

DESIDERIO, ROBERT
Broken Promises: Taking Emily Back
Jonathan Stone: Threat Of Innocence
Original Sin
She Stood Alone
Stop At Nothing

DEUTSCH, KURT
Moment Of Truth: Cradle Of Conspiracy

DEVANE, WILLIAM
Chips, The War Dog
Murder C. O. D.
Nightmare In Columbia County
Obsessed
Preppie Murder, The
Presidents Child, The
Prophet Of Evil: The Ervil Lebaron Story
Rubdown
Timestalkers
Woman Named Jackie, A

DEWHURST, COLLEEN
Between Two Women
Danielle Steel's Kaleidoscope
Glitter Dome, The
Johnny Bull
Lantern Hill
Sword Of Gideon
Those She Left Behind

DEY, SUSAN
Angel In Green
Bed Of Lies
I Love You Perfect
Lies And Lullabies
Whose Child Is This? The War For Baby
....Jessica

DHIEGH, KHIGH
James Clavell's Noble House

DI BENEDETTO, TONY
Kojak: The Price Of Justice

DIAMOND, REED
O Pioneers

DiAQUINO, JOHN
Seaquest Dsv

DiBIANCO, LOUIE
Mafia Princess

DICKINSON, ANGIE
Fire And Rain
Hollywood Wives
Once Upon A Texas Train
Police Story: The Freeway Killings
Prime Target
Stillwatch
Touch Of Scandal, A
Treacherous Crossing

Wild Palms

DICKSON, NEIL
Freedom Fighter
Murders In The Rue Morgue, The

DIEHL, JOHN
Glitz

DILLON, KEVIN
When He's Not A Stranger

DILLON, MELINDA
Judgment Day: The John List Story
Shattered Innocence
Shattered Spirits
Space
State Of Emergency

DIOL, SUSAN
Road Raiders, The

DISPINA, TERESA
For The Love Of My Child: The Anissa
....Ayala Story

DISTEFANO, JAMES
Running Against Time

DIXON, DONNA
Beverly Hills Madam

DIXON, IVAN
Perry Mason: The Case Of The Shooting Star

DJOLA, BADJA
Christmas On Division Street

DOBSON, KEVIN
Casey's Gift: For Love Of A Child
Conviction Of Kitty Dodds, The
Dirty Work
Fatal Friendship
House Of Secrets And Lies, A
Money, Power, Murder
Sweet Revenge, A

DOBSON, PETER
Killer Rules
What She Doesn't Know

DODSON, JACK
Return To Mayberry

DOHERTY, SHANNEN
Blindfold: Acts Of Obsession
Obsessed

DOMBASLE, ARIELLE
Lace I I

DONALDSON, LESLEH
Special People

DONOHOE, AMANDA
It's Nothing Personal
Shame
Substitute, The

DONOVAN, TATE
Into Thin Air
North Beach And Rawhide
Nutcracker: Money, Madness And Murder

DOODY, ALISON
Duel Of Hearts

DOOLEY, PAUL
Guess Who's Coming For Christmas
Mother Of The Bride
State Of Emergency
When He's Not A Stranger

DORFF, STEPHEN
Always Remember I Love You
Do You Know The Muffin Man?
Son's Promise, A

DOTRICE, ROY
Children Of The Dark
Lady Forgets, The

DOTY, JUDITH
When The Time Comes

DOUGLAS, BRANDON
Children Of Times Square
Chips, The War Dog
Father's Homecoming, A

DOUGLAS, DONALD
Diana: Her True Story

DOUGLAS, KIRK
Amos
Inherit The Wind
Queenie
Secret, The

DOUGLAS, PAVEL
Passport To Murder

DOURIF, BRAD
Rage Of Angels: The Story Continues
Vengeance: The Story Of Tony Cimo

DOWLING, KATHRYN
Ultimate Betrayal

DOWN, LESLEY-ANNE
Arch Of Triumph
Indiscreet
Ladykillers
Night Walk
North And South
North And South, Book 3: Heaven And Hell

DOWNEY, JR., MORTON
Revenge Of The Nerds: The Next Generation

DOWNEY, ROMA
Devlin
Getting Up And Going Home
Woman Named Jackie, A

DOYLE, DAVID
Maybe Baby

DRAKE, LARRY
Murder In New Hampshire: The Pamela
....Smart Story
One More Mountain
Too Good To Be True

DRAKE, PAUL
Poker Alice

DRAPER, POLLY
Danielle Steel's Heartbeat

DRAPER, WYLIE
Jacksons: An American Dream, The

DRESCHER, FRAN
Love And Betrayal

DREYFUSS, RICHARD
Prisoner Of Honor

DRYER, FRED
Day Of Reckoning
Hunter

DUBOIS, MARTA
Generation
Johnnie Mae Gibson: F B I

DUCHOVNY, DAVID
Baby Snatcher
Red Shoes Diaries

DUDIKOFF, MICHAEL
Woman Who Sinned, The

DUFF, HOWARD
Love On The Run
Roses Are For The Rich
Settle The Score

DUFFY, JULIA
Children In The Crossfire
Cover Girl And The Cop, The
Love Boat: A Valentine Voyage, The
Maybe Baby
Menu For Murder

DUFFY, PATRICK
Children Of The Bride
Danielle Steel's Daddy
Murder C. O. D.
Too Good To Be True
Unholy Matrimony

DUGAN, DENNIS
Shadow Chasers
Toughest Man In The World, The

DUKAKIS, OLYMPIA
Fire In The Dark
Lucky Day
Sinatra

DUKE, PATTY
Absolute Strangers
Always Remember I Love You
Amityville: The Evil Escapes
Call Me Anna
Everybody's Baby: The Rescue Of Jessica
....Mcclure
Family Of Strangers
Fatal Judgment
Fight For Life
George Washington I I: The Forging Of A
....Nation
Grave Secrets: The Legacy Of Hilltop Drive
Killer Among Friends, A
Last Wish
Matter Of Justice, A
No Child Of Mine

One Woman's Courage
Perry Mason: The Case Of The Avenging Ace
Time To Triumph, A

DUKE, ROBIN
Hostage For A Day

DUKES, DAVID
Held Hostage: The Sis And Jerry Levin Story
Josephine Baker Story, The
Kane And Abel
Sentimental Journey
She Woke Up
Turn Back The Clock
War And Remembrance
War And Remembrance, Part I I
Wife, Mother, Murderer

DUNAWAY, FAYE
Agatha Christie's Thirteen At Dinner
Beverly Hills Madam
Casanova
Cold Sassy Tree
Columbo: It's All In The Game
Silhouette

DUNCAN, SANDY
Miracle On I-880
My Boyfriend's Back

DUNDARA, DAVID
Journey To The Center Of The Earth

DUNN, KEVIN
Taken Away

DUNNAM, STEPHANIE
Independence

DUNNE, GRIFFIN
Love Matters
Secret Weapon

DUNOYER, FRANCOIS
Fatal Image, The

DUNSMORE, ROSEMARY
After The Promise
Liar, Liar
Miles To Go . . .

DURNING, CHARLES
Case Closed
Death Of A Salesman
Dinner At Eight
Kennedys Of Massachusetts, The
Man Who Broke 1,000 Chains, The
Prime Target
Roommates
Unholy Matrimony
When A Stranger Calls Back

DUSENBERRY, ANN
He's Not Your Son

DUVALL, ROBERT
Lonesome Dove
Stalin

DUVALL, SHELLEY
Lily
Mother Goose Rock 'n' Rhyme

DYSART, RICHARD
Day One
L. A. Law
Last Days Of Patton, The
Malice In Wonderland
Marilyn & Bobby: Her Final Affair
Moving Target
Six Against The Rock

DZUNDZA, GEORGE
Babymaker: The Dr. Cecil Jacobson's Story
Brotherly Love
One Police Plaza
Something Is Out There
Terror On Highway 91
What She Doesn't Know

EASTERBROOK, LESLIE
Taking Of Flight 847: The Uli Derickson
....Story

EASTON, MICHAEL
Shadow Of A Stranger

EASTWOOD, JAYNE
Partners 'N Love

EBERSOLE, CHRISTINE
Acceptable Risks
Dying To Love You
Gypsy

EBSEN, BUDDY
Stone Fox
Working Trash

ECCLES, AIMEE
J. O. E. And The Colonel

ECKHOUSE, JAMES
Moment Of Truth: Why My Daughter?

EDEN, BARBARA
Brand New Life: The Honeymoon
Eyes Of Terror
Hell Hath No Fury
Her Wicked Ways
I Dream Of Jeannie: 15 Years Later
I Still Dream Of Jeannie
Opposites Attract
Secret Life Of Kathy Mccormick, The
Stepford Children, The
Visions Of Murder
Your Mother Wears Combat Boots

EDSON, RICHARD
Love, Cheat And Steal

EDWARDS, ANTHONY
El Diablo
Going For The Gold: The Bill Johnson Story

EDWARDS, LUKE
I Know My First Name Is Steven
Not Of This World
Yarn Princess, The

EDWARDS, STACY
Glory Days

EDWARDS, VINCE
Dirty Dozen: The Deadly Mission

EGAN, EDDIE
Out Of The Darkness

EGGAR, SAMANTHA
Ghost In Monte Carlo, A
Love Among Thieves
Secrets Of Lake Success

EGGERT, NICOLE
Just One Of The Girls

EGI, STAN
Hiroshima: Out Of The Ashes

EICHHORN, LISA
Blind Justice
Pride And Extreme Prejudice

EIKENBERRY, JILL
Assault And Matrimony
Cast The First Stone
Chantilly Lace
Family Sins
Inconvenient Woman, An
L. A. Law
Living A Lie
My Boyfriend's Back
Parallel Lives
Secret Life Of Archie's Wife, The
Stoning In Fulham County, A
Town Torn Apart, A

EILBACHER, LISA
Blind Man's Bluff
Deadly Deception
Deadly Matrimony
Joshua's Heart
Manhunt: Search For The Night Stalker
Monte Carlo

EISENBERG, NED
Murderous Affair, A: The Carolyn Warmus
....Story

ELAM, JACK
Detective In The House
Once Upon A Texas Train
Where The Hell's That Gold

ELIZONDO, HECTOR
Burden Of Proof, The
Courage
Finding The Way Home
Forgotten Prisoners: The Amnesty File
Murder: By Reason Of Insanity
Out Of The Darkness
Your Mother Wears Combat Boots

ELLIOTT, DENHOLM
Camille
Love She Sought, The
Mrs. Delafield Wants To Marry
One Against The Wind

ELLIOTT, SAM
Blue Lightning, The
Conagher
Death In California, A
Fugitive Nights: Danger In The Desert
Gettysburg
Houston: The Legend Of Texas

Quick And The Dead, The

EMILFORK, DANIEL
Riviera

ENGLUND, ROBERT
Infidelity

ENRIQUEZ, RENE
Hostage Flight

EPPS, OMAR
Daybreak

EPSTEIN, ALVIN
Doing Life

ERBE, KATHRYN
Breathing Lessons

ERMEY, R.LEE
French Silk

ESPY, WILLIAM
In Like Flynn

ESTABROOK, CHRISTINE
One Special Victory

ESTES, ROB
Lady Against The Odds

ESTEVEZ, RENEE
Dead Silence

ESTRADA, ERIK
Dirty Dozen: The Fatal Mission
Earth Angel
She Knows Too Much

EVANS, JACK
Bad Attitudes

EVANS, LINDA
Dynasty: The Reunion
Gambler Returns: The Luck Of The Draw
I'll Take Romance
Last Frontier, The

EVANS, RICHARD
Deadly Care

EVANS, TROY
Green Dolphin Beat

EVE, TREVOR
Corsican Brothers, The
Presidents Child, The
Shadow Chasers

EVERETT, CHAD
Thunderboat Row

EVERHARD, NANCY
China Lake Murders, The
This Gun For Hire

EVIGAN, GREG
Columbo: A Bird In The Hand
Lady Forgets, The
Lies Before Kisses
One Of Her Own
P. S. I Luv U
Scene Of The Crime

EWART, JOHN
Which Way Home

FABARES, SHELLEY
Deadly Relations

FAHEY, JEFF
Blindsided
Curiosity Kills
Hit List, The
In The Company Of Darkness
Iran: Days Of Crisis
Parker Kane
Sketch Artist

FAIRCHILD, MORGAN
Based On An Untrue Story
How To Murder A Millionaire
Menu For Murder
Paper Dolls
Perry Mason: The Case Of The Skin-Deep
Scandal
Street Of Dreams
Writer's Block

FAIRFIELD, HEATHER
Deadly Silence, A
Sins Of The Mother

FAISON, SANDY
Eight Is Enough Wedding, An

FALK, LISANNE
Dead Silence

FALK, PETER
Columbo: A Bird In The Hand
Columbo And The Murder Of A Rock Star
Columbo - Caution: Murder Can Be
....Hazardous To Your Health
Columbo: Death Hits The Jackpot
Columbo Goes To College
Columbo: It's All In The Game
Columbo: No Time To Die
Columbo: Undercover

FARACY, STEPHANIE
Classified Love
Only Way Out, The

FARENTINO, DEBRAH
Back To The Streets Of San Francisco
Equal Justice
Revenge Of Al Capone, The
She Was Marked For Murder
Sherlock Holmes Returns
Whereabouts Of Jenny, The

FARENTINO, JAMES
Common Ground
Family Sins
Honor Thy Father And Mother: The
....Menendez Murders
In The Line Of Duty: A Cop For The Killing
Miles From Nowhere
Naked Lie
One Woman's Courage
Red Spider, The
Sins
Summer To Remember, A

That Secret Sunday
When No One Would Listen
Who Gets The Friends?

FARINA, DENNIS
Blind Faith
Case Of The Hillside Strangler, The
Corpse Had A Familiar Face, The
Cruel Doubt
Disappearance Of Nora
Drug Wars: The Cocaine Cartel
One Woman's Courage
Open Admissions
People Like Us

FARNSWORTH, RICHARD
Fire Next Time, The
Red Earth, White Earth

FARR, JAMIE
Combat High
For Love Or Money

FARRELL, MIKE
Deadly Silence, A
Incident At Dark River
Private Sessions
Silent Movie
Vanishing Act
Whereabouts Of Jenny, The

FARRELL, SHARON
Sworn To Vengeance

FARRELL, TERRY
Danielle Steel's Star

FAULKNER, JAMES
Just Another Secret

FAUSTINO, MICHAEL
Judgment

FAWCETT, FARRAH
Between Two Women
Burning Bed, The
Criminal Behavior
Margaret Bourke - White
Nazi Hunter: The Beate Klarsfeld Story
Poor Little Rich Girl: The Barbara Hutton
....Story
Small Sacrifices
Substitute Wife, The

FAY, MEAGAN
Your Mother Wears Combat Boots

FELDON, BARBARA
Get Smart Again

FENN, SHERILYN
Dillinger

FERNANDES, MICHAEL
Seeds Of Tragedy

FERRELL, CONCHATA
Backfield In Motion
Deadly Intentions... Again?
Eye On The Sparrow
North Beach And Rawhide
Opposites Attract
Your Mother Wears Combat Boots

FERRELL, TYRA
Better Off Dead

FERRER, JOSE
Blood And Orchids
Hitler's S S: Portrait In Evil
Seduced

FERRER, MEL
Dream West
Outrage

FERRER, MIGUEL
Broken Badges
C. A. T. Squad: Python Wolf
Cruel Doubt
In The Shadow Of A Killer
Royce
Shannon's Deal

FERRERO, MARTIN
Shannon's Deal

FERRIGNO, LOU
Death Of The Incredible Hulk, The
Incredible Hulk Returns, The
Trial Of The Incredible Hulk, The

FERRY, DAVID
Sadie And Son

FIELD, CHELSEA
Birds I I: Land's End, The
Complex Of Fear
Murder C. O. D.
Nightingales
Royce

FIELDS, KIM
Facts Of Life Down Under, The

FINCH, JON
Riviera

FINDLAY, JAMES
Girl From Tomorrow, The

FINE, TRAVIS
Menendez: A Killing In Beverly Hills
They've Taken Our Children: The Chowchilla
....Kidnapping

FINLAY, FRANK
Sakharov

FINLAY-McLENNA, STEWART
Christy

FINN, JOHN
Posing: Inspired By Three Real Stories

FINNEY, ALBERT
Endless Game, The
Image, The

FIORENTINO, LINDA
Neon Empire

FIRTH, COLIN
Camille
Hostages

FIRTH, PETER
Incident, The

Prisoner Of Honor

FISHER, CARRIE
Liberty
Sweet Revenge

FISHER, FRANCES
Attack Of The 50ft. Woman
Cold Sassy Tree
Lucy & Desi: Before The Laughter
Praying Mantis
Promise To Keep, A

FISHER, TRICIA LEIGH
Strange Voices

FITZGERALD, GERALDINE
Circle Of Violence: A Family Drama
Do You Remember Love?
Night Of Courage

FLANAGAN, FIONNULA
Death Dreams
Ewok Adventure, The
Scorned And Swindled
White Mile

FLANAGAN, MARKUS
Sunset Beat

FLANDERS, ED
Danielle Steel's Message From Nam
Final Days

FLANERY, SEAN PATRICK
Young Indiana Jones Chronicles: The Curse
....Of The Jackal

FLECK, JOHN
River Of Rage: The Taking Of Maggie
....Keene

FLETCHER, ALAN
Mercy Mission: The Rescue Of Flight 771

FLETCHER, LOUISE
Final Notice
Hoover
In A Child's Name
Karen Carpenter Story, The
Nightmare On The Thirteenth Floor
Summer To Remember, A

FLYNN, MICHAEL
Evil In Clear River

FLYNN, STEVEN
And Then There Was One
High Price Of Passion, The
Without Warning: The James Brady Story

FOCH, NINA
In The Arms Of A Killer
Outback Bound
Shadow Chasers

FOLLOWS, MEGAN
Back To Hannibal: The Return Of Tom
Sawyer And Huck Finn
Cry In The Wild: The Taking Of Peggy Ann
Inherit The Wind
Second Chances
Sin Of Innocence

FONDA, PETER
Reason To Live, A

FONTAINE, JOAN
Crossings

FOOTE, HALLIE
Habitation Of Dragons, The

FORBES, BRENDA
Laura Lansing Slept Here
Mrs. Delafield Wants To Marry

FORD, BETTE
Lucy & Desi: Before The Laughter

FORD, FAITH
Poisoned By Love: The Kern County Murders

FORD, GLENN
Final Verdict

FOREST, DELPHINE
Marcus Welby, M. D.: A Holiday Affair

FORKE, FARRAH
Journey To The Center Of The Earth

FORMBY, NICOLA
Women Of Windsor

FORREST, FREDERIC
Against The Wall
Beryl Markham: A Shadow On The Sun
Citizen Cohn
Deliberate Stranger, The
Habitation Of Dragons, The
Little Girl Lost
Lonesome Dove
Margaret Bourke - White
Precious Victims
Right To Kill?

FORREST, STEVE
Gunsmoke: Return To Dodge
Hollywood Wives

FORSYTHE, JOHN
Dynasty: The Reunion
On Fire
Opposites Attract

FORSYTHE, WILLIAM
Kiss To Die For, A

FOX, COLIN
Woman On The Run: The Lawrencia
....Bembenek Story

FOX, EDWARD
Anastasia: The Mystery Of Anna
Crucifier Of Blood, The
Hazard Of Hearts, A
Robin Hood

FOX, JAMES
Beryl Markham: A Shadow On The Sun
Doomsday Gun
Fall From Grace
Heart Of Darkness

FOX, JORJAN
Missing Persons

FOX, MICHAEL J.
Family Ties Vacation
Poison Ivy

FOXWORTH, ROBERT
Double Standard
Face To Face
For Love And Glory
Return Of Desperado, The
With Murder In Mind

FOXX, REDD
Ghost Of A Chance

FRANCIOSA, TONY
Blood Vows: The Story Of A Mafia Wife
Stagecoach

FRANCIS, ANNE
Love Can Be Murder
My First Love
Poor Little Rich Girl: The Barbara Hutton
....Story

FRANCIS, GENIE
North And South
Perry Mason: The Case Of The Killer Kiss

FRANGIONE, NANCY
Sharing Richard

FRANK, BEN
Assassin
Shattered Innocence

FRANK, CHARLES
Letter To Three Wives, A

FRANK, GARY
Deliver Them From Evil: The Taking Of Alta
....View
Nurses On The Line: The Crash Of Flight 7
Unspeakable Acts
Untamed Love

FRANKEL, MARK
Season Of Giants, A

FRANKEN, STEVE
Bring Me The Head Of Dobie Gillis

FRANKLIN, BONNIE
Sister Margaret And The Saturday Night
....Ladies

FRANN, MARY
Eight Is Enough: A Family Reunion
Fatal Charm
I'm Dangerous Tonight
Single Women, Married Men

FRANZ, DENNIS
Deadly Messages
In The Line Of Duty: Standoff At Marion
Kiss Shot
N. Y. P. D. Mounted

FRASER, BRENDAN
Guilty Until Proven Innocent

FRASER, BRENT
Spooner

FRASER, DUNCAN
Call Of The Wild

FREEMAN, J.E.
Memphis

FREEMAN, MORGAN
Atlanta Child Murders, The
Clinton And Nadine
Fight For Life
Resting Place

FRELICH, PHYLLIS
Love Is Never Silent

FRENCH, VICTOR
Highway To Heaven
Little House On The Prairie - Bless All The
....Dear Children

FREWER, MATT
Day My Parents Ran Away, The

FRICKER, BRENDA
Sound And The Silence, The

FROST, LINDSAY
Calendar Girl, Cop Killer? The Bambi
....Bembenek Story
Danielle Steel's Palomino
In The Shadow Of A Killer
Lady In A Corner
Stop At Nothing
When We Were Young

FROST, SADIE
Cisco Kid, The

FUDGE, ALAN
Too Young To Die?

FULLER, KURT
Capital News
Stormy Weathers

FULLER, PENNY
Baby Snatcher
Danielle Steel's Star
George Washington I I: The Forging Of A
....Nation
Rio Shanon
Two Mrs. Grenvilles, The

FURRH, CHRIS
Family For Joe, A

FURST, STEPHEN
If It's Tuesday, It Still Must Be Belgium

FUTTERMAN, DAN
Class Of '61

GABOR, EVA
Return To Green Acres

GAIL, MAX
Can You Feel Me Dancing?
Child Lost Forever, A
Intimate Strangers
Killer In The Mirror
Man Against The Mob
Other Lover, The
Outside Woman, The

Sodbusters
Tonight's The Night

GALECKI, JOHNNY
Family Torn Apart, A

GALLAGHER, MEGAN
And Then She Was Gone

GALLAGHER, PETER
I'll Be Home For Christmas
Inconvenient Woman, An
Love & Lies
Murder Of Mary Phagan, The
White Mile

GALLEGO, GINA
Personals

GALLIGAN, ZACH
Psychic
Surviving

GALLOWAY, CAROLE
Town Torn Apart, A

GALLOWAY, DON
Return Of Ironside, The

GALLOWAY, JANE
Moment Of Truth: Broken Pledges

GAMMON, JAMES
Father Of Hell Town
Middle Ages

GARBER, TERRI
North And South, Book 3: Heaven And Hell

GARBER, VICTOR
Liberace: Behind The Music

GARCIA, ANDY
Clinton And Nadine

GARDENIA, VINCENT
Tragedy Of Flight 103: The Inside Story, The

GARDNER, AVA
Harem
Long Hot Summer, The

GARDNER, MARTIN
Memphis

GARLAND, BEVERLY
Finding The Way Home

GARLICK, SEAN
Fortress

GARLINGTON, LEE
Conviction Of Kitty Dodds, The
Dying To Love You
Killing In A Small Town
Kiss Of A Killer
When No One Would Listen
Yarn Princess, The

GARNER, JAMES
Barbarians At The Gate
Breathing Lessons
Decoration Day
Glitter Dome, The
Heartsounds

My Name Is Bill W.
Promise
Space

GARR, TERI
Deliver Them From Evil: The Taking Of Alta
....View
Fresno
Fugitive Nights: Danger In The Desert
Intimate Strangers
Mother Goose Rock 'n' Rhyme
Pack Of Lies
Quiet Little Neighborhood, A Perfect Little
....Murder, A
Stranger In The Family, A

GARRONE, RICCARDO
Killer Rules

GARTH, JENNIE
Brand New Life: The Honeymoon
Danielle Steel's Star
Lies Of The Heart: The Story Of Laurie
....Kellogg

GARTIN, CHRISTOPHER
Aaron's Way
Danielle Steel's Changes
Matters Of The Heart

GARVIE, ELIZABETH
Diana: Her True Story

GASSMAN, VITTORIO
Abraham

GAUTHIER, DAN
N. Y. P. D. Mounted

GAUTHIER, VINCENT
Nazi Hunter: The Beate Klarsfeld Story

GAUTIER, DICK
Get Smart Again
This Wife For Hire

GAZZARA, BEN
An Early Frost
Blindsided
Downpayment On Murder
Letter To Three Wives, A
Lies Before Kisses
Love, Honor & Obey: The Last Mafia
....Marriage
People Like Us
Police Story: The Freeway Killings

GEARY, ANTHONY
Impostor, The
Kicks

GEER, ELLEN
Town Bully, The

GEER, KEVIN
Sweet Bird Of Youth

GEESON, JUDY
Secret Life Of Kathy Mccormick, The

GELMAN, KIMIKO
Rags To Riches

GENDRON, FRANCOIS-ERIC
Lethal Exposure

GEORGE, SUSAN
Jack The Ripper

GERAGHTY, MARITA
To Save A Child

GERARD, GIL
E. A. R. T. H. Force
Final Notice
For Love Or Money
International Airport
Stormin' Home

GERROLL, DANIEL
Eyes Of A Witness

GERSHON, GINA
Sinatra

GERTZ, JAMI
This Can't Be Love

GETTY, ESTELLE
Copacabana

GETZ, JOHN
Majority Rule
Untamed Love

GIBB, CYNTHIA
Drive Like Lightning
Gypsy
House On Sycamore Street, The
Karen Carpenter Story, The
Sin And Redemption
When We Were Young
Woman Who Loved Elvis, The

GIBB, CYNTHIS
Twist Of The Knife, A

GIBBEL, KEN
Elvis And Me

GIBBS, MARLA
Menu For Murder

GIBSON, HENRY
Around The World In 80 Days

GIELGUD, JOHN
Camille
Man For All Season, A
Romance On The Orient Express
War And Remembrance
War And Remembrance, Part I I

GILBERT, MARCUS
Chameleons

GILBERT, MELISSA
Babymaker: The Dr. Cecil Jacobson's Story
Blood Vows: The Story Of A Mafia Wife
Choices
Donor
Dying To Remember
Family Of Strangers
Forbidden Nights
House Of Secrets
Joshua's Heart

Killer Instinct
Little House On The Prairie - Bless All The
....Dear Children
Lookalike, The
Shattered Trust: The Shari Karney Story
With A Vengeance
With Hostile Intent
Without Her Consent

GILBERT, SARA
Sudie And Simpson

GILLIAM, SETH
Assault At West Point

GILLILAND, RICHARD
Bad Attitudes
Challenge Of A Lifetime
Just My Imagination
Killing In A Small Town
Not In My Family

GILLIN, HUGH
Elvis And Me

GILLING, REBECCA
Blue Lightning, The
Danger Down Under

GILYARD, CLARENCE
Walker, Texas Ranger

GIMPEL, ERICA
Case Closed

GINTY, ROBERT
Hawaiian Heat

GIRARDOT, ANNIE
Mussolini: The Decline And Fall Of Il Duce

GISH, ANNABETH
Lady Against The Odds
Last To Go, The
Silent Cries
When He's Not A Stranger

GIVENS, ROBIN
Beverly Hills Madam
Penthouse, The
Women Of Brewster Place, The

GLASER, PAUL MICHAEL
Attack On Fear
Single Bars, Single Women

GLASS, RON
Perry Mason: The Case Of The Shooting Star

GLEASON, JACKIE
Izzy And Moe

GLEASON, JOANNA
Born Too Soon
Boys, The

GLEASON, PAUL
Fourth Story
Supercarrier

GLENN, SCOTT
As Summers Die
Intrigue
Outside Woman, The

Past Tense
Shadowhunter

GLESS, SHARON
Honor Thy Mother
Letting Go
Outside Woman, The
Separated By Murder

GLOVER, DANNY
Lonesome Dove
Mandela
Queen

GLOVER, JOHN
Apology
Assault At West Point
Breaking Point
David
Dead On The Money
Drug Wars: The Cocaine Cartel
El Diablo
Grass Roots
Hot Paint
Majority Rule
Moving Target
Nutcracker: Money, Madness And Murder
South Beach
Traveling Man
Twist Of Fate
What Ever Happened To Baby Jane?

GLOVER, JULIAN
Treasure Island

GOETZ, PETER MICHAEL
Karen Carpenter Story, The
Promise
Right To Die

GOING, JOANNA
Columbo: No Time To Die

GOLD, TRACEY
Dance Till Dawn
Labor Of Love: The Arlette Schweitzer Story
Reason To Live, A

GOLDBERG, WHOOPI
Kiss Shot

GOLDBLUM, JEFF
Framed
Lush Life

GOLDEN, NORMAN
On Promised Land
There Are No Children Here

GOLDIN, RICKY PAUL
Love Lives On

GOLDONI, LEILA
Victims For Victims - The Theresa Saldana
....Story

GOLDRING, DANNY
Two Fathers: Justice For The Innocent

GOLDWYN, TONY
Iran: Days Of Crisis
Love Matters
Taking The Heat

GOMEZ, CARLOS
Kiss To Die For, A
Silhouette

GOODEVE, GRANT
Eight Is Enough: A Family Reunion
Eight Is Enough Wedding, An

GOODING, JR., CUBA
Daybreak

GOODRICH, DEBORAH
Liberace

GOODWIN, KIA JOY
Strapped

GOORJIAN, MICHAEL
David's Mother
Flood: Who Will Save Our Children?

GORDON, EVE
Boys, The
Secret Passion Of Robert Clayton, The
Whereabouts Of Jenny, The

GORDON, KEITH
Combat High
Single Bars, Single Women

GORG, GALYN
Nightingales

GORMAN, CLIFF
Doubletake
Forget Me Not Murders, The
Internal Affairs
Murder In Black And White
Murder Times Seven
Terror On Track 9

GORMAN, ROBERT
Deception: A Mother's Secret
Where Pigeons Go To Die

GOSSELAAR, MARK-PAUL
Saved By The Bell-Hawaiian Style

GOSSETT, JR., LOUIS
Carolina Skeletons
El Diablo
Father Clements Story, The
Father & Son: Dangerous Relations
Gathering Of Old Men, A
Guardian, The
Josephine Baker Story, The
Keeper Of The City
Ray Alexander: A Taste For Justice
Return To Lonesome Dove
Roots: The Gift

GOULD, ELLIOTT
Bloodlines: Murder In The Family
Stolen: One Husband
Vanishing Act

GOULD, HAROLD
Get Smart Again
Mrs. Delafield Wants To Marry

GOULET, ROBERT
Based On An Untrue Story

GOWEN, PETER
Investigation: Inside A Terrorist Bombing

GRACEN, ELIZABETH
Death Of The Incredible Hulk, The
Eighty-Three Hours 'til Dawn

GRAF, DAVID
Town Bully, The

GRAFF, TODD
Framed

GRAHAM, CURRIE
Survive The Night

GRAHAM, GARY
Danger Island

GRAMMER, KELSEY
Beyond Suspicion
Dance Till Dawn

GRANGER, STEWART
Hazard Of Hearts, A

GRANT, BETH
Fall From Grace

GRANT, DAVID MARSHALL
Dallas: The Early Years

GRANT, FAYE
Omen I V: The Awakening

GRANT, HUGH
Our Sons

GRANT, LEE
Citizen Cohn
Hijacking Of The Achille Lauro, The
In My Daughter's Name
Mussolini - The Untold Story
She Said No
Something To Live For: The Alison Gertz
....Story

GRANT, RODNEY A.
Son Of The Morning Star

GRAVES, PETER
If It's Tuesday, It Still Must Be Belgium

GRAY, DAVID BARRY
Blind Faith

GRAY, ERIN
Addicted To His Love
Norman Rockwell's Breaking Home Ties
Perry Mason: The Case Of The Avenging Ace

GRAY, LINDA
Accidental Meeting
Entertainers, The
Highway Heartbreaker
Kenny Rogers As The Gambler I I I: The
....Legend Continues
Moment Of Truth: Broken Pledges
Moment Of Truth: Why My Daughter?
To My Daughter With Love

GRAY, SPALDING
Zelda

GREEN, KERRI
Tainted Blood

GREENBUSH, BILLY
Elvis And Me

GREENE, ELLEN
Dinner At Eight

GREENE, GRAHAM
Cooperstown
Last Of His Tribe, The

GREENE, LORNE
Alamo: 13 Days To Glory, The

GREENE, MICHELE
Double Standard
Heart Of A Child
Moment Of Truth: A Child Too Many
Nightmare On The Thirteenth Floor
Perry Mason: The Case Of The Notorious Nun
Posing: Inspired By Three Real Stories
To My Daughter

GREENHALGH, DAWN
Doing Life

GREENWOOD, BRUCE
Adrift
Bitter Vengeance
Destination: America
Great Pretender, The
Heart Of A Child
In The Line Of Duty: The FBI Murders
Little Kidnappers, The
Spy
Summer Dreams: The Story Of The Beach
....Boys
Twist Of Fate
Woman On The Run: The Lawrencia
....Bembenek Story

GREENWOOD, JOAN
Ellis Island

GREGG, JOHN
Captain Cook

GREGORY, NATALIE
Alice In Wonderland

GREIST, KIM
Duplicates
Payoff

GREY, JENNIFER
Case For Murder, A
Criminal Justice
Eyes Of A Witness
Murder In Mississippi

GREY, JOEL
Marilyn & Me
Queenie

GREYEYES, MICHAEL
Geronimo

GRIECO, RICHARD
Born To Run
Sin And Redemption

GRIER, PAM
Mothers' Right, A: The Elizabeth Morgan
....Story

GRIFFITH, ANDY
Crime Of Innocence
Diary Of A Perfect Murder
Fatal Vision
Matlock: The Witness Killings
Return To Mayberry
Under The Influence

GRIFFITH, MELANIE
Alfred Hitchcock Presents

GRIFFITH, THOMAS IAN
Rock Hudson

GRIFFITHS, LINDA
Passion And Paradise
Town Torn Apart, A

GRIFFITHS, SUSAN
Marilyn & Me

GRIMM, TIM
Overkill: The Aileen Wuornos Story

GRIZZARD, GEORGE
Caroline?
David
Deliberate Stranger, The
False Witness
Iran: Days Of Crisis
That Secret Sunday

GRODIN, CHARLES
Fresno

GROENENBERG, EDWARD
Starcrossed

GROH, DAVID
Broken Vows

GROSS, MICHAEL
Connecticut Yankee In King Arthur's Court, A
Family Ties Vacation
Firestorm: 72 Hours In Oakland
In The Line Of Duty: Manhunt In The
....Dakotas
In The Line Of Duty: The FBI Murders
In The Line Of Duty: The Price Of
....Vengeance
Letter To Three Wives, A
Right To Die
Snowbound: The Jim And Jennifer Stolpa
....Story
Vestige Of Honor
With A Vengeance

GROSS, PAUL
Due South

GRUBBS, GARY
Foxfire
Guilty Of Innocence: The Lenell Geter Story

GUEST, LANCE
Favorite Son

GUEST, NICHOLAS
What Price Victory?

GUGINO, CARLA
Murder Without Motive: The Edmund Perry
....Story

GUILLAUME, ROBERT
Penthouse, The
Perry Mason: The Case Of The Scandalous
Scoundrel

GUINAN, FRANCIS
Lies Of The Heart: The Story Of Laurie
....Kellogg
Mortal Sins

GUNN, MOSES
Bates Motel
Memphis
Murder Times Seven
Perfect Harmony
Women Of Brewster Place, The

GUNTON, ROBERT
Bride In Black, The

GUTTERIDGE, LUCY
Christmas Carol, A
Hitler's S S: Portrait In Evil
Woman He Loved, The

GUY, JASMINE
Killer Among Us, A
Queen
Stompin' At The Savoy

GWILYM, MIKE
Plot To Kill Hitler, The

GWYNNE, FRED
Kane And Abel
Murder By The Book
Vanishing Act

GWYNNE, MICHAEL C.
Seduced

HAAG, CHRISTIAN
Condition: Critical

HAAS, LUKAS
Perfect Tribute, The
Ryan White Story, The
Shattered Spirits

HACK, SHELLEY
Bridesmaids
Casualty Of War, A
Kicks
Not In My Family
Single Bars, Single Women
Taking Back My Life: The Nancy
....Ziegenmeyer Story

HAGAN, MOLLY
Shootdown

HAGMAN, LARRY
Dallas: The Early Years
Staying Afloat

HAID, CHARLES
Children In The Crossfire
Deadly Silence, A
Dreamer Of Oz, The

Fire And Rain
Fire Next Time, The
For Their Own Good
Great Escape I I: The Untold Story, The
Man Against The Mob: The Chinatown
....Murders
Revenge Of Al Capone, The
Six Against The Rock
Weekend War

HAID, DAVID
Winner Never Quits, A

HAIDUK, STACY
Round Table, The
Seaquest Dsv

HAIM, COREY
Just One Of The Girls
Time To Live, A

HALE, BARBARA
Perry Mason Mystery, A: The Case Of The Lethal
Perry Mason Mystery: The Case Of The Wicked Wives
Perry Mason Returns
Perry Mason: The Case Of The Avenging Ace
Perry Mason: The Case Of The Defiant Daughter
Perry Mason: The Case Of The Desperate Deception
Perry Mason: The Case Of The Fatal Fashion
Perry Mason: The Case Of The Fatal Framing
Perry Mason: The Case Of The Glass Coffin
Perry Mason: The Case Of The Heartbroken Bride
Perry Mason: The Case Of The Killer Kiss
Perry Mason: The Case Of The Lady In The Lake
Perry Mason: The Case Of The Lost Love
Perry Mason: The Case Of The Maligned Mobster
Perry Mason: The Case Of The Murdered Madam
Perry Mason: The Case Of The Notorious Nun
Perry Mason: The Case Of The Poisoned Pen
Perry Mason: The Case Of The Ruthless Reporter
Perry Mason: The Case Of The Scandalous Scoundrel
Perry Mason: The Case Of The Shooting Star
Perry Mason: The Case Of The Sinister Spirit
Perry Mason: The Case Of The Skin-Deep Scandal
Perry Mason: The Case Of The Telltale Talk Show Host

HALL, DAISY
I'm Dangerous Tonight

HALL, DEIDRE
Woman On The Ledge

HALL, DIEDRE
Reason To Live, A
Take My Daughters, Please

HALL, JERRY
Bejeweled

HALL, KEVIN PETER
Misfits Of Science

HALL, PHILIP BAKER
Spirit, The

HALL, RICH
True Blue

HALLHUBER, ERICH
Captain Cook

HALMER, GUNTHER
Candles In The Dark

HAMEL, VERONICA
Baby Snatcher
Conviction Of Kitty Dodds, The
Deadly Medicine
Disappearance Of Nora
Shadow Of Obsession
She Said No
Stop At Nothing
Twist Of Fate

HAMILL, MARK
Earth Angel

HAMILTON, ANTONY
Mirrors

HAMILTON, CARRIE
Hostage
Mother's Justice, A

HAMILTON, ERIN
Plaza Suite

HAMILTON, GEORGE
Columbo - Caution: Murder Can Be
....Hazardous To Your Health
Monte Carlo
Poker Alice
Two Fathers' Justice
Two Fathers: Justice For The Innocent

HAMILTON, LINDA
Club Med
Go Toward The Light
Secret Weapons

HAMILTON, MURRAY
Last Days Of Patton, The

HAMILTON, RICHARD
Plymouth

HAMLIN, HARRY
Deadly Intentions... Again?
Deceptions
Deliver Them From Evil: The Taking Of Alta
....View
Dinner At Eight
Favorite Son
Favorite Son
In The Best Of Families: Marriage, Pride And
....Madness
L. A. Law
Laguna Heat
Poisoned By Love: The Kern County Murders

HAMMOND, NICHOLAS
Trouble In Paradise

HAMMOND, VINCENT
Frankenstein: The College Years

HAMPTON, PAUL
Never Forget

HAN, MAGGIE
Murder In Paradise

HANCOCK, JOHN
Streets Of Justice

HANDY, JAMES
Appearances
Drive Like Lightning
False Arrest
Popeye Doyle

HANEY, ANNE
Blind Justice
Matlock: The Witness Killings

HANNAH, DARYL
Attack Of The 50ft. Woman

HARDEN, MARCIA GAY
Fever
In Broad Daylight
Sinatra

HARDIN, MELORA
Miles From Nowhere

HARDISON, KADEEM
Dream Date

HAREWOOD, DAVID
Bermuda Grace

HAREWOOD, DORIAN
Amerika
God Bless The Child
Guilty Of Innocence: The Lenell Geter Story
Kiss Shot
Polly--Comin' Home
Viper

HARKER, SUSANNAH
Crucifier Of Blood, The

HARKINS, JOHN
This Gun For Hire

HARMON, DEBORAH
Prince Of Bel Air

HARMON, MARK
After The Promise
Deliberate Stranger, The
Dillinger
Fourth Story
Long Road Home
Prince Of Bel Air
Shadow Of A Doubt
Sweet Bird Of Youth

HARPER, JESSICA
When Dreams Come True

HARPER, ROBERT
Murder Ordained
Outback Bound

HARPER, TESS
Christy
Daddy
In The Line Of Duty: Standoff At Marion
Incident At Dark River
Little Girl Lost
Summer To Remember, A
Unconquered
Willing To Kill: The Texas Cheerleader Story

HARPER, VALERIE
Drop-Out Mother
Execution, The
People Across The Lake, The
Perry Mason: The Case Of The Fatal Fashion
Stolen: One Husband
Strange Voices

HARRELSON, WOODY
Bay Coven
Killer Instinct

HARRINGTON, LAURA
Linda

HARRIS, CYNTHIA
Pancho Barnes
Special Friendship, A

HARRIS, DANIELLE
Don't Touch My Daughter

HARRIS, DAVID
Badge Of The Assassin

HARRIS, ED
Last Innocent Man, The
Paris Trout
Running Mates

HARRIS, JOSHUA
Locked Up: A Mother's Rage

HARRIS, JULIE
Single Women, Married Men
They've Taken Our Children: The Chowchilla
....Kidnapping
Too Good To Be True
When Love Kills: The Seduction Of John
....Hearn
Woman He Loved, The

HARRIS, LEONORE
Lena: My 100 Children

HARRIS, MEL
Burden Of Proof, The
Child Of Rage
Cross Of Fire
Desperate Journey: The Allison Wilcox Story
Grass Roots
Harry's Hong Kong
My Brother's Wife
Spider And The Fly, The
Ultimate Betrayal
With Hostile Intent

HARRIS, NEIL PATRICK
Cold Sassy Tree
Family Torn Apart, A
Home Fires Burning

Snowbound: The Jim And Jennifer Stolpa
....Story
Stranger In The Family, A

HARRIS, RICHARD
Abraham

HARRISON, GREGORY
Angel Of Death
Bare Essentials
Breaking The Silence
Caught In The Act
Dangerous Pursuit
Duplicates
Family Torn Apart, A
Fresno
Hot Paint
Lies Of The Heart: The Story Of Laurie
....Kellogg
Oceans Of Fire
Red River
Seduced

HARRISON, REX
Anastasia: The Mystery Of Anna

HARROLD, KATHRYN
Dead Solid Perfect
Deadly Desire
Man Against The Mob

HARRY, DEBORAH
Intimate Stranger

HARRY, JACKEE
Crash Course
Double Your Pleasure

HART, DAVID
In The Heat Of The Night

HART, ROXANNE
Last Innocent Man, The
Living A Lie
Samaritan: The Mitch Snyder Story
Tagget
Vengeance: The Story Of Tony Cimo

HARTLEY, MARIETTE
Child Of Rage
Diagnosis Of Murder
Murder C. O. D.
My Two Loves
One Terrific Guy
Passion And Paradise
Perry Mason: The Case Of The Telltale Talk
Show Host
Silence Of The Heart

HARTMAN, LISA
Bare Essentials
Beverly Hills Cowgirl Blues
Fire: Trapped On The 37th Floor
Full Exposure: The Sex Tapes Scandal
Not Of This World
Operation, The
Red Wind
Return Of Eliot Ness, The
Roses Are For The Rich
Search For Grace
Take, The

Two Thousand Malibu Road
Without A Kiss Goodbye

HARVEY, DON
Better Off Dead
Mission Of The Shark

HASKELL, PETER
Columbo - Caution: Murder Can Be
....Hazardous To Your Health

HASSELHOFF, DAVID
Baywatch: Panic At Malibu Pier
Bridge Across Time
Cartier Affair, The
Knight Rider 2000
Perry Mason: The Case Of The Lady In The
Lake

HATCHER, TERI
Dead In The Water
Lois & Clark: The New Adventures Of
....Superman

HAUER, RUTGER
Amelia Earhart: The Final Flight
Blind Side
Deadlock
Escape From Sobibor
Voyage

HAUSER, WINGS
Bump In The Night
Sweet Revenge, A

HAVERS, NIGEL
Lie Down With Lions

HAWKES, JOHN
Roadracers

HAYEK, SALMA
Roadracers

HAYES, HELEN
Highway To Heaven
Murder With Mirrors

HAYS, ROBERT
Murder By The Book
Running Against Time

HEALY, PATRICIA
Sweet Poison

HEAMES, DENIS
Aftermath: A Test Of Love

HEARD, JOHN
Cross Of Fire
Dead Ahead: The Exxon Valdez Disaster
Necessity
Out On A Limb
Spoils Of War
There Was A Little Boy

HECHT, PAUL
I'll Take Manhattan

HECKART, EILEEN
Stuck With Each Other

HEDAYA, DAN
Double Your Pleasure

Whereabouts Of Jenny, The
HEDREN, TIPPI
Birds I I: Land's End, The

HELGENBERGER, MARG
Blind Vengeance
China Beach
Death Dreams
In Sickness And In Health
Lie Down With Lions
Through The Eyes Of A Killer
Tommyknockers, The
When Love Kills: The Seduction Of John
....Hearn

HELLMAN, OCEAN
Anything To Survive

HELMOND, KATHERINE
Deception: A Mother's Secret
Grass Roots
Perfect Tribute, The
When Will I Be Loved?

HEMINGWAY, MARIEL
Amerika
Desperate Rescue: The Cathy Mahone Story
Into The Badlands
Steal The Sky

HEMMINGS, DAVID
Beverly Hills Cowgirl Blues
Harry's Hong Kong
Three On A Match

HEMSLEY, SHERMAN
Camp Cucamonga
Combat High

HENDERSON, FLORENCE
Bradys, The
Very Brady Christmas, A

HENDERSON, JO
Fatal Judgment
Terrorist On Trial: The United States Vs.
Salim

HENDERSON, MAGGIE
Indiscreet

HENNER, MARILU
Ladykillers
Stark

HENRIKSEN, LANCE
Reason For Living: The Jill Ireland Story
Streets Of Justice

HENRY, BUCK
Keep The Change

HENRY, GREGG
Great Pretender, The
Staying Afloat
Stoning In Fulham County, A
White Lie

HEPBURN, AUDREY
Love Among Thieves

HEPBURN, KATHERINE
Laura Lansing Slept Here

Man Upstairs, The
Mrs. Delafield Wants To Marry
This Can't Be Love

HERD, RICHARD
Fall From Grace
My First Love

HERRMANN, EDWARD
Fire In The Dark
Murrow
So Proudly We Hail
Sweet Poison

HERSHBERGER, GARY
Columbo Goes To College
Love She Sought, The

HERSHEY, BARBARA
Abraham
Killing In A Small Town
Paris Trout
Return To Lonesome Dove
Stay The Night

HERTFORD, CHELSEA
Darkness Before Dawn

HESS, SUSAN
Dress Gray
What Price Victory?

HESSEMAN, HOWARD
Call Me Anna
Diamond Trap, The
Murder In New Hampshire: The Pamela
....Smart Story
Quiet Killer
Silence Of The Heart
Six Against The Rock

HESTON, CHARLTON
Crash Landing: The Rescue Of Flight 232
Crucifier Of Blood, The
Little Kidnappers, The
Man For All Season, A
Nairobi Affair
Original Sin
Proud Men
Treasure Island

HEWLETT, DAVID
Penthouse, The

HEXUM, JOHN ERIK
Cover Up

HICKEY, WILLIAM
Hobo's Christmas, A

HICKMAN, DWAYNE
Bring Me The Head Of Dobie Gillis

HICKS, CATHERINE
Hi Honey -- I'm Dead
Laguna Heat
Running Against Time
Souvenir
Spy

HIGGINS, ANTHONY
Lace I I
Sherlock Holmes Returns

HIGGINS, JOEL
Laura Lansing Slept Here
Threesome

HILL, ARTHUR
Christmas Eve
Guardian, The
Murder, She Wrote
Perry Mason: The Case Of The Notorious Nun

HILL, CHARLES C.
Waco & Rhinehart

HILL, DANA
Combat High
Silence Of The Heart

HILLERMAN, JOHN
Around The World In 80 Days
Assault And Matrimony
Hands Of A Murderer
Street Of Dreams

HINCHLEY, PIPPA
Fergie And Andrew: Behind The Palace
....Doors

HINDLE, ART
Liar, Liar
World's Oldest Living Bridesmaid, The

HINES, GREGORY
T Bone N Wessel
White Lie

HINGLE, PAT
Everybody's Baby: The Rescue Of Jessica
....Mcclure
Gunsmoke I I I: To The Last Man
Kojak: The Price Of Justice
L B J: The Early Years
Lady From Yesterday, The
Manhunt For Claude Dallas
Not Of This World
Stranger On My Land
Town Bully, The

HIPP, PAUL
Liberace: Behind The Music

HIRSCH, ANDY
In A Child's Name

HIRSCH, JUDD
Betrayal Of Trust
Brotherly Love
Detective In The House
First Steps
Great Escape I I: The Untold Story, The
She Said No

HIRT, CHRISTIANNE
Double Standard

HOAG, JUDITH
Murder In High Places

HODGE, PATRICIA
Secret Life Of Ian Fleming, The

HOFFMAN, DUSTIN
Death Of A Salesman

HOFMANN, ISABELLA
Independence
Town Bully, The

HOLBROOK, HAL
Behind Enemy Lines
Bonds Of Love
Day One
Dress Gray
I'll Be Home For Christmas
Mario Puzo's The Fortunate Pilgrim
Perry Mason Mystery, A: The Case Of The Lethal
Plaza Suite
Sorry, Wrong Number
Three Wishes Of Billy Grier, The

HOLDER, GEOFFREY
Ghost Of A Chance

HOLLAND, ANTHONY
Christmas Comes To Willow Creek

HOLLIMAN, EARL
American Harvest
Gunsmoke: Return To Dodge
P. S. I Luv U

HOLLY, LAUREN
Archie: To Riverdale And Back Again
Dangerous Heart
Picket Fences

HOLM, CELESTE
Jessie
Murder By The Book

HOLM, IAN
Borrowers, The

HONG, JAMES
Karen Carpenter Story, The

HOOD, DON
Blind Vengeance

HOOKS, ROBERT
Supercarrier

HOOTKINS, WILLIAM
Return Of Sherlock Holmes, The
Waco & Rhinehart

HOPE, LESLIE
Caught In The Act

HOPKINS, ANTHONY
Arch Of Triumph
Great Expectations
Guilty Conscience
Hollywood Wives
Mussolini: The Decline And Fall Of Il Duce
Tenth Man, The
To Be The Best

HOPKINS, BO
Blood Ties
Houston: The Legend Of Texas
Smokey Mountain Christmas, A

HOPPER, DENNIS
Doublecrossed
Heart Of Justice, The

Nails
Paris Trout

HORDERN, MICHAEL
Secret Garden, The

HORNEFF, WIL
Yearling, The

HORSFORD, ANNA MARIA
Baby Brokers
Killer Among Us, A
Murder Without Motive: The Edmund Perry ....Story
Taken Away

HORSLEY, LEE
Corpse Had A Familiar Face, The
Crossings
Danielle Steel's Palomino
Face Of Fear, The
French Silk
Infidelity
Single Women, Married Men
When Dreams Come True

HORST, JASON
Broken Angel

HORTON, MICHAEL
My Father, My Son

HORTON, PETER
Children Of The Dark

HOSEA, BOBBY
Mantis

HOSKINS, BOB
Mussolini: The Decline And Fall Of Il Duce
World War I I : When Lions Roared

HOSSACK, ALLISON
Night Owl

HOUSEMAN, JOHN
Lincoln

HOWARD, ALAN
Casualty Of War, A
Just Another Secret
Pride And Extreme Prejudice

HOWARD, ARLISS
Hands Of A Stranger
I Know My First Name Is Steven
Iran: Days Of Crisis
Those Secrets
Till Death Us Do Part

HOWARD, KEN
Agatha Christie's The Man In The Brown Suit
Hart To Hart Returns
He's Not Your Son
Mastergate
Moment Of Truth: To Walk Again
Murder In New Hampshire: The Pamela ....Smart Story
P. S. I Luv U
Rage Of Angels: The Story Continues

HOWARD, RON
Return To Mayberry

HOWARD, TREVOR
Christmas Eve
Peter The Great

HOWELL, C. THOMAS
Curiosity Kills
Dark Reflection
Into The Homeland

HUBLEY, SEASON
Child In The Night
Christmas Eve
London And Davis In New York
Shakedown On The Sunset Strip
Steel Justice
Stepfather I I I
Three Wishes Of Billy Grier, The
Under The Influence
Unspeakable Acts
Vestige Of Honor

HUBLEY, WHIP
Devlin

HUDDLESTON, DAVID
Blacke's Magic
Tracker, The
When The Bough Breaks

HUDSON, ERNIE
Broken Badges
Dirty Dozen: The Fatal Mission
Love On The Run
Wild Palms

HUDSON, ROCK
Las Vegas Strip Wars, The

HUFF, SHAWN
Secrets Of Lake Success

HUFFMAN, DAVID
Children In The Crossfire

HUFFMAN, FELICITY
Stephen King's Golden Years

HUGHES, BARNARD
Day One
Hobo's Christmas, A
Home Fires Burning
Incident, The
Night Of Courage

HUGHES, BRUCE
Danger Down Under

HUGHES, MIKO
Dark Reflection

HUGHES, WENDY
Donor
Heist

HULCE, TOM
Murder In Mississippi

HUNSAKER, ED
Moving Target

HUNT, HELEN
In The Company Of Darkness
Incident At Dark River

Into The Badlands
Murder In New Hampshire: The Pamela
....Smart Story

HUNT, LINDA
Room, The
Room Upstairs, The

HUNTER, HOLLY
Crazy In Love
Gathering Of Old Men, A
Positively True Adventures Of The Alleged
Texas Cheerleader Murdering Mom, The
Roe Vs. Wade
With Intent To Kill

HUNTER, KIM
Bloodlines: Murder In The Family
Scene Of The Crime

HUNTER, RONALD
Internal Affairs

HURT, JOHN
Investigation: Inside A Terrorist Bombing

HURT, MARY BETH
Baby Girl Scott

HUSSEY, OLIVIA
Corsican Brothers, The
Psycho I V: The Beginning

HUSTON, ANJELICA
Family Pictures
Lonesome Dove

HUSTON, CAROL
Shooter

HUSTON, JOHN
Alfred Hitchcock Presents

HUTTON, LAUREN
Fear
Perfect People
Scandal Sheet
Timestalkers

HUTTON, TIMOTHY
Zelda

HYDE-WHITE, ALEX
Ironclads
Supercarrier

HYLANDS, SCOTT
Ordeal In The Arctic

IDLE, ERIK
Around The World In 80 Days

IMAN,
Lies Of The Twins

IRELAND, KATHY
Danger Island

IRIZARRY, VINCENT
Jackie Collins' Lucky Chances

IRONSIDE, MICHAEL
Black Ice
Deadly Surveillance
Deadman's Revenge

Marked For Murder

IRVING, AMY
Anastasia: The Mystery Of Anna

ISOBEL, KATHARINE
Yes, Virginia, There Is A Santa Claus

ITO, ROBERT
American Geisha

IVANEK, ZELJKO
Aftermath: A Test Of Love
Our Sons

IVES, BURL
Poor Little Rich Girl: The Barbara Hutton
....Story

IVEY, DANA
Child Lost Forever, A

IVEY, JUDITH
Decoration Day
Her Final Fury: Betty Broderick, The Last
....Chapter
Long Hot Summer, The
On Promised Land
We Are The Children

JACKO,
Highwayman, The

JACKSON, ANNE
Baby M
Out On A Limb

JACKSON, GLENDA
Sakharov

JACKSON, GORDON
Lady And The Highwayman, The

JACKSON, JOHN M.
Black Widow Murders: The Blanche Taylor
....Moore Story
Line Of Fire: The Morris Dees Story
Sudie And Simpson
Switched At Birth

JACKSON, KATE
Adrift
Armed & Innocent
Empty Cradle
Quiet Killer
Stranger Within, The

JACKSON, SAMUEL L.
Against The Wall
Assault At West Point

JACOBI, DEREK
Secret Garden, The
Tenth Man, The

JACOBS, LAWRENCE-HILTON
Jacksons: An American Dream , The

JACOBY, BOBBY
Day My Parents Ran Away, The

JAECKEL, RICHARD
Supercarrier

JAFFE, SETH
Stark

JAFFE, TALESIN
Child's Cry

JAKUB, LISA
Rape Of Dr. Willis, The

JAMES, DALTON
Substitute, The

JAMES, GENNIE
Christmas Gift, The
Secret Garden, The

JAMES, JOHN
Dynasty: The Reunion
Haunted By Her Past
Partners 'N Love
Perry Mason: The Case Of The Ruthless
Reporter

JAMES, SHEILA
Bring Me The Head Of Dobie Gillis

JAMES, STEVE
C. A. T. Squad
Mantis

JARRE, KEVIN
Gotham

JARVIS, GRAHAM
Cry For Help: The Tracey Thurman Story, A

JASON, PETER
From The Dead Of Night

JENKINS, DANIEL
Florida Straits

JENKINS, KEN
Homefront

JENKINS, REBECCA
Harvest For The Heart
Till Death Us Do Part

JENKINS, RICHARD
Out On The Edge
When You Remember Me

JENNINGS, BRENT
In The Line Of Duty: The Price Of
....Vengeance

JENNINGS, JUANITA
Laurel Avenue

JENNINGS, WAYLON
Stagecoach

JETER, MICHAEL
When Love Kills: The Seduction Of John
....Hearn

JILLIAN, ANN
Ann Jillian Story, The
Convicted: A Mother's Story
Heart Of A Child
Killer In The Mirror
Labor Of Love: The Arlette Schweitzer Story
Little White Lies
Macshayne: Winner Take All

Mario And The Mob
Original Sin
Perry Mason: The Case Of The Murdered
Madam
White Lie

JILOT, YOLANDA
J F K: Reckless Youth

JOHANSSON, PAUL
Laker Girls, The

JOHNSON, ANNE-MARIE
Dream Date
In The Heat Of The Night
Jackie Collins' Lucky Chances

JOHNSON, ASHLEY
Men Don't Tell

JOHNSON, BEN
Bonanza: The Return
Chase, The
Dream West
Wild Horses

JOHNSON, BEVERLY
Cover Girl Murders, The

JOHNSON, BRAD
American Story, An
Birds I I: Land's End, The
Cries Unheard: The Donna Yaklich Story
Ned Blessing: The Story Of My Life And
....Times

JOHNSON, CLARK
Starcrossed

JOHNSON, DON
Long Hot Summer, The
Miami Vice

JOHNSON, GEORDIE
Stranger In The Mirror, A

JOHNSON, GEORGANN
Our Family Honor
Shattered Dreams

JOHNSON, JAY
Broken Badges

JOHNSON, LAURA
Marked For Murder
Murderous Vision
Nick Knight

JOHNSON, MARK W.
Separated By Murder

JOHNSON, MICHELLE
Woman Scorned: The Betty Broderick Story

JOHNSON, PENNY
Columbo - Caution: Murder Can Be
....Hazardous To Your Health
Night Visions

JOHNSON, RICHARD
Crucifer Of Blood, The
Treasure Island

JOHNSTON, GRACE
God Bless The Child

JOHNSTON, JOHN DENNIS
Miracle In The Wilderness

JONES, DEAN
Fire And Rain
Saved By The Bell-Hawaiian Style

JONES, EDDIE
Final Appeal

JONES, HENRY
Codename: Foxfire - Slay It Again, Sam

JONES, JAMES EARL
Atlanta Child Murders, The
Confessions: Two Faces Of Evil
Heat Wave
Las Vegas Strip Wars, The
Last Elephant, The
Last Flight Out
Percy & Thunder

JONES, JEFFREY
George Washington I I: The Forging Of A
....Nation

JONES, RENEE
Jessie

JONES, SAM
Highwayman, The
Spirit, The

JONES, TOMMY LEE
April Morning
Broken Vows
Gotham
Lonesome Dove
Stranger On My Land
This Park Is Mine

JORDAN, RICHARD
Manhunt: Search For The Night Stalker
Murder Of Mary Phagan, The

JORDON, JAMES CARROLL
London And Davis In New York

JOSEPH, RON
Stones Of Ibarra

JOURDAN, LOUIS
Beverly Hills Madam

JOY, MARK
Night Walk

JOYNER, MICHELLE
Bonnie And Clyde: The True Story
Passion For Justice, A: Hazel Brannon Smith
....Story

JUDD, NAOMI
Rio Diablo

JULIA, RAUL
Alamo: 13 Days To Glory, The
Florida Straits
Mussolini - The Untold Story
Richest Man In The World: The Aristotle
....Onassis Story

JUMP, GORDON
On Fire

Perry Mason: The Case Of The Lost Love

JURASIK, PETER
Crash: The Mystery Of Flight 1501
Lily
Peter Gunn

KAAKE, JEFF
Nasty Boys
Seeds Of Tragedy

KACZMAREK, JANE
Christmas Gift, The
I'll Take Manhattan
Right Of The People, The
Spooner
Three Kings, The

KAHN, MADELINE
For Richer, For Poorer

KALEMBER, PATRICIA
Danielle Steel's Kaleidoscope
Little Girl Lost
Shattered Trust: The Shari Karney Story

KAMM, KRIS
Heroes Of Desert Storm
Shattered Innocence

KANALY, STEVE
Scene Of The Crime

KANE, CAROL
Burning Rage
Drop-Out Mother
When A Stranger Calls Back

KAPELOS, JOHN
For The Love Of Aaron
Nick Knight

KAREN, JAMES
Shattered Dreams

KARLEN, JOHN
Babycakes
Calendar Girl, Cop Killer? The Bambi
....Bembenek Story
Cover Girl And The Cop, The
Daddy
In A Child's Name
Nightmare On The Thirteenth Floor
Welcome Home, Bobby

KARLIN, MIRIAM
Attic: The Hiding Of Anne Frank, The

KASH, LINDA
Partners 'N Love

KASPER, GARY
J. O. E. And The Colonel

KATT, WILLIAM
Perry Mason Returns
Perry Mason: The Case Of The Avenging Ace
Perry Mason: The Case Of The Lady In The
Lake
Perry Mason: The Case Of The Lost Love
Perry Mason: The Case Of The Murdered
Madam
Perry Mason: The Case Of The Notorious Nun

Perry Mason: The Case Of The Scandalous Scoundrel
Perry Mason: The Case Of The Shooting Star
Perry Mason: The Case Of The Sinister Spirit
Swimsuit

KAUFMAN, DAVID
Last Prostitute, The
Your Mother Wears Combat Boots

KAVA, CAROLINE
Guilty Until Proven Innocent
Nobody's Child

KAY, DIANNE
Eight Is Enough: A Family Reunion

KAYE, CAREN
Poison Ivy

KAYE, LILA
Return Of Sherlock Holmes, The

KEACH, JAMES
Good Cops, Bad Cops

KEACH, STACY
Intimate Strangers
Mickey Spillane's Mike Hammer: Murder
....Takes All
Mission Of The Shark
Mistral's Daughter
Revenge On The Highway
Rio Diablo

KEAN, GREG
Summer Dreams: The Story Of The Beach
....Boys

KEANNE, KERRIE
Hot Pursuit

KEATON, DIANE
Amelia Earhart: The Final Flight
Running Mates

KEATS, STEVEN
Lies Of The Heart: The Story Of Laurie
....Kellogg

KEEN, DIANE
Agatha Christie's Thirteen At Dinner

KEITH, BRIAN
Alamo: 13 Days To Glory, The
Lady In A Corner
Murder, She Wrote

KEITH, DAVID
Gulag
Guts And Glory: The Rise And Fall Of Oliver
....North
If Tomorrow Comes
Liar's Edge
Whose Child Is This? The War For Baby
....Jessica

KELLER, MARTHE
Nightmare Years, The
Young Catherine

KELLER, MARY PAGE
Deception: A Mother's Secret
Revealing Evidence

Those She Left Behind

KELLERMAN, SALLY
Boris And Natasha
Drop Dead Gorgeous
Secret Weapons

KELLEY, SHEILA
Deconstructing Sarah
Fulfillment Of Mary Gray, The

KELLY, DANIEL HUGH
Macshayne: The Final Roll Of The Dice
Night Of Courage

KELLY, JAMES
Marilyn & Bobby: Her Final Affair

KELLY, MOIRA
Daybreak
Love, Lies And Murder

KELSEY, LINDA
Attack On Fear
Baby Girl Scott
Nutcracker: Money, Madness And Murder
Place To Be Loved, A

KEMP, JEREMY
Prisoner Of Honor

KEMP, MARTIN
Murder Between Friends

KENNEDY, GEORGE
Kenny Rogers As The Gambler I I I: The
....Legend Continues
Liberty
What Price Victory?

KENNEDY, MIMI
Baby Girl Scott
Homefront

KENSIT, PATSY
Fall From Grace

KERCHEVAL, KEN
Keeping Secrets

KERNS, JOANNA
Big One: The Great Los Angeles Earthquake
Blind Faith
Bunny's Tale, A
Captive
Deadly Intentions... Again?
Desperate Choices: To Save My Child
Nightman, The
Not In My Family
Preppie Murder, The
Rape Of Richard Beck, The
Shameful Secrets
Stormin' Home
Those She Left Behind

KERR, DEBORAH
Reunion At Fairborough

KERR, JAY
American Harvest

KERSHAW, WHITNEY
Longarm

KERWIN, BRIAN
Against Her Will: An Incident In Baltimore
Bluegrass
Switched At Birth
Wet Gold

KESTNER, BOYD
Amy Fisher: My Story
Somebody's Daughter

KIDDER, MARGOT
Body Of Evidence
Glitter Dome, The
One Woman's Courage
Picking Up The Pieces
Vanishing Act

KIELY, MARK
Tears And Laughter: The Joan And Mielissa
....Rivers Story

KIGER, ROBBY
Still Crazy Like A Fox

KILBOURNE, WENDY
Turn Back The Clock

KILEY, RICHARD
Absolute Strangers
Bad Seed, The
Do You Remember Love?
Final Days
Gunsmoke: The Last Apache
If Tomorrow Comes
Mastergate
My First Love
Separate But Equal

KILMER, VAL
Gore Vidal's Billy The Kid
Man Who Broke 1,000 Chains, The
Murders In The Rue Morgue, The

KILNER, KEVIN
Danielle Steel's Heartbeat
Murder In Paradise

KIMBROUGH, CHARLES
Weekend War

KING, ERIK
Missing Persons

KING, MORGANA
Deadly Intentions

KING, PERRY
Danielle Steel's Kaleidoscope
Disaster At Silo 7
I'll Take Manhattan
Jericho Fever
Only One Survived
Perfect People
Roxanne: The Prize Pulitzer
Shakedown On The Sunset Strip
Something To Live For: The Alison Gertz
....Story
Stranded
Stranger In The Mirror, A

KING, VANESSA
Liar, Liar

KINGSLEY, BEN
Murderers Among Us: The Simon Wiesenthal
....Story

KINNEY, TERRY
J F K: Reckless Youth

KINSKI, KLAUS
Timestalkers

KIRKLAND, SALLY
Double Deception
Double Jeopardy
Haunted, The
Heat Wave
Woman Who Loved Elvis, The

KITAEN, TAWNY
California Girls

KITCHEN, MICHAEL
Crossing To Freedom

KLEIN, ROBERT
Poison Ivy
This Wife For Hire

KLENCK, MARGARET
My Father, My Son

KLUGMAN, JACK
Odd Couple, The

KNELL, DAVID
Jailbirds

KNEPPER, ROBERT
E. A. R. T. H. Force
Getting Out

KNIGHT, SHIRLEY
Mothers Revenge, A
To Save A Child
When Love Kills: The Seduction Of John
....Hearn
With Intent To Kill

KNIGHT, TUESDAY
Two Thousand Malibu Road

KNOTTS, DON
Return To Mayberry

KNOX, TERENCE
Chase
City Killer
J. O. E. And The Colonel
Lucky Day
Mothers' Right, A: The Elizabeth Morgan
....Story
Murder Ordained
Overexposed
Snow Kill

KOBER, JEFF
Desperate Rescue: The Cathy Mahone Story
Matter Of Justice, A

KOCHER, NAOMI
Target Of Suspicion

KOEHLER, FREDERICK
He's Fired, She's Hired

KOPELL, BERNIE
Combat High
Get Smart Again
Love Boat: A Valentine Voyage, The

KOPINS, KAREN
Archie: To Riverdale And Back Again

KORF, MIA
Silent Witness: What A Child Saw

KORMAN, HARVEY
Based On An Untrue Story
Crash Course

KOTTO, YAPHET
Chrome Soldiers
Corpse Had A Familiar Face, The
Harem
In Self Defense
It's Nothing Personal
Playing With Fire
This Park Is Mine

KOVE, MARTIN
Higher Ground

KOWANKO, PETE
Gifted One, The

KOWANKO, PETER
Starcrossed

KOZAK, HARLEY JANE
Beyond Control: The Amy Fisher Story

KOZLOWSKI, LINDA
Favorite Son

KRABBE, JEROEN
Secret Weapon

KRAMER, ERIC
Incredible Hulk Returns, The

KRAMER, STEFANIE
Bridge Across Time
Coins In The Fountain
Hunter

KREBS, SUSAN
News At Eleven

KRIGE, ALICE
Double Deception
Dream West
Iran: Days Of Crisis
Max And Helen
Second Serve
Wallenberg: A Hero's Story

KRISTEL, SYLVIA
Casanova

KRISTOFFERSON, KRIS
Amerika
Another Pair Of Aces: Three Of A Kind
Blood And Orchids
Christmas In Connecticut
Last Days Of Frank And Jesse James, The
Miracle In The Wilderness
Pair Of Aces
Sodbusters

Stagecoach
Tracker, The
Trouble Shooters: Trapped Beneath The
....Earth

KROEGER, GARY
Columbo: Death Hits The Jackpot

KRUPPA, OLEK
Last Elephant, The

KUPCINET, IRV
Father Clements Story, The

KURLANDER, TOM
Moment Of Truth: Stalking Back

KURTZ, SWOOSIE
Baja Oklahoma
Guilty Conscience
Image, The

KURTZ, SWOOZIE
Positively True Adventures Of The Alleged
Texas Cheerleader Murdering Mom, The
Time To Live, A

KUZYK, MIMI
Blind Justice
Family Sins
I Know My Son Is Alive
Miles To Go . . .
Nightingales
Wolf

KWAN, NANCY
James Clavell's Noble House
Miracle Landing

LA PAGLIA, ANTHONY
Black Magic
Criminal Justice
Frank Nitti: The Enforcer
Keeper Of The City

LaBELLE, PATTI
Unnatural Causes

LABIOSA, DAVID
Private Sessions

LABORTEAUX, MATTHEW
Shattered Spirits

LABORTEAUX, PATRICK
Prince Of Bel Air

LADD, CHERYL
Bluegrass
Broken Promises: Taking Emily Back
Crash: The Mystery Of Flight 1501
Crossings
Dancing With Danger
Danielle Steel's Changes
Dead Before Dawn
Deadly Care
Death In California, A
Fulfillment Of Mary Gray, The
Girl Who Came Between Them, The
Jekyll & Hyde
Locked Up: A Mother's Rage
Romance On The Orient Express

LADD, DIANE
Bluegrass
Celebration Family
Crime Of Innocence
Hush Little Baby
I Married A Centerfold
Lookalike, The
Shadow Of A Doubt

LaFLEUR, ART
Penalty Phase

LAHTI, CHRISTINE
Amerika
Crazy From The Heart
Fear Inside, The
Good Fight, The
Love Lives On
No Place Like Home
Single Bars, Single Women

LAKE, RICKI
Babycakes
Chase, The

LALA, JOE
Take, The

LAMB, TIFFANY
E. A. R. T. H. Force

LAMPERT, ZOHRA
Izzy And Moe

LANCASTER, BURT
Barnum
On Wings Of Eagles
Phantom Of The Opera, The
Scandal Sheet
Separate But Equal

LANDAU, MARTIN
By Dawn's Early Light
Legacy Of Lies
Max And Helen
Neon Empire
Something To Live For: The Alison Gertz
....Story
Twelve O' One (12: 01)

LANDERS, AUDREY
Popeye Doyle

LANDESBERG, STEVE
Mission Of The Shark

LANDI, SAL
Marilyn & Me

LANDO, JOE
Dr. Quinn, Medicine Woman

LANDON, JR., MICHAEL
Bonanza: The Return

LANDON, MICHAEL
Highway To Heaven
Us

LANDRY, LANTZ
No Place Like Home

LANDSBURG, VALERIE
One Of Her Own
Terror In The Night

LANE, DIANE
Descending Angel
Lonesome Dove
Oldest Living Confederate Widow Tells All

LANE, MARK
There Are No Children Here

LANG, PERRY
Betrayed By Love
Revealing Evidence

LANG, STEPHEN
Babe Ruth
Darkness Before Dawn
Death Of A Salesman
Gettysburg
Murder Between Friends
Stone Pillow
Taking Back My Life: The Nancy
....Ziegenmeyer Story

LANGE, HOPE
Cooperstown

LANGE, JESSICA
O Pioneers

LANGE, TED
Love Boat: A Valentine Voyage, The

LANGELLA, FRANK
Doomsday Gun
Liberty

LANGENKAMP, HEATHER
Tonya & Nancy: The Inside Story

LANSBURY, ANGELA
Love She Sought, The
Mrs. 'Arris Goes To Paris
Murder, She Wrote
Rage Of Angels: The Story Continues
Shell Seekers, The
Shootdown

LANTEAU, WILLIAM
Shadow Of A Doubt

LAO, KENNY
Vestige Of Honor

LaPAGLIA, ANTHONY
Past Tense

LaPLACA, ALISON
In The Nick Of Time

LARA, JOE
Tarzan In Manhattan

LARROQUETTE, JOHN
Convicted
Hot Paint
One Special Victory

LASCHER, DAVID
Cries Unheard: The Donna Yaklich Story
Flood: Who Will Save Our Children?

LASKAWY, HARRIS
Necessity

LASKY, KATHLEEN
Getting Gotti

LATESSA, DICK
Izzy And Moe
Shattered Trust: The Shari Karney Story

LATHAM, LOUISE
Crazy From The Heart
Fresno
Haunted, The
In The Best Of Families: Marriage, Pride And
....Madness
Love Lives On

LAUGHLIN, JOHN
If Tomorrow Comes
Memphis
Streets Of Justice

LAUPER, CYNDI
Mother Goose Rock 'n' Rhyme

LAUREN, ASHLEE
Untamed Love

LAUREN, TAMMY
Desperate For Love
I Saw What You Did
People Across The Lake, The
Stepford Children, The

LAURIA, DAN
Big One: The Great Los Angeles Earthquake
David
Dead And Alive
From The Files Of Joseph Wambaugh: A Jury
Of One
Howard Beach: Making The Case For Murder
In The Line Of Duty: Ambush In Waco
Overexposed

LAURIE, PIPER
Go Toward The Light
Lies And Lullabies
Love, Mary
Promise
Rising Son
Twin Peaks

LAUTER, ED
Cartier Affair, The
Stephen King's Golden Years

LAVIN, LINDA
Lena: My 100 Children
Place To Call Home, A

LAW, SALLYANNE
Women Of Windsor

LAWRENCE, MATHEW
Popeye Doyle

LAWRENCE, MATTHEW
David
Joshua's Heart
Summer My Father Grew Up, The
With A Vengeance

LAWRENCE, SCOTT
Laurel Avenue

LAWSON, DENIS
Bejeweled

LAWSON, RICHARD
Double Your Pleasure
Johnnie Mae Gibson: F B I

LEACHMAN, CLORIS
Danielle Steel's Fine Things
Double, Double, Toil And Trouble
Facts Of Life Down Under, The
Fade To Black
Going To The Chapel
In Broad Daylight
Little Piece Of Heaven, A
Love Is Never Silent
Miracle Child
Without A Kiss Goodbye

LEADER-CHARGE, FREDRICK
Broken Cord, The

LEARNED, MICHAEL
Aftermath: A Test Of Love
Deadly Business, A
Gunsmoke: The Last Apache
Keeping Secrets
Mercy Or Murder?
Murder In New Hampshire: The Pamela
....Smart Story
Roots: The Gift
Walton Thanksgiving Reunion, A

LeBLANC, MATTHEW
Anything To Survive

LEE, CHRISTOPHEER
Death Train

LEE, JONNA
Shattered Innocence

LEE, MICHELE
Fatal Image, The
Letter To Three Wives, A
My Son Johnny
Single Women, Married Men
When No One Would Listen

LEE, SHERYL
Love, Lies And Murder

LEEDS, MARCIE
Wheels Of Terror

LeGUALT, LANCE
Three On A Match

LEHNE, FREDERIC
Amityville: The Evil Escapes
Billionaire Boys Club
Love Is Never Silent

LEHNE, JOHN
Johnnie Mae Gibson: F B I

LEIBMAN, RON
Christmas Eve
Many Happy Returns

Terrorist On Trial: The United States Vs.
Salim

LEIGH, JENNIFER JASON
Buried Alive

LEIGH, STEVEN
In Love And War

LEISURE, DAVID
Goddess Of Love
Perfect People

LeMAT, PAUL
Blind Witness
Burning Bed, The
In The Line Of Duty: Standoff At Marion
Into The Homeland
Long Time Gone
Night They Saved Christmas, The
On Wings Of Eagles

LEMBECK, MICHAEL
Danielle Steel's Heartbeat

LEMMON, JACK
For Richer, For Poorer
Life In The Theater, A
Murder Of Mary Phagan, The

LEMMONS, KASI
Court - Martial Of Jackie Robinson, The

LENNOX, ANNIE
Room, The

LENZ, KAY
Hitler's Daughter
Murder By Night

LEO, MELISSA
Carolina Skeletons
Silent Witness

LEONI, TEA
Counterfeit Contessa, The

LERNER, MICHAEL
Comrades Of Summer
Hands Of A Stranger
King Of Love, The
Omen I V: The Awakening
This Child Is Mine

LESTER, TERRY
Blade In Hong Kong
In Self Defense

LETHER, SHELLI
Born To Run

LETHIN, LORI
Brotherly Love
Diary Of A Perfect Murder

LEVINE, TED
Dead And Alive
Fulfillment Of Mary Gray, The
Last Outlaw, The
Murder In High Places

LEVITCH, ASHLEE
I'll Fly Away

LEVITT, JOSEPH GORDON
Gregory K

LEVY, EUGENE
Partners 'N Love

LEWIS, CHARLOTTE
Bare Essentials

LEWIS, DAWN
The Race To Freedom: The Underground
....Railroad

LEWIS, EMMANUEL
Lost In London

LEWIS, GEOFFREY
Dallas: The Early Years
Day Of Reckoning
Gunsmoke: The Last Apache
Matters Of The Heart
Pancho Barnes
Spenser: For Hire

LEWIS, JENNY
Line Of Fire: The Morris Dees Story
Runaway Father

LEWIS, JERRY
Fight For Life

LEWIS, JULIETTE
Too Young To Die?

LEWIS, RICHARD
Danger Of Love, The

LIFFORD, ERIC
Paris Trout

LIGHT, JUDITH
Betrayal Of Trust
Dangerous Affection
In Defense Of A Married Man
Men Don't Tell
My Boyfriend's Back
Ryan White Story, The
Wife, Mother, Murderer

LINDEN, HAL
Blacke's Magic
Dream Breakers

LINDFORS, VIVECA
Ann Jillian Story, The
Secret Weapons

LINDLEY, AUDRA
Perry Mason: The Case Of The Lady In The
Lake

LINDSEY, GEORGE
Return To Mayberry

LINEBACK, RICHARD
Woman With A Past

LINN-BAKER, MARK
Bare Essentials
Going To The Chapel

LINNEY, LAURA
Blind Spot

LIPPER, DAVID
Moment Of Truth: Broken Pledges

LIPSCOMB, DENNIS
Moonlighting

LIPTON, PEGGY
Fatal Charm
Spider And The Fly, The

LISI, VIRNA
Christopher Columbus

LITHGOW, JOHN
Baby Girl Scott
Boys, The
Glitter Dome, The
Last Elephant, The
Love, Cheat And Steal
Resting Place
Traveling Man
World War I I : When Lions Roared
Wrong Man, The

LITTLE, CLEAVON
Lincoln
Separate But Equal

LITTLE, MICHELLE
Bluffing It

LIVELY, ERNIE
Overkill: The Aileen Wuornos Story

LIVELY, JASON
Gunsmoke I I I: To The Last Man

LIVELY, ROBYN
Not Quite Human I I

LLOYD, CHRISTOPHER
Cowboy And The Ballerina, The
Dead Ahead: The Exxon Valdez Disaster
T Bone N Wessel

LLOYD, ERIC
Seasons Of The Heart

LLOYD, KATHLEEN
Waco & Rhinehart

LLOYD, NORMAN
Amityville: The Evil Escapes

LO BIANCO, TONY
Ann Jillian Story, The
Body Of Evidence
In The Shadow Of A Killer
Jessie
Lady Blue
Palace Guard
Police Story: The Freeway Killings
Ten Million Dollar Getaway
True Blue
Welcome Home, Bobby

LOCKHART, JUNE
Danger Island
Night They Saved Christmas, The
Whisper Kills, A

LOCKLEAR, HEATHER
Body Language

City Killer
Fade To Black
Her Wicked Ways
Highway Heartbreaker
Jury Duty: The Comedy
Rich Men, Single Women

LOCKLIN, LORYN
Night Visions

LOCKWOOD, VERA
Infidelity

LOGGIA, ROBERT
Afterburn
Dream Breakers
Echoes In The Darkness
Intrigue
Lifepod
Mercy Mission: The Rescue Of Flight 771
Nurses On The Line: The Crash Of Flight 7
Streets Of Justice
Touch Of Scandal, A
White Mile
Wild Palms

LOLLOBRIGIDA, GINA
Deceptions

LONDON, JEREMY
I'll Fly Away

LONG, SHELLEY
Fatal Memories
Message From Holly
Voices Within: The Lives Of Truddi Chase

LONSDALE, MICHAEL
Souvenir

LOOKINLAND, MIKE
Bradys, The

LOPEZ, FERNANDO
Killer Instinct

LOPEZ, JENNIFER
Second Chances

LOPEZ, MARIO
Saved By The Bell-Hawaiian Style

LOPEZ, PRISCILLA
For The Love Of My Child: The Anissa
....Ayala Story
Intimate Strangers

LORD, MARJORIE
Side By Side

LOREN, SOPHIA
Aurora
Courage
Mario Puzo's The Fortunate Pilgrim

LORING, GLORIA
Convicted: A Mother's Story

LOUGHLIN, LORI
Doing Time On Maple Drive
Empty Cradle
One Of Her Own
Place To Call Home, A
Stranger In The Mirror, A

LOVE, VICTOR
Return Of Desperado, The

LOWE, CHAD
April Morning
Candles In The Dark
Captive
Silence Of The Heart
So Proudly We Hail
There Must Be A Pony

LUCAS, JOSHUA
Charles And Diana: Unhappily Ever After
Class Of '61

LUCCI, SUSAN
Anastasia: The Mystery Of Anna
Between Love And Hate
Bride In Black, The
Double Edge
French Silk
Haunted By Her Past
Lady Mobster
Mafia Princess
Woman Who Sinned, The

LUCKINBILL, LAURENCE
One Terrific Guy

LUCKING, WILLIAM
J. O. E. And The Colonel
Ladykillers
Naked Lie
Napoleon And Josephine: A Love Story

LUKE, KEYE
Blade In Hong Kong

LUMBLY, CARL
Back To The Streets Of San Francisco
Eyes Of A Witness
Mantis
On Promised Land
Out Of The Darkness

LUND, DEANNA
Red Wind

LUNDY, JESSICA
Over My Dead Body

LUNER, JAMIE
Moment Of Truth: Why My Daughter?

LuPONE, PATTI
L B J: The Early Years
Water Engine, The

LYMAN, DOROTHY
Tears And Laughter: The Joan And Mielissa
....Rivers Story

LYNCH, KATE
Ann Jillian Story, The
Easy Prey

LYONS, PHYLLIS
Casualties Of Love: The Long Island Lolita
....Story
Love, Honor & Obey: The Last Mafia
....Marriage

LYTHGOW, GENE
When A Stranger Calls Back

MACCHIO, RALPH
Last P. O. W? The Bobby Garwood Story
Three Wishes Of Billy Grier, The

MACCORKINDALE, SIMON
Obsessive Love

MACGRAW, ALI
Gunsmoke: The Long Ride Home
Survive The Savage Sea

MACHT, STEPHEN
Blind Witness
Fear Stalk
Moment Of Truth: A Child Too Many
My Boyfriend's Back
Strange Voices

MACINTOSH, KEEGAN
For The Love Of Aaron

MACLACHLAN, KYLE
Against The Wall
Dream Breakers
Roswell
Twin Peaks

MACLAINE, SHIRLEY
Out On A Limb

MACLEOD, GAVIN
Love Boat: A Valentine Voyage, The

MACNAUGHTON, ROBERT
Place To Call Home, A

MACNEE, PATRICK
Club Med
Sorry, Wrong Number

MACNICOL, PETER
Johnny Bull

MACVITTIE, BRUCE
Night Visions

MACY, BILL
Columbo: It's All In The Game
Water Engine, The

MADIGAN, AMY
And Then There Was One
Lucky Day
Roe Vs. Wade

MADSEN, MICHAEL
Baby Snatcher
Our Family Honor

MADSEN, VIRGINIA
Bitter Vengeance
Gotham
Hearst And Davies Affair, The
Ironclads
Linda
Long Gone
Love Kills
Murderous Affair, A: The Carolyn Warmus
....Story
Mussolini - The Untold Story

Third Degree Burn
Victim Of Love

MAGUIRE, TOBEY
Spoils Of War

MAHAFFEY, VALERIE
They

MAHER, BILL
Out Of Time

MAHONEN, MICHAEL
Conspiracy Of Silence

MAHONEY, JOHN
Favorite Son
Image, The
Secret Passion Of Robert Clayton, The
Ten Million Dollar Getaway
Trapped In Silence

MAITLAND, BETH
Plaza Suite

MAJORS, LEE
Bionic Showdown: The 6 Million Dollar
....Man/Bionic Woman
Cover Girl Murders, The
Cowboy And The Ballerina, The
Danger Down Under
Fire: Trapped On The 37th Floor
Return Of The 6 Million Dollar Man & Bionic
....Woman
Smokey Mountain Christmas, A

MAKO,
Hawaiian Heat
Hiroshima: Out Of The Ashes
Murder In Paradise

MALDEN, KARL
Absolute Strangers
Back To The Streets Of San Francisco
Fatal Vision
Hijacking Of The Achille Lauro, The
My Father, My Son
They've Taken Our Children: The Chowchilla
....Kidnapping
With Intent To Kill

MALINGER, ASHLEY
To My Daughter With Love

MALKOVICH, JOHN
Death Of A Salesman
Heart Of Darkness

MALONE, DOROTHY
He's Not Your Son
Peyton Place: The Next Generation

MANCUSO, NICK
Burning Bridges
Danielle Steel's Message From Nam
Fatal Exposure
For The Love Of Aaron
King Of Love, The
Lies Before Kisses
Somebody's Daughter

MANCUSO, SAM
Only Way Out, The

MANDAN, ROBERT
Perry Mason: The Case Of The Lost Love

MANDRELL, BARBARA
Burning Rage

MANDYLOR, COSTAS
Picket Fences

MANILOW, BARRY
Copacabana

MANOFF, DINAH
Babies
Classified Love
Cover Girl And The Cop, The
Maid For Each Other

MANTEGNA, JOE
Comrades Of Summer
State Of Emergency
Water Engine, The

MANTEL, BRONWEN
Barnum

MANTOOTH, RANDOLPH
Bridge Across Time

MARCIANO, DAVID
Due South

MARCOUX, TED
Danielle Steel's Message From Nam
Eyes Of Terror
Nightman, The

MARCUS, BILL
Long Time Gone

MARCUS, RICHARD
Jesse

MARGOLYES, MIRIAM
Orpheus Descending

MARIN, CHEECH
Cisco Kid, The

MARINARO, ED
Amy Fisher: My Story
Dancing With Danger
Diamond Trap, The
Passport To Murder
Sharing Richard
Tonight's The Night

MARK, MARKY
Substitute, The

MARKEL, DANIEL
For Love And Glory

MARLOWE, SCOTT
No Place Like Home

MARSH, JEAN
Bejeweled
Connecticut Yankee In King Arthur's Court, A
Corsican Brothers, The

MARSHALL, E.G.
At Mother's Request
Hijacking Of The Achille Lauro, The
Oldest Living Confederate Widow Tells All

Tommyknockers, The
Under Siege

MARSHALL, MELISSA
Girl From Tomorrow, The

MARSHALL, PAULA
Flash, The

MARSHALL, PENNY
Challenge Of A Lifetime
Odd Couple, The

MARTELLS, CYNTHIA
Blind Spot

MARTIN, ANDREA
Boris And Natasha

MARTIN, BARNEY
Us

MARTIN, DEAN PAUL
Misfits Of Science

MARTIN, JOHN
Moment Of Truth: Stalking Back

MARTIN, KELLIE
Christy

MARTIN, KIEL
Convicted: A Mother's Story
If It's Tuesday, It Still Must Be Belgium

MARTIN, NAN
Proud Men

MARTIN, PAMELA SUE
Bay Coven

MARTINEZ, A
Criminal Behavior
Deconstructing Sarah
In The Nick Of Time
Manhunt: Search For The Night Stalker
Not Of This World

MARTYN, GREG
Ellis Island

MASON, MADISON
Omen I V: The Awakening

MASON, MARSHA
Dinner At Eight
Surviving
Trapped In Silence

MASON, TOM
Final Appeal
Nightmare In The Daylight
Our Family Honor

MASSEY, ANNA
Anna Karenina

MASTERS, BEN
Deliberate Stranger, The
James Clavell's Noble House
Kate's Secret
Keys, The
Riviera
Running Mates
Street Of Dreams

MASTERSON, MARY STUART
Love Lives On

MASTRANTONIO, MARY ELIZABETI
Mussolini - The Untold Story

MASUR, RICHARD
Adam: His Song Continues
Burning Bed, The
Cast The First Stone
George Mckenna Story, The
Higher Ground
Obsessed With A Married Woman
Roses Are For The Rich
Search For Grace
Settle The Score
Stephen King's It
Story Lady, The
Third Degree Burn
When The Bough Breaks
Wild Horses

MATHESON, TIM
Bay Coven
Blind Justice
Buried Alive
Dying To Love You
Harmful Intent
Joshua's Heart
Kiss To Die For, A
Little White Lies
Littlest Victims
Obsessed With A Married Woman
Quicksand: No Escape
Relentless: Mind Of A Killer
Shameful Secrets
Stephen King's Sometimes They Come Back
Target Of Suspicion
Trial And Error
Warm Hearts, Cold Feet
White Lie
Woman Who Sinned, The

MATHEWS, CARMEN
Last Best Year, The

MATHIS, SAMANTHA
Extreme Close-Up
To My Daughter

MATLIN, MARLEE
Bridge To Silence

MATTHAU, WALTER
Against Her Will: An Incident In Baltimore
Incident In A Small Town
Incident, The
Mrs. Lambert Remembers Love

MATTHEWS, DAKIN
Criminal Behavior
Jailbirds
My Brother's Wife
Out On The Edge
Revolver

MATTHEWS, DeLANE
I'll Take Romance

MATTSON, ROBIN
False Witness

MATUSZAK, JOHN
Dirty Dozen: The Fatal Mission

MAXWELL, PAUL
Intrigue

MAY, DEBORAH
Call Me Anna

MAYER, CHRISTOPHER
Glitter

MAYO, WHITMAN
Father Of Hell Town

MAYRON, MELANIE
Ordeal In The Arctic
Other Women's Children
Wallenberg: A Hero's Story

MAZZELLO, JOE
Desperate Choices: To Save My Child

MCANALLY, RAY
Jack The Ripper

MCARTHUR, ALEX
Desperado
Desperado: Badlands Justice
Drug Wars: The Cocaine Cartel
L. A. Takedown
Return Of Desperado, The
Shoot First: A Cop's Vengeance

MCBAIN, ROBERT
Indiscreet

MCCAFFREY, JAMES
Viper

MCCAIN, FRANCES LEE
Can You Feel Me Dancing?
First Steps
Lookalike, The
Rape Of Richard Beck, The
Scandal In A Small Town

MCCALLUM, DAVID
Behind Enemy Lines
Freedom Fighter
Shattered Image

MCCALMAN, MACON
Independence

MCCANN, SEAN
High Price Of Passion, The

MCCANTS, REED
Road Raiders, The

MCCARTHY, KEVIN
Duplicates
In The Heat Of The Night
Long Journey Home, The
Midnight Hour, The
Passion And Paradise
Poor Little Rich Girl: The Barbara Hutton
....Story

McCASHIN, CONSTANCE
Love On The Run
Nightmare At Bitter Creek
Obsessive Love

McCAY, PEGGY
Deadly Care
Winnie
Woman On The Run: The Lawrencia
....Bembenek Story

McCLANAHAN, RUE
After The Shock
Agatha Christie's The Man In The Brown Suit
Baby Of The Bride
Children Of The Bride
Danielle Steel's Message From Nam
Dreamer Of Oz, The
Liberace
Little Match Girl, The
Mother Of The Bride
Take My Daughters, Please
To My Daughter

McCLARIN, CURTIS
Murder Without Motive: The Edmund Perry
....Story

McCLOSKEY, LEIGH
Accidental Meeting
Trouble Shooters: Trapped Beneath The
....Earth

McCLURE, DOUG
Cover Up
Deadman's Revenge

McCOOK, JOHN
Codename: Foxfire - Slay It Again, Sam

McCORD, KENT
Accidental Meeting

McCORMICK, MAUREEN
Very Brady Christmas, A
Very Brady Christmas, A

McDERMOTT, DYLAN
Fear Inside, The
Into The Badlands
Neon Empire

McDONALD, CHRISTOPHER
Fatal Exposure
Little Girl Lost
Red Wind
Telling Secrets

McDONNELL, MARY
American Clock, The

McDONOUGH, KIT
Letting Go

McDONOUGH, MARY
Walton Thanksgiving Reunion, A

McDOWALL, RODDY
Deadly Game
Heads
London And Davis In New York

McDOWELL, MALCOLM
Arthur The King
Gulag
Monte Carlo
Seasons Of The Heart

McENTIRE, REBA
Gambler Returns: The Luck Of The Draw
Man From Left Field

McFARLAND, JOEY
Kids Like These

McGANN, MARK
John And Yoko: A Love Story

McGAVIN, DARREN
American Clock, The
Baron And The Kid, The
Child In The Night
Diamond Trap, The
Perfect Harmony

McGILL, BRUCE
Last Innocent Man, The

McGILLIS, KELLY
Bonds Of Love
Grand Isle
In The Best Of Families: Marriage, Pride And
....Madness
Sweet Revenge, A

McGINLEY, TED
Linda
Revenge Of The Nerds: The Next Generation

McGOOHAN, PATRICK
Of Pure Blood

McGRADY, MICHAEL
Child Lost Forever, A

McGRATH, MATT
Cruel Doubt

McGREGOR, RICHARD
Your Mother Wears Combat Boots

McGUIRE, DOROTHY
American Geisha
Amos

McGUIRE, MICHAEL
Shakedown On The Sunset Strip

McHATTIE, STEPHEN
Jonathan Stone: Threat Of Innocence

McILWRAITH, DAVID
Mothers, Daughters And Lovers

McKEAN, MICHAEL
Classified Love
Father's Homecoming, A
Hider In The House

McKEE, LONETTE
Dangerous Passion

McKELLAR, DANICA
Camp Cucamonga
Moment Of Truth: Cradle Of Conspiracy

McKELLEN, IAN
And The Band Played On

McKEON, DOUG
At Mother's Request
Heart Of A Champion: The Ray Mancini Story

McKEON, NANCY
Baby Snatcher
Cry For Help: The Tracey Thurman Story, A
Facts Of Life Down Under, The
Firefighter
Lightning Incident, The
Love, Honor & Obey: The Last Mafia
....Marriage
Poison Ivy
Strange Voices
This Child Is Mine

McKERN, LEO
Murder With Mirrors

McLAFFERTY, MICHAEL
Trade Winds

McLARTY, RON
Spenser: For Hire

McMILLAN, KENNETH
Acceptable Risks
Our Family Honor

McNAMARA, BILLY
Sworn To Vengeance

McNAMARA, BRIAN
On Fire
Sadie And Son
Storm And Sorrow
Triumph Over Disaster: The Hurricane
....Andrew Story

McNAMARA, WILLIAM
Doing Time On Maple Drive
Honor Thy Mother
Wildflower

McNEIL, ROBERT DUNCAN
One More Mountain

McNICHOL, KRISTY
Baby Of The Bride
Children Of The Bride
Love, Mary
Mother Of The Bride
Women Of Valor

McPEAK, SANDY
Taking Of Flight 847: The Uli Derickson
....Story

McQUEEN, CHAD
Search And Rescue

McRANEY, GERALD
Armed & Innocent
Blind Vengeance
City Killer
Easy Prey
Fatal Friendship
Hobo's Christmas, A
Love And Curses . . . And All That Jazz

Murder By Moonlight
People Across The Lake, The
Scattered Dreams: The Kathryn Messenger
....Story
Vestige Of Honor
Where The Hell's That Gold

McSHANE, IAN
Evergreen
Great Escape I I: The Untold Story, The
Murders In The Rue Morgue, The
War And Remembrance

McWILLIAMS, CAROLINE
Shattered Vows
Sworn To Silence

MEADOWS, STEPHEN
Price She Paid, The
Sunstroke
Trade Winds

MEILLON, JOHN
Outback Bound

MELDRUM, WENDEL
Due South
Hush Little Baby

MELL, RANDLE
Stranger In The Family, A

MELONI, CHRISTOPHER
When Will I Be Loved?
Without A Kiss Goodbye

MEREDITH, BURGESS
Night Of The Hunter
Outrage
Wet Gold

MEREDITH, DON
Police Story: The Freeway Killings

MERRILL, DINA
Fear
Hot Pursuit

MERRITT, THERESA
Miracle At Beekman's Place

METZLER, JIM
Love Kills
Murder By Night

MEYER, BESS
Quiet Victory: The Charlie Wedemeyer Story

MEYERS, ARI
Kids Don't Tell
Picking Up The Pieces

MEYERS, KIM
Sitter, The
When He's Not A Stranger

MICHAS, JASON
Stone Fox

MICHELE, MICHAEL
Trade Winds

MICHELL, KEITH
Captain Cook

MICKELBURY, DENISE B.
Time To Triumph, A

MIDKIFF, DALE
Blackmail
Cry For Help: The Tracey Thurman Story, A
Dallas: The Early Years
Elvis And Me
Marla Hanson Story, The
Plymouth
Shoot First: A Cop's Vengeance
Sins Of The Mother

MIDLER, BETTE
Gypsy

MILANO, ALYSSA
Candles In The Dark
Casualties Of Love: The Long Island Lolita
....Story
Crash Course
Dance Till Dawn

MILES, JOANNA
Right To Die

MILES, SARAH
Ghost In Monte Carlo, A
Harem
Queenie

MILES, VERA
Hijacking Of The Achille Lauro, The

MILIAN, TOMAS
Nails

MILLER, AUBREE
Ewoks: The Battle For Endor

MILLER, CHARLES
Little Kidnappers, The

MILLER, DENISE
Private Sessions

MILLER, JASON
Deadly Care
Touch Of Scandal, A

MILLER, LARRY
Frankenstein: The College Years

MILLER, LINDA
Elvis And Me

MILLER, MARK THOMAS
Blue Deville
Misfits Of Science

MILLER, SAM
Fergie And Andrew: Behind The Palace
....Doors

MILLER, TAYLOR
Overexposed

MILLER, TY
To My Daughter

MILLS, ALLEY
Jonathan: The Boy Nobody Wanted
Tainted Blood

MILLS, DONNA
Barbara Taylor Bradford's Remember
False Arrest
He's Not Your Son
In My Daughter's Name
Intimate Encounters
Lady Forgets, The
My Name Is Kate
Outback Bound
Presidents Child, The
Runaway Father
World's Oldest Living Bridesmaid, The

MILLS, HAYLEY
Back Home

MILLS, JOHN
Frankenstein
Murder With Mirrors

MILLS, JULIET
Stranger In The Mirror, A

MIMIEUX, YVETTE
Fifth Missile, The
Obsessive Love

MINNELLI, LIZA
Parallel Lives
Time To Live, A

MIRREN, HELEN
Red King, White Knight

MITCHELL, DONNA
Spenser: For Hire

MITCHILL, SCOEY
Miracle At Beekman's Place

MITCHUM, CARRIE
Dead Silence

MITCHUM, JOHN
Jake Spanner, Private Eye

MITCHUM, ROBERT
Brotherhood Of The Rose
Family For Joe, A
Hearst And Davies Affair, The
Jake Spanner, Private Eye
Reunion At Fairborough
Thompson's Last Run
War And Remembrance
War And Remembrance, Part I I

MIYORI, KIM
Fire: Trapped On The 37th Floor
John And Yoko: A Love Story
Journey To The Center Of The Earth
When The Bough Breaks

MODEAN, JAYNE
Street Hawk

MODGLIN, DARA
Time To Triumph, A

MODINE, MATTHEW
And The Band Played On

MOFFAT, DONALD
Babe Ruth

Bourne Identity, The
Danielle Steel's Kaleidoscope
Lily
Majority Rule

MOFFETT, D.W.
Counterfeit Contessa, The
Danielle Steel's Fine Things
Dream Breakers
In The Deep Woods
Lies And Lullabies
Palace Guard
Passion For Justice, A: Hazel Brannon Smith
....Story

MOLL, RICHARD
Combat High

MONETTE, RICHARD
Murder By Night

MONTGOMERY, BARBARA
Polly--Comin' Home

MONTGOMERY, BELINDA
Aaron's Way
Casey's Gift: For Love Of A Child
Stone Fox

MONTGOMERY, ELIZABETH
Amos
Black Widow Murders: The Blanche Taylor
....Moore Story
Corpse Had A Familiar Face, The
Face To Face
Sins Of The Mother
With Murder In Mind

MONTGOMERY, LEE
Midnight Hour, The

MOODY, LYNNE
Atlanta Child Murders, The
Lost In London
Toughest Man In The World, The

MOONEY, DEBRA
Too Young The Hero

MOORE, ALVY
Return To Green Acres

MOORE, JULIANNE
Cast A Deadly Spell
Money, Power, Murder

MOORE, MARY TYLER
Finnegan Begin Again
Heartsounds
Last Best Year, The
Lincoln
Stolen Babies
Thanksgiving Day

MORALES, ESAI
On Wings Of Eagles

MOREAU, NATHANIEL
Kissing Place, The

MORELLI, ROBERT
Sadie And Son

MORGAN, DEBBI
Guilty Of Innocence: The Lenell Geter Story

MORGAN, HARRY
Against Her Will: An Incident In Baltimore
Blacke's Magic
Incident In A Small Town

MORGAN, KELLY
Gunsmoke: One Man's Justice

MORIARTY, MICHAEL
Born Too Soon
Frank Nitti: The Enforcer

MORIN, D. DAVID
Broken Promises: Taking Emily Back

MORITA, PAT
Amos
Babes In Toyland
Las Vegas Strip Wars, The

MORLEY, ROBERT
War And Remembrance

MORRIS, ANITA
Smokey Mountain Christmas, A

MORRIS, GARRETT
Maid For Each Other

MORRIS, HOWARD
Return To Mayberry

MORRIS, JUDY
Last Frontier, The

MORRIS, KATHY
Rise & Walk: The Dennis Byrd Story

MORRIS, PHIL
Jackie Collins' Lady Boss

MORSE, BARRY
Fight For Life
Return Of Sherlock Holmes, The
Reunion At Fairborough

MORSE, DAVID
Brotherhood Of The Rose
Cross Of Fire
Cry In The Wild: The Taking Of Peggy Ann
Downpayment On Murder
Miracle On I-880
Shattered Vows
Six Against The Rock
Winnie

MORTON, JOE
Challenger
Equal Justice
Howard Beach: Making The Case For Murder
Legacy Of Lies
Terrorist On Trial: The United States Vs.
Salim

MOSCOW, DAVID
I'll Be Home For Christmas

MOSES, MARK
Tracker, The

MOSES, RICK
Pleasures

MOSES, WILLIAM R.
Perry Mason Mystery: The Case Of The
Wicked Wives
Perry Mason: The Case Of The All-Star
Assassin
Perry Mason: The Case Of The Defiant
Daughter
Perry Mason: The Case Of The Desperate
Deception
Perry Mason: The Case Of The Fatal Fashion
Perry Mason: The Case Of The Fatal Framing
Perry Mason: The Case Of The Glass Coffin
Perry Mason: The Case Of The Maligned
Mobster
Perry Mason: The Case Of The Musical
Murders
Perry Mason: The Case Of The Poisoned Pen
Perry Mason: The Case Of The Ruthless
Reporter
Rock Hudson

MOSS, ELISABETH
Midnight's Child

MOTT, ZACHARY
Guilty Until Proven Innocent

MR. T,
Toughest Man In The World, The

MUELLER, MAUREEN
She Woke Up

MULDAUR, DIANA
Agatha Christie's Murder In Three Acts
Locked Up: A Mother's Rage
Perry Mason: The Case Of The Fatal Fashion
Return Of Sam Mccloud, The

MULGREW, KATE
Danielle Steel's Daddy
Fatal Friendship
For Love And Glory
Roots: The Gift
Roses Are For The Rich

MULHARE, EDWARD
Knight Rider 2000

MULHERN, MATT
Terror In The Night

MULKEY, CHRIS
Deadbolt
Runaway Father

MULL, MARTIN
California Girls
Day My Parents Ran Away, The

MULLAVEY, GREG
Not Quite Human II
Who Gets The Friends?

MULLIGAN, MARY
Two Fathers: Justice For The Innocent

MULLIGAN, RICHARD
Babes In Toyland

Guess Who's Coming For Christmas
Lincoln
Poker Alice

MULRONEY, DERMOT
Daddy
Family Pictures
Heart Of Justice, The
Last Outlaw, The
Long Gone
Sin Of Innocence
Unconquered

MURCELO, KARMIN
Right To Kill?

MURNEY, CHRISTOPHER
Murder By The Book

MURPHY, MICHAEL
Dead Ahead: The Exxon Valdez Disaster

MURPHY, ROSEMARY
Woman Named Jackie, A

MURPHY, TIMOTHY PATRICK
With Intent To Kill

MURRAY, DON
Brand New Life: The Honeymoon
Mistress
Something In Common
Stillwatch
Touch Of Scandal, A

MURRAY, SEAN
River Of Rage: The Taking Of Maggie
....Keene

MUSANTE, TONY
Nutcracker: Money, Madness And Murder
Rearview Mirror

MUTI, ORNELLA
Casanova

NABORS, JIM
Return To Mayberry

NADER, MICHAEL
Great Escape I I: The Untold Story, The
Jackie Collins' Lucky Chances
Lady Mobster
Nick Knight

NATWICK, MILDRED
Deadly Deception

NAUGHTON, DAVID
Goddess Of Love

NAUGHTON, JAMES
Birds I I: Land's End, The
Cosby Mysteries, The
Necessity
Sin Of Innocence

NAVIN, JOHN
Toughest Man In The World, The

NEAL, PATRICIA
Caroline?

NEEDHAM, TRACEY
Bonnie And Clyde: The True Story

Lush Life
Prophet Of Evil: The Ervil Lebaron Story

NEESON, LIAM
Sworn To Silence

NEGODA, NATALYA
Comrades Of Summer

NEILL, SAM
Amerika
Family Pictures
Fever
Kane And Abel
Leap Of Faith
One Against The Wind

NELLIGAN, KATE
Diamond Fleece
Kojak: The Price Of Justice
Love And Hate: A Marriage Made In Hell
Shattered Trust: The Shari Karney Story
Spoils Of War

NELSON, CRAIG T.
Alex: The Life Of A Child
Drug Wars: The Camarena Story
Extreme Close-Up
Fire Next Time, The
Murderers Among Us: The Simon Wiesenthal
....Story
Ride With The Wind
Switch, The
Ted Kennedy, Jr., Story, The

NELSON, ED
Peyton Place: The Next Generation

NELSON, JOHN ALLEN
Quantum Leap

NELSON, JUDD
Billionaire Boys Club
Blindfold: Acts Of Obsession
Hiroshima: Out Of The Ashes

NELSON, TRACY
Fatal Confession: A Father Dowling Mystery
Glitter
Highway Heartbreaker
If It's Tuesday, It Still Must Be Belgium
Kate's Secret
No Child Of Mine
Pleasures
Ray Alexander: A Taste For Justice
Tonight's The Night

NELSON, WILLIE
Another Pair Of Aces: Three Of A Kind
Last Days Of Frank And Jesse James, The
Once Upon A Texas Train
Pair Of Aces
Stagecoach
Where The Hell's That Gold
Wild Texas Wind

NEMEC, CORIN
For The Very First Time
I Know My First Name Is Steven
My Son Johnny

NERO, FRANCO
Windmills Of The Gods
Young Catherine

NETTLETON, LOIS
Brass
Manhunt For Claude Dallas

NEUWIRTH, BEBE
Without Her Consent

NEWBERN, GEORGE
I Spy Returns

NEWHART, BOB
Entertainers, The

NEWLEY, ANTHONY
Outrage

NEWMAN, BARRY
Fatal Vision
My Two Loves

NEWMAN, LARAINE
This Wife For Hire

NEWSOM, DAVID
Homefront
Trouble Shooters: Trapped Beneath The
....Earth

NEWTON-JOHN, OLIVIA
Mom For Christmas, A

NGOR, DR. HANG S.
In Love And War

NICHOLAS, DENISE
On Thin Ice: The Tai Babilonia Story
Supercarrier

NICKSON, JULIA
Around The World In 80 Days
Harry's Hong Kong
James Clavell's Noble House

NIELSEN, BRIGITTE
Murder By Moonlight

NIELSEN, CONNIE
Voyage

NIELSEN, LESLIE
Blade In Hong Kong
Chance Of A Lifetime
Fatal Confession: A Father Dowling Mystery

NIGHY, BILL
Agatha Christie's Thirteen At Dinner
Hitler's S S: Portrait In Evil

NIMOY, LEONARD
Never Forget
Sun Also Rises, The

NIPOTE, JOE
Viper

NIXON, CYNTHIA
Face Of A Stranger
Love She Sought, The

NOBLE, CHELSEA
Little Piece Of Heaven, A

NOBLE, JAMES
Archie: To Riverdale And Back Again
When The Bough Breaks

NOGULICH, NATALIJA
Out On The Edge

NOLAN, KATHLEEN
Switch, The

NOLAN, TOM
Jessie

NORDLING, JEFFREY
Baby Brokers
Quiet Killer
Shooter

NORMAN, SUSAN
Knight Rider 2000
Tower, The

NORRIS, CHUCK
Walker, Texas Ranger

NORTH, SHEREE
Scorned And Swindled

NORTON, JUDY
Walton Thanksgiving Reunion, A

NOSEWORTHY, JACK
Place For Annie, A

NOTH, CHRISTOPHER
In The Shadows, Someone Is Watching

NOURI, MICHAEL
Between Two Women
Black Ice
Danielle Steel's Changes
Exclusive
Eyes Of Terror
In The Arms Of A Killer
Psychic
Quiet Victory: The Charlie Wedemeyer Story
Rage Of Angels: The Story Continues
Shattered Dreams

NOVAK, KIM
Alfred Hitchcock Presents

NUNN, BILL
Silent Witness: What A Child Saw
White Lie

O'BRIAN, HUGH
Gambler Returns: The Luck Of The Draw

O'BRIEN, TOM
Love & Lies

O'CONNOR, CARROLL
Brass
Convicted
Father Clements Story, The
In The Heat Of The Night

O'CONNOR, GLYNNIS
Conspiracy Of Love
Deliberate Stranger, The
Sins Of The Father
To Heal A Nation
Too Good To Be True

O'CONNOR, HELEN
Girl From Tomorrow, The

O'CONNOR, TIM
Peyton Place: The Next Generation

O'FARRELL, CONOR
Back To The Streets Of San Francisco
Moment Of Truth: A Child Too Many

O'HERLIHY, GAVIN
Tailspin: Behind The Korean Airlines Tragedy

O'HURLEY, JOHN
Seduction: Three Tales From The Inner
Sanctum

O'KEEFE, MICHAEL
Bridge To Silence
Disaster At Silo 7
Fear
In The Best Interest Of The Child
Unholy Matrimony

O'LEARY, WILLIAM
Flight Of Black Angel
In The Line Of Duty: Ambush In Waco

O'NEAL, GRIFFIN
Children Of Times Square

O'NEAL, RON
North Beach And Rawhide
Playing With Fire

O'NEAL, RYAN
Man Upstairs, The
Small Sacrifices

O'NEAL, TATUM
Woman On The Run: The Lawrencia
....Bembenek Story

O'NEILL, DICK
Secret Life Of Kathy Mccormick, The

O'NEILL, ED
Popeye Doyle
Whereabouts Of Jenny, The

O'NEILL, JENNIFER
Chase
Cover Girl Murders, The
Cover Up
Full Exposure: The Sex Tapes Scandal
Glory Days
Invasion Of Privacy
Personals

O'QUINN, TERRY
Born Too Soon
Deliver Them From Evil: The Taking Of Alta
....View
Don't Talk To Strangers
Good Fight, The
Heart Of A Child
Last To Go, The
Macshayne: Winner Take All
Roe Vs. Wade
Sexual Advances
Shoot First: A Cop's Vengeance
Stranger On My Land

Wild Card
Women Of Valor

O'REILLY, CYRIL
Matlock: The Witness Killings

O'ROSS, ED
Dreams Of Gold: The Mel Fisher Story
Tailspin: Behind The Korean Airlines Tragedy

O'SULLIVAN, JAMES
Flight Of Black Angel

O'SULLIVAN, MAUREEN
Habitation Of Dragons, The
With Murder In Mind

O'TOOLE, ANNETTE
Alfred Hitchcock Presents
Broken Vows
Copacabana
Danielle Steel's Jewels
Dreamer Of Oz, The
Guts And Glory: The Rise And Fall Of Oliver
....North
Kennedys Of Massachusetts, The
Kiss Of A Killer
Love Matters
Mothers Revenge, A
White Lie

O'TOOLE, PETER
Crossing To Freedom

OGILVY, IAN
Anna Karenina

OH, SOON-TECK
Red Spider, The

OKUMOTO, YUJI
Murder In Paradise
Only One Survived

OLANDT, KEN
Impostor, The
Supercarrier

OLDHAM, WILL
Everybody's Baby: The Rescue Of Jessica
....Mcclure

OLIN, KEN
Good Night, Sweet Wife: A Murder In Boston
I'll Take Manhattan
Stoning In Fulham County, A
Telling Secrets
There Must Be A Pony
Tonight's The Night

OLIVIER, LAWRENCE
Peter The Great

OLMOS, EDWARD JAMES
Mario Puzo's The Fortunate Pilgrim
Menendez: A Killing In Beverly Hills

OLSEN, ASHLEY
Double, Double, Toil And Trouble
To Grandmother's House We Go

OLSEN, MARY KATE
Double, Double, Toil And Trouble
To Grandmother's House We Go

OLSEN, MERLIN
Aaron's Way

OLSON, JAMES
North Beach And Rawhide
One Police Plaza

ONORATI, PETER
River Of Rage: The Taking Of Maggie
....Keene
With Hostile Intent

ONTKEAN, MICHAEL
In A Child's Name
In Defense Of A Married Man
Kids Don't Tell
Legacy Of Lies
Right Of The People, The
Twin Peaks
Whose Child Is This? The War For Baby
....Jessica

ORBACH, JERRY
Broadway Bound
In Defense Of A Married Man
Love Among Thieves
Out On A Limb
Perry Mason: The Case Of The Musical
Murders

ORMOND, JULIA
Stalin

ORR, MOLLY
Message From Holly

OSBORNE, MADOLYN SMITH
Deadly Intentions
If Tomorrow Comes
Plot To Kill Hitler, The
Rose And The Jackal, The

OSTERWALD, BIBI
Stillwatch

OUTERBRIDGE, PETER
Drop Dead Gorgeous

OVERALL, PARK
Overkill: The Aileen Wuornos Story
Precious Victims

OVERBEY, KELLIE
Wife, Mother, Murderer

OXENBERG, CATHERINE
Roman Holiday
Rubdown
Still Crazy Like A Fox
Swimsuit

PACULA, JOANNA
Black Ice
Breaking Point
E. A. R. T. H. Force
Escape From Sobibor

PAGE, GERALDINE
Nazi Hunter: The Beate Klarsfeld Story

PAGE, HARRISON
Columbo: Undercover

PALANCE, JACK
Keep The Change

PALMER, BETSY
Goddess Of Love
Still Not Quite Human

PALTROW, GWYNETH
Deadly Relations

PANKIN, STUART
Different Affair, A

PANTOLIANO, JOE
Dangerous Heart
El Diablo
Through The Eyes Of A Killer

PARIS, CHERYL
Columbo And The Murder Of A Rock Star

PARK-LINCOLN, LAR
Children Of The Night

PARKER, COREY
At Mother's Request
Broadway Bound
I'm Dangerous Tonight

PARKER, ELEANOR
Dead On The Money

PARKER, JAMESON
Dead Before Dawn
She Says She's Innocent
Who Is Julia?

PARKER, MARY LOUISE
Place For Annie, A
Too Young The Hero

PARKER, NOELLE
Amy Fisher: My Story

PARKER, NORMAN
Leap Of Faith

PARKER, SARAH JESSICA
Equal Justice
Going For The Gold: The Bill Johnson Story
In The Best Interest Of The Children

PARKINS, BARBARA
Peyton Place: The Next Generation

PARKS, JAMES
Blind Vengeance

PARKS, MICHAEL
China Lake Murders, The
Dangerous Affection

PARSEKIAN, TOM
Shattered Vows

PARSONS, ESTELLE
Open Admissions
Private Matter, A

PARTON, DOLLY
Smokey Mountain Christmas, A
Wild Texas Wind

PASCO, ISABELLE
Deep Trouble

PASDAR, ADRIAN
Grand Isle
Lost Capone, The

PASTORELLI, ROBERT
Harmful Intent
Yarn Princess, The

PATRIC, JASON
Toughlove

PATTERSON, LORNA
Impostor, The

PATTERSON, NEVA
Women Of Valor

PATTON, WILL
Deadly Desire
Dillinger
Gathering Of Old Men, A
In The Deep Woods

PAUL, ADRIAN
Cover Girl Murders, The

PAUL, ALEXANDRA
Death Train
Laker Girls, The
Perry Mason: The Case Of The Musical
Murders

PAUL, DON MICHAEL
Search For Grace

PAULIN, SCOTT
Appearances
Deadly Medicine
Dreams Of Gold: The Mel Fisher Story
To Heal A Nation
Tricks Of The Trade
White Hot: The Mysterious Murder Of
....Thelma Todd

PAX, JAMES
Nasty Boys

PAYMER, DAVID
Love, Mary
Pleasures

PAYNE, BRUCE
Cisco Kid, The

PAYS, AMANDA
Dead On The Money
Flash, The
I Know My Son Is Alive
Parker Kane

PECK, CECELIA
Portrait, The

PECK, GREGORY
Portrait, The

PEEPLES, NIA
My Name Is Kate

PELDON, ASHLEY
Child Of Rage

PELIKAN, LISA
Bunny's Tale, A

PELUCE, MEENO
Detective In The House

PENA, ELIZABETH
Fugitive Among Us
Roommates
Shannon's Deal

PENGHLIS, THAAO
Lookalike, The
Under Siege

PENNY, JOE
Blood Vows: The Story Of A Mafia Wife
Danger Of Love, The
Jake And The Fatman
Operation, The
Perry Mason: The Case Of The Shooting Star
Roses Are For The Rich
Terror In The Night
Whisper Kills, A

PEPPARD, GEORGE
Man Against The Mob
Man Against The Mob: The Chinatown
....Murders

PEREZ, ROSIE
Criminal Justice

PEREZ, TONY
For The Love Of My Child: The Anissa
....Ayala Story

PERKINS, ANTHONY
Daughter Of Darkness
I'm Dangerous Tonight
In The Deep Woods
Napoleon And Josephine: A Love Story
Psycho I V: The Beginning

PERKINS, ELIZABETH
For Their Own Good

PERKINS, EMILY
Anything To Survive

PERKINS, MILLIE
Broken Angel
Murder Of Innocence
Other Lover, The
Penalty Phase
Shattered Vows
Strange Voices

PERLMAN, RHEA
Dangerous Affection
Place To Be Loved, A
Spoils Of War
To Grandmother's House We Go

PERLMAN, RON
Blind Man's Bluff
Stoning In Fulham County, A

PERRINE, VALERIE
Sweet Bird Of Youth

PERRY, JOHN BENNETT
Independence
Last Fling, The
Nightingales

She Knows Too Much

PERSKY, LISA JANE
Sharing Richard

PETERS, BERNADETTE
David
Fall From Grace
Last Best Year, The

PETERS, BROCK
Broken Angel
Secret, The
To Heal A Nation

PETERSEN, WILLIAM
Keep The Change
Kennedys Of Massachusetts, The
Long Gone
Return To Lonesome Dove

PETERSON, AMANDA
Fatal Charm
Hell Hath No Fury
Love And Betrayal
Posing: Inspired By Three Real Stories

PETERSON, CASEY
Us

PETRUZZI, JOE
Secret Weapon

PEYSER, PENNY
Still Crazy Like A Fox

PHELAN, SHAWN
Caroline?
Miles From Nowhere

PHELPS, PETER
Baywatch: Panic At Malibu Pier

PHILBIN, JOHN
Resting Place

PHILLIPS, CHYNNA
Comeback, The
Moving Target
Roxanne: The Prize Pulitzer

PHILLIPS, JONATHAN
Max And Helen

PHILLIPS, JULIANNE
Getting Up And Going Home
Only Way Out, The

PHILLIPS, LOU DIAMOND
Three Kings, The

PHILLIPS, MICHELLE
Assault And Matrimony
Rubdown
Secrets Of A Married Man
Trenchcoat In Paradise

PHILLIPS, SIAN
Ewoks: The Battle For Endor

PHILLIPS, WENDY
Appearances
Gifted One, The
Homefront
Macshayne: The Final Roll Of The Dice

Macshayne: Winner Take All

PHOENIX, RIVER
Circle Of Violence: A Family Drama

PICARDO, ROBERT
China Beach
Fatal Deception: Mrs. Lee Harvey Oswald
She Says She's Innocent

PICKETT, CINDY
Amerika
Echoes In The Darkness
I Know My First Name Is Steven
Into The Homeland
Plymouth
Wild Card

PICKLES, CHRISTINA
Hijacking Of The Achille Lauro, The
Revenge Of The Nerds I V: Nerds In Love

PICKUP, RONALD
Attic: The Hiding Of Anne Frank, The
Jekyll & Hyde

PIDDOCK, JAMES
Women Of Windsor

PIERCE, BRADLEY
Ride With The Wind

PIGOTT-SMITH, TIM
Agatha Christie's Dead Man's Folly

PILEGGI, MITCH
Three On A Match

PINCHOT, BRONSON
Between Two Women
Jury Duty: The Comedy

PINTER, COLLEEN
Woman On The Ledge

PISTONE, KIMBERLEY
Blue Deville

PITT, BRAD
Too Young To Die?

PLACE, MARY KAY
Bed Of Lies
In The Line Of Duty: The Price Of
....Vengeance
Out On The Edge

PLANA, TONY
Case Of The Hillside Strangler, The

PLANK, SCOTT
Dying To Remember
L. A. Takedown

PLAYTEN, ALICE
Cosby Mysteries, The

PLEASENCE, DONALD
Great Escape I I: The Untold Story, The
Room, The

PLESHETTE, JOHN
Lies Of The Twins
Shattered Innocence
Welcome Home, Bobby

PLESHETTE, SUZANNE
Alone In The Neon Jungle
Battling For Baby
For Love Or Money
Kojak: The Belarus File
Leona Helmsley: The Queen Of Mean
Stranger Waits, A
Twist Of The Knife, A

PLIMPTON, MARTHA
Chantilly Lace
Daybreak

PLOWRIGHT, JOAN
On Promised Land
Place For Annie, A
Stalin

PLUMB, EVE
Bradys, The
Very Brady Christmas, A

PLUMMER, AMANDA
Last Light
Miss Rose White
True Blue
Whose Child Is This? The War For Baby
....Jessica

PLUMMER, CHRISTOPHER
Crossings
Danielle Steel's Secrets
Ghost In Monte Carlo, A
Hazard Of Hearts, A
Souvenir
Young Catherine

PLUNKETT, MARYANN
Littlest Victims

PODEWELL, CATHY
Earth Angel

POGUE, KEN
Due South
Harvest For The Heart

POINDEXTER, LARRY
I'll Take Romance

POITIER, SIDNEY
Separate But Equal

POLLAK, CHERYL
For The Very First Time
Marla Hanson Story, The
Sin And Redemption

POLLAN, TRACY
Abduction Of Kari Swenson, The
Baron And The Kid, The
Children Of The Dark
Danielle Steel's Fine Things
Dying To Love You
Special Friendship, A

POLO, TERI
Phantom Of The Opera, The

POLSON, JOHN
Dadah Is Death

PONCE, LUANNE
Moment Of Truth: Stalking Back

PONTI, EDOARDO
Aurora

POPE, PEGGY
Roses Are For The Rich
Toughest Man In The World, The

PORTNOW, RICHARD
Original Sin

POSPIL, ERIC
Other Women's Children

POST, MARKIE
Beyond Suspicion
Glitz
Scene Of The Crime
Stranger At My Door
Tricks Of The Trade
Triplecross

POSTON, TOM
Fresno

POTTS, CLIFF
International Airport

POTTS, JONATHAN
Conspiracy Of Silence

POUGET, ELY
L. A. Takedown

POUNDER, CCH
Common Ground
Disappearance Of Christina, The
Ernest Green Story, The
For Their Own Good
Lifepod
Murder In Mississippi
Psycho IV: The Beginning
Third Degree Burn

POWERS, ALENANDRA
Matter Of Justice, A

POWERS, ALEXANDRA
Dangerous Pursuit
Tonya & Nancy: The Inside Story

POWERS, STEFANIE
At Mother's Request
Beryl Markham: A Shadow On The Sun
Burden Of Proof, The
Deceptions
Hart To Hart Returns
Love And Betrayal
Mistral's Daughter
She Was Marked For Murder
Survive The Night
When Will I Be Loved?

POWNALL, LEON
Love And Hate: A Marriage Made In Hell

PRAED, MICHAEL
Writer's Block

PRATT, DEBORAH
Three On A Match

PRESS, LAURA
Barnum

PRESSMAN, LAWRENCE
Diary Of A Perfect Murder
Little Girl Lost
Street Hawk
Three Wishes Of Billy Grier, The
To My Daughter With Love
Victims For Victims - The Theresa Saldana
....Story
White Hot: The Mysterious Murder Of
....Thelma Todd

PRESTON, J.A.
Court - Martial Of Jackie Robinson, The
Steel Justice

PRESTON, KELLY
Perfect Bride, The

PRESTON, MIKE
Hot Pursuit

PRESTON, ROBERT
Finnegan Begin Again
Outrage

PRICE, ANNABELLA
Good Night, Sweet Wife: A Murder In Boston
Murder Ordained
Roe Vs. Wade
Roots: The Gift

PRICE, KENNETH
John And Yoko: A Love Story

PRIMUS, BARRY
Stillwatch

PRINCIPAL, VICTORIA
Beyond Obsession
Blind Witness
Burden Of Proof, The
Don't Touch My Daughter
Mistress
Naked Lie
River Of Rage: The Taking Of Maggie
....Keene
Seduction: Three Tales From The Inner
Sanctum
Sparks: The Price Of Passion

PRINE, ANDREW
Scattered Dreams: The Kathryn Messenger
....Story

PRINGLE, JOAN
Visions Of Murder

PROCHNOW, JURGEN
Danielle Steel's Jewels
Fire Next Time, The
Forbidden
Murder: By Reason Of Insanity
Robin Hood

PROSKY, ROBERT
Heist
Home Fires Burning
Into Thin Air
Murder Of Mary Phagan, The

PROTHEROE, BRIAN
Not A Penny More, Not A Penny Less

PRYCE, JONATHAN
Barbarians At The Gate

PRYOR, NICHOLAS
Into Thin Air

PULLIAM, KESHIA KNIGHT
Connecticut Yankee In King Arthur's Court, A
Little Match Girl, The
Polly--Comin' Home

PULLMAN, BILL
Crazy In Love

PURCELL, LEE
Betrayed By Innocence
Incredible Hulk Returns, The
Long Road Home
Secret Sins Of The Father
To Heal A Nation

PURL, LINDA
Accidental Meeting
Addicted To His Love
Body Language
Danielle Steel's Secrets
In Self Defense
Outrage
Pleasures
Spies, Lies And Naked Thighs
Under Cover
Web Of Deceit

PUTCH, JOHN
Street Of Dreams

QUAID, RANDY
Dead Solid Perfect
Evil In Clear River
Frankenstein
L B J: The Early Years
Murder In The Heartland
Roommates

QUAYLE, ANTHONY
Bourne Identity, The

QUINLAN, KATHLEEN
American Story, An
Blackout
Children Of The Night
Last Light
Operation, The
Stolen Babies
Strays
Trapped

QUINN, AIDAN
An Early Frost
Lies Of The Twins
Perfect Witness
Private Matter, A

QUINN, ANTHONY
Old Man & The Sea, The
Richest Man In The World: The Aristotle
....Onassis Story
This Can't Be Love

QUINN, ELIZABETH
Sound And The Silence, The

QUINN, FRANCESCO
Old Man & The Sea, The

QUINN, J.C.
Secret Life Of Archie's Wife, The

QUINN, VALENTINA
Old Man & The Sea, The

QUO, BEULAH
American Geisha

RACHINS, ALAN
Jackie Collins' Lady Boss
L. A. Law
She Says She's Innocent

RAFFIN, DEBORAH
James Clavell's Noble House
Lace I I
Threesome

RAGSDALE, WILLIAM
Frankenstein: The College Years

RAILSBACK, STEVE
Bonds Of Love
Good Cops, Bad Cops
Separated By Murder
Sunstroke

RAINES, CRISTINA
Generation

RAINEY, FORD
Who Is Julia?

RAINEY, JAMIE
Clarence

RALPH, SHERLY LEE
Codename: Foxfire - Slay It Again, Sam

RAMBO, DACK
Paper Dolls

RAMIREZ, JUAN
Missing Persons

RAMSEY, ROBIN
Dadah Is Death

RAMUS, NICK
Geronimo

RANDALL, ETHAN
Bad Attitudes

RANDALL, LEXI
Heidi
In The Best Interest Of The Children
Sarah, Plain And Tall
Skylark

RANDALL, TONY
Agatha Christie's The Man In The Brown Suit
Hitler's S S: Portrait In Evil
Odd Couple, The

RANDOLPH, JOHN
Right Of The People, The
Vital Signs

RANSOM, TIM
Last To Go, The
They've Taken Our Children: The Chowchilla
....Kidnapping

RASCHE, DAVID
Silhouette

RASHAD, PHYLICIA
David's Mother
False Witness
Jailbirds
Polly--Comin' Home
Uncle Tom's Cabin

RASKIN, JONATHAN
Rockabye

RASULALA, THALMUS
Blind Vengeance

RATLIFF, GARETTE
Her Secret Life

RATZENBERGER, JOHN
Camp Cucamonga
Going To The Chapel
Timestalkers

RAY, ANDREW
Passion And Paradise

READ, JAMES
Celebration Family
North And South, Book 3: Heaven And Hell
Poor Little Rich Girl: The Barbara Hutton
....Story
Web Of Deceit

REDGRAVE, LYNN
Bad Seed, The
Jury Duty: The Comedy
My Two Loves
What Ever Happened To Baby Jane?

REDGRAVE, VANESSA
Man For All Season, A
Orpheus Descending
Peter The Great
Second Serve
They
What Ever Happened To Baby Jane?
Young Catherine

REED, JAMES
North And South
North And South, Book 2

REED, OLIVER
Christopher Columbus
Ghost In Monte Carlo, A
Lady And The Highwayman, The
Prisoner Of Honor
Return To Lonesome Dove

REED, PAMELA
Born Too Soon
Caroline?
Scandal Sheet
Woman With A Past

REED, ROBERT
Bradys, The
Very Brady Christmas, A

REED, SHANNA
Babymaker: The Dr. Cecil Jacobson's Story
Coins In The Fountain
Don't Talk To Strangers
Mirrors
Moment Of Truth: Stalking Back

REES, ROGER
Tower, The

REEVE, CHRISTOPHER
Anna Karenina
Bump In The Night
Death Dreams
Great Escape II: The Untold Story, The
Mortal Sins
Nightmare In The Daylight
Rose And The Jackal, The
Sea Wolf, The

REEVES, KEANU
Brotherhood Of Justice, The
Under The Influence

REEVES, PERREY
Mothers, Daughters And Lovers
Plymouth

REGALBUTO, JOE
Beyond Obsession
Fatal Judgment
Leona Helmsley: The Queen Of Mean
Street Hawk
That Secret Sunday
Writer's Block

REGEHR, DUNCAN
Danielle Steel's Once In A Lifetime
Gore Vidal's Billy The Kid

REID, DAPHNE MAXWELL
Long Journey Home, The

REID, FIONA
Mark Twain And Me

REID, FRANCES
Mercy Or Murder?

REID, KATE
Christmas Eve
Death Of A Salesman

REID, TIM
Perry Mason: The Case Of The Silenced Singer
The Race To Freedom: The Underground ....Railroad

REILLY, CHARLES NELSON
Three Kings, The

REINHOLD, JUDGE
Black Magic
Four Eyes And Six Guns
Promised A Miracle

REISER, PAUL
Tower, The

REKERT, WINSTON
World's Oldest Living Bridesmaid, The

REMAR, JAMES
Brotherhood Of The Gun
Deadlock
Indecency
Night Visions

REMICK, LEE
Bridge To Silence
Dark Holiday
Jesse
Mistral's Daughter
Nutcracker: Money, Madness And Murder
Of Pure Blood
Rearview Mirror
Toughlove

REMSEN, BERT
Who Is Julia?

REYNOLDS, BURT
Man From Left Field

REYNOLDS, DEBBIE
Battling For Baby
Perry Mason: The Case Of The Musical Murders
Sadie And Son

REYNOLDS, MICHAEL J.
Sadie And Son

REYNOLDS, ROBERT
Daughter Of Darkness

REYNOLDS, RYAN
My Name Is Kate

REYNOLDS, SIMON
Deadly Betrayal: The Bruce Curtis Story

RHODES, DONNELLY
Penthouse, The

RHYS-DAVIES, JOHN
Desperado: Badlands Justice
Gifted One, The
Great Expectations
James Clavell's Noble House
Little Match Girl, The
Nairobi Affair
Under Cover
War And Remembrance

RIBISI, VONNI
Promised A Miracle

RICH, ADAM
Eight Is Enough: A Family Reunion

RICH, CHRISTOPHER
Archie: To Riverdale And Back Again

RICHARD, LITTLE
Mother Goose Rock 'n' Rhyme

RICHARDS, ARIANA
Disaster In Time

RICHARDS, BEA
As Summers Die

RICHARDSON, IAN
Barbara Taylor Bradford's Remember
Plot To Kill Hitler, The

RICHARDSON, LA TANYA
Shameful Secrets

RICHARDSON, NATASHA
Hostages
Zelda

RICHARDSON, SALLI
I Spy Returns

RICHMOND, BRANSCOMBE
Jericho Fever

RIEGERT, PETER
Barbarians At The Gate
Ellis Island
Gypsy
Middle Ages

RIFKIN, RON
Courage
Evergreen

RIGG, DIANA
Hazard Of Hearts, A
Mrs. 'Arris Goes To Paris

RIGG, REBECCA
Fortress
Mercy Mission: The Rescue Of Flight 771

RILEY, LARRY
Badge Of The Assassin

RINELL, SUSAN
One Terrific Guy
Pals

RINGWALD, MOLLY
Something To Live For: The Alison Gertz ....Story
Stephen King's The Stand
Surviving

RITTER, JOHN
Danielle Steel's Heartbeat
Dreamer Of Oz, The
Last Fling, The
Letting Go
My Brother's Wife
Only Way Out, The
Prison For Children
Stephen King's It
Summer My Father Grew Up, The
Tricks Of The Trade
Unnatural Causes

RIVERA, CHITA
Mayflower Madam

RIVERS, JOAN
How To Murder A Millionaire
Tears And Laughter: The Joan And Mielissa ....Rivers Story

RIVERS, MELISSA
Tears And Laughter: The Joan And Mielissa ....Rivers Story

ROBARDS, JASON
Atlanta Child Murders, The
Chernobyl: The Final Warning
Enemy Within, The
Heidi
Inconvenient Woman, An
Inherit The Wind
Johnny Bull
Laguna Heat
Last Frontier, The
Long Hot Summer, The
Mark Twain And Me
Norman Rockwell's Breaking Home Ties
Sakharov

ROBARDS, JR., JASON
Perfect Tribute, The

ROBBINS, BRIAN
One Terrific Guy

ROBERTS, DORIS
If It's Tuesday, It Still Must Be Belgium
Mom For Christmas, A
Remington Steele: The Steele That Wouldn't
....Die

ROBERTS, ERIC
Descending Angel
Fugitive Among Us
Lost Capone, The
Love, Cheat And Steal
Love, Honor & Obey: The Last Mafia
....Marriage
To Heal A Nation
Voyage

ROBERTS, PERNELL
Perry Mason: The Case Of The All-Star
Assassin

ROBERTS, TONY
Different Affair, A

ROBERTSON, CLIFF
Dead Reckoning
Dreams Of Gold: The Mel Fisher Story

ROBERTSON, JENNY
Danger Of Love, The
Danielle Steel's Message From Nam
Little Piece Of Heaven, A
Nightman, The
Notorious

ROBERTSON, KATHLEEN
Survive The Night

ROBINSON, ANDREW
Lady Forgets, The
Liberace
Not My Kid
Rock Hudson

ROBINSON, BUMPER
Spirit, The

ROBINSON, CHARLIE
Crash Course

ROCCO, ALEX
Badge Of The Assassin

How To Murder A Millionaire
Love, Honor & Obey: The Last Mafia
....Marriage

RODRIGUEZ, MARCO
Trial: The Price Of Passion

RODRIGUEZ, PAUL
Hi Honey -- I'm Dead

ROEBUCK, DANIEL
Killing Mind, The

ROGERS, KENNY
Gambler Returns: The Luck Of The Draw
Kenny Rogers As The Gambler I I I: The
....Legend Continues
Macshayne: The Final Roll Of The Dice
Macshayne: Winner Take All
Rio Diablo
Wild Horses

ROGERS, MIMI
Bloodlines: Murder In The Family
Deadlock
Fourth Story
Hider In The House
Kiss To Die For, A
Lady Killer
Paper Dolls

ROGERS, WAYNE
American Harvest
Bluegrass
Drop-Out Mother
He's Fired, She's Hired
I Dream Of Jeannie: 15 Years Later
Lady From Yesterday, The
Miracle Landing
One Terrific Guy
Passion And Paradise

ROHNER, CLAYTON
Snow Kill

ROLLE, ESTHER
To Dance With The White Dog

ROLLINS, JR., HOWARD E.
Children Of Times Square
In The Heat Of The Night
Johnnie Mae Gibson: F B I
With Murder In Mind

ROMAN, SUSAN
Special People

ROMANO, ANDY
Victim Of Love: The Shannon Mohr Story

ROMANUS, RICHARD
Entertainers, The

ROMERO, NED
Stranger On My Land

RONEY, JOHN
Barnum

ROOKER, MICHAEL
Afterburn

ROONEY, MICKEY
Bluegrass

RORKE, HAYDEN
I Dream Of Jeannie: 15 Years Later

ROSE, JAMIE
Brotherhood Of The Gun
Columbo: Death Hits The Jackpot
Lady Blue

ROSS, CHARLOTTE
She Says She's Innocent

ROSS, DIANA
Out Of The Darkness

ROSS, KATHARINE
Conagher

ROSSELLINI, ISABELLA
Last Elephant, The
Lies Of The Twins

ROSSI, LEO
Kids Don't Tell
Out Of Time

ROSSOVICH, RICK
Gambler Returns: The Luck Of The Draw

ROTH, GEORGE
Tailspin: Behind The Korean Airlines Tragedy

ROTH, TIM
Heart Of Darkness
Murder In The Heartland

ROUNDTREE, RICHARD
Bonanza: The Return
Christmas In Connecticut
Fifth Missile, The

ROURKE, MICKEY
Last Outlaw, The

ROWAN, KELLY
Adrift

ROWE, DOUGLAS
Writer's Block

ROWLANDS, GENA
An Early Frost
Betty Ford Story, The
Crazy In Love
Face Of A Stranger
Montana
Silent Cries

RUBES, JAN
Descending Angel

RUBIN, JENNIFER
Drop Dead Gorgeous
Fear Inside, The

RUBINEK, SAUL
Liberace: Behind The Music

RUBINSTEIN, JOHN
American Clock, The
In My Daughter's Name
Liberace
Still Crazy Like A Fox
Two Mrs. Grenvilles, The
Voices Within: The Lives Of Truddi Chase

RUCK, ALAN
Shooter

RUNNINGFOX, JOSEPH
Geronimo

RUNYON, JENNIFER
Blue Deville
Quantum Leap

RUSCIO, AL
Lady Mobster

RUSCIO, ELIZABETH
Positively True Adventures Of The Alleged
Texas Cheerleader Murdering Mom, The

RUSH, BARBARA
Web Of Deceit

RUSLER, ROBERT
Stephen King's Sometimes They Come Back
Tonight's The Night

RUSS, TIM
Dead Silence
Heroes Of Desert Storm

RUSS, WILLIAM
Crazy From The Heart
Drive Like Lightning
Long Hot Summer, The
Middle Ages
Nasty Boys
Promise To Keep, A
Sexual Advances

RUSSO, JAMES
Desperate Rescue: The Cathy Mahone Story
Double Deception
Illicit Behavior
Intimate Stranger

RUSSOM, LEON
Crash Landing: The Rescue Of Flight 232
Hostage
Long Road Home
Moment Of Truth: Broken Pledges
Private Matter, A

RUTTAN, SUSAN
Deadly Matrimony
Deadly Medicine
Kicks
Quiet Little Neighborhood, A Perfect Little
....Murder, A
Scorned And Swindled
Take My Daughters, Please
Triumph Of The Heart: The Ricky Bell Story
Without Warning: Terror In The Towers

RYALL, DAVID
Revolver

RYAN, FRAN
Father Of Hell Town

RYAN, JERI LYNN
Nightmare In Columbia County

RYAN, MITCHELL
Penalty Phase

RYAN, TIM
China Beach
Jackie Collins' Lucky Chances
Lightning Incident, The

SABATO, ANTONIO
Moment Of Truth: Why My Daughter?

SABELLA, ERNIE
Copacabana

SADLER, WILLIAM
Bermuda Grace
Face Of Fear, The
Tagget

SAGAL, KATEY
She Says She's Innocent

SAINT, EVA MARIE
Danielle Steel's Palomino
Fatal Vision
I'll Be Home For Christmas
Kiss Of A Killer
Last Days Of Patton, The
Norman Rockwell's Breaking Home Ties
People Like Us

SAINTE-MARIE, BUFFY
Broken Chain

SAITO, JAMES
Blood And Orchids
To Be The Best

SALDANA, THERESA
Victims For Victims - The Theresa Saldana
....Story

SALINGER, DIANE
Street Of Dreams

SALINGER, MATT
Blood And Orchids
Deadly Deception
Manhunt For Claude Dallas
Second Chances

SALMI, ALBERT
Jesse

SALT, JENNIFER
Out Of The Darkness

SAMMS, EMMA
Agatha Christie's Murder In Three Acts
Bejeweled
Connecticut Yankee In King Arthur's Court, A
Dynasty: The Reunion
Harmful Intent
Lady And The Highwayman, The
Shadow Of A Stranger

SAMS, JEFFREY
Green Dolphin Beat

SAN GIACOMO, LAURA
For Their Own Good
Stephen King's The Stand

SAND, PAUL
Last Fling, The

SANDA, DOMINIQUE
Nobody's Children

SANDER, CASEY
Summer Dreams: The Story Of The Beach
....Boys

SANDERS, HENRY
Rainbow Drive

SANDERS, JAY O.
Hostages
Nobody's Children

SANDERSON, WILLIAM
Man Who Broke 1,000 Chains, The

SANDOVAL, MIGUEL
Dancing With Danger

SANDS, JULIAN
Crazy In Love
Room, The

SANFORD, CLARK
Stranger Within, The

SANTIAGO, SAUNDRA
Miami Vice

SANTOS, JOE
Deadly Desire
Sinatra

SAPP, CAROLYN
Miss America: Behind The Crown

SARA, MIA
Blindsided
Call Of The Wild
Daughter Of Darkness
Judith Krantz's Till We Meet Again
Queenie

SARAFIAN, RICHARD
Sex,Love, And Cold Hard Cash

SARANDON, CHRIS
Liberty
Mayflower Madam
Murderous Affair, A: The Carolyn Warmus
....Story
Stranger Within, The
This Child Is Mine

SARANDON, SUSAN
Mussolini: The Decline And Fall Of Il Duce
Women Of Valor

SARRAZIN, MICHAEL
Passion And Paradise

SAVAGE, FRED
Christmas On Division Street
When You Remember Me

SAVAGE, JOHN
Nairobi Affair
Shattered Image
Silent Witness

SAVALAS, TELLY
Cartier Affair, The
Dirty Dozen: The Deadly Mission

Dirty Dozen: The Fatal Mission
Kojak: The Belarus File
Kojak: The Price Of Justice

SAVIANO, JOSH
Camp Cucamonga

SAVIDGE, JENNIFER
Shootdown

SAXON, JOHN
Payoff

SBARGE, RAPHAEL
Back To Hannibal: The Return Of Tom
Sawyer And Huck Finn
Billionaire Boys Club
Cracked Up
Prison For Children

SCACCHI, GRETA
Camille

SCALIA, JACK
After The Shock
Casualties Of Love: The Long Island Lolita
....Story
Club Med
Deadly Desire
Donor
I'll Take Manhattan
Illicit Behavior
Jackie Collins' Lady Boss
Other Lover, The
Remington Steele: The Steele That Wouldn't
....Die
Runaway Father
Shadow Of Obsession
Shattered Image
Torch Song
With A Vengeance
Wolf

SCARABELLI, MICHELE
Deadbolt

SCARWID, DIANA
After The Promise
J F K: Reckless Youth
Night Of The Hunter

SCHAEFFER, REBECCA
Out Of Time

SCHALLERT, WILLIAM
Bring Me The Head Of Dobie Gillis
Mrs. Lambert Remembers Love

SCHEDEEN, ANNE
Cast The First Stone

SCHEIDER, ROY
Seaquest Dsv
Somebody Has To Shoot The Picture

SCHELL, MAXIMILAN
Miss Rose White

SCHELL, MAXIMILIAN
Abraham
Candles In The Dark
Peter The Great
Stalin

SCHERRER, PAUL
Honor Thy Mother

SCHIFF, ERIC
Toughlove

SCHLATTER, CHARLIE
Stormy Weathers

SCHNEIDER, EDITH
Of Pure Blood

SCHNEIDER, JOHN
Christmas Comes To Willow Creek
Desperate Journey: The Allison Wilcox Story
Highway Heartbreaker
Outback Bound

SCHOELAN, JILL
When A Stranger Calls Back

SCHREIBER, AVERY
Shadow Chasers

SCHRODER, RICK
Blood River
Call Of The Wild
Lonesome Dove
Miles From Nowhere
My Son Johnny
Out On The Edge
Reason To Live, A
Return To Lonesome Dove
Son's Promise, A
Stranger Within, The
Terror On Highway 91
To My Daughter With Love
Too Young The Hero

SCHULTZ, DWIGHT
Child Of Rage
Killer Among Us, A
Last Wish
Menendez: A Killing In Beverly Hills
Perry Mason: The Case Of The Sinister Spirit
Victim Of Love: The Shannon Mohr Story
Woman With A Past

SCHWEIG, ERIC
Broken Chain

SCHYGULLA, HANNA
Casanova

SCOFIELD, PAUL
Anna Karenina
Attic: The Hiding Of Anne Frank, The

SCOGGINS, TRACY
Hawaiian Heat

SCOLARI, PETER
Fatal Confession: A Father Dowling Mystery
Fire: Trapped On The 37th Floor
Perfect Harmony
Perry Mason: The Case Of The Glass Coffin
Ryan White Story, The

SCOTT, CAMPBELL
Perfect Tribute, The

SCOTT, GEORGE C.
Choices

Christmas Carol, A
Descending Angel
Finding The Way Home
Last Days Of Patton, The
Murders In The Rue Morgue, The
Mussolini - The Untold Story
Pals
Ryan White Story, The

SCOTT, KATHRY LEIGH
Murrow

SCOTT, TASHA
Kiss Shot

SCOTT, TIM
Ned Blessing: The Story Of My Life And
....Times
Town Bully, The

SEAGROVE, JENNY
Deadly Game
In Like Flynn

SEALE, DOUGLAS
Rags To Riches

SECOR, KYLE
In The Line Of Duty: Standoff At Marion
Inherit The Wind
Outside Woman, The
Shootdown

SEDGWICK, KYRA
Family Pictures
Miss Rose White

SEGAL, GEORGE
Endless Game, The
Many Happy Returns
Not My Kid
Seasons Of The Heart
Taking The Heat

SEGALL, PAMELA
Pleasures

SELBY, DAVID
Grave Secrets: The Legacy Of Hilltop Drive

SELLECCA, CONNIE
Brotherhood Of The Rose
Downpayment On Murder
House Of Secrets And Lies, A
Last Fling, The
Miracle Landing
P. S. I Luv U
Passport To Murder
People Like Us
Second Chances
Turn Back The Clock

SENECA, JOE
Gathering Of Old Men, A
Samaritan: The Mitch Snyder Story

SERNA, ASSUMPTA
Day Of Reckoning

SESSIONS, JOHN
Sweet Revenge

SEVERANCE, JOAN
Another Pair Of Aces: Three Of A Kind
Illicit Behavior

SEYLER, MICHELE
Classified Love

SEYMOUR, JANE
Angel Of Death
Are You Lonesome Tonight?
Crossings
Dr. Quinn, Medicine Woman
Heidi
Jack The Ripper
Matters Of The Heart
Obsessed With A Married Woman
Passion For Justice, A: Hazel Brannon Smith
....Story
Praying Mantis
Richest Man In The World: The Aristotle
....Onassis Story
Sun Also Rises, The
Sunstroke
War And Remembrance
War And Remembrance, Part I I
Woman He Loved, The

SEYMOUR, PHILIP
Yearling, The

SHACKELFORD, TED
Baby Of The Bride
Dying To Remember
Harvest For The Heart
Spider And The Fly, The

SHAMATA, CHUCK
On Thin Ice: The Tai Babilonia Story

SHANDLING, GARRY
Mother Goose Rock 'n' Rhyme

SHANKS, MIKE
When The Time Comes

SHANNON, MICHAEL J.
Ted Kennedy, Jr., Story, The

SHARIF, OMAR
Harem
Lie Down With Lions
Mrs. 'Arris Goes To Paris
Peter The Great

SHARKEY, RAY
Behind Enemy Lines
Chrome Soldiers
Good Cops, Bad Cops
In The Line Of Duty: Street War
Neon Empire
Revenge Of Al Capone, The
Take, The

SHATNER, WILLIAM
Broken Angel
Family Of Strangers
North Beach And Rawhide
Secrets Of A Married Man

SHATTUCK, SHARI
Laker Girls, The

SHAVER, HELEN
Fatal Memories
Many Happy Returns
Mothers, Daughters And Lovers
Pair Of Aces
Poisoned By Love: The Kern County Murders
Ride With The Wind
Survive The Night
This Park Is Mine
Trial And Error

SHAW, MARTIN
Investigation: Inside A Terrorist Bombing

SHAW, STAN
Court - Martial Of Jackie Robinson, The
Three Kings, The
When Dreams Come True

SHEA, JOHN
Baby M
Case Of Deadly Force, A
Do You Know The Muffin Man?
Hitler's S S: Portrait In Evil
Lady Killer
Lois & Clark: The New Adventures Of
....Superman
Notorious
Small Sacrifices

SHEEDY, ALLY
Chantilly Lace
Fear
Lethal Exposure
Lost Capone, The
Ultimate Betrayal
We Are The Children

SHEEHAN, DOUG
In The Line Of Duty: The FBI Murders
Mom For Christmas, A
Stranger In My Bed

SHEEN, MARTIN
Atlanta Child Murders, The
Consenting Adult
Gettysburg
Guardian, The
Guilty Until Proven Innocent
Last P. O. W? The Bobby Garwood Story
Matter Of Justice, A
News At Eleven
Out Of The Darkness
Samaritan: The Mitch Snyder Story
Shattered Spirits

SHEFFER, CRAIG
Babycakes

SHEPHERD, CYBIL
Baby Brokers
Moonlighting

SHEPHERD, CYBILL
Long Hot Summer, The
Memphis
Secrets Of A Married Man
Seduced
Stormy Weathers
Telling Secrets

There Was A Little Boy
Which Way Home

SHEPPARD, W. MORGAN
Seduction: Three Tales From The Inner
Sanctum

SHERIDAN, JAMEY
Killer Rules
Murder In High Places
My Breast
Shannon's Deal
Stephen King's The Stand

SHERIDAN, NICOLETTE
Deceptions
Jackie Collins' Lucky Chances
Somebody's Daughter
Time To Heal, A

SHIELDS, BROOKE
Diamond Trap, The
I Can Make You Love Me: The Stalking Of
....Laura Black
Wet Gold

SHIELDS, NICHOLAS
Liar's Edge

SHILOA, JOSEPH
Lion Of Africa, The

SHIPP, JOHN WESLEY
Baby Of The Bride
Flash, The
Green Dolphin Beat

SHIRE, TALIA
Blood Vows: The Story Of A Mafia Wife
For Richer, For Poorer
Mark Twain And Me

SHOOP, KIMBER
Extreme Close-Up

SHOR, DAN
Elvis And The Colonel: The Untold Story

SHOW, ROBIN
Forbidden Nights

SHRINER, KIN
Obsessive Love

SHROYER, SONNY
Scattered Dreams: The Kathryn Messenger
....Story

SHUE, ELISABETH
Blind Justice

SIDNEY, SYLVIA
An Early Frost
Finnegan Begin Again
Pals

SIEBERT, CHARLES
Shakedown On The Sunset Strip

SIEMASZKO, CASEY
Chase, The

SIEMASZKO, NINA
Baby Brokers

SIERRA, GREGORY
Donor
Something Is Out There

SIGNORELLI, TOM
Bride In Black, The

SIKES, CYNTHIA
Oceans Of Fire

SIKKING, JAMES B.
Desperado: Badlands Justice
Doing Time On Maple Drive
Too Good To Be True

SILVER, RON
Billionaire Boys Club
Blind Side
Father's Revenge, A
Forgotten Prisoners: The Amnesty File
Kane And Abel
Lifepod
Trapped In Silence

SILVERMAN, JONATHAN
Broadway Bound
Challenge Of A Lifetime
For Richer, For Poorer
Traveling Man
Twelve O' One (12: 01)

SILVERSTONE, ALICIA
Torch Song

SIMMONS, JEAN
Dark Shadows
Great Expectations
Inherit The Wind
Perry Mason: The Case Of The Lost Love

SIMON, PAUL
Mother Goose Rock 'n' Rhyme

SIMPSON, FREDDIE
Thunderboat Row

SINGER, MARC
Deadly Game
Sea Wolf, The

SINGER, RAYMOND
Leona Helmsley: The Queen Of Mean

SINISE, GARY
Stephen King's The Stand

SIROLA, JOSEPH
Wolf

SISTO, ROCCO
Doing Life

SIZEMORE, TOM
American Story, An

SKERRITT, TOM
Child In The Night
China Lake Murders, The
Getting Up And Going Home
Heist
In Sickness And In Health
Miles To Go . . .
Moving Target

Nightmare At Bitter Creek
Picket Fences
Poker Alice
Red King, White Knight
Touch Of Scandal, A

SLATE, JEREMY
Whisper Kills, A

SLATER, CHRISTIAN
Desperate For Love

SLATER, HELEN
Twelve O' One (12: 01)

SLATTERY, JOHN
Under Cover

SLOYAN, JAMES
Vital Signs

SMALL, RON
Trial And Error

SMART, JEAN
Fight For Jenny, A
Just My Imagination
Locked Up: A Mother's Rage
Overkill: The Aileen Wuornos Story
Seduction In Travis County
Yarn Princess, The
Yearling, The

SMITH, ALEXIS
Death In California, A
Dress Gray
Marcus Welby, M. D.: A Holiday Affair

SMITH, CEDRIC
Penthouse, The

SMITH, COTTER
Armed & Innocent
Desperate Journey: The Allison Wilcox Story
Equal Justice
Last Prostitute, The
Message From Holly
Midnight's Child
Place To Be Loved, A
Rape Of Richard Beck, The
With Hostile Intent

SMITH, JACLYN
Bourne Identity, The
Cries Unheard: The Donna Yaklich Story
Danielle Steel's Kaleidoscope
Florence Nightingale
In The Arms Of A Killer
Lies Before Kisses
Love Can Be Murder
Night They Saved Christmas, The
Nightmare In The Daylight
Rage Of Angels: The Story Continues
Rape Of Dr. Willis, The
Sentimental Journey
Settle The Score
Windmills Of The Gods

SMITH, KURTWOOD
Nightmare Years, The

SMITH, LANE
Blind Vengeance
Challenger
False Arrest
Final Days
Killer Instinct
Lois & Clark: The New Adventures Of
....Superman
Place To Call Home, A

SMITH, LEWIS
Fulfillment Of Mary Gray, The

SMITH, REX
Street Hawk

SMITH, SAVANNAH
Sweet Revenge, A

SMITH, SHAWNEE
Brand New Life: The Honeymoon
Crime Of Innocence
Easy Prey
I Saw What You Did

SMITROVICH, BILL
Gregory K
Labor Of Love: The Arlette Schweitzer Story

SMITS, JIMMY
Broken Cord, The
Cisco Kid, The
Dangerous Affection
Glitz
L. A. Law
Tommyknockers, The

SNODGRESS, CARRIE
Reason To Live, A
Rise & Walk: The Dennis Byrd Story
Woman With A Past

SNYDER, ARLEN DEAN
Summer Dreams: The Story Of The Beach
....Boys
Wheels Of Terror

SNYDER, DREW
Parker Kane

SNYDER, SUSAN MARIE
Betrayed By Innocence

SOMERS, SUZANNE
Exclusive
Keeping Secrets
Rich Men, Single Women
Seduced By Evil

SOMMARS, JULIE
Matlock: The Witness Killings

SOMMER, JOSEF
Betty Ford Story, The
Hostages
Money, Power, Murder

SORBO, KEVIN
Condition: Critical

SORCEY, JULIET
Mom For Christmas, A
Taken Away

SORENSON, LINDA
Many Happy Returns

SORVINO, PAUL
Betrayed By Innocence
Don't Touch My Daughter
Perry Mason Mystery: The Case Of The
Wicked Wives
Surviving
With Intent To Kill

SOUL, DAVID
Cry In The Wild: The Taking Of Peggy Ann
Fifth Missile, The
Harry's Hong Kong
In The Line Of Duty: The FBI Murders
Perry Mason: The Case Of The Fatal Framing
So Proudly We Hail

SOUTENDIJK, RENEE
Murderers Among Us: The Simon Wiesenthal
....Story

SPACEK, SISSY
Place For Annie, A
Private Matter, A

SPACEY, KEVIN
Doomsday Gun
Fall From Grace
When You Remember Me

SPADER, JAMES
Starcrossed

SPANO, JOE
Bloodlines: Murder In The Family
Brotherhood Of Justice, The
Cast The First Stone
Deep Dark Secrets
Disaster At Silo 7
Fever
Flood: Who Will Save Our Children?
For The Very First Time

SPANO, VINCENT
Afterburn

SPEARS, MICHAEL
Broken Cord, The

SPENCER, JOHN
From The Files Of Joseph Wambaugh: A Jury
Of One
In The Arms Of A Killer
When No One Would Listen

SPIELBERG, DAVID
Sworn To Silence

SPRADLIN, G.D.
Carolina Skeletons
Houston: The Legend Of Texas
Nutcracker: Money, Madness And Murder
Resting Place
Robert Kennedy And His Times
Shoot First: A Cop's Vengeance
Telling Secrets

SPRINGFIELD, RICK
Dead Reckoning
In The Shadows, Someone Is Watching

Nick Knight
Silent Movie

SRIDE, JOHN
Agatha Christie's Thirteen At Dinner

ST. JOHN, MICHELLE
Geronimo

STACK, ROBERT
Perry Mason: The Case Of The Sinister Spirit
Return Of Eliot Ness, The

STACY, JAMES
Matters Of The Heart

STAFFORD, NANCY
Moment Of Truth: A Child Too Many

STAHL, NICK
Incident In A Small Town

STALLONE, FRANK
Crossing The Mob

STAMOS, JOHN
Captive
Daughter Of The Streets
Disappearance Of Christina, The

STANLEY, FLORENCE
Maybe Baby

STANTON, HARRY DEAN
Against The Wall
Payoff

STAPLETON, JEAN
Agatha Christie's Dead Man's Folly
Fire In The Dark
Ghost Mom
Habitation Of Dragons, The
Mother Goose Rock 'n' Rhyme

STAPLETON, MAUREEN
Last Wish
Liberace: Behind The Music
Miss Rose White
Private Sessions
Sentimental Journey

STARNES, ANDREW
Armed & Innocent

STARR, MIKE
Frank Nitti: The Enforcer
Ten Million Dollar Getaway

STEEL, AMY
First Steps
Jake And The Fatman
Perry Mason: The Case Of The Reckless
Romeo
Red Spider, The

STEEN, JESSICA
Great Pretender, The
Homefront
To Save The Children

STEENBURGEN, MARY
Attic: The Hiding Of Anne Frank, The

STEIGER, ROD
In The Line Of Duty: Manhunt In The
....Dakotas
Passion And Paradise
Sinatra
Sword Of Gideon

STEPHENS, JAMES
Follow Your Heart
Pancho Barnes
Perry Mason Mystery, A: The Case Of The
Lethal

STERLING, PHILIP
Death Of The Incredible Hulk, The

STERN, DANIEL
Court - Martial Of Jackie Robinson, The
Weekend War

STERNHAGEN, FRANCES
At Mother's Request
Follow Your Heart
She Woke Up
Stephen King's Golden Years

STEVENS, CONNIE
Bring Me The Head Of Dobie Gillis

STEVENS, CRAIG
Marcus Welby, M. D.: A Holiday Affair
Supercarrier

STEVENS, MORGAN
Criminal Behavior
Deep Dark Secrets
Roses Are For The Rich

STEVENS, STELLA
Man Against The Mob

STEVENSON, COLETTE
Freedom Fighter

STEVENSON, MCLEAN
Class Cruise

STEVENSON, PARKER
Are You Lonesome Tonight?
Baywatch: Panic At Malibu Pier
Cover Girl And The Cop, The
Probe
Shadow Of A Stranger
That Secret Sunday

STEWART, AMY
Mark Twain And Me

STEWART, BARBARA
Our Family Honor

STEWART, CATHERINE MARY
Follow Your Heart
Murder By The Book
Ordeal In The Arctic
Passion And Paradise
Perfect Harmony
Psychic
Sea Wolf, The
With Intent To Kill

STEWART, JEAN-PIERRE
Napoleon And Josephine: A Love Story

STEWART, PATRICK
Death Train

STIERS, DAVID OGDEN
Bad Seed, The
Final Days
Final Notice
Hoover
How To Murder A Millionaire
Kissing Place, The
Last Of His Tribe, The
Perry Mason: The Case Of The Avenging Ace
Perry Mason: The Case Of The Lady In The Lake
Perry Mason: The Case Of The Lost Love
Perry Mason: The Case Of The Shooting Star
Perry Mason: The Case Of The Sinister Spirit
Wife, Mother, Murderer
Without A Kiss Goodbye

STILLER, BEN
Working Trash

STOCK, BARBARA
Spenser: For Hire
Trade Winds

STOCK-POYNTON, AMY
Gunsmoke I I I: To The Last Man
Gunsmoke: One Man's Justice
Guts And Glory: The Rise And Fall Of Oliver
....North

STOCKWELL, DEAN
Fatal Memories
In The Line Of Duty: The Price Of
....Vengeance
Kenny Rogers As The Gambler I I I: The
....Legend Continues
Quantum Leap
Shame
Son Of The Morning Star

STOCKWELL, JOHN
Billionaire Boys Club

STOLTZ, ERIC
Foreign Affairs
Heart Of Justice, The
Roommates

STONE, CHRISTOPHER
Dying To Remember

STONE, DEE WALLACE
Addicted To His Love
Hostage Flight
I'm Dangerous Tonight
Moment Of Truth: Cradle Of Conspiracy
Prophet Of Evil: The Ervil Lebaron Story
Search And Rescue
Sin Of Innocence
Stranger On My Land
Witness To The Execution

STONE, ROB
Crash Course

STORKE, ADAM
In My Daughter's Name

STOWE, MADELINE
Blood And Orchids

STRAIGHT, BEATRICE
Robert Kennedy And His Times

STRASBERG, ANNA
Mario Puzo's The Fortunate Pilgrim

STRASSER, ROBIN
Baby M
Glitz

STRASSMAN, MARCIA
Haunted By Her Past
Shadow Chasers

STRATHAIRN, DAVID
Judgment
O Pioneers

STRATTON, CHARLIE
On Thin Ice: The Tai Babilonia Story

STRAUSS, PETER
Brotherhood Of The Rose
Eighty-Three Hours 'til Dawn
Flight Of Black Angel
Fugitive Among Us
Kane And Abel
Men Don't Tell
Penalty Phase
Peter Gunn
Proud Men
Thicker Than Blood: The Larry Mclinden
....Story
Trial: The Price Of Passion
Under Siege
Yearling, The

STRICH, ELAINE
Stranded

STRICKLAND, GAIL
Barbara Taylor Bradford's Remember
Silent Cries

STRUTHERS, SALLY
In The Best Interest Of The Children

STUDI, WES
Broken Chain

SUCHET, DAVID
Agatha Christie's Thirteen At Dinner
Gulag
Last Innocent Man, The

SULLIVAN, SUSAN
Rage Of Angels: The Story Continues

SUROVY, NICOLAS
Stark
Wolf

SUTHERLAND, DONALD
Oldest Living Confederate Widow Tells All
Quicksand: No Escape
Railway Station Man, The

SUTHERLAND, KIEFER
Brotherhood Of Justice, The
Last Light

Trapped In Silence

SUTORIUS, JAMES
Columbo Goes To College
My Breast
Whisper Kills, A

SVENSON, BO
Dirty Dozen: The Deadly Mission

SWANK, HILARY
Cries Unheard: The Donna Yaklich Story

SWANSON, GARY
Triplecross

SWAYZE, DON
Beyond Suspicion

SWAYZE, PATRICK
North And South
North And South, Book 2

SWEENEY, D.B.
Lonesome Dove

SWENSON, INGA
Nutcracker: Money, Madness And Murder

SWIT, LORETTA
Dreams Of Gold: The Mel Fisher Story
Execution, The
Hell Hath No Fury
Killer Among Friends, A

SYLVESTER, HAROLD
Double Your Pleasure
In The Line Of Duty: A Cop For The Killing
Love And Curses . . . And All That Jazz

SZARABAJKA, KEITH
One Woman's Courage
Stephen King's Golden Years

TALBOTT, MICHAEL
Going To The Chapel
Miami Vice

TAMBOR, JEFFREY
Quiet Little Neighborhood, A Perfect Little
....Murder, A
Three Wishes Of Billy Grier, The

TAMBURRELLI, KARLA
Counterfeit Contessa, The

TANDY, JESSICA
Foxfire
Story Lady, The
To Dance With The White Dog

TARANTINA, BRIAN
Resting Place

TAYBACK, VIC
Three Kings, The

TAYLOR, BENEDICT
Duel Of Hearts

TAYLOR, BUCK
Gunsmoke: Return To Dodge

TAYLOR, ELIZABETH
Malice In Wonderland
Poker Alice

Sweet Bird Of Youth
There Must Be A Pony

TAYLOR, HOLLAND
In The Best Of Families: Marriage, Pride And
....Madness
Perry Mason Returns
Rape Of Dr. Willis, The

TAYLOR, JOSH
Class Cruise
Secret Life Of Kathy Mccormick, The
Woman On The Ledge

TAYLOR, LILI
Family Of Spies

TAYLOR, MARK
Murder 101

TAYLOR, MESHACH
Double, Double, Toil And Trouble

TAYLOR, REGINA
I'll Fly Away

TAYLOR, ROBERT
Steel Justice

TAYLOR, ROD
Danielle Steel's Palomino

TAYLOR-YOUNG, LEIGH
Napoleon And Josephine: A Love Story
Who Gets The Friends?

TENDLER, MESSE
Secret, The

TENNANT, VICTORIA
Under Siege
War And Remembrance
War And Remembrance, Part I I

TERLESKY, JOHN
Battling For Baby
Longarm
When He's Not A Stranger

TERRY, JOHN
Killing In A Small Town
Miracle Child
Seduction: Three Tales From The Inner
Sanctum
Silhouette

TESTI, FABIO
Only One Survived

TEWES, LAUREN
China Lake Murders, The

THAYER, BRYNN
Comeback, The
Ghost Of A Chance
Triumph Over Disaster: The Hurricane
....Andrew Story

THICKE, ALAN
Jury Duty: The Comedy
Not Quite Human I I
Perry Mason: The Case Of The Shooting Star
Still Not Quite Human

THIESSEN, TIFFANI-AMBER
Killer Among Friends, A
Saved By The Bell-Hawaiian Style

THINNES, ROY
Blue Bayou
Dark Holiday
Dark Shadows

THOMAS, BETTY
Prison For Children

THOMAS, DANNY
Side By Side

THOMAS, DAVE
Boris And Natasha

THOMAS, HENRY
Beyond Obsession
Psycho I V: The Beginning
Taste For Killing, A

THOMAS, KRISTIN SCOTT
Endless Game, The
Framed
Secret Life Of Ian Fleming, The
Tenth Man, The

THOMAS, MARLO
Consenting Adult
Held Hostage: The Sis And Jerry Levin Story
Nobody's Child
Ultimate Betrayal

THOMAS, PHILIP MICHAEL
False Witness
Fight For Jenny, A
Miami Vice

THOMAS, RICHARD
Common Ground
Crash Landing: The Rescue Of Flight 232
Final Jeopardy, The
Go Toward The Light
I Can Make You Love Me: The Stalking Of
....Laura Black
Linda
Mission Of The Shark
Precious Victims
Stephen King's It
To Save The Children
Walton Thanksgiving Reunion, A
Yes, Virginia, There Is A Santa Claus

THOMAS, ROBIN
Haunted By Her Past
Memories Of Murder
Personals
Rape Of Dr. Willis, The

THOMAS, SERENA SCOTT
Bermuda Grace
Diana: Her True Story

THOMERSON, TIM
Intimate Stranger

THOMPSON, FRED DALTON
Bed Of Lies
Stay The Night

THOMPSON, JACK
Last Frontier, The
Trouble In Paradise

THOMPSON, LEA
Montana
Stolen Babies
Substitute Wife, The

THOMPSON, SADA
Fear Stalk
Home Fires Burning
My Two Loves

THOMSON, KIM
Hands Of A Murderer

THORNTON, NOLEY
Danielle Steel's Fine Things
Heidi

THRELFALL, DAVID
Casualty Of War, A
Diana: Her True Story

THUNDER, RINO
Miracle In The Wilderness

THURMAN, UMA
Robin Hood

TICOTIN, RACHEL
Deconstructing Sarah
From The Files Of Joseph Wambaugh: A Jury
Of One
Keep The Change
Rockabye
Thicker Than Blood: The Larry Mclinden
....Story

TIERNEY, MAURA
Crossing The Mob

TIGHE, KEVIN
Betrayal Of Trust
Better Off Dead
Caught In The Act

TILLY, JENNIFER
Heads

TILLY, MEG
In The Best Interest Of The Child

TOBOLOWSKY, STEPHEN
Deadly Medicine

TODD, BEVERLY
Different Affair, A

TODD, RUSSELL
High Mountain Rangers

TODD, RYAN
Mrs. Lambert Remembers Love

TODD, TONY
Last Elephant, The

TOLBERT, BERLINDA
International Airport

TOLKAN, JAMES
Leap Of Faith
Sunset Beat

Weekend War

TOM, HEATHER
I'll Take Romance

TOMEI, CONCETTA
China Beach

TOMEI, MARISA
Parker Kane

TOMITA, TAMLYN
Hiroshima: Out Of The Ashes

TOMLINS, JASON
Live: From Death Row

TOOTOOSIS, GORDON
Call Of The Wild
Stone Fox

TOPOL,
Queenie

TOPPANA, PETA
Which Way Home

TORN, RIP
Another Pair Of Aces: Three Of A Kind
April Morning
Atlanta Child Murders, The
Columbo: Death Hits The Jackpot
Dead Ahead: The Exxon Valdez Disaster
Destination: America
Dream West
Execution, The
Hoover
King Of Love, The
Laguna Heat
Manhunt For Claude Dallas
My Son Johnny
T Bone N Wessel

TORRES, GINA
Mantis

TORRES, LIZ
Miracle At Beekman's Place

TOUSSAINT, BETH
Blackmail

TOUSSAINT, LORRAINE
Case Of Deadly Force, A
Lies And Lullabies

TOUZET, CORINNE
Danielle Steel's Jewels

TOWNSEND, BARBARA
George Mckenna Story, The

TRACEY, IAN
Conspiracy Of Silence

TRACY, JILL
Over My Dead Body

TRAINOR, MARY ELLEN
Fear Stalk

TRAVANTI, DANIEL J.
Adam: His Song Continues
Aurora
Eyes Of A Witness

Howard Beach: Making The Case For Murder
In The Shadows, Someone Is Watching
Missing Persons
Murrow
My Name Is Kate
Tagget

TRAVIS, NANCY
Harem
I'll Be Home For Christmas

TREMKO, ANN
Adventures Of Brisco County Jr., The

TREVOR, CLAIRE
Norman Rockwell's Breaking Home Ties

TRISKA, JAN
World War I I : When Lions Roared

TRITT, TRAVIS
Rio Diablo

TROTTER, KATE
Clarence

TROUP, RONNIE
Where Pigeons Go To Die

TSURUTANI, BRADY
Hiroshima: Out Of The Ashes

TUBB, BARRY
Billionaire Boys Club
Consenting Adult
Without Her Consent

TUBNEY, ANNE
Orpheus Descending

TUCCI, MICHAEL
Chance Of A Lifetime

TUCCI, STANLEY
Revealing Evidence

TUCK, JESSICA
Lifepod

TUCKER, MICHAEL
Assault And Matrimony
Casey's Gift: For Love Of A Child
Day One
In The Nick Of Time
Secret Life Of Archie's Wife, The
Spy
Too Young To Die?
Town Torn Apart, A

TUNNEY, ROBIN
J F K: Reckless Youth

TURMAN, GLYNN
Secrets Of A Married Man
The Race To Freedom: The Underground
....Railroad

TURTURRO, JOHN
Mario Puzo's The Fortunate Pilgrim

TWEED, SHANNON
Liar's Edge
Longarm

TWEED, TERRY
High Price Of Passion, The

TWIGGY,
Diamond Trap, The

TYRRELL, SUSAN
If Tomorrow Comes
Thompson's Last Run

TYSACK, MARGARET
Young Indiana Jones Chronicles: The Curse
....Of The Jackal

TYSON, CICELY
Acceptable Risks
Duplicates
Heat Wave
Intimate Encounters
Oldest Living Confederate Widow Tells All
Playing With Fire
Samaritan: The Mitch Snyder Story

TZUDIKER, BOB
Waco & Rhinehart

ULRICH, KIM
Blood Ties

UNDERWOOD, BLAIR
Cover Girl And The Cop, The
Father & Son: Dangerous Relations
Heat Wave
Murder In Mississippi

UNDERWOOD, JAY
Not Quite Human I I
Still Not Quite Human

UNKNOWN, JACKEE
Women Of Brewster Place, The

URICH, ROBERT
Amerika
And Then She Was Gone
April Morning
Blind Faith
Blind Man's Bluff
Comeback, The
Deadly Relations
Defiant One, The
Double Edge
Eighty-Three Hours 'til Dawn
Lonesome Dove
Mistral's Daughter
Murder By Night
Night Walk
Quiet Little Neighborhood, A Perfect Little
....Murder, A
Revolver
Scandal Sheet
She Knows Too Much
Spenser: Ceremony
Spenser: For Hire
Spenser: Pale Kings And Princes
Spooner
Stranger At My Door
Survive The Savage Sea
To Save The Children

USTINOV, PETER
Agatha Christie's Dead Man's Folly
Agatha Christie's Murder In Three Acts
Agatha Christie's Thirteen At Dinner
Around The World In 80 Days

VACCARO, BRENDA
Deceptions
Paper Dolls
Red Shoes Diaries
Stolen: One Husband

VALENTINE, ANTHONY
Father's Revenge, A

VALENTINE, KAREN
Children In The Crossfire
He's Fired, She's Hired
Perfect People

VALENTINE, SCOTT
After The Shock
Dangerous Pursuit
Going To The Chapel
Secret Passion Of Robert Clayton, The
Without Her Consent

VALLONE, RAF
Christopher Columbus

VAN ARK, JOAN
Always Remember I Love You
In The Shadows, Someone Is Watching
Menu For Murder
My First Love
Shakedown On The Sunset Strip
Tainted Blood
Terror On Track 9

VAN BUREK, NICHOLAS
Clarence

VAN DYKE, BARRY
House On Sycamore Street, The
Twist Of The Knife, A

VAN DYKE, DICK
Daughters Of Privilege
Diagnosis Of Murder
Ghost Of A Chance
House On Sycamore Street, The
Twist Of The Knife, A

VAN DYKE, JERRY
Fresno
To Grandmother's House We Go

VAN HORN, PATRICK
Between Love And Hate
Rio Shanon

VAN NOSTRAND, AMY
Flood: Who Will Save Our Children?
Kids Like These

VAN PATTEN, DICK
Eight Is Enough: A Family Reunion
Eight Is Enough Wedding, An
Jake Spanner, Private Eye
Midnight Hour, The

VAN PATTEN, JAMES
Dirty Dozen: The Deadly Mission

VAN PATTEN, JOYCE
Breathing Lessons
Maid For Each Other
Malice In Wonderland
Picking Up The Pieces
Under The Influence

VAN PATTEN, TIM
Dress Gray

VAN PATTEN, VINCE
Dirty Dozen: The Deadly Mission

VAN PEEBLES, MARIO
Blue Bayou
Child Saver, The
Children Of The Night
In The Line Of Duty: Street War
Stompin' At The Savoy
Triumph Of The Heart: The Ricky Bell Story

VAN VALKENBURGH, DEBORAH
C. A. T. Squad: Python Wolf
Going For The Gold: The Bill Johnson Story

VANCE, COURTNEY
Percy & Thunder
The Race To Freedom: The Underground
....Railroad

VANCE, DANITRA
Cover Girl And The Cop, The

VANITY,
Memories Of Murder

VARGAS, JOHN
Seduced By Evil
Unnatural Causes

VAUGHAN, PARIS
Laker Girls, The

VAUGHAN, PETER
Bourne Identity, The
Monte Carlo

VAUGHN, NED
Chips, The War Dog

VAUGHN, ROBERT
Desperado
Prince Of Bel Air

VELEZ, EDDIE
Children Of The Night
From The Files Of Joseph Wambaugh: A Jury
Of One

VELJOHNSON, REGINALD
Bride In Black, The
Grass Roots

VENTON, HARLEY
Blood Ties

VENTURE, RICHARD
Family Sins
Second Serve

VEREEN, BEN
Lost In London

VERICA, TOM
Babymaker: The Dr. Cecil Jacobson's Story

VERNON, JOHN
Hostage For A Day
Sodbusters
Woman Who Sinned, The

VERNON, KATE
Daughters Of Privilege
House Of Secrets

VERRELL, CEC
Supercarrier

VIHARO, ROBERT
Palace Guard

VILLARD, TOM
Swimsuit

VINCE, PRUITT TAYLOR
I Know My First Name Is Steven

VINCENT, JAN-MICHAEL
Six Against The Rock
Tarzan In Manhattan

VISCUSO, SAL
This Wife For Hire

VISITOR, NANA
Father's Homecoming, A
Spirit, The

VOIGHT, JON
Chernobyl: The Final Warning
Last Of His Tribe, The
Return To Lonesome Dove

VON DOHLEN, LENNY
Love Kills

VON SYDOW, MAX
Christopher Columbus
Hiroshima: Out Of The Ashes
Kojak: The Belarus File
Red King, White Knight

VON ZERNECK, DANIELLE
Survive The Savage Sea

VOYAGIS, YORGO
Mario Puzo's The Fortunate Pilgrim

WAGNER, JACK
Moving Target

WAGNER, LINDSAY
Babies
Bionic Showdown: The 6 Million Dollar
....Man/Bionic Woman
Child's Cry
Convicted
Danielle Steel's Once In A Lifetime
Evil In Clear River
Fire In The Dark
From The Dead Of Night
Jessie
Message From Holly
Nightmare At Bitter Creek

Nurses On The Line: The Crash Of Flight 7
Other Lover, The
Passions
Return Of The 6 Million Dollar Man & Bionic
....Woman
Shattered Dreams
She Woke Up
Stranger In My Bed
Taking Of Flight 847: The Uli Derickson
....Story
This Child Is Mine
To Be The Best
Treacherous Crossing

WAGNER, NATASHA
Substitute, The
Tainted Blood

WAGNER, ROBERT
Danielle Steel's Jewels
Deep Trouble
False Arrest
Hart To Hart Returns
Indiscreet
Love Among Thieves
There Must Be A Pony
This Gun For Hire
Windmills Of The Gods

WAGNER, THOMAS
Marilyn & Bobby: Her Final Affair

WAHL, KEN
Gladiator, The
Search For Grace

WAITE, RALPH
Crime Of Innocence
Red Earth, White Earth
Sin And Redemption
Walton Thanksgiving Reunion, A

WAKEHAM, DEBORAH
Long Time Gone

WALKEN, CHRISTOPHER
Sarah, Plain And Tall
Skylark

WALKER, ALLY
True Blue

WALKER, ERIC
Ewok Adventure, The

WALKER, KATHRYN
Murder Of Mary Phagan, The
Private Sessions

WALKER, LOU
Passion For Justice, A: Hazel Brannon Smith
....Story

WALKER, MARCY
Babies
Midnight's Child
Overexposed
Palace Guard
Return Of Desperado, The

WALLACE, GEORGE D.
Haunted, The

WALLACE, LEE
Last Wish

WALLACE, WILLIAM
Danger Down Under

WALLACH, ELI
Legacy Of Lies
Murder: By Reason Of Insanity
Something In Common
Teamster Boss: The Jackie Presser Story

WALSH, M. EMMET
Broken Vows
Deliberate Stranger, The
Love & Lies
Murder Ordained
Resting Place
Right Of The People, The

WALSH, SYDNEY
Trenchcoat In Paradise

WALSTON, RAY
For Love Or Money
I Know My First Name Is Steven
Pink Lightning
Red River

WALTER, JESSICA
Aaron's Way
Execution, The
Killer In The Mirror
Round Table, The

WALTERS, SUSAN
In The Line Of Duty: A Cop For The Killing

WANAMAKER, SAM
Heartsounds
Running Against Time
Sadie And Son
Shell Seekers, The

WARD, FRED
Cast A Deadly Spell
Florida Straits
Four Eyes And Six Guns

WARD, JONATHAN
Father's Homecoming, A

WARD, RACHEL
And The Sea Will Tell
Black Magic
Double Jeopardy
Fortress

WARD, SELA
Bridesmaids
Child Of Darkness, Child Of Light
Double Jeopardy
Killer Rules
King Of Love, The
Rainbow Drive

WARD, SOPHIE
Macgyver: Lost Treasure Of Atlantis

WARD, WALLY
Children Of The Night
Combat High

WARDEN, JACK
Dead Solid Perfect
Still Crazy Like A Fox
Three Kings, The

WARFIELD, EMILY
Beyond Obsession
Bonanza: The Return

WARFIELD, MARLENE
Child's Cry

WARLOCK, BILLY
Honor Thy Father And Mother: The
....Menendez Murders
Swimsuit

WARNER, DAVID
Cast A Deadly Spell
Desperado
Hitler's S S: Portrait In Evil

WARNER, MALCOLM-JAMAL
Father Clements Story, The

WARNER, RICK
Too Young The Hero

WARREN, JENNIFER
Paper Dolls

WARREN, KIERSTEN
False Arrest
Grave Secrets: The Legacy Of Hilltop Drive

WARREN, LESLEY ANN
Apology
Baja Oklahoma
Evergreen
Family Of Spies
Fight For Jenny, A
In Sickness And In Health
Mothers Revenge, A
Seduction In Travis County
Willing To Kill: The Texas Cheerleader Story

WARREN, MICHAEL
Child Saver, The

WASHINGTON, DENZEL
George Mckenna Story, The

WASS, TED
Pancho Barnes
Sins Of The Father
Sparks: The Price Of Passion
Triplecross
Triumph Over Disaster: The Hurricane
....Andrew Story

WASSON, CRAIG
Strapped

WATERS, JOHN
Which Way Home

WATERSTON, SAM
Assault At West Point
David's Mother
Enemy Within, The
Fifth Missile, The
Finnegan Begin Again
I'll Fly Away

Lantern Hill
Lincoln
Love Lives On
Nightmare Years, The
Room Upstairs, The
Terrorist On Trial: The United States Vs.
Salim

WATERSTREET, ED
Love Is Never Silent

WATSON, ALBERTA
Relentless: Mind Of A Killer

WATSON, MILLS
Prime Target

WAXMAN, AL
I Still Dream Of Jeannie
Quiet Killer

WEATHERS, CARL
Dangerous Passion
Defiant One, The

WEAVER, DENNIS
Bluffing It
Disaster At Silo 7
Going For The Gold: The Bill Johnson Story
Return Of Sam Mccloud, The

WEAVER, FRITZ
Blind Spot
Death In California, A
Dream West
Hearst And Davies Affair, The
Ironclads
Under Siege

WEAVER, JASON
Jacksons: An American Dream , The

WEBB, CHLOE
China Beach
Lucky Day
Silent Cries

WEBB, GREG
Baron And The Kid, The

WEBBER, ROBERT
Assassin
Cover Up

WEBER, STEVEN
Betrayed By Love
Deception: A Mother's Secret
In The Company Of Darkness
In The Line Of Duty: A Cop For The Killing
Kennedys Of Massachusetts, The

WEDGEWORTH, ANN
Right To Kill?
Stranger Waits, A

WEINTRAUB, CARL
Coins In The Fountain
Sorry, Wrong Number

WEISSER, MORGAN
Extreme Close-Up
Long Road Home
Stay The Night

WEISSER, NORBERT
Seeds Of Tragedy

WEITZ, BRUCE
Babe Ruth
Baby M
Cry For Help: The Tracey Thurman Story, A
Deadly Silence, A
If It's Tuesday, It Still Must Be Belgium
Rainbow Drive
Reason To Live, A

WELCH, RAQUEL
Right To Die
Scandal In A Small Town
Tainted Blood
Torch Song
Trouble In Paradise

WELD, TUESDAY
Circle Of Violence: A Family Drama
Scorned And Swindled
Something In Common

WELDON, ANN
Out Of The Darkness

WELDON, CHARLES
Case Closed

WELLER, PETER
Apology
Rainbow Drive
Substitute Wife, The

WELLES, JESSE
Stranger Waits, A

WELLIVER, TITUS
Lost Capone, The

WELLS, CARRIE
Bad Seed, The

WELLS, DAVID
Over My Dead Body

WELSH, KENNETH
Adrift
Deadly Betrayal: The Bruce Curtis Story
Getting Gotti
Love And Hate: A Marriage Made In Hell
Mothers' Right, A: The Elizabeth Morgan
....Story
Spider And The Fly, The
Woman On The Run: The Lawrencia
....Bembenek Story

WELSH, MARGARET
Killer Among Friends, A
Shadow Of A Doubt

WENDT, GEORGE
Hostage For A Day

WERT, DOUG
Roswell

WEST, TIMOTHY
Tragedy Of Flight 103: The Inside Story, The

WESTON, JACK
If Tomorrow Comes

WETTIG, PATRICIA
Silent Movie
Taking Back My Life: The Nancy
....Ziegenmeyer Story

WHALEY, FRANK
Fatal Deception: Mrs. Lee Harvey Oswald

WHALIN, JUSTIN
Fire Next Time, The

WHEATLEY, LEO
Little Kidnappers, The

WHEATON, WIL
Last Prostitute, The

WHELCHEL, LISA
Facts Of Life Down Under, The

WHITAKER, FOREST
Criminal Justice
Enemy Within, The
Last Light
Lush Life

WHITE, BETTY
Chance Of A Lifetime

WHITE, DEVOREAUX
Room Upstairs, The

WHITE, RHONDA STUBBINS
Laurel Avenue
Out Of The Darkness

WHITE, RON
Harvest For The Heart

WHITE, VANNA
Goddess Of Love

WHITEHEAD, PAXTON
Child Of Darkness, Child Of Light
Chips, The War Dog
Twelve O' One (12: 01)

WHITFIELD, LYNN
Cosby Mysteries, The
Johnnie Mae Gibson: F B I
Josephine Baker Story, The
State Of Emergency
Stompin' At The Savoy
Taking The Heat
Thicker Than Blood: The Larry Mclinden
....Story
Triumph Of The Heart: The Ricky Bell Story

WHITMAN, STUART
Stillwatch

WHITMORE, JAMES
Favorite Son

WHITMORE, JR., JAMES
Hunter
Tricks Of The Trade

WHITTON, MARGARET
Summer My Father Grew Up, The

WICKES, MARY
Christmas Gift, The
Fatal Confession: A Father Dowling Mystery

WIDMARK, RICHARD
Blackout
Cold Sassy Tree
Gathering Of Old Men, A
Once Upon A Texas Train

WIKES, MICHAEL
Liberace: Behind The Music

WILCOX, LARRY
Perry Mason: The Case Of The Avenging Ace
Rich Men, Single Women

WILCOX, SHANNON
Triplecross

WILDE, CYNTHIA
Lena: My 100 Children

WILDER, JAMES
Confessions: Two Faces Of Evil
Cracked Up
Grass Roots
Night Owl
Tonya & Nancy: The Inside Story

WILHOITE, KATHLEEN
Broken Promises: Taking Emily Back

WILLARD, FRED
Sodbusters

WILLIAMS, AMIR JAMAL
Silent Witness: What A Child Saw

WILLIAMS, ANSON
I Married A Centerfold

WILLIAMS, BARBARA
Indecency
Peter Gunn
Spenser: Ceremony
Spenser: Pale Kings And Princes

WILLIAMS, BARRY
Bradys, The
Very Brady Christmas, A

WILLIAMS, BILLY DEE
Courage
Dangerous Passion
Impostor, The
Jacksons: An American Dream , The
Marked For Murder
Percy & Thunder
Return Of Desperado, The
Right Of The People, The

WILLIAMS, CHINO "FATS"
Parker Kane

WILLIAMS, CINDY
Earth Angel
Perry Mason: The Case Of The Poisoned Pen
Tricks Of The Trade
When Dreams Come True

WILLIAMS III, CLARENCE
Against The Wall
Highwayman, The

WILLIAMS, JOBETH
Adam: His Song Continues

Baby M
Chantilly Lace
Child In The Night
Final Appeal
Jonathan: The Boy Nobody Wanted
Kids Don't Tell
Murder Ordained
My Name Is Bill W.
Sex,Love, And Cold Hard Cash
Victim Of Love

WILLIAMS, KEITH
Blue Bayou

WILLIAMS, KELLI
Snowbound: The Jim And Jennifer Stolpa
....Story

WILLIAMS, MONTEL
Perry Mason: The Case Of The Telltale Talk
Show Host

WILLIAMS, PAUL
Night They Saved Christmas, The

WILLIAMS, STEVEN
Revolver

WILLIAMS, TIMOTHY
Welcome Home, Bobby

WILLIAMS, TREAT
Bonds Of Love
Deadly Matrimony
Drug Wars: The Camarena Story
Echoes In The Darkness
Final Verdict
Hoover
Max And Helen
Parallel Lives
Third Degree Burn
Till Death Us Do Part
Water Engine, The

WILLIAMS, VANESSA
Full Exposure: The Sex Tapes Scandal
Jacksons: An American Dream , The
Perry Mason: The Case Of The Silenced
Singer
Stompin' At The Savoy

WILLIAMSON, MYKEL T.
Killer Among Us, A

WILLIAMSON, NICOL
Sakharov

WILLINGHAM, NOBLE
Quiet Victory: The Charlie Wedemeyer Story
Road Raiders, The
Shooter
Unconquered

WILLIS, BRUCE
Moonlighting

WILSON, ELIZABETH
Conspiracy Of Love

WILSON, LAMBERT
Frankenstein

WILSON, MARA
Time To Heal, A

WILSON, ROGER
Can You Feel Me Dancing?

WILSON, SHEREE J.
News At Eleven
Walker, Texas Ranger

WILSON, STUART
Her Wicked Ways
Romance On The Orient Express
Wallenberg: A Hero's Story

WILTON, PENELOPE
Borrowers, The

WIMMER, BRIAN
China Beach
Dangerous Pursuit
Honor Thy Mother
Kiss Of A Killer
World's Oldest Living Bridesmaid, The

WINDOM, WILLIAM
Attack Of The 50ft. Woman
Back To Hannibal: The Return Of Tom
Sawyer And Huck Finn
There Must Be A Pony

WINFIELD, PAUL
Eighty-Three Hours 'til Dawn
Guilty Of Innocence: The Lenell Geter Story

WINFREY, OPRAH
There Are No Children Here
Women Of Brewster Place, The

WING, LESLIE
Cowboy And The Ballerina, The
Perry Mason: The Case Of The Reckless
Romeo

WINKLER, HENRY
Absolute Strangers
Only Way Out, The

WINNINGHAM, MARE
Betrayed By Love
Better Off Dead
Crossing To Freedom
Eye On The Sparrow
Fatal Exposure
God Bless The Child
Intruders
Love Is Never Silent
Love & Lies
She Stood Alone
Those Secrets
Who Is Julia?
Winner Never Quits, A

WINTER, ED
Christmas Gift, The
Held Hostage: The Sis And Jerry Levin Story
Mickey Spillane's Mike Hammer: Murder
....Takes All

WISE, RAY
Secret Life Of Archie's Wife, The

Taking Of Flight 847: The Uli Derickson
....Story

WITHERSPOON, REESE
Desperate Choices: To Save My Child
Wildflower

WITHROW, GLENN
Naked Lie

WITTNER, MEG
Higher Ground

WOHL, DAVID
Island Sons

WONG, B.D.
Good Night, Sweet Wife: A Murder In Boston

WONG, VICTOR K.
Forbidden Nights

WOOD, ANDY
Probe

WOOD, ELIJAH
Day - O

WOODARD, ALFRE
Blue Bayou
Child Saver, The
L. A. Law
Mandela
Sweet Revenge, A
Unnatural Causes

WOODBINE, BOKEEM
Strapped

WOODLAND, LAUREN
Willing To Kill: The Texas Cheerleader Story

WOODS, JAMES
Badge Of The Assassin
Boys, The
Citizen Cohn
In Love And War
Jane's House
My Name Is Bill W.
Promise

WOODS, JOHN
At Mother's Request

WOODS, MICHAEL
Blindfold: Acts Of Obsession
Double Edge
Omen I V: The Awakening

WOODS, NAN
Betty Ford Story, The
China Beach

WOODS, ROBERT S.
Chase

WOODWARD, EDWARD
Agatha Christie's The Man In The Brown Suit
Arthur The King
Hands Of A Murderer
Over My Dead Body
Uncle Tom's Cabin

WOODWARD, JOANNE
Blind Spot

Breathing Lessons
Do You Remember Love?
Foreign Affairs
Passions

WOOLDRIDGE, SUSAN
Crossing To Freedom

WOOLVETT, JAIMZ
Deadly Betrayal: The Bruce Curtis Story

WOPAT, TOM
Burning Rage
Christmas Comes To Willow Creek
Just My Imagination

WORTH, IRENE
Forbidden

WRIGHT, GORDIE
Prison For Children

WRIGHTMAN, ROBERT
Stepfather I I I

WUHL, ROBERT
Percy & Thunder

WYATT, JANE
Amityville: The Evil Escapes

WYNTER, DANA
Return Of Ironside, The

YAGHER, JEFF
One Of Her Own

YARLETT, CLAIRE
Staying Afloat

YATES, CASSIE
Detective In The House

YESSO, DON
Empty Cradle

YOAKAM, DWIGHT
Roswell

YORK, JOHN J.
Thunderboat Row

YORK, KATHLEEN
Gregory K
Thompson's Last Run

YORK, MICHAEL
Duel Of Hearts
Fall From Grace
Judith Krantz's Till We Meet Again
Lady And The Highwayman, The
Sword Of Gideon

YOTHERS, TINA
Crash Course
Family Ties Vacation
Laker Girls, The

YOUNG, BRUCE A.
Three On A Match
What Ever Happened To Baby Jane?

YOUNG, BURT
Columbo: Undercover
Double Deception

YOUNG, CHRIS
Breaking The Silence

YOUNG, DEY
Murder 101
Not Quite Human I I

YOUNG, KAREN
Drug Wars: The Cocaine Cartel
High Price Of Passion, The
Summer My Father Grew Up, The
Ten Million Dollar Getaway

YOUNG, LORETTA
Christmas Eve
Lady In A Corner

YOUNG, NORMA
When Dreams Come True

YOUNG, ROBERT
Conspiracy Of Love
Marcus Welby, M. D.: A Holiday Affair
Mercy Or Murder?

YOUNG, SEAN
Blood And Orchids
Sketch Artist
Witness To The Execution

YOUNG, WILLIAM ALLEN
Outrage

YOUNGBLOOD, JACK
C. A. T. Squad
C. A. T. Squad: Python Wolf

YOUNGBLOOD, ROB
Elvis And The Colonel: The Untold Story

YOUNGFELLOW, BARRIE
Lady From Yesterday, The

YOUNGS, GAIL
Last Days Of Frank And Jesse James, The

YULIN, HARRIS
Daughter Of The Streets
Last Hit, The

ZABRISKIE, GRACE
Black Widow Murders: The Blanche Taylor
....Moore Story
House Of Secrets And Lies, A
Miracle Child

ZAL, ROXANA
Daughter Of The Streets
Deadly Relations
Everybody's Baby: The Rescue Of Jessica
....Mcclure

ZAMMIT, EDDIE
Long Time Gone

ZANE, BILLY
Case Of The Hillside Strangler, The

ZANE, LISA
Babe Ruth
Dark Reflection

ZAPATA, CARMEN
Broken Angel

ZERBE, ANTHONY
Independence
One Police Plaza
Richest Man In The World: The Aristotle
....Onassis Story
To Save A Child

ZIMBALIST, JR., EFREM
Trade Winds

ZIMBALIST, STEPHANIE
Agatha Christie's The Man In The Brown Suit
Breaking The Silence
Caroline?
Celebration Family
Incident In A Small Town
Jericho Fever
Killing Mind, The
Letter To Three Wives, A
Love On The Run
Personals
Remington Steele: The Steele That Wouldn't
....Die
Sexual Advances
Story Lady, The

ZMED, ADRIAN
Victims For Victims - The Theresa Saldana
....Story

ZOBEL, RICHARD
Parker Kane

ZORICH, LOUIS
Death Of A Salesman

ZUNIGA, DAPHNE
Stone Pillow

NOTES